JOHN RANELAGH

The author has been a Commissioning Editor at Channel 4 Television. His two previous books were on Ireland, and he was Associate Producer of the BBC series *Ireland – A Television History*.

He now lives in Granchester, Cambridge.

John Ranelagh

THE AGENCY

The Rise and Decline of the CIA

sceptre

First published in Great Britain in
1986 by Weidenfeld and Nicolson
Limited

Sceptre edition 1988

Sceptre is an imprint of Hodder and
Stoughton Paperbacks, a division of
Hodder and Stoughton Limited.

British Library C.I.P.

Ranelagh, John
    The Agency: the rise and decline
of the CIA.
    1. United States – Central Intelli-
gence Agency – History
    I. Title
    327.1′2′0973   JK468.I6

    ISBN 0-340-41230-5

Printed and bound in Great Britain
for Hodder and Stoughton Paperbacks, a division of Hodder and
Stoughton Limited, Mill Road, Dun-
ton Green, Sevenoaks, Kent TN13
2YA (Editorial Office: 47 Bedford
Square, London WC1B 3DP) by
Richard Clay Limited, Bungay, Suffolk. Photoset by Rowland Photo-
typesetting Limited, Bury St
Edmunds, Suffolk.

Contents

Photo insert follows page 224.

Preface

I wrote this book in pursuance of an intuition: that the CIA was not as contemporary demonology depicted it. I was also responding to the fact that there was no book giving an overview of the agency. I took it for granted that every great power must have a system of intelligence. It was clear that the history of the growth of American intelligence was woven into the story of the United States' suddenly becoming the greatest power in the world. In the course of researching and writing this book I encountered many specific surprises but nothing to alter my original assumption, which in itself may be surprising to many. All in all, I believe the CIA has been representative of the United States, with the same strengths and weaknesses. Significantly, several major investigations of the agency have demonstrated that it has almost invariably acted on the orders of the President or his appointed supervisors. When it has failed to meet with the approbation of its investigators, it has always been because of confused instructions or understandings. The CIA has not been the rogue elephant of excited journalists and politicians.

The CIA is, of course, a secret agency. We are never likely to know its complete history. Those who accept its purpose—the never fully acknowledgeable security objectives of the United States—should not be surprised by its secrets.

A NOTE ON SOURCES

The bibliography will show the literature on intelligence that I have gratefully drawn upon. In particular I would like to single out the Church Committee report, *Alleged Assassination Plots*, and the *History of the CIA*, by Anne Karalekas, in Book IV of its findings. Thomas Powers' *The Man Who Kept the Secrets* was a valuable work. The Freedom of Information Act has enabled me to consult many thousands of documents. Where a document is referred to in a footnote or a source note, unless otherwise specified it comes through FOIA. There is nothing like this act in any other country, and it tells us something about the United States and the context within which the CIA works. It is a testament to democratic self-confidence. In Chapter 19, the Top Secret Reagan Transition Team report, with its information about espionage performance and systems and its analysis of the intelligence community, was given to me individually and is not in the public domain. I did not approach the CIA itself in the course of writing this book, except on three occasions when I telephoned for press information. I felt that it was necessary to maintain a certain distance from the agency to establish the book's integrity.

The book took form and life once I began to interview the several hundred people who were to be so generous with their time, their records, and their patience over the last four years. I was told much without recrimination and regret, and I sensed the agency as an institution from the tone of these conversations. At all times I have acknowledged interview material. For obvious reasons I have not been able to name all those I have consulted and interviewed, but in every case the material I have quoted was sent to the person interviewed for checking. In some cases I heard no further and have accordingly chosen to regard silence as approval.

ACKNOWLEDGMENTS

John A. Bross gave me constant support, encouragement, advice, and friendship, and I owe him an enormous debt of gratitude. This book in important respects was made possible by him.

Timothy Dickinson was a mine of advice, illumination, guidance, and knowledge of the American scene. To him too I owe an enormous debt.

John Taft opened his work and research to me, making available the draft of his forthcoming book on U.S. foreign policy and the men who made it. I am also deeply grateful to him for limitless and unconditional hospitality and generosity.

Lawrence Houston, Walter Pforzheimer, and R. Jack Smith gave me unstintingly of their time, knowledge, and help. Walter's knowledge of intelligence literature was of great benefit. Larry placed the experience of his extraordinary career and his exceptional memory at my disposal. Jack was painstaking in his attention to detail and accuracy. Together with John Bross they have informed my story.

Jeremy Isaacs gave me his support and encouragement. For his flexibility and confidence, and for giving me time off, I shall always be grateful.

Kay Murphy Halle made me welcome at all times and introduced me to her friends, who were everywhere. Her endorsement made a real difference to many people. John Carbaugh opened doors for me I did not know existed and gave me his own acute commentary on intelligence issues. Joseph Persico and David C. Martin both gave me advice and useful guidance. Richard Belfield, Sig Cohen, Nicholas Fraser, Jonathan Hill, Michael Jones, Gus MacDonald,

Deirdre McMahon, Jean Newington, and my sister Bawn all helped with arguments, corrections, and information. They gave me a net of support. My researchers, Martha Page, Susannah Seely, and Fiona Gore, were invaluable. They provided much of the material I have used.

Michael Shaw and James Oliver Brown at Curtis Brown were bastions of encouragement and common sense. Without their help and friendship I doubt if this book would have been written. Alice Mayhew, Ann Godoff, and Henry Ferris at Simon and Schuster were stimulating, friendly, and constructive in all aspects of the enterprise. Alice courageously backed and shaped the project from the start. To my wife, Elizabeth, as ever I owe most thanks of all.

I am particularly grateful to Samuel Halpern and Walter Pforzheimer for many of the corrections made in the paperback edition of this book.

The opinions and any inaccuracies in the following pages are mine alone.

John Ranelagh
Washington, DC

Introduction

"Some time ago a cattle rancher told me about a huge snake holed up in a cave," said Lee, a CIA agent in Bolivia in the late 1950s. "He said that snake was over ten meters long; it had eaten, at the very least, ten Indians. He said the snake came out of his hole every three months, threw himself in a big loop around a steer, dragged him into the river, drowned him, and devoured him. Then the snake would slip into the cave and sleep it off for another three or four months. The rancher wanted that snake captured if possible and carted off to a zoo, since it was certainly the largest snake in existence. For the next few months that snake was the subject of conversation at every embassy cocktail party. But how do you capture a snake over thirty feet long? Finally someone came up with a scheme. We had quite a long cotton-picking sack made in Lima. We had a giant zipper sewn into each end. Our plan was to use tear gas to drive that snake out of his hole into the sack and zip it up. We appointed a head zipper man and a tail zipper man. I was to oversee the entire operation, and to carry a .357 Python pistol in case something went wrong.

"Well, we went to the ranch and got ready. We took a long pole along with the idea that when we got the snake inside the sack and zippered up we'd tie the sack to the pole, and then, by placing the pole between two jeeps, get the snake to the railroad."

"Just a minute, Lee," said David Atlee Phillips, a colleague to whom Lee was telling the story.

"I'm telling you the God's honest truth," Lee insisted. "Well, we got everything set and shot tear gas into the hole. The snake coughed and thrashed around in there and then came barreling out. He saw daylight at the end of the sack we were holding at the mouth of the cave and headed for it. The zipper men stood their ground and zippered that snake right up. The flaw in our scheming was that we made the sack too roomy. When the snake discovered it was trapped, it dashed its body against the side of the sack with such force that it split the sack almost from one end to the other. The next thing I knew, it was out and headed toward me. I finally got off a shot into the snake's head when it was about twelve yards away. It made a big loop with its body, hit a hardwood tree about the size of a small telephone pole, and shattered the tree like

15

matchwood. Then the snake fell over into the jungle, where I was able to put two more shots into its head. We measured this snake and found it was thirty-four feet, three inches in length!"

"Lee," said Phillips, his credulity strained too far, "you're a damned liar."

Lee, who before he had joined the CIA had been a national pistol-shooting champion, took Phillips into his backyard and brought out the snakeskin from his garage. It was the biggest snakeskin Phillips had ever seen, but he still doubted Lee's story of how he had ended up with it. Some years later, in late 1967, Phillips was at a Washington party where he fell into conversation with Darwin Bell, the deputy assistant secretary for international labor affairs, who had served in Bolivia while Lee was there. "Did you know Lee?" Phillips asked him.

"Certainly did. Knew Lee well."

Phillips recounted the tale of the snake in tones of amused disbelief. "To this day," he said in conclusion, "he claims they made a canvas sack with zippers at both ends. Now, did you ever hear anything about that?"

"Mr. Phillips," said Darwin Bell, looking straight into Phillips' eyes, "I certainly have heard about that. *I* was the tail zipper man."[1]

The story of CIA agents and future deputy assistant secretaries of labor gripping specially made canvas sacks and trying to capture one of the world's longest snakes in the jungle of Bolivia strains credulity even for those wanting to believe. However, unusual as it was, other comparable CIA stories that were equally well attested made it difficult to dismiss and more believable than if it had come from the folklore of IBM or the U.S. Marines. The idea of the button-down technocrats of IBM personally trying to capture a snake with guns, tear gas, zippers, and canvas strains credulity past the breaking point. The idea of the Marine Corps analyzing how to save the snake by using tear gas rather than an explosive charge also presses the story too far. But in the CIA, which had men and women who would be at home in both IBM and the Marine Corps, the story could be accepted for what it was: true. It could be accepted not only by CIA people but also by outsiders, because the CIA was special, elite, secret, and different. It could be anything, and there was a strong sense until the mid-1960s that it could do anything too.

A PUBLIC SECRET

The headquarters of the Central Intelligence Agency is in Langley, Virginia. In 1980 the agency had a staff authorization of 16,500 and an annual budget of $750 million.* It is the most public of the world's secret intelligence

---

*The CIA's staffing and budgets have remained secret. Under William Casey the agency's budget is reported to have increased at a rate of 17 percent annually since 1980 (*Newsweek*, October 10, 1983, p. 30).

services, having its own press office—something no European intelligence agency would dream of having. The headquarters building is set on approximately 219 acres of flat, partially wooded country on the banks of the Potomac about eight miles northwest of downtown Washington, DC. For the first fifteen years of its life the agency was housed in a number of office buildings in Washington and in the World War II prefabricated huts along the reflecting pool and around the Lincoln Memorial. This scattered its departments and made coordination and administration difficult. One of the driving ambitions of Allen Dulles, the director of Central Intelligence from 1953 to 1961, was securing a centralized headquarters site and building. Langley was the result of his effort. When it was first built, its turnoff on the George Washington Parkway was marked with an overhead sign that said simply "C.I.A." When in 1961 the attorney general, Robert F. Kennedy, who was also President Kennedy's overseer of the agency, saw the sign, he reacted with consternation and ordered that it be taken down. To him the Central Intelligence Agency was a secret agency and should not advertise its presence on the highway. What he forgot was that the Langley building was known to all. Indeed, its size made it a useful landmark to pilots flying into Washington's National Airport. For years afterward everyone in Washington knew that the turnoff on the parkway marked "Federal Highway Administration" (the neighboring complex to the agency) was the one to take to the CIA. Under Nixon the overhead sign came back with an additional marker: "Central Intelligence Agency/Intelligence Community Staff/Federal Highway Administration/Next Right."

Completed in 1961, the Langley headquarters is now showing its age, not only in terms of styling and design—it is more concrete than glass and has a squared, blocklike construction—but also in terms of wear and tear. It was built at a time when the agency was much more action-oriented than it is today and when it also had a smaller staff. Now that several thousand CIA officers are no longer working secretly abroad, their offices can no longer be used by others in their absence. Office space is at a premium and overcrowding is a constant problem. As a result, CIA "colonies" have spread into the nearby towns and the suburbs of Washington, thus negating the initial attraction of having a centralized CIA headquarters. Arising once more is the problem the Langley building was meant to solve: different departments in different places naturally strengthen the tendency toward competing fiefdoms which exists in any large organization. In 1982 a $46 million extension was approved so that the agency could once again try to function on one site.

The compartmentalization of functions and departments for security purposes—the administrative consequence of the need-to-know principle (that people should be told only what they need to know for each particular job and are never told the whole story)—is exacerbated by the physical design of the Langley building. The organization of the agency also contributes to the tendency to create individual fiefdoms and to the internal coordination problems faced by every director of Central Intelligence. It also creates headaches for those working with the CIA. The air force, cooperating closely with the agency on the U-2, satellite, and SR-71 projects, often found that obtaining even straightforward project-related information was like trying to get blood from a stone. It was not simply bureaucratic rivalry that was involved, it was the complications of physically contacting one office or another, of knowing which office or officer to approach, of knowing the geography of the agency and Langley.

CIA officers, for example, could work for years without ever knowing precisely where the head of counterintelligence worked or what he looked like. The counterintelligence head of the agency for twenty years was the legendary James Jesus Angleton, a thin man with hawklike features who habitually wore a homburg when he went out. One officer in 1954, who in spite of four years' service had never seen Angleton, asked a colleague to point him out. While they were walking to the cafeteria together one day his friend said, "There he is!" and with a nod of his head pointed out a short man with stooped shoulders and a shuffling gait. "That's him. That's Angleton." "So that's the fabulous Angleton," said the officer. Fourteen years later, having pointed out the small shuffling man to others, the officer, now a division chief, met Angleton for the first time. He was six feet tall, "a man who looks like his ectoplasm has run out," with a sallow and sensitive face. His desk was always littered with papers with red *Priority* stickers on them. A *Priority* sticker was guaranteed to galvanize a division chief into action, but they didn't faze Angleton.[2] He was known as the "Delphic oracle" in the agency and was one of the few who knew where the different offices were and how to cut through them. Few others had this overview or the authority to circumvent the agency's internal security mechanisms, even though on many occasions the inability of others to cut through resulted in bureaucratic turmoil that belied the verse from the Gospel according to Saint John inscribed on the marble wall of the main lobby at Langley: "And ye shall know the truth and the truth shall make you free."

Of course the purpose of the CIA was not so much to inform everyone who worked for it or with it of the truth; frequently operations demanded the exact opposite. The agency has one main client, the President of the United States, who is also the agency's boss. Agency people are the President's men. Their basic job is to find out the truth and tell it to the President. Some die in the process, as witnessed by the fifty small stars carved into the marble walls in the main lobby at Langley, each star representing a CIA officer who lost his or her life in the service of the United States. Most agency people pass through the lobby every morning, going to work at the same time as other Washington office workers and in the evening going home at the same time too. Most agency people are on the overt side and can tell their friends for whom they work, although they cannot talk about the work itself. They are in the directorates of Science and Technology, Management and Services, or Intelligence.

They may be on the Historical Staff or in the office of the general or legislative counsel. The Directorate of Operations—the clandestine side of the agency—contains the espionage and counterespionage agents and the covert operators whose identities are kept secret. These people often cannot tell their families what they do and for whom they work, although in recent years the number of people in this group has dropped sharply in step with reduced agency operations. Inside Langley the atmosphere reminds one far more of the Department of the Treasury or a research institute than what the imagination might conjure up for the world of James Bond. Bond's world is an unreal world, and the CIA is very much in the real world.

Through the main lobby, across the agency's emblem in marble on the floor—a sixteen-pointed star on a shield with the head of a bald eagle in profile on top, set in a circle, with *Central Intelligence Agency* written on the top rim and *United States of America* on the bottom—the offices and corridors begin. There are seven stories in the Langley building, with the agency's most senior officers and the offices of the director of Central Intelligence and support staffs at the top. Other floors bear no particular relationship to the agency's command structure. The first floor includes the library, the medical staff and a small medical facility, the staff credit union, the travel offices, the cable secretariat, and the cafeterias. The main cafeteria is partitioned into two units: one for staff, who show their badges to armed guards when entering, and the other for visitors—thus ensuring that a chance sighting of a CIA officer by an outsider will not occur. The CIA's "supergrades"—the highest-paid, most senior officers—have a separate dining room in the seventh-floor executive suite, but even they have to pay for their meals: there is no such thing as a free lunch at Langley.

Armed guards standing at the point where the main lobby joins the rest of the building check passes with the aid of a computerized system instituted in 1977. In the corridor behind the lobby are five elevator banks. One elevator is separate, for the personal use of the director of Central Intelligence, whisking him from the garage in the basement to his office suite on the seventh floor. To reach this elevator, one turns to the left at the computerized-pass checkpoint just before entering the corridor behind the main lobby, walks through the visitors' area, and then turns right. It is a single unit operated by a key. The elevator banks are color-coded, each cutting out certain floors the others service, and the office compartmentalization begins. Corridors are lettered on each floor—"A" corridor, "B," and so on—and rooms are numbered and lettered: 5G44, for example, would denote room 44 on corridor "G" of the fifth floor. The corridors are painted off-white and kept bare. Only the doors to offices—painted bright red and blue and yellow—add color. Offices tend to be small, with all but the most senior officers in eight-by-twelve- or twelve-by-fourteen-foot rooms. Junior officers in some of the agency's divisions may find themselves sharing rooms.

About one-third of the agency's total full-time staff serve overseas on a tour system, most of them under the umbrella of the State Department, doing research, reports and analysis on the spot. Some, serving usually under cover as businessmen, run agents and covert activities abroad. Today there are very few of these. Thirty years ago they numbered over one thousand. The change is symptomatic of the change in the agency over the years and of the change in America's perceptions of secret service. Today the CIA is a mature bureaucracy, with all the strengths and weaknesses of being established in the framework of government. In the early years the CIA was a fledgling organization, new to the American concept of government, fighting for a place in the government bureaucracy. It had a mission to roll back communism and saw itself not so much as the analyst but rather as the special forces of the Western world. Today the agency sees itself—and is seen by the President—as the analyst, and this is where its strength now lies. Thirty years ago, when President Eisenhower decided that the regime of Jacobo Arbenz in Guatemala should be overthrown, he turned to the CIA to do it. Today, when President Reagan decides the regime in a Caribbean statelet should be overturned, he sends in the marines.

The agency's can-do quality has declined with the decline in the exercise of U.S. power. In the intervening years the CIA has become the other voice of U.S. foreign policy, frequently talking to the people the State Department finds it difficult to talk to. This was already happening in the late 1950s. While the State Department had cordial relations with the government of France, the CIA was secretly helping Algerian nationalists in their fight for independence. Frantz Fanon, the Algerian philosopher of revolution, was flown to Washington and treated at CIA expense for the cancer that would eventually kill him.[3]

Whether it was fighting snakes or bureaucratic battles in Washington or colonial powers in the Third World or whether it was dealing with the intricate sophistication of the U-2 and satellites, the CIA was a force to be reckoned with behind its conventional exterior and its internal compartments. "We want you to go out and support the noncommunist left in Latin America," said Vice-President Hubert Humphrey to John McCone, the director of Central Intelligence, and his senior agency officers during Humphrey's first visit to Langley early in 1965. "Fine, Mr. Vice-President," said McCone, "we'll do what the President wants. But if it gets out, it could blow up in our faces. Will we be supported if that happens?" McCone, Humphrey, and President Lyndon Baines Johnson all knew that the agency did have the power to bring the noncommunist left to office in the countries of Latin America. McCone's question had to do with something else: If it got out that the CIA was supporting the left, would the President disown it? Would it be accused of acting on its own, of being a rogue elephant, of being made up of a bunch of pinko Ivy League elitists using the American taxpayer's money against the American taxpayer's wishes? Humphrey laughed. He understood the question precisely.

President Johnson had just asked him to settle a steel dispute only to find that the President had undercut him by reaching a settlement without telling him, leaving Humphrey looking foolish and ineffective with the labor unions and management. "What?" he said. "You expect to be backed? Hell, they won't even back *me!*"[4] But the CIA had the strength to do what it was asked to do and to survive the consequences of finding itself up a creek without a paddle.

AGENTS IN PLACE

The first generation of senior CIA people, the "Founding Fathers," came in the main from the Ivy League colleges and the East Coast Establishment. The bulk of early staffers came from schools such as City College of New York, New York University, Fordham, Michigan, UCLA, and had served in the Army and Navy departments during the war. They had served in the Office of Strategic Services (the OSS), the World War II precursor of the CIA. This was a mature generation with a wide range of experience gained before the war started. Many had been lawyers; some had been journalists; others had taught at universities or had pursued postgraduate degrees. They recognized that the creation of the Central Intelligence Agency in 1947 was an opportunity for the nation. America had never had a peacetime intelligence organization like the CIA before, and it clearly represented a new window on the future within the government. Able people who had experience and wanted to serve their country found the CIA attractive. They also understood that within a new bureaucracy they could have a large say in their career patterns, and, since the agency was established by law as a presidential arm, this say would come from a privileged position. Behind the founding generation came another generation eight or ten years younger. Entering the war straight from college, they usually served in the OSS. They joined the agency for the same reasons as their seniors.

In 1950, the five thousand or so people in the CIA came from backgrounds that were broadly OSS, the Federal Bureau of Investigation (itself noted for its high-quality personnel), and the military services. In addition, some lawyers, academics, public relations people, and journalists were involved. This group dominated the agency right through the 1960s. By 1955, following a reorganization and under the demands of the Korean War, the agency expanded to about fifteen thousand people.* The latest recruits were

---

*The CIA staffing has remained at about 15,000 to 18,000. In recent years more women have been recruited, but the agency has never had a high proportion of women staffers. In 1981 Bernice Turbeville, who had a thirty-six-year career in the CIA (starting in 1946 in the Central Intelligence Group, a forerunner organization), sued the agency for sexually discriminating against her and 500 other women staffers (*The Sunday Times,* January 3, 1982).

In 1985 the agency launched a recruiting drive in American universities. At the University of Southern California career-opportunities director Sharon Slavin observed: "The CIA can offer graduates a fairly independent job with a high degree of responsibility—and they can become spe-

different from those who came before them. They were more likely to be from the West or from midwestern universities than from the East Coast Establishment, and once again they were younger. There were often other differences too. Out of necessity, their mind-set was more technical than that of the first two groups. As the process of intelligence collection became increasingly involved with airplanes, tapping landlines, and electronic eavesdropping rather than with having agents in place, the agency needed more electronics experts, engineers, and scientists to do its work.

In the 1960s, as the demands of the Vietnam War pushed the agency more toward analysis and away from operations (which were conducted by the military), another generation came in. It was the generation that was fighting the Vietnam War, and it reflected the tensions of the time. Nearly all the agency's whistle-blowers—the people who after leaving the CIA wrote exposés of their time there—came from this generation. In some ways this generation was reminiscent of the first. Many of the recruits came from the finest East Coast families and were motivated to join the agency out of a patriotic desire to serve their country. Others joined because it was better to be in the CIA, they thought, than in the paddy fields of Vietnam fighting "gooks." Since the early 1970s the agency has advertised for recruits in newspapers, turning away from the old way of recruiting through recommendation or introduction via its alumni or friendly academics.

Today's generation is bright and professional and represents a cross section of the more highly educated groups in the United States. The pay of current CIA employees is much lower than what they could receive if they joined law firms, banks, and other private-sector businesses (although for analysts pay is better than in academia). Nevertheless it is good by U.S. government standards. This has always been the case, by intent. Allowances are generous, as are pensions. The staff credit union is attractive. There is a bonus system, and salaries at the top compete with the best in government. In 1952, as the agency began its big personnel expansion, a career service program was developed by the Directorate for Administration (DDA), which now has a staff of approximately fifty-five hundred. The DDA controls the agency's internal organization and services, including the communications staff and systems. It came up with a reasonably flexible, compassionate program that attempted to institutionalize a certain freewheeling spirit. People could choose the directorate within which they wanted to serve, and the door was always left open for internal movement and for movement outside the agency when a total mismatch

---

cialists within two or three years." Chris Shinkman, careers director at Stanford University, said: "There's been a pretty dramatic change since the seventies. Ten years ago the CIA wouldn't have been able to stay on the campus. There would have been a big demonstration against their presence." Patti Volz, CIA public affairs spokesman, said that in 1984, "We had a record 150,000 job applications" and that this was "the highest ever." Only one in seventeen applicants was successful (*Daily Express*, March 29, 1985).

took place. Of course systems are always inadequate for the human condition, and despite the best efforts of the DDA, the complexions of the different generations caused problems. "There was some animosity against the Eastern Establishment set," recalled one former deputy director for administration:

> I can think of some people in pretty senior positions when I was serving through the years who felt their further advancement had been inhibited because they didn't go to this school or that school or they weren't invited to this party or that party or their words weren't given sufficient credence because they were not part of the inner set. There was some of that, but it disappeared as time went by because you don't have the same kind of people today that you had twenty years ago. You take a hard look at the leadership of the agency today and you will find little hint of the Eastern Establishment—it's gone.[5]

This sort of thing was only to be expected. If it had not been the Eastern Establishment, there would have been another bogey. The "Knights Templar," as the agency's top brass were called by some during its first twenty years, all came from a small group of the "Founding Fathers" and, with relatively few changes, had been running the agency almost from the start during this period.[6] This had far more to do with their generation's participation in World War II than with the schools or parties they attended. Members of the same generation were to be found running other government agencies and private-sector businesses for the same long period. Since they were all about thirty years old in 1947 and in senior positions because of the express train of war, it was not surprising that they should dominate for so long. In the course of this domination the "Templars" lost the aura they had had in their OSS days during the war. No longer were they seen as a fashionable regiment. Rather, they were now part of a bureaucratic—although extremely talented—government agency. "Everything begins in mystery and ends in intrigue," remarked Charles Péguy, a radical Catholic writer of the left in France before World War I, and from having been very special and mysterious in the 1940s and 1950s, the agency became relatively ordinary and bureaucratic by the early 1970s as the founding generation retired.

ACADEMICS ANONYMOUS

From the beginning the agency has had an academic tone, which is imparted by its analysts, who are now also its driving force. It was the analysts who always made certain that the agency was able to express itself academically while relying on the power of understatement. They functioned coolly and deliberately despite CIA operations that were neither academic nor cool. This approach stemmed in part from an acute awareness of European intelligence models and was shared by agency leaders. Interestingly, the CIA's friends abroad do not see the agency as a quintessentially American institution (which it is), and in America it is viewed at times as dangerously cosmopolitan. All this characterizes academia as well, especially Ivy League academia.

At first the analysts were topped by the Board of National Estimates (known colloquially within the agency as the "College of Cardinals"), composed of "the great and the good" from within the intelligence community and extending to the Foreign Service, civilian life, and the military services. In the Directorate of Intelligence (DDI) were the analytical officers—a high proportion of whom had doctorates and other advanced degrees—who were responsible for summarizing all the information available in their own areas (which could be countries, regions, or technical, economic, or military subjects). From these summaries came the National Intelligence Estimates—papers on problems, subjects, and questions of policy—which were assessed by the Board of National Estimates and then submitted by the director of Central Intelligence to the President on request or on the director's own initiative.

Today about thirty-five hundred people are in the DDI, which spends about 10 percent of the agency's total budget, but the original structure has broken down. The Board of National Estimates was eliminated in 1973, and its job of assessing the evidence and the conclusions of the National Intelligence Estimates and making recommendations to the director was taken over by National Intelligence officers, who were individually responsible for all aspects of the Estimates they wrote. The review function was placed outside the agency in the hands of the National Foreign Intelligence Board (the heads of the intelligence community, previously the United States Intelligence Board) and the President's Foreign Intelligence Advisory Board (presidential appointees drawn from "the great and the good" of academia, business, government, and the military). In 1976 Gerald Ford abolished the Advisory Board and set up the Intelligence Oversight Board to monitor the legality of intelligence operations; President Reagan subsequently brought back the Advisory Board. At all times the concern of successive presidents and of the intelligence community as a whole has been to ensure accurate reporting and good judgments, free of political or commercial influence. (See Appendix IX.)

The changes in the organization of intelligence have marked the changes in the CIA. From being a unique intelligence agency it has gradually come to be challenged on its own ground: by the Defense Intelligence Agency, by the State Department, and by some private institutions. By and large, the CIA's analytical system and the review procedures have worked well in preventing external pressures from influencing judgments and in keeping the agency ahead of its competitors. The Directorate of Science and Technology (DDS&T), created in the early 1960s to keep the air force from encroaching on the technical intelligence-collection systems developed by the agency (the U-2 and satellites, in particular), succeeded in its task and also performed a useful analytical function. Its approximately fifteen hundred people are, however, essentially engaged in developing new and improved collection systems and devices. It was first named the Directorate of Research but this was changed to DDS&T. In the wake of the Cuban missile crisis, its people reflected the intensity of the moment. They wanted to work to prevent a war and to win one if it broke out. It was widely accepted, for example, that the scientific research of most interest was military. As a result the DDS&T attracted high-quality people (although we can now see that the really innovative research involved unraveling the biochemical secrets of the chromosome). Under Albert ("Bud") Wheelon, its second head, the DDS&T was a powerful bureaucratic player.

One of the early problems of both the DDI and the DDS&T was attracting people of the right caliber, given the secrecy of the agency's work. How could they attract the highflying young engineers or political scientists who could find more rewarding careers in academia or business in terms of both remuneration and public prestige? The agency could not depend on moments of national intensity or emergency for its long-term recruitment. Allen Dulles, the director under whom the agency filled out, always maintained that it was wrong to bottle up the agency's intellectuals. He argued that they should be able to publish their work in declassified forms so that they could gain the respect of their peers. In an important way Dulles himself provided the lead by agreeing to be interviewed by *Time* while he was director of Central Intelligence. (His photograph graced the magazine's front cover.)

Today many of the analysts publish their findings in academic journals and are acknowledged by name in the CIA reports and papers on which they have worked. This has been an important factor in the agency's ability to attract people, along with the appeal of patriotism, the mystique surrounding the agency, and the fact that the CIA's information is far more detailed, wide-ranging, and up to date than that available outside. CIA analysts have always known more about more than their peers on the outside, and their knowledge—inevitably—stays with them throughout their entire career. On both sides of the house—the analytical side and the covert side—these attractions have appealed to very able young men and women ever since the agency began.

DIRECTOR IN CHIEF

The director of Central Intelligence wears three hats. He not only is head of the CIA but also serves as the head of the intelligence community of which the CIA is only one part. He is also the President's chief intelligence officer. Richard Helms, director from 1966 to 1973, put it this way: "As the director of Central Intelligence I was chairman of the United States Intelligence Board and the principal intelligence adviser to the President of the United States, as well as the head of the Central Intelligence Agency."[7] The directors are presidential appointees, as are the deputy directors of Central Intelligence, and their appointments are ratified by the U.S. Senate. It is a post that existed before the creation of the CIA and is separate from the agency, although running the CIA is the single most important part of the job.

Between 1946 and 1987 there were fourteen directors of Central Intelligence. Four have been admirals; two have been generals. Five of the fifteen deputy directors during this period have been generals; two have been admirals. (See Appendix X.) There has always been a strong military interest in the CIA, reflected in this military contingent. This was to be expected since the agency inevitably treads heavily in areas of military concern and since the director of Central Intelligence and his deputy, as the President's chief intelligence officers, coordinate and oversee the whole U.S. intelligence effort. That turnoff sign on the George Washington Parkway that said "Central Intelligence Agency" and "Intelligence Community Staff" indicated this dual role of the DCI. The sign has been changed: the staff is no longer housed in Langley. It has never been part of the CIA: it serves the DCI in his role as overseer.

Because of the central and powerful role of the director, to understand the CIA and the world within which it operates it is necessary to examine closely the personality and policies of each man who has held the office.

The relationship of the agency and the director to the rest of the intelligence community has been at the center of countless bureaucratic battles. It was not simply as a new concept that centralized intelligence had to fight for a place in government, but also as a bureaucracy requiring funding and competing with much longer established intelligence departments in the armed forces, the FBI, the Treasury, and the State Department. This battling competition at times was thought to challenge the integrity of the National Intelligence Estimates and the agency's analytical function. Periodic accusations were made that the CIA had geared an Estimate or colored its reporting in order to achieve some bureaucratic or political purpose. Said Major General George Keegan, who, as a former head of air force intelligence, was an old agency rival:

> Affecting the quality of the product is something totally undocumented in the public record. The competition between the bureaucracies is a process that occurs in all the liberal democracies to some degree. It has to do with permanency of status, relative importance of position, dominant influence. It has to do with job security and the enhancement of the traditional perquisites of service high in the echelons of large government where the expenditures are vast. In the case of the CIA and very able elitists generally, they bring to this their good education, the fact that they are very articulate, and their outside connections in the form of a vast legal/lobbying apparatus permanently in place, constantly selling the CIA. And because the military were much bigger and more involved in missions and much better and much more experienced when the CIA started, how do you operate in the face of all that and acquire the kind of position and prestige that you need? It led to internecine warfare of the worst kind.[8]

Keegan was speaking in 1984. But the web of influence and connection to which he referred was at the very heart of the CIA, mirroring the social and professional world of the gentlemen who founded it.

A GENTLEMAN'S CALLING

"Gentlemen do not read each other's mail," Henry Stimson said shortly after his appointment as secretary of state in 1929.* He had just learned that the United States had maintained a highly successful code-breaking unit, known as the Black Chamber, ever since the end of World War I. He disapproved of the operation and closed it down. It had solved more than forty-five thousand cryptograms and at one time or another had broken the codes of countries as diverse as China, Cuba, France, Great Britain, Germany, Japan, and the Soviet Union.† Prying into other people's secrets, however, was not, in Stimson's view, for gentlemen or the United States. But what is a gentleman? And what might Henry Stimson have meant?

Broadly defined, there are two kinds of gentlemen. A gentleman can be one who has money and polite social graces or he can be born into the social class of gentlemen. In both cases being a gentleman is being a member of an elite.

"In America," said Alexis de Tocqueville in 1835, "there are no nobles or literary men, and the people are apt to mistrust the wealthy; lawyers consequently form the highest political class and the most cultivated portion of society. They have therefore nothing to gain by innovation, which adds a conservative interest to their natural taste for public order. If I were asked where I place the American aristocracy, I should reply without hesitation that

*There is some question whether Stimson ever actually said this. But the sentence and its authorship were ascribed to him during his lifetime, and he never denied them.

†Herbert O. Yardley, the head of the Black Chamber, was a genius of cryptanalysis. His job was "to read the secret code and cipher diplomatic telegrams of foreign governments—by such means as we could. If we were caught it would be just too bad!" On one occasion, Yardley rashly informed one of Stimson's less principled predecessors that he could break the Vatican's diplomatic code. Noticing a look of shock on his superior's face, he quickly added, "I personally feel that it is unethical for us to inquire into the Vatican's secrets."

Yardley's Black Chamber was funded jointly by the State and War departments, so Stimson's withdrawal of support forced its closure. It closed shop on October 31, 1929. Yardley found no employment for his talents elsewhere in the government, and, driven by financial desperation, he wrote the story of the Black Chamber in a series of popular articles in *The Saturday Evening Post.* They were subsequently published in a best-selling book in 1931. (In Japan alone the book sold more than thirty-three thousand copies, provoking massive indignation by its revelations that America had been reading Japan's most secret diplomatic communications.) A follow-up book was impounded by federal marshals in a dramatic raid on the New York offices of Macmillan and Company in February 1933. In 1938 Yardley was hired by Chiang Kai-shek to read the codes of the Japanese then invading China. His last role in life was as a professional poker player; in 1957—a year before he died—he published *The Education of a Poker Player.* For an account of Yardley's Black Chamber, see Herbert O. Yardley, *The American Black Chamber* (New York: Random House, 1931).

it is not among the rich, who are united by no common tie, but that it occupies the judicial bench and the bar." In the 150 years since he placed lawyers on the pinnacle of American society, a great deal has changed. Innovation, rather than conservative interest, has become the lawyer's hallmark, keeping pace with the changes that have happened in and to America. But socially, de Tocqueville was right. In Britain, the term "Esquire" formally denotes to the present day that someone is a gentleman. In America the term today is a social designation that someone is a lawyer.*

Technically, a gentleman is a member of a class in the social order of aristocratic Britain connected to nobility and agriculture rather than to a profession or trade. A gentleman is someone in that group of men without titles immediately below knights. It is a social position, having more to do with birth and manners than with money. Typically, younger sons in titled families are in this group. They have to make their own way and cannot depend on the inheritance of family wealth. They may become merchants or enter the professions, but they will still cling to the ideal of country life and money from the land. In the days of the European empires, emigration and colonial service were often chosen outlets for this group. George Washington was an English gentleman.

To John Waller, a gentleman who had been in the wartime Office of Strategic Services (known, significantly, as "Oh So Social") and who retired in the mid-1970s as inspector general of the Central Intelligence Agency, "A gentleman is somebody who doesn't buy clothes: he has them."[9] To him being a gentleman meant a combination of inherited money and social standing. Gentlemen such as John Waller provided the leadership of the CIA and its predecessor organizations: when the agency was set up in 1947, about one third of its senior officers came from the Ivy League/Wall Street background of the OSS. What Stimson had failed to understand in 1929 was that intelligence was a sophisticated and intellectual business and no longer simply a prying matter. What he probably meant was that American gentlemen had no need to pry: the world was other people, and America was separate from it.

ATTORNEYS AT WAR

One of the basic elements in American society in the early twentieth century was the acceptance of the most ruthless forms of competition, matched by

---

* Alexis de Toqueville, ed. Phillips Bradley, *Democracy in America* (New York: Knopf, 1966), p. 278. For the use of "Esquire" see *Debrett's Correct Form* (Kingston upon Thames, England: Debrett, 1971), pp. 119, 322–26: "In New York, Washington, Boston, Philadelphia, and Baltimore, and generally in the eastern part of the United States, 'Esq.' after the name denotes an attorney at law, and as such appears on a letter heading or list, but this usage is less common in other parts of the United States. In Department of State usage, the term is reserved for Foreign Service officers serving abroad, and is not usually given to attorneys."

a noninterventionist doctrine of government. The most dramatic aspect of President Roosevelt's New Deal was its overturning of this long-standing government role. Nonintervention by government was an expression of the idealistic side of American life: the idea that the rights of individuals are supreme. Freedom in America has always meant that someone has the right to punch someone else if he wants to as long as he is prepared for the consequences. Freedom in Europe, the Old World, is freedom *from* such action. In America people are free to do things; in Europe people are free from things. The American freedom in its turn largely derived from the absence of the "health of the state" attitude, which is a consequence of war and international struggle. From the outset the United States reversed the ordinary European consciousness of the state's needing constant inoculations of military, police, and political power to maintain its health. Both the Declaration of Independence and the Constitution make this clear. America was the state with weak neighbors and an expanding, unthreatened frontier. Opportunity was its characteristic. International struggle was at a distance. Great cities and corporations could be (and were) brought into being within a generation. The people who organized opportunities in a new world where the rules were to be made were lawyers. An understanding of the Central Intelligence Agency, the group of gentlemen who do read other people's mail, can be gained from an understanding of lawyers.

Lawyers have always constituted a significant proportion of all CIA employees, and as a result, a legal orientation of organized American intelligence has colored the agency's methods and operation from the start. William Donovan, a New York lawyer and the "father" of the CIA, consciously drew upon his legal background and connections in forming his model for an American secret intelligence agency. In 1929 the idea of the United States as a spying nation was disconcerting to many. Of course there had been American spies in the Revolutionary War, the Civil War, the First World War; but while this was acceptable during war, it was not acceptable during peace and did not seem necessary. People in and out of government were used to being spied upon by foreign countries—they expected no less of the old countries they had left to create America—but they had not given any real thought to the process of spying themselves on other countries. America had chosen isolation, secure in its own wealth and the vastness of its own terrain. The intelligence interests of the United States outside America were long-term, far away, and of a self-evident nature.

What presidents, chiefs of staff, and secretaries of state wanted to know about the outside world was: Could any power compromise American supremacy in the Western Hemisphere? Was there a likelihood that countries sharing the same continent would unite against American interests? Would the United States face a hostile united Europe or a threat from the China/Japan/Southeast Asia bloc? While there was an interest in the old empires' falling so that American commercial concerns and American democracy (the idealism was always important) could penetrate them, America always left the resolution of these problems to the empires themselves. Although American business may have had a hand here and there in encouraging colonial independence, American government, for the most part, stayed out of the struggle.

At home, however, spying was not unusual. The requirements of the legislative and political processes in an intensely combative democratic arena where the rights of individuals were always measured against the power of government and were always used to challenge the complexity of regulations gave an intensity to the democratic right to information. Obtaining information that affected people's personal lives, and a pervasive concern for the interests of individuals, lent to the class of lawyers a very special place in American life. It was small wonder that when it came to the business of intelligence after Pearl Harbor, America was more ready than people might think for "dirty work." Law firms were gauged by the wealth and influence of their clients, which led to the wealth and influence of the firms themselves. A senior partner in a law firm hardly ever appeared in a courtroom; he owed his position to the clients he had or could bring to a firm and to the confidence those clients had in him as a fixer. He was a master drafter of legal instruments, a mercenary of the most formidable power, which was exactly what society expected him to be. He could make wills; break wills; outflank contracts; change and evade laws.

The range and resourcefulness of such people was never to be underestimated. They were formidable, possessing the qualities of intellectual precision and highly sophisticated practical competence—the same qualities required in intelligence work. They were used to acting as buffers and shields for their clients from the outside world, paying people off when necessary, influencing legislation and legislators, acting as cutouts in business deals of all kinds. A partner in any successful law firm knew where secrets were buried and had a network of informants from all walks of life to supply him with information. During World War II men like these joined the OSS and made deals with criminal elements in occupied Europe and the Far East to facilitate Allied victory. In the 1960s men like these in the CIA made deals with criminals in attempts to assassinate Fidel Castro. There was a reservoir of experience in predatory conduct in America, reaffirmed by the experience of World War II. Bankers, lawyers, industrialists had engaged in ruthless competition and conspiratorial activity at home and abroad for several generations, just like their British, French, and German counterparts. This experience contributed to the creation of a sophisticated intelligence establishment. Psychologically, a large number of Americans in positions of power and influence were always prepared for dirty work. These men were no innocents.

So it should have come as no great surprise when in 1976 the United States Senate Select Committee to Study Governmental Operations with Respect to Intelligence Activities (the Church Committee) revealed that since 1947 the gentlemen of the CIA had read other Americans' mail; had tried to murder foreign leaders; had organized the destabilization of the governments of other countries; had planned and executed invasions of other sovereign states; had tested drugs on unwitting Americans and foreigners; and in other ways had upset the self-perceptions of Americans. The shock was that America had been acting like everyone else.*

MODERATE MORALITY

The revelations of the Church Committee resulted in a popular reassessment of what America stood for. In the first place, the genuine idealism of most Americans—their determination to make the new world a better world, with a simpler and more straightforward life than the tradition-ridden countries of Europe—had been compromised. After the shock wore off, Americans simply accepted that their country had more in common with other countries than they had thought. Second, the political and geographical isolation of the United States which had characterized its first hundred and fifty years was set firmly in the past. Communication advances—airplanes, radio, television, telex, satellites—and the extent of American power had brought this about. World War I had been America's first major foray across its great defenses, the Atlantic and the Pacific. Lindbergh's flight across the Atlantic had taken place in 1927;† America entered World War II fourteen years later; the atom bomb was used for the first time four years after that; the first satellite was launched only twelve years later. The rapidity with which America expanded into a wider world, and the way in which the wider world expanded upon America, had simply left many Americans behind, politically, culturally, and morally. In 1976 many Americans were still clearly in an America they thought was purer than the world outside, purer than the one the Church Committee revealed to them. In a country of individualists, individual wrongdoing somehow seemed more real and more wrong.

After the mid-1950s there was an ever-increasing difference in perspective between the seasoned unenthusiasts of the CIA, with their cool eyes and long horizons, and other public officials, with their short-term objectives and constant search for immediate answers. As this difference developed, the agency's professionals did what professionals do in every field: they developed their own ethical standards. What will a lawyer not do for a client? What will a doctor do to keep a patient alive who is begging to die? What will a CIA man do to defend American interests? The answer came out of experience and was very sophisticated. It owed a great deal to the experience of lawyers, combining a

---

* People who had accepted the bomber offensive against Germany and the atomic bombing of Japan during World War II did not like hearing about attempts to kill Fidel Castro.

† There were, of course, earlier flights, but his was the first solo flight. In a nation of individuals it was an individual success: Lindbergh was a star.

belief in the exactitude and flexibility of law with a willingness to push law all the time—testing it, restricting it, making it.

CIA officials were ingenious, very determined, and invisible, straining hard not to be an invisible government but servants of American interests acting—with restraint—in (for America) a new world of secrecy. Out of this came a qualitative ethic in which success was based on judgment, analysis, and the pursuit of limited ends. It was an ethic in which liberal democratic ideals were the engine of activity. It held that ends justified means, and means colored ends, and all means were available. It was American, seeking a democratic sanction all the time. It would be wrong to see the ethics of the CIA as those either of mercenaries or of fresh-faced farm boys.

THE WILSONIANS

A generation earlier the American governing elite had shared a similar perception, in many ways enshrined in Woodrow Wilson's Fourteen Points, his basis for the peace after World War I: national self-determination; representative government; democratic principles; an end to empires; free trade; and a legalistically formulated system of international relations dependent on enlightened public opinion, whereby disputes between nations would be resolved in a league of nations dedicated to peaceful coexistence. Wilson's liberalism assumed that white peoples were capable of self-government and therefore should have it. But he did not think Black Africa could govern itself. When he spoke of an end to empire he had in mind the German and Austro-Hungarian empires because they denied European self-determination. He was ambivalent about the British and French empires (which were not in Europe). This ambivalence in turn reflected the fact that he was an Anglophile southerner, conscious of his Protestant Northern Irish roots, identifying with Britain in world affairs. It was this element in his approach to the world and America's place in it that helped pave the way for America following the British and French imperial presence in Southeast Asia after 1955.

Wilson's supporters were the carriers of a motivating idealism in U.S. foreign policy which long antedated Wilson, a liberal internationalist view of the world and America's place in it, as demonstrated by the effect of the United States' entry into World War I in 1917 and its instrumental role in devising the postwar peace in 1919. In those three years America proved what many European leaders had recognized for some time: that its weight in the scales of the balance of power (in 1917 still an entirely European affair) would guarantee victory for whatever side it was on. Winston Churchill was able to look back on hearing the news of the Japanese attack on Pearl Harbor and say, "So we had won after all."[10]

What the Wilsonians never fully realized was that it was America's sheer military and economic strength, and not their idealism, that was effective in the balance of power. They saw American economic power as the reward for virtue. Their security and self-confidence were the mainsprings of their internationalism. They insisted on putting a moral gloss on material matters, but they sensed that there were enormous possibilities intimately linked to the prospects of American life. The inheritors of Wilsonian idealism were the young men who had fought or who identified with those who had fought for the rights of national self-determination and democratic values in 1917 and 1918.

More than twenty years later, in the 1930s and 1940s, they were a far more disillusioned generation, more ready to accept that American power had a legitimate part to play in securing the ideals that had not been achieved. They would not acknowledge that their ideals of a new, liberal, democratic world order requiring no balancing power to sustain it could never be universally applied. Rather, they saw their failure as the result of a betrayal by the American public (or at least its representatives) in opting out of the League of Nations and international involvement just when Woodrow Wilson was about to secure a substantial element of his ideal world order with the Paris peace treaties of 1919. There was also a feeling among Wilsonians and others that in 1919 Europe had outsmarted America, had cynically used American boys and American money to shore up the Old World. Twenty years later, much of the support for the America First movement was not support of fascism or German or Italian imperial dreams but a heartfelt American sense that the cunning, manipulative, cynical old European empires should not drag America into their mess again.

NEITHER WAR NOR PEACE

America had saved what was left of the Old World in 1917–19, but in that victory the Old World had begotten terrible children. Between 1919 and 1923 European cynicism and American naïveté had thrown away the big chance to improve the world. For the United States, opting out of the League of Nations and a return to isolation were the results. So in 1941, when America entered World War II, there was a strong feeling among Americans that they would have to do it all again, only this time the task would be much more difficult. In 1945 this was confirmed. People understood that Hitler's empire could have prevailed had he had the atomic bomb. They also understood that Stalin could create a worldwide empire with one. Many Americans said, "Never again. Never take the risks of isolation again: rather take the risks of engagement." This was the spirit of the founding generation of the CIA, of the North Atlantic Treaty Organization, of the Marshall Plan.

This generation was coming of age in 1945. Having been through war, they had a double sense of trying to avoid the suffering of war and of trying to avoid the colossal risk that war would happen again. They saw that the same

sort of mobilized effort required of everyone in war was now required of the political and professional elites (always much the same thing) in an effort to
maintain America in a situation of neither war nor peace. A Hitler empire
could have stretched through fourteen time zones, and then where would
America have been? In 1945 a Stalin empire stretched through twelve time
zones and seemed poised on the borders of two more. If Hitler had managed to
do so much in the 1930s without being fully noticed, what might Stalin do?
He had already killed tens of millions of his own people and moved nation-
sized populations around with few noticing.

At the same time, the generation imbued with the ideals of Wilson clung
to the notion that a better world could be achieved. The difference between
1919 and 1945 was that people now recognized that to achieve their goals they
had to deal with the world as it was and not simply as they would wish it to be.
In the 1940s everything came together to give the CIA its opportunity, and the
agency's founding fathers seized it.

COOL WARRIORS

The generation that made the United States enter international espionage
and covert action and establish the CIA was by 1941 rising to supreme power.
Its members had been born in the period 1885–95: Dean Acheson (1893), secretary of state under Truman; Robert Lovett (1895), lawyer, banker, "fixer"
par excellence, served as Truman's secretary of defense and was later Kennedy's *éminence grise*; James Forrestal (1892), secretary of the navy under
Roosevelt, also secretary of defense under Truman and one of the first cold
warriors; John Foster Dulles (1888), lawyer and Eisenhower's secretary of state,
promised the liberation of eastern Europe and the threat of massive nuclear retaliation against the Soviet Union; his younger brother, Allen (1895), again a
lawyer and the CIA's longest-serving director; Walter Bedell Smith (1891), Eisenhower's chief of staff during World War II, ambassador to the Soviet
Union, the third director of the CIA, and subsequently undersecretary of state;
Dwight D. Eisenhower (1890). Harry S Truman (1884), William J. Donovan
(1883), and Franklin Delano Roosevelt (1882) were born just outside the decade. All experienced the excitement and hopes of World War I. Acheson had
been a naval officer; Lovett and Forrestal had served as naval aviators.* John

---

*Naval aviators were the most glamorous officers during World War I because of the cour-
age required to carry out their hazardous missions. Exceptional people were required to fly the
wood, wire, and canvas biplanes from the primitive carriers that were their takeoff and landing
fields. On every flight the aviators faced the prospect that they would not find their ship and
would be lost at sea. They also faced the dangers of fog, storms, insufficient fuel, and the knowledge that if they ditched in the ocean, there was little chance of rescue. When F. Scott Fitzgerald
wrote his short story "The Rich Boy," his central character was someone who had been a naval
aviator in World War I.

Foster Dulles had worked with "The Inquiry," Woodrow Wilson's secretariat during the Paris peace negotiations in 1919. Harry Truman had fought as a lieutenant and then as a captain in an artillery unit on the western front. William Donovan fought in the trenches in France, becoming America's most highly decorated officer for his bravery under fire. Franklin Roosevelt was assistant secretary of the navy throughout the war.

Out of the experience of these men in the years between the end of the first and the start of the second world war came three strongly held convictions upon which they based their policies as they came to power. The first conviction grew out of what had happened to America in 1919 when, in their view, America had been outsmarted by the British and the French in the postwar settlement and had reacted by withdrawing to its continental boundaries. They were determined that this would never happen again. Their second conviction was tied to the events of Munich in September 1938 when Hitler was let loose by the tired, dispirited, cynical politicians of the old empires. Loose, the aggressor gained one step, then another, and soon compound interest was working for him. In 1965 as Lyndon Johnson wrestled with the question of whether or not to order a huge increase in American involvement in Vietnam, one of the factors that influenced his decision was Munich. "I feel there is a greater threat to start World War III if we don't go in," Henry Cabot Lodge said to the President. "Can't we see the similarity to our indolence at Munich?"[11] They were also convinced that democracy was a viable governing alternative; the idea that people can get together and make deals based on idealism as well as selfish interest and hard-nosed pragmatism appealed to them on a number of different levels. These convictions underpinned the attitudes and activities of the governing elite of the United States from 1941 until the late 1970s.

During World War II the governing elite understood the strength of America: the whole concept of massive retaliation as a threat was based on the recognition of massive strength. They also understood the importance of mobilizing this strength powerfully and efficiently, not simply to win battles but also to be in a position to achieve their vision of a new, liberal, democratic international order with America in the lead. Thus it was essential throughout the war years and immediately afterward for them as civilians to retain control of the levers of American power. They could not allow the military to assume the unchallenged right to this power for achieving narrow war aims, as they had done in all previous conflicts. The elite sought to retain the power in their hands for the much greater purpose of reshaping the world. They saw 1945 as a great moment in which to remake the world. Aware of the threat to the democratic model posed by the Soviet Union, they nevertheless felt bound by their idealism to try to remake the world in cooperation with the Soviets. Because of its role in bringing down Nazi Germany they were prepared to view Russia as the most respected of nations. In part this was the reason why America tried hard to avoid the across-the-board confrontation of the cold war until 1947.

But at the same time, they knew that it might be impossible to cooperate with Russia, so they also took steps to ensure that failed attempts would not return America to isolation. Idealism and pragmatism were combined. As it became clear that any hopes of cooperation were misplaced, and as Europe's postwar fragility became more apparent, they focused their energy on securing for America the senior partnership in a world economic and political system that did not include Russia. They knew that America would have to be willing and able to act alone. They also knew that it would have to be prepared. It was a complicated business involving simultaneous and sometimes contradictory steps, and for it to work it had to be tightly controlled.

Along with this postwar sense of opportunity came protracted—sometimes vicious—interdepartmental battles for control of the agencies of the cold war. The most notable battles involved the military and their supporters over the quasi-military Coordinator of Information Office, its successor agency, the Office of Strategic Services, and finally the CIA. Because the exercise of power in America was personal in nature—because the right telephone calls from the right people could make or break a career and because the right family connections made far more than a social difference—a feuding, vitriolic quality characterized much of the struggle. Betrayal and feelings of betrayal were widespread.

The creation of the CIA represented a victory for the governing elite, but the struggle in turn had a vital effect on the nature of the agency. On the one hand, it was the vehicle of the civilian elite; on the other hand, it was an agency practiced in all the martial arts, experienced in war and bureaucratic infighting. Above all, it represented the very public-spirited determination of the governing elite not to let America be surprised or outsmarted by the old European empires or the new Soviet one, and their deep belief in American democracy as the best system for the expression of both the self-interest and the natural altruism of every individual.

—1—

Cruel Necessity
1939-1941

The Central Intelligence Agency was William Donovan's idea. The complexion, the dominant themes, the concept, and the role of the agency can all be traced to him. The reliance on the East Coast Establishment was his habit. The fight for the bureaucratic place close to the President was a fight he started. The notion of centrally coordinating all United States intelligence activity in peacetime was his. The concept of United States intelligence activity *in* peacetime was his. He was a member of the generation that had fought on the western front in World War I and then for twenty years had watched with mounting horror and frustration as isolationist America stood aside from the attempt by the old empires, France and Britain, to stem the rush of the new fascist/communist, militaristic, totalitarian empires of Russia, Italy, Japan, and Germany. World War I, America's ever-growing worldwide interests, and a real concern for democracy and democratic values motivated Donovan and many others. Unlike many Europeans in the 1920s and 1930s, he was not convinced that democracy was doomed. He wanted to fight for democracy and had no interest in putting his chips on one of the totalitarian alternatives; he knew that American power if released from isolation could stem the totalitarian tide and make the world safer for democracy.

He was one of the first "modern" Irish-Americans, no longer interested in fighting the battles of the "old country" from which their families had originally come but anxious to establish their new country, with both its idealism and its commercial interests, in the world. Modernism represented a willingness to cast off isolation and engage in world affairs. The years 1941-45 provided an intense experience of the "otherness" of other nations. Americans had been shocked (far more so than the British) by the encounter with completely alien despots and their actions: Japanese pilots prepared to crash planes loaded with explosives into ships; Hitler prepared to exterminate millions of helpless civilians. The outside world entered the American consciousness as a strange and potentially dangerous place, quite unlike America. Donovan was one of the first to possess this sense and to act on it. He recognized that America was inextricably entwined with the rest of the world and therefore had to learn about that world and defend itself from possible attacks.

Donovan's grandparents had emigrated from Ireland, impoverished and uneducated. This did not affect Donovan's attitudes, and while he was brought up and remained a Roman Catholic, he was a staunch member of the Republican party in New York (where to be Irish was synonymous with being a Democrat) and a firm Anglophile. He was a successful lawyer and he established the law firm known today as Donovan, Leisure, Newton and Irvine, at Two Wall Street, in the heart of Manhattan's financial district. In 1973, sixteen years after his death, the firm moved uptown to 30 Rockefeller Plaza. "He was a morally good man," recalled James R. Murphy, an old friend who worked closely with him in the Office of Strategic Services. "He had a very strict moral code. He was very careful about his personal life, physically and healthwise. He was inclined to overweight: he liked big steaks. I heard gossip during the war that Donovan was a drunk—I actually heard people saying that—but I don't think he ever touched a drop of alcohol, not in all the years that I knew him. He wouldn't drink wine or beer or any kind of alcohol. He was not a good, practicing Catholic, but still he was a Catholic. He believed in it."[1] Like many people for whom chance or ambition acts to distance them from their roots, Donovan was extremely socially conscious. It was not that he was a snob; it was rather that he liked well-connected, wealthy, influential people. He wanted to be all these things himself, and he bent every fiber to the task. He had an immense ambition to get to the top in wealth and power. He had a romantic view of success and was insufficiently inoculated against the charms of the upper class, a trait that fueled suspicion in Washington that the British had an ascendancy over him. He was also a man of adequate hardness, willing to pay the price for what he wanted. But because he wanted so much, he was always afraid of defining his ambition in specific terms, and so he tended in practice to substitute hard work and energy for his overall objectives, which were never quite achieved.

In 1940 Donovan fastened firmly onto intelligence as the mast on which to raise his flag. He won the Distinguished Service Cross, the Distinguished Service Medal, and the Medal of Honor for battlefield exploits in France in 1918. As early as 1935 he had sensed that another war was likely and that America would again be involved. After war started in Europe in 1939, he cast around for a military job, warning that America would be and should be drawn into the conflict on the side of the Allies, wanting again to play a part. His war heroism had made him a national figure, and his views attracted attention. "In an age of bullies, we cannot afford to be a sissy," he declared to the American Legion in his typically down-to-earth way.[2] At the age of fifty-three, however, active combat was unlikely for him, so he applied his efforts to establishing a coordinated intelligence agency. In June 1940, as Nazi armies were rapidly forcing the collapse of France, Donovan turned down an offer from his friend Frank Knox to be undersecretary of the Department of the Navy. (Knox, a Republican, had just been made secretary of the navy by the Democratic president Franklin Roosevelt as part of an effort to broaden his administration in the face of the war in Europe.) Instead, in July 1940, at a meeting at the White House with Knox, Henry Stimson, also a Republican and Roosevelt's secretary for war, and Cordell Hull, the secretary of state, Donovan agreed to travel to Britain to assess morale and military capabilities and to examine British intelligence and counterintelligence methods.* Out of this meeting, Donovan's trip, and his report on it came America's first centralized intelligence organization and Donovan's own launching as America's spy master.

THE BRITISH SECRET INTELLIGENCE SERVICE

Behind the meeting at the White House and Donovan's trip was one of the most important coups of the British Secret Intelligence Service. Britain desperately wanted the participation of the United States in the war, and Winston Churchill set this as his foreign-policy priority from his first days as premier. Short of actual entry into the war, American economic support for the British war effort was sought, as was American cooperation with British Intelli-

---

*For an explanation of the relationship between Knox, Roosevelt, and Donovan, see Anthony Cave Brown, *Wild Bill Donovan: The Last Hero* (New York: Times Books, 1982), pp. 141, 148–149. Donovan had traveled abroad several times in the previous years, making reports to the War Department on political, industrial, and military matters. In 1935, after a European trip, he wrote to the army's chief of staff, General Douglas MacArthur, with whom he had served in the Rainbow Division in France, that he thought Italy's invasion of Ethiopia might have widespread repercussions. At the end of 1935 he was in Europe again, meeting Mussolini in Rome and securing from him permission to visit Italian units in Ethiopia and Libya. His report to the War Department after this trip was highly praised.

In 1937 he attended German army maneuvers and examined German tanks and artillery. In 1938 he toured Czechoslovakian defenses in the Sudetenland, visited Yugoslavia and Italy, spent time at the Ebro River front during the Spanish civil war, and again attended German military maneuvers. In 1939, convinced that war was likely soon, he visited Holland and Belgium (where he thought Hitler would probably attack), Germany, Denmark, Norway, and Sweden. His instincts were right, although his judgment was not: he concluded that war would not actually break out in 1939, although Britain would face "an exciting summer" (Thomas Troy, *Donovan and the CIA* [Frederick, MD: University Publications of America, 1981], p. 28). In 1940 Donovan was considered by President Roosevelt for a job in his administration and was recommended to Roosevelt by Knox as secretary for war.

gence.* This cooperation was much more easily obtained than might have been expected, because President Roosevelt was deeply anti-Nazi and lent his personal support to the secret exchange of information. Still, securing the cooperation was a key purpose of British intelligence in 1940.

American intelligence was uncoordinated and fragmented. In 1929, after Stimson had closed down the Black Chamber, the armed services and the State Department had only a spasmodically effective code-breaking operation. It did not seem to the British—or, for that matter, to anyone else—that American policy makers had recognized the need for intelligence. By 1940 President Roosevelt and some of his top advisers had in fact recognized this need, but to those outside the American governing elite this was not yet apparent. So the British devoted considerable energy to convincing the President and his administration that America needed a coordinated intelligence service. What was a long way off was the recognition by Roosevelt and his administration that America might need a centralized, national intelligence service. This was something that Donovan, in part prompted by William Stephenson, a Scottish-Canadian millionaire, boxing champion, World War I flying ace, and international financier and industrialist, did recognize. Stephenson was British Intelligence's man in America and an unofficial channel between the British and American governments, unaffected by diplomatic protocol.

William Stephenson was William Donovan's sort of man. He was glamorous, well connected, and certifiably brave. He was ten years younger than Donovan, which enabled Donovan naturally to assume the lead in their relationship as it developed after May 1940 when Stephenson was appointed by the British Secret Intelligence Service as their liaison with the American intelligence services. His appointment had the personal approval of President Roosevelt.[3] One of the first things he urged through his personal contacts with Roosevelt's advisers and with J. Edgar Hoover, with whom at first he principally cooperated,[4] was that someone should be sent to Britain to make an independent assessment of Britain's will and ability to continue the war. The American ambassador to the Court of St. James's, Joseph P. Kennedy, was

---

*Discussions about defense matters had taken place between Britain and the United States since early 1937 but had rarely included intelligence concerns and then only between the two navies. The British director of Naval Intelligence in 1938 supplied the American naval attaché in London with information about the Japanese navy. The British were given technical help in exchange. From early 1939 the diplomatic services of the two countries began to exchange information, with the British Foreign Office detailing intelligence that indicated that Nazi Germany was planning to attack the Netherlands. During the summer of 1939 State Department information about the secret negotiations that resulted in the Nazi-Soviet Pact of August 1939 was passed to London. This was the sum total of U.S.–U.K. exchanges when war between Britain and Nazi Germany broke out in September 1939. Early in 1940 the chief of the British Secret Intelligence Service, Colonel Stewart Menzies, acted to extend secret Anglo-American contact. With the approval of the prime minister, Neville Chamberlain, and President Roosevelt, Menzies informally approached J. Edgar Hoover, seeking a working cooperation with the FBI. Hoover, who was personally anti-Nazi, welcomed Menzies' approach.

known to be pessimistic about Britain's chances, and the British wanted somehow to reassure Roosevelt that the country would not collapse. This was the background to the July 1940 meeting between Donovan, Knox, Stimson, and Hull at the White House.

On July 14 Donovan sailed from New York to England. Stephenson, who at this stage had not met Donovan personally, emphasized in his cables to London the importance of the trip. British Intelligence should "bare their breasts" to Donovan, he said.[5] More than that happened: in London, Donovan dined with Churchill and met King George VI and members of the war cabinet. He had extensive briefings from the principal British military commanders. Colonel Stewart Menzies, the chief of the British Secret Intelligence Service, acted as his host, staying in daily contact with him and making sure that Donovan saw whomever he wanted and was told whatever he wanted to know. When Donovan left Britain on August 3, he had a real grasp of British capabilities.* Back in America, he in turn briefed the leading members of Congress and spent two days with President Roosevelt. To everyone he said that Britain was determined to resist and would probably survive but that British military equipment was deficient and American aid was vital to the British war effort. Later, after Roosevelt agreed to American destroyers being given to the Royal Navy in exchange for American rights to British bases in the Atlantic, Lord Lothian, the British ambassador in Washington, commented that "Donovan helped a lot."[6]

BIG BILL AND LITTLE BILL

One of the ways Donovan helped was by putting his legal training and the resources of his law firm to work reviewing legal precedents in order to find a way to circumvent the need for congressional approval of the destroyers-for-bases deal. It was a classic example of an American lawyer's activity: finding ways of doing things through the back door. The way that he found was through the powers conferred on the President as commander in chief. He continued to focus on these powers as he developed his arguments for a centralized U.S. intelligence service. Another way Donovan helped was by putting his name to a series of articles written by Edgar A. Mowrer—a *Chicago Daily News* reporter who had joined Donovan for part of his time in Britain—which

---

*Among the things shown to Donovan by the British were their new, top-secret invention of radar, their newest interception planes, and their coastal defenses. He was also briefed on British propaganda and psychological warfare methods, and he was particularly intrigued by the details of one of Britain's most closely guarded secrets: the use of captured German spies as counteragents and playbacks—the "Doublecross," or "XX" system. But apparently he was not told about the British effort to unravel the secrets of the German Enigma cipher machine (Corey Ford, *Donovan of OSS* [Boston: Little, Brown, 1970], p. 91).

warned of the dangers of a Nazi fifth column operating in the United States.
Attracting enormous publicity, the articles catapulted Donovan into the center
of public attention. The combination of the public and the confidential Donovan made him particularly effective in Washington, with its keen understanding of the connection between publicity and power. Lord Lothian certainly
understood this. He dropped a clear hint that if Ambassador Kennedy were to
be replaced, Donovan would be a welcome appointment in his stead.[7]

Donovan met Stephenson soon after returning from his British trip, and
they got along very well, soon becoming real friends. As the autumn progressed
the two men spent more and more time together discussing plans for centralized, coordinated U.S. intelligence. They soon became known as "Big Bill"
Donovan and "Little Bill" Stephenson; in Donovan's case, "Big Bill" competed with an earlier nickname, "Wild Bill."* A certain amount of controversy
has surrounded the relationship of the two Bills, one view being that Donovan
was, in effect, Stephenson's agent even before his trip to Britain.[8] Although
this relationship was most unlikely, contemporary allegations that he was a
British stooge did Donovan and his ideal of a centralized American intelligence
agency real damage in 1945. The other view is that Donovan was self-moti-
vated and that his trip to Britain was simply the result of pressures upon Roosevelt to determine U.S. policy toward Britain after the fall of France, when
Nazi power looked invincible. It is now clear that Donovan was his own man at
all times and not, as one writer has stated, a man "put in place" by William
Stephenson.[9] It is also true, however, that the personal and professional relationship between the two Bills gave Stephenson, through Donovan, a real influence on the development of American intelligence.[10] Yet Britain, in
pursuing the war against the Axis powers in 1940, had no alternative but to
look to America for support. Even if Stephenson had not existed, Britain would
have found someone else of comparable ability and influence for secret liaison
work with Washington. Stephenson's success was achieved more by accident
than design, and in all probability Donovan would have succeeded in establishing at least a partially successful coordinated American intelligence effort
without British help.

In December 1940 Donovan again traveled to Britain, this time at the direct instigation of Stephenson. If the British "were to be completely frank with

*Donovan's "Wild Bill" nickname has given rise to various legends. In 1916 Donovan was
called by a New York National Guard cavalry troop, which he helped organize, to serve on the
Mexican border against the alleged banditry of Pancho Villa. It was there, according to his
brother Vincent, that Captain Donovan won the nickname "Wild Bill." As his men rested after
an exhausting ten-mile march, Donovan was reported to have encouraged them to further effort
with the words "Look at me, I'm not even panting. If I can take it, why can't you?" He received
this answer from the ranks. "We ain't as wild as you are, Bill" (Ford, *Donovan of OSS*, p. 12).
Ford states that the nickname may also have originated in Donovan's football days at college, in
World War I, or in that of another William Donovan, who was a baseball pitcher (for the Detroit
Tigers). This Donovan walked six and hit one in the first three innings of the deciding game of
the 1909 World Series.

Colonel Donovan," Stephenson had cabled London beforehand, "the latter would contribute very largely to our obtaining all that we want from the United States."[11] In London he had a long interview with Winston Churchill at 10 Downing Street, and, carrying high-level introductions from the British leader, visited the Mediterranean, North African, and Balkan war zones. He was away for three months, and his trip was paid for by the British; they had seen the value of having a private channel to the White House. The day after his return to New York on March 18, 1941, Donovan spent an hour with the President, and evidence suggests that it was then that he first broached the idea of centralized intelligence to Roosevelt.* Again his confidential report to the President was matched by a public report in a national broadcast on March 26, drawing attention once more to the secret side of war. Nazi successes, he declared on the radio, had been helped by "political sapping and disintegration," just as "in our schoolbooks . . . we read that the soldiers of ancient days prepared for the taking of a city by first undermining its walls."[12]

At the same time, Donovan was using his influence to press for the creation of a new civilian intelligence agency to coordinate all U.S. intelligence efforts and analyze all intelligence information.† It was the start of an enormous

---

*See Troy, *Donovan and the CIA*, pp. 41–42, for Donovan's interview with Roosevelt. On his trip Donovan visited Gibraltar, Malta, Egypt, the North African front in Libya, Greece, Bulgaria, Yugoslavia, the Albanian front, Cyprus, Palestine, then back to Egypt, to Iraq, Egypt again, back to Malta and Gibraltar, to Spain, Portugal, Ireland, and Britain before returning home. In Britain he was impressed by the commandoes and the newly formed Special Operations Executive responsible for sabotage activities overseas. The subject of intelligence increasingly dominated his mind, and he was fascinated by the British approach, with its combination of special operations and guerrilla and commando work and its intelligence research, collection, and analysis.

The British were operating in places that they or their allies knew intimately. The United States, on the other hand, knew little about the rest of the world. Although in the past America had used information gained from multinational corporations to piece together details about other countries, by and large it was a nation that stood in the darkness of its own isolation. Donovan wanted to end this limitation and make America's vision—and grasp—truly global. He committed himself to eliminating America's blind spots and to making America equal to the world and not just to particular parts of it. This was an unprecedented move and a real leap forward for intelligence, putting it at the forefront of America's rise to globalism. As a result the focus of intelligence shifted from the order-of-battle and military information commonly used during World War I to a post–World War II examination of entire societies in complex, long-term analysis.

† Troy, *Donovan and the CIA*, p. 40. Donovan's influence within the Roosevelt administration increased with his second trip. Everybody knew that he had the President's ear and was entrusted with top-secret work by him. His ideas on intelligence, based upon his observations of the British system, were comprehensive and persuasive. "Donovan is the first man I have talked to that I would be willing to really back," said the secretary of the treasury, Henry Morgenthau, Jr., to his staff on March 20 after meeting Donovan. "[He] has been for a week actually in the trenches up in Albania. He was down in Libya when they took that last town, whatever the last town was. He was with Wavell for over a week. He was with Eden in Cairo. He has been twice in England. He has been in Spain and he has been in Portugal. I think he knows more about the situation than anybody I have talked to by about a thousand percent. And he is not discouraged" (ibid., p. 40).

bureaucratic battle that has still not been resolved. Each of the existing intelligence agencies, particularly the military ones, felt it should be the preeminent agency.* The army and navy especially resisted Donovan's proposals, with their traditional dislike of civilians meddling in military matters. The most important principle for any military commander is the security-of-forces principle—the protection of his forces from the enemy—and intelligence is a key element in this. The idea of civilians being involved has always been anathema to the military, who feel they know their business best and know how best to use intelligence for their specific purposes. The military was also convinced that if intelligence were controlled by civilians, in due course war policy would be too. In their view, civilian producers of intelligence produced civilian-minded intelligence.

ROOSEVELT, THE MILITARY, AND AMERICAN OPINION

Donovan, however, was one of those enjoying the support of the President. This was crucial in 1940, and it was to be crucial to the CIA later on. It was to determine the place of centralized intelligence in the government bureaucracy, and it was to establish that a central intelligence agency was designed to serve the President directly and not simply the secretaries of state, war, or defense. It meant that intelligence was within the executive branch in government, enjoying greater freedom and flexibility than other government agencies, which, for legislative and historical reasons, had to secure congressional approval for new initiatives or had their budgets determined by political pressures.

On April 4 President Roosevelt asked the heads of army and navy intelligence and J. Edgar Hoover to discuss the institution of a British system of intelligence coordination in case of war. They all knew that Roosevelt intended to appoint Donovan either their overall head or the head of a separate agency to which they might have to report, and they lobbied against the idea.† It did

---

*The different agencies were Army Intelligence (G-2), the Office of Naval Intelligence, the FBI, the State Department, the Customs Service, the Secret Service, the Immigration Service, the Federal Communications System Service, and the Treasury's Foreign Funds Control Unit.

† Donovan was not the first person to argue for centralized, coordinated intelligence. In the spring of 1929 John A. Gade, a banker and diplomat, proposed something of the sort to the Office of Naval Intelligence (ONI), suggesting an intelligence agency immediately answerable to the President. His model was also British Intelligence, in which various sources reported to a central unit in constant touch with the prime minister. Nothing came of Gade's proposal. In mid-1939 an Intelligence Coordinating Committee consisting of the FBI, the ONI, and G-2 (army intelligence) was set up to work out programs for investigating foreign espionage and sabotage in the United States. By mid-1940 the intelligence agencies themselves realized the desirability of centralization and agreed "that undercover intelligence activities should be coordinated." J. Edgar Hoover independently proposed to Roosevelt that the FBI set up a Special Intelligence

not change Roosevelt's determination to create a new agency and to appoint Donovan to run it. He asked Donovan to make him a proposal for coordinating American intelligence, and throughout April Donovan worked on a paper, consulting the heads of the existing agencies as he did so. On April 26 he presented his recommendations to the President. They were sophisticated, far-reaching, and heavily dependent on Donovan's experience as a lawyer and on what he knew of the British Secret Intelligence Service. He also demonstrated an acute awareness of Washington politics and bureaucratic rivalries.

In April 1941 the average American was glad the United States was not involved in the war. Six months earlier Roosevelt had won his third term as President, promising that American boys were not going to be sent into any foreign wars. Roosevelt's support for Britain, therefore, had to be very carefully managed. So too did any steps, such as a reform or revitalization of American intelligence, which could be construed as indicating that, despite his promises, the President was secretly preparing for war. In this context Donovan as a Republican was an advantage to Roosevelt. The President also had another advantage: the genuine loathing of the heads of the military services and of J. Edgar Hoover for the Nazis. None of them was tempted to leak the President's plans to the press. They were all patriotic. In turn, Donovan framed his proposals in a way that appealed to his patron in the matter, the President, but also accommodated the worries of the other agencies.

The President should control a new agency, said Donovan, and have discretion over its funds, which should remain secret. But the new agency should not "take over the home duties now performed by the FBI, nor the intelligence

---

Service with FBI agents abroad. This led Roosevelt to divide the fields of espionage and counter-espionage abroad: the FBI in the Western Hemisphere and the navy in the Pacific; the army in Europe, Africa, and the Panama Canal Zone. Hawaii was a joint army-navy area. In November 1940 the State Department established a Division of Foreign Activity Correlation. It was small and concentrated on gathering information about foreign visitors and political leaders from all sources, but it was ill-equipped to appraise the capabilities and intentions of foreign countries. For a discussion of the bureaucratic background, see Ray S. Cline, *The CIA Under Reagan, Bush and Casey* (Washington, DC: Acropolis Books, 1981), pp. 34-39.

The first reaction of the army to Donovan's proposals came when the proposals were only a rumor. Brigadier General Sherman Miles heard news of Donovan's campaign on April 8 and alerted the Army Chief of Staff, General George C. Marshall: "In great confidence ONI tells me that there is considerable reason to believe that there is a movement on foot, fostered by Col. Donovan, to establish a super agency controlling *all* intelligence. This would mean that such an agency, no doubt under Col. Donovan, would collect, collate and possibly even evaluate all military intelligence which we now gather from foreign countries. From the point of view of the War Department, such a move would appear to be very disadvantageous, if not calamitous" (quoted in Troy, *Donovan and the CIA*, p. 42). Marshall made a counterproposal for a Joint Intelligence Committee, made up of the heads of the U.S. intelligence agencies (excluding the FBI), which would meet daily and exchange information. But General Miles of G-2 objected to this suggestion and proposed a clearinghouse instead. Eventually, in October 1941, the secretary of war and the secretary of the navy agreed to a reduced version of the Joint Intelligence Committee consisting only of the army and the navy. For details of the anti-Donovan lobbying operation, see Troy, *Donovan and the CIA*, pp. 44-51.

organizations of the Army and the Navy." It should, however, have sole responsibility for overseas intelligence work, and it should coordinate, classify, and interpret for the President information from all sources. An advisory committee to monitor the agency's activities should be appointed and should consist of officials of at least assistant-secretary level from the departments of State, War, the Navy, the Treasury, and Justice. It should be involved in "the interception and inspection . . . of mail and cables; the interception of radio communication; the use of propaganda to penetrate behind enemy lines, the direction of active subversive operations in enemy countries." The final section of Donovan's report detailed the workings of the British Secret Intelligence Service, with its linking of foreign and domestic intelligence activity through the private office of the prime minister.[13]

It was clear that Donovan was proposing a similar operation geared to American requirements, focusing on the Oval Office and the theory of the President as commander in chief, so suited to the policies of Roosevelt's New Deal. His proposals would find a ready acceptance among New Dealers, who welcomed the idea of centralized power as the best means of attaining political and social objectives. They were also geared to the perceptions about the outside world, which in 1940 and 1941 looked very dangerous. Germany had overrun Europe. Japan was overrunning the Far East. German elites ran many of the countries of Latin America. Communist Russia was allied to Nazi Germany. American communists were in positions of power and influence in some states and universities.[14] No one knew what would happen next. Would Nazi Germany leap the Atlantic? Would Japan leap the Pacific? Would the next step in technology be the transatlantic bomber? What would happen if Britain surrendered? Would the Royal Navy end up in German hands? America's governing elite was well aware that if the Royal Navy suddenly collapsed, America would no longer have a buffer against the Nazi war machine. Despite three thousand miles of ocean, it would be vulnerable. These worries fired the emotional drive of the period, increasing the sense of urgency.

Donovan himself did not maneuver for the job of running the agency he proposed; he was still attracted by the prospect of renewing his military career in the event that America entered the war. Stephenson, however, had other ideas. He spent a lot of time pushing at doors that were already open, and he was anxious to urge Donovan as far as he could toward intelligence, where his own influence could be brought to bear through the American. He cabled Menzies at the beginning of May that he was "attempting to maneuver Donovan into accepting the job of coordinating all U.S. intelligence."[15] He had already played a vital part in Donovan's proposal, not only by suggesting the organization of a new agency but also by writing some of Donovan's report.

By the end of May, Donovan seems to have come round, declaring that Little Bill had "intrigued and driven him to the job."[16] He gave Roosevelt an additional paper, fleshing out his April proposal, arguing for a close working relationship between strategy and information and stressing the importance of coordinating economic warfare as well. "It is essential that we set up a central enemy intelligence organization, which would itself collect either directly or through existing departments of Government, at home and abroad, pertinent information concerning potential enemies." This information, he argued, should be analyzed not only by military experts but also by scholars, economists, psychologists, scientists, and technicians. The organization should be headed by a coordinator responsible directly to the President and advised by the heads of the other intelligence agencies. Just before lunch on July 11, 1941, accompanied by his friend Frank Knox and the President's legal draftsman, Ben Cohen, Donovan met Roosevelt in the Oval Office and was appointed coordinator of information. His instructions were to implement the proposals he had put forward. He was to act as the President's chief intelligence officer and coordinate the analysis and collection of information. He told William Stephenson the news immediately, and the British agent cabled London the same day. "You can imagine how relieved I am," he reported, "after three months of battle and jockeying for position in Washington that our man is in a position of such importance to our efforts."[17]

COORDINATOR OF INFORMATION, 1941

The creation of the Office of the Coordinator of Information (COI) along the lines proposed by Donovan was an event of major political importance. The United States had never before had a peacetime, civilian, centralized intelligence agency incorporating military concerns. Its creation was a significant step on two fronts. First, it meant that America was turning its back on isolationism. The country's leaders had recognized that America could not stand aside from the wider world. They had seen that the world outside it could have a direct effect on America: the war had affected trade, stirred up passionate feeling, and demanded that America take at least minimum steps to protect herself. Second, it was an important expansion of presidential power. Ben Cohen, who was responsible for drawing up the legal documents implementing the President's decision, understood that the new agency was not simply another New Deal organization. It was the result of executive fiat, drawing upon the President's authority as commander in chief, cutting through the balances among the executive, legislative, and judicial powers established by the Constitution. This was not trumpeted at the time—Roosevelt made no mention of his powers as commander in chief before Pearl Harbor—but it was the start of the emergence of the presidency as the preeminent governmental arm. When America entered World War II, the requirements of war began to highlight this development, which finally became what Arthur M. Schlesinger, Jr., called "the imperial presidency."

It is noteworthy that the first assertion of special presidential power was over the area of secrecy in government in peacetime. Thirty-five years later it was through the area of secrecy that the presidency would start to have its wings clipped by Congress. At all times Congress had the right to establish financial appropriations (which meant that it could effectively circumscribe the agency and the President) and, with the necessary majorities, overrule presidential moves. It did not exercise these rights in 1941 and for three decades following, because of the assumptions and attitudes of the time. There was a feeling that fifth columns were at work, conspiring against American interests. This feeling convinced Congress that it was necessary for the President to appropriate to himself vital intelligence information. Later there was a different feeling: that as long as secrecy was about foreign affairs, it was better not to know. This feeling was also apparent in 1941—Donovan constantly stressed that the purpose of his plans was the collection of information from abroad and the carrying out of operations that would be conducted or directed abroad—and it was strengthened when America entered the war.

Throughout this period there was a sense that both peace and war were possible and that it was necessary to plan for both. Although there was hope that the clock could be put back and America might remain uninvolved, no one suspected there could be an ambiguous state of neither war nor peace. No one questioned the right of the President or of military commanders to keep their plans and battle objectives secret. It was an epoch in which hero-leaders were willingly followed by a mass public that represented the nation's first radio generation. Hero-leaders could now be heard by their publics directly and simultaneously. Everybody sensed that immense impersonal forces had been unleashed.

On October 30, 1938, in a CBS broadcast, Orson Welles's Mercury Theater presented a radio play of H. G. Wells's *War of the Worlds.* Minutes after it had begun, its realism caused a nationwide panic. Over 1.2 million people took to the streets in fear that Martians really had landed. "Things have happened so thick and fast since my grandfather's day," said one person affected by the broadcast, "that we can't hope to know what might happen now."[18] The whole incident was symptomatic of the moment. Donovan's proposals, which were the blueprint for centralized intelligence in America to the present day, were framed in an atmosphere of tension, with a sense of impending conflict and an awareness that America needed to know a great deal more about the world if it were to maintain the democratic and liberal principles under attack from totalitarian governments.

Although only 252 words long—everything was left in general terms—the executive order setting up the COI captured much of this feeling. Money would come from the President's secret funds, thus avoiding detailed congressional scrutiny. The full job description of the director of COI, the President and Donovan agreed, should not be in writing. Instead, an all-embracing phrase summed it up: he was "to carry out, when requested by the President, such supplementary activities as may facilitate the securing of information important for national security."* Within the administration the meaning of all this was perceived in bureaucratic terms, which led to continuing friction between Donovan and the other intelligence agencies. "All the regular Army and Navy people were very suspicious of Donovan," according to James R. Murphy, a former law clerk of Donovan's who joined COI as Donovan's executive assistant. "They were always sure he would show up in some way or take away some of their jurisdiction. They figured if they let him come into their bailiwick, he'd be likely to take it over, he was so energetic and dynamic once he'd get on the trail of something." Their suspicions had justification, recalled Murphy. "The unwritten part of COI was the President's direction to Donovan to organize an undercover service. The other agencies did try to cooperate and coordinate with Donovan and his staff—it seems they were more willing to do it before Pearl Harbor than they were after it. But right from the beginning it was understood by those of us who were there that the important part of Donovan's job was to organize an intelligence service."[19]

Donovan's legal training and his method of preparing a case influenced the actual form of the COI and from it the subsequent central intelligence organizations. From the outset his background was reflected in the emphasis on analysis of information and not simply its collection. Donovan overwhelmed people with his information. In his law cases he would assemble all the relevant information he could find and then devote himself to analyzing it (not always very well). From this analysis would come his argument and his evidence, each point being carefully prepared and exhaustively sustained by the material he had assembled. A Donovan case was legendary in New York law circles for being encyclopedic in its approach. His weak sense of the crucial point in an argument was matched by his overpowering evidence. He had the American tendency to reach for quantity in a crisis rather than subtlety of approach. His arguments were lined up like field guns standing wheel to wheel, firing one after the other. And he brought the same emphasis on mass collection and analysis to the new organization. It was an area COI could shine in, largely be-

---

*Troy, *Donovan and the CIA*, pp. 70, 423. COI was an unequivocally civilian organization. Donovan agreed with the secretary for war, Henry Stimson, that his would be a civilian job rather than one tied into the military. (Military ties would have provided considerable advantages in terms of securing resources but would have made COI subject to military control and more distant from the President.) A clause of the executive order stated that the director of COI, "with the approval of the President," could have access to all other government departments, agencies, and sources of information, providing he did not "in any way interfere with or impair the duties and responsibilities of the regular military and naval advisers of the President as Commander in Chief of the Army and Navy." The executive order itself was not released to the press. Instead, when Stephen T. Early, the President's press secretary, announced the news of the creation of COI in mid-July 1941, he stayed away from specifics, later explaining that he had done so because much of the order was unclear in its meaning and was likely to lead to considerable questioning.

cause, initially, American intelligence collection was threadbare. The FBI had some agents in Latin America, the army and the navy had some attachés in North Africa, Europe, and the Far East, and that was about it. There were not ten Americans in June 1941 who had even rudimentary espionage skills, and from the start Donovan looked to the British for help and guidance.

For the British the creation of COI by no means marked the end of their interest. Their primary source of intelligence came from signals interception. So did America's. But because of their greater experience and sophistication, the British knew that a substantial number of America's cryptographic systems were compromised. This meant that the British were always anxious about giving their top secrets to America, but in order to have influence in Washington and in order to secure American confidence, they had to give something. The result was a masterpiece of juggling throughout the war, with the British constantly finding ways of giving information to the American armed services and the COI and its successor, the Office of Strategic Services, without revealing their real sources. Donovan was their favored conduit for information exchange, and he was probably personally informed by the British of their worries in the matter.

To the British, fighting for survival, nothing was worth compromising their sources of information. Signals intelligence overshadowed all their intelligence efforts. Its focus was the code-breaking units at Bletchley Park, which from 1940 onward managed to decipher many of the most secret German communications. Protecting this operation was Britain's intelligence priority throughout the war. At the same time they had to use their intelligence information in exchange for American assistance in other areas and to help Donovan establish COI, since effective and friendly American intelligence was very much in Britain's interests. Neutral America had sources denied to Britain. America in the war had enormous resources that would benefit Britain, releasing British resources to concentrate on British priorities.

Donovan threw himself into his new job with gusto. He was convinced that America's entry into the war on the side of the British was inevitable, and he spent his time trying to convince the army and navy that they should start preparing for it. For his part, he was preparing a methodology for American intelligence operation in the event of war. He had a wave theory that he expounded with great vehemence. There were three waves, he said: the first was the collection and analysis of information; the second was commando action to test enemy defenses; and the third was the invasion force. In each wave, intelligence played a vital role. Information needed to be marshaled for the first wave and used for a continuous propaganda offensive designed to unsettle and demoralize the enemy, thus beating the Nazis at their own game. In the second wave, accurate intelligence would inform and guide a campaign of guerrilla activity, subversion, and commando action. The third wave would be based upon the accumulated knowledge and experience of the first two. It was another

Donovan blueprint for the future and was to be followed by the CIA in Guatemala and Cuba fifteen and twenty years later.

The problem was that while Donovan's ideas were proper for war, they were more difficult to apply in peacetime. A propaganda campaign against an opponent in peacetime was one thing; launching an invasion force or a guerrilla campaign against him was another. And even on the first wave there were problems. Donovan disagreed with Robert Sherwood (a presidential speech writer and Pulitzer Prize-winning playwright who joined COI as head of the propaganda office): while Sherwood felt strongly that America's voice to the world should speak the truth, Donovan believed that America's voice should say whatever helped America.

The people Donovan collected for COI in 1941 were typical of those who were to dominate the CIA later. "He recruited a lot of people out of the social class which he looked up to," said one man who knew Donovan well in New York. "The result was that he hired some of the most incredible jerks!"[20] Others took a different view, among them James Murphy:

> Socially, financially, we had quite a gathering of Ivy League Wall Street people. Most of them whom I had contact with were very able people and made important contributions whenever they were called upon—Henry Morgan and Junius Morgan and Bill Vanderbilt. They worked hard. They came down to Washington and they kept regular hours and they paid their own expenses. Most of them didn't draw any salaries. They were anxious to do whatever they could do. Some of them were good at opening doors. Junius Morgan belonged to all the best clubs in London and had friends in high places there. There were lots of others who were hardworking, honest, loyal, motivated Americans.[21]

Archibald MacLeish, the noted poet and literary critic who was head of the Library of Congress, helped organize the "brain bureau"—a group of academics and specialists responsible for intelligence analysis. James Roosevelt, the President's son, transferred from the Marine Corps to COI to act as Donovan's emissary to the White House and other government departments. Colonel G. Edward Buxton, a personal friend of Donovan's from their days together in the American expeditionary Rainbow Division in France during World War I, joined as Donovan's unofficial deputy. He was one of the very few people Donovan trusted completely. It was generally recognized, and he used to say it of himself, that he cleaned up after Donovan. Donovan had the ideas; Buxton did the work.* Two Hollywood film directors, John Ford and Merian C. Cooper, joined to make films and devise effective presentation methods. Other recruits included writers, bankers, and diplomats. Their head-

---

*Buxton had been Sergeant York's commanding officer in World War I and had persuaded York not to be a conscientious objector.

quarters was established in the old State, War, Navy Building (now the Executive Office Building) beside the White House. Then it moved to the Apex Building before settling in the old public health office buildings in Foggy Bottom, beside the Potomac.

The first months of COI's existence were spent in organizing and detailing budgets.* Apart from its lack of intelligence-collection skills, COI did not have much time for collection as it recruited people and found offices. Here the British stepped in, anxious that the new agency should make its mark in intelligence as quickly as possible. In December the British set up a training school for COI people at a farm near Toronto, Canada. They provided Donovan with advice and information on any subject he requested. British intelligence officers were lent to COI, and COI officers were sent to work with Military Intelligence in Britain. William Stephenson was the contact. Donovan later said Stephenson taught COI everything it ever knew about foreign intelligence.

It would be a mistake, however, to think of COI as a clone of British Intelligence. It was heavily indebted to British experience, advice, and information, but it had a life of its own. David Bruce, who served as Donovan's liaison officer in London later in the war, made this point in 1946 when arguing for a postwar intelligence agency:

> Despite lack of cooperation from American intelligence services, COI had little difficulty in establishing the closest and most friendly relationships with foreign secret intelligence agencies. In this way it provided the War, Navy and State Departments with masses of material heretofore unknown to them. . . . The British, thoroughly familiar with our deficiencies, volunteered, in enlightened self-interest, to teach us their techniques, and to make us free of their information from all sources. As our armies, air forces and fleets began to fight abroad, our operational, as distinguished from our strategical intelligence, developed rapidly and successfully. American Army and Navy officers, the majority of whom were not professionals, aided by civilian specialists, adapted British operational intelligence techniques to their own requirements, frequently improving on them.[22]

In particular, Donovan's emphasis on research and analysis, in combination with operational objectives, gave COI a unique character. (See Appendix II.)

Despite his success in molding COI to the form he wanted, Donovan did not succeed in creating an all-embracing centralized intelligence agency. J.

---

*COI's first theoretical budget was $1,454,700, to be supplied from the President's secret funds of $100 million per year. Neither Ben Cohen nor Harold D. Smith, the director of the budget, expected COI to exceed this figure by any large amount. The consequences of Donovan's plans, however, were expensive, and by the end of August, COI was asking for a financial allocation of $10 million in its first year. Behind this request were not merely Donovan's plans but also the hardheaded administrative expertise of Thomas G. Early, an old Washington hand, who had joined COI as Donovan's assistant responsible for management and finance. By September, COI had a staff of forty and was advertising for more. For this background, see Troy, *Donovan and the CIA*, p. 77.

Edgar Hoover referred to the COI as "Roosevelt's folly" and made it clear to William Stephenson that its existence was not to affect their relationship. He also secured Roosevelt's approval for his proposal that the FBI, rather than COI, should continue to operate in South America. Nelson Rockefeller, appointed by Roosevelt as coordinator of inter-American affairs at the same time Donovan was appointed coordinator of information, won his fight to keep COI out of propaganda in South America. The armed services managed to retain their tactical and strategic intelligence interests, although in September and October 1941 the army and the navy gave COI their undercover intelligence operations.* The need for centralization was not yet clear to senior policy makers and the armed forces. "Owing to the attitude of the older services," David Bruce observed, "COI never reached its highest potential of success in intelligence. Much information that should have been made available to it for synthesis and analysis was withheld for purely captious reasons. MIS [Military Intelligence Service], for instance, refused to grant COI access to British reports on interrogation of German prisoners of war in the United Kingdom."[23]

---

*COI's analytical effort was, perhaps, its main achievement. With Archibald MacLeish, Donovan surveyed the staff and facilities of the Library of Congress. The first organizational charts of COI were drawn up by MacLeish's people. When COI was created, the library formed a Division of Special Information exclusively for it. Staffed by scholars drawn from universities, the new division was charged with research and analysis of a multidisciplined nature. The president of Williams College, Dr. James Phinney Baxter III, was chosen by Donovan to head the unit and the COI Board of Analysts. The board was composed of eight scholars, and its job was to review analysis and test conclusions and evidence. Specialist divisions—economics, geographical areas, psychology—reported to the board.

The system as planned was that the Library of Congress Division of Special Information would coordinate scholarship from within the library and academic centers, bringing it to bear on the policy options facing the President. Division reports would be refined by the Board of Analysts and, separately, by COI experts with access to secret information. Then Donovan himself would present the report to the President. It did not actually work this way—the board was soon by-passed—but the concept of research and analysis geared to practical and effective purpose survived. For the background, see Troy, *Donovan and the CIA*, pp. 84–109.

Donovan also emphasized the importance of radio as "the most powerful weapon" in the "psychological attack against the moral and spiritual defenses of a nation." He set up the Foreign Information Service within COI as an outright propaganda agency and monitoring service. It was staffed mainly by journalists. Beginning operations on August 1, 1941, it listened to Axis broadcasts and supplied U.S. news agencies and broadcasters with news stories and analysis. COI was also concerned with economic warfare, but this never became a significant element in its operations. A special operations group was established for espionage and covert actions. Its first step was to set up an Oral Intelligence Unit in New York to debrief refugees from fascist Europe and to collect from them items of clothing, papers, and personal belongings that agents might be able to use when operating in Europe. A Domestic Morale Unit was planned to survey American opinion, as was a commando group and a Visual Presentation Branch responsible for eye-catching filmed reports.

For the relationship between J. Edgar Hoover and William Stephenson, see Hyde, *The Quiet Canadian*, pp. 26–27, and William R. Corson, *The Armies of Ignorance: The Rise of the American Intelligence Empire* (New York: The Dial Press/James Wade, 1977), p. 140. For the territorial battles, see Troy, *Donovan and the CIA*, pp. 16–20, 103–104. For the military handover of undercover intelligence, see Corson, *The Armies of Ignorance*, pp. 145–147.

PEARL HARBOR

Before COI had a chance to take much shape, everything changed. The Japanese attack on Pearl Harbor on December 7, 1941, followed by Nazi Germany's and Fascist Italy's declarations of war against the United States on December 10, rapidly brought a wider appreciation of Donovan's arguments for centralized intelligence. Pearl Harbor caught the United States unprepared, not because intelligence agencies had no information indicating where and when the attack would take place (they had), and not because President Roosevelt, anxious to enter the war, suppressed the information (he did not), but because no one had put the information together and analyzed it accurately. Despite his title as coordinator of information, and despite the fact that by December 1941 Donovan's organization had taken over military undercover activities, it was not actually the repository of centralized intelligence and Donovan was not one of those with any advance information about Japanese intentions. Knowledge was centered in the Office of Naval Intelligence and the War Department, which, since the 1920s and the Black Chamber, had successfully broken the key Japanese military and diplomatic codes. Despite the importance of this major cryptanalytical operation, called Magic, Donovan was kept in ignorance of it.

Important intercepts, the raw material itself rather than the analyzed product that Donovan saw as essential, were passed directly to the President and his top advisers.* By 1939 the most secret Japanese code, named Purple by its U.S. Navy decrypters, was being used to keep Japanese embassies and diplomats informed about their government's policies and to send them instructions on negotiating positions. In August 1940 the Office of Naval Intelligence finally succeeded in breaking Purple. It took time to decode the messages, and several days usually passed before the President could be given an English text. By December 1941 the Magic operation had revealed fairly clearly that Japan was planning war and that the United States might be attacked at some point. But no one thought that Hawaii would be a target; it was far away from Japanese bases, and the risk of failure would be great. America's great defensive barrier to the west, the Pacific, was assumed to provide all the protection rea-

---

*This is a recurring theme in intelligence; raw material may look very convincing and may appear to contain precise information, but without knowledge of its source and the conditions influencing the information, it is potentially dangerous. It might be forged, or it might be from a double agent, or the intention might be to have it intercepted. It might be apparently unimportant on its own but vitally important when placed with other information. Donovan had all this in mind when he spoke about coordinated intelligence and the importance of research and analysis. As well as to the President, Magic raw material was passed to the secretaries of state, war, and the navy—in 1941 Cordell Hull, Henry L. Stimson, and Frank Knox, respectively—General George C. Marshall, the Chief of Staff, and Admiral Harold R. Stark, the Chief of Naval Operations. For the story of Magic, see David Kahn, *The Codebreakers* (London: Sphere Books, 1977), pp. 25–32, and Ronald Lewin, *The American Magic* (London: Penguin, 1982).

sonably required. The Philippines were thought to be a far more likely target, or perhaps further invasions by Japan of Thailand or the Dutch East Indies. As dawn broke in Hawaii on December 7, the U.S. naval base at Pearl Harbor was not on war alert.

Of the many repercussions the attack on Pearl Harbor had, none was greater than that on intelligence. The complete disorganization of the United States government revealed by Pearl Harbor won the argument for a director of central intelligence and a central intelligence agency. Everyone from the President on down saw that the continuing fragmentation of American intelligence had precluded adequate warning of the attack. Nearly two years later Donovan summed up the situation before Pearl Harbor. "The intelligence agencies of the United States were not geared to the demands of a World War," he said. "They had been caught unprepared. There was no overall general intelligence service which collected and analyzed information on which decisions should be made and plans formulated. There was no coordination of our various agencies of information, nor of the information itself. There was no Secret Intelligence nor Counter-Intelligence Service for working in enemy territory. There was no plan to meet these needs."[24] Donovan himself learned of the attack several hours after it took place through a telephone call from James Roosevelt, who was at the White House.

The United States had been caught napping when it could have been and should have been alert and prepared. Pearl Harbor provided the kind of argument politicians have to respond to, thus accelerating the development of centralized intelligence. It brought everything out into the open and made possible actions that had not been possible before. For the first time the President was expressly granted extensive powers to wage war in secret as well as in the open. It made secrecy in America's interests something everybody now wanted. "The attack on Pearl Harbor," said David Bruce, "startled us like some gigantic dissonant firebell in the night of our false security. We felt betrayed and indeed we were. We were betrayed by the complete failure of our intelligence agencies. Any intelligence service worthy of the name should have foretold this event."[25]

The breaking down of the deeply held prejudice that, in the words of Lieutenant General Hoyt S. Vandenberg, one of the first postwar directors of Central Intelligence, "there was something un-American about espionage and even about intelligence generally" was one of the key effects of Pearl Harbor. In evidence to the Senate Armed Services Committee in 1947 Vandenberg said:

The Pearl Harbor disaster dramatized [the need for a coordinated intelligence program] and stop-gap measures were adopted. I feel that the people of this country, having experienced the disaster of Pearl Harbor and the appalling consequences of a global war, are now sufficiently informed in their approach to intelligence to understand that an organization such as [the CIA], or the intelligence divisions of the armed services, or the FBI, cannot expose certain of their activities to public gaze. . . . Before Pearl Harbor we did not have an intelligence service in this country comparable to that of Great Britain, or France, or Russia, or Germany, or Japan. We did not have one because the people of the United States would not accept it. . . . There was a feeling that all that was necessary to win a war—if there ever were to be another war—was an ability to shoot straight. One of the great pre-war fallacies was the common misconception that, if the Japanese should challenge us in the Pacific, our armed services would be able to handle the problem in a matter of a few months at most. All intelligence is not sinister, nor is it an invidious type of work. But before the Second World War, our intelligence services had left largely untapped the great open sources of information upon which roughly 8o percent of intelligence should normally be based. I mean such things as books, magazines, technical and scientific surveys, photographs, commercial analyses, newspapers and radio broadcasts and general information from people with a knowledge of affairs abroad. What weakened our position further was that those of our intelligence services which did dabble in any of these sources failed to coordinate their results with each other."[26]

The intelligence failure was also a consequence of America's isolation, its "island state" psychology. "Our comparative geographic isolation," David Bruce observed five years later, "led us, erroneously, to consider ourselves invulnerable to attempts against our sovereignty. Our immediate concern was with internal affairs; the alarums and excursions of foreign wars seemed to us infinitely remote and somewhat ridiculous."[27] The President and his senior advisers knew that the sense of American invulnerability was an illusion, but the American electorate and Congress did not know this, nor did they want to think that America was vulnerable. Isolationism had been popular, so much so that Roosevelt had to tread very carefully in his efforts to provide embattled Britain with military aid in 1940 and 1941. Twenty years earlier, despite Wilson's efforts, America had withdrawn from world affairs and, ostrichlike, had put its head in the sand, hoping that the troubles of the world would pass it by. Pearl Harbor was a very rude awakening, shattering decades of illusion. No one would easily catch America unprepared again.

—2—

In the Service
of a Republic
1942-1945

The war suited William Donovan right down to the ground. He was in his element, constantly trying to get closer to the smell of cordite, rushing around the world setting up intelligence stations and approving covert operations. He was a romantic, and the glamour of uniforms and bravery strongly appealed to him. He had a habit of walking on the balls of his feet, "like a halfback who might suddenly swerve,"[1] and the impression he created everywhere was of bustling physical and intellectual energy. Half his schemes were brilliant; the other half were silly. This was Donovan's real problem: no one minds a dynamo of energy as long as his judgment is right, and Donovan's often was not. On one occasion he pressed President Roosevelt to receive Otto von Habsburg, the pretender to the Austrian throne, who had ideas about the anti-Nazi underground in Hungary. Roosevelt sensibly refused. The Habsburgs represented a pre–World War I world that the smaller nations of eastern Europe and the Balkans wanted to leave in the past. Receiving Otto would have seriously alarmed the Czechs, the Yugoslavs, the Hungarians, and the Russians concerning Allied intentions for the postwar world. On another occasion Donovan sent the President a proposal for building oil pipelines from plywood. He proposed sending Errol Flynn to Dublin to attempt to secure air and naval bases in neutral Southern Ireland.

Donovan was not alone in the matter of concocting madcap schemes: President Roosevelt himself took top honors with an idea that the Japanese were afraid of bats. Instead of finding out from reliable sources whether or not this was true (it was not), Roosevelt instructed Donovan to develop a way to take advantage of this supposed national phobia. For several years the COI and then the Office of Strategic Services cooperated with the Army Air Corps to catapult and parachute bats out of bombers flying over Japan. The experiments were ended only because the bats persisted in freezing to death at the high altitudes flown by the bombers.[2]

In the Washington power structure, where the conduct of subversive warfare and the debate about the shape of the postwar world were primary focuses, Donovan was an important figure. From the first days of America's entry into the war he was making suggestions to extend American influence in the Middle East—a traditional British preserve—after the war. Like Roosevelt, Donovan had no time for the old empires. Although he was attracted by the pomp and ceremony, by London clubland, by aristocracy and imperial titles, he was all too aware that the old empires had failed to stop totalitarian tyranny. Moreover, they had a selfish outlook on the world, viewing their possessions as their private concerns and shunning interference from outsiders. They wanted no part of free trade and the exchange of information and ideas. Throughout the war, despite the close collaboration with the British on all fronts, the top American policy makers knew well that in the postwar world, in which America would be firmly placed, there would be a struggle with their erstwhile allies. If anything, Donovan was too much of an Anglophile, an allegiance he would suffer for as the war came to an end and America stood on the threshold of its inheritance through victory—world power.

Among all Donovan's efforts, keeping the ear of the President was all-important. At the time of Pearl Harbor, Roosevelt received reports from ten different intelligence agencies, of which COI was just one. This was partly because there had been no intelligence coordination and partly because Roosevelt never trusted any one man or institution. When he agreed to the establishment of COI (and its successor, the OSS), he was agreeing to the creation of another channel of influence rather than to the replacement of existing ones. He never tried, for example, to force the FBI, the State Department, or the military to create a centralized intelligence service; this was something Donovan—not the President—tried to achieve. The protagonists of centralized intelligence liked to talk as if Donovan were successful, but in truth, Roosevelt never gave him the support he needed to succeed.[3]

Roosevelt used to describe himself as a quarterback, and he was correct: he liked to position himself while others around him quarreled and competed for his favor. From his point of view, Donovan was simply another competitor in the ring. Roosevelt was a cold and calculating man. When he died and his wife, Eleanor, found that he and Lucy Mercer Rutherford had been having a relationship for years with the connivance of everybody, she was furious. Eleanor had broken off conjugal relations with him in 1917, so her fury was somewhat surprising, causing her friends and family to take her anger seriously. Her daughter, Anna, said, "Mama, you must remember that father was a very lonely man." She had put her finger on her father's core. Roosevelt was an elementary man, with a boundless appetite for power. He had amazing charm, which he used unhesitatingly for his own advantage. He had a handful of relatively principled opinions centered on the need for a humane political-economic system and on the desirability of the preeminence of the United States. He had a limited intellectual drive, with little disinterested curiosity. The distinguished Washington commentator Arthur Krock considered Jack Kennedy to belong to a whole order of intelligence above Roosevelt's. Roosevelt once said that his great source of information about the outside world was his stamp collection. He was interested in acquiring information only to the extent that he could use it as a manipulative tool. His strength (apart from enormous courage, revealed by the way in which he dealt with his crippling polio) was an almost complete lack of personal or intellectual commitment. He was an improviser, who neither sought consistency nor believed in preparing for the future before it was absolutely necessary. This was the nature of the President who established Donovan as coordinator of intelligence. Donovan never realized the complex of calculation and improvisation behind the charm.

Donovan made the mistake of thinking that his drive for centralized intelligence under Roosevelt would be successful. He saw the creation of the Joint Chiefs of Staff in February 1942 as the umbrella grouping under which COI could act as overall intelligence coordinator. He realized that in war the armed forces would predominate and that it would be wise to link COI to military activity. This also appealed to him personally, giving rise to one of the basic themes of modern American intelligence: the commitment to political, psychological, and paramilitary action. Two weeks after Pearl Harbor, Donovan proposed to the President that COI take over "unorthodox warfare," outlining his wave theory in the process. The fruits of intelligence as analyzed by COI would inform planning and help shape propaganda. Propaganda would be the arrow that would initially penetrate enemy territory. Then special operations in the form of sabotage and fifth columns would follow. Commando raids and behind-the-lines harassment would be the prelude for invasion.*

*From *War Report of the OSS*. Prior to Pearl Harbor, Donovan made no formal request for authorization of guerrilla operations. After Pearl Harbor he constantly recommended to the President that subversive activities and guerrilla units be considered in strategic planning. A memorandum to the President on December 22, 1941, clearly indicates the importance he placed on propaganda: "I fear, however, that there may be no suggestion that an integral and vital part of such plan would be the preparation and conditioning of those people and those territories where the issue is to be fought." Propaganda was something Roosevelt was also interested in. Roosevelt, ever the politician, used radio effectively to by-pass Congress and journalists, reaching out to the American electorate directly. Propaganda was seen fundamentally as the opportunity to talk directly to the enemy peoples and to those in the countries occupied by them.

For a discussion of the bureaucratic maneuvering in the weeks following Pearl Harbor, see William R. Corson, *The Armies of Ignorance* (New York: The Dial Press/James Wade, 1977), pp. 164–168; Rhodri Jeffreys-Jones, *American Espionage: From Secret Service to CIA* (New York: Free Press, 1977), p. 165; and Thomas F. Troy, *Donovan and the CIA* (Frederick, Md.: University Publications of America, 1981), pp. 131–134. One of the first things the Joint Chiefs did was to urge the integration of COI with the military high command. Early in March 1942

One of Donovan's first specific propaganda proposals was to encourage the Japanese to attempt to achieve impossible war goals—to undertake military actions that would overextend their resources and demoralize the national spirit. Roosevelt was receptive to these proposals, which were numerous enough to keep Donovan in the President's mind. (Occasionally the constancy of Donovan's ideas created a mild backfire. In April 1942, for example, Roosevelt remarked that he was thinking of putting Donovan "on some nice, quiet, isolated island where he could have a scrap with some Japs every morning before breakfast . . . [and] would be out of trouble and entirely happy.")[4] Another imaginative Donovan idea was the creation of a war room designed for the President. This room would epitomize Donovan's integrated intelligence concept and would be a key element in COI's visual-presentation branch, whose purpose was to illustrate intelligence analysis and information in eye-catching ways. The idea was publicized in an article by Arthur Krock in *The New York Times* on October 8, 1941. The room would contain, wrote Krock, "a huge globe, lighted from within," upon which could be traced the progress of the war as well as plans and quantitative information, so that "the tired mind of the President" could easily assimilate the information.[5] The plan was for an entire building devoted to the presentation of information, with twelve "theater rooms," each concentrating on a particular theater of war, an "economic room," an "inner sanctorium" for the most secret matters, and a "big room" where the major aspects of the world situation could be displayed. There would be a car ramp so the President could drive directly into the building.

Donovan asked for $3.8 million for the project, known as Q-2. Roosevelt personally approved $2 million.[6] Control of Q-2 was bitterly contested by the military, who saw that it would provide not only direct access to the various elements of COI but also to the policy makers—particularly the President—for whoever controlled it. Behind the contest lay a view of intelligence as a coin of influence rather than as a repository of secrets whose existence was not to be revealed. The Q-2 idea generated considerable debate, but ultimately the project never got past the planning stage. It was vetoed by the Secret Service, whose job was to protect the President. The Secret Service argued that if Q-2 were built anywhere except in the White House, the President would be vul-

---

they commissioned a study of the ways the military services could best use the facilities of COI. The study analyzed each element of COI, and, beginning with the observation that COI was not fully efficient because it was not sufficiently integrated with the military, it proceeded to suggest the dissolution of the organization. Just because the concept of coordinated, centralized intelligence was accepted, this did not mean that Donovan, the father of the concept, should have anything to do with it, as far as the military were concerned. Donovan countered with a separate proposal for cooperation between COI and the Office of Naval Intelligence, the army's G-2, and the new Army Air Force's A-2. The Joint Intelligence Committee, formed by the Joint Chiefs and consisting of representatives of the army, navy, State Department, Board of Economic Warfare, and COI, might have provided a coordinating group that COI could dominate (it appears that Donovan hoped that this would happen), but it soon disintegrated into subcommittees and paper.

nerable to personal attack as he drove along a regular route from the White House to the war room and back.

BUREAUCRATIC BATTLES

During the first months of 1942 Donovan showed his mettle as a bureaucratic fighter in dealing with the military. One of the reasons he wanted a military rather than a civilian alliance during the war was that intelligence and subversive activities would have to be geared to military interests. Worried about the consequences of placing military security and operations in the hands of civilians, the military proposed to the President that the various components of COI be split among the military services.* Donovan argued for the retention of COI as a complete organization under the control of the Joint Chiefs. The particular stumbling block in negotiations between Donovan and the Joint Chiefs was the control of covert operations. Donovan argued that they could not be run on traditional military lines; individuals with imagination rather than large military staffs were required. Donovan fought tenaciously to retain control of the Special Service units he set such store by. He won because he assured the military that groups and agents behind the lines would ultimately be dependent upon military support and would not operate without the approval of the theater commander. The result was an agreement between the Joint Chiefs and COI at the end of March 1942, leading to Donovan's writing to the President supporting a proposal of the Joint Chiefs for integrating COI with the military.[7] Ten weeks went by before anything happened. The State Department and the Bureau of the Budget also had ideas about the nature of intelligence and what should happen to COI during the war, and they were lobbying Roosevelt too.

In the State Department the assistant secretary of state, Adolf Berle, took an interest in intelligence. A veteran of World War I military intelligence, Berle now had personal clout in the Roosevelt administration as a friend of the President, a staunch Democrat, and an early New Dealer. Not wanting to see the State Department being elbowed aside by the war, he fought for control of propaganda. With the support of Nelson Rockefeller and J. Edgar Hoover he took complaints about Donovan's activities directly to the President. "It would be of help to us," he said in January 1942, "if we knew exactly what picture the President had of Bill's functions."[8] J. Edgar Hoover took more abrasive action when confronted with COI actions that he believed stepped on the FBI's terri-

---

*Major General George V. Strong, G-2 in 1942–44, vehemently opposed OSS and nearly succeeded in strangling it at its birth. He called it "a hydra-headed organization" under "an ambitious and imaginative Director" who was "constantly at war with other Government agencies." When COI came to an end, Strong argued that there should be no replacement agency (Troy, *Donovan and the CIA*, pp. 147, 205). J. Edgar Hoover was another antagonist. In 1924, when Donovan was assistant attorney general, he opposed Hoover's appointment as director of the FBI in an action Hoover never forgot.

torial toes. When he discovered one evening that COI agents had broken into the Spanish Embassy in Washington to photograph documents they thought might reveal secret Spanish support for Nazi Germany, he ordered several squad cars to go to the embassy and sound their sirens outside, forcing the COI men to flee. But while Hoover had no objections in principle to clandestine activity, Berle had scruples, and their budding alliance faltered on Berle's idealism—a harbinger of things to come in the 1960s and 1970s.

Berle was a third-generation American, imbued with the German liberalism of the 1848 revolutions, the failure of which had driven his grandfather to emigrate. His opposition to Donovan's COI was based on a feeling that government can easily be corrupted. It was the highly developed instinct of an intelligent man who understood that organizations can get out of control. "Paranoid work" was what Berle called espionage and subversive warfare, and he wanted to be rid of it altogether. "Navigating the rapids in the next few months is going to be difficult, if not impossible," he said in February, "and it will require pretty careful steering to remain both honest and American, and at the same time see that all of the interests which have marched together are kept together, going in the same direction and for an ultimate victorious, and I hope somewhat idealistic, end."[9] These feelings were shared to some extent by Robert Sherwood, head of COI's propaganda group, the Foreign Information Service, who wrote to Harold Smith, director of the Bureau of the Budget, on March 7, 1942, proposing that the Information Service leave COI and, with other information agencies, be formed into a new Office of War Information. Smith thought this was a very good idea and proposed it to Roosevelt.

Had Donovan chosen the right allies in the Joint Chiefs? Or would the civilian arguments of Berle, Rockefeller, Hoover, and Smith—representing as they did major agencies of government—prevail? The answer would govern the future development of American intelligence. By mid-June, Roosevelt had made up his mind. Victory in the war was his priority now rather than involvement in Washington intrigues and battles. Convinced that an Office of War Information would be more effective than different departments and agencies giving out uncoordinated information, he established the office. COI lost its Foreign Information Service. At the same time, Roosevelt rejected the idea of breaking up COI any further, accepting the recommendation of Donovan and the Joint Chiefs for the integration of COI with the military. On June 13, 1942, the military Office of Strategic Services (OSS), replacing COI, was established by a presidential military order. William Donovan was appointed its director.* Donovan had sided with the winning team, but in doing so he had helped set the parameters of American intelligence within the context of war.

*Military Order, June 13, 1942:

(1) The office of Coordinator of Information established by Order of July 11, 1941, exclusive of the foreign information activities transferred to the Office of War Information by Executive Order of June 13, 1942, shall hereafter be known as the Office of Strategic Services, and is hereby transferred to the jurisdiction of the United States Joint Chiefs of Staff.

After the war the idea of a peacetime centralized, civilian intelligence agency would be more difficult to achieve. Because of this decision, intelligence would be seen as a military activity. The battle to control intelligence was not between elected representatives and unelected appointees. Rather, it was between two sets of appointees: the military on one side and a combination of the FBI and the State Department on the other.

The new arrangement with the OSS under the jurisdiction of the Joint Chiefs of Staff, however, also had long-term advantages. The OSS was only nominally military. Not everyone in it had a rank, and even those who did found that rank bore little relationship to responsibility. Moreover, its people were not subject to direct orders from anyone outside OSS except in theaters of war. Donovan recognized the importance of these new arrangements "in having our Joint Chiefs of Staff do something which has never been done in our military history. That is, to take in as part of their organization a civilian unit."[10] The outcome of this relationship was crucial, for it was the military that ultimately shielded the idea of centralized intelligence after the war. By making a point of working harmoniously with the military during the war, Donovan avoided damaging bureaucratic battles with them and gained quiet support for his ideas (although not for him personally) in the early postwar years. The military wanted intelligence as long as it was *theirs*.*

Viewed by politicians as an entrenched bureaucracy and not as a group that could compete with them in elective politics, the military was seen at one and the same time as no political threat and as crucially important to anyone wanting a solid base of political and bureaucratic influence in Washington after 1945. They possessed the prestige of victory, and as the cold war with the Soviet Union progressed into a series of arms races, they exercised considerable pull in Congress. Agreeing to locate a military installation or sign an arms contract with a firm in a particular congressional district or state could attract a

---

(2) The Office of Strategic Services shall perform the following duties: (a) Collect and analyze such strategic information as may be required by the United States Joint Chiefs of Staff. (b) Plan and operate such special services as may be directed by the United States Joint Chiefs of Staff. (3) At the head of the Office of Strategic Services shall be a Director of Strategic Services who shall be appointed by the President and who shall perform his duties under the direction and supervision of the United States Joint Chiefs of Staff. (4) William J. Donovan is hereby appointed as Director of Strategic Services.

Donovan had a personal interview with Roosevelt before the order was made, and he argued for the Joint Chiefs' proposal. Roosevelt, Donovan later recalled, said, " 'They'll absorb you.' I said, 'You leave that to me, Mr. President!' I knew the rumors that were going around that JCS wanted to get us under their control and then tear the agency apart piece by piece and scuttle me, but I explained to Roosevelt that the JCS were the ones who would win the war, so that was the place for the agency to be." For background information, see Troy, *Donovan and the CIA*, pp. 118–164, 427.

*The military was never homogenous, and Donovan had powerful enemies, such as General Strong, in certain military quarters. Donovan's friends in the military, who included General George Marshall and the high command in Washington, tended to be oriented toward Europe. Field and theater commanders were often suspicious of the OSS (although there were some notable exceptions).

great deal of congressional support. With military loyalties usually transcending the passing moments of political life, military officers are often entrusted by presidents with sensitive jobs and with jobs of long-term importance to the nation. Richard Nixon used General Alexander Haig in this way; Eisenhower and Truman used General Walter Bedell Smith. (Truman used Smith as ambassador to Russia and as an early and very important director of Central Intelligence; Eisenhower used him as undersecretary of state, where, rumor had it, his job was to report on John Foster Dulles, the secretary of state.) President Reagan used General Vernon Walters as a roving troubleshooter and emissary.

OFFICE OF STRATEGIC SERVICES, 1942

In December 1942 the Joint Chiefs finally agreed to a directive for the OSS, putting it officially into the business of sabotage, espionage, counterespionage, and covert action—hallmarks that were to stay on in the CIA. In October 1943 the Joint Chiefs extended the OSS charter, acknowledging the agency as international in scope and charging it with another responsibility, also to become a CIA characteristic. "The Office of Strategic Services," the Joint Chiefs directed, "is responsible for the execution of all forms of morale subversion including false rumors, 'freedom stations,' false leaflets and false documents, the organization and support of fifth column activities by grants, trained personnel and supplies and the use of agents, all for the purpose of creating confusion, division and undermining the morale of the enemy."[11] The loss of the Foreign Information Service had made very little difference. Propaganda had military use, so the OSS would engage in it. In the bustle of war it was not noticed that a secret agency could in practice do anything unless it was specifically prohibited from doing so. This was to be another OSS legacy to the CIA. It did not matter if there was an Office of War Information responsible for propaganda; if its operating requirements included propaganda, the OSS would provide the propaganda itself.

In meeting its wide-ranging brief, by war's end the agency had about twenty-five thousand people on its books, some permanent, some temporarily attached to it. Despite its growing ranks, the OSS lacked a formal hierarchy—a situation that often caused great confusion to outsiders. Noncommissioned OSS men were sometimes in charge of operations involving commissioned officers in subordinate roles. Arthur M. Schlesinger, Jr., a U.S. Army corporal in the OSS, and several colleagues were responsible for the OSS Reports Section in Paris after the liberation of France in 1944. Schlesinger personally took the initiative in rejecting a plan proposed by the American communist Noel Field and backed by the OSS chief in Switzerland, Allen Dulles, to ally with German communists in forming a German anti-Nazi underground.[12] In Yugoslavia an OSS lieutenant in the American mission to Tito asked by a colonel to encode a message protested that it could wait until the next day's radio contact. The colonel tried reasoning: "I'll admit it's not much fun coding but that's true of lots of things in the army. Orders, after all, are orders in the army." "Army?" the lieutenant asked. "Did you say army? Hell, man, we're not in the army. We're in the OSS."[13]

At the end of the war in Europe the OSS mounted an operation code-named Paperclip to seize German scientists and prevent them from falling into the hands of the Russians.* When OSS Lieutenant Mroz, who was dispatched with a unit on this operation, confronted an American lieutenant colonel in the field who would not cooperate, Mroz pulled a gun on the colonel and managed to round up the scientists he was after. He was subsequently court-martialed. Donovan testified for him, although in fact he was personally deeply offended by Mroz's flouting of army discipline. "I'd rather have a young lieutenant with guts enough to disobey an order," said Donovan in Mroz's defense, "than a colonel too regimented to think and act for himself."[14] The freewheeling style of the OSS was a real attraction, generating a postwar mystique about it and intelligence.

The "Oh So Social" catchphrase of the OSS was matched by another—the "Oh So Socialist." While a staunch Republican, Donovan never allowed his political views to interfere with the running of the agency. "I'd put Stalin on the OSS payroll if I thought it would help us defeat Hitler," he said.[15] Ex-communists, communists, Marxists, socialists—all were employed in the OSS, a fact seized upon by opponents and stoutly defended by Donovan. "You can have an organization that is so secure it does nothing," he said after the war. "You have to take chances . . . If you're afraid of the wolves, you have to stay out of the forest."[16] Members of the Abraham Lincoln Brigade, which had been sponsored by the American Communist party to fight against fascism in Spain during the 1936–39 civil war, were used by the OSS as behind-the-lines agents. They were some of the best agents in the war. An OSS Labor Branch, under a Chicago attorney, Arthur Goldberg—who would later become President Kennedy's secretary of labor, a Supreme Court justice, and ambassador to the United Nations—maintained contacts with labor unions in occupied Europe. Anticommunists were also in the agency. Prince Serge Obolensky and a number of fiercely anticommunist Russian émigrés formed a clique. Paul Mellon, scion of the great industrial family, and his brother-in-law, David Bruce, a millionaire in his own right, joined the Morgans and William Vanderbilt in the OSS.

---

*Paperclip was the operation that brought Wernher von Braun and his team of V-1 and V-2 experts to the United States. Dr. Arthur Louis Hugo Randolph, who in 1984 renounced his U.S. citizenship and returned to Germany to avoid extradition hearings, was one of these scientists. He had controlled the slave-labor factory in the Harz mountains, Mittlewerk Dora, during World War II, having joined the Nazi party in 1931 and the paramilitary SA (storm troopers) in 1933. In 1984 charges were brought against him for war crimes. In the thirty-five years he worked for the U.S. Army and the National Aeronautic and Space Administration he designed the Pershing missile and supervised production of the Saturn 5 rocket, which put the Skylab space station into orbit and twelve Apollo astronauts on the moon. He was awarded the Distinguished Service Medal, NASA's highest honor (*The Washington Post*, November 4, 1984).

Recruitment was fairly evenhanded within the conventions of war agencies, but it was possible for those inclined to do so to see plots of the left and of the right. One OSS officer, who had worked with the Italian resistance, later made an impassioned complaint charging that the agency was filled with

> Republican businessmen who sported themselves in the OSS enjoying the thought of sending packages of arms, money, food, etc., by parachute, but who didn't really care if they got there during this or the next moon, while all the time poor devils in the mountains slaved at building fires in the snow, waiting, hoping, night after night, till the whole village, the whole mountain, the whole countryside, knew what was about to happen, and by the time the parachute *did* drift to earth, some "bulgar" had betrayed the operation, and the Fascists and the Germans would be waiting on the spot ready to kill and maim the partisans who were doing their best to aid the Allied cause.[17]

A completely different view was expressed by another OSS officer, who learned in June 1944 that he had been selected for an undercover mission in Italy "and that a friend in the government who wanted at least a few soldiers on it who were both anti-fascist and anti-communist had dropped my name in the hat.... Shortly thereafter OSS dropped me as being 'too anti-communist.' "[18] Hilaire du Berrier, a right-wing American journalist, interned by the Japanese for three years before being rescued by an OSS team near the end of the war and recruited as an Indochina expert, served for some months in the agency and then resigned, complaining that OSS's "left wing, through its directness of purpose and teamwork, managed to squeeze those on the right out of the organization."[19] The vast majority of OSS people, however, like Donovan, submerged their politics in pursuit of the war effort.

A large number of America's most distinguished public servants since the war had their first government-service experience in the COI and OSS. Four directors of Central Intelligence were OSS officers: Allen Dulles, who was an OSS agent in Switzerland; Richard Helms, who served in England, France, and Germany; William Colby, who fought in OSS teams behind the lines in France and Norway; and William Casey, who served for a period in London.

> My introduction to OSS was to be rushed off to a training camp in the Maryland countryside known as Area E [recalled Richard Helms]. There we were warned to use only first names, to try to spy out the backgrounds of our classmates, and to learn how to handle ourselves in life or death situations. Col. Fairbairn, once of the Shanghai police, later trainer of the famed British commandos, taught us the deadly arts, mostly in hand-to-hand combat. Within fifteen seconds I came to realize that my private parts were in constant jeopardy. I will not describe the unpleasant techniques taught, except to point out that Fairbairn's method of dealing with a hysterical woman was to grab her lower lip, then give her a resounding slap on the face. If the fear of being disfigured by move #1 did not sober her up, move #2 might. In short, the good Colonel's theory was that gentlemanly combatants tended to end

up dead, and he persuaded us that this was the proper attitude in the area of self-defense. If some of us brought a tough outlook into CIA a few years later, it is hardly surprising.[20]

Men such as Helms became the founding fathers of the CIA. Others achieved distinction elsewhere. David Bruce, OSS chief in London during the war, later served as ambassador to France, West Germany, the United Kingdom, and NATO. He was the chief negotiator at the Paris peace talks of 1970–71, which led to the American withdrawal from Vietnam, and chief of mission to Peking before full diplomatic relations were restored by Richard Nixon. Presidential advisers Walt Rostow, Arthur Schlesinger, Jr., Douglass Cater, and Carl Kaysen all served in the OSS.

The activities of the OSS were varied and widespread. Early on it faced administrative difficulties because of the British Secret Intelligence Service (SIS), which sought—successfully—to establish its preeminence. "In the beginning, we had nothing but what they furnished us," recalled James Murphy.[21] On the operational side it was the same. The British Special Operations Executive (SOE), responsible for organizing and supplying resistance groups, worked as the senior partner with the OSS. Reginald Spink, deputy head of SOE's Danish section in 1942, reported that "SOE and OSS were fully integrated in Baker Street [SOE's London headquarters] in the later stages of the occupation. OSS loyally accepted SOE's prior interest, seniority and longer experience of the territory, and relations between British and American as well as Danish officers in the section were never anything but cordial."* There were, of course, exceptions, but in general the OSS accepted

---

*Letter to the editor, *Times Literary Supplement*, October 19, 1984, p. 1187. As far as the British were concerned, OSS had little to offer in intelligence matters. When America entered the war, the British had already been fighting for over two years. They were dealing with myriad intelligence organizations of governments-in-exile and were afraid that the new and inexperienced OSS would muddy the waters. On August 4, 1942, reflecting these worries, the OSS was ordered by the Joint Chiefs to carry out no operations without the consent of the theater commander, as Donovan had agreed when OSS was set up. The British had pressed the Joint Chiefs to exercise even greater control over the OSS than this, but Donovan's argument that the OSS should have independent rights also carried weight. The OSS was an intelligence arm of the United States and should be able to conduct itself independently of the British. Still, the Joint Chiefs' order was seen by the OSS as "playing into the hands of SIS in the latter's efforts to curtail the development of an independent American SI Service."

After the successful Allied invasion of North Africa in 1943, OSS operations worked more happily from Algiers under an American theater commander, away from the control of the British and SIS. This in itself was, of course, a reflection of the balance of power between the British SIS and SOE and the OSS during the war: OSS was frozen out of the most important fields. Its largest military detachment, Detachment 101, operated in Burma, away from the war's center. Its operational centers were in such places as Algiers, on the fringe of warfare. Not until the period immediately preceding D-Day did the British allow OSS to mount its own operations in Europe. In the eastern Mediterranean, centered in Cairo, relations with the British were particularly uneasy, leading to the creation in February 1943 of a joint controlling committee to arbitrate disputes. For the background, see F. H. Hinsley, E. E. Thomas, C. F. G. Ransom, and R. C. Knight, *British Intelligence in the Second World War* (London: Her Majesty's Stationery Office, 1981), Vol. 2, pp. 53–54, and the *War Report of the OSS*, Vol. 2, pp. 6–8.

British seniority up to D-Day (June 6, 1944), although operationally there was a lack of trust between them. If the OSS appointed a lieutenant as a liaison officer or in command of an OSS operation, the British would appoint a captain. The British wanted the OSS as a partner, but a junior one.

The situation started to change after D-Day, when the far greater resources of OSS began to be deployed, and in some war theaters OSS effectively took charge. In the Far East this was generally the case by 1945. In the Middle East and the Adriatic area, particularly in Greece, the OSS took over supply responsibility (under overall SOE control). In 1945 when SOE withdrew its teams from Greece, the OSS was left with six of its own groups in place. "Our very close relations with British intelligence remained good but not nearly as close," said Lawrence Houston of this period. "Our interests were growing apart in the Middle East."[22] The one-two relationship, however, also had advantages for both organizations. On the one hand, it enabled the British Secret Service to concentrate on their priorities while enjoying the much larger global spread and resources of the OSS. On the other, it gave the OSS much more than access to SOE training camps in Canada and instructors like Colonel Fairbairn. It gave them British intelligence about the Caribbean and Latin America (from which the OSS was excluded by the FBI) and the benefit of British experience and analysis. When the British Secret Service scored its most important intelligence coup of the war—the breaking of the top-security German codes, known as the Ultra secret—they shared their information with OSS counterintelligence (X-2). "Our first access to cable information was from the British," said James Murphy, OSS counterintelligence head. "Until we made the arrangement with the British to have access to Ultra, G-2 [U.S. Army intelligence] would never even let us read the digest of the Japanese Magic material! With Ultra, things began to change. The British set it up and monitored it. We had a very secure system."

Donovan, however, was not particularly interested in this side of the intelligence business. He far preferred the thrills of commando and guerrilla operations on the one hand and the intellectual excitement of research and analysis on the other. He was a classic intuitionist. According to James Murphy:

> He thought that if you used your talents and research facilities properly, you could outsmart the enemy simply by the use of brainpower. He did not give a lot of worth to professionalism in intelligence gathering, such as secret intelligence. When I was operating a counterespionage facility, he used to complain now and again saying, "You people are becoming too professional!" I knew what he meant: he thought we were relying too much upon information gathered, without relying upon our intellectual capacity in analyzing it and making proper use of it. He did not pay a lot of attention to the traffic of Magic or Ultra. It may be that he distrusted it, but it never had an important role in his mind.[23]

Tension between the intelligence-analysis and intelligence-collection functions of secret agencies is nearly always present. Thirty years later this conflict had a dramatic effect on the CIA when Admiral Stansfield Turner, President Carter's director of Central Intelligence, chose to emphasize collection at the expense of analysis. Many people won and lost jobs on a large scale in consequence, and the controversy sparked a public debate on the relative merits of collection and analysis. Richard Helms referred to the debate as "the interplay between humans and gadgets,"[24] and argued strongly, in the Donovan tradition, that there is no substitute for analysis: collection should never become an end in itself.

Some of the Donovan traditions dominated not only the OSS but the first twenty-five years of the CIA.* Apart from gathering together a collection of extremely able, unusually talented people, valuing research and analysis, and focusing on paramilitary activity, Donovan handed on a can-do, try-anything philosophy. He considered plans to kidnap Hitler in 1944 and actually authorized an attempt to capture Mussolini, but a German special operations team beat him to it.† He was willing to buck systems and to allow good people to use their wits and judgment. This hallmark of the OSS was passed on to the CIA.

Richard Helms, when a young lieutenant in the OSS, met Donovan for the first time in Washington in 1944 after a very difficult scandal in London involving the British, the Free French intelligence service, and General Charles de Gaulle, the Free French leader. At their headquarters on Duke Street the Free French had illegally imprisoned people who they suspected were double agents infiltrated by the Nazis into their forces. Some, it was rumored, were tortured to death. When one suspect managed to escape, he brought personal charges against de Gaulle, which the French leader refused to acknowledge. Although the accuser ultimately dropped the charges, the situation created enormous difficulty for the British judicial system. Helms, a junior officer, with no involvement in the scandal, suddenly found himself in the thick of it:

> Colonel Passy, whose real name was André de Wavrin, had been under fire in London for what were known as the Duke Street murders. Frenchmen under interrogation had allegedly died in the basement of the Free French intelligence headquarters. A few days before, Colonel Atherton Richards, a senior OSS officer, phoned me out of the blue, verified that I had been a newspaperman and could speak French, informed me that I was to join him and two

---

*Some of Donovan's qualities were not handed on. He had a short attention span; the CIA does not. He had a willingness to rush into things; the CIA does not. Donovan's OSS was full of excitement; the CIA is full of chilly professionalism.

†Mussolini was arrested and imprisoned in a mountain hotel by right-wing Italians in 1944. He was rescued in a brilliant glider raid by Otto Skorzeny, commander of a special SS detachment, and brought to Germany before returning to German-occupied northern Italy as head of a Nazi puppet regime there.

other officers as an escort group to take Colonel Passy and two French subordinates on a tour of the United States. My assignment was to ensure that there was *no* press coverage. At the airport to greet the French visitors I approached General Donovan with considerable trepidation, and the following exchange took place: "General Donovan, what about publicity in connection with this visit?" "We don't want any." "I know, but what if some newspaperman asks me whether it is true that Colonel Passy is in this country?" "That's what *you're* here for, Lieutenant." And the general walked away. There was no press coverage.[25]

THE UNCERTAIN ALLY

Donovan was entirely dependent on the President for his bureaucratic power. Thus when he apparently decided in late 1944 that the Red Army in occupied territory should become an intelligence target for the United States, he found himself without support, because Roosevelt would not agree. This did not stop Donovan from monitoring the Russians, but it did stop him from developing any significant capacity against them. Lieutenant Colonel Paul West, Donovan's representative in Greece (who had entered the country to prepare the way for OSS operations despite the attempts of the British theater commander to keep him out), reported communist efforts to dominate the resistance movement early in 1944. According to West, the communists were trying to subvert Greek royalist groups and control contacts between the Greek resistance and the Allies.[26] In Rumania in the autumn of 1944 an OSS mission under the command of Frank Wisner, a former Wall Street lawyer who became one of the OSS's top operatives, began one of the first operations against the Russians in what was to become the cold war. At the end of September 1944 Major Robert Bishop, who was one of Wisner's officers in Bucharest, contacted a top-secret unit of Rumanian intelligence that, ever since the Russian revolution of 1917, had penetrated the underground Rumanian Communist party. Since this unit was unknown to the Russian intelligence services, the information it provided was considered highly reliable. Its agents supplied Bishop with convincing evidence of Soviet plans to take over the country, despite the fact that in August 1944 King Michael of Rumania had broken with Nazi Germany, obtained an armistice with the Soviet Union, and declared war on Germany.

For nearly a year the "Bishop traffic," as it was called, detailed Russian plans not only in Rumania but in eastern Europe as a whole. It revealed that, despite Stalin's assurances to the contrary, the Soviet Union actually planned to force the creation of a pro-Soviet Eastern bloc between Russia and the West in Europe after the war. Wisner, who would later become one of the CIA's arch cold-war hawks, immediately grasped the significance of the Bishop traffic and pressed for measures to counteract the Soviet plans, but to no avail. When Wisner was transferred from Bucharest in March 1945, the Bishop traffic also ended. Somehow the Russians had found out about the OSS operation. They arrested the Rumanian intelligence officers involved—who were never seen again.[27] Because of such experiences, Donovan was convinced earlier than many others of the coming struggle with the Soviet Union.

The clearest demonstration of Donovan's awareness of the Soviet threat came through an extraordinary intelligence coup. In November 1944 the OSS mission in Sweden obtained some fifteen hundred pages of Soviet codes, including their intelligence codes, from the Finnish intelligence service. The Russians did not know that the codes had been compromised and were still using them. Nevertheless, after informing Roosevelt of this coup and of the potential value of the codes, Donovan was ordered by the President to hand back the material, uncopied, to the Russians. Instead, Donovan secretly photographed the codes. These copies were later used by the FBI to decode postwar Russian communications.[28] The intelligence gathered provided evidence against the British traitor Donald Maclean and the Rosenberg spy ring. This affair, as well as the growing volume of reports from OSS agents in Europe warning of Soviet-backed communist attempts to dominate resistance movements, with an eye to political control in the postwar world, convinced Donovan that the Soviet threat was real.* By the winter of 1944 he had begun on his own to prepare for East-West confrontation. It was the start of what was in effect a secret foreign policy, which found form only when America formally recognized the cold war in 1947.

It was ironic that Donovan was also one of the few high government officials in the West who really tried to cooperate with Soviet intelligence. In December 1943, while on a visit to Russia, he discussed with his Soviet counterparts a plan to exchange OSS and Russian missions in Washington and

---

*Edward Stettinius, the secretary of state, opposed the purchase of the Soviet codes from the start. Upon learning that Donovan had gone ahead with the purchase, Stettinius protested directly to Roosevelt. According to Stettinius' notes, Roosevelt told him "to see that the Russians were informed of this matter at once." By February 15, 1945, the original pages of codes had been turned over to the Soviet ambassador in Washington, Andrei Gromyko. In another case, Donovan demonstrated that his anti-Naziism was greater than his fear of the Soviet Union. Wilhelm Hoettl, deputy chief of the Gestapo's foreign intelligence section, offered the OSS his Balkan spy network shortly before the Nazi surrender in 1945. In June—nearly four weeks after V-E Day—Donovan tested Hoettl's radio links to see if there really were any Nazi agents left behind in the area. Two responded. Instead of using them, however, Donovan informed the Soviets, having decided that Hoettl's "ulterior motive in turning over [the] network to [the] U.S. was [the] hope that it be used against Russia and thus embroil the two nations with resultant German gain." George Marshall was disturbed by Donovan's unilateral action in this affair. So was Eisenhower's G-2, General Edwin Sibert. Some of those at the very top of U.S. decision making by the summer of 1945 were already taking harder cold-war attitudes, being prepared to work with former Nazis against the Soviet Union. For the story of Donovan's relationship with the Russians, see Bradley F. Smith, *The Shadow Warriors: OSS and the Origins of the CIA* (New York: Basic Books, 1983), pp. 330–359.

Moscow. The purpose was to cooperate on sabotage operations behind the German lines. Although the idea was supported by Averell Harriman, the American ambassador in Moscow, who thought it would provide an unparalleled opportunity for a U.S. government team inside Russia, it did not survive. The project was undermined by suspicions that arose within both the Russian and the U.S. intelligence communities. The Russians seem to have had second thoughts about their decision to let the OSS inside their intelligence apparatus. And both Admiral William Leahy, President Roosevelt's Chief of Staff, and ex-President Herbert Hoover quashed the idea in Washington on the grounds that the Soviets would have everything to gain from the arrangement.[29] Donovan was not particularly concerned; his attempt to cooperate with the Russians had placated the left in Washington.

Perhaps not surprisingly, the Russians had a long-standing mistrust of the Western Allies. Britain and America had sent armies to fight with the White Russians against the communist Red Army after World War I. The Soviet Union had provided the moment for Hitler to start World War II by signing the Nazi-Soviet Pact in August 1939. For the first two years of the war Stalin was Hitler's ally. They had invaded Poland together, dividing the country between them. In addition, Stalin had invaded and annexed the unallied, neutral states of Estonia, Latvia, and Lithuania. He had ceased to be Hitler's ally only when the Nazi invasion of Russia began on June 22, 1941, without a declaration of war. Having been forced by Hitler to join Britain and America, Stalin was always suspicious that the democracies might conclude a separate peace with Germany and then turn on him, or else spin out the war against Hitler until Russia and Germany had exhausted each other. He was constantly pressing Churchill and Roosevelt to open a second front in the west to take pressure off his armies, which, even in victory, were suffering grievous losses in the east. What was perhaps more surprising was that Westerners were not suspicious of Stalin in return and did not understand the Soviet Union's clear purpose of expanding into Central Europe in order to establish buffer satellite states on Russia's western border. This purpose had guided Russia's European policy since the Congress of Vienna in 1815 and was revealed by the Bishop traffic to be a continuing thrust. And while there was some fear that Stalin might conclude a separate peace with Hitler, there was little awareness of Russia's historic ambitions.

SPY MASTER

Allen Dulles, the best placed of all OSS operatives, with headquarters in Berne, Switzerland, gave the Russians most cause for worry during the war because of the secret lines of communication he maintained with Nazi Germany concerning what the Nazis perceived as a mutual Soviet threat. Starting at the end of 1942, as the Nazis were repeatedly defeated and pushed back by the

Red Army in the East, they promulgated a new policy position to the West. According to the Nazis, if the Western powers joined together with Russia to attack and destroy Germany, there would be nothing to stop the Russian occupation of Central and eastern Europe after the war ended. It was a thought that went back to 1918–19, when German communists were considered to be about to take over the ruins of Germany. In late 1944, when Adolf Eichmann tried to negotiate the release of Hungarian Jews to the Western Allies in return for food, medical supplies, and trucks, he stated that the supplies would be used to support the German war against Russia. Even though the German analysis of the postwar world was accurate, Britain and America would not accept a deal like this with the Nazis, which would have allowed them to sit back and watch Germany and Russia finish each other off.

On the other hand, nurturing the hope within Nazi Germany that the Western Allies might be amenable to an accommodation in the form of an agreement with the German opposition to the Nazis, or even (as Himmler, the head of the SS, came to believe possible) with the SS or Nazi government itself, had tactical advantages. It could open avenues of information and intelligence valuable to the war effort, and it could have an effect on German morale. Accordingly, Allen Dulles maintained secret lines of communication with the German military leadership, German military intelligence—the Abwehr—and the German SS and Wehrmacht commanders in the field. In the course of this activity the suspicions of the Russians were aroused, as was their opposition. They had signed the Nazi-Soviet Pact and were concerned that the Western Allies might in turn agree to a pact with the Nazis against them. Such worries illustrated the importance placed upon intelligence by all sides.

Dulles, who would later become the fifth and longest-serving director of Central Intelligence, was a mild-mannered lawyer, a partner with his brother John Foster Dulles in the prestigious New York law firm Sullivan and Cromwell when he joined the COI as head of its New York office in October 1941. At that time he was one of the handful of Americans with espionage experience, having served as an American agent in Switzerland during World War I. There an episode occurred that he frequently spoke of in later years. He had contacts with a number of revolutionaries in Switzerland and across the border into Austria. One day he had a message from a Russian revolutionary, Lenin, asking for a meeting to discuss an important development. Dulles did not find the time to see Lenin, who then was an apparently insignificant Russian exile. Not surprisingly, Dulles regretted this decision ever after. Lenin, it was later discovered, had just been approached by the Germans, who offered to transport him secretly back to Russia, where he would organize a revolution and make peace with Germany, releasing millions of German soldiers for the war on the western front. In retrospect, it seems clear that he wanted to inform Dulles of this and probably offer another deal. Dulles never forgot this incident, and as a result always made a point of seeing anyone who called.

Before his World War I assignment in Switzerland, Dulles had been a schoolmaster in India, where he developed a healthy dislike of the British Empire. He loved the world of intelligence and was one of the first to support Donovan's ideas in 1940. Unlike Donovan, however, Dulles was principally interested in espionage rather than special forces and research and analysis. He also had the personal ambition of one day running an American centralized intelligence agency—an ambition that led to a complex relationship with Donovan and other leading OSS men such as David Bruce, whom he saw as rivals. His ambition took him back to Switzerland at his own request. Although Donovan offered to make him head of secret intelligence in western Europe under David Bruce in London, Dulles refused, stating that he did not want to work "with a lot of generals looking over my shoulder."[30] He arrived in Switzerland in 1943 with a $1 million letter of credit, a suitcase, and two suits. There he worked happily without generals.

It took Dulles a long time to establish himself in Switzerland because, unknown to him, his intelligence output was being checked against the British Ultra information and unfortunately was found wanting. "All news from Berne these days is being discounted 100% by the War Department," Donovan cabled him in April 1943. In January 1944 he was warned that his material "disagrees with reports we have received originating from other sources and parts of it were months old. . . . Your information . . . is now given a lower rating than any other source. This seems to indicate a need for using the greatest care in checking all your sources."[31]

Dulles' principal source was a high-level diplomat in the German Foreign Ministry, Fritz Kolbe, to whom he gave the code name George Wood. Kolbe had first approached the British in Switzerland but had been rejected by them; they thought he was a German disinformation agent, someone who would feed them misleading information. British misgivings of Kolbe played a part in coloring Washington's view of Dulles' material. In particular, Washington thought that Kolbe was seeking to build his credibility with accurate information so that he would be in a position to mislead the Allies at a crucial moment, probably around D-Day, the date and place of which were a primary focus of German intelligence during 1943 and the first half of 1944. From his first meeting with Kolbe, however, Dulles believed he might be genuine. Kolbe explained that he was a member of an anti-Nazi underground within the German administration. During the following eighteen months Kolbe gave Dulles over sixteen hundred copies of telegrams, letters, and synopses of messages between the German Foreign Ministry and German embassies all over the world. Dulles regarded this information as being of the highest value and forwarded it to Washington for analysis. There he hit snags based on British suspicions. Sir Claude Dansey, deputy head of British SIS, considered Kolbe's material "obviously a plant, and Dulles had fallen for it like a ton of bricks."[32]

The head of SIS's Iberian section, Harold "Kim" Philby, revealed after the war to have been a Soviet agent since the mid-1930s, constantly denigrated Kolbe's reports and the anti-Nazi underground generally.[33] Philby's remarks were consistent with Russia's postwar plan. The Russians did not want "good" Germans to overthrow Hitler and make a separate peace; they wanted the complete defeat of Germany and a buffer zone of conquered countries in Central Europe between Russia and the West. Dulles committed himself to Kolbe. "I now firmly believe in the good faith of Wood," he wrote in a cable to Donovan on December 29, 1943, "and am ready to stake my reputation on the fact that these documents are genuine."[34] He had the courage of his convictions and consistently defended his judgment and Kolbe's motives. In April 1944 an OSS analyst in Washington, aware that the thrust of Kolbe's material was in accord with German propaganda concerning Soviet advances in the East, which if unchecked would result in Soviet power extending well into Europe, sent a message to Dulles asking, "Could this data have been planted with a view to developing a viewpoint which could influence operations in such a way as to affect [Germany] vitally?"[35] Dulles, well aware that this possibility existed, was also satisfied that the Russians *were* a future danger and was happy to collect information about Soviet intentions and order of battle. "I feel that genuine opportunities may be lost to us if we are unduly suspicious," he told Washington in May 1944.[36]

After the plot against Hitler's life failed in July 1944, Kolbe fell silent. Nazi security became so tight that he was no longer able to travel to Switzerland. But the questions he had raised were in many ways more important than the material he had passed. The first question—Was Kolbe's material genuine?—was answered by checking it against information from other sources, a procedure that was to become one of the basic steps of intelligence analysis in both OSS and the CIA. This cross-checking showed that Kolbe's material was genuine but added little to what was already known by Churchill and Roosevelt and their senior military commanders. Ultra was already giving the Allies access to Germany's most closely held secrets: Hitler's strategic and operational plans. Eighteen years later the information passed to Britain and America by Colonel Oleg Penkovsky from within Soviet military intelligence was cross-checked in the same way against satellite and U-2 photographs.

The second question—How can intelligence avoid the extremes of excessive caution and excessive haste in order to seize real opportunities as they arise?—can be answered only through judgment. This question is at the heart of the debate about intelligence collection and analysis. By emphasizing collection at the expense of analysis, human judgment is reduced, the quality of interpretation is changed, and intelligence loses an important element of "feel" and atmosphere.* During the war it could be argued that Ultra had this effect

*In 1983 Richard Helms declared:

If there is a weakness in our intelligence apparatus, it is in our ability to figure out what the leaders of a foreign power are going to do in any given situation. For example, it is open knowledge in our government that we do not know how the Saudi royal family arrives at its

on the British. Today it is argued that satellite and electronic intelligence collection has dangerously displaced intelligence judgment and analysis. "I think that a real criticism of British intelligence during the war," said Gerhard Van Arkel, an OSS officer with Dulles in Switzerland, "was that they were overly suspicious of the motives of the people with whom they had to deal, and the consequence was that as far as I was concerned the three best agents that Allen Dulles had were rejected by the British. They were absolutely priceless agents. The British had turned them all down, and it was Allen Dulles' wit that picked them up."[37]

Apart from Kolbe, Dulles had two other principal agents, Hans Bernd Gisevius and Fritz Molden. Molden was the son of a professor at the University of Vienna, and through his father's friends and colleagues had developed a network of well-placed informants in Austria, Hungary, Czechoslovakia, Rumania, and Yugoslavia. He was a dedicated anti-Nazi and spent most of the war on the run, having deserted from the Wehrmacht. He used to cross into Switzerland on foot over the Alps, never carrying a scrap of paper on him. He remembered everything. "He would tell me about railroads, order of battle, supplies, foodstuffs, prices—everything," said Van Arkel. "His memory was absolutely phenomenal. He and I would work together for thirty-six hours without stopping. Then he would go to Paris or Caserta or some other place to talk to someone else, and then he would cross the Alps again, maybe going to Milan, dress himself up as a German Gestapo agent or something, catch a train to Vienna, get more information from his father, make the trip back to Milan, and then into Switzerland to see us. He made about half a dozen trips."[38] Molden was one of the first to bring the Allies details of the German V-1 and

---

decisions. The same applies to the Russian leadership. In that case we may not even divine for some time that a decision was made, let alone the nature of it.

Arkady Shevchenko, the Russian defector from the United Nations, recently wrote that American followers of Kremlin politics have a regrettable lack of understanding about how the Soviet leaders think, how they act behind the scenes, and how they make decisions. The attacks on our embassy in Iran and the political infighting which brought on the taking of the hostages were surprises born of an inadequate grasp of Ayatollah Khomeini's bigotry and zealotry. To this day the varied patterns of Islamic thought are mysterious to our American minds.

I could go on and on, but you have my point. As a country we must develop a far deeper knowledge of other people's culture, religion, politics than we possess today. Believe it or not, we are still essentially a provincial nation. ("Remarks at Donovan Award Dinner," May 24, 1983)

Helms's perspective is clear: American intelligence is perhaps too content to rely on technology at the expense of analysis. Too often human judgment is set aside when gadgets can provide useful answers. As a result, proper understanding, or "feel," is sacrificed, leaving intelligence operations out in the cold when gadgets cannot discern actions, policies, and attitudes. What Helms might have added was that America is still a rationalist power that believes it can make deals on a logical basis. When it meets irrational powers such as Khomeini's Iran or Qadaffi's Libya, America's rational approach falls apart, as does its indomitable strength. In Vietnam the American war effort collapsed on the irrationality of the North Vietnamese, who were willing to fight until extinction.

V-2 rocket site at Peenemünde, which he collected from German and Austrian scientists who his father knew were working on Nazi secret projects. After the war Molden married Allen Dulles' eldest daughter, Joan. Although the marriage was short-lived, he remained Dulles' close friend and stayed in touch with him throughout the 1950s.[39]

Gisevius, like Kolbe, was a member of the anti-Nazi underground. He was a close friend of Admiral Wilhelm Canaris, head of German military intelligence, and, it seems, was used by the admiral (who was anti-Nazi) to pass information to the Allies.* He was a very brave man, and from the outset of the war contemplated high treason. His motive, like that of most other members of the anti-Nazi underground, was not ideological—he was not a communist or religious opponent of Naziism—but was rooted in traditional German patriotism. "I will not demean myself by being a common thief, stealing trivia from office filing cabinets," he said to Dulles, "but I will give you a list of every general in Germany who wishes to see Hitler dead, and I will help you communicate with them. In the meantime, I will tell you when my friends are planning to assassinate the Führer."[40] To prove his trustworthiness he revealed to Dulles that Abwehr cryptanalysts had broken some OSS and U.S. State Department codes. The British already knew this (they also had broken the American codes), which was one of the reasons why they were always anxious to protect their communications intelligence sources from the Americans. Gisevius also revealed that some British diplomatic codes had been broken by the Abwehr and that there was a German agent inside the British Embassy in Turkey. Independently of Fritz Molden, he gave Dulles details of the V-1 and V-2 rocket programs.†

---

*There is some debate as to whether Canaris consciously helped the Allies during the war. One writer, Rupert Allason, writing as Nigel West (*Unreliable Witness* [London: Weidenfeld and Nicolson, 1984], pp. 18–38), argues that Canaris "deliberately passed important strategic intelligence to the Allies, albeit via an 'unspoken understanding,'" and is supported in this view by some other investigators and British wartime intelligence officers. Gerhard Van Arkel (interview, November 11, 1983) was more cautious:

> Canaris wasn't an agent, but he knew what was going on. He protected Hans Gisevius any number of times. But whether he was a British agent, or was prepared to use any means to topple Hitler, is more difficult to judge. He was willing to treat with the British. He was anti-Nazi. I am inclined to think that he was pro-Allies. But a British agent? That's an entirely different question. He was involved in the July 20 plot. They were all working in the interests of Germany as they saw it, and were after Hitler because they thought he was ruining Germany.

After the war Donovan personally saw to it that Canaris' widow received a pension from the U.S. government, implying that Donovan valued whatever Canaris had done for the Allies.

In secret testimony to the House Government Operations Committee in June 1947, Dulles said that Canaris and his deputy had been in direct touch with him while he was OSS chief in Switzerland. Dulles also said that about ten percent of the Abwehr turned against Hitler in disgust and because of his treatment of the Russians (*The Washington Post*, September 29, 1982).

†The German spy in the British Embassy in Ankara was Elyesa Bazna, the ambassador's valet, who was given the code name Cicero by the Germans. He secured a great deal of secret information by stealing the ambassador's keys and photographing the contents of his safe. The

After the Casablanca Conference in January 1943, when President Roosevelt announced that he would accept nothing less than the unconditional surrender of the Axis powers, it was clear to Gisevius that collaboration with Dulles would be entirely in the Allies' interest; it was unlikely that Germany would avoid military defeat and occupation. This testing moment came right at the start of Gisevius' relationship with Dulles. A Nazi before the war and a member of the Gestapo (he served in the German Consulate in Zurich under Foreign Ministry cover), Gisevius put aside any allegiance he might have felt toward the Nazi regime and became increasingly passionate in his rejection of Nazism and plans for a new Germany after the war. Following the failure of the July 20, 1944, plot against Hitler, most members of the anti-Nazi underground, including Admiral Canaris, were rounded up and executed by the Gestapo. Gisevius, with Dulles' help, escaped. In the Nuremberg war trials he gave damning evidence against the Nazi leaders.

"THE SECRET SURRENDER": ITALY, 1945

In February 1945 Dulles masterminded one of the most important secret negotiations of the war: the surrender of German and Italian forces in Italy. It was called Operation Sunrise, and it started when the German military commanders in Italy approached Dulles through SS General Karl Wolff to discuss surrender terms. Like nearly all Dulles' informants during the war in Switzerland, General Wolff was a "walk-in." The operation commenced not with action on the part of Dulles or the OSS but as a result of an independent action taken by others. In later years, as the CIA was to discover, walk-ins often provided the best intelligence, as they had clear motivation for their actions. They were not bought and therefore were not likely to change sides if the ante was raised. Moreover, they had no need to elaborate or invent stories for their paymasters in order to justify their contracts. Dulles' skill lay in effectively directing these contacts while maintaining the security of his own operation. "It was a funny thing in Switzerland," recalled one of Dulles' staff there, "but all the intelligence agents knew each other. We all ate at the Bellevue Hotel. At one table would be all the Polish agents, at another would be the Nazi agents,

---

Germans, however, could never quite believe their luck and did not accept Cicero's material as completely genuine: they thought the British knew Bazna was a spy and were planting false documents in the safe for him to photograph. Acting on Gisevius' tip-off, the British revamped security at the embassy and dismissed all the Turkish staff there. Bazna had resigned before this happened, planning to live on the £250,000 paid him by the Germans. Unfortunately for him, he had been paid in forged banknotes (Vincent and Nan Buranelli, *Spy/Counterspy: An Encyclopedia of Espionage* [New York: McGraw-Hill, 1982], pp. 21–22).

    After the war, Dulles confirmed that he had received information about Germany's missile program from sources close to Canaris (*The Washington Post*, September 29, 1982).

another would have all the British, another the Americans. We all knew each other, and there was an unwritten rule that you respected each other's private life."[41] In such an atmosphere, keeping secrets was a real achievement. Keeping Operation Sunrise secret was especially difficult because of the scale of what was involved and the hundreds of people on both sides who had to know something about it. If Hitler or the German high command had learned about it from one of their agents in Switzerland, there is no doubt that there would have been another bloodletting, similar to that which followed the July 20, 1944, plot.

Dulles first learned about the intention of the German commanders in Italy to surrender when he received a telephone call from Major Max Waibel of Swiss military intelligence on February 25, 1945. Waibel, who was the liaison with Allied intelligence services in Switzerland, asked for an urgent meeting with Dulles. During a dinner meeting that evening Waibel told Dulles that he had been approached by two businessmen, one Italian and one Swiss, with a peace proposal that he thought Dulles should take seriously. "It was just another peace feeler from the Italian front," thought Dulles at the time. "I must admit that my immediate reaction was not enthusiastic."[42] What was more, Dulles knew that there were several peace feelers coming from various factions in Germany, all of which were being very carefully handled so as not to alarm the Soviet Union.* He had been deeply disappointed by the failure of the July plot the previous year and was convinced of future conflict with the Soviet Union, as one of his staff recorded. Learning of the arrest of the plotters, he sorrowfully outlined his view of the future: he "had always hoped that through

---

*The most important of these peace feelers had begun in the summer of 1944 when Donovan himself had discussions in Rome with the German ambassador to the Holy See, Baron Ernst von Weizsäcker. The meeting had been arranged by the Vatican contacting the OSS. Von Weizsäcker floated a proposal for the surrender of German forces in the west while they continued to fight the Russians in the east. This was rejected by Donovan; it was exactly what the Russians feared and exactly what the Casablanca Conference had vetoed. Contact was maintained with Von Weizsäcker, who, after Canaris' arrest following the failure of the July plot, became the most important secret link to the German general staff.

In January 1945 Von Weizsäcker told his OSS contact that the German Chief of the General Staff, General Heinz Guderian, and the supreme commander of all German forces in the west, Field Marshal Gerd von Rundstedt, were prepared to surrender. Donovan kept the White House, the War Department, and the Allied commander in chief in western Europe, General Dwight D. Eisenhower, fully informed of these peace feelers. It was decided to do nothing until after the Yalta Conference, from February 4 to 11. Dulles had been involved in this peace feeler as well. He held discussions with a German diplomat, Alexander Constantin von Neurath, who acted as an emissary for the German commander in chief in Italy, Field Marshal Albert Kesselring, a party to the Guderian/Von Rundstedt proposal. The Yalta Conference reaffirmed Allied determination to secure the unconditional surrender of all German forces, and this effectively brought the separate peace feelers to an end. See Leonard Mosley, *Dulles: A Biography of Eleanor, Allen and John Foster Dulles and Their Family Network* (New York: Dial Press/James Wade, 1978), pp. 174–175; Anthony Cave Brown, *Bodyguard of Lies* (New York: Bantam Books, 1976), pp. 728–769; and *Wild Bill Donovan: The Last Hero* (New York: Times Books, 1982), pp. 728–731.

a sudden downfall of Hitler, the war would be ended before the Soviet Russians entered Berlin. A quick peace agreement with a democratic German regime would have prevented that. But now all was lost: the continuation of the war would provide the Russians with a pathway to the Elbe in the heart of Europe. American policy had suffered a terrible defeat."[43]

Dulles' thoughts mirrored those of Donovan in Washington. While dealing with the various German peace feelers, Donovan was planning a postwar central intelligence agency, which he saw in terms of confrontation with the Soviet Union. Donovan wrote a memorandum to Roosevelt about his plans, only to find it leaked to the press. He blamed a jealous J. Edgar Hoover, but later on Walter Trohan, the journalist responsible for the story, said he had been tipped off by one of Roosevelt's aides at the President's instruction.[44] Just two and a half weeks before Sunrise began, headlines in American newspapers screamed, "Donovan Proposes Super Spy System for Postwar New Deal/Would Take over FBI, Secret Service, ONI and G-2 to Watch Home, Abroad/Project for U.S. Super-Spies Disclosed in Secret Memo/New Deal Plans Super Spy System/Sleuths Would Snoop on U.S. and the World/Order Creating it Already Drafted/New Deal Plans to Spy on World and Home Folks, And Super Gestapo Agency is Under Consideration."[45] Not surprisingly, with all this going on, Dulles was suspicious and pessimistic about Major Waibel's businessmen. Nevertheless, no doubt mindful of his Lenin experience, Dulles agreed to meet them.

The first meeting between Dulles and Waibel's contacts was not a success. The two businessmen said they were in touch with the German commander in chief in Italy, who was willing to surrender. They claimed that SS General Wolff, in charge of the SS armies in northern Italy, was also involved. As a member of the SS, Wolff belonged to the most fanatical Nazi group. He was known to be close to Himmler (who was trying to negotiate a surrender himself). Wolff was also reputed to be the German commander responsible for the Nazi "Redoubt," the area in the Austrian and Tyrolean Alps said to be where the Nazis planned their last stand. This information made Dulles skeptical. However, Washington was mesmerized by the Redoubt, although there was little evidence that the Germans had any plans for one. The Redoubt idea was seen by some as more likely to be a Russian deception to encourage Eisenhower to deflect his advance toward Austria and southern Germany and away from Berlin and the German heartland. "Possibly these reports were planted by the Russians with the intention of inducing Eisenhower to do exactly what he did, which was to cut south instead of going directly for Berlin, to cut the Germans off from the Redoubt," said Van Arkel. "Obviously Eisenhower believed the information we were sending in, and he acted accordingly. It was to the Russian interest to stop him going to Berlin, and it's certainly possible that some smart Russian agent decided that this was a way to deflect Eisenhower to the south. It's the kind of mystery you're left with."[46]

Dulles decided to test the peace feeler but not to tell Donovan or anyone else about it. He would take advantage of being free of generals to act on his own initiative. "An intelligence officer in the field is supposed to keep his home office informed of what he is doing," he later explained. "That is quite true, but with some reservations, as he may overdo it. If, for example, he tells too much or asks too often for instructions he is likely to get some he doesn't relish, and, what is worse, he may well find headquarters trying to take over the whole conduct of the operation." He asked the businessmen to secure the release of two Italian partisans recently captured by the Germans and in the hands of the Gestapo—Feruccio Parri in Verona and Antonio Usmiani in Turin. He made their release his condition for negotiating with SS General Wolff, who was in charge of the peace move on the German side. "I proposed, therefore, that General Wolff, if he wanted to see me, should give evidence of the seriousness of his intentions by releasing these two prisoners to me in Switzerland. In asking for Parri I realized that I was asking for probably the most important Italian prisoner the SS held . . . Yet if these men could be released, the seriousness of General Wolff's intentions would be amply demonstrated. Also, I had deliberately chosen two men who were imprisoned in different places in Italy to test out the extent of Wolff's authority."[47]

On March 8, 1945, Parri and Usmiani were driven by SS officers to the Swiss-Italian border at Chiasso and handed over to an officer from Major Waibel's staff with a request that they be taken to Dulles "with the compliments of General Wolff."[48] Wolff had clearly demonstrated the seriousness of his intentions. Some hours later Wolff himself crossed into Switzerland and traveled to Berne, where he spent the evening with Dulles, convincing him that this peace feeler would yield results, avoiding loss of life and further destruction in Italy and possibly shortening the war in Europe. Wolff made no demands about the disposition of Germany, his colleagues, or himself after the war. On the contrary, he stated that his commanders in Italy were prepared to surrender unconditionally. Dulles now informed Washington and Allied headquarters at Caserta, and Major Generals Lyman L. Lemnitzer, U.S. Army, Field Marshal Alexander's deputy Chief of Staff, and Terence Airey, British Army, flew to Switzerland to talk to Wolff themselves.

Just as with earlier peace feelers, the Sunrise negotiations alarmed Stalin when he learned about them some weeks later. On April 5 he wrote Roosevelt an acrimonious letter. "You affirm that so far no negotiations have been entered into," he declared. "Apparently you are not fully informed. As regards my military colleagues, they, on the basis of information in their possession, are sure that negotiations did take place and that they ended in an agreement with the Germans, whereby the German commander on the Western Front . . . is to open the front to the Anglo-American troops and let them move east, while the British and Americans have promised, in exchange, to ease the armistice terms for the Germans."[49] Stalin was right in saying that negotiations had been entered into (although when Roosevelt had given his assurance to the contrary, he had not known about Dulles' secret) but was wrong about their nature. He was expressing his own paranoia, not the substance of the Sunrise negotiations. His fears meant, however, that if Sunrise were to proceed, it had to do so with great caution. The war was obviously nearing an end, and there was no need for accommodation with any Germans to secure victory. All that a local surrender would achieve would be the saving of life and an end to destruction: important, yes, but not vital. What Stalin failed to understand—and was probably constitutionally incapable of understanding—was that in the two great democracies of the United States and Britain, leaders and governments would have to face the electorate soon after war was over and would have to justify their actions in ending the war in the light of Nazi atrocities. They would not have been able to justify favorable arrangements with one set of Nazis in April 1945.

Before the matter was resolved between the Big Three, on April 12 Roosevelt died. He was succeeded as President by Harry S Truman, whom FDR had kept out of many of the important war decisions. While Truman came to grips with the presidency, Operation Sunrise bogged down. Within eight days Truman came to a decision, relayed by cable to Dulles by the Joint Chiefs of Staff on April 20: "JCS direct that OSS break off all contact with German emissaries at once. Dulles is therefore instructed to discontinue immediately all such contacts . . . in view of complications which have arisen with the Russians, the US and British governments have decided OSS should break off contacts; that JCS are so instructing OSS; that the whole matter is to be regarded as closed and that Russians be informed . . ."[50] Three days later, unaware of this change in American attitude, Wolff, through Major Waibel, asked Dulles "immediately to arrange for the capitulation of all the German forces, Wehrmacht and SS, in North Italy."[51]

Dulles frantically asked for guidance from the JCS, but all they could suggest was that the Swiss act for him. Waibel agreed personally to start negotiations, thus buying Dulles time to get Washington to change its mind. For two days Waibel talked to Wolff in Lucerne, to which he had traveled, as he thought, to complete unconditional surrender. Wolff became more and more suspicious as Dulles failed to appear. On April 25 he returned to Italy to command his forces, then engaged in a fierce defensive fight against the Allies, who had launched a major offensive on April 9 along the river Po, south of Bologna. On April 27 Truman reversed his earlier decision and gave instructions for Wolff's surrender to be accepted at Allied headquarters in Caserta, with the Russians to be invited as witnesses. The following day all Axis forces in northern Italy—SS, Wehrmacht, Kriegsmarine, Luftwaffe, and Italian Fascist—surrendered.[52]

OSS WORLDWIDE

Operation Sunrise had been very unusual, far more dependent upon the circumstances of the end of the war and Dulles' diplomatic skills than upon any well-conceived clandestine operational plan. In other parts of Europe and elsewhere—in North Africa, the eastern Mediterranean, the Balkans, and the Far East—OSS men and women had begun to cut the teeth of a full-fledged American intelligence service. European theater operations had taken priority because of the Allies' Germany-first policy. But from an early point, OSS was also active in all war theaters, with the exception, in 1945, of General Douglas MacArthur's and Admiral Chester W. Nimitz's Pacific area. MacArthur was reported as being "satisfied with his own intelligence unit," and Nimitz was reported as having "spurned OSS cooperation in the Pacific theater."[53] Under David Bruce, OSS London had established effective contacts with the intelligence arms of the Free French, Polish, Czechoslovak, Norwegian, Belgian, and Dutch governments. The Dutch proved a very useful source of information for Far Eastern operations.

On May 9, 1942, Donovan submitted a memorandum to the President arguing that the OSS should be allowed to extend its operations into South America, reserved so far to the FBI and Nelson Rockefeller's Coordinator of Inter-American Affairs agency. Roosevelt had preferred to create competition between Hoover, Rockefeller, and Donovan through this arrangement rather than give Donovan overall control. It was typical of Roosevelt to play people and agencies against each other in this way, and it prevented Donovan from ever achieving his ambition—a truly coordinated and centralized intelligence agency. OSS achieved theoretical rights to some South American operations in its final directive from the Joint Chiefs of Staff in October 1943.[54] But not until the CIA was created in 1947 was the FBI really challenged in South America.

Quite rapidly, as the pace of the U.S. war effort increased, OSS headquarters in Washington came to act more as a coordinating center for the various OSS branches under the control of the different theater commanders. Over time, theater relationships between OSS units and military commanders in the field became more important than relationships between these units and OSS headquarters. By 1944, within eighteen months of its creation, OSS had an intelligence-collection network that spanned the globe. Masterminded by Donovan, this network was closely tied into the U.S. armed forces but in most areas remained free of military hierarchy. In cooperation with the State Department, prior to the invasion of North Africa, OSS covert installations began to function in Casablanca, Tangiers, and Algiers and were later extended to Marrakech, Rabat, Alexandria, and Cairo. The Allied invasion of Italy in 1943 was supported by OSS commando units in Corsica and, on the mainland, in Bari and Naples.*

*In the European and Mediterranean theaters, good working relations with the British were vital. The British provided most of the communications intelligence. OSS operations were carefully coordinated with military requirements. The British attempt to lead the OSS, however, was by no means easy and was often not successful. In the Mediterranean the British were tempted into overselling their strategic conceptions to the Americans and even into undertaking opera-

In May 1942 OSS entered the Far East theater with what was to become its largest unit. Bases were set up in India, Burma, and Ceylon. Reconnaissance units of the OSS operated out of K'un-ming and Chungking in mainland China, performing missions for General Chennault's Fourteenth Air Force. OSS Detachment 101, billeted on a tea plantation in the Brahmaputra valley, supported a complex of jungle outposts dotted over upper Burma and extending as far south as Lashio and Mandalay. Thailand, the Japanese stronghold in the Far East, was successfully infiltrated by an OSS group that ran Operation Ruth out of the heart of Bangkok. (Ruth was the code name given to the Thai prime minister, who was put in office by the Japanese but was in fact an Allied agent controlled by OSS.)[55]

These operations in Indochina represented a significant moment in the institutional history of American intelligence. They were an enormous expansion of the scope of intelligence into unconventional warfare. Although initial expansion in this area had already occurred in Europe with resistance groups, what happened in Burma and Thailand set the stage in earnest for the cold-war operations of the late 1940s and 1950s. It was a new world for intelligence. Politics, intelligence, and war met. In addition, technology—the light airplanes, the backpack radio—made a different combination of choice and operation possible.

As OSS developed its worldwide network, two of its departments—the Foreign Nationalities Branch (FNB), in New York, and the Research and Analysis department, centered at OSS headquarters in Washington—became increasingly involved with the practicalities of Donovan's conception of intelligence work. The diversity of OSS operations, ranging from guerrilla and commando units to the academic analysis of information, gave OSS a character and self-awareness different from those of any other intelligence organization. Thus the FNB, responsible for establishing contacts with leaders of foreign-oriented organizations formed in the United States, soon found it very difficult to distinguish between its right to collect information and actually operating within the United States with its contacts and organizations.* As early as April

---

tions the Americans would not collaborate in. See *Times Literary Supplement*, October 12, 1984, review by John Keegan of F. H. Hinsley, E. E. Thomas, and C. F. G. Ransom, *British Intelligence in the Second World War* (London: Her Majesty's Stationery Office, 1984), Vol. 3.

*Library of Congress, FNB Papers, Memorandum by "A.J.H.," July 23, 1942:

The multitude of various national organizations, the presence in the U.S. of representatives of practically all political groups and parties who are active at home, the great masses which formed the milieu from which these organizations were formed, have created in the U.S. a kind of microcosm of each European country with the same aspirations, interests, conflicts, etc. . . . Contacts have to be handled by experienced workers of FNB who can meet the European leaders on their own ground . . . It is absolutely futile to entrust this task to people who are primarily interested in collecting information . . . After one or two interviews, the foreign representatives get resentful and sulky. They approach the Allied Governments for help in a common fight, they intensely dislike being treated as sources of information only.

1942 Donovan found it necessary to try to clarify the position, both for administrative reasons and for the sake of relations with the FBI. In so doing he marked out the area of domestic operation that has ever since dogged the politics of U.S. intelligence agencies: "We are not policemen," he wrote, "we are not concerned with sedition, secret meetings, sabotage and betrayal. That is the province of the FBI . . . The province of this Branch . . . is foreign politics . . . as they are unfolding within the U.S."[56]

The branch itself, with its special position as a domestic arm of OSS concerned almost entirely with foreigners and foreign politics, took the lead in resolving the dilemma between collection and operation by firmly looking to the outside world, avoiding the temptation to enter the province of the FBI. An FNB document of September 1, 1943, stated its global scope: "peace will not be long enduring until either our way of thought and life, or somebody else's, becomes general and controlling in the world. . . . It is immediately plain that, so far as we may be impelled into any definite campaign to win others over to our democratic way, we are a nation of nations peculiarly well-equipped for the undertaking."[57] Despite Donovan, at least part of the OSS clearly saw a future in which the United States could be the world's policeman.

THE DEPARTMENTAL BLUEPRINT

Research and Analysis (R&A), as Donovan all along envisaged, proved in practice to be the heart of OSS intelligence. It was also a feature unique to the OSS, although it was subsequently copied by many other organizations. What was unexpected about OSS Research and Analysis was its remarkably effective use of publicly accessible information. Highly trained scholars and analysts extracted information from academic works, journals, magazines, newspapers, and the files of U.S. corporations with overseas operations. From sources such as these, R&A provided exact details of the North African train systems. It accurately predicted that the crunch for the Nazis would come in the area of manpower and not, as was widely assumed, in the area of food production. The R&A specialists reached this conclusion by reading journals, examining statistics on German agricultural exports, and noting obituaries. This realization was critically important to the Allies, since it revealed that destruction of German industry, communications, and urban centers by bombing would take a heavy toll on the Germans as scarce manpower was brought in to make repairs. Other major analysis efforts demonstrated that the Axis powers would probably be able to maintain sufficient supplies of gasoline, oil, and lubricants for their needs despite Allied bombing. By studying casualty lists in German newspapers, R&A accurately estimated German U-boat and battle casualties.[58] The truth of these studies was shocking to the military: the idea that "egghead" intellectuals could tell them something of practical use was a revelation.

This kind of work not only demonstrated the value of research and analysis but also provided another way of checking secret intelligence by comparing it with hard evidence gathered from published sources. Later on Dr. Ray Cline, who served in OSS R&A and became deputy director for intelligence of the CIA, argued that the respect for scholarship established in the OSS and continued in the CIA gave U.S. intelligence a marked intellectual superiority over the KGB: "The most valuable OSS legacy that endured was Donovan's belief in the value of bringing able people from all walks of life into intelligence work. He lifted intelligence out of its military rut, where it had little prestige and little dynamism, and made it a career for adventurous, broad-minded civilians. This tradition carried down to CIA, which regularly recruited some of the most able graduates from U.S. universities to learn the intelligence business."[59]

Donovan also made it the job of intelligence to organize and apply the United States' new interest in every aspect of the world's people, events, cultures, geographical boundaries, politics, and so on. As a result, intelligence was expected to be omniscient and omnicompetent as it represented American society and prepared the United States to do battle with other societies. Donovan set out to make this so. The CIA took the OSS experience one step further by feeding back into the academic pool much of its research work—as long as sources were not jeopardized. Consequently the CIA became more integrated with the academic world as a whole than its predecessor had been. By 1966 the CIA could almost consider itself a mini research institute: half its analysts had advanced degrees; one third had doctorates.[60]

During the 1960s and 1970s, when the CIA was repeatedly criticized as an aberrant U.S. institution, R&A retained its value as a respectable and respected element. After the Bay of Pigs disaster in 1961 the CIA reiterated its view of the importance of research and analysis and played down the importance of its operational activities. Fortunately for the agency, this argument had the advantage of probably being correct. In 1963 Alexander Orlov, a Soviet spy who defected to the United States, commented that the secret intelligence work and clandestine information gathered through research and analysis differentiated American intelligence efforts from those of the Russians, who still believed in the primacy of old-fashioned spying as the basis of intelligence.[61]

The Foreign Nationalities Branch and R&A fitted into a complex organizational structure. The OSS Special Operations branch required an organizational pattern that was completely military in form and was as closely tied to military commanders in the various war theaters as it was to OSS HQ. In contrast, R&A was based almost completely at HQ and had a definite collegiate air to it.* The Secret Intelligence (SI) branch, while also at OSS HQ in Wash-

---

*William Colby, head of the CIA from 1973 to 1975, was critical of this and argued that the separation of the R&A scholars from the clandestine operatives encouraged and exacerbated the

ington, was a tightly knit small group of security-conscious officers who saw bureaucratic checks as important for secrecy. OSS outposts in war theaters were patterned on the Washington structure, with adjustments made for local needs. The political necessity to work with the various intelligence agencies of Allied governments and to create liaisons with government agencies and departments at home further complicated OSS's administrative system. Donovan, never an enthusiastic administrator, depended upon his deputy, Colonel G. Edward ("Ned") Buxton, to keep the OSS house in order. Two other deputy directors of OSS worked with Ned Buxton and Donovan, who was as often in Washington as he was visiting OSS posts around the world.

These administrators were responsible for the OSS Planning Group and Planning Staff and were charged with the duty of coordinating the three main OSS functions: (a) intelligence, consisting of R&A, Secret Intelligence, counterespionage and liaison work (X-2); (b) operations, consisting of sabotage, guerrilla warfare, psychological warfare, and related activities; and (c) schools and training. A chief of services supervised the work of the offices of budget, procurement, and finance. In addition, eighteen other offices, not assigned to any subordinate command, were effectively controlled by Donovan's own staff directly. In practice this compartmentalization helped maintain security and fostered strong branch loyalties within OSS. Each branch had its own secret files, which were available to personnel in other branches only on an official "need to know" basis. Donovan himself was not told the names of some of his most successful agents, nor did he seek to learn them. It was a system that worked, and although it developed out of the need to organize and administer the many disparate elements in the OSS, the system was subsequently used in the CIA as well. (See Appendix III.)

Donovan's personal fascination with gung-ho military exploits provided another kind of OSS legacy for the CIA. Both the American public and the OSS staff associated OSS success with guerrilla and commando activities, reflecting the special experience of wartime. However, because of the political competition OSS faced from the British (who, as we have seen, were glad to cooperate in counterintelligence matters but tried hard to subordinate OSS to its own intelligence agencies in the field), the FBI, and MacArthur and Nimitz in the Pacific, OSS grew in a misshapen way, filling gaps where others had not ventured. Burma, where Detachment 101 operated, was certainly not the center of the war; Algiers, Casablanca,[62] Marrakech were not exactly vital war zones either. Donovan knew that the value of these operational activities was limited.

Although he was personally more interested in operations, Donovan real-

---

growth of "two cultures" within the intelligence profession, divided from and often hostile to each other (William Colby and Peter Forbath, *Honorable Men: My Life in the CIA* [New York: Simon and Schuster, 1978], p. 61).

ized the importance of code-breaking. In a conversation late in 1941 with Otto Doering, a law firm partner and COI/OSS colleague, he observed that crypt-analysis as an intelligence source so overshadowed human espionage that unless he was granted access to the intercept material, his secret intelligence service would be doomed to play a small, subordinate role in the intelligence war. Well aware that British Intelligence, not OSS, possessed Ultra and that the War and Navy departments, not OSS, had broken the secret Japanese codes, Donovan did everything he could to avoid seeing OSS relegated to the background in the intelligence community. He established a cover company, the FBQ Corporation,[63] to act as a COI and then an OSS cryptanalysis unit; he made contacts with anti-Axis groups of all kinds; he cultivated relationships with other intelligence agencies, including the Soviet NKVD, with which OSS had regular contact toward the end of the war;* and he mounted behind-the-lines combat operations, linking OSS with the prestige attached to the military for winning the war. These efforts were successful, for by war's end OSS had gained the experience necessary to provide the United States with a first-rate peacetime intelligence service. The agency had acquired operational and intelligence know-how and had developed a professional, highly skilled staff. By 1945 OSS had clearly demonstrated its potential, and even though it had been kept at the periphery of military activity, everyone involved in intelligence realized its value and would fight all the harder for control of intelligence in the following years.

Some of the most effective OSS operations during the war were carried out by the Morale and Special Operations departments of the Psychological Warfare division. In North Africa several assassinations were authorized, including, it was rumored within OSS, that of Vichy French Admiral Darlan. This foreshadowed later CIA assassination attempts in which OSS's wartime experience and methods were carried over into peacetime. Morale Operations used the postal links between neutral Sweden and Nazi Germany to implicate a number of Germans regarded as particularly effective in pursuing the war against the Allies, in the July 20, 1944, bomb plot to kill Hitler. After the Gestapo and SS uncovered the forged evidence of complicity, they executed several men on suspicion of involvement in the plot. In this case and in others like it the OSS successfully used the enemy to do its work.

THE PARAMILITARY TRADITION

The war in Europe had two major fronts: the northern European front culminated in D-Day 1944 and the eventual push into Germany; the southern

---

*French intelligence was the first foreign intelligence agency with which OSS London developed a liaison; it was followed by the Poles, the Belgians, the Norwegians, the Dutch, and the Czechs. The Belgians and the Czechs proved disappointing, while the OSS liaison with Poland ultimately proved unproductive (*War Report of the OSS*, Vol. 2).

European front used North Africa as a springboard for the invasion of Italy and southern France. The war in southern Europe was considered a secondary war by the Allied high command and so never received all the resources it might have. The objective of the Allies in southern Europe was to pin down and tie up Axis troops and resources, keeping them from being deployed in areas more important to the Allies. OSS played a very important part in this war. Its Secret Intelligence and Special Operations units developed a very effective resistance movement in German-occupied northern Italy, forcing the Germans to travel along the major roads and railways and to camp in the towns, thus leaving the countryside effectively free. They were supported by OSS Operational Groups, which operated in uniform behind enemy lines. It was an important achievement and a vindication of Donovan's dreams for commando-style units.

Jedburghs (a British idea)—led by units of OSS or British SOE and made up of teams of guerrilla fighters drawn from the forces of the governments-in-exile of Axis-occupied countries—performed some courageous missions behind enemy lines in the weeks before and after D-Day. Their mission was to prevent the Germans from consolidating their forces in France after the Allied landings. William Colby led one such team in France and went on to lead a larger Operational Group in Nazi-occupied Norway in 1945. Groups such as Colby's played an important part in the psychological as well as the practical war against the Axis powers, demonstrating that OSS had varied and effective services to offer theater commanders. In Europe, OSS supported underground resistance groups that softened up target areas prior to such amphibious invasions as those code-named Torch, Anvil, and Overlord.* In the Far East, even greater emphasis was placed on guerrilla and commando activities. An OSS unit in Burma closely cooperated with regular Allied forces as it operated as an irregular military force. In 1944, OSS cost approximately $100 million, largely because of its straightforward military expenditures.

Although the Allies would have won World War II without the OSS and, for that matter, without the British SIS or the Soviet NKVD (this does not deny the importance of Ultra to Britain in 1940 and 1941 and Magic's role in winning some vital battles in the Pacific), OSS did provide real help in speeding the end of the war. In North Africa, OSS Operational Groups facilitated Allied landings and ultimate victory. In southern France and northern Italy, OSS groups tied up entire German divisions, denying the Germans the front-line reinforcements they needed, sometimes at vital moments; Jedburgh-coordinated Maquis activity in France after D-Day effectively prevented the Second SS Panzer Division from reaching Normandy in time to affect seriously the Allied beachhead (although Allied air superiority probably would have secured the beachhead in any event). The OSS (and others) supported Tito's

---

*Torch was the invasion of North Africa in 1943, Anvil was the invasion of southern France in 1944, and Overlord was the Normandy invasion.

partisans in Yugoslavia and guerrilla units in Greece. Although, it must be said, all these activities were secondary to the major war effort, they helped keep Axis intelligence efforts spread thin and enabled the Allies to draw an accurate picture of the enemy based on large-scale observation.

By 1945, however, many in the OSS were aware that the part they had played had not been central. Looking back on the effort nearly forty years later, James R. Murphy, head of OSS's X-2 (counterintelligence), considered that OSS "contributed a great deal to the principle of gathering, researching, coordinating, analyzing information in one central place and disseminating it wherever it would do the most good." Murphy continued his recollection: "I was in Paris with a British MI-6 officer, Malcolm Muggeridge, months before the Germans surrendered, having a few drinks. I remember—he was enjoying himself in Paris—I said, 'Malcolm, the war isn't over yet. I don't think we should start celebrating this early.' 'Oh,' he said, 'don't give it a thought. There is nothing that you or I or any of these people can do that is going to shorten the war one day. From now on it is all over, and we may as well admit it and enjoy ourselves.' I guess he was right."[64]

NEW FRIENDS

Under Donovan the OSS tried everything. Its weakness was that like any new organization, it was trying everything for the first time. Donovan realized that for OSS to survive, it had to pay its way with the military and the White House through tactical exploits—Operational Groups, Jedburghs, Detachment 101—although he personally was more interested in the problems of the future and specifically in the question of permanent U.S. intelligence capability. As much as anything else, OSS was successful merely by virtue of its having been created in the first place—bringing with it a new American awareness and understanding of the place of the United States in the world—and that it stayed in business during the war. "Looking back on it now," Dr. William Langer, a senior OSS analyst, was to say, "perhaps Bill Donovan's greatest single achievement during the war was to survive."[65] A further, though mixed success lay in its legacy: the institutionalization in the CIA of centralized intelligence analysis within the fabric of the government. "For me and many of my friends," Richard Helms remarked about Donovan in 1983, "his most important contribution was to found, defend and operate the first integrated intelligence organization in U.S. history. He was truly the father of American intelligence. Before him our efforts were trivial."[66]

The OSS legacy also had another facet. Under Donovan the agency took some of the first steps in the cold war with the USSR, at times walking a thin line between Allied interests in winning the war and Donovan's perceptions of U.S. postwar interests. Thus he secretly copied the Russian codes the OSS purchased from the Finns (had this been known, the repercussions on the OSS surely would have been great, although the Russians must have assumed that they had been copied) and maintained OSS access to the communications traffic between Marshal Malinovsky in Bucharest and his superiors in Moscow from late 1944 until the war's end. Donovan also took some very dubious action when, in the spring of 1945, he secretly authorized OSS to make an intelligence target of Soviet intentions in the Balkans. The nature of this move was so clearly cold-war that he gave the order verbally and not in writing. "During that time," recalled Lawrence Houston, who was acting deputy head of the OSS in the Middle East theater, "came the first directive Donovan put out to change our intelligence targets from strictly German and Middle East to Russian intentions in the Balkans. That was the first time Donovan had put out such a directive: it was about April 1945. The new head of the Secret Intelligence branch came out and he brought this by word of mouth. Donovan wouldn't put it in writing."[67] Within weeks of the end of the war in Europe, suspicion of Russia secured special privileges and exemptions for General Reinhard Gehlen, head of the Abwehr's Foreign Armies East (Fremde Heere Ost—FHO) section and responsible for military intelligence about the Soviet Union.

For Gehlen the war had been a tremendous personal success story. In 1942, three days before his fortieth birthday, and with the rank of lieutenant colonel in the Wehrmacht, he was placed in command of FHO—a move he did not welcome. Before then he had served as a staff officer on the operational side: he was the head of strategic planning of the Wehrmacht's Operation Branch Group I covering the Russian front. Within two weeks of his appointment he made a significant impact. He reorganized FHO, closely tying it to military functions instead of geographical areas. Like Donovan, he placed great value on research and analysis work and sped up the intelligence-collection and -analysis processes. Also, again like Donovan, he paid attention to the presentation of his conclusions, using graphic illustrations, maps, and colored diagrams.

In 1944 Gehlen was promoted to general, becoming one of the few who reached the rank without significant operational experience at the front during the war. However, careful examination of the record shows that Gehlen's reputation was not deserved. His reports tended to equivocate, so that he could always claim credit for predicting an attack or other major events on the front, and in some cases his forecasts were completely wrong.[68] What was important in 1945, however, was that he had an excellent reputation, not only in the German Army but also among the Allies. Toward the end of May 1945, about two weeks after the German surrender, Gehlen gave himself up to the U.S. Army in Bavaria and, to his consternation, was described as "just another Nazi."[69] A month later Brigadier General Edwin L. Sibert, G-2 of the U.S. Twelfth Army in Germany, came across Gehlen's name in the prisoner roster.

Realizing that he might have useful information, he personally debriefed him. During their sessions together Sibert was more and more impressed by the German, particularly by his forecasts of Soviet policy in postwar Europe. According to Gehlen, Stalin would keep Poland in the Soviet fold, and Czechoslovakia, Bulgaria, Hungary, and Rumania would become Soviet satellite states. Unless the Western Allies were clearly resolute in their determination to see a free Germany, Gehlen warned, the Soviet Union would even risk war to secure control of the whole country. Gehlen told Sibert that he would be willing to give the Americans a hoard of corroborating FHO documents, which he had hidden away, in return for freedom for himself and members of his staff in various POW camps. On his own authority Sibert agreed and established Gehlen at the headquarters of U.S. forces in Germany in Wiesbaden. Gehlen then led Sibert to his hidden documents in the Bavarian Alps. "Here," he said, touching one of several steel cases, "are the secrets of the Kremlin. If you use them properly, Stalin is doomed."[70]

Gehlen produced a summary of his Kremlin secrets, including a list of OSS men who, he claimed, were members of the U.S. Communist party. He also included profiles of the Soviet leadership and items of Kremlin gossip, strongly hinting that he had a source high in the Russian administration. His most useful information, in fact, was the Soviet order of battle at the time of the German collapse. At this point Sibert decided he had enough evidence to convince his superiors to go along with Gehlen, and he informed General Walter Bedell Smith, Eisenhower's Chief of Staff at Supreme Headquarters, Allied Forces Europe (SHAFE), of his contact. Since Eisenhower had forbidden fraternization with Germans and was involved in increasingly difficult talks on cooperation with Marshal Zhukov, Bedell Smith gave his own consent to Sibert to continue the Gehlen operation. Sibert then informed Donovan, Dulles (who had moved from Switzerland to become OSS head in Germany), and the War Department in Washington. All agreed on Gehlen's value as a source of information and intelligence to the United States. (Gehlen was also able to offer the U.S. the prospect of an intelligence network in eastern Europe, since some FHO agents had been left behind as the Wehrmacht retreated.) When Gehlen's car was ambushed and hit by a bullet, they realized even more the importance of his information. Shortly afterward Gehlen and three members of his staff were secretly flown on Bedell Smith's plane to Washington, where he arrived on September 20, 1945—the same day that President Truman signed an executive order giving Donovan ten days to disband the OSS.

—3—

Fear and Emergency 1945-1947

"As soon as we found ourselves at war with the Germans, on the same side as the Russians," George Kennan has observed, "then our feelings toward them changed entirely."[1] During the first years of the war there was an almost euphoric attitude toward the Soviet Union among the great mass of Americans. President Roosevelt felt he could more easily make a deal with Russia than he could with the British Empire, which he saw as a rival, and his wife, Eleanor, and the Vice-President, Henry Wallace, were both pro-Russian—in Wallace's case to a marked degree. Walter Duranty, *The New York Times* correspondent in Moscow, who won two Pulitzer Prizes for reporting and who was universally held to be *the* expert on Soviet affairs, was considered by Joseph Alsop to be an apologist/propagandist for the Soviet system. Alsop charged that on at least one occasion Duranty filed a completely false account of the Stalin-induced starvation in the Ukraine in which perhaps five million people died. "The Duranty cover-up, for that is what it was," said Alsop, "also continued thereafter; and no one of consequence told the terrible truth."[2] The climate of opinion in the United States between 1941 and 1944 willed a heroism on the Soviet Union and on Stalin. By 1944 only a handful of men, among them William Donovan, thought otherwise, seeing the Soviet Union as a foreign despotism reaching out and really affecting American interests, with its supporters using the cover of the common cause to penetrate deep within the institutional infrastructure of the United States.

As early as September 1944 Donovan was conducting a major campaign for the survival of OSS in peacetime. He saw Russia as the future enemy and recognized that American isolationism was over: there could be no postwar withdrawal from the politics of the world. On September 17, 1944, at the request of General Walter Bedell Smith, he completed a report entitled "The need in the United States on a permanent basis as an integral part of our military establishment of a long-range strategic intelligence organization with attendant 'subversion' and 'deception of the enemy' functions." Donovan argued the need for the OSS or "a new but similar agency" to remain after the war on equal terms with the military as the "fourth arm" of the fighting services, with "a status equal to that of the army, navy and air force."* He was convinced that such an intelligence organization was something that the United States would definitely need on an active basis and not merely as a potential that could be activated as needed. Six days later, Harold D. Smith, the director of the Bureau of the Budget, sent Donovan a copy of a letter from Roosevelt asking for plans for the liquidation of war agencies. Smith wanted to know how Donovan proposed "to convert from a war to a peace basis or to liquidate, as the case may be."[3]

Without being able openly to state his fears about future relations with Russia, Donovan was hamstrung in his arguments. The climate of American opinion would not take kindly to suggestions that one of America's allies in war would soon be an enemy in peace. Apart from official Washington's emotional identification with the Soviet Union as a new revolutionary power whose back had been forced to the wall by Nazi Germany, the governing elite knew that the view of Russia as an enemy of the West was a key element in Nazi propaganda. If Donovan advanced this argument, he would be accused of playing into Nazi hands. So he concentrated instead on historical and bureaucratic justifications for a postwar centralized intelligence agency, emphasizing the inadequacy of American intelligence at the time of Pearl Harbor, recommending a permanent peacetime organization established "to gather and correlate information of military value in time of war" but limited to areas outside the Americas.[4] For him, America and the world were entwined. He believed that there was going to be a much greater degree of interpenetration than most people recognized. This in turn, Donovan saw, meant a different kind of intelligence, both in terms of institution and of capacity, because it would be addressing a truly closed society—the Soviet Union.†

*Thomas F. Troy, *Donovan and the CIA* (Frederick, Md.: University Publications of America, 1981), p. 218. Nothing came of this report, probably because there were powerful forces against continuing the OSS in any form after the war. Also, by arguing for parity with the military, Donovan was proposing an agency that would compete strongly for resources without accepting military control. So it was not surprising that the military—with some individual exceptions like Bedell Smith—opposed his proposal.

†Donovan in 1944 was much more accurate than even he imagined. Within eight years the CIA was funding newspapers in Italy and a cultural magazine in England. Along with the FBI, it was wrestling with the problem of Americans who were Soviet spies. The extent to which the capacity requirements of intelligence changed to the monitoring of whole societies from an emphasis on military and political strategy was demonstrated by the U-2 photographs that revealed Soviet cities previously unknown in the West. Assessing a closed society was a new problem.

TOWARD PEACETIME INTELLIGENCE

Donovan was forced to talk in terms of military concern; if he suggested that political concerns would, in fact, be paramount in the postwar world, the cause of peacetime centralized intelligence would be vulnerable to the question, "What political concerns?" Any coherent answer would have an anti-Russian or anti-British, -French or -Dutch imperial bias. But by focusing on military concerns as justification for peacetime centralized intelligence, he ran the risk of alienating the military, who, with reason, pointed out that military concerns were the military's business. In the military's view, an efficient military intelligence service could easily be centralized within the War Department after the war. Donovan was also up against the traditional military resistance to civilian intelligence dealing with military matters.

Typically, Roosevelt asked a number of people for advice about postwar intelligence, ostentatiously giving equal weight to each reply. John Franklin Carter, a New Deal journalist and an intimate of Roosevelt's, had been running a small clandestine intelligence group for FDR since 1941. He came across Donovan's proposal in reply to Harold Smith and immediately warned the President against it. The OSS, said Carter, had probably been "penetrated" by British Intelligence, and he recommended himself and his small group for the job of postwar intelligence coordination. The origins of the OSS, which owed a great deal to British Intelligence, were now catching up with Donovan. The OSS director, asked by the President to comment on Carter's warning, was told by one senior OSS officer that he had to say something about "our present national dependence upon British Intelligence," indicating that Carter had drawn blood. Not only was Donovan finding that he had to justify OSS instead of arguing the case for postwar intelligence but also he was being drawn into squabbles about unessential issues and arguments about theoretical bureaucratic boundaries in postwar Washington. On November 7 he sent Roosevelt a reply to Carter, dismissing the allegation that OSS had been penetrated by the British, stating that OSS had "maintained the integrity of our organization" and was "an independent American Intelligence Service."* "Our

---

*Donovan was deluding himself if he really believed OSS had not been penetrated. The FBI in 1942 began to document what amounted to a communist colony within OSS, listing six people (whose names have been removed from the document, released under the Freedom of Information Act) as being involved (Sheffield Edwards, director of security, CIA, to J. Edgar Hoover, director, FBI, May 12, 1955). Much more significant, some months after the formation of COI "Little Bill" Stephenson gave Donovan a map showing Nazi German plans for the reorganization of South America, assuring him that British Intelligence had stolen it from a German courier later killed by the Gestapo for his bungling. In fact, the map was a clever forgery by British Intelligence, and Donovan was used to secure Roosevelt's acceptance of it. The plot succeeded, at the time helping Donovan build his prestige as a spy master.

On October 27, 1941, Roosevelt's address to the annual Navy Day dinner was broadcast. "I have in my possession a secret map, made in Germany by Hitler's government—by planners of the new world order," he announced. "It is a map of South America and a part of Central America as Hitler proposes to reorganize it. The geographical experts of Berlin have ruthlessly

allies and our enemies," he declared, "know less about our inner workings than we do about theirs." Eleven days later he followed this up with a new proposal that he sent directly to Roosevelt. The control of intelligence in peacetime, he now suggested, should be "under the direction and supervision of the President" and should be taken away from the military.[5]

This proposal immediately evoked widespread resistance. Various military men consulted by the White House described it as "dangerous." The United States had never had a President directing as well as supervising intelligence. Donovan no doubt calculated that the concept would appeal to Roosevelt and that he would need the President's energetic support for his ideas. Roosevelt had just been reelected for a fourth term, but people around him knew that he was dying. Donovan may have been attempting to secure Roosevelt's "yes" to wave under the nose of the next President. He was making an abrasive push with his proposal, depending entirely on Roosevelt's sanctioning of it before he died. He must have known it would stir up enemies who, as it turned out, could kill the idea if he failed to convince Roosevelt in time. A "central intelligence service," Donovan urged, should be under a director who should have virtually absolute authority in intelligence matters and coordination, subject only to the President. The director would work with an advisory board consisting of the secretaries of state, war, and the navy, and others whom the President might wish to appoint. Donovan knew that in order to survive, the new intelligence organization would have to be able to adapt readily to the changing world.

In December the Joint Chiefs sent Roosevelt their counterproposal. The advisory board outlined by Donovan should be a supervisory board for a postwar "Central Intelligence Authority," which, they said, in time of war would be controlled by the military in the same way as the OSS. Here matters rested while the interested parties waited anxiously for the President to decide whether or not there should be a peacetime intelligence agency, and if so, whether or not it should be centralized and under White House, State Department, or military control.* Donovan's proposal and the Joint Chiefs' counter-

---

obliterated all the existing boundary lines, bringing the whole continent under their domination. . . . This map makes clear the Nazi design not only against South America but against the United States as well." American opinion was outraged. The plan inferred from the map would put German bombers within range of Florida. A week later the Senate repealed the Neutrality Acts, and the House of Representatives followed, giving Roosevelt a free hand to wage covert war on Britain's side. It was a British Intelligence coup of the first order, accomplished through the manipulation of Donovan himself. James R. Murphy, at the time Donovan's executive assistant, said that if Donovan had suspected the map was not authentic he would never have forwarded it to the President (*The Times* [London], April 2, 1985).

*Troy, *Donovan and the CIA*, pp. 227–247. Brigadier General George V. Strong and Major General Clayton Bissell, the new head of G-2, both described Donovan's proposal as "dangerous" and urged the liquidation of the OSS at the end of the war. The Interdepartmental Intelligence Committee, established by Roosevelt in 1939, said Strong, had "covered the Western Hemisphere for intelligence purposes in an eminently satisfactory manner without any advertising, publicity or self-seeking." Bissell declared that Donovan's director of centralized intelligence proposal later would become the basis of the CIA. But, at the time, they were seen more as shots in a bureaucratic battle. Donovan pressed his arguments with the White House and the Joint Chiefs. On April 12, 1945, before any-thing had been resolved, Roosevelt died, and Vice-President Harry S Truman moved into the top job.

Truman was something of an unknown quantity in April 1945. Roosevelt had taken him on as his running mate in the 1944 election for political reasons. Henry Wallace had been dropped from the ticket because he had bruised rela-tionships with the congressional leadership, he was very left-wing, and Roose-velt considered that he had not done a good job as Vice-President. Various Democratic luminaries competed for the vice-presidential nomination, but Roosevelt chose Truman (who had not sought the nomination) because he was popular in the Congress and was a loyal Democrat acceptable to the party as a whole. He was a compromise candidate who was not well known outside of Congress and his home state of Missouri, which he had represented in the Senate since 1935. His great quality was resilience. He was a simple but not a humble man. His sense of intellectual adequacy—which was strong, retrospec-tively adding to his reputation—was sustained by a naïve awareness of being a student of history. He was fortified by his position, not by a sense of his own destiny, and since his position was President, he did not falter.

Truman was a man of business transacting the affairs of state rather than dealing with global abstractions. He never lost sight of the fact that the Presi-dent's first duty is to make up his mind. He did not formulate contingencies, and he never agonized over any decision. He was, in an Emersonian sense, a representative man. John F. Kennedy's subordinates felt that in serving him they were serving a very unusual man. Harry Truman's subordinates felt they were serving a typical American. His simplicity, coupled with the necessary vanity of a man taking on major tasks, saw him through. He was able to step from the public to the private with ease; for him there was no difference. He deferred to the creative professionals around him, though not in an uncritical

---

would have too much power and that his personal views could color analysis. At a meeting of the Joint Chiefs' Joint Intelligence Committee on December 22, 1944, Bissell told those present:

This man tells the President, tells any department of the government, the final evaluation, because the charter says one of his prerogatives is that he gives final synthesis. When he is through with it, that is the end . . . Every bit of intelligence located anywhere else is dupli-cated in this central agency. If he doesn't have it, he certainly isn't prepared to do the final evaluation; if he does have it, you have eliminated largely the necessity for other agencies. You can let them play with it, but he is the one who says what it means . . . this man doesn't have to take anybody's advice. . . . Such power in one man is not in the best interest of a democratic government. I think it is in the best interest of a dictatorship. I think it would be excellent for Germany, but I don't think it fits in with the democratic set-up we have in this country, where you run things by checks and balances.

The Joint Chiefs' reply to Donovan's proposal was redrafted five times before finally being sent to the President. In the first draft the proposed postwar agency was called for the first time the Central Intelligence Agency.

fashion. James Forrestal, the navy secretary, and Dean Acheson, undersecretary of state, both leading influences in the formation of postwar foreign policy, might press for anti-Soviet measures, but Truman's refusal to be rushed and his personal hope for a return to the ways of peace acted as a brake.

IN THE GRINDER: THE END OF OSS

In mid-April 1945 an end to the war with both Germany and Japan was in sight. Truman wanted to think about peace, not continuing hostilities. He had an instinctive distrust of secret organizations, and was content to follow the advice of the Bureau of the Budget on winding down wartime agencies. He delegated responsibility for deciding the question of peacetime centralized intelligence to his staff and Harold D. Smith.[6] Donovan knew what the decision would be. He thought that Roosevelt would have accepted his plan, but Truman would surely reject it. He was in Paris on the day Roosevelt died. Colonel Ned Buxton spoke to him that evening. "What will happen now to OSS?" Buxton asked. "I'm afraid it's the end" was Donovan's reply.[7]

Donovan's fear, however, did not stop him from continuing to fight for postwar centralized intelligence, even though the odds against success rapidly increased. On February 9, 1945, a front-page banner-headline article by Walter Trohan in the *Chicago Tribune*, the New York *Daily News*, and the *Washington Times-Herald* had revealed Donovan's postwar plans in detail. It was a leak and a hatchet job, connected at the time to J. Edgar Hoover. All three newspapers were conservative in outlook, deeply suspicious of the New Deal. In May, Trohan broke two more anti-OSS stories concerning General MacArthur's and Admiral Nimitz's refusals to have OSS in their areas. The headlines read "OSS Is Branded British Agency to Legislators" and "British Control of OSS Bared in Congress Probe."* In the gossip columns OSS was hailed again as "Oh So Social" and "Oh So Secret" and referred to as "The Glamour Set."[8] At about the same time, Truman received a report detailing accusations (some of them true) of corruption, inefficiency, nepotism, insecurity, orgies, and recklessness against OSS and OSS officers.† Donovan, faced with another outcry against his

---

*Washington Times-Herald, May 18 and 19, 1945. The New York Times, in contrast, argued for Donovan's proposals. On February 13, 1945, following the first leak, this newspaper denounced the comparison of Donovan's proposed intelligence service with the Gestapo and pointed out that bureaucratic rivalries were involved. In the opinion of the Times, the President would have to intervene to forestall a return to the prewar situation, when each service looked after its own intelligence and there was no coordination: "failure to support the proposal," the editorial concluded, "would lay open the country to grave dangers from without."

†The report was commissioned secretly by Roosevelt (Donovan's faith in FDR was almost certainly misplaced), and was conducted by a Colonel Richard Park, Jr. Park listed over a hundred accusations against the OSS and OSS personnel and recommended that Donovan be replaced and the OSS be broken up. For the background, see Troy, Donovan and the CIA, p. 282, and Anthony Cave Brown, Wild Bill Donovan: The Last Hero (New York: Times Books, 1982), pp. 792–793.

agency, decided that the best thing he could do would be to ride out the storm. He sent various reports of OSS successes to Truman but otherwise took no strong countermeasures that spring.[9]

By early August 1945 Donovan clearly saw that OSS in its wartime form definitely would not survive the war, and he prepared for its liquidation. But this did not stop him from continuing to argue for "the establishment for the first time in our nation's history of a foreign secret intelligence service which reported information as seen through American eyes" and to emphasize that research and analysis were "an integral and inseparable part of this service."[10] He declared that he wanted to return to private life. People close to him considered that his failure to convince the President of the need for a postwar intelligence agency along the lines of OSS had both distressed and disillusioned him deeply. It was as if he recognized that he might be an impediment to his own proposal and wanted to make it absolutely clear that neither self-aggrandizement nor personal publicity was part of his reasons for urging a peacetime successor to the OSS. He threw himself into preparing for the Nuremberg war crimes trials instead. Truman agreed to his appointment as a member of the American prosecuting team, and for the rest of his life, apart from a stint as ambassador to Thailand, Donovan stayed with the law.*

With the writing on the wall for the OSS clearly visible, Donovan authorized the release of OSS success stories to the press—Allen Dulles gave an edited account of Operation Sunrise to *The Saturday Evening Post*—in an attempt to generate public support for a similar postwar agency. It was to no avail. On September 13 Truman decided that the OSS would end.† Within the bureaucracy the State Department volunteered to take over OSS Research and Analysis (and laid claim to taking the lead in peacetime intelligence). The War Department agreed to oversee the winding down of OSS operations. On September 20 Harold D. Smith placed an executive order dissolving the OSS in front of Truman, who "glanced over the documents and signed."‡

---

*The question of why Donovan dropped out of the intelligence scene after the war lingers on. The ambassadorship was clearly a pat on the head for the child being sent to bed early. Donovan was seen as an enthusiastic amateur, with a good eye for material, but not as a good proceduralist. He was respected, but he was not consulted in the same way that Dean Acheson or Clark Clifford were applied to between and after their periods of government service. All his precedents were not followed: the OSS precedent respected by the CIA was its research and analysis, not its operations, to which Donovan was most attached despite the fact that he had been instrumental in establishing the research-and-analysis function.

†On September 5 Truman made it clear to Harold D. Smith that he wanted the various secret agencies substantially cut down, at the very least. Some days later Smith's Committee on Agency Liquidation made the recommendation "to dispose of OSS by a transfer of its research staff to State and its clandestine activities and administrative facilities to the War Department." Truman decided to accept this recommendation "even if Donovan did not like it" (Bradley F. Smith, *The Shadow Warriors* [New York: Basic Books, 1983] p. 406).

‡Ibid., p. 407. Also see *The New York Times*, September 21, 1945, editorial by Arthur Krock, in which he says that some of the OSS's activities had been made public to persuade the American people that a skilled and unified intelligence department is essential to the mainte-

The fragmentation of OSS meant the end of wartime intelligence coordination attempts. Over the next five months Truman was to change his mind completely, becoming an ardent advocate of centralized, coordinated intelligence in the face of failed hopes and dreams. There was probably a personal element in his decision as well. "I always thought Truman abolished OSS because the Joint Chiefs of Staff said 'Let's get rid of this guy Donovan. He's a pain in the ass. He's all over the place.' That must also have been buttressed by the end of the war and the feeling of 'Let's get rid of it all. Let's get back to peace,' " reflected Tom Braden, an old OSS man.[11] "Truman and Donovan never got along," remembered James R. Murphy. "They had no regard for each other. Truman was in World War I as a captain; Donovan came out as a colonel. Donovan got all the decorations. Donovan was a Catholic Republican. Truman was a Democratic Baptist. They never saw eye to eye on anything."[12]

From September 20, 1945, to January 22, 1946, one of the fiercest bureaucratic battles Washington has ever known raged over intelligence: what it should be, who should have it, and who should control it. As a result of the experience of the war and of OSS, all the parties involved—the State and War departments, the services, and the advocates of a civilian central intelligence agency—knew what they wanted and what was involved. Some, such as James Forrestal and the Joint Chiefs, wanted military intelligence to be an arm of the military establishment; some (Donovan, for example) wanted a great civilian intelligence agency; and, like Harold D. Smith, some wanted only better policing of the rival services and looked to a director who could knock heads together in the President's name.

The backdrop to the intelligence struggle was the debate about a unified Department of Defense, which was going on simultaneously. The mood was for greater centralization. The questions were: Would a "central intelligence agency" really be just that or simply represent a reduction of existing fragmentation? If there was to be a central agency, who would control it? "Between the September abolition of OSS and January 22, 1946," recalled Lawrence Houston, who was to become CIA general counsel for twenty-six years, "I witnessed one of the toughest bureaucratic fights—tougher than I'd ever seen before; as tough as anything I saw afterward—about the future of the intelligence services. At the time, the State Department thought the conduct of peacetime intelligence impinged on foreign affairs, so they ought to be in charge; the army thought they were the pros and therefore they should be in charge; and the navy vaguely supported the army."[13]

Faced with this line-up, the two elements of OSS that remained—Re-

nance of peace and that its work would lie outside the fields of the services, the State Department, and the FBI. Truman, in writing to Donovan to notify him of the decision, maintained that the fragmentation of OSS represented "the beginning of the development of a coordinated system of foreign intelligence within the permanent framework of the government." In other words, as far as Truman was concerned, pre-1941 represented a permanent state; no regard was given to the war experience or the consequences of victory.

search and Analysis, under Dr. William Langer in the State Department, and the operations side, under Brigadier General John Magruder in the War Department, where it was now called the Strategic Services Unit (SSU) and was charged with concluding OSS operations—found themselves in the bureaucratic meat grinder. By 1947 Research and Analysis had declined from 1350 people to only about 500, while the SSU dropped to about 800 from its 1945 level of 9000.[14] This decline, while in part reflecting the reluctance of the Truman administration to accept a need for peacetime intelligence greater than that existing at the time of Pearl Harbor, did not reflect the determination of the supporters of centralized peacetime intelligence. Magruder and a number of other quietly influential officers in the War Department, in the face of strong pressure for military control of a centralized agency, adopted the concept of an independent and nonpolitical civilian service for peacetime intelligence, keeping it alive in military circles and lending to it the military's prestige from victory.

Despite having the job of winding down OSS operations, Magruder, in fact, continued some operations in Southeast Asia and China. He made a conscious effort to keep the best of OSS in SSU. Allen Dulles and Richard Helms, for example, stayed on in Germany at Magruder's request, making the transition to peacetime intelligence operations there.* An intellectual, Magruder came from an army family and was himself a regular officer. In a number of subtle ways he tried to convince officials of the value of peacetime intelligence. He organized an official history of OSS; the idea for it was approved in mid-1946, and the project was completed in September of that same year. The history was circulated within the bureaucracy, where it played an influential role in gaining support for Donovan's original concept of coordinated intelligence. Both halves of the OSS—Magruder's in the War Department and Langer's in the State Department—kept closely in touch with each other and with old OSS hands outside. Langer developed a comprehensive biographical index of all former American intelligence personnel for future reference. The coherence of former OSS people, and the fact of OSS's simple division between the State and War departments in 1945, meant that under one name or the other the essence of OSS survived into the postwar years.[15]

THE CENTRAL INTELLIGENCE GROUP, 1946

The combination of the developing cold war and Truman's changing perception of the Soviet Union—factors outside the bureaucratic struggle—ulti-

---

*Dulles went back to the law firm of Sullivan and Cromwell in 1946. Magruder had high-level support from James Forrestal and the Joint Chiefs, who, in their December 1944 memorandum to Roosevelt, accepted the need for peacetime centralized intelligence. They saw Magruder as not so much keeping the OSS alive as making an excellent case for the military to control postwar intelligence. In fact, once he was appointed, Magruder fought for an independent, centralized civilian intelligence agency.

mately advanced the cause of central intelligence. Intimately bound to this was a view of America's postwar role in world affairs, which in turn was supported by the immediate postwar experience. Russian armies, in contrast to American and British ones, had been kept on an offensive footing in Europe after 1945. By the end of the year Truman and senior officials had come to realize that the Russians saw the Western allies as enemies. No one had expected enmity to intensify so quickly, and part of the sense of urgency of the time lay in coming to grips with this new and unwanted confrontation.

Truman focused on the immediate problem characteristically. He examined the recent past for instructive lessons. He reached the conclusion that if Russian occupation/manipulation of eastern Europe continued and Russian imperial ambitions succeeded in China (Mao Tse-tung was seen as a Soviet stooge, not as an independent national communist leader), America would have to be prepared to intervene to protect "free" countries everywhere. The war experience had taught that efficiency lay in elite organizations and in slimmed-down decision making. These lessons led Truman to order an appraisal of U.S. national security in January 1946. Eighteen months later a new post, that of secretary of defense, was created in charge of the "National Military Establishment." Also created was the Central Intelligence Agency.*

On January 22, 1946, while the appraisal of national security was under way, Truman issued a directive creating a Central Intelligence Group (CIG), jointly funded and staffed by the departments of State, War, and the Navy. The September 1945–January 1946 fight over intelligence was over: there would be a peacetime intelligence apparatus, which was coordinated and centralized under the overall control of the President, just as Donovan had conceived. The CIG was under the direction of a director of Central Intelligence, who was a presidential appointee advised by an Intelligence Advisory Board made up of the heads (or their representatives) of the military and civilian intelligence agencies. The director of Central Intelligence was responsible to the National Intelligence Authority, consisting of the secretaries of state, war, and the navy, and a presidential representative. The job of the director was to correlate and evaluate intelligence and to "perform such other functions and duties related to intelligence affecting the national security as the President and

---

*Truman's directive was sent on January 22, 1946. It created the National Intelligence Authority, to ensure that "all Federal foreign intelligence activities be planned, developed and coordinated so as to assure the most effective accomplishment of the intelligence mission relating to the national security" (Troy, *Donovan and the CIA*, pp. 346, 464–465).

Truman did not suddenly change his mind about peacetime intelligence. In the fall of 1945 he asked one of his advisers, Clark Clifford, to think about the creation of a central intelligence agency in peacetime. Truman's concept was for a civilian agency—he had a traditional dislike of military domestic involvement—and he wanted an authoritative source of intelligence. So those interested in controlling intelligence in the winter of 1945–1946 were battling for control of something that was going to happen (interview, Clark Clifford, May 21, 1985).

the National Intelligence Authority may from time to time direct."[16] At the time, covert operations were not envisaged: the new arrangements were seen far more as a Washington bureaucratic affair. Dirty tricks to match Soviet dirty tricks were still to come. There were also to be "no police, law enforcement or internal security functions . . . exercised under this directive." Truman was quite clear: he was not going to tolerate anything that his political opponents could term an "American Gestapo."

On January 23, 1946, the day after his directive was circulated, Truman appointed Rear Admiral Sidney W. Souers the first director of Central Intelligence. Truman was tired of having numerous people giving him briefings and their views on world affairs, and he wanted one source to which he could look with confidence. Souers was a reserve officer who in private life was a St. Louis banker and businessman. During the war he had served as deputy chief of naval intelligence. A journalist who interviewed him shortly after his appointment asked, "What do you want to do?" thinking he might hear what the government's intelligence priorities were. Souers, who was sitting behind Donovan's old desk, chuckled and said, "I want to go home."[17] He was James Forrestal's recommended choice for the new job.[18] He was a good administrator, got along well with Truman (he later became a Truman crony), and agreed with Forrestal that the Soviet Union presented the greatest single threat to the security of the United States.

Souers did not have a clear policy function to perform (and perhaps Truman did not intend that he should have). His appointment was a response to increasing fears and perceptions of the time: that the United States was faced by a new enemy, the Soviet Union, which was intent on global expansion by overt and covert means. This should have given Souers an enormous job of organizing on several levels simultaneously, but he was not given the authority or the resources to do so. Both his appointment and the CIG were an interim affair on the path toward the CIA. By being director, however, he gave force to the idea of peacetime intelligence. What remained in the balance was whether the military, the State Department, or the White House would control it. Powerful forces were at work preparing the ground for a unified Department of Defense, and Souers, as a Forrestal protégé, would have worked easily from within such a department. He would also work equally easily from within the White House, as his friendship with Truman was to show.

The feuding between the State, War, and Navy departments over controlling intelligence was what strengthened the arguments for a new, independent civilian agency with presidential backing so that it could centralize information. The problems of the emerging cold war were also new, and the creation of an autonomous agency was an authentically American response. The eventual outcome, however, was by no means certain when Souers accepted the appointment. He agreed to take the job for six months, and he soon found himself completely outmaneuvered by the established agencies. Far from heading an independent Central Intelligence Group, Souers was the administrative director of an interdepartmental group answerable to a committee, the National Intelligence Authority, a situation in which he was outranked by Fleet Admiral William D. Leahy, Truman's representative, and outclassed by the three secretaries. In the one hundred and forty days that Souers was director of Central Intelligence—January 23–June 10, 1946—the National Intelligence Authority met three times and issued three directives, each of which made clear that they were in charge.

Donovan, who had wanted a civilian intelligence service independent of other departments, regarded Truman's arrangements as an "advance," which indeed they were.[19] But they were also within the framework of government: the three secretaries and Admiral Leahy actually controlled the director and the Central Intelligence Group, who were not directly responsible to the President or to Congress.[20] Truman had made the critical decision to take peacetime intelligence seriously—this had been the big battle. Now the battle would be about coordination and control. Would American intelligence remain the prerogative of the operating departments, fragmented and geared to battlefield and day-to-day concerns? Or would it be centralized, under presidential control, geared to strategy and long-term policy?

THE STATUTORY BACKGROUND

The battle for control began immediately. The armed services were dead set on having their own system and fought doggedly to prevent civilian interference. They had the great advantage of enormous prestige from the war, while the advocates of a centralized, fundamentally civilian intelligence agency had the disadvantage of being tied to OSS—an agency unpopular in the Truman White House.* The armed services, however, also had a major disadvantage: they were involved in an extraordinarily vitriolic feud involving peacetime pecking orders and the question of whether or not there should be a separate air force (until 1947 there was only an Army Air Force). Many senior military officers in all service branches were dismissed or reassigned before the dust settled—moves that severely reduced the military's overall bureaucratic effectiveness. Admiral Leahy, Truman's Chief of Staff, was guided by the December 1944 Joint Chiefs' recommendations, which were not much removed from Donovan's. There was a good deal of common ground, therefore, between the advocates of military control and the advocates of presidential control on the organization of peacetime intelligence.

*Admiral Leahy, who had Truman's ear, detested Donovan and had resented OSS throughout the war. He consistently argued for military control of intelligence and found in Truman a President who had a natural preference for military formations. For Truman's views on this, see his *Memoirs: Years of Trial and Hope 1946–1952* (New York: Doubleday, 1956), pp. 55–58.

During his six months as director of Central Intelligence, Souers completed one of the most important stages in determining the nature of centralized intelligence: an investigation of the statutory background and requirements for a comprehensive peacetime agency. Behind this lay the reports of two very influential bodies, whose recommendations were by 1946 already playing a central role in the debate on intelligence—the Eberstadt and Lovett committees. In June 1945, in the midst of the struggle over the future of the OSS, James Forrestal, the strong-minded, driven, ambitious, sensitive, publicity-conscious navy secretary, took a personal interest in the question of a unified Department of Defense. He commissioned Ferdinand Eberstadt, an old friend and, like Forrestal, a New York investment banker, to report on the subject from a navy perspective (as secretary of the navy, Forrestal did not want his department or position to lose out in any new arrangements).

Three months later, on September 25, 1945, Eberstadt recommended, among other things, the creation of a civilian Central Intelligence Agency answering to a National Security Council that was to advise the President.[21] Forrestal took up the committee's proposal for a CIA, and this, together with Eberstadt's conclusions about the navy's position in a Department of Defense, prompted the secretary of war, Robert P. Patterson, in mid-October, to appoint the Lovett Board to advise him on his response to Forrestal and Eberstadt. Robert A. Lovett was assistant secretary of war for air under Patterson, and he was instructed to make certain that the positions of the army and of the soon to be separate air force were considered. Lovett reported on November 3, 1945, essentially endorsing Eberstadt's proposals for a civilian Central Intelligence Agency, adding an Intelligence Advisory Board, consisting of the representatives of military intelligence, to advise the director of Central Intelligence. The CIA itself, said Lovett, should "operate as the sole collection agency for all departments . . . in the foreign espionage and counter-espionage fields."[22] These two reports and Donovan's 1944 memorandum effectively launched the CIA.

Immediate administrative and military concerns dominated the approach to central intelligence in 1945. Long-term, analytic questions were not yet asked. Rather, the debate about intelligence reflected what was already beginning to happen in the secret espionage warfare in Europe. Soviet and American military intelligence competed to collect German scientists, engineers, and technicians. Agents and informers on both sides were kidnapped and sometimes murdered. There was ruthless fighting to control political, labor, and professional groupings of all kinds. It was a tense, dangerous, murky year. The people who realized they were dealing with a continuing struggle (who by the end of 1945 included Truman and most senior government officials) faced the practical difficulty of keeping wartime institutions going and retargeting them in the post V-E and V-J Day euphoria of peace and the demand to bring the boys home.

The American public was not prepared for a continuing struggle. Peace still meant peace, demobilization, business as (prewar) usual. There was still the hope that a deal could be made with Russia and confrontation avoided. No one thought in 1945–50 that a central intelligence agency would be a final undertaking. The CIA was to become frozen in place because the circumstances of the period—the condition of neither war nor peace—remained unchanged for the next fifteen years. The notion of intelligence as a career in itself was still not present; everyone thought of it as a continuation of war service. Truman's decision to support the creation of the CIA and its immediate predecessor, the CIG, was a politician's response to an emergency that, it was considered, had to be resolved soon either by peace or by war. What was ignored was the legal operating position. In war a President enjoys enormous legal freedoms; in peace the position is quite different. What would be the position if the CIA killed someone? In war the question would not be asked. In peace it certainly would be.

Recognizing the need for a proper legal background, Souers appointed Lawrence Houston, on loan from the Strategic Services Unit, as CIG's general counsel. "All the personnel at CIG were lent by other departments," Houston recalled. "It had no hiring and firing powers of its own—that was one of its drawbacks." In fact, the group was seen as being more of a small coordinating team than an overall commanding or operating agency. "We went to the books and found there was a statute which said there could not be an organization set up in the executive branch for more than one year without statutory background. There was no statutory background at all. That February we started to go to work and put together what might be legislation for an equivalent peacetime organization. The work was based quite a bit on Donovan's 1944 memo. We looked at all the legal problems we could think of that had turned up in the running of OSS and put them in a concept paper and a long administrative draft."[23] On June 13, 1946, three days after Souers retired as director of Central Intelligence, Houston submitted his report to the new director, Army Air Force Lieutenant General Hoyt S. Vandenberg. It was entitled "Administrative Authority of CIG" and declared that the Central Intelligence Group had "purely a coordination function with no substance or authority to act on its own responsibility in other than an advisory and directing capacity." After January 1947, Houston pointed out, it was questionable whether CIG could legally continue without legislation.[24]

At this stage attention was focused on the relationship the proposed Central Intelligence Agency would have with the President. As commander in chief the President was considered to have the authority necessary to establish and control a peacetime intelligence agency—if additional legislation were passed. Though correct, this view took insufficient note of the role of Congress in controlling intelligence activities. It was just one more step in the concentration of power in the hands of the President that began during the New Deal and World War II. This was by no means obvious at the time, and Congress itself showed little interest in interfering. The focus in Washington was not on how to return to a pre-Pearl Harbor peace but on how to come to terms with America's new world position.

The change in Truman's own perceptions was symptomatic of this national mood. No longer was he trying to restore what he imagined to be the prewar administrative arrangements, as he had set out to do in April 1945. He had an emotional attitude, not an operational objective. Now he was concerned with creating new worldwide institutions instead of simply enlarging the responsibilities of existing ones. Just like any President, he needed institutions that could help him deal with the dawning problems of the day. He had little sense of the day becoming years. The CIA, with its world theater of operations, was part of this change, and, as with any great institution, it was to mirror the general pattern of its creative culture. It was set against a background of enemies within and without, a world to be remade, a fantastic increase in the momentum of scientific and technical advances, a new American world outlook and responsibility, a quivering sense of emergency and of speed.

At first, however, Truman followed through with Roosevelt's plans to trim the wartime administration back to its peacetime level, and authorized a rapid demobilization. The Republican party built upon its opposition to the New Deal, calling for greater retrenchment and curtailment of presidential power and, by and large, a return to isolation. The hope for peace channeled ordinary people's thoughts away from the harsh realities of the postwar world. It was not until Russia's aggressive behavior in eastern Europe became clear that the attitude of Americans began to change. People realized—perhaps for the first time—that there would be a battle for peace, just as there had been during war. They began to remember the force, five years earlier, of the pro-Nazi enemy within that had campaigned to keep the United States isolated from Britain's struggle. People remembered the August 1939 Nazi-Soviet Pact and the fashionableness of the left, the popular front, and communism during the Spanish civil war. They wondered if the left might not have learned from the right, if the Soviets might not be spying and plotting in the same way the Nazis had done.

These thoughts brought with them a posteuphoria depression that gripped the nation. Despite America's spirit of victory, there was no escaping the Soviet repression in eastern Europe. Churchill had consistently warned Roosevelt and then Truman that the Soviet Union would be an enemy in peace, but the Americans believed that they could deal with Stalin. Shortly after being appointed secretary of state by Truman in June 1945, James F. Byrnes said that the "Soviet Union has a right to friendly governments along its borders," while the undersecretary of state, Dean Acheson, spoke of "a Monroe Doctrine for Eastern Europe."[25] These men were convinced that their democratic ideals could function in postwar world affairs. They believed that honest dealings with the Russians would secure an equally honest exchange. Ten years later Truman explained why this attitude changed: "Victory had turned a difficult ally in war into an even more troublesome peacetime partner. Russia seemed bent upon taking advantage of war-shattered neighbors for imperialistic ends. The whole balance of power in the Far East had shifted. Most of the countries of Europe were bankrupt, millions of people were homeless and starving, and we were the only nation that could come to their help. . . . We were witnessing the transformation of the United States into a nation of unprecedented power and growing capacity."[26] By 1946 more and more Americans, with their President at the fore, felt they were sailing in uncharted seas and that war might be the "normal" state of affairs. They believed that peace would be short-lived and that they had to get America ready not simply for another war but for a rapid and complete victory that would finally ensure the end to war. The moment was unforgiving. There would be no excuse for them to hide behind if they did not deal with the world as it was rather than as they wished it to be.

This sense of urgency possessed the second director of Central Intelligence. General Vandenberg had been one of World War II's glamour "flyboys" and was clearly on his way up. He was young—forty-seven years old in 1946—boyish, and handsome. He was well connected (his uncle was Senator Arthur H. Vandenberg, the powerful Republican who became chairman of the Senate Foreign Relations Committee the following year) and ambitious.[27] His goal was to be nothing less than the Chief of Staff of the prospective independent air force. Souers had played a major part in choosing his successor, seeing in Vandenberg someone who would promote the cause of central intelligence.* Within ten days of taking up his new job Vandenberg produced a draft

---

*Troy, Donovan and the CIA, p. 359. The path to the CIA was by no means smooth. Congress remained suspicious of the need for peacetime intelligence well into 1946. On April 10, 1946, The New York Times (throughout in favor of Donovan and the concept of centralized peacetime intelligence) reported in scathing terms the decision of the House Appropriations Committee to deprive the State Department of $4 million for its Intelligence and Research unit in 1947 on the grounds that intelligence work amounted to political and economic reporting and should be performed by other units of the department. Two weeks later, on April 24, the newspaper ran an editorial criticizing congressional obstacles to intelligence and a new centralized agency and arguing that Congress was paying too much attention to accusations of Red infiltration into the State Department during the war.

The opposition of "small minds" was losing the United States the experience of war. On May 26, 1946, The New York Times criticized the National Intelligence Authority for its vulnerability to interdepartmental jealousies and internal conflict among its members and for not making provision for an elite group of clandestine agents for special emergencies. The article pointed out that it would be politically disastrous if American secret agents were caught by a foreign power and turned out to be attached to the State Department or the uniformed services. Secret agents were needed, but they had to stay secret and ultimately "deniable." On September 16 Donovan attacked the National Intelligence Authority (NIA) and the existing intelligence setup generally. The NIA was "phony," he said. It was meant to head an integrated intelligence service, but it did not. "It contains the same logrolling elements of the State Department, the Army and the Navy that have made the intelligence service the 'Little Orphan Annie' of the government since time began," he declared. "All we need is the American way of being on the level, but not letting anyone push us around" (see The New York Times, September 17, 1946).

National Intelligence Authority directive aimed at strengthening the Central Intelligence Group. Reflecting Vandenberg's desire not to have intelligence by committee, the draft directive gave the director of Central Intelligence control of all intelligence—including clandestine collection—and appointed him "executive agent" of the NIA to ensure that policies were implemented. A watered-down version based on Vandenberg's draft was issued as NIA Directive No. 5 in July 1946, but it was already apparent that Lawrence Houston was right: an effective, independent, centralized intelligence agency needed the underpinning of separate legislation. Houston's June 13, 1946, administrative draft became the focus of attention over the next six months as the Truman administration prepared to create a new intelligence agency within a framework of a reorganized pattern of national defense.

CENTRAL INTELLIGENCE AGENCY

By the spring of 1947 the cold war was in full swing. Newspapers were full of stories about the investigation of why and how the United States had been caught by surprise at Pearl Harbor. It was implied that in 1941 fifth-column spy rings had existed, which had disturbing contemporary parallels.[28] Ominous tales of worldwide Soviet ambitions filled front pages. Letters and editorials reflected a growing anticommunist feeling. Against this background a bill proposing unified control of the armed services (including a new, separate air force) in a new National Military Establishment, and a Central Intelligence Agency under the supervision of a National Security Council was sent to Congress on February 27, 1947. Giving evidence for the bill, Vandenberg made telling reference to the prewar public and government hostility to intelligence activity, linking it directly with America's lack of preparedness at Pearl Harbor. Few demurred. The attitude that refused to sanction the reading of other people's mail was completely changed. As the *Christian Science Monitor* put it, "It is generally agreed that a good intelligence service is the first line of military defense today. 'Aha!' says the average American. 'Spies!' Yes, spies—such as all the major nations of the world maintain in order to know what the others are up to. There is no use being coy about the subject."[29]

Although sentiment was on Vandenberg's side, a last stand was made by the old opponents of central intelligence in the bureaucracy. This fight was probably orchestrated by J. Edgar Hoover, whose FBI would now lose the Latin American intelligence monopoly held by its Special Intelligence Service, which it had fought to keep from Donovan throughout the war. Walter Trohan and the conservative press published stories (inspired in part probably by leaks from Hoover) echoing the 1944 and 1945 allegations that the CIA would be an American Gestapo.[30]

The opposition failed, and the National Security Act came into effect on July 26, 1947. A Central Intelligence Agency was created, responsible directly to the President through a National Security Council (NSC), which replaced the National Intelligence Authority.* It was a partial vindication of Donovan's centralized civilian-intelligence concept (although exactly what the new agency would do was not yet clear). Both the NSC and the NIA were compromise arrangements. The NIA had been an intermediary between the director of Central Intelligence and the President. The NSC was, theoretically, in a different position. In the new arrangement it was advisory to the President, who was its head. The CIA technically reported directly to the President through the director, its chief and a presidential appointee.

The gap in Donovan's thinking occurred because he failed to recognize that most Presidents were less concerned with intelligence than he was, so the President was unlikely to be very involved in intelligence matters, and thus the council would inevitably dominate the agency. It is always easier to involve the President on paper than it is in day-to-day affairs. Similarly, the ostensible powers of the agency and of the director could not always be applied: in particular, the director was to be the President's chief intelligence officer, with theoretical oversight of all intelligence activities of the U.S. government, but in practice this has never been fully established. Directors were to serve as civilians, even if they were military officers. This stipulation was inserted by a Congress anxious not only to free peacetime intelligence from military control but also to make sure that the new agency would not become another military

---

*Vandenberg had played a very important part in securing the legislation. He completely agreed with Donovan's concept of an integrated intelligence service incorporating a research and analysis function, and he tried hard to establish the director of Central Intelligence (DCI) as *the* coordinator of American intelligence, as Donovan had envisaged. In November 1946, for example, five months after his appointment as DCI, Vandenberg was laying claim to comment on State Department reports and analyses, sending memoranda directly to the President on subjects of traditional State Department concern:

In discounting the possibility that a French Government could be formed excluding the Communists, Ambassador Caffrey asserts (No. 5624, 14 November) that the Communists now have sufficient strength to seize power in France whenever they may deem it desirable to do so. . . .

The chief obstacle to such a *coup* would be the French Army and its habitual loyalty to regularly constituted authority of whatever political coloration. . . . Thus, although the Communists have an undoubted capability to precipitate civil war in France, it is unlikely that they could at present succeed in a *coup d'état.* It is agreed that, in any case, the Communists have no present motive for a resort to force, since they have more to gain by continued participation in the Government and further infiltration, with a view to obtaining power ultimately by political means. . . .

It is also agreed that any decision to resort to force would be made in Moscow rather than in Paris and would be based on overall Soviet/Communist interests rather than the prospects of the Party in France. In such case, the Party would resort to force regardless of local considerations. The continuing penetration of the French administrative structure is therefore a matter of utmost gravity, even though there is no immediate prospect of an attempted *coup.* ("Memorandum for the President," November 26, 1946, from Hoyt S. Vandenberg, Lieutenant General, USA)

voice. By the same token, Congress determined that no military officer could become secretary of defense: this was later modified for General George C. Marshall, but only for him. Congress wanted civil authority.

Many of the features of the Office of Strategic Services and the Central Intelligence Group were incorporated in the CIA, as were some lessons from OSS experience. The new agency was to be an intelligence and not an operations organization: the lesson of the OSS was that operations were "war"; intelligence was neither war nor peace. Operations stirred up heat and smoke, and their embers often started unwanted fires elsewhere. (Only later, after its foundation, did the agency come to have a covert-action capacity.)[31] The functions of the CIA were to make recommendations for the coordination of intelligence; to correlate and evaluate intelligence from all quarters relating to the national security; to perform services of common concern to all the government's intelligence organizations as determined by the National Security Council; and "to perform such other functions and duties related to intelligence affecting the national security as the National Security Council may from time to time direct." It was specifically denied "police, subpoena, law-enforcement powers or internal security functions." The director of Central Intelligence—separately from the agency he now headed—was charged with responsibility for the security of sources and methods of intelligence.[32] This latter provision was put into the act at the insistence of the army's G-2, and it was motivated by the military's mistrust of a civilian agency. For the director of Central Intelligence this created a serious ambivalence, as Richard Helms was to learn: he might one day have to choose between protecting a source or a method and misleading (if only by inference) or lying to Congress.

4

Dawn Like Thunder
1947-1948

On May 1, 1947, as the National Security Act was going through Congress, Truman announced the appointment of Rear Admiral Roscoe H. Hillenkoetter to succeed Vandenberg, whose ambition to be Chief of Staff of the new air force was fulfilled. Hillenkoetter became the third director of Central Intelligence and the first head of the CIA. At the time of his appointment he was serving as naval attaché in Paris. During the war he had worked under Admiral Nimitz as staff officer responsible for intelligence in the Pacific Theater of Operations. He was a longtime regular officer, and, like Donovan, an early cold warrior. He made a point of studying the writings of Marx, Lenin, and Stalin and liked to quote them at length to make a point.

Straddling the transition from fragmented to more centralized intelligence, Hillenkoetter's principal job was to secure the acceptance of the CIA within the bureaucracy and to try to reduce the departmental feuding that had preceded its creation. In this he faced a very tricky problem. He had to deal with Vandenberg's attempt to become the "executive agent" of the National Intelligence Authority. As executive agent, the director of Central Intelligence would have had day-to-day superiority over the heads of the other intelligence agencies. The National Security Act accorded the director a superior position but did not specify in what ways he should exercise control apart from the general instruction to coordinate and evaluate all intelligence. The new National Security Council, composed of the same people (or their representatives) as the old National Intelligence Authority, inherited the executive-agent proposal and was prepared to implement it. It was so bitterly opposed by the military and the State Department, however, that Hillenkoetter asked that it be dropped in the interests of goodwill. Once Forrestal saw that the CIA would not be controlled by his Department of Defense (he had been promoted from secretary of the navy to secretary of defense in July 1947), he was prepared to let the military pull its teeth. General George C. Marshall, secretary of state since January 1947, had always seen intelligence as a military staff activity and was suspicious of civilian intelligence. He too was prepared to see the new agency's powers reduced.

Hillenkoetter's decision was a serious step back from the position Vandenberg had fought for, and indeed no director of Central Intelligence since has ever been able to dominate the intelligence community in the way that the title and the legal outline of the job imply. It was also a significant step away from Donovan's concept; the minute a director proposed to act as *the* director of Central Intelligence, the attempt met with such resistance that it collapsed. If Truman had fully comprehended the idea of really centralized intelligence, he would have intervened for Vandenberg and Hillenkoetter, but he was conspicuous by his absence from the quarrel. Under the circumstances, Hillenkoetter was probably right not to press the executive-agent point. He was outclassed and outranked in the same way Souers had been; and goodwill was vital if the new CIA was to get off the ground in Washington. But it was the one occasion since the creation of the post on which a director might have obtained the practical administrative authority to run the whole of American intelligence.* Over the next five years Hillenkoetter and his successor managed to establish the director of Central Intelligence as more than an equal of the chiefs of military intelligence but not superior to the director of the FBI and certainly subservient to the secretaries of defense and state. No one ever intended that the DCI should be superior to these cabinet members, but in bureaucratic terms, if the DCI were executive agent of the National Security Council, he would have had more independence and freedom from pressure.

The new agency had a slow start. A year after its inception *The New York Times*, more in anger than in sorrow, was still describing U.S. intelligence as "one of the weakest links in our national security," singling out the old problem of bureaucratic rivalry between the State Department and the CIA, the FBI and the CIA, and the Department of Defense and the CIA, and the overlapping and duplication of activity that resulted as a principal cause of weakness.[1] In part this slow beginning reflected Hillenkoetter's rather quiet approach to Washington infighting. Before serving in the Pacific with Nimitz he

---

*Both John McCone, under President Kennedy, and James Schlesinger, under President Nixon, were given presidential backing as overall heads of the intelligence community, but they never developed the practical means to enforce it. Although William Casey was given cabinet rank by President Reagan, the rank still did not give the DCI administrative control. Casey was in the position to argue as an equal with other cabinet members, who, naturally, took it upon themselves to speak—as equals—for their intelligence departments. The only way to gain this control would be to centralize all intelligence under the DCI—something that nobody thinks is a good idea. The military, after all, tend to be best at military intelligence and have a proper interest in having their own intelligence services.

had worked briefly in the Office of the Chief of Naval Operations, and for the last eighteen months of the war he had been back in Washington, first as assistant director of training and then as director of planning and control in the personnel bureau of the Navy Department. He knew how Washington worked, and he was no innocent in bureaucratic battling. This was no guarantee that he would win every battle, however. When, for example, during his first year, he had a bitter argument with army intelligence about the control of agents overseas, Hillenkoetter won the battle for the CIA in theory. But in practice the army still ran its own agents. In another dispute, the CIA and the State Department disagreed over the CIA's use of embassies and State Department communications systems. This argument, which was to simmer for decades, led, according to press reports, to "open name calling" between the two organizations in April 1948.[2]

The complete collapse of public order in Colombia during the inter-American conference in Bogotá in March–April 1948, when thousands of people were killed, caused the first investigation of the work of the CIA. The violence had been building up for eight years, and it was extraordinary that the conference should have been held in Bogotá at all. Hillenkoetter was called to testify before the House Executive Expenditures subcommittee on April 15 about allegations that the CIA had failed to warn the State Department that there might be violence in Bogotá during the conference. It was an early example of the fact that the agency was expected to monitor whole societies. Hillenkoetter demonstrated that the CIA had warned the State Department that there might be unrest but that an officer there had dismissed the warning.[3] In South America, where the CIA was directed under the National Security Act to take over from the FBI, there were frequent reports of CIA officers arriving in FBI offices only to discover the FBI's files burned and the FBI agents gone. Hoover explained that the FBI had to take these drastic steps because the CIA was not sufficiently "security conscious."[4]

"The Abwehr gets better treatment from the FBI than we do," Donovan once remarked during the war.[5] And while it could not be said that after 1945 the Soviet secret services were favored above the CIA by Hoover's FBI, it was not until after Hoover's death that relations between the two organizations became amicable and cooperative. Hoover was a lifelong enemy of the agency, seeing it as a rival and competitor, and there was, unfortunately, some evidence to support Hoover's contention that the CIA was insufficiently security conscious. In the autumn of 1947, for example, two ex-OSS men attached to the CIA in Rumania made clumsy contact with an anticommunist group, which led to the arrest and trial of all the Rumanians involved.[6] Other similar stories of CIA ineptitude circulated in Washington and in the press (often, no doubt, planted by Hoover). As a result, Hillenkoetter spent a great deal of his time trying to reassure congressmen and the White House that all was well with the new agency.

At the inaugural meeting of the National Security Council on December 19, 1947, Directive NSC 4, "Coordination of Foreign Intelligence Measures," was issued. It required the secretary of state to coordinate anticommunist propaganda activity, and a secret annex, NSC 4A, instructed the director of Central Intelligence to supplement this with covert psychological warfare. James Forrestal, now secretary of defense, was behind this secret instruction.* He was worried by the prospect of a communist or communist/broad left victory in the forthcoming Italian elections, and he saw the CIA as offering a means of secretly influencing the elections in the interests of the democratic parties, in particular the Christian Democrats. Not only did this establish a long-running American support for several Italian political parties and politicians, it also brought the CIA into covert political operations—influencing and molding societies—in addition to its intelligence and espionage function.†

Hillenkoetter was concerned about the legality of NSC 4A. He knew that covert operations had been in no one's mind when the National Security Act was passed, and so he asked Lawrence Houston, who had stayed on from the Central Intelligence Group to be the CIA's first general counsel, and his deputy, John Warner, to study the act and report back on the question. Said Houston: "Hillenkoetter sent me a note asking if we had the legal authority to undertake these covert operations. We wrote back an opinion that we could find nothing in the specific language of the legislation that specifically gave us authority for such activities. Section 5 of the 'powers and duties' clauses of the act was not sufficient. Hillenkoetter then asked was there any way, and we wrote another opinion saying that if the President gave us the proper directive and the Congress gave us the money for those purposes, we had the administrative authority to carry them out. So that's how we got into covert operations."[7] With Truman's backing and with money voted by Congress in the general subvention to the agency, NSC 4A became the proper directive.‡ A Special Procedures Group, charged with implementing the requirements of the

*Forrestal had initially opposed the creation of a unified Department of Defense, but Truman, with considerable finesse, secured Forrestal's support (and administrative and bureaucratic ability) for the new arrangements by appointing him first secretary of defense (interview, Clark Clifford, May 21, 1985).

†The noncommunist left as well as parties in the center and on the right received support (and probably still do) not only through the CIA but also through the State Department. Payments were made to help individual politicians defray their election expenses. Printing costs of posters, leaflets, and pamphlets were met. Anticommunist newspapers received help. The Soviets offered Italian communists the same sort of support. It was early communist successes in local elections and in controlling parts of the Italian (and French and German) trade union movement that prompted Forrestal and the National Security Council to decide on direct intervention. See Ray S. Cline, *Secrets, Spies and Scholars: Blueprint of the Essential CIA* (Washington, DC: Acropolis Books, 1976), p. 102, and Thomas Powers, *The Man Who Kept the Secrets* (London: Weidenfeld and Nicolson, 1979), p. 29.

‡It should be noted at this point that while the chairmen of the concerned congressional committees knew in general how much money the agency was getting and how it was spending it, the average congressman did not know.

directive, was set up within the CIA's Office of Special Operations on December 22, 1947.[8]

COVERT-ACTION CAPABILITY

Behind these moves lay a broad agreement in Congress and the administration that covert action capability was necessary. Earlier in 1947, while the National Security Act was being debated, Allen Dulles as a private citizen submitted a memorandum to the Senate Committee on Armed Services arguing that the CIA "should have exclusive jurisdiction to carry out secret intelligence operations."[9] This memorandum sparked a discussion within the administration on the question of covert operations which resulted in the decision by General George C. Marshall to keep the State Department apart from these operations. Marshall was not opposed to covert operations—quite the contrary—but he realized that if American diplomacy were integrated with American espionage, U.S. foreign policy could be compromised. This was the orthodox State Department view. At times during the debate on peacetime central intelligence this view brought the department into forceful opposition to the concept of the CIA, effectively removing the State Department from contention as the agency of central intelligence coordination.*

The State Department was the weakest of the Washington bureaucracies. No President ever really trusted it. For the first one hundred and seventy years of the existence of the United States the State Department was obviously more interested in the world outside America, while most Americans were interested only in America. To make matters worse, as with every foreign office, it traditionally held the long view of foreign affairs, while presidents were far more concerned with the short and medium views dictated by democratic politics. Marshall knew all this, and he used his influence to place the State Department in a position to have knowledge of covert operations, as well as a say in their management through his membership of the National Security Council. He was careful not to overextend his influence by trying to claim more.

*This was not to say that the State Department was opposed to intelligence per se. Dean Acheson in mid-1945 was emphasizing to the secretary of state, James F. Byrnes, "the importance of properly amalgamating the new wartime agencies dealing with intelligence and information into the Department" (Dean Acheson, *Present at the Creation* [New York: W. W. Norton, 1969], p. 120). Acheson was one of those who saw the need for coordinated intelligence, and he wanted his State Department to control it. His influence in this respect upon General Marshall resulted in the creation of the Office of Policy Coordination (OPC) under State Department control but funded by the CIA. (See pp. 133–38.) Marshall was conducting a two-track policy: one through the State Department, which was conventionally diplomatic; the other through the OPC, which was a secret war capacity answering to him and a vehicle through which he could effectively overrule the director of Central Intelligence. If the CIA would not do something he wanted, OPC would, thus forcing the agency's hand.

Simultaneously, James Forrestal was increasingly concerned with combating Soviet covert operations around the world. He came to the conclusion that neither the State Department nor the military establishment was equipped for covert operations, espionage, and counterespionage, and he asked Hillenkoetter if the CIA could undertake such activities. This prompted the process leading to NSC 4 and NSC 4A. Allen Dulles' idea—the Donovan idea—found its first peacetime form in the Special Procedures Group. From this point on, the CIA was perceived by successive administrations as the action-oriented (as opposed to the "passive" State Department) agency of American foreign policy. According to one CIA man, starting with Truman, every President has "endorsed the wisdom of trying to frustrate Soviet—or other communist—subversive political activities by giving covert assistance to those who would oppose communist aims."[10] Their vehicle for this has been the CIA.

James Forrestal was one of the driving forces behind the rapid emphasis on covert action. He was as driven a man as Jack Kennedy, with the education but not the fortune to sustain his ability and ambition. He was also an enigmatic man. John O'Hara, an extraordinary chronicler of the American obsession with social class, considered Forrestal a friend but said he never understood him. Forrestal was also a man who lived between several worlds. He was a Catholic who married a Protestant. He was a Wall Street Democrat. He was an intensely competitive man who, in his early thirties, had his nose smashed while boxing a few rounds at a New York athletic club. He was drawn to strange situations and friends in both his personal and public lives. He was always ready to take drastic action. During the early part of World War II he rented his house at 27 Beekman Place in Manhattan, one of New York City's most exclusive areas. When he decided he wanted it back before the lease expired, he asked his tenants to find another place to live. They agreed but said that they needed to stay until they found a new place. Almost immediately they started receiving phone calls at odd times from odd people. One mysterious caller asked them, "When do you want the hearse to come round?" Despite their insistence that there was some mistake, a hearse actually arrived in front of the door.[11] It was never clear that Forrestal was behind these calls, but there was strong circumstantial evidence that he was.

He was physically and intellectually highly strung. His extreme nervousness heightened his perception of everything, and he thought in extreme terms. Printed on a card he kept on his desk in the Pentagon was this statement: "We will never have universal peace until the strongest army and the strongest navy are in the hands of the most powerful nation." From mid-1944 he was convinced that the Soviet Union would be the most formidable postwar threat to American interests, and he propounded this view among the Western Allied leadership.[12] He was one of the very first American cold warriors, determined to carry the fight for American interests and ideals to the enemy.

At its start the CIA was conceived in slightly different terms, not so much as an interventionist organization but as a defensive, protective one. The inquiry into the agency's performance in warning of the Bogotá riots was in line with this original concept: the CIA was to warn America of troubles ahead rather than to intervene to prevent them. This changed with the Italian elections, and intervention increasingly became the agency's keynote.* The transition was smooth, for the CIA was an institution formed in changing times and marked by flexibility. Created originally as an emergency institution to deal with a climate somewhere between war and peace, the CIA represented the determination on the part of the governing elite not to repeat history and not to allow America to retreat once more into its own hemisphere.

Hillenkoetter successfully channeled the currents of the time in ways that

---

*On December 22, 1963, *The Washington Post* published an article signed by Harry S Truman which stated:

> For some time I have been disturbed by the way the CIA has been diverted from its original assignment. It has become an operational arm and at times a policy-making arm of the Government. . . . I never had any thought when I set up the CIA that it would be injected into peacetime cloak and dagger operations. Some of the complications and embarrassments that I think we have experienced are in part attributable to the fact that this quiet intelligence arm of the President has been so removed from its intended role that it is being interpreted as a symbol of sinister and mysterious foreign intrigue. . . . We have grown up as a nation, respected for our free institutions and for our ability to maintain a free and open society. There is something about the way the CIA has been functioning that is casting a shadow over our historical position, and I feel that we need to correct it.

The article was apparently written by David Noyes, Truman's assistant, who in early June 1965 told General Pat Carter, the then deputy director of Central Intelligence, and his executive assistant, Enno H. Knoche, that he and not Truman had written the article and that "It is highly doubtful whether President Truman ever saw the article prior to its publication, as he was already beginning to age considerably at that time" (quoted in "What Did Truman Say About CIA?," Central Intelligence Agency, *Studies in Intelligence*, n.d.). Despite this, the sentiments did coincide with Truman's at the time, as his personal diary confirmed. Truman never found it difficult to rewrite history, and the real point—as Allen Dulles said to the former President on April 17, 1964—was that Truman had authorized the steps that took the CIA into operations and "cloak and dagger" work. Dulles produced a record of his talk with Truman for Lawrence Houston on April 21, 1965:

> I then reviewed with Mr. Truman the part he had had in supplementing the overt Truman Doctrine affecting Greece and Turkey with the procedures largely implemented by CIA to meet the creeping subversion of Communism, which could not be met by open intervention, military aid, under the Truman plan. I reviewed the various covert steps which had been taken under his authority in suppressing the Huk rebellion in the Philippines, of the problems we had faced during the Italian elections of 1948, and outlined in some detail . . . the organization of the Free Europe Committee and Radio Free Europe, keeping hope alive in the Satellite countries, etc. . . .
>
> I pointed out the number of National Security Actions (Action #4 and Action 10-2) which he had taken which dealt with covert operations by the CIA. He studied attentively the *Post* story and seemed quite astounded at it. In fact, he said that this was all wrong. He then said that he felt it had made a very unfortunate impression. . . . At no time did Mr. Truman express other than complete agreement with the viewpoint I expressed. (Ibid.)

Truman authorized the first covert actions personally and took the lead in the National Security Council discussion that preceded the establishment of the Office of Policy Coordination to carry out covert operations directed against secret communist subversion, arguing strongly for it.

supported the new CIA. Especially important during this period was the growing paranoia about communists, who were suspected of being everywhere and of seeking world domination. This fear was behind the Bogotá inquiry, and it directly affected the agency's intelligence mission. Thirty-five years later Senator Frank Church observed: "When the CIA succeeded the OSS, Stalin replaced Hitler as the Devil Incarnate. Wartime methods were routinely adopted for peacetime use. Nearly all our postwar Presidents shared the same view: the war was not over, it had merely changed from hot to cold. The Soviet Union had become the enemy, the world was up for grabs."[13] The decent world had been taken by surprise in the 1920s and the 1930s. Pearl Harbor had shocked America. It was in this climate that the CIA had to fulfill its three missions. First, it was to provide intelligence to avoid surprises. Second, it was to provide the intelligence of secrets—finding things out about other people and other countries. And third, it had to manage organizations and countries whenever and wherever necessary. With a world up for grabs and with the Soviet Union taking what it could get, the CIA was charged with laying the U.S. claim. The atmosphere was of a dawn like thunder. The realization was clear that if it failed, the whole world might be lost.

Elitism was another current that Hillenkoetter channeled for the agency's benefit, making the agency simultaneously attractive and powerful. The sheer eliteness of the CIA needs to be remembered. It was structured to deal with a world that was plastic to whatever came along. It was meant to be alive to the range of possibilities in the political world, the scientific world, the technical world, the espionage world. Its early strength lay in its people and their contacts rather than in its bureaucratic pull. The late 1940s were not only the years of the intensive cold war, they were also the years of incredible possibilities. In the minds of air force generals, for example, flying saucers were not only possible, they were also investigated as Soviet spy vehicles. Present at the time was an overwhelming feeling that anything could happen, and thus there was a need for institutions that could deal with any eventuality. And since there was no great historical perspective in the republic, people were being called upon to reinvent the world in those years.

Everything was new; everything had to be reconceptualized. People felt the melting pot had only just begun to bubble. The CIA was at the center of this. It had a presence that is hard to recapture now that so many people are in the "greatness" business. It existed at a time when it was relatively easy to predict who would achieve the next great success in any particular field. The complexity of today's world makes this almost impossible. The world was centered on far fewer places than it is now. Television coverage was slight. Newspapers and radio were more regionalized. Although people read or heard about events and discoveries, there were not many eloquent voices interpreting what was going on. The eloquent voices that there were, such as Walter Lippmann's, were not very good at conveying the sense of urgency, excitement, and fear of the time. And with little understanding of the resilience of the world economy, people looked to an elite group of government officials they believed were the only ones who could energize and rebuild the world.

Despite the enormity of the task they faced, the elite were confident that they could remake the world, creating a better, more secure place in the process. It was to be a free-trade world; the United States thought of itself as a natural exporter and as a country that would profit from the international division of labor. Averell Harriman, U.S. ambassador to Russia during World War II and a leading Democrat; Dean Acheson, another leading Democrat, who had been undersecretary of state (1945–47) and then secretary of state (1949–53) under Truman; and George Marshall devoted a great deal of time and energy formulating these free-trade objectives. The General Agreement on Tariffs and Trade, signed by twenty-eight nations in Geneva on October 30, 1947, was a cornerstone in this new world. The elite also saw the new world in democratic terms. The United Nations was created to make sure that the world had learned the lessons of the 1920s and 1930s. This too was a cornerstone. The concept of collective security in the form of precise and purposeful alliances was a third cornerstone.

In this new world there was no longer any such thing as a faraway country about which little was known. Vietnam was no longer just a country rich in rubber and tin. It was now the gateway to Southeast Asia—an area of vast political and economic potential. There was also a sense that people were being connected to each other by new communications technology. The 1940s witnessed the first generation of politicians who regularly flew from place to place: Neville Chamberlain and Franklin Roosevelt were the first British and American heads of state to use airplanes. Conferences bringing together representatives from every part of the world were now possible—even on short notice—and became a feature of World War II. The technology also transmitted an awareness of how quickly the world can work, how quickly a battle could be lost. The events of 1940 made an impression that stayed with this generation of politicians. In May 1940 France was considered the greatest military power in the world; one month later it stood defeated, unable to withstand the new war technology of the German blitzkrieg. As a result of this experience, the postwar governing elite wanted an organization that could quickly assess a place or a series of events or discoveries barely heard of and perhaps act on that assessment in ways not prescribed in any textbook. It all led to the CIA.

There was a painful feeling, dating back to the 1939–41 period, that a great democracy could not respond in a timely, purposeful, subtle way to changing world events. Roosevelt had taken pains to convince public-opinion leaders to support the New Deal and U.S. aid to Britain at the start of World War II before publicly announcing his policy, because he did not trust the untutored democratic instinct. His successors have generally followed suit.[14] This sense pervaded the atmosphere when the CIA was formed. As a result, the CIA took shape as a "nonbureaucracy." It was an institution with the least invest-ment in the past or the status quo. Whether it was developing a new airplane or a new foreign policy, it was to take an innovative, nontraditional approach. The benefits of this new organization were clear. Where the United States was unpopular the CIA would quietly operate in the backwater. Without a big stick in sight, agents could tap the vanguard of revolutionary power by forming relationships with opposition leaders, revolutionaries, and guerrillas. This had occurred during the war when OSS agents parachuted into such countries as Yugoslavia, Italy, and Vietnam to fight alongside men and women who later became opposed to the United States.* Flexibility was the keynote of the CIA. It carried none of the bureaucratic baggage that encumbered other agencies, and it had the capacity to take seriously new world forces. This is exactly what the governing elite wanted from the new agency and what the United States had to do if it were to become the world's leading postwar power.

TRUMAN INTERVENES

By January 1948, six months after its creation, the CIA was fighting the enemy. In Vienna and in Berlin there was what amounted to a war of spies be-tween the British and Americans on one side and the Russians on the other. Throughout western Europe bitter struggles were being waged for control of labor unions, newspapers, publishing houses, pressure groups, and professional bodies.† With armies of little use in these areas, the CIA was looked to as the country's shadow warrior. In the Philippines the Hukbalahaps, a communist-backed guerrilla group, was challenging the government established there by the United States after the Japanese surrender. In the northern Iranian prov-ince of Azerbaijan, Soviet agents were fomenting separatist unrest despite

---

*Ho Chi Minh assisted the OSS in organizing an intelligence network throughout Indo-china in 1945. He reported on developments within Mao Tse-tung's Chinese Communist party as well as on the political situation in Vietnam. One OSS/SSU officer in Vietnam in 1945–46 negotiated an arrangement with Ho for his future cooperation with the United States but never received approval from Washington to clinch the deal. Had America later decided to support Ho instead of the French in Vietnam, the ground would have been laid. For a detailed explanation of U.S. involvement with Ho, see Archimedes L. A. Patti, *Why Vietnam? Prelude to America's Al-batross* (Berkeley, CA: University of California Press, 1981).

†The emphasis on penetrating professional bodies at this time was indicated by Maurice Oldfield, a senior British Intelligence officer who rose to become director general of MI-6. He spent the early 1950s in the Far East and studied the tactics of Mao Tse-tung's intelligence chief, K'ang Sheng. In 1979 Oldfield expressed an interest in meeting Richard Deacon, author of *A History of the Chinese Secret Service.* "Maurice Oldfield would very much like to meet you," Deacon was told by the bursar of All Soul's College, Oxford, where Oldfield had retired. "He says he was interested in your diagnosis of K'ang Sheng. He claims that it was K'ang Sheng who even-tually convinced Mao Tse-tung that the Russians in the early 1950s had obtained control of the Chinese Institute of Mathematics and that by doing so they threatened to acquire total control of Chinese technology and make the People's Republic dependent upon the USSR" (Richard Dea-con, *"C"—A Biography of Sir Maurice Oldfield* [London: Macdonald, 1985], p. 100).

agreements with Britain and the United States that they would refrain from such activity. In China, Mao Tse-tung's communist army was steadily advancing to power at the expense of the pro-American Chiang Kai-shek. CIA agents were soon at work in almost every area of conflict. Many of the agents who had had OSS experience during the war brought a derring-do quality to whatever they were engaged in. This was sometimes appropriate and sometimes not. What worked in a hot war was often not right for peacetime. The currents that were channeled into the CIA had started some years earlier with the shock of Pearl Harbor and the experience of American power mobilized by the war.

It is essential to understand the foreign policy and international politics of the early postwar years, because they gave the CIA its drive. The combination of an atmosphere of urgency and fear, and an almost instinctive reliance on action in a crisis was the background to the Truman Doctrine and his administration's decision to engage the Soviet Union. There was, of course, an inevitability to Truman's decision. After 1940, American military and economic strength had kept Britain in the war. After 1941, American military and economic strength had enabled the Soviet Union to blunt the edge of the Nazi attack. After Hiroshima and Nagasaki, American military power had quickly established America's dominant position among the Allies. From 1945 to 1951 the United States kept its allies at arm's length over Japan and the Far East, making what was in effect a unilateral peace in the area. Its ability to do so was based on its sheer military power.

The growing action-oriented power of the United States led almost inevitably to the decision to engage the Soviets: it was a conflict the United States simply could not back down from. This changing balance of world power was not immediately accepted by Britain. In 1947 Britain sought to use American strength to secure British interests in retaining the empire. When, in a British Foreign Office meeting that included the British foreign secretary, Ernest Bevin, and some members of his staff, the American Marshall Plan to give massive economic aid to Europe was announced, the reaction was questioning. "What does Marshall mean?" staff members asked. Not sure of the implications, they wondered what he wanted. Bevin was furious. "Ask him what he means?" he roared. "Ask him what he means? *Tell him what we want!*"[15] George Marshall, Harry Truman, and other members of the American governing elite considered that old empires that clung to their colonies despite growing nationalist movements were creating conditions that would inevitably lead to communism. In their attempts to restore monarchies and prewar political conditions, these empires were standing in the way of democratic processes. "Gentlemen, it is not Soviet communism I fear, but rather British imperialism," Truman remarked to Senator Burton K. Wheeler some weeks after becoming President.*

---

*Quoted by Sidney Hook in *Freedom At Issue*, No. 35, March/April 1976. There was always an ambivalence toward the British Empire. In certain areas and respects, Americans re-

In 1947 the opposing forces of the old British Empire and the new nationalism came together in Greece. Britain wanted America to undertake the cost of fighting communist guerrillas who opposed the restored Greek monarchy, thus enabling Britain to concentrate its resources elsewhere, especially in the eastern Mediterranean and Egypt. On Friday, February 21, 1947, Lord Inverchapel, the British ambassador in Washington, spoke to Dean Acheson on the telephone. He had two urgent messages from the British government, and he wanted to know if it would be possible to see the secretary of state at once. Acheson explained that it would not be possible because Marshall had already left for a speaking engagement at Princeton University's bicentenary celebrations. In order to observe protocol, Inverchapel arranged instead for his first secretary, H. M. Sichell, to convey the messages to the State Department. When he arrived at State Department headquarters, Sichell was met by a State Department officer of appropriate rank, Loy Henderson, director of the Office of Far Eastern and African Affairs. He handed Henderson two papers. One was about Greece, baldly stating that unless the Greek government received $200 million immediately, the country would almost certainly fall to communist guerrillas. The other was about Turkey, a country also vulnerable to communist pressure. Both papers made clear that Britain could no longer continue its support to both countries and was itself in dire financial straits. It was the British government's considered view that the United States must either step in or accept the consequences of British withdrawal.[16]

Dean Acheson saw this moment as an apocalyptic emergency. After a flurry of State Department and White House activity over the weekend, the President decided that the United States had to intervene. On Monday, Truman, Marshall, and Acheson met the congressional leaders to secure their support for aid to Greece and Turkey.

> I knew we were met at Armageddon [Acheson recalled]. My distinguished chief, most unusually and unhappily, flubbed his opening statement. In desperation I whispered to him a request to speak. This was my crisis. For a week I had nurtured it. These congressmen had no conception of what challenged them; it was my task to bring it home. Both my superiors, equally perturbed, gave me the floor. Never have I spoken under such a pressing sense that the issue was up to me alone. No time was left for measured appraisal. In the past eighteen months, I said, Soviet pressure on the Straits, on Iran, and on

---

garded it highly and supported it. Most informed Americans considered that British imperialism in Africa was beneficial and that without the British presence there most of the continent would slip back into darkness. When Britain gave independence to India, many people in Washington were concerned that India might slide into the Soviet orbit. It struck them that Britain had miscalculated and that the British imperial interest in India should have been maintained in some direct way. In the Far and Middle East it was a different story. The energy and enterprise of Far Easterners, and the oil wealth of the Middle East, prompted Americans to support colonial independence in these areas. The British Empire was seen, overall, as being badly managed rather than as a "bad thing."

northern Greece had brought the Balkans to the point where a highly possible Soviet breakthrough might open these continents to Soviet penetration. Like apples in a barrel infected by one rotten one, the corruption of Greece would infect Iran and all to the east. It would also carry infection to Africa through Asia Minor and Egypt, and to Europe through Italy and France, already threatened by the strongest domestic Communist parties in Western Europe. The Soviet Union was playing one of the greatest gambles in history at minimal cost. It did not need to win all the possibilities. Even one or two offered immense gains. We and we alone were in a position to break up the play. These were the stakes that British withdrawal from the eastern Mediterranean offered to an eager and ruthless opponent.

A long silence followed. Then Arthur Vandenberg said solemnly, "Mr. President, if you will say that to the Congress and the country, I will support you and I believe that most of its members will do the same." Without much further talk the meeting broke up.[17]

Truman was shocked by the British messages.* He saw them in terms of another Munich, of Britain backing away from responsibility again and taking the line of least resistance. At the end of August 1945, only days after V-J Day, he had rejected British appeals for an extension of Lend-Lease because of opposing congressional views. In July 1946 he had authorized a fifty-year $3.75 billion loan to Britain, which, he thought, would end U.S. aid to Europe. His views on this issue accurately reflected those held by Roosevelt toward the end of World War II. Gladwyn Jebb (later Lord Gladwyn), a contemporary British diplomat, summarized Roosevelt's stand: "President Roosevelt's views at that time were very hazy, I think, and Roosevelt of course was only anxious to get on good terms with the Russians. Roosevelt didn't think anything, as you know, of the British Commonwealth and Empire. . . . He just wanted to make a deal with Uncle Joe over a division of the world."[18]

It took Truman about a year to realize that Uncle Joe was stolidly following Trotsky's dictum of "neither war nor peace." Through a steady consolidation of gains and encroachment whenever the opportunity arose, Stalin was incorporating bits and pieces of territory into the Soviet sphere. Outright rapaciousness by the Soviets in their occupied zone in Germany and the countries of eastern Europe was the first sign. This was followed by Russia's refusal to conduct democratic elections in the territories it controlled; its refusal to contribute to reconstruction in Europe; its maintenance of a large army that looked uncommonly like an army of occupation in the countries where it was posted (the army's size would have elicited no comment if it had been based only in Russia); its obstructionism in the United Nations and other international organizations; growing evidence of its involvement in a concerted attempt to subvert democratic processes and organizations in western Europe;

*The messages were a "watershed moment," said Clark Clifford. "Truman agonized over the decision to engage. It was a brave decision, and the right one. There was still tremendous isolationist pressure" (interview, Clark Clifford, May 21, 1985).

and its guerrilla campaigns in the Balkans, Greece, and China. The combination of these events and policies changed Truman's perceptions of the Soviets. This change was confirmed with a vengeance as evidence mounted of Soviet espionage activity in the United States and Britain. The messages that Sichell delivered to Loy Henderson forced Truman finally to accept the fact that the United States had to either "put up" or "shut up." Its choice was clear: it had to try to stem what was regarded as a steady, powerful communist advance or withdraw again into isolation.

In fact, Truman had little choice. The cost of the war in all sorts of different ways was seen by Americans generally as an investment in the future of the world. There was also a strong idealistic element involved: Russia, like Britain, had been a wartime ally and had paid an enormous price in suffering and destruction for victory. Truman wanted an end to this suffering. He, Roosevelt, and others believed that the old empires and the cynical balances of power that existed among them should be swept away in favor of a new system of international cooperation and understanding. The United Nations was the immediate postwar symbol of this American vision, and for a while it was coupled with a widespread desire for a continuation of the wartime spirit of alliance. In September 1946 Henry Wallace, Truman's secretary of commerce, received a warm reception when he said: "To make Britain the key to our foreign policy would, in my judgment, be the height of folly. Make no mistake about it: the British imperialist policy in the Near East alone, combined with Russian retaliation, would lead the United States straight to war. . . . The real peace treaty we now need is between the United States and Russia."[19]

Unlike the audience, Truman was furious with these remarks and dismissed Wallace from his administration. Wallace later ran for the presidency against Truman on the grounds that Truman was a warmonger and Russophobe. By then the President and his administration considered Russia an enemy. "Wallace is a pacifist 100 percent," said Truman. "He wants us to disband our armed forces, give Russia our atomic secrets and trust a bunch of adventurers in the Kremlin Politburo. I do not understand a dreamer like that. The German-American Bund under Fritz Kuhn was not half so dangerous. The Reds, phonies and the parlor pinks seem to be banded together and are becoming a national danger. I am afraid they are a sabotage front for Uncle Joe Stalin."[20]

Observing these events from the sidelines, John Foster Dulles, at the time the Republicans' leading foreign-policy specialist, noted that Wallace's sentiments reflected "the attitude towards the Soviet Union which we all had when we began negotiations."[21] At the State Department, Dean Acheson combined George Kennan's views and Winston Churchill's private warnings on the Russian menace into a May 1946 policy paper, which declared: "The Soviet Union operates on a world-wide basis. . . . Each move in its foreign policy is carefully planned and integrated with moves on other fronts."[22]

The change noted by John Foster Dulles was an enormous one. It reflected a complete shift in U.S. government thinking and in popular perceptions. In 1945 there had been a unique American view that war was like a game of football, requiring no follow-up. Americans wanted peace. It was with the greatest reluctance that Truman and his administration came to accept the fact that Western democratic values as well as national rights faced an aggressive threat from the Soviet Union, even if that threat itself was motivated by fear of Western aggression. The CIA was one of the outcomes of this new awareness.

In 1945 America was the only country capable of dealing with Russia and communism. This was clear to Truman, but he had no idea what was likely to happen next, and he had no effective mechanism for finding out what was happening. He was painfully aware, however, that with the invention of missiles and long-range bombers, America was as vulnerable as any other country to attack.

Truman thought in specific, immediate terms about America's involvement with the world. For him, it was all primitively simple: America had been caught with its pants down in 1941, and it must never happen again. He had seen the greatest man he knew, Franklin Roosevelt, tricked by the Russians. And he himself had been a victim of Russian duplicity. Repeatedly he saw his attempts to douse the flames of conflict throughout the world undermined by the Soviet Union.

Truman was very proud of being a soldier. Bad eyesight had stopped him from getting into West Point as a young man, and he always regretted this. He had fought well during World War I, and he had remained involved in the military as a colonel in the National Guard. He thought in terms of military requirements. For him intelligence was such a requirement. For Forrestal and Acheson, who took a longer, less emergency-oriented view of the situation, intelligence was a weapon of siege, for long-term endurance, rather than a weapon for immediate war. They saw intelligence as a vital element in the capacity to endure, to keep the U.S. shield of defense permanently raised.

At the end of 1945 Forrestal told journalists, "To me the fundamental question in respect to our relations with Russia is whether we are dealing with a nation or a religion."[23] He followed this line of thinking with a memorandum in January 1946 entitled, "Dialectical Materialism and Russian Objectives," in which he noted, "We are trying to preserve a world in which a capitalistic-democratic method can continue, whereas if Russian adherence to truly Marxian dialectics continues, their interest lies in the collapse of this system."[24] Forrestal's analysis seemed confirmed when, on February 9, 1946, Joseph Stalin publicly stressed the incompatibility of capitalism and communism and even went so far as to imply that future wars between the capitalist-democratic countries and the communist countries were inevitable. It was, said *Time* magazine, "the most warlike pronouncement uttered by any top-rank statesman since V-J Day."[25] On his return to Washington after three years as ambassador in Moscow, Averell Harriman expressed his conviction that one object—perhaps the object—of Soviet foreign policy was to extend communist ideology to other parts of the world. Supreme Court Justice William O. Douglas, a leading liberal, told Forrestal that Stalin's speech was "the declaration of World War III."[26] There were other indications that Douglas might have been right.

THE WORLD DIVIDED

Unlike the Western powers, which virtually disarmed after 1945, the Soviet Union maintained a massive military strength of over three million men. In Iran, Stalin gave the first sign that he might use these forces. Under the terms of the 1943 Tehran Agreement involving Russia, Britain, and America, Britain and Russia would withdraw their troops from Iran within six months of the end of the war. In 1945 Britain withdrew. Russia did not. Truman was furious. He ventilated his feelings in a letter he wrote (but did not send) to his secretary of state, James F. Byrnes, on January 5, 1946:

> Iran was our ally in the war. Iran was Russia's ally in the war. Iran agreed to the free passage of arms, ammunition and other supplies running into millions of tons across her territory from the Persian Gulf to the Caspian Sea. Without these supplies furnished by the United States, Russia would have been ignominiously defeated. Yet now Russia stirs up rebellion and keeps troops on the soil of her friend and ally—Iran. There isn't a doubt in my mind that Russia intends an invasion of Turkey and the Black Sea Straits to the Mediterranean. Unless Russia is faced by an iron fist and strong language, war is in the making. Only one language do they understand—"How many divisions have you?" . . . I'm tired of babying the Soviets.[27]

Stalin backed down only after Britain moved a brigade to Basra on the Iran-Iraq border and the United States threatened to intervene directly. The iron fist and strong language had worked.

Decisive American action worked in the eastern Mediterranean too. Stalin demanded a permanent base in the Dardanelles and the cession of the northeastern provinces of Turkey to the Soviet Union. In April 1946 he explained his demands to General Walter Bedell Smith, the new American ambassador: "Turkey is weak," he said, "and unfriendly to us. . . . It is a matter of our own security."[28] By August, Truman felt it necessary to send the battleship *Missouri* and an aircraft-carrier task force to Istanbul and this succeeded in quieting Stalin.

Soviet attempts to expand elsewhere, however, remained unaffected. Eastern Europe was firmly under Soviet control, making America feel impotent. The Baltic states of Latvia, Estonia, and Lithuania had been annexed by Stalin in 1940. Now parts of Finland, Rumania, Poland, Germany, and Czechoslovakia were added to them, bringing within the borders of the USSR an additional 180,000 square miles and a population of 24 million. Poland, eastern Germany, Hungary, Czechoslovakia, Bulgaria, Rumania, Yugoslavia, Albania—the small nations that loomed so large in Wilson's Fourteen Points less than thirty years earlier and that comprised an area of 393,500 square miles, with a population of nearly 92 million—were either occupied directly by the Red Army or controlled by communist-influenced governments. Despite promises, Russia ignored demands for free elections in nearly all these countries.

On May 12, 1945, four days after V-E Day, Churchill, using his famous "iron curtain" metaphor for the first time, warned Truman of the dangers the democracies faced. "I am profoundly concerned about the European situation," he said. "What will be the position in a year when the British and American armies have melted . . . when Russia may choose to keep two or three hundred [divisions] on active service? An iron curtain is drawn down upon their front. We do not know what is going on behind."[29] William Donovan and James Forrestal were already there, as shown by the order in the spring of 1945 to the OSS by word-of-mouth to alter its intelligence target from the collapsing Axis powers to the Soviet Union.[30] Now Truman had joined them. He needed a coordinated way of knowing what was going on behind the Russian curtain, and he agreed to the creation of the CIA for this purpose.

The victorious Allies overthrew a demonstrable tyranny in 1945. In the process of winning a long, bitter war, they believed that they had defeated forever the forces of evil and darkness. Victory was great and good news. Japan and Germany, once powerful war machines, now stood completely defeated. But hanging over this joy was the atomic bomb, which brought with it the frightening knowledge that the world was utterly changed. "I am become Death, the shatterer of worlds," J. Robert Oppenheimer, the mastermind of the bomb, quoted to himself as he saw the first mushroom cloud rise over the New Mexico desert during the test of the bomb.* In Santa Fe, one hundred and twenty-five miles away, a blind girl looked up and asked, "What was that?" as the light flash went by. On hearing the news of the successful bombing of Hiroshima, Truman said: "This is the greatest thing in history!"[31] Yet within two years it was apparent that, all along, the atomic secret, the heart of power, the incredible key to a new world, had been deeply penetrated by Soviet agents. Truman wanted the CIA to be able to meet the Russians on every level, including espionage.

*Quoted in William Manchester, *The Glory and the Dream: A Narrative History of America* (New York: Bantam Books, 1975), p. 378. Oppenheimer had two passages from the Bhagavad-Gita in mind, the other being: "If the radiance of a thousand suns were to burst into the sky, that would be the splendor of the Mighty One." "Good God!" a senior military officer present said, "I believe those long-haired boys have lost control!" The test had been given the code name Trinity, referring to the fact that there were only three bombs in existence, one being used in the test. In August 1945, the United States had a manufacturing capacity of three atom bombs a month.

In 1946, only the United States knew how to make an atomic bomb—a fact that gave the Anglo-American alliance an insurmountable edge over the Soviets in any military confrontation. This advantage was short-lived. A week after Stalin's 1946 statement that East-West confrontation was inevitable, news broke of the arrest of twenty-two people involved in a Soviet spy ring in Canada. They were charged with the theft of atomic secrets for the Soviet Union.[32] Igor Gouzenko, a code clerk in the Soviet Embassy in Ottawa, defected in the autumn of 1945, bringing with him hundreds of documents detailing the activities of an extensive network of Soviet spies in Canada, the United States, and Britain. From Gouzenko came a trail that eventually led to the arrests of the Rosenbergs and the German-born British atomic scientist Klaus Fuchs. When some of the first arrests were announced, the full extent of Soviet penetration of the most closely held secret in the West was still not apparent. What frightened people was the link the first arrests made between Soviet activity and the world communist movement. It was as if Forrestal's question of whether the West was dealing with a nation or a religion had been answered: it seemed it was dealing with both.

COSTS OF ENGAGEMENT

On February 22, 1946, a week after news of the spy ring broke, George F. Kennan, American chargé d'affaires in Moscow, sent an eight-thousand-word telegram to his superiors in the State Department, arguing, as he had done in the past, that the Soviet Union represented a real, aggressive, long-term threat to the West.[33] It was a view that found a suddenly receptive audience in Washington, put forth just as the Russian threat was beginning to be seen. The overwhelming majority of people assumed that there would be another recession and that disintegration and war would follow once more. Within nine months of V-E Day, de Gaulle had resigned in France; Churchill had been rejected by the British electorate, who were emotionally drained and physically exhausted from the war effort; a guerrilla war was being waged in Greece; communists were taking over eastern Europe, and it looked as if Italy and France might be the next to go.

These world events raised certain critical questions in Kennan's mind. What were the Russians doing and what was their motivation? What was going on in Poland? In Hungary? In China? Was the wartime resistance network of the Communist party in France and Italy gearing up to take over? As he answered these questions in his telegram, Kennan raised the specter of a worldwide communist threat. According to Kennan, the communists viewed the world as split between capitalism and socialism—two systems that cannot peacefully coexist, as Stalin himself had declared. He believed that the Soviets were taking every opportunity to weaken the West in the confident knowledge that capitalism would collapse of its own internal tensions. Kennan emphasized that this Soviet view had not been reached by an objective study of the West; rather, it was a new way of justifying traditional Russian needs, particularly its autocratic system of government. Marxism "is the fig leaf of their moral and intellectual respectability. Without it they would stand before history, at best, as only the last of that long succession of cruel and wasteful Russian rulers who have relentlessly forced their country on to ever new heights of military power in order to guarantee external security for their internally weak regimes."[34]

This meant that Soviet aggression was essential to Soviet survival and that the United States and the West as a whole could do little to reduce Soviet hostility. According to Kennan, it also meant that the Soviets would use everything possible, including "an underground operating directorate of world communism, a concealed Comintern tightly coordinated and directed by Moscow to reach their goal of world domination."[35] The Soviet Union was a "political force committed fanatically to the belief that with US there can be no permanent modus vivendi, that it is desirable and necessary that the internal harmony of our society be disrupted, our traditional way of life be destroyed, the internal authority of our state be broken, if Soviet power is to be secure."[36] Kennan's advice was to do what was necessary to resist communist attempts to subvert, discredit, and overthrow Western institutions and to wait out the Soviets until internal changes within Russia produced changes in Soviet perceptions and policy. He gave voice to a crucial intellectual grouping that considered cold war necessary and manageable and something to be managed before it gave way to all-out war. This formed another current in the creation of the CIA, and its ability to take a long view reflected this management concept.

Kennan's telegram became a blueprint for United States cold-war policy. His views were embraced by most high officials in Washington, although Donovan and others had no use for what they regarded as Kennan's defensive approach. They argued that U.S. policy should be active and not simply seek the containment of the communist threat. This dissenting opinion was held by the CIA, the institution created to counter Soviet espionage and subversion. Nevertheless Kennan's reception in Washington was, in his own words, "nothing less than sensational." Truman and most of his cabinet read the telegram. Forrestal had it reproduced and made required reading for higher officers in the armed forces. As Kennan later observed, his telegram arrived at "one of those moments when official Washington . . . was ready to receive a given message."[37] More hard-line anti-Soviet speeches and statements began to emerge from the administration after this, but none was more aggressive than a semiofficial speech made in March 1946 by Winston Churchill, no longer British prime minister but a private citizen on a private visit to the United States.

Churchill arrived in the United States in January for a long vacation in Florida. At President Truman's invitation he agreed to speak at Fulton, Missouri, on March 5, with Truman on the platform beside him. In close con sultation with Truman, Churchill wrote a speech that was to become world-famous: "From Stettin in the Baltic to Trieste in the Adriatic, an iron curtain has descended across the continent. Behind that line lie all the capitals of the ancient states of central and eastern Europe. Warsaw, Berlin, Prague, Vienna, Budapest, Belgrade, Bucharest and Sofia, all these famous cities and the populations around them lie in the Soviet sphere and all are subject in one form or another, not only to Soviet influence but to a very high and increasing measure of control from Moscow." He went on to say that while he did not believe the Soviet Union wanted actual war, it did want "the fruits of war and the indefinite expansion of their power and doctrines. . . . I am convinced that there is nothing they admire so much as strength, and there is nothing for which they have less respect for than military weakness."[38]

Most observers agreed that Churchill had voiced what Truman privately thought. It was, said *Time* magazine, a "magnificent trial balloon."[39] The handling of the Iranian and Turkish crises by the administration demonstrated that Truman had decided to stop babying the Soviets. Opinion polls showed that Americans overwhelmingly endorsed this new approach to their wartime ally. Whether Americans would also underwrite the costs involved—financial as well as moral—was by no means clear.[40]

On March 12, 1947, Truman addressed a joint session of Congress. He wanted, as he put it, to "scare hell out of the country" in order to obtain political and financial backing for the United States' leadership role in the cold war. The inciting event was Britain's message that it could no longer afford to support the fight against communism in Greece and Turkey. Truman accepted the burden, and in his speech to Congress he called for $400 million in military and economic assistance for Greece and Turkey. He also enunciated the "Truman Doctrine" to "support free peoples who are resisting attempted subjugation by armed minorities or by outside pressures." Freedom, Truman declared, was threatened by "totalitarian regimes," and the United States must not falter in leading the West, otherwise "we may endanger the peace of the world—and we shall surely endanger the welfare of our own nation."[41] Both Democrats and Republicans in Congress agreed. Political and financial support was given to the President, who used it overtly in Greece and Turkey and covertly in France and Italy, through the CIA, to support the democratic center-right and center-left political parties.

The cold war, which for some began in 1944 at the height of World War II, took its toll of several government leaders. James Forrestal paid a high personal price in the struggle to contain Soviet expansion. Forrestal resigned as secretary of defense in March 1949, having increasingly exhibited signs of mental breakdown over the previous twelve months.* On his last day as secre-

---

*His resignation had been forced by Truman, who had learned that Forrestal had been talking to Republicans at a time when it looked as if they might win the 1948 presidential election. Forrestal's ambition was enormous, and it probably influenced his nervous collapse.

tary he returned from a House Armed Services Committee presentation to him and sat rigid at his desk in the Pentagon for hours. An aide took him to his home in Georgetown and called his close friend Ferdinand Eberstadt, who came around. Communists, Jews, and certain people in the White House were out to "get" him, Forrestal told Eberstadt, and they had finally succeeded. Realizing that his friend was seriously ill, Eberstadt immediately arranged for an air force plane to fly Forrestal to Hobe Sound, Florida, where Robert Lovett and some others were holidaying. When he got off the plane that evening in Florida, Forrestal was met by Lovett. "Bob," he said, "they're after me." He attempted suicide some days later. Once, walking along the beach, he pointed to a row of metal sun-umbrella sockets in the sand and said to his companion, "We had better not discuss anything here. Those things are wired and everything we say is being recorded." He frequently declared that the communists were planning to invade the United States and was deeply anxious about communist infiltration and influence. He was admitted to Bethesda Naval Hospital, where, on May 22, in the middle of transcribing Winthrop Mackworth Praed's translation of Sophocles' chorus from *Ajax*, he left his room and used a pajama cord to hang himself from a storeroom window. The cord broke, and he fell to his death.[42] To many his tragic death was a symptom of the cold-war struggle.

Others were catapulted to prominence by the fears and demands of the moment. In April 1947 Marshall appointed George Kennan, recalled from Moscow early in 1946, as head of the Policy Planning Staff in the State Department, which was charged with finding ways of helping western Europe combat the Soviet threat. Marshall had concluded that support for European economies was a vital measure in the defense of democratic values in the West. It was Kennan's job to formulate a specific plan to provide this support. He recommended a long-range program of economic assistance to eradicate the poverty and social distress that were the seedbeds of communist support.[43]

Out of this program came the Marshall Plan, outlined by the secretary of state in the commencement address at Harvard University on June 5, 1947. Marshall proposed the complete reconstruction of the European economies, financed mostly by the United States but to be worked out among equals. To an important degree Marshall's speech was a last attempt at reconciliation with the Soviets; no distinction on political grounds was drawn and the offer was couched in purely humanitarian terms.* Britain and France took the lead in

*"Our policy is directed not against any country or doctrine," said Marshall, "but against hunger, poverty, desperation and chaos. . . . Its purpose should be the revival of a working economy in the world so as to permit the emergence of political and social conditions in which free institutions can exist." See also Truman, *Memoirs: Years of Trial and Hope: 1946–1952* (New York: Doubleday, 1956), pp. 112–116. Dean Acheson played a major role in drafting Marshall's speech and outlined what became known as the Marshall Plan a month earlier in a speech of his own. Marshall launched the Plan in his speech because Truman decided not to make the speech himself on the grounds that Marshall's personal popularity would give the Plan more chance of

coordinating European response; the Soviet Union, its satellites, and Finland and Czechoslovakia chose to remain apart. In March 1948 Congress approved a massive $5.3 billion aid program for a first year. Together with the Truman Doctrine, the Marshall Plan represented a revolutionary shift in American perceptions. For the first time in peace the United States had committed its military and economic strength to the support of nations outside its hemisphere. It had done so in order to prevent the continuing expansion of the Soviet Union and the spread of communism.

COVERT ACTION BEGINS: OPC AND OSO

On June 18, 1948, six days before the Russians began the Berlin blockade, another of George Kennan's recommendations, this time involving the CIA, was implemented. Based on what was seen as a CIA success in Italy one month earlier (the Christian Democrats were elected to form a new government) and the fact that in Washington the agency was given credit for this, Kennan recommended the creation of another organization to manage covert operations. After considerable debate within the administration, the National Security Council, which still saw the CIA essentially as a coordinator of intelligence rather than as an intelligence operative, finally agreed to Kennan's proposal after George Marshall and Dean Acheson had both backed it. The CIA's right to conduct operations was not in question; it was simply that no one thought that operations were its main concern. Another organization, whose main focus would be operations, seemed like a good idea, particularly if its activities were coordinated by the National Security Council.

Seven months after agreeing to the NSC 4 and 4A directives, the council approved a new directive, NSC 10/2, superseding them. Citing the "vicious covert activities of the USSR, its satellite countries and communist groups to discredit the aims and activities of the US and other Western powers," the new directive authorized the creation of an Office of Special Projects, soon renamed the Office of Policy Coordination, to combat Soviet and communist activity generally. The new office was limited only by the requirement that its opera-

---

being passed by Congress. Acheson also played a major part in drafting Truman's address to Congress in what became known as the Truman Doctrine. In Washington, on January 10, 1952, Churchill expressed his view that the Marshall Plan had been an act of extraordinary generosity. He was speaking at a private lunch with the press, which included Arthur Sulzberger of *The New York Times*. "What other nation in history," asked Churchill, "when it became supremely powerful, has had no thought of territorial aggrandizement, no ambition but to use its resources for the good of the world? I marvel at America's altruism, her sublime disinterestedness." Sulzberger replied after a short silence during which it was clear that Churchill was deeply moved, "I think, Prime Minister, it was hard-headedness on our part. I mean it was thought out, not emotional. Anyway, I hope it was, because emotion soon passes, whereas a thought-out plan might last" (Lord Moran, *Winston Churchill: The Struggle for Survival* [London: Sphere, 1968], p. 386).

tions be "so planned and conducted that any US government responsibility for them is not evident to unauthorized persons and that if uncovered the US Government can plausibly disclaim any responsibility for them."[44] The message the United States was sending its secret warfare operative was quite plain: Don't get caught—but if you do get caught, be sure that no mud can stick in Washington. It took no account of what people might do if they were captured and tortured. It showed how simplemindedly the intelligence conflict was undertaken. One day mud would stick in Washington, as everyone who knew about intelligence understood. During the 1960s, after the shooting down of the U-2 spy flight over Russia and the disaster of the Bay of Pigs, the naïve nature of this message became painfully clear to every CIA agent. In the late 1940s, however, such a directive passed without much notice or discussion.

From the start the Office of Policy Coordination (OPC) was an anomaly. It was paid for and staffed by the CIA. Its head was appointed by the secretary of state and reported to the secretaries of state and defense, by-passing the director of Central Intelligence. It was a clumsy arrangement. Frank Wisner, who had served in Germany in 1945 in the OSS office under Allen Dulles, was appointed to head the OPC. Along with Dulles and some other influential men outside the administration, Wisner had been instrumental in making the case for a covert-action organization. As OPC's head he was ideal. He possessed the experience, operational instincts, activist temperament, and sheer physical energy required to establish and develop the office. He was a Mississippian with money and he had succeeded as a Wall Street lawyer. Described almost unanimously by those who knew him as brilliant, Wisner had independent wealth and professional and social contacts that gave him an edge over many of his contemporaries. He was a leading member of an informal group of ex-OSS people (Allen Dulles was another) who maintained their interest in intelligence and were anxious to see that the "right" American peacetime intelligence system developed. Their intelligence model was based on Donovan's ideas and combined both analysis and operations, as Allen Dulles had proposed to Congress in 1947. Lawrence Houston recalled:

> Frank Wisner had been instrumental in setting OPC up, and, as opposed to myself, who had been convinced that the postwar intelligence problem was the one we should concentrate on, he went into the political-action field. OPC was obviously designed for covert action and not intelligence from the start. It was a major complication for us in the CIA. OPC was under the policy control of State but with the CIA responsible for quarters and rations. We had to support them, house them, employ their people, pay them and theoretically had no control over their activities. This was a very troublesome situation. It all happened in the wake of the Italian elections and at the time we were engaged in a very major effort to achieve the proper coordination and improvement of the intelligence aspect. This was considered by the management of the CIA, by Hillenkoetter and those of us around him, to be almost

the primary objective at that time. It was very frustrating, and Hillenkoetter found it almost impossible to get the backing he needed.[45]

The State Department and the Department of Defense were at logger-heads over which department would control and implement the Marshall Plan and the Truman Doctrine. OPC was very much a State Department weapon in this battle, and the CIA's interests were secondary. Neither the secretary of state nor the secretary of defense—the two key people on the National Security Council—was interested in Hillenkoetter's efforts to establish the CIA's position at the expense of their departments. The result was two new intelligence services, the CIA and OPC. Hillenkoetter was never able to resolve this return to duplication because of the bureaucratic battling that prevented the National Security Council from making a clear policy choice. What was more, with George Marshall's backing, OPC obtained all the money it needed, thus reducing the amount available to the CIA.[*] OPC also had a well-defined mission (although this was never spelled out in writing), arising out of postwar conditions and the Italian elections: it was to develop German democracy and support resistance groups in eastern Europe in preparation for a "hot" war, which was generally thought to be coming.

The derring-do quality of the OSS found a ready home in OPC as it unleashed a flood of agents and anti-Soviet propaganda in Europe. In contrast, the more circumspect CIA, concentrating on administrative matters in Washington and on intelligence research and analysis rather than on operations, seemed to Wisner to be "a bunch of old washerwomen exchanging gossip while they rinse through the dirty linen." This view had its equally forceful counterpoint in the CIA.[46] "The clandestine operators in the CIA considered themselves the pros of clandestine action," said Lawrence Houston, "and the OPC as a bunch of amateurs who didn't exercise good tradecraft."[47] Within a year OPC had five foreign stations, employed 302 agents, and had a budget of $4.7 million. By 1952 OPC had forty-seven foreign stations, a staff of 2812 plus 3142 contract personnel, and a budget of $84 million.[48]

In Germany, OPC's main area of operation, conflicts between the Western allies and the Soviets were growing. Tension centered around the "German question." The Russians did not want a reunited Germany outside their control; the West feared a Soviet-controlled Germany would become not simply a political satellite but a military one as well. The most immediate concern was the irregular methods adopted by the Soviets in matters of technical and industrial intelligence. At the Potsdam Conference, which lasted for a year beginning in September 1945, agreement had been reached among the British,

---

[*]See Acheson, *Present at the Creation*, pp. 127, 157–163, 214, for an insight into the position of the State Department and the question of centralized as opposed to fragmented intelligence. Acheson blamed Secretary of State James F. Byrnes for "muffing" the State Department's chances of controlling centralized intelligence.

French, Americans, and Russians for an inter-Allied control system for all German scientific institutions. Allied scientists and intelligence officers together were to collect and analyze the complete output of Germany's wartime scientific and technical research, including the blueprints of secret weapons and armament improvements.[49] It was often necessary for search parties to unearth plans from steel safes and strong rooms beneath mounds of rubble in bombed German cities. The Western experts cooperated closely, making their findings and reports freely available to their Soviet counterparts.

But the Soviet control zone of Germany (later East Germany) was closed to the West, and Soviet experts sent all their discoveries straight to Moscow without sharing them. More than two thousand German scientists and technicians were sent to Russia, many never to return. Research centers in the Soviet zone—the Kaiser Wilhelm Institute in Berlin (atomic research), the rocket-development and -testing station at Peenemünde, rocket-manufacturing plants in Brandenburg, optical and precision instrument plants in Thuringia—were combed and dismantled for reconstruction in the Soviet Union. The Potsdam Agreement for German reparations "for damage, destruction, loss and suffering the Soviet people had endured during the War" was used by the Soviets to take these and large quantities of German machinery from their zone in addition to the 25 percent of capital equipment in the metallurgical, chemical, and machine industries of the Western zones they were also entitled to. Soviet expeditions into the Western zones to collect their share of these industries were used by the Soviet secret police and military intelligence for espionage and political subversion purposes. Any German working for the Western allies seemed to be a target for the Soviets as part of a design to conquer Europe from within by fomenting unrest and political collapse.[50]

The Soviets already had the framework of an espionage organization in western Germany: they had preserved the communist Rote Kapelle (Red Orchestra), one of the most effective anti-Nazi networks of the war, and continued to use it after the Nazi surrender. Within days of the war's ending in Europe, Lavrenti Beria, chief of the Soviet secret police, the NKVD, and Stalin's right-hand man, set up headquarters at Karlshorst, in East Berlin, and in Austria at Baden, just outside Vienna. In Berlin, NKVD General Ivan Serov, who would later succeed Beria, was in charge of recruiting informers and establishing new spy rings in the West.[51] Soviet military intelligence, GRU, was based on the outskirts of Berlin. Full advantage was taken of postwar dislocation to infiltrate the Western zones and intimidate opponents.

The division of Germany gave hostages to both sides in the form of war records and divided families and possessions. A person facing a denazification court could easily be blackmailed into playing along with Soviet or Western intelligence. Heinz Felfe, who rose to a senior position in the Gehlen organization, the Bundesnachrichtendienst (BND—the Federal Intelligence Service), was revealed in 1961 as a Soviet agent. He had been in the SS during the war and had worked on Himmler's staff and did not admit this to the BND. The records of his Nazi career, which fell into Russian hands in 1945, were almost certainly used to blackmail him. It was a nasty, brutal time. Soviet defectors to the West—there were many in the postwar years—were made the special target of the NKVD's Section for Terror and Diversion (until 1946 called SMERSH, an acronym for the Russian phrase meaning "death to spies").* Before the wall was built on August 13, 1961, Berlin was known as "kidnap town" in intelligence circles because of the frequency with which East German security police would drag someone across the line into East Berlin to the averted gaze of passersby, hardened by years of tension.[52]

The Office of Policy Coordination and the CIA's Office of Special Operations entered battle on this field. Agents were briefed and given false papers and sent on missions throughout the Eastern bloc, including into the USSR itself, where for several years after the war a Ukrainian resistance movement continued to fight the Red Army.[53] This was a major and fascinating undertaking. The Ukraine was an acknowledged part of the USSR, so the operations were tantamount to war. It demonstrated the determination with which the United States entered the cold war. It also demonstrated a cold ruthlessness: the Ukrainian resistance had no hope of winning unless America was prepared to go to war on its behalf. Since America was not prepared to go to war, America was in effect encouraging Ukrainians to go to their deaths.

Wisner organized a successful operation to encourage doctors and other professional people to leave the East for the West. The Office of Special Operations developed relations with the embryonic West German Federal Intelligence Service of General Reinhard Gehlen, which had grown under U.S. Army auspices. It was to become West Germany's principal military intelligence organization.† Early on, Gehlen managed to place an agent close to the East

---

*In one form or another, and under different names, SMERSH has existed ever since the Russian revolution of 1917. Since 1946 the section has been called by other names. A SMERSH agent, acting upon Stalin's direct orders, killed Trotsky in Mexico in 1940. Two SMERSH agents, Nicolai Khokhlov and Bogdan Stashinski, defected to the West—Khokhlov in 1953 and Stashinski in 1961—bringing with them various assassination devices (a cyanide-pellet electric gun; a prussic-acid sprayer) and information about the section.

†The importance of the Gehlen organization, and the fact that liaison was maintained with it despite its penetration by the Soviets, lay in the position of West Germany within NATO. West Germany was, and remains today, NATO's weakest security link. Massive penetration by East Germany of every aspect of West German society was aided by the large number of refugees from the East and by the fact that one West German in five had relatives behind the iron curtain, thus providing opportunities for blackmail. In April 1961 the West German minister of the interior revealed to the Bundestag the extent of the East German espionage effort. There were, he estimated, approximately 16,000 East German agents in West Germany. Between 1950 and 1960, 2186 agents had been caught and convicted on treason charges; 19,000 more had confessed to espionage missions but were not prosecuted. It would be surprising if the West did not have similar penetration of East Germany.

For background on the Gehlen organization and intelligence work in West Germany, see Sanche de Gramont, *The Secret World* (New York: Putnam's, 1962), pp. 455–460; David Wise and Thomas B. Ross, *The Espionage Establishment* (New York: Random House, 1967), pp.

German leader, Walter Ulbricht, and in the spring of 1949 one of his agents secured the plans and test-flight records of Russia's first jet plane, the MiG 15.[54] It was an opportune success, because in their major effort—the penetration of the USSR itself—the CIA and OPC both met with almost complete failure.

In June 1948 the Joint Chiefs of Staff had briefed the CIA on their principal requirement: early warning of Soviet military plans, particularly of mobilization. It was with this in mind that agreement had been reached with the army over a liaison with the Gehlen organization. It tied into the CIA's analytical strength, since Gehlen's speciality was order-of-battle information—the tabulation of enemy units, their dispositions and their strengths. OPC in contrast developed ties with the U.S. Air Force and émigré groups, concentrating on bringing what amounted to actual warfare to the Soviets. As a result, the failure to place agents within the Soviet Union (which was not apparent for several years, since the Russians successfully doubled nearly every agent sent into the USSR) did not harm the agency's standing in Washington. It was still understood that the CIA's emphasis was not on operations. What mattered was that a determined effort was being made to penetrate Russia; it was an action-oriented rather than a results-oriented time. With the exception of a handful of spies in the 1950s and 1960s, the Soviet Union did not really open up to Western intelligence until the advent of the U-2 and satellites.

OPERATION SILVER

The border with the iron curtain in Europe was quite a different matter in intelligence terms. There was always useful order-of-battle, signals, and communications intelligence to be had from one source or another. In Vienna, second only to Berlin as a point of East-West conflict, British and American intelligence working in cooperation scored a particular success. The Imperial Hotel on the Ringstrasse, the inner ring road, on which the state buildings of the Austro-Hungarian Empire were located, was the headquarters of the Soviet occupation forces in Austria after the war. Until May 15, 1955, Austria remained occupied by the four wartime allies. On that day the Austrian State Treaty came into effect, by which all four countries withdrew their forces and Austria became an independent neutral state. Until that time the clandestine conflicts that characterized Berlin also typified Vienna. For the British and Americans the targets were the same: the penetration of Soviet operations and

115–125; and Reinhard Gehlen, *The Service: The Memoirs of General Reinhard Gehlen* (New York: World Publishing, 1972), a rather self-serving account of his career. For a more critical view, see Heinz Hohne and Hermann Zolling, *The General Was a Spy* (New York: Coward, McCann & Geoghegan, 1972), which argues that Gehlen was far less efficient and effective than people thought. This book prompted Gehlen to publish his memoirs.

Soviet order-of-battle intelligence. What went on in the Imperial Hotel was, accordingly, a major intelligence target. By 1951 the CIA Vienna station had a blueprint of the underground cables and communications routes between the Soviet command in the hotel and Moscow. Using information gleaned from city plans and other sources, Carl Nelson, an officer in the CIA's Office of Communications, was able to put this blueprint together. Unknown to Nelson, British MI-6 had been tapping the lines since 1949, thanks to a brilliantly simple operation, code-named Silver.[55]

One of the characteristics of the old European empires had been their administrative centralization. Just as in the ancient Roman empire, where it was said all roads led to Rome, in the Russian, German, French, and Austro-Hungarian empires of the nineteenth and early twentieth centuries, all major roads and telephone lines converged on the various imperial capitals. Up until the 1950s, for example, a telephone call from Algiers to neighboring Tunis in North Africa was routed through Paris. If you wanted to tap into telephone communications between these two cities (and in some cases even within the cities themselves), you could do it in faraway Paris. Realizing this, the British found that they could monitor Soviet communications by linking into landlines near a private house in the Schwechat suburb of the Austrian capital. They purchased the house, brought in engineers, and tunneled seventy feet under a nearby highway to the telephone cables. Needing a cover for the comings and goings at the house, MI-6 decided to open a shop selling Harris Tweed. To their consternation, Harris Tweed proved very popular with local people, and MI-6 agents found their hands full running a successful shop when they needed to be in the cellar listening in to Soviet conversations.

Other unusual problems interfered with Silver. One involved a schoolgirl who acted as a messenger. Her job was to hand over the recordings of the taps to an MI-6 officer she met at prearranged times and places in Schoenbrun Park. (These meetings also provided MI-6 with an opportunity to see if the girl was followed and Silver therefore compromised.) At one such prearranged meeting a vigilant Viennese policeman arrested the MI-6 man on suspicion of child molestation. Once such problems were resolved, however, Silver ran smoothly until Carl Nelson started his own operation. To prevent increasing the dangers of exposure, the British had to tell Nelson about Silver. From then on it was run cooperatively.

Operation Silver had greater importance than that of obtaining communications intelligence. Changes in radio technology had made the interception of radio traffic far more difficult than it had been during World War II. Ultra-high-frequency shortwave communications had replaced lower-frequency longer-wave methods for government and military security. Ultra shortwaves with higher frequencies (UHF) traveled in straight lines like lines of sight. Unless an intercept could be placed directly along such a line, these communications were secure. In contrast, older, longer-wave transmissions were more diffuse and vulnerable to the bounce effect of the Heaviside layer, or iono-sphere (a magnetic belt in the outer atmosphere), and could be monitored from far away. The result, a CIA Office of Communications report noted, was the creation of "gaps in our intelligence coverage which were particularly un-fortunate during the period of cold war escalation."[56] Silver, therefore, enabled the British and the Americans to keep pace with developments in the Soviet control zone in Austria as well as with overall Soviet policy in the East-West border areas, despite the fact that their general intelligence coverage was re-duced. CIA involvement enormously enhanced the benefits of Silver, espe-cially because of a discovery Carl Nelson had made.

Nelson found that Sigtot, a cipher machine made by Bell and used for U.S. government communications, was not secure. His discovery was to re-main a closely guarded secret for over twenty years, being referred to obliquely in CIA documents in these terms: "The Office of Communications, in the course of its continuing efforts to provide secure communications for the Agency, became aware of a principle which, when applied to target communi-cations, offered certain possibilities."[57] In testing CIA signals for security pur-poses, Nelson found that as Sigtot electrically encrypted messages, it gave off echoes of the clear text down the line up to twenty miles away. While the United States rapidly abandoned Sigtot for another machine, Nelson investi-gated whether Soviet communications were vulnerable in the same way. The answer, he found, was that they were. Using this discovery in Vienna, the CIA was easily able to break a whole range of Soviet codes as well as to amass, through the MI-6 intercepts and five more CIA taps in Vienna, a wealth of practical information. (For security reasons, the British were not told of Nel-son's discovery.) The most important fact that emerged was that the Russians did not plan an invasion of the Balkans through its satellites to reassert control over Tito in Yugoslavia. Tito had been denounced as a deviationist by Stalin on June 28, 1948, after the Yugoslav leader made it plain that Stalin's road to socialism was not for him and that Yugoslavia, although communist in princi-ple, was willing to be a friend to the West.* After the Korean War started, in June 1950, this information was particularly valuable for those deciding U.S. troop deployments in Europe and the Far East.

For the CIA the Vienna intelligence coup had additional significance. It gave the agency the opportunity to demonstrate its expertise, and in the pro-

---

*There was an interesting debate within the American and the British foreign-policy estab-lishment on how to deal with Tito. To many he was a communist, and the "break" with Stalin was simply a ruse to confuse and draw in the West. To others, his break with Stalin was genuine. "Tito may be a scoundrel," said the British foreign secretary, Ernest Bevin, "but he's our scoun-drel." See Acheson, Present at the Creation, pp. 327, 332–334, and George F. Kennan, Memoirs, 1935–1950 (New York: Pantheon Books, 1967), p. 366. Kennan immediately recognized the break as genuine and played a vital part in swinging the State Department and the President around to supporting Tito's communist Yugoslavia. The event was to provide an interesting parallel with the Sino-Soviet split in the 1960s.

cess came up ahead of British Intelligence, the model for the agency. It proved that espionage was a practical benefit to U.S. decision makers. It also showed that the CIA would meet the principal requirement placed upon it: providing accurate information about Soviet intentions.* These successes were vitally important to the new institution. And while it was the activist quality of the Office of Policy Coordination and the more circumspect agent recruitment and functioning of the Office of Special Operations that attracted attention, it was the cool intelligence analysis of the CIA's Office of National Estimates that really established the agency within the administration.†

Recognizing the importance of intelligence analysis and research was Donovan's special contribution to intelligence. The CIA was distinctive among the intelligence services of the world in emphasizing these aspects. The analysis of the Vienna intelligence helped answer one of the burning questions that Truman faced in the late 1940s and early 1950s: Would the Soviets bank on war weariness and isolationist pressure to keep America away from real war in Europe despite demonstrations to the contrary in Greece and Turkey and Korea? The agency did not think so.‡ It was the clearest voice saying that com-

---

*The CIA's intelligence failure in not accurately predicting the Korean War or the Chinese involvement in that war were in part offset by the success in Vienna, which lasted until 1955, when Austria was left by the Russians and the other wartime allies.

†For a discussion of the Office of National Estimates and its work, see Chapter 6.

‡This was an early CIA view, buttressed by the Vienna intelligence rather than made by it. On November 7, 1947, for example, Hillenkoetter advised the President:

> During recent weeks there have been signs of a marked deterioration in the Communist political position in Western Europe. The process apparently began with the announcement of the "Truman Doctrine." It has been accelerated by Soviet-Communist efforts to defeat the European recovery program. In tacit recognition of the trend, the Kremlin appears to have abandoned its once promising attempt to bring Communist Parties to power in Western Europe by conventional political processes, and to be reverting to prewar techniques for the creation and exploitation of an eventual "revolutionary situation." This reversion will further antagonize the people of Western Europe and ultimately reduce the Communist following there to the hard core of militants. It implies Soviet recognition that the postwar opportunity to win Western Europe by political action has now been lost. . . .
>
> Despite the prevalence of anti-Communist sentiment throughout Europe, the Communists can maintain their control of the Satellite States for an indefinite period, and the Communist Parties of Western Europe are still dangerous, particularly in France and Italy. Communist propaganda against the recovery program will be unrelenting. The Communist Parties will exploit every political opportunity afforded them. The significance of the change in the Communist position is that there no longer appears to be any prospect of Communist accession to power in France and Italy by conventional political processes and that the future Communist program in those countries will be primarily revolutionary in character.

Hillenkoetter went on to say that the USSR had its hands full with its eastern European satellites, and despite its conventional military superiority, it was highly unlikely to risk starting another European war for Germany, Austria, France, or Italy. In Hillenkoetter's view, the Soviets still perceived these countries as recovering from the cost of World War II, vulnerable economically to the tune of the Marshall Plan's billions, and certainly not in a position to contribute to the greater wealth of the Soviet empire.

All the information above is from "Memorandum for the President," November 7, 1947, from R. H. Hillenkoetter, rear admiral, USN, director of Central Intelligence.

munism and the Soviets would seek to advance by means other than frontal attack. The agency throughout the 1950s considered it unlikely that the Soviets
would push west in Europe with tanks and infantry. It had a view of the Soviets
as being hard and bitter but not reckless. In the late 1950s the CIA was the
calmest voice on Soviet offensive capabilities and intentions after the first Soviet intercontinental rockets had been deployed. Overall, it was more accurate
than inaccurate in its analysis. In the early 1950s it said that war with Russia
was not likely to be started by Russia; by the late 1950s it was seen to have
been correct. This gave the CIA real influence, because it was listened to at the
highest levels during Eisenhower's presidency. Eisenhower's principal objective was to keep the peace, and as the agency quietly proved to him to be the
people who were competent in intelligence, its standing went up.

—5—

Double Trouble
1945-1951

On September 3, 1949, a B-29 belonging to the U.S. Air Force Long Range Detection System, on patrol eighteen thousand feet over the North Pacific, identified a radioactive cloud. Immediately the entire detection system, made up of airplanes specially fitted with monitoring equipment—radar and radio stations and intelligence sources of all types—went into high gear. Over the next week the system tracked the cloud across Canada and the North Atlantic to the British Isles, where it was picked up and monitored by the Royal Air Force. The CIA reported each stage of this operation to President Truman.[1] The evidence, analyzed by CIA scientists as well as by specialists in the air force, the Atomic Energy Commission, and universities, was conclusive: between August 26 and 29 the Russians had exploded an atomic bomb somewhere on the Asiatic mainland. The Soviets too now had the ultimate weapon of terror.

Seven months later, after exhaustive research, the CIA Office of Reports and Estimates presented the first analysis of the implications of Soviet possession of the atomic bomb for the security of the United States. It was not a National Intelligence Estimate; the agreement of the other intelligence agencies to its conclusions had not been secured, and so the agency had decided to proceed on its own. The CIA reaffirmed its view that the Soviet Union was unlikely to start another "hot" war now that they had the secrets of the bomb and summarized its overall perception of the Soviet threat:

> There would appear to be no firm basis for an assumption that the USSR presently *intends* deliberately to use military force to attain a Communist

143

world or further to expand Soviet territory *if this involves war with a poten-tially stronger U.S.* An analysis of the Stalinist concepts which motivate So-viet leaders, as opposed to an interpretation of their motives and actions in the light of Western concepts, suggests strongly that the preferred objective of Soviet policy is to achieve a Soviet-dominated Communist world through revolutionary (the term "revolutionary" is used to connote all means short of all-out war involving the US) rather than military means. . . .

The presently active Soviet threat to US security, therefore, while in-cluding the ever-present danger inherent in Soviet military power, appears to be a Soviet intention and determination to hasten, by every means short of war, the economic and political disintegration of the non-Communist world. . . .

In terms of this approach to their objectives, the role presently assigned by Soviet leaders to Soviet military power appears to be: (1) defense in the world power situation, accompanied by preparations for the eventuality of war; (2) intimidation in support of their revolutionary program; and (3) where consistent with their objectives, local use against military and eco-nomic forces already weakened by Communist subversion, but not in aggres-sion that would automatically involve war with the US.

The Soviets, in the agency's opinion, would probably not change their ob-jectives or their methods now that they had the bomb. The big difference was that war could now involve devastation of the U.S.: "It is not yet possible to estimate with any precision the effects of the Soviet possession of the atomic bomb upon the probability of war," but "a capability for effective direct attack upon the continental US must be considered to increase the danger that the USSR might resort to military action to gain its objectives. . . . The continental US will be for the first time liable to devastating attack."[2]

The analysts were talking about the prospect of atomic missiles and bombers. America had already been subjected to devastating Soviet spying.

THE ATOM SPIES

The successful testing by the Soviets of an atomic bomb was far ahead of all Western predictions. Truman and his advisers knew that sooner or later the Russians would develop their own bomb, but they were all surprised at how soon it actually came. Their surprise turned to horror when it emerged that in all probability the Russian success was not simply the result of brilliant, origi-nal engineering but was also due to successful espionage in the United States. As the search began for the security leak, a whole series of apparently disparate trails converged in a highway of deceit and double cross.

In September 1945, Prime Minister Mackenzie King of Canada made a hurried visit to Washington to speak confidentially to President Truman. He told him about Igor Gouzenko's information concerning Soviet espionage activity in Canada, the United States, and Britain. Information was included about a Soviet atom-bomb spy network and the probable involvement of at least one U.S. State Department official. "It would not be surprising," Truman observed about Soviet espionage in Canada and Britain. "There must be similar penetrations by the Russians into the conditions in the United States."[3] He was right. The FBI was ordered to investigate.

Agent Bill Harvey was in charge of the FBI's first big break in the investigation. He was a solidly built man with an ever-spreading girth and large, cop's eyes. He possessed an extremely independent mind that made him stand out in J. Edgar Hoover's buttoned-down bureau. Harvey's upbringing in a small midwestern town made him feel out of place in sophisticated Washington society—a factor that would be significant in a later spy case. As a spy catcher he was in the first rank. When Elizabeth Bentley, a homely, nondescript woman, confessed to FBI agents in New York that she had been the courier of an extensive Soviet spy network in Canada and the United States, Harvey traveled from Washington to supervise her interrogation. During two weeks of questioning, Bentley named over one hundred people in Soviet spy nets. "Fifty-one of these persons were deemed of sufficient importance to warrant investigative attention by the Bureau," Harvey's report stated. "Of those 51 individuals, 27 were employed in agencies of the U.S. government," including one State Department official named Alger Hiss.* At this stage the FBI considered Bentley's evidence against Hiss her most important. She was the second person to name Hiss as a spy.

In 1939 Whittaker Chambers, an ex-courier for a Soviet espionage ring in the United States, had warned Adolf Berle, assistant secretary of state, that Hiss was a Soviet spy.† Possibly assuming that they still lived in a world of gen-

---

*Elizabeth Bentley disclosed the existence of two Soviet spy networks in the United States. One was headed by the Treasury economist Nathan G. Silvermaster; the other by Victor Perlo of the War Production Board. These networks had members in the Justice Department, the Foreign Economic Administration, the Board of Economic Warfare, and the State Department. FBI and OSS investigators uncovered more members of the networks in the War and Navy departments, the Office of War Intelligence, and in the OSS itself. Bentley named Harry Dexter White in the Treasury, who had collaborated with Maynard Keynes to create the postwar international monetary system. In April 1944 White had been instrumental in the U.S. government's decision to hand over U.S. Treasury plates to the Soviet Union to print occupation currency, ultimately costing the American taxpayer $225 million. See Paul Johnson, *A History of the World from 1917 to the 1980s* (London: Weidenfeld and Nicolson, 1984), p. 458. For the FBI report, see David C. Martin, *Wilderness of Mirrors* (New York: Ballantine Books, 1980), p. 27.

†Chambers also named Hiss's wife, Priscilla, and brother, Donald, as Soviet spies. At about the same time William C. Bullitt, the American ambassador in Paris, warned Dr. Stanley Hornbeck, Hiss's superior as head of the Far Eastern Division in the State Department, that the French had evidence that both Alger and Donald Hiss were Soviet agents. Hornbeck questioned Alger, who denied the allegation to Hornbeck's satisfaction.

Berle's role was interesting. It seems he was not prepared to put faith in anything Whittaker Chambers said. In 1939 the Roosevelt administration was purging people who were seen as communists or procommunist. Berle, who was anticommunist, probably felt that Chambers was a

tlemen (something the bohemian and bisexual Chambers could not claim to be), or that Hiss was unlikely to be associated with someone like Chambers, Berle did not investigate the charge. Hiss's brother, Donald, was a partner in Dean Acheson's law firm and had acted as Acheson's assistant. Hiss was one of the Establishment. A graduate of Johns Hopkins and Harvard Law School, he was Ivy League. He had served for a year as law clerk to Supreme Court Justice Oliver Wendell Holmes. When Berle had relayed Chambers' accusation against Hiss to Roosevelt, "the President had laughed."[4] This perception changed after Gouzenko's and Bentley's evidence was gathered. Without naming Hiss, Gouzenko had spoken about a Soviet "agent in the United States in May, 1945, who was an assistant to the then Secretary of State, Edward R. Stettinius"—a description of Hiss's job at the time.[5] Hiss, while constantly denying the allegations against him, agreed to leave the State Department in 1946. He became president of the Carnegie Endowment for International Peace in New York.

Despite the Gouzenko and Bentley information, the FBI was unable to obtain evidence that would stand up in court against those named. Harvey could not understand why the spy rings had fallen so quiet or why further evidence had dried up. Only several years later did he realize that Gouzenko's defection and Bentley's testimony had prompted the Russians to close down the rings, believing correctly that they had been compromised. In July 1947, after nearly two years of frustrating work and little success, Harvey resigned from the FBI. Within weeks he was in the CIA's Office of Special Operations, back on the spy trail. He brought with him something the CIA desperately needed: a knowledge of counterespionage methods and a knowledge of FBI operations, agents, and methods. "We liked Bill and he was one of us," recalled an old FBI friend, "but as far as Hoover was concerned, he was the enemy."[6]

For two years Harvey concentrated on building up his counterespionage Staff C. Then, in 1949, there was movement on the Gouzenko-Bentley spy trails. In part this was prompted by the fall of China to Mao Tse-tung's communists. Despite $2 billion in aid to Chiang Kai-shek's Kuomintang Nationalists, China had experienced a revolution over which the United States had no control. But it was the Soviet possession of the atom secret that really prompted movement. The fear that Russia planned a war against the West took on a new and terrifying dimension. A year earlier, on June 23, 1948, the Soviet blockade of Berlin had begun, lasting until May 12, 1949. Now, less than four months after the end of the blockade, strategists on both sides of the iron curtain had to address for the first time the prospect of actual atomic war. With renewed vigor the FBI and Harvey's Staff C attacked the problem of unearthing the Soviet spies. After all, if the secrets of the Manhattan Project,

---

distraction and was jealous of Hiss. Berle was an austere man possessed of strong public-service instincts; if he had thought there really was a spy in the State Department, he would have acted to expose him.

America's most closely guarded wartime secret, could be betrayed to the Russians, what else had been betrayed? What was safe?

Having failed to resolve the problem of how to identify Soviet spy rings in America in 1945, Harvey decided that his net had to be cast farther. He went back over the books, looking for clues in the testimony of earlier defectors, trying to piece together the rings and what they had done. The fifteen hundred pages of Soviet codes Donovan's OSS men had secured in November 1944, which Donovan had secretly copied, provided the next break. The sheer volume of messages cryptanalysts had to decipher meant there was a four-year backlog of work. Thus in 1949 a message sent by a Soviet agent in New York to Moscow in 1945 was deciphered for the first time. The message contained the complete text of a private telegram from Churchill to Truman, and it revealed that a Soviet spy with high-level security clearance had been in the British Embassy in Washington at the time. The deciphered message was so accurate that it included the embassy's reference numbers, which were part of the copy sent to the White House.

As more messages were deciphered, it became clear that this spy had regularly passed British and American secrets to his Soviet spy master in New York. Other deciphered messages confirmed the Gouzenko-Bentley information; there had been a major leak from the Manhattan Project.* It was obvious to the CIA and the FBI that they were no longer dealing with isolated spies, but with a well-organized and interconnected Soviet espionage effort in Canada, Britain, and the United States. This interconnection was crucial to Harvey, for he reasoned that if the British or Canadian spy network could be broken and its secrets revealed, then the information gained might help break the American spy network too. And so it was.

The first indication of the identities of the atom spies came from two further decrypts, both of which pointed to the same man. The first was a message indicating that one of the Soviet agents had a sister at an American university; the second was a message containing a verbatim report to Moscow detailing in

---

*The book of Soviet codes that Donovan had secured was incomplete; many pages were burned or missing. The codes were so complex that even though fifteen hundred pages remained either intact or usable, the job of decipherment was extremely difficult. The job was made more arduous by the lack of computer assistance. At the time, computers were not commonplace in cryptanalysis, so thousands of man-hours were required to do the job. A Soviet slip helped the decrypting effort. It was discovered that the Soviets, either through an oversight or overconfidence in their system, had sent a duplicate set of additive references to some of their embassies. An additive reference was a number chosen by a page-and-line reference to books, magazines, journals, newspapers, and any other publications that were generally available. These additive references would be learned by an agent beforehand. In themselves they would not raise suspicion—they might, for example, take the form of a reference to a verse from the Bible. These figures, each one intended to be unique to a particular agent, were added to the base code, effectively making each message possess all the qualities of a "one-time pad" code. By sending out a duplicate set of additives, the Soviets gave the United States the opportunity to make a comparison, and, as a result, more messages were deciphered. See Martin, *Wilderness of Mirrors*, pp. 41–42, and David Kahn, *The Codebreakers* (London: Sphere, 1973), pp. 199, 368–370.

scientific terms progress made on the atom bomb during the war. Klaus Fuchs, a German-born British physicist on the Manhattan Project, whose sister Kristel had been at Swarthmore College, immediately became the prime suspect. When the FBI put this information together with that given by Gouzenko, suspicion hardened. The mounting evidence led to Fuchs's arrest on February 2, 1950, at Harwell, England, where he was working at the Atomic Energy Research Establishment.

An idealist, Fuchs never seemed to realize the nature of his crime. He gave MI-5 a complete rundown of his activities and contacts during his interrogations. This was passed to J. Edgar Hoover, who reported to the President that he had "just gotten word from England that we have gotten a full confession from one of the top scientists who worked over here, that he gave the complete know-how of the atom bomb to the Russians."[7] Fuchs identified Harry Gold, a naturalized American citizen of Russian birth, as his contact. Gold, who lived in Philadelphia, had first come to the attention of the FBI as a result of Elizabeth Bentley's information, but as with so many others in 1945, no hard evidence could be found against him. When faced with Fuchs's charges, Gold maintained his innocence, declaring that he had never been near Los Alamos, where the Manhattan Project was centered. When his home was searched and a brochure from the Santa Fe Chamber of Commerce was found, he was proved a liar on that score. When he finally cracked, he gave the FBI a list of all his contacts. The evidence he supplied led directly to the arrest in 1950, trial, conviction, and execution in 1953 of Julius and Ethel Rosenberg for conspiracy to commit espionage.[8] The atomic spy ring was broken.

By 1953 Harvey's Staff C, the FBI, and British Intelligence had unraveled far more than the Soviet atom network. Information gained from Fuchs, Gouzenko, and other defectors as well as from decryption successes provided leads to a mass of Soviet spies in Britain and America. In 1949, when Harvey decided to reexamine the evidence from defectors, he discovered that as early as 1938, General Walter Krivitsky, a former principal agent of Soviet military intelligence for western Europe who had defected to the United States, had supplied some information on Soviet spies. Although Krivitsky's knowledge of Soviet spying in America was vague, he had detailed knowledge of Soviet spies in Britain. Early on, Krivitsky told Isaac Don Levine, who collaborated on his memoirs, that "he had knowledge of two Soviet agents who had been introduced into the British service." One of these he named as "King." The other he could not name, but he knew something of his characteristics, which "were that of a young Scotsman who had been imbued with communism in the early thirties, and who subsequently was induced to enter the service of British diplomacy."[9] Krivitsky also told his State Department debriefers of another Soviet agent who was a British journalist and had reported from Spain on the Spanish civil war.[10] Harvey connected this information with the evidence of the security leak from the British Embassy in Washington. In 1941 Krivitsky was found dead in his New York hotel room—murdered, it was later believed.[11]

PHILBY

After 1948 the decryption of Soviet codes became much more difficult. In part this was due to the espionage of William Weisband, a clerk in the Armed Forces Security Agency, who sold the Russians information that the Americans possessed their code book, thus causing the Russians to change their codes. Although the FBI tracked down Weisband two years later, they decided not to prosecute him; they did not want to reveal to the Russians how much they knew about their codes and activities.* Meeting with Harvey and James Jesus Angleton, another CIA counterespionage expert, who had been trained in Britain during the war and served in the OSS in Italy, was Harold "Kim" Philby, the British Secret Intelligence Service's official contact with the CIA in Washington, where he served under the cover of first secretary at the British Embassy. He was also responsible for working with the FBI on the cases arising from the decrypted Soviet messages. He came, as Angleton remembered, "with the fanciest recommendations you could get from the British government."[12]

Philby was very well connected. The post of liaison officer in Washington was one of the most important in the British secret service. It was comparable to being an ambassador and executive officer combined. The person holding the job had to make decisions on a day-to-day basis, committing the British government to cooperate with the United States on operations. As a result, he had to understand both British and American policy goals as well as the extent of both countries' intelligence efforts. Philby had regular briefings from the leadership of the CIA and the FBI, and, as all who knew him remarked, was very well informed about British and CIA operations. In 1951, when it became obvious that Philby was a Soviet agent and almost certainly the "British journalist" referred to by Krivitsky in 1938 (Philby had covered the Spanish civil war for the London *Times*), it was also obvious that he had been the Soviet's most important spy. According to a later FBI report, Philby "knew of the interrogation of Fuchs as well as the full cooperation given by him . . . yet no action was taken by the Soviets to save any American members of the espionage ring which ultimately was uncovered as a result of the Fuchs revelations."[13] Another report speculated similarly: "Philby and his Russian spy chiefs in Moscow even knew that the FBI planned to arrest the Rosenbergs [but] chose to sacrifice them, most probably to keep Philby's identity a secret."[14]

---

*Martin, *Wilderness of Mirrors*, p. 46. The same approach was taken with decryption information in the Rosenberg case. Then too the FBI decided not to present their decrypts implicating the Rosenbergs in Soviet spying, so as to protect their sources. As a result, the conviction of the couple was based upon flimsier evidence than could have been the case.

Philby knew that the CIA and the British were setting up a Committee of Free Albanians, whose purpose was to free Albania from the grip of Enver Hoxha, the communist dictator. He knew about plans to support east European resistance groups and to parachute agents into the Soviet Union. Michael Burke, an Office of Policy Coordination officer then organizing anticommunist resistance groups behind the iron curtain, recalled:

> When I first met Philby in London in March 1950, I was aware that he was legitimately privy to my assignment; what surprised me was his easy familiarity with operational matters. Frankly, too, I was pleasantly surprised and flattered that a man of his rank would invite me to dine with him privately.
>
> We decided on Wheelers in Dover Street, ate sole and drank Meursault, and talked easily and freely about all manner of things. His considerable charm was disarming, his slight stutter sympathetic, his face almost handsome in a neglected way. He gave the appearance of wasting no more time shaving or combing his hair than he did with his clothes, which were unfashionable and unpressed. Entirely likeable and very much at home in and on top of his profession, Philby's surface persona seemed to go right to his core. His social class and his education at Westminster School and Cambridge University presumed loyalty and commended him to the Establishment. It was unthinkable to suspect that those traditional credentials would conceal a Soviet agent, and the degree of self-control, of self-discipline demanded of Philby to sustain his enormous deception over so long a period of time is immeasurable.[15]

Life in Washington must have been extremely tense for Philby as the decrypting of Soviet messages proceeded, moving closer and closer to uncovering his colleague in deceit, Donald Maclean, known as "Homer" in the Soviet codes. It must have been excruciating for him when another colleague in treachery, the homosexual, alcoholic (all three drank like fish), and indiscreet Guy Burgess sent him this message in 1950: "I have a shock for you. I have just been posted to Washington." (The head of Foreign Office Security had recommended Burgess' posting to Washington, since "his eccentricities would be more easily overlooked in a larger Embassy than a smaller one.") Burgess went on to suggest that he share a house with Philby when he arrived.[16] Philby's agreement to this arrangement was his first mistake. Burgess, an unreliable ally at the best of times, was bound to come unstuck sooner or later, and Philby was lighting a fuse leading directly to himself by taking him in. His arrival signaled the end for both of them.

James Angleton returned from Italy to join the CIA's Office of Special Operations in 1947. (Philby described him as "the driving force of OSO.") He worked with Harvey's Staff C to track down Soviet spies in America. Both men collaborated closely with Philby from September 1949, when he arrived in Washington. "We formed the habit of lunching once a week at Harvey's," recalled Philby about Angleton, "where he demonstrated regularly that overwork was not his only vice. He was one of the thinnest men I have ever met, and one of the biggest eaters. Lucky Jim! After a year of keeping up with Angleton, I took the advice of an elderly lady friend and went on a diet, dropping from thirteen stone to about eleven in three months."[17] At these lunches, and at other meetings, Philby was kept abreast of progress on identifying "Homer."

Not knowing what to do, and not receiving any pertinent advice from his Russian contact, Philby decided that he should try to deflect the investigation to protect Maclean. This was his second mistake; the pressure was telling. By trying to protect Maclean, he was bound to draw attention to himself if anything went wrong. In August 1945 he had acted to protect himself, Donald Maclean, and Guy Burgess when a senior Soviet intelligence officer in Istanbul, Konstantin Volkov, made contact with the British, telling them that he had knowledge of two Soviet agents in the British Foreign Office and of another in MI-6. When papers dealing with the case were given to Philby, he alerted his Russian contact in London and then delayed Volkov's defection, giving the Russians the time they needed to arrest him. An internal inquiry conducted at the time by MI-6 concluded that Volkov's planned defection had probably been given away by an indiscreet diplomat. Five years later Philby realized that he himself would be open to suspicion if anyone connected a deflection of the "Homer" investigation with the Volkov case: "One day, any day, somebody in London or Washington would look into his shaving mirror and find inspiration there. Once investigation of the diplomats started, it would certainly yield the right answer sooner or later. The great question was: How soon? How late?"[18] Very soon, was the answer.

The British were the first to suspect Philby of treachery. During 1947 Philby served in Turkey and may well have been an officially sanctioned contact with the Russians. Later, when he was in Beirut, he kept a photograph of himself on the Russian side of the Turkish border with Mount Ararat in the background—evidence that he was very friendly with the Russians, to say the least. Before the cold war started in earnest he may have continued his contacts with official approval. The information gathered from both Gouzenko and Volkov forced the British to search for a Soviet spy in their own intelligence organization. Gouzenko had spoken of an agent in British intelligence, as had Volkov, who insisted that news of his wish to defect be addressed to the highest level of the British Secret Intelligence Service, so convinced was he that the Soviet agent might compromise him. By early 1951 the British apparently focused on Philby as the Soviet spy. In all likelihood they hoped to use him as a disinformation agent, quietly moving him away from areas of real importance and sensitivity and out of his Washington post. Before anything could be done, however, Bill Harvey and Jim Angleton, aroused by their own suspicion of Philby's treachery, began pursuing Philby themselves. This impetuous unilateral action on the part of the Americans forced the British to recall Philby and show their hand.[19]

In America, Bill Harvey was the first to look into his shaving mirror one day and find inspiration there. One evening at a dinner Philby gave in the spring of 1951, Burgess grossly insulted Bill Harvey's wife. One of Burgess' party tricks was to draw cartoons of the guests, and Libby Harvey begged him to draw one of her. The result was a caricature of a drunken Mrs. Harvey, legs spread, crotch bared, and her dress around her waist. Both Bill and Libby were furious. This sort of "humor" was far too sophisticated for them. Bill had to be taken out of the house and walked around the block by Jim Angleton to cool off.* He never forgot the incident, and Burgess, linked with Philby, stayed in his mind.

Meanwhile Philby, sensing that events were coming to a head, either decided to try to protect himself or was directed by Moscow to do so at the expense of Maclean. He pointed out the obvious to his superiors in London: they might be able to track down "Homer" by comparing the records of diplomats stationed in Washington between the relevant dates of the "Homer" intercepts (1944–45) with Krivitsky's evidence.† When the comparison was made, Donald Maclean was one of six possible suspects. Additional decrypted information pinned him down as the spy.[20] Maclean's Scottish name (the family was originally Scottish, but Donald was brought up in south Wales) tied him to Krivitsky's information, and his position in the Foreign Office tied him to the information provided by Gouzenko and Volkov. Between 1944 and 1948 he served as first secretary at the British Embassy in Washington, and in 1951 he was head of the American desk in London.

Burgess, who had been sent back to London for disgraceful behavior in Washington, was asked by Philby to warn Maclean that the net was closing on him and that he should flee.[21] Maclean was also warned by Anthony Blunt, another well-connected Soviet agent in London, that his arrest was imminent. On the evening of Friday, May 21, 1951, Maclean fled to Russia. Burgess fled along with him, although his departure was not part of any plan. He apparently decided on his own to end his career as a spy and to go to Russia with Maclean. Burgess' action meant that Philby would almost certainly be discovered too.[22]

---

*Martin, *Wilderness of Mirrors*, p. 50. By all accounts, Libby Harvey was well on the way to becoming an alcoholic at this stage. Bill Harvey was moving up in the world and developing a reputation for womanizing. He was also developing an excessive liking for the bottle. Libby simply could not keep up, and drink was her answer. At Philby's dinner party the Harveys were both fairly well oiled by the time Burgess took out his pen, and Bill and Libby no doubt had some responsibility for the scene that developed. They were divorced in 1954.

†Kim Philby, *My Silent War* (London: Grove Press, 1968), p. 130. Philby also tried a red-herring suggestion on SIS. Sir Robert ("Bobby") Mackenzie, the security officer of the Washington embassy, reasoned that the code name "Homer" indicated that another suspect, Paul Gore-Booth, who fitted Krivitsky's description of one of the Foreign Office spies just as well as Maclean and was a classics scholar to boot, was the one most likely to be a spy. In addition, "Homer" in its Russian form "Gomer" was similar to "Gore." Philby passed the suspicion on: "It was a neat bit of work, good enough, I hoped, to give London pause for a few days." Bruce Page, David Leitch, and Phillip Knightley, *Philby: The Spy Who Betrayed a Generation*, pp. 258–259, show that from August 1950 Philby must have known that Maclean was conducting his treachery on borrowed time. Diplomats at the Washington embassy and British Foreign Office security officers knew that Maclean was the suspect from the requests for information about him that were made by the investigators. "We never used his name to each other. It was just understood who it was," recalled one senior official later (ibid., p. 259).

It was not until the following Monday that the British realized what had happened and alerted Washington. Philby received word of the defection in this way: "One morning, at a horribly early hour, Geoffrey Paterson, MI-5's Washington liaison, called me by telephone. He explained that he had just received an enormously long Most Immediate telegram from London. . . . When I reached the Embassy, I went straight to Paterson's office. He looked gray. 'Kim,' he said in a half-whisper, 'the bird has flown.' I registered dawning horror (I hope). 'What bird? Not Maclean?' 'Yes,' he answered. 'But there's worse than that. . . . *Guy Burgess* has gone with him.' At that my consternation was no pretence."[23] When Harvey heard the news, he put the pieces together.

On June 13, 1951, three weeks after Maclean's and Burgess' flight, Harvey submitted a five-page memorandum to the head of Special Operations, stating categorically that Philby was a Soviet agent. He tied Philby not only to Burgess and Maclean (Philby was one of the few people who knew about the "Homer" investigation) but also to the mysterious Volkov case six years earlier. Harvey's insight was built on a number of factors, some relevant, others not. The insult to his wife, his sense of social inferiority compared to the sophisticated Philby and Burgess, his police training, and his experience with the layers of deception involved in the Bentley case all led to one inescapable conclusion: *Philby was a Russian spy!* Five days later Jim Angleton reached the same conclusion, which he also communicated in a memorandum. While not directly naming Philby as a spy, he recounted Philby's connection with Burgess and suggested his suspicion between the lines.[24]

General Walter Bedell Smith, Hillenkoetter's successor as director of Central Intelligence since October 7, 1950, sent both memoranda to London and demanded that Philby be recalled within the week. He informed Sir Stewart Menzies, the head of the British Secret Intelligence Service, that the CIA had declared Philby persona non gratissima. "Fire Philby or we break off the intelligence relationship" was his terse message.[25] Philby realized that as long as he maintained his innocence, no matter what the evidence against him, he could not be proven guilty of being a Soviet agent. The same considerations that had kept the FBI from revealing the full evidence against Weisband would operate in his favor too. As a result, until he left for Moscow on January 23, 1963—twelve years after his treachery was suspected—he remained free, never trusted again but never quite condemned either. Just before his departure he admitted some responsibility for tipping off Burgess and Maclean but little else. Not until his memoirs, *My Silent War*, were published in 1968 did he admit what everyone had suspected seventeen years earlier.*

---

*The CIA put Philby's treatment down to the British "old boy" system. See, for example, Michael Burke, *Outrageous Good Fortune* (New York: Little, Brown, 1984), pp. 152–153:

MI6 moved protectively in its traditional old-boy fashion. Philby resigned in 1951 to spend five years in the shadows, his loyalty still stoutly defended by British colleagues, and was put on hold both by them and by his Soviet controllers. In 1956 he surfaced as a Mideast correspondent for the London *Observer* and the *Economist*, his appointments arranged by MI6

After the Burgess and Maclean episodes, and after Philby "resigned" from the Secret Intelligence Service, subsequent analyses determined that Maclean had detailed knowledge of certain aspects of wartime planning for economic and political conditions in postwar Europe; that he knew the precise nature of Anglo-American intelligence agreements with NATO; that he knew about uranium requirements for atomic-energy schemes; that he had had access to certain diplomatic codes; and that he knew Allied high policy during the Korean War.

By 1955 the suspicions of the roles Burgess and Maclean might have played in the U.S. intelligence failure over the Korean War were made public. Magazine and newspaper articles speculated on "How two spies cost US Korean War"[26] by informing Red China, through their Russian contacts, that the United Nations forces in Korea would not retaliate against Red China itself if Red Chinese troops entered the war. This assertion may well have been accurate. Truman's refusal to allow MacArthur to retaliate directly against Red China eventually prompted MacArthur's dismissal. According to Roy Medvedev, a Russian historian who knew Maclean in Moscow and who later left Russia for life in the West, Maclean occasionally "made reference to certain historic events which he seemed to have influenced,"[27] and in this context he discussed Korea.

In the summer of 1950 the North Korean army's attack on the South quickly placed the South Koreans on the defensive in an enclave by the sea, leaving 90 percent of the country in North Korean hands. General MacArthur's landing at Inchon, far to the North Korean rear, turned the tables, and the North Korean troops of Kim Il Sung were driven back toward the Chinese border. According to Medvedev, Stalin then (at the end of 1950) insisted on Chinese intervention, but Mao Tse-tung hesitated, afraid that MacArthur might invade China and even use the atomic bomb on Chinese military and industrial targets.

Maclean, back in London as head of the American desk in the British Foreign Office after his time in Washington, was privy to the secret communications between the British and American governments. Because both countries were part of the United Nations force in Korea, sensitive intelligence information was exchanged between them. Thus Maclean was in a position to know of President Truman's October 9, 1950, order to MacArthur that "In any case you will obtain authorization from Washington prior to taking any military action against objectives in Chinese territory."[28] In addition, Maclean would have had a fairly accurate knowledge of American/United Nations policy for

friends. Then one night in 1963, Philby failed to show up for a dinner date at a friend's home in Beirut. He simply vanished. The British were at last closing in, and Philby's nerve began to crack under the now unbearable strain. His Russian handlers actioned the long-laid plan to spring him, and Philby decamped to Moscow.

pursuing the war and would have known that an invasion of China or the use of atomic weapons was not planned. He does not seem to have known, however, about the plans for the Inchon landing. After his defection Maclean indicated that he had passed policy information (rather than military plans) to his Soviet masters, who in turn had informed the Chinese. If so, he must have acted very quickly and the Russians and Chinese even more quickly: on October 11 the Chinese announced that they could not stand by if U.N. forces crossed the 38th parallel; from October 26, Chinese troops were identified as fighting alongside North Koreans; and on November 26 Chinese armies crossed the Yalu River and attacked MacArthur.

Whether or not Maclean did actually affect the outcome of the Korean War was of secondary importance to the CIA. The crucial fact was that a Soviet spy, Maclean, was well placed to affect the course of the war. "There can be little doubt that [the] final period of his work for the KGB was of considerable value to them," estimated Robert Cecil, an ex-colleague in the Foreign Office:

> Chinese intervention in the Korean War in mid-October 1950 had much intensified Cold War tensions, including tension between the USA and her principal allies. The wish of MacArthur to carry the war to the PRC led to fears in London that he might induce Truman to employ the A-bomb. In December 1950 Attlee went at short notice to Washington with the intention of averting this danger. Among the secret papers, which I unearthed in Maclean's filing cabinet after his flight, was a copy of the Prime Minister's report to Cabinet on his visit. On the other hand, neither Burgess nor Maclean would have been privy to operational decisions and it is hard to give credence to MacArthur's later complaint that they had frustrated his efforts by disclosure of his plans to the enemy. In any case, there was no premature disclosure of his most spectacular surprise operation, the seaborne landing at Inchon in mid-September 1950.[29]

Despite all this, Maclean was not as deadly a spy as Philby. While Maclean's base of operations was the "open" area of national strategy, where a secret is not a secret for very long because each country's intentions soon become obvious, Philby's was a world made up of informal, high-level social contacts with FBI and CIA people as well as formal briefings with those in power, including the director of Central Intelligence himself. Philby's personal popularity in London and Washington during the last four years of his intelligence career had succeeded in opening many doors. Consequently it was never fully possible to assess the damage he had done, because no one was sure just how much he actually knew.

In all probability Philby knew more than was comfortable but less than was imagined. As a Soviet agent he had been a loner, with not much of a Soviet network around him. When a crisis came, he was forced to depend upon his own intervention (as he did in the Volkov affair) or on the drunken and irresponsible Burgess. No doubt his Soviet masters stood in a certain awe of him, never really giving him orders, depending instead on Philby to determine his own activity. His intimate knowledge of operations and operational methods undoubtedly contributed to the deaths of several hundred people.

Philby's treachery successfully compromised one particular Anglo-American intelligence operation, involving the attempted overthrow of Enver Hoxha's communist regime in Albania. This was originally a British Secret Intelligence Service operation, started in 1946; the CIA joined the affair in 1949. Philby, who had not yet been posted to Washington, became the operation's joint coordinator. After being transferred to Washington in September 1949, Philby stayed abreast of developments and undoubtedly gave the Soviets full details of the operation. In the late 1960s, after the London *Sunday Times* conducted a full-scale investigation of Philby's treachery, the paper's editor, Harold Evans, wrote:

> The enterprise was doomed, because at the center of the campaign against Albania, sitting in Washington on the Anglo-American Special Policy Committee, was Kim Philby. We pieced together the story of the Albanian expedition, which had lain secret for seventeen years, by finding survivors: at least 300 men lost their lives. . . . The first big "drops" of men who would lead the revolution were infiltrated into Albania by sea and air in spring 1950. "They always knew we were coming," one of the few who lived told the *Sunday Times* researcher. The infiltrators were shot, the local people who helped them were forcibly resettled in another area.[30]

Another, similar operation was probably compromised by Philby. This involved American and British support for the Ukrayinska Viyskova Organizatsiya (UVO), the fighting arm of the Ukrainian nationalist movement, which had been a thorn in Stalin's side since the late 1920s. Although British and American agencies provided supplies and trained agents to the UVO (material and men were parachuted into Russia and the Ukraine), most were captured. By 1961 the Soviets had completely destroyed the UVO and executed most of its leaders.[31]

Although both Albania and the Ukraine were victories for the Soviets, they never let the world know about them. The reason behind their silence was clear. The operations demonstrated that the West was prepared to use covert action to subvert communist regimes in eastern Europe and to disrupt the Soviet Union itself. The Soviets did not want nationalists and anticommunists behind the iron curtain to know that they might receive practical assistance from the Americans and the British.* The British and the Americans, on the

---

*In *My Silent War*, for example, Philby makes no mention of the Albanian operation, although he must have counted it as one of his greatest coups.

other hand, were not interested in publicizing their failures. "The Albanian operation was the first and only attempt by Washington to unseat a Communist regime within the Soviet orbit by paramilitary means," observed Harry Rositzke, who in the 1950s conducted CIA intelligence operations into eastern Europe and the Soviet Union. "It taught a clear lesson to the war planners: Even a weak regime could not be overthrown by covert paramilitary actions alone."[32] The significant point about Albania was that there were no Soviet divisions within the country or on its borders; paramilitary action might have worked there. The defeat of the Albanian operation was seen as a result of treachery at the heart of the Anglo-American effort, and therefore the validity of paramilitary operations elsewhere in Europe was not questioned. It took the Polish, German, and Hungarian uprisings in 1956 to give the lie to paramilitary theory: where there were Soviet divisions it would require NATO divisions to dislodge them, not paramilitary ones.

Philby's most important effect was on the Anglo-American intelligence relationship. For years after his discovery as a Soviet agent the relationship was full of bitterness and suspicion. Tom Braden, an early CIA officer, recalled how Philby's treachery affected him:

> I had been in the British army for three years. I'd volunteered in 1940 straight out of college, and I was in the British army in Africa and then in Italy. Then I transferred in early 1944. So I had very strong natural affinities for someone who called me from the British embassy. I'd say "Come on in." This guy called and he was over, working for SIS. He identified himself and wanted to know what my Division was doing. He came in and chatted with me briefly, and I took him up to meet Allen Dulles—just "How do you do?"—and took him back to my office. And then I got a phone call from Allen while he was in the office telling me to watch it, don't tell him anything. This was a shock to me. The wartime alliance that I had always considered as strong as the Rock of Gibraltar was full of suspicions and bitterness and worry and concern.*

---

*Interview, Tom Braden, November 14, 1983. Major General Kenneth Strong, who during the war had served as Eisenhower's intelligence officer, was temporarily transferred by the British Ministry of Defense to SIS to act as its link with the CIA after Philby. He was trusted by Bedell Smith and soon became a familiar sight at the CIA headquarters at 2430 E Street NW, Washington 25, DC (the old Central Intelligence Group headquarters), where he was known as "the hangman's dilemma" and "the chinless wonder" because of his receding chin. Apparently Bedell Smith wanted to appoint Strong as his deputy to take charge of all foreign intelligence operations but could not secure the approval of Truman or the National Security Council (Leonard Mosley, *Dulles: A Biography of Eleanor, Allen and John Foster Dulles and Their Family Network* [New York: Dial Press/James Wade, 1978], pp. 270–272).

Ten years later the British Secret Intelligence Service liaison officer in Washington, Maurice Oldfield, found that he still had to deal with the effects of the British traitors on the Anglo-American intelligence relationship:

> I took a bet with myself that the names of Burgess and Maclean would be mentioned to me within a month of my arriving in Washington. So I had taken every chance to study all re-

The intelligence relationship with the British was also muddied by cultural, stylistic, and experiential differences that made a clash almost inevitable. World War II had provided a concentrated learning experience for the United States. By 1945 America was fully aware of the world outside its own hemisphere and was instinctively responding to it in a practical, immediate manner. This need for immediate action affected the CIA's handling of Philby. The pressure to take decisive action against him came from Washington, not London. Britain's sophisticated longer perspectives were set aside. British instincts of crisis management, honed over centuries, were not understood. The idea of trying to feed Philby misleading information so as to confuse the Russians, or of placing him in a less sensitive post while building the case against him and assessing the damage he had caused (as was done, in effect, by the British with the traitor Anthony Blunt), was not even thought of in Washington.

Instead, the CIA seemed obsessed with finding the answers to some rhetorical questions: How could Philby have done it? How did he manage to disguise his true allegiance? How could he have betrayed friends and allies? Recalling the events and attitudes that surrounded the Philby case over thirty years later, Michael Burke, who was involved in the Albanian affair, reflected how the revelation of Philby's deceit stunned the U.S. intelligence community. When Burke was posted as a station chief in Europe early in 1951, he and his wife, Timmy, were given various farewell dinner parties. One party given by Philby stood out:

> Ironically, the largest, jolliest, and wettest of these parties was given by the Philbys on February 24, 1951, at their home on Nebraska Avenue. Timmy and I and Ken Downs, the only people without cars and awaiting a taxi, were the last to leave. Downs, still carrying one more martini for the road, fell from the porch into a thick hedge, landed flat on his back, and held up his glass triumphantly to show that he hadn't spilled a drop. The Philbys and we cheered him extravagantly from the top step. We all hugged one another in semidrunk camaraderie, rescued Downs from the bushes, and left the Philbys awash in bonhomie. It was that kind of party, not at all the kind of party Philby had arranged for our agents returning to their homeland. . . .
>
> It was virtually impossible for me to reconcile the Philby I knew and liked with the Philby I did not know and recoiled from. I could understand his having become a Communist in the despairing British political climate of

---

ports concerning those two. I wanted to have all the answers. Sure enough within two weeks I was shown a memorandum of the American Joint Chiefs of Staff, which stated that regarding inquiries into the affairs of Burgess and Maclean "in 1955 little or no action has been taken to prevent repetition of these mistakes." To which Admiral Arthur Radford had added his own comment that Burgess and Maclean "were apparently protected by others in high places, some allegedly still in key positions." (Quoted in Richard Deacon, "C"—A Biography of Sir Maurice Oldfield [London: Macdonald, 1985], p. 119)

the early 1930s, and I could comprehend his renouncing his country; however dubious, it was in a sense an abstract, a personal, decision. What I could not assimilate was the magnitude of his treachery, for Philby's direct action had betrayed and caused the deaths of an untold number of men who counted him an ally.[33]

—6—

Among the Ruins
1947-1951

Clarifying problems and accurately estimating the nature and course of events—the CIA's most important responsibilities—were given additional prominence by the discovery of the spies in Britain and America. The facts of Soviet espionage and subversion in the West transformed political assumptions and helped the CIA establish itself as a long-range institution. Democrats and Republicans alike began to realize that the cold-war struggle with Russia might last throughout several presidential terms, if not for decades. They also began to realize that the Soviet Union was not simply a geopolitical opponent. As Philby, Burgess, Maclean, the Rosenbergs, and Whittaker Chambers clearly demonstrated, the Soviets were intent on far more than geographical conquest: they sought to destroy democratic confidence as well. With spies in the inner sanctuary of its democracy, America suffered a sense of violation; it no longer felt secure from within. As a result, the question James Forrestal posed in 1945—Is the Soviet Union a nation or a religion?—took on a new pertinence. For the first time the United States faced the reality that it had enemies within its boundaries, who, if unchallenged, would steal America's strength.

During the 1948 presidential election the idea of enemies within was pushed hard by Republicans. It held a large measure of truth. Three years later Senator Joseph McCarthy would take the idea to destructive and malicious extremes, exaggerating the fact that Whittaker Chambers and Elizabeth Bentley were giving evidence about *Americans* who spied for the USSR because of their dedication to the ideal of a communist utopia. Richard Bissell, a brilliant young economist who became instrumental in securing congressional support for the Marshall Plan and in implementing this support during the late 1940s and early 1950s, had previously been on Truman's White House staff. There he was involved in a bitter struggle over communist agents in the bureaucracy and in the labor unions. Bissell described the struggle in this way:

> Immediately after the war there was an interlude, mercifully a short one, when there was a very important struggle in the United States between communist domination of the American left and noncommunists. I was in the middle of that. At that time I was on the White House staff mediating labor disputes, and it was quite fascinating to watch the process where communist-leaning leadership in the unions was defeated and driven out. There weren't many people—unless they were in public affairs—in that era who knew about the struggle and where it went on and what happened. That was the moment when the principal adviser to the head of the Steelworkers' Union was a member of the Communist party; it was a moment when the Electrical Union's top leadership was communist-dominated.[1]

Bissell eventually joined the CIA, where he masterminded the U-2 and Bay of Pigs operations. He retired from the agency as deputy director of plans.

Cord Meyer, another future senior CIA officer, was also involved in this pre-McCarthy struggle with internal subversion. Meyer, who left Yale to enlist in the marines in 1942, served as a lieutenant in the Pacific, where he was seriously wounded. In 1945 he was part of the American team setting up the United Nations organization. His boss on this assignment was Alger Hiss. "Hiss struck me at the time as a disciplined if somewhat arrogant State Department official," Meyer wrote in his memoirs, "and nothing about him gave the remotest indication that there would later be allegations that seemed persuasive to me that he could once have been one of the Soviets' most important agents of influence within the American government. In those days, of course, I hardly knew the Russian secret police existed."[2]

Meyer's innocence reflected the innocence of the entire nation. It was followed abruptly by the shock of discovering enemies within. As the United Nations came into being, Meyer, who had also taken a private interest in the American Veterans Committee, became involved in a battle with American communists for control of the committee. The battle lasted over three years, ending in November 1948 with a noncommunist victory:[3]

> My participation in this struggle provided a unique opportunity to learn at first hand the strengths and weaknesses of Communist organizational strategy. As nothing else could, it gave me an understanding of how formidable is that dedicated man, the Communist true believer, and it taught me never to underestimate the potential strength of a disciplined Communist minority. It revealed the techniques of covert infiltration and control, through which Communists have too often captured organizations from those who awoke

too late to these dangers. In microcosm, our struggle was an extension of the political battle being waged then in Western Europe between the democratic left and the mass Communist parties of Italy and France. My role in this small skirmish made me realize how much was at stake on the larger stage.[4]

Although not numerically strong during the 1930s, American communists had the ability and discipline to infiltrate America's leading institutions. Many of the private and government institutions that eventually became havens for communists were not even in existence before 1932. The rapid growth of the great improvised institutions of the New Deal and of the war made them extremely vulnerable to penetration. As a result, communists soon found their way into positions of power throughout America. They were visible in Hollywood, labor unions, the OSS, the American Veterans Committee, and the Washington bureaucracy. At one point an organized communist minority had virtually taken over the state of Minnesota in the mid-1930s.[5]

Most communists were not Soviet agents but were more sympathetic to the totalitarian Soviet cause than to American democracy. Many came to communism and then left it. While it was fashionable to be a communist on campus in the mid-1930s, it was no longer fashionable by 1948. The close attachment many Americans had to communism made the Hiss case hit home. When Hiss was found guilty in 1950 of lying about his association with a communist spy network, it was clear that he was only one of hundreds of government officials who had similar communist leanings.* As people tried to escape from their communist pasts, there was a sense in the nation of incredible ambiguity and crossing forces which dissolved perspectives. Keeping one's head, remaining cool, was difficult during those years. Such men as Bissell and Meyer, who joined the CIA in February 1954 and October 1951 respectively, did not believe that all communists were Russian spies controlled from Moscow. Although they knew that some communists were Soviet agents, and they considered communism to be a generally repugnant philosophy, they accepted the right of every person to hold his own political opinion. For them the enemy would become Russia as a state, using communism for its advancement. If the state could be contained, communism could be contained by democratic virtue and other means. This cool, dispassionate look at events, unusual at the time, was to become a CIA trademark.

---

* There is a theory that Hiss's accuser, Whittaker Chambers, never really left the party and that Hiss was thrown to the wolves because he had outlived his usefulness. The Soviets were in the position to gain from the publicity of the case. The late 1940s saw a wave of defectors to the West, who were busy revealing the true nature of Stalin's Russia. Drawing attention to Hiss served as a useful counteraction to this and drew attention away from others who remained hidden. There is an account of an acrimonious meeting between Chambers and Henry Luce, the owner of *Time* magazine, on which Chambers worked after the war. "Whittaker, I have to ask for your resignation." "All right, Harry, but why?" "You were a communist!" "But, Harry, you knew I was." "I didn't think you were a Soviet agent." Long pause. Then, dramatically, Chambers replied, "Harry, there are moments when I despair for my country" (interview, November 17, 1984).

By 1950 the fear of enemies within and Soviet espionage activity weighed heavily on public opinion; Americans now supported the cold war.* Senator Vandenberg and other Republicans abandoned their isolationist attitudes, adopting instead a position of continued U.S. involvement in the postwar world. They represented the cutting edge of the large constituency that believed the United States had to remain involved with the world after victory in 1945. Between 1945 and 1950 people came to accept the idea that life was never going to be "normal" again. If America was to control its own destiny, it would have to cease hoping for a return to the prewar world. More than that, it had to recognize its position as the world's greatest power. For with this vision, engagement now meant hardheaded international dealing with the Soviets. In the five years since the end of World War II, Americans in both major parties, including many who had been America Firsters before Pearl Harbor, had come broadly to accept the Wilsonian view that the world was manageable and that America could manage it. This was coupled with an almost religious belief that America's decision not to join the League of Nations after World War I was a sin for which amends needed to be made.

It was the hardheaded quality of this view that was instrumental in shaping the CIA and placing such importance on the National Intelligence Estimates its staff produced. If America was to engage in the cold war on behalf of what the governing elite saw as liberal, democratic values, it had to have the best information and assessments possible across the whole range of human activity. Above all, America had to inform itself. This was Truman's interest in intelligence. It was the best way to ensure independence of thought and action and the best way to ensure the maintenance of idealistic values. Against this background the Estimates became the focal point of U.S. intelligence activity.

BLUEPRINTS FOR ACTION

In April 1949 National Security Council Directive 68 (NSC-68) channeled this new resolve into guidelines that established American defense and foreign policy for the next thirty years. It summed up the awareness of the time. America, it held, was the greatest power in the Free World and had moral, political, and ideological imperatives to uphold free institutions and free countries worldwide. The directive estimated that the Soviet Union devoted

---

* These fears were justified. In 1947 Alexander Foote, a Soviet agent who was a member of the anti-Nazi communist "Lucy" network in Switzerland during the war, was sent to Mexico after training in Moscow by the "Razvedka," or GRU—the Soviet military intelligence. He defected to the West on his way there. "At the beginning of 1947," Foote stated, "I was informed that I was to be entrusted with the rebuilding of a Razvedka network in the USA from an HQ that I was to establish in Mexico. I was told that all Resident Directors of Soviet espionage had been withdrawn from activity in the territory of Russia's cobelligerents in June 1941, and that numerous dormant sources of information in the USA were to be reactivated" (quoted in Richard Deacon, *"C"—A Biography of Sir Maurice Oldfield* [London: Macdonald, 1985], pp. 83–84).

13.8 percent of its gross national product to defense, while America devoted
only 6–7 percent. "The Kremlin is inescapably militant," NSC-68 stated. "It is
inescapably militant because it possesses and is possessed by a world-wide revolutionary movement, because it is the inheritor of Russian imperialism, and
because it is a totalitarian dictatorship. . . . It is quite clear from Soviet theory
and practice that the Kremlin seeks to bring the free world under its domination by the methods of the cold war."[6] In the opinion of the National Security
Council, the Soviet Union "mortally challenged" the United States and sought
its destruction. The struggle was seen as a traditional one between states. To
meet this challenge the council recommended a rapid buildup of U.S. defenses. In its view, America could afford to spend up to 20 percent of its annual
gross national product for defense and security purposes. The directive was debated for a year and then issued in April 1950.

Guidelines did not constitute a global master plan, however, and over the
next decades the CIA, the Defense Department, and the State Department
slowly filled in gaps. For the CIA the expansiveness of NSC-68 was balanced
to a certain extent by the recommendations of a report on agency functioning
that was commissioned by Truman in the autumn of 1948. Truman appointed
a committee of three to conduct a complete investigation of the agency. Allen
Dulles was chairman. He was joined by William H. Jackson, who would later
become a deputy director of Central Intelligence, and Mathias Correa, an assistant to James Forrestal during the war. All three were based in New York,
and all three were lawyers. The report they produced was presented to the National Security Council in January 1949. It was to become the blueprint for
CIA organization and operation. In its most important statement it pinpointed
the need to create a centralized intelligence organization from the numerous
small, *ad hoc* institutions that now existed, each reflecting the particular emergencies that had produced them. They took a longer view of what dangers were
likely to arise rather than simply trying to deal with the dangers that were recognized at the time.

The Dulles report called for the creation of five divisions to replace the
multitude of offices in the CIA. The organization's disorganization was no secret; it was mirrored in the agency's lack of centralization. Dulles emphasized
the need for the director of Central Intelligence to be recognized as *the* coordinator of intelligence and for the Central Intelligence Agency to act as a coordinating agency rather than as yet another intelligence department. The five
proposed divisions were: Estimates, which was considered a crucial division
upon whose performance the future of the agency would be judged; Research
and Reports, which would provide the raw material for Estimates and monitor
current intelligence information requiring speedy reporting and analysis; Operations (covert action, espionage, and counterintelligence); Coordination,
which would link the CIA with the other government intelligence agencies and
departments that had intelligence components; and Administration, which
would take care of the CIA's housekeeping needs.

Noting the random nature of the agency's activities during its first year, Dulles recommended that it should concentrate instead on the functions assigned by or derived from National Security Council directives. In particular, said Dulles, the agency should "discard" intelligence production work that was "superfluous or competitive with the proper activities of departmental intelligence" elsewhere in government. He criticized the agency for not having promoted interagency coordination and cooperation, for not having exercised better "leadership, imagination and initiative," and for not having conducted "continuous examination" of the other intelligence agencies and their work. Dulles singled out covert operations, espionage, and counterintelligence as areas requiring clear objectives and careful, professional implementation.

Coordination was the essence of the report. Dulles stressed it as the major responsibility of the agency. It was, he declared, the job of the CIA to synthesize information and coordinate intelligence activity. The report also recommended that the public be made aware of the CIA's role as a coordinator of intelligence—a role that would enable the agency to "cover up rather than to uncover the secret operations entrusted to it."[7] It avoided the big question: What were the interests and objectives of the United States and how should intelligence fit in? Instead it concentrated on methods. Only later, when he was director of Central Intelligence, did Dulles answer the question through his deployment of resources. Then it was seen that for him American interests lay in managing the world and that American intelligence should operate covertly to prepare the ground for overt American management or, if necessary, for covert management itself.

Dulles was in effect arguing that the CIA should become the sieve through which all intelligence reporting was filtered. The operations the agency conducted should be at the direct instigation of the National Security Council, the supervising body in intelligence, and should, he implied, require the agency to become a professional service. By being professional, of course, the agency would be able to secure effective autonomy. The National Security Council was not a full-time board, and the more active and effective the agency was, the less attention would the council be able to give to each item. The eight-year-old debate about centralized and coordinated intelligence was behind Dulles' report, along with two new factors. When Hillenkoetter succeeded Vandenberg as director of Central Intelligence, he was given the additional task of establishing the CIA in relation to the other agencies of government, not simply those involved in intelligence. Therefore placing the agency within the bureaucracy was vitally important. To make sure it was not treated as a poor relation of any other agency or department, it had to secure its special connection with the President. Making the agency the principal arm of the National Security Council would help achieve this. The President chaired the council, which in turn was advisory to the President. Thus if the CIA became the agency through which NSC directives were implemented, its bureaucratic position would be strong.

Dulles was fully aware of all this. Hillenkoetter's main problem was that he could never obtain clear policy guidelines from the President or the National Security Council. This was not surprising: everybody was trying to come to terms with the new postwar perceptions of America's role in the world, and it was not until NSC-68 was issued that guidelines were established. The State and Defense departments effectively defined intelligence requirements, and if they could not agree, the CIA and the director of Central Intelligence suffered. One of the results of the poorly defined situation that existed before NSC-68 was issued was the creation of the Office of Policy Coordination to conduct political action abroad. Yet all the while the CIA already had a perfectly adequate vehicle for political action in its Office of Special Operations. It meant that suddenly there were two competing clandestine bodies. The creation of OPC was symptomatic of the sense of urgency that gripped the Truman administration to respond to the Soviet threat at all levels all over the world. It was also a move by George Marshall to secure State Department interests in intelligence.

As a result of these pressures, Hillenkoetter was never given the time he needed to establish the CIA and himself as the central coordinator of American intelligence. The title "Central Intelligence Agency" belied the fact that the agency was not the nation's preeminent intelligence agency. It was *meant* to be, but it was still too new, and the bureaucratic interests of the State and Defense departments, represented on the National Security Council by cabinet members who outclassed the director of Central Intelligence (the DCI attended meetings but was not a member of the council), made it very difficult for Hillenkoetter to put into practice the original intentions that had created the agency. Lawrence Houston later reflected:

> Hillenkoetter was underrated. He was not a tremendously forceful guy, but he was by no means stupid, as people very often implied. About four months after Bedell Smith took over, in his morning meetings I remember him saying, "I don't know how on earth Hilly got as far as he did." Hillenkoetter had found it very difficult to get the backing he needed. It was the time when Secretary of State Acheson and Secretary of Defense Johnson weren't talking to each other, and they were the key people on the NSC as far as intelligence was concerned. And as long as they weren't getting on, Hillenkoetter found it very difficult to get things resolved.[8]

The other element behind the Dulles report was the 1948 presidential election. The Republican candidate, Thomas E. Dewey, governor of New York, had made a point of challenging Truman on his apparently lackluster performance in foreign affairs and in dealing with the mounting evidence of communist subversion at home. In August, three months before the election, Whittaker Chambers testified at a hearing of the House Un-American Activities Committee that he had been a member of a communist underground network, which also included Alger Hiss, a senior State Department officer. China was obviously falling to Mao Tse-tung. To many Americans it seemed as if America was unable to stem the advance of the Soviet empire. On November 3, the day after the election, an editorial in the *Detroit Free Press* echoed widespread feeling when it called on Truman to appoint John Foster Dulles, Dewey's foreign-policy adviser, as secretary of state in place of George Marshall. It was a time when to survive in politics it was essential to be an anticommunist.

Truman's ability as a politician was demonstrated in the quietly effective way he dealt with these forces. In preelection moves he appointed Allen Dulles to head the committee investigating the CIA; Allen's brother could not easily criticize that. He also responded forcefully to the Berlin blockade with the Berlin airlift, an action that challenged and ultimately defeated the Soviet move. The Truman Doctrine and the Marshall Plan also provided convincing evidence of his staunch determination to support the "free peoples" of the world. The Dulles report came out of the tensions of a hard-fought election campaign and represented a wide area of political agreement on foreign policy and the conduct of the cold war. NSC-68 and its longevity, spanning three Republican and four Democratic administrations, represented the same consensus. Had Dewey, not Truman, won the election, the Dulles report would probably have been no different; the election debate had been about improving American responses, not about whether or not to respond.

The CIA was *the* agency of this new commitment. Backed by an across-the-board agreement on the need for the United States to engage the Soviet Union at all levels, the CIA was attractive to highfliers. It was significantly strengthened by NSC-68. It was an elite agency, staffed by elite people. Hillenkoetter was the unsung hero of this bureaucratic achievement, though his successor, Bedell Smith, was usually given the principal credit. Under Hillenkoetter, as the Dulles report observed, the CIA had been an *ad hoc* body with a fragile position in government. There was no certainty in this period that the creation of the National Military Establishment and the CIA with the 1947 National Security Act would not result in the military's taking over the agency. In his quiet way Hillenkoetter maintained the CIA as an independent agency, using his own military connections to keep the State Department at bay and to show military colleagues that the CIA's independence had advantages for them. They responded favorably to his assertions that the agency's estimate and analytic functions could play a crucial role in securing military appropriations. Later on, as the cold war eased, it became clear that this role could cut the other way. But in the decade following 1947, when there was no question that America should have a strong defense capacity, the CIA's independent support for policies involving military interests came to carry considerable weight in government and in Congress.

The feeling that the United States was involved in a battle with communism for control of the world helped Hillenkoetter place the agency at the cutting edge of the cold war. To function in this role the agency had to operate at a senior bureaucratic level that made it superior to the individual armed services in intelligence matters. (The armed services were always regarded with suspicion when it came to their intelligence analysis because they seemed always to argue for still more money for new weapons systems.) In policy matters the CIA was in a special position because of its connection with the President. Also, its newness made it different from the other agencies and departments, as did the fact that it already had very powerful bureaucratic enemies in the Defense and State departments and in the FBI. So the agency looked to the President and secretly carried out the President's will in return for his support.

Hillenkoetter established the agency in this relationship and so did Truman. In contrast, the departments of State and Defense, as well as the FBI, restricted by edicts of public policy, could never conduct secret operations for the President. The State Department could not maintain diplomatic requirements and actively support noncommunist parties in the Italian elections, but the CIA could ignore diplomatic requirements and do so. The State Department could estimate Soviet intentions in the Far East; so could the CIA. But the CIA had the added advantage of being able to obtain in covert ways information and contacts not always conveniently available to ambassadors.

During the initial years of the cold war the belief was that the future would be filled either with war or with a crisis lasting ten to twelve years. Once it became apparent that the Soviet Union was a long-term enemy, the governing elite changed many of its basic attitudes, including those it held toward government bureaucracies. Congressional attitudes also changed, and instead of being reluctant to maintain a large navy and a tiny army, an enthusiastic Congress was now willing to support an enormous military establishment with a host of enormous ancillary programs. Any agency or department that found itself on the high ground of policy formation and implementation possessed vast patronage and influence. It was also assured of still greater opportunity ahead.

Hillenkoetter's achievement was to put the CIA on the bureaucratic high ground, making it a place where individual and collective efforts counted. He created an environment that was attractive to serious and able people who felt that a mortal danger was at hand and who wanted to serve their country as it faced this danger. It helped that the military and the established bureaucracies were now at a distance. "For several years after the National Security Act was passed," said Lawrence Houston, "there was an attempt, particularly from the military intelligence services, to keep the DCI down to one amongst equals. Vandenberg had seen the job almost as commander. What we came up with was the DCI as *primus inter pares*—the principle of preeminence—because while each one of them faced a challenge from their secretary if they did anything he did not like, the DCI was the one who went straight to the National Security Council and the President."[9]

At the same time that the Dulles report was presented and NSC-68 was being drafted, another important assessment of intelligence organization was under way. The United States Intelligence Board (USIB)—the coordinating body of all the intelligence agencies in government, consisting of the heads of the agencies, with the director of Central Intelligence as chairman—commissioned Dr. Vannevar Bush, director of the Office of Scientific Research and Development under Roosevelt and Truman, to recommend ways of linking all the intelligence bureaucracies.[10] This step was taken at the initiative of James Forrestal in one of his last acts before resigning as secretary of defense. Bush recommended that the director of Central Intelligence be recognized by the heads of the other intelligence agencies as being what his title implied: responsible for coordination of all intelligence functions and activities. The report was a turning point, and in many ways it was Hillenkoetter's finest hour. Lawrence Houston attended the USIB meeting when Bush's report was discussed and said later:

> The other intelligence services were squabbling amongst themselves and with us and not admitting the priority of the DCI. The G-2 was carrying on a rearguard action against the legislation, and there was a clique in G-2 that was violently opposed to any cooperation with CIA. The military members of the board kept pressing for the concept that the DCI was one amongst equals and had no preeminence. We were claiming that under the statute he was given the position of preeminence, although not of command. Among the staff of the board was a regular army colonel who was the most vociferous in pressing for the one-amongst-equals concept. It got so bad that Hillenkoetter finally got the ear of Forrestal, who asked Dr. Bush to look into the situation. He did look into it and wrote a devastating report on the situation to Forrestal. Hillenkoetter got this letter out at one of the meetings and read it to us, and there was a deathly hush around the room. General Chamberlain, the G-2, looked up and said, "Hilly, what's all this about? You're the boss." And the colonel down at the end of the table turned absolutely green.[11]

This was the moment when the other agencies realized that the CIA was not only there to stay but that it had impressive bureaucratic clout. Houston put his finger on the reason: only the CIA could turn directly to the President without having to go through a bureaucratic hierarchy. The CIA was an executive arm of intelligence and, as it would emerge, of policy. These roles provided the agency with impressive bureaucratic protection as long as it realized that it served only one President at a time. Its advantage to the President was that it was the newest and least bureaucratized agency of government and as such provided him with a means of having a secret and forceful foreign policy, able to take steps like interfering in the Italian elections, without going through more cumbersome and public channels.

ANALYSIS

As Truman's struggles to understand world affairs increased, so did his reliance on the intelligence provided by the CIA. Within six months of its creation the agency was consciously taking a broad view of events, drawing parallels in its analysis with the prewar world and committing itself to definite statements. "The future Communist program," the analysts predicted in November 1947, "will be primarily revolutionary in character."* Two years were spent producing the first National Intelligence Estimate on the Soviet Union (this excessive period of time was more an indication of lack of internal coordination than of a "cool" approach to problems), although several analytical papers on particular aspects of Soviet affairs were produced in the interim.[12]

In August 1947 the Office of Reports and Estimates evaluated a memorandum written "by the Chief of Mission of one of the Soviet Satellite Countries," as a covering note explained, carefully maintaining the confidentiality of the source. The note also explained that "the official in question does not know that this paper was obtained as it was microfilmed and then returned to his safe." The memorandum was translated and studied, with its analysis reflecting the no-nonsense approach that was to characterize the agency. The analysis cautiously began (the analysts had not been given any details either):

> Lacking information concerning the source, especially the motivation which resulted in the submission of the paper and the date submitted, it is analyzed on its contents and the conclusion it produces in the informed reader. . . . It

---

* Central Intelligence Agency, "Memorandum for the President," November 7, 1947, from R. H. Hillenkoetter, Rear Admiral, USN, director of Central Intelligence. This was an interesting observation given the growing fear at the time that there might be a "hot" war with the Soviets. Everywhere but in western Europe, communism was entwined with revolutionary and national movements. The Eurocommunist movement of the 1970s in which the Italian, French, and Spanish Communist parties in particular publicly declared their independence of Moscow was ultimate confirmation of part of this early CIA judgment.

European communists had come to see that the choice for them was between conventional and revolutionary action. By choosing the former they were in effect saying they were nationalists first and communists second. Not until the early 1960s did Americans and Europeans shrug off the feeling that there would be another great economic depression. This change in assumption was the background to the political change Eurocommunism represented. Communist parties, however, always have a third choice: to go the way their prophets (Marx, Engels, Lenin) directed and do whatever might be necessary to secure power. The awareness that despite appearances in 1939 the national Communist parties of Europe had supported Stalin after the Nazi-Soviet Pact was signed underpinned the suspicion of the Soviets on the part of such men as Forrestal, Acheson, and Truman in government and of James Angleton in the CIA.

Western Communist parties became "national" during World War II and were not revolutionary after 1945. By not being aware of this, the analysts were also in part making a questionable judgment. The postwar dislocations were still obscuring analysis. Revolutionary noise and pressure for revolution were being interpreted as revolutionary action. In Italy, where revolutionary action by communists was a strong possibility in 1947–48, U.S. intervention in support of constitutional parties through the CIA, and strong Italian government antirevolutionary action, prevented it from occurring.

is not believed that the paper is a plant.... That the source, if in a position to *know* about conversations and "bitter struggle" in the Politburo, would pass on this information, seems almost incredible, but further exploitation certainly is indicated. Examination of the style, spelling and idioms makes it apparent that the paper either was written in English by someone thinking in the French language or was translated literally from the French.[13]

In the tradition established by the OSS, the CIA's research and analysis was focused on the precise information contained in this and similar documents. Its conclusion in this case that the information should be accepted was based on a careful analysis of the document itself and on the full force of the agency's collected knowledge. Analysts determined that the source was probably Rumanian or Hungarian, since both countries used French as their language of diplomacy. The textual and linguistic analyses that went into this opinion were only part of the methodology commonly used by the CIA.*

From the start the CIA was actively conducting analyses and estimates of major importance to the foreign and defense policies of the United States and the Western allies. It assimilated the intelligence information drawn from the various government agencies to reach a conclusion. On December 15, 1947, Hillenkoetter submitted to the President a detailed report, "Status of the Soviet Atomic Energy Program," which, since the full impact of the Soviet spy ring was not yet known, estimated that the Soviets were still some years away from developing their own atomic bomb. Six months later, a year before the Soviets did explode their first atom bomb, Hillenkoetter wrote another report to Truman, pinning down the Estimate even more:

> In the interval since the 15 December 1947 report ... no information has been received that necessitates changes in the argument of that report.... It continues to be impossible to determine its exact status or to determine the date scheduled by the Soviets for the completion of their first atomic bomb. It has been learned, however, that in the summer of 1947 the highest Soviet authority was seriously disturbed by the lack of progress.
>
> On the basis of the evidence now in our possession it is estimated that the earliest date by which it is remotely possible that the USSR may have completed its first atomic bomb is mid-1950, but the most probable date is believed to be mid-1953.

* This type of analytical work had been pioneered by the OSS. During the war Gerhard Van Arkel was asked to research the "application of Cutter's formula to the basin of the Rhine at Basel." Van Arkel said:

I had no idea what Cutter's formula was. I had to go to the library, look up Cutter's formula, find out what it was, and then find somebody that might know. Cutter's formula is a calculation of the depth of the stream and the flow of the water and it tells you something about the amount of water that will go through a given stream in a given period of time. It was terribly important to the engineers who were planning on pontoon bridges across the Rhine, and they were very fearful that the Germans were going to blow up some dam up the Rhine at the time of the spring floods and wash out any pontoon bridges that had been put across the Rhine (interview, November 11, 1983).

Further discussions with geological consultants, further literature studies, and such information as has been received from the field lead to the conclusion that previous estimates of the total reserves of uranium available to the USSR were low. As a result, the estimated production of bombs has been increased. It is now believed that the maximum number of bombs in the Soviet stockpile in 1955 will not be more than 20 if the first bomb is completed in 1953, or not more than 50 if it is completed in 1950.[14]

Except for air force intelligence, all other interested intelligence agencies agreed that the CIA's estimate on the development of the Soviet atomic bomb was essentially correct. In the opinion of the air force, "it is possible that the Soviets are at present on the brink of success in the development of an atomic bomb."[15] However, the air force was not prepared to push this view and accepted the consensus that 1950 was the earliest the Soviets might have their own bomb. This disagreement between the air force and the CIA in 1947 was one of a series. In 1946 the Central Intelligence Group had argued with the Army Air Force about Soviet strategic bomber capabilities, which resulted ultimately in the "bomber gap" debate; this, along with the later "missile gap" disagreement, was to become one of the major intelligence controversies of the 1950s.

THE "BOMBER GAP"

The "bomber gap" debate started because the Central Intelligence Group held that once the Russians had developed their atomic bomb, they would need bombers in order to be able to use their bombs. The air force at this stage was much less certain of Soviet intentions and capabilities as far as atomic bombs and strategic bombers were concerned and had focused its attention on conventional Soviet capabilities and intentions in Europe. Air force views soon changed, however, and by late 1947 were more hawkish on the Soviet atomic and strategic bomber threat than anyone else. In 1948 a Soviet defector revealed that the USSR was planning a strategic air force with planes based upon the American B-29. This information seemed confirmed when at the 1948 May Day parade in Moscow a fly-past of a new Russian bomber, the TU-4, took place. The new plane looked remarkably like the B-29.[16] If the Soviets could build a strategic bomber in such a short time, reasoned the air force, then Soviet atomic and bomber capabilities were probably far more advanced than had been thought. This was the ground for the "bomber gap" argument with the CIA. The agency, having been more concerned than the air force about Soviet strategic bombers initially, was much cooler about the threat later on, recognizing that the air force view was based on observation and defector information that had not been confirmed by evidence of real strategic capability—no TU-4 had been observed flying long distances nonstop, for example.

Six years later, at the 1954 May Day parade, another observation was made by the U.S. Air Force attaché at the Moscow embassy, Colonel Charles E. Taylor. He saw a new, much larger Soviet bomber, the Bison, in fly-past formation. The following year Taylor reported a whole squadron of Bisons in the fly-past. The air force was convinced that Taylor's sightings had confirmed their earlier deduction that the Soviets were far more advanced than the CIA had conceded and that there was a far greater Soviet threat to the security of the United States in consequence. By 1959, the air force estimated, the Soviet Union would have a strike force of over one thousand bombers.[17] General Curtis E. LeMay, the air force Chief of Staff, used this estimate to argue for an ever bigger B-52 strike force, despite increasing evidence that there was no "bomber gap" at all. LeMay's argument resulted in a lingering distrust of air force intelligence within the CIA and the other military services.

Colonel Taylor had in fact observed a clever (though ultimately self-defeating) Russian deception. The Bison, like the TU-4, was much less impressive than it looked. Both planes had shorter ranges and less powerful engines than their American counterparts, the B-29 and the B-52, and both planes were being produced in much smaller numbers than Taylor and air force intelligence thought. At the May Day parades the Russians had simply flown the same planes by in different formations, giving Taylor the impression that there was a squadron of Bisons in 1955 at the fly-past when, in fact, there were only eight. Not until 1953 did the Soviets develop jet engines capable of fifteen-thousand-pound thrust, the minimum necessary for effective strategic bomber performance.

This information was gleaned by CIA analysts working from their desks in Washington, using literature studies and economic intelligence. The Soviet Union's industrial-production base was not capable of building over one thousand Bison bombers by 1959, they argued. There were not enough machine-tool production lines or aluminum forges to do the job in the USSR. Wire hangers, obtained from the cabin closet of an Aeroflot passenger plane, provided supporting evidence for the CIA's view. The hangers, in common with Western practice, were made out of metal scrap from the plane. Analysis of the metal in the hangers suggested that Soviet metallurgy was not advanced enough to build bombers of the necessary high performance or range. In 1956 the U-2 spy plane finished the argument with its photographs showing that the Soviets did not have a large bomber fleet. The Soviet strategic bomber force, the CIA declared in 1957, consisted of between ninety and one hundred and fifty planes.[18]

CONSENSUS AND DISSENT

The early debate over the Soviet atomic bomb and the "bomber gap" quickly gave the Estimates their standard format. If another agency did not concur with the CIA, then if it insisted, its view and the reason for it would become a footnote. The argument of an Estimate would not be diluted to encompass all views, but at the same time the drive toward achieving a consensus meant that only really important differences would not be ignored. On September 13, 1948, Hillenkoetter issued a directive based on the experience of the CIA's first year, establishing the method of interagency coordination in National Intelligence Estimates:

> Departmental participation in the preparation of national intelligence reports and estimates is undertaken to ensure that authorized recipients (a) are presented with national intelligence that comprises all the best available expert knowledge and opinion; (b) are aware, in the case of disputed points, of the views of the departments on substantive matters within their special fields of responsibility and interest.... Dissent published in a national intelligence paper should present a distinct difference of opinion on which CIA and the dissenting intelligence organization have found it impossible to agree.[19]

The Dulles report four months later supported Hillenkoetter's effort to establish the DCI's and CIA's preeminence in this field:

> A national intelligence report or estimate as assembled and produced by the Central Intelligence Agency should reflect the coordination of the best intelligence opinion, based on all available information. It should deal with matters of wide scope relevant to the determination of basic policy, such as the assessment of a country's war potential, its preparedness for war, of its strategic capabilities and intentions, its vulnerability to various forms of direct attack or indirect pressures.... The principle of the authoritative national intelligence estimate does not yet have established acceptance in the government. Each department still depends more or less on its own intelligence estimates and establishes its plans and policies accordingly.[20]

It was to take some time and another director before the CIA's reports and Estimates achieved the status called for by Hillenkoetter and stressed by Dulles. Throughout this period of intense cold war, certain elements of intelligence combined to thwart the accomplishment of this goal. The perception was that the problems facing the country were military ones as reflected in the language of the Dulles report. Terms such as "assessment of a country's war potential," "preparedness for war," and "direct attack" set the tone for the report. Flowing from this perception was the problem that the CIA was involved in military estimating and had to compete in areas in which the military were expert. Accordingly, the problems dealt with and the conclusions reached by Estimates generally reflected military concerns and were by and large of a short-term nature. This was exemplified after General Lucius D. Clay, the U.S. commander in Germany, made this warning on March 5, 1948, a month after what was in effect a communist coup overthrowing democracy in Czechoslovakia: "I have felt and held that [war] was unlikely for at least two years. Within the last few weeks, I have felt a subtle change in Soviet attitude which I cannot define but which now gives me a feeling that it may come with dramatic suddenness."[21] Not surprisingly, the CIA echoed a consensus of this view when it reported to the President on March 16 that war was improbable only through the next sixty days.[22]

The following day in an address to a joint session of Congress, Truman called for the passage of the Marshall Plan and the restoration of conscription. He went on to declare:

> One nation has not only refused to cooperate in the establishment of a just and honorable peace, but—even worse—has actively sought to prevent it. . . . Since the close of hostilities, the Soviet Union and its agents have destroyed the independence and democratic character of a whole series of nations in Eastern and Central Europe. . . . The tragic death of the Republic of Czechoslovakia has sent a shock wave through the civilized world. . . . There are times in world history when it is far wiser to act than to hesitate. There is some risk involved in action—there always is. But there is far more risk involved in failure to act.[23]

Truman was making it quite clear that the United States would be prepared for war should the Soviets attempt aggressive action beyond their existing boundaries. CIA Estimates inevitably shared this atmosphere, which was to last for the next six or seven years.

The drive to achieve consensus on the part of the CIA, while natural enough, was not universally welcomed within the agency. Some in the agency believed that although a consensus on any particular issue might be correct, it was also important for other views which might not have been footnoted to be considered and put to the President and the National Security Council.[24] Morale in the Office of Reports and Estimates was affected by the conviction that consensus was not always in the nation's best interest. Hillenkoetter, who was determined to organize the Estimates and reports so that they would contribute to the agency's position in government, did not pay much attention to these doubts. He was more interested in formalizing the Estimates—gearing them toward having a direct effect on policy making while maintaining the footnoting principle he had defined in his September 1948 directive—than in the more *ad hoc* procedures inevitably involved in sustaining differences of opinion.[25]

Once again, achieving this goal took time. One of the earliest Estimates, issued on September 1, 1947 (still referred to as a "CIG Situation Report"), was on the subject of Norway. It was a general survey, without any particular direction. Reading like an institutional summary of the affairs and prospects of any country, it dealt with the political and economic situations of Norway, its foreign affairs, and military position. It also included appendices oriented toward military concerns, covering topography and climate, significant communications facilities, population statistics and characteristics. Although the Estimate was more like an academic treatise than a concise report, readers found a pervasive message of possible war. The summary prefacing the paper opened with this statement: "Norway's political influence, economic resources, and military strength are negligible from the point of view of United States security. Its strategic significance lies in its geographical location as a potential base for operations in the North Atlantic and northwestern Europe." The summary concluded: "Any threat to peace arising from Norway's actions, either unilateral or in concert with other Scandinavian states, is extremely remote and can almost be dismissed."[26] The report took forty-one pages, including five appendices and six chapters, to reach these conclusions. No doubt Hillenkoetter wondered at the egghead approach of such reports and knew the off-putting effect they would have on his military colleagues, let alone on a busy President.

EFFECTIVE REPORTING

By October 1947 Hillenkoetter was already sharpening up the CIA's reports. Responding to Forrestal's and Truman's wishes to play hardball with the communists in the Italian elections due in the spring of 1948, the Office of Reports and Estimates produced an analysis, "The Current Situation in Italy," which, unlike the earlier Norway report, came to only four concise printed pages. Instead of investigating all potential developments the report concentrated on Soviet and Italian communist intentions and activities:

> The stability of the existing Government depends primarily on its ability to obtain adequate economic support from the United States. Given interim aid sufficient to avert acute distress during the winter, it should be able to maintain its position until the general elections in April. The communists and Nenni Socialists will continue their vigorous effort to intensify existing difficulties and dissatisfactions with the purpose of thoroughly discrediting the existing Government. . . . Assuming that the present Government survives the winter, the outcome of the April elections will depend not only on the results of interim aid, but also on the prospects for the success of the European recovery program. Favorable developments in this regard would operate to the decided advantage of the Government. Adverse developments and the consequent disillusionment would enhance the possibility of a Communist electoral victory.[27]

From reports such as these the CIA's Office of Special Operations determined operational objectives in the financial and propaganda support for the

Italian Christian Democrats. Starting at the end of 1947, once its legal authority in this area was established, the CIA began its cold-war tradition of covert action (as opposed to espionage), which was to culminate in the Bay of Pigs affair.

Hillenkoetter added to the specific Estimates and reports an overview series of reports entitled "Review of the World Situation as It Relates to the Security of the United States." Although originally varied in their frequency, these reports ultimately spawned a weekly digest series that were concise statements of the administration's current thinking. During the late 1940s and early 1950s they reflected the same presumption-of-war attitudes found in other Estimate documents and tended to focus on the immediate concerns of policy makers rather than on longer-term issues and prospects. The third review, CIA 3, issued on December 17, 1947, summarized for the President the world situation as it had developed since CIA 2, issued on November 14:

> Since our last report, the Communists, under Soviet direction, have launched a concerted campaign of disorders, strikes, and sabotage in France and Italy.... The primary Soviet objective is to defeat the European recovery program by bringing about a sufficient degree of economic deterioration: (a) so greatly to increase the cost of the recovery program to the U.S. that the U.S. Congress and the public will reject it; and (b) to cause the collapse of the French and Italian centrist Governments. To obtain this objective, the USSR is risking the political popularity of the Communist Parties in France and Italy and will depend thereafter, if necessary, on a hard core of militants, possibly operating underground.[28]

Europe was not the only area of CIA concern, although it was the main one. The review also observed communist activity (always seen as Soviet-directed or -inspired) in the Far and Middle East—areas where the collapsing old empires were creating vacuums or alienating nationalists in their colonies who might look to Russia for support. The Dutch were ceasing to be a seaborne empire almost overnight. The British were concentrating on their African possessions and withstanding communist–nationalist movements in Malaysia. They had pulled out of India in 1947. The French were seriously attempting to restore their prewar empire without accommodating nationalist aspirations. Mao Tse-tung was increasing his control in China, area by area, week by week. Red was creeping over the maps in Washington. There was an assumption that the prosperity of the developed countries depended upon special relationships with colonies.

In the Middle East there was a convulsion with long-term implications: Israel was formed, and the Arabs and their oil were becoming more and more important in political and economic terms. Events seemed to be moving at as great a speed as during the war. This was the tone of the CIA's reports. "An increase in Soviet activities in the Far East may be motivated in part by the

Kremlin's desire to divert world attention from possible Soviet reverses in Europe," warned the December 1947 review. "In the Middle East the USSR is resuming its pressure on Iran. It is evidently planning to exploit fully the Palestine situation. . . . The Middle East rather than the Far East probably occupies second priority to Western Europe as an objective of Soviet expansion." Throughout there was a strong sense of new forces being unleashed or pent up, of a malevolent Soviet presence everywhere, of the world up for grabs.

Particular situations and economic conditions were also reported. The increase in coal production in Britain and Germany was linked to its likely effect on steel production in both countries—again a military interest—and the Soviet Union's grain harvest of 1948, the best since 1941, was singled out as a potential economic weapon, since wheat exporting could "be used to better advantage politically than at present." The Gravesend Parliamentary by-election in Britain provided a platform for a concise political report:

> The Labor Party's narrow victory in the recent significant Gravesend Parliamentary by-election confirms earlier evidence of a swing away from Labor, but it also indicates that the swing does not have the landslide proportions suggested by the preceding municipal elections. Among the national electorate, the Labor Party appears to retain a slender majority. The prestige and cohesion of the Government have improved as a result of the recent Cabinet changes and the increase in coal and steel production. Basically, however, the stability of the Labor Government rests on the ability of British industry to fulfill [its] export goals, the willingness of the people to accept a reduced standard of living, and the realization of substantial direct or indirect dollar benefits under the European recovery program.

Similar reports were given on France, where a reactionary government under General de Gaulle was seen as a more likely prospect than a communist government; on Italy, where a communist-inspired and -led general strike was considered probable, followed by communist guerrilla activity by the "well trained partisan groups which achieved considerable popularity through their war-time resistance activities"; on Germany, where politics reflected not "any lack of desire for unity on the part of the Germans but . . . a continuing skepticism regarding unity on Soviet terms"; on Austria, where "the USSR is continuing to rely chiefly on economic pressure in its attempt ultimately to reduce Austria to the status of a Satellite"; on the USSR itself, which was considered to be on the threshold of an economic revival, with the prospect of "some rise in the general standard of living" (the Kremlin was concerned with "the persistence, even among members of the party, of capitalist ideology"); on the USSR's satellite states, where events would soon show CIA analysis to be wrong—"The Kremlin is not yet willing to risk the political and economic consequences of ordering the Czechoslovak Communists to use the ruthless tactics successfully employed in the other satellite countries"; on Poland, which was seen to be almost completely dominated by communists, with the Roman Catholic Church there under attack; and on Yugoslavia, which was seen as "gradually emerging as the dominant Satellite in southeastern Europe."

In Europe, the CIA's analysts perceived, there was a continuity of the clandestine spirit—similar to the continuity of the OSS spirit in the agency itself. People had had the time of their lives in the resistance during the war. The resistance movements had been composed of elites, and the communists were part of the resistance. This inheritance meant a great deal to the intelligence people of both sides, and it was continued by both sides in various ways: the Philby/Burgess/Maclean/Blunt group was an elite; the Jewish opposition within the USSR was another. The Soviet Jewish penetration of the highest levels of Israeli society in the 1950s and 1960s was yet another elite grouping. In 1945–47 western Europe looked like a wounded city, with rubble slowly being cleared, exposing the subterranean power complexes that provided the base for postwar clandestine activity. By 1947 these complexes were in use in Yugoslavia and Greece, enabling the CIA to identify, support, and exploit professional and clandestine elites attached to the power networks of Europe.

The core of the analysis being applied to all these countries was the absolute acceptance of Soviet communist aggression and malevolent Soviet intentions. Behind it all there was an expectation of war—not that war was inevitable, but that it was likely and that the United States had to be prepared for it.[29] What was more, the United States, it was felt, might well have to fight another war alone, without the support of its allies France and Britain. Analysts saw the former plagued by political extremism and communist disruption and the latter in the hands of a Labour government presiding over economic decay and possibly not very sound in its ideological stance toward Russia. In the Near and Middle East, CIA analysts concentrated on the evidence of Soviet involvement in the Greek civil war, in which "neither side, however, is believed capable of obtaining a decisive victory in the near future." Palestine, on the brink of being partitioned to create the modern country of Israel, was seen by the analysts as a hotbed of unrest where the Soviets would seize any opportunity to secure advantage.

In particular, the analysts pointed to the growing disillusionment of Arabs with Western support for a Jewish state in Palestine. "Faced with rapidly increasing anti-US feeling," the review noted, "executives of US oil companies in the Middle East believe that they may be forced to suspend operations. . . . There is increasing evidence that the USSR intends to utilize Palestine as a base for penetration of the Middle East." As events over the next thirty years were to show, the CIA was correct in linking Arab political perspectives to U.S. oil interests and in recognizing that U.S. support for Israel would involve repercussions in other areas.

However, wider implications were not drawn at this time. The more sophisticated linkages, which the diplomatic and intelligence services of the old empires would naturally have made, were still missing from the CIA's (and for that matter from the State Department's) armory. The situation in Iran, for example, was seen as essentially political, with no indication that Iranian oil would one day be a significant force in the politics of the Middle East or that Iran would play a part in Russia's traditional territorial ambitions to its south to obtain a warm-water port and a handle on Arab oil fields. On points like this the CIA's early analysis reflected the transformation of the United States in international affairs and its lack of experience in handling international as opposed to localized situations. Europe was slightly different because of the connections that existed between U.S. and European politics and people. There was a natural European orientation in America that was reflected in the thinking of CIA analysts.

India and Pakistan, the two new dominions within the British Commonwealth, formed from the old Indian Empire's Moslem population in Pakistan and Hindu population in India, were thought to be on an inevitable collision course because of age-old religious differences. (These predictions eventually proved to be accurate.) The importance of both countries to the West was to become increasingly clear. For the British Empire, India (then incorporating Pakistan) was the powerhouse supplying at any time a massive army to sustain British imperial interests anywhere in the world. Britain's reliance on Indian manpower was demonstrated in Burma, North Africa, and Europe during World War II. With independence India became the world's largest democracy and was second only to China in population. If India entered the communist camp after 1949, approximately three quarters of the world's population would be aligned against the West. West Pakistan possessed similar strategic significance. It bordered Afghanistan, Iran, Tibet, and India; had an Indian Ocean coastline; and, as a Moslem nation, had a strong connection to the Moslems of southern Russia. The existence of Pakistan was therefore seen as a potential counter to any Indian moves toward Russia (its political ally in clashes with China), and vice versa.

In December 1947 the review restricted itself to reciting facts and political attitudes about these countries; the more thoughtful analyses were still to come. Similarly, the review only hinted at the imminent collapse of Chiang Kai-shek's National Government in China. More significant, however, the review also hinted at something that was accepted only fifteen years later in the West: that the Chinese communists were not mere puppets of the Soviet Union and that there might even be serious differences between them: "Despite the present precarious position of the National Government, the USSR is probably not ready to abandon its 'correct' attitude. The USSR is not likely to give open assistance to the Chinese Communists because it would undoubtedly arouse Chinese antiforeign sentiments and would thus impede Communist progress. The USSR, in fact, has recently made conciliatory gestures toward the National Government at the same time that it was reported putting strong pressure on that Government to support the Soviet position on a Japanese peace treaty."

The Japanese peace treaty was also the subject of the report on Japan. Analysts believed that the Soviet Union would not sign the treaty unless it was given veto powers to overrule any objectionable provision. Since, in the CIA's view, the Soviets believed that the "U.S. intends to make Japan a strong springboard" against them, Japan was seen as an almost inevitable cold-war site. Dealing with Korea, the review stated that the "optimism of the moderate groups concerning the chances of a definitive UN solution of the Korean problem is beginning to show a marked decline." In the CIA's view, a continuing postwar partition of the country was indicated: "The USSR appears to be making preparations to accord full recognition to the North Korean puppet regime." A North Korean invasion of the South, or Chinese participation in a Korean war, was not considered by the CIA or, at that point, by anyone else.

Additional CIA analyses of the Far East suggested a strong likelihood of a coup in the Philippines that would "adversely affect US strategic interests." They also pointed to instability in Southeast Asia generally that "continues to provide opportunity for Soviet exploitation of the growing nationalist and antiwestern sentiment among the native peoples. . . . In French Indochina, the continued efforts by the French to eliminate by force the Communist-dominated government of the Vietnam Republic has strengthened native loyalty to the Vietnam government and has intensified the already widespread hatred of the French." In addition, trouble with communists in Burma was seen as jeopardizing the stability of the newly independent state; nationalism in Thailand (still called Siam), with its consequent anti-Westernism, was viewed in terms of its possible negative effect on U.S. commercial interests in the area; and nationalists in Indonesia were seen as likely to upset Dutch plans for a United States of Indonesia.

Latin America was one bright spot in the CIA view of the world. According to the review, "the extensive support which the US can now expect from Latin America on important issues with respect to the USSR is indicated by the sentiment favoring coordinated anti-Communist action throughout the hemisphere and the continuing tendency of Latin American governments to take anti-Communist action on their own initiative." A temperate note was nevertheless sounded: "This increase in anti-Communist activity, however, is not wholly the result of a general and growing hostility to the Soviet Union; it stems in part from a desire to obtain favor and possible financial assistance from the US." The report stated that strength in Latin America had not suffered substantially as a result of anticommunist activities of Latin American governments, although in labor unions the noncommunist left was thought to be gaining ground. The review concluded with the observation that there was "no reason to believe . . . that Communist capabilities for espionage or sabotage in the area have been materially reduced." Thus stood the world in mid-December 1947 as far as the CIA was concerned. On one side was the United States assuming the role of defender of the West. On the other was a relentless Soviet empire intent on seizing every opportunity for expansion.

Four months later, in April 1948, another review took a slightly less belligerent view of the Soviet Union. However, it retained the CIA's established position that the United States was involved in a cold-war struggle of international proportions. Unlike the earlier review, this one was not coordinated with the intelligence organizations of the State Department, the army, navy, or air force. In Hillenkoetter's drive to distinguish the CIA for its independent approach, he decided to have reviews prepared separately; they no longer followed the coordinating procedures of Estimates and reports. As in December, the review concentrated its attention and detailed reporting on Europe. Of the review's eight summary points, only two—concerning the inevitability of war in Palestine and the intensification of "Communist diversionary activity in the Far East"—dealt with other areas.[30] Until the Vietnam War in the 1960s this focus characterized CIA analytical activity. Africa, the Middle East, and the Far East received detailed attention only at times of crisis.

Russia's belligerent intentions colored every judgment made in the report. To the CIA the Soviets were a familiar and recognizable threat to liberal democracy as well as to U.S. free-trade interests. This view of Russia as aggressive and warlike held widespread credibility not only in America and in the CIA but throughout the West. Russia was viewed as distrustful of Western efforts to maintain cooperation among the wartime allies. Moreover, the CIA knew that in Russia's view capitalism and communism could not coexist. The survival of one system meant the ultimate defeat of the other. The dominant conviction in Washington was that Russia should not become stronger, that subversion should not win Europe for Russia, that the general changes of the world should not be left to communism to exploit, and that some sort of developed world entente should exist for the purposes of free trade and mutual association. America still had a stronger feeling for ideological harmony than any other Western country. There was a sense that the interests of the United States were for order and the interests of the Soviet Union were for anarchy and violence. This feeling unified conservatives who believed in order and One-Worlders who wanted a liberal, disciplined world where everyone desired the same things. Free-traders who believed the United States would prosper in proportion to its opportunity to trade also embraced the objective of order. They were all determined not to allow the period after World War I to repeat itself.

This determination colored the CIA's analysis, which was still moralist and contained assumptions of perpetuity that compromised it. No one, for example, had worked out how rapidly Britain was going to drop out of the first rank of powers. No one recognized the future of Japan. No one really gave adequate weight to the enormous differences between Russia and China. The sense of emergency, focusing on the Soviet Union, seemed to push everything else aside.

WAR FEAR

The fear that the Soviet Union would start another war was the major concern of CIA analysts in the late 1940s. A series of papers on possible flash points and Soviet capabilities and intentions resulted. On April 28, 1948, the CIA's Office of Reports and Estimates produced an Estimate covering "a program that might be resorted to by the USSR in Germany in an effort to cause the Western powers to leave Berlin, to consolidate the Soviet hold over Eastern Germany, and to extend Soviet influence into Western Germany."[31] The Estimate had been sparked by the Soviet walkout from the four-power discussions on the future of Germany and by the Soviet actions that would soon culminate in the Berlin blockade. It concluded that the USSR would probably establish a separate East German state, that it would try to force the Western allies out of Berlin, and that it would pressure Western Germany into becoming part of a Soviet-dominated Germany. Although this Estimate was backed by the intelligence arms of the State Department, army, navy, and air force, it was clear from the report that the CIA was still trying to establish itself as a separate policy-making force in Washington. This statement of CIA views was included: "CIA has believed and continues to believe that the USSR might encourage the Peoples' Congress to organize a future 'national' administration and establish a *de facto* Government for the Eastern Zone while propagandistically claiming to speak for all the country. . . . CIA has believed and continues to believe also that in preparation for the new 'government,' the USSR would attempt to discredit the ACC [Allied Control Commission]."[32]

Statements such as these were far from daring and instead were similar to the projections of the State Department, but in the coded language of Washington's bureaucratic politics, they were clear challenges to the traditional supremacy of the State Department in foreign-policy formation. There was little the State Department could do at this time, however. With Washington once again seriously considering the prospect of war, military interests dominated, and the CIA, headed by a rear admiral, staffed by many former military officers, and focused on military concerns, seemed more immediate and relevant in its reports.

A report, presented on July 15, 1948, as a supplement to an earlier Estimate, "Possibility of Direct Soviet Military Action During 1948," was typical of CIA estimating at this time.[33] The report concluded that the Soviet Union would be unlikely to attempt an invasion of western Europe and the Near East even though, it was believed, it was militarily capable of doing so. In the CIA's view the costs of this exploit, in military and economic terms, would be too great for the Soviets to risk. Only if the Western allies agreed to peace soon after the fighting began could the Soviets hope to win. A formal dissent was included in the Estimate from air force intelligence, which held that although the CIA's conclusions were logical, they were products of Western thinking. The air force argued that despite the dangers and hardships involved, the USSR might believe victory was possible and launch an invasion of western Europe and the Near East. The air force concluded that U.S. preparations to prevent or counter such action should not be relaxed. In its private view the CIA's position was not strong enough to secure political support for the military rearming and expansion the air force felt was necessary.

At this level the CIA was obviously playing hardball. It could not afford to lose the support of the military in its Estimates, and while the "defection" of the air force was significant, reflecting as it did the tensions facing Hillenkoetter in his attempt to establish the director of Central Intelligence as the President's chief intelligence officer, it was not critical. As long as Hillenkoetter carried with him two of the services on an Estimate, he was safe enough. A year later, in April 1949, Hillenkoetter reaffirmed his military bona fides with a memorandum to the National Security Council titled "Atomic Energy Program of the USSR." The memorandum developed, he stated, as "a result of discussion of a paper submitted by the Director of Intelligence, United States Air Force." In it he recommended that since "it is generally agreed that Russian intent and plans to engage in aggressive warfare will be influenced by the progress she can make in her atomic energy program," the United States should improve its air defenses and attack abilities.[34]

Three months later, on the eve of the Soviet success in exploding their first atomic device, Hillenkoetter sent a top-secret special report to the President, "Status of the USSR Atomic Energy Project." While quite erroneously maintaining that the Soviets would be unable to produce an atomic bomb until the mid-1950s, the report further sustained air force interests by suggesting that by mid-1957 the Soviet Union might have as many as one hundred and fifty bombs stockpiled.[35] Similarly, an Estimate on the German railway system published on August 2 had useful implications for army and navy re-equipping if the German railway system was to be properly exploited by the United States in the event of a military emergency. A note of dissent from the army was confined to the observation that the CIA was overly optimistic about the capabilities of the German railway system, implying even greater importance to military preparations for an emergency.[36]

A VIEW OF THE WORLD

Soviet intentions in Europe were not the only subject of detailed reports and Estimates; they were just the main subject. On July 18, 1949, an Estimate was prepared on the Tudeh party in Iran, which saw the party as "for all practical purposes, the Communist Party of Iran.... As a more or less conspiratorial group, however, the Tudeh organization is well fitted to further Soviet policy by undertaking sabotage, work stoppages, and disturbances" and could provide a pretext for Soviet intervention in Iran.[37]

China was also the subject of periodic reports, starting with a major situation report in May 1948. Unlike the CIA's work on Soviet atomic bomb development, this report summarized the Soviet Union's role in China and its implications for the future:

> In the Chinese civil war, the USSR thus far has refrained from overt material assistance to the Chinese Communists and, in accordance with the Sino-Soviet Treaty of 1945, continues to recognize the National Government as sovereign in China. It is apparent, nevertheless, that Soviet sympathies lie with Chinese Communists who, because of their ideological affinity with Soviet Communists, are in effect an instrument for the extension of Soviet influence.... Should US aid be provided to the National Government, the USSR might adopt a more conspicuous role in Chinese affairs....
>
> In the resultant ascending spiral of support and counter-support by the US and the USSR, the advantage both in terms of cost and effectiveness of aid would lie with the USSR, largely because of the vitality of the Chinese Communist movement and the favorable geographic position of the USSR. Such a course of events would also increase the possibility of a direct clash of interests in China between the US and the USSR.[38]

There was much less of a hint in this report than in the December 1947 review of an awareness of any real differences between Mao Tse-tung's Chinese Communist party and Stalin's Soviet Communist party. Nevertheless the grasp of international connections and medium-to-long-term political implications was already much surer. In October 1949, following the collapse of the National Government in mainland China and its removal to Taiwan, an Estimate was prepared that, with considerable levelheadedness, concluded that there was no survival potential for noncommunist regimes in China.[39]

Britain's notification of withdrawal from Greece and Turkey in February 1947 generated, more than two and a half years later, in December 1949, an Estimate on the possibility that Britain would abandon its overseas military commitments.[40] The conclusion was that Britain's financial difficulties would be the determining factor in the country's decision to withdraw or stay but that Britain would make every effort to avoid taking drastic action. Again, as it turned out, this was a fair assessment, which recognized the overriding motivating element in the affairs of modern Britain: economic considerations. On subjects of this nature the quality of the Office of Reports and Estimates was maintained because of the superb academic backgrounds of the analysts involved. (Most came from Ivy League colleges.) Analysts were grouped according to regional divisions of the world. Their work was supervised by staff editors responsible for preparing the CIA's Estimates and reports in consultation with their opposite numbers in the State Department, the army, navy, and air force, as well as other agencies with an interest in a particular subject (e.g. the FBI, the Atomic Energy Commission, and the Treasury).

As the Estimate on Norway showed, the analysts' first efforts reflected their Central Intelligence Group habit of producing overly long academic reports. This changed in 1948 when Hillenkoetter encouraged reports and Estimates to reach specific, tightly worded conclusions. Dissents—the form the footnoting principle took—were kept to a minimum, but because of the dominance of military concerns in cold-war policy, the CIA tended to compromise readily with military intelligence and to produce work that basically supported military interests. In itself this was a reflection not only of the bureaucratic imperatives facing a new agency trying to establish itself at the apex of policy making in foreign affairs but also of the mind of the time: Senator McCarthy was in full spate by mid-1950; Mickey Spillane was selling millions of books with brutal anticommunist themes; the United States had created the North Atlantic Treaty Organization and was rearming with a perception of imminent war with the Soviet Union; Soviet spies were beginning to be dug out of the woodwork.

INTELLIGENCE FAILURES

Mistakes were also made, some too important to ignore—notably the agency's failure clearly to predict the outbreak of the Korean War. Some papers warning of the possibility had been presented to the National Security Council but not in terms sufficient to capture the council's attention.[41] It was a situation too reminiscent of Pearl Harbor: an "enemy" had massed its forces and launched a successful surprise attack without the United States' being prepared. The CIA's overriding purpose was to prevent another Pearl Harbor, and the North Korean attack on South Korea on June 25, 1950, was too close a parallel to pass without changes being made.*

In December 1945 the Moscow Conference between the wartime allies had agreed to the division of Korea into two zones divided at the 38th parallel, the northern zone to be administered by the Soviet Union and the southern by the United States. The intention, as far as the United States, Britain, France, and China were concerned, was to see a unified, peaceful, independent Korea. Within months it became obvious that this was not the Soviet intention, and on October 1, 1946, the United States reasserted to Russia its determination to stay in South Korea until the whole of the country was united and free. A year

---

* It should be said that there was a fear that South Korea might start a war. Dean Acheson on January 12, 1950, had said that South Korea was not in the U.S. defense perimeter, and this may have encouraged the North to attack.

later the United Nations agreed that elections for a united Korean government should be held in Korea in the spring of 1948. The Russians refused to accept this agreement.

In May 1948 elections under United Nations supervision were held in the South but not in the North, and a government under the nationalist Syngman Rhee was elected. On August 15 Syngman Rhee declared the independence of the Republic of Korea in the South; on September 9 a People's Republic was announced in the North. Both republics claimed sovereignty over the whole of Korea. On June 29, 1949, the United States completed the withdrawal of its forces from the South. A United Nations Commission on Korea, set up earlier in 1949, reported on September 2 that there was a real danger of civil war as both sides prepared to achieve unification by force. On June 25, 1950, North Korea invaded the South.

Even after the invasion the Office of Reports and Estimates in the CIA did not come up with a coordinated Estimate on the situation in Korea, and Hillenkoetter's advice to the President and the National Security Council took the form of personal memorandums. Four days after the invasion he sent a somewhat inconclusive note to Truman containing the contradiction that "Morale of southern army ranks is good" but "According to the US Embassy, the Koreans are dispirited. . . . The south Korean army, which has all of its forces committed, is reported to have lost about 50 percent of its combat effectiveness and police groups are now being used in combat."[42] On July 2 another memorandum to the President from Hillenkoetter stated that the American ambassador to South Korea had reported that "as a result of the arrival of US ground forces, there is no question of Southern Korean determination to carry on."[43] The following day he revealed how skimpy CIA intelligence was about the real situation in Korea: "Although press reports state that Northern columns have by-passed Suwon, there are no official reports of large-scale Northern operations during the past twenty-four hours. . . . Some progress appears to have been made in re-assembling and consolidating Southern remnants."[44] Information of this nature was freely available in *The New York Times*.

William Bundy, who joined the agency in the spring of 1951, remembered the opaque intelligence picture provided by the CIA at the time:

> When the agency was set up one of the charges in the legislative charter was that it should prepare National Intelligence Estimates utilizing every available source of intelligence. But that had not really been done or turned to by people involved in high policy in the 1947–50 period. Intelligence was generally in the doldrums in that period. A high percentage of the top people in the war years had left. R&A of OSS had been disbanded as such and some of its people had ended up in State and some in the CIA. The director of Central Intelligence—Hillenkoetter and Vandenberg before him—did not have much clout or, it's fair to say, much expertise. Organization was haphazard.

All this showed up acutely in the failure to predict the attack on Korea in 1950.[45]

At a moment of crisis the CIA was seen to be seriously lacking in the intelligence it had been created to provide. It was not surprising, therefore, that on August 2, the New York *Herald Tribune* carried a hard-hitting article on failures in the U.S. intelligence system, listing five in addition to Korea:

1. Failure to predict the "Fall of Czechoslovakia";
2. Failure to foresee "Tito's defection" from Moscow;
3. Failure to predict the "Fall of the Chinese Nationalists";
4. Failure to foresee the Israeli victory in Palestine;
5. Failure to judge the mood of the Latin American states at the Bogotá Conference of 1948.

In many ways the article was a rehash of the earlier *New York Times* articles in July 1948, which criticized the agency for overlapping with other government agencies.[46] The articles also cited intelligence failures in eastern Europe and in the analytical process.

This time, because of the intelligence failure in Korea, the CIA had to take these allegations seriously. As a result, Hillenkoetter sent a personal and confidential note to the President refuting the *Herald Tribune* charges.[47] On Czechoslovakia, he argued, in September 1947 "CIA pointed out that the Czechoslovak Communists were pursuing a deliberate policy designed to 'weaken if not destroy' the National Front government. On 13 October 1947 CIA estimated that the Kremlin had abandoned its program of parliamentary cooperation with non-Communist parties and had reverted to the original program of control and support of international revolutionary Communism. Four days before the coup, CIA estimated that the Czechoslovak Communists might well precipitate a political crisis, resulting in the breakdown of the National Front government." It was a defense, but between the lines Hillenkoetter admitted that the CIA's analysis had not been as precise as he now might have liked.

He was more adamant in rejecting the allegation that the CIA had failed to predict the split between Tito and Russia. "Tito did not defect," he wrote, "he was expelled from the Cominform on 28 June 1948. In May 1948, CIA noted that Tito was taking energetic steps to purge the Yugoslav Communist Party of diversionists, and on 10 June reported that the Yugoslav Government was groping for a policy which would make it once again 'the Balkan spearhead of evangelical and expansionist Communism.' When Yugoslavia defied the USSR on 20 June by insisting that the Danube Conference be held at Belgrade, CIA estimated the Kremlin faced a serious problem in reconciling within the satellite states the conflict between national interests and international Communism." Similarly, he defended the CIA's role in predicting the fall of the Chinese Nationalists. According to Hillenkoetter: "CIA predicted the elimination of Nationalist China from the mainland time after time. ORE 77-48 (December 1948) estimated that 'The rapid disintegration of the Nationalist Army indicates that organized resistance to the military forces of the Chinese Communist Party will probably cease within a few months.' "

Dealing with the question of Palestine, where bloody conflict had erupted between Jews and Arabs before the declaration of the state of Israel, Hillenkoetter straightforwardly admitted misjudgment: "CIA did not overestimate the capabilities of the Arab forces. However, CIA failed to anticipate that the Jews would receive such extensive outside aid that Israeli military capabilities would be greatly increased. CIA also failed to predict that the truces imposed by the UN would prevent implementation of the Arabs' long-range attrition tactics. CIA correctly estimated that Arab-Israeli hostilities would occur as a result of partition and that the resultant instability throughout the Near East would seriously affect US strategic interests." Hillenkoetter dismissed the final charge that the CIA failed to judge the mood of the Latin American countries at the Bogotá Conference as "a rehash of previously reported mis-statements."

More interesting than Hillenkoetter's reply to the specific *Herald Tribune* allegations, however, was his concluding statement defending the CIA within the practical situation in which it had to work:

> In a fairly accurate account of U.S. Intelligence operations, the article characterizes as "duplication" the simultaneous examination of the basic documents by CIA and the other intelligence agencies. It ought to be pointed out, however, that such duplication is inevitable and desirable inasmuch as CIA examines these documents from the standpoint of national security whereas each of the other intelligence agencies examines them from the standpoint of departmental responsibilities. The article correctly charges that the services withhold planning and operational information from CIA and that this hampers CIA in fulfilling its mission. Under the pressures of the Korean situation there has been some improvement in this matter. CIA recognizes the danger . . . that the services have a tendency to reflect their own interests in their intelligence estimates. For this reason, CIA strives to maintain in its estimates an objective, balanced view, and to keep U.S. national security, rather than departmental interests, as the dominant consideration.

Two months later Hillenkoetter was posted to a command in the Pacific, and General Walter Bedell Smith, Eisenhower's wartime Chief of Staff and more recently U.S. ambassador in Moscow, was appointed the second director of the CIA and the fourth director of Central Intelligence. His priority, as a result of the weaknesses shown up by the Korean conflict, was to reorganize and sharpen the CIA's estimating procedures.

—7—

Terra Nostra
1950–1953

General Walter Bedell Smith is generally regarded by CIA people as having been one of the best if not the best director the agency ever had. He rose from the ranks to the top of the army before joining the CIA. He was not a West Pointer—he came up the hard way. Although small in stature, he possessed a magnetism that made him stand out in any gathering. He was plagued by ulcers, which gave him a notoriously bad temper. His nickname, "Beetle," was spoken with as much affection as respect. Ray Cline recalled of Smith: "When Truman appointed him to replace Hillenkoetter in October 1950, Smith approached the job with determination. He was a shrewd, dynamic man with broad experience and absolutely no tolerance for fools. It was often said he was the most even-tempered man in the world—he was always angry. . . . He had an intimidating personality and was a perfectionist. Largely self-educated, he had a photographic memory, encyclopedic knowledge, and shrewd judgment about people and ideas."[1]

Smith had the personal prestige as director of Central Intelligence not to invite but to command the heads of the military intelligence services to attend meetings he called and to stay until they had agreed on a conclusion to an intelligence question. One deputy director of intelligence, looking back, said:

> Bedell Smith put us on our feet originally because of his tremendous prestige as Eisenhower's G-3 at the end of World War II. He established our position in relation to the military. He treated the generals and admirals who were G-2s and A-2s and the ONI representatives as schoolboys. He'd make fun of

them in front of all of us. It was embarrassing sometimes. He'd known them and he'd seen them when they'd made mistakes and he could lacerate them with a phrase in no time at all. He certainly established us. He set up the Board of National Estimates and the Office of National Estimates. He made it possible for us to produce coordinated Estimates—something we'd been trying to do for years. He established a proper administrative facility for the whole of the agency rather than have each office do its own. He was a formidable man. I don't think he knew anything about operations, and the kind of thing we had to do in the later years of the cold war would have made him very ill at ease.[2]

According to Lyman Kirkpatrick, briefly chief of operations in the Directorate of Plans under Frank Wisner during Smith's tenure:

The agency, when Smith took it over, was very well described by Tracy Barnes as "a group of warring feudal baronies." Smith did not try to get too deeply into the details of what was going on, but he tried to organize the agency and to select the people who were competent to do the job he wanted done. If they couldn't do the job he wanted, he'd change them. There was an advertising slogan for a moving company that used to be very popular: "Don't make a move without calling—." The slogan went around the agency during the Smith regime, "If you can't find your furniture, you've been moved by Smith." It tells you how speedily he operated. He changed just about the entire top echelon of the agency in a couple of months. He was a tough and very able director.[3]

In the summer of 1950 Smith underwent an operation for the removal of his stomach ulcers. He was then fifty-five years old, and the surgery, which cut away a large portion of his stomach, had a dramatic effect on him. When he came in as director of Central Intelligence in October he weighed only about a hundred and thirty-five pounds. But in spite of his bad health, he responded to what he considered his country's need in time of war—cold war, but war nevertheless—and for many his example was one to follow. When he asked Professor William L. Langer, who had headed OSS research and analysis (which Smith had used during the war and greatly respected), to give up the opportunity of a professorship in history at Harvard and join him in Washington to reshape CIA's Office of Reports and Estimates, Langer felt he had no option but to agree. William Bundy, who joined the agency as an analyst in the spring of 1951, recalled:

In October 1950 Smith recalled Langer, who was then in the middle of writing his two definitive books on how we got into the war. Smith gave Langer first call on all the personnel on the analytic side of the agency and permission to approach anyone else he thought he might need. They tentatively allocated a strength of two hundred people for this. Langer had a wonderful nasal accent from Dorchester, Massachusetts, and he replied, "I can't possibly do it with more than twenty!" What was then established was the Board of National Estimates, which was composed of senior people—retired, distinguished academics: some from State; some with other government service; some of the top people from the war who had been with the Central Intelligence Group—and they were the judging panel. The Soviet Union was our prime preoccupation.[4]

The result of the Smith-Langer partnership was to establish the CIA, in the words of Harry Truman, as "an efficient and permanent arm of the Government's national security structure. . . . No President ever had such a wealth of vital information made available to him in such a useful manner as I have received through CIA."[5]

The achievement of Langer and Smith in reorganizing CIA's analytical and estimating procedures was one of the most important in the agency's history. It enabled the agency to overcome the stigma of "failure" that had become increasingly associated with it during the Korean War. The reforms carried out under Smith cemented the agency's position in the policy-making apparatus of the U.S. government. The attention given to providing concise and relevant papers and Estimates had a great deal to do with Smith's success in this respect. The President and senior government officials did not want voluminous reports, and certainly not in the highly charged atmosphere of the period when the questions being asked were "Will the Soviet Union attack?" "Is Korea the first step in a general Soviet offensive?" "Are the Chinese going to attack?" "Is the Soviet Union going to take over Iran?" They wanted crisp answers, and Smith and Langer saw to it that they had them. As William Bundy remembered:

> Bedell Smith made it clear that the staff were not to write research papers. They were to give the situation with certain fundamentals as necessary. I remember one occasion when Bedell Smith said, "Don't start that paper on China by saying 'China is a great land mass'!" People could always get that from someone else. A paper would go in draft to the Board of National Estimates, and the board would first cross-examine rigorously the staff who drafted it, and then they'd bring in the representatives from the other agencies. Then the board would approve the paper. It would usually have been seen by Bedell Smith a little before it was finalized. He treated the findings of the board with enormous respect.
>
> The real contributors to the process were State, the military services, and the CIA as coordinator. Beetle established the principle that they would not waffle on an agreement. If someone didn't agree, OK, but Smith was not going to fudge his language to produce mush. The Estimate was the Estimate of the director of Central Intelligence. Disagreement could be footnoted. It did not happen most of the time, but on the Soviet strength Estimates the army and the air force would always disagree with each other. Their appro-

priations hinged on it. Human nature hasn't been repealed, and G-2s were very seldom powerful enough not to reflect their service point of view. If the Estimate said the Soviets were building six hundred heavy bombers, the army would disagree; if it said two hundred, the air force would disagree.

Under Beetle the Estimates got to the top-policy people, and on certain subjects they had great effect. Smith reflected absolutely no army prejudice when he was DCI. He was a very tough fellow. He was no great stylist, but he went straight to the heart of the matter. He and Langer would not take junk by way of drafting.[6]

Smith's blueprint for the reorganization and refocusing of the agency was the Dulles report. He placed William H. Jackson, one of the codrafters of the report, as his second-in-command as deputy director. He also had the Central Intelligence Act of 1949 to fall back on.

THE ACT OF 1949

Although it was passed in what *The New York Times* called an atmosphere of "dense mystery,"[7] the Central Intelligence Agency Act was not considered particularly important in 1949. Over the years, the act emerged as a linchpin of CIA operations, giving Bedell Smith the legal backing for many controversial activities as well as with simplified administrative and financial practices. "It took time to evolve the central intelligence concept," observed Lyman Kirkpatrick. "It is a very fine-sounding phrase, but you simply don't issue a presidential edict—which was what was done originally—saying that there will be a central intelligence agency which will have coordinating authority over all other intelligence agencies, and expect it to happen overnight. The military intelligence agencies, the State Department, and the FBI were simply not going to accept that on the basis of an edict. Teeth were finally put into the edict by the passage of a new law and the appointment of a new director, Smith, who had the integrity, the personality, and the rank that were needed."[8]

The act also established Congress' authority to regulate the CIA, although it left vague Congress' oversight of the CIA's clandestine activities. That for thirty years Congress did not exercise this authority was a separate matter; the 1949 act provided the text of congressional power, and it could always be built upon: "Notwithstanding any other provisions of law, sums made available to the Agency by appropriation or otherwise may be expended for purposes necessary to carry out its functions. . . . The sums made available to the Agency may be expended without regard to the provisions of law and regulations relating to the expenditure of Government funds; and for objects of a confidential, extraordinary or emergency nature, such expenditure to be accounted for solely on the certificate of the Director. . . . "[9] This gave the director great freedom and was couched in terms to enable clandestine activity to be conducted with security. It also meant that the CIA did not have to account for its expenditure of unvouchered money (i.e., the DCI's discretionary funds).

As an executive arm, and without formal oversight procedures, the agency had a great deal of financial and operational freedom. Tom Braden, a senior operations officer in the early 1950s, recalled the practical effect:

> It never had to account for the money it spent except to the President if the President wanted to know how much money it was spending. But otherwise the funds were not only unaccountable, they were unvouchered, so there was really no means of checking them—"unvouchered funds" meaning expenditures that don't have to be accounted for. . . . If the director of CIA wanted to extend a present, say, to someone in Europe—a Labour leader—suppose he just thought, This man can use fifty thousand dollars, he's working well and doing a good job—he could hand it to him and never have to account to anybody. . . . I don't mean to imply that there were a great many of them that were handed out as Christmas presents. They were handed out for work well performed or in order to perform work well. . . . Politicians in Europe, particularly right after the war, got a lot of money from the CIA. . . .
>
> Since it was unaccountable, it could hire as many people as it wanted. It never had to say to any committee—no committee said to it—"You can only have so many men." It could do exactly as it pleased. It made preparations therefore for every contingency. It could hire armies; it could buy banks. There was simply no limit to the money it could spend and no limit to the people it could hire and no limit to the activities it could decide were necessary to conduct the war—the secret war. . . . It was a multinational. Maybe it was one of the first.[10]

The importance of this was noted by the CIA's general counsel, Lawrence Houston: "Provisions of unvouchered funds and the inviolability of such funds from outside inspection is the heart and soul of covert operation."[11]

In the British system the constitutional position of the Crown as head of state as well as part of the legislative process (the British Parliament is made up of the Commons, the Lords, and the Crown: no legislation is possible without the participation of all three), coupled with the absence of a written constitution, has meant that the British Secret Intelligence Service could operate without reference to Parliament and without specific legal background. In the United States, where the framework of the state is based upon a fine balance of powers among the executive, legislative, and judicial branches, with each element enjoined in the Constitution jealously to guard its particular powers, the existence of a clandestine intelligence and espionage service presented special problems. How would each branch be sure that another was not using this service improperly? Would such a service be used to project to preeminence one branch over the others?

The answers have never been certain, but in 1949, in the fury of the cold war, a tacit agreement was reached that no one would look too closely at the CIA. On April 18, 1948, Hillenkoetter appeared before the House Armed Services Committee, testified for the legislation and effectively summarized the position: "It was thought when we started back in 1946, that at least we would have time to develop this mature service over a period of years—after all, the British, who possess the finest intelligence in the world, have been developing their system since the time of Queen Elizabeth. Unfortunately, the international situation has not allowed us the breathing space we might have liked, and so, as we present this bill, we find ourselves in operations up to our necks, and we need the authorities contained herein as a matter of urgency."[12]

Twenty-five years later, when Lawrence Houston retired from the CIA, William Colby, then director of Central Intelligence, in his farewell speech to Houston, ascribed to him the credit for the 1949 act:

> The law as passed then [said Colby] was quite a triumph in its description of the need for an intelligence agency and the role it is to play in American society, and Larry Houston is the basic author of it. . . .
> There had to be arrangements for secrecy. Our normal legislation requires that all employees be open, and that our records be available for scrutiny by any member of the Congress, and so forth, and it was impossible to run an intelligence service if this was going to be the situation. So Mr. Houston produced, for instance, the CIA law of 1949, which gave the Director certain authority to certify the expenditure of money without the normal review that is given to regular appropriations; gave the Director authority to terminate the employment of individuals when in his judgment it is in the interests of the security of the United States, without the normal appeals and open review. If we were going to keep our identities and our activities secret, we could not subject them to normal open appearances throughout the land. . . . What Mr. Houston really is, is the father of intelligence law.*

THE DIRECTORATE OF INTELLIGENCE

By the time Bedell Smith became DCI, the CIA's operations were even more extensive than in 1949. However, the way in which information was put

---

* Quoted in Central Intelligence Agency, *Studies in Intelligence*, "Lawrence Houston," 1974. Colby was speaking at the presentation to Houston of the National Security Medal and the CIA's Distinguished Intelligence Medal on February 1, 1974. Colby also cited the "Wiretap Act" as a Houston achievement, which "seemed to establish recognition of a constitutional principle [by saying] that nothing in this bill shall limit the Constitutional power of the President to take such measures as he deems necessary to obtain foreign intelligence information deemed essential to the security of the United States." All this was said in the midst of the post-Watergate furor about the CIA. Colby was then anxious to stress that the law was the CIA's guideline and that Congress had agreed to the agency's secrecy. Colby was wrong about the director's authority to terminate employment stemming from the 1949 Act: it came from Section 102(c) of the 1947 National Security Act.

to use in reports and Estimates was seen by Smith and the top echelon of policy makers as being of overriding importance. At the same time that he invited
Langer back into intelligence analysis, Smith was taking organizational steps to
improve matters. The weaknesses in the estimating and reporting procedures,
which Hillenkoetter had pointed out in his August 1950 memorandum to
Truman, defending the CIA against the *Herald Tribune*'s criticism, echoed
some of the findings of the Dulles report. Bedell Smith did not seek to dis-
member and then reassemble the agency's organization; rather he chose to direct it firmly at the targets set for it by the 1947 National Security Act and
National Security Council directives and not duplicate the activity of other
agencies. (See Appendix IV.)

Smith gave Langer a free hand in managing the research and analytical
side of the agency. Langer wanted a small analytical staff—whom he selected
from all parts of the agency—so that administration would not consume too
much time.[13] The Office of Reports and Estimates was abolished and the Office of National Estimates (ONE) created partially in its stead, headed by
Langer. It was organized on two levels. The small upper tier, known officially
as the Board of Estimates and unofficially within the agency as the "College of
Cardinals," was based directly on the OSS system and composed of distinguished academics and others. It too was headed by Langer. The job of these
experts was to test, by debate and interrogation, the Estimates written by the
second level, known as the Estimates Staff. In charge of this second tier was
Ray Cline, who had served under Langer in the OSS. The job of the Estimates
Staff was to make suggestions for National Intelligence Estimates; analyze all
available information; compose Estimates and reports and generally coordinate
their findings with other agencies. The staff also produced National Intelligence Surveys, separate from the Estimates. These encyclopedia-like documents contained a wide range of information on foreign countries and acted as
a source book within the agency.

After being processed through this system Estimates were presented to
the Intelligence Advisory Committee, composed of the heads of the armed
services' intelligence departments, the FBI, the Department of State's Office of
Intelligence and Research, and the Atomic Energy Commission. This committee, which was chaired by the director of Central Intelligence, had been
formed in 1947 and was part of Hillenkoetter's struggle to establish the preeminence of the DCI and the CIA. Under Bedell Smith, Hillenkoetter's objective
was achieved. This system remained in operation for the next twenty-five years,
proving itself, in the words of the Church Committee in 1976, as "by far the
best analytical organization for the production of finished intelligence within
the government."[14]

The Office of National Estimates was part of the Directorate of Intelligence, a new directorate, established by Smith in January 1952. Working with
ONE were the Office of Research and Reports, formed in November 1950

alongside ONE, and the Office of Scientific Intelligence, created by Hillen-koetter in 1949. Although ONE was the most important element in this trium-virate, the other offices provided the driving force of analytical work. They conducted basic research, cooperating closely with the Estimates Staff and the staffs of other intelligence agencies, particularly the military. In August 1952 the military succeeded in restricting the work of the Office of Scientific Intelli-gence to basic research and medicine, away from weapons development, which the military regarded as its special concern.

A fourth office, the Office of Current Intelligence, was created in 1951 to supply quick analysis and reports in response to fast-moving events. The new directorate encompassing these offices was headed by a new deputy director for intelligence (DDI), one of three additional deputy directorships created by Smith. Loftus Becker, a young lawyer, was the first DDI. (Langer, whom Smith had wanted for the post, did not want the administrative burden.) Becker stayed for just over a year and was succeeded in 1953 by Robert Amory, a Harvard Law School professor. After Langer returned to academia in 1952, the Board of Estimates was chaired by Sherman Kent. Kent, who had served as Langer's deputy, remained with the Board of Estimates for sixteen years, until 1968, and was to become the father figure of CIA research and analysis.

The relationship the board and the Estimates Staff had with academia under Langer and then Kent carried forward Donovan's original conviction that the best brains in America could be gathered and put to work on strengthening the country's national intelligence system. Starting in the 1960s, this brain pool was seen by people outside the agency as corruptive and sinister, lending to the CIA a sense of infinite connection and omniscience. To many the agency was a sort of Moby Dick, a master of the deep recesses of secrecy and information, occasionally surfacing but for periods never long enough to make its size and shape fully clear.

In fact, much of the work of the academics within and outside the CIA was unexceptional. For example, Max Millikan, a professor of economics from MIT, organized the Economic Research unit within the Office of Research and Reports during 1951 and 1952 to analyze economic conditions within the Soviet Union. Millikan returned to MIT's Center for International Studies in 1953, building a close link with the CIA there. Academics who answered the CIA's call did so out of a patriotic desire to serve their country and out of a self-interested desire to obtain privileged, top-class information unavailable to them in the normal course of their university work. The mystique of the CIA and the general awareness that the agency played a part in the formation of U.S. foreign policy also attracted highfliers. As Ray Cline recalled, the CIA that Bedell Smith had

fashioned in the 1950s carried out its mission in a romantic atmosphere of adventure that no amount of disclaimer could deflate. Of course at least one-half of the CIA's staff members, a number that ultimately peaked at about 18,000, were engaged in clerical, secretarial, and routine administrative duties normally about as exciting as dishwashing. It made no difference; exceptionally bright men and women fresh from high school or college flocked to take jobs no different from those in the Pentagon or other civil service organizations, performed their duties with a sense of excitement because the work often dealt with important events and glamorous faraway places, and, even more, because they had a chance, in due course, of being sent to some exotic foreign locale. . . . Such was the mystique of the CIA that when any employee refused to disclose the precise nature of his work or, indeed, for whom he worked other than "for the U.S. Government," people assumed that the employee was deeply involved in dangerous undercover deeds.[15]

William Colby captured the peculiar atmosphere surrounding clandestine operations and agents that drew so many talented young people to the CIA:

Considering the missionary zeal, sense of elitism and marvelous camaraderie among my colleagues [in clandestine activities] . . . one can see how easy it would have been for me to drop out of [the outside] world and immerse myself exclusively in the cloak-and-dagger life. And some of my colleagues at the Agency did just that. Socially as well as professionally they cliqued together, forming a sealed fraternity. They ate together at their own special favorite restaurants; they partied almost only among themselves; their families drifted to each other, so their defenses did not always have to be up. In this way they increasingly separated themselves from the ordinary world and developed a rather skewed view of that world. Their own dedicated double life became the proper norm, and they looked down on the life of the rest of the citizenry. And out of this grew what was later named—and condemned—as the "cult" of intelligence, an inbred, distorted, elitist view of intelligence that held it to be above the normal processes of society, with its own rationale and justification, beyond the restraints of the Constitution, which applied to everything and everyone else.[16]

Bedell Smith was very aware of the "Oh So Social" element in the agency, although when he came in as director in 1950, it had not reached the peculiar position Colby described. On the operations side in particular there were a number of dubious security risks and dilettantes, and in his first month Smith fired about fifty employees on these grounds. The criterion was simple. "I don't care whether they were blabbing secrets or not," he declared. "Just give me the names of the people at Georgetown cocktail parties."[17]

THE DIRECTORATE OF PLANS

The second of the new deputy directorships created by Smith in his reorganization was filled by Allen Dulles, who among all the CIA's top leaders was the most interested in undercover deeds and the most aware of the mystique of clandestine activities. On January 2, 1951, Dulles came aboard as deputy director responsible for OSO and OPC, anxious to implement the recommendations that he, William Jackson, Smith's direct deputy, and Mathias Correa had submitted to the National Security Council in January 1949. The amalgamation of OSO and OPC into a single office, the Directorate of Plans, clearly under the control and direction of the director of Central Intelligence, had been one of the strongest recommendations of the Dulles report. But it did not happen as quickly as Dulles wanted, in spite of his efforts.[18]

This lack of action was due in part to the unease that existed between the two offices. Instead of forcing a merger between OSO and OPC, Bedell Smith chose to proceed more diplomatically, achieving the merger by mutual consent instead. Using the sheer force of his personality, Smith had already achieved a major bureaucratic victory. Within days of taking office he simply declared that Wisner and OPC would henceforth be under his sole administrative and policy control and would not take orders from the State Department. Lawrence Houston recalled the situation: "It was an impossible situation for the CIA not to be responsible for a large and rapidly growing and influential staff under it. It was resolved in typical style by Smith in 1950 as one of his first acts. He called Frank Wisner and myself in and said OPC would have to come under the control of the DCI. Frank didn't argue. I think he knew Smith had squared it at the proper levels. And so we went up to my office and in fifteen or twenty minutes we drafted a paper and we took it back to Smith, and he said, 'I don't need a paper—just do it!' "[19]

The two offices worked better together after this, but as separate units within the CIA they still duplicated each other in certain respects and competed for information and agents. The interoffice rivalry was fueled by several factors. In the first place, Wisner had picked his OPC staff with considerable care, reaching back into his OSS and New York law days to select the best people he could find. Inevitably these people tended to come from Wisner's own circle and often were independently wealthy—Ivy League–educated lawyers and bankers. OSO people, in contrast, tended to be more career-oriented—a fact that made them objects of derision in the eyes of the more cavalier OPC. They were looked down on by OPC people as losers—those who clung to government service after the war because they could not get good jobs outside. Second, as Richard Bissell, who became deputy director of plans in 1958, explained, "There always were two philosophies about clandestine operations, and they could be associated with OSO and OPC. OSO had an emphasis on high professionalism, with very tight security and the maintenance of espionage and counterespionage. OPC placed a great deal more emphasis on covert action and was probably less professional and less secure."[20]

The rivalry was also fueled by major salary differences that existed between the two offices. Thanks to Wisner's ability to convince Secretary of State Marshall, when OPC was set up in 1948, that a high pay scale was necessary to attract the best people, OPC pay scales were much better than in OSO. Recruitment for OPC and OSO was also different. While OSO tended to recruit people from within the CIA or allied government agencies, OPC drew its staff from prestigious universities—Harvard, Brown, Princeton—where Wisner in his search for the best people had mobilized ex-OSS academics to keep a lookout for likely recruits. In this way foreign students as well as Americans were recruited to work for the CIA. In 1976 one former CIA officer reportedly remarked (prematurely, as it turned out), "By 1985 we'll own 80 percent of the Iranian government's second and third level of officials"[21] as a result of this early recruitment method. Between 1949 and 1975 approximately one million foreign students and millions more American students had been scrutinized by CIA recruiters for the agency.[22] During the 1960s this method of recruitment was viewed with great suspicion by outsiders who feared the influence of an "invisible government" of the CIA.

Because of this continuing unease between OSO and OPC, Smith appointed the popular and effective Dulles as deputy director of plans (DDP) in December 1950 and followed this up by merging the two offices from July 1, 1952. As Richard Helms, who at the time of the merger was one of the top officers in OSO, said of the situation:

> The worst feature of the competition was that often we were competing for the same agents. For example, if there is a little man in a town in France or Germany who has the kind of access that you want, are you going to use him to pass out leaflets? Are you going to use him to plant stories in newspapers? Are you going to use him for intelligence purposes? What are you going to use him for? If you've got competing services, they're obviously going to start to bid for him for their own different purposes. It might happen subtly, quietly, but "I'll pay you fifty dollars!" and "I'll pay you a hundred dollars!" That's what was disastrous.[23]

Frank Wisner, who had been Dulles' deputy as head of OPC, had become DDP ten months earlier in August 1951 when Dulles was promoted to replace William Jackson as Smith's deputy director of Central Intelligence. Richard Helms from OSO became Wisner's number-two man as chief of operations.

Lyman Kirkpatrick had done much of the spadework for the merger over the previous twelve months.

> It was a very traumatic period in the agency [he recalled]. General Smith called me in one day and said "Kirkpatrick, we are going to have one operational office in this agency, and you are going to see it's done!" That was the start of what then lasted for over a year of constant work and negotiation and bargaining back and forth. We wanted to stop the constant feuding and bickering between the two offices. The CIA and the United States were being exploited. We were being fed information that was purely fic-

tional. There is one thing in the intelligence area that will always be true: there are refugees desperate to make a living. So when they reach Paris or London or West Berlin or wherever, suddenly the idea occurs to them that they should go up to a garret and type intelligence reports about their native lands. These have to be tracked down to discover if they are truth or fiction.

Usually these refugees are very knowledgeable, so what they have to say sounds very true to the innocent. In the earlier stages it was not realized that most of the refugee groups were penetrated, but as the counterintelligence and counterespionage effort of the agency improved, it became more and more clear. The difficulty was trying to persuade the people who were dealing with these groups that they were phonies. The price of having an intelligence operation is that the operator is very reluctant to yield even if his contacts are phony, because they are so valuable and important to him.[24]

Kirkpatrick himself caught polio in 1952 and was out of the running when Smith made the new appointments in the Directorate of Plans.*

A third directorate Smith created in 1950 was the Directorate of Administration (DDA), which in addition to running the personnel affairs of the agency was responsible for agency communications and logistical support for covert operations abroad. By 1953 the DDA included the CIA's audit branch, general counsel's department, the Office of Security (responsible for internal security and staff monitoring), the comptroller's department, and the agency's own medical service, which was involved with staff health matters. The two most prominent elements in the Smith scheme, the Directorate of Intelligence and the Directorate of Plans, were securely supported by the Directorate of Administration, whose job it was to ensure that plans worked and that policies could be practically and legally implemented. The overwhelming majority of

---

* In 1952 Kirkpatrick was a front runner for the very top positions within the agency. Along with Dulles, Wisner, and Helms, he was an OSS veteran and was close to Bedell Smith, having served as his executive assistant, moving into OSO as assistant director under Dulles with Richard Helms as his deputy. In the spring of 1952 the signs were that Bedell Smith had decided that Kirkpatrick should become Frank Wisner's number two as chief of operations in the DDP. In the summer, before the merger of the two offices actually took place, Kirkpatrick set off on a tour of the agency's stations abroad to deliver the merger plans in person to OSO and OPC field staffs. In Bangkok, doctors later decided, Kirkpatrick caught polio. By all accounts, he had had an aggressively successful career in the agency up to this point. He combined a good brain with a strong, handsome physique. He was tall—over six feet—and physically dominating, with an articulate and confident manner, and was obviously going places. In the weeks before he set off on his world tour he was seen working hard at home digging a swimming pool.

The tensions at work and physical tiredness may have weakened him, making him more vulnerable to illness. He returned to Washington from Thailand and went straight into a hospital. When he came out seven months later, in March 1953, he was in a wheelchair, crippled for life. Richard Helms had stepped into the post of chief of operations, and while Kirkpatrick was welcomed back, it was clear that Helms had overtaken him in the promotion stakes. Kirkpatrick seems to have felt this keenly, and colleagues generally noticed more than a physical change in him. He was considered to be ruthlessly ambitious after 1953, almost as if he were compensating for his disability by trying to prove himself a better and more astute administrator and political operator than anyone else.

CIA resources, however, went into the clandestine operations and covert activities carried out by the Directorate of Plans. While about 20 percent of the agency's budget and 40 percent of the agency's personnel were involved in research, analysis, reporting, and administration, the remaining 80 percent of the budget and 60 percent of the people were involved in the Directorate of Plans.[25]

Nearly all the activities that would later embarrass the CIA began during the Bedell Smith period, under the auspices of the Directorate of Plans. With the acceptance by the Department of State of Smith's control over Frank Wisner and OPC in October 1950, the agency assumed full responsibility for covert operations. It now had two clear purposes: to prepare National Intelligence Estimates and to conduct extradiplomatic activity worldwide. NSC 68 gave the agency additional support for these activities. It consisted of a series of decisions framing the policy of containment of the Soviet Union and its allies. It represented a summing up of the perceived Soviet threat and the steps that would be taken to deal with it. The Soviet Union was not superhuman, and it could be restrained by resolute opposition at all levels—political, economic, diplomatic, clandestine—and by clearly signaling that the United States would use its military strength to counter further Soviet encroachments if need be.[26] Along with the Korean War, this directive had a massive effect on American military procurement, increasing appropriations for defense from about $15 billion in 1950 to about $50 billion two years later. Part of this increase went straight to the CIA for espionage and covert operations of all sorts, some on a very large scale.

MIND CONTROL

One of the first fruits of Smith's merger of the OPC and OSO was a group of projects known from 1953 as MKUltra. Most of the projects dealt with drug or counterdrug research and development; they had been prompted by a CIA analysis of confessions in Stalin's show trials and in particular by the public "confession" of Cardinal Mindszenty of Hungary on February 3, 1949. Mindszenty was obviously a broken man when he confessed, and the CIA was interested in how he had been broken. As the Korean War progressed and a few captured American servicemen began to make radio propaganda broadcasts for the communists and to sign statements calling for an end to U.S. involvement in the war, senior CIA people concluded that the Soviets had perfected a way of capturing the minds and the wills of people, thus making them utterly responsive to Soviet commands. People really were standing up in communist courts and admitting to the most extraordinary charges. It was a phenomenon that the agency investigated in detail.

This was a period when the horror of the Nazi death camps was recent and in everyone's mind, and it seemed to many of the best and brightest in

U.S. government service that another, similar, totalitarian threat faced the world. Just as the previous generation of people in power had come to terms with the mass bombing of civilians, the new generation had to face up to the prospect of ever more refined technical evils. Being involved in this way showed the CIA to be in the context of its time, sharing the concerns of society, not removed from them.[27] These concerns were reflected in the following CIA analysis:

> Since the notorious Moscow trials of 1937, overt Russian judicial procedure has been noteworthy for the dramatic trials in which the defendants have exhibited anomalous and incomprehensible behavior and confessions. Characteristics and manner of the defendants, and formulation and delivery of the confessions, have been so similar in a large number of cases as to suggest factitious origin. Most noteworthy and incredible has been the recent "confession" of His Eminence Cardinal Mindszenty while on trial in the People's Court of Hungary. . . .
>
> The evident incongruities prompted this study. . . . It became apparent at the outset of the study that the style, context and manner of delivery of the "confessions" were such as to be inexplicable unless there had been a reorganization and reorientation of the minds of the confessees. There is adequate historical experience to establish that basic changes in the functional organization of the human mind cannot be brought about by the traditional methods of physical torture—these, at the most, achieve a reluctant, temporary yielding and, moreover, leave their mark upon the victim. Newer or more subtle techniques had, therefore, to be considered . . . :
>
>   a. Psychosurgery: a surgical separation of the frontal lobes of the brain.
>   b. Shock method: (1) electrical (2) drug: metrazol, cannabis, indica, insulin, cocaine.
>   c. Psychoanalytic methods: (1) psychoanalysis (2) narcoanalysis and synthesis (3) hypnoanalysis and synthesis.
>   d. Combinations of the foregoing.[28]

For the next twenty-three years, under one name or another, the CIA was involved in researching ways of controlling human behavior.[29] The first effort was named Project Bluebird.

During World War II the OSS conducted drug experiments, including one for a "truth drug" with cannabis. Military hospitals had noticed that some anesthetics made soldiers speak freely while they were unconscious. The first field test was carried out on an unsuspecting underworld figure, August Del Gracio, a member of the Charles "Lucky" Luciano crime family in New York. Del Gracio was involved with the OSS attempt to arrange, through Luciano, underworld Italian-American help in preparing the way for the invasion of Sicily and for the protection of New York docks and shipyards against enemy sabotage. He was given a number of cigarettes heavily laced with cannabis, and as he smoked them he was questioned about underworld activities to see how freely he talked under the influence of the drug. After several sessions cannabis was deemed to be a tongue loosener.[30]

Bluebird started before the OPC/OSO merger and while Hillenkoetter was still DCI. Directed by Sheffield Edwards, head of the CIA's Office of Security, whose job it was to protect agency personnel and facilities from penetration, the project was aimed at determining whether interrogation teams consisting of a psychiatrist, a lie detector expert and hypnotist, and a technician would obtain better results with drugs than with other interrogation methods. A month after the start of the Korean War a team traveled to Tokyo to interrogate four people—probably suspected double agents. The results it achieved were considered successful. In October 1950 further experiments were carried out by Bluebird teams, probably on captured North Koreans. When Bedell Smith became DCI, Project Bluebird came under the auspices of Allen Dulles. It was coordinated with other similar research work in the agency aimed at developing what was in effect a human robot. This work, Project Artichoke, was carried out by the CIA's Office of Scientific Intelligence and was officially described as intending to "exploit, along operational lines, scientific methods and knowledge that can be utilized in altering the attitudes, beliefs, thought processes, and behavior patterns of agent personnel. This will include the application of tested psychiatric and psychological techniques including the use of hypnosis in conjunction with drugs."[31] Both Project Bluebird and Project Artichoke arose from the CIA's growing frustration at its inability to penetrate iron curtain countries with agents, and its fear of enemies within.

The failure of the CIA and the British Secret Intelligence Service to place agents in Albania had generated a major spy scare within the agency. It was obvious that the penetration effort had been betrayed, but at the time no one knew by whom. It was not until Kim Philby was discovered to be a Soviet agent that the answer was known. Meanwhile the search for the betrayer consumed a good deal of time on both sides of the Atlantic. Thirty-three years later this was vividly recalled by Tom Braden: "It was Albania that Allen and Bedell were trying to investigate and where they tried to run down the leak, and I think it was Albania as far as the agency was concerned that led to the uncovering of Philby. They were very, very disturbed by Albania at that time. They were investigating it up and down and back and forth and left and right and center. Frank Wisner was blamed for Albania—that was something he might have done while he was in OPC still over at State. But they were onto it by then, which must have been about 1950."[32]

This search, combined with the revelations of the extent of the Rosenberg spy ring, the uncovering of Philby, and the defection of Burgess and Maclean, caused the agency to institute lie detector tests for all agency personnel and to conduct research into drugs, hypnosis, and interrogation methods under the MKUltra programs as a later CIA internal report described:

As a result of several years' effort devoted primarily to attempts at penetration of denied areas through various black techniques, the Agency has concluded that the vehicle of legal travel offers greater opportunities to place controlled agents within denied areas. In addition, far greater emphasis must and will be placed in the future upon long range agent operations and penetration of key Communist organizations. . . .

In the case of long range operations, lapse of time alone will erode motivation. There is, therefore, the immediate requirement for the development of every technique that can be devised to precondition the agent mind and to create within him a viable and long lasting motivation impervious to lapse of time and direct psychological attacks by the enemy.[33]

Because of the "extreme sensitivity of the techniques and substances employed" in the project, Artichoke was kept on the strictest need-to-know basis within the agency.[34] Along with Bluebird experiments, Artichoke work was conducted in the field in Germany and the Far East and in a U.S. Navy facility acquired by the agency in the Panama Canal Zone. Agents and their families who for some reason needed to escape from Europe and find new lives and identities were housed at this facility. Several suspected double agents were also there, and these men provided the MKUltra projects with their guinea pigs. Within a short time rumors circulated within the Directorate of Plans that some suspected double agents were killed during MKUltra experiments. Going as far as they did, these experiments made the CIA's decisions to attempt to assassinate foreign leaders ten years later seem somehow ordinary within the covert side of the agency.

In April 1953, with the CIA now under the direction of Allen Dulles, Richard Helms, Frank Wisner's number-two man, proposed a "program for the covert use of biological and chemical materials"[35] in experiments for the control of human behavior. This time Americans were used as guinea pigs. An arrangement was made with a Dr. Harris Isbell, head of a drug treatment center in Lexington, Kentucky, to test various drugs supplied by the agency on addicts in his care. In this case (though not in other tests elsewhere) the testees were informed and their consent obtained.[36] The drug d-lysergic acid diethylamide (LSD) interested the agency experimenters most during this period. In one instance Dr. Isbell kept seven men on LSD for seventy-seven days—a feat that even the most hardened "acid head" of the 1960s would have balked at. Of course at this stage the medium- and long-term effects of the drug were not known. The object of the tests was not to examine the immediate effect of the drugs but to see if their use could help control people for long periods of time and at long distances. The spectacle of people's behavior being controlled in Soviet show trials indicated that the Russians had perfected such techniques.

Some thought that George Kennan's loss of temper at Tempelhof airport in Berlin on his way to London from Moscow, where he was ambassador in September 1952, was an example of Soviet success in long-range control. Reporters were at the airport, and they questioned Kennan about policy and life in Russia. Then one young reporter asked him if American diplomats in Moscow had many social contacts with Russians. Stalin's increasing paranoia and the tensions of the cold war had resulted in the Russians' ending virtually all social contacts and isolating Western diplomats in their embassies. Kennan himself had just come through a particularly trying time, including the discovery of a Russian bugging device in the Great Seal of the United States in his study. He wrote later on:

> The question itself annoyed me. Had the man been born yesterday? The regime of isolation applied to Western diplomats in Moscow had been in existence for at least two decades. How could a reporter not know that? Why, I thought to myself, must editors send people of such ignorance to interview ambassadors at airports?
> "Don't you know," I asked, "how foreign diplomats live in Moscow?"
> "No," he replied. "How do they?"
> "Well," I said, "I was interned here in Germany for several months during the last war. The treatment we receive in Moscow is just about like the treatment we internees received then, except that in Moscow we are at liberty to go out and walk the streets under guard."[37]

On October 3 Kennan was declared persona non grata by the Soviets. His outburst in Berlin had been used by them to discredit him personally and to embarrass the United States. His answer was "slanderous," a "rude violation," "hostile." The comparison Kennan made between Nazi Germany and the Soviet Union was taken as indicative of the attitude of the United States. As Kennan himself was the first to admit, "Nowhere would I be likely to find full understanding for what I had done, or full support."[38] He had broken the rules of diplomatic behavior, damaged his career, and worsened—if possible—relations with the USSR.

The effects of Dr. Isbell's tests on drug addicts, however, showed that they did not respond to control for long periods of time or at long range, away from the test centers. Since this could be explained by the fact that the testees were all hardened drug addicts anyway, it was decided in 1953 to administer drugs to unsuspecting "normal" people.[39] Many of the various MKUltra programs were coordinated under Dr. Sidney Gottlieb, deputy head (1962–66) and then head of the CIA's Technical Services Staff (TSS). Gottlieb reported to Frank Wisner and Richard Helms in the Directorate of Plans. He worked closely with the Office of Security (which was interested in his results for vetting CIA employees) and the army's Chemical Corps research and bacteriological warfare center, at Fort Detrick, in the foothills of the Maryland Appalachians.

From April 13, 1953, the date on which the coordinated MKUltra project was approved by Allen Dulles,[40] a host of programs came under Gottlieb's umbrella. There were the Bluebird and Artichoke experiments already under way. There was Project Chatter, a navy program that had begun in autumn

1947 and was an attempt to identify and test truth drugs in response to reports "of 'amazing results' achieved by the Soviets."[41] There was MKNaomi, a program set up in May 1952, in which the CIA's Technical Services Staff cooperated with the Army Chemical Corps Special Operations Division at Fort Detrick in the production of biological chemical weapons and substances for the agency's operational use.[42] MKDelta, a special procedure for governing the use of MKUltra materials abroad, started in 1952 by Allen Dulles and Frank Wisner with Bedell Smith's approval, also came within Gottlieb's responsibility.[43] In all there were eventually 149 MKUltra subprojects and 33 additional subprojects funded under MKUltra but having nothing to do with behavioral modification, toxins, or drugs.[44]

The MKUltra programs provide an example of the way the agency was prepared to engage the world at all levels. Its analysts were concerned with everything that happened in foreign societies; its scientists and technicians were involved in the most speculative areas of applied science, technology, medicine, and psychophysical research. The U-2 project, which began in 1954, resulted in an airplane that at the time was at the frontiers of aeronautic engineering. The doctors and biologists in the Technical Services Staff working on MKUltra subprojects were ambitious to press the frontiers of their disciplines even further, to the point of "executive action" capability—the agency's in-house euphemism for assassination.

MKUltra Subproject 142 was "a small biological program of electrical brain stimulation involving some new approaches to the subject. . . . The reason for separating this work financially from the other efforts of [blanked out] on the Agency's behalf is to allow it to engage in some very practical experiments at some point in the work which would present security problems if this effort were to be handled in the usual way. Some of the uses proposed for these particular animals would involve possible delivery systems . . . or for direct executive action type operations as distinguished from the eavesdropping application."[45] Subproject 94 was similar. "The purpose of this subproject," a CIA memorandum for the record stated, "is to provide for a continuation of investigations on the remote directional control of activities in selected species of animals. Miniaturized stimulating electrode implants in specific brain center areas will be utilized."[46]

Such projects resulted in dogs, cats, and monkeys being used as guided microphones and bombs. "Initial biological work on techniques and brain locations essential to providing conditioning and control of animals has been completed," a report on Subproject 94 declared in October 1960. "The feasibility of remote control of activities in several species of animals has been demonstrated. The present investigations are directed toward improvement of techniques."[47] By April 1961 Gottlieb's staff had "a 'production' capability."

At the present time we feel that we are close to having debugged a prototype system whereby dogs can be guided along specified courses through land areas out of sight and at some distance from the operator. . . . In addition to its possible practical value in operations, this phenomenon is a very useful research tool in the area of the behavioral sciences. Dr. [blanked out] is taking appropriate action to exploit our knowledge of this area and provide adequate background for the development of future Agency applications in the general areas of Influencing Human Behavior, Indirect Assessment and Interrogation Aids.[48]

Victor Marchetti, who in the mid-1960s worked as special assistant to the deputy director of the CIA, recalled one guided-animal experiment:

> One of the problems with an audio device in the wall or under the mat is that, like cameras, they take a picture of what *they* see and not what *you* see in your mind's eye. Human beings have a cochlea in our ears masking out noise, so we can have conversations at a cocktail party. But if you tape a cocktail party, you get all the noise and you can't make out conversations. So they worked on an audio device that had the ability to mask out noise. Then they got this idea: let's stop trying to make a cochlea—let's use a real cochlea. Cats have cochleas. So if they wired up a cat, he could mask everything out. That's what they did. They trained him to listen to conversations and not to listen to all the background noises.
> A lot of money was spent. They slit the cat open, put batteries in him, wired him up. The tail was used as an antenna. They made a monstrosity. They tested him and tested him. They found he would walk off the job when he got hungry, so they put another wire in to override that. Finally they're ready. They took it out to a park and pointed it at a park bench and said, "Listen to those two guys. Don't listen to anything else—not the birds, no cat or dog—just those two guys!" They put him out of the van, and a taxi comes and runs him over. There they were, sitting in the van with all those dials, and the cat was dead![49]

In retrospect, it is clear that Gottlieb's work lit a fuse to a time bomb that was to explode in the 1970s, destroying a good deal of the agency's image as a proper defender of American values in the public mind. Projects designed to develop methods and devices that could kill or control people at long distance and that, during nearly two decades, involved hundreds of people, some outside the agency on contract, sooner or later were bound to leak. One project that led to the death of a participating scientist made publicity almost certain since his family naturally pressed for full disclosure of the facts behind his death.

THE CASE OF FRANK OLSON

On November 18, 1953, ten scientists working on MKUltra and Army Chemical Corps projects, including Gottlieb and two other CIA personnel, gathered in a log cabin by a lake in the Appalachians for one of their twice-yearly informal weekend conferences to discuss their work. There, as recounted in the agency's subsequent investigation of what occurred, "according to a statement made by an Agency employee present to the then Director of Security of the Agency, it was decided to experiment with the drug LSD. A very small dose of LSD was placed in a bottle of cointreau and eight of the ten persons present had a drink. Two of the individuals present did not drink the cointreau since one was a teetotaler and the other had a heart condition."[50] Although there was a conflict of testimony on this point, the agency investigation determined that Gottlieb conducted this experiment on his colleagues with their prior knowledge. His action resulted in the suicide a month later of Frank Olson, an army civilian scientist working at Fort Detrick. The CIA report explained the background:

> Files of this Agency reflect a conflict with respect to the administering of the LSD since a memorandum written by the then Inspector General of the Agency indicates that the individuals present were not told that the drug was LSD until some 20 minutes after its ingestion. However, this memorandum does indicate that an Agency representative had discussed the possibility of an unwitting use of the drug and that Army representatives had agreed that this would be a valuable experiment. After the ingestion of the drug, a definite effect was seen on the group in that they became boisterous and "happy." The Army civilian, who later committed suicide, complained of wakefulness that evening.[51]

In the weeks following the experiment Olson appeared mentally depressed and, according to his family, experienced personality changes. Realizing that something was seriously wrong with him, Gottlieb sent Olson for psychiatric treatment in New York. After treating him five or six times in the course of a week, his doctor decided to place Olson in Chestnut Lodge, a sanatorium near Rockville, Maryland. At 3:20 A.M. on the night before Olson and his CIA companion were to leave New York, where they were staying at the Statler Hotel, Olson crashed through the closed window in his hotel room, falling ten floors to the sidewalk below. His companion woke in time to see the suicide but not prevent it. Gottlieb reported what happened to Allen Dulles, who ordered Lyman Kirkpatrick, as the inspector general of the CIA, to make an investigation and report. Kirkpatrick concluded that a reprimand was in order and, by implication, that the LSD experiment had caused Olson to commit suicide:

> Although Dr. Gottlieb knew all of the individuals who received the drug, he obviously was not aware of their medical records. Therefore, only one individual was excluded from the experiment because of a heart condition. Gottlieb was not aware that over a period of five years Olson had apparently had a suicidal tendency. . . .

It is apparent that there is a strong possibility that the drug was a trigger mechanism precipitating Olson's suicide. . . .

Uncontrolled experiments such as these conducted by TSS could seriously affect the record and reputation of the Agency. . . .

Using employees of another agency could seriously jeopardize our relationship with that and all other agencies should this become known. . . .

The Deputy Chief TSS should be reprimanded for his poor judgment shown in this instance. . . .

Chief TSS should be admonished to exercise tighter supervision and control over the use of this drug and should render periodic reports to DD/P on its use and the results.[52]

Lawrence Houston, CIA's general counsel, who was also involved in the investigation, recorded that he was "not happy with what seems to me a very casual attitude on the part of TSS representatives to the way this experiment was conducted and to their remarks that this is just one of the risks running with scientific experimentation."[53] Olson's widow, Alice, was first told that her husband had died of a "classified illness" and then that he had jumped or fallen out of a window. Not until the Church Committee hearings in 1975 did she and her family learn the truth, and they were naturally very bitter about it. In 1976, in addition to the full pension she had received since her husband's death, Congress passed a bill to pay $750,000 to her in compensation, and the family received a personal apology from President Ford.

Olson was one of the first people known to have died as a result of CIA activity. There may have been others in Germany, Japan, Korea, and the Canal Zone, but what made the Olson case special was that he was an American, uninvolved in espionage and engaged in work *for* the United States, not against it. In addition, as Lawrence Houston noted, his death had serious implications for those concerned about the attitude of Gottlieb and the Technical Services Staff toward human life. It was not simply a question of the risks of scientific experimentation; the experiment had been entirely unscientific and cavalier, and even if Olson had not subsequently committed suicide or complained about being used as a guinea pig, Gottlieb and his superiors should have been aware of the wider implications. The lack of this awareness was demonstrated conclusively when Kirkpatrick's recommendation that they be reprimanded was watered down by Allen Dulles to letters criticizing bad judgment. Even these slaps on the wrist were kept, quite formally, off the record and were not recorded in personnel files.[54]

PLANS AND TOXINS

Seven years later Gottlieb was in Africa on another approved CIA mission to kill Patrice Lumumba, the Congolese nationalist leader, with bacteria that would generate a fatal disease.[55] Before Gottlieb could accomplish his goal the

Congolese leader was captured and killed, probably by his rival, Mobutu. Gottlieb was involved in other attempts to assassinate foreigners; he developed toxins to poison Fidel Castro[56] and impregnated a handkerchief with poison to attempt to kill an Iraqi colonel.[57] Although all these cases involved the use of poisons and drugs, they were considered at that time to be different from Olson's case. They were justified by the fact that their victims were enemies of the United States and that the deaths of these men would prevent greater bloodshed. Looking back on these assassination attempts, Richard Bissell, the deputy director of plans in 1960 to whom Gottlieb reported, remarked: "Killing people is wrong, but it happens, and if someone had polished off Idi Amin it would have saved a lot of people a lot of grief. But at the same time it must be a decision in the hands of people you can trust and who will not take such a decision lightly."[58]

Gottlieb and Bissell at their different levels in the agency did not act alone. They consulted colleagues and were confident that they had presidential sanction. The important point was that they were officers of an agency within which the idea of killing people and manipulating people in the national interest was accepted. Years later, in 1975, one CIA officer deeply involved in the LSD experiments described the climate in which he had worked: "It is awfully hard in this day and age to reproduce how frightening all of this was to us at the time, particularly after the drug scene has become as widespread and as knowledgeable in this country as it did. But we were literally terrified, because this was the one material that we had ever been able to locate that really had potential fantastic possibilities if used wrongly."*

Before these resulting moral and institutional conundrums were faced, the MKUltra programs spawned a firm base for subsequent public paranoia, not only about the nature and purposes of their research and experiments but in the involvement of academia. In its LSD research alone, for example, doctors and medical researchers at Columbia Presbyterian Medical Center and Mount Sinai Hospital in New York, Boston Psychopathic Hospital, the Addiction Research Center in Lexington, Kentucky (Dr. Isbell's center), the University of Rochester, the University of Oklahoma, and the University of Illinois Medical School used CIA funds, channeled to them through the Josiah Macy, Jr., Foundation and the Geschickter Fund for Medical Research, to conduct their experiments. Many researchers did not know that they were working for the CIA, a fact that fueled widespread suspicion of the agency in academic circles during the 1960s and 1970s and sustained the general impression of the agency as a hidden monster.

To ordinary Americans the later perception of a monster at work was subsequently reinforced by the release in the 1970s under Freedom of Information

---

* Joint Hearing, *Project MKUltra*, pp. 72–73. In the late 1940s and early 1950s there were persistent reports that the Soviet Union was engaged in intensive efforts to produce LSD and to purchase the entire world supply of the chemical. The pressure for a "defensive" American program was considerable.

legislation of CIA internal memorandums on the MKUltra, Artichoke, and Bluebird projects. A November 26, 1951, memorandum on Artichoke read:

> When to use "Artichoke." Heretofore it has generally been thought that "Artichoke" or the "Artichoke" techniques should only be used as a last resort or when all other means have failed in a particular problem or series of problems. . . .
> This is not in any sense the only time that "Artichoke" can be used. . . .
> (1) The "Artichoke" techniques could successfully be used immediately upon the development of a case as a starting point for the obtaining of information or as a quick determinant as to what is necessary to be done in a particular problem.
> (2) "Artichoke" could be used at any given point in the development of a case. . . .
> (3) "Artichoke" can always be used as a last resort when all or nearly all the attempts at obtaining information have failed or when a subject is completely recalcitrant or particularly stubborn.[59]

Artichoke merged into Bluebird as the programs developed along similar lines and expanded as more sections of the CIA became involved. The purpose remained the same: to achieve successful brain control at long distances over long periods of time. *The Manchurian Candidate*, the novel and film of the 1950s, and *Telefon*, a 1970s novel and film, accurately portrayed the goals of this program (although ascribing them to KGB agents in America). In *The Manchurian Candidate*, a brainwashed American is triggered to assassinate his father when he sees a certain playing card. In *Telefon*, Soviet agents placed up to twenty years earlier in locations close to important U.S. military installations are triggered by coded telephone calls to perform suicide missions destroying these installations. These brain-control techniques were also viewed by those involved in the Artichoke program as interrogation aids. Early on, this became an added purpose of the program, even though these techniques put life at risk.

This disregard for life was not unusual at the time, since many in the agency considered life a commodity of war. While it was always preferable for foreigners' lives to be at risk, Americans were also involved.* While the CIA's actual techniques were not clear, it is known that they involved drugs, hypnosis, and electric shock. Memorandums written at the time indicate that some had overtones of physical torture:

> "What General Facilities should 'Artichoke' Have in the Field?"
> (A) Ideally, "Artichoke" could best be operated in a hospital or a hospi-

---

* Dr. Isbell's experiments were conducted on blacks, apparently because at that time drug addiction was overwhelmingly a black problem, not because of racial considerations. Sid Gottlieb's experiment with Dr. Olson and others was conducted in part because of the selective group involved in Dr. Isbell's work.

tal-type area. However, this is generally not possible in view of the present attitude of hospital authorities, military or otherwise.

(B) In the event that hospital-type facilities could not be procured, it would then be best to carry out "Artichoke" operations in a safe house or safe area. . . .

(C) For technical reasons, it is best to have two adjoining rooms with a bath also adjoining or very close by. . . .

(D) The adjoining room mentioned above is essential for the setting up of technical equipment, i.e., recording devices, transformers, etc. . . .

(E) The bathroom is essential for two reasons. The first is that the "Artichoke" doctor in handling the case needs water for various purposes, and second is that occasionally the "Artichoke" technique produces nausea, vomiting, or other conditions which make bathroom facilities essential.[60]

This kind of interrogation by Artichoke teams does not appear to have occurred on a large scale, although for years these teams were available both in the United States and abroad.

Sodium pentothal, known in popular fiction as a "truth drug," was tested and used in the Artichoke program, eventually becoming a staple interrogation drug in security services around the world. The drug was first tested in the CIA's Bluebird program during the summer of 1950 under conditions of 90–100-degree heat, extremely high humidity, and no air conditioning. The clinical reports of the tests, which also included experimentation with other chemical solutions, reveal some of what was involved. In the first of six separate tests completed during the experiment,

the drug . . . was sodium amytal intravenously, 5% solution at the rate of 1 cc a minute. The stimulant employed was benzedrine intravenously at the rate of 1 cc a minute plus 10 mg given orally at the completion of the technique. The intravenous injection was begun at 13.32. At 13.42, 9.4 cc had been administered. At 13.45 the Subject was sound asleep. It was possible to arouse him but in order to obtain the exact state desired intravenous benzedrine, as a stimulant, was administered. At 14.05 he was accessible, but his speech was quite thick. . . . The Subject had amnesia as to his conversations under the influence of the medication. The test was regarded as successful.

The second test also used a 5 percent solution of sodium amytal: "The desired effect of the medication was obtained. The Subject was interrogated under simulated enemy conditions and he was quite violent upon occasions during the interrogation as he was convinced that the interrogators were his enemies." Tests three and four involved different amounts of sodium amytal and benzedrine, and the final two tests involved sodium pentothal. In the fifth test, "a 2½% solution [of sodium pentothal] was given intravenously" in conjunction with the stimulant benzedrine:

The medication was effective as to the desired results. It is believed that when this particular drug, sodium pentothal, is used, the method employed in this case is best, that is, after the initial stage of impaired consciousness be produced, it is advisable to give intermittently small amounts of the drug in order to maintain the desired state. When using sodium amytal, however, due to the more prolonged effect, it is not so necessary to inter-space minute doses in this way. The advantage of sodium pentothal is that it is much easier to have the man back in his normal state in a comparatively short time but it is not certain that the amnesia will be as definite as in the use of the longer acting drug. In this particular case, amnesia for the interrogation was produced. Also sodium pentothal is slightly more dangerous than sodium amytal in the more rapid production of respiratory failure.[61]

The sixth test used sodium pentothal in conjunction with the stimulant Coramine. In all the tests, stimulants were necessary to counter the depressive effects of the sodium amytal and pentothal, keeping the effect of the drugs in balance. Although the dangers to life were recognized, the agency decided that the risks were worth it. However, it also decided to subject only foreigners, many of whom were known or suspected of being Soviet agents or double agents, to the experiments. If these drugs were to be used at a later time, it was thought by those involved that the interrogation subjects would probably be Soviet agents or defectors. The original testing of sodium amytal and sodium pentothal was probably conducted at the CIA's Canal Zone base, and the CIA was aware that any future use of these drugs would have to take place outside the United States to avoid breaking U.S. laws.

Different interrogation techniques came under careful CIA scrutiny during the early 1950s, partially in reaction to McCarthy's red scare, the revelations of widespread Russian spying, and what were seen as agency intelligence failures during the Korean War. Interrogation linked to intelligence information and security was of special interest in the atmosphere of security paranoia generated by the Rosenbergs, Burgess, Maclean, and Philby. One Bluebird/Artichoke study in 1951 exemplified these attitudes:

Our principal goal remains the same as it was in the beginning: the investigation of drug effects on ego control and volitional activities, i.e., can willfully-suppressed information be elicited through the aid of drugs affecting higher nervous centers? If so, which agents are better for this purpose? What are the initial signs and symptoms of drug effects? Can these be recognized by the subject or observers? We now add to these the following: Can these signs and symptoms be taught to security officers so that they can detect the use of such agents in themselves or others? Practical purposes of this study are to gain information which will permit us to detect what work of a similar nature may be in progress in enemy hands (to be judged in escaped or returned prisoners).[62]

Studies also attempted to develop antidotes to truth drugs; to learn how to guard against infiltration by people whose brains might be controlled by others (as in *The Manchurian Candidate* and *Telefon*); and to protect people in possession of important information from giving that information away without being aware of what they were doing. In retrospect we can see how much these studies were linked to the realities of the times: American and other United Nations servicemen captured by the North Koreans and Chinese in Korea were subjected to brainwashing techniques that, in one case at least, may have resulted in the placement of an important communist spy in British intelligence: George Blake. The agency's worries about "ego control and volitional activities" were not misplaced, although the extremes to which CIA experiments were taken without doubt were.

Largely because of General MacArthur's criticisms of the CIA, the public was convinced that the intelligence failures to predict the start of the Korean War and Red China's subsequent entry into the war were the agency's fault. In May 1951 MacArthur claimed that the CIA had told him that Red China would not intervene in the war. President Truman flatly contradicted MacArthur, stating in public that in November 1950 the agency warned of the danger of a Chinese attack across the Yalu River.[63] Although the agency needed the President's support far more than MacArthur's, its public image was damaged by the incident. In December 1950 *Time* magazine reported that a passage from Shakespeare was being quoted in military circles to denigrate the CIA. This passage almost certainly came from MacArthur, probably the only U.S. general sufficiently familiar with Shakespeare to quote him:

King John:	How goes all in France?
Messenger:	From France to England never such a power for any foreign preparations was levied in the body of a land. The copy of your speed is learn'd by them; for when you should be told they do prepare, the tidings come that they are all arrived.
King John:	Oh, where hath our intelligence been drunk? Where hath it slept?[64]

What was not publicly known at the time was that Burgess and Maclean might have played a part in Red China's decision to enter the war.

Within the CIA the defection of Burgess and Maclean and the certainty that Kim Philby was also a Soviet agent acted as a spur to the Bluebird/Artichoke programs. Suspected Soviet use of mind-altering drugs helped explain willingness of these British agents to spy for Russia. With the Korean War on, brain-control techniques had a real purpose: to detect Soviet agents still under cover and to place brain-controlled U.S. spies in the communist world. Faced by the problem of having dangerous spies at the heart of the Anglo-American alliance, the CIA was doing its best, through the Bluebird, Artichoke, and

MKUltra programs, to detect and counteract them and to create spies of its own.

THE MIGHTY WURLITZER

The Korean War led the agency farther down the paramilitary and covert-operations road traveled first by Donovan's OSS and then by Frank Wisner's Office of Policy Coordination. The agency's definition of covert operations was straightforward enough: "Any clandestine operation or activity designed to influence foreign governments, organizations, persons or events in support of the United States' foreign policy."[65] It was used, however, in combination with the 1947 National Security Act and the 1949 Central Intelligence Agency Act, to indulge in all sorts of activities, not all of them straightforward. The effort to influence the 1948 Italian election was the first major covert operation, closely followed by the Albanian operation with the British. In 1950, some months before the North Korean attack on South Korea, the agency established a base in Formosa/Taiwan, under the guise of a company called Western Enterprises, Inc., to train Nationalist Chinese guerrillas for raids on the communist-controlled mainland.[66] At the same time, major financial subsidies were paid to the anticommunist cultural organization known as the Congress for Cultural Freedom and to the Center for International Studies at the Massachusetts Institute of Technology.[67]

In 1951 the agency began tapping telephones in the United States in an attempt to find the source of leaks of classified information. Over the following fourteen years it monitored the conversations of twenty-one people, all but two of whom were or had been CIA employees.[68] Financial support at this time was given to West German labor unions through the good offices of Walter Reuther, head of the United Auto Workers Union, and his brother Victor, a resident of West Germany.[69] Starting in 1952, key individuals in foreign governments, including pro-Western politicians, military men, and civil servants also received large-scale CIA support.[70] In 1952 the National Student Association started receiving CIA funds, which ultimately totaled $3.3 million before ending in 1966.[71] Radio Free Europe and Radio Liberty, which started in 1950 and 1951 respectively, beamed news and propaganda into eastern Europe from bases in western Europe. Although technically privately managed and owned, these radio networks received the vast bulk of their $30–$35 million a year combined budgets from the CIA.[72]

Following the tradition started by Donovan, paramilitary special operations were encouraged in this period as well. On November 9, 1952, two CIA agents were captured in China, where they were attempting to lead and organize anticommunist guerrilla bands.[73] For three years, starting in 1950, Colonel Edward Lansdale, on loan to the agency from the air force, led a team of advisers to the Philippines and successfully helped the Philippine leader,

Ramón Magsaysay, overcome the communist-backed Huk guerrillas.[74] In Korea itself, as the war progressed, CIA agents mirrored many of the activities of their OSS predecessors.

General Douglas MacArthur's well known antipathy toward civilian intelligence agencies (during World War II, he effectively excluded the OSS from the Pacific Theater) was still a problem for the CIA in 1950 with the advent of the Korean War. However, after Shanghai fell to the communists in 1949, the CIA moved to Japan where a reluctant MacArthur, as allied governor of Japan and U.S. military commander in the Far East, agreed that the CIA could operate in his command area. Hans Tofte, a Dane who escaped Nazi-occupied Europe in 1940, had enlisted in the British Army, rising to the rank of major in India. He then resigned his commission to join the OSS, in which he organized support for anti-Nazi guerrillas in the Balkans, joined OPC in 1950, and was sent to Japan to organize CIA operations in the Far East. With headquarters near Tokyo, Tofte and his team of six agents set up an escape and evasion system for airmen shot down over Korea and the Sea of Japan. It involved occupying two islands and manning them with CIA personnel; placing agents across Korea who could act as guides and provide hideouts for lost airmen, and report information by radio and code to headquarters; using fleets of small boats for the same purposes, under cover of smuggling and black market operations; briefing pilots on procedures and escape techniques; and securing $700,000 in gold bars for downed airmen to use as bribes and payments in gold-conscious Korea.

Tofte's operation was multifaceted and complex and had even greater ramifications. It found and trained guerrillas to operate in North Korea; debriefed returned airmen and captured North Koreans (in the process, Bluebird and Artichoke methods were probably tested); and used the old OSS Flying Tiger squadron, now incorporated in the CIA-owned company, Civil Air Transport, as a private air force based in Japan and Korea to support and carry out some CIA operations.* Driven by the impetus of war, CIA activities

---

* Civil Air Transport (CAT) was started by Major General Claire L. Chennault and Whiting Willauer acting in a private capacity, with the support of the Nationalist Chinese government of Chiang Kai-shek and the United Nations Relief and Rehabilitation Administration. Willauer had worked for Chennault in the Far East during the war, and his personal financial and legal contacts in New York helped back the project. It was conceived as an effort to withstand communist advances in China in 1946 at the time when the debate about a central intelligence agency and how to respond to the Soviet threat (seen as including Mao Tse-tung's forces in China) was unresolved.

The origins of CAT highlight the divergence between public American policy, which in Truman's first year was directed toward establishing a harmonious world order, and the conviction of many powerful and influential men that Truman's policy was misconceived and that the United States would have to take steps to counter Soviet encroachments worldwide. In many ways the Office of Policy Coordination came out of this "private" effort. For the story of CAT, see William M. Leary, *Perilous Missions: Civil Air Transport and CIA Operations in Asia* (University, AL: University of Alabama Press, 1984).

Chennault and Willauer sold CAT to OPC for $950,000. (For the details of CAT ownership, see ibid., pp. 109–112.) When the CIA liquidated CAT in 1973, the U.S. Treasury received about $30 million in net receipts. "That was one of our more successful business ventures," said

stretched into China, Manchuria, and the Russian naval base at Vladivostok. These "closed" areas were successfully penetrated with Korean and Chinese CIA agents. Psychological-warfare methods used during World War II were revived, and Tofte even made a commercially successful Japanese propaganda film to incite anti-Soviet feelings in Japan. Korean and Chinese communications were intercepted and their codes broken, giving United Nations commanders accurate information about enemy plans. A Norwegian freighter carrying medical supplies to North Korea was pirated in a joint CIA/Nationalist Chinese operation.*

Colorful and successful operations won the agency growing respect in Washington and in military circles. The range of activities involved also demonstrated the enormously varied work of the agency and its ability to grow rapidly and flexibly. OPC, responsible for many of the headline-grabbing operations of the agency at this time, was justifiably described by Frank Wisner as "the mighty Wurlitzer": it could play military and diplomatic tunes; it could mount operations, control newspapers, influence opinion. These characteristics made the Office of Policy Coordination a microcosm of the CIA itself; its varied staff and activities as diverse as guerrilla fighting and the analysis of academic journals gave it a reputation as a multifaceted organization. By mid-1953, after the OPC-OSO merger into the Directorate of Plans, the new clandestine service group was spending almost $200 million annually.[75]

Bedell Smith had realized one of the central factors governing the agency's life: really important intelligence only rarely came from clandestine activities, but it was clandestine activities that caught the imagination and attention of the agency's political masters in the White House and Congress. By understanding and catering to this preoccupation the agency would benefit in terms of both prestige and financial appropriations. Victor Marchetti, who spent fourteen years in the CIA, the last four in the office of the director of Central Intelligence before leaving in 1969, reflected on this point: "Once I got upstairs and started working for Helms, I found out how the agency really

Lawrence Houston, who had been instrumental in setting up OPC/CIA's ownership of CAT in 1950. "We had all sorts of other operations backed by corporate structures—it might have been almost a notional one, a name on a door, or a corporate structure for which we picked directors from outside and lawyers to represent them who were all thoroughly briefed on what this was about and what the objects were and who fitted the operation into their corporate bases" (interview, Lawrence Houston, November 9, 1983). For an example of this, see pp. 600–603 on the *Glomar Explorer*, a CIA ship built and operated by Howard Hughes's Summa Corporation.

* Interview, Hans Tofte, July 15, 1983. Joseph C. Goulden, *Korea–The Untold Story of the War* (New York: McGraw-Hill, 1982), pp. 462–475, gives a glowing account of Tofte's exploits. Others say Tofte's account is overblown. *Final Report*, I, p. 145, indicates that the CIA's activities during the Korean War were not altogether successful: most operations never came to fruition, and $152 million worth of foreign weapons and ammunition were acquired for use by guerrilla groups that never existed. However, the point was not wholly whether particular operations succeeded or not but that the agency saw itself as being properly involved in such a range of activities and was seen in Washington and in military circles as being properly involved.

works. I found out that one boasted of intelligence but what rings the cash registers is clandestine operations, and within clandestine operations it isn't spying: it's covert action—overthrowing governments; manipulating governments; doing this, that, and the other, including assassinations. And in order to achieve these goals, anything goes. I could see how it worked. I was dealing with Congress and the White House."[76]

Marchetti became disaffected with the agency, and five years after leaving, with a journalist, John D. Marks, he published a major exposé of the CIA called *The CIA and the Cult of Intelligence*. The book caused a furor among Marchetti's old colleagues, many of whom had not realized the extent of the CIA's operations or that suborning foreign officials and plotting assassinations had a basis in fact. The book was published at the time of greatest popular indignation with the secret activities of government—during the withdrawal from Vietnam and the start of various congressional investigations into the CIA. Although it was written with a clear purpose to expose and with a sense of moral outrage that the United States should be involved in dirty work, there was a strong indication that it was also accurate. Before the book was published the agency demanded the deletion of 339 passages; a court agreed that 168 passages should be cut. Both the agency action and the court reaction suggested that Marchetti knew his facts. If he had written fiction, the agency would have had little cause for concern.

As a result of the exploits of men such as Tofte and the strengthening of cooperation between the agency and the military brought about by the Korean War, the standing and influence of the covert-action side of the CIA increased throughout the 1950s and was periodically revitalized by additional anticommunist operations. After the Korean War the communist menace was perceived in more general and worldwide terms. It was no longer believed that communism was a threat to only those geographic areas bordering China and the USSR. The CIA changed its operations and attitudes in accordance with this new perception. Its emphasis began to shift from Europe and from crisis management to a worldwide effort to forestall and contain what was seen as communist aggression. In some ways this represented a return to the early days of the agency, when concern about the possible results of the May 1948 Italian elections had prompted anticommunist covert operations starting nearly a year earlier.[77]

OPC/OSO

The first steps in this new effort were taken in October 1950 with OPC coming fully under CIA control. On October 21, 1951, National Security Council Directive 10/5 replaced the earlier 10/2 directive as the basis for the agency's covert actions. Clearly prompted by the requirements of the Korean

War, this new directive provided the agency with the authority to conduct covert activity on a larger scale. Few budgetary constraints limited the agency's ability to meet the ever-increasing demand for intelligence information.[78] The agency's research and analysis operation was reorganized to meet this demand, concentrating on communist nations. The Office of Research and Reports grew from 461 staffers in July 1951 to 766 in February 1953; because of the Korean War, covert operations increased sixteenfold between January 1951 and January 1953, with OSO doubling in personnel size to about 1200 and OPC growing to about 6000 in the same period.[79] On the analytical side, economic intelligence was instituted with the formation of the Economic Intelligence Committee, a subcommittee of the Intelligence Advisory Committee. The job of this committee was to produce reports that used the best available foreign economic information. Its methods were similar to those used to prepare and scrutinize National Intelligence Estimates. By the end of 1953 there were 3338 people in the Directorate of Intelligence as a whole.[80]

On the covert side, the organizational structure always reflected the character and interests of Allen Dulles, who served first as deputy director of plans (in effect the number-two spot in the agency under Bedell Smith), then, beginning in January 1951, as the deputy director for Central Intelligence (the official number-two spot), and, finally, as director, from 1953 until 1961. Dulles was known inside the agency as "The Great White Case Officer," because of his interest in clandestine activities and covert operations. As DDI he often spent hours debating and monitoring operational details with operatives, letting appointments slip by, much to the annoyance of the agency's analytical staff, who correctly perceived that Dulles was not really interested in research and analysis. Dulles also failed to provide the agency with the precise, organized policy direction it needed to fill in the broad objectives set forth by the National Security Council in both NSC 10/2 and NSC 10/5. These directives stated in bold terms the necessity for meeting the Soviet challenge head on but failed to specify how this should be done.

Divergent demands pulled at the covert side of the CIA as well. Despite the merger with OSO, OPC people were geared to the needs of the State and Defense departments and allowed these departments more say in operations than OSO people. The State Department had encouraged political action and propaganda activity; the Defense Department had tended to think in terms of paramilitary and guerrilla operations. OSO people, on the other hand, were geared to secret intelligence, espionage, and counterespionage. Dulles' temperament had fueled competition between the two offices, so that at the time of their merger in the Directorate of Plans, pet projects and madcap schemes abounded, Tom Braden recalled:

> The big thing that was occupying everybody's mind was how to merge the CIA and the OPC. Frank Wisner had been ordered to leave the State Department, where he was running OPC, and come over and run the OPC

inside the CIA. When Allen Dulles came in as the number-two man under Bedell Smith, Frank was disappointed, because Frank thought that as head of OPC he ought to be named the deputy director of plans. He wasn't, and Allen was put in over his head.

The general flavor in the agency, reflecting back on some conversations with Allen and some things he said, was "We have to get hold of OPC"; that "Wisner was running wild"; that he had operations going on that were not any good; that he had hired a lot of people who were flamboyant but risky. There were two guys, they were both working for Wisner, and they went down to Madison Avenue and Forty-second Street in New York, got a drill bit, roped the area off, drilled a helluva hole in Madison Avenue, and walked off! I think they were just showing how versatile they were. It was prankster stuff.

But there were more serious breaches of what people thought a responsible agency should do. One of the chief of these—I remember Allen talking about this, I remember Bedell Smith blowing his top about it—had to do with an army in Burma. Wisner had okayed it, and in charge was an army colonel. I just happened to be going up to see Allen Dulles one day when I heard the most violent tongue-lashing being delivered through the door next door—this was down at the old headquarters in O Street—Bedell Smith roaring. He had picked up a *New York Times* that morning, and there was a story about this army in Burma, and Bedell was vastly disturbed by it, and he fired the colonel on the spot with much invective and sergeant's language. The colonel went down the hall in tears—I saw him. Later I heard Bedell had sent after him and apologized for his rudeness, but the colonel did indeed quit the agency at that point, asking Bedell if he could, in lieu of an apology, have a battalion in Korea, and Bedell arranged that instantly, so he went off to be a colonel in Korea.*

If covert operations were going to be a fact of life, Bedell Smith had determined that they should be tightly controlled and professionally conducted. For

---

* Interview, Tom Braden, November 14, 1983. In 1951 the Burma army was recruited from Chiang Kai-shek's Chinese Nationalist Army in Taiwan and paid for by OPC. The soldiers were transported to northern Burma to mount guerrilla raids into China. The probable reason for Bedell Smith's anger was that Wisner may not have informed him of the operation, since it was at a time when OPC was still pushing for bureaucratic independence. It could also have been because news leaked out. President Truman had refused Chiang Kai-shek's offer to participate in the Korean War because he was anxious to contain communism without ending up in another world war. Along with Dean Acheson, he considered that Chiang Kai-shek's involvement could well expand the war and force America to defend Taiwan while its own troops were engaged in Korea. Thus by using Nationalist Chinese troops in Burma, OPC was risking exactly what Truman wanted to avoid. In addition, it was risking Burmese neutrality. Fortunately these fears were never realized and the "ChiNat 'Li Mi'" operation, as it was known (after the Chinese general/war lord/opium trader Li Mi, in command of the army), did not result in an expansion of the Korean War or in a diplomatic incident. Li Mi's army never fought successfully; it rapidly became a drug-producing operation instead. OPC could never admit this, and for years afterward, even after the OSO-OPC merger, CIA personnel hatched elaborate plans for the army, knowing full well they were engaged in nonsense but not prepared to jeopardize careers and bureaucratic position by admitting to so monumental a mistake.

this reason he had forced the merger of OSO and OPC before he left the agency and Allen Dulles succeeded him.

The pranks and serious excesses within covert-action operations were very much a symptom of the emergency sense of the period. David Atlee Phillips, who worked as a CIA agent in South America in the early 1950s before joining the agency as an officer in 1954, remembered one particular prank. One day in early 1955 he was walking down the corridor of K Building, one of the wartime prefabricated huts along the reflecting pool in Washington, DC, where the CIA was housed. A colleague stopped him, waving a memorandum:

> "I've got it! I've got it!" he shouted, thrusting the paper in my face. "The greatest psychological warfare operation in history! The Soviets will never recover. Russian morale will plummet, never to be restored. The Communist system will totter!"
>
> I read the title of the memorandum: OPERATION PENIS ENVY.
>
> With fantastic ardor, he explained his scheme. "First, we make millions of contraceptives! Condoms!"
>
> I was aghast. "CIA will manufacture condoms?"
>
> "Yes," he said, eyes gleaming. "Rubbers. Millions and millions. Not just ordinary ones, but giant-sized. Immense!" He spread his hands in the gesture fishermen use to describe the one that got away.
>
> "Rubbers four feet long?" I stammered.
>
> "Exactly. Then we drop them all over the Soviet Union. Planes flying everywhere, from St. Petersburg to Vladivostok! We'll drop them by the millions!"
>
> "You are totally demented," I said. "What possible good will that do?"
>
> "Oh, it's not the rubbers." He leaned toward me, his eyes wide with enthusiasm. "It's the propaganda—it's what we will say. You see, on each one will be printed in Russian:
>
> MADE IN USA, MEDIUM SIZE!"
>
> Shaken, I returned to the office. . . . Len laughed. "He's kidding. It's his standard performance for newcomers. He's really a brilliant guy, just a little bored. He has a lot of fun with that act."[81]

John M. Maury, a senior agency officer who was chief of the Soviet Division in the Directorate of Plans in the early 1960s, chief of station in Greece, and then the agency's legislative counsel before retiring in the mid-1970s, identified the concern of the agency's cool professionals about covert action:

> In the early Fifties there was much talk about how something called the "international Communist conspiracy" had been the main instrument for spreading Soviet influence throughout Eastern Europe and paving the way for Communist takeovers in other parts of the world. Accordingly, it was suggested by eminent Washington statesmen that we should fight fire with fire and develop a subversive capability of our own which would roll back the Iron Curtain to prewar Soviet frontiers, and perhaps stimulate nationalist up-

risings among the peoples of the Baltic States, Byelorussia, and the Ukraine. The late Chip Bohlen has noted the fallacy in this thesis by pointing out that the Kremlin has not gained effective control of a foot of territory since 1917 without the use or threat of superior force, and that covert action, while a useful supplement to overt military and diplomatic measures, can never be a substitute for them. In the early days of the Agency, however, a general failure to appreciate this point led to a certain amount of excessive and romantic zeal, and a corresponding amount of concern and suspicion among those who feared that ill-considered political action ventures might get out of hand.[82]

In many ways the covert-action staff's idealized view of itself was personified by Desmond FitzGerald. He was one of OPC's Far East specialists, charming, wealthy, and well connected, coming from the same Irish-American Boston background as the Kennedys (he was a personal friend of Robert F. Kennedy). From early on he was the agency's senior spokesman for agents in the field. He was a diplomatic proponent of the "can-do" philosophy that characterized CIA operations right into the 1970s. During the Korean War, manpower and energies were concentrated in the Directorate of Plans' Far East Division under Colonel Richard Stilwell, with FitzGerald as his executive officer. When Stilwell left the agency to take up an army command in Korea, FitzGerald in practice ran the division, and eventually became its head after the OSO-OPC merger. "Don't be so wet," he said to a relatively inexperienced subordinate who wondered about the ethics of some operation during the Vietnam War in the 1960s. This classic preppy put-down revealed the drive that possessed him and many of the covert-action staff.[83]

FitzGerald was one of the agency's highfliers, rising to become deputy director of plans in 1965, only to die of a heart attack two years later. He made his name in the early 1950s, smoothly organizing a multitude of covert operations during the Korean War from the CIA base in Taiwan, which itself had more than six hundred operatives providing guerrilla training, support facilities, aircraft reconnaissance, radio broadcasting, and propaganda activity of all kinds. First as deputy head and then as head of the Far East Division based in Taiwan, FitzGerald established good working relationships with another CIA highflier from the other side of the house, the chief in Taipei, Ray Cline.[84]

Cline's career in the agency was unusual. Before World War II he had won a scholarship to study history at Harvard, and from there had won a fellowship to Oxford University. Returning to America in 1940, he went back to postgraduate work at Harvard and the following year was elected a junior fellow in the university's Society of Fellows, along with Arthur Schlesinger, Jr., and McGeorge Bundy, later President Kennedy's national security adviser. He was an intellectual, but he also had an activist streak that in 1943 led him to the OSS. There, using his Harvard connections, he joined the Office of Current Intelligence in the R&A branch, ending as chief of current intelligence.

He returned to academic history after the war, coming back into intelligence in 1949 when he joined the CIA. At first he continued on the analytical side, but after becoming an assistant to Dulles, he was increasingly attracted to covert operations. Being appointed station chief without an operations background was noteworthy, and he was one of the very few people in the agency who had real experience in working on both sides of the house. In 1962 he returned to Washington and was appointed deputy director of intelligence.

JUST WARS

During the 1950s the major long-term project of the Far East Division was to keep communists from power in the Philippines. The project started with a short, sharp success that was to have enormous repercussions on the pattern of CIA operations. Lieutenant Colonel Edward G. Lansdale was sent to Manila as chief of OPC in the area in 1950, under the cover of being an adviser to the Philippine army but in reality to develop an effective counter to the burgeoning communist Hukbalahap insurgency, which began in 1948. The Huks were founded in 1942 as a "people's army" to fight against the Japanese, but unlike other anti-Japanese guerrillas, they refused to surrender their arms to the Philippine government when the war ended. By 1950 they controlled most of the countryside in central Luzon and even part of Manila. Lansdale devised a sophisticated combination of military, political, and psychological measures to defeat the Huks, centering on his identification of Congressman Ramón Magsaysay as a decent and honest alternative to communists on the left and corrupt politicians who had cooperated with the Japanese during the occupation. He advised Magsaysay personally and "provided him imaginative political counsel and other forms of Agency help"[85] in the form of money, propaganda leaflets, posters, and broadcasts. This was essentially the same sort of help that had been provided to De Gasperi and the centrist political parties in Italy in 1948. In this situation Americans had the added advantage of being looked upon as liberators and friends. By putting himself firmly behind Magsaysay, Lansdale identified the Filipino with American prestige and success.

On August 31, 1950, Magsaysay was named secretary of national defense of the Republic of the Philippines. In close cooperation with Lansdale and the CIA, Magsaysay went on to launch an effective military and psychological campaign against the Huks that made him a national hero long before the presidential elections in 1953. The Huks were offered the alternatives of relentless war or economic well-being in the form of resettlement and property ownership. CIA analysis was that the Huks would give up only if they were offered something they wanted more than the satisfaction they obtained from resisting authority from their base in the hills. Magsaysay himself realized the effectiveness of this approach, being the son of a blacksmith who had risen from poverty. "If a farmer owns his own piece of property," he used to say, "he will resist anyone who tries to take it away from him."[86] With Lansdale, he instituted an Economic Development Corps, through which Huks who surrendered were given a tract of land, a house, tools, seeds, and a cash loan to be repaid over a five-year term.

George Aurell, who took over as Far East Division chief in 1952 just after the OPC-OSO merger, could never understand Lansdale's methods. One CIA operative in Washington at the time remembered that Aurell "never felt comfortable about any of this. He used to come over to our Plans office and unburden himself. . . . 'What in hell is an intelligence agency doing running a rural resettlement program?' he used to ask. 'I'm glad to help fight the Huks, but is it our job to rebuild a nation?' "[87]

Lansdale, FitzGerald, and Allen Dulles were satisfied that rebuilding nations was part of the CIA's job. The finesse of Lansdale's approach, however, lay in his allowing the people of the country to do the job themselves, with Americans directing and helping from a back seat. Aurell and—as events were to show—many others in the agency had a cruder philosophy of blasting and destroying their opposition. They were more interested in securing victories in military terms than in political or psychological ones. Nation-building sounds grandiose now, but it did not then to the "big" thinkers. Serious people saw the stricken world as needing gluing together again, and if the United States did not do it, someone else would, and the world might have to endure decades of further suffering. Allen Dulles, presiding over the agency's involvement with world affairs, was harnessing it to the perceptions of the time.

Lansdale and his team, while being sophisticated about popular support, did not think they could win without some fighting. As the 1953 presidential elections in the Philippines approached, Magsaysay was encouraged to use the Philippine army to attack the Huks as well as to protect the resettlement program, support for which was nonexistent outside the Department of Defense. The technique of working through second and third parties was developed by Lansdale in the Philippines into a high art of counterinsurgency, becoming a feature of CIA methodology. Philippine army units were even disguised as Huks at times, attacking villages, so as to generate more support for the government and greater resistance to the Huk appeal.[88] At the same time, Magsaysay's political message was refined. Filipinos were told that a change was needed: their country could not survive in freedom without some economic reform. This could be done—the resettlement program provided a model—and the country could become an example of democracy in action for the other nations of Southeast Asia to follow. Two public organizations were formed to help carry this message to the electorate: the National Movement for Free Elections, supported by CIA funds and various pro-Magsaysay civic groups, and the Magsaysay for President movement. By the time the election took place in September 1953, Magsaysay had achieved real popularity among Filipinos for his success in fighting the Huks and in dealing with the rural conditions that had contributed to Huk appeal.

Magsaysay's victory was hailed by *The New York Times* as making the Philippines "the showcase of democracy in Asia," and President Eisenhower was quoted as declaring, "This is the way we like to see an election carried out."[89] Lansdale and his team viewed this as public tribute to their effort and working methods. They were to go on and apply them in Vietnam next, beginning the major policy decision of the United States to take over from the old empires in Southeast Asia rather than ally itself with the burgeoning nationalist and independence movements identified as the major new force in the area by CIA analysts during preceding years. It was also to herald a continuance of the shift in attention away from Europe and toward the East.

The change from concentration on Europe came about in part because Europe was rapidly becoming more organized, secure, and stable. In part it was because of Soviet and Chinese advances elsewhere, and partly it was because more and more was being found to need attention: a politician here, a newspaper there, a labor union, a student organization. Through its involvement in the monitoring and the operations that flowed from this discovery, the CIA was globalized. It was responding to a widening view in Washington, as well as to bureaucratic imperatives. (Its job was to engage with the outside world at all levels, so it engaged.) The Directorate of Plans spearheaded much of this involvement.

By 1953 Frank Wisner's agents stationed in Europe had also achieved some notable successes. They had recruited a host of influential secret informants, including a Soviet police chief in the Russian Zone of occupied Austria, a monsignor in the Vatican, a French cabinet minister, and the mistress of a senior aide to Marshal Tito of Yugoslavia. However, efforts to secure and place agents behind the iron curtain in the Soviet Union and in the occupied countries of eastern Europe generally had failed. These failures prompted not only the Bluebird, Artichoke, and eventually MKUltra projects but also a serious effort on the part of the Office of Policy Coordination to establish what amounted to private armies of émigré Ukrainian, Polish, Rumanian, and Bulgarian groups for possible armed missions.

OPC sent agents into the Soviet Union and eastern Europe by sea, land, and air from Norway, Sweden, Finland, Germany, Greece, Iran, Turkey, and Japan, all with the mission of setting up networks and reporting on military and political affairs in the Soviet Union and the Soviet bloc. None of these agents met with any long-term success, and many were arrested soon after their arrival, either never to be heard from again or else to be used as players in the classic double-cross system developed by the British during World War II. As a result of Soviet success in turning some agents as well as OPC tendencies to revert to World War II OSS-style methods under the pressure of constant demands from Washington for information, ambitious paramilitary operations were also conducted, the most serious of which took place in Poland.

In the summer of 1950 Poland seemed to U.S. defense strategists to be one of the weakest elements in the Soviet system. Hundreds of thousands of Poles had elected to remain in the West after 1945 rather than return to a communist-controlled Poland. Also, after 1945 thousands more emigrated or fled to the West, bringing with them all sorts of information about conditions in the country and about anticommunists still there. Using such connections, contact was made by OPC with two émigré Polish nationalist organizations, the Polish Political Council in London and the Freedom and Independence movement (known as WIN from its Polish initials). WIN claimed substantial support and an organization within Poland. The CIA was unable to check this claim effectively because agents sent in were quickly captured by the authorities. Those who were not caught provided some confirmation of WIN's claims. Despite the uncertainties, Wisner decided to persevere with WIN, and money, arms, ammunition, and radios were secretly airdropped to WIN groups in Poland. During 1951 WIN claimed to be advancing steadily toward becoming an effective fighting force able to delay the Soviet advance into western Europe that was considered to be even more likely with the advent of the Korean War. By 1952 WIN was asking for more and more support, claiming 500 active and 20,000 partially active members, as well as 100,000 others who would be ready for service in the event of war.[90] They even asked that an American general be sent to help them organize.

What Wisner and his colleagues did not realize was that by mid-1947 the Polish security forces had penetrated WIN completely and turned some of its leaders, although its representatives in the West did not know this. Polish radio revealed the full extent of the fiasco on December 27, 1952, providing the Soviets with a major propaganda coup. To some of those involved it was the end of an effort to make the Russians do something in Poland to counter WIN which would provide further anti-Soviet propaganda. It was another demonstration that lives were a commodity of the cold war. "Many entered CIA so soon after World War II, which was regarded as a 'just' war," said David Atlee Phillips, "that they didn't worry too much if civilians were killed in the process. This feeling remained in CIA for a long time afterwards. We were soldiers in a 'just' war."[91]

The sense of being engaged in a "just" war permeated U.S. government thinking, preventing some lessons from being learned. The failure of WIN did not stop the encouragement of wholly unjustified hopes among European émigré and refugee groups. The determination with which the governing groupings had so recently accepted the challenge of global competition and confrontation with the Soviet Union meant that setbacks would not be allowed to interfere with policy. Enthusiasm was not yet touched by disappointment.

The lesson of WIN was badly learned by the agency and by Washington generally. The November 1952 American presidential election campaign had been marked by extremely belligerent anticommunist talk on the part of Eisenhower and Richard M. Nixon, his running mate. By publicizing the WIN affair, Moscow no doubt sought to demonstrate to the new President that if he really hoped for military resistance to communist governments in eastern Europe, he had better think again. It also shocked the proponents of paramilitary operations in the CIA and the National Security Council, especially since the WIN collapse coincided with the last radio messages from CIA-trained operators in the Ukraine. Lists of émigrés willing to fight the Soviets in the event of war were kept up for some years, but eventually even those were abandoned. But the real lesson—that the United States was not prepared to launch a war to liberate eastern Europe—was not recognized by those who hoped to benefit from it. It would take uprisings in East Berlin and Hungary before European hopes of paramilitary action sponsored by the CIA or of straightforward military action by the United States were finally dashed.

—8—

The Wounded Peace
1953–1956

By 1953 three major changes had taken place in Washington. First, Dwight D. Eisenhower had been elected President; he was the first Republican to grace the White House since Herbert Hoover had taken office twenty years earlier. Even though Eisenhower was an adopted Republican rather than a staunch party man, his election signified the second major change: the acceptance by the American electorate of the Republican party as forward-looking, no longer isolationist, with a belligerent anticommunist attitude. This unmistakable message was put to the American public during the 1952 presidential election campaign by Eisenhower, Nixon, and, in a cautious way, by John Foster Dulles, the new secretary of state. The third major change was the appointment of Allen Dulles, John Foster's brother, as director of Central Intelligence, replacing General Walter Bedell Smith, who became undersecretary of state.

Eisenhower played a key role in all these changes. Indeed, despite the popular perception that his presidency was run by an "Ike-Dulles" team, Eisenhower dominated not only the personalities of his administration but also the policies. "I would say that the three agencies in Washington that really find it very hard to work if they feel they are out of the President's eye are the Joint Chiefs, the CIA, and the State Department," McGeorge Bundy, later to be Kennedy's intelligence adviser, has observed. "They like to be in the main line of presidential favor. When we came in, I would say that Allen put great stock in having direct access to the President."[1] Eisenhower understood the importance of bureaucratic pecking orders and privileges, and as President he paid close attention to his appointments.

Like other Presidents who had actually overseen combat, Eisenhower had no wish to enter another war. In this respect his policies were traditionally Republican; it had been the Democrats, not the Republicans, who brought America into World War II and Korea. Refusing to enter an all-out arms race with the Soviet Union, he chose instead to concentrate fiscal resources on maintaining U.S. preparedness. He placed special emphasis on elite forces such as the Strategic Air Command, which could carry out a massive nuclear retaliation if the country were attacked. To use the language of the time, he wanted "more bang for the buck."

John Foster Dulles had played a leading part in Eisenhower's election campaign, taking full advantage of the Korean conflict to speak about the "liberation" of eastern Europe rather than the mere "containment" of communism. However, Dulles' actions as secretary of state were more cautious than his words. While he spoke about a foreign policy that would take the United States to the brink of war but not to war itself, he actually negotiated Soviet withdrawal from eastern Austria in 1955 and developed a series of military and economic pacts linking the United States to Spain (1953) and forming the Southeast Asia Treaty Organization (1954). In April 1955 he also helped negotiate the Baghdad Pact, leading to the Central Treaty Organization in 1959, although the United States never officially acceded to either. However, the art of "brinkmanship," as it was known in the press, depended upon forceful negotiation, and this is where the Central Intelligence Agency came in. The CIA played a crucial role both as the other voice of U.S. foreign policy and as the arm of hidden force with which the United States could take direct action without the overt use of its uniformed services. By involving the CIA as closely as possible in the implementation of U.S. policy, John Foster Dulles could keep options open and the Soviets guessing. With Allen as director, he could be certain of using the agency as a finely tuned instrument to achieve foreign-policy goals.

Walter Bedell Smith did not want to leave his post as director of Central Intelligence. By all accounts it was a job he enjoyed and was extremely good at. His departure as DCI was anticipated because of his ill health and not simply because a new President was coming in. There was already a strong sense that the position of director should be on a par with that of director of the FBI, a position J. Edgar Hoover had already held under three Presidents and through six elections before Eisenhower, establishing the tradition that the leadership of the FBI was above party politics. There was a very strong move within the agency to secure Donovan's appointment as Smith's successor, but it came to nothing for two reasons. First, John Foster wanted his brother, Allen, in the job, and Allen wanted the job too. From his position of power, John Foster was able to override all objections to his relationship with his brother and to Allen's lack of interest in the research and analytical work that was so important to the agency's bureaucratic survival. Second, Donovan was an Anglophile and a Europhile, and American world dominance was still being resisted by Britain, the old empire.

AGAINST BRITAIN

Anglophilia ran wide but never deep in America, even among the New England Establishment. No American President, for example, including Eisenhower, could be described as an Anglophile. Jack Kennedy's father, as U.S. ambassador at the Court of St. James's, was convinced in 1938–40 that Britain was a degenerate, dissolute empire facing its inevitable decline. Franklin Roosevelt had a clear vision of the old British, Dutch, and French empires collapsing in the face of national and ideological forces they could no longer contain and of American industrial strength as the new banker of Western liberal democracy.

There was something else involved as well: social differences, competition, and snobbery. Jack Kennedy's grandfathers, both of whom had dubious careers, were part of an Irish-American community more loyal to its members than to the law, with a bitter memory of what they perceived as British injustice and cruelty in Ireland. The great flood of European migrants to the United States following the suppression of liberal-national uprisings in 1848 brought with it a common dislike of colonialism. Franklin Roosevelt's grandfather owned large estates in China and Vietnam, including a large part of Saigon, having built a shipping company in competition with British, Dutch, and French interests, plying a phenomenally lucrative trade in opium. FDR would have been an enormously rich man had the French not suppressed the trade. British and European aristocrats and gentlemen, whose families had frequently made their money in similar ways only several generations earlier, were quite prepared to marry American money but would never fully accept Americans as social equals. Winston Churchill's American mother, Jenny Jerome, suffered the gossip of London society. "A bunch of supercilious snobs" was the description of the British by Joseph Smith, a CIA officer in Singapore in the early 1950s.[2] Wilsonian liberalism developed in reaction both to the old empires and to a sort of social imperialism identified with them.

Richard Nixon in his memoirs reflected upon his experience of colonial peoples and found himself more in tune with Joseph Smith than he would have realized. Describing a trip he made as Vice-President in 1953 with his wife to a number of Asian countries he said:

Both Pat and I had a tremendous amount of personal contact with the people wherever we went. One day in the Philippines we shook hands with more than five thousand students at a 4-H exhibition. Later, as I walked through heavy crowds at a factory, my Filipino escort touched my arm and said,"That man back there, Mr. Vice-President, said, 'He is not afraid to shake my hand even if my shirt is dirty!' " I shall never forget the look of quiet pride in my escort's face. . . .

Today it may hardly seem a revelation that the peoples of Asia wanted to be treated with respect; but it was a lesson that the European nations did not learn sufficiently well or sufficiently soon in the years after World War II. In Hong Kong, the best run and most prosperous of the Asian cities I visited, I asked a local Chinese leader how the people would vote if offered independence. Without hesitation he said, "They would vote for independence by ten to one." I asked him why this was so, since the British presence had obviously materially benefited the people. He replied, "There is a saying that when the British establish a colony they build three things, in this order: a church, a racetrack, and a club to which Orientals cannot belong. That is an exaggeration but it is based upon a truth, and that is why we would always choose to be independent."

For better or worse, the colonial empires were disintegrating. The great question in the 1950s was who would fill the vacuum. Japan had the potential but was prohibited from doing so by the postwar treaties. None of the other countries in the region had the military and economic resources to defend itself unaided against Communist infiltration and subversion. It was clear to me that if the United States did not move, the Chinese or the Soviets, acting with or through the local Communist insurgent groups in each country, certainly would. The question, therefore, was not *whether* but *how*.[3]

The strongest emotion the Americans had about the old European empires was one of distrust. American isolationism was a way of avoiding being drawn into the machinations of the Old World while at the same time protecting the base from which American exporters and entrepreneurs competed with European interests for economic gains. Isolationism never meant a self-denying ordinance on opportunity: quite the contrary. From the turn of the century there was a strong sense that it would be an age of American achievement. Americans did not see America only as a weary titan forced to pick up the pieces of a disintegrating world in 1919 or in 1945. They also saw a wider world that offered opportunity and advantage. American power was accepted as a fact. The question was what kind of great power America should be.

In the decade after World War II, this was resolved from a position of strength: the United States was viewed by all as the mightiest power the world had ever known. The generation in power seized the available opportunities and were as determined as Franklin Roosevelt had been when he vowed not to repeat the mistakes made by President Wilson and the Congress after World War I. By 1944 Roosevelt and Congress had a unified vision of the future, consisting of a global system with the United Nations at its center. Through this organization the United States could act as needed, secure in the knowledge that the acceptance of the principles of the U.N. Charter by countries throughout the world would enable it to compete and win against the competition. The Roosevelt administration had already recognized America as the world's great power but hoped to exercise this power indirectly. "England is really broke," the secretary of the treasury, Henry Morgenthau, told Roosevelt in August 1944. "This is very interesting," Roosevelt replied only half-jokingly, according to Morgenthau. "I had no idea England was broke. I will go over there and make a couple of talks and take over the British Empire."[4]

The wish to use American power indirectly was a policy mainspring initiated by President Wilson and carried on by his successors. It emerged from their recognition that the old empires were essentially inefficient mechanisms for commercial purposes. If internationally accepted principles of law and conduct could be established, the expense and encumbrance of maintaining an empire could be avoided. Within days of becoming President, Woodrow Wilson stated his conviction that American capitalism could provide a model and a method for reforming the world, although in this case he was addressing the development of Latin America only. There should be a new system, Wilson held, based on "orderly processes of just government based upon law, not upon arbitrary or irregular force," on the "consent of the governed," and on alliance with "those who act in the interest of peace and honor, who protect private rights." In a subsequent newspaper interview he identified the enemies of this approach and in the process voiced the deep American distrust of the Old World. "The concessionaries and foreign interests must go. Not that foreign capital must leave Central America, but that it shall cease to be a dominant special interest. . . . Who commonly seeks the intervention of the United States in Latin American troubles? . . . Always the foreign interests, bondholders or concessionaries."[5] "European financiers and contractors" in Wilson's opinion were the principal threat to his concept. In November 1913 a British diplomat accurately foresaw the consequences of Wilson's policy when he said:

> With the opening of the Panama Canal it is becoming increasingly important that the Governments of the Central American Republics should improve, as they will become more and more a field for European and American enterprise: bad government may lead to friction. . . . The President did not seem to realize that his policy will lead to a "de facto" American protectorate over the Central American Republics; but there are others here who do, and who intend to achieve that object. . . . It seems to me that we have neither the intention nor the power to oppose this policy.[6]

Under Truman, those who did recognize the consequences of Wilsonian idealism in practice came into their own. Once in power, they faced the reality that the indirect exercise of American power did not really work. Indeed, it accomplished what Wilson feared; it enabled European capital to gain greater footholds throughout the world. Realizing this, they faced the next question: How direct would the exercise of American power have to be to achieve practical success? When on Friday, February 21, 1947, Lord Inverchapel, the British ambassador in Washington, supplied Dean Acheson with the two papers stating Britain's decision to withdraw from Greece and Turkey, Britain was not consciously handing over world leadership to the United States or surrendering its imperial ambitions. Rather, it was calculating correctly that America would take over the cost and the responsibility of keeping Greece and Turkey free from communism, leaving Britain to concentrate on sustaining the empire and commonwealth.

To Truman and his administration, however, the British withdrawal from the eastern Mediterranean was another wily move to secure the intervention of the United States in sorting out British troubles. In Truman's view, Britain was banking on America's new perception of the need to combat communism, and in the process it was effectively securing additional American funding for British attempts to hold on to as much of its empire as possible. The British calculation was confirmed in U.S. eyes when the National Security Council submitted a report to the President on March 22, 1949, dealing with U.S. objectives with respect to Greece and Turkey "to counter Soviet threats to US security." The conclusion of the council was that "It is in the interest of US national security that neither Greece nor Turkey fall under communist domination. In existing circumstances US aid and support are essential if this is to be prevented." The prospect of war with the Soviet Union was behind the whole affair:

> Military decisions with respect to Greece and Turkey should be made in the light of the over-all world situation and the defense needs and potentialities of the Middle East and Eastern Mediterranean areas as determined on the basis of US strategic interests, and not primarily as a contribution to the solution of the problem in those countries.... US policy on military aid to Turkey, or other military programs with respect to Turkey, should be based on the necessity of supporting and strengthening Turkish efforts to oppose communist pressure, and on possible utilization of Turkey for US strategic purposes in the event of conflict with the USSR.[7]

From 1945 onward it was obvious that British indecision over withdrawal from empire (the British Conservative party strongly opposed the Labour party's decolonization moves) would inevitably involve a clash with the United States. There was cutthroat political and economic competition developing in the Third World, Arabia, and Iran, just as there was between France and the United States in the Far East. "The future foreign interests of the United States will be in the Western Hemisphere and in the Pacific,"[8] Truman declared in September 1945. His expectation was that China under Chiang Kai-shek would take Japan's place as the dominant power in the Far East, providing at last a stable, vast market for American business to exploit and from which to exploit other markets in the East. John Carter Vincent, a State Department China expert, told a British diplomat in Washington in November 1945, "We are endeavoring to get businessmen back into China for their sake and for China's sake."[9] He meant American businessmen.

Ten years earlier there had been a tremendous Anglo-German trade war against American interests in Latin America, with British businesses making deals and concessions to Germans in an effort to gain their backing for a crumbling British economic position in the subcontinent. There was an awareness that while with Britain trade had followed the flag, with the United States trade itself rather than the flag would flourish. Instead of having the flag directly follow trade, the Central Intelligence Agency was given the responsibility to achieve the same result indirectly. In addition, the awareness of inevitable postwar competition and possible confrontation between Britain and America was focused in intelligence instead of in public diplomacy. The United States saw Britain as a declining power and so was prepared to be conciliatory to a certain degree in public, using the CIA as necessary to secure American objectives in private. In the late 1950s and early 1960s the U.S. mission in Lusaka compared in size to the Soviet one and was certainly not there to bolster a fading British presence. The period between 1946 and 1956 represented a series of *ad hoc* British schemes to find a world slot similar to the one it had held before the war. It was only after Prime Minister Sir Anthony Eden lost his nerve during the Suez crisis in 1956 and withdrew from Egypt that Britain began seriously to reconsider its imperial role.

The uncovering of the Soviet British spy network also played a major part in the deterioration of Anglo-American relations, seriously damaging British influence in Congress, providing reasons for countering Britain's undoubted channel to the legislature. The homosexual aspect of the Burgess-Maclean affair was very useful in all sorts of corners in Washington bureaucratic warfare, as McCarthy's attacks on the State Department were to show. In the early 1950s McCarthy and his supporters charged that there were a hundred and ten homosexual State Department officers based in Taiwan. When the bisexual Whittaker Chambers was added to the list of spies, it was easy to equate homosexuality with communism and treachery. This paranoid atmosphere scored points for McCarthy within the Washington bureaucracy and Congress. The British spies brought about the widespread feeling that the British social and governmental systems were compromised.

With America's trust in Britain greatly diminished, the traitors provided a natural opportunity to remove the incipient competition between Britain and America to a safe area within which Britain was on the defensive. These collisions and consciousnesses of the time effectively ruled out the appointment of Bill Donovan to head the CIA or, for that matter, any agency of foreign policy. Although never voiced, Donovan's Anglophilia was probably the reason for his rejection by Roosevelt and then Truman in 1944–45. Allen Dulles, Eisenhower's choice as Bedell Smith's replacement, had the avuncular manner and style of a British patrician but was no Anglophile. After leaving Princeton in

1912 he traveled to India at the height of the British Raj, teaching English in Allahabad, in the Central Provinces. There he experienced both the life of a sahib "with five Hindu servants and people pulling punkahs back and forth," as his sister, Eleanor, later remembered, and the life of the suppressed Indians, hating Britain. He learned Hindi and Sanskrit and attended underground nationalist meetings. He was introduced to the Nehru family and was much impressed by the early feminism and fervent nationalism of Vijaya Lakshmi Nehru. Dulles' opinion of the British was formed by his encounter with their empire in India. Alliance with Britain was, however, likely and, as his uncle Robert Lansing put it, "It would not do, therefore, to let our controversies reach a point where diplomatic correspondence gave place to action."[10] He did not have to like the people he had to work with, and this was his view of Britain.

EISENHOWER'S MEN

Allen Dulles also saw the traitors as symbolic of what was happening to Britain. They represented the moral and political decline of a country living beyond its means and cracking apart. They were left-wing, homosexual, alcoholic, and none of them could be dismissed as unrepresentative radicals embittered by struggle. They were people in conflict who could not resolve their relationship to authority and therefore undertook self-destructive antisocial activity. Men such as Dulles felt there was an inbred quality to British life and were not taken in by the charm of British clubland. Miles Copeland, an ex-CIA officer, accurately reflected this feeling when he described the Lambton–Jellicoe affair of 1973:

> Following the Lambton–Jellicoe affair, in which two members of the British nobility were discovered to have been consorting with call girls, a security commission was formed to ascertain the extent to which the British Government's security had been endangered. Members of the commission, under Lord Diplock, concentrated on the question of whether or not either of the unfortunate peers might have blurted out TOP SECRETS while engaged in postcoital pillow talk—and, whether the fact that one of them was smoking pot during intercourse had a bearing. They dealt only summarily with the question of possible blackmail, since it was apparent to all of them that the lords, both basically good and honest men despite the errancy in question, would have scoffed at any blackmailer.*

---

* Miles Copeland, *The Real Spy World* (London: Sphere, 1978), p. 17. Copeland goes on to say that British security officials "must have been appalled" by the naïvete of the Diplock Commission's report, since they knew well that "some espionage services make extensive use of prostitutes," who are used to put their targets into compromising situations so that they can be blackmailed. "Can you imagine," he writes, "Lambton, with a puff on his joint, saying 'Darling, I

Copeland viewed the Diplock Commission's naïve approach to a potentially major security scandal as indicative of British amateurism. He also saw a tie between the inbred and dissolute aristocracy and Britain's ruling groups. In 1973 the Earl Jellicoe, son of the Admiral of the Fleet who had fought the great naval battle of Jutland during World War I, was the Conservative government's leader of the House of Lords; Viscount Lambton was a government minister in the Ministry of Defence, the son of the fifth Earl of Durham. In the same way that Lords Jellicoe and Lambton could be used to embarrass British government in 1973, so the British traitors provided a symbolic rite of passage for Britain in 1953. Understanding this, Dulles had the feeling that a new great power was absorbing and replacing an old one in a kind of Whitmanesque continentalism. Anglophiles such as Bill Donovan were set aside by those who shared this perception.

With Eisenhower and Allen and John Foster Dulles the CIA achieved the role it wanted: playing point for the United States to ensure that accurate predictions could be made about the plans and policies of other countries. It was not in the position to do whatever was necessary to secure American ambitions and interests. Agency people prided themselves on their toughness. They were well financed and in no danger of cracking. They were the storm troops of the cold war, in harmony with the mood of the country at the time. "We were under war conditions," recalled George Humphrey, Eisenhower's secretary of the treasury, "and we were in war."[11] Eisenhower's election was a reflection of this mood. He was regarded as an efficient soldier who won wars and as a President who could make peace in Korea and deal with Stalin. In March 1953, five months after the presidential election, Stalin died, forcing Eisenhower to make judgments about the Soviet Union's future course of action. Even if he believed that Stalin, with the experience behind him of American resolve in World War II, Berlin, and Korea, had not been actually interested in "hot" war and that his belligerent posture had been for domestic purposes only, he had no way of knowing what Stalin's successors would do. Similarly, if he believed that Stalin's death had simply prevented him from taking a planned, final step of war, he could not know whether his successors would opt for peace.

The answer came from the CIA. Analysts firmly declared that the new Soviet rulers would concentrate on domestic matters and on securing internal control and would not chance new or risky ventures in foreign policy.[12] It was a crucial judgment heralding the future of a stable, divided Europe and meaning that the cold-war struggle would move elsewhere. Eisenhower accepted this analysis for practical purposes but, along with John Foster Dulles, maintained a cold-war ideology. He assumed, as Dulles told the Senate during his confir-

---

simply must tell you about the new X5-11'—or the prostitute having the faintest idea what he was talking about even if he did?"

mation hearings, that there would be "irreconcilable conflict"[13] between Soviet communism and Western values. This, of course, denied a certain flexibility in foreign policy as conducted by the State Department, but provided the CIA with an opportunity to pursue the second, more liberal voice of American intentions abroad.

The character of Eisenhower was a powerful component in the molding of the CIA. His methods and the procedures of administration and consultation he established determined the CIA's own *modus vivendi*. He was the dutiful apprentice who notices more than dutiful apprentices should notice. He was an obedient subordinate—watchful, patient, and resourceful. He was a man whose ambition was restricted by his resources, so he could never afford to put a foot wrong. His ambition was reflected in an extraordinary temper and a profanity that constantly brought him to the brink of trouble. For him life was a constant assault on Olympus. He was a man of great ability, resolved never to let his emotions run away with him. He would never slap a soldier, as George Patton did, or play at being an emperor, as Douglas MacArthur did. Murray Kempton used to say that Eisenhower had been brought up on small army posts playing cards with the consistently richer notables of the town, and in order to win he had to be calm, imperturbable, and shrewd.

Of all Presidents, Eisenhower valued the facts of power over the appearances of power. He was able to concentrate on being really powerful (and therefore publicly not very exciting) because he judged—correctly—that the American public would back him on his record. He was more concerned to prevent things from becoming worse than he was to make things better. He did not want any more killing; he knew war was terrible. He was a democrat, with little prejudice, calling himself a liberal conservative. He prided himself on being able to get on with everyone; hence his remarkable belief in conference diplomacy. He was enlightened, uncreative, and proud. He valued professionalism, and he came to value and to respect the CIA as an agency more professional about its job than most of the other agencies and departments. He involved the agency at every level of foreign-policy debate. He rewarded the agency by supporting the building of its headquarters in Langley and giving it a platform of respectability in government by the manifest attention he paid to its reports and to Allen Dulles.

McCARTHY, DULLES, AND THE CIA

Eisenhower's support of the CIA was also established by the activities of Senator Joseph McCarthy. In the summer of 1953, within months of Allen Dulles' appointment as DCI, McCarthy announced that he had reason to believe that there were more than one hundred communists in the CIA and that he was going to root them out. The "worst situation" of all, he said, existed in the CIA.[14] No doubt he had reason to expect the CIA to run as scared as the

State Department had in March 1953, when John Foster Dulles issued a press statement along with McCarthy, endorsing a blatant piece of interference in foreign affairs by the senator.* Most people ran scared from McCarthy in those days.† Even Bedell Smith, testifying in a libel case between McCarthy and Senator William Benton of Connecticut, succumbed to the prevailing atmosphere and declared that there were communists in the CIA. "They are so adroit and adept," he said, "that they have infiltrated practically every security agency in the Government."[15] "The McCarthy underground," as Lyman Kirkpatrick termed it, was also fed reports on the agency by disgruntled ex-personnel. "We had cases where individuals would be contacted by telephone and told that it was known that they drank too much," Kirkpatrick recalled, "or were 'having an affair,' and that the caller would make no issue of this if they would come around and tell everything that they knew about the Agency."[16]

McCarthy's cynical and ruthless manipulation of popular fears of communism, his willingness to cap outlandish accusations with even more outlandish ones and to use the prestige of the Senate in an irresponsible political campaign designed to bring him personal glory rather than to root out genuine communist infiltrators in the bureaucracy, carried the nation with him for some years. To his surprise, the CIA under Allen Dulles and with the personal backing of Eisenhower was not cowed by his accusations when he went after a CIA officer, William P. Bundy.

The CIA was, of course, in a stronger position than other Washington institutions, since it was a secret agency operating under a presidential umbrella. Personnel information could reasonably be regarded as secret (overall staff size and names of employees were protected by statute), so McCarthy would have had to devote considerably more energy to the CIA than he did to the State Department, where the same considerations were not generally applied. McCarthy had his "underground" in the State Department but not among serving officers in the CIA. In addition, the President would not stand idly by in the face of such attacks, since the agency was at the heart of U.S. activity in the cold war.

Undeterred, McCarthy nevertheless launched his attack on July 9, 1953. Shortly after 9:00 A.M. on that day Roy M. Cohn, the chief counsel to

* McCarthy announced that he had "negotiated" an agreement with Greek shipping interests not to ship goods to communist countries, and that he had achieved this without consulting the State Department or being advised by anyone there. There were many other examples of John Foster Dulles' State Department caving in to McCarthy pressure. Scott McLeod, a McCarthy hanger-on who had been an FBI officer in Manchester, New Hampshire, was appointed by John Foster Dulles as State Department personnel and security officer. Dulles even cleared the appointment of ambassadors with McLeod. On the one occasion when this was not done—when Charles E. Bohlen was appointed ambassador to the Soviet Union—McCarthy caused so much trouble (casting suspicion on Bohlen for having been Roosevelt's interpreter at Yalta) that Dulles refused to have photographs taken of himself with Bohlen.

† Despite the fact that his Marine Corps record during the war showed that he had flown few combat missions or even qualified as an air gunner, McCarthy claimed that he had and in 1951 asked for and in 1952 was granted by a Democratic administration the Distinguished Flying Cross, normally awarded for twenty-five combat missions.

McCarthy's Permanent Subcommittee on Investigations, telephoned Walter Pforzheimer, the CIA's legislative counsel, to say that the subcommittee wished to have William P. Bundy, assistant to the deputy director of intelligence, appear before it at 10:45 A.M. that same day. Cohn had heard that Bundy had recently been recommended for "a top, top clearance" by the agency. He also knew that Bundy had contributed to the Alger Hiss defense fund some years earlier. The implication was that Bundy might be another Hiss. Pforzheimer went straight to the deputy director of intelligence, Robert Amory. Allen Dulles was at a meeting of the National Security Council at the White House, which Eisenhower had forbidden anyone to interrupt. As Amory remembered it:

> When Pforzheimer called, I had to stall for time—about two hours. I told Bundy to call his wife, tell her to pack for a trip to New England by auto and not to answer the phone again. About fifteen minutes after Bundy had gone, well before most of the office staff had arrived, I swore the few who had seen him to deny he'd been in, called Cohn and said "Unfortunately Bundy left on leave on a motor trip." When Allen returned about 11:00 I immediately reported what I had done and he approved. Soon after, he got to Nixon, who agreed to get McCarthy to call off his dogs.[17]

As it turned out, the decision to instruct Bundy to take leave was crucial to what followed. Pforzheimer covered up in conversations with Roy Cohn, but when he was subpoenaed later that day, he told Allen Dulles that if he, Pforzheimer, was called before the subcommittee, he would not commit perjury and deny on oath that Bundy had been sent on leave. "I made it very plain to Allen that I would not commit perjury and that if I was asked if Bundy was on duty, I would have to say that although I did not see Bundy, I did know that we had put Bundy on leave. I was in on the arrangements." When Pforzheimer was subpoenaed, Dulles firmly stated that, with its secrets, the agency had to investigate its own and that McCarthy was not going to be allowed to interfere.* Favorable publicity followed. Although this pleased Dulles personally—

---

* "I didn't mean anything to Dulles," Pforzheimer later explained. "Bundy did. Bundy was social. He was married to the daughter of Dean Acheson. Dulles played the social game really hard. I didn't mean anything to him: I was just a guy. If it had been just me, I think I would have gone down the drain. Of course it was clear that Bill wasn't involved in any loyalty matter—he gave two $200 checks to the Hiss Defense Fund. That was explainable and he explained it. He was part of the Acheson law firm and Donald Hiss was a partner. They were all batting for Alger. I don't think there is any doubt that Dulles was a little annoyed and surprised when I told him, 'I will not commit perjury on this.' If the agency had been going down the drain, I'd have to rethink my position, but not for this. It wasn't an agency matter that would affect the running of the agency if I had testified. It was that simple. If the positions were reversed, he wouldn't have done the same for me. I'm convinced of that, knowing how the man worked. It was that simple" (interview, Walter Pforzheimer, April 2, 1984). As against this view, Dulles must have recognized that the attack on Bundy was an attack on the CIA. Both Robert Amory and William Bundy firmly reject any assertion that Dulles acted for "social" as opposed to professional reasons. They

he loved public praise—a note was distributed within the CIA calling for the incident to be downplayed. There was no point in goading Joe McCarthy either.[18]

Richard Nixon, who had worked with McCarthy in the Senate before becoming Vice-President, had enlisted the support of the other Republicans on McCarthy's subcommittee and had told McCarthy that he would be outvoted if he continued to pursue Bundy or the CIA: "I told McCarthy that I had seen Bundy's performance in several National Security Council meetings and he seemed to me a loyal American who was rendering vital service to the country."[19] McCarthy sent off a face-saving letter to Dulles asking him to fire Bundy if the investigation of him sustained any doubt about his loyalty, and let the matter drop.[20]

The "top, top clearance" which Roy Cohn had heard that William Bundy was being checked for was a "Q" clearance for atomic-energy secrets, which he needed as a result of Eisenhower's repositioning of the National Security Council to oversee atomic as well as intelligence work. In the summer of 1952 Allen Dulles (then still deputy director of Central Intelligence) made Bundy his assistant for council work. Bundy found that the council had little to do with Estimates at that period, but with the presidential elections that autumn, he was assigned to prepare a briefing book on CIA activities and assessments for the candidates—Eisenhower, the Republican, and Adlai Stevenson, the Democrat. "Bedell Smith said on his own initiative, I believe," said Bundy, "that we should have a black briefing book that pulls together all our prevailing judgments on every key issue that will be available for whoever wins the election. I edited like mad, pulling together stuff and getting new stuff written. We had one, maybe two black books. It was an example of professionalism. It was delivered to the Eisenhower people at the Commodore, and I don't believe a page of it was read. But the fact that it was done forced us to assess our inventory."[21]

Eisenhower had a proclivity for orderly staff work, so the internal assessment of its inventory had the bonus of making the CIA better prepared for the new President's rearrangements. In particular, Eisenhower put the National Security Council on a different footing, at the center of his administration's pursuit of the cold war. Bundy looked back on his experience:

> It had been a ratifying mechanism for decisions reached between the President, Acheson, Marshall, and Lovett. With everyone working so closely together, it was almost superfluous. But then the Eisenhower people made the NSC process the centerpiece of the whole policy process. It met regularly

---

see Dulles as having as his basic concern the protection of a loyal agency subordinate. Bundy had informed the agency before he took up his job there about the checks to the Hiss Defense Fund (letter, Robert Amory to author, February 22, 1985, and William Bundy to author, March 6, 1985).

once a week. Its role was systematized. The subject matter and the schedule were worked out. It was a superb arrangement. It put a great premium on what we were doing. It was the time that intelligence was most systematically plugged into what was really read at the top—much more so than in the Kennedy period.

This new focus on the NSC meant that Estimates were more systematically reviewed by the council and wedded to policy formation; as Bundy put it:

We had a system whereby the production of the Estimates was scheduled a month ahead or two weeks ahead of the policy papers. We would digest the Estimates so that they were going right into the NSC policy papers. Eisenhower had developed this in his staff during the war. What is the subject we are going to talk about? What is the decision we are trying to make? What are the supporting papers? In that first year and a quarter of the Eisenhower administration he ran through the whole gamut of issues systematically and set up a policy.[22]

It was important that this was done for another reason too: Allen Dulles' lack of interest in the Estimates. The agency and Dulles were lucky that under Sherman Kent's direction the Estimates could be relied upon to be authoritative and responsible. It was Bedell Smith's legacy in this as in the other areas of agency activity that Dulles inherited.

Allen Dulles' personal preference for operations did not mean that he ignored the Estimates. He occasionally challenged the findings of a National Intelligent Estimate (NIE) before he presented it. This happened in 1956 when an Estimate on the Polish political situation predicted that unrest in eastern Europe would not spread to Poland. Dulles thought otherwise, and he was proved correct.

He had his own eyes and ears, and he had a stream of visitors from war contacts and so on [remembered Bundy]. He would always receive a visitor. He used to say that it was because when he had been in Berne in 1917 he had missed a chance to meet Lenin, so if somebody interesting came along he'd be whisked up to the director's office. Allen enjoyed that sort of thing. He was picking up a certain amount of low gossip, but he was also picking up a feel for things, getting away from a dependence on paper that could turn into an ivory tower.[23]

The intelligence relationship with the British was an additional help to the CIA analysts. Based on a secret agreement between the Old Central Intelligence Group and British SIS in 1946, there was close cooperation between the British decrypting center at Bletchley Park, in Buckinghamshire, and later, when it moved, at Cheltenham, in Gloucestershire, and the National Security Agency at Fort Meade, Maryland. There was also close cooperation on intelligence Estimates between the CIA's Office of National Estimates and the British Joint Intelligence Bureau headed by Bedell Smith's old friend, Major General Sir Kenneth Strong (he was knighted in 1952). From 1953 a senior officer from the Directorate of Intelligence sat in on some British estimates as CIA Estimates liaison officer in London. Estimates dealing with the concerns of the British Empire and Commonwealth did not involve this officer and were treated by the British as very much their own. There was no similar British liaison officer in Washington, although Strong visited Washington for short periods for high-level consultation on coordination and the substance of intelligence judgments. The cooperation was sufficiently strong to survive not only the Burgess-Maclean scandal but also Philby's exposure as a traitor. William Bundy regularly came across both the British JIC papers and the hard contrast of Sherman Kent's NIEs:

> I found the British work very useful in a lot of ways: There was a very much more relaxed use of language, more discursive, more stylistic feel to the British papers. Ours were crude and had no flowing style in the literary sense— which was not surprising after they had been through the coordination process! We always tried to write them with a certain amount of style, but we were always entirely resigned to having any style disappear. But the conclusions tended to be more precise in our papers, and it got to the point where we were using certain words in what we hoped was a clearly understood sense. If it was said something was "probable" it meant it was between 50 and 75 percent; "almost certain," 75 to 90 percent. Sherman Kent even put out a numerical equivalent so that when we used a word, somebody could see what it meant. Similar precision was not a British habit. Conclusions were less hard. They presumed a great deal of literacy. Ours was for consumption up and down the shop: military minds could grasp it.[24]

With this backup on the substantive side, Allen Dulles was able to devote himself to the agency's clandestine operations. As deputy director under Bedell Smith, he had paid a great deal of attention to operational matters, at times himself recruiting people he perceived as able to bring the war to the enemy. Cord Meyer was recruited into OPC by Dulles personally in late 1951. He was representative of a major element in the CIA's founding generation. He acted on his beliefs, becoming the ultimate character witness to the agency's liberalism. Few people believed in American justice and individualism as strongly as Meyer did. He was deeply committed and as a result was never invisible: his World Federalist beliefs had made him a controversialist in print after 1945. He possessed the New Deal idealism of government service, so when the call came to engage in a struggle for American liberalism in a world up for grabs, Meyer responded:

> Looking back, I think that the impression Allen Dulles made on me was the decisive factor in my final decision to join the CIA. Behind his jovial and

bluff exterior, he struck me as having a searching and undogmatic mind and a cosmopolitan and sophisticated knowledge of the world. . . . It seemed to me that an organization that had such a man in one of its top positions was one well worth working for. In the years that followed, I was to learn that in addition to his other qualities, he was a loyal and courageous friend in time of trouble.[25]

Meyer soon had the opportunity to find out just how loyal Dulles was. In September 1953, soon after his attack on the CIA through Bundy, McCarthy (who was close to J. Edgar Hoover) pressed the FBI to aim its sights at Meyer. By then, however, Dulles had learned that it was possible for the agency to withstand McCarthy. He refused to allow the FBI to interrogate Meyer, and insisted that the CIA itself would deal with allegations that Meyer might be another Hiss. An internal investigation cleared Meyer:

On Thanksgiving Day, I received a call from Allen Dulles with the good news that my secret trial had ended in acquittal. On the basis of a joint recommendation from the general counsel and the director of security, he had found my continued employment with the agency "clearly consistent with the national security." He congratulated me on the outcome. . . . He could have sought to protect himself by convening a hearing board as a way of sharing the responsibility of decision, but he spared me the prolonged agony and expense of such a procedure.[26]

News of the stand Dulles had taken with Meyer naturally spread throughout the agency and Washington. Morale zoomed, as did the agency's ability to attract high-quality recruits. The agency's reputation also benefited by inevitable comparisons with the State Department, where Allen's brother was seen as less willing to defend his staff from McCarthy's incursions.

John Foster Dulles had a more difficult job of protecting his people at the State Department than Allen had at the CIA. Also, he did not feel the same loyalty to the State Department that Allen felt for the agency, of which he was a founding father. It was not "John Foster Dulles' State Department," but it was "Allen Dulles' agency." The State Department did have a number of known homosexuals as well as some senior officers who were regarded as "soft" on communism. Several members of this second group, who were senior analysts and diplomats in the China section, had become disgusted by the corruption of the Kuomintang regime of Chiang Kai-shek and welcomed Mao Tse-tung's communist government as an improvement for the people of China. McCarthy latched onto this while also zeroing in on the homosexuality of some State Department officials.

Do I feel badly about what happened to State? [said Walter Pforzheimer.] They had it coming to them. They colonized one on the other. They had the homosexual problem. But don't forget that undersecretary Sumner Welles was a raving homosexual. He brought in people. Alger Hiss—the whole crew—were his appointees, pretty much. Roosevelt was pretty fond of Sumner Welles, but when members of the Congress went to him and said, "Look, we're just back from Alabama and Sumner Welles was found *in flagrante delicto* with a colored porter on the train," Roosevelt had to let him go. Did Joe overdo it? Sure he did. But he did have something to go on.*

Owen Lattimore, a professor at Johns Hopkins University and a noted expert on China whose books and articles had greatly influenced a whole generation of State Department officials, was one of the men singled out for a particularly vicious attack by McCarthy, although he had never been in the State Department. John Stewart Service, John Paton Davies, John Emmerson, and Oliver Clubb, all in the China section, fell foul of McCarthy for being "soft" on communism, and either left or had their careers blighted. Emmerson, who stayed in the State Department, never gained the ambassadorial rank and posts to which his talents should have entitled him. Service and Clubb were fired by John Foster Dulles, not so much because of their judgment: even though Chiang Kai-shek's regime was corrupt, the communists in China were not the answer as far as the Eisenhower administration was concerned, and those who thought they were had to go.

Allen Dulles in the CIA took a different line, with the result that China expertise within the agency was soon much better than within the State Department: McCarthyism had the unforeseen effect of helping the CIA become a major player in the later implementation of foreign policy in Asia. Also involved were the internal personnel changes brought about by the Korean War. A new group of people from good universities (not all were monied, Ivy League graduates, or ex-OSS) were hired to deal with the storm of demands for analysis and information. This meant that under Bedell Smith and Allen Dulles the CIA in key ways replaced the State Department in policy development. This suited John Foster Dulles, because with his brother in charge, he did not have to worry about a challenge to his own position. He knew that the CIA would effectively do his bidding. It also suited Allen Dulles, whose interests lay else-

---

* Interview, Walter Pforzheimer, April 2, 1984. Sumner Welles had been compromised—though not publicly—in this way in 1943. The story was the talk of Washington, and Roosevelt reluctantly had to fire him. Richard Rovere in *Senator Joe McCarthy* (London: Metheun, 1959), p. 124, says:

> And there was more nastiness. McCarthy soon found a way of spicing his disquisitions with sex. He had discovered that homosexuality was regarded as a factor in security judgments, and he worked this for what it was worth, which was quite a bit. It gave lesser demagogues, who realized that the Communists-in-government issue could never be taken from him, a corner of McCarthyism to work for themselves. A subcommittee of the District of Columbia Committee was set up to investigate "sexual deviates" (I believe this ugly phrase was invented at that time) in government. . . . The District Police set up a special detail of the Vice Squad "to investigate links between homosexuality and Communism."

where. His agency's increased prestige gave him a fairly clear field in clandestine activities.

STUDENTS AND LABOR

Cord Meyer masterminded one of Allen Dulles' more sophisticated secret operations. In 1954 Tom Braden, who had headed the International Organizations Division in the Directorate of Plans, resigned from the CIA, and Dulles appointed Meyer as his successor. His job was to build on the work of Braden, Wisner, and the OPC of Bedell Smith to support organizations, individuals, newspapers, and periodicals throughout the world, including the International Confederation of Free Trade Unions; the Italian centrist political parties; such politicians as Willy Brandt in Germany and De Gasperi in Italy; and magazines such as *Encounter*, to prevent their being penetrated and influenced by communists as well. Braden recalled:

> Journalists were a target, labor unions a particular target—that was one of the activities in which the communists spent the most money. They set up a successful communist labor union in France right after the war. We countered it with Force Ouvrière. They set up this very successful communist labor union in Italy, and we countered it with [another union]. . . . We had a vast project targeted on the intellectuals—"the battle for Picasso's mind," if you will. The communists set up fronts which they effectively enticed a great many— particularly the French—intellectuals to join. We tried to set up a counterfront. [This was done through funding of social and cultural organizations such as the Pan-American Foundation, the International Marketing Institute, the International Development Foundation, the American Society of African Culture, and the Congress of Cultural Freedom.] I think the budget for the Congress of Cultural Freedom one year that I had charge of it was about $800–$900,000, which included, of course, the subsidy for the Congress's magazine, *Encounter*. That doesn't mean that everybody that worked for *Encounter* or everybody who wrote for *Encounter* knew anything about it. Most of the people who worked for *Encounter* and all but one of the men who ran it had no idea that it was paid for by the CIA.*

---

* Interview, Tom Braden, in Granada Television program *World in Action: The Rise and Fall of the CIA*, Part I. See also *The New York Times*, February 14–28, May 8–15, 1967, and Thomas W. Braden, "I'm glad the CIA Is 'Immoral,' " *Saturday Evening Post*, May 20, 1967.

In his article Braden said that he had personally given Walter Reuther of the United Automobile Workers Union $50,000, that a CIA agent was "placed" in the Congress of Cultural Freedom, and that *Encounter* was not merely subsidized but that one of its editors was an agent. On May 9 Melvin Lasky announced that he had decided to stay on as editor of *Encounter* and regretted the resignations of his coeditors Stephen Spender and Frank Kermode. Spender and Kermode maintained that Lasky had lied to them about the source of some of the magazine's funds. On May 14 Michael Josselson, executive director of the Congress of Cultural Freedom, announced his resignation after assuming full responsibility for accepting CIA funds since 1950.

The early struggle was particularly bitter in two areas: the trade unions in Europe and the world student movement. The World Federation of Trade Unions, formed at the suggestion of the Soviet Union in 1945 in the immediate postwar euphoria, attracted the support of both the British Trades Union Congress and the American Congress of Industrial Organizations (CIO). But it proved to be a Soviet communist-front organization, and in 1949 the British and Americans left, forming the rival International Confederation of Free Trade Unions with secret CIA support. Officials of the Congress of Industrial Organizations—like executives in many other American professional organizations and businesses at the time—willingly helped channel CIA funding and propaganda into the new body. After the bitter struggle against communists in the American labor unions, it was natural for the CIA to go to those who had had the experience of this struggle for help in fighting communists in foreign labor unions.

Allen Dulles personally pushed for this sort of involvement, probably aware of the significant part played by American labor union contacts in Europe during World War II through OSS. As Tom Braden recalled:

> I did not initiate the activities of the agency with the CIO. The guy who did that was Allen. Allen was very much interested in the labor movement and the labor potentiality, and although I came from that corner and was idealistically prolabor since the days of the New Deal, I didn't have the concept that Allen did. The first job I was given when I got to the agency, even before

---

The battle for the intellectuals was undertaken by Braden and then Meyer on difficult ground. The authoritarianism required by the mobilization for war was reflected in the immediate postwar electoral appeal of socialist and communist parties, all implying that victory had come from effective socialist or communist principles of mobilization, which could now be applied to peacetime conditions. Democrats in France and Italy were not passive in the face of this challenge (although Braden and his colleagues, it would seem, assumed that they were), and themselves campaigned against the totalitarian left. In both countries there were social democrats with long histories of antitotalitarianism. However, the attraction of communism in these countries immediately after the war was aided by the sense that communist Russia had endured great hardships in the war against Nazi Germany and it was now "their" turn: the turn of those who had made sacrifices.

In Britain there was also a disquiet and revulsion from empire (reflected in the attitudes of Philby, for example), and a loss of confidence in the governing elite. In 1936 Oxford undergraduates had voted in a famous student debate against fighting for "King and Country." In 1940 George Orwell could write:

The English intelligentsia . . . take their crockery from Paris and their opinions from Moscow. In the general patriotism of the country they form a sort of island of dissident thought. England is perhaps the only great country whose intellectuals are ashamed of their own nationality. In left-wing circles it is always felt that there is something disgraceful in being an Englishman and that it is a duty to snigger at every English institution from horse racing to suet puddings. It is a strange fact, but it is unquestionably true that almost any English intellectual would feel more ashamed of standing to attention during "God save the King" than of stealing from a poor box. (*The Lion and the Unicorn* [London: Gollancz, 1941)], p. 95)

the division that I headed was created, was that Allen wanted me to stay in touch with the labor guys, which I did. I got to know the people at the CIO better than the people at the American Federation of Labor, which in December 1955 merged with the CIO.

There was a guy named Mike Ross that ran the CIO and Jay Lovestone ran the AFL side. Irving Brown ran around Europe organizing things, and Jay Lovestone sent the money. Allen was giving Lovestone money long before I came into the agency, and I think he was doing only what had been done before. I think the AFL/CIO interest in protecting the docks in Marseilles and things like that antedated the establishment of the agency. The secret funding of the AFL and CIO by the CIA I have always thought predated the agency. I suspect it was done by the OSS or the army or State Department.[27]

Apart from supporting democratic trade unionism worldwide through the AFL and CIO and the International Confederation of Free Trade Unions, the CIA, first under Bedell Smith and then under Allen Dulles, directed particular attention to labor unions in France and Italy. In both countries large unions were under communist control—a fact that played a major part in securing communist control of the World Federation of Trade Unions. The Soviet and eastern European unions were able to work through French and Italian officials to control the federation. To counteract this, a major clandestine effort was launched to secure pro-Western people in key union positions. This was backed by a detailed analysis of labor unions and political developments in both countries. Donovan's lesson—that research and analysis should underpin operations—had been well learned.

The people involved in developing this connection with noncommunist unions in France and Italy were, like Tom Braden and Cord Meyer, politically liberal or, like Jay Lovestone, ex-communists. Only in the CIA, of all government agencies, could these people have received such protection from public scrutiny as the McCarthy anticommunist fever grew. And only in the CIA would they have been allowed to take part in clandestine work. Lovestone was born in Lithuania, emigrating with his family to New York when he was a young boy. There he grew up in the same Jewish, left-wing circles as the Rosenbergs, becoming general secretary of the Communist Party of the United States of America in the 1920s. "Lovestone was a veritable Tammany chieftain among us Communists," wrote an ex-colleague. "One of his most successful methods was to call a comrade into his office, tell him extremely confidential information, obtaining in return a solemn promise that the matter would not be disclosed to a soul. In that way he won the support of numerous Party members who believed they were particularly favored by him."[28]

Lovestone was also a principled man, and the terrors of Stalin's Russia eventually brought him to a strong anticommunist sensibility. In the OSS during the war he worked to generate labor resistance to the Axis in Europe and North Africa. After the war he grew close to George Meany, general secretary and later president of the AFL and then the AFL–CIO, identifying communists in the American labor movement and acting as a link man between the AFL–CIO and the CIA. In his position as director of the International Affairs Department of the AFL–CIO, Lovestone also directly affected American labor's foreign-policy stance. In this he worked closely not only with Meany but also with Arthur J. Goldberg, with whom he had cooperated during the war when Goldberg was head of the OSS Labor Branch.

Like Lovestone, Arthur Goldberg came from Jewish left-wing Russian émigré stock. A lawyer specializing in labor law, he became general counsel of the CIO after the war, working with Walter Reuther to purge communists. Goldberg was one of the chief engineers of the AFL–CIO merger in 1955, remaining general counsel of the new body. With Walter Reuther he was instrumental in securing labor support for Kennedy in 1960, being rewarded with the cabinet post of secretary of labor. The connection with men like Lovestone and Goldberg cemented the relationship between American labor and U.S. foreign-policy goals through the CIA.

The effort to counteract the communist influence in European and world trade unionism met with mixed success. Free labor unions wedded to the principles of democratic procedures have become the hallmark of western Europe. But this feature of European labor probably would have happened in any case as long as the political environment of the West was democratic. In the Third World and Latin America the authoritarian attractions of communism were more readily accepted, and there was a fluctuating membership in the International Confederation of Free Trade Unions from those quarters. In January 1962 President Kennedy accepted advice from Cord Meyer, Arthur Goldberg, George Meany, Jay Lovestone, and others, and appointed a Labor Advisory Committee for the Alliance for Progress, under George Meany's chairmanship. This committee was to make recommendations on how best to "win" Latin American labor. It pressed for U.S. participation in the newly formed American Institute for Free Labor Development, and its advice was accepted.

The purpose of the institute was to combine American labor and business in supporting training programs for labor union officials and anticommunist propaganda of all sorts in Latin America. Its setting up was organized by the CIA, but once the institute was in motion, the CIA dropped out. It was funded jointly by the AFL–CIO, the Agency for International Development, and by large multinational corporations, including the Chase Manhattan Bank, Pan American World Airways, IBM World Trade Corporation, Standard Oil of New Jersey, Coca-Cola Export Corporation, and Pfizer International. Cord Meyer had had the original idea for the institute in the late 1950s, and since its inception over two hundred thousand Latin American labor union officials have been trained at its center at Front Royal, Virginia. It has been one of the more successful CIA ventures, indirectly organizing a very sophisticated collaboration between government, business, and labor, carrying out a clear policy conceived as being in the external interests of the United States. Presumably it also had the additional advantage of providing the CIA with informants and agents throughout the labor unions of South and Central America.*

Cord Meyer's other principal achievement during the Dulles era was in a similar field—the student movement. Here too the motive for CIA involvement was combating Soviet and communist influence. It was a job only the CIA could do. Behind the veil of secrecy the CIA could support the noncommunist left and work with democratic socialists through officers who were themselves liberals and democrats.[29] Tom Braden put the point precisely: "In the early 1950s, when the cold war was really hot, the idea that Congress would have approved many of our projects was about as likely as the John Birch Society's approving Medicare."[30] In the light of clear evidence that the Soviet Union was seeking to infiltrate and control various kinds of international student bodies, just as they had the World Federation of Trade Unions, Allen Dulles decided in 1954 that the American National Student Association, the Congress for Cultural Freedom, and a host of other anticommunist organizations should be heavily funded. The International Union of Students (IUS), founded in 1946 in Prague, at a time when there was no representative American student body, was manipulated by the Soviets in the same way as the trade union federation. The first Soviet vice-president of the IUS was Aleksandr Shelepin, later chief of the KGB.[31]

In the summer of 1947 the United States National Student Association (NSA) was formed as a representative American student organization. The following year, when the IUS failed to condemn the communist takeover in Czechoslovakia, the NSA broke with the IUS and in 1950 helped form the rival International Student Conference (ISC) with noncommunist European student unions. Then, from the perspective of American and democratic interests, as Cord Meyer described it,

> the ISC was inevitably compelled to defend itself against Communist attacks and to compete with the Communists for the allegiance of the emerging student population of the less developed countries. At the beginning, the struggle was decidedly unequal. The Soviet national student union and the international operations of the IUS headquarters in Prague were backed by virtually unlimited funds from the treasury of the Soviet Union. Owing a supranational allegiance to the Soviet Communist Party, disciplined young

---

* The connections with foreign labor groups and leaders fostered by the institute demonstrated an American sense of continuity with other nations. The United States, as a nation of nations, with millions of Poles, Germans, Czechs, Lithuanians, Ukrainians, as "new" Americans, has always had an intimacy with other countries. Spanish and Portuguese Americans gave the institute and its work a feeling of being much less foreign to those who attended its courses. After World War II as world attention turned toward America, this intimacy provided an intelligence opportunity which was taken enthusiastically, whereas before 1941 it had not been.

party activists throughout the world provided an interlocking directorate through which to influence the decisions of national student federations on matters ranging from policy positions to the selection of delegates, to the orchestration of propaganda campaigns.

Viewing things from this perspective, it was natural for the CIA to support the ISC and the NSA. A founder member of the ISC subsequently joined the agency and successfully made the case for support: "In the United States at that time, the fund-raising climate was not propitious for an organization that on most issues took a line that was definitely on the left in the political spectrum. The private foundations were intimidated by the hysteria that Senator McCarthy was generating. . . . The State Department was equally reluctant to provide grants from its limited budget for cultural affairs, and the open receipt of government funds would have damaged the reputation for independence that the NSA had found valuable in dealing with foreign students."[32]

Under Meyer, support was vastly extended, and the CIA's annual funding of the NSA quickly reached a level of approximately two hundred thousand dollars.[33] By 1955 the ISC (which received a large proportion of the NSA subsidy in dues) represented students in fifty-five countries. Over the fifteen years of CIA–NSA collaboration a number of foundations, student exchanges, and propaganda exercises were involved. The 1961 Helsinki Youth Festival, organized by the International Union of Students, was successfully boycotted by the International Student Conference, much to the pleasure of the agency and Robert Kennedy, the attorney general of the United States, who took a close interest in CIA activity in this area.[34]

The difficulty the agency found with the National Student Association was—ironically—its democratic nature: every few years its leadership changed. This necessitated telling a series of newly elected senior NSA officers about the association's secret CIA support. All went well during the 1950s and early 1960s, when American students were overwhelmingly supportive of their government's stand in the cold war. But attitudes changed during the 1960s as the post-World War II "baby boom" generation entered college and began to examine critically America's presence in Vietnam.[35] In February 1967 the radical, left-wing *Ramparts* magazine published three articles by an NSA officer revealing the CIA connection. In the months following, American newspapers—notably *The New York Times* and *The Washington Post*—pursued the story, and more and more information about the agency's contacts with public bodies, the labor movement, and business began to emerge.[36]

This publicity had two effects. First, it embarrassed the agency and had bureaucratic repercussions in Washington. Second, it revealed the extent of the agency's shadowy hand in a multitude of areas, nearly all of them started under Allen Dulles as either deputy director or director of Central Intelligence. A scholarship program for Algerian students was financed by the CIA between

1958 and 1962 because the government felt unable to offer open support for students involved in anti-French activities.[37] In this case the "other voice" of U.S. foreign policy was speaking. While the United States foresaw the inevitable demise of the French empire, the State Department could not openly sanction the student opposition. This was left to the CIA. In a similar vein, students at the Free University of Berlin were recruited by the CIA during the 1950s and 1960s, and one, Marvin W. Makinen, was arrested in the Soviet Union in July 1961, having boasted to friends that he was working for American intelligence.[38] The Hobby Foundation of Texas, the Independent Research Service, and many other private foundations were used as CIA conduits for funds going to organizations in the United States and abroad.[39]

Not all the foundations involved knew that they were being used in this way, and not all the organizations being supported realized that the money they received was from the CIA.[40] In many cases the funding went to organizations considered leftist and sometimes anti-American, a demonstration of Allen Dulles' flexibility and willingness to support anticommunists of any kind. CIA money was passed through the J. M. Kaplan Fund, a private foundation,* to the Institute of International Labor Research, which was engaged in training Latin American politicians on the democratic left. When the relationship was revealed in 1967, Norman Thomas, chairman of the institute and the leader of the American Socialist party, protested his ignorance of the CIA's involvement, saying, "This CIA thing is the strangest thing I've ever heard of. . . . We always thought the CIA was fighting against us."[41] Liberal American students like Gloria Steinem were involved in a CIA operation to send hundreds of American students to the World Youth festivals in Vienna in 1959 and Helsinki in 1961 as unofficial observers and lobbyists. When this was revealed in 1967 Steinem said she approved of the CIA effort in this operation because it was the work of liberals "who were far-sighted and cared enough to get Americans of all political views to the Festival."[42]

COUNTERINTELLIGENCE

The formal and informal links employed by the agency in its support of anticommunists and democrats worldwide gave it not only an extraordinary range of contacts but also an aura of omniscience. Dulles used both these elements to the full, especially in developing the CIA's counterintelligence branch under James Angleton.

Counterintelligence is a very specialized form of intelligence activity. Its

---

* In 1971, Jack Kaplan's nephew, in jail in Mexico convicted of murder, was lifted from prison by helicopter in an extraordinary escape of which nothing more is publicly known. Kaplan's fortune was based on molasses in the 1920s.

purpose is to identify hostile foreign intelligence operations and then prevent them from passing intelligence information, or destroy them, or turn them to advantage, while at the same time protecting its own country's intelligence operations. The sophistication required for effective counterintelligence was instinctively appealing to Dulles and to Angleton. The two men had an especially close professional relationship, and although the Counterintelligence Staff was part of the Directorate of Plans, Angleton reported directly to Dulles. He was known as "No Knock" in the higher levels of the agency because he was able to walk in to see Dulles whenever he wanted. The basis of Angleton's effort was good research, and here the connections with universities, business, labor, students, and professional bodies, pioneered by the OSS under Donovan and expanded by the agency, came into significant use.

Two separate subdivisions of the staff were formed by Angleton, one composed of a Research Section and a Liaison Section, to provide support for counterintelligence operations, and the other the Office of Security, through which the responsibility of the Directorate of Plans for protecting agency personnel and installations was discharged. The Research Section compiled information from all quarters in ways designed to facilitate operations, while the Liaison Section was responsible for contacts with foreign intelligence services. "There are no friendly services," one staff specialist was quoted as saying. "There are services of friendly foreign powers."[43]

Friendship between the metropolitan centers of power did not necessarily mean friendship at the edges; there was definite operational conflict, for example, with the British in Africa and in Iran, and with the French in Algeria and the Far East. Friendship between America and Israel did not prevent the Israeli Air Force from attacking the USS *Liberty* during the 1967 Middle East War. The *Liberty* was on an intelligence-gathering mission off the Israeli coast, and the subsequent accumulation of evidence suggests that the attack was at the instigation of Israeli Intelligence, frightened that the Americans might use information collected by the *Liberty* to force Israel into an unsatisfactory peace.[44]

However, no counterintelligence organization can operate in total isolation, so cooperation with others was essential. In this respect the British Secret Intelligence Service has always been the CIA's foremost partner, not simply because of the war alliance and its help in creating OSS and CIA but also because Britain operates the only other friendly international network. Historical reasons also made the connection between the CIA and the British different from the CIA's contacts with other services. It was not really through governments that this connection worked but through bureaucrats who shared the wartime collaboration experience and many common purposes, including the containment of the Soviet Union; combating communist political activity and subversion in the West; and acting as early warning systems for their respective governments in the event of potential conflicts of interest.

Ray Cline, who from October 1951 until November 1953 was one of the CIA's Estimates liaison officers with British intelligence in London, found that there was a real spirit of mutual understanding and, despite the Burgess-Maclean and Philby scandals, trust. "I often used to be in their offices," he recalled. "They'd say 'This has a code sign which means it is not for Americans, but I can't be bothered to lock it up!' "[45] British openness was, of course, in British interests, as Cline has pointed out: "The British, recognizing the importance of keeping the United States actively engaged in an effort to contain Soviet disruptive thrusts, were extraordinarily open and cooperative with Americans in intelligence matters. They provided not only most of their highest-level joint intelligence estimates but also supplied the station chief in London with most of their clandestine intelligence MI-6 reports."[46] As Cline describes it, this connection also benefited the CIA:

There was no other major service in the world with which to collaborate. The Germans were penetrated more badly. The Israelis had a limited service of high quality. If we were to have any serious collaboration, we had to have it with the British. We had early on split the world with the Brits on code-breaking and monitoring. It would cost us millions to pick up the load on just monitoring open broadcasts. We had a lot of benefits from the operation and I would argue it was well worth taking the risks we took.

Now there was at the same time a feeling that they were stuffy, British old boy stuff, that they were careless. But then they argued that we could go and operate our machines and so on, but that they with their smaller service did about as well. And they did. I thought so, though a lot of my colleagues did not.

The people who criticized only had one major argument in their favor: the unique case of the Cambridge cell—Blunt, Philby, Burgess, Maclean. It could happen in America too: feelings of utopianism, alienation, depression in the 1930s. It was an historical accident. When we didn't have an intelligence system, our problems were in government. We had Hiss—not as bad as the Philby case, but there. Take out the Philby group and what have you got? A few penetrations of the Government Communications Headquarters in Cheltenham. Martin and Mitchell were just as bad. I don't think our system worked any better except for the one damning thing of the Cambridge cell.*

---

* Interview, Ray Cline, July 25, 1983. William Martin and Bernon Mitchell were both cryptologists and employees of the National Security Agency. They were homosexual. In 1958 they both joined the Communist Party—unknown to the NSA—and in 1960 they defected to the Soviet Union, causing an inevitable upheaval in the NSA and its security clearance procedures. Homosexuality is generally considered to have been the cause of their actions: their work in the NSA would have shown them that the Soviet Union was engaged in activity more repugnant morally than anything the United States did.

In 1983 an employee of the British Government Communications Headquarters, Geoffrey Prime, was arrested on charges of espionage for the Soviet Union. Subsequently, it was considered that Prime did real damage to Western security by enabling the Russians to identify weak communications links into which the British and Americans were electronically eavesdropping.

It was Angleton's job to ensure that the agency was not penetrated by the likes of Philby and company and to maintain contact with other services. During the 1950s, particularly strong connections (though none involving the same collaboration as with the British) were made not only with the western European services but with the Turkish, South African, Yugoslav, Taiwanese, and Thai intelligence organizations as well. Through Angleton, signals intelligence—Sigint—would be exchanged by the CIA for more detailed local information, which would always be analyzed not only for its political content but also to try to obtain penetration agents.

Allen Dulles was keen on penetration agents. He had experienced their value firsthand in Switzerland during World War II, and he made their recruitment a prime CIA target. Despite the risks involved—notably that such agents could be "turned"—Dulles' judgment ultimately was vindicated. Reflecting on Dulles' period as head of the agency, John McCone, his successor as DCI, stated in 1963: "Experience has shown penetration to be the most effective response to Soviet and [Eastern] Bloc Services."[47] However, this success was not achieved overnight. It was not until 1952 that the agency or any other Western intelligence service was able to put a Soviet official in place. In that year Major Popov, assigned to the secret Glavnoe Razvedyvatel'noe Upravlenie (GRU, or Chief Intelligence Directorate of the General Staff) in the Soviet-occupied section of Austria, dropped a letter into the car of an American diplomat in Vienna. "I am a Russian officer," wrote Popov, "attached to the Soviet Group of Forces Headquarters in Baden Bei Wien. If you are interested in buying a copy of the new table of organization for a Soviet armored division, meet me on the corner of Dorotheergasse and Stallburgasse at 8:30 P.M., November 12. If you are not there I will return at the same time on November 13. The price is 3000 Austrian schillings."[48] It was a classic "walk-in" case, similar to Dulles' experience with Fritz Kolbe during World War II, which became a precedent for American intelligence. "The piercing of secrets behind the Iron and Bamboo Curtains," wrote Dulles in 1963, "is made easier for the West because of the volunteers who come our way. . . . There is a large band who have come over to us from communist officialdom for highly ideological reasons. They have been revolted by life in the communist world and yearn for something better. Hence, for these cases I use the term 'defector' sparingly and then with apology. I prefer to call them 'volunteers.' "[49]

Dulles imprinted on the minds of newcomers to the business of agent-handling the legend "It's the walk-in trade that keeps the shop open." William Hood, Popov's case officer in the CIA, summed up the Russian's contribution as a spy for the United States until his arrest in 1958 and execution in Moscow the next year: "For six years he trundled bales of top-secret information out of the secret centers of Soviet power. In the process he shattered the Soviet military intelligence service, caused the transfer of the KGB chief (a four-star general and one of the most powerful men in the USSR), and saved the United States half a billion dollars in military research."[50]

The arrest of Popov did not affect efforts to obtain more agents and informants. Against the backdrop of the pledge of the Eisenhower administration to "liberate" Europe, the CIA's Austrian station was ordered to raise the possibility of forming a "small, tightly-knit resistance group of like-thinking comrades" around Popov. It was also to work with the German station to formulate ways "to shake the Hungarian government to its knees."[51] Both endeavors were recognized as the height of folly by the operatives on the ground and were quietly put on the back burner. They preferred to concentrate on securing additional penetration agents and debriefing the flood of defectors that made their way to the western zones of Germany and Austria.

A year after Popov's walk-in, an officer serving under him, Major Deriabin, who was security officer of the Russian colony in the Soviet zone in Vienna, walked through the gates of the American Kommandantura in Vienna and asked for asylum. Deeply disillusioned with the Soviet system, Deriabin held nothing back. He was the highest-ranking Soviet officer to have defected since the war, and he had knowledge not only of the KGB organization in Vienna (it was spying on Soviet military intelligence!) but also of the Kremlin intrigue that had followed Stalin's death.* His principal importance, however, lay in the fact that he was able independently to corroborate Popov's information, providing the agency with the best possible check on the intelligence it was receiving.

In 1954 Soviet defectors to the West included the KGB chief in Australia, Vladimir Petrov; Yuri Rastvorov, a KGB officer stationed at the Soviet Embassy in Tokyo; Nikolai Khokhlov, a member of the SMERSH section of the KGB—the assassination section—who defected in West Germany; and Joseph Swialto of the Polish intelligence service, who defected in West Berlin. Over the years scores of defectors from the Soviet Union and eastern Europe contributed to the agency's knowledge of Soviet plans and activities, often enabling vital cross-checking to take place. Emigrants to the West also helped in this effort, providing the agency with information as well as clothes and documents, reminiscent of the OSS experience with refugees from Nazism. Peter Karlow, an original CIA officer in the OSO, who organized a semi-independent Technical Services section in Germany during the early 1950s, reporting directly to Richard Helms, found emigrants especially useful:

We broke the code for the Czech identity documents. The Soviet system controls human lives through pieces of paper. They had identity docu-

---

* For purposes of simplicity, I have referred to the KGB throughout rather than follow the various changes of name the Soviet intelligence/secret police organization underwent. It began in 1917 as the CHEKA, personally established by Lenin as a successor to the old Czarist secret police. It was redesignated the GPU in 1922. The following year it became the OGPU. In 1934 it became the NKVD. In 1946, the MVD. In 1954 it received its present designation as the KGB, the Committee for State Security.

ments—work papers; living papers; travel papers; police papers—all coded, and the codes must match. You could not move without reregistering each one of these things, and if you were out of line and your code numbers did not match who you professed to be—whammo! We could produce documents that could get you in and out, and until they went back to the files to check, nobody would suspect. It was a terrific point of pride to me that while some agents were captured, they were not captured because of their documents.[52]

Behind all this activity was the drive emanating from Washington to light the fires of resistance to communism worldwide.

GEOPOLITICS

The public foreign-policy positions adopted by the Eisenhower campaign during the 1952 presidential election inevitably led to brinkmanship over Korea, the new administration's most pressing foreign problem. Korea was seen as part of an undivided, global Soviet communist threat that was more ideological than national in character and purpose. In John Foster Dulles' words, Soviet policy in Korea presented the prospect of "irreconcilable conflict" without "any permanent reconciliation" between the political and commercial freedom of the West and the centralized, undemocratic system of the East. Free elections in a united Korea were Eisenhower's first demand in April 1953, followed by an end to communist guerrilla activity in Malaysia and South East Asia; United Nations responsibility for controlling and inspecting disarmament agreements; free elections in a united Germany; free choice of government for the nations of eastern Europe; and a treaty to restore Austria's independence. If these demands were not met in some way, the threat was implicit: America would begin building its arsenal in preparation for an East-West conflict. This was expressed by a banner *New York Times* headline on April 17, 1953, the day after John Foster Dulles had testified before the Senate Foreign Relations Committee. The headline read: "Dulles Bids Soviets Cooperate or Face Vast West Arming." This foreign-policy approach caused a real flutter in the dovecotes of European foreign ministries.

Winston Churchill, prime minister again since 1951, was aware of how marginal Britain's "great power" status was and how that margin would be eroded if America and Russia really did enter into conflict or an expensive arms race, so he fought to dampen cold-war ardor. A year earlier when he had visited Truman to seek American help for the British economy, he had reflected on Britain's decline. "In Washington they will feel we are down and out," he confided to his doctor. "We have to tell them that if the rearmament is not spread out over a longer time the nations of Western Europe will be rushing to bankruptcy and starvation. When I have come to America before it has been as an equal. If, late in the war, they spoke of their sacrifices we could retort by saying that for a year and a half we fought alone; that we had suffered more losses. They have become so great and we are now so small. Poor England! We threw away so much in 1945." "I realize," he said in Washington, "that England is a broken and impoverished power, which has cast away a great part of its Empire and of late years has misused its resources."[53]

In an attempt to keep Britain at the top table of world affairs, on May 11, 1953, Churchill warned Eisenhower against seeing problems as undivided and global. Instead he urged détente and assurance to the Russians that the security of the Soviet Union would be respected, thus establishing British distance from the United States. This was emphasized by a declaration that Britain would protect its own interests without help from "the United States or anyone else."[54] In Washington this was seen in terms of another Munich, a British willingness to sell out for selfish purposes, a visibly dying empire compromising the general interests of freedom for its own selfish imperialism. From the American perspective the British showed a lamentable disposition to compromise at the wrong times and places and to be truculent at the wrong times and places too. Eisenhower did not change his views and reaffirmed America's stance toward Russia. "The world happened to be round," he was reported as saying at a news conference on May 14, "and it had no end and he didn't see how you could discuss the problems, the great basic problems of today, which were so largely philosophical in character, without thinking in global terms."[55] The idea of containment, in essence defensive, combined with a conservative Wilsonianism, in Eisenhower's view was not sufficient to deal with what was perceived as a purely aggressive communist threat.

Public brinkmanship at first had some success. Toward the end of May 1953 John Foster Dulles hinted to Peking that if the Korean War were not ended, the United States might use the atomic bomb. In less than two weeks the Chinese and North Koreans agreed to the basic American peace plan, dividing Korea near the 38th parallel, which brought peace in the form of an armistice signed on July 27. It was not a united Korea with free elections, but it was an end to fighting and a demonstration that the threat of using superior force worked. However, simultaneously another message was being received from East Germany which showed that brinkmanship would not always be successful unless atomic war was accepted as a consequence—something that the Eisenhower administration had always been careful to stress was not part of its plan. On June 16 three days of anticommunist demonstrations and riots began in East Berlin and spread throughout East Germany.* Radio Free Eu-

---

* News of the riots in East Berlin on June 17, 1953, reached CIA Washington late that evening in the form of a cable from the CIA base in Berlin requesting authority to distribute weapons to the rioters. The chief of the division responsible for CIA activity in eastern and Central Europe, John A. Bross, drafted a reply directing the Berlin base to encourage expressions of sympathy and praise for the courage of the rioters (who were mostly students), to circulate offers of asylum in West Berlin, but not to distribute weapons. The cable was cleared with the deputy director for plans, Frank Wisner, and released on his authority in Allen Dulles' absence. Subse-

rope led a chorus of support for the protests. Then Soviet armored divisions moved to suppress the revolt, and there was no move from the West to counteract them. The liberation of Europe, which John Foster Dulles had spoken about so passionately in 1952, was not going to take place with American or western European troops in the picture. When on August 8 Georgi Malenkov, Stalin's successor as premier of the Soviet Union, announced that Russia had successfully exploded a thermonuclear (hydrogen) bomb, the prospects of brinkmanship dimmed even more. As a policy it would work when dealing with less powerful foes, but now with the one foe that mattered, it would not work unless the prospect of nuclear war was accepted. The speed of Soviet nuclear-weapon advances between 1945 and 1953 and the Soviet ability not simply to imitate but also to innovate brilliantly— as demonstrated by Sakharov's development of the improved hydrogen bomb, which was a step ahead of America in 1953—made Americans generally aware of the need to run fast simply to stay in the same place, and to run head down if they were to be ahead. This realization meant that the CIA's operational abilities were to become an increasingly important element in the cold-war struggle.*

In 1953 and 1954 two of the CIA's clandestine operations—the overthrow of left-wing governments in Iran and Guatemala—met with spectacular success, vindicating the agency's connection with foreign policy. Using the total arsenal of the Directorate of Plans—sabotage, propaganda, paramilitary actions, political action—the operations succeeded with a minimum of fuss, bloodshed, and time expended. In the process the agency established itself as the most effective instrument in the secret brinkmanship of the cold war, becoming ever more important as the State Department moved back toward containment as the means of dealing with the Soviets. The Iranian operation

---

quently officials in the Eisenhower administration were unhappy about the CIA's failure to do more to make trouble for the Soviets by distributing arms and promoting the spread of violence in East Germany. Wisner and Bross felt that any such action would have led inevitably to useless bloodshed, given the obvious unwillingness of the United States to go to war to protect the rioters. Despite considerable grumbling, no real effort was made to reverse this decision (letter, John A. Bross to author, April 8, 1985).

* See *Final Report*, IV, pp. 42–43, for a concise summary of the perceptions of U.S. government at the time and the role of the CIA:

The extent to which the urgency of the Communist threat had become a shared perception is difficult to appreciate. By the close of the Korean War, a broad consensus had developed about the nature of Soviet ambitions and the need for the United States to respond. In the minds of government officials, members of the press, and the informed public, the Soviets would try to achieve their purposes by penetrating and subverting governments all over the world. The accepted role of the United States was to prevent that expansion. Washington policy makers regarded the Central Intelligence Agency as a major weapon—both offensive and defensive—against communism. By 1953, the Agency's contributions in the areas of political action and paramilitary warfare were recognized and respected. The CIA alone could perform many of the activities seemingly required to meet the Soviet threat. For senior government officials, covert operations had become a vital tool in the pursuit of United States foreign policy objectives.

also established that the United States, in secret more than in public, was no friend of the old empires and, given the choice, would opt to support national movements unless they were communist.

IRAN AND GUATEMALA

In 1953 Iran was the focus of two struggles: one between the United States and the expansionist policies of the Soviet Union and the other between the United States and the British attempt to maintain its empire and a world role. Two years earlier these struggles were precipitated by an Iranian nationalist movement, led by Muhammad Mussadegh, which came to power and effectively undercut the authority of the young shah Muhammad Reza Pahlevi, who had ruled under the British eye since 1941. British interests in the country were paramount, politically centering on the security of the British Empire—the prevention of Russian expansion to the Indian Ocean and the Gulf—and economically centering on Iran's oil, which, through the Anglo-Iranian Oil Company (AIOC), was one of Britain's principal suppliers. The company had been founded in 1901 by an English entrepreneur who was given a sixty-year oil-production monopoly throughout most of the country. The British government bought a substantial share of the company, which entered into contracts to supply the Royal Navy. The shah enjoyed production royalties from the company, which were increased in 1933 when the original monopoly was renegotiated and extended to 1993.

In 1951 Mussadegh nationalized the company, arguing that Britain had received more in profits and corporate taxation than Iran had received for the exploitation of its natural resource. Shortly after this John Foster Dulles toured the Middle East and reached the conclusion that Western influence was declining in the area and that Soviet influence was gaining. The British, he considered, "interpret our policy as one which in fact hastens their loss of prestige in the area" and were to some extent justified in this interpretation. His answer was United States involvement and a political/diplomatic effort to convince the Arab countries that America was not on the side of the British and French empires.[56] His instrument was the CIA.

Early in 1951, following nationalization of the Anglo-Iranian Oil Company, the British began pressing Mussadegh for compensation. British pressure took the form of a cruiser anchored in the Gulf of Abadan, which frightened off the oil tankers of other countries, effectively blockading Iranian oil exports. Mussadegh maintained his position despite the calamitous effect of the British blockade on the Iranian economy. Truman and the secretary of state, Dean Acheson, afraid that the dispute would ultimately affect world oil supply and prices and that it could possibly involve the Soviet Union, pressed Britain to be temperate and not to resort to force. "Only on the invitation of the Iranian government," Acheson told the British ambassador in Washington, "or Soviet military intervention, or a communist *coup d'état* in Tehran, or to evacuate British nationals in danger of attack, could we support the use of military force."[57]

Attempts to mediate the situation failed, and while not wanting to return to the prenationalization status quo, Washington did want to secure Western interests in the Iranian oil supply. This was also seen as an opportunity to extend American commercial interests into a lucrative new market at the heart of the British imperial economic order. The British, on the other hand, played up the political dangers of Soviet expansion. Anxious to secure American backing in their effort to repossess Iranian oil, they emphasized Mussadegh's left-wing proclivities. The British proposed and Eisenhower and Dulles accepted in 1953 a cooperative venture to replace Mussadegh. It was agreed, however, to operate clandestinely.

American participation came only after rumors of a Soviet-Iranian loan and the prospect of a Soviet-Iranian alliance began to circulate. Kermit Roosevelt, grandson of Theodore Roosevelt, an OSS veteran and an early covert-operations man in the CIA, was put in charge of Operation Ajax. "The original proposal for AJAX came from British Intelligence after all efforts to get Mossadegh to reverse his nationalization of the Anglo-Iranian Oil Company had failed," Roosevelt wrote later in his memoir of the operation. "The British motivation was simply to recover the AIOC oil concession. We were not concerned with that but with the obvious threat of Russian takeover."[58] The operation was essentially formulated by the Dulles brothers, working together, on June 25, 1953, at a meeting in John Foster Dulles' office in the State Department.*

At this meeting Allen Dulles, with Kermit Roosevelt in attendance, presented a CIA plan for the overthrow of Mussadegh. It had been drawn up by Roosevelt in consultation with the British and was very simple. It called for an internal *coup d'état* in Iran based on analyses made by the CIA and British Intelligence that there were powerful groupings in the country that could easily be brought to overthrow Mussadegh. After Allen Dulles and Kermit Roosevelt

---

* Apart from the Dulles brothers and Roosevelt, present were Walter Bedell Smith, now undersecretary of state, with a personal inclination in favor of clandestine operations; H. Freeman ("Doc") Matthews, one of Bedell Smith's deputies; Robert Richardson Bowie, director of the State Department's Policy Planning Staff, professor of law and then of international relations at Harvard, and later, during Admiral Stansfield Turner's period as DCI, deputy to the director, with responsibility for Estimates and analysis; Henry ("Hank") Byroade, the assistant secretary of state for the Near East, Africa, and South Asia, subsequently ambassador to more places than anyone else in the history of the State Department; Ambassador Robert D. Murphy, deputy undersecretary of state for political affairs, who organized the clandestine side of Operation Torch during World War II; Secretary of Defense Charles Wilson; and Loy Henderson, the U.S. ambassador to Iran, who flew back to Washington especially for the meeting. These were the men who masterminded the other clandestine voice of U.S. foreign policy in Iran. To this day they represent not only the sort of people involved in this kind of operation but also the offices concerned with secret activities: the departments of State and Defense and the CIA. All three sent their National Security Council representatives to the meeting, thus ensuring that correct approval and reporting procedures would be followed.

outlined their plan, detailing the cooperation with British Intelligence, which included British communications control in Cyprus and the use of British agents in Iran, John Foster Dulles asked each person present for his opinion. Doc Matthews and Bob Bowie of the State Department were noncommittal. The rest supported the scheme with varying degrees of enthusiasm, Roosevelt recalled:

> [Loy Henderson, the ambassador to Iran] was, without question, a key person in the meeting. . . . Loy's position was clear, and clearly unhappy. A gentleman himself, he preferred dealing with his foreign colleagues in a gentlemanly fashion. But Henderson was one of a small band of distinguished foreign-service officers of that era who understood the realities of life in the world we live in. He feared that Iran under the leadership of Mussadegh was slipping under Russian control. He believed that this would be a grave blow to the West and would constitute an eventual danger to U.S. national security.

All the men present would have been considered "gentlemen." John Foster and Allen Dulles, Bob Bowie, and Ambassador Murphy were all lawyers. All the men came from or had joined the Washington Establishment. But all were prepared for dirty work if necessary. Henderson summed it up. "I don't like this kind of business at all," he said. "You know that. But we are confronted by a desperate, a dangerous situation and a madman who would ally himself with the Russians. We have no choice but to proceed with this undertaking. May God grant us success." "That's that, then," said John Foster Dulles, "let's get going!" With these words the CIA began its operation to secure American control in Iran.[59]

Within two months Operation Ajax succeeded in overthrowing Mussadegh and bringing Iran firmly into the West's orbit. The operation's fundamental assumption, that in a showdown between the shah and Mussadegh (especially if Mussadegh had Russian backing) the army and the people would for reasons of loyalty back the shah, was proved correct. The cost was minimal—less than two hundred thousand dollars—and the risk, while significant, was no greater, in the agency's estimation, than if nothing were done. Before the operation went into action Roosevelt took the step of deciding who, exactly, should replace Mussadegh. He chose General Fazlollah Zahedi, who had been arrested in 1941 by the British, suspected of being pro-Nazi, and interned in Palestine for the rest of the war.

According to Roosevelt, when the British officials in Washington on the operation, led by Sir Patrick Dean, a senior Foreign Office official, heard the news they were nonplussed:

> There was a moment's silence. Foster and Bedell had no idea whom I was talking about. The British knew only too well. . . .
> Foster looked at me and then at our British visitors. In his deliberate

drawl he asked, "Well, what do you think of that?" The British hesitated, but clearly it was up to the Foreign Office, represented by Pat Dean, to reply.

Pat cleared his throat. "I'm sure we shall have to refer it to London for comment." After a brief pause he added: "If this is what you and the Iranians feel is necessary, I don't see that we have much choice." He gave me a questioning look.

"I'm afraid that's right, Pat. Zahedi is not our selection, I promise you that. But we do think that the Shah must choose his own Prime Minister. And Fazlollah Zahedi appears to be his choice." I added once again that our Iranian contacts assured us, for what it was worth, that the general was not anti-British. . . .

I took our British friends directly back to Allen's office at 2430 E Street. There, in an effort to put them at ease, tea was served. (Probably the British would call it tea only out of politeness; it came in small tea bags and was not the best I've ever had.) Once they had got it down, I raised the question that had been plaguing me. Who *were* their principal representatives of whom they were so proud? . . . Mr. Cochran [one of the British officials] spoke almost formally, as I had just done in Foster's office. "Our especial allies are a couple of top-flight fellows. . . . We refer to them as Nossey and Cafron. . . ."

And here I must confess that I allowed professional scruples to overcome what moral scruples I might have felt. Now that I was sure that [our agents] were truly ours and ours alone, I was not about to disclose them to the British.*

Perhaps he did not need to; perhaps the British realized that by seeking American help they had ensured that American interests would come first.

In September, Roosevelt's Operation Ajax was completed. Mussadegh was dismissed and arrested. Zahedi became prime minister. The Anglo-Iranian Oil Company was not restored. Instead a nationalized company known as the National Iranian Oil Company was formed. This was operated by an international consortium in which British Petroleum (formerly Anglo-Iranian) held 40 percent; Royal Dutch Shell 14 percent; Gulf, Mobil, Standard Oil of New Jersey, Standard Oil of California, and Texas Company 7 percent each; nine other American oil companies a total of 5 percent, and the Compagnie Française des Petroles 6 percent. In all, American oil interests held 40 percent of the new consortium—the same percentage as the British, who until 1951 had controlled all of Iran's oil.

Although the Iranian operation was a stunning CIA success, Kermit Roosevelt sensed that it might have dangerous implications—and indeed it had. The wrong conclusions were drawn in Washington about the nature and use of

---

* Roosevelt, *Countercoup*, pp. 122–24. The British gave the correct names of their principal agents, and so Roosevelt was saying he knew that his agents were not the same. This is not certain. The British agents were native Iranians belonging to the commercial middle class with influence in the bazaars of Tehran. Through them rumors were spread which in a matter of days generated popular demonstrations in support of the shah and against Mussadegh.

covert operations, and these conclusions eventually led to the Bay of Pigs disaster. Roosevelt summed up his feelings in this way:

> Foster Dulles had been so pleased and mesmerized by the success I'd had in Iran that he just figured I could solve any problem anywhere in the world. I tried to explain to him very carefully just why it was we'd succeeded in Iran: because careful studies had convinced us that first and foremost the army and secondly the people wanted the same things we did. Under those circumstances it's possible to achieve the results you want. This was something that could be done without sending the marines in. When I reported to the White House, I could see Foster Dulles sitting there, very prominently placed, licking his chops. I said to the group when I'd finished that this operation had succeeded because the people, but most of all the army, wanted the same thing we did and therefore it was something that could be done by clandestine means. And I said, if you don't want something that the people and the army want, don't give it to clandestine operations, give it to the marines. And Foster Dulles sat there, just obviously not accepting that at all.
>
> He called me in from time to time and placed other burdens on me, and most of them I rejected. Finally it got to the point where I said, it just can't go on this way so I'm going to quit. And I will say that Allen Dulles was entirely in agreement with me. He was very much Foster's younger brother—he did basically what Foster wanted him to do—but in this particular case, even though he didn't stand up and be counted, he told me he was in agreement with me.*

Within a few weeks of returning to Washington after the Iranian exploit Roosevelt was offered command of the CIA's second major covert operation: bringing down the government of the apparently left-wing Jacobo Arbenz in Guatemala. He refused the offer, preferring more sophisticated operations in Arabia and Egypt. The scheme to replace Arbenz, however, went ahead at John Foster Dulles' urging and with the enthusiastic support of an increasingly confident CIA. In the agency's collective mind, Roosevelt's success in Iran proved the effectiveness of covert action, and now it would be tried again. The

---

* Interview, Kermit Roosevelt, November 8, 1983; see also Roosevelt, *Countercoup*, pp. 208–210. Roosevelt reported on his mission directly to Eisenhower, John Foster Dulles, Allen Dulles, General Andrew Goodpaster, Eisenhower's chief of staff, Admiral Radford, the chairman of the Joint Chiefs of Staff, and Charles Wilson, the secretary of defense. He also reported directly to the British prime minister, Winston Churchill, who at the time was recovering from a stroke at 10 Downing Street. Churchill kept dozing off, and Roosevelt spent two hours with him, telling him the story between dozes. "When he woke up again I described my final meeting with the Shah, the bringing in of Prime Minister Zahedi and my emphatic statement that they must not consider themselves in any way obligated to us. At this point Churchill was hardly overwhelmed with enthusiasm, but he raised no objection."

Roosevelt had used very few people in Ajax. "Well, agency personnel, I would say six to eight at the most. And the money that was available there, well, I can't remember but I think we had seven to eight hundred thousand dollars available, of which we used during the course of the operation maybe ten thousand dollars" (interview, Kermit Roosevelt, in Granada Television program, *World In Action: The Rise and Fall of the CIA*, Part II).

relationship between the United Fruit Company and Guatemala was similar to that between the Anglo-Iranian Oil Company and Iran. It had a monopoly on the country's shipping, communications, and railroad operations and was the largest commercial entity there. Unlike Anglo-Iranian Oil, however, United Fruit did not get on that well with the natives. Arbenz, who had come to power as the country's second democratically elected president in March 1951,* found that his political base depended on continuing the social and economic reform instituted by his predecessor. This was compounded by the militancy of the small but important Communist party and the large, effective labor groupings that supported Arbenz and on whose votes he relied.

The situation brought about a polarization in Guatemalan politics between Arbenz on one side and the strong, agrarian, commercial, conservative opposition on the other. In 1953 Arbenz confiscated the United Fruit Company's holdings. John Foster Dulles heeded the company's complaints and pressed Arbenz for compensation. Arbenz refused, largely because the country could not afford to pay proper compensation, and he also refused to take the matter to the International Court of Arbitration at the Hague. This cleared the way for action. On the diplomatic front, the State Department secured a condemnation of Guatemala's actions from the Tenth Inter-American Conference meeting in March 1954. Secretly, plans that had been made by the CIA in 1952 to overthrow Arbenz by supporting Guatemalan exiles and mercenaries in Nicaragua were dusted off and expanded.† Colonel J. C. King, chief of the Western Hemisphere division in the CIA's Directorate of Plans, was put in charge after Roosevelt turned the offer down. King had more faith in military approaches to covert operations than in sophisticated political ones. He put the CIA into action by organizing a "revolt" in the town of Salamá, a provincial capital not far from Guatemala City. Two hundred guerrillas held the town for seventeen hours before being arrested after a brief gunfight in which four of the guerrillas were killed. King was pulled off the operation, and Frank Wisner was given direct charge.

Wisner took stock of the project and determined to demonstrate the way in which Donovan's ideas of first softening up a target with sabotage, propaganda, and commando raids and then following through with a thoroughgoing attack could be used in peacetime. He named the project Operation Success and placed Tracy Barnes, his deputy, in control. His choice of field commander was Colonel Albert Haney, the CIA station chief in Korea, who while

---

* The election took place on November 13, 1950, and the inauguration occurred four months later. Arbenz obtained 65 percent of the 400,000 votes cast.

† Truman approved Operation Fortune in 1952 by which Arbenz was to be overthrown with the backing of Nicaragua under Anastasio Somoza García. Colonel King was put in charge of the operation by Bedell Smith. He used United Fruit Company ships to carry arms and ammunition to a group of Guatemalan exiles in Nicaragua. The venture was also supported by Trujillo in the Dominican Republic and Jiménez in Venezuela. However, when David Bruce, undersecretary of state, learned of the plan, he opposed it as illegitimate and convinced Dean Acheson, secretary of state, to persuade Truman to cancel the operation.

a counterintelligence specialist in Korea had gained valuable experience in paramilitary and commando operations. King, miffed at his removal from the project, tried to convince Wisner, Barnes, and Haney that his way of doing things had been best: working in collaboration with the United Fruit Company and looking to the Guatemalan army to oust Arbenz themselves. "If you think you can run this operation without United Fruit, you're crazy!" King told Haney. He told Wisner that the idea of using guerrillas to overthrow a government had not worked in Korea and that now Haney would "be starting a civil war in the middle of Central America." "Do we want another Korean War right at our doorstep?" he asked, and argued for a massive program of military aid to the Guatemalan army in exchange for toppling Arbenz.

Wisner passed King's objections to Allen Dulles, who consulted his brother. Then, at a cocktail party for his chief lieutenants at his home in Georgetown, Allen Dulles relayed the decision to go ahead as planned.

"Colonel," he said to Haney, "there's one question I want to ask you. Do you really think you can succeed?"

"Sir," Haney answered, "with your help we can win."

Dulles grinned and slapped his hands on Haney's shoulders. "Then go to it, my boy," he said, laughing. "You've got the green light." Without a word J. C. King strode out of the room.[60]

Even so, Dulles reckoned that the plan had only about a 40 percent chance of success. Between January and mid-June 1954 the CIA spent, by some estimates, about $20 million, organizing a guerrilla army and a secret air force, setting up secret radio stations, and finding a leader—Colonel Carlos Castillo Armas—to replace Arbenz. On May 15 the CIA was able to confirm that a Swedish freighter, the *Alfhem*, had delivered 15,424 cases of Czech military supplies at Puerto Barrios, Guatemala's east-coast port.

This news shook Washington and removed any remaining restraints on Operation Success. With air support, Armas launched an attack on Guatemala City on June 18 and within days overthrew Arbenz.* In Washington everyone

---

* The President took a very close interest in the operation throughout. He was, after all, a soldier by training and was interested in covert operations. In the middle of the putsch Armas found the Guatemalan army pushing him back and no popular uprising in his support. For the operation to succeed at that stage required either air support or the marines. Eisenhower met with the Dulles brothers and Henry Holland, assistant secretary of state for inter-American affairs, who "made no secret of his conviction that the United States should keep hands off, insisting that other Latin American republics would, if our action became known, interpret our shipment of planes as intervention in Guatemala's internal affairs."

Holland's view was rejected by Eisenhower and the others, and the President asked Allen Dulles, "What do you think Castillo's chances would be without the aircraft?"

"About zero."

"Suppose we supply the aircraft . . . ?"

"About 20 percent."

When the meeting ended, Eisenhower again turned to Allen Dulles: "Allen, the figure of 20 percent was persuasive. . . . If you had told me that the chances would be 90 percent, I would have had a much more difficult decision."

was delighted. John Foster Dulles hailed the Armas government in glowing terms, and President Eisenhower asked the CIA for another personal briefing. David Phillips, who had run the clandestine anti-Arbenz "Voice of Liberation" radio station, recalled the White House visit and Allen Dulles' preparations:

"Tomorrow morning, gentlemen," Dulles said, "we will go to the White House to brief the President. Let's run over your presentations." It was a warm summer night. We drank iced tea as we sat around a garden table in Dulles' back yard. The lighted shaft of the Washington Monument could be seen through the trees. . . . Finally Brad rehearsed his speech. When he finished Allen Dulles said, "Brad, I've never heard such crap." It was the nearest thing to an expletive I ever heard Dulles use. The Director turned to me: "They tell me you know how to write. Work out a new speech for Brad. . . ."

We went to the White House in the morning. Gathered in the theater in the East Wing were more notables than I had ever seen: the President, his Joint Chiefs of Staff, the Secretary of State—Allen Dulles's brother, Foster—the Attorney General, and perhaps two dozen other members of the President's Cabinet and household staff. . . .

The lights were turned off while Brad used slides during his report. A door opened near me. In the darkness I could see only a silhouette of the person entering the room; when the door closed it was dark again, and I could not make out the features of the man standing next to me. He whispered a number of questions: "Who is that? Who made that decision?"

I was vaguely uncomfortable. The questions from the unknown man next to me were very insistent, furtive. Brad finished and the lights went up. The man moved away. He was Richard Nixon, the Vice President.

Eisenhower's first question was to Hector: "How many men did Castillo Armas lose?" Hector said only one, a courier. . . . Eisenhower shook his head, perhaps thinking of the thousands who had died in France. "Incredible. . . ."

Nixon asked a number of questions, concise and to the point, and demonstrated a thorough knowledge of the Guatemalan political situation. He was impressive—not at all the disturbing man he was in the shadows.

Eisenhower turned to his Chief of the Joint Chiefs. "What about the Russians? Any reaction?"

General Ridgeway answered. "They don't seem to be up to anything. But the navy is watching a Soviet sub in the area; it could be there to evacuate some of Arbenz's friends, or to supply arms to any resisters."

Eisenhower shook hands all around. "Great," he said to Brad, "that was

---

Allen was equal to the situation. "Mr. President," he said, "when I saw Henry walking into your office with three large lawbooks under his arm, I knew he had lost his case already."

Apart from the airplanes, the key to Operation Success was the psychological and propaganda onslaught on Arbenz and his government, so that they believed Armas was far stronger and more popular than he was and that he was far more successful than was actually the case in the first days of his putsch. (Dwight D. Eisenhower, *The White House Years: Mandate for Change 1953-1956* [New York: Doubleday, 1963, pp. 425-426]).

a good briefing." Hector and I smiled at each other as Brad flushed with pleasure. The President's final handshake was with Allen Dulles. "Thanks, Allen, and thanks to all of you. You've averted a Soviet beachhead in our hemisphere." Eisenhower spoke to his Chief of Naval Operations. "Watch that sub, Admiral. If it gets near the coast of Guatemala we'll sink the son-of-a-bitch." The President strode from the room.[61]

So it was "our hemisphere," a transformation of the Monroe Doctrine, which has been asserting U.S. protection for revolutionary change against the empires, with no intention of America ever going beyond its borders or colonizing itself. It was also "our CIA" that had done the job. From Iran and Guatemala "both the agency and Washington policymakers acquired a sense of confidence in the CIA's capacity for operational success," as the Church Committee was to observe twenty years later in addressing some of the consequences.[62]

The nature of Arbenz's government, however, meant that Operation Success launched both the CIA and the United States on a new path. Mussadegh in Iran was left-wing and had indulged in talks with Russian diplomats about possible alliances and treaties. Arbenz, on the other hand, had simply been trying to reform his country and had not sought foreign help in this. Thus by overthrowing him, America was in effect making a new decision in the cold war. No longer would the Monroe Doctrine, which was directed against foreign imperial ambitions in the Americas from across the Atlantic or the Pacific, suffice. Now internal subversion—communism from within—was an additional cause for direct action. What was not said, but what was already clear after the events in East Germany the previous year, was that the exercise of American power, even clandestinely through the CIA, would not be undertaken where Soviet power was already established. In addition, regardless of the principles being professed, when direct action was taken (whether clandestine or not), the interests of American business would be a consideration: if the flag was to follow, it would quite definitely follow trade.

The whole arrangement of American power in the world from the nineteenth century was based on commercial concerns and methods of operation. This had given America a material empire through the ownership of foreign transport systems, oil fields, estancias, stocks, and shares. It had also given America resources and experience (concentrated in private hands) with the world outside the Americas, used effectively by the OSS during World War II. American government, however, had stayed in America, lending its influence to business but never trying to overthrow other governments for commercial purposes. After World War II, American governments were more willing to use their influence and strength all over the world for the first time and to see an ideological implication in the "persecution" of U.S. business interests.

Guatemala was a case in point. Iran provided an arena that enabled the United States to operate both on principled grounds—it was combating a threatened extension of Soviet power—and on commercial grounds—it was subsuming the fifty-year-old British oil monopoly. Guatemala was spoken of in the same principled terms (although John Foster Dulles admitted that it was "impossible to produce evidence clearly tying the Guatemalan government to Moscow")* and served as a warning to the rest of the Americas that U.S. interests as perceived in Washington would enjoy U.S. protection.†

---

* Blanche Weisen Cook, *The Declassified Eisenhower—A Divided Legacy of Peace and Political Warfare* (New York: Doubleday, 1981), p. 269. This was said by John Foster Dulles in May 1954 at a meeting with the ambassadors of Brazil, Panama, El Salvador, Uruguay, and other Latin American states. However, he also said that if the Soviet Union were allowed to "establish a puppet state in this hemisphere" without the support or "threat of the Red Army," it would be "a tremendous propaganda victory" for communism. Such a victory, he said, would weaken American "assurances to states in Asia and in Europe that we would support them in their efforts to eliminate communism . . . because of our demonstrated inability to prevent the establishment of a communist puppet state in our own hemisphere."

† U.S. companies moved back into Guatemala right away. One of Armas' first actions was to introduce investment guarantees. The United Fruit Company was given back most of its expropriated property.

—9—

Cry Havoc
1956

It was outside the Americas that the struggle with world communism took place during the 1950s, although at times it had its base in the United States itself.* The various schemes for "operating or influencing international organizations in every field where Communists fronts had seized ground," as Tom Braden put it, "and in some where they had not even begun to operate,"[1] began in 1952 under Allen Dulles. In Senate testimony William Colby acknowledged that between 1953 and 1973 the CIA "conducted several programs to survey and open selected mail between the United States and two Communist countries." According to a secret Senate note by Colby, these programs were based in New York and San Francisco and were directed against mail to China and the Soviet Union. Their purpose, said Colby, was "to identify individuals in active correspondence with Communist countries for presumed counter-intelligence purposes"; "to learn the foreign contacts of a number of Americans of counter-intelligence interest," and "to determine the nature and extent of censorship techniques."[2]

Operating within the United States had been difficult for the agency ever since 1944, when the journalist Walter Trohan compared Donovan's plans for a postwar intelligence organization to an "American Gestapo." It was also dif-

---

* There were two separate struggles: the ordinary struggle of any nation for its own interests (the Iranian operation could be seen primarily in these terms) and the ideological struggle with communism for possession of the world. The double helix of these struggles involved the agency intimately: it was intelligence business.

ficult because the United States was considered FBI territory.* A territorial battle was avoided initially when the man in charge of the program, James Angleton, made the case that the mail-opening operation was a necessary backup to the CIA's foreign operations. (Angleton knew that this "hot pursuit" argument would be hard to turn down.) The FBI was not informed of the mail openings, which were officially known in the CIA as Project HTLingual, until 1958, when it requested permission to mount a similar operation of its own and was told by the then postmaster general that the CIA had been opening mail for five years.[3]

A compromise was struck, and from 1958 the agency shared the information it gained from HTLingual with the bureau. This was the most direct CIA operation in the United States, and it raised both legal and bureaucratic difficulties, which eventually came to a head in the 1970s. It was not, however, the only U.S.-based operation the CIA ever mounted. The agency also engaged in a number of indirect activities in conjunction with police forces and universities, where it funded research consultancies and covert training programs. In all cases the fundamental basis for the agency's domestic operations was its responsibility for national security and its need for a safe area— a sanctuary—where training and experience could be gained for its foreign operations.

Although the range of agency activities was essentially established under Hillenkoetter and Bedell Smith, it was filled out by Allen Dulles. In one respect, however, Dulles differed substantially from both his predecessors: he did not seek to impose either himself or the agency as the coordinator of U.S. intelligence. He preferred instead to work alone, depending upon his close personal relationships with America's governing elite. The fact that HTLingual existed for five years before the FBI learned of it was a case in point. (It is important to remember that the bureau did not uncover the operation but was informed of its existence.) Complain though J. Edgar Hoover might, Allen Dulles was secure: his brother was secretary of state, and they both had Eisenhower's backing. The official relationships that existed between the three were secondary to their personal connections, especially the one that existed between Allen and John Foster. Allen Dulles probably never quite realized how important it was to him that his brother was secretary of state until 1959, when John Foster died. Until then one telephone call, one meeting at home could sort out problems or resolve policy, with Allen and the agency scrupulously loyal to his brother's and the President's decisions.

"I had some project that had to do with a publication—I think it was in

---

* Through these programs the CIA was backing into the forbidden territory of domestic operations. Mail from Soviet agents in the United States would not have been sent directly to Moscow: it would have been sent to innocuous addresses in neutral countries such as Switzerland, which would act as "cut-outs." So the result of the programs was that the agency was in effect monitoring the mail of the American Communist party.

France," said Tom Braden, giving an example of the power in Allen Dulles' relationship with his brother:

> I went over to the French desk in the State Department, saw the chief at the French desk, told him I was going to do this in France, and he objected. And I remember I was astonished because it was not a very important expenditure—it was a few hundred thousand dollars for a publication, and the communists had one just like it, so there was every good reason for doing it. But I didn't argue with the man, because I knew what could happen. And I went back and I went up to the director's office, and I said, "Allen, French desk in the State Department doesn't want to do this." And Allen said, "What?!" then picked up the phone: "Foster, one of your people seems to be a little less than cooperative." That's power.[4]

With this sort of contact and support, it was not surprising that Allen felt no need to assert his dominance in intelligence; he was given it by the man who mattered most to him and the country. He knew very well that if he ever had a problem with someone in the FBI or the Pentagon, he always had one huge advantage they did not have: a brother in the cabinet. It also meant that Allen was able to concentrate on covert operations—the part of his job he enjoyed most and for which the President had the most praise and John Foster the most respect.

COVERT ACTION

The CIA's success in Iran and Guatemala colored Washington's general view of the agency and promoted the Directorate of Plans (DDP) in importance within the agency. Because of Dulles' personal preference for clandestine activity, Frank Wisner, the DDP, had easy and frequent access to him. Wisner was Dulles' friend and colleague from OSS days in 1945, and both men enjoyed spending time together concocting plans and schemes. Between 1953 and 1961 the clandestine side of the agency enjoyed an average of 54 percent of the agency's total annual budget. During the Korean War its average funding was even higher, and from 1950 on, the number of personnel increased both directly within the DDP and indirectly in the supporting departments: Administration, Personnel, Communications, Logistics, Security, and Training.[5] Between 1953 and 1963 the DDP evolved into a distinct department within the agency and, as a result, received special treatment. Its evolution reflected the change of battleground with Russia into the clandestine world, away from uniformed armies. With secrecy required to protect covert operations, top agency officials were the only ones allowed to scrutinize the directorate. This too gave the DDP an advantage over the other directorates. In addition, the DDP's internal financial and political strength increased with every successful operation.

The DDP's ascendency was in sharp contrast to the haphazard management arrangements of Dulles and Wisner, neither of whom was very interested in the art of bureaucracy, or "man management," and both of whom believed strongly that the whole nature of covert operations and clandestine activity required informal rather than formal routines. They recognized the agency as a young organization, untrammeled as yet by the entrenched bureaucratic attitudes of Washington, attractive to the best and the brightest, and valued by the President and the secretary of state for its flexibility and the rapidity with which it could respond to and resolve problems such as those in Iran and Guatemala. Division chiefs such as Desmond FitzGerald were encouraged to take initiatives, to be buccaneers. At times Allen Dulles and Frank Wisner took on this swashbuckling role themselves, setting up task forces and endorsing projects without consulting or informing other sections of the agency that should have been involved. Richard Bissell recalled:

> After I became DDP I began to see Allen's managerial practices from a slightly different standpoint. He would quite often call someone who was two or three echelons down from me. He would call them about a cable that had come in, and he would sometimes tell them how to answer it. I finally blew up at Allen and said "That's just no way to run a railroad! You must go through my office." Allen's instant reaction on the phone was quite violent. He said "I'm going to speak to anybody I want to in this agency about anything I want to speak to them about. The rules are very simple: if I tell a branch chief or a division chief of yours to respond to a cable in a particular way, and they write a cable, it will of course come across your desk for approval, and if you don't agree with it you can take it up with me. If your people haven't been telling you about their conversations with me, that's because you're not enforcing the rules!" He was right. I came to live with it, and I realized it was part of his way, and it was a perfectly good way to run the place.*

The secrecy the DDP maintained in order to protect the security of its operations and agents caused the directorate to be viewed with suspicion by the Directorate of Intelligence analysts, who had no way of gauging the reliability of a source, simply because they knew nothing about it. This problem contributed to one of the most important developments in modern American intelligence—the turning away from human sources to nonhuman ones in the form of electronic and communications intelligence. "With the passage of time,"

---

* Interview, Richard Bissell, July 18, 1983. The comptroller's office was responsible for scrutinizing the DDP's budgetary expenditure, but under Dulles, special activities were excluded. The inspector general's office, established in 1951 with the job of monitoring the agency's activities, was restricted in its dealings with the DDP until 1957, when Dulles gave way. Throughout this period the DDP maintained its own inspection staff—an example itself of the way in which Dulles and Wisner set up staffs that duplicated the work of other staffs in the agency, achieving even greater compartmentalization through a multiplicity of "self-sufficient" units and departments.

Richard Helms said, looking back to the 1950s, "a distortion threatened to change the character of our work. The collectors with technical gadgets began to disparage the efforts of the human collectors. The new cry from the gadgeteers was, 'Give us the money and leave it to us.'

"And indeed, why take risks running spies when gadgets would tell you what you wanted to know? But therein lay a fallacy. And the debate over the elements of that fallacy is with us today and will inevitably crop up from time to time in the future. Why? Because gadgets cannot divine man's intentions."[6] In the 1950s, however, the advent of electronic gadgetry enabled Dulles to establish the agency's independence from the other intelligence agencies of government, which for a period pressed hard for the CIA's clandestine service to be at their disposal too so that they could conduct their own operations. By concentrating on old-fashioned human intelligence in the DDP, Dulles allowed electronic and communications intelligence to expand elsewhere, notably in the Department of Defense and the National Security Agency. As spies in the skies and space proliferated, the pressure on Dulles to hire out CIA espionage agents was greatly reduced.

After the Korean War and the exploits in Iran and Guatemala, covert action substantially increased. These actions not only provided America with a forceful foreign-policy lever and politically attractive results; they also gave it a method of dealing with the political and propaganda battles waged by the Soviet Union. After Korea there was a change in the way the United States perceived the Soviets. No longer was a direct "hot war" feared. Rather the reality of a prolonged cold war was accepted, with the result that methods were needed to play a covert game of handball with the Russians. The CIA was accepted as the natural vehicle for America's counterthrust.

FOCUS ON LATIN AMERICA

During Eisenhower's first full meeting of his cabinet designate, eight days before his inauguration, the draft of his inaugural address was discussed. He wanted to say that Moscow had moved from being the capital of autocracy to being the cockpit of revolution. Henry Cabot Lodge, who was to be U.S. ambassador to the United Nations, wondered delicately if Eisenhower should use the word "revolution":

> *Henry Cabot Lodge:* Lots of people won't like to hear that word revolution. . . . A lot of people would like to have a revolution and it might help revolutions in some parts of the world as it is now.
>
> *Eisenhower:* I would like to make that change. In Mexico today they still talk about revolution like the second coming of the Lord. While it hasn't worked too well, nevertheless it is better than they had.

Charles Wilson: We had a little revolution in our country, a peaceful
   one.
Eisenhower: Little?
John Foster Dulles: We had a violent one.
Wilson: I think we are going to have an American renaissance now.[7]

The renaissance was back to the frontier, only this time the frontier was the
rest of the world. The frontier mentality of direct action and the seizing of opportunities was rekindled. Since both the suppression as well as the fueling of
revolution was part of this, Eisenhower and his team thought it best not to
mention revolution at all. They recognized that there was no point in being
caught in public in a contradiction. They did not want revolutions that interfered with American interests; they did want revolutions that interfered with
Russian ones.

South and Central America were seen as areas of paramount American interest. Their raw materials were of economic and military importance, and
their countries' votes in the United Nations were important politically; before
the Guatemalan operation John Foster Dulles felt it necessary to canvass Latin
American support. President José Figueres Ferrer of Costa Rica, a moderate socialist, made Washington anxious because of his liberalism. His policies allowing communists as well as noncommunists to enjoy political asylum in Costa
Rica were considered close to outright opposition to American interests. Conditions in Latin America, John Foster Dulles told Congress in 1953, "are
somewhat comparable to conditions as they were in China in the mid-thirties
when the Communist movement was getting started. They were beginning to
develop the hatred of the American and the Britisher, but we didn't do anything about it. . . . Well, if we don't look out, we will wake up some morning
and read in the newspapers that there happened in South America the same
kind of thing that happened in China in 1949."[8]

Using the same forthright terms he had used earlier to impress the Truman administration concerning Russia, George Kennan provided the blueprint
for American action in Latin America in 1950. According to Kennan, Latin
America's importance to the United States was threefold: to protect "our raw
materials," to prevent the "military exploitation of Latin America by the
enemy," and to prevent "the psychological mobilization of Latin America
against us." Moreover, Latin America would be the last area of support left to
the United States if Europe turned anti-American. As a result, declared Kennan, American policy toward Latin America had to put U.S. security interests
first. "The final answer might be an unpleasant one," he concluded, "but . . .
we should not hesitate before police repression by the local government. This
is not shameful, since the communists are essentially traitors. . . . It is better to
have a strong regime in power than a liberal government if it is indulgent and
relaxed and penetrated by communists."[9]

By the end of 1954, thirteen of the twenty countries of Latin America were military dictatorships. As strong regimes that could deliver American requirements for raw materials and political support, they in turn enjoyed the support of the United States. The CIA was the channel of support, training police forces, temporarily assigning advisers, exchanging information and intelligence.[10] In Costa Rica, by 1955 the only democracy in Central America, Figueres' refusal to be stampeded into schemes of nationalization and expropriation and his willingness to conduct business as usual with American firms resulted in only a half-hearted CIA attempt to replace him. Articles were placed in Costa Rican papers; Figueres' own telephone was bugged; Costa Rican political parties, politicians, labor unions, and labor leaders were compromised. It soon emerged that there was no real need to replace Figueres quickly, so such methods were enough to keep him unsettled and thereby focus his attention on his own political survival rather than on making moves toward Russia. In 1958 Figueres left power, and his nominee to succeed him was defeated in that year's presidential election.[11]

INTELLIGENCE ADMINISTRATION

It was in Europe, however, that the major clandestine activities were conducted during the 1950s, and, as in the late 1940s, these activities were underwritten by a set of administrative devices geared to provide the agency with both the support and the rationale it needed in the cold war. In July 1954 Eisenhower commissioned Lieutenant General James Doolittle—the swashbuckler of the air force—to report on the agency's covert activities and to "make any recommendations calculated to improve the conduct of these operations." Doolittle completed his report in two months with the very active support and cooperation of Allen Dulles. It was expected to be a hard-nosed, action-oriented report, and it was. It summarized in sixty-nine pages American cold-war attitudes in the mid-1950s after Korea:

> The acquisition and proper evaluation of adequate and reliable intelligence on the capabilities and intentions of Soviet Russia is today's most important military and political requirement. . . .
>
> Because the United States is relatively new at the game, and because we are opposed by a police state enemy whose social discipline and security measures have been built up and maintained at a high level for many years, the usable information we are obtaining is still far short of our needs.
>
> As long as it remains national policy, another important requirement is an aggressive covert psychological, political and paramilitary organization more effective, more unique and, if necessary, more ruthless than that employed by the enemy. No one should be allowed to stand in the way of the prompt, efficient and secure establishment of this mission. . . .

It is now clear that we are facing an implacable enemy whose avowed objective is world domination by whatever means and at whatever cost. There are no rules in such a game. Hitherto acceptable norms of human conduct do not apply. If the United States is to survive, long-standing American concepts of "fair play" must be reconsidered. We must develop effective espionage and counterespionage services and must learn to subvert, sabotage and destroy our enemies by more clever, more sophisticated and more effective methods than those used against us. It may become necessary that the American people be made acquainted with, understand and support this fundamentally repugnant philosophy.*

Following this through, the report recommended that "every possible scientific and technical approach to the intelligence problem" should be explored, since the closed society of the Eastern bloc made old-fashioned human espionage "prohibitive" in terms of "dollars and human lives." The CIA was properly placed in the organization of the government, said the report; and the laws relating to its functions were deemed sufficient to enable it to undertake the task of penetrating the closed East. Numerous recommendations were made for more efficient internal administration, including procedures to check over personnel, reduce costs, and increase cooperation between the clandestine and analytical sides of the agency:

We have made a study of the educational and experience background of the 34 key people in the Agency's chain of command. From this the following composite figures emerge: all are natural born US citizens; they range in age from 38 to 66 yrs, averaging 47.9 years; 32 are married; 17 have 1 or more dependent children; 21 are wholly dependent on government salary; all 34 are college graduates; 15 have advanced degrees. Twelve have had 1 or more years' business experience; all but 6 have served in the US Armed Forces; 15 have had intelligence experience (O.S.S., Armed Forces, etc.) prior to 1947; and 10 have had specialized C.I.A. training. Of this group 32 have had 3 years or more service with C.I.A., 20 have had 5 years or more, and 15 have been with the Agency for the full 7 years since it was established.

Of the total CIA staff as of June 30, 1954, "males make up 58 percent of total, females 42 percent; average age is 34.2 years and two-thirds are in the 25–39-year age bracket. As for education, approximately 68 percent of the total are high school graduates, some 47 percent have B.A. (or equivalent) degrees, and about 24 percent have done postgraduate work or possess advanced degrees."

* *Report on the Covert Activities of the Central Intelligence Agency*, September 30, 1954, the "Doolittle Report." "Fundamentally repugnant" was a code phrase. Every great combination of people is stained with blood: America itself had been won by "fundamentally repugnant" revolutionary, Mexican, civil, and Indian wars. Its use by Doolittle showed a fear of public opinion, of what Americans might think if they knew what was being done in their name. In the 1980s, a decade after the reports of the Church Committee, which assumed that Americans would find dirty work "fundamentally repugnant," the assumption was much less certain.

In addition, 73 percent of the total had some foreign-language training or experience.

Although, the report stated, this talent pool contained some dead wood, it nevertheless made it possible for the CIA to be the foremost agency for conducting the "fundamentally repugnant," ruthless cold war against Soviet Russia.* It was matched by a new National Security Council directive, NSC 5412, which gave secret though formal substance to the agency's command to reconsider the American concept of fair play and to be more clever, sophisticated, and ruthless than the enemy.

Under the previous governing NSC directive, NSC 10/2, dating back to 1948, weekly meetings between the President's senior consultants in the White House, State and Defense departments, and the CIA's assistant director for policy coordination were held. It was a somewhat informal system, and meetings tended to take up new projects in advance of their formal presentation (if they were presented at all) to the National Security Council. Under Hillenkoetter, Bedell Smith, and Allen Dulles, no real restriction of CIA activities resulted, largely because of the attitudes of the time as demonstrated in the Doolittle Report, the agency's growing competence and list of successes, and the personal pull with the President of two of the directors, Bedell Smith and Allen Dulles.

For Eisenhower the CIA was the chief instrument for carrying the cold war to the enemy, and he kept a close eye on it personally. It was controversial, and things could go wrong. Allen Dulles' authority derived from the President's close attention. Doolittle had given Eisenhower a critical verbal report on Dulles as part of his investigation of the agency's covert activities. He said that Dulles' principal strength was "his unique knowledge of his subject; he has his whole heart in it," but he was a bad organizer and the quality of his subordinates was poor. Having his brother as secretary of state, said Doolittle, was "unfortunate." Eisenhower replied that he thought it was "beneficial." Doolittle said that Allen Dulles was "too emotional for the job," and that his "emotionalism was far worse than it appeared on the surface." Eisenhower said that he had never seen Allen Dulles "show the slightest disturbance" and that

---

* Recruitment came under closer scrutiny in 1967. By this stage the agency's base of recruitment had shifted from the eastern schools such as Harvard and Yale to the universities of the Midwest and to the armed forces. A study in 1967, following complaints by a civil-rights activist, revealed that there were fewer than twenty blacks among approximately 12,000 nonclerical CIA employees. Efforts to hire more blacks were unsuccessful (Victor Marchetti and John D. Marks, *The CIA and the Cult of Intelligence* [New York: Knopf, 1974], pp. 237–238).

The agency has remained resolute in its unwillingness to employ homosexuals. In 1980 a homosexual employee of the National Security Agency was allowed to keep his job and security clearances: the first case of its kind in the U.S. intelligence community (*International Herald Tribune*, December 31, 1980). In contrast, in 1983 an aerospace contract worker sued the CIA after he disclosed his homosexuality in a routine security check and was fired. The CIA's guidelines, "Policy on Certain Sexual Conduct," suggest that homosexuality is a "personality disorder." The worker protested that "I feel I'm the victim of the old guard embedded in the bureaucracy—people with homophobic values" (*Newsweek*, November 28, 1983).

"here is one of the most peculiar types of operation any government can have, and it probably takes a strange kind of genius to run it."[12]

Doolittle, whose bravery (he led the first bombing raid on Tokyo in 1942) was touched with recklessness, had simply managed to confirm Eisenhower's complete support for Allen Dulles and the CIA, which was doing what the President wanted, even if he did not say so when challenged. Proposals originating in the agency were usually endorsed as a result of the President's control of and confidence in the agency.[13] Eisenhower set a trend for presidents to rely upon the CIA to do their bidding instead of trying to bend the State and Defense departments to their will. Between 1948, when covert action was first authorized, and 1955 there was no formal method of approval. But as covert actions multiplied, the set of understandings and working relationships involved between the agency, the White House, the State and Defense departments, and the National Security Council came to be seen as needing a proper framework.

The National Security Council met this need with NSC 5412/1 and NSC 5412/2, in March 1955 and November 1955 respectively. Together, these directives instituted control procedures for covert action and clandestine activities. A group of "designated representatives" was established, made up of nominees of the President and the secretaries of state and defense, to review and approve projects. This procedure survived right into the 1970s. Under Eisenhower and Kennedy it was called the "5412 Committee" or the "Special Group." Under Johnson it became the "303 Committee," after the room in the White House Annex where it met. Under Nixon it was called the "40 Committee," following the number of the new directive by which it met. Throughout, the same core of people were represented. The chairman of the Joint Chiefs of Staff either attended himself or sent an observer, as did others on an *ad hoc* basis, depending on projects and policies. The National Security Council proper approved projects referred to it by the committee. These projects came through the committee on behalf of the President, who, particularly in the cases of Kennedy, Johnson, Nixon, and Ford, was effectively represented by the assistant to the President for national security affairs, a position held successively by McGeorge Bundy, Walt Rostow, and Henry Kissinger.

In addition to the Special Group, Eisenhower set up two other groups to facilitate cooperation between the CIA and other government agencies and departments and to act as political watchdogs for the President—a sort of anti-banana-skin brigade. In January 1956 he created the President's Board of Consultants on Foreign Intelligence Activities (PBCFIA), composed of retired senior officials (generals Doolittle, Omar Bradley, and John E. Hull as well as Admiral Sidney Souers sat on the first board) and distinguished members of the professions (David Bruce, former ambassador; William B. Francke, former secretary of the navy; Henry Wriston, president of the Council on Foreign Relations and former president of Brown University). Eisenhower set up the board partly to head off closer scrutiny of intelligence gathering.[14]

The board had no administrative authority—it was an advisory group to the President directly—and so, while it made administrative recommendations, they were often not carried out. In December 1956 and again in December 1958 it recommended that Allen Dulles appoint a chief of staff to administer the agency and coordinate the other intelligence groupings—a clear reflection of the awareness of Dulles' unconventional management and failure to dominate U.S. intelligence in bureaucratic terms. Dulles was able to withstand the board's recommendation both times. When, however, the board accepted completely the idea that the director of Central Intelligence was the President's chief intelligence officer and made recommendations supporting this view, Dulles was happy to stand squarely behind the board's decision. In 1957 the board recommended that communications intelligence be centrally coordinated under the DCI. This was implemented in 1958 with the creation of the United States Intelligence Board (USIB), chaired by the DCI. The USIB replaced the Intelligence Advisory Board—the interdepartmental coordination group dating from 1947—and the United States Communications Intelligence Board, dating from 1946 and on which the DCI had only observer status and no vote.[15]

After the Bay of Pigs affair, President Kennedy changed the board of consultants into the President's Foreign Intelligence Advisory Board (PFIAB), a part-time board composed of distinguished private citizens whose job it was to report to the President on the performance, progress, and problems of those involved in U.S. intelligence. Over the years members of the PFIAB included Edward Teller, the Nobel prize-winning "father of the H-Bomb"; Edwin H. Land, an engineer of genius, of the Polaroid Corporation; Dr. William O. Baker, an electronic communications expert, vice-president in charge of research with Bell Laboratories; Nelson A. Rockefeller, an expert on Latin America and psychological warfare; John Connally, former governor of Texas and a real "can-do" man; former Ambassador Clare Booth Luce; Robert W. Galvin, chairman of Motorola, Inc.; and Leo Cherne, an authority on refugees and displacement, executive director of the Research Institute of America.

The first chairman of the PFIAB was James R. Killian, Jr., a great academic administrator, a man of powerful resourcefulness, president of MIT, who had also chaired the PBCFIA under Eisenhower. He was succeeded in 1968 by General Maxwell D. Taylor, a war hero with a sure eye for publicity. Taylor had retired as Army Chief of Staff in 1959 and in 1960 publicly protested at Eisenhower's refusal to accept his advice about conventional forces; he had then become Kennedy's military adviser and chairman of the Joint Chiefs of Staff. When Taylor retired in May 1970, he was succeeded as chairman of the board by Admiral George W. Anderson, Jr., a fierce right-winger, who had not been reappointed by Kennedy as chief of naval operations and had instead been sent as ambassador to Portugal.[16] It was through such people and with such mechanisms that CIA activities were approved and reviewed and information about them transmitted to the necessary places. It was a shadowy system in which the director of Central Intelligence could usually secure the necessary sanctions for projects without anyone else, except the President or his designated representative, being too sure about what was involved.

This system caused enormous confusion to those in the 1970s who tried to investigate the CIA's activities, particularly because when it came to the questions about attempted assassinations, the presidents involved—Eisenhower and Kennedy—were dead. Moreover, their national security advisers tended to have hazy memories about some decisions or else were apparently entirely ignorant of them, and the CIA officials were perceived as having a natural preference for stressing that their actions had been properly approved at all times. Ultimately the CIA's statements were accepted as true, although at times there may have been an excess of zeal on the part of agency officers. The control systems that operated up to the mid-1970s were those which in substance had been formulated during Eisenhower's presidency, with Allen Dulles as director of Central Intelligence, and they reflected the unspoken agreement in governing circles in the 1950s not to scrutinize intelligence activities closely.

CONGRESS

For the first thirty years of its existence the agency's relationship with Congress was very informal indeed. In essence, the DCI and his close colleagues dealt personally and informally with the chairmen of the important and relevant Senate and House committees (Foreign Affairs, Appropriations, Armed Services), and other senators and congressmen who were "friends" or who had significant political influence in areas important to the agency in Washington. This worked because the agency was trusted, its directors were respected, and it was seen as being America's principal defense against the subterranean machinations of world communism. One of the most explicit demonstrations of the widespread trust of the agency occurred on April 14, 1971. The then director of Central Intelligence, Richard Helms, in a rare speech (authorized by the President) given to the American Society of Newspaper Editors, asked the nation "to a degree take it on faith that we too are honorable men devoted to her service."* He was applauded by his audience. They were newspapermen, and they accepted Helms' word; few felt there was sufficient evidence to challenge it.

Allen Dulles' friendly, warm, outgoing personality had helped develop

* *The New York Times*, April 15, 1971. Helms went on to say that the CIA was not a law unto itself: "We do not target on American citizens. . . . The Central Intelligence Agency is not and cannot be its own master. It is the servant of the United States Government, undertaking what that Government asks it to do under the directives and controls the Government has established. We make no foreign policy." This was an interesting moment: Helms clearly felt the need to defend the agency from allegations to the contrary and also felt the ground shifting under his feet as American opinion began to focus on the CIA as the representative of dark, undemocratic secrecy in American government. In many ways this speech marked the end of the period of trust.

and sustain these relationships enormously, creating an atmosphere of trust around the office of DCI. His style was to appear voluntarily before a group, usually informally constituted, and give a *tour d'horizon* that tended to blur agency activity and foreign policy. Senator Leverett Saltonstall of Massachusetts, a former member of the Senate Armed Services and Appropriations Committees, succinctly described the working practice: "Dominated by the Committee chairmen, members would ask few questions which dealt with internal agency matters or with specific operations. The most sensitive discussions were reserved for one-to-one sessions between Dulles and individual Committee chairmen."[17]

Not all Senators were happy with these arrangements, however, and in 1955 and 1961 attempts were made, first by Senator Mike Mansfield and then by Senator Eugene McCarthy, to establish a formal Congressional Oversight Committee of the CIA. Both failed, fundamentally because the agency, as conceived and operated, was the President's, not Congress', and also because informal congressional briefings divided senators and congressmen on the subject. Nearly thirty years later, looking back on these attempts, Senator William Fulbright saw a definite scheme by the agency and its friends in Congress to prevent any formal oversight from taking place. The chairmen of the committees—Senator Richard Russell of the Senate Armed Services Committee; Congressman Carl Vinson of the House Armed Services Committee; Congressman Clarence Cannon of the House Appropriations Committee—and other influential people, notably Clark Clifford, one of Truman's closest advisers and perhaps Washington's leading lawyer, operated to keep Congress away from close scrutiny of the agency's activities. Senator Richard Russell, who in the 1950s and early 1960s was the power man in the Senate, established with Clark Clifford an unofficial committee to which top CIA people reported informally; he used the existence of this setup to stave off the creation of a formal oversight system.[18] "He's quite right," said Lawrence Houston, the CIA's general counsel until 1973, about Fulbright's view:

> Senator Russell wouldn't let anyone else in. One of our difficulties over the years was to get people to understand CIA problems in the Senate. The Senate would hear from the army and the State Department and the other services, but they didn't trust any of them. They trusted the director to give them an objective intelligence appraisal of what was going on around the world. That was the strength of our position, but it was also the weakness. Seldom could we get them to concentrate on what we were doing and why we were doing it. The House paid a lot more attention, particularly in the Appropriations Committee. Our appropriations were gone over as thoroughly as any appropriations. Cannon was chairman of the Appropriations Committee most of the time, and he established that we would bring to him any detail and he would question or have the committee question us. They knew our appropriations, line by line. Sure, they were hidden in the defense budget,

but to get in there they had to pass the committee. But we couldn't get the Senate interested.[19]

Reluctance to endanger operations was one reason for this lack of interest. Another was the strength of the congressional committee system. The chairmen of key committees wielded enormous power, which was enhanced by their private and personal conversations with the CIA. These chairmen were naturally reluctant to have their power and influence watered down by wider congressional and public involvement.* When Congress came close to changing the system, the power men in Washington went into operation. Thus the Doolittle Committee was inspired by a congressional commission, chaired by former President Herbert Hoover, surveying the executive branch in 1954. The commission, mindful of secrecy, delegated a small subgroup, under General Mark Clark, to review the relationship of the intelligence organizations to the executive. Foreseeing public congressional hearings dealing with, among other aspects of intelligence, the CIA's covert operations and clandestine activities, President Eisenhower then used his influence to secure the Hoover Commission's agreement to a separate report on the CIA's Directorate of Plans, which would be presented to him personally. This was the Doolittle Report. Since General Clark's group did not duplicate its area of study, Congress did not have its own full investigation of the CIA, and it did not try to; Eisenhower's wishes were respected. This was the way power and influence operated in 1950s Washington.

The Hoover Commission recommended both a congressional oversight committee drawn from the House and the Senate and an advisory board to the President composed of private citizens. This latter recommendation was effectively implemented with the President's Board of Consultants on Foreign Intelligence Activities, but the oversight proposal was not. The Church Committee's brief *History of the CIA* in 1976 concentrated on this question of congressional review of the agency, quoting at length from the Senate debate in 1955 on Senator Mansfield's resolution to implement the Hoover Commission's recommendation on oversight. Mansfield met fierce opposition from senators Russell, Hayden, and Saltonstall of the Armed Services and Appropriations committees, who were reluctant to concede their privileged relation-

* Traditionally, wrote John Maury in his 1974 article "CIA and the Congress," written for the agency's in-house *Studies in Intelligence*, the older members of the oversight committees used their seniority to monopolize the oversight function. Also, because of other assignments and responsibilities "they have only limited time and energy to devote to their Intelligence Subcommittee responsibilities." They also tended to be conservative and hawkish, while the younger members, excluded from these prestigious committees, tended to be liberal and dovish. "The Agency can ill afford to be closely identified with either," Maury concluded. "CIA and the Congress" was declassified in 1980 and printed in the *Congressional Record* on September 18, 1984, as a tribute to Maury by Senator Barry Goldwater. Maury had been chief of the Soviet Division 1954–62 and chief of station in Athens 1962–68. He was the agency's legislative counsel 1968–74.

ship with the agency. An exchange between Mansfield and Saltonstall at the time was indicative of the majority view in the Senate, which ultimately defeated both Mansfield and, six years later, McCarthy:

> *Mr. Mansfield:* I know the Senator from Massachusetts speaks from his heart, but I wonder whether the question I shall ask now should be asked in public; if not, let the Senator from Massachusetts please refrain from answering it: How many times does the CIA request a meeting with the particular subcommittees of the Appropriations Committee and the Armed Services Committee, and how many times does the Senator from Massachusetts request the CIA to brief him in regard to existing affairs?
>
> *Mr. Saltonstall:* I believe the correct answer is that at least twice a year that happens in the Armed Services Committee, and at least once a year it happens in the Appropriations Committee. I speak from my knowledge of the situation during the last year or so; I do not attempt to refer to previous periods. Certainly the present administrator and the former administrator, Gen. Bedell Smith, stated that they were ready at all times to answer any questions we might wish to ask them. The difficulty in connection with asking questions and obtaining information is that we might obtain information which I personally would rather not have, unless it was essential for me as a Member of Congress to have it. . . . It is not a question of reluctance on the part of the CIA officials to speak to us. Instead, it is a question of our reluctance, if you will, to seck information and knowledge on subjects which I personally as a Member of Congress and as a citizen, would rather not have, unless I believed it to be my responsibility to have it because it might involve the lives of American citizens.[20]

Allen Dulles listed the disadvantages of a formal congressional oversight committee for the National Security Council, influencing the council and senior members of the administration against it. However, although Mansfield's resolution was defeated, it did lead to a halfway accommodation. In 1956 Senator Russell formed a CIA subcommittee of the Armed Services Committee, and the following year the Senate Appropriations Committee followed suit. In both cases senators Richard Russell, Styles Bridges, and Robert Byrd were members, and they often conducted the business of both subcommittees at one meeting. Other senators were sometimes involved—Senator Carl Hayden, chairman of the Appropriations Committee from 1955 to 1969, usually sat in; senators Leverett Saltonstall and Lyndon Johnson sometimes attended as members of the Armed Services subcommittee. In the House of Representatives, as Lawrence Houston has remarked, information on the CIA was more organized. Congressman Carl Vinson established a formal CIA subcommittee of the House Armed Services Committee. Congressman Clarence Cannon on the House Appropriations Committee monitored the agency with an informal special group of five congressmen that advised the committee proper.

The reluctance of the legislators to press the CIA for information about operations and operational plans was entirely understandable. They knew that the agency's job was to combat the Soviet Union and the worldwide spread of communism on the terms set out by General Doolittle in his report to the President. They preferred to be able to plead ignorance of specific information so that they would not find themselves compromised politically. CIA officials were content with this arrangement; they made it clear that they would provide the information asked of them, and if it was not asked, so be it. For over twenty-five years the system worked. The exposés of the 1970s served to confirm only that the more that was known about the agency and its activities the less effective America would be in meeting the Soviet Union on equal terms and the more difficult it would be to convince Americans of the need to operate a more sophisticated and clever espionage and counterespionage service than that used against the United States.

KHRUSHCHEV'S SECRET SPEECH

The year 1956 was in many ways the time when the CIA matured in the perception of its users into a sophisticated espionage as well as counterespionage service. It began with a real shock: Khrushchev's denunciation of Stalin at the Twentieth Party Congress in February. The speech was important for two reasons. First, it marked the rise to power of Khrushchev himself, emerging from the collective leadership that had succeeded Stalin. Second, it marked a crucial turning point in the Soviet Union as it shook off the dead end of Stalinism—inefficient economic management, the virtual extinction of the intellectual classes, and the loss of popular acceptance not only in Russia and its satellite countries but also for the Communist parties elsewhere in the world.

Since the USSR was and still is a "closed society" where information is equated with power and therefore kept secret, Western diplomats and intelligence officers spend much of their time trying to divine the meaning of public utterances to determine what they represent about the power structure. Khrushchev's speech, delivered to a closed session of the party congress, was not circulated, and the copies that did exist were guarded by the KGB as the reaction to it within the Communist Party of the Soviet Union and the parties of the Eastern-bloc countries was gauged. Obtaining a copy of the actual speech became a major objective for the State Department and the CIA. As versions of fragments of the twenty-thousand-word text, which Khrushchev had spent half a day delivering, began to appear in March, the pressure on Allen Dulles to deliver an authentic text mounted.

The deputy director for intelligence, Robert Amory, was one of those to whom Dulles turned for help.* "In the words of the ancient bawdy ballad, he offered 'half his kingdom and the royal whore, Hortense' to whoever brought him home the bacon," recalled Amory.[21] Frank Wisner, Amory's opposite number as deputy director of plans, tried to obtain a copy of the speech, and in April, about two months after Khrushchev's tirade, Wisner's agents came up with a text. So did James Angleton. Wisner's people had scoured their contacts in the eastern European Communist parties and received—reputedly from a Polish source—a copy of an abridged text distributed to communist leaders in the Eastern bloc. Angleton, using his close personal contact with Israeli intelligence, managed to obtain a full text from inside Russia—reputedly through a Jewish Soviet communist reporting to Israel.† The texts matched, so the CIA knew they had a genuine copy of the speech. This was confirmed by Ray Cline, who then was working in the Office of Current Intelligence:

> Wisner decided to let me read and judge the precious document. The denizens of the DDP lived on the other side of the Lincoln Memorial from the DDI elements of the CIA. Their home was a dismal row of World War II temporary buildings labeled J, K, and L, now destroyed, but then stretching the whole length of the reflecting pool from 17th to 23rd Streets. There was not a great deal of intercourse between the two areas, mainly because of DDP clannishness and fierce tradecraft indoctrination in security. Occasionally representatives met, however, and I went down to the reflecting pool to give my views on the secret speech. I remember a solemn conclave chaired by Wisner with Angleton representing the DDP professionals' judgment of the

---

* Amory and the CIA generally had a warm relationship with the Yugoslavs, and so it was to Belgrade that a request for Khrushchev's speech was made:

I suggested that I be permitted to try a direct, overt secret approach to the Yugoslav foreign office on the knowledge that their party had been furnished an official text and that the country was on the receiving end of hundreds of millions of US military and economic aid. . . . My visit to the Yugoslav foreign office with Ambassador Riddleberger went well, and both of us thought we'd succeeded in our pitch. We later learned that Foreign Minister Kardelj had recommended to Marshal Tito that the Khrushchev speech be turned over to us on assurance that we could and would disguise whence it had been obtained but that the Marshal had, on the insistence of his hard-line Minister of the Interior, Rankovich, turned down the recommendation. (Robert Amory, "Hungary '56—A Subjective/Objective Account.")

† Ray S. Cline, *The CIA Under Reagan, Bush and Casey* (Washington, DC: Acropolis Books, 1981), p. 185. See also William R. Corson, *The Armies of Ignorance: The Rise of the American Intelligence Empire* (New York: Dial Press/James Wade, 1977) p. 367; Stephen E. Ambrose, *Ike's Spies—Eisenhower and the Espionage Establishment* (New York: Doubleday, 1981), p. 237; *The New York Times*, November 30, 1976. Angleton claimed that the source for the speech was not paid and had given it to the agency for ideological reasons. Cline said a copy was obtained "at a very handsome price." The securing of two separate copies would explain this discrepancy, as would a presumed desire on the part of both men to protect the sources.

Charles E. Bohlen, at the time U.S. ambassador in Moscow, recorded in his memoirs that at the end of May 1956, he "received from Washington the text of a document obtained by the Central Intelligence Agency in Warsaw. After careful study, I concluded that in all probability it was an authentic copy" (Charles E. Bohlen, *Witness to History, 1929–1969* [New York: W.W. Norton, 1973], pp. 398–399).

speech. I was vastly outnumbered, but I was able to provide convincing, and most welcome, internal evidence that the text we had was an authentic account of what happened at the 20th Party Congress and that much of it was Khrushchev's own colorful prose. This made everyone happy.*

The question that was faced next was what to do with the speech now that they had it. There was intense argument about this, the result of which brought to a head the political realities of the time in contrast to the aspirations voiced by John Foster Dulles and others during the 1952 election campaign.

Ray Cline argued for publication in full. "I made what I thought was an eloquent plea to make the speech public. I said that it would provide scholars and students interested in the Soviet Union invaluable insights into the real workings of Stalinist Russia. I also said it was a rare opportunity to have all the critical things we had said for years about the Soviet dictatorship confirmed by the principal leader of the Soviet Politburo. The world would be treated to the spectacle of a totalitarian nation indicted by its own leadership."[22] Frank Wisner and James Angleton argued against this view and instead proposed that the speech be exploited by feeding selected bits of it to particular audiences in order to create a specific impact rather than a general reaction. "They kept saying they wanted to 'exploit' the speech rather than simply let everybody read it," remembered Cline.

Behind this argument was a covert-action plan, Red Sox/Red Cap, being organized by the Directorate of Plans at the CIA's training center in West Germany, outside Munich. It involved émigrés and refugees from Hungary, Poland, Rumania, and Czechoslovakia who were being trained in paramilitary methods for operations inside eastern Europe. In April 1956 they were "not up to snuff," in Angleton's words,[23] and so he and Wisner wanted to delay the release of the speech to help Red Sox/Red Cap operations. They considered that publication of the speech would trigger unrest in eastern Europe which Red Sox/Red Cap could exploit. Matters rested there until June 2, when Allen Dulles, working on a speech with Cline, made a decision:

> Suddenly, in the way he often moved from one topic to a quite unrelated one, Dulles swung his chair around to look intently at me and said, "Wisner says you think we ought to release the secret Khrushchev speech." I related my reasons for thinking so, and the old man, with a twinkle in his eye, said, "By

---

* Cline, *The CIA*, p. 186. In a series of articles in *The New York Times* in December 1977 it was claimed that the CIA's published text was only an expurgated version prepared for eastern Europe, from which some thirty-four paragraphs of material on future Soviet foreign policy had been deleted. Although the text made available to U.S. newspapers was an expurgated version, another text containing the deleted material was circulated by the CIA to other newspapers around the world. This material, claimed *The New York Times* articles, had been forged by CIA counterintelligence experts (John M. Crewson and Joseph B. Treaster, "CIA: Secret Shaper of Public Opinion," *The New York Times*, December 25–27, 1977). However, Moscow never denied the authenticity of the CIA text.

golly, I am going to make a policy decision!" He buzzed Wisner on the inter-com box, told him that he had given a lot of thought to the matter, and wanted to get the speech printed. Frank Wisner agreed, a little reluctantly but graciously, and Allen then phoned Foster Dulles at State to give him the same views he had given Wisner. Foster concurred, the speech was sent over to State and given directly to *The New York Times*, which printed the whole text on June 4, the following Monday.[24]

Publication of the speech certainly caused a buzz in Eastern Europe as well as in the West. On June 28, workers in Poznań, Poland, started a militant strike; forty-four workers were killed before it was suppressed. By October there was a general political crisis in the Eastern bloc. However, to link the publica-tion of the speech in the West to the start of this crisis would be too strong. The crisis was generated by the speech itself and the freedom the Communist parties and governments of the Eastern bloc thought it heralded for *them*. Khrushchev had spoken of the evils of Stalin and indicated political and eco-nomic liberalism in place of Stalin's totalitarianism. When the Soviet satellites put this to the test, they found that what might apply for Russia itself was not intended for them and that Russian security interests militated against any dra-matic changes in eastern Europe.*

What publication of the speech did do was to confirm in many people's minds the evils of Stalin and the political, economic, and social benefits of the West. However, it had a different effect on China. It made Mao Tse-tung begin to diverge significantly from Russia, since he preferred the control exer-cised by Stalinist communism as well as its ideological base. Like Stalin, Mao Tse-tung believed that communist societies should tolerate no divergence or opposition and that individuals who stand in the way must expect to be crushed. The speech publicly demonstrated that Soviet communism was inse-cure, divided, and had, by Khrushchev's own admission, harbored and nur-tured evil. Perhaps, though, Dulles' real reason for opting for publication was that he needed a headline story of his own to counteract a headline story of the Russians: they had discovered the Berlin Tunnel.

THE BERLIN TUNNEL

Operation Silver in Vienna in 1951 gave rise to a similar operation in Berlin in 1953—Operation Gold. As early as 1948, both army intelligence and

---

* The choice that faced Khrushchev was either to relax or further increase repression in Russia. He chose to relax it. The Soviet leaders were emotionally exhausted men who had been preying on each other for decades. It was time to make peace, to deintensify relations among themselves. If they kept up the degree of ferocity that had characterized Stalin's regime, the more ferocious would be the younger men waiting their chance to take over.

Major General William Donovan, head of the wartime Office of Strategic Services, leaving the White House on March 15, 1945, after one of his last conferences with the dying President Roosevelt. *(UPI/Bettmann)*

Big Bill and Little Bill: Seventeen years after the war, Sir William Stephenson – "Little Bill" – director of the British Security Coordination Office in the United States from 1940 to 1945, and as such a key figure in the establishment of American centralised intelligence, was the first non-U.S. citizen to be awarded the Medal of Merit, the nation's highest civilian honor. From left to right: General William J. ("Big Bill") Donovan, presenting the medal in Sir William's suite at the Dorset Hotel in New York; Colonel Edward G. ("Ned") Buxton, Donovan's wartime deputy; and Robert Sherwood, playwright and wartime propaganda expert. *(UPI/Bettmann)*

"And ye shall know the truth": Christian Democratic and pro-American posters on a pillar in Rome's Piazza Colonna Galleria during the 1948 Italian election. The cost of such posters was frequently met by secret CIA funding intended to counterbalance similar Soviet support for left-wing parties. Fears that the Communists might win the election prompted the Truman administration to enter covert operations through the CIA's Office of Special Operations and Office of Policy Coordination, and support for democratic newspapers and parties in Italy was the first result. *(Wide World Photos)*

Bogotá, April 15, 1948: The downtown section of the capital of Colombia seen in the wake of fierce riots that disrupted the Bogotá conference, which eventually negotiated the charter for the Organization of American States. The CIA was accused of inadequate political analysis for failing to predict the likelihood of civil strife during the conference, but was able to shift the blame to the State Department. The accusation, however, signified the background expectation that the CIA was to monitor the entire world. *(Wide World Photos)*

Above left: James Forrestal in 1940 when he was appointed an administrative assistant to President Roosevelt. He was to become secretary of the navy and Truman's secretary of defense. He was one of the principal men behind U.S. involvement in the cold war, and the strain probably pushed him to suicide in 1949. *(Wide World Photos)*

Above right: SS General Karl Wolff, who negotiated the surrender of Axis forces in northern Italy in 1945 through Allen Dulles, OSS chief in Switzerland, photographed in 1947 while being tried for war crimes at Nuremberg. *(Wide World Photos)*

Aid to Greece and Turkey: After Britain informed the United States in February 1947 that it could no longer afford to maintain its effort to prevent communist takeovers in Greece and Turkey, Truman decided to intervene. Giving evidence in support of this decision to the Senate Foreign Relations Committee on March 13 are, from the left: Acting Secretary of State Dean Acheson; Secretary of War Robert P. Patterson (standing); Committee Chairman Senator Arthur H. Vandenberg; Secretary of the Navy James V. Forrestal (standing); and Senator Tom Connally. *(Wide World Photos)*

The "Bomber Gap" bomber: The Soviet TU-4 in flight in a scene from a Russian newsreel captured in Korea, according to the Department of Defense, and released on January 3, 1951. The plane was a copy of the American B-29 and was first seen in the 1948 May Day fly-past in Moscow. Worries that the bomber was as effective as the B-29 (it was not) and was being produced in large numbers prompted the USAF to press for more funding to prevent a bomber gap. *(Wide World Photos)*

"Kill me": Former Premier Mohammed Mussadegh of Iran challenges a military tribunal in Tehran to "Kill me," pointing to his throat on November 10, 1953. Mussadegh, who liked to do business from his bed, is also seen wearing his favored garb of pajamas and bathrobe. He had been dismissed by the shah earlier in the year in a royalist coup engineered jointly by the British Secret Service and the CIA following his nationalization of the Anglo-Iranian Oil Company. *(Wide World Photos)*

Lieutenant Colonel Jacobo Guzman Arbenz delivering his inaugural address as president of Guatemala on March 15, 1951. He was overthrown in a CIA-organized coup in 1954. A quarter of a century later, viewing growing civil unrest in the country, a U.S. official reportedly observed: "What we'd give to have an Arbenz now." *(Wide World Photos)*

Left to right: General Walter Bedell Smith, undersecretary of State and outgoing director of Central Intelligence; Allen Welsh Dulles, incoming director; and General Omar Bradley, chairman of the Joint Chiefs of Staff, leaving the White House on January 29, 1953, after attending a National Security Council meeting. *(Wide World Photos)*

Above: Kim Philby in his mother's apartment at a 1955 press conference he called to celebrate being formally cleared of being the "third man" who tipped off Maclean and Burgess that they were suspected of being Soviet spies. *(UPI/Bettmann)*

Right: The passport photographs of Donald Maclean (left) and Guy Burgess released by the British government on August 29, 1951, three months after they had fled to the Soviet Union. *(UPI/Bettmann)*

The German-born British physicist Klaus Fuchs, being greeted by his nephew on arriving at Schoenefeld Airport, East Berlin, on June 23, 1959. He had been discharged earlier in the day from a British prison after serving nine years and three months of a fourteen-year sentence for giving atomic-bomb secrets to the Soviets. *(Wide World Photos)*

The Berlin Tunnel: The meticulous
engineering of the tunnel is demonstrated
in this Soviet photograph taken from just
beyond the chamber where the East
German landlines were intercepted and
their messages sent back to the
American end of the tunnel in West
Berlin through the cables on the bottom
right of the passage. The sandbags along
either side, held in place by wires, were
for soundproofing and insulation.
(Sovfoto/Eastfoto)

The start of the cold war in space:
In response to the Soviet Sputnik in
October 1957, President Eisenhower
gave high priority to the U.S. space
effort. Coordinated by the CIA's brilliant
Richard Bissell, deputy director for
plans from the fall of 1958, Weapons
System 117L was a joint CIA-Air Force
photo-reconnaissance satellite project.
Publicly referred to as the "Discoverer"
weather system, but known as "Corona"
in the agency, it was operational after a
series of initial failures by early 1962.
　　Each satellite was launched from
Vandenberg Air Force Base in a bullet-
shaped heat-resistant reentry capsule on
top of an Agena rocket with a Thor
booster, as shown in this 1959 photograph
of one of the first (unsuccessful) attempts.
(UPI/Bettmann)

End of an era: Francis Gary Powers, pilot of the U-2 shot down by the Soviets in May 1960, was released nearly two years later in exchange for Rudolf Abel, a Russian spy arrested in New York in 1957. Holding a model of the shot-down U-2, Powers testified to the Senate Armed Services Committee on June 3, 1962, about the flight and his capture and imprisonment in the Soviet Union. By then, the first photo-reconnaissance satellites were already operating over the USSR and U-2 flights were no longer necessary. *(UPI/Bettmann)*

President John Fitzgerald Kennedy proclaims a naval blockade against Cuba, October 22, 1962. *(Wide World Photos)*

the CIA became interested in the benefits of tapping Soviet and eastern European landlines. As the tension of the cold war mounted, it became evident that an operation of this kind might produce the information needed to fill gaps in intelligence. Debriefings of German scientists returning to the West from Russia, where they had been taken to work after World War II, revealed that the Russians were moving to UHF signals for their most important and secret communications. However, because of the vulnerability to interception of the older long- and short-wave radio communications, the Russians, like the Americans, had gone back to using landlines as well, which were secure unless they were physically tapped. Thus tapping into landlines, as was done in Operation Silver, could provide important intelligence information.

Carl Nelson's discovery that echoes of the clear text being enciphered could be picked up from the cable carrying the encoded message when Bell's Sigtot cipher machine was used resulted in a technique that could be applied to Soviet-bloc landline communications too. Put together, these factors gave the CIA a chance not only to score an intelligence victory but also to score a bureaucratic victory over the emerging National Security Agency, which depended upon radio communications intercepts for its information at that stage. The Soviet use of landlines cut the NSA off.

In 1953, according to the CIA's official history of the operation, "exploratory discussions were held in Washington to plan the mounting of an attack on Soviet landlines in East Germany with special emphasis to be placed on the Berlin area."[25] Part of the discussion was with the British, who, as had happened with Silver in Vienna, first had the idea of trying the same thing in Berlin and had proposed another joint effort to the CIA. The most important Soviet landline circuits were pinpointed in Berlin, and a tap was placed on a prime target circuit in East Berlin. Even if a tap was discovered, there would be no evidence that anything but the *enciphered* messages were being collected. The clear-text echo was still known to only very few people.

When Allen Dulles was told of Carl Nelson's discovery he immediately grasped its importance and, as with Operation Silver in Vienna, ordered that "in the interests of security, as little as possible concerning the project would be reduced to writing. It is probable that few orders have been so conscientiously obeyed," remarked the official history. Throughout the Gold operation the British never knew Carl Nelson's secret. With Philby warm in Allen Dulles' memory, he was determined not to risk there being another British traitor. What attracted Dulles to cooperate with the British was his respect for their professional skill. "They saw us as Greeks to their Romans," recalled one British Secret Intelligence officer involved with Gold.[26] The British were to carry out the analysis of half the material. The CIA considered the British to be expert in accurately judging the content of Soviet military and political communications. Despite Philby, despite having fewer resources, and despite being dependent in obvious ways on the American intelligence community, the British were still valued by the agency. British analysis was very good. Its lack of resources made British Intelligence emphasize quality over quantity.*

Having established the viability of the technique with Operation Silver, after months of study and debate the organizers drew up a plan calling for a tunnel approximately five hundred yards long into East Berlin to intercept the landlines running from the Soviet Air Force headquarters at Karlshorst to Berlin. It was to be drilled from the southern West Berlin suburb of Altglienecke, a remote area that contained a "squattersville" of shacks and hovels constructed from rubble by refugees from East Berlin and East Germany. Allen Dulles approved the plan, and Operation Gold was under way.

It was a major undertaking. The tunneling had to be done secretly under the feet of Soviet troops and East German guards. The earth removed had to be carted away without drawing attention. The site entrance had to be small enough not to attract undue interest from across the zone border. The tunnel itself had to be constructed in such a way that there was no sign of it on the surface, no subsidence at all. The work had to be done with an absolute minimum of noise. During construction and afterward the tunnel had to be ventilated—not just for the benefit of the people working there but also for the electronic equipment and transformers that would be placed inside, generating a great deal of heat in the enclosed space. Because it would be impossible to drive ventilation shafts up to the ground at regular intervals without risking discovery, air had to be pumped into the tunnel at its mouth and then be drawn out again after circulating along its length. It had to be air-conditioned so that it did not heat up the earth around and above it. All in all, it was a massive engineering challenge.

Both the British and the Americans tested whether the undertaking was practicable by boring tunnels for experiment. The British test tunnel and tap chamber was dug at the Royal Engineers' establishment at Longmore, in England, and blind men and blind dogs were used to walk over it to determine if there was any slight change underfoot as a result of the digging. The test tunnel passed this trial. In Colorado the Americans experimented with digging and ventilation techniques. "The first question, 'Could the tunnel be dug?,' was never really a debatable one—those concerned more or less decided that given sufficient money and personnel the job could be done," reported the official history. The final cost of the tunnel came to between $25 and $30 million.

Bill Harvey, who was now the CIA's top man in Berlin, was given the

---

* Roger Hilsman, a West Pointer who had served in guerrilla operations during the war and was to become Kennedy's assistant secretary of state for Far Eastern affairs, expressed the American view of British Intelligence in colorful terms: "To most of us," he wrote in 1956, "the words *strategic intelligence* evoke an image of a cool and competent British agent matching wits with the enemy, including a beautiful but dangerous woman, necessarily a brunette, while they roar through the Balkan night on the gaily lighted Orient Express" (*Strategic Intelligence and National Decisions* [Glencoe, IL: Free Press, 1956] p. 17).

overall command. The division of labor between the CIA and British Intelligence was agreed upon. The CIA would "(1) procure a site . . . and drive a tunnel to a point beneath the target cables . . . (2) be responsible for the recording of all signals produced . . . (3) process in Washington all of the telgraphic material received from the project." The British would "(1) drive a vertical shaft from the tunnel's end to the targets; (2) effect the cable taps and deliver a usable signal to the head of the tunnel for recording; and (3) provide for a . . . center . . . to process the voice recordings from the site."[27]

Available plans indicated that the cables were buried about eighteen inches deep along the side of the Schoenefelder Chaussee, a heavily traveled highway that was the principal link between East Berlin and Karlshorst. The top of the vertical shaft needed to be close to the surface of the highway in order to give the tapping crew room to work below the ceiling of the shaft, and the whole structure had to be strong enough to support the weight of heavy traffic, since the tunnel and tap chamber lay directly beneath the highway. The official history states:

> Considerable care was devoted to insulating the tap chamber to prevent its acting like a huge drum. In spite of the insulation, it was a weird sensation to be in the chamber when an iron-shod horse trotted across it. We also suffered some anxious moments one foggy morning when the microphone in the tap chamber gave forth with a continuous series of dull thuds. After the sun burned away the fog, visual observation showed that the East German police had set up a temporary automobile checkpoint directly over the chamber. The "thuds" the microphone picked up were caused by the police officer in charge stomping his feet on the road surface to keep warm.

The U.S. Army Corps of Engineers in Berlin built a massive semiunderground warehouse close to the border, large enough to hold the 3100 tons of earth excavated from the tunnel, which ran 1476 feet, with a 78-inch diameter. The warehouse in turn was to act as a disguise for a radar intercept station—the official cover for the site. When the site was built less than 100 yards from the border, the comings and goings, the delivery of electronic equipment, and the earth removal fitted the construction of a major radar intercept station directed at spying on Soviet air force communications. It was just the sort of thing the Russians and East Germans might expect, and in any case, they had to assume that their communications were being intercepted—all governments and military formations have to make this assumption, which is why codes are used.

From the Russians' point of view, the only thing that mattered was the security of their codes, or so they thought. George Blake, a senior British MI-6 officer in Berlin who later turned out to be a Russian spy, knew about the tunnel after it was constructed but not about Carl Nelson's echo-effect discovery. So even when he informed his Soviet masters of the operation, as he must have done, their thoughts would have been directed at their code security. Moreover, they would not have wanted to jeopardize Blake by taking precipitate action against the tunnel, so they allowed the operation to continue. According to the official history:

> Careful visual observation was maintained and tunneling operations stopped each time the German guards walked over the tunnel on their regular patrols. Pumps were installed to take care of the excess water. Observation logs were maintained, and since the highway under observation was the main road from East Berlin to the Schoenefeld Airport, considerable Order of Battle information was obtained. It was also possible to estimate quite accurately the relative importance of individuals visiting East Berlin by observing the security precautions taken by the East Germans and the Soviets.[28]

The tunnel was bored with its bottom 20 feet below the surface, leaving 13½ feet of earth between the top of the tunnel and the ground. "The lack of an adequate base line made the surveying problem especially difficult," the official history recorded. "No one had ever tunneled [that distance] under clandestine conditions with the expectation of hitting a target two inches in diameter and 18 inches below a main German/Soviet highway. There were those who manifested certain reservations on the feasibility of so doing." Ingenious attempts were made to ensure pinpoint accuracy. "The engineers decided at one point that an object of known size in the East Zone would be useful as a reference point, so a baseball game was organized with the objective of knocking a baseball as far into the East Zone as possible. This scheme was frustrated by the friendliness of the East German guards who kept returning the baseball."

Finally two CIA agents in army uniform made one of the regular military trips into East Berlin, arranged to have a flat tire at the desired point, and left behind a tiny radio reflector that enabled precise measurements to be made, and "the engineers expressed confidence that they knew their position when the tunnel was completed to a point which could be contained in a six-inch cube. They were correct." This done, the work progressed rapidly from August 1954. A steel ring of the correct diameter, 6½ feet, fitted with hydraulic jacks around the circumference, was placed at the tunnel face and pressed forward after every two inches of excavation, the space behind being secured with steel liners bolted in place.

The tunneling took nearly seven months. During the work Bill Harvey, well known to the Soviets as a CIA man, visited the site at night, taking every precaution not to be followed. "Major General Ben Harrell, chief of staff for the Army command in Berlin, recalled a nighttime tour of the tunnel with Harvey. 'Harvey and I drove way across Berlin and went into a parking area and changed cars. It was real cloak and dagger as far as I was concerned. . . . Coming back, Bill asked me to come up and have a drink. He poured me a full glass of scotch without anything else in it. When I finally got home, my wife asked me where I'd been.' Covered with mud and reeking of alcohol, Harrell could only offer the lame response, 'I've been out with Bill Harvey on business.' "[29]

On February 25, 1955, the tunnel was finished. To guard against the possibility that excess humidity might affect the electronic equipment, the section of the tunnel immediately adjacent to the tap chamber was insulated and sealed to form, in effect, a closed room:

> Vapor barriers were erected and, in addition, a heavy "anti-personnel" door of steel and concrete was constructed to seal off the tunnel some 15 yards from its terminal end. . . . This door bore the following inscription neatly lettered in German and Cyrillic. "Entry is forbidden by order of the Commanding General." It was reasoned that this sign might give pause to Soviet and/or German officials and gain time. As a matter of fact, there were those communist individuals who considered the posting of this sign as one of the most audacious aspects of the entire undertaking. . . . From the beginning it was realized that the duration of the operation was finite. Considerable thought was given to the posture the U.S. Government would adopt upon the tunnel's discovery.[30]

Knowing this, the CIA based its decision to go ahead with Operation Gold on an expectation of significant intelligence benefits. This turned out to be justified. In fact, the CIA's initial decision to prepare personnel and equipment to exploit only a percentage of the anticipated take was far too cautious. The three landline cables tapped into carried a "1 + 4 system" of one telegraph and four telephone lines. Each line could carry up to four communications at a time. Six hundred Ampex tape recorders in the warehouse collected the tapped communications, amounting to 1200 hours per day and using up 800 reels of tape. So much tape was used that CIA buyers had to go to great lengths not to distort the supply-and-demand balance in the U.S. audiotape market! Planeloads of tapes were ferried out of Berlin each week for analysis in Washington and London.

"The task of translating and analyzing the messages thus intercepted was monumental," remembered Ray Cline.[31] The sheer physical labor required of those involved in the tapping, decrypting, and analyzing was enormous. "The moisture in the air caused by the breathing and perspiration of the technicians doing the tapping operation forced the suspension of the operation several times to permit the air conditioning equipment to dehumidify the chamber."[32] In Washington, fifty CIA officers fluent in Russian and German worked in a windowless room of forty-five square feet in the "Hosiery Mill," a prefabricated hut in Washington Mall so nicknamed because of the wires into it for communications intelligence. The floors sagged under the weight of machinery needed for their work, and the whole building was clad in steel to prevent the escape of electronic emissions that might be picked up. "The deputy chief of the processing section briefed them on the need for security. 'It is greatly in your interest not to know where any of the material you are processing is coming from,' he began. Even so, 'for the opposition to stop the flow, all they would have to know is that we have this many Russian and German speakers together.' "[33] The translators and analysts had to work two weeks on and one day off to keep up with the flow.

A small processing unit was maintained in Altglienecke to permit on-the-spot monitoring of engineering circuits for the protection of the project and scanning of the more productive circuits for "hot" intelligence. The job of quickly picking up important messages which had no "echo effect" was undertaken by a painstakingly recreated Soviet decoder, which its CIA operators named "The Bumblebee." Like its namesake, the Soviet system, which was antiquated, buzzed with activity, from playback to recording to rerecording to teleprinting. It broke down the channels of each circuit into separate recordings at a speed four times faster than the intercepted messages had been transmitted. The clear-text echo was electronically pried away from the encoded messages and printed out at a hundred words a minute. These texts were then taken from the teleprinters and given to the Russian and German translators.

On April 21, 1956, eleven months and eleven days after the first message had been processed, the tunnel was discovered. "Analysis of all available evidence," the official history states, "—traffic passing on the target cables, conversations recorded from a microphone installed in the tap chamber, and vital observations from the site—indicates that the Soviet discovery of [the tunnel] was purely fortuitous." An early CIA postmortem document explained the discovery as due to "unfortunate circumstances beyond our control—a combination of the fact that one of the cables was in very poor physical condition (this was known from the beginning) and a long period of unusually heavy rainfall. It appeared that water entered the cable in sufficient quantity to make it inoperative, thus necessitating digging up sections of the cable and causing discovery of the tap."[34] Due to the sheer volume of information collected during the tunnel's operation, it took the CIA another two years and five months—until September 30, 1958—to process the backlog of messages.

The plans made for the expected day of discovery revolved around the calculation that news of the tunnel would be seen as a tribute to Western ingenuity and, in the cold-war atmosphere, would do no harm to the United States in the court of public opinion. This reflected a change in cold-war perceptions: it was no longer seen as a hand-to-hand struggle but had become instead a series of less intense propaganda and intelligence coups. The CIA history of the operation stated:

> In retrospect it is probably correct to say that, among those most actively concerned with the project's management, a consensus developed that the Soviets would probably suppress knowledge of the tunnel's existence rather

than to admit to the world that Free World intelligence organs had the capability of successfully mounting an operation of this magnitude. In other words, it was felt that for the Soviets to admit that the U.S. had been reading their high level communications circuits would cause the Soviets to lose face. Perhaps fortunately, fate intervened, and as a possible consequence the Soviet course of action was exactly contrary to expectation.

Fate took the form of the absence of the commandant of the Soviet Berlin garrison on April 21, 1956. The acting commandant was in charge. The official history continues:

> There is some reason to believe that he (for whatever reason) was forced to make a personal decision on a course of action without benefit of advice from Moscow. At any rate his reaction was unexpected in that he invited the entire Berlin press corps to a briefing and tour of the tunnel and its facilities. As a result the tunnel was undoubtedly the most highly publicized peacetime espionage enterprise in modern times prior to the "U-2 incident." Worldwide reaction was outstandingly favorable in terms of enhancement of U.S. prestige.

To prove the point, the history contains an analysis of world press coverage of the affair. On May 1, 1956, *The Washington Post* ran an editorial headlined "The Tunnel of Love" which hailed "Yankee ingenuity" and observed that "the probable result of all this has been to give the anticommunist resistance in East Germany a good deal of amusement and encouragement." On May 7 *Time* magazine ran a story entitled "Wonderful Tunnel," which quoted a Berlin editor saying to a U.S. official: "I don't know whether your people dug that wonderful tunnel or not, but whoever it was, let me say I think it was too bad it was found. It's the best publicity the US has had in Berlin for a long time."

Within Washington the intelligence obtained through the tunnel was respected and very useful. Through Carl Nelson's discovery the CIA learned that the Russians had a spy in the British Intelligence station in Berlin, although his identity (George Blake) was not discovered for several more years. Allen Dulles had the problem of alerting the British without giving Nelson's secret away. A great deal of practical day-to-day information also resulted from Gold. It confirmed, for example, that the East German railways were in severe disrepair. This information reduced the possibility of a surprise Soviet attack on Berlin. It provided detailed order-of-battle information and enabled accurate assessments of Soviet military movements and dispositions to be made. It also provided the sort of primary and secondary information with which to gauge the accuracy of political judgments about Soviet and Eastern-bloc politics, plans, and policies. Most important, it meant that the United States and Berlin would have been alerted early to any Soviet intentions of attacking the West. However, other communications interceptions also provided these early warnings, and so the discovery of the tunnel was not a major setback. Allen Dulles must have been pleased with the favorable publicity that ensued but also worried by the decline in morale within the CIA. Disappointed by the tunnel's discovery and the sudden end to the operation after years of hard work, many CIA people were depressed and disheartened. Dulles needed a positive headline story to restore the spirit of the agency, and the Khrushchev speech gave it to him.

THE SUEZ CRISIS

While the publicity about the Berlin tunnel and the Khrushchev speech was still settling, a dramatic crisis cut to the heart of the Western alliance, leaving the CIA offstage. British, French, and Israeli forces in a carefully coordinated operation, the details of which, by all accounts, had been kept officially secret from the United States (privately, senior British officers had kept their American counterparts informed), launched an invasion of eastern Egypt in the Sinai and the Suez Canal area at the end of October 1956. It was to turn out to be the last gasp of the old empires as they tried to hold onto direct control of the vital communication route of the canal, which connected Britain and France with Iranian oil, Indian and Far Eastern markets and colonies, and eastern Africa more economically and efficiently than the old sea route around the Cape of Good Hope. In 1955, 67 million tons of oil had moved through the canal to Europe. Winston Churchill had presaged the invasion in 1953 when he warned that Great Britain would defend its own interests, particularly in the Middle East, where Egyptian national pride threatened British control of the Suez Canal, without the help of "the United States or anyone else."[35] This was fair enough; the United States was quite happy not to be too closely associated with the colonial concerns of the old empires and in any event was more interested in the emerging national movements across the world and preventing their alliance with the Soviet Union.

In July 1955 at the Geneva Summit meeting Eisenhower had proposed his "open skies" initiative, whereby the United States and the Soviet Union would allow overflights to photograph and monitor each other's military arrangements and would exchange plans of military facilities. This was in part an attempt to reduce European worries about the stationing of U.S. nuclear weapons on their territory, and Eisenhower's hope was based on the apparent thaw in Russian attitudes with their agreement to leave Austria when they had signed the Austrian Peace Treaty in May. However, the Russians wanted something else in exchange for leaving Austria: confirmation of their security and control in eastern Europe and of the sovereignty of their satellites. The result was that the Summit achieved nothing specific but left the Soviets frustrated. In their minds, they had "given up" Austria and received nothing in return. Their next step, as John Foster Dulles correctly foresaw, would certainly be indirect action, working through emerging national movements to upset Western arrangements in the Near and Middle East and South Asia.[36]

Among U.S. policy makers there was conflict over how to match the Russians. The Asiatic experts were stressing the need to support emerging nationalist forces in the Far East. The European experts were arguing that there was a real danger of weakening and alienating the European powers, making them ripe for the left, by supporting nationalists in their empires. The timing of Suez, however, cut through this; it was seen in Washington as an attempt to manipulate American policy through the U.S. elections (in November 1956 there was a presidential election), and Eisenhower personally was furious at being misled by British and French political leaders, who did not tell him their plans. It was not surprising, therefore, that America proved itself willing to push aside Britain and France as it rushed to meet this new threat to American and Western interests. The old empires, in their dissolute last throes, were not to be allowed to jeopardize democratic interests as they wrestled desperately with their inevitable loss of empire, endangering the future for short-term advantage. All this was to become clear with the 1956 Suez crisis.

There had been an earlier instance of the fundamental dissonance between the purposes of America and the old empires when, in 1954, the French withdrew from Vietnam after the fall of Dien Bien Phu. The collapse of the French cleared the deck, in a way, making America's subsequent policy in Southeast Asia easier; American support could be given to anticommunist nationalists without being inevitably associated with the French. But when Ho Chi Minh made it clear that communism was vital to his nationalism, American support was given to his opponents, and by 1956 the United States had replaced France as the Western power in Vietnam. In Egypt during the same period something very similar had happened, with oil, nationalism, communism, and the decline of the old empires all being involved. The oil issue made the Suez Canal of major importance, since so much of Europe's economic life depended on a steady oil supply through the canal. Egypt therefore became an important pawn in international relations. In December 1955 the United States and Britain had offered help in building the Aswan Dam to Colonel Gamel Abdel Nasser, the young nationalist Egyptian leader who in 1952 had led a military *coup d'état* against the corrupt regime of King Farouk.* No

---

* Nasser had been helped to power by the CIA: Kermit Roosevelt had advised and funded the coup leaders in secret and against the British policy of trying to make the monarchy of King Farouk work. To the Dulles brothers, however, British attempts to hold onto colonial prototypes were more than an invitation to communist nationalists: they were a directive to them. For a colorful account of Roosevelt's Egyptian exploits, see Miles Copeland, *The Real Spy World* (London: Sphere, 1978), pp. 60–64, and *The Game of Nations* (New York: Simon & Schuster, 1969), pp. 62–64. For a more detailed account of the CIA's role in Egypt in the early 1950s, see Wilbur Crane Eveland, *Ropes of Sand* (New York: W. W. Norton, 1980), pp. 95–105, 125. While acknowledging CIA involvement, Eveland wryly recalled Kermit Roosevelt's modesty on the subject,

doubt Nasser's agreement to buy arms from Czechoslovakia three months earlier had prompted the Anglo-American initiative. But while Britain saw this effort as a carrot to entice Nasser to a pro-Western stance that would guarantee oil supplies through the canal, John Foster Dulles and the Eisenhower administration saw it as part of a long-term effort to win nationalists to the anti-Soviet balance of forces in the world.

Earlier, in 1954, the different objectives of Britain and America in the Middle East conflicted in secret over the Buraimi Oasis. In the affair Saudi Arabia sought possession of the oasis from the two states that owned it, Oman and Abu Dhabi, both of which were under British control, though technically independent. Saudi Arabia was far more oriented toward America than Britain because of the investment there of the omnipresent American oil consortium, Aramco. King Saud and his brother, Prince Faisal, sought American help in obtaining the oasis, promising any oil concessions that resulted to Aramco. Allen Dulles decided to try to arrange the deal and sent Kermit Roosevelt, fresh from his 1953 Iranian triumph, to Saudi Arabia as his covert ambassador. Roosevelt first tried to fix an election in the oasis area, packing it with Saudis and offering the local sheik an air-conditioned Cadillac for his support. This failed—the local sheik was brother to the Abu Dhabi ruler—and so Roosevelt tried outright bribery to the tune of $90 million in gold (to be supplied by the CIA, Aramco, and the Saudis) if the sheik would cede his oasis to the Saudis, "preventing the [British-controlled] Iraq Petroleum Company from operating in the disputed territories and leaving the field open to Aramco."[37] The sheik asked for a written guarantee of this, and when he was not given one he in-

---

implying that it was disingenuous: "In 1972 I discussed with Kim Roosevelt Copeland's allegation that the CIA had arranged Farouk's ouster. Then profiting from his company's representation of the shah and the Saudis in Washington, Kim had become modest. He claimed that he'd never have been able to gain the confidence of his customer monarchs if he'd really ousted Farouk" (p. 98).

The British were also active in Egypt. In 1953 they recruited Mahmoud Khalil, chief of Nasser's air force intelligence, and over the next four years paid him over £150,000. On December 23, 1957, Nasser announced that Khalil had all along been his agent and revealed British attempts to reestablish King Farouk on the Egyptian throne (Richard Deacon, "C"—A Biography of Sir Maurice Oldfield [London: Macdonald, 1985], pp. 110–12).

Roosevelt ascribed the attempt to oust Nasser to the British. "The proposal was that an operation be mounted against Nasser, and the U.S. Government's position was very reserved," he recalled. "We said we agreed in principle that this would be a good idea but we were not satisfied that the appropriate conditions existed to carry it out successfully." The proposal was for Nasser to be "replaced by a palace revolution," said Roosevelt, "and of course we didn't see—we couldn't identify the palace revolutionaries who were willing to undertake it with any chance of success. There were always people who you know are willing to have a crack at something, but you've got to judge their capabilities" (interview, Kermit Roosevelt, in Granada Television program, World in Action: The Rise and Fall of the CIA, June 1975, Part II). Shortly after this, Roosevelt quit the agency and joined Gulf Oil because he considered that large-scale covert operations were wrong and involved a dangerous misconception on the part of John Foster Dulles about the nature and possibilities of intelligence operations (interview, Kermit Roosevelt, November 8, 1983).

formed the British, who took the case to the International Court in Geneva. Despite CIA attempts to bribe the arbitrators in Geneva, the British won the case, and the oasis stayed with Oman and Abu Dhabi.

Roosevelt was not blamed by Allen Dulles—he had done his best. Both Dulles brothers had simply been trying to replace British influence and commercial interests with American ones. Influence was most important; they wanted to win emergent nationalists to the anticommunist cause. John Foster Dulles' first trip overseas after becoming secretary of state had included a visit to Nasser, whom he had tried to convince of America's concern with communism and the Soviet Union while distancing America from traditional British and French interests in the area. "How can I go to my people," Nasser asked him, "and tell them I am disregarding a killer with a pistol sixty miles from me at the Suez Canal to worry about somebody who is holding a knife a thousand miles away?"[38] Dulles' answer was to offer Nasser American money for his pet project of building the Aswan Dam, and CIA expertise.[39] Nasser played along for a while, but by mid-1956 domestic political pressure had forced the United States more and more clearly to the side of Israel, seen by the Arab states as their mortal enemy.

In April 1956 Egypt, Saudi Arabia, Syria, and Yemen formed an obviously anti-Israel military alliance. In May, Nasser recognized Mao Tse-tung's communist China, withdrawing recognition from Chiang Kai-shek. Together, this made it very difficult for John Foster Dulles to convince Congress to fund the Aswan Dam. In addition to opposition from the Israeli and China lobbies, Foster Dulles also had to deal with southern senators and representatives who opposed the project on the grounds that it would enable Egypt to produce and export cotton that was cheaper than the cotton produced in their home districts. As a result of these pressures Dulles publicly announced American withdrawal from the dam project on July 19. It was a damaging blow to Nasser's prestige at home. His reply one week later was to nationalize the British-controlled Universal Suez Canal Company.

In 1950 Britain, France, and the United States had agreed to a declaration speaking against the use of force to resolve problems in the Middle East and stating that in the event of war it would "not involve the United States on the side of Israel."[40] In 1954, following his coup against King Farouk, Nasser had reached an agreement with Britain by which British technicians would operate the Suez Canal but British troops guarding it would leave in 1956, with the proviso that they could return if Turkey, Egypt, or any Arab country were attacked by a country other than Israel. Nasser's nationalization of the Canal Company was legal and was also within the terms of the 1950 and 1954 agreements. However, it meant that he had sole control over a major economic channel to Europe. When he refused to share control (a proposal made by John Foster Dulles), Britain and France decided to take advantage of American hostility to Nasser and reassert their Egyptian interests. Dulles was privately informed of their general plans but not of any details. Israel would attack Egypt, and Britain and France would move in to "protect" the canal.

Dulles chose to stick to the terms of the 1950 declaration and distanced the United States from the plot of which—officially—he knew nothing. On October 29, 1956, Israel launched a surprise attack on Egypt, and over the next few days rapidly occupied the Sinai Peninsula. On October 30 Britain and France delivered ultimatums to Egypt and Israel to stay away from the canal. This was a calculated deception: it was aimed against the Egyptians, who had to reject the demand, for in order to counter the Israelis, they had to move military formations and supplies across the canal. British and French bombers then attacked Egyptian military targets, and their forces made landings at the Mediterranean end of the canal and occupied a zone on either side.

The CIA supplied detailed reports of these actions with some of the first operational flights of the U-2 spy plane. (The first operational flight had taken place in the summer of 1956 to photograph British and French naval preparations in Malta for the Suez invasion.) One flight over Cairo International Airport photographed Nasser's air force lined up on the tarmac. By the time the U-2 had swung round to fly over again, the second set of photographs showed the airport devastated and Nasser's planes destroyed. During the flight the Israelis had attacked. By November 6 British and French units were only days away from securing complete control of the area, and the Israelis controlled most of Egyptian Sinai.

November 6 was presidential election day, and three days earlier John Foster Dulles had undergone emergency surgery for the cancer that would eventually kill him. The British and French had chosen one of the most difficult periods in the tenure of any American President for their Suez operation, with the threat of making Eisenhower look weak to his electorate if he publicly opposed their plans. To make matters worse, they had gone ahead with the Suez operation after uprisings had broken out in Hungary against the communist regime there. It seemed to Eisenhower and his officials that Britain and France were being unscrupulous and selfish in moving without formally consulting the United States at the time of the administration's greatest political weakness and in deflecting attention and potential resources away from exploiting Soviet troubles in eastern Europe.

Khrushchev also saw an opportunity to take advantage of the split between the Western allies and Eisenhower's involvement in the election. He proposed a joint Russo-American settlement in the area and warned Britain and France that unless they quickly withdrew, Russia would use force on the side of Egypt. Eisenhower saw this as a fast Soviet move to extend Russian influence and power in the Middle East, to distract attention from Hungary, and to undercut America's bid to be the new nationalists' friend. Accordingly, he blunted the proposal by siding with the Soviet Union in the United Nations in passing a resolution condemning the Anglo-French action, and determined that "we should be promptly ready to take any kind of action that will mini-mize the effects of the recent difficulties and will exclude from the area Soviet influence."[41]

This bought time and made it clear to the Soviets that if they intervened, so would America. Tremendous pressure was exerted on the British and French to withdraw. Oil supplies from Latin America were cut off, and dollar support for the pound and the franc on international exchanges was with-drawn, resulting in a serious run on both currencies and consequences of fiscal austerity in both countries. By December 22 the French and British forces had caved in to this pressure and withdrawn, being replaced by a United Nations force as an interim measure before the canal was handed back to Nasser. Rus-sia and America had staked out their future conflict and it had no room for third parties. The Third World (which included most of the old colonies) would be the battleground. Apart from anything else, the prospect of liberating them was more certain than the 1952 election hope of liberating Europe.

The attempt to salvage American interests in Egypt failed. Nasser's anti-Israel position would brook no positive relationship with anyone who sup-ported Israel. In a gesture of defiance, Nasser used CIA money—reputedly part of $12 million given to his colleague General Naguib, who had been a coleader of the coup against King Farouk—to build the Cairo Tower, known privately to Nasser and his friends as the "CIA Monument," and "Roosevelt's erec-tion," after Kermit Roosevelt's efforts in Egypt. Bribery on a massive scale had been a hallmark of the CIA in the Middle East. Similar amounts were repu-tedly paid to the mother of King Hussein of Jordan; an estimated $40 million to King Saud of Saudi Arabia; additional amounts to his brother, Prince Faisal; and millions more to key officials throughout the Middle East. Naguib fell out with Nasser, who confiscated his CIA monies.[42]

After the Suez affair Nasser's Egypt became more and more entwined with the Soviet Union. His successor, Anwar Sadat, conducted a diplomatic revolution after the 1973 war with Israel, reaching a *modus vivendi* with Israel and receiving in return major American military and economic aid. More tra-ditional diplomatic methods were suited to the extraordinary complex of Egyptian foreign policy, and the CIA's enormous expenditure there was vir-tually fruitless: Prince Faisal took CIA money but was secretly a Nasser sup-porter and informant; King Hussein of Jordan enjoyed major private British support and in any event did not invite his mother's participation in govern-ment.

On the eve of the October 29 Israeli attack in the Sinai, which triggered the Suez crisis, the CIA had not been able to secure any precise official infor-mation about the Anglo-French-Israeli plans, despite American friendship and aid to all three countries. The first news of an imminent attack came from "a low grade [confidential] message from the U.S. Military Attaché in Israel to the G-2 of the Army in Washington," remembered Robert Amory:

It said: "Just thought you ought to know that my driver—a reservist with one arm and one leg missing and blind in one eye—has been called to the colors!" I read the message that Friday morning when I got into my office at about 7:30 A.M. and immediately realized it meant an attack. Mobilizing to that degree was more than defensive. It indicated mobilization for aggressive purposes: the Jordanian army was not that strong a threat to Israel that double amputees had to be called up, so it had to mean that they were going to attack Egypt. Since, from sundown on Friday to the same time on Saturday was the Sabbath, the chances were for an attack on Monday morning. When I showed it to Allen I commented it was a general mobilization, and he said the Watch Committee (the early warning subcommittee of the U.S. Intelligence Board) should be called. I said I'd already called a meeting on an hour's notice and was on my way to it. On Saturday, in a conference in Foster Dulles's office, I alluded to the cable and he struck a sentence or two out of the campaign speech (his only one) he was about to make that evening in Dallas, lest what he said be taken as meaning that the U.S. had been officially notified.*

Amory's accurate interpretation of the implications of the intercepted telegram and his resulting action benefited the agency. It meant that when the Israelis did attack shortly after midnight on Monday, October 29, John Foster Dulles and the Washington bureaucracy knew that the CIA had correctly called the shots. Inside the agency, however, the fact that the intelligent analysis of information lay behind their achievement did not deflect them from their interest in covert operations. It was the events taking place in eastern Europe at the same time as Suez which generated a reassessment.

HUNGARY

From mid-April 1956, immediately following Khrushchev's secret speech, the CIA's Directorate of Plans noticed signs of ferment in the satellite countries. Robert Amory, while on a trip to Europe trying to secure a copy of the speech, was also assessing developments, particularly in Poland and Hungary, with the help of friendly intelligence services in Sweden, Germany, Austria, and Yugoslavia. Poland and East Germany showed the first signs of active po-

---

* Interview, Robert Amory, Jr., November 9, 1983, and letter, Amory to author, February 22, 1985. See also Leonard Mosley, *Dulles—A Biography of Eleanor, Allen and John Foster Dulles and Their Family Network* (New York: Dial Press/James Wade, 1978), pp. 414–415, for a somewhat sanitized version of the telegram and the debate within the State Department and the CIA over Amory's prediction. In the agency, James Angleton, known to be particularly close to the Israeli Mossad, was asked for his opinion and apparently said, "Amory's speech may sound alarming, but I think I can discount it. I've spent the last evening and most of the early hours with my Israeli friends in Washington, and I can assure you that it's all part of maneuvers and is certainly not meant for any serious attack. There is nothing in it. I do not believe there is going to be an attack by the Israelis." This was on Friday, October 26 (ibid.).

litical unrest, with strikes and demonstrations throughout the summer, but it was to be in Hungary that the real test of what Khrushchev might have meant or would allow took place.

The historical background to the Hungarian communist regime was a central element in the Hungarian revolt of 1956. In October 1944 Russian armies advanced into Hungary, where they met stiff resistance from German SS divisions and their Hungarian equivalents. Between October and February 1945, when the Soviet armies finally overcame this resistance, the Nazis conducted a furious purge of the large Jewish population of the country, which up until then had been largely spared. Jews in Hungary provided much of the country's professional expertise in all fields, and their persecution seriously affected Hungary's ability to administer and tend to its people. The Arrow Cross, fascist formations that ran Hungary in the last days of the war, played a large part in the attack on the Jews, but with the Soviet occupation of Hungary, many of its members joined the new, communist-controlled secret police, the AVH. During the next four years a multiparty government, dominated by the social democratic Small Holders party and also including communists, held power.

In April 1949, using the AVH, the communists purged the government and declared a Popular Front, which they dominated. Three months later a further, internal purge placed the government firmly in the hands of hard-line Stalinists led by Matyos Rakosi, "a squat bald-headed man, whom Joe Alsop would have dubbed toadlike and whom Stalin called behind his back 'arsehead.'"[43] Under Rakosi, the AVH became an arm of repression. Its regular force, which numbered a hundred thousand, was augmented by perhaps a million other members—informers, clerks, administrators—all of whom sustained a cult of Rakosi, aping that of Stalin. The Hungarian Politburo even went so far as to decree that the word "wise" be used solely to describe Rakosi. After Stalin's death Rakosi was replaced briefly by Imre Nagy, who sought to liberalize the regime. In 1955 Rakosi came back and Nagy went into exile. In 1956, after the June workers' demonstrations in Poznań, Poland, were suppressed by the Polish Army, Rakosi determined to nip potential Hungarian demonstrators in the bud and prepared to clamp down on dissenters. Instead, much to his surprise, just after outlining his plans to his Politburo on July 18, Anastas Mikoyan, a member of the Soviet Politburo and Soviet minister for foreign trade, suddenly and unexpectedly came into the meeting and ordered Rakosi to resign. Rakosi telephoned Khrushchev for confirmation and then dutifully resigned.

The Russians felt that the backlash in world opinion after Poznań put at risk the new initiative set forth in Khrushchev's secret speech—an initiative that sought to overturn the Stalinist defensive fears of encirclement which saw eastern Europe as a protective buffer zone to be strictly controlled. Instead, the satellites were to be used to develop wider opportunities for Soviet foreign policy, not the least of which was an appeal to the Third World. Crackdowns were not the best advertisement for this new thrust. Rakosi was replaced by Erno Gero, another hard-liner, who had the advantage of not yet being publicly identified as such. Imre Nagy, whose popularity increased by the day because of his earlier liberalizing reforms, was excluded from returning to power. The popular mood in Hungary was not prodemocratic or anticommunist. On the contrary, people were content to live under communism as long as their personal liberties and economic prosperity were assured.

The same could not be said about Poland, where traditional national prejudices identified communism with Russia and its puppet regimes and, as a result, rejected communist control. After the Poznań riots Wladyslaw Gomulka spearheaded a rapid de-Stalinization program in Poland, frightening hard-liners, who on October 19 called upon the Russians to send in the Red Army to contain what they saw as imminent revolt. Khrushchev flew to Warsaw, mobilized Soviet troops, and denounced Gomulka's changes. Gomulka, similar to Nagy in his political views but a more determined politician, publicly countered to a crowd of four hundred thousand with a fierce attack on Stalinism and promises of even more reforms. The tumultuous support he received made it clear to the Russians and the hard-liners that they would have to take on the Polish people if repression were reinstated.

In Washington all this was seen as a potential flashpoint for World War III. Since his return from Europe in May, Robert Amory, the DDI, closely monitored developments:

> I was able to help the US Government keep up-to-date and way ahead of the wire services and intelligence and diplomatic cables through my friendship with the charming and extraordinarily talented war correspondent Marguerite Higgins, who had many friends in the leading Polish newspaper *Tribuno Ludo*. Sitting in her office with an open telephone line to the *Tribuno's* and freely identified as a top CIA officer, I had virtually real-time solid information leaked to the Polish editors by their friends on the Warsaw Politburo and gladly passed on to encourage US assistance in case the Soviets cracked down. . . .
>
> I asked for and promptly got an appointment with Buz Wheeler, the brilliant operations head and later Chairman of the Joint Chiefs of Staff. On entering his office I said "General, do you realize that World War III may be hours away?" He replied, "We're following the situation closely." I said, "If the Polish situation explodes, their army will fight against the Russians with the desperate valor of Kosciusko and Bor-Komorowski—25 divisions strong and the land war balance in Eastern Europe will be decisively tipped in our favor if material support can only be given them." To his credit because military intelligence hewed to the line that monolithic communism would never shatter, he then and there called in his staff and went to work on a crash analysis and planning program.[44]

In Hungary the news of Gomulka's successful resistance to Soviet threats launched a series of demonstrations. Demands grew for Nagy's return and the arrest of Rakosi. Gero countered by arresting Nagy and loosing the AVH against the demonstrators on October 23. Within hours workers had joined students in protests, the AVH had started machine-gunning the crowds, and the army and police had been called in to help restore order but had instead given their weapons to demonstrators. At almost exactly the same time, at Sèvres, a few miles down the Seine from Paris, the final arrangements were made for the Anglo-French-Israeli attack on Egypt.

In Hungary on the following day, October 24, the demonstrations had turned into an uprising. The Hungarian Politburo recalled Nagy to replace Gero and forced him (an AVH officer trained a pistol on him) to ask the Russians for assistance. At daybreak Soviet tanks rolled into Budapest. Over the next ten days events seesawed. Then Khrushchev realized that the Anglo-French invasion of Suez, the American presidential election, and the obvious tensions among the Western allies meant that he could crush the Hungarian revolt with nothing but political repercussions. Many in the CIA, including Frank Wisner, were already aware that the circumstances would enable Khrushchev to succeed. Wisner was so furious with the situation that it affected his health. He was outraged to think that Britain and France, placing their hopeless imperial ambitions in the Middle East to the fore, had effectively sabotaged the best chance (as he saw it) since 1945 to wrest eastern Europe from Soviet control. Wisner pressed Allen Dulles to release the Red Sox/Red Cap groups and allow the CIA's covert-action arm to go into operation, directly supporting the Hungarian resisters.

At first Dulles was sympathetic, but as the Anglo-French Suez affair unfolded, caution set in, and Egypt rather than Hungary became the priority. State Department and CIA analysts, while less willing than military intelligence to view the communist world as a monolith, took the view that the communist regimes in eastern Europe would not be toppled by internal unrest.[45] Gomulka in Poland had kept reform within the communist camp; in Hungary the people were not seeking an alternative to communism. Robert Amory explained:

> Intelligence reports reaching Washington showed that the Soviet Army was assembling a large force, gathering troops from Rumania and all over the Ukraine and moving them toward the Hungarian frontier. It was only logical for us to conclude that, with war a fact in the Near East, the Kremlin had decided to put its satellite backyard in order and quickly without worrying about any niceties. Appalled by the combination of a God-given chance to witness a significant roll-back of this iron curtain by the unaided guts and verve of the Magyar people and a sense of helpless foreboding at what would happen to them if the Russians felt certain that the West would not lift a finger, some of us on the NSC planning board who could turn their attention

from the opéra bouffe being played out on the sand dunes of Suez and at the UN tried to come up with a strategy that might conceivably work.[46]

The introduction of NATO troops into Hungary was dismissed on the grounds that the Soviets, who enjoyed shorter supply lines in the area, could at least match them—there were more Soviet troops and weapons in Central Europe than NATO could muster—and such a move would heighten the risk of World War III. It could also put at risk the continued existence of a free and united Austria, only in its second year of restored sovereignty. Soviet weakness lay in its nuclear-weapons inferiority, the unity of Hungarian resistance—the Hungarian army had merged with the resisters—and the centralization of its rail and road marshaling points. "It was easy to see," Amory recalled, "that the rail and road links into Hungary from the east are tenuous and could be virtually put out of operation by what is now called a surgical nuclear strike limited to Lvov in Soviet-annexed Poland and selected passes in the mountains of Russian Ruthenia and western Rumania."[47]

This was the line of action Amory recommended, arguing that massive preemptive use of nuclear weapons would also prevent World War III:

Was this a possibility for consideration by rational and civilized people? . . . Consider the following facts: on March 1, 1954, the United States' first true fusion (i.e. megaton) weapon had been successfully tested in the Pacific, and in the following 2½ years a significant stockpile had been assembled. The Soviets had boasted of developing a thermo-nuclear bomb, but our detailed analysis of their early tests showed them to be merely fusion-boosted fission devices. Only in November, 1955, less than a year before the period we are discussing did they produce the first successful fusion device and, in the intervening months, they could only have assembled a modest arsenal of fusion weapons. Thus, the relative strategic balance in these doomsday weapons stood more favorable to the United States than it would ever again.

So I drafted a one-page ultimatum for the President and Secretary of State to consider, calling for a halt to all further Soviet reinforcement of its forces in Hungary on pain of our taking military measures at our disposal, etc. etc., and gave it to Allen Dulles to pass to his brother. I said that if Khrushchev were to ask Marshal Zhukov if he was ready for nuclear war with the United States, the latter would have to answer no; hence, the ultimatum by itself might well work.[48]

Wisner supported this line of reasoning but throughout was constantly pressing for conventional direct and covert action too. Since the period before the Suez crisis Wisner had been in Germany and Austria and was affected by local feeling. In close communication with his brother at all times, Allen Dulles came out against the arguments of both men. "How can anything be done about the Russians, even if they suppress the revolt, when our own allies are guilty of exactly similar acts of aggression?"[49] asked Allen Dulles. In his report Wisner referred to the need to liberate eastern Europe and roll back Soviet forces, both of which were goals set forth in the 1952 presidential campaign. He also made clear that the CIA had been planning for just this sort of situation in 1956. Allen Dulles introduced the political reality that with the presidential election on, it was not the moment to do much else besides talk.

What had happened was that just as Red Sox/Red Cap operations were being readied, events went much faster, overtaking the plans before any policy decision was made on the principle of whether or not the United States should prepare and foment revolutions in eastern Europe. Wisner flew to Vienna and witnessed the collapse of his and the Hungarian dreams from as close a vantage point as he could. Returning to Washington, he hit the bottle and began a descent into a personal hell, as Richard Bissell remembered:

> I saw him in all the stages of the onset of the depression; then there was recovery, then recurrence. It was set off really by his presence in Vienna during the Hungarian uprising. It was very noticeable when he came back that he was in a manic, overexcited state. He was relieved for three or four months—that term was never used, but that in effect is what it amounted to—and Dick Helms was acting DDP. Frank went into an institution, and within a relatively few months he was able to return to the job and to all appearances was in good form and became again an active DDP. Then the second incident started—after he had been on a trip around the world, I think—in any case, he had been out in the Orient. He drew dramatic attention when on a Fourth of July weekend quite a group of us were staying down at the Nitzes' place on the Potomac and Frank arrived a day after the rest of us. He had bolts of material that he had bought, Thai silks and things for the ladies. It didn't take five minutes to see that another manic phase was developing. He spoke very fast—loquacious, excessively outgoing. Fairly soon after that it became clear that he again had to take a leave of absence for a while. That was in '58.*

WORDS, NOT DEEDS

Part of Frank Wisner's "mighty Wurlitzer" operation in the DDP included Radio Free Europe (RFE), which played an increasingly frantic part as events in Hungary reached their climax. Cord Meyer, who succeeded Tom Braden as head of the CIA's International Organizations Division in Septem-

---

* Interview, Richard M. Bissell, Jr., July 18, 1983. Wisner's collapse may have occurred for another reason. Red Sox/Red Cap and the support given to Polish and Hungarian hopes were the work of ruthless men. Were Red Sox/Red Cap intended for a "hot" war with the Soviets, risking the use of nuclear weapons in the cause of eastern European liberation? Or were they a tease to sucker the Soviets into acting more repressively and brutally in the satellite countries in order to secure propaganda victories for the West? A moral question of importance was involved either way, and Frank Wisner may have been finally destroyed by it. He had also contracted hepatitis in Greece in 1956, and this undoubtedly contributed to his breakdown.

ber 1954, had direct charge of the agency's relationship with the staffs of Radio Free Europe and Radio Liberty. He continued Braden's policy of insisting on journalistic freedom for both radio networks, rejecting periodic attempts to use them for overt propaganda or disinformation campaigns.[50] In the summer of 1956 Radio Free Europe's American advisers in Munich, digesting the reports they received from journalists returning from visits behind the iron curtain, from émigrés and from local radio broadcasts they could pick up from satellite countries, determined that events were moving toward a confrontation with the Russians in Poland and Hungary. They warned Meyer in Washington of the volatile situation.

Meyer recalled what happened next:

> When I tried to convey this impression of approaching crisis to the State Department and intelligence analysts in Washington, they were inclined to be skeptical and tended to assume on the basis of past experience that the communists would remain firmly in control. Allen Dulles was later to criticize me for not having brought RFE's advice more forcefully to his personal attention and that of senior policymakers. I admit to not having been sufficiently sure of my case to challenge the prevailing consensus directly. It was a salutary lesson in the reality that not all wisdom resides in Washington and that access to even the most secret intelligence is no guarantee against human error.[51]

When Khrushchev's secret speech was published in *The New York Times*, both Radio Liberty and Radio Free Europe beamed its contents repeatedly into the Soviet Union and eastern Europe. When the Poznań riots took place Radio Free Europe responded with caution, advising Poles that an insurrection would be suicidal and supporting Gomulka's line as the best hope of preventing a Soviet invasion. This was recognized by the Gomulka regime, which removed the internal jamming of RFE broadcasts so that its moderating voice could be heard. Jan Nowak, the head of the Polish section at RFE, was largely responsible for this approach. He had fought against the Germans in Warsaw in 1944 during the last desperate uprising and was one of the last to escape to the West. He was personally concerned that the Poles keep their heads and not adopt a romantic stance that would lose them the modest improvements obtained by Gomulka. He never assumed that there was a realistic chance of American or NATO aid to Poland.

When it came to Hungary, however, it was a different story at RFE. By November 3, 1956, Soviet allegations were being made that RFE broadcasts were inciting Hungarians to violence. Over the next six months several investigations were made into this charge: tapes of broadcasts were reviewed and their contents analyzed. Meyer conducted an agency investigation that cleared the Hungarian section and RFE generally of the charge. Two independent investigations were made that reached the same verdict—one by the West German government at the personal instruction of Chancellor Konrad Adenauer, another by the Council of Europe. However, what did emerge from these studies and became increasingly clear as the Hungarian revolt grew was that the RFE Hungarian broadcasts contained a far more partial and hysterical tone than the earlier RFE broadcasts to Poland. By transmitting without comment local broadcasts from Hungary that frequently carried appeals for help, rumors of help, and diatribes against Rakosi, Gero, and the Soviets, RFE imbued them with an importance that sustained Hungarian hopes of U.S. intervention.[52] The lessons were learned, and when it came to the liberal "Prague Spring" of the Dubček regime in Czechoslovakia in 1968, which was crushed by Soviet tanks, it was the Nowak approach that was taken. Propaganda had its place but not in the driving seat. Covert operations had their place too: against those who could not threaten major war, not against those who could. Donovan's OSS days were war days, and the methods developed then did not always translate as easily to peace.

All this was at last recognized in the wake of the Hungarian revolt. The steady movement of the agency away from a "war" mind to a "hard and bitter peace" mind was confirmed. In the founding years of the agency Europe was in ruins and nothing was certain. By 1956 lines had been drawn. Western Europe was stable; eastern Europe was Russian. The Third World was the principal area of contest, and there was a sense that the shape of the world would be determined not, after all, in Europe, but elsewhere. It was easier than many thought it would be for the agency to accept these lessons because it was already moving into the future mainstay of intelligence: electronic and mechanical devices that had little to do with people.

—10—

Planes, Plans, Plots
1955–1961

Richard Bissell was the man who guided the CIA into the new age of intelligence. He was one of the first to realize that accurate factual information, rather than simply accurate political intelligence, was essential for the proper assessment of conflict and tension in a world under the thrall of nuclear weapons, and to turn this recognition into a bureaucratic program. In the process he engineered an intellectual and management revolution in intelligence. As was proved during the 1962 Cuban missile crisis, precise factual information enabled analysts quickly to determine the practical effects of tactical and strategic political moves and the nature and basis of diplomatic maneuvers.

Bissell was also one of the first to identify the way to obtain this information: by deploying to the full the technological advances being made in electronics, flight engineering, space research, and computer science and by establishing parallel programs to develop methods and equipment for intelligence purposes. He put together resources and talent in a concerted, continuing way without acceding to the passions of the moment. His was not a burst of wartime enthusiasm or need but a dispassionate management of problems in a strategic way, designed to be effective and long-lasting. It was unusual for such a result-oriented agency as the CIA to have a man of such farsighted intellect in its governing group.

In 1954 the Intelligence Advisory Board, the official interagency intelligence coordination body, was studying ways to improve the systems that provided advance warning of enemy attack on the United States. It was presented with a report from a committee it had established to look into the threat of any such surprise attack. The Killian Committee was chaired by James Ryan Killian, Jr., president of MIT and head of the army's Scientific Advisory Panel. A subcommittee chaired by Edwin H. Land of the Polaroid Corporation was responsible for discovering ways of accurately monitoring Soviet military capabilities and dispositions. Land's subcommittee made two recommendations. It proposed that a new airplane be developed that could fly higher than Soviet antiaircraft missiles along a north-south path across the USSR without refueling; it also proposed that a high-definition camera be developed and placed aboard. The board accepted Land's proposals, and on December 1, 1954, Eisenhower gave his approval.

Allen Dulles asked his special assistant, Richard Bissell, who had joined the agency only a few months earlier, to take charge of the CIA's involvement in the project. At a meeting in the office of the head of air force research and development Bissell brought the project under CIA control by agreeing to pay its full cost—an estimated $22 million—from the Discretionary Fund of the director of Central Intelligence.[1] In this way Congress would not be involved, nor would it need to be informed. This was important because of the extreme secrecy of the whole project. If news of it leaked out, the Soviets might have time to develop effective antiaircraft missiles or other devices. Once the plan was actually in operation flying over the Soviet Union, the CIA expected the Russians to develop these missiles, but in the time it might take them to do so, valuable information would be obtained.[2] The plane was called the U-2 and was regarded as one of the most highly classified projects in the agency. Bissell ran it as a self-contained operation within the CIA. Even its designation "U" was chosen to shield its real purpose: "U" stood for utility.

BISSELL AND THE U-2

The CIA's leading role in fostering such a technical intelligence project was a new development. Under Bedell Smith the agency had been offered the opportunity of becoming America's principal communications interception center but had rejected it. Bedell Smith had considered that the agency's role in communications intelligence was primarily analysis, and he did not want to be responsible for thousands of acres of real estate around the world and thousands of employees who, in most cases, would be under the direct control of the military. The result was the creation in 1952 of the National Security Agency, with headquarters at Fort Meade, Maryland, responsible for U.S. government communications and for communications interception on a global scale. Within three years of its creation the NSA was making its mark in the manner of Herbert Yardley's Black Chamber thirty years earlier. This time, however, the Vatican's codes (let alone anyone else's) certainly were not safe. Not to be overtaken by the new arrival in the intelligence fraternity, Allen Dulles and Richard Bissell recognized that the U-2 project would maintain the agency's comparative position as a sophisticated collector of intelligence by technical means—depending on humans to the most limited degree. This was underlined by the project's self-contained separation from the rest of the agency, an arrangement that Bissell used all his extraordinary ability and experience to achieve.

An economist by training, Bissell had studied at the London School of Economics in the early 1930s under Harold Laski and was reputedly the first professor to teach Keynesian economics in the United States (in 1936, at Yale). He was also one of the principal organizers of Allied shipping during the war. Once the war ended, he became one of the mainstays of the Marshall Plan and is credited with having "sold" the plan on Capitol Hill. Following that, he had worked briefly in the Truman White House. He was a friend of Frank Wisner and knew Allen Dulles socially. He was also a friend of the junior senator for Massachusetts, John F. Kennedy. He was well connected, an American patrician, and brilliant. Allen Dulles' choice of Bissell as his special assistant was inspired. What was more surprising, perhaps, was that a man of Bissell's ability should have been attracted to the work of the CIA. In later years another of his friends, John Kenneth Galbraith, would write of him:

> Bissell was an economist of ability and intelligence and an early Keynesian, who, in the New Deal days, had held himself aloof from the political enthusiasms of the time. Keynes was one thing; liberal politics was something else. In consequence, his professional competence, combined with his inner conservatism, made him highly acceptable to the businessmen who were associated in later years with the Marshall Plan, and he was a particularly influential figure in its management and success. He went on to join Allen Dulles in the belief that communism anywhere called for an automatic and often unthinking response and that a system so evil allowed of indecency in return.[3]

That sense of the "enemy within" that Bissell observed from close quarters while he was working in the White House during the late 1940s was a powerful motivating force. This was shared by his colleagues in the CIA and the upper levels of the Eisenhower administration: "Soviet Capabilities and Intentions with Respect to the Clandestine Introduction of Weapons of Mass Destruction in the U.S." was one of the last CIA National Intelligence Estimates to be completed under Eisenhower in 1960, in retrospect revealing the penetrating fears of the governing elite.[4] Bissell was also a pioneer technocrat—neither a liberal nor a conservative (Galbraith was wrong on this point). His passion was for detachment, to remove belief and emotion from situations. He epitomized what Eisenhower (and the CIA) wanted the CIA to be. He had a powerful sense of the New World and was very much a master of his time, fully conscious of political and intellectual currents. One of these was a faith in technology and an almost awed assessment of its capabilities.

As with the fear of "enemies within," the faith in technology was another attitude Bissell shared with the most senior levels of government. An incident told by Robert Keith Gray, Eisenhower's cabinet secretary, demonstrated this:

> During a Cabinet meeting in 1959 a beam of brilliant light suddenly pierced one end of the room. From my place at the Cabinet table it seemed to me to be coming from the top corner of the Washington Hotel. Some of us on the staff had witnessed a demonstration a month earlier of a scientific development which makes it possible to hear a conversation carried on in a car or room blocks away by "shooting" a ray of light off a window. I sent word to the Secret Service men on guard outside the Cabinet room, there was the sound of running in the halls, and the light soon disappeared. It may have been only the sun reflected off a polished hotel window.[5]

The Eisenhower staff and cabinet were not composed of piano-wire neurotics; they were solid Republicans of the quietest kind. But ever since Pearl Harbor their world had been continually shaken, and they were prepared to think that the Russians might be ahead all the time. They saw technology as having the answer to practical requirements. It was a view Bissell appealed to, and it provided a sense of excitement too.

Bissell's originality and administrative experience came together with the U-2 project. He immediately began with a separate, special group housed a short distance away from the agency's headquarters, then at E Street. He made arrangements for the group's cable traffic, both incoming and outgoing, to be handled separately. Bissell explained:

> Normally the agency's cable traffic came into the Station Division, and at that point a selection was made of what copies to send to Allen and the others. The cable distribution was handled there. In the case of our traffic, which had a special designation, all of it came to the Project Office, and the Project Office did the distribution—and there was very little distribution. I don't know if to his dying day Allen ever realized that a volume of traffic, which may have been as much as 10 percent of the agency's total, was going on in this way without him having direct access to it in the sense of distribution of important messages by the communications system.[6]

On December 1, 1954, Bissell's staff was formally designated as the Development Project Staff. The project staff had its own administrative officer, an accountant, and a contracting officer. It wrote its own contracts, kept its own books and handled its own administration and security. At its peak, the staff had about 225 people. "The largest group was security," recalled Bissell. "Perhaps it would have been about thirty security officers. And we had a fairly big communications group. Our communications from the field to Washington went through military channels, but our encryption and decryption separated it even from the rest of agency traffic. We planned to have three detachments to fly, which would have meant about 675 people overseas, about 200 in Washington, and about 150 either out at Edwards Air Force Base or in Utah."[7]

Bissell persuaded President Eisenhower to allow the U-2 to use the Federal atomic testing grounds in Utah so that the project would automatically enjoy the highest security clearances throughout government under the Atomic Energy Commission and would have its own secret air base. At Edwards, pilots were trained by the Strategic Air Command. Within eight months of taking over the project Bissell supervised the first flight of a U-2. It was a remarkable achievement. The plane had been built from scratch, and it was breaking entirely new aeronautical ground, flying higher and longer than any plane had ever flown.

The man who designed the U-2 was Clarence L. "Kelly" Johnson, president of Lockheed. He had already designed some of America's most successful warplanes, including the P-38 fighter/bomber and the F-104 Starfighter. He had drawn up plans for the Killian Committee, having had the idea for such a plane himself in the first place and being convinced of its usefulness for American national security. Verification of information about Soviet military capabilities had been the stumbling block in U.S. intelligence. The U-2 would change all that. Recognizing this, Kelly Johnson chose to develop the plane for government rather than commercial use. In turn the agency followed traditional practice, commissioning private contractors for the work rather than undertaking it itself or through another government agency. Lockheed was the natural choice as the project contractor, given Johnson's involvement in the conception of the U-2. They agreed to develop the plane for $22 million on a standard 9 percent profit basis, with a rider that if the cost was less, Lockheed would have a larger profit; if it came in for more, their profit would be less.

Within days of securing control of the project Bissell instructed Johnson to build a prototype. At a secret workshop near Burbank, California—Lockheed's "Skunk Works"—the first plane was built. It turned out to be at the leading edge of technology; nearly everything about it involved new technology or significant advances on existing technology. A new fuel was specially developed for it by Shell, commissioned by Bissell through General James H. Doolittle, who was then on the Shell board. Unusual features of the design included an all-metal airframe; a light, extremely flexible wing with gliderlike qualities; specially designed Pratt & Whitney turbojet engines; and outrigger wheels that jettisoned on takeoff (on landing, the plane tipped onto a downturned wing).

The second original element in the U-2 project was the camera. Edwin H. Land's subcommittee had realized that a completely new camera would have to be developed to make the U-2 plane's flying abilities effective for intelligence. A wide-angle-lens camera was invented, capable of very-high-definition photography through seven apertures that were able to cover a 125-mile width of land in one frame. It required a 180-inch lens, which meant that the air scoop, which in Johnson's original idea was to run centrally through the fuselage of the plane, had to be altered. The size and weight of the lens precluded a central scoop. Johnson's solution was air scoops on either side, which, he later said, probably worked better than that of the original design. Land himself invented a new film—Eastman Kodak tried and failed—because the weight and thickness of the 4000 frames needed for each reconnaissance trip with eight hours of filming meant that existing film stock would be too bulky and heavy to be carried. He came up with a strong, thin, lightweight film stock that suited the requirements of the plane, of the camera, and of definition quality. It was stored in two counterbalancing rolls that moved one after the other frame by frame, thus maintaining the plane's weight balance.

A story was circulated after the flights became public that the CIA had shown President Eisenhower a U-2 photograph of himself playing golf in Augusta, Georgia, and that the President was able to pick out a golf ball in the photograph. Whether this was true or not, the fact was that Land's camera and film in Kelly Johnson's plane provided extraordinarily detailed photographs. In July 1956 a U-2 maintained a bird's-eye view of the Soviet Aviation Day flypast over Moscow, and the resulting photographs helped solve the "bomber gap" dispute. The world saw the results of the achievement during the Cuban missile crisis when President Kennedy published U-2 photographs of Soviet missiles and missile-site building in Cuba, clearly revealing, even to the untutored eye, that his assertions of Soviet missile deployment were true.

Approximately $19 million was spent developing the plane—$3 million less than was budgeted—and in only seventeen months after Johnson received the go-ahead from Bissell the U-2 was operational. Although generally smooth, the project was not without hitches. One of the main problems involved the engines, which were procured for the project by the air force. Pratt & Whitney J-57 engines were chosen and then development work was carried out to improve their performance. Although the first improved engine was successfully tested and declared combat-ready by Strategic Air Command's Engine Assessment unit, when it was mounted on the prototype, it demonstrated an alarming tendency to flame out in the thinner upper atmosphere. Bissell remembered:

> I was sitting in my office one day when the phone rang and I was told that a U-2 on a training mission from Nevada which was to take it over eastern Tennessee and back had had a flame-out. It had happened within the previous five minutes and the U-2 was going to make an emergency landing in Albuquerque. I called the base commander at Albuquerque and made arrangements with him to handle the crash landing for security. He got his troops out there just in time, screened off the area into which the pilot made a dead-stick landing, and no one ever found out what we were up to.[8]

A new, improved batch of J-57s that had very stable combustion in thin air was ready for the first detachment of U-2s. Just over two years after the first operational flights in the summer of 1956, a new and more powerful engine, the J-75, replaced the J-57.[9]

Nine months after the prototype's first flight on August 6, 1955, the first operational deployment of a U-2 wing targeted against the Soviet Union, consisting of four planes, six pilots, and about two hundred support staff, was in place in Turkey. Altogether, a fleet of twenty-two airplanes was eventually built and stationed at U.S. Air Force bases in Turkey, Germany, Japan, Taiwan, and England, as well as in Norway and Pakistan.[10] The pilots were all civilians, with military service backgrounds, under contract to the CIA.

The first operational flights over the Middle East and the Mediterranean were conducted in May and June 1956, and these planes were used to photograph the Anglo-French-Israeli preparations for their Suez venture. In June, President Eisenhower personally authorized the first flights over the Soviet Union from Turkey to Norway, allowing only ten days of flights in the first instance. Anxious to interpret this to secure the maximum number of flights, Bissell tried to have the ten-day stipulation understood as ten flying days after the first three days of the period were washouts because of bad weather:

> I was given permission by the President to fly missions for a period of ten days, starting on a certain date. It was then left to me to decide within that ten-day period what we were to do. We had about three days in the beginning of bad weather, so I said to Andy Goodpaster [Eisenhower's chief military aide], "I assume ten days means ten good days?" He said, "Absolutely not! Your permission expires on July 5." I was very disappointed.
>
> Every time after that we would get permission for each individual mission. The procedure was that we would say what we wanted. We would get the pro forma of U.S. intelligence advice—the U.S. Intelligence Board representing the community—and then there was a meeting in the Oval Office with President Eisenhower. I can't remember a case when it wasn't along with John Foster Dulles, the secretary of defense, or the deputy secretary of defense, quite often the Chiefs of Staff, Allen Dulles, Cabell [General Charles Pearré Cabell, Allen Dulles' DDCI], Goodpaster, and myself. We would lay out the missions and make as good a case as we could in terms of security in flying it and what we wanted to find out. The missions were in-and-out missions, and the targets were pretty carefully selected.[11]

Each flight had a specified set of targets, and repetition of targets from flight to flight was avoided. The first U-2s had a range of 2200 miles, but within three years this was increased to 3000 miles. Pilots had authority to deviate from their flight course but not from their altitude. The U-2 could fly over 13 miles high, and the normal altitude during an operational flight was over 70,000 feet.[12] (The official world altitude record for flying was 65,889 feet at that time.) Bissell recalled:

In one case a pilot used his authorization to deflect from his course. He was flying over Turkistan, and off in the distance he saw something that looked quite interesting and that turned out to be the Tyuratam launch site—and unlike almost every other target we went after, not even the existence of that had been suspected. I don't think anything had as yet been fired from there—I may be wrong—and he came back with the most beautiful photographs of this place, and within about five days the photo-interpreters had built a cardboard model of the whole Tyuratam site—roads, railway sidings, feeder roads, everything.[13]

As time went on, U-2 operations expanded. Some flights over the USSR originated in Lahore and Peshawar, Pakistan; Atsugi, Japan; Wiesbaden, Germany; Lakenheath, England; and Bodø, Norway. Flights over China originated in Taiwan. As flights continued, a mass of information accumulated not only about Soviet military targets but also about the detailed geography of the Soviet Union. Navigation was conducted by fixing on a group of known radio transmitters in different locations in the USSR. The U-2 was a difficult plane to fly and navigate even when the best pilots were at the controls. Their wingspan was 80 feet and their fuselage 49 feet 7 inches long, making them look more like sailplanes than jet planes. Later models had a 103-foot wingspan and a fuselage length of 63 feet. With such a configuration—the wingspan gave the planes their ability to fly high but, as with an oil tanker, made maneuvering slow—sharp turns were impossible and there was a high risk of not being able to steer out of a steep dive.

Pilots had to spend hours in prepressurization and pressurization preparations on pure oxygen before each flight in order to reduce the nitrogen content of their blood. At high altitudes nitrogen can cause the "bends," a problem familiar to deep-sea divers which results in dizziness, blackouts and possibly crippling damage to joints. In flight, special pressure suits were worn. The cockpits were small and cramped, and since flights could last over ten hours, fatigue was a major problem. Despite special diets of low-residue foods, toilet requirements sometimes made flights extremely uncomfortable. Although the operational speed of a plane was about 500 mph, at 70,000 feet or more only about 8 mph separated this speed from the stalling speed—a fact that made clear concentration imperative for the pilot at all times.

From the very first flight over Russia from Incirlik in 1956 (over Moscow and Leningrad to Bodø in Norway), Russian radar tracked the planes. Over the next four years they periodically complained about the flights through diplomatic channels, and undoubtedly Eisenhower weighed the political repercussions each time. He knew that the Russians would sooner or later develop a method of shooting down one of the planes. Lawrence Houston realized this at the outset and therefore wanted to be sure that the project was worth the risk. In his view it was: "I realized that sooner or later something would happen, so I asked the air force for an estimate of U-2 performance after the first flights.

They said the U-2 information had forced them to completely retarget the USSR."[14]

Eisenhower kept the political and military benefits of the project under constant review. Most of the flights were conducted during a two-year period between 1956 and 1958, by which time the bulk of military information had been assembled. In 1959 only a very few flights took place. When Francis Gary Powers' U-2 was shot down in May 1960, ending the flights over Russia, there had been only two previous CIA flights that year. In total, about twenty American flights were conducted by the CIA over the Soviet Union between 1956 and 1960, but Bissell wanted more, and he organized them in an ingenious way. The constraint on the number of flights was the specific approval President Eisenhower insisted on giving—or not giving—for each one. To overcome the presidential restriction, Bissell approached the British with a plan for the Royal Air Force and the British Secret Intelligence Service to undertake U-2 missions of their own (Allen Dulles was aware of this and all similar overtures):

> My theory was to set up a system whereby there would be another chief of state who could give consent, namely the British prime minister. So I approached the RAF, and, needless to say, they were eager to be in on the act. My real problem was this—it was a very difficult negotiation—they said, "If we're partners in this, that will require the approval of the prime minister and the President." I said, "Not at all. That's not the play. We're not going to call it that kind of partnership. There will be missions that the United States will run and missions that the United Kingdom will run. And I want it to be perfectly clear that the United Kingdom can run missions without detail from Washington and Washington can run missions without detail from London." The RAF got the point, and we got it set up.[15]

Five U-2 planes were acquired by the British and based in Cyprus and Turkey. Bissell was overall coordinator. "I was—probably wrongly as I look back at it—satisfied with British security, especially dealing with the RAF. I think there is still a nonrational element in American feelings about the RAF. I always thought of them as highly efficient."[16] Bissell also approached Chancellor Adenauer of West Germany and the French prime minister with proposals similar to the one he made to the British. Adenauer was receptive, and a U-2 base was established at Wiesbaden, West Germany, although in this case under CIA control. His approach to the French, in a personal meeting with the French prime minister, was less fruitful. He never pursued the proposal, largely because suspicions about French security were so great. "I'm sure if I'd asked Jim Angleton before approaching the French," Bissell later reflected, "he would have said, 'Oh, for the love of God, don't ever tell them even that the thing exists, let alone get them involved!' "[17]

Equipping Britain and West Germany with U-2s was an unadulterated power play on the part of Allen Dulles and Richard Bissell. Although everybody knew about it at the highest levels of government, they could not do anything about it unless the President was prepared to take the matter up with other heads of state. Bissell really was running "an empire within an empire," as he termed it, and with great success. Bissell said:

> We did learn things that were valuable, but consider another element that was involved. If you're in the Kremlin and you know that the United States can overfly any part of the USSR with complete impunity and that there's nothing that you and the Kremlin can do to stop it, does this not, as long as it continues, put a brake on overambitious friends? Because if a reconnaissance plane can overfly, how sure can you be that a bomber couldn't overfly? We had a crude bomber out of it. It couldn't have done much, actually; it couldn't carry nuclear weapons because of their weight. But we thought of this as something which someday might be useful.[18]

Gary Powers' U-2 flight on May Day 1960 was prompted by the Soviet advances in missile technology over the previous two and a half years. On August 26, 1957, the Russians successfully launched their first intercontinental missile, following it six weeks later on October 4 with the launch of the first satellite into space, the Sputnik. This demonstration of Soviet technical sophistication put a temporary halt to U-2 flights. If the Russians could get into space before the Americans, then they could probably shoot down a U-2. These developments had not caught Washington completely by surprise; the U-2 flights had provided evidence of Soviet development in missile technology, and analysts knew that the Tyuratam launch site was not built for existing Soviet missiles.

The surprise lay in the speed at which Soviet technology was developing. Analysts in the State Department and the CIA were not prepared for the rapidity of these developments, just as years earlier analysts had failed to predict the Soviet's rapid development of an atomic and then a hydrogen bomb. Powers' flight was plotted to fly from Incirlik directly over the Tyuratam site, then north to Sverdlovsk (Russia's main atom research center) and Plesetsk, which communications intercepts indicated was a base for the new SS-6 intercontinental ballistic missiles, which the Soviets were known to be deploying. The flight was planned to end in Bodø, Norway. Said Bissell:

> It was routine. We had been phoned by either the secretary of state or the President himself. My recollection is that we had authorization to fly this particular mission up to two weeks before the Summit [Eisenhower and Khrushchev had agreed to meet in May], and then our authorization expired. My recollection is that we were sitting there for several weeks waiting for a break in the weather over the target areas in northern Russia, and finally the break came and the mission was authorized. The only connection between

the timing of that mission and the Summit was that our authority to fly the mission would have expired within a matter of days because of the Summit. It was the judgment of the political advisers that up to whatever the date was we were not endangering the Summit. Whenever I got permission to fly, believe me we flew whenever the weather permitted.[19]

Khrushchev canceled the Paris Summit with American, British, and French leaders when the U-2 was shot down, probably because he suddenly found that with growing dissent in eastern Europe and a growing rift with China, he needed to demonstrate to hard-liners in the Politburo that he too was a hard-liner. Since summits are for deals and concessions, Khrushchev was anxious to avoid this one. However, in his memoirs the Russian leader blamed the U-2 flight directly: "The meeting collapsed just before it was to begin because the Americans sent one of their U-2 spy planes over our territory and we shot it down—a landmark event in the history of our struggle against the American imperialists who were waging the Cold War."[20] In the inquiry that followed, considerable attention focused on the question of why the Russians had canceled the Summit rather than use the incident and their capture of Gary Powers to secure concessions in their interests. The conclusion was that domestic political requirements forced Khrushchev's hand—not that it needed much forcing—and that he had opportunistically seized upon the incident to shore up his position at home, never very secure even in the best of times.

Powers reported on his flight after his return to America in February 1962, following his exchange for a Russian spy, Rudolf Abel.* About four hours after takeoff he felt a "push" from behind that sent the plane into an inverted spiral. He had loosened his harness for comfort, so when the push occurred he went forward, and his legs were caught under the instrument panel. "My God, I've had it now!" he exclaimed.[21] The centrifugal force of the spinning plane kept him in this position. Frightened he would lose his legs if he used the ejector seat, he unbolted the canopy and levered himself out. He was unable to connect the wires activating the destruct system for the plane; the wires had to be unscrewed and then reconnected to a button switch.† After bailing out, Powers decided that he preferred to take his chances rather than commit suicide with a pin concealed in a silver dollar, coated with shellfish toxin; this was always a voluntary matter. He was, he said, treated properly by the Russians, who interrogated him at length.[22]

* After his return Powers worked for Lockheed as a test pilot, which had been his cover when flying for the CIA. He divorced his first wife and married a CIA psychologist (*The Nation*, May 27, 1968).

† When Powers gave evidence to the Senate Armed Services Committee hearing, he was not asked whether he was under mandatory order to destroy his plane. The destructor mechanism was a particularly sensitive area for the CIA. The agency's cover stories were based on the assumption that Powers had activated the destructor mechanism. David Wise and Thomas B. Rose. *The Invisible Government* (New York: Vintage, 1974), p. 124.

He felt afterward that he had been able to hold some things back from them, especially names of people and places. But having the crashed plane as well, the Soviets clearly had all the information they needed about the U-2 and its capabilities. So ended the U-2 flights over Russia. The plane and the Development Project Staff, however, continued to operate. Right into the 1980s U-2 flights were conducted over China and elsewhere around the globe under CIA auspices. By 1960 Bissell's Project Staff unit had also greatly expanded operations in other directions. The Church Committee's 1976 history of the agency recorded:

> The U-2 marked the beginning of the agency's emergence as the intelligence community's leader in the area of technical collection capability. Soon after the first U-2 flight in 1955 Bissell moved quickly to organize the research and development of follow-on systems. The agency never attempted to establish its own technological R&D capability. Instead, it continued to utilize the best private industrial manpower available. In large part this arrangement accounts for the consistent vitality and quality of the agency's technical R&D capability, which remains unsurpassed to this day.[23]

This tribute pinpointed the importance of the U-2 project as far as the CIA was concerned; it put the agency firmly at the top of the new world of technical collection of intelligence.

Rudolph Abel, the man Gary Powers was exchanged for, was a colonel in the KGB who had lived in Canada and the United States with forged papers and a false identity for ten years before being arrested by the FBI in New York in 1957. From 1948 he organized and ran a network of Soviet agents in the United States, using the cover of being an artist and photographer with the name Emil R. Golfus. Abel was a perfectly competent artist, and after his arrest he drew the Christmas cards for Leavenworth prison, where he was held. He delighted in sending them to the CIA men he knew. His deputy from 1953 was another KGB man, Reino Hayhanen, who turned out to be not only lax in his duties but extremely dangerous to the Russian cause: he drank, chased women, misappropriated KGB funds and failed to complete assignments. Recalled by Moscow, Hayhanen traveled as far as Paris, where he defected to the Americans. When he was interviewed at the U.S. Embassy by a CIA man, Hayhanen gave the details of Abel's cover, which resulted in the spy master's arrest within days.

Abel never admitted that he was a spy and would only confirm that he was an illegal immigrant. Although he was defended in court by James Donovan, who had been a prosecutor at Nuremberg, Hayhanen's evidence and the evidence of spy equipment found in Abel's flat convinced the court of Abel's guilt. Donovan then argued that Abel should not be sentenced to death, because one day an American agent might be arrested in Russia and it would be useful to be able to make an exchange. Four years later Donovan's argument was vindicated when Abel was exchanged for Gary Powers.* However, the days when spies such as Abel were of prime importance to intelligence-gathering efforts were coming to an end. In their place was the U-2 and the successor systems Bissell was devising.

"MISSILE GAP"

Two years after the initiation of the U-2 project the Development Project Staff began another, similar program, called at first the A-12 project, then the XF-12, and finally the SR-71: a supersonic spy plane. It took much longer than the U-2 to deploy—nearly ten years elapsed from the start of the project in August 1956 to the deployment of the first SR-71 wing in 1966, compared to the U-2's seventeen months—but it was a far more sophisticated machine. It could fly higher, at over 85,000 feet, than the U-2 and could cruise at speeds greater than mach 3.[24] It is still in use, and holds the world record for sustained altitude flying at 85,069 feet. Almost simultaneously, starting in July 1956, the air force began a program code-named WS-117L†: America's first spy satellite project.

The launch of the Soviet Sputnik on October 4, 1957, sent a shiver through American public opinion which the development of the WS-117L and the SR-71 was not capable of countering at the time. Both systems were secret and, although far in advance of any Soviet equivalents in technological terms, were some years away from being operational. So all the average American knew was that the Soviets had far more sophisticated rockets than had been realized. The Soviet SS-6 rocket that had put the Sputnik into orbit was obviously capable of intercontinental flight from the USSR to the U.S.A. The Sputnik itself was seen as having a bombing potential. The fact that the American Atlas missile, already being deployed, was more powerful than the SS-6 and was capable of sending a one-ton payload into space was ignored. The popular perception was that the Russians had not simply caught up with America but had overtaken America too.

The Eisenhower administration, knowing that the Soviet achievement was far more show than substance and having earlier decided to concentrate on achieving technological superiority over the Russians rather than headline-grabbing exploits, was far more sanguine about the SS-6 and Sputnik.[25] Politically, however, the ground had been laid for the "missile gap" that John F. Kennedy was to use to effect in his 1960 presidential campaign and that the air

---

* James Donovan stayed in regular touch with Abel in prison at Abel's request. The spy began to receive letters from his "wife" in East Germany, which, of course, were screened and which in any case Abel insisted that Donovan read. It was through this communication that the suggestion was made by Abel's "wife" for a swap for Powers, and the arrangements were made by Donovan.

† The WS prefix stands for "Weapons Systems."

force was to use—just as it had used the "bomber gap"—to obtain larger appropriations.

Eisenhower's apparent complacency in the face of the lurid politics of the "missile gap"—the fear that the Soviets would rain thermonuclear bombs on the United States with supermissiles and satellites, and that Eisenhower was not doing enough to reduce the gap—masked a cool assessment of the realities of the situation. The launch of Sputnik coincided with the CIA's pricking of the air force's "bomber gap" arguments with U-2 photographs. The same evidence showed Eisenhower that there was no great Soviet intercontinental missile force and that the few SS-6s the Soviets had built were being used for the space effort.

But the problem was political. The Democrats, sensing popular support for assertions that there was a "missile gap" in favor of the Soviets, continued to press for more money for missiles. They had started a "missile gap" campaign in 1956 when Senator Stuart Symington had charged that the U.S. lagged seriously behind Soviet guided-missile development and production. Symington had no specific evidence for his charge, but in the cold-war atmosphere of the time it had effect. Eisenhower had managed to dampen the charge by assuring Congress and the American public at his press conferences that the scientific community could not absorb any additional funds: they were doing all that could be done to stay ahead in the missile race. "I'll wager my life I can sit on any base we've got," he said, "and in the next ten years the Russians can't hit me with any guided missile."[26] After the launch of Sputnik, however, even Eisenhower's assurances were not enough. In the 1958 midterm elections, Democrats scored points and won votes with the "missile gap."

The CIA was in the middle of this political debate. In 1954 its analysts had estimated that the Soviet Union would not be in a position to deploy intercontinental ballistic missiles for about five years. This was a view that the air force rejected. A year earlier the detonation of the Soviet hydrogen bomb ahead of all Western expectations had convinced the air force that the Soviets were further advanced in most areas than had been conceded by the CIA. This attitude had colored air force estimates during the "bomber gap" debate, and it colored them during the "missile gap" debate as well. Air force estimates of a large Soviet intercontinental missile force were leaked to the press. Eisenhower used Allen Dulles to try to convince congressional leaders and opinion formers that there was no "missile gap" and that the air force arguments should be seen as having more to do with their appropriations than with a real Soviet missile threat. But Dulles was not able to reveal the U-2 information or the A-12 program and so was not convincing in his assertions. In addition, CIA analysts were to some extent swayed by the Sputnik launch, and in 1958 Estimates held that the Soviets might be ahead of the United States in intercontinental missile development. In 1959 Estimates were even saying that the Soviet Union might have up to fifteen hundred intercontinental ballistic missiles by 1963—more than twice the number planned by the United States for its own missile force.[27]

By the time of the 1960 presidential election, however, the CIA had modified these conclusions. The evidence from all sources by then had convinced the CIA that they were facing a parallel to the "bomber gap" and that the Soviets were far less advanced in missile technology and deployment than the air force and their own earlier Estimates had held. There might be only about two hundred Soviet intercontinental ballistic missiles by 1963 according to the agency's 1960 Estimate, "Soviet Capabilities and Intentions."[28] This had no effect on the presidential election, however, and Kennedy made full use of air force leaks and earlier conclusions to sustain "missile gap" allegations in his campaign.

SPACE SPIES

Within the intelligence community the "missile gap" debate resulted in a further extension of CIA power. In the first place, it saw the agency's right to contest military estimates about military matters confirmed. Second, because of the political imperatives following the Sputnik launch, Eisenhower wanted to see rapid advances in the WS-117L project to still public fears about Soviet missile and satellite superiority. The CIA, responsible for the extraordinarily rapid development and operational use of the U-2, was the obvious candidate to speed up development of WS-117L, and in February 1958 it was agreed to transfer the project to joint CIA/air force supervision. Ultimately this project, which was headed once again by Richard Bissell, would become Dulles' most important undertaking for the agency. In that same month USAF General Shriever, Bissell's deputy for the project, appeared before the Senate and made public the satellite program. WS-117L was developing Corona, a reconnaissance satellite that would be put into space by a Thor intermediate-range ballistic missile, said Shriever, and it would send back to earth a recoverable photographic capsule. Corona, he went on to say, was expected to be operational by the spring of 1959.[29]

Bissell's impressive record with the U-2 underpinned Shriever's statement. Corona was a fin-stabilized reconnaissance satellite rather than the earth-orbiting type the Russians developed with Sputnik, and eventually it did its job, providing photographs deep into most of Russia. Those parts of Russia that the satellite could not reach were subject to U-2 flights such as the one flown by Francis Gary Powers. Within a year of the last U-2 flight, however, American advances in space technology made even the most remote areas of the Soviet Union accessible to photo-satellite reconnaissance. The major problem that affected the space spying effort in these early years was the recovery of the photographic capsules, which had to be parachuted to sea or land for collection and which were therefore vulnerable to bad weather conditions and technical difficulties in the release and collection systems.[30]

Corona's problems—which included electrical malfunctions in the various stages of the launch rocket; radio failures in the photographic capsules' trigger mechanism; failure of the capsule parachute to open; and ground radar and radio defects that made it impossible to find some capsules that successfully reentered—caused President Eisenhower to become extremely frustrated and at one point to scold Bissell for the delays. Under severe political and public pressure to develop an American counterpart to the Soviet Sputnik, the President considered revealing the existence of the U-2 but decided not to on the promise of Corona's success. Since satellites could not be hidden from the public, they were heavily publicized in order to improve the image of the United States throughout the world. In this case the public was told that the Corona satellites were weather/scientific satellites called Discoverer. The first satellite was successfully launched on February 28, 1959 (the fact that it spun out of control in space was not publicized). Bissell had to endure the failure of fifteen of the next sixteen launches—the fourteenth Discoverer was successful in August 1960—and there was a frantic race to make the system dependable.* This was achieved by January 1961 and the program was under way.

As Bissell recalled, his second great success was not easy:

> It was a most heartbreaking business. If an airplane goes on a test flight and something malfunctions, and it gets back, the pilot can tell you about the malfunction, or you can look it over and find out. But in the case of a recce satellite, you fire the damn thing off and you've got some telemetry, and you never get it back. There is no pilot, of course, and you've got no hardware, you never see it again. So you have to infer from telemetry what went wrong. Then you make a fix, and if it fails again you know you've inferred wrong. In the case of Corona it went on and on.[31]

At the same time another satellite system known as Samos (Satellite and Missile Observation System) was being developed by the air force. Although it too met problems similar to those encountered by Corona/Discoverer, the first Samos satellite was successfully put into orbit on January 31, 1961. In his memoirs George Kistiakowsky, Eisenhower's special assistant for science and technology, recorded what this new system could do. "There would be ten television channels to the ground and a library of information so complete that a general sitting at his easy chair in the Pentagon, by just pressing a button will be able to see on a screen the complete display of current military activities televised from anywhere in the world."[32] As a result of satellites, a wealth of photographic material began to flood into the CIA in 1961. These pictures revolutionized the analytical work being done, although progress was slow. It took

---

* Discoverer 2 was launched successfully on April 13, but its photograph capsule reentered incorrectly because of a timing error, falling over northern Norway (it may have been found by the Russians). Discoverers 3 and 4 failed to achieve orbit. Discoverer 5 ejected its photograph capsule farther into space.

months for analysts to digest the first thousand photographs Samos 1 sent back before the results could be incorporated in Estimates.

IN TECH WE TRUST

The success of these satellites brought a serious conflict to the fore. Worries were expressed within the agency about the effects of "mechanical" intelligence on traditional intelligence methods. On one side of this debate were such people as Richard Helms, who believed that "gadgets cannot divine man's intentions." On the other were Richard Bissell and his followers, who believed that gadgets were preferable to agents. The basic problem was an institutional one: as long as exceptional people are involved and aware of the dangers of overdependence on gadgets, "mechanical"—technical—intelligence has great advantages. But when the ability of those involved lessens, the apparent security and technical accuracy of detailed photographic and electronic information easily encourages a shift away from painstaking analysis, including speculative assessments, in favor of staying only with what is certain.

Clearly the easy option is to reduce or totally dismiss the need for speculative assessments. A photograph of a person or a missile is always more attractive to people who are wary of the dangers of hazarding a judgment, particularly since the intelligence gathered through technical means is often so detailed. "Any time I look at any of the photographs," Bissell said, "I am still impressed. We took a picture of the U.S. Capitol Building and when we enlarged a triangle of it, we could see a small section where they were working on the dome. There was another taken over Butte, Montana, of a football game. You could see all the players, even if you couldn't see the ball itself. And remember that this was taken from a hundred miles up."[33]

With Corona/Discoverer providing this detail, it was not surprising that there was a feeling in the agency that the day of the gadgets was at hand. The failure of the United States to place many spies in good positions behind the iron curtain despite repeated attempts encouraged the reliance on technical intelligence even more. Richard Helms admitted this point when he said:

Many who had served in OSS became the foundation of the operational or clandestine section of the new CIA when its doors opened in September 1947. We had been trained to work against the Nazis, the Japanese, the Italians, and we had done so. Now we were to confront the Eastern Bloc, adversaries little understood but certainly tough, at least in the intelligence field. Then came the People's Republic of China. For some years we used the same methods, learned from the British in World War II, that had been tried and proven. But the Soviet Bloc in peacetime, particularly the Russians themselves—suspicious, disciplined, possessed of a formidable security police— proved a tough nut to crack. Then in the late fifties technology came to the rescue. First the U-2 brought photographs with a mind-boggling volume of detail on Soviet arms and weapons systems. Close behind came the first photographic satellites. And the intelligence explosion of the century was on, a relentless stream of detailed data which turned analytical work on these so-called "denied areas" from famine to feast. Our best Russian agents, Popov and Penkovsky, suddenly seemed pale and inadequate.[34]

The information provided by the U-2 and the satellites had another vitally important effect. For the first time it was possible to verify arms-limitation agreements with the Russians. "Missile gaps" and "bomber gaps" were resolved by U-2s and satellites. For nearly twenty years after the U-2 and the Sputnik were realities, only political impediments stood in the way of arms agreements. (This began to change in the 1970s when Soviet improvements in their camouflage techniques provided some protection from discovery by American spy satellites of new weapons systems, making arms agreements again more difficult.) Ray Cline was sent as a member of the U.S. team to the first Summit meeting in July 1955 at Geneva. It was Cline's function to provide daily intelligence reports directly to Eisenhower and the secretary of state, John Foster Dulles. As Cline recalled in 1980, Eisenhower was already aware of how the prospective U-2 could be used to verify arms-limitation agreements:

Eisenhower tried to achieve a diplomatic breakthrough on the basis of his foreknowledge of the U-2 by proposing an open-skies mutual inspection pact based on aerial reconnaissance of each other's territory. In the eternal hopeful American spirit, he tried to make a gesture of good will and was sharply rebuffed by Khrushchev. I was standing outside the conference room when this extraordinary, farsighted proposal was made, and I learned from Ambassador Chip Bohlen, Eisenhower's interpreter at the session, as soon as they emerged, that the Russians had called the open-skies proposal nothing but an American espionage trick. I wonder if they ever regretted it in the next years as the U-2s began doing unilaterally over the USSR what Eisenhower had proposed they do on a reciprocal basis. It is ironic that the peace of the world now depends to a remarkable degree on the unilateral U.S. and Soviet technical means of monitoring arms agreements that have evolved from this U-2 technology of 1955. In any case the balance of strategic nuclear power that protects U.S. security is guaranteed by U.S. intelligence efforts, based on the photographic techniques the CIA officers began working on 25 years ago.[35]

The rapid advances in space and aerial reconnaissance had repercussions in the organization of intelligence analysis and dissemination. In particular, they created a renewed need for photo-interpreters, who had played such an important part in choosing targets for the strategic bombing campaign of 1944–45 against Nazi Germany. In 1953 Dulles created a group of about twenty interpreters in the CIA's Directorate of Intelligence. Aware that the volume of U-2 photographs would dramatically increase the burden of photo-interpretation work, Bissell arranged in 1955 an informal committee, the Ad Hoc Requirements Committee (ARC), consisting initially of representatives from the National Security Agency, the Joint Chiefs of Staff, and the State Department. The role of the committee was to coordinate resources for this work. Eventually over twelve hundred agency employees were involved in the interpretation of photo-reconnaissance material.

In 1960, with the Discoverer and Samos material in prospect, ARC was replaced by a formal subcommittee, known as the Committee on Overhead Reconnaissance (COMOR), of the United States Intelligence Board. COMOR was responsible for the development and operation of all aerial reconnaissance systems. In 1961 the CIA, still the principal interpretation and analysis center, combined with the military to create the National Photographic Interpretation Center under the director of Central Intelligence. By maintaining its central role in these arrangements, the agency developed a close interrelationship with the other departmental intelligence services (the air force, for example, launched the satellites; the CIA interpreted and analyzed the information, so each was dependent on the other) and established its claim to a major portion of the funding for the whole of US intelligence.[36]

THE HARE AND THE TORTOISE

Richard Bissell, who had been behind all these developments, by 1958 was the golden boy of the CIA and Allen Dulles' favorite. He had foreseen that space reconnaissance was the future and had taken the initiative in pioneering, at first in cooperation with the air force, the Corona project.[37] Following the realization in the agency that Frank Wisner was indeed having a mental breakdown in the summer of 1958, Allen Dulles asked Bissell to take over Wisner's job as deputy director of plans. Bissell accepted. He was the heir apparent. Bissell said later:

> It happened that all the time I was there Allen's deputy was Pearré Cabell, an air force general. Cabell was a man whom I came greatly to like and greatly to admire. He had an intense loyalty to the agency and to Allen. He was very supportive. With the U-2 project going on, Cabell was profoundly interested in it, and I dealt with him intensively on it. I almost invariably took the problems on that operation to him, if only to ask for his advice, and he was invariably supportive. He was never interfering. It's hard for me to say enough for that gentleman in this relationship. Here was I, an academic economist, running an aircraft development program and an aircraft operation, and there he was, a general in the air force who had flown God knows how many planes and was highly intelligent and had been in the intelligence business.
>
> Cabell had a human quality that was staggering, although he never got

much credit for it. One of the reasons, I guess, is that I am the person who knew about it and there really wasn't much way that anybody else could know. He was condemned by Allen's *modus operandi*—reaching way down for information on any given subject; quite often not going through channels—Allen's wide connections and prestige outside the agency; Allen's long connection with intelligence. By all of this Cabell was condemned to what would have been for many a difficult and eclipsed role, and despite that, I think he performed extraordinarily well and that he quietly added a real element of strength.[38]

Others were not so supportive or happy with Bissell's appointment as DDP. Lyman Kirkpatrick, who hoped to become DDP himself and one day, no doubt, DCI, was not pleased at all. Nor was Richard Helms, who remained as chief of operations, the number-two officer in the Directorate of Plans.

Bissell and Helms were very different people. Apart from an early try at journalism Helms had spent his entire career since 1942 in intelligence. He served first in the OSS, then in 1945–47 in the Strategic Services Unit and the Central Intelligence Group, and then in the CIA's Office of Special Operations, staying on the clandestine side in the DDP. He was an institutional man, completely loyal to the agency, interested in the role of intelligence in U.S. decision making and government, anxious to perfect the bureaucratic arrangements within the CIA and between the agency, the White House, Congress, and the other departments of government. He matched this with a very powerful professional loyalty to those he worked with and with a personal expertise in intelligence use. "Intelligence always has a policy effect," he remarked, "no matter what you say to a policy maker. If three horses die in Berlin, that has a policy effect, because they want to find the foot fever that caused it. You can't divorce intelligence from policy. The only thing you can do is what I did, which was to try not to get into the actual policy-making process by trying to influence it one way or the other."[39] Ray Cline summarized Helms' contribution in this way:

> Dick was the perfect model of the cool, well-informed professional manager of agent networks and case officers, the agent handlers of the CIA's stations. A case officer is the CIA officer, usually an American citizen, who maintains contact with the clandestine agents themselves, usually non-Americans, who provide the hard-to-get data that fills in the gaps of what cannot be obtained from overt sources or by technical means of collecting intelligence. Helms knew this arcane world, especially in Europe, better than anyone except Allen Dulles himself.[40]

In contrast, Bissell did not concern himself with such matters, regarding them as essentially secondary to the main purpose of U.S. intelligence, which, in his view, was to protect the United States and further American interests. He did not care which particular part of the bureaucracy did what and he had no commitment to using people instead of machines as spies. In his view, if U-2s, SR-71s, and spy satellites could provide an accurate picture of Soviet order-of-battle activities, then there was less reason to risk lives obtaining it.

Between them the two men represented the traditions of intelligence and the future of intelligence: Bissell, the brilliant generalist with a touch of genius; Helms, the manager, the professional, with a cool mastery both of detail and of policy. It was a team that could have worked very well. Dulles had many of Helms's attributes, and he worked well with Bissell. But Helms and Bissell did not get along. Helms felt keenly that Bissell was a late arrival who did not know as much as he should. "There was a large element of philosophic difference," Bissell later reflected, "and the trouble was that the philosophic difference did not get brought out and discussed. If I had been more effective and had tried to draw him in more, and if he'd been willing to be drawn in more, he could have given wise counsel. I sure as hell needed it. I don't think I knew at the time I needed it."[41]

As a result, Helms's reaction behind Bissell mirrored the position of Cabell behind Dulles. Bissell, with two starry, seminal successes behind him, confident of his relationship with Allen Dulles and confident of his own abilities, let Helms simply fill in without paying attention to what Helms must have felt. It was not so much Bissell's arrogance that caused this—what arrogance Bissell had was entirely justified, and this was recognized by all who knew him—but his headlong pursuit of goals based on a wrong assumption of complete understanding on the part of those he worked with. Bissell assumed Helms would advise and support without specific direction. Helms did offer support, but he kept his advice to himself. The story is told of Helms being so isolated and undervalued as Bissell's deputy that one day in 1959 when an officer in the counterintelligence staff came to see him, Helms asked, "What's new?" The counterintelligence officer was amused: Helms was chief of operations in the DDP and James Angleton, head of counterintelligence, reported (or so it was thought) to him and Bissell. "You mean _you_ don't know?" Helms raised both hands and, baring his teeth in a grimace, said in German, "Aber keiner sagt mir 'was!"—"No one tells me anything!" Later Helms's exasperation became more apparent. "Why don't you take it up with Wonder Boy next door?" he would ask when someone came to him with something he knew Bissell would want to handle himself.[42]

Despite the limitations he placed on Helms, Bissell allowed him to run the agents. This was not surprising, since it was an area Bissell knew very little about, and what he did know he did not value. In his view, agents were of limited value to the intelligence-gathering effort. At best they could provide only a worm's-eye view of things, and the cost-effectiveness of agents historically was low. In part, this low return was a result of the fierce competition for agents that characterized the early OSO-OPC rivalry. It was also caused by the agency's failure to place high-level agents behind the iron curtain. It was a "denied area," in Helms's phrase, as far as agents and operations were concerned, which Bissell's U-2 and follow-on systems had to a very large extent overcome.

When Colonel Oleg Penkovsky of the Red Army's intelligence wing, the GRU, made his approach to the British in 1961 and they told the CIA, Bissell was deeply suspicious. "How do we know this guy is on the level?" he asked Jack Maury, head of the Soviet Division in the DDP. Throughout the Cuban missile crisis in 1962, Penkovsky's information proved enormously valuable. (The exact capabilities of the Soviet missiles came from him: every major city in the continental United States except Seattle would be threatened by Soviet missiles once the Cuban emplacements were complete.) Subsequently, on the *cui bono* principle, more support was given to Bissell's view (though Bissell himself came fully to respect Penkovsky and appreciate what he had done). In any event, it was only a matter of time before Soviet advances in rocket technology placed all American cities under threat.[43]

The major philosophic difference between Bissell and Helms became apparent in the Bay of Pigs operation, which began toward the end of the Eisenhower administration and erupted in the early days of the Kennedy presidency. It was the culmination of the faith in covert operations after the Iran and Guatemala successes: a covert operation so enormous that everyone knew about it. To Bissell this did not matter as long as its goals were achieved. For Helms the lack of secrecy was a major worry, jeopardizing not only the particular operation but also other operations, as it made the agency's undercover activities notorious. Against this, however, it is important to remember the time at which it was all happening. Richard Nixon put it in perspective:

> Before Sputnik, before the missile age, the U.S. had an enormous advantage because of the way that an airplane could deliver atomic weapons to the Soviet Union. Now we still have those planes, but on the other hand the Soviet Union, rather than trying to match us in airplanes, which they could never have done, moved ahead to missiles. And so under the circumstances then you wouldn't have any warning time—maybe thirty minutes—before any kind of a war would come about. So I would say what Sputnik meant was that it made even more vital the necessity of having very close communications between the two superpowers, even though they totally disliked each other, totally disagreed, because you are not going to have the time to have any conversations and so forth prior to a confrontation that could lead to war.[44]

This need for communication and for extremely accurate calculations of policy resulted in overwhelming support within the top echelon of the governing elite for Bissell's approach. What is more, Bissell's push for the future was not at the expense of tradition: the Directorate of Plans under him continued with enthusiasm the operations and plans Frank Wisner had left behind.

SHADOW WARS

Beginning in 1955 and until 1959 the CIA had a $25 million contract with Michigan State University to conduct a covert police-training program for the South Vietnamese, with five CIA officers operating as members of the university staff for this purpose.[45] In November 1957 Eisenhower approved direct CIA aid to rebel Indonesian army colonels based on the island of Sumatra who opposed the regime of President Sukarno of Indonesia, and he had also begun a Guatemala-style plan to overthrow him. Sukarno had shown himself to be too procommunist. The Communist party of Indonesia had attracted about one-quarter of the votes cast in Indonesia's 1955 elections, and so Sukarno argued they should have one-quarter of the posts in the cabinet. Simultaneously he was moving from a democratic system to one that he described as "guided democracy." This was enough for the CIA to go into action.[46] Joseph Burkholder Smith, deputy chief of the FE/5 Branch of the DDP, related one of the operations the agency used to undermine the Sukarno regime:

> We had been ringing as many changes on the theme of Sukarno's communist proclivities as we could for the past several months. . . . We developed, in this last regard, the theme that Sukarno's well-known swordsmanship had trapped him in the spell of a Soviet female agent. His succumbing to Soviet control, we implied, was the result of her influence or blackmail or both.
> Exploiting Sukarno's sexual appetite in this way was a tricky theme. His conquests didn't disturb Indonesians too much. In Indonesian society a woman's place is in the bed. And it was the Prophet Mohammed who promised his faithful warriors that he would furnish heaven with beautiful black-eyed houris to provide them eternal happiness if not eternal rest. However, what we were saying was that a woman had gotten the better of Sukarno. Being tricked, deceived, or otherwise outsmarted by one of the creatures God has provided for man's pleasure cannot be condoned. Also, we were interested in the impact of this theme outside Indonesia, for our purpose was to present Sukarno in as unfavorable and unsympathetic a light as possible. If he were deposed by our friends the colonels, we wanted the world to agree with us that Indonesia would be better off. . . .
> We had, as a matter of fact, considerable success with this theme. It appeared in the press around the world.[47]

The CIA built further on the sex theme in an attempt to topple Sukarno from power. Why not make a blue movie, which could be clandestinely distributed in Indonesia and elsewhere, showing Sukarno engaged in his favorite activity? Sheffield Edwards, the CIA's chief of security, was roped in. Through his friendly contacts with the Los Angeles police he obtained a grainy black-and-white film with a swarthy, apparently Mexican man and a rather seedy woman amorously embroiled. Smith and other officers involved in planning Sukarno's downfall viewed the film in Washington and decided it wouldn't do.

What they needed was a film with a man who looked like Sukarno and a be-lievable sex goddess, and they decided that they would have to produce it themselves, since the talent available for blue movies did not meet their stan-dards. Various men were scrutinized, but none was right. Despite wide-ranging searches, they could not find a candidate for the part of a "beautiful blond So-viet agent," and they had equal difficulty with a Sukarno look-alike:

> Los Angeles's supply of blue films suited our purpose, we thought, because they included dark male subjects, like the Mexican, who might be made to look like Sukarno with a little touching up. The problem was the female part-ner. They did not use the talent in blue films in Los Angeles in those days that could compare with that of a decade later. We saw no likely candidates for the beautiful blond Soviet agent.
>
> We hadn't too much luck with a likely Sukarno either. One idea we had was to ask the Los Angeles police department to find us a dark and bald male lead. Sukarno never permitted himself to be photographed without his *pitji*, the traditional black cap worn by Malayan and Indonesian male Moslems, lest his balding head be seen. We figured he surely didn't wear his *pitji* in bed. We thought we would expose his vanity while we were exposing him. We saw a number of bald Chicanos but no Sukarnos. Finally, we decided that we would try to develop a full-face mask of Sukarno. We planned to ship this out to Los Angeles and ask the police to pay some blue film star to wear it during his big scene.[48]

An untitled film was made, and still photographs were taken for distribution in the Far East.

A less complicated effort of a similar nature was directed against a Philip-pine senator, Claro Recto, because he—like Sukarno—was perceived as being a communist sympathizer. In 1957 Joseph Smith dealt with this also:

> He had been labeled a Chinese communist stooge, an agent infiltrated into the Philippine Senate (shades of Senator Joe McCarthy), and, I discovered, he had been subjected to various dirty tricks. As I went through the files, I found something that absolutely astounded me. I saw a sealed envelope marked "Recto Campaign." I opened it and found it filled with condoms, marked "Courtesy of Claro M. Recto—the People's Friend." The condoms all had holes in them at the place they could least afford to have them.
>
> I tried to find out what purpose the condoms had been supposed to serve. The best I could do was to learn that they were distributed to show how Recto would let you down. This crude locker-room prank made me feel a little better about my days as a pornographer. Our Sukarno pictures, after all, could have well been real if anyone had ever been able to hide a camera in a hotel room he occupied.[49]

The days of Donovan's OSS psychological-warfare operations must have seemed old hat in comparison to the blue movies and strategically placed holes of 1957.

More in keeping with OSS-style special operations, closer contacts were also developed with the rebel Indonesian colonels in Sumatra, culminating not only in sending them arms but also in CIA pilots flying B-26 bombers—just as had been done in Guatemala—on missions in support of the rebels. In February 1958 the colonels declared themselves the government of Indonesia while Sukarno was on a visit to Japan, and the CIA put its back into making the rebel government succeed. "I think it's time we held Sukarno's feet to the fire," Frank Wisner had declared two years earlier, and the time had now arrived.* Sukarno, however, showed himself to be far more forceful and competent in crisis than had been thought. Within five months, following his ordering of his forces into action, the colonels' government collapsed. After Allen Pope, the pilot of a CIA B-26, was shot down and captured by Sukarno's troops on May 18, having mistakenly bombed a church and killed most of the congregation,[50] the CIA decided, in Allen Dulles' words, "that we must disengage."[51] When Sukarno released Pope four years later following a personal plea from Robert Kennedy, it marked the end of one of the CIA's first major covert-action failures.

Although officially the United States denied any involvement with the rebels, the Indonesians knew full well who had been behind the colonels. They elected to play the affair quietly, however, calculating that there was more benefit to be had from official American gratitude than from official American hostility. At the same time the Eisenhower administration was becoming increasingly concerned with Red China, so Sukarno's nonaggressive attitude met with acceptance as a diplomatic effort was launched by John Foster Dulles to win support for American interests in the Far East. Foreign-aid assistance was increased in the area from 1957, with the bulk going to Burma, Indonesia, and South Vietnam; this was the carrot as far as U.S.–Indonesian relations were concerned. The stick was the threat—implemented in March 1959—of U.S. restrictions on the import of crude oil. Once Sukarno demonstrated that he

---

* Joseph B. Smith, *Portrait of a Cold Warrior* (New York: Ballantine Books, 1976), p. 197. Sukarno had left for a tour of foreign capitals on January 6, 1958, flying to Cairo on January 12:

> The only station that was able to bug his telephone was, of all places, Cairo. Evidently, we had some remnants of the operational capabilities there that had helped Kim Roosevelt put Nasser in power. . . . We learned . . . that Gamal Nasser was a prude by Sukarno's standards.
>
> Almost as soon as Sukarno had settled in his hotel room, he called Nasser. He greeted his friend effusively and suggested Nasser come right over to the hotel. "I have three gorgeous Pan American stewardesses here with me and they'd like to have a party," Sukarno said. There was an awkward pause at the other end of the line. Then Nasser replied curtly that he couldn't accept the invitation and slammed down the phone.
>
> We had given some thought to recruiting one of the Pan Am girls when we learned that he was chartering a plane from the company for the trip, but finally dismissed the idea as unproductive. We already knew enough about his sex life, and unless we had been able to give the girl a lot of training we figured we wouldn't find out much of intelligence value. We were relieved to know now that we hadn't missed an orgy involving Sukarno and Nasser with all the possibilities the mere thought of such a thing brought to mind. (Ibid., pp. 237–238.)

was happy to exist in financial and economical cooperation with the United States rather than with Red China or the Soviet Union, Washington was content to let him rule at home as he wished.

The CIA had disengaged from supporting the Indonesian rebels just before Richard Bissell took over as DDP, but other operations started by Frank Wisner continued. As the Sumatran colonels collapsed, the CIA was busy establishing a secret base at Camp Hale, near Leadville, Colorado, where agency personnel began training troops of the Dalai Lama for guerrilla incursions into Tibet, occupied by Red China since 1951. Once the Tibetans were trained and equipped, they were flown back to India and Nepal, where they launched raids into their homeland. After a Tibetan revolt against the Chinese occupation failed in 1959, an increasing number of the Dalai Lama's supporters as well as the Dalai Lama himself escaped to India, where they were given sanctuary. At Camp Hale, as Victor Marchetti remembered, training continued:

> Although the CIA officers led their Tibetan trainees to believe that they were being readied for the reconquering of their homeland, even within the agency few saw any real chance that this could happen. Some of the covert operators who worked directly with the Tibetans, however, came to believe their own persuasive propaganda. Years later, they would flush with anger and frustration describing how they and their Tibetans had been undone by the bureaucrats back in Washington. This phenomenon of "emotional attachment" is not rare in the clandestine business, but is particularly prevalent in special operations. The officers who engage in special ops often have a deep psychological need to belong and believe. This, coupled with the dangers and hardships they willingly endure, tends to drive them to support extreme causes and seek unobtainable goals. Several [of those involved in Tibet] would turn for solace to the Tibetan prayers which they had learned during their years with the Dalai Lama.[52]

For several more years these CIA-trained Tibetans conducted spot raids against Chinese facilities. The raids were planned by CIA officers and sometimes led by CIA contract mercenaries. The regional agency proprietary air force, Civil Air Transport (CAT), flew missions in support of these raids. (CAT's B-26s had been used in Indonesia, and Allen Pope was a CAT employee.) Companies such as CAT, Southern Air Transport (based in Miami), Air America, Air Asia, and Intermountain Aviation were owned and operated by the CIA to provide air support under commercial cover to CIA and other U.S. government agency operations. One CAT-supported raid into Tibet returned with a major intelligence haul of official Chinese government papers detailing the problems the Chinese faced in Tibet and revealing that, in their own estimation, Mao Tse-tung's Great Leap Forward—his attempt at a Soviet-style economic plan—had failed in several crucial respects. "As incredible as it may seem in retrospect," said Marchetti, who was working in the director's office at the time, "some of the CIA's economic analysts (and many other officials in Washington) were in the early 1960s still inclined to accept much of Peking's propaganda as to the success of Mao's economic experiment. The acquisition of the Tibetan documents was a significant contribution to the resolution of this particular debate within the U.S. intelligence community."[53] By the late 1960s, however, the Tibetan operations were more of an embarrassment than a source of important information, and they were wound down.

DEADLY BUSINESS

With involvement in such a range of activity, it was not surprising that the Directorate of Plans was also involved in assassination plots against foreign leaders. Soldiers and civilians of other governments had by 1960 been killed on a relatively large scale by CIA–backed invasions, rebellions, and guerrilla attacks. Death was not foreign to the CIA. The question was: Would the death of a particular person advance U.S. aims? The answer was that in some cases it would. From this conclusion came a limited number of proposals for the agency to take "Executive Action."[54]

There is no clear evidence to show conclusively whether each particular assassination plot, including those on the lives of Patrice Lumumba in the Congo, Fidel Castro in Cuba, and Colonel Abdul Kassem in Iraq, was authorized personally by the President of the United States or not. But in each case the CIA was involved with assassination plans. The agency was also closely associated with plotters who assassinated Rafael Trujillo in the Dominican Republic, Ngo Dinh Diem in Vietnam, and General René Schneider in Chile. The muddying of the CIA name as a result of these assassinations was the inevitable consequence of these associations. In each case the people involved would probably have been killed by the plotters even if the CIA had not existed. Ironically, the plotters were successful in their murderous exploits while the CIA, with all its sophistication, was not.

The Senate inquiry into the CIA, chaired by Senator Frank Church of Idaho, found that no foreign leader was ever directly assassinated by the CIA[55] but that "American officials encouraged or were privy to coup plots which resulted in the deaths of Trujillo, Diem and Schneider."[56] It also found that the CIA's own attempts at assassination represented a failure on the part of the agency rather than any change of mind. William Colby, director of Central Intelligence from 1973 to 1976 and a longtime CIA officer before that, had to weather the storm of criticism the agency received in the post-Watergate years which was spearheaded by the Church Committee inquiry. Commenting on these failed assassination attempts, Colby remarked:

It wasn't for want of trying, I have to say. Castro gave George McGovern in 1975 a list of the attempts made on his life—there were about thirty by that time—as he said, by the CIA. McGovern gave it to me and I looked through it and checked it off against our records and said we could account for about five or six. The others—I can understand Castro's feeling about them because they were all ex-Bay of Pigs people or something like that, so he thinks they're all CIA. Once you get into one of them, then bingo!—you get blamed for all the rest. We didn't have any connections with the rest of them, but we'd never convince Castro of that.[57]

Although assassination is always an option, it is a risky weapon of state. Foreign leaders may retaliate in kind (President Johnson was convinced that Castro was behind John F. Kennedy's death for precisely this reason), and there is no guarantee that the replacement will be any better than the original. It was during the period of Richard Bissell's tenure as deputy director for plans, however, that CIA–backed assassinations were actually attempted.[58] In January and March 1960, formal, highly secret discussions took place in a subcommittee of the 5412 Committee, the "Special Group," about assassination planning. Fidel Castro was the target. By March 10, 1960, formal and informal secret discussions had advanced to the stage at which assassination could be discussed, even if only by clear inference, at a meeting of the National Security Council, with the President in the chair. The minutes of the meeting report: "Mr. Dulles said some anti-Castro leaders existed, but they are not in Cuba at present. The President said we might have another Black Hole of Calcutta in Cuba, and he wondered what we could do about such a situation. Mr. Dulles reported that a plan to affect the situation in Cuba was being worked on. Admiral Burke suggested that any plan for the removal of Cuban leaders should be a package deal, since many of the leaders around Castro were even worse than Castro."[59] Four days later, at a meeting of the Special Group in the White House, Allen Dulles and J. C. King, chief of the CIA's Western Hemisphere Division charged with anti-Castro operations, discussed "the effect on the Cuban scene if Fidel and Raul Castro and Che Guevara should disappear simultaneously."[60]

Years later, the surviving participants in these National Security Council and Special Group meetings testified to the Church Committee that assassination was neither discussed nor considered. Ray Cline, however, familiar with the language of secret minutes and the CIA's relationships with the President, the NSC, and the other departments of government, considered that the terminology used suggests that "the assassination of Castro, his brother Raul, and Che Guevara was at least theoretically considered."[61] This being so, and despite the Church Committee's conclusion that "there was insufficient evidence from which the Committee could conclude that Presidents Eisenhower, Kennedy, or Johnson, their close advisers, or the Special Group authorized the assassination of Castro,"[62] it seems, at the very least, that the Cuban leader's death would not have made Eisenhower unhappy. As a soldier, Eisenhower would have been most likely to consider assassination dispassionately—after

all, he had been used to it in war—and to approve it if its results were beneficial. John A. Bross, one of the longest-serving and most senior agency officers,
summed up the attitude in Washington: "[T]he decision to proceed or not to
proceed must be made on the basis of a rational assessment of the consequences."[63]

This attitude was more likely to be that of Eisenhower and Allen Dulles
than Bissell's. Certainly Richard Bissell was in no doubt that he had been
asked by Eisenhower through Dulles to arrange a capability for assassinating
foreign leaders as a last resort. Arranging such a capability was a responsibility
he accepted. Using it was something he would not have done without approval. Bissell explained:

> One circumstance that, I think, confuses accounts of these matters, especially
> as they become more public and therefore less sophisticated, is that people
> don't clearly distinguish between the decision to prepare for a possible course
> of action and the decision to pursue that course of action. I authorized if I
> didn't actually decide to make the preparations. I have full responsibility for
> that. It was my view then and now that it would have been deficient not to
> have prepared an option that had been identified in the case of extreme af-
> fairs.[64]

Ray Cline supported this view:

> The CIA's becoming engaged in planning assassinations was not a momen-
> tary aberration on the part of the handful of men who were involved. In Jan-
> uary . . . Bissell ordered William Harvey, a veteran station chief, to set up a
> "standby capability" for what was called euphemistically "Executive Ac-
> tion," by which was plainly meant a capability for assassination of foreign
> leaders as a "last resort." Harvey was a colorful figure, a former FBI man who
> carried a pistol at all times when posted abroad, something unique among the
> CIA officers. I am sure he believed that it was patriotic, even moral, to kill a
> foreign ruler when ordered to do so by his superiors for reasons of U.S. secu-
> rity. Many of the romantic so-called "cowboy" types of covert action officers
> would have accepted this proposition, and in 1960–61 many officials outside
> the CIA would have subscribed to it as well. In any event, the responsible
> officers in the CIA, Harvey and Bissell, were convinced at the time that the
> White House had orally urged the creation of an assassination planning ca-
> pability as a contingency precaution. The written record does not clearly
> demonstrate this to be either true or untrue.[65]

There is strong evidence to suggest that President Eisenhower actually
approved the attempted assassination of Patrice Lumumba in the Congo in
1960. "The chain of events revealed by the documents and testimony is strong
enough to permit a reasonable inference that the plot to assassinate Lumumba
was authorized by President Eisenhower," declared the Church Committee,
although it then went on to hedge: "Nevertheless, there is enough countervail-
ing testimony by Eisenhower Administration officials and enough ambiguity

and lack of clarity in the records of high-level policy meetings to preclude the Committee from making a finding that the President intended an assassination effort against Lumumba."[66] Minutes of the Special Group on August 25, 1960, and of the National Security Council on September 21, 1960, state, "It was finally agreed that planning for the Congo would not necessarily rule out 'consideration' of any particular kind of activity which might contribute to getting rid of Lumumba."[67] The minutes also report Allen Dulles declaring in the presence of the President, "Mobutu appeared to be the effective power in the Congo for the moment but Lumumba was not yet disposed of and remained a grave danger as long as he was not disposed of."[68] Such phrases as "getting rid of" and "disposed of" in official minutes clearly indicate that fairly forceful action was being contemplated. Implied were such drastic actions as killing and burying. The English language has many other words and phrases that would indicate less while still conveying the idea that making Lumumba politically ineffective was desirable.

Lumumba attracted this lethal attention in large part because of his own role in the chaos afflicting the newly independent Belgian Congo. It was a consequence of the growing flight from empire as the old empires realized that if they did not give way to nationalism, one way or another their colonies would become too expensive to retain. In 1945 four African countries were independent: Egypt, which was controlled by Britain, the Dominion of South Africa, Liberia, and Ethiopia. In 1957, in the wake of Suez, Britain began dismantling its empire by granting independence to the Gold Coast, renamed Ghana, the first black African state to receive independence.

In 1960 sixteen new independent African nations were created, including the Belgian Congo, renamed the Republic of the Congo (and usually called Congo-Leopoldville to distinguish it from its neighbor, the ex-French colony now also a republic, known as The Congo or Congo-Brazzaville). Belgium had granted independence to its huge central African colony without preparing its people for the responsibilities of independence: fewer than twenty Congolese had received higher education, and the civil service and army were controlled by Belgians, as was the country's economy, after independence. Belgium was gambling that by calling the country independent it could still manage to collect the benefits of a colony without the responsibility. Within weeks of independence the Belgian plan failed. In July 1960 black troops in the Congolese army rebelled. There was a bloodbath, with many natives and European settlers losing their lives and property. The Belgian government sent paratroops to restore order.

The Congolese government of President Joseph Kasavubu and Prime Minister Patrice Lumumba appealed to Eisenhower for help. He directed them to the United Nations, which, with the United States and the Soviet Union voting together, decided to respond by sending a UN peacekeeping force to the area. The Eisenhower administration calculated that a multilateral UN force would be the best way to keep the Soviet Union out.[69] Unilateral

U.S. intervention might have provoked a Soviet intervention in response. In the midst of this Belgium encouraged and supported the secession from the Congo of its richest province, Katanga, in the south, where the Belgian mining company, Union Minière du Haut Katanga, like Aramco in Saudi Arabia, effectively owned the economic infrastructure. Lumumba made it clear that he would take aid from anyone to help regain Katanga and force Belgian withdrawal. In Washington this was seen as further evidence that Lumumba, who had always had a left-wing bent, was looking to the Soviet Union for help. Allen Dulles summarized the American view at a National Security Council meeting on July 21: "Mr. Dulles said that in Lumumba we were faced with a person who was a Castro or worse. Mr. Dulles went on to describe Mr. Lumumba's background which he described as 'harrowing.' It is safe to go on the assumption that Lumumba has been bought by the communists; this also, however, fits with his own orientation."*

As the evidence increased that Lumumba would gladly accept Russian support and that Russia was anxious to give it, and as reports filtered into Washington of Lumumba's irrational, undisciplined behavior—he smoked hemp, indulged in witchcraft, and asked the State Department for a white, blond prostitute to stay with him at Blair House, the President's guest quarters, while he was visiting Washington at the end of July—President Eisenhower, according to a member of the NSC staff, "said something—I can no longer remember his words—that came across to me as an order for the assassination of Lumumba. . . . I remember my sense of that moment quite clearly because the President's statement came as a great shock to me. . . . I have come to wonder whether what I really heard was only an order for some such political action. All I can tell you with any certainty at the present moment is my sense of that moment in the Cabinet Room of the White House."[70]

On August 25, 1960, Allen Dulles sent a cable to Lawrence Devlin, the CIA station chief in Leopoldville. Cables carrying the personal signature of the DCI are rare in the CIA and signify the special importance of the contents. According to CIA people and the Church Committee, Dulles' message in this cable was in effect saying, "Who will rid me of this turbulent priest?" This message authorized an assassination plot (a plot was the first step, actual assassination the next):

In high quarters here it is the clear-cut conclusion that if Lumumba continues to hold high office, the inevitable result will at best be chaos and at

* Church Committee, *Alleged Assassination Plots* (New York: W. W. Norton, 1976), p. 57. Over 10,000 U.S. troops were in the Congo as part of the UN peacekeeping force. From September, in response to a request from Lumumba, direct Soviet help began to arrive, including Russian troops, planes, technicians, and weapons. It was not surprising that Washington felt that Lumumba might be turning the Congo into a second Cuba. A counterargument is advanced that Lumumba tried to secure United States help first but that America's suspicions of him and refusal to act directly outside the United Nations forced him into Soviet hands.

worst pave the way to Communist takeover of the Congo with disastrous consequences for the prestige of the UN and for the interests of the Free World generally. Consequently we conclude that his removal must be an urgent and prime objective and that under existing conditions this should be a high priority of our covert action. To the extent that Ambassador may desire to be consulted, you should seek his concurrence. If in any particular case, he does not wish to be consulted you can act on your own authority where time does not permit referral here.[71]

The inexactitude of the phraseology in all the written documents concerning assassinations makes it impossible, as Ray Cline has pointed out, to be absolutely certain of any particular statement. This is because of the concept of "plausible denial," which became the bureaucratic method of protecting the President and senior officials. The idea was to report (rather than to present) potentially embarrassing matters and decisions in ways that would enable the President and others to deny knowledge or responsibility. It was the administrative mirror-image of the CIA's proprietary companies: everyone involved knew he/she was working for (or on the receiving end of) the CIA, but if, for example, a pilot were shot down (as Allen Pope was), the CIA, the President, and the State Department would deny any involvement in the affair. All that could be proved was that the pilot was working for a registered company.

"In the conduct of foreign affairs," said Eisenhower, the originator of the plausible-denial concept, "we do so many things we can't explain." He was speaking in November 1954 to Senator Knowland in the Oval Office. Knowland had not forgotten the promises to "liberate" eastern Europe that had been made during the 1952 presidential campaign and was pressing for action. "There is a very great aggressiveness on our side that you have not known about," Eisenhower went on, "and I guess that is on the theory of why put burdens on people that they don't need to know about." Eisenhower had turned on his secret recording device for this conversation. He continued, telling Knowland that he knew "so many things that I am almost afraid to speak to my wife." The CIA, said the President, was "very active, and there are a great many risky decisions on my part constantly . . . but I do try to spare other people some of the things I do."[72] The difference between Eisenhower and some of his successors was that for him plausible denial was a presidential prerogative and he was not prepared—as he said—to let others carry the burden. He would deny something if he considered it politic or beneficial to do so, but if he had to, he would also own up rather than blame subordinates.

Eisenhower was caught in such a plausible denial by Khrushchev when the U-2 was shot down in May 1960. The Russians did not reveal for two weeks that they had captured Powers and had the wreckage of his plane. Operational procedures called for the pilot to activate the self-destruct mechanism of the plane before bailing out, and if captured, to stick to a cover story of having lost his memory or being blown off course. On the assumption that this is what had happened or that Powers was dead, Eisenhower at first refuted Soviet statements that they had shot down an American spy plane, denying that the United Sates was involved. Then the Russians produced Powers and the wreckage of the plane, and the President publicly admitted that he had lied.[73] Richard Bissell described plausible denial as "circumlocutious" ways of reporting:

> The fact that Allen knew about the assassination plot and did not forbid it would have been a circumlocutious matter. What is very difficult for anybody to understand is that if you say in however veiled or murky terms that you are going to do something, and if the terms aren't so murky that the listener doesn't know what you're going to do, and if you don't receive a negative and you think it will advance the cause, you go ahead and do it. And so you were never explicitly authorized, but you have to add that the whole system was set up so that the chief of state doesn't have to authorize things explicitly.[74]

For Bissell (who was on a sailing holiday in mid-August 1960 when the decision to organize an assassination plot against Lumumba was apparently made) and for the others concerned in the agency Allen Dulles' cable of August 26 to Lawrence Devlin in Leopoldville said, in effect, " 'The President has let it be known that he wants this guy taken care of permanently.' I have always been at pains to say that I am perfectly certain that the President would have vastly preferred to have him taken care of some way other than by assassination, but he regarded Lumumba as I did and a lot of other people did: as a mad dog who was doing nothing constructive and potentially most destructive, and he wanted the problem dealt with. And that's what Allen said in the strongest terms to the station chief."*

On September 5, Lumumba was dismissed from the Congo government by Kasavubu. Three weeks earlier, reportedly with Soviet encouragement, Lumumba had broken with the United Nations and had told UN Secretary General Dag Hammarskjold that the Congo had lost confidence in him personally; according to Lumumba, he was conspiring with Belgium. Congolese troops began arresting UN officials. The Soviet Union was invited by Lumumba to intervene directly instead. Kasavubu saw this as an attempt by Lumumba to usurp power completely. It was seen by the United States and, indeed, by most of the United Nations, including Hammarskjold, not only as a personal bid for power but also as a rejection of UN principles and a move toward further civil

---

* Interview, Richard M. Bissell, Jr., July 18, 1983. See also *Alleged Assassination Plots*, p. 53, which quotes testimony from then Undersecretary of State Douglas Dillon about Lumumba: "He would never look you in the eye. He looked up at the sky. And a tremendous flow of words came out. He spoke in French, and he spoke it very fluently. And his words didn't ever have any relation to the particular things that we wanted to discuss. . . . You had a feeling that he was a person that was gripped by this fervor that I can only characterize as messianic. . . . He was just not a rational being."

war. The Kasavubu-Lumumba conflict was soon overshadowed by a successful military coup led by Mobutu, apparently orchestrated in part by the CIA and Belgian intelligence agents in Leopoldville. Lumumba, however, remained an active participant in the Congo's affairs; he had the backing of the Congo Parliament and his own loyal troops and goon squads. It was against this background that the final decision was made to assassinate Lumumba, probably at the time of the September 21 National Security Council meeting, when Allen Dulles spoke of "disposing of" him.

During September Dr. Sidney Gottlieb, the CIA's resident toxic-substance expert who had gained his reputation in the MKUltra, Artichoke and Bluebird drug programs, was asked by Richard Bissell to make preparations for an assassination attempt. After collecting various toxic biological materials that would produce a disease indigenous to that part of Africa, he took them in late September to Lawrence Devlin in Leopoldville with the instruction that Devlin use them to kill Lumumba. "When asked if he had considered declining to undertake the assignment to provide technical support to an assassination operation," the Church Committee reported fifteen years later, Gottlieb stated: "I think that my view of the job at the time and the responsibilities I had was in the context of a silent war that was being waged, although I realize that one of my stances could have been . . . as a conscientious objector to this war. That was not my view. I felt that a decision had been made . . . at the highest level that this be done and that as unpleasant a responsibility as it was, it was my responsibility to carry out my part of that."[75]

To avoid identification with the assassination, the CIA trained two professional killers, neither of whom were American, to carry it out. The men were trained separately in the United States, and neither man knew of the other's existence. Both met with Lawrence Devlin in Leopoldville, where they were each given one of Gottlieb's toxic biological kits. Realizing that the assassination operation would take time and would be complicated, requiring minute attention to detail, Devlin asked for a case officer to supervise the affair. Bissell asked Justin O'Donnell, the head of an operations unit in the DDP, to be that case officer and explained the plan. O'Donnell, a Roman Catholic, was not prepared to kill Lumumba. "I told him that I would absolutely not have any part of killing Lumumba," O'Donnell said. "I told him in no way would I have any part in the assassination of Lumumba . . . and reasserted in absolute terms that I would not be involved in a murder attempt."[76]

O'Donnell's was a very different view from that held by Bissell and Gottlieb, who saw the operation not only as being in the best interests of the United States (that was something all three could agree on) but as being ordered by their commander in chief in—as Gottlieb testified—a war atmosphere. O'Donnell could not accept assassination morally unless, it is to be presumed, a state of actual war existed. In one sense O'Donnell's attitude was a harbinger of attitudes to come, although it is difficult to understand what he was doing in the operations side of the CIA, given the attitudes of his colleagues and the working atmosphere in which U-2 pilots were issued suicide pills, pins, or needles they were expected to take in order to avoid capture.

O'Donnell agreed to go to the Congo, not to supervise Lumumba's assassination but to see that he was handed over to Mobutu by the UN peacekeeping force that held him in custody. (Lumumba had taken refuge with the UN force after the military coup.) Since it was obvious that Lumumba's life would be seriously at risk in such circumstances, O'Donnell's attitude appeared somewhat self-serving. He was not prepared to be involved in a direct attempt on Lumumba's life, but if the Congolese did it themselves, then all right. "It would have been a Congolese being judged by Congolese for Congolese crimes," is how he put it.[77] To cover himself for the record, however, O'Donnell went to see his immediate boss, Bill Harvey, and Bissell's deputy, Richard Helms. "In the Agency," he explained later, "since you don't have documents, you have to be awfully canny and you have to get things on record, and I went to Mr. Helms' office, and I said, 'Dick, here is what Mr. Bissell proposed to me,' and I told him that I would under no conditions do it, and Helms said, 'You're absolutely right.' "[78]

Helms, who knew the plausible-denial game and who knew that Bissell would not have started an assassination attempt without Dulles' and the President's approval, remained silent. He spoke to no one about O'Donnell or what O'Donnell had told him. No doubt his feelings toward Bissell also played a part, as his biographer, Thomas Powers, has suggested. This was something "Wonder Boy" was keeping to himself and had not involved Helms in at all. If it went well, fine. If it didn't, then Bissell would have some answering to do, and since O'Donnell was obviously a weak link, already the chances were that something would leak out, so better to stay out of it.[79]

Despite these plans, Lumumba was not assassinated through the efforts of the CIA or by the CIA's killers. (The Church Committee was satisfied that there was no CIA involvement in the murder.) He broke away from UN custody on November 27, determined to lead his supporters against Mobutu and the UN force. He was captured by Mobutu's troops three days later. On January 17, 1961, he was flown to Elisabethville, the capital of the secessionist Katanga province, and he was murdered (probably by Mobutu supporters) there within hours of his arrival.[80] It was five days before the inauguration of John Fitzgerald Kennedy as the thirty-fifth President of the United States. Lumumba's supporters and opponents all felt that the new President might force the Congolese leader's release—criticism of Eisenhower's involvement as subverting genuine independence in the Congo had figured in Kennedy's election speeches—so doubtless Lumumba's death was considered by his opponents as the best way out before the new President could act.

In Eisenhower's last year three other foreign leaders were considered by the CIA as targets for assassination: Colonel Abdul Kassem in Iraq, President Rafael Trujillo, the dictator of the Dominican Republic, and Fidel Castro in

Cuba. Like Lumumba, Kassem and Trujillo were killed by their domestic opponents before CIA plans were completed. Kassem was killed by a firing squad; Trujillo was ambushed and assassinated on May 30, 1961, by men who used guns supplied by the CIA. Gottlieb was involved in the Kassem operation. He impregnated a handkerchief with some toxic substance and then sent the handkerchief to the colonel by mail. The deadly parcel arrived after the colonel's execution, but since no one is known to have died as a result of opening it, presumably the toxin's strength had waned in the post. Plans involving the possible assassination of Trujillo were drawn up in December 1960. However, their status was not settled by the time President Kennedy took office in January 1961.

In December 1959 the first steps were taken to assassinate Castro when Allen Dulles approved a memorandum stating that "thorough consideration be given to the elimination of Fidel Castro. . . . Many informed people believe that the disappearance of Fidel would greatly accelerate the fall of the present Government" in Cuba.[81] Bissell then began to organize with Colonel J. C. King "a capability to eliminate Castro if such action should be decided upon."[82] By September 1960 this assassination capacity was organized and an assassination plan formulated. Included was a scheme that had the agency and the Mafia working together to assassinate Castro. (The Mafia was involved out of its own self-interest. They hoped to regain the extensive interests they had lost in Cuba when Castro took power.) Nothing further had been done to implement this plan by the time Kennedy was inaugurated.

AUTHORIZATIONS

The central question facing the CIA was whether it or the National Security Council required the formal approval of the new President to continue operations approved by his predecessor or whether presidential approval, once given, was taken as sustaining that operation until its completion. The answer is clear in the military: an army acts under orders and implements orders until they are specifically rescinded or replaced by other orders. If a general is killed or replaced in the middle of a battle, his army does not wait until his successor repeats or changes his orders, it just gets on with those orders and the battle. So, it seems, was the case with the Central Intelligence Agency. When asked this question, McGeorge Bundy, President Kennedy's national security adviser, said: "That's one of the troubles about covert operations. By definition, you limit the circle and you restrict it to people whose other obligations make it difficult for them to second-guess. You really are reliant on the internal disciplines of the agency. In that sense, making sure the things the President has not authorized do not happen is the job of the director, and only gets done if he does it. But, I'm not sure we were as meticulous in testing that question as we should have been."[83]

Richard Helms, on the other hand, argues that proper reporting and authorizing procedures existed and were followed. From the earliest days of the agency, the 5412 Committee or its equivalent approved or disapproved operations to protect the President from direct involvement, "so that if something went sour and the President wanted to sacrifice all these fellows, they could be sacrificed because they were appointees. A President is elected for four years. We don't have a parliamentary system and you can't get rid of a President for having made a bad call, and therefore he has to be insulated from certain things." Concerning plausible denial, in other words, "It was not necessarily presidential authority that backed these things, it was the authority of these officials." Since "these officials"—the 5412 Committee or its equivalents—consisted of representatives of the secretaries of defense and state (or the secretaries themselves), the director of Central Intelligence and the President's national security adviser, it is a moot point whether it would be simply their authority behind CIA operations. As appointees, they enjoyed delegated presidential authority. However, in Helms's view, the agency would obtain its permission from this group and make periodical reports about operations as they took form and unfolded, "and certainly if there was a change in the administration, the agency would come back to make sure the operation was satisfactory to the new administration."

Helms, as a director of Central Intelligence who held office under two presidents, no doubt operated in this way. But in 1960 another DCI was in place and things may well have been different:

The agency says that the President is its sun, moon, and stars and that it does nothing without specific approval. That's what they told the new administration [said McGeorge Bundy], but what they never said was that there are some things you don't spell out. The two propositions don't hang together. You cannot really say you are the President's men and then say that of course there are some things we do for him that we don't tell him about. It was a careless or inaccurate reliance, if you like, looking back on it, on these assurances that was part of the trouble. I had that serene confidence that we knew what was going on until the assassination stories began to appear years later.

For Helms this was not quite the position; the 5412 Committee or its equivalents approved operations. "If they did not approve an operation, then we would not attempt to carry it out. That is not to say that the national security adviser would not go up the back stairs and tell the President what we had decided to do and ask 'Do you have any objections?' " It was the committee's job to authorize, and it could always change its mind. Thinking back on the reporting system he remembered, McGeorge Bundy said:

There is a terrible danger that if you don't really listen extremely hard and have a relationship of mutual trust that is very close, you can get a situation where what you think you are authorizing is in fact rather different from what the agency will believe it is free to do under that authorization. The tendency to believe that "higher authority" will not mind a little inventive enlargement on what it has intended to authorize is endemic among covert operations, and I repeat that the best way of ensuring that no such liberties are taken is to have a line authority that guards against them. White House staff supervision is very much a second-best method.

The role of the director of Central Intelligence changed during the Eisenhower presidency. From being the President's man in the intelligence community of the United States, the *primus inter pares* that Lawrence Houston had spoken of and that both Hillenkoetter and Bedell Smith had tried hard to establish, under Dulles the DCI became another player. Instead of being an impartial overseer of U.S. intelligence operations and activities, he was master of a major element of collection, analysis, espionage, and operation. He was head of an agency spending hundreds of millions of dollars, constantly fighting bureaucratic battles to maintain the CIA's position in relation to competitors for funds and its role—the military services, the Atomic Energy Commission, the Treasury—and could not be expected to control them all. His effectiveness and success depended directly upon his relationship with the President, to whom, under the terms of the National Security Act, he was directly responsible and from whom, ultimately, he received his authority. In this, however, he was again a competitor: the Joint Chiefs of Staff and the State Department had identical imperatives and competed fiercely for Presidential favor.

In practice, under Dulles it became clear that the director of Central Intelligence could not be expected to exercise anything resembling command authority over the secretary of defense or the secretary of state. If a secretary of defense decided not to spend any money on overhead reconnaissance, the DCI had a responsibility to go to the President and complain, but it did not mean he would win the argument and it might mean that he had to spend his own money instead. There was another reality as well: if a director of Central Intelligence ever had a real showdown with a secretary of defense or a secretary of state without first being sure he had the President's support, he could not win. The secretaries have the power, the budget, the deal in the Congress. "Congressmen are naturally interested all the time for things in their local constituencies which the military can grant, for favors which State can grant," said R. Jack Smith when considering this question. "So if it comes to that kind of contest, the director can never win."[84]

None of this bothered Allen Dulles very much, particularly because with his brother as secretary of state (until his death in 1959), he did not have to worry about access to the top of the government. In addition, he had Eisenhower's complete confidence. In 1960 the President's Board of Consultants on Foreign Intelligence Activities suggested that the director of Central Intelligence be separated from the Central Intelligence Agency and act solely as the President's chief intelligence officer and coordinator of U.S. intelligence overall. Nothing happened, in part because the board was advisory, removed from administration; in part because of Allen Dulles' personal standing and success as DCI; and in part because President Eisenhower, who, on a personal level, frequently urged Dulles to exert more initiative in overseeing intelligence, nevertheless supported Dulles fully in what he did, even if Dulles defined his role in a limited way. "I'm not going to be able to change Allen," Eisenhower was recorded in a CIA history as declaring. "I have two alternatives, either to get rid of him and appoint someone who will assert more authority or keep him with his limitations. I'd rather have Allen as my chief intelligence officer with his limitations than anyone else I know."[85]

—11—

On the Beach
1961

"What would you think if I ordered Castro to be assassinated?" President Kennedy asked a *New York Times* reporter in a private conversation in the Oval Office ten months after his inauguration. The reporter, Tad Szulc, had returned from Cuba, where he had held several long conversations with Castro. In November 1961 he was asked by a special assistant to the President to brief the attorney general, Robert F. Kennedy, on his impressions of Castro and Cuba (starting in April 1961 Bobby Kennedy had special responsibility for anti-Castro operations in the Kennedy administration) and, at the attorney general's request, met the President too. Szulc told the President that the assassination of Castro would not necessarily cause a change in the Cuban system and that in his personal view the United States should not be party to murders and political assassinations. "I agree with you completely," said the President, who then went on for some minutes to make the point that both he and his brother felt very strongly that moral considerations should preclude the United States from ever resorting to assassination.

"JFK then said he was testing me, that he felt the same way," Szulc's notes of the meeting record, and "—he added 'I'm glad you feel the same way'— because indeed US morally must not be part[y] to assassinations. JFK said he raised question because he was under terrific pressure from advisers (I think he said intelligence people, but not positive) to okay a Castro murder. Said he was resisting pressures."[1] "Well, that's the kind of thing I'm never going to do," said Kennedy. "We can't get into that kind of thing, or we would all be targets," he repeated some days later.[2] "There are occasions when I

349

would go a long way to protect the President of the United States from certain kinds of embarrassment," said Richard Bissell, and discussing assassination plots with the President in the Oval Office was something he would not do.[3] Richard Helms expressed similar feelings: "I think that any of us would have found it very difficult to discuss assassinations with a President of the United States. I just think we all had the feeling that we were hired to keep those things out of the Oval Office."[4] Despite the feelings of these top CIA officers, it is plain that the President himself had no such inhibition.

Jack Kennedy—though less so than his brother Bobby—was a driven man. Their father, Joseph, who even at home was referred to as "The Ambassador," had been President Franklin Roosevelt's appointee to the Court of St. James's. He was an extremely wealthy man—not as wealthy as a Mellon or a Rockefeller or a Du Pont but wealthy enough to spend tens of millions of dollars on his sons' political ambitions. These political ambitions were nurtured by the father: it was a drive for power. In the Kennedy family the more powerful a son became, the more the father loved him. They were all vehicles for power, with even their bodies thrown onto the scales. "The Ambassador" and Jack competed with each other for girl friends and mistresses. The family developed a rough and bloody version of touch football, in which winning had less to do with points than with physical courage. They enjoyed other people's discomfort. William Manchester, a longtime Kennedy friend, recalled:

> You once asked Jack the secret of his romantic triumphs. With that charming tact he reserved for friends, he said: "Some guys have got it, and some haven't. You haven't got it." It was the kind of answer the question had deserved. Jack would lay it on you that way, enjoy your discomfort, and then give you something you had always wanted and never dared to ask for. In this case it was an invitation to spend a weekend in Hyannis Port, the fief of his father, the powerful, ruthless, and unbelievably opulent Joseph P. Kennedy. . . .
>
> If you had known what lay ahead, you would have spent a week *training*. Around the house members of the Kennedy tribe darted back and forth, playing tag, kick-the-can, and, of course, touch football, all with a teeth-grinding physical tenacity, pushing themselves to the limits of endurance, and sometimes beyond the pale of fair play, in order to win. Win what? It didn't matter; they had been raised to compete, to finish *first*. Rose, who seemed to be completely dominated by the ambassador, explained serenely: "My husband is quite a strict father; he likes the boys to win at sports and everything they try. If they don't win, he will discuss their failure with them, but he doesn't have much patience with the loser." That was putting it gently. If they lost, and he felt they hadn't made their best effort, they would be sent from the dinner table in disgrace. . . .
>
> In most families, boys are warned not to pick on their younger brothers. Joe Kennedy believed in muscular laissez-faire. . . . Jack was the same; when Teddy was small, he was afraid to leave his bedroom, because he knew Jack was waiting to smack him over the head with a pillow. . . .

Yet everyone who came to know them was struck by the abiding love between parents and children, between brothers and sisters.[5]

For the whole of his adult life, when Jack met his father he greeted him in an unconventional way. Jack would make a fist, and his father would put his hand over it.

The drive to win, the belief in muscular laissez-faire, the will to go beyond the pale of fair play, the veneration of courage all drove Jack Kennedy to assemble an action-oriented White House staff. Foreign affairs had been a constant backdrop throughout the 1960 election campaign, more so than it had during the 1956 campaign.* On May 1 the Russians had shot down the U-2, within weeks catching Eisenhower in a web of outright lies. Eisenhower had flown to Paris for the Summit Conference some days later only to be publicly humiliated by Khrushchev, who called him a "hypocrite" and a "liar" over the U-2 incident. The regime of Syngman Rhee in South Korea was overthrown by civil riots. Fidel Castro nationalized all American property in Cuba and announced an alliance with the Soviet Union. Khrushchev warned that Russia would destroy the United States if America made any attempt to attack Castro. Disarmament talks in Geneva collapsed. Soviet influence in Africa was established in Egypt and appeared to be growing amidst the chaos and bloodshed of the Congo. The Japanese withdrew an invitation to Eisenhower to pay a state visit, much to the President's embarrassment, because they could not guarantee his safety after weeks of anti-American demonstrations in Tokyo and elsewhere. The cumulative effect of all these events left Kennedy and his supporters with the feeling that a tired President and an equally tired Republican party were stumbling through their last days in office as America and the world waited for a new, young, dynamic leader to take the reins of power in an effective and forceful way.

In 1960 Kennedy was twenty-six years younger than Eisenhower, who celebrated his seventieth birthday three weeks before the presidential election. Richard Nixon, Eisenhower's vice-president for eight years, had an uphill struggle (which he lost by the narrowest percentage of popular votes in American presidential election history—114,000 votes out of 68.3 million votes cast) trying to meet Kennedy's attacks on the "failure" of the Eisenhower administration to recognize the force of emerging nationalism in the Third World—a failure that allowed Soviet influence to grow. A typical Kennedy campaign speech began in this way: "I don't run for the office of the presidency to tell you what you want to hear. I run for the office of President because in a dangerous time we need to be told what we must do if we are going to maintain our freedom."[6] Kennedy spoke of chaos in Africa, of the disintegration of American foreign policy, of the stagnant economy, of the problems of bored and drifting young people. "When Jack laid it out like that," remembered Man-

---

* In 1956, rather than a constant backdrop in foreign affairs there had been a detonation with Hungary and Suez.

chester, "you felt challenged. We were perhaps the last liberal patriots to stride down the campaign trail. This was our country, and it was on the wrong track, and we were going to set it right."[7]

Kennedy was a young and vigorous cold warrior, willing to rethink traditional arguments and reexamine traditional positions in an effort to stop the spread of communism. American power was to be recognized and used in full to meet this end. Although Eisenhower and John Foster Dulles had spoken of "massive retaliation," they used American power with cautious selectivity. Kennedy, who was less experienced and less wise, was far more excited by the opportunities American power offered. He played Kennedy touch football in the arena of foreign affairs with as much vigor and determination as he played it at home.

Many of the liberal patriots who found Kennedy's message so appealing were in the Central Intelligence Agency, including Richard Helms, William Colby, Cord Meyer, R. Jack Smith, John A. Bross, and Ray Cline. These men were at ease with those people with whom the State Department was uncomfortable. They believed in the New Deal principle of mobilization and in democracy. Kennedy's appeal was to an intensive, emotionally and intellectually mobilizing atmosphere, a pride in clear-minded ruthlessness for particular purposes. He was a child of World War II, separating himself from his isolationist father. He was influenced by the ideals of Wilson and the New Deal, but he wanted to make his own mark. He was a management man, although he had never managed anything in his life. For him management was an ideology in itself and of the time; claiming to possess the technical skill validated the approach to power. It also stated an independence from earlier doctrines and earlier presidents, all of whom, it was implied, were fuddy-duddy.

Allen Dulles, whose manner could easily be taken as fuddy-duddy, seems to have recognized the Kennedy interest in vigor and management early on and took steps to exploit it. "In early 1961, Dulles and Bissell moved rapidly to demonstrate their power and skill to the key Kennedy men," recalled Harris Wofford, special assistant to Kennedy for civil rights, and he continued:

> The CIA Director invited some dozen White House aides close to the President to a dinner and long evening at Washington's little-known Alibi Club with the top ten CIA men. After most had relaxed with several cocktails, the inside stories of past secret exploits were recounted; it was heady wine. Bissell was asked to introduce himself and talk about his work. "I'm your man-eating shark," he said. CIA man Robert Amory thought that Bissell had set just the right note, that it was good to have got "a head start on State," and that Dulles had been correct: the New Frontiersmen would respond best to a "New Yorkerish type of précis." Speed was certainly one of the skills Kennedy appreciated. He liked shortcuts. Before long, McGeorge Bundy reported to Amory that the President had said, "By gosh, I don't care what it is, but if I need some material fast or an idea fast, CIA is the place I have

to go. The State Department takes four of five days to answer a simple yes or no."[8]

From its inception the CIA was a magnet for the best and the brightest entering government service. The analysts who joined the CIA were consummate professionals who thought matters through in a far more intellectual way than their counterparts at the departments of State and Defense. Those drawn to the CIA learned about the world behind the world of appearances; there was no place in government that had better information. The agency in the mid-1960s represented, in Stewart Alsop's phrase, "the triumph of the prudent professionals."[9]

R. Jack Smith gave an example of the analytical approach that was the CIA's hallmark: "I remember once we were dealing with the Air Force on the question of a certain Russian bomber that did not have the range to fly to the USA and back to the Soviet Union. The Air Force maintained it was to fly one-way missions. We just could not accept the Soviet Union flying an airplane they had spent so much time, energy and blood producing, and letting it fall somewhere in Arkansas or Mexico."[10] In another instance the analysts came up with a technique for counting tail numbers. The Russians were trapped by their methodology: when an airplane came out of a hangar it had a tail number on it, and the analysts were able to work out the sequence and figure out how many the Russians produced in a series. For an administration interested in *doing* things, in energizing a world it saw as passive without American action, the CIA—and its professional President's men—was an obvious place to get things done. "Welcome aboard," a young CIA recruit was told in 1950, "you've just joined the cold war arm of the U.S. government."* Under Kennedy this arm was to have a fist at the end of it.

THE BAY OF PIGS

Castro's Cuba was the first to feel this fist. The plans for the Bay of Pigs invasion and various assassination attempts on Castro had been drawn up dur-

---

* Joseph B. Smith, *Portrait of a Cold Warrior* (New York: Ballantine Books, 1976), p. 53. "First of all," Smith was told, "let me explain what I meant by saying you've just joined the cold war arm of the U.S. government. We're not in the intelligence business in this office. We're an executive action arm of the White House that's trying to counter the Sino-Soviet bloc by using the same covert tactics they do, because the top level of government has decided this is essential if the cold war isn't going to turn hot" (ibid., pp. 53–54). This was the effect of the "Munich model": the more little things the Russians got away with, the more they would get away with. It was also the American response: the view that the Russians were deeply afraid of America, and, if countered at a low level, Russian aggression would not go higher. There was an additional element behind this application of the "Munich model": the proof of manhood, of coming of age. If America was perpetually vigilant, with brave people on the night watch, the Russians would take note and moderate themselves.

ing Eisenhower's last year. One of Eisenhower's trademarks—a trademark of the General Staff mind—both as Allied commander in chief in Europe during World War II and as President, was that he would have plans drawn up for a wide range of possibilities but would not necessarily implement them. This was the case with Hungary in 1956. It was also the case with Lumumba. Despite appearances and campaign propaganda, Eisenhower had plans under way in 1960 to deal with the problems Kennedy was making political mileage from.

One of these problems was the "missile gap," which, Kennedy maintained, gave the Soviets a tactical nuclear capability superior to America's. Russia had more missiles, said Kennedy, and so could deliver more nuclear warheads. This meant that Russia could match America missile for missile and also threaten other countries without jeopardizing its standoff with the United States. "At the Pentagon they shudder when they speak of the 'gap,' " wrote Joseph and Stewart Alsop in their newspaper column in 1958, launching the controversy, "which means the years 1960, 1961, 1962, and 1963. They shudder because in these years, the American government will flaccidly permit the Kremlin to gain an almost unchallenged superiority in the nuclear striking power that was once our specialty."[11] In fact, the CIA confirmed to Eisenhower that the United States was well ahead of the Soviets, who were actually experiencing grave difficulties and long setbacks in their development of an operational intercontinental ballistic capability.[12] The U-2 photographs had provided extremely detailed information on Soviet advances and capabilities, identifying nuclear test areas at Novaya Zemlya and Semipalatinsk, the antiballistic missile test site at Sary-Shagan, the missile test sites at Kapustin Yar and Tyuratam, and the weapons factory near Alma-Ata.

Starting in mid-1958, the CIA's Board of National Estimates was encouraged by Sherman Kent and Allen Dulles to concentrate on estimating Soviet missile capabilities. In January 1960 Allen Dulles briefed the National Security Council on the contents of a National Intelligence Estimate on the subject, which concluded that mid-1961 was the moment when the United States might be most vulnerable to Soviet attack if the "worst case" analysis was correct, because American offensive and defensive systems would still be incomplete. Still, according to George Kistiakowsky, Eisenhower's scientific adviser, to those in the know at the time, "in fact the missile gap doesn't look to be very serious."[13] Nevertheless, in the closing weeks of his presidential campaign Kennedy voiced loudly the public's fears of a missile gap that might lead to another Pearl Harbor if America were not careful.

Nixon, unable to use the top-secret information the CIA had provided that the gap was imaginary, had to keep silent. For the same reason his rebuttals were also limited when Kennedy promised to aid Cuban exiles and rebels who sought Castro's overthrow. Nixon could not reveal the plans for the invasion of Cuba by a CIA-directed and -supported Cuban exile force without jeopardizing the plan's success. Two years later, in his book *Six Crises*, Nixon used this situation as an example of the "disadvantage that confronts a candidate who also represents an incumbent administration."[14] As a CIA man, aware of the whole story and sympathetic to Nixon's dilemma, put it: "At the time I credited Nixon with doing a good job when he denounced Kennedy's statement, pointing out that we couldn't intervene in Cuban affairs because of our treaty commitments to nonintervention in Latin American affairs and because of the UN charter. It was Nixon's job to uphold the principle of presidential plausible denial of covert operations."[15]

The Cuban operation was the most overt of any the CIA had conducted so far. It began in 1959 and by mid-1960 had developed to a Guatemala-style covert operation for the overthrow of the Castro government. The course of events in Cuba preceding the CIA plans was the same as in Guatemala: a politically elite group that had been excluded from power took over the control of government. Only after this was accomplished did the new leaders spell out their anti-American and anti-American-business "national liberation" policies. Castro's manifesto, which called for democracy and social justice, appealed to both Cuban nationalism and American idealism. The only extreme left-wing influences in these early years were Castro's brother Raul and Raul's Argentinian friend Ernesto "Che" Guevara. In seeking power, however, Castro and his followers came to value the propaganda importance of a "philosophy" and the tactical importance of espousing social reform; peasants were more willing to harbor those who promised land reform and prosperity than those who taxed them into greater poverty.

When he came to power Castro turned his back on the promises he had made. He refused to incorporate in his regime those officials who had been (in his own words) "honest," refused to hold elections, and refused to spread the patronage of power beyond his own loyal followers. The result was the alienation of the politically conscious middle classes, the Cuban democrats, from whom Castro had come and to whom Castro made his first appeals for support. The loyalists that remained were not numerous enough or well educated enough to administer the country, so Castro turned to the communists for help. Their experience in running labor unions made them invaluable to Castro, especially since they were not in competition with him for popularity and would make deals in return for power. He was never a "prisoner" of the communists. He was a *caudillo de izquierda*, a totalitarian leader of the left and personally anti-American. Neither Moscow nor the Cuban Communist party needed to prod Castro. This led to the hostility between Cuba and America.

In May 1959, after less than five months of power, Castro nationalized American property, offering compensation in the form of twenty-year bonds. America demanded better terms, but Castro refused to negotiate.[16] He also began sending out guerrilla invasion teams to the Dominican Republic, Panama, Haiti, and Nicaragua. It was clear to Washington that a new and dangerous dictator was ensconced in Cuba and that he was already challenging—as George Kennan had outlined in Rio de Janeiro in 1950—American interests in the Caribbean and Central America.

From the beginning the CIA kept a close eye on Castro and the progress of his revolution. They decided to plan for his "elimination" as early as December 1959. (President Batista fled Cuba on January 1, 1959, leaving Castro with an open field.) On January 13, 1960, a meeting of the Special Group agreed that the CIA should start "covert contingency planning to accomplish the fall of the Castro government." By March, Colonel J. C. King had organized a task force to plan for Castro's overthrow and had made it clear that assassination was also being considered. By July authorization was actually cabled to the CIA's Havana station for the assassination of Raul Castro, only to be withdrawn within hours. By September Robert Maheu, an ex-FBI officer turned private investigator and free-lance CIA agent, approached underworld leaders John Rosselli, Santos Trafficante, and Sam Giancana with a deal to kill Castro for $150,000.[17]

After Maheu left the FBI in 1954 he occasionally worked for the CIA. In Rome he bugged Aristotle Onassis' room for the agency and prevented the Greek shipping tycoon from securing a monopoly to carry Saudi Arabian oil by leaking the information to a local newspaper. He had also produced the pornographic film of Sukarno for the agency. His connections extended into the underworld, and when he was approached by a former FBI associate in the CIA's Office of Security to arrange for the Mafia—that loosely connected, disparate criminal grouping—to kill Castro, Maheu turned to a Hollywood acquaintance, John Rosselli, an underworld fixer in Las Vegas and southern California, for help. When Rosselli realized at an early stage that the CIA was behind the approach, he notified his boss, Giancana, the Mafia chief in Chicago and the Midwest, and Trafficante, a leading criminal boss in Cuba. Both Trafficante and Giancana willingly involved themselves in the plans, which depended upon exiled anti-Castro Cubans to carry out the actual killing or killings. (It was never clear if only Fidel Castro was to be killed or if Raul Castro and Che Guevara were also targeted for assassination.)[18]

Rosselli, Trafficante, and Giancana were a high-powered trio. Rosselli's Mafia roots dated back to the early 1920s when he was a member of Longy Zwillman's gang in New Jersey. From there he moved to Chicago, where he joined Al Capone and became an expert in labor racketeering and extortion. After Capone's arrest and imprisonment for income-tax evasion in 1931 Rosselli made his way to Hollywood, where he organized the International Alliance of Theatrical Stage Employees and Moving Picture Machine Operators as an extortion racket. In California he served four years of a ten-year sentence for extortion. Giancana had an even more sensational underworld career. He started out as a bodyguard to a hit man, Jack "Machine Gun" McGurn, one of the prime suspects in the St. Valentine's Day massacre in which Al Capone wiped out the rival Bugs Moran gang in Chicago. Trafficante gained notoriety in Cuba for staging some of the most perverted live sex shows in the Americas. His business ability also gained respect within the Mafia, as did his ability to keep Batista's government away from his operations. Undoubtedly all three men believed that the Maheu/CIA approach could be of enormous benefit to their criminal activities, especially since a mistress of Giancana's was also sharing a bed with the President-elect of the United States.

Judith Campbell met Jack Kennedy for the first time on February 7, 1960, at the Sands Hotel in Las Vegas while Kennedy was campaigning for the Democratic nomination. They were introduced by Frank Sinatra. Four weeks later Campbell became Kennedy's mistress after meeting him for the third time.[19] From the start Giancana must have calculated that it would be useful to have evidence of Kennedy's infidelity, and after the November 1960 election he undoubtedly believed this even more, seeing Campbell as a link in a chain involving the President and the CIA. He proposed marriage to Campbell in the winter of 1962, knowing that she was still having the affair with Kennedy. (She said no.)

In late October 1960 Giancana tested his CIA link, arranging for Maheu to bug the hotel room in Las Vegas occupied by one of Giancana's other girl friends, on the grounds that she might reveal the Castro assassination plans, which he had apparently told her about. The bugging equipment was discovered in the hotel, the FBI was called in, and the CIA was forced to protect Maheu, citing "national security" as the reason the FBI should drop its prosecution.[20] To his friends Giancana said he had arranged for the bug "to determine the occupant's relationship with Giancana's girl friend"[21] and indicated that the CIA was closely involved with him. The incident seriously embarrassed the CIA. It also prompted Hoover to reveal to the CIA that news of their anti-Castro plans was widespread. Hoover wrote to Richard Bissell on October 18:

> During recent conversations with several friends Giancana stated that Fidel Castro was to be done away with very shortly. When doubt was expressed regarding this statement, Giancana reportedly assured those present that Castro's assassination would occur in November. Moreover, he allegedly indicated that he had met with the assassin-to-be on three occasions. . . . Giancana claimed that everything has been perfected for the killing of Castro, and that the "assassin" had arranged with a girl, not further described, to drop a "pill" in some drinks or food of Castro's.[22]

The methods being considered for the assassination included some of Dr. Gottlieb's legendary potions. The first pills Gottlieb produced were rejected because they would not dissolve in water. In February 1961 Rosselli was given a second batch of pills containing botulinum toxin, which did dissolve. In March and April two attempts were made to use the pills to kill Castro, but each failed because the Cubans involved had "cold feet." Later other assassination plans were made using poison pens, bacterial powder in a diving suit, and a poison dart gun. All of these attempts were conducted during Kennedy's presidency and ended when he died.

Once again the question of whose authority was behind the assassination attempts is raised. Kennedy himself was obviously aware that Castro's assassination was being discussed and was happy to discuss it himself in the Oval Office even if the CIA was not. McGeorge Bundy, President Kennedy's national security adviser, either urged Richard Bissell to establish an "executive-action" capability in April 1961 or else raised no objections to such a capability in the CIA when told about it by Bissell. Walt Rostow, another security adviser, may also have urged Bissell to set up an assassination team.[23] It is not clear, however, whether Bundy, Rostow, or indeed any member of Kennedy's staff was briefed at this early stage of the new administration about the specific plans to assassinate Castro. In any event, Bissell and the CIA were satisfied that they could go ahead and develop such a capability—it was given the cryptonym ZR/Rifle—although actually using it would be another matter entirely, requiring specific approval.

In the first months of Kennedy's presidency, however, after Gottlieb's pills failed to reach their target (these attempts do not appear to have been sanctioned by Kennedy or any of his staff; they were probably leftovers from the last days of the Eisenhower administration, which would have "understood" Castro's death at the hands of underworld agents backed by the CIA), attention was focused on a major covert operation that, if successful, would make Castro's assassination less attractive: the Bay of Pigs operation to land anti-Castro Cuban troops in Cuba, where they would announce a government in opposition to Castro which the United States could then recognize and support.

Planning for the Bay of Pigs operation started under Eisenhower in March 1960. As Bissell recalled:

> What was approved was a plan to take about twenty-five Cuban refugees, young and well motivated, and train them in sabotage and communications techniques—train them to be guerrillas—then to insert them into Cuba. In the first class there were twenty-five, and in subsequent classes there might have been thirty to forty-five, not more than that. The design was a classic World War II underground activity. Our operation was to train eventually up to seventy-five or more individuals who would first of all have communications techniques and equipment, and second, have some skills in sabotage. Their primary function was to enter the country, join guerrilla groups or resistance groups already there, and put them in direct communications with an external headquarters, partly to exercise command control and partly to enable them to receive logistic supplies by boat and aircraft.[24]

Drawing on previous experience, Bissell's directorate based the plan on three elements of operation: first, an effective communications system to an external base, just as the French underground had with London during World War II; second, a dependable means of resupply by air, sea, or land, or a combination of all three; and third, security within the guerrilla organization brought about by dividing it into cells and having safe houses and dependable routes for moving from one location to another.

Very quickly Kermit Roosevelt's argument that covert action had to be finely geared to the conditions in the country, and the compromise of the Guatemalan operation, were set aside for a full-blooded World War II model underground-movement plan. As Bissell explained:

> The original conception of training guerrilla leaders and organizing communications for guerrilla groups actually in Cuba grew a little bit into the notion that once we had developed a true underground on the World War II model, with the capability of receiving people and equipment in small numbers and amounts, and moving them around, we would detonate an uprising in a small way with possibly a hundred people or two groups of a hundred people landing at different points on the coast. As soon as it was formulated, that plan began to come apart. At this early stage I wasn't paying much attention to it—the plan originated in the division as typically operational plans do—I knew it, but I wasn't paying very much attention to it.[25]

Tracy Barnes, Bissell's special assistant for the operation, was masterminding plans at this stage, along with Colonel King. A training ground was obtained in the Panama Canal Zone, and construction was begun on a base. All of this took time, and while the original landing-force plan called for the groups to start training in July 1960, by September neither the base nor the training had begun. After this delay, trainees arriving in Panama were put through the training program in late 1960. Some of the first to finish were successfully landed on Cuba's north coast. Air drops of supplies followed, although as Bissell ruefully remembered, they did not always wind up in the correct hands: "We think we may have made one successful air drop, but in most cases it was Castro's people who received it."[26]

Given the training and Castro's success in tracking down many of the infiltrators, by December 1960 two things were clear. First, the chances of inciting an uprising were rapidly diminishing as Castro took an ever firmer grip on power. Early estimates that the Cuban people would rise up against Castro (never very likely—Castro was popular) were completely out of date. Second, President Eisenhower's authority for the operation would no longer be sufficient: the new President would also need to give his agreement, because the operation would be taking place during the new presidency. There was not a serious problem with Kennedy, however. During his first meeting as President-elect with Eisenhower on December 6, 1960, Kennedy wanted to talk about Cuba and the national security setup and its operations. Eisenhower recalled this meeting:

> I explained to him in detail the purpose and work habits of the Security Council. . . . I said that the National Security Council had become the most important weekly meeting of the government: that we normally worked from

an agenda, but that any member could present his frank opinion on any subject, even on those that were not on the formal agenda. I made clear to him that conferences in the White House are not conducted as committee meetings in the legislative branch. There is no voting by members and each group has one purpose only—to advise the president on the facts of particular problems and to make him such recommendations as each member may deem applicable.[27]

Both before and after this meeting Kennedy received several CIA briefings on the Cuban plans from Allen Dulles. By March 1961 the plan had developed into a military landing with a brigade—"La Brigada"—of about fifteen hundred men, armed with tanks, supplied by ships, and with an air force to destroy Castro's planes and armor and "soften up" target areas.* When Eisenhower actually left office, there was no operational plan: the one that was attempted had unraveled because of the delays. Kennedy was uncertain and somewhat hesitant about the operation, but given his campaign promises, he went ahead."It was a sort of orphan child JFK had adopted from the Republicans—he had no real love and affection for it," Allen Dulles later recalled. "[He] proceeded uncertainly toward defeat—unable to turn back—only half sold on the vital necessity of what he was doing, surrounded by doubting Thomases among his best friends."[28]

The Kennedy plan was a military operation. Earlier thoughts of instigating and supplying guerrilla activity were completely abandoned. Bissell's military adviser for the operation, a marine colonel named Jack Hawkins who was temporarily assigned to the CIA at Dulles' request to provide military expertise, devised the new plan under Tracy Barnes's supervision.† These two men did not make a particularly good team. Hawkins was too much a military man, too close to military methods, without much imagination. After it was decided to launch the brigade invasion, Hawkins was still talking of using eight hundred to nine hundred people. He had not fully considered how many more would be needed for supply purposes once the landing was completed, not realizing that military support mechanisms had to be specially planned and that he could not rely on anything happening automatically.

Barnes was one of the glamour boys of the agency, sharing a background similar to Bissell's. A graduate of Groton, Yale, and Harvard Law School, he was a handsome and athletic man. He had served in OSS during the war and,

---

* The members of the brigade referred to it as "Brigade 2506" after the number of a recruit who was killed making a parachute jump in training.

† The position of the Joint Chiefs was never clear. Hawkins was regarded as a top marine colonel, and his assignment to the operation was regarded by the CIA as evidence of joint participation in it by the chiefs. The chiefs did not see it this way, but the misunderstanding was not clarified at the time. Afterward "a very senior Admiral" told John A. Bross that "the assignment of the colonel was rather like a prominent hostess who lends her cook to a friend. If the cook burns the potatoes the hostess is sorry but hardly considers it her personal responsibility" (interview, John A. Bross, November 8, 1984).

like William Colby, had been parachuted behind enemy lines in France after D-Day. The war's end found him serving under Allen Dulles in Switzerland, and the two men remained firm friends. Within the CIA, Barnes was seen by colleagues as somewhat erratic, owing his senior position more to his social connections and friendship with Allen Dulles than to ability. Barnes and Hawkins were more familiar with making plans than with carrying them out. Barnes was excited by the prospect of success and did not seriously consider the prospect of failure. Hawkins did what he was told and assumed that if he was not specifically asked to do something, someone else would be doing it.

While these plans were being made Bissell was also heavily involved in the Corona/Discoverer project and the development of the SR-71. His chief of operations, Richard Helms, had distanced himself from the Cuban plan, worried that, successful or not, it would bring only notoriety to the agency. He even went so far as to air his doubts to Roger Hilsman, director of the State Department's Bureau of Intelligence and Research, indicating that the Cuban operation was mushrooming out of control. He claimed that Bissell had taken the project over for himself and was keeping Robert Amory (deputy director of intelligence) and Sherman Kent away from it.* Behind this was a growing difference between Bissell and Helms, leading to top-level agency discussions over Helms's future. The possibility of transferring Helms to London, where he would take over Frank Wisner's job as station chief, was raised. (The position was soon to be vacated by Wisner, who had become increasingly depressed.)[29] It was felt that Helms could not work productively with Bissell and was not

---

* Hilsman had been a distinguished World War II guerrilla officer and had rescued his own father from a Japanese prison camp. He was a highly intelligent, well-educated West Pointer. After the war he left the army, studied government, and became a professor of international affairs at Columbia. He joined the Kennedy administration and became assistant secretary of state for Far Eastern affairs. Helms was power-playing by going to Hilsman. He was also going to someone who was tough and who knew from personal experience what was involved in the Cuban plan: Hilsman could have argued effectively with Hawkins about military matters.

With Bissell's appointment as DDP Helms had become increasingly isolated from the covert-action programs, which more and more interested Bissell. Since covert action was the "fast track" within the agency, this isolation could have adversely affected Helms's career.

There was a precedent for taking the Cuban operation out of channels and handling it separately. Guatemala had been handled that way, and Bissell had played a part in that. In 1961 Bissell was clearly expected to succeed Allen Dulles as DCI. He knew the President, Bobby Kennedy, and McGeorge Bundy personally and belonged more or less to their generation rather than to Allen's. Dulles may very well have reasoned that it made sense to give Bissell a very loose rein: both the Iranian and Guatemalan operations had been substantially delegated and had worked. But there is still a question: Where was Dulles? At the crucial moments in the implementation of the plan Allen Dulles was not around. If the involvement of the DDI and Sherman Kent was important, it was Allen Dulles' responsibility to see that they were involved. At the same time it should be noted that Bissell, as DDP, had access to (and was responsible for obtaining most of) the data bearing on the depth and extent of internal resistance to Castro. What were missing, therefore, were the analytic facilities of the Directorate of Intelligence. Whether or not the involvement of the analysts in the detailed planning of the operation would have made a difference, John McCone, Dulles' successor as DCI, thought it might have and saw to it that their involvement in operations planning became an established feature of CIA methodology.

part of the "team." Especially disturbing was his lack of enthusiasm for the Cuban operation, which, Dulles believed, would establish the CIA's reputation with the new President and get rid of Castro too.

Helms' professional judgment and cool temperament enabled him to ride out this storm. He kept his position by sticking to basics. He insisted that James Angleton's counterintelligence section should be involved in maintaining the internal security of the Cuban operation.* He concentrated on running agents efficiently worldwide and confined himself to administrative requirements. On those rare occasions when he was asked for an opinion he provided hardheaded observations. Helms' reservations about the Bay of Pigs operation were well known to his friends within the agency. He advised some to stay away from the operation; he told others in no uncertain terms that if they even spoke to anyone on Bissell's team, he would never have anything to do with them again. "Bastard" is what he began calling Bissell in private.[30]

Impatient with the delays in the plans and with the backbiting politics of the office, Bissell and Barnes pressed ahead. They were determined to mount the operation as quickly as possible, aware that Castro probably knew all about it and that the Soviets were supplying Cuba with military equipment, including planes. In February 1960 Castro had signed a trade agreement with the USSR, eliminating Cuba's reliance on the American market for its sugar revenue. Further agreements were signed with East Germany and Poland. In July 1960 Soviet weapons began to arrive in Havana, and Khrushchev made his startling announcement: "In a figurative sense, if it became necessary, the Soviet military can support the Cuban people with rocket weapons."[31] Seven months later, after numerous delays, it was not surprising that Bissell and Barnes were anxious to act. One of the last moves Eisenhower made before leaving office was to break off diplomatic relations with Cuba, preparing the ground for U.S. recognition of a "provisional government" and speedy action should Kennedy decide to go ahead. The more time that passed without action, the more difficult it would be to maintain security and the better armed and prepared Castro would be.

The operational plan, although by no means perfect, was serviceable. It could have worked and probably would have worked had President Kennedy not interfered once it was under way. Bissell had convinced McGeorge Bundy of the virtue of the new plan: a landing to establish a beachhead with a defendable perimeter would be made. The landing force would be capable of

---

* This job became especially difficult after a CIA courier lost a briefcase full of secret CIA papers, including a list of agents and contacts in Cuba! It was difficult also because of the indiscretion of some of the participants. A secretary whose brother was in the FBI was staying in a hotel room next to Gerry Droller (who used the cover name "Frank Bender"), the CIA linkman with the Cuban exile leadership in Miami, where "La Brigada" was being assembled. When she overheard Droller discussing the operation she made notes and passed them to her brother, thus enabling J. Edgar Hoover to score points at the agency's expense.

maintaining its own air defense. Once the beachhead was secure, the Cuban government-in-exile, the anti-Batista, anti-Castro democrats waiting in Florida, would return and be recognized by the United States. Allen Dulles and Richard Bissell are clear that neither they nor anyone else in the CIA told the President that the landing of an exile force in Cuba was expected to trigger massive uprisings all over Cuba and bring down Castro.* Once the new "government"

---

* Lucien S. Vandenbroucke, "The 'Confessions' of Allen Dulles: New Evidence on the Bay of Pigs," Vol. 8, No. 4, *Diplomatic History* (Fall 1984), p. 367. Richard M. Bissell, Jr., "Response to Lucien S. Vandenbroucke's 'The "Confessions" of Allen Dulles: New Evidence on the Bay of Pigs,' " Vol. 8, No. 4, *Diplomatic History* (Fall 1984), pp. 379–380:

> [The] most discussed alleged misconception was the expectation that a successful landing would promptly detonate internal revolts within Cuba on a useful scale, and that these would facilitate consolidation of the beachhead and ultimate overthrow of the regime. . . .
> As Allen Dulles has stated more than once . . . it was neither his expectation nor that of those in charge of the operation that extensive internal resistance or uprising was to be expected until a beachhead had been seized, consolidated, held against attack by conventional forces, and endured whatever siege Castro could mount for at least some days.
> What was contemplated was a period in which the brigade's aircraft would totally dominate Cuban airspace, operating out of the strip on the beachhead, and would be used against strategic military targets (any remaining aircraft and armor), telecommunications (the telephone system relied heavily on microwave towers), and transportation. Radio transmissions from the beachhead would be used both to create confusion and to advertise Castro's inability to recapture it. Small diversionary landings would be made at remote locations on the island. Only after a week or more of this treatment was it anticipated that internal resistance might begin to materialize, probably more in the form of guerrilla action than of an uprising.
> The president, or other policymakers, may have formed an exaggerated impression of the contribution to be expected from spontaneous rebellion on the island, but there is no support in the record for the view that the CIA indulged in or promulgated such unrealistic optimism.

For a different view, see Arthur M. Schlesinger, Jr., *A Thousand Days: John F. Kennedy in the White House* (Boston: Houghton Mifflin, 1965), pp. 223-227:

> We all in the White House considered uprisings behind the lines essential to the success of the operation; so too did the Joint Chiefs of Staff; and so, we thought, did the CIA. . . . Obviously no one expected invasion to galvanize the unarmed and unorganized into rising against Castro at the moment of disembarkation. But the invasion plan, as understood by the President and the Joint Chiefs, did assume that the successful *occupation* of an enlarged beachhead area would rather soon incite *organized* uprisings by armed members of the Cuban resistance. . . .
> When questioned early in April about the prospects of internal resistance, instead of discounting it, which seems to have been [the view of Dulles and Bissell], they claimed that over 2500 persons presently belonged to resistance organizations, that 20,000 more were sympathizers, and that the Brigade, once established on the island, could expect the active support of, at the very least, a quarter of the Cuban people.

For Allen Dulles' only public statement of the CIA's view at the time, see Allen W. Dulles, *The Craft of Intelligence* (Westport, CT: Greenwood Press, 1977), p. 169: "Much of the American press assumed at the time that this action was predicated on a mistaken intelligence estimate to the effect that a landing would touch off a widespread and successful popular revolt in Cuba. . . . I know of no estimate that a spontaneous uprising of the unarmed population of Cuba would be touched off by the landing."

had established itself and was recognized, the plan was for its "army," with some overt U.S. support, to advance on Havana and take over the country. Together with Bundy, Bissell sold this plan to the President, telling him the exiles had a "good fighting chance, and no more."* They did not need to oversell it, they just sold it.[32]

Unfortunately, a serious misapprehension that flawed the plan was not recognized until it was too late: Kennedy had a much more limited understanding of military operations than his predecessor. General David M. Shoup, an independent-minded marine who disliked foreign interventions, sobered up White House discussions of the operation by asking Kennedy and his advisers, "Do any of you gentlemen know how big Cuba is?" Then, as they watched, he took an overlay of Cuba and placed it on top of a map of the United States. Kennedy and his team were surprised to see that Cuba was much bigger than Long Island. It stretched 800 miles from Washington, DC, to Chicago, a fact that in Shoup's view made an invasion a major undertaking. He had another overlay with a red dot, and he placed this one over Cuba. "What's that?" he was asked. "That, gentlemen, represents the size of the island of Tarawa," said Shoup, "and it took us three days and eighteen thousand marines to take it."†

The problem was that Kennedy did not have Eisenhower's understanding of what was and what was not required to make the operation a success. All he understood was that he should take it seriously, and this made him increasingly nervous. He began insisting that the operation be trimmed back for political reasons.

Neither Eisenhower nor Kennedy wanted the attempt to unseat Castro to be seen as an American operation. Both wanted Cubans to handle the actual fighting and logistics so that American recognition and support for the new "government," once it was set up, would be considered respectable. Accordingly the operation was planned so as to avoid any discernibly American support. However, America's dissociation from the invasion became increasingly

---

* Quoted in Vandenbroucke, "The 'Confessions' of Allen Dulles," p. 367. Dulles considered that it was simply untrue to say (as Theodore C. Sorensen and Arthur M. Schlesinger, Jr., had maintained publicly) that the Cuban venture failed because the CIA misled Kennedy into approving an ill-conceived plan. The real cause of the failure, in Dulles' view, was the lack of "determination to succeed" evidenced by the White House. Dulles believed that Kennedy, fearing "some unpleasant political repercussion," consistently tried to reduce the visibility and scale of the operation, eventually fatally weakening the plan. Theodore C. Sorensen ("Kennedy's Worst Disaster: Bay of Pigs," Look, August 10, 1965, pp. 43–50) and Arthur M. Schlesinger, Jr. ("The Bay of Pigs: A Horribly Expensive Lesson," Life, July 25, 1965, pp. 65–70) argue that Kennedy's military and intelligence advisers seriously misled the President on the prospects of the invasion force and the logistical requirements of the force.

† Shoup, who had won the Medal of Honor at Tarawa, was commandant of the Marine Corps, and had Kennedy decided to involve American armed forces directly, it would have been Shoup's men who would have borne the brunt of fighting on the beachhead. His bravery in World War II impressed Kennedy, as did his forthrightness. He was to become Kennedy's favorite general. See David Halberstam, The Best and the Brightest (Greenwich, CT: Fawcett Crest, 1973), p. 85.

difficult to achieve as the pressure to launch the operation mounted. In the drive to get the invasion started Bissell and Barnes found it impossible to come up with the cover stories needed by the B-26 bombers that were providing the air support. As a result of this failure, there were direct connections between the planes, their pilots, and the CIA.

In order to avoid political embarrassment should this connection become known, Kennedy intervened to reduce the role of the B-26s and air support generally. Eisenhower, in contrast, had worried that not enough time was being allowed to train "La Brigada." He preferred to postpone the invasion to provide the necessary training time and to give Kennedy the opportunity to review the plan when preparations were complete. This was typical of Eisenhower. He had gained a reputation in the army for preparing fully for contingencies and for refusing to be stampeded into hasty or risky decisions. Kennedy, however, excited by the possibilities and unfamiliar with military complexities, preferred to go ahead as quickly as possible, modifying arrangements only where his political antennae warned of danger.

It was also Kennedy's decision to go for a military as opposed to a traditional covert operation. He threw out the detailed system of committees and staff work instituted by Eisenhower and sought direct control himself, establishing a "War Room" in the White House, insisting on detailed personal briefings, himself telephoning desk officers in the State Department and the CIA for information. A study of the Operations Coordinating Board completed two days before Kennedy took office and named after the board's chairman, Mansfield Sprague, had strongly recommended the continuation of the board (Eisenhower's method of overseeing foreign operations as they were implemented). The report was scrapped and the board abolished two days after Kennedy's inauguration. A network of what came to be called "floating crap games" was substituted for the planning and program-approval system that had been laboriously built up and fine-tuned under Eisenhower. The new system was one that gave the new President much greater apparent control.[33]

David Atlee Phillips, who had organized the anti-Arbenz radio station that broadcast to Guatemala during the coup there, was involved in a similar operation with the Bay of Pigs. His work in Guatemala successfully confused the Arbenz administration and created a sense of depression and defeat in Arbenz before he was actually ousted. With the same purpose in mind, Phillips established an anti-Castro "Cuban" radio station—Radio Swan—on Swan Island, located between Cuba and Central America, and stayed in close touch with the organizers of the landing:

> At the very beginning of April . . . I went to the War Room of the paramilitary officers, an inner sanctum within the inner sanctum of the Cuba task force. . . .
> "There's been a change in the plan," Colonel Alcott said. "Trinidad is

out. Now we are going to land here." The colonel touched an area on the coast one hundred miles west of Trinidad. I squinted to read the fine type. Despite years in Cuba, I had never heard of the place.

"Bahía de Cochinos?" I laughed. This really must be April Fool. "How can we have a victorious landing force wading ashore at a place with that name? How can propagandists persuade Cubans to join the Brigade at the 'Bay of Pigs'?"

The colonel was not concerned with the exigencies of psychological warfare. "That's the new plan," he repeated. . . . "The first ships to land will carry tanks."

"Tanks!" I was stunned. "We're going to mount a secret operation in the Caribbean with tanks?"

"That's right," said the colonel. "A company. Three platoons of five each, and two command tanks." . . .

What had been conceived as a classic guerrilla warfare operation with individual fighters carrying their own weapons had been converted only a few weeks before D-Day into an amphibious landing of tanks on Cuban beaches. *Dean Rusk had persuaded President Kennedy that political risks made unacceptable the plan of landing near a town where women and children might be hurt and where there was no airstrip which could explain the flights of exile B-26 planes.*[34]

D-Day was to be April 17, 1961. Kennedy asked the Joint Chiefs of Staff to review the plans in February, and they reported back that "La Brigada" seemed capable of handling the operation.[35] On April 4 Kennedy polled his advisers.* With the single exception of Senator Fulbright, they agreed that the invasion should proceed.

However, as Arthur M. Schlesinger, Jr., later recalled, a cold-war atmosphere pervaded White House discussions on Latin America at this time, with the result that the communist threat to Latin America was seen in the same terms as the Nazi-Fascist menace there in the 1930s.[36] Latin America was regarded with such disdain that it was seen as a patsy for any strong, totalitarian threat. Throughout the period, there was constant talk of prewar "appeasement" in the White House; the "Munich model" was a feature of Kennedy attitudes. The new administration was not going to cave in to threats or bullies and was going to act forcefully to meet them in the field. The President gave his approval for the invasion to proceed, reserving his right to change his mind and the plans later if need be.

Kennedy's decision reflected the tone of his entire presidency; he and his

---

* Secretary of State Dean Rusk; Secretary of Defense Robert McNamara; Secretary of the Treasury Douglas Dillon; General Lyman Lemnitzer, chairman of the Joint Chiefs of Staff; Thomas C. Mann, assistant secretary of state for inter-American affairs; Adolf Berle, chairman of the Kennedy Task Force on Latin America; Arthur M. Schlesinger, Jr., special assistant to the President specializing in Latin American affairs; Richard Goodwin, a member of the Latin America Task Force and Kennedy's personal White House staff; and Senator William Fulbright.

advisers shared a tendency to choose action over inaction. The more cautious counsels of Fulbright and, later, Adlai Stevenson were out of step in the 1961 White House. One CIA man, who had voted for Kennedy and was intimately involved with the Bay of Pigs operation, believed this was a key point: "Kennedy was surrounded by a lot of action-oriented people like Mac Bundy who wanted to go forward, not backward. He was overwhelmed by them, and both the President and Bobby Kennedy listened to them when they perhaps should have listened to the cautious counsels of Fulbright. Everybody in the White House was involved. The agency and the White House went down the road together. Arthur Schlesinger was involved. There were eight, nine, or ten people in the White House constantly phoning for reports."[37]

As the men of "La Brigada" with their ships, tanks, and supplies sailed from Guatemala, where they had been trained in a secret camp, Kennedy's political worries increased. When Adlai Stevenson, ambassador to the United Nations, learned of the operation around April 10, he strongly argued to the President that the invasion would cause an outcry in the United Nations which would result in a loss of support for the Alliance for Progress, the Kennedy scheme for combating Marxism in the Americas by identifying the United States with indigenous democratic progressive movements. The undersecretary of state, Chester Bowles, also opposed the plan when he found out about it. After the invasion a story circulated in Washington that when Bobby Kennedy ran into Bowles in the White House, he jammed three fingers into Bowles's stomach and told him in a level, tough voice that "he, Bowles, was for the invasion, remember that, he was for it, they were all for it."[38]

Perhaps Bobby also was nervous, realizing that the failure of the invasion would be linked directly to the President. Bobby was a Boston-Irish politician. He saw Bowles as a prissy New Englander who had to be made to understand that when things are bad you need group loyalty and should act as a group. Bowles was not going to get out of it as far as Bobby was concerned. Jack Kennedy took exactly the same view. In a postmortem session McGeorge Bundy reminded the President that Arthur Schlesinger had written a memorandum opposing the Bay of Pigs expedition. "Oh sure," said Kennedy. "Arthur wrote me a memorandum that will look pretty good when he gets round to writing his book on my administration. Only he better not publish that memorandum while I'm still alive."[39]

The plan hinged on destroying Castro's planes—Castro had made the mistake of concentrating his air force at one base—and supporting the invasion force from the air. When all was said and done, this would ensure some measure of military success for "La Brigada" even if the invasion failed politically. Part of the CIA's calculation was that when it was seen that the United States was involved, Cubans would fall away from Castro.

The first air strike was scheduled for April 15. On April 12 President Kennedy publicly stated that the United States would not intervene militarily in Cuba. On April 13 he ordered that the air strike had to appear as if it had originated in Cuba with defecting Castro pilots rather than with exile planes from Central America. This was done, with a cover story prepared at the last minute to explain two B-26 bombers, actually flown from Nicaragua, landing in Key West, Florida, as if they had defected from Cuba having shot up their own airfields. One newsman noticed that there was still protective tape over their machine guns: they had not been fired.

At the United Nations, Raul Roa, the Cuban foreign minister, denounced the bombings and the cover story as an American plot. Adlai Stevenson, not having been told any details and under the impression that Kennedy had decided to delay the operation, made an emotional and effective speech refuting Roa's charges. Kennedy asked Bissell what the last moment would be when he could cancel the invasion. He was told midday on Sunday, April 16. When the time came Kennedy gave the green light. However, hours later he ordered that there be no air strike. According to some sources Kennedy changed his mind after Stevenson, furious at being misled over the April 15 "defectors'" air strike, insisted on Sunday afternoon that the invasion be canceled. Unable to cancel the whole operation, Kennedy halted the air strike. Other sources say that Dean Rusk told the President the same afternoon that after the UN debate, air strikes that could be linked to the United States would seriously embarrass American diplomacy in Latin America.[40] In the end the air strikes, which had already caused political difficulties and were likely to cause more, were canceled by the President without regard to their military necessity.

To a man, every participant in the CIA agreed that this decision was fatal to the operation. "Those of us working in the operation did not expect the Cuban people to rise up and throw Castro out," said David Atlee Phillips. "In the event, the lack of air cover was crucial."[41] "Kennedy began to insist on the operation being trimmed back," said Richard Helms, "and when they finally took the air cover away, they had denuded it. Whether it would have worked according to the original plan I have no idea. But one thing is for sure: it had no chance of working the way it was finally whittled down."[42] And according to Richard Bissell:

> The plan called for strategic bombing to take out the whole telephone system, which was a microwave system, so you knock down some pylons and take out some communication lines—railways, bridges—and attack the big installation to the south of Havana, where most of Castro's armor was parked. Meanwhile you would suppress any Castro aviation on the airfields and any naval activities; there was one Castro naval vessel on the south coast which we thought might have made trouble. And it seemed possible to do all these things if Castro's planes were knocked out, if we did have complete command of the air. And we had a reasonable force of B-26s. There was a clear understanding, at least as far as I was concerned, that the force would not be strong enough to take the island over from Castro: it would have to

rely on other kinds of things. What we were talking about was strategic air action giving rise to extreme disorganization and disorientation in the regime—this was the Guatemala example. We had eighteen operational B-26s and crews. The expectation was that we would be able in three strikes to hit around forty targets.

Some days before the operation, strike number two was canceled, and that put us back. We expected eighteen sorties on the first and maybe fifteen on the second. Then on the Friday, Kennedy dropped a bombshell when he told me he didn't want the first strike on Saturday in full force, he wanted a muted strike. I said, "What, exactly, does that mean?" and he said, "I have to leave that to you, but I don't want you to use full force." So that cut down to eight or nine sorties. And then on the Sunday afternoon he canceled the third strike entirely. So from an expectation of some forty sorties, we were down to eight or nine actually accomplished. I cannot avoid the impression that if we'd had anything like the forty sorties, we really would have knocked out Castro's air. We would have been more effective by a factor of four. I think that did have a definite bearing on the outcome.[43]

Effective air cover and command were essential for the success of the amphibious operation, Bissell and Allen Dulles agreed. "I didn't see to it," said Dulles afterward, "that everyone understood beyond doubt that air cover for the landing was an 'absolute' prerequisite."[44] "Why did the Americans fail?" a newsman asked Fidel Castro some years later. "They had no air support," he replied.[45] The lack of air support was the visible sign that Kennedy had lost his nerve and would not follow through.

"La Brigada" landed without air cover or the strategic bombing Bissell had planned to precede the landing, fought for three days, and surrendered to Castro's army after 114 of its number had been killed—about one man in ten of the force—and more wounded, thirty-six of whom later died. Within hours of the landing at dawn on Monday, April 17, at Zapata, on the Bay of Pigs, Castro's planes, unopposed in the air, sank two Brigade transports, one of which carried most of the Brigade's ammunition. Kennedy approved an air strike on Tuesday morning, but low clouds protected the targets. Three of the B-26s were shot down and others were damaged.

On Tuesday night the President hosted a black-tie dinner for congressmen at the White House. The dinner was interrupted when Bissell sent word that he had to see Kennedy. Starting at midnight, Bissell argued with the President for two hours that air cover was essential and that since the B-26 pilots were exhausted after hours of futile flying on Tuesday, and since several planes had been lost or damaged, U.S. Navy planes on the U.S.S. *Boxer*, about fifty miles from the Bay of Pigs, should be called in to give supportive action. "Kennedy and his aides were still dressed in evening clothes," remembered Phillips, who was there with Bissell. "Rusk voted no, as did civilian White House aides. The military advisers were for it. Kennedy chose to compromise.

The navy jets, the President said, could fly over the beach the next morning for one hour, to protect landing craft and to permit the Brigade B-26s to strike again at Castro's air force and the Cuban ground forces which were converging on the beach."[46] The next morning there was a mistiming, and the B-26s arrived while the *Boxer's* fighters were still on deck. Two more B-26s were shot down. At sea the Brigade supply ships were subjected to unimpeded attack by Castro's air force; the President had ordered that while U.S. planes could protect Brigade B-26s and ships, they could not fire at Cuban planes or ground targets. Peter Wyden, a historian of the operation, described the result:

> The Navy airmen on the carrier *Essex* had been confined to a maddening spectator role. On Tuesday Commander Mike Griffin landed his "Blue Blasters" A4D jet on the flight deck and came up to the bridge to report to Captain Searcy. Griffin had just overflown the beach area and helplessly watched the Brigade being driven back to the sea. Searcy was shocked by the pilot's appearance. Griffin's face was blue. Tears were running down it without restraint. He was so angry and upset that it took a couple of minutes before he could utter a word. "I hate to see a grown man cry, but I didn't blame him," Searcy said later. The captain was "surprised" that some of the pilots didn't take the battle into their own hands and drop bombs against orders. He "wouldn't have blamed them."[47]

The location of the invasion also contributed to the failure. Moving the landing area from the coastal town of Trinidad to the Bay of Pigs only weeks before the operation had left little time to research the terrain. Shoals and reefs that had not been properly charted impeded the landing of the invasion force and the supply transports that came later. In addition, the Zapata marshland made ground movement difficult. It quickly became clear that the Bay of Pigs was not a suitable beachhead from which to expand and within which a "provisional government" could be established. "The preferred landing site at Trinidad had been changed," Allen Dulles later argued, "*without a full realization at the top* that this greatly reduced the 'guerrilla' alternative since it was far removed from the area in the Escambray, the best guerrilla territory, and also by being a more quiet landing reduced the chance of bringing about a revolt or defections to the landing places. In fact the [invasion] required a well-publicized landing so that the people of Cuba ... could have a clear knowledge of what was in progress."[48] In Richard Bissell's opinion, moving the landing site had a fatal effect once Kennedy decided not to involve U.S. forces directly, because the marshland seriously reduced the ability of "La Brigada" to retreat into the Escambray mountains.[49]

These difficulties could have been overcome, however, if the Brigade had received substantial military support; but this was not to happen for understandable political reasons. "The clear and grave mistake that was made by everybody involved in the operation," said Richard Bissell, "—it was made very much by me and Allen; it was made by Kennedy himself; it was made by Rusk; it was made by just about everybody—was this: we came to believe that if an operation couldn't be tied in a court of law to the U.S. government, it would be disclaimable, and that that was important."[50]

Kennedy was only ninety days into his presidency and still enjoyed a remarkably friendly relationship with the press (this began to change only in 1963). *The New York Times* had the story of America's involvement with the Cuban exiles and "La Brigada" days before the landing took place and decided to suppress it in the national interest.[51] However, as events were to demonstrate, the United States was too closely involved in the operation to disavow it, whether it succeeded or not. The political naïveté of this view was extraordinary; everybody would know the United States was behind the operation. Richard Bissell said:

> The fact of the matter is that the press had been full of stories that a landing was planned. There was no way it could have been carried out without ninety-nine people out of every hundred in the entire world attributing it correctly to the U.S. government. The question I raise with hindsight—I can't say I was wise about it at the time—is, "What the hell do you think you're doing buying used B-26s that are obsolescent instead of some more modern aircraft? What were we doing by not using some long-range fighters to protect the B-26s? What were we doing by refusing to allow perhaps fifty U.S. volunteers to go in with the Brigade, for stiffening and direction and training? What did we buy with all the hocus-pocus?" My point is that even when Kennedy said he was not going to have U.S. troops in uniform, under the U.S. flag, involved in the invasion, I should have said "All right, but then at least we've got to use our full resources to train and arm and equip the Cuban outfit so that when the day comes at least they'll have everything going for them."[52]

In Bissell's view, this was the most serious misconception of the operation:

> The first, most pervasive, and, I would argue, most damaging misconception was that the covert character of the operation could be maintained. . . . It was this misconception that gave rise to a whole sequence of requirements and limitations on operational flexibility in the interest of preserving the impression of the operation as a strictly Cuban affair. Thus there was to be no use made of facilities, personnel, or up-to-date equipment which could have been made available only by the U.S. government and would, if revealed or captured, constitute proof of official U.S. sponsorship.[53]

At that time Bissell and other CIA officers were becoming increasingly concerned about the effect of the air strike restrictions on the success of the operation, but they all decided to stay aboard and do their best. David Atlee Phillips recalled one discussion before the landing:

"You gentlemen are masquerading as experts in overthrowing a government," Bill said caustically. "Have any of you entertained the notion that this damned thing might not work?" We were all uncomfortable. Bill, with his customary candor, had broached what many of us had contemplated but all of us left unsaid. Cliff clamped his cigar in his teeth. Len squirmed in his chair, adjusting his artificial leg. Colonel Alcott appeared to be offended.

Abe removed his bifocals and cleaned them thoroughly with his napkin. "What can we do?" I asked Bill.

"Not go back," Bill said. "We cannot go back to Quarters Eye. We can stay right here and drink brandy, and when Bissell shows up in Cliff's office there will be no one to run the show. Without us, it won't go."

It was quiet for a long time. Finally Cliff finished his brandy.

"Come on," he said, "let's go back."

"Why?" someone asked.

"You know why," the task force chief said. *"Because we're good soldiers, that's why."**

Bissell himself, well aware of the prospects of failure, persuaded people not to quit. Plans were too far along to be abandoned. They might as well stay and try to make the best of it.[54] "I think neither Colonel Hawkins nor myself," said Bissell, "seriously contemplated calling the whole thing off. This is probably where we made the big mistake. But one becomes emotionally and psychologically committed, and things have a momentum of their own."†

Allen Dulles later conceded that neither he nor anyone else in the CIA attempted to correct Kennedy's belief that the landing would be a quiet affair because they calculated (incorrectly, as it turned out) that the President would do what was necessary for the operation to succeed once it was underway:

> [We] never raised objections to repeated emphasis [by the President] that the operation: a) must be carried through without any 'combat' action by the U.S.A. military forces; b) must remain quiet [and] disavowable by the U.S. government; c) must be a quiet operation yet must cause internal revolt vs. Castro and create a center to which anti-Castroites will defect. . . . [We] did not want to raise these issues—in an [undecipherable word] discussion— which might only harden the decision against the type of action we required. We felt that when the chips were down—when the crisis arose in reality, any action required for success would be authorized rather than permit the enterprise to fail.

* Phillips, *The Night Watch*, p. 104. "Colonel Alcott" is the pseudonym Phillips uses for Colonel Hawkins. "Bill" is Dick Drain, an operations officer. "Abe" is Jim Flannery, Bissell's staff officer for the operation. "Len" was Flannery's deputy. "Cliff" was the task force chief. Quarters Eye was one of the temporary buildings erected during World War II in the Mall by the reflecting pool between the Lincoln Memorial and the Washington Monument. It was the headquarters of the CIA planners. Quarters Eye itself faced the Potomac off Ohio Drive. See also Peter Wyden, *Bay of Pigs: The Untold Story* (London: Jonathan Cape, 1979), pp. 158–160, who places the lunch at Napoleon's Restaurant in Washington, DC.

† Interview, Richard M. Bissell, Jr., July 18, 1983. These were gentlemen at work, faced with the traditions of speaking out or not speaking out and having to deal with those who violated the code. A gentleman keeps his word, Bissell was saying.

In a sense we were right. If only half the military help had been made available to get the Brigade and its equipment safely ashore that was later shown in trying to rescue and later liberate the Brigade, there would have been a good chance of success.

We believed that in a time of crisis we would gain what we might lose if we provoked an argument. . . . I have seen a good many operations which started out like the B[ay] of P[igs]—insistence on complete secrecy—noninvolvement of the U.S.—initial reluctance to authorize supporting actions. This limitation tends to disappear as the needs of the operation become clarified.*

President Kennedy needed to be "educated." Eisenhower had placed a heavy reliance on covert operations by the CIA, establishing a tradition that Kennedy never showed any signs of wanting to change. It was reasonable to expect that Kennedy would follow Eisenhower's lead; he made it clear often enough that he was interested only in success. And in his personal advisers Kennedy had highly intelligent men who prided themselves on alerting him to the nuances of situations. Allen Dulles and the CIA were simply doing what they were asked to do. They were being good soldiers, anxious to keep nonexperts from interfering in their plans once the operation was approved. If Kennedy did not want the operation to take place, he always had the option of canceling it.

It was not decisiveness but indecisiveness that led to failure. There was a failure of nerve all around once the operation had started. Tracy Barnes later told a story about how he was standing outside Dean Rusk's office when Rusk, who was with Bissell and Pearré Cabell, the deputy director of Central Intelligence, telephoned Kennedy. Both CIA men argued strongly with Rusk to convince Kennedy of the need for the planned second air strike which the

---

* Quoted in Vandenbroucke, "The 'Confessions' of Allen Dulles," pp. 369–370. It would be wrong to interpret Dulles' statement as meaning that the CIA had taken a policy-making role unto itself unknown to the President or other senior policy makers. He was concerned with the integrity of operational planning and execution once the operation itself had been approved. Vandenbroucke argued this point: "They appear to have assumed the unauthorized role of de facto policy-makers, acting as if, in the covert war against Castro and communism, key decisions rested with them rather than with the nation's elected leaders" (ibid., p. 371).

Bissell pointed out:

This is an allegation about motives. As such, it can be neither proved nor disproved. . . . Vandenbroucke is entirely correct, however, in pointing out that an eager operational group, presenting a plan of action, can and must be expected to put on its best face. If there are to be operational plans in government, or elsewhere, there have to be enthusiastic people to conceive them, develop them, submit them for approval, and become advocates in the process. For these people to put their best foot forward in policy discussion, so long as the facts and the assumptions on which projections rest are honestly and accurately presented, does not constitute the willful misleading of the policymakers who must finally decide whether the plans are to be carried out (Bissell, "Response to Lucien S. Vandenbroucke," p. 380).

It should also be noted that the whole operation was preceded by widespread leaks and publicity, so many of Kennedy's worries had in fact been overtaken by the time he gave approval for the operation to commence.

President had just canceled. "I'm not signed on to this," Kennedy had said. Only "overriding considerations" would make him change his mind. Rusk had agreed with Kennedy and had himself urged cancellation. Bissell, who was particularly worried by the cancellation, told Rusk that "the landing was committed. It was too late to call it off." The success of the operation required the air strike.

"Well, all right," Rusk finally agreed. "I will call the President again." Kennedy wanted to know if the planned second air strike was really necessary for the operation, which was then under way, to succeed. Rusk said that he considered the strike would be "important, but not critical. . . . But I am still recommending that we cancel." He listened to Kennedy for a moment and then turned to Cabell.

"Well, the President agrees with me, but would you, General Cabell, like to speak to the President?"

"Well, you've put it to the President a second time," Cabell replied. "I don't think he's going to override your recommendation."

Bissell tried to press the point. "Do you think he realizes I agree with you?" he said to Cabell.

Cabell shrugged. "There's no point in my talking to the President."

It was over: the cancellation stood. Rusk rang off.*

Bissell stated:

> There was no negligent failure by the intelligence and military advisers to inform President Kennedy and other senior policymakers about weaknesses in the invasion plan, with the exception of the absence of a contingency plan for an initial defeat.
>
> There were, to be sure, assumptions which turned out to be inaccurate but nevertheless represented the best honest judgement of those in charge of the operation. For instance, the president was never told that the brigade's air arm was potentially inadequate for its task, but this was because the project planners' analysis was defective, to their ruin, and not because either facts or

---

* Quoted in Wyden, *Bay of Pigs*, pp. 199-200. Where was Dulles? This was a vital moment. Bissell, "Response to Lucien S. Vandenbroucke," p. 379:

> As the process of whittling away the authorization for strategic air attacks continued during the planning phase, it was difficult for the operators to specify the exact minimum level of activity that would be adequate but below which cancellation of the project should be recommended. The inherent margin of error and uncertainty is much too large to permit such a black or white operational judgment. In the event, the project's military commander believed after the D-2 strike that the attempt was worth making, with the one additional full-strength strike planned and authorized until late on D-1 for D-day. By the time it was canceled, the brigade was already entering the Bay of Pigs. The Taylor Committee report was probably correct in concluding that Cabell and Bissell were negligent in failing to make a last attempt to persuade the president by telephone to reverse his decision. Be that as it may, it can hardly be claimed that those in charge of the operation either suffered from this particular misconception or tolerated it in policy discussions. They thought themselves overruled on the basis of political considerations.

judgements were being concealed. The overriding example was the failure of the agency to call attention to the absurdity of attempting to maintain plausible disclaimability, which the policymakers should have been able to judge for themselves, or the costs in terms of operational effectiveness that this policy imposed. . . .

Many of us, like Dulles himself, believed there was a possibility that, in the event of trouble, restrictions would be relaxed, possibly even on the use of U.S. aircraft. The profound hope and expectation in the CIA was that there would not be a crisis which would call for such a drastic policy change. There was never any trace of a conspiratorial alternative operational plan based on the assumption that the president's hand would be forced.[55]

The end of the operation was confirmed in Washington on Wednesday, April 19. As David Phillips remembered:

> The task force officers in Quarters Eye were in direct communication with the Brigade commander on the beach. Cliff, who had known the commander and many of the Brigade officers, was white with remorse and fatigue. Colonel Alcott held one hand across his face, as if hiding. Len scratched his wrists viciously; blood stained his cuffs and darkened his fingernails. Bill left the War Room; later he said he had vomited in a wastebasket.
>
> The Brigade commander radioed that he was standing in the shallows. "I have nothing left to fight with. . . . Am headed for the swamp." He cursed. The radio was dead. It was over.[56]

For the CIA, however, it was far from over. Allen Dulles and Richard Bissell were held primarily responsible for the failure.* Dulles was given time to resign with dignity, which he did seven months later. Bissell, despite being a Kennedy friend, first learned that his resignation also was expected from James "Scotty" Reston, *The New York Times* Washington correspondent and a Kennedy intimate, who had been told the news by the President at a White House dinner before anyone else. The official word came from Allen Dulles and McGeorge Bundy. "I went in to see Kennedy, and by that time I had been told it was definite," recalled Bissell. "It wasn't to see him to discuss it—it was in effect to say goodbye. He said, 'In a parliamentary government I would resign. In this government the President can't and doesn't and so you and Allen must go.' The unstated but obvious and valid premise was that where there has been a major boo-boo, somebody has to go."[57]

Before Bissell could officially resign he was asked in December 1961 by John McCone, the new DCI, to stay on as DDP for a while. McCone's wife had died, and the new director was unsure whether he would remain in the job.

---

* The man most responsible for inadequacies in the operational plan and for not alerting his civilian superiors in the CIA to them was Colonel Hawkins. He was brought in as the expert and he did an inexpert job.

He wanted Bissell to support him while he was there and to provide an element of continuity. In the new year, with the backing of the President, McCone asked Bissell not to leave the CIA after all but to stay on as deputy director for science and technology (DDS&T). Bissell's extraordinary achievements with the U-2, Corona/Discoverer, and the continuing development of the A-12/XF-12/SR-71 had, in the balance, more than offset any mistakes he had made in organizing the Bay of Pigs invasion. After thinking about McCone's offer for a few days Bissell decided to reject it and leave the agency as planned. Part of the reason he said no was that DDS&T was a less important position than deputy director for plans, the unofficial number-two spot in the agency. In an organization as tightly knit as the CIA it would have been uncomfortable for Bissell to be removed from operations he knew so much about. Particularly sensitive were the operations involving the post-Bay of Pigs attempts to kill Castro.*

CASTRO

Within days of the Bay of Pigs collapse President Kennedy privately admitted his share of responsibility for it. He blamed himself for listening to experts rather than reaching his own conclusions and, alone with his wife, broke down and cried. He told William Manchester that he could see but two consolations for the blunder:

> The first was that he had lost all illusions about the Joint Chiefs' infallibility. Their future opinions would be received skeptically, subjected to ruthless scrutiny, and weighed against the judgment of experienced civilians. The second consolation arrived on May 3, two weeks after the calamity. Kennedy was remarking on the difference between British and American forms of democracy. Had he been prime minister in England, he said, his government would have fallen and he would have been evicted from his home. At that point [his secretary] arrived with an advance copy of the latest Gallup poll. The figures showed an unprecedented 83 percent of the American people behind him. He tossed it aside and sighed. "It's just like Eisenhower," he said. "The worse I do, the more popular I get."[58]

Elspeth Rostow, observing her husband as he returned from the White House exhausted and exhilarated by the post-Bay of Pigs crisis, said to him, "You

---

* After leaving the agency Bissell came back on contract to undertake a study of some National Security Agency operations that had been commissioned by the director of Central Intelligence and the Department of Defense. The chief cryptanalyst at the NSA told John A. Bross that "after working with Bissell for several weeks, [he concluded that] in his entire career he had met only one other individual with Bissell's capability to assimilate and correlate complex data" (interview, John A. Bross, November 8, 1984).

know what you all are? You are junior officers of the Second World War come to responsibility."*

Discharging this responsibility in relation to the CIA fell to Robert Kennedy, who within days was inside the agency's headquarters grilling everyone involved. On Friday, April 21, President Kennedy phoned General Maxwell Taylor, who had retired from the army as Chief of Staff under Eisenhower and then written a book, *The Uncertain Trumpet*, criticizing U.S. defense policy, and asked him to come to Washington the next day. In the Oval Office on Saturday, Taylor, who at the time was president of the Lincoln Center for the Performing Arts in New York, supervising its construction, accepted the President's request to head a presidential investigation into the Bay of Pigs affair. At about the same time Lyman Kirkpatrick, the inspector general of the CIA, initiated an inspector general's investigation within the agency. Tracy Barnes organized an in-house DDP postmortem investigation as well.

Everybody recognized that the Bay of Pigs was a major turning point for the CIA and for the new administration. To the Kennedys the CIA now seemed like a windmill, and they felt that they might have been spun into trouble by the agency. "It is a hell of a way to learn things," said Kennedy, "but I have learned one thing from this business—that is, that we will have to deal with CIA. McNamara has dealt with Defense; Rusk has done a lot with State; but no one has dealt with CIA."[59] On another occasion he said, "I've made a terrible mistake,"[60] and he immediately took steps to punish the agency. He began by redefining its mandate, transferring paramilitary actions to the Department of Defense and restricting the size of the Directorate of Plans within the CIA. He also threatened to reduce the CIA's budget.[61]

The Kennedys, however, were in love with the clandestine world. "Robert

---

* Quoted in Wyden, *Bay of Pigs*, p. 306. Joseph Burkholder Smith, an officer in the DDP not involved in the Bay of Pigs, with hindsight blamed his colleagues in the agency for "arrogance."

The Cuban task force claimed that when President Kennedy and his advisers had ruled against the involvement of any back-up U.S. air support on April 5, 1961, they knew the doom of the invasion forces had been sealed. Why didn't they tell the President they thought they were going to fail ten days later? Why didn't they tell him that the invasion should be called off?

A second flaw in all of us, in those days of great adventure, was career opportunism. "If you win you'll be known as the second Ed Lansdale," someone told me during the Philippine election campaign of 1959 . . . . Bissell would have been the next Director of the CIA if he successfully engineered the Bay of Pigs operation. All the officers down the line were keenly aware of what a victory over Castro would mean to them.

Smith goes on to say that subsequently, with the exceptions of Bissell and Dulles, everyone connected with the Bay of Pigs seemed to be promoted and favored within the agency (Smith, *Portrait of a Cold Warrior*, pp. 320, 346). He did not understand that the operation might have failed because of Kennedy's decisions or that it is the nature of institutions to disguise failure. See also Phillips, *The Night Watch*, p. 113. Phillips tendered his resignation to Bissell after the operation, and Bissell replied by dictating a memorandum for Phillips' personnel file recommending him for promotion.

Kennedy, in his shirtsleeves, delved into the inner workings of the agency," recalled one CIA man who was grilled by Bobby about his part in the Bay of Pigs. "In the end he did not shake it up as his brother had wanted, but fell in love with the CIA and the concept of clandestine operation."[62] Jack Kennedy realized, as he told Clark Clifford—an influential and trusted Kennedy adviser and Democratic power broker—"I have to have the best possible intelligence"[63] and soon reversed his decision to punish the CIA. Both brothers saw that alone of the agencies of government the CIA was willing to take action and had tried to do in Cuba what the President wanted (the subsequent White House-inspired attempts to overthrow Castro bore witness to this fact). The Bay of Pigs failure meant that the agency would not resist tighter control. Rejection of the agency was not necessary: the windmill was theirs to turn and direct. They were determined to make it work under their close direction.

Robert Lovett, who had served on Eisenhower's President's Board of Consultants on Foreign Intelligence Activities and who had been consistently critical of the agency's organization under Allen Dulles, was called in by Kennedy for advice. Lovett told him the CIA was badly organized, dangerously amateurish, and excessively costly. In his view, it should be cut down, reorganized, and restricted. It should run, he said, in a hard-boiled fashion.[64] The President decided that his brother Bobby should head the CIA; he was tough enough and dependable enough to do the job. Bobby refused, convinced that his appointment to a nonpolitical post would not be wise: "Allen Dulles handled himself awfully well," Bobby recalled, "with a great deal of dignity and never tried to shift the blame. The President was very fond of him, as I was. . . . The President spoke to me about becoming head of the CIA, and I said I didn't want to become head of the CIA and I thought it was a bad idea to be head of CIA, in addition, because I was a Democrat, and brother."[65] The President gave his brother informal responsibility over the whole intelligence community instead, and after months of searching, John McCone was appointed to succeed Allen Dulles.

McCone had no connection with the Kennedys and was a Republican. He had worked as an assistant to James Forrestal in 1947 and had been closely involved with the creation of the CIA. He was a convert to Catholicism and, like Kennedy, was a determined cold warrior, seeing communism as evil. Further changes took place with the 5412 Committee, chaired by General Maxwell Taylor, which was given special oversight of CIA covert action. Richard Helms, whose career had been based on secret-intelligence expertise rather than on covert operations, replaced Bissell as DDP. Eisenhower's Board of Consultants, which had disbanded with Kennedy's inauguration, was reconstituted as the President's Foreign Intelligence Advisory Board, with James R. Killian, Jr., as chairman and Clark Clifford as a member. Clifford succeeded Killian as chairman in 1963.

One of Kennedy's first actions as President had been to call up Allen

Dulles and ask to be introduced to America's "James Bond." He loved the Ian
Fleming thrillers and was much taken by the character and style of the suave
British agent. The request was an indication of what was to be the nature of
the Kennedy administration. It was concerned with virile action and it was
prepared to give action men great scope. Only toward the end of his presidency
did Kennedy begin to question the objectives and the nature of derring-do.
Neither he nor his brother ever understood the strength of restraint: their be-
quest from Eisenhower. Instead they regarded Ike as having been an old and
ineffective President who had not realized America's potential to change the
world. They were determined to use the potential fully.

Bobby Kennedy concentrated his attention on the 5412 Committee, announcing it was going to direct the CIA's covert activities. He apparently believed that his efforts would reverberate within the agency, improving its
organization and management and making it more hard-boiled and tough in
the process. Bobby Kennedy wanted to achieve what the CIA had failed to
do—remove Fidel Castro from power. Precisely because of the Bay of Pigs failure, Bobby was determined to prove that the United States and President Kennedy could pursue a course of action—in this case the elimination of
Castro—until they achieved success. The Taylor and Kirkpatrick reports on
the Bay of Pigs were of some help in establishing institutional strengths and
weaknesses and areas for reform, but the major force for toughening up the
agency and making it even more effective was Bobby Kennedy himself, backed
by his brother, the President.*

The Taylor Commission report focused on administrative rather than operational matters and courageously did not shy away from looking at the role of
the White House in the affair. "Top level direction was given through ad hoc
meetings of senior officials," the report stated, "without consideration of operational plans in writing and with no arrangement for recording conclusions and
decisions reached . . . . By acquiescing in the Zapata plan, they gave the impression to others of approving it. . . . They reviewed the successive changes of
the plan piecemeal and only within a limited context, a procedure which was
inadequate for a proper examination of all the military ramifications."

The report went into the question of the canceled air strikes, blaming the
CIA and—between the lines—the White House in equal measure, condemning "the failure to make the air strike plan entirely clear in advance to the President and the Secretary of State. . . . [T]he President and senior officials had
been greatly influenced by the understanding that the landing force could pass

---

* There was an element of a grudge fight with Castro. The Kennedys were not geopoliti-
cians; they felt that if one stitch were dropped, the whole weave might unravel. They had an
acute fear that the Russians were willing and able to march and were beginning to show their
hand. They sensed that once Russia reconstructed after the years of Stalin and the devastation of
World War II, it would be Hercules unchained. That reconstruction, they felt, was now close to
completion.

to guerrilla status if unable to hold the beachhead."[66] (This smacks of hindsight: from February onward the plan was to establish a beachhead and a "provisional government" that would then be recognized and supported by the United States.) Lyman Kirkpatrick's report covered much the same ground but from a different, more personalized perspective. Within the agency it had the effect of a bomb blast. Twenty-five years later it was still under lock and key in its entirety, while only parts of the Taylor report were now held back.

Perhaps the Bay of Pigs simply came at a time when the agency's luck had run out, as some of its officers thought; if it had not been the Bay of Pigs, it would have been something else. The habit of success had grown within the agency under Eisenhower, undermining necessary pessimism. But even if this was the case, it was not what the reports focused on. The Taylor report took a management-consultancy line. Kirkpatrick's report, in contrast, looked at the personalities of the agency in the light of the Bay of Pigs. In 1961 it was generally believed that Lyman Kirkpatrick wanted to head the CIA despite the fact that he had been paralyzed from polio for over ten years. Something had changed in him after his polio attack. Before then he was one of the team, a gentleman player. Kirkpatrick in his wheelchair, however, was no longer seen as someone whose path to the very top of the CIA would be effortless, especially after Allen Dulles moved him out of the Directorate of Plans (which spent approximately 80 percent of the CIA's total budget in the 1950s and which was where all the action really was) and into the bureaucratic sideline of the inspector general's office. "The IG staff wasn't the way to go to fame and glory," one CIA man said. "It was where you put somebody who had blotted his copybook somewhere along the way."[67]

Kirkpatrick showed enormous personal energy and application, as if determined to prove that this handicap should have no bearing on his career. His Bay of Pigs report was his opportunity to show his worth, and he grasped it with absolute ruthlessness. Completed in five months, the report was viewed by those few within the agency who read it as professionally shabby. The agency expected to be peeled like an onion after the Bay of Pigs, and Kirkpatrick's report sustained the expectation. Instead, the Kennedys realized that a consequence of the Bay of Pigs was that the CIA was suddenly vulnerable and therefore controllable, and they moved in. If Kirkpatrick had calculated that his report would become a Kennedy blueprint for the onion peeling and that he would be made director to implement his report's recommendations, he was wrong.

Kirkpatrick's delivery of the report cemented the view of him as ambitious. He gave the report directly to the DCI-designate, John McCone, while Allen Dulles was still director and therefore still his boss. According to the stories that surround the incident, after McCone's appointment was announced, he visited the agency and then went to National Airport to board a plane for his home in Los Angeles. Kirkpatrick either chased out to the airport after McCone or sent somebody to hand the report personally to him. According to Angleton, who closely followed the affair at the time, McCone "read it on the way back to California, and when he got off the plane he obviously began to see that something was up." McCone saw that a power play was probably afoot and that Kirkpatrick was trying to "double-cross his Director, carrying on a feud with the clandestine side." Arriving home, McCone, according to Angleton, "called Kirkpatrick and asked whether he had given a copy to Dulles. When the answer came 'No,' he became quite rude and ordered him to give a copy to Dulles since he was still Director."[68] Dulles was furious with Kirkpatrick, not simply because—as Kirkpatrick later admitted—he had handled the presentation of the report incorrectly but also because the contents were a hatchet job, with Dulles and the Directorate of Plans as its victims. McCone apparently concurred. When he took over as director, he ordered all but one copy of Kirkpatrick's report destroyed and locked that one surviving copy in the director's safe.

In 1972 Kirkpatrick published an article in the *Naval War College Review* that apparently reflected the findings of his report. He criticized the planners for not having consulted—before the invasion—Sherman Kent or Robert Amory's analysts on the Cuban political situation. In an informal brainstorming session with the Cuban analysts a couple of months before the landing Tracy Barnes had been given the analysts' view that the Cuban army would be loyal to Castro: they had no evidence that it would not be.[69] According to Kirkpatrick, this conclusion should have been formally presented and the planners should have been required to take account of the analysts' findings and judgments. The article also criticized President Kennedy and his senior advisers for not having informed themselves better and for not having thought through the consequences of their decisions on the plan as it developed. The operation's internal security was virtually nonexistent, said Kirkpatrick, and nearly everybody knew what was going on.[70]

McGeorge Bundy, who had offered Kennedy his resignation after the Bay of Pigs, said after reading the report, "Well, that casts quite a different light on things."[71] The CIA, in Kirkpatrick's view, bore most of the blame, and the Kennedy White House could be forgiven for having paid attention to the experts. He was trying to play in an obvious way what he saw as the Kennedy game. Standing back from the ill-fated operation now, one can see that it was more a White House failure than a CIA one. The agency had reached a state at which others wanted to hitch a ride on it: the Zapata plan had all the marks of too many cooks. It stands in stark contrast to the highly focused, minimally staffed sequence of agency successes in Iran, Egypt, the Middle East, Guatemala, and with the U-2. The imperatives of the Kennedy administration—vigor, decision, speed—had been substituted for the longer, cooler view of the agency. This had not happened under Truman and Eisenhower, and it did not happen later under Johnson and Nixon. It had more to do with the Kennedy experience of being the little boy in the candy store not knowing what to do when told he owns the store. In the past their father or their wealth and connections had always bailed the Kennedys out, but not this time. The Bay of Pigs was theirs. At the time, as far as the White House was concerned, Bundy told friends, the Bay of Pigs failure was not very important or serious. It was just "a brick through the window."[72]

Of course it was not just a brick through the window, and Kennedy and his advisers knew it. The Soviet Union would read the failure as a fault of indecision on the part of a new, young President and move quickly to exploit this weakness. Khrushchev's public belligerence and boasting of growing Soviet military strength increased tension dramatically. He told every Western visitor he met in Moscow that Russian missiles were ready to force the Western allies out of West Berlin. Almost daily incidents in Berlin increased U.S. fears that the situation would explode. The 450 nuclear missiles in the U.S. arsenal were now perceived in political terms as entirely inadequate, despite the CIA's demonstration to the President that they were not. The secretary of defense, Robert McNamara, who was known as a "number cruncher," hardware man, and management efficiency expert, was forced to pledge to end a missile gap that did not exist. While it was clear that the United States' 450 missiles were more than adequate for Western defensive and offensive purposes, he had to argue for 500 more. The Joint Chiefs of Staff, excited by the idea of a missile gap, had wanted 2500–3000 more, but Bundy had checked around quietly and found that there was no need for such an increase in military strength. But there was a need, in the face of growing cold-war tensions, for an increase on political grounds, so McNamara hit upon the idea of increasing the number of missiles while leaving their destructive power—throw-weight—at the same level as the existing 450 missiles, thus being able to argue to the Russians that America was not starting a new arms race. "Same bang for more bucks" in effect. Why? asked President Kennedy. "What about it, Bob?"

"Well, they're right," said McNamara, referring to those who said the 450 missiles were all that were needed.

"Well, then, why the 950, Bob?" the President queried.

"Because that's the smallest number we can take up on the Hill without getting murdered," McNamara replied.[73]

The Bay of Pigs was already costing far more than the CIA's estimate of $50 million.[74] When later in the year Carl Kaysen of the National Security Council Staff told the President that the Russians had resumed atmospheric testing of nuclear weapons, Kennedy, reflecting the frustrations of the year, said, "Fucked again."[75]

12

Touch Football
1961-1965

"If you needed someone to carry out a murder," said Richard Helms, "I guess you had a man who might be prepared to carry it out."[1] Helms made this statement in 1975 to the Church Committee as he was giving evidence on CIA involvement with assassination plots during his tenure as chief of operations and deputy director for plans ten to fifteen years earlier. He was referring to one of the paid assassins who had gone to the Congo in 1960 to try to kill Lumumba and who was part of the ZR/Rifle project to develop an "Executive Action" capability under Bill Harvey's supervision in the Directorate of Plans. There is no evidence that the paid assassin ever actually carried out an assassination or, for that matter, that the CIA ever succeeded in assassinating anyone. However, as William Colby remarked, it was not for want of trying.

In 1961, spurred on by Bobby Kennedy's constant prodding, the CIA made a concerted effort to have Castro killed. It renewed its association with Maheu, Rosselli, and Giancana and directed Dr. Gottlieb to come up with more toxins and devices to poison the Cuban leader. The renewed attempt to kill Castro was run by Bill Harvey within the CIA. It was conducted as a top-secret adjunct of Operation Mongoose—the name given to the continuing effort to secure Castro's overthrow—overseen from the White House by Bobby Kennedy. The attorney general supervised Mongoose with the seasoned Edward G. Lansdale, a covert-action expert who, with Maxwell Taylor, was the Kennedys' personal choice for the job. The new assassination plans began in November 1961.

The Mongoose effort came directly from the pre-Bay of Pigs attempts to kill Castro. The attorney general, Robert Kennedy, apparently first learned of

the CIA underworld connection from J. Edgar Hoover. (The news of this connection genuinely infuriated Kennedy:* he had publicly pledged to fight organized crime, and Giancana was one of those he had named as a target for
Justice Department investigation.) Hoover, like many others, realized that the
Bay of Pigs failure had placed the CIA in a weak position and took advantage
of it. From the earliest days of the OSS he had fought a bureaucratic battle
against any other department or agency that he perceived as trespassing on FBI
territory.†

After the Bay of Pigs, Hoover decided to win favor with the new administration by homing in on the Kennedys' distrust of their "experts." He also put
the Kennedys on the defensive by showing that he knew a thing or two about
Jack Kennedy's personal life. Colonel Sheffield Edwards, the CIA director of
security, was in close contact with the bureau about Maheu's bugging case in
Las Vegas and in the spring of 1961 was involved in trying to persuade the
Justice Department not to prosecute Maheu. On May 22, 1961, the memorandum summarizing the case was sent by Hoover directly to the attorney general:

> Colonel Edwards advised that in connection with CIA's operation against
> Castro he personally contacted Robert Maheu during the Fall of 1960 for the
> purpose of using Maheu as a "cut-out" in contacts with Sam Giancana, a
> known hoodlum in the Chicago area. . . . Colonel Edwards said that since
> this is "dirty business" he could not afford to have knowledge of the actions
> of Maheu and Giancana in pursuit of any mission for CIA. . . . Mr. Bissell, in
> his recent briefings of General Taylor and the Attorney General and in con-
> nection with their inquiries into CIA relating to the Cuban situation told the
> Attorney General that some of the associated planning included the use of
> Giancana and the underworld against Castro.[2]

This must have made Bobby Kennedy aware that something murky was going
on if he did not already know it, but there is no conclusive evidence—once
again—that he realized that an assassination plot was involved. A year later,
however, he certainly did realize what was happening and lent his weight
to it.

---

*Thomas Powers, *The Man Who Kept the Secrets: Richard Helms and the CIA* (New
York: Knopf, 1979), p. 155. Lawrence Houston, recalling a meeting a year later on May 7, 1962,
with Robert Kennedy, said, "Kennedy was mad. He was mad as hell. But what he objected to was
the possibility it would impede prosecution against Giancana and Rosselli. He was not angry
about the assassination plot, but about our involvement with the Mafia." Despite his anger, Robert Kennedy had known about this involvement for at least a year and, although attorney general,
had done nothing about it. Perhaps he saw the information as another opportunity to berate the
agency, keeping it on the defensive and anxious to please. In 1961, however, he was genuinely
angry about the connection with the Mafia, seeing it as another example, after the Bay of Pigs, of
CIA incompetence.

†Interestingly, he was happy for others to take on drug enforcement and narcotics work, reasoning that the inevitable offer of huge sums of money in bribes would undoubtedly corrupt
many agents. The CIA took on the major work of fighting the narcotics trade instead.

THE KENNEDYS, BILL HARVEY, AND OPERATION
MONGOOSE

On May 7, 1962, Richard Helms, Lawrence Houston, and Sheffield Edwards met Robert Kennedy in the attorney general's office and briefed him about the CIA's connections with the underworld in the attempts to kill Castro. Two days later, Robert Kennedy told Hoover about this conversation, and Hoover wrote a note of what he was told: "Robert A. Maheu, a private detective in Washington, D.C., to approach Giancana with a proposition of paying $150,000 to hire some gunmen to go into Cuba to kill Castro."[3] On May 14 Houston and Edwards wrote a memorandum of their May 7 meeting with the attorney general which indicated that nothing of this nature was discussed. The Church Committee decided that this memorandum "may be . . . intended to be false to serve as a 'cover' for the real facts. Alternatively, the memorandum may just have resulted from the apparent confusion between Houston and Edwards and a general reluctance to detail in writing something like an assassination operation."[4] Aside from this, all other evidence suggests that assassination was discussed and that Bobby Kennedy knew about it and instructed the CIA to carry it out. Whether Bobby Kennedy informed his brother the President of the assassination attempts we do not know, but the presumption must be that he did: the brothers were too close, the matter was too important for him to keep to himself. It also seems clear that much earlier, in October and November 1961, both the President and the attorney general had a good idea that plans were being made to kill Castro and overthrow his regime. In all probability President Kennedy was behind these moves.

Richard Helms recalled that in October or November that year "the Agency was instructed to get going on plans to get rid of Castro by some device which obviously would have to be covert because nobody had any stomach anymore for any invasions or any military fiascos of that kind." The atmosphere, he said, was "pretty intense, and I remember vividly it was very intense. . . . Nutty schemes were born of the intensity of the pressure. And we were quite frustrated. . . . No doubt about it, it was white heat."[5] During the same period Bill Harvey's executive assistant on Mongoose was told by Richard Bissell that he had been to the White House for a meeting and was "chewed out in the Cabinet Room of the White House by both the President and the Attorney General for, as he put it, sitting on his ass and not doing anything about getting rid of Castro and the Castro regime."[6] Robert McNamara remembered: "We were hysterical about Castro at the time of the Bay of Pigs and thereafter, and there was pressure from JFK and RFK to do something about Castro."[7]

President Kennedy's instructions for Operation Mongoose were to assess and implement whatever schemes were appropriate to get rid of Castro and his government. Killing Castro was within the scope of its assignment. On January 19, 1962, the attorney general addressed the 5412 Committee, stressing the President's interest in getting rid of Castro. It was "the top priority in the U.S. government—all else is secondary," declared Bobby Kennedy. "No time, money, effort, or manpower is to be spared. . . . Yesterday . . . the President had indicated [to the attorney general] that the final chapter had not been written—it's got to be done and will be done."[8] By this stage the attorney general was quite happy with the Mafia involvement; anything to get rid of Castro.

Within the Kennedy administration Bobby's determination to remove Castro (many who were not in on the secret nevertheless suspected he was trying to have the Cuban killed) was well known by mid-1962. "The Attorney General was the driving force behind the clandestine effort to overthrow Castro," said Harris Wofford. "From inside accounts of the pressure he was putting on the CIA to 'get Castro,' he seemed like a wild man who was out-CIAing the CIA. I also heard accounts of how avidly he was advancing counter-insurgency as the answer to the Communists in Vietnam. During this period Robert Kennedy would import Green Berets for weekends at Hyannis Port. They would demonstrate their prowess in swinging from trees and climbing over barricades."[9]

The Mongoose team came up with thirty-three different plans to do "something" about Castro. Included in these schemes were intelligence collection, the use of armed force, and biological and chemical attacks on the Cuban sugar crop. One of the more creative plans involved an attempt to convince Cuba's large Roman Catholic population that the Second Coming was soon and that Christ would return in Cuba if the Cubans got rid of Castro, the anti-Christ, first. This particular idea was Lansdale's. He had conducted a similar scheme in the Philippines during the anti-Huk campaign, using helicopters fitted with loudspeakers to broadcast to primitive tribesmen from the sky. In the case of the more advanced Cuba, rumors were to be circulated in the country that the Second Coming was actually going to take place in Cuba very soon. Once these rumors had taken hold and, it was hoped, generated a popular uprising against Castro, a U.S. submarine off the Cuban coast would fill the night sky with star shells. This display would be taken as indicating that Christ was on his way by the natives, who would promptly complete the overthrow of Castro. "Elimination by illumination," was what Walt Elder, McCone's executive assistant, termed this scheme, which was too fanciful even for the Mongoose team and was not implemented.[10]

None of the Mongoose plans resulted in Castro's overthrow, however, and the Kennedys became increasingly restless. Bill Harvey complained that Lansdale and Taylor were demanding too many reports from him and his team, Task Force W, tying them up in administration.[11] Bobby Kennedy kept up a barrage of memorandums and phone calls to the CIA, often bypassing the chain of command and speaking directly to junior officers as he pressed for action and results against Castro. But the fundamental problem was the same one that had bedeviled the Bay of Pigs: Castro would not be toppled by guerrilla action or unsupported landings. Nothing short of direct American military action would defeat him.

Bill Harvey remembered that because of the chaotic state of Mongoose plans in August 1962 which resulted from the pressures on his team, he did not feel that he needed to brief John McCone about the assassination plots. He assumed that McCone would know about them anyway, he said, since by then attempts to remove Castro had been going on for two and a half years. As far as Harvey was concerned, the pressure was coming from the White House and top Kennedy aides by-passing the DCI. He recalled attending a meeting of the Special Group Augmented on August 10, at which Robert McNamara asked the group to "consider the elimination or assassination of Fidel," and that the next day,

> [i]n connection with a morning briefing of John McCone, the question again came up and I expressed some opinion as to the inappropriateness of this having been raised in this form and at that forum, at which point Mr. McCone stated in substance that he agreed and also that he had felt so strongly that he had, I believe, the preceding afternoon or evening, personally called the gentleman who had made the proposal or suggestion and had stated similar views as to the inappropriateness and that [McCone] said in addition . . . if I got myself involved in something like this, I might end up getting myself excommunicated.[12]

John McCone was a devout Roman Catholic, personally opposed to assassinations, with a healthy concern for his immortal soul. Both Bill Harvey and Richard Helms, the two men in charge of anti-Castro operations within the agency, used this as a reason for not discussing assassinations with the director. They agreed they would not tell McCone in any detail of their plans unless he asked them point blank. They considered that McCone's Catholicism—unlike that of the Kennedys—was serious and that it would be better not to tell him about the assassination plans, particularly because there was no need to; they were receiving their instructions from the attorney general, the President's brother.

Although McCone was the director of Central Intelligence, he was not a necessary part of the chain of command in this operation. None of the available documents indicate that McCone knew about assassination plans from 1961 to 1963, although as the Church Committee hearings revealed, it is hard to accept that he did not suspect something. Mongoose came to an end in October 1962 with the Cuban missile crisis, although throughout 1963 attempts continued to subvert the Castro government and to kill Castro. It was not until August 1963, after the *Chicago Sun Times* carried an article linking the CIA with Giancana, that McCone asked Helms for a report. Helms gave him a copy of the Houston/Edwards memorandum of May 14, 1962, which stated that attempts to kill Castro had been terminated before McCone became DCI.

McCone was relieved. "Well," he said, "this did not happen during my tenure," and he handed the memorandum back to Helms without any particular comment.[13] It must also be said that Bobby Kennedy was effectively in charge of the CIA's covert operations at this stage, acting as the executive head of the Directorate of Plans. There seems to have been an unwritten understanding with McCone that this should be so. Castro and killing were Bobby's business. When Richard Helms, the DDP, had evidence of Cuban involvement with Latin American guerrilla movements, he went straight to Bobby with it, bypassing McCone.[14]

As the Cuban missile crisis mounted in October 1962, Robert Kennedy instructed McCone to stop all operations against Cuba: he did not want to give the Russians any excuse for their attempt to place nuclear weapons in Cuba. Despite these instructions, Harvey approved two landings in Cuba by CIA-trained Cubans from Task Force W in Miami. The agents involved were simply put in place, Harvey argued; they had not been instructed to carry out any operations. McCone was livid and removed Harvey from any association with Mongoose and Task Force W. McCone had lost his patience with Harvey, who had gone too far once too often. Irritated by Harvey's flamboyance, McCone had wanted to fire him on several earlier occasions but had been dissuaded from doing so by Helms. Harvey had also upset the Kennedys with his directness. On one occasion in the White House War Room during the Cuban missile crisis, Bobby Kennedy grabbed an important message straight from the decoder and started to leave the room with it. All the identifications were on the message, and it was a CIA message, Harvey's message. So Harvey grabbed it back from the attorney general, and there was a scene. Harvey kept the message, but he was never asked back to the War Room again.[15]

In early 1963, after a few months without an assignment, Harvey was sent to Rome as station chief. Task Force W was disbanded by early 1963 and replaced by a new CIA group called the Special Affairs Staff, headed by Desmond FitzGerald, who left the leadership of the DDP's Far Eastern Division to take it over. The White House-controlled plans against Castro, however, continued relatively unaffected by this administrative shuffling. At least six major CIA operations were carried out inside Cuba by CIA Cuban teams in 1963, each of which was aimed at disrupting government and damaging industry and agriculture. In February 1963 Harvey's last act in the Cuban saga was to have dinner with Rosselli in Miami to tell him that the operation was over, the CIA-underworld link severed.

FitzGerald took up the attempt to kill Castro directly, using some extraordinary devices invented for that specific purpose. One of FitzGerald's ideas was for an exploding seashell, made by the Technical Services Division, to be placed on the sea floor at the place Castro was known to swim. Another was for Castro to be given a diving wet suit impregnated with one of Dr. Gottlieb's toxins. This too was handled by the Technical Services Division, which carefully coated the inside of a new wet suit with poison. Delivering it to Castro, however, presented a problem. How could Castro be given the suit without arousing suspicion? FitzGerald's answer was to give the suit to James B. Donovan, who had been Abel's lawyer and the go-between in the Abel-Powers exchange and who now was negotiating the release of the Bay of Pigs Brigade members captured by Castro. This posed another problem: should Donovan be told of the poison in case he was tempted to try the suit on himself or should the agency take the risk that nothing would happen? The answer came when Donovan, ignorant of the CIA's plans, bought a wet suit himself as a present for Castro. The CIA suit was destroyed.*

Another scheme involved the use of a major in the Cuban army, Rolando Cubela, who had been a CIA "asset" since 1961. Cubela was close to Castro but was ambitious and willing to attempt a coup that could result in Castro's death. He asked for sniper's rifles and poisons. FitzGerald met him personally in Paris on October 29, 1963. A month later, on November 22, Cubela was given a poison pen capable of injecting Castro but rejected it, demanding something more sophisticated.[16] President Kennedy was killed that same day in Dallas.

Ten years later, when paranoia about the CIA and secrecy in general was rife, a flood of books and articles suggested that Kennedy's death was the result of a conspiracy or conspiracies. Some theorists held that the CIA was responsible for his death. Bobby Kennedy at the time asked McCone "if they had killed my brother, and I asked him in a way he couldn't lie to me, and they hadn't."[17] Some Kennedy aides wondered if Bobby's aggression and "out-CIAing the CIA" in efforts to oust and kill Castro or to convict Teamsters Union leader Jimmy Hoffa of criminal activities had not been behind his brother's murder. "Had his all-out efforts to destroy the Mafia, including Sam Giancana and those who thought they had bought protection by working with the CIA to kill Castro, caused them to kill the President?" wondered Harris Wofford. "Or was it the result of his drive against Jimmy Hoffa and the Teamsters leader's criminal connections? Could it even be something as absurd as Sam Giancana's jealousy over Judith Campbell? Was it Castro's retaliation, or that of anti-Castro Cubans?"[18]

"When I was young in Texas, I used to know a cross-eyed boy," President Johnson said, according to Bobby Kennedy. "His eyes were crossed, and so was his character. That was God's retribution for people who were bad and so you

---

*"One idea was to dust Castro's shoes, if he chanced to leave them outside his hotel room, with thallium salts in the expectation that this would cause his beard to fall out and destroy his charisma," records Arthur M. Schlesinger, Jr., *Robert Kennedy and His Times* (London: Futura, 1979), p. 518. A pretty German girl, Marie Lorenz, may have been recruited by the agency for an assassination attempt on Castro. She was Castro's mistress for some years, starting in 1959. She also seems to have been the mistress of an ex-Castro supporter turned anti-Castro expatriate, Frank Fiorini (who changed his name to Sturgis and figured in the Watergate burglary ten years later). She claimed in 1976 that the CIA approached her and offered her money to kill Castro. She agreed, and Sturgis gave her two poison capsules, which she hid in a jar of cold cream. She returned to Havana and Castro's bed, but "I couldn't find the capsules. They had melted. It was like an omen. . . . I thought, 'To hell with it. Let history take its course' " (quoted ibid).

should be careful of cross-eyed people because God put his mark on them. Sometimes I think that, when you remember the assassination of Trujillo and the assassination of Diem, what happened to Kennedy may have been divine retribution."[19] To Leo Janos of *Time*, Johnson said that Kennedy "had been operating a damned Murder, Inc., in the Caribbean."[20] To Howard K. Smith of CBS News, Johnson declared, "Kennedy was trying to get Castro, but Castro got to him first."[21]

Castro was with a French journalist when news of Kennedy's death came through. He was shocked and saddened. He had been telling the journalist, "Personally, I consider [Kennedy] responsible for everything, but I will say this: he has come to understand many things over the past few months," and had suggested that he would be happy to coexist peacefully with the United States. *"Es una mala noticia"*—"This is bad news"—he repeated over and over when the news came in.[22]

After Kennedy's death the CIA's direct attempts to kill Castro ceased. Support continued for Cubela in his plans to mount a coup and for the Cuban exiles, but in the autumn of 1964, when Cubela again asked for a sniper's rifle, he was told that the CIA wanted nothing more to do with his plans to kill Castro. The word had come from the Johnson White House that the new President wanted no part in assassinations.

"CUBA II"

The principal consequence of the Bay of Pigs was its effect on U.S.–Soviet relations.* Nikita Khrushchev read the affair as meaning that the Soviet Union could gain a firm foothold in the Americas, which would undermine U.S. influence in the Third World. On April 22, 1961, immediately after the defeat of the invasion force, President Kennedy met Eisenhower at Camp David to ask his advice. The day before, Eisenhower had met Allen Dulles at Kennedy's request as well and had been briefed in detail by the CIA Director. Kennedy's

---

*The Bay of Pigs did not represent a general overreaching or favoring of large-scale paramilitary operations on the part of the agency. Small, low-key operations were under way at the same time. In Brazil, for example, in 1960 some antigovernment conspirators led by General Olympio Murao made contact with the local CIA station. They were given money, advice, and weapons to overthrow President João Goulart. They were also given assurances that the United States would recognize a military government. On April 1, 1964, Murao launched a bloodless and successful coup. Goulart was deemed too leftist and pro-Castro in Washington.

In British Guyana, after the colonies' Marxist prime minister, Dr. Cheddi Jagan, won his third successive election victory in 1961, the CIA organized a subversion campaign through manipulation of Guyana's labor movement. After two years of riots, arson, and strikes (including the longest general strike in history—ten weeks), Jagan fell. The CIA had financed the subversion campaign, and a CIA agent, Howard McCabe, working under cover of the London-based Public Services International labor secretariat's educational office in Guyana (which he established), masterminded the operation. In both Brazil and Guyana, the CIA's efforts compared to those earlier in Iran and Guatemala.

own analysis of what had gone wrong agreed exactly with Allen Dulles': there was a failure of intelligence and there were errors in logistics, timing, and tactics. The problem that the President now faced, as the ex-President realized, was how the Russians would react. Eisenhower wrote about Kennedy in his diary after this meeting:

> He believes that the two great powers have now neutralized each other in atomic weapons and inventories but that in numbers of troops, and our exterior communications as opposed to the interior communications of the communists, we are relatively weak. He did not seem to think that our great seapower counteracted this situation completely. . . .I told him from my own position I could not offer any advice—I could just say that as a generality in order to keep your position strong at the conference table you had constantly to let the enemy see that our country was not afraid. We believe in what is right and attempt to insist upon it.*

Khrushchev had the same basic idea but detected that Kennedy might not understand that he could not bluff about being strong and unafraid. He either had to be both and be prepared to use his strength fearlessly—risking war in the process if necessary—or else effectively he would be weak and afraid. He saw the Bay of Pigs as indicating that Kennedy did not understand that to have power you had to be prepared to use it. Moreover, he felt that Kennedy had a major weakness: an overriding determination to appear to be right, even at the expense of U.S. influence. Khrushchev was a bully and had a strong sense of weaknesses in others. "Of all the leaders I have met," said Richard Nixon, "I disagreed with none more vehemently than Nikita Khrushchev. And yet none earned my grudging respect for his effective exercise of raw power so consistently. That he was the Devil incarnate, many would concede. That he was an ominously able Devil, few could dispute."[23] Khrushchev's memoirs record:

> After Castro's crushing victory over the counter-revolutionaries we intensified our military aid to Cuba. We gave them as many arms as the Cuban army could absorb. . . .
> Castro came out with a declaration that Cuba would follow a Socialist course. . . . We welcomed Castro's victory, of course, but at the same time we were quite certain that the [Bay of Pigs] invasion was only the beginning and that the Americans would not let Cuba alone. . . .

---

*Robert H. Ferrell, ed. *The Eisenhower Diaries* (New York: W. W. Norton, 1981,), pp. 386–387. The situation in Laos—communist-backed guerrillas versus the U.S.-supported government—was one of the principal issues discussed by Eisenhower with Kennedy in the post-1960 presidential-election transition period. Eisenhower's advice was to support and train the Laotians and Thais (who, according to the domino principle, were seen as also being vulnerable to communist takeover) so they could withstand attacks on their own rather than turn to the United States for direct intervention.

We were sure that the Americans would never reconcile themselves to the existence of Castro's Cuba. They feared, as much as we hoped, that a Socialist Cuba might become a magnet that would attract other Latin American countries to Socialism. Given the continual threat of American interference in the Caribbean, what should our own policy be? This question was constantly on my mind, and I frequently discussed it with the other members of the Presidium. Everyone agreed that America would not leave Cuba alone unless we did something. We had an obligation to do everything in our power to protect Cuba's existence as a Socialist country and as a working example to the other countries of Latin America. It was clear to me that we might very well lose Cuba if we didn't take some decisive steps in her defense.[24]

His solution was to defend Castro with Soviet strategic nuclear missiles. Early in October 1962 this was recognized in Washington as being too important a threat to ignore.

The Soviet buildup in Cuba began in 1960 with substantial amounts of conventional weapons being provided for the Cuban army, along with Soviet technicians and military personnel for training programs. By early 1962 this had expanded to include training for Cuban pilots and the supply of about sixty MIG jet fighter aircraft. "This phase," reported a Special National Intelligence Estimate early in October, "was largely completed by February 1962 with the result that Cuban forces were much better prepared to handle incursions upon their territory."[25] Between July and mid-September the CIA reported that some seventy ships had delivered various types of military supplies and construction equipment and SA-2 surface-to-air missiles to strengthen Cuban air defenses.

However, at this stage Khrushchev's willingness to play brinkmanship was not recognized, and the Board of National Estimates agreed that while "the USSR could derive considerable military advantage from the establishment of Soviet medium and intermediate range ballistic missiles in Cuba, or from the establishment of a Soviet submarine base there," the Russians would not raise the stakes too high and "the establishment of a submarine base would be the most likely. Either development, however, would be incompatible with Soviet practice to date and with Soviet policy as we presently estimate it. It would indicate a far greater willingness to increase the level of risk in U.S.–Soviet relations than the USSR has displayed thus far, and consequently would have important policy implications with respect to other areas and other problems in East-West relations."[26]

One year earlier, on August 13, 1961, Khrushchev had given a portent of things to come in Berlin with the sudden construction of the Berlin Wall. It was a demonstration that Russia was willing to take strong unilateral action to achieve its tactical and strategic political goals. It was also a demonstration that Khrushchev believed he could bully Kennedy.

Six weeks earlier the two leaders had met for the first time, in Vienna.* It was at this meeting that Kennedy finally realized that the Bay of Pigs had directly influenced Khrushchev's attitude toward him, making the Soviet premier believe that he could stare the young President down. Averell Harriman, Kennedy's roving ambassador and wartime U.S. ambassador to the Soviet Union, advised Kennedy to rise above Khrushchev's belligerence and not try to match it at the Summit. Khrushchev, he predicted, would attack and see if he could get away with it. If Kennedy matched him, Khrushchev would be forced to do something to prove that *he* was strong and unafraid and meant what he said.

Harriman's was a lone voice on this occasion. Kennedy's other advisers— Rusk, Bundy, Charles Bohlen, Llewellyn Thompson, George Kennan—said that he should stand up to Khrushchev to show him that he was tough and that the Bay of Pigs was just a brick through the window and not a reflection of Kennedy's will. Some went further: the Summit was an opportunity firmly to close the Bay of Pigs episode and show Khrushchev that Kennedy had learned the lesson and would be strong and resolute if anything like it ever happened again. A confrontation was to be encouraged, therefore, to show Khrushchev that Kennedy had an iron will.

At the end of the Summit Kennedy gave Scotty Reston an exclusive interview. "Pretty rough?" Reston asked. "Roughest thing in my life," said Kennedy. He had taken the hard line and was clearly shaken by the result. He told Reston that he had decided to take a different approach to the meeting and to go it alone. Unlike Eisenhower, who had always been accompanied by John Foster Dulles at summits and turned to him for answers, Kennedy had briefed himself thoroughly and confronted Khrushchev without the help of Rusk or anyone else. "I propose to tell you what I can do, and what I can't do," he opened, "what my problems and possibilities are and then you can do the same." Khrushchev replied with a violent, vituperative attack on American "imperialism" and the Western presence in Berlin. If the Western allies did not vacate West Berlin, he threatened, missiles would fly and tanks would roll. This attack continued until Kennedy finally replied in kind. Kennedy told Reston:

> I've got two problems. First, to figure out why he did it, and in such a hostile way. And second, to figure out what we can do about it. I think the first part

*Khrushchev, however, was apparently already in secret contact with Kennedy, as several mysterious incidents testified. In September 1961 Pierre Salinger had a secret meeting in New York with Georgi Bolshakov, editor of *USSR*, a Soviet English-language magazine, and apparently a top KGB agent. Salinger was given a twenty-six-page letter from Khrushchev for Kennedy. Theodore Sorensen recounted a similar episode when Bolshakov handed him a letter folded inside a newspaper as they were walking along a Washington street. The Soviet ambassador knew nothing of the letters. (See David Wise and Thomas B. Ross, *The Espionage Establishment* [New York: Random House, 1967], p. 71.)

is pretty easy to explain. I think he did it because of the Bay of Pigs. I think he thought that anyone who was so young and inexperienced as to get into that mess could be taken, and anyone who got into it, and didn't see it through had no guts. So he just beat hell out of me. So I've got a terrible problem. If he thinks I'm inexperienced and have no guts, until we remove those ideas we won't get anywhere with him. So we have to act. . . . Now we have a problem to make our power credible, and Vietnam looks like the place.[27]

Kennedy's analysis was correct, but Khrushchev also had ideas about the place for confrontation: Cuba. He was locked into a collision course with Kennedy.

Cuba was not Kennedy's chosen ground for demonstrating his strength to Khrushchev: Southeast Asia was. Vietnam, Cambodia, Laos, Thailand were countries less emotive, less in the American consciousness than Europe and the Caribbean. In July 1961, after returning from the Vienna Summit, Kennedy announced a 25 percent increase in American military strength, and within two years he approved an increase of from five hundred to ten thousand American military "advisers" in Vietnam. The Bay of Pigs, the Vienna Summit, and the Berlin Wall had impelled him to the Eisenhower-Dulles view of communism as a global menace. He now believed that Berlin, Vietnam, and Cuba were all related and that every communist move had to be countered and defeated. American power would be used to the full in the process. "Who would want to read a book about disasters?" Kennedy said in the autumn of 1961, reflecting on his performance so far to a reporter who wanted to write about his first year in office.[28] When in October 1962 the Russian buildup in Cuba was confirmed as including nuclear weapons, he was determined not to have another disaster.

The first indication that Soviet missiles would be sent to Cuba came from Cuban exile debriefing in Miami and from a CIA U-2 reconnaissance flight over the island in August 1962 which came back with photographs showing that a surface-to-air missile site was being built. These photographs warned Washington that the Russians were moving away from conventional military support for Castro and generated the Special National Intelligence Estimate of early October, which held that ground-to-ground missiles would probably not be installed. On October 14 another U-2 flight returned with photographs of a ballistic-missile launch site under construction at San Cristobal.

The CIA went into high gear as the photographic evidence came in. Ray Cline, now deputy directory of intelligence, coordinated a comprehensive interagency intelligence collection and analysis program to discover the precise facts. His effort gave the agency one of its historical highlights, injecting it into the center of decision making throughout the crisis. Kennedy, already impressed by the agency's performance in the wake of the Bay of Pigs and satisfied that it was responding to his wish to unseat Castro, gave McCone and

Cline his backing.* "The photo experts alerted me as to what they had found late in the afternoon of Monday, October 15," Cline recalled, "and my missile experts assured me we were seeing a major investment in nuclear missiles that would double the number of nuclear warheads the USSR could fire on the United States." Cline immediately warned the White House that there was a crisis. The next day he took the U-2 photographs and showed them to the President.[29]

The work of Cline and his analysts was vital. Accurate information was essential for the President in order to force the removal of the Soviet weapons from Cuba without over- or underestimating the consequences of each step. It was important for another reason as well. John McCone, on a hunch, had some days earlier decided that the Russians were placing missiles in Cuba and had so warned the President. Cline was now able to back up his boss and enhance the reputation of the agency too. R. Jack Smith, head of the Office of Current Intelligence at the time, recalled McCone's early role:

> In September McCone remarried and went to Nice on his honeymoon. We had just begun to get some evidence that something more than antiaircraft missiles were going in, from agent reports and refugees who said the Russians were building a big force to attack the United States. We needed U-2 overflights to establish this, and so we got authorization. McCone had all along said that the Russians were not putting in antiaircraft missiles just for the fun of it: they were putting them in to defend something, and that was missile capability or something of that sort. That was his reasoning. What was wrong with it was that it did not consider the nature of Soviet military production. You could see the heavy hand of the bureaucrats frequently at work.
>
> It turned out that the SA-2 missile they were building was a tremendous success. They were being produced like clockwork, and they worked. They sprinkled the Soviet Union with SA-2s, and all up and down the Soviet Union the most improbable places had SA-2 units. It got to be ludicrous. Militarily, it didn't make any sense. It looked as though they had them to give out like candy, and that tended to indicate they were putting SA-2s into Cuba. It would make the Cubans feel great. An SA-2 missile is fairly long, and to the untrained eye it looks like one hell of a weapon. It looks like it could fly from here to Alaska.
>
> But they weren't surface-to-surface missiles, they were surface-to-air missiles, and all the reports we had indicated that they were all that were going in. It didn't necessarily mean that they were going to put in offensive missiles protected by these things. It did to McCone, though. He sent this hot wire back from his bridal suite saying that the Soviets were going to put some of their own offensive missiles in there and we'd better get out and find them.

*Cline had succeeded Robert Amory as DDI in March 1962. After the Bay of Pigs, Cline considered, "in other ways the CIA was working well under McCone and had won its way back into the good graces of the President."

At about that time we did find them. But McCone was a hero because he had called it ahead of us.[30]

McCone was lucky. His guess was ahead of the evidence (bad weather had delayed U-2 flights until October 14), but because Cline showed that he had been accurate, McCone's voice—and through him the CIA's—gained strength within the administration.

By October 19, more U-2 flights provided evidence that nine medium-range (1100-mile) and intermediate range (2200-mile) ballistic missile sites and twenty-four antiaircraft missile sites were being built. Another Special National Intelligence Estimate revised earlier conclusions and declared:

> A major Soviet objective in their military build-up in Cuba is to demonstrate that the world balance of forces has shifted so far in their favor that the US can no longer prevent the advance of Soviet offensive power even into its own hemisphere. . . .
>
> It is possible that the USSR is installing these missiles primarily in order to use them in bargaining for US concessions elsewhere. We think this unlikely, however. . . . US acceptance of the strategic missile build-up would provide strong encouragement to Communists, pro-Communists, and the more anti-American sectors of opinion in Latin America and elsewhere. Conversely, anti-Communists and those who relate their own interests to those of the US would be strongly discouraged. It seems clear that, especially over the long run, there would be a loss of confidence in US power and determination and a serious decline of US influence generally.[31]

The Estimate came down against a naval blockade of Cuba, since it would place the Soviets "under no immediate pressure to choose a response with force," and in favor of an invasion and occupation of Cuba, which, in the CIA analysts' view, "would be more likely to make the Soviets pause in opening new theaters of conflict than limited action or action which drags out." The next day another Special National Intelligence Estimate maintained this position but concluded: "Finally, we believe that, whatever course of retaliation the USSR elected [to take against a U.S. blockade or military occupation of Cuba], the Soviet leaders would not deliberately initiate general war or take military measures, which in their calculations, would run grave risks of general war."[32]

Within the administration the CIA view that the United States should respond militarily, removing Castro from power and occupying Cuba, was supported by a strong and influential group. By October 16 some of the sites were only a week away from completion, and it was estimated that about 80 million Americans might be only days away from death. The Joint Chiefs of Staff at first unanimously favored a military strike. So did Dean Acheson, who was called upon for advice. Munich in 1938, that constant Kennedy fear, was used by these people to argue against a blockade, which, they said, "would not neutralize weapons already within Cuba . . . and it would mean another Munich."[33]

Outside the administration, with the midterm congressional elections due in the first week of November, Republicans, led by Senator Kenneth Keating of New York, were giving warnings about the Soviet buildup in Cuba and challenging Kennedy to do something about Castro. (They expressed these concerns even though they did not know yet that nuclear missiles were being installed; this was still a closely held secret within the administration, and Kennedy did not announce the crisis publicly until October 22.) On October 16 a National Security Council group met and constituted itself as the "Excom" group ("Executive committee of the NSC"). For the next thirteen days the members of this group monitored developments minute by minute and advised the President what to do.

Bobby Kennedy, who chaired the Excom group, was a "dove" from the start, favoring a blockade. Along with most of the group, he considered some action was required, but he wanted to defuse tension as well if possible. "I now know how Tojo felt when he was planning Pearl Harbor," he said in a note to his brother on the first day of the crisis as they listened to the arguments for and against a military strike.[34] George Ball and Robert McNamara, the two other leading doves on Excom, slowly succeeded, with Bobby Kennedy's support, in convincing the group to favor a blockade instead of direct military intervention. Although John McCone strongly favored the military occupation proposal at the start, he eventually came around to accept the blockade proposal.[35]

As the intelligence coordinator within the administration for the crisis, pulling information from all sources, the CIA was able to demonstrate its allround expertise. Colonel Oleg Penkovsky, who by that time had been passing Soviet military information to the West for over a year, enabled the CIA to provide exact information about the capabilities of the Soviet missiles and equipment being sent to Cuba. "The information he had provided on types of Soviet missiles," wrote Ray Cline later, "proved invaluable to U.S. intelligence analysts during the Cuba missile crisis."[36] Cline spearheaded the agency's analytical role:

> We got the critical evidence in time for the President to digest it in private, with only his closest advisers aware of what we had found. This is a luxury that permits policymakers to examine options thoroughly, ready their moves in secret, and act firmly to deal with the dangers that intelligence has uncovered. . . .
>
> McGeorge Bundy felt free to show the closely-held Khrushchev-Kennedy correspondence not only to Ambassador Llewellyn Thompson for analysis and action on preparing responses but also to me as Deputy Director (Intelligence) at the CIA, for vetting to garner any light it shed on Soviet pol-

icies and intentions. This sharing of diplomatic correspondence of the highest sensitivity with the CIA analytical component made it possible for me to guide intelligence output into matters directly germane to policy issues of the moment.[37]

This effort, combined with the photographs obtained during the U-2 flights and McCone's accurate guess, won for the agency all the ground it had lost with the Kennedys. Although the CIA's analysts until quite late felt that strategic nuclear missiles would not be placed in Cuba, this was understood: it was the rational conclusion.[38] Khrushchev's belligerence and deception (he had told Kennedy through the Soviet ambassador in Washington that he would do nothing to embarrass the President during the congressional election campaign and that he had no intention of installing strategic missiles in Cuba),[39] added to the fact that there was no direct evidence of the presence of Soviet offensive missiles, meant that others were more cautious than McCone. Looking back, R. Jack Smith pointed out:

> The argument the estimators in the Office of National Estimates were putting forward was that the Soviets would not put in offensive weapons, because it would not enhance their strategic capability very much, and it did not. When the U-2 overflights showed that offensive weapons were being put in, we showed a very small percentage of their total land-based missile capability was involved, perhaps 6 to 8 percent of the total land-based missiles in the Soviet Union against the United States. And seen from that perspective, it did not seem to us a very worthwhile gamble. And it didn't to them either. Khrushchev took them out because we said, "Get them out of there!"*

---

* Interview, R. Jack Smith, July 23, 1983. One of the problems at the start of the crisis was accurate intelligence from U-2 flights being delayed because of bad weather. After the authorization for the flights had been obtained, no flights were made for three weeks over San Cristobal because cloud cover obscured large areas of western Cuba. U-2 flights had been carried out over parts of Cuba on August 29, September 5, 17, 26, and 29, October 5 and 7. The CIA recommended the flight over western Cuba on October 4; it was approved on October 10 and took place on October 14. On Thursday, October 18, Bobby Kennedy recorded "estimates by our intelligence community placed in Cuba missiles with an atomic warhead potential of about one-half the current ICBM capacity of the entire Soviet Union" (Robert F. Kennedy, *Thirteen Days: A Memoir of the Cuban Missile Crisis* [New York: Signet, 1969], p. 35). Twenty years after the crisis General Maxwell Taylor recalled that, at the time, nuclear war was thought unlikely to result: "I never heard an expression of fear of nuclear escalation on the part of any of my colleagues. If at any time we were sitting on the edge of Armageddon, as nonparticipants have sometimes alleged, we were too unobservant to notice it" (*The Washington Post*, October 5, 1982).

The consequence of America's superior nuclear strength, Richard Helms has suggested, was Russian determination to match if not exceed that strength:

> Jack McCloy, who was then advising President Kennedy on disarmament, tells about sitting on a fence at his house in Connecticut with Kuznetsov, the deputy foreign minister, arranging the withdrawal of the IL-28 bombers that were still there after the missiles had been removed. And Kuznetsov turns to him and says, "All right, Mr. McCloy, we will get the IL-28s out as we have taken the missiles out. But I want to tell you something, Mr. McCloy. The Soviet Union is not going to find itself in a position like this ever again." And it was at

Getting the missiles out of Cuba was Kennedy's most significant foreign-policy success. He was prepared to risk war with the USSR if he had to in order to make Khrushchev back off and withdraw and stop thinking he could bully the United States, and he delivered an ultimatum saying so to the Soviets.* The Excom group worked under the most intense political and psychological pressure, as R. Jack Smith observed:

> They were extraordinarily deliberate, very cautious. They had the evidence on Monday, and they made their decision the following Saturday night. They brought in everybody. The thing about the Kennedy White House was they threw out all the machinery—the National Security Council machinery went out the window. It was too cumbersome, they felt. They didn't like it. The Kennedys resembled something between a Harvard seminar and a touch-football game. They called in McCloy, Acheson, all these old-timers, men of stature and judgment, and they by-passed the standard mechanism. It was all done right in the White House.[40]

On October 26 Khrushchev replied, offering to remove the missiles in return for an American pledge not to invade Cuba. The next day he sent another reply, demanding the dismantling of U.S. Jupiter missile sites in Turkey. After detailed consultations with Cline's analysts about Khrushchev's political situation, Soviet capabilities and plans, and the psychology of the Soviet leadership, the Excom group, prompted by Robert Kennedy, made the crucial decision to ignore the second reply and answer the first, accepting the demand to promise not to invade Cuba if the missiles were removed. No undertakings were given about Turkey in reply, but the American missiles there were removed later. Sixteen Soviet ships, some with crated missiles lashed to their decks, turned round in mid-Atlantic to return to Russia. The crisis was over.

Khrushchev had lost, and as a result the Soviet Union faced public humiliation throughout the world. Two years later, almost to the day, Khrushchev was completely ousted from power, spending the remaining seven years of his life in isolated retirement. Kennedy, in contrast, benefited enormously from the resolution of the crisis, enjoying massive popular support and for the first time having international charisma. He was able to use this to steamroller

---

that point, if you look back, that the Russians started their big surge in strategic weapons. Various members of the Kennedy administration who stayed over into the Johnson administration never believed that the Soviets would go for a force that was larger than the U.S. had. And yet that's exactly what they've done. I'm not laying this at anybody's door. The events of life led there. But . . . if you look at it with a cold eye, you can say that this probably wasn't a golden moment for American foreign policy. (*Newsweek*, November 28, 1983)

* As he waited for the Russian reply to his ultimatum over Cuba he discussed with Bobby "the still unfulfilled commitments and guarantees the British had given to Poland" in 1939 (Kennedy, *Thirteen Days*, p. 62). He was determined to act forcefully and to effect. British appeasement was not for him.

through Congress, despite powerful military and political opposition, the first U.S.–Soviet nuclear test-ban treaty the following year. "My brother is not going to be the Tojo of the 1960s," Bobby Kennedy said to George Ball, endorsing his arguments for a blockade—and with Cuba he was not.[41] But the experience did have the consequence of accelerating America's involvement in Southeast Asia.

PENKOVSKY

GRU Colonel Oleg Penkovsky played a vital part in the Cuban crisis. He was a spy and was handled jointly by the British and the CIA. In 1961, toward the end of Dulles' tenure as DCI, Penkovsky had approached Greville Wynne, a British businessman in Moscow who was on the fringes of British Intelligence, and said that he would like to contact Western intelligence. Later in the year, Penkovsky traveled to Britain with a Soviet trade delegation and in London met officers of MI-6 and the CIA. He convinced them of his disillusionment with Soviet society and his sincere wish to become a penetration agent for the West. For approximately eighteen months Penkovsky reported on the highest levels of Soviet policy making and handed over top secret documents on Soviet plans, intelligence activities, military developments, and satellites.

The CIA paid Penkovsky three hundred dollars a month into a Swiss account, but he was an ideologically motivated man. He had a particular eccentricity: he wanted to be formally recognized as a spy. In England on a visit with a Soviet trade delegation, he spent an afternoon with Greville Wynne at Windsor where he saw the Queen not far away. Wynne said later:

> Her Majesty was standing just a few yards away, dressed in casual country clothes, leaning against a Land Rover with a couple of Corgis in the back. I could barely restrain him from attempting to rush up and speak to her. "In the Soviet Union a head of state would never move about so freely!" he exclaimed. "I must talk with her, Greville. She ought to know what I am doing for the cause of peace. I'm sure she will speak to me." It was only with difficulty that I held him off, trying to make him understand that she could not under any circumstances be involved in what we were doing, it just didn't work that way.[42]

But Penkovsky was determined to meet the Queen, becoming obstinate about it at his next debriefing session. "Finally, one of the CIA men sitting in on the session cleared his throat and said, 'Well, look, Alex, I know our President isn't quite the same as the Queen, but how would you like to meet him instead?' "

Twenty-four hours later Penkovsky and Wynne flew to Washington to meet Kennedy. The CIA and MI-6 had to time the journey exactly so that

Penkovsky would not be missed by the delegation. As it was, the round trip and the meeting took eighteen hours and was a considerable risk.[43] It would never have been undertaken had not Penkovsky's eccentric craving for recognition as a spy been so strong that his continuing espionage depended upon its being satisfied. When the two men arrived at the White House, President Kennedy was waiting for them. "I've heard about the work you've done for us. I'd just like to add my personal thanks, and the thanks of the United States," he said to Wynne. Turning to Penkovsky, he drew him aside with a hand on his arm and said, "Oleg Penkovsky, I want to assure you, from what I know about the situation with the Soviet Union, that I am very aware of all that you've done to help the cause of peace in the world, not only for the West, but for the sake of your own people as well. If only it were possible to tell everyone of the efforts you have made, the name of Oleg Penkovsky would be acclaimed throughout the world. You know very well that we wish no harm to the Russian people, that we are concerned solely for peace on earth."[44]

The meeting lasted thirty minutes, and Kennedy spent almost the entire time with Penkovsky. Wynne said:

> The problem now was that having met the President of the United States, Alex was now more determined than ever to be received by the Queen." Wanting to avoid ruffled feelings, the Intelligence chiefs made an alternative proposal. As a token of their good faith, he could, if he wished, be immediately appointed to the rank of colonel in the British army. The CIA, never to be outdone, made a similar offer. Alex was so pleased when it was suggested that the next briefing be held in full military dress, that he gave his eager assent. That session, in fact, was entirely taken up by a reception in his honour to celebrate his simultaneous appointment in the armed forces of the two nations. Photographs to commemorate the occasion were made of Alex first in his British uniform, then in his American one. These pictures, tragically, were later to provide damning evidence against Alex at his trial when the KGB found them in a secret drawer of his desk in his Moscow flat. It is indicative of how much they must have meant to him that he kept these with him despite the appalling risk.[45]

Penkovsky was still insistent on meeting the Queen, however, and was finally mollified only when Earl Mountbatten of Burma, the Queen's cousin, agreed to meet him and let him visit him at home.

While much of Penkovsky's information was factual, accurate, and important, some of it was of less high quality and struck MI-6 and the CIA as gossipy and half-understood remarks picked up in Soviet military bars and canteens. When this was considered in light of Penkovsky's carelessness about his own security, some counterintelligence experts in both services thought he might be a Soviet disinformation agent. James Angleton was for a long time convinced of this. Maurice Oldfield, the MI-6 liaison officer in Washington

(1960–64) and later head of the British Secret Intelligence Service (1973–78), devoted great energy to convincing the CIA and President Kennedy of Penkovsky's real value. He arranged for all the Russian's information to be analyzed by British experts before being passed to Washington, and with patience and results convinced most doubters of Penkovsky's *bona fides.*

The information Penkovsky gave on Soviet missile development showed that the Soviet Union in 1962 could not yet attack the United States with intercontinental nuclear weapons. He confirmed that the chief of Soviet missile forces and three hundred officers had been killed when a Soviet missile had exploded at a test site. His information had a direct effect during the Cuban missile crisis, helping to convince Kennedy that Khrushchev would back down because of poor Soviet missile technology. Penkovsky's information also helped pinpoint Soviet missile sites in Cuba.[46] In 1963 Penkovsky was arrested by the Soviets, as was Greville Wynne, his contact. Both men were tried for espionage and found guilty. Penkovsky, according to Soviet sources, was shot immediately after his trial; Wynne was imprisoned for nearly a year before being exchanged for Gordon Lonsdale, a Soviet spy imprisoned by the British.

LEGEND

When, immediately after the Cuban missile crisis, the Kennedy administration sought to reduce tension with the Soviet Union by reducing CIA covert operations against Cuba, many of the Cubans exiled in America, who had cooperated with the agency and were ambitious to overthrow Castro themselves, greeted the change in policy with fury. Weeks later, in January 1963, the administration changed its mind again. Bobby Kennedy saw to it that Desmond FitzGerald replaced Bill Harvey and that the CIA was instructed to increase covert operations against Castro. FitzGerald changed the name of Task Force W to "Special Affairs Staff." Contact was made with Major Rolando Cubela—in an operation code-named AMLASH by the agency, which was to secure the overthrow of Castro—and Castro's assassination was discussed.*

Shortly after this Castro gave a press conference at which he stated that American agents were meeting with terrorists who planned to assassinate Cuban leaders, and he declared that Cuba would answer in kind. On September 12, 1963, the CIA informed the Special Group that there was a strong probability that Castro would retaliate in some way but not by attacking American officials within the United States. Cubela was given more encourage-

---

* Richard Helms was to testify that the post–Bay of Pigs attempts to kill Castro were one of the biggest mistakes of his career. "I have apologized for this," he said to the House Select Committee on Assassinations in September 1978. "I can't do any more than apologize on public television that it was an error of judgment on my part. There was great pressure on us at that time to try to find connections in Cuba. For my part in this and to the extent I had anything to do with it, I am heart sorry. I cannot do any more than apologize"(House Select Committee on Assassinations, *Investigation of the Assassination of President John F. Kennedy,* Vol. IV, p. 181).

ment to mount a coup against Castro, and although it was never clear if he was being asked to kill Castro too, on November 22, when he was offered a poison-pen device he was also told he would be given rifles with telescopic sights. Assassination was clearly in the air, not only in Dallas, where Oswald that day shot John F. Kennedy.*

Oswald, who had served as a radar operator in the U.S. Marine Corps, "defected" to the Soviet Union in 1959. He returned to America in June 1962 with a Russian wife and Marxist views. He was interviewed by the FBI three times between his return and September 1963, when he went to Mexico City and visited the Soviet and Cuban embassies. The CIA observed him with a Soviet KGB officer there, but because of bureaucratic inefficiency he was not interviewed by the FBI or the CIA on his return from this visit. For months prior to November 22 he was also observed in contact with pro- and anti-Castro Cuban exile groups. Six days after Kennedy's death J. Edgar Hoover disciplined seventeen FBI personnel, including one assistant director, for serious investigative deficiencies in the handling of the Oswald case. The Warren Commission under Chief Justice Earl Warren, investigating the assassination, was not told this.

The FBI publicly declared that Oswald, acting alone, had killed Kennedy. It made no effort to investigate the questions of possible Cuban government or

---

*In September 1978 a CIA inspector general's report on plotting against Castro, compiled in 1967, was released to the House Committee on Assassinations investigating the death of President Kennedy. The report said:

> It became clear very early in our investigation that the vigor with which schemes were pursued within the agency to eliminate Castro personally varied with the intensity of the U.S. Government's efforts to overthrow the Castro regime. . . . We cannot overemphasize the extent to which responsible agency officers felt themselves subject to the Kennedy administration's severe pressures to do something about Castro and his regime. The fruitless and, in retrospect, often unrealistic plotting should be viewed in that light.

The report made the point that "bringing about the downfall of a government necessarily requires the removal of its leaders from positions of power, and there is always the risk that the participants will resort to assassination. Such removals from power as the house arrest of a Mussadeq or the flight of a Batista should not cause one to overlook the killings of a Diem or of a Trujillo by forces encouraged but not controlled by the U.S. Government."

"The AMLASH operation," said Helms, "was designed to try and get this man to organize a political action operation and a military operation to get rid of Castro. It was he who kept saying that the fastest way to do this is to kill the man. But this doesn't mean that the agency was interested in that aspect of the thing and the primary reason for being in touch with him was quite the opposite. We were trying to do various things to rein him in." Well, perhaps, but Helms goes on to say, "It was a hypodermic syringe they had given him with something called Black Leaf-40 in it. This was in response to AMLASH request that he be provided with some sort of a device whereby he could kill Castro. He returned this device on the spot to the case officer. The case officer brought it back to Washington and that was the end of the plot." A CIA officer who had served as an assistant to Desmond FitzGerald in 1963 testified: "The AMLASH operation prior to the assassination of President Kennedy was characterized by the Special Affairs Staff, Desmond FitzGerald and other senior CIA officials as an assassination operation initiated and sponsored by the CIA" (*Investigation of the Assassination of President John F. Kennedy*, Vol. IV, pp. 128, 130–31, 173, 174, 195).

Cuban exile involvement in the assassination. The Warren Commission was not told by the CIA or the FBI about the CIA attempts to assassinate Fidel Castro, although it must be said that Allen Dulles (who knew about some of them) was a member of the commission and was therefore in a position to judge the relevance of this information. Dulles, who had ceased being director in 1961, did not know about the contact with Cubela and the encouragement given to him. The Cubela plot was more significant to the work of the Warren Commission than the earlier plots because it seemed to have sparked Castro's reprisal threat. (Some CIA people thought that Cubela was a Castro man all along acting as an *agent provocateur* and that he could be traced back to the CIA and Robert Kennedy.)*

Oswald's contacts with anti-Castro Cubans were also not revealed to the Warren Commission. After the Bay of Pigs the CIA had employed Cubans who had taken part in missions elsewhere, often working as pilots for CIA proprietary companies or flying operations in Africa. No doubt the agency was anxious not to arouse suspicion that it might have had prior knowledge of Oswald's plans (there is no evidence that it did) through its Cuban contacts. Subsequently CIA officials who had been involved with Cubela testified to the Senate Church Committee in 1975 that they had not thought their contacts with him relevant to Kennedy's assassination, while others, who had conducted the CIA's internal investigation of Kennedy's death, testified that had they known of their agency's contacts with Cubela, their findings might have been different. In the middle of the Warren Commission's hearings, Yuri Ivanovich Nosenko defected to the CIA with his declaration that the KGB had not been involved with Oswald.

Yuri Nosenko first contacted the CIA in the spring of 1962 in Geneva while he was acting as chief security officer for the Soviet delegation to the disarmament talks. He said he was prepared to become a CIA spy in Russia, rather than a defector, because his family was in Russia and he wanted to stay there. On January 20, 1964, he was again in Geneva with the Soviet disarmament delegation, and he contacted the CIA once more. This time he wanted to defect. He told his CIA contact that he had been responsible for monitoring the KGB's relationship with Lee Harvey Oswald. Less than two months had elapsed since Kennedy's death, and the CIA officer thought it suspicious that Nosenko had not only changed his mind about defecting but had done so at such a time with such convenient information. The information was too important, however, to be delayed, and it was relayed to Langley immediately.

Nosenko was debriefed on Oswald in Geneva. The KGB, he said, had de-

---

* Desmond FitzGerald met Cubela on October 29, 1963, and, responding to a prior request from the Cuban for some official sanction for his plot, told him that he was "the personal representative" of Robert Kennedy and that the United States government would support Cubela's coup.

cided that Oswald was of no interest to them in 1959 when he had asked for Soviet citizenship and had urged him to return to America. Oswald reacted by attempting suicide, so the KGB relented and gave him residential permission in Minsk, where he stayed until 1962, when he returned to America. When Oswald visited the Soviet Embassy in Mexico City in September 1963 he applied for a visa to return to Russia, but when the application was routinely passed to the KGB in Moscow, Nosenko said he had recommended that it be turned down. When Oswald shot Kennedy, panic broke out in Moscow, and Nosenko said he was put in charge of a KGB investigation of its connections with Oswald. Nosenko's claim, therefore, was that he was one of the people who could talk authoritatively about Oswald and the KGB. He offered to testify before the Warren Commission.

In Washington, Richard Helms (as DDP, in overall charge of the case) and David Murphy (in direct charge as head of the Soviet Russia Division of the directorate) recognized that Nosenko's information had to be presented to the Commission, and when some days later Nosenko was suddenly ordered back to Moscow, Helms authorized his reception in the U.S. as a defector. On February 4 Nosenko was flown from a United States air base in Germany to Washington. Helms informed the FBI, the State Department, the Defense Intelligence Agency, the military intelligence services, and the National Security Agency that Nosenko had defected. On February 26 the FBI questioned Nosenko about Oswald and the Kennedy assassination. Parts of his testimony were circumstantially confirmed by an FBI source, code-named Fedora, a KGB officer working under diplomatic cover at the United Nations in New York who later was revealed as a KGB double agent all along. Without waiting for the CIA's conclusions, J. Edgar Hoover sent Nosenko's statement to the Warren Commission.

This caused a bitter row between the CIA and the FBI. The CIA and the Warren Commission at the time were concerned that the Soviets or the Cubans might have been involved in some fashion with Kennedy's death and had made this an area of primary focus. "Since Nosenko was in the agency's hands this became one of the most difficult issues to face that the agency had ever faced," said Richard Helms. "Here a President of the United States had been murdered and a man had come from the Soviet Union, an acknowledged Soviet intelligence officer, and said his intelligence service had never been in touch with this man and knew nothing about him. This strained credulity at the time. It strains it to this day."* Helms considered it imperative to inform

---

* *Investigation of the Assassination of President John F. Kennedy*, Vol. IV, p. 12. Peter Bagley, deputy head of the Soviet Russia Division (referred to as "Mr. D.C." in the transcripts of his testimony), made an additional point: Was it not extraordinary that Nosenko should happen to be at all the right places at all the right times in the Oswald case?

We were not able to check inside the USSR, as the Warren Commission noted. We didn't have other sources in the KGB who were connected with the Oswald case. But then how

the chief justice of the agency's reservations about Nosenko's claims in April.*
The misgivings were based on a number of points, summarized in a staff report
of the House Select Committee on Assassinations in 1978:

1. Many of the leads provided by Nosenko had been of the "give-away"
   variety, that is information that is no longer of significant value to the
   KGB, or information which, in the probable judgment of the KGB,
   is already being probed by Western intelligence, so that there is more
   to be gained from having a dispatched agent "give it away" and
   thereby gain credibility.
2. A background check of Nosenko—of his schooling, military career
   and his activities as an intelligence officer—led U.S. officials to suspect Nosenko was telling them a "legend," that is, supplying them
   with a fabricated identity. Certain aspects of Nosenko's background
   did not "check out," and certain events he described seemed highly
   unlikely.
3. Two defectors who had preceded Nosenko were skeptical of him.
   One was convinced Nosenko was on a KGB mission, the purpose of
   which was to neutralize the information he had provided.
4. Information Nosenko had given about Oswald aroused suspicions.
   The chief of the Soviet Russia Section had difficulty accepting the
   statements about Oswald, characterizing them as seeming "almost to
   have been tacked on or to have been added, as though it didn't seem
   to be part of the real body of the other things he had to say, many of
   which were true."[47]

---

lucky we were to have even one inside source on Oswald inside the KGB. Of the many thousands of KGB men around the world, CIA had secret relations with only one, and this one
turned out to have participated directly in the Oswald case. Not only once, but on three separate occasions: When Oswald came to Russia in 1959; when he applied for a visa from
Mexico to return to Russia; and again after the assassination when the Kremlin leadership
caused a definitive review of the whole KGB file on Oswald. How many KGB men could say
as much? CIA was thus unbelievably lucky to be able to contribute to the Warren report. In
view of other suspicions of Nosenko, the keyword in that last sentence is "unbelievably."
(Ibid., Vol. XII, p. 596)
* Richard Helms later testified to what he said to the chief justice:

It is my recollection that what I said to the Chief Justice was that we don't know what this
man represents but we cannot vouch for him. In other words, we cannot vouch for him positively, and therefore I think the Warren Commission should take into consideration the fact
that we cannot vouch for him and therefore we cannot sign off, if you like, on what he has
said as being true, and that in all fairness to the Commission this obviously sets in question
the statement which the FBI passed to the Warren Commission about Nosenko's comments right after his defection about Oswald, and that I took as close to a middle position as
I could. In other words, I didn't use any excessive language, I didn't attempt to dramatize
this. I just said we can't establish his bona fides. And that is our responsibility and I am
sorry. . . . I don't think [the chief justice] was pleased to hear this. He was perfectly reasonable about it and said, "Thank you, and I will inform my colleagues on the Commission
about this; I appreciate your having told us, and we will be guided accordingly" (Ibid., Vol.
IV, pp. 101–102).

In other words, the CIA thought that Nosenko was either a genuine defector, whose intentions had been known to the KGB before he defected, and that the KGB had manufactured the Oswald story so that Nosenko would innocently relate it when he defected; or that Nosenko was a KGB disinformation agent, as Anatoly Golytsin, one of the two previous defectors referred to in the report, was convinced.

Some of the best supporting evidence for thinking that Nosenko was on a KGB mission to discredit other defectors and mislead the Warren Commission about Oswald and the KGB came from the discrepancies in Nosenko's account of his career.* The Warren Commission decided not to refer to Nosenko's testimony to the FBI and the CIA in their final report and not to receive testimony directly from him either. For nearly three years, from April 1964 to Sep-

---

* Oswald had clearly been given favorable treatment in the Soviet Union and may well have worked for the KGB. But suspicion of KGB complicity in Kennedy's assassination was almost certainly unjustified. Nevertheless Nosenko may have been a plant, dispatched to help the KGB keep its distance from allegations of involvement. Bitter internal argument surrounded Nosenko's information. Peter Bagley was one of Nosenko's principal interrogators and was early on convinced that he was a disinformation agent and not a true defector. Fifteen years later in congressional testimony Bagley said:

> A KGB paper of this period stated that just catching American spies isn't enough, for the enemy can always start with new ones. Therefore, said this KGB document, disinformation operations are essential. And among the purposes of such operations, as I recall the words of the document, the first one mentioned is "to negate and discredit authentic information the enemy has obtained." I believe that Nosenko's mission in 1962 [when he first made contact with the CIA] involved just that: covering and protecting sources threatened by [Golytsin's] defection. . . .
>   If Nosenko *is* a KGB plant, as I am convinced he is, there can be no doubt that Nosenko's recited story about Oswald in the USSR is a message from the KGB. That message says, in exaggerated and implausible form, that Oswald had nothing whatever to do with the KGB, not questioned for his military intelligence, not even screened as a possible CIA plant. . . . By sending out such a message, the KGB exposes the fact that it has something to hide. . . . That something may be the fact that Oswald was an agent of the KGB.

During questioning, Bagley was asked by Representative Floyd J. Fithian whether or not he would "rule out the possibility that even though the KGB had nothing to do with the assassination . . . they would spend this kind of energy or effort personally to convince us they had nothing to do with it."

To this Bagley replied:

> I think it is entirely conceivable. If you accept the hypothesis, the supposition, the speculation that in fact they had something to hide, and that something might have been—perhaps he had a code name, perhaps he was a sleeper agent—they obviously couldn't expect as much from him coming back to the United States with a Soviet wife, they couldn't expect him to be elected President, but at the same time, they may have said, "We will get in touch with you in time of war," or they may have recruited him by saying, "We will get in touch with you by the following procedures." This is pure speculation. But then if he is on their rolls as a sleeper agent or for wartime sabotage or something of that sort, they would be absolutely shocked to hear their man had taken it upon himself to kill the American President. I would think their reaction could very well be of the sort you suggest. They might indeed change the mission of another man on another operation in order to get this message over to us that they really had nothing to do with it (*Investigation of the Assassination of President John F. Kennedy*, Vol. XII [March 1979], pp. 578, 641).

tember 1967, Nosenko was kept in strict isolation in Spartan conditions and interrogated as if he were a KGB agent on a disinformation mission. No one resolved whether Nosenko was telling the truth or not. David Murphy and Richard Helms were convinced that he was not, although whether he himself thought his story was true was a different matter. Other officers on the Counterintelligence Staff became convinced that Nosenko was genuine.

In 1967 the Soviet Russia Section of the staff wrote a 900-page report based on the interrogations of Nosenko and concluded that he was a disinformation agent. A year later it was reduced to 447 pages and formally sent to Helms. This, of course, presented Helms with a major difficulty. If Nosenko was a disinformation agent, the KGB had had a closer connection with Oswald than was admitted and therefore may have had some part in the killing of President Kennedy. Consequently, the Warren Commission's report, submitted to the President in September 1964, which concluded that Oswald had acted alone and that there was no conspiracy, would have to be set aside and the investigation reopened. The results for Soviet-American relations could be dire.

Faced with this dilemma, Helms decided that there should be another assessment of the case by an outsider, and Bruce Solie, a member of the Office of Security, was called in to write a critique on the handling of Nosenko. Solie spent a year preparing his final report, including nine months of interrogating Nosenko from three to five days a week. At the same time he removed Nosenko from his confinement and treated him in a generally friendly fashion. In 1968 he came to the conclusion that Nosenko was probably supplying valid intelligence and was who he claimed to be. In essence, the Nosenko case rested there, unresolved.* Two entirely different conclusions were reached from the

---

* In 1977 the then DCI, Admiral Stansfield Turner, launched another investigation of the Nosenko case in an attempt to reach a clear conclusion. It was conducted by a retired CIA officer, John L. Hart, who also became convinced that Nosenko was genuine.

Hart argued that "the handling of Nosenko by the Central Intelligence Agency was counterproductive from the time of the first contact with him in Geneva in 1962, and that it continued in a manner which was counterproductive until the jurisdiction over the case was transferred to the CIA Office of Security in late 1967, specifically in August of that year." He maintained that Nosenko's information was mistranslated and misunderstood and that it was never properly realized by his interrogators or by Nosenko himself that his knowledge was inevitably circumscribed by the compartmentalization of the KGB. Nosenko, said Hart, believed that his information was true and complete. The fact that it was not was not Nosenko's fault and should not have meant that his interrogators assumed he was a disinformation agent. Said Hart:

I, like many others, find Mr. Nosenko's testimony incredible. I do not believe, I find it hard to believe, although I, as recently as last week, talked to Mr. Nosenko and tried to get him to admit that there was a possibility that he didn't know everything that was going on. I find it very hard to believe that the KGB had so little interest in [Oswald]. Therefore, if I were in the position of deciding whether to use the testimony of Mr. Nosenko on this case or not I would not use it. . . .

I was once upon a time chief of what we can call the Cuban Task Force, long after the Bay of Pigs, within the agency. At some point I was asked whether I knew anything, whether I thought there had been an attempt to assassinate Castro. I said in all good faith that I didn't think there had. I had absolutely no knowledge of this. It had been kept from me,

same evidence, and each conclusion was persuasively argued and supported by strong evidence.[48] The affair meant that at a central point in the contest with the Soviets the CIA was operating in a fog. Not being able to decide about Nosenko showed that the agency had not come to terms with the KGB: it was divided on the question of KGB integrity and Soviet resolution. Could the KGB really train their agents to stick to a false story under interrogation for over twenty years, and to live a false life as well? Those who considered Nosenko a disinformation agent were saying "Yes, they can." Those who considered Nosenko genuine were less overawed by the Soviets, less complicated in their reasoning, and more American in their suspicion of sophistication and complexity. Within the CIA, the differences of opinion about Nosenko were several years in the future. So was Kennedy's death when, on November 29, 1961, John McCone was sworn in as the sixth director of Central Intelligence.

SETTLING DOWN

The Cuban missile crisis not only reestablished the CIA in White House favor (as far as Bobby Kennedy was concerned, this happened soon after the Bay of Pigs as he became aware of the agency's capabilities) but also gave it a significant voice in policy making.* This was the achievement of the agency analysts and of John McCone, who, like Allen Dulles, put his unique stamp on the position of DCI. Both men defined the role of DCI in basically the same way despite their different interests. For them the DCI was master of the house, a buffer between the White House, or the State or Defense departments, or Congress, and the staff of the agency. Allen Dulles' stand against

---

possibly because my predecessor several times removed had taken all the evidence with him. I didn't know about it, but I said it in good faith. And I think it is very possible that an officer of Nosenko's rank might have functioned within the KGB and not known everything which was going on in regard to [Oswald].

Hart said that the evidence that Nosenko lied about his career was the result of bad translating: "Into the transcript was put the fact that Mr. Nosenko said he had graduated from the Frunze Military Academy. He never said this. He never said this at all, but it was held against him that he had said this. That is an example of the type of evidence which was used against him in assessing him" (*Investigation of the Assassination of President John F. Kennedy*, Vol. II, pp. 489, 492, 511).

Peter Bagley strongly rejected Hart's arguments. Nosenko made "evasions, contradictions, excuses, whenever we pinned [him] down [including on his] accounts of his career, of his travels, of the way he learned the various items of information he reported, and even accounts of his private life. . . . All of those irregularities point to the same conclusion: That Nosenko was sent by the KGB to deceive us. . . . For the KGB does send false defectors to the West, and has been doing so for 60 years" (ibid., Vol. XII, p. 592).

* "A main factor in restoring the CIA to a place of prestige and active participation in the policy process," said Cline, "was the services it performed during the Cuba missile crisis of 1962" (Ray S. Cline, *The CIA Under Reagan, Bush and Casey* [Washington, DC: Acropolis Books, 1981], p. 219).

Senator McCarthy was a prime example of this. John McCone's insistence that Khrushchev was lying over Cuba and that the Soviet Union was developing an offensive capability there was another. He may have had to force his view on the agency, but he would brook no criticism of his people's performance, and his own performance enhanced theirs. After McCone, directors tended to be far more influenced by Presidents rather than the other way around.*

McCone came to the CIA as an outsider. He was a millionaire with a background in private industry who had amassed his fortune during World War II. Trained as an engineer, he had risen to the position of executive vice-president of the Consolidated Steel Corporation. He had gone on to found his own engineering firm and during World War II had become a major U.S. constructor of ships and aircraft. Under Eisenhower he served as undersecretary of the air force and in 1958 became chairman of the Atomic Energy Commission. He was a staunch Republican and was appointed DCI after the Kennedy administration had conducted an exhaustive search to find a replacement for Allen Dulles. By appointing a Republican, Kennedy was saying in effect that he was not trying to extend his personal influence further than it should properly go (he had already offended many people's sense of propriety by appointing his brother attorney general and then giving him enormous authority within the entire administration) and that he considered the director of Central Intelligence to be above party politics even though he was a presidential appointee. One of Kennedy's first announcements as President-elect in 1960 was that he intended to keep both Allen Dulles and J. Edgar Hoover in his new administration; he acknowledged that their jobs should not change willy-nilly after each election.

McCone had other strengths as well. In complete contrast to Dulles, he was far more interested in the analysis and intelligence-collection activities of the CIA than in its clandestine and covert activities. This analytical ability is what Kennedy realized he could have used during the Bay of Pigs. In effect, the authority to approve covert operations was brought into the White House and taken out of the hands of the CIA with McCone's appointment. In part be-

---

* Up to 1965 the agency was a political asset for the President because of its recognized ability, involvement in policy, and prestige. After 1965 the very secrecy of the agency became a liability to presidents as the American public became increasingly disenchanted with the Vietnam War and tended to blame government secrecy for the involvement, seeing secrecy as undemocratic. "If we'd had a say when the decisions were made to go in, we wouldn't have gone in," was the popular perception in the late 1960s.

The agency survived this disrepute because Vietnam reduced its competitors, the State and Defense departments, to the same condition, leaving the presidency with only the White House—the presidency itself. Nixon bankrupted the presidency, leaving government generally with the job of starting again to win prestige and respect. The director of Central Intelligence, as a presidential appointee, was always liable to be influenced by a President. But whereas before the mid-1960s being director brought with it the prestige of the agency, after the mid-1960s that prestige was greatly lessened, and directors found themselves more dependent on the prestige of the presidency and their connection with it as far as the American public and the bureaucracy were concerned.

cause of what had happened at the Bay of Pigs, the President wanted to be firmly in control of covert operations. This change was also brought about by the growing recognition that covert operations were no longer unusual or exceptional; they were commonly used in the conduct of U.S. foreign policy and required higher-level control and review. Those involved in the control and review process remained the same as under Eisenhower. They included the President, his national security adviser, the Joint Chiefs, the secretaries of State and Defense or their representatives, the director of Central Intelligence, and various others who did not necessarily hold any official position in the administration. The 5412 Committee, frequently referred to as the Special Group, since it was a subgroup of the National Security Council, continued but for only a short time. After April 1962 it basically ceased for the remainder of the Kennedy presidency.

In place of the 5412 Committee came the Special Group on Counterinsurgency (CI) and the Special Group (Augmented). The Special Group (CI), established in January 1963, had only three members: General Maxwell Taylor, the President's military adviser; McGeorge Bundy, the President's assistant for national security affairs; and Robert Kennedy, the attorney general. The Special Group (Augmented) was set up after the Bay of Pigs and was responsible for only one operation, Mongoose, 'which it supervised until Mongoose ended in October 1962. During the thirteen months of its existence its members included Robert Kennedy, Maxwell Taylor, and McGeorge Bundy, along with Roswell Gilpatric, deputy secretary of defense; U. Alexis Johnson, deputy undersecretary of state; General Lyman Lemnitzer, chairman of the Joint Chiefs of Staff; and Allen Dulles, followed by John McCone, as DCI.

As a result of these changes, procedures were streamlined, and control and authority were concentrated in the hands of Robert Kennedy, Taylor, and Bundy. This was further confirmed when during 1963, as covert operations multiplied in Cuba, Laos, Vietnam, and Africa, the CIA was required to seek approval of all projects on a "cost and risk" basis. Until then the director of Central Intelligence, working within the guidelines and directives of the National Security Council, had the power to decide whether or not to submit a project for approval or review to the Special Group or the 5412 Committee.

By 1960 the proliferation of operations and activities meant that within the agency, approvals were delegated to station chiefs and division chiefs under the deputy director for plans (until then either he or his assistant had personally approved every project) as a matter of administrative necessity. Cost and risk governed what the chiefs could approve without further referral, and only sensitive projects were referred to the DDP, his assistant, or the DCI. This was changed in 1963, and the Special Group (Augmented) took on the approval and reviewing function. No specific criteria were approved in writing, but the agency regarded twenty-five thousand dollars as a threshold cost for a project, and, as a matter of course, all projects at that level or above were submitted to the Special Group for approval.[49]

The changes in approval and review procedures, concentrating authority in the White House, were matched in another way by the agency's move in the autumn of 1961 from its scattered complex of buildings along the Mall and in downtown Washington to Langley, Virginia. Allen Dulles had fought a long, hard battle to establish a permanent site for the CIA. He knew that his agency needed its own headquarters to complete its integration into the Washington bureaucracy. He also argued that a new building would increase security and improve efficiency. In 1958 he won his fight, and after various sites in Washington, DC, were turned down (no one site was large enough), 125 acres of partially wooded land were obtained eight miles from the Capitol along the Potomac to the northwest.

By 1961 the building, which cost $46 million and had space for about 15,000 people, was complete. The architect had never been told exactly how many people would use the building (agency staffing was classified information) and was forced to infer this from the building dimensions he was given. As a result of the architect's misjudgments, years of minor heating and air-conditioning problems resulted. The architect was brought to court by the CIA, but his argument that he was never given the necessary information convinced the court: the CIA lost the case. Within a short time various sections of the agency, as they expanded or were pushed out by expansion elsewhere, left the building and established themselves back in Washington or in the vicinity of Langley, particularly at Tysons Corner, a small town about six miles from the new headquarters, west along the Dolley Madison Boulevard. Today the agency has a constellation of sites all around Langley.[50]

John McCone, under whom many of these changes took place, brought to the job of DCI the skills of a manager, a keen intelligence, and a strong personal self-confidence. One of his achievements was to secure from President Kennedy a directive unequivocally stating that the director of Central Intelligence was not a second-level bureaucrat but a principal participant in the administration, on a par with the secretary of State or of Defense. This directive, which came in a letter from Kennedy dated January 16, 1962, immediately became a crucial document in the history of the agency. What Allen Dulles had achieved by personal stature and connections, McCone institutionalized for the agency.* In part the letter read:

> In carrying out your newly-assigned duties as DCI, it is my wish that you serve as the government's principal foreign intelligence officer, and as such

---

* Despite his stature and connections, on October 18, 1957, *U.S. News and World Report* ranked Allen Dulles as only thirty-fourth on the protocol list. This ranking was determined by salary, and the DCI's salary was in Category V of the Executive Pay Scale, four levels below that of the cabinet. In effect this meant that at any official Washington social event the DCI was placed well down the table. Theoretically, it could influence the willingness of people to talk and listen to him, though neither Bedell Smith nor Dulles ever had much of a problem with making their positions clear.

that you undertake as part of your responsibility, the coordination and effective guidance of the total U.S. foreign intelligence effort.

As the government's principal intelligence officer, you will assure the proper coordination, correlation, and evaluation of intelligence from all sources and its prompt dissemination to me and to other recipients as appropriate. In fulfillment of these tasks, I shall expect you to work closely with the heads of all departments and agencies having responsibilities in the foreign intelligence field. . . .

As head of the CIA, while you will continue to have overall responsibility for the agency, I shall expect you to delegate to your principal deputy, as you may deem necessary, so much of the direction of the detailed operation of the Agency as may be required to permit you to carry out your primary task as DCI.[51]

The detailed administrative concern exhibited in this letter suggests that Kennedy wrote it at McCone's prodding. "Directives always look bigger to the recipient," said McGeorge Bundy about this one. "Probably McCone persuaded the President to do it."[52] McCone had a very clear idea of his role as DCI as opposed to his role as head of the CIA. He would scrupulously report intelligence information and analysis to the President as objectively as possible and then, only if asked, would venture his personal or political opinion.

For the analytical side of the agency McCone's appointment was like a new dawn. McCone had little time for covert operations and emphasized the DDI over the DDP. He considered the Directorate of Plans to be too powerful within the agency and he therefore sought to reduce its power. This suited Kennedy. It meant that McCone did not fight Kennedy's control: Bobby was the President's man for operations separately from McCone. McCone spent a long time going over personnel records, meeting his staff, and talking to people before selecting his principal lieutenants.

Richard Helms, the professional's professional, was McCone's choice as Bissell's successor as deputy director of plans, not only because he provided important continuity but also because his area was tradecraft—maintaining contact with agents—running agents—rather than operations. Ray Cline was promoted to become deputy director of intelligence. Lyman Kirkpatrick remained as inspector general. R. Jack Smith became head of the Office of Current Intelligence under Cline. John A. Bross, a senior DDP operator, was brought in to handle agency coordination problems.* Sherman Kent, head of the Office of National Estimates, and Ray Cline took on pivotal roles in the

---

* McCone reconstituted the administrative position of comptroller, giving it strong program-review authority over the entire agency to foster internal cohesion. This job he gave to John A. Bross. He made Lyman Kirkpatrick the first executive director, a new position recommended by Kirkpatrick in a study of the director's office he conducted in 1961. In 1963 Kirkpatrick combined the roles of executive director and comptroller and Bross was appointed to a new position, deputy to the director for National Intelligence Program Evaluation, with the prime function of coordinating the intelligence community.

agency as McCone gave new energy to the Estimates. Lawrence Houston, the CIA's general counsel since its inception, was also heavily relied on by McCone. Desmond FitzGerald became the recognized spokesman for the covert-action specialists. Robert Bannerman, promoted from within the Office of Security, became its head. Bannerman had played a vital part in policing internal CIA security during the McCarthy years, and as a member of the agency's founding generation, he knew the agency and its people very well. James Angleton continued as head of Counterintelligence. Army Lieutenant General Marshall S. Carter came in as DDCI. (See Appendices I and V.)

This was McCone's team, and he expected them—as directed by the President—in effect to run the agency on a day-to-day basis. This was not to say that McCone himself did not take a detailed interest in everything—he did—but he relied on this group of senior officers for his staff work.[53] Cline recalled:

> McCone liked to get his principal subordinates together at nine A.M. every day to listen to a short review of current intelligence and any pressing business of the day, then to acquaint us with his activities, ideas, and instructions. He was deadly serious most of the time, but he recounted his adventures at the White House level in detail with great skill, which frequently occasioned a little humor. He enjoyed the laughs if they did not get in the way of dispatching the day's business. As I got to know him better, I learned that he had a warm and sentimental side beneath the stern Scots exterior, although it surfaced only from time to time and usually when we were far away from the daily grind.[54]

These nine o'clock morning meetings became a standard feature of the CIA's management, being continued by most of McCone's successors.

The most revealing difference between McCone and Allen Dulles was that McCone hated being called a "spy master," a title Dulles had gloried in. Spies were far less interesting to him than technical collection methods—the U-2, the SR-71 program, the satellites—and the job of analyzing intelligence and managing the whole range of the agency's resources and activities. Said Ray Cline:

> His sharp, penetrating queries kept everyone in the CIA on his toes, and he had little patience with imprecision, or slowness in producing results. He demanded instant, full briefings on anything that caught his attention, and he absorbed more from complex briefings than any senior official I have ever worked with. He always did his homework, was anxious to learn, and, although strongminded, willing to adjust his opinions in the light of evidence and reasoned judgment. In the agency his attitude was reflected in a widely repeated, true story: When a staff officer looked at a memo from McCone requesting a vast amount of information, he said in dismay, "I suppose you want it all tomorrow?" Without blinking, McCone replied, "Not tomorrow,

today—if I wanted it tomorrow, I would ask for it tomorrow." Actually he was reasonable about deadlines, but he demanded a lot of work.[55]

Other stories circulated emphasizing McCone's confident approach and his determination to get rid of the old-boy atmosphere of the Dulles years. On his last day as DCI, Allen Dulles left the agency in the director's limousine, a specially constructed car with sophisticated communications equipment built in. McCone, who had come out to see Dulles off, turned around as the car pulled away and told his aides that he wanted a similar car to be ready for him the following morning. The car was provided after the agency's technical staff worked all night converting one for him. He had Dulles' office intercom system, which enabled senior officers to communicate with the director without going through secretaries or assistants, taken out; McCone's staff would operate through proper channels. To make the point entirely clear, he ordered that the door from his office to the deputy director's office be bricked up and painted over one night. The new DDCI, Marshall Carter, saw at once what McCone was saying and had a fake hand put on the wall where the door had been, as if it had been cut off when the door was slammed shut.[56] "Jolly John" was the ironic nickname McCone was soon given at Langley.

President Kennedy's interest in taking covert-operation planning and control into the White House and McCone's interest in management and analysis set the CIA firmly on the course charted by Richard Bissell—that of technical intelligence. The emphasis on management and the split control naturally encouraged dependence on systems and technique. Looking back on the agency in 1983, Richard Helms argued fiercely against this development. "Even if computers can be programmed to think," he said, "they will not necessarily come to the same conclusions as Mr. Andropov. And if they should, how would we know? There is no substitute for old-fashioned analysis performed by old-fashioned brain power any more than there is a substitute for sound judgment based on adequate facts."[57]

The Cuban missile crisis, however, convinced the White House that technical intelligence, in the form of U-2 photographs, was preferable to human espionage. Diplomatic, military, and intelligence experts had assured President Kennedy that Khrushchev would not attempt to sneak intermediate-range ballistic nuclear missiles into Cuba. It was not until U-2 photographs confirmed that missiles were actually being installed that the President had the hard evidence he needed to act. However, the lesson that was learned—that gadgets are more reliable than people—ignored one of the great lessons of World War II intelligence: that gadgets and technical-intelligence information are only as effective as the people handling them. In October 1962 the U-2 photographs provided the evidence of the missile sites because of the analysts' work in interpreting them. But to Bobby Kennedy in particular the hard evidence that convinced the world that the Russians had lied and irresponsibly increased the risk of nuclear war was due to technical collection. Richard Helms made this point:

> I asked Attorney General Kennedy, who was the President's honcho on matters Cuban, why the White House was not making more of an issue of Cuban weapons support to dissidents and opposition elements in other Latin American countries. He replied, "The President needs hard evidence that this is going on." Again that term "hard evidence." Did it have to be a photograph? Perhaps not. That time the human collectors came to the rescue. On a *finca* in Venezuela a large arms cache was discovered, the purpose of which was to arm a group intent on mounting a coup in Caracas. In this cache were sub-machine guns of Belgian manufacture with holes the size of a 50 cent piece braised on the stock. Skilled agency technicians were able to recover for a few seconds the insignia which had been braised away, long enough to photograph it. The official seal of Castro's Cuba emerged. Triumphantly, a colleague and I marched down to the AG's office, gun in a brief case. A half hour later we were ushered into the Oval Office, Bob Kennedy having made the appointment for me to present the "hard evidence." I apologized to President Kennedy for bringing such a mean-looking weapon into his presence. He laconically replied, "Yes, it gives me a feeling of confidence." Three days later he was dead.[58]

Plugging the information collected from the government's various intelligence agencies into the CIA's analytical operation was John McCone's major administrative task.

> The man who did more than any other to improve the quality of our reporting and estimating [said R. Jack Smith] was John McCone. I have sat for as long as three hours in Allen Dulles' outer office waiting to get to see him about an Estimate about a Soviet missile program which was going to be presented the next day and which he was going to sign his name to, and he was in there going over some operation that took his fancy in Iran or Hungary or wherever. When we would go up to see Dulles the night before the big meeting of the United States Intelligence Board, we would be there for a four o'clock appointment, and we would sit out there—six or eight of us—sometimes to seven-thirty while he was talking to someone about some operation. He never would have read the Estimate. He would say things like "Why can't we write as well as the British?" Or he'd find a sentence beginning with a "However," and he'd say, "I don't think you should start a sentence with a 'However.'" Really nit-picking, not a real interest in it.
>
> McCone would set a meeting at four o'clock, and we would walk through the door at four o'clock and he would have read the Estimate. He'd say, "I have three questions on this Estimate, and here they are—one, two, three." And "How would you defend your judgment that this is the case?" And you would defend it. He never overrode anybody. He had a marvelous mind, very disciplined, hard, clean, beautifully controlled, and a marvelous memory.[59]

For the analysts McCone was bliss. He took them seriously and presented their advice forcefully. Throughout the Cuban missile crisis it was the strength and accuracy of the CIA analysts that was looked to by the Excom group and that impressed the President and his brother Bobby. More than anything else it was this strength, McCone's commitment, and McCone's ready entrée to the Kennedy White House that established the agency with renewed vigor and influence after the Bay of Pigs.

VIETNAM: MAKING POWER CREDIBLE

Analysis, by definition, is removed from operations. Although it is based on experience and historical analysis and may be expected to determine and influence actions, ultimately it should be dispassionate, objective, and uninvolved. The intelligence that results from analysis deals with the way things *really* are, which frequently is not the way policy makers want them to be. Policy concerns, on the other hand, deal with setting and seeking desirable objectives. They involve the changes government leaders *want* to make. As might be expected, clashes between intelligence and policy are common. A classic example of this involved Hitler in the last years and especially the last months of World War II. Driven by his own desires for a German empire, Hitler would not listen to the factual reports of German defeat presented by his generals and intelligence experts. Not daring to tell him the truth, they left him in the Führerbunker in Berlin moving nonexistent armies on the map as the Russians fought their way closer to his refuge, street by street.

In 1956, before the Suez crisis, CIA analysts accurately predicted the events that would take place (not a very difficult task, since many members of the British general staff were openly telling their American counterparts what the British government was up to). Despite the presence of this intelligence information in the Estimates, the Eisenhower administration was caught by surprise when Britain, France, and Israel invaded Egypt.[60] Because of the administration's own policy bias, its members chose not to heed clear CIA warnings of an impending crisis. This is a perennial problem for the CIA: it does the work, provides the information and analysis, and watches helplessly as its intelligence falls on the deaf ears of policy makers. All too often what the CIA says is not absorbed until it is too late.

This discrepancy between policy and intelligence became increasingly acute as the United States pledged itself to deeper and deeper involvement in Vietnam. As *The Pentagon Papers*—the official, top-secret history of the United States' role in Indochina—later showed, apart from the earliest period in 1963–64, the agency's analysis was consistently pessimistic about U.S. involvement in South Vietnam's war against communist guerrillas supported by North Vietnam. In spite of this, first President Kennedy and then President

Johnson poured hundreds and then thousands of U.S. troops into the war, first as support for the South Vietnamese military forces and then as front-line units, as policy diverged from reality and as domestic political considerations were, naturally enough, placed before conditions in Vietnam. Ironically, this process began in the Kennedy White House among those who prided themselves on being realists and who insisted on quantifying everything before making policy decisions. The members of this group—including Rusk, McNamara, Bundy, and Rostow—stayed on after Kennedy died to fight the war under Johnson. In retrospect, their problem was that they often concentrated on details, losing sight of the big picture.

Peer de Silva, the CIA chief of station in Vietnam during 1964–65, vividly recalled his first taste of a full-scale Military Assistance Command Vietnam (MACV) briefing dominated by the secretary of defense, McNamara, early in 1964. It was conducted at the Combat Operations Center in Saigon. McNamara sat at the head of the table and began scribbling notes on a pad of yellow paper even before the briefing began. As a series of colonels presented MACV's view of the war, McNamara scribbled on, only infrequently pausing to listen to a particular officer, ask a question, and then go back to his pad.

> The briefing concluded, McNamara dropped his pencil, pushed his chair back from the table, and began to bombard at large the MACV senior staff, present in the room. How many more strategic hamlets have been constructed since I was last here? How many more yards of barbed wire for these new hamlets have been issued since my last visit? What are the newest POL [petroleum, oil, and lubrication] requirements for ARVN [Army of the Republic of Vietnam]? Tire requirements? I sat there amazed, and thought to myself, what in the world is this man thinking about? This is not a problem of logistics and, in any event, there are plenty of people here at MACV fully competent to handle the matériel side of the war. This is a war that needs discussion of strategic purpose and of strategy itself. What is he talking about? . . .
>
> The man simply had no comprehension of the nature of the conflict in Vietnam, let alone any idea of how it should be handled. As time wore on, he demonstrated that he believed only in the application of military force. A rational man himself, he tended to view the world as being populated by rational people; surely once the Vietcong perceived the fact that an overwhelming American military force could not be stopped, McNamara logically believed, then they would, as rational men, cease their violence. How wrong he was.[61]

De Silva was not the only person in the CIA worried by the nature of America's growing Vietnam involvement: practically everyone in the agency was worried. In the early years, between 1963 and 1965, the worry was about the nature of the involvement, not about the involvement itself. Only later, after 1965, was there growing concern in the agency (and elsewhere) about whether America should be in Vietnam at all. President Eisenhower had consistently warned against military engagement on the Asian mainland. The Korean War had shown that massive resources of men and matériel could be mobilized rapidly and effectively by opponents on the mainland—their supply lines were much shorter than those of the Americans—and that communism had successfully identified with nationalist movements there that were fighting the post-World War II British, Dutch, and French efforts to maintain their empires.

Eisenhower's policy—which, as usual, included a host of contingency plans, some of which called for direct U.S. military involvement—was to do the minimum necessary, short of actual involvement, to support pro-Western regimes in the area. When he handed the presidency over to John F. Kennedy, his greatest concern was Laos. Before he left office he authorized CIA support for the government and for anticommunist hill tribes but refused to allow any significant U.S. military presence. What worried him when he spoke to Kennedy in December 1960 and again in January 1961 was that the new President might give way to the institutional forces pressing for more direct involvement and that even being involved to the extent America was in 1960 might be a mistake.

Eisenhower had started the direct involvement some years earlier. In 1954 Colonel Edward Lansdale arrived in Saigon straight from his success against the Huks in the Philippines. Allen Dulles told him that he was to "enter into Vietnam quietly and assist the Vietnamese, rather than the French, in unconventional warfare [and] to undertake paramilitary operations against the enemy and to wage political-psychological warfare" in collaboration with the South Vietnamese.[62] In January 1954 Eisenhower sent fifty B-26s to Vietnam to help the French defend Dien Bien Phu. It was a necessary diplomatic move, as was America's paying for a considerable part of the French effort in Vietnam. But the whole business infuriated Eisenhower. He thought the French were incompetent militarily in choosing to make a stand at Dien Bien Phu, and he also thought their attempt to maintain their imperial ambitions was an open invitation to the communists to gain advantage. So, despite French pleas, he kept America at arm's length from the war in Vietnam. Lansdale had limited success in Vietnam. His major achievement was forestalling a coup against Ngo Dinh Diem, the nationalist anti-French South Vietnamese prime minister who until October 1955 served under the pro-French Emperor Bao Dai. Although by 1960 there were several hundred U.S. military advisers to ARVN, Eisenhower was not prepared to let the United States become involved to any greater extent.

President Kennedy did not see the world in the same terms. He was a moderate successor to the Wilsonians, possessed of Wilsonian idealism, believing that there were common assumptions of justice and order in the world which America could impose. He was also a committed cold warrior, absolutely determined to prevent further communist expansion and in 1963 still smarting from the Bay of Pigs, the Vienna Summit, and the Cuban missile crisis. It was time to go on the offensive, show these communists what the United States could do if it put its mind to it, and Vietnam seemed the right place. It was an arrogance, born of ignorance of what the world really was like, assuming that American energy and power, applied with conviction, would change an essentially passive world. At the fateful moment, when the United States could have disengaged itself from Vietnam without political embarrassment, there was a President in the White House looking for opportunities to assert American strength.

Kennedy wondered during 1963 whether he was in fact right in deciding that Vietnam was the place for the exercise of this strength, and some of his close associates subsequently were convinced that he would have pulled out had he lived. But his own character and domestic political considerations militated against this actually happening. In 1964 the Republican presidential candidate, Barry Goldwater, ran on a strong prowar plank, and it would not have suited Kennedy—just as it did not suit Johnson—to face the electorate with the promise of complete disengagement. In addition, in September 1963 McNamara was promising Kennedy that with the proper American effort the war in Vietnam would be won by the end of 1965. No one was listening to the CIA or its analysts. Ray Cline recalled:

> McCone and I talked a lot about the U.S. involvement in Vietnam, and we both agreed in advising that intervention there would pay only if the United States was prepared to engage in a long, difficult process of nation-building in South Vietnam to create the political and economic strength to resist a guerrilla war. The CIA's estimates and other analytical papers in the entire Kennedy-Johnson era were soberer and less optimistic than those of the Defense Department, particularly those of McNamara. . . .
>
> I remember once—in the Lyndon Johnson period—being asked by Bundy to have the CIA prepare an objective analysis of the results of the U.S. Air Force bombing of North Vietnam. He said "Everyone agrees your analysts are the only honest guys in town, and we need to know the truth." . . . Over a period of time [our] work demonstrated that little progress was being made in slowing down the North Vietnamese infiltration of the South. The CIA was the bearer of bad tidings throughout the Vietnam war, and was not very happily received by any of the policymakers who tried to make the Vietnam intervention work. The intelligence was sound, but the policy was not firmly based on the evidence.[63]

This central clash between policy and intelligence had been controlled by Eisenhower. His method of administration, by committees and through staff work, bent the bureaucracy to his service. Things might take time, but by and large they were done in the way the President wanted. Eisenhower did not plan an invasion of Cuba in the Oval Office—he left that to those responsible for carrying it out—and he would never even have thought of dealing with the Cuban missile crisis only from the Oval Office. There were systems in place, people responsible, and he would look to them to do their jobs according to his direction. He would not have tried to do their jobs himself. Always keeping a distance from tactics, he was free to ponder strategy, and through him the CIA's analysts had a clear effect on policy.

Early in 1954 Eisenhower made it clear that the National Security Council—as he was to tell Kennedy seven years later—was the most important single unit in his administration; it was the fulcrum between policy and intelligence. He also made clear that intelligence, which had proved its value to him during World War II, was to play a central role in his policy making. However, he complained that there were two things wrong with the intelligence he was receiving. First, there was no clear distinction being made between Soviet capabilities and actual intentions. Second, there was no proper perspective of the Soviet threat; it was not being matched with American capabilities and intentions. What Eisenhower wanted was a "net" estimate, what the military called a "commander's estimate," in which everything that was known about a problem was put together, each element being measured off against another, until a best guess could be made in those areas where there was still uncertainty.[64]

Before Eisenhower took office the Board of National Estimates under Bedell Smith organized regular annual Estimates on problems facing the United States year after year, notably Soviet capabilities and intentions. Frequently these reports were long, detailed, and finely balanced, the results of years of work by CIA scholars and information collectors. "National Intelligence Estimates," said Lyman Kirkpatrick, "are perhaps the most important documents created in the intelligence mechanisms of our government. . . . An NIE is a statement of what is going to happen in any country, in any area, in any given situation, and as far as possible into the future."[65]

In terms of readability they represented a quantum improvement over those produced during Hillenkoetter's tenure. Despite this, they probably were not read very carefully, or, at most, their summaries were considered. Presidents are kept busy dealing with domestic as well as international political questions all the time, having to spend as much time shaking hands as studying strategic threats. Only when a problem becomes acute is expert advice really listened to, and if "wrong" or inadequate advice is given, the experts may never be listened to again. This was the problem that faced the Joint Chiefs and the CIA after the Bay of Pigs when Kennedy resolved to control everything from the Oval Office in the future. Despite the CIA's performance during the Cuban missile crisis, it was a view Kennedy held to.

When it came to Vietnam, agency analyses were initiated by Eisenhower and heeded by him. Under Kennedy and most particularly Johnson, however, the CIA's reporting, increasingly at odds with policy, became more and more difficult for the President to bear. From the perspective of the Oval Office, it was not helping to *win* the war. All the CIA efforts in the war—including the work of its chiefs of station in Vietnam, its intelligence reporting of Vietcong operations and intentions, its help to the South Vietnamese, its development of Operation Phoenix to identify and make ineffective Vietcong operatives and supporters—could not hide the fact that on the big question the CIA was not a member of the team: it refused to go along with policy makers' hopes that the war was winnable. By elevating the importance to the system of accurate intelligence Eisenhower made possible this independent stand by the CIA on such a vital matter.

Eisenhower was not the only one responsible for the CIA's ability to take an independent stand. It was also the directors of the agency and their analysts who saw to it that every statement could be documented and that the principle of footnoting was maintained so that differences were acknowledged. They also realized that being the President's men did not mean going along with the President all the time. However, the pressures to agree with the President's policies—no matter how divorced they were from the reality of CIA intelligence—did have an effect on the Estimates and directly influenced the efforts of the CIA to fight for its place in the bureaucracy.

John McCone was the first director to feel this pressure after Kennedy's death. President Johnson operated in a way different from Kennedy's and had extremely different interests. Kennedy liked to *start* his day with a CIA intelligence summary; the agency invented a special publication tailored for him, the "President's Intelligence Checklist," giving the current intelligence of interest, laced now and again with titbits and humor. Since Johnson, who lacked Kennedy's wit, liked to *end* his day with an intelligence rundown, the checklist was redesigned for him and made more solemn. While Kennedy would make comments on his checklist and telephone Ray Cline or Jack Smith—or even junior officers—for more details or perhaps to discuss stories that appeared in the newspapers but not in the checklist, getting feedback from Johnson was nearly impossible. The CIA were not even sure he read his checklist. While Kennedy offered McCone ready access to the Oval Office, Johnson paid little attention to intelligence, and National Security Council meetings became even more occasional than under Kennedy. While Kennedy was prepared to listen to unwelcome information, Johnson was not. According to Ray Cline:

> As the Vietnam war became more worrisome, Johnson retreated more and more from orderly reviewing of evidence and systematic consultation. Kennedy had converted Eisenhower's methodical NSC process to a fast-break, executive task-force process, which worked well if the President really focused on the problem. Lyndon Johnson further narrowed the circle of participants in the NSC to the principals, whom he began to meet at a weekly luncheon—Dean Rusk, McNamara, and Bundy, who was replaced later by Walt

Rostow. There were other groups: but this was the critical policy forum, and intelligence did not have a place at the table.[66]

John McCone was not invited. Personally wealthy and with wide cultural and business interests, he did not need the job of DCI and saw no reason to continue in it if the President would not speak to him because he brought bad news or did not get along with him. So he resigned. Johnson appointed Vice Admiral William F. Raborn, Jr., as McCone's successor, with Richard Helms as the deputy director, on April 28, 1965.

Raborn inherited an effective, well-managed agency that was well established in the bureaucracy but fighting for presidential favor. He was attractive to Johnson because he had been in charge of the navy's successful *Polaris* nuclear submarine missile program, bringing it in on time and within budget and winning friends on Capitol Hill. Raborn had a reputation as a manager and a systems man, not an ideas man. Johnson must have calculated that Raborn would make sure that the agency did his bidding and find some way of making its Vietnam views more palatable. Unfortunately Raborn was not equipped to deliver the agency to Johnson or "sell" it on Capitol Hill. Unable to grapple with the intricacies of intelligence or international affairs, he was viewed within the agency with suspicion and quickly with derision too. The stories of his ineptness abounded. "It was very embarrassing for Helms," recalled one man close to the DCI's office at the time, "because when there were NSC meetings, for instance, Mac Bundy would call up from the White House and say, 'The President wants to be sure that the director brings Mr. Helms with him.' Now, this was always very embarrassing to the director. It could not warm the cockles of his heart toward his deputy when the White House said, 'Look, for Christ's sake, don't show up without your deputy, who can tell you what to do!' Which in effect was what was happening."[67] Another ex-colleague remarked:

> Raborn is a very simple man, a patriot from the word go. He was a career navy officer who at one point saw his career go down in flames. He was at sea in his carrier and there was a fire and explosion below decks. After that the navy sidelined him. He finally got the job of working the *Polaris* program, which the dominant navy admirals at the time were not very happy with—they wanted big ships, carriers, nuclear submarines—and he brought the *Polaris* program in something like twenty-four months ahead of schedule. He did it with a management technique of strict accountability, a kind of systems analyst approach. His picture was on the cover of *Time*.
>
> Raborn retired in 1963 and went out to Palm Springs and bought a large house overlooking the eleventh fairway and played golf all day. When Lyndon Johnson said, "Admiral, I want you to come and run the CIA," two years later—why, hell, he would have run through fire to be there: he was a real patriot. On the platform at the swearing-in ceremony, after the President had

said some kind things about him, about how he'd searched the country over and the only man he could find really capable of running it was "Red" Raborn, there he was with tears trickling down his cheeks and coming off his chin in steady little drops. They really were.[68]

As director of Central Intelligence, however, Red Raborn caused a lot of other people to cry with frustration. "Who's this fellow Oligarchy anyway?" he once asked. One former associate remembered:

> In those days we had pseudonyms for everything, and certain high-level government agencies had cryptonyms with a KU digraph, and Raborn couldn't remember these. Most directors don't care—there is always a guy outside the door who writes in the true name for the director. So one day he sent for this guy, his executive assistant—a longtime CIA man but an Annapolis graduate like Raborn, so he could swim in the same pond—and Raborn said to him, "I've told you. I want those cryptonyms translated!" And the guy said, "But, Admiral, I've done it." "No, you haven't!" He said, "I'm sorry if I haven't. If you show me where, I'll translate it." "What is this KUWAIT?" asked Raborn. What do you do? You gasp.[69]

"He was Director of Central Intelligence for only a year," records the Church Committee History, "and his impact on the agency was minimal."[70] In that year, from April 28, 1965, to June 30, 1966, a great deal happened to the agency as Johnson, with Raborn not prepared to upset him, involved the CIA more and more in the conduct of the Vietnam War. Although the Estimates did not change, the agency found itself fully embroiled on the operations side.

The decolonization of Africa in the early 1960s generated a dramatically increased American interest in the continent. It also generated an increase in the scale of clandestine activities carried on there by the CIA. Third World countries generally were seen first by Kennedy and then by Johnson as a new battleground for the United States and the Soviet Union. (This changed in 1972 with the recognition of Red China by the United States; and with its admission to the United Nations, a new player was seen to have entered the contest against Russia.) There was a universal assumption that the USSR would seek to control the new states and make the same identification with nationalism it had made in Southeast Asia. Before 1960 the African continent was divided between the European and Middle Eastern divisions of the agency. In 1960 a new Africa Division was formed, and CIA stations in the continent mushroomed, increasing by 55.5 percent between 1959 and 1963. A comparable increase took place in Latin America as the United States belatedly realized that a country need not be a recent ex-colony to be in the Third World. Castro's attempts to export the Cuban revolution to Peru, Bolivia, and Colombia were met by a 40 percent increase in the size of the agency's Western Hemisphere Division between 1960 and 1965.

In 1962 the CIA began what was to become a large-scale involvement in Southeast Asia, concentrating on Laos and Vietnam. In Laos the support that Eisenhower had authorized was increased to regular air supply of anticommunist government troops and hill tribesmen, paramilitary training programs, and a growing number of U.S. personnel on the ground. Ultimately a secret war was effectively fought in Laos, with CIA support for hill tribesmen being geared to bringing them into the fight against the Vietcong rather than simply helping the tribes resist the Pathet Lao, the Laotian communists. The calculation was that this would force the North Vietnamese and the Vietcong to divert men and resources from the war in South Vietnam. By the mid-1960s there were approximately ten thousand American Special Forces troops and CIA officers controlling an army of about thirty thousand (mainly tribesmen), all paid for by the CIA from its secret appropriations. By 1970 the secret war had effectively been won by the Pathet Lao and North Vietnamese, but—as the CIA had calculated—at significant cost to the communist effort in South Vietnam.*

---

* The CIA referred to the hill tribes as "Meos" although there were, in fact, several different tribes. But the complexity of being accurate about the tribes was considered inappropriate for Washington briefings and discussion. In 1973 Senator Stuart Symington claimed to be shocked and surprised when the Senate Foreign Relations Committee learned about the secret war in Laos. Questioning William Colby about CIA Indochina operations, Symington said in response to Colby's assertions of presidential authority for CIA actions, "What you can really call the CIA, then, is 'The King's Men' or 'The President's Army'?"

"I do not think this is the case, Mr. Chairman," replied Colby. "I think the CIA is an intelligence agency."

"I know you know that much of the CIA operation in Laos had as much to do with intelligence as the production of carpets in the United States," Symington retorted. "This is what worries the American people. They find something going on for years, killing a lot of people, about which they had no idea."

Symington had a very good idea of what had been happening in Laos, and his "shock" in 1973 was viewed with undisguised scorn in the agency. He had been regarded as an agency "friend" and had been briefed about the war as early as September 1966. He visited the country and was a houseguest of Ted Shackley, the CIA chief of station in Vientiane, and personally invited Shackley to testify before the Senate Armed Services Committee on October 5, 1967. At that time Symington praised the CIA effort in Laos as a sensible way to fight a war (Thomas Powers, *The Man Who Kept the Secrets* [New York: Knopf, 1979], pp. 178–179).

In 1968 President Johnson ordered an end to all air operations in Southeast Asia, and this drastically reduced the supplies to the secret army in Laos, resulting in their ultimate rout. (It also resulted in the loss of nine spy teams in North Vietnam; intelligence operations in 1968 were regarded as marginal to domestic politics and international relations.) During Nixon's presidency support for the secret army was renewed but to no strategic effect. It had been too weakened.

The CIA has been accused of involvement in the Asian drug trade through General Vang Pao, the leader of the Laotian secret army, who traded in opium, at times using CIA planes. See Alfred A. McCoy, *The Politics of Heroin in South-East Asia* (New York: Harper & Row, 1972), for an anti-CIA account of the agency's role in this episode. The Church Committee investigated allegations that the CIA was actively involved in the drug trade and found no evidence that it was.

Chou En-lai at the same time was organizing the export of Chinese opium to Vietnam and the United States in an effort to demoralize American troops. Chou admitted this to Nasser in 1965, saying, "The effect this demoralization is going to have on the United States will be far

In South Vietnam, which was always the principal battleground, the agency developed closer and closer relationships with the native police and military forces with training programs and the development of Vietnamese Special Forces units. The country had become a republic in October 1955 when Diem, following a referendum, replaced the Emperor Bao Dai as president. In 1965, after McCone's departure, the CIA found itself even more deeply involved in full-scale paramilitary and intelligence assistance to South Vietnam, paralleling the increasing U.S. military commitment there.[71]

greater than anyone realizes" (Schlesinger, *Robert Kennedy and His Times*, p. 520). Castro was similarly engaged, apparently, trying to promote drug addiction in the United States through Santos Trafficante, who was rumored in the Cuban exile community in 1961 to be a Castro agent (ibid.).

—13—

Agency Agonistes 1965–1968

"When you walk down that hall," said Raborn to his startled staff, "I want to see the wind move."[1] With McCone's departure, the message to the agency was clear: Respond positively to the President's wishes or else risk being broken up or disregarded by him. "Johnson's only interested in dossiers on who's doing what to whom," complained one important CIA man about the work he was doing to make the President happy.[2] Raborn had registered the message and was determined that his people should race to do the President's bidding. During 1965, as the President became increasingly involved with the Vietnam War, the CIA conducted an increasing number of operations in Vietnam, requiring more and more agency personnel to sustain the effort. As the pressure to perform mounted, Raborn caved in to the natural bureaucratic urge to deploy more resources there. The best staffers understood that career advancement depended on a stint in Vietnam. Station chiefs in posts outside the war zone often had to go to great lengths to keep their best people from transferring to Vietnam.

It was to take nearly twenty years after the French withdrawal from Vietnam in 1955 before Americans realized that they were seen as another colonial power and not as the introducers of democracy and liberalism. The end had come to the age of consent, in colonial countries, to government by Europeans—and by Americans. This was a view that specialists on the analytical side of the agency had come to, but it was swept aside in the general enthusiasm for the war effort as American liberals in government resolved to show that they were not soft on communism. Unfortunately, in Vietnam this meant backing an undemocratic ruler, Ngo Dinh Diem.

Diem was as strong a ruler of South Vietnam as was possible in the circumstances. Since 1955 he had been in power with U.S. support. At first the support was financial and diplomatic, based on John Foster Dulles' determination that while the old empires were to be replaced by national groupings, these groupings should not be communist. "What shall we do about those bastards out there?" Frank Wisner once asked complainingly about the French in Vietnam in the early 1950s.[3] As he saw it, the obdurate French were playing straight into the hands of the communists, forcing communism on Vietnamese nationalism. The Southeast Asia Treaty Organization (SEATO), formed on September 8, 1954, at America's urging, provided an umbrella under which American efforts to secure anticommunist, antiimperial nationalist governments in Cambodia, Laos, and Vietnam (all three specifically protected by SEATO) could be conducted without facing British or French diplomatic opposition. After America's other alliance initiative in the area, the ANZUS pact, whereby the United States effectively replaced Britain as the guarantor of Australia and New Zealand, and after the French military defeat in their war against Vietnamese communists, the Viet Minh, at Dien Bien Phu in 1954, both old empires recognized the dominance of American power over their own in Southeast Asia, and fell into line with it.

When in July 1955 Diem announced that the elections agreed to in the Geneva Accords ending French control in Vietnam would not be held, the United States backed him. Neither America nor Diem's government had signed the Accords, Dulles argued, and so were not bound by them. Diem no doubt realized that if elections were held throughout Vietnam as planned, he would lose to Ho Chi Minh.[4] Diem was still establishing his government and had inherited not only officials but also those groups that had collaborated with the French. Ho Chi Minh, on the other hand, was *the* nationalist leader and had actively fought the French and, before them, the Japanese. "We are confronted by an unfortunate fact," said John Foster Dulles to the cabinet before the congressional hearings on SEATO in Washington; "most of the countries of the world do not share our view that Communist control of any government anywhere is in itself a danger and a threat."[5] His implication was clear: America might have to act alone against communists. He added the official force of the United States to it when he announced that the Monroe Doctrine was being extended to Asia. The doctrine, originally aimed against European interests in the Americas, was now being used to police the borders of the noncommunist world.

The first test of this new determination came in the Red Chinese threat to the islands of Quemoy, Matsu, and the Tachens in the Formosa Straits between the mainland and Taiwan. A small island of the Tachen group was occupied by Mao's troops in January 1955. Eisenhower declared that this action required no counteraction, because the island was not important to the defense of Taiwan, but at the same time he secured a congressional resolution giving him authority to use U.S. military force if necessary. The message hit home. China realized that if it continued its aggression, it would face direct American opposition in support of Taiwan. Sporadic shelling of Quemoy from the Chinese mainland continued, but landings on the Tachens stopped. Six months later Diem knew that he would enjoy the same backing in his effort to establish his anticommunist government in South Vietnam.[6]

Eight years later the Kennedy administration had a different view of Diem, though not of the overall policy instituted by Eisenhower and Dulles. Diem had shown himself to be not only anticommunist but antidemocratic as well. He had stopped agrarian reforms in the interests of the old French empire landlord class. He had arrested political opponents and concentrated power and wealth in the hands of his brother, his brother's wife, Madame Ngo Dinh Nhu, and himself. Discontent resulted in genuine, though limited, support for anti-Diem guerrillas and guerrilla attacks. In 1960 North Vietnam, seeing an opportunity to overthrow Diem by guerrilla activity, established the National Liberation Front to give encouragement to anti-Diem elements in the South and to focus opposition in communist hands. The next year, Viet Minh (or Vietcong, as the communists came to be called) guerrilla strength in the South reached ten thousand (by CIA estimate) and Red China began funneling arms and supplies to the guerrillas.

By the time John F. Kennedy became President, a genuine civil war was developing in South Vietnam, and, quite reasonably, Diem was seen as being largely responsible for creating this opportunity for his enemies. In May 1961, following an election in South Vietnam which Diem won convincingly, Kennedy sent Vice-President Lyndon Johnson on a fact-finding trip to the country.[7] Johnson, whose knowledge of foreign affairs was limited and whose interest in foreign policy was even smaller, came back a big fan of Diem's. He called him the "Winston Churchill of Asia," recognizing a determined politician when he saw one.

The trouble was that Diem's political ability was obscured by his political liability to the United States. If America were to sustain a South Vietnamese government facing serious dissent and subversion, policymakers in Washington thought it had to be a government that deserved support in the eyes of the Free World. Certain norms of justice had to be upheld throughout the world, even if the Vice-President did not understand this point.

In October 1961 another White House fact-finding mission went to Vietnam, headed by General Maxwell Taylor and Walt Rostow. The Taylor-Rostow report that resulted argued for full support of Diem for meeting communist insurgency with South Vietnamese counterinsurgency and for an increasing number of American military advisers to back up the counterinsurgency effort. Simultaneously, pressure should be applied to make Vietnam more democratic. As a result, the President's top advisers effectively agreed with the President that Vietnam was the place to make a stand against communism. They disagreed only about whether to support Diem or some other South Vietnamese leader and about the nature of American support: whether it should remain fundamentally advisory and at a distance or whether it should become a full-scale military affair. Against this was the advice of some military commanders who, like Eisenhower, feared military commitments on the Asian mainland, and some senior State Department hands who gave first priority to European affairs and were anxious that the United States not be sidetracked by African or Asian concerns. The SEATO countries also made it clear that although Vietnam enjoyed their protection, if Diem could not deal with the domestic unrest he himself had helped generate, then he would have to face the consequences alone.

Kennedy himself confided in some friends and journalists at the time that he had doubts about the domino theory, which was being advanced to justify greater American involvement. He also admitted that when Red China became a member of the nuclear club, as it inevitably would, it would exert a dominant influence throughout Asia regardless of what the United States did in Vietnam. A *New York Times* editorial in October 1961 echoed the weight of opinion, however, when it denounced what it termed "communist aggression" in South Vietnam and declared, "The present situation is one that brooks no further stalling."[8] In February 1962 Kennedy committed the United States directly when he established the Military Assistance Command, Vietnam, under General Paul Harkins. From that point on there was no easy return. The Pentagon had an ever-increasing stake in the war. "It is fashionable in some quarters," said a future chairman of the Joint Chiefs of Staff, General Earle G. Wheeler, in November 1962, "to say that the problems in Southeast Asia are primarily political and economic rather than military. I do not agree. The essence of the problem is military."[9]

The advice of George Ball that the conflict in South Vietnam was political and that what mattered was the attitude of the people there toward their own government was pursued in tandem with the military effort. When Diem proved consistently unwilling to institute more relaxed domestic policies and to implement land reform, he was viewed first as a stumbling block that negated American efforts to help him and then as a major impediment: The war could not be won, it was considered, if the government on whose behalf the war was being fought was unpopular. The hearts and minds of the South Vietnamese people had to be behind the war effort.

THE VIETNAM ESTIMATE

By 1961 the CIA's accumulated knowledge about Vietnam was considerable. Since 1953 Vietnam had been one of the countries covered by an annual National Intelligence Estimate produced by Sherman Kent and his team.

The first, presented to President Eisenhower on June 4, 1953, analyzed the French colonial war in the country and the prospects of a Red Chinese invasion in support of Ho Chi Minh. "If present trends in the Indochinese situation continue through mid-1954," the Estimate predicted, "the French political and military position may subsequently deteriorate very rapidly."[10]

The next year, after the fall of the French garrison at Dien Bien Phu on May 7, 1954, agency analysts wrestled with the question of U.S. intervention on the side of France. American military support had been vital to the French war effort, and American financial support had met 78 percent of the cost of the war in Vietnam. On April 7 President Eisenhower publicly opposed a negotiated settlement to end the war on the grounds that it would lead to a communist-controlled Vietnam and a "falling row of dominoes" in Southeast Asia. John Foster Dulles urged direct U.S. military involvement, and the CIA was asked to estimate reactions to the use of nuclear weapons by the United States in Vietnam. Dulles, Richard Nixon, Secretary of Defense Charles E. Wilson, and all the Joint Chiefs except the army's General Matthew Ridgway urged the use of nuclear weapons.

Eisenhower rejected the use of what he termed "those terrible things" on both moral and political grounds. He pointed out that it would be the second time in less than a decade that the United States had used nuclear weapons against Asians. He was completely supported in his views by the CIA. "The Chinese would take whatever military action they thought required to prevent destruction of the Viet Minh. . . . U.S. use of nuclear weapons in Indochina would hasten the ultimate decision whether or not to intervene." The Estimate was presented on June 15, 1954, the same day that France was notified, at Eisenhower's instructions, that the time for American intervention had passed. France had lost the war. America would pick up the pieces and assume the burden of supporting South Vietnam—a policy recommended by the National Security Council and agreed to by the President on August 20. Futile French attempts to keep their empire from disintegrating had not only opened a door to a communist takeover of North Vietnam but also made the environment ripe for communism in Indochina. A clean break with the past was essential if America was to find a viable constituency among noncommunist nationalists in the area.[11]

First hopes of a new beginning in Vietnam centered on the national elections agreed to by France, Britain, the Soviet Union, Red China, Cambodia, Laos, and North and South Vietnam in the Geneva Agreements of July 20, 1954. These hopes were soon dashed, however, with the CIA reporting less than a month later that "if the scheduled national elections are held in July, 1956, and if the Viet Minh does not prejudice its political prospects, the Viet Minh will almost certainly win." In September, Ngo Dinh Diem was identified by the agency analysts and by Colonel Edward Lansdale, already in Saigon for over a year, as the best anticommunist bet, "the only figure on the political scene behind whom genuine nationalist support can be mobilized." While Diem, in the CIA's judgment, was "confronted with the usual problems of inefficiency, disunity, and corruption in Vietnamese politics," he had the character and ability to overcome them and the benefit of "considerable unorganized popular support, particularly among Catholic elements in South Vietnam."

In the view of the agency, however, "early and convincing" support was necessary for Diem to have a chance of success. This Estimate influenced Eisenhower, and on October 23 he wrote to Diem offering American aid,

> provided that your Government is prepared to give assurances as to the standards of performance it would be able to maintain in the event such aid were supplied. . . . The Government of the United States expects that this aid will be met by performance on the part of the Government of Vietnam in undertaking needed reforms [so that it will be] so responsive to the nationalist aspirations of its people, so enlightened in purpose and effective in performance, that it will be respected both at home and abroad and discourage any who might wish to impose a foreign ideology on your free people.[12]

Diem accepted the aid but, as the CIA regularly began to report, showed no interest in reform. On the contrary, Diem opted for tighter controls and increased repression. But, as the CIA also pointed out, no other South Vietnamese leader enjoyed the same support as Diem or, in the analysts' view, was as effective an administrator. With Saigon flourishing, the hope was that economic prosperity would prove more effective than democratic practices in combating Ho Chi Minh's appeal. Diem was demonstrating what could be done in contrast to communist totalitarianism.

The view that Diem represented an acceptable alternative was commonly held during the early Eisenhower years and was reflected in the CIA Estimates. The 1959 Estimate on Vietnam described the South, where "the standard of living is much higher and there is far more freedom and gaiety . . . than the North, where the standard of living is low; life is grim and regimented; and the national effort is concentrated on building for the future," as being a country where prosperity, stability, and Diem would survive "for many years." There was, however, growing opposition to the regime because of Diem's failure to carry out agrarian reforms. According to CIA analysts, his refusal to tolerate political opposition was alienating the country's educated elite. Moreover, by concentrating power in his own hands he was creating enemies out of potentially useful and important political partners.[13]

This was the overview Kennedy inherited. From it came his idea that if only Diem continued everything he was doing for the country's economic prosperity and, in addition, could be pressured to fulfill American hopes of a "free people" in South Vietnam, then South Vietnam would be a good battlefield on which to discredit and possibly throw back communism. In a way, when President Kennedy told Scotty Reston in Vienna that he would confront the communists in Vietnam, he was repeating the same fatal mistake the French had made at Dien Bien Phu: he was choosing somebody else's anvil on which to crush somebody else's enemies. It was not a failure of intelligence, as some later charged, that brought Kennedy to this decision but a failure on Kennedy's part to use information.

The President was not reading the Estimates, which, though generally optimistic about Diem, made it perfectly clear that without social and economic reform, Diem's castle was built on sand. Within fifteen months of the Taylor-Rostow report, American uniformed troops were fighting on the ground, and the U.S. Air Force was bombing and strafing Vietcong positions in South Vietnam. Quite understandably, Diem took this as support for him and his regime and intensified his internal repression. In turn this made the question of Diem an important one: he was getting in the way. Somebody else's fight had become America's fight. America would also be on the anvil.

DEATH IN SAIGON

Within the CIA everyone understood that, despite doubts, their job was to help win the war in Vietnam. Both sides of the house, the analysts and the clandestine operators, bent their backs to the task. Operators in Vietnam developed and managed schemes to win the hearts and minds of the South Vietnamese people, emphasizing the importance of improving the military operation in the countryside and making the intelligence capability of MACV and ARVN more effective. Analysts in Saigon and Washington put their efforts into painstakingly detailed reporting of specialized aspects of the war as well as into analyses of the medium- and long-term prospects.

This increasing U.S. involvement had a drawback. By taking over the military, political, and diplomatic dimensions of the war, the United States was showing an alarming disregard for local conditions. The first demonstration of this, which had a major and lasting effect, was with Diem. "We were rapidly discovering that the tiger we were backing in Vietnam was more a Tammany tiger than a disciple of Thomas Jefferson," recalled George Ball, who in 1963 was undersecretary of state and from the outset an opponent of direct involvement in Vietnam.

> Kenneth Galbraith, who had visited Saigon at the President's request, had told me in unambiguous terms that Diem was an insurmountable obstacle to success. . . .
> During a demonstration in May, Vietnamese soldiers killed nine Buddhists; then, in protest against Diem, a monk, Quang Duc, poured gasoline over his head and burned himself to death on a crowded Saigon street while other bonzes formed a circle around him. By the end of October, there had been seven fiery bonze suicides. . . .
> In August, Nhu engineered a midnight raid against the Buddhist pagodas. Intelligence reports increasingly identified him and his wife with the

communists, and I thought it likely that the Nhus were deliberately trying to destroy the Saigon government to advance their own personal power. How could we hope to fight a successful war when Diem was under such poisonous influence? How could the United States continue to identify itself with a regime that behaved with such brutality and crass disregard of world sensitivities?[14]

The answer was to replace the Diem family with a South Vietnamese leadership that would command more widespread support and behave in a more democratic or at least humanitarian manner.

Henry Cabot Lodge, appointed U.S. Ambassador to South Vietnam on June 27, 1963 (he arrived on August 21 and presented his credentials to Diem on August 26), rapidly concluded that Diem and the Nhus were real obstacles to winning the war, and in August he pressed Washington to support anti-Diem generals in Saigon. On August 24 a cable drafted by Averell Harriman, undersecretary of state for political affairs, Roger Hilsman, now assistant secretary for Far Eastern affairs, and Michael Forrestal, McGeorge Bundy's assistant in the White House, was sent to Lodge in Saigon authorizing him to tell a group of South Vietnamese generals that if they overthrew the Diem regime the United States would recognize their new government. It was a green light for a coup and before it was sent had been cleared directly with the President and with virtually everyone else involved, including the secretary of state, Dean Rusk. General Marshall Carter, deputy director of Central Intelligence, was phoned by Roger Hilsman and told that the President had decided to send the cable (Carter took the call on McCone's behalf).[15]

John Richardson, the CIA's chief of station in Saigon, was approached at about the same time by General Duong Van Minh ("Big Minh"), who outlined a plan to assassinate Nhu and another of Diem's brothers. Richardson reported this to Ambassador Lodge, recommending that "we do not set ourselves irrevocably against the assassination plot." John McCone, however, made it very clear that assassination was not something the CIA should be involved in. "We cannot be in the position of stimulating, approving, or supporting assassination," he declared in a cable to Saigon on September 5 on hearing of Big Minh's plans. "We cannot be in position actively condoning such course of action and thereby engaging our responsibility therefor," he repeated in another cable a day later. McCone met privately with the President and Bobby Kennedy, taking the position that

our role was to assemble all information on intelligence as to what was going on and to report it to the appropriate authorities, but to not attempt to direct it. . . . I felt that the President agreed with my position, despite the fact that he had great reservations concerning Diem and his conduct. I urged him to try to bring all the pressure we could on Diem to change his ways, to encourage more support throughout the country. My precise words to the President, and I remember them very clearly, [were] "Mr. President, if I was manager of a baseball team, I had one pitcher, I'd keep him in the box whether he was a good pitcher or not." By that I was saying that, if Diem was removed we would have not one coup but we would have a succession of coups and political disorder in Vietnam and it might last several years.[16]

McCone was echoing the basic thrust of the CIA's analysis, but once again it was not heeded. If there was going to be a coup, it should have been obvious to everyone that Diem would be overthrown and quite possibly killed and that no one would take the risk of mounting a coup just to remove Diem's brother, Nhu. Ambassador Lodge pointed this out in a cable to the President on 30 August: "To be successful, this operation must be essentially a Vietnamese affair with a momentum of its own. Should this happen you may not be able to control it, i.e., the 'go signal' may be given by the generals." Lucien Conein, the CIA liaison with the coup plotters in Saigon, told one of the generals that the United States was opposed to assassination and received the reply, "All right, you don't like it, we won't talk about it anymore."

On November 1 the coup began. The generals telephoned Conein and asked him to bring all the cash he had available to their headquarters. He went there with $42,000, which the generals said would be used to buy supplies and to pay death benefits to those killed in the coup. Conein stayed in the coup headquarters until Diem telephoned his willingness to surrender early in the morning of November 2. In midmorning he returned to the generals' headquarters, following orders from the President to locate Diem, and was told that Diem and Nhu were dead.[17] "If you get killed in the course of a coup," Richard Helms later reflected, "I don't know if you call that assassination. When they killed Mohammed Daoud, the chief of state in Afghanistan during a Soviet-engineered coup, was he assassinated or was he killed in connection with a coup? We were not responsible for Diem. He was killed by his own people for very simple political reasons. Any other way of having a transition of power in Vietnam without this killing would have been far better in the end."[18] Having studied the evidence, after interviewing McCone, Helms, Conein, and many others, the Church Committee agreed. "There is no available evidence," their report stated, "to give any indication of direct or indirect involvement of the United States" in the deaths of Diem and Nhu.[19]

With Diem's death South Vietnam spiraled steadily into greater political instability. Although Diem, a Roman Catholic, might have alienated the Buddhists, he could at least call on the support of South Vietnam's large Roman Catholic population. The various generals who succeeded him enjoyed ever smaller circles of support, rapidly becoming almost entirely intramilitary leaders rather than national politicians with a strong base of public support. For a while after 1963 this did not seem to matter, as South Vietnam's leaders were seen by others as—and were—fronting an American war and an American-controlled government. But in the late 1960s and early 1970s, as the United States sought to escape with some semblance of dignity from what had become a quagmire, it faced the problem of a South Vietnamese government reluctant to accept withdrawal proposals. Another serious problem encountered by the United States was the obvious political weakness of post-Diem regimes, which meant that it was unrealistic to expect any particular arrangement to stick.

Once the war was under way, the CIA, while not suppressing its pessimistic analysis, emphasized its efforts to contribute to successful solutions. William Colby, chief from 1963 to 1967 of the Far Eastern Division of the DDP, which at the time was its largest division, tried in 1964 to organize a rotation system for CIA officers in Vietnam on the grounds that officers from other geographic areas should share the burdens and dangers there. He approached John McCone with his plan. "Mr. Colby," said McCone coldly, looking at him with steely eyes, "the President believes that Vietnam is the most important task this nation faces, and wants our very best men assigned there, and I do not want to hear any more talk of sharing the duty with less qualified ones."[20]

PHOENIX

The best the CIA could do was to run various counterinsurgency programs, collect intelligence on North Vietnam, the Vietcong, and South Vietnam, and train the South Vietnamese in paramilitary techniques.* The thrust of the agency's operational effort was to generate Vietnamese resistance in the countryside to the Vietcong. Its lack of success had more to do with Vietnamese conditions and the Vietcong and North Vietnam's determination to win the war at any cost than with its plans or methods. Since the early 1950s, with the exceptions only of Guatemala in 1954 and the Bay of Pigs in 1961, the

---

* CIA analysis of intelligence was closely involved with military tactics and operations. In 1970 CIA analysts determined that an influenza outbreak could have military benefits for MACV and ARVN. They constructed "a model of the direction of the influenza epidemic. Tchepone was a key junction on the Communist roadnet which extends into Southern Laos—if Tchepone became infected, the disease would move from Binh Tram north and south in Laos and back to North Vietnam," explained an analyst in an article, "Intelligence Implications of Disease," in CIA, *Studies in Intelligence*, n.d. Presumably steps were taken to ensure that Tchepone became infected. The article stated:

> It was estimated that in the primary infected area of Quang Binh Province the epidemic peak would occur about 30 January 1971 and in the secondary infected area south of Tchepone the peak would be about mid-February 1971. An overall 50 percent infection rate was calculated for VC/NVA personnel in those areas and it was estimated that about one-half of those infected would be incapable of performing normal duties for about a week. . . . During February 1971, South Vietnamese army units entered Laos and conducted extensive operations near Tchepone and other areas in and near the primary infectious zone. Unfortunately, these operations took place just after the predicted time for the peak incidence. Combat effectiveness of committed VC/NVA forces probably was affected to a lesser degree by the declining rate of influenza during February. This aspect was, however, difficult to quantitate.

CIA had moved away from performing guerrilla, paramilitary, and counterinsurgency operations. Instead, it trained and advised others about operations, itself concentrating on intelligence collection and analysis. Operation Phoenix, devised by Robert W. Komer, an ex-CIA Middle East analyst who had left the agency to join the National Security Council staff, became the centerpiece of this training and advisory effort in Vietnam. In March 1966 President Johnson appointed Komer as a special assistant to be the President's man in Vietnam, and in mid-1967 he came up with a joint CIA-MACV program called ICEX (Intelligence Coordination and Exploitation) as part of a general attempt to secure greater interagency cooperation.

This was the Phoenix program, called "Phung Hoang" in Vietnamese. Although not a CIA operation, it enjoyed full CIA support and was supervised by William Colby, who left the agency to become the number-two man in Komer's Civilian Operations Revolutionary Development Staff (CORDS) in Saigon, responsible for the program. Phoenix's purpose was to identify and then remove Vietcong personnel hidden within the civilian population of South Vietnam. Its agents were Vietnamese. It rapidly achieved a reputation as a terror and assassination program and became the favorite target of those increasingly disenchanted with the war. These antiwar critics were convinced that the CIA was single-handedly and secretly implementing policies repugnant to the American public.

As a result of his involvement with Phoenix, Robert Komer soon gained the nickname "Blowtorch," which stuck. Of all its revealed secrets, the CIA's connection with this operation as well as the trickle of evidence implicating the agency in assassination plots against foreign leaders lent the greatest support to public fears that the CIA was a rogue elephant, uncontrolled and uncontrollable. What was not generally perceived was that the agency was a presidential tool, acting under the direction of and in coordination with other U.S. government agencies—in this case the armed forces. In addition, agency critics ignored the fact that Congress at all times had the power to legislate against the war and particular operations in it, including intelligence operations. It could have put a halt to Phoenix, but it never did.

Phoenix was a well-conceived program badly executed. As the war in Vietnam developed, analysts in the Pentagon and the CIA came to have a detailed knowledge of the Vietcong infrastructure. The Vietcong were organized along traditional communist lines. Each province had what amounted to a governing body, called the Current Affairs Committee, under which were a number of different organizations. The main Vietcong organization was the Province Unit, the military/guerrilla arm engaged in ambushes and fighting. Others were the Secret Police, the Ban-an-ninh; the Medical Service; the Military Proselytizing Unit—there were about eleven main units in the average province. Naturally enough, MACV concentrated on the Province Unit, tending to leave the others aside.

The Ban-an-ninh, however, were a formidable grouping in their own right and engaged in assassinations, terror, and kidnappings as well as running a massive espionage operation against the South Vietnamese armed forces and government. The threat posed by the Ban-an-ninh (an estimated twenty-five thousand strong, with one of the largest espionage operations—perhaps thirty thousand agents—in the history of warfare) had become much more apparent during 1965 as American involvement in the war brought a better knowledge of Vietnamese conditions. Phoenix was an attempt to combat the Secret Police and the other Vietcong support organizations by identifying their members, welcoming defectors, capturing members, and killing members. "In my view," said one analyst who supported the program, "if you've got the KGB in there and it's a wartime situation, you're nuts not to kill them. There was a Ban-an-ninh assassination team trying to zap a bunker during the Tet offensive. They were zooming around in a car trying to find out where the bunker was. You're not going to kill these guys? You're nuts not to. And so, yes, we were trying to kill these people inside the Vietcong organization who were this sort of threat."[21]

As support organizations, the Vietcong subgroups also were absolutely vital to the Province units and the Vietcong war effort. Without them a Vietcong regiment hidden on a mountainside or in a swamp might survive for only days until their water and food supplies ran out. With the support groups, Vietcong regiments survived in hiding for months. Thus combating these organizations eventually came to be seen by MACV as important too. The trouble was that the drive to quantify everything in the war resulted in a demand for quotas, and soon the Phoenix groups were infiltrated by the very people they were trying to defeat and were turned by them against the South Vietnamese government. "Quite often I found the reports I was submitting being used for one person located in one spot at one time being either assassinated on the spot or brought in for interrogation and tortured to death without any second opinion whatsoever," recalled Barton Osborne, a MACV intelligence officer responsible for overseeing Phoenix in one area:

> I found examples in my own nets of Vietnamese reporting people to whom they owed money or had long-standing family fights or had personal arguments: turning names over to their control for neutralization of the individual with whom they had some disagreement. We had one agent in Kontum Province south of Da Nang who was neutralized because he was reported to another agent . . . as being under suspicion as a V.C. because his activities were irregular, and when he was assassinated I had quite a problem covering that up in the paperwork. . . .
> There was simply an awful overcrowding of the province interrogation centers. The process of bringing these people in and interrogating them, the process of even considering legal recourse, was just too overpowering, considering the mania of the body count and the quotas assigned for V.C.I. [Vietcong infrastructure] and neutralization. So quite often it was a matter of

expediency just to eliminate a person in the field rather than deal with the paperwork. . . .

At the height of the body-count mania, the point of success in the neutralization of V.C.I. was the body count. It was one of the only indexes we had in a very kind of muddled situation. People who were just complicit were good for ten thousand or more piastres on the presentation of a head or an ID card or an ear to identify them. . . . It was a very wild kind of program. There were an awful lot of vendettas being carried out with Phoenix license.[22]

As a CIA analyst put it, "They assassinated a lot of the wrong damn people."[23]

CIA officers were closely involved in planning Phoenix and in analyzing the information that came from Phoenix teams. The regional and provincial officers supervising things reported to the CIA as well as to CORDS; the interrogation centers were financed by the CIA, and every person who ran Phoenix from Saigon was assigned to the program from the agency.[24] It was not the CIA, however, that was responsible for the excesses of Phoenix (although the agency clearly condoned what was happening). Ruthless members of the South Vietnamese government and armed forces willingly did all the dirty work themselves. The agency and its people were in a high-leverage situation, like investment bankers physically removed from the operations they have funded—making things possible but not dirtying their hands. They were institutional consultants, friends at court, organizers of Vietnamese countersubversion.

The CIA did not have hundreds of third-grade enthusiasts it could send into the jungles of Vietnam to shoot village headmen they thought might be with the Vietcong: this was just not the agency's business. It was an organization deploying comparatively few people, all of whom could be trusted. It was operating on ground controlled by MACV or the South Vietnamese, who were as willing to spill blood as the Vietcong. (Bloodline feuds resulting in assassination were common among the Vietnamese, and Phoenix reflected the fact.) It was the South Vietnamese who killed the Diem brothers, just as it was the South Vietnamese who pushed Vietcong prisoners out of American-built airplanes over the South China Sea and the Vietcong who spitted babies in village compounds to terrorize villagers into hiding and feeding them and acting as informers. The techniques of torture were familiar to the CIA, but the experience of World War II had demonstrated that information gained by brutal methods is unsound. An injection of sodium pentothal would have faster and better results than a hammer or a blowtorch or suffocation with a wet towel.

Behind Phoenix lay a history of CIA counterterrorist activity in Vietnam, which, because of the use of Vietnamese mercenaries, at times had greater similarity to Vietnamese than to American interrogation techniques. The first Counter Terror (CT) program was started by William Colby in 1965. (The CT units were later called the Provincial Reconnaissance Units, emphasizing the concentration on winning the war in the countryside.) The program was funded and masterminded by the CIA although conducted by South Vietnamese security forces. It was described by Wayne Cooper, a former State Department official who spent about eighteen months as an adviser to the South Vietnamese internal-security apparatus: "It was a unilateral American program, never recognized by the South Vietnamese government. CIA representatives recruited, organized, supplied and directly paid CT teams, whose function was to use Viet Cong techniques of terror—assassination, abuses, kidnappings and intimidation—against the Viet Cong leadership."[25]

Provincial interrogation centers were constructed with CIA funds in each of South Vietnam's forty-four provinces. Phoenix took over these centers and incorporated most of the CT teams. As a result, the program started with a tarnished image, which virtually defeated its purpose; the Vietnamese identified it with torture and terror. Two years after its inception Colby found it necessary to issue a directive explaining Phoenix activity. He made it clear that torture and assassination were not part of the purpose of Phoenix. He was prompted to do so after learning that someone assigned to Phoenix had applied for transfer because he feared that the program was immoral. What was apparent from this directive was the same problem that had bedeviled the earlier Counter Terror program. "If U.S. personnel come in contact with activities conducted by Vietnamese which do not meet the standards of land warfare," said Colby, "they are certainly not to participate further in the activity. . . . If an individual finds the police-type activities of the Phoenix program repugnant to him, on his application, he can be reassigned from the program without prejudice."[26]

It was obvious from Colby's directive that something was very wrong with Phoenix. A program director would not make such a statement unless there was a problem with the fundamental program itself or with the public perception of it. In his memoirs Colby defended the Phoenix program:

> Didn't it, in fact, undertake to organize and supervise an assassination campaign in its attempt to destroy the Viet Cong Infrastructure, and in the process wind up murdering some 20,000 people, many of them innocents? That is a charge that has been hurled at Phoenix—and at me—repeatedly in recent years. And the short answer to it is: No. . . .
>
> To some degree I am responsible for the 20,000 figure gaining popular currency. At a 1971 Congressional committee hearing, at which I was asked to testify on Phoenix, I reported that under the program from 1968 to 1971 some 17,000 had chosen amnesty, some 28,000 had been captured, and some 20,000 had been killed. But the word was "killed," not "assassinated," and I want to clarify that the vast percentage of these—over 85 percent—were killed in combat actions with Vietnamese and American military and paramilitary troops and only about 12 percent by police or other security forces. What's more, most of the latter deaths occurred in fights when the VCI

cadre, whom the police were trying to round up and capture, resisted arrest, fled, or otherwise defended themselves.[27]

RIVALRIES

The agency's intelligence-collection and -dissemination operations were also embroiled in battles with the military. Robert Komer's pressure for inter-agency coordination and exchange of information in part reflected a decade-old feud between the air force and the CIA. When Richard Bissell took over the U-2 program in 1954–55, the air force had agreed readily enough because it was then concentrating on building up its delivery capability, especially the Strategic Air Command (SAC) with its fleet of B-52s and bombs to go with them. B-52s were expensive, as were SAC's overall operational requirements, which included the cost of personnel, bases, and supplies. As a result the air force accepted without much difficulty the CIA's takeover of the U-2.

At the time, the whole U-2 idea was futuristic in the extreme. Long-range flying was still in its formative stages. Technical intelligence was still thought of only in terms of communications interception. There was little expectation that in just eighteen months Bissell would develop a plane that could fly non-stop across the Soviet Union. The air force reasoned that it was much wiser to save its money for more important, practical matters. It also reasoned that, ulti-mately, air force pilots would be behind the controls if the plane were suc-cessful. However, the speed of Bissell's success and the dramatic change that U-2 photography made in intelligence information and analysis (in Richard Helms's words, it turned intelligence operations from a famine into a feast) made the air force quickly regret its decision to leave the U-2 to the CIA.

When Bissell capitalized on the U-2 to lead the way into intelligence sat-ellites and the next generation of spy planes, the SR-71, the air force became increasingly determined to regain first a piece and then the whole of the action. One air force general, who battled with the CIA on this score for nearly twenty years, summarized the air force view:

A lot of Dick Bissell's key decisions, particularly the one on the U-2, were less a reflection of his brilliance and his authoritarian manner than the total abdication of responsibility of General Le May in the Strategic Air Command who was so caught up in his narrow little world—budgets, fight-ing the bureaucracy, trying to buy B-52s—that the proposition of spending tens of millions on building a spy plane was just simply anathema to the old bastard. So Bissell had carte blanche. He didn't have to argue about money. Le May had to account for every dollar bill.

Dick Bissell had no accounting to do: he had millions of dollars to spend any way he wanted. He had security mechanisms in place to protect him in the bureaucracy. He managed projects through compartments, and the CIA continued this after he'd gone. With the SR-71 we worked with them, and the number of compartments they built around it made it almost impossible for us to do our jobs and made it inevitable that their influence would grow. We just had one helluva time surviving in the bureaucratic rat race—a race which the air force, the military, for a long time lost, not because the CIA was out to swindle them but because the air force had defaulted.[28]

The battle reached its height between 1963 and 1965 when the air force sought jurisdiction over the CIA's photographic reconnaissance programs in space. In 1961 the CIA, air force, and navy reached an agreement for cooperation on overhead reconnaissance which in essence left the agency in control of the collection program. At about the same time the National Aeronautics and Space Administration (NASA, created in 1958) was given responsibility for the overall U.S. space program, and intercontinental ballistic missiles became a reality. These developments meant that the air force's bombers and Strategic Air Command were no longer the prime American military defense. So the air force dug in, determined not to have space photographic reconnaissance programs snatched away too. Its trump was that the CIA's program was dependent on the air force in terms of missiles, bases, launch sites, and manpower, and while some in the agency argued for a further expansion to give the CIA complete control, most acknowledged that the air force should have a share. "These factors complicated an already complex rivalry," observed the Church Committee history:

> Control by one agency or another involved more than budgets, manpower, and access to photography. A decision would affect the nature of the reconnaissance program itself. Given its mission, the Air Force was interested in tactical information, which required high resolution photography. The CIA, on the other hand, was committed to procuring national intelligence, essentially long-range strategic information. This required an area search capability, one with broad coverage but low resolution. Also at issue was the question of who would determine targeting and frequency of coverage, i.e., the establishment of requirements. If the Air Force assumed responsibility, its decisions would reflect its tactical orientation: if the agency decided, national intelligence requirements would havè precedence.[29]

In August 1965 a deal was struck giving the secretary of defense overall control of the space photographic-reconnaissance programs, with the director of Central Intelligence having the right to establish collection requirements and to appeal to the President if he disagreed with the secretary.[30] While this settled matters at the top, on the ground in Vietnam the interagency rivalry continued, expressing itself in lack of cooperation and the refusal to exchange information at senior levels. Major General George Keegan, chief of air force intelligence in Vietnam for two years in the late 1960s, described the frustrating situation:

My biggest problem in Southeast Asia was not General Giap [the North Vietnamese military commander], it was the CIA in the first instance and the National Security Agency in the second. I spent more time, more resources more intellectual energy, fighting those two bureaucracies for the privilege to do the things—legal things—that I had to do to support my air commander to conduct effective air operations against Hanoi, and at every inch of the way I was hamstrung. They were interceding with the President, with the secretary of defense, with influential senators. I couldn't get the reconnaissance that I wanted, where I wanted it, even though the air force owned the reconnaissance. I couldn't use the U-2, the SR-71, the drones, the signals eavesdropping without going through internecine battles in Washington.[31]

On one particular occasion in 1967 the CIA and the air force ended up spying on each other's activities as they wrangled about how best to stop the flow of men and supplies along the Ho Chi Minh Trail into South Vietnam from the North. Keegan recalled the incident:

> I finally found where 90 percent of the enemy's supplies were flowing: through two mountain passes. I determined what was moving through them, I intercepted communications, and I broke codes (which I was forbidden to do but which nobody else would do for me: it was part of the big bureaucratic struggle). My superiors were interested but in a way that maximized what was being kept by the accountants in the Pentagon—the numbers of trucks "killed" every day. In that process the CIA took it on itself to prove to the President that no matter what we bombed, the enemy was by-passing us. That was the sine qua non of the CIA. And in order to do that, they put their agents in my targeting organization until I got rid of them. And then when I got onto the two passes and was able really to zero in on them and prove that I could block them—which we did for three weeks—the CIA went to great extremes to prove the enemy was still by-passing us, sending reports through their own private channels to Washington.
>
> Then I discovered what else they were doing. They had sent some road-watch teams into the mountains behind enemy lines, and they were sending back signals listing the number of trucks going through the passes. I had the photography eight times a day to prove that no trucks were moving through the passes, so I was aware once again that somebody was lying. I was denied permission several times to send some air force people in by parachute to observe the passes. It was absolutely forbidden by the CIA. So I finally parachuted some teams in on my own. They found what the CIA road-watchers were reporting as trucks *observed* were trucks *heard*—they're not seeing or counting any trucks. And what they're hearing, it turns out, are the trucks that are blocked and can't move going across the road from one camp to another to avoid the bombing, and each move from east to west and back was being counted as a truck to the south.[32]

Other Vietnam difficulties also reflected Washington rivalries. The relationship between the CIA and the Military Assistance Command, Vietnam, was constantly under strain. By 1965 the CIA station in South Vietnam had developed an increasingly effective program for training anticommunist cadres—"People's Action Teams" (PAT)—of South Vietnamese who had suffered or whose families had suffered at the hands of the Vietcong. After training, the teams operated in the countryside just like the Vietcong. Over a five-month period three teams killed over one hundred and fifty Vietcong and captured about two hundred more with their weapons. The teams' losses in the same period were six dead and about twenty wounded; there were no desertions.[33] The high motivation and success of the teams naturally drew the attention of MACV. "We don't know what you're doing with these people," a MACV officer said to the CIA station chief, "but they're the only local Vietnamese force of any value at all, and they're damned valuable at that."[34]

General Maxwell Taylor, who succeeded Henry Cabot Lodge as ambassador to South Vietnam in May 1964 (Lodge had asked to be replaced so that he could take part in the Republican election campaign that year),* became a strong supporter of the program and insisted that General Westmoreland (who succeeded Harkins as MACV commander in June 1964) receive a personal briefing about it. This was the start of another interagency conflict. Westmoreland saw the program both as a potential threat to the manpower resources MACV might need to call on and as an armed effort that properly belonged under MACV rather than CIA control. "If they don't wear uniforms," a member of Westmoreland's staff asked the CIA station chief, "how can you tell your own men from the farmers?"

"You can't, but neither can the Vietcong."

"They've got to be made to look like soldiers and act like soldiers," declared a MACV general.

"I and my staff deal with the matter of Vietnamese manpower acquisition in the form of the draft and the allocation of this manpower into the ARVN, Vietnamese Air Force, Navy units, and the Regional and Popular Forces," Westmoreland stated, having decided fully to control the war in Vietnam and make the South Vietnamese (who were weak and severely disorganized after Diem's death) completely subservient to American command:

> We also deal with the Interior Ministry concerning the amount of manpower needed to keep the National Police up to strength and, in some cases, to enlarge it. Now, here comes the PAT. Most of us at MACV agree that although it is new, it is increasingly successful and effective and may provide the key to a Vietnamese problem we haven't been able to lick. But the PAT

*Lodge had been Nixon's running mate in 1960. In 1964 he won the New Hampshire primary on an unsolicited write-in vote. He came second to Nelson Rockefeller in Oregon, his only official entry in the primaries. He decided not to seek the Republican nomination and resigned his Saigon post to campaign for Governor William Scranton of Pennsylvania in an attempt to prevent the nomination from going to Senator Barry Goldwater. He returned to Saigon as ambassador in 1965, serving an additional two years there. After Nixon's election in 1968 Lodge was sent to the Paris peace talks on Vietnam but left when they became deadlocked.

team needs manpower and that has already been apportioned out to the elements I have named. Two questions come out of this: manpower for the PAT program must be carved out of somebody else's hip. O.K., whose? Then, and this may be the toughest question of all, which American element is best suited to support the Vietnamese in their development of the PAT program? CIA or MACV?[35]

"We in CIA felt at the time that our appraisal of the situation in Vietnam was the right one and that our approach to the Vietcong program was substantially correct," recalled Peer de Silva. "Conversely, we felt that MACV in appraising the situation in South Vietnam in purely military terms was off on the wrong track. However, the massive nature of MACV's resources and influence left the CIA anguished and impotent. Though we never stopped trying, our efforts to change the course of action being taken by MACV were rather like trying to stop the inexorable advance of a glacier."[36] By November 1966 MACV had charge of the People's Action Teams, and the agency's paramilitary efforts were concentrated on behind-the-lines work with hill tribes along the Ho Chi Minh Trail and in Laos.

Ambassador Taylor gave General Westmoreland broad support in the jurisdictional wrangle over the People's Action Teams. Taylor saw Westmoreland as his protégé from army days and shared with him the view that the war should be an American war, as formal a military affair—rather than a guerrilla affair—as possible. Both men believed this would force the enemy to be more formal in turn and thus to fight on American terms. The Tet offensive, launched by the North Vietnamese and Vietcong in 1968, represented the major success achieved by this approach. The Vietcong and North Vietnamese launched a traditional military offensive. But, although defeated, the effect was simply to force the guerrillas back to guerrilla warfare and convince the North Vietnamese that their major effort had to be diplomatic and propagandistic.

Both in Washington and in Vietnam, the requirement to go along with a war the analysts were pessimistic about winning and the operatives were certain was being fought in the wrong way caused tremendous strain in the CIA's relationships with the White House, other agencies, the U.S. ambassador to South Vietnam, and MACV. Once again the agency was isolated within the bureaucracy, its dependence upon the ear and the favor of the President apparent, with no other important allies in the policy-making process. Its voice, in addition, was only occasionally heeded by the President, who found himself trapped by the determination of the Vietcong and the obstinate refusal of the North Vietnamese to make a deal, leaving him with only two options: to withdraw and face severe political and diplomatic humiliation or to increase the pressure in Vietnam by escalating the war. At each point the arguments for escalation seemed more attractive than humiliation. Behind each escalating step that brought more troops and hardware into the war was the hope that the North Vietnamese and the Vietcong would finally be driven to the conference table. If this failed, the least the President hoped for was more time to convince the American public to support him and his war effort again in the next presidential election.

After each setback the CIA would gain little by saying "I told you so" or by continuing to emphasize the futility of the war. The CIA's frustration became clear when Daniel Ellsberg, a contract analyst in the Rand Corporation, leaked *The Pentagon Papers* to *The New York Times*. The *Papers* were a comprehensive collection of the minutes, speeches, and policy documents that lay behind the growing U.S. involvement in the war, and they revealed, among many things, that the CIA's advice and predictions were more accurate than anyone else's. "All the way through the Vietnam War," said R. Jack Smith, "we said the most uncongenial things that possibly could be said. *The Pentagon Papers* revealed that. My son said to me, 'Father, did you have anything to do with those CIA papers?' and I said yes, and I was very proud. The agency held its head high."[37]

Holding its head high while the events covered in *The Pentagon Papers* were going on was not so easy, however. Particularly troublesome was the CIA's relationship with the State Department. CIA officers posted abroad frequently enjoyed diplomatic cover as embassy officials—"political affairs officers," "analysts," and sometimes even attachés or ambassadors. In Vietnam the CIA chief of station was a political officer on the embassy staff (depending on the ambassador, he was sometimes a "special assistant" as well), and was thus formally under the ambassador's authority. As the war escalated, successive ambassadors insisted on this subservient relationship while successive chiefs of station tried to avoid it.

This relationship was symptomatic of the more important subservient policy position the CIA found itself in. CIA operatives in Vietnam were not being asked to conduct an alternative, secret foreign policy or covert operations that might be publicly embarrassing. Rather, they were compelled to contribute to policies and operations devised and controlled by the State Department and the Pentagon, the ambassador and MACV, which the CIA thought were wrong or misconceived. If the agency mounted an independent operation of its own, as it did with the People's Action Teams, and it was successful, it was immediately taken over by someone else.

In other embassies, at other times, relationships were different. During the early 1960s Kennedy's ambassador to India, John Kenneth Galbraith, made it clear to the CIA station chief, Harry Rositzke, that the ambassador was in control and then simply established areas of operation for the CIA in India and let Rositzke do his job. When David Bruce was ambassador to Germany during the 1950s he had a similar relationship with John A. Bross, the chief of station. Bruce told Bross that he did not want to hear the sound of a spade digging in the hands of the CIA without his approval.[38] But in Saigon the tensions between the CIA and the State Department were obvious when in 1964 Peer de Silva took up his appointment as station chief after Ambassador Henry Cabot Lodge successfully pressed for the recall of John Richardson, the previous chief, who had strongly opposed the decision to encourage a coup against Diem.[39] What followed was a silly (but all too common in bureaucracies) struggle between Lodge, McCone (who was about to be replaced by Admiral William Raborn as DCI), and De Silva. De Silva recalled later:

> McCone didn't want any further difficulties between his station chief and the ambassador; the war was quite enough trouble as it was. . . .
>
> During an otherwise pleasant luncheon and without ever looking directly at me, Lodge went out of his way to emphasize to John McCone that he neither wanted nor needed a new CIA station chief, gesturing in my direction. . . . Wearing a tight little smile, McCone, who had no great affection for Lodge, mused that unless the ambassador really had cause for refusing my assignment, he, as director, felt he must insist. . . .
>
> Cabot Lodge had lived in the official residence, a very large but exceedingly unattractive structure not far from the Cercle Sportif. . . . He was not happy with this house and as soon as Richardson departed, he had John's house redecorated and promptly moved in himself. The deputy chief-of-mission in turn moved from his house to the former Residence, leaving his old house empty; it was here that we were to live. . . .
>
> My secretary buzzed me to tell me that Ambassador Lodge wanted to see me at once. In his office on the top floor, he saw me without delay. He motioned me to sit in a chair and stood up to pace slowly back and forth before a window. "I'm sure you remember our luncheon yesterday at my house and I want you to understand I have nothing against you personally. I simply do not want a new station chief, but that's now beyond arguing. There are, however, two things I want you to do without delay. . . . First, you will have noticed that on the door of your office there is a large brass plaque bearing the title 'Special Assistant to the Ambassador.' I don't want to see that plaque on your door when you get back. . . . Second, you have inherited from your predecessor a very large and long black Chevrolet sedan. That car is newer and longer than my official car. Get rid of it."[40]

Under Raborn, De Silva was not about to receive the sort of intercession from Washington that would straighten Lodge out. Raborn had a hierarchical view of the world that included a natural deference to secretaries of state and ambassadors. Moreover, he was psychologically unwilling to act at the level McCone had established for the director under Kennedy. He also had in front of him the model of McCone's defeat. As director, McCone had attempted to stand up to the other agencies and to argue with the President. When he failed, he was effectively forced to retire.

But Raborn had far greater weaknesses than McCone. He was not a success on the Hill. He failed to impress senators and congressmen that he had a grasp of foreign affairs, let alone the complex political and diplomatic relations with other countries. This was too important a failure for Johnson to ignore: it was vital to the war effort that the director be an effective member of the team, able to convince Congress of the war's viability. Within the agency the resistance to Raborn grew daily as he was perceived to have little grasp of operations and analysis and to be unable to present agency views strongly. By the end of 1965 the top officers in the CIA, led by Ray Cline, began to press for Raborn's removal. At Washington dinner parties and on the Georgetown circuit Red Raborn was ridiculed, his statements repeated, his influence undermined. "It was obvious that something had to be done about Raborn and someone had to be sacrificed to do it," recalled a colleague, "and Ray did it. He ended up as chief of station in Germany. Ray put himself on the line to salvage American intelligence. Somebody had to; it really was getting that bad."[41]

Raborn's deputy director, Richard Helms, was waiting in the wings to take over. Thinking back, Helms said:

> When Raborn was made director and I was made deputy director, Johnson called me in and told me what he was going to do. He said, "I'm putting Raborn in there as a temporary measure, and I want you to go to all the meetings with him and I want you to get yourself up to speed and then I think what I'll do is appoint you at some time in the future." A year or so later he provided another block in this picture when he said, "The reason I appointed Raborn was that you weren't known in town. You were a professional intelligence officer. Nobody on the Hill knew you much—none of the newspapermen knew you, none of the public knew you, and I wanted to give you a chance to come to the surface and so I put somebody in there who could take care of the agency and deal well with Capitol Hill and all the rest of it, and I hardly foresaw that Raborn wasn't going to do all that much good." When I was finally appointed director, Johnson announced it at a press conference; he didn't tell me he was appointing me. I heard it from the newspaper people who called me up![42]

Another element in Johnson's decision to appoint Helms, the first professional CIA officer to hold the post, was that he needed a reliable director immediately. It had taken nearly six months to find a replacement for John McCone after he said he wanted to go, and Raborn had been the result. In 1966 Johnson did not have the time or the inclination for another search, which might also turn up the wrong man. In Helms he had what he needed: a professional, indebted to the President personally for having advanced him, who was able to handle himself well in public and who had an impressive track record on the Hill.[43]

A TEXAN IN A RAINSTORM

Lyndon Johnson was a highly intelligent man who had clear ideas about where he was going and what he was doing. He was an idealist with a strong vision. The "Great Society" program of domestic social reform was the essence of his dream and effort. He really believed in an America of equal opportunity. He was also unexpectedly loyal to ideals, a trait he proved when he gave himself the mission of securing Kennedy's reforming legislation, logjammed in Congress at the time of his death, despite the fact that as Vice-President he had been lukewarm about a great deal of it. The Vietnam War was another such inheritance, and Johnson—completely at home in America but lost abroad—again was loyal to the ideal of containing communism in Southeast Asia. The best and the brightest men whom Kennedy had collected to oversee the war in a way overwhelmed Johnson with their brains and academic qualifications. He found it easier to leave foreign affairs to them: they knew about it and he did not, and in any case everyone agreed that they were bright, so it should be all right. As George Ball observed:

> He was constantly aware—particularly in the presence of his sophisticated, elegantly educated advisers—that he had acquired his education, such as it was, from the Southwest State Teachers College.
> Yet much of his strength lay in his individuality and in the fact that his manners and expressions had not been honed by the debilitating polish of a more self-conscious environment. His speech gained force as an instrument of persuasion by the vividness of his metaphors, since, like all men of elemental eloquence, he spoke in images. He had, he would say, been as busy as a man with one hoe and two rattlesnakes. Or he might describe someone at a meeting as making as much noise as a crazy mule in a tin barn, or dismiss a man with the ultimate language of mistrust: "I'd never go to a water hole with him!" When we were heading into the harsher days of Vietnam his constant advice was that we should "hunker down like a jackass in a rainstorm." . . .
> As a good politician, Johnson thought more in terms of people than ideas and he enjoyed gossip about people. Sometimes he would press me for comments on my colleagues. . . . He was neither inhibited nor charitable in his evaluation of his closest associates. . . .
> His voice took on a sharp edge—"You know, I can use raw power"—drawing the words out harshly and making a tight fist—"I can use raw power as well as anyone. You've seen me do it, George. But the difference between John [Connally] and me is that he *loves* it. I *hate* it." Perhaps he's right about Connally, I thought—although I didn't really know him well—but, as for LBJ hating to use raw power—on that point I had grave doubts.[44]

Richard Helms observed, commenting on presidential behavior:

> One of the things that is the key to any discussion of intelligence is the style of the individual President. And they just change from one to the other. So if Johnson does it one way, Nixon wants to do it another way. Kennedy does it that way, Nixon does it this way. Each President when he comes in wants to put his stamp on the government. That is a characteristic stand. If one gives white-tie dinners, another wants to give them with open-necked shirts. John-

son loved people. He liked them around. There is another factor too. Every President has only twenty-four hours to be both chief of state and chief of government. They have a helluva lot of functions to perform which have nothing to do with running the government of the country, so time is really squeezed. This means they have to delegate.[45]

Johnson oversaw what was happening in Vietnam during his Tuesday lunches and frequent "special meetings," even though he tried to leave the actual winning of the war to his advisers—Bundy, Rostow, McNamara, Rusk, and the Joint Chiefs.

Helms's inheritance was an agency fully engaged in the policy debates surrounding the Vietnam War, itself with a view on policy but expected to contribute impartially to the debate all the same. Helms's task was not an easy one: he had to walk a tightrope between giving unpalatable advice and information and simultaneously proving that the agency was inside the reservation as far as the war was concerned. He also had the important task of restoring agency morale, which had suffered from the frustrations of the Raborn period, during which the agency lost out to the air force and the Defense Intelligence Agency in the bureaucratic wrangle over technical intelligence.

It was an age of managers and technocracy, when such battles were important. Greater faith was instinctively placed in machines and systems than in men. McNamara's drive to quantify everything was symptomatic of the time. John F. Kennedy, lunching with André Malraux, expressed his view that many problems were technical problems and declared that the real issue of the contemporary world was the management of industrial society—a problem, in Kennedy's view, not of ideology but of administration. "They are very sophisticated judgments which do not lend themselves to the great sort of 'passionate movements' which have stirred this country so often in the past," said Kennedy. "How can we look at things as they are, not through party labels, or through position labels, but as they are?"[46] In such an age the expectation was that the agency would look at things as they were and come up with practical, hardheaded solutions. Its performance in this respect governed its bureaucratic position after the budget cuts and redeployment of functions it had suffered in the wake of the Bay of Pigs and after the lost bureaucratic battles under Raborn.

There was another tension as well. Despite Johnson's adherence to technocratic principles of man-management and systems analysis, his character and political inclinations were quite different from Kennedy's. Johnson had the politician's tremendous weakness of wanting access to other politicians, of acting on people, thinking in terms of traitors and agents-in-place, feeling much more secure and much more triumphant if "his" people were there. It was a reflection of the quarrels that go on within society, escape from them being manifested in the perpetual urge either to substitute for or to improve the human element. Kennedy's substitute was management-as-a-science; Johnson's was a political thirst to improve people, to have human assets everywhere, and this meant that ultimately he rejected Kennedy's attempt to substitute for the human element. In both cases there was no tolerance for interlopers or those whose reasoning brought them into disagreement.

From Kennedy on, presidents have had an almost pathological resentment of press criticism and a paranoia about press leaks. Soon after taking office Kennedy stopped the White House subscription to the *New York Herald Tribune* and expected everyone around him to follow suit. Johnson went a step further and ordered FBI investigations of even minor leaks. As Helms recalled:

> Johnson enjoyed appointing people and surprising everybody. He didn't want to appoint "Mr. Leak," and if you wanted to thwart a guy in this town who was going to get a job, all you had to do was leak it to the newspapers, and as soon as Johnson read it he'd say, "I'm not going to appoint this fellow. He can't keep his mouth shut!" He went to great lengths. When he appointed Raborn and me, he had us fly down to the ranch, and he was going to have the signing of this education bill down there, which was one of the great breakthroughs. They had the signing of the bill outside in the schoolyard where he had gone to school, and there were lots of dignitaries and the press around. And when that was over, when everybody was milling around, he suddenly grabbed us both and walked to the rope where the press was and said, "I've got another announcement to make," and he announced our appointments. The press was furious because at that time they were about half a mile from a telephone. He enjoyed that.[47]

Thus, as the Vietnam War was raging, as public and agency disenchantment with the war was growing, and as agency frustration was mounting because the advice and warnings presented by the analysts were consistently ignored, Helms had to prove continually that he was the President's man. The CIA's dependence on presidential support was the lever Helms used to keep his people in line.

Kennedy's search to see things for what they really were was spearheaded by Robert McNamara and McGeorge Bundy (succeeded in 1966 by Walt Rostow). Both men looked to the CIA for dispassionate analysis on Vietnam. The State Department, the bureaucracy with the long view, benefited in Washington power terms from having the civilian side of the war under its wings, but it was (and is) never really trusted by any President, simply because its view always goes beyond the elected presidential terms. No secretary of state since 1945 has ever been able to control the State Department. This enabled the CIA to move forward quietly in the foreign-policy arena under presidential wings, very much within the terms set by the President and with its operations side at the President's disposal for quick results.

The appeal of the CIA to the President was of the doer—doing things for him, making him shine—and it was the agency's major strength, although the Bay of Pigs seriously weakened it in this respect. Helms was determined not to repeat that mistake. He left Vietnam operations in the hands of the ambassador and MACV while he concentrated on other operations and the analysis and above all on getting things right, on looking at things as they really were.

In 1965 Johnson made two decisions that cemented the Vietnam War as an American war: in February he approved the bombing of North Vietnam, and in July he agreed to send large numbers of American troops into the war zone. Under Raborn the CIA had little to do with either decision. Although the agency produced Estimates and papers that counseled against escalation, its advice was ignored, and Raborn, who was determined to do nothing to upset policy, never fought for the agency view. After Helms was sworn in as director on June 30, 1966, the context for seeing things as they really were was much more limited. The crucial decisions had been made. The job was to see those decisions through and estimate consequences and alternatives while being removed from what was really happening (an American commitment to military victory, which refused to acknowledge that defeat was likely). Consequently the job was on a purely political level: the public's *perceptions* of the war and the President's appreciation of those perceptions.

This meant that the agency's analytical ability, despite everything, would be its best card to play in the policy power game. This was recognized by Helms, who geared the analysts to the problems of solving existing policy questions rather than suggesting different policies.* Said Ray Cline:

> Up to about 1965/66, estimates were not seriously biased in any direction. I think when the Vietnam War pressures began to get so high under Johnson, the pressure to give the right answers came along. I left in 1966 for overseas and came back to the State Department, which was different, but I felt I was coming under increasing pressure to say the war in Vietnam was winnable, and I didn't. When Raborn came back from the White House, where the pressures must have been unbearable, he'd say, "My God! They're all going to Vietnam. How can we do more? How can we find another five hundred people to get out there?" His aim was to please the President.
>
> The pressure came on Vietnam from Mac Bundy originally, although Mac was always very supportive and fair. He would come to me and say, "You're the only honest man in town: tell me what you think." The pressure

* In 1967 Helms was urged by his staff to review the whole community's intelligence collection, with emphasis on technical collection systems. Since this field involved the military to a considerable extent, Helms decided to authorize a study only of the CIA's in-house needs. A senior agency officer, Hugh Cunningham (Rhodes Scholar, ex-DDP officer, ex-Board of National Estimates), carried out the survey. He concluded that there was too much duplication in the collection of intelligence and that this was making the job of intelligence analysis and policy making more difficult. He was especially critical of the military intelligence-collection programs. CIA directorates did not escape criticism either, and several deputy directors complained to Helms that Cunningham's report seemed to diminish the importance of their work (Victor Marchetti and John D. Marks, *The CIA and the Cult of Intelligence* [New York: Laurel, 1980], pp. 84–85).

got stronger after Mac left. Walt Rostow was anxious to have the reports come out well, and he did believe in bombing and just couldn't believe that it wasn't effective, as we were reporting it. It was pressure from the White House, and I could see the squeeze coming.[48]

In 1965 Cline was asked by McNamara and Bundy, with the President's permission, to conduct an in-house study of the "Rolling Thunder" tactical bombing campaign in Vietnam. His report was pessimistic. On the basis of his work John McCone stated to the National Security Council that the bombing had "not caused a change in the North Vietnamese policy. . . . If anything, the strikes to date have hardened their attitude." If the bombing continued, said McCone, American public opinion would probably turn against the war as escalating military moves proved ineffective, and the United States would find itself on a track of increasing commitment with limited effect. He therefore argued strongly against being "mired down in combat in the jungle in a military effort that we cannot win, and from which we will have extreme difficulty in extracting ourselves."[49]

A year later, with McCone gone, McNamara made essentially the same request to Helms, asking for a continuous study of the effectiveness of bombing in Vietnam, much to the fury of the Pentagon and the Defense Intelligence Agency.[50] The Rolling Thunder analysis was conducted entirely by the agency; other agencies and the armed services had no right of consultation in it, so the analysts could be tougher, undeterred by footnotes. Officially, therefore, these reports were not Estimates, but they came from the same general background and were regarded—despite their pessimism—as authoritative. According to R. Jack Smith, who wrote many of the reports:

> Helms never stopped taking our reports down, and McNamara never stopped believing them as long as he was in the United States. When he got over to Vietnam, something strange happened! The first time he asked us to do the Rolling Thunder analysis, I asked him if he wanted us to get together with his Pentagon people or the air force people who were running the program and find out from them what their view was of our findings. "No, no," he said. "I know what their view is. I want to know what your bright people think." At the very end I understand one time LBJ said to him, "You don't believe that crap, do you, Bob?" and he said, "Yes, Mr. President, I do." But he would go out to Vietnam, and he'd get that treatment that the military boys put on so well, and perhaps he felt that if he were to take a line that was pessimistic, it would be detrimental to the effort.
>
> I don't think that LBJ, who was a very intelligent man in his own field, ever grasped what this war was like and what it was about. Nor did the military. The greatest mistake was to send in a tremendous number of troops, which we did in 1965. It imposed all kinds of burdens on the economic system. It required the military to draft people to fight a most difficult war to understand rather than doing what the British did on the northwest frontier: fighting a holding-action with professional troops for seventy-five years. Viet-

nam could have gone on a long time that way. But the professionals liked it. They said "Don't knock it, it's the only war we've got!" They enjoyed being able to use their weapons, find out how capable they were, what their tactics were like, and so on.[51]

With the Rolling Thunder study and McNamara's support within the White House and the bureaucracy, the agency under Helms came back into the thicket of policy. Helms started to attend Johnson's Tuesday lunches. Since there had never been any clear decision under Kennedy or Johnson on exactly what the war aims of the United States were in Vietnam, apart from a general statement about containing communism, it was difficult for the President and the military to focus on objectives other than victory. In the words of Lyndon Johnson when he returned from his visit to Vietnam as Vice-President in 1961, the war was being waged because "The battle against communism must be joined in Southeast Asia with strength and determination to achieve success there—or the United States, inevitably, must surrender the Pacific and take up our defense on our own shores."[52] The result was that when it came to the analysis, Helms correctly saw that the agency's views could be effectively expressed in relation to specific military actions and objectives, since that was all that there was to focus on once it was decided not to keep on challenging the war itself. This, inevitably, led to a major clash with the military.

THE POLITICS OF NUMBERS

The bombing campaign instituted in 1965 was Johnson's main hope for turning the war America's way. The ability of the air force to deliver massive payloads of bombs accurately was the trump that, it was hoped, would either force the enemy to the negotiating table or else so severely reduce the enemy's fighting ability that the ground forces would win. At the start of the bombing the agency was, as usual, pessimistic about the effect. In December 1965 the CIA was asked its view on the pressure by the Joint Chiefs of Staff for bombing the port of Haiphong and the gasoline storage facility there. "Although there presumably is a point at which one more turn of the screw would crack the enemy resistance to negotiations," the agency said, "we do not believe the bombing of the Haiphong facility is likely to have such an effect." In March 1966 the agency identified "the will of the regime as a target system" for the bombing of North Vietnam, coming as close as it ever did to being hawklike in Raborn's last days. By September, under Helms, the agency's analysts were definite: the bombing was having only a marginal effect. As Helms's biographer put it:

Thereafter the CIA never again promised much result from the air war, nor, for that matter, did McNamara. CIA's position gradually jelled around a single strategic assumption: Hanoi intended to exhaust U.S. patience with the war, and no amount of bombing could do enough damage to force them to call it off. Paper after paper—on proposals to hit Haiphong, or to concentrate on lines of communication, or to restrict the bombing to the southern panhandle below the 20th parallel—ended with the CIA's belief the step would not "decrease Hanoi's determination to persist in the war."[53]

"We just can't fight this kind of war," Helms said to a colleague, "not against a fanatically committed bunch of guys who don't need anything except a bag of rice on their backs." To another, who asked him in June 1968 if the air force was right about its bombing statistics, he said, "Sure, as far as it goes. Look: before the bombing they used to send three men south to get two in place. Now they have to send five. We're willing to lose planes, they're willing to pay in manpower. So it doesn't make a particle of difference. In terms of bodies it makes a difference. There are more dead bodies. But in terms of net result, it doesn't make a damn bit of difference."[54] Although these were Helms's views and the view of the agency, they were never presented quite so forcefully in papers and Estimates. John Huizenga, the last head of the Board of National Estimates, said:

> In doing Estimates about Vietnam, the problem was that if you believed that the policy being pursued was going to be a flat failure, and you said so, then you were going to be out of business. In expressing such an opinion you would lose all influence. You'd be written off as unprofessional or irrelevant or some such euphemism. When a subject becomes as passionately divisive as Vietnam became within the country and within the government, the sort of thing a National Intelligence Estimate is meant to be becomes impossible. During calmer periods, when you have a substantial political consensus in the country about foreign policy, the job is easier, but then of course, it's less needed. When it's really needed is when you have a divisive issue.[55]

In order to deal with the deep divisions over Vietnam, reflected in major contradictions in Estimate footnotes, Sherman Kent and his successor as head of the Board of National Estimates, Abbott Smith, began to assemble analysts from different parts of the agency to report on contentious issues and to hear each one out. Arguments that withstood such investigation and cross-questioning were collected to provide the core for each Estimate, and this, along with detailed backup information, was then tested on the other agencies involved. Sam Adams, a young Harvard graduate who started off in the agency as an analyst on Africa before moving over to Vietnam, was responsible for one of the most thoroughgoing intra-agency debates on the military conduct of the war.

The MACV order of battle for the Vietcong and North Vietnamese was arranged in four categories: regulars, guerrilla self-defense units (containing Vietcong soldiers), service troops, and political cadres. By 1967 the MACV total for these categories was 270,000. However, in 1966 a number of documents captured from the Vietcong indicated they were having a serious problem with desertions. Adams concluded from these documents and other snippets of information that the Vietcong desertion rate was between 50,000 and 100,000 a year, much higher than previously thought. When this was put together with MACV's "body count" figures of enemy dead and captured, which totaled 150,000, Adams reasoned that the remaining enemy strength was no more than 20,000 to 70,000. It was too easy, and Adams decided he had better investigate more. In 1961, he found, the CIA's and the U.S. military's official estimate of Vietcong strength was 10,000, while some CIA officers and U.S. advisers on the ground in Saigon estimated the strength at 18,000.

More detailed order-of-battle breakdowns came with the establishment of MACV, but there were still differences:

> I made a series of discoveries [said Adams] that three of the four order-of-battle categories hadn't been looked at for a period of anywhere from two to six or seven years. Basically, the only number that changed for a long period was the regulars—the guys with uniforms and pith helmets and little red stars attached. The other ones, the guerrilla self-defense, the service troops, and the political cadres, hadn't changed for a long time. In a guerrilla war, we hadn't tried to discover the number of guerrillas! We carried roughly 100,000 guerrillas for years.[56]

Analyses of additional captured documents brought Adams to a figure of 330,000 guerrillas instead, higher than MACV's total and higher than any previous CIA estimate. Regular troop numbers were also higher, he reckoned, giving a new total of more than double the CIA's and MACV's official count. In Saigon, MACV seemed to be coming to a similar conclusion early in 1967. That year Adams transferred to the staff of George Carver, another young analyst appointed by Helms to be his special assistant for Vietnamese affairs, and went to Honolulu for an order-of-battle conference with MACV, called by General Earle Wheeler, chairman of the Joint Chiefs of Staff. There Colonel Gains Hawkins, MACV's order-of-battle expert, opened by saying, "You know, there's a lot more of these little bastards out there than we thought there were," and gave a figure of 500,000, close enough for compromise with Adams' count of about 600,000.[57] Essentially, this was where the trouble really started.

If MACV's total of 270,000 enemy fighters in Vietnam was seriously challenged or changed to a significant degree, it would have dramatic political consequences. With 270,000, the bombing, desertions, and the body counts would eat into the figure just as Adams had thought at first, and this could be used to encourage the belief that the war could be won. If the number was 500,000 to 600,000 despite the bombing, the body counts, and the desertions, winning the war would be seen by Americans as much more difficult than they had been told. On top of this, President Johnson had determined that the year

1967 would see a breakthrough in Vietnam (the following year was election year).

No one wanted to tell Johnson that a breakthrough would be roughly twice as hard as previously expected. He knew that without a breakthrough, or an obvious major success, he might lose the 1968 election. Johnson wanted the estimates of enemy strength kept low for domestic political purposes. "These figures at the time and in the context of the Vietnam War," said Adams, "were a political bombshell because everybody was watching numbers. TV shows every week were showing how many bad guys and how many good guys were being killed and wounded. The revelation that the enemy force we faced was twice as big as we thought was bound to have political repercussions."* By May 1967, when the Board of National Estimates came to the annual Estimate on Vietnam, the Pentagon's position had hardened.

The problem was referred to the director, Richard Helms, who was formally responsible for the Estimates and took them very seriously. Helms did three things. First, he organized a detailed in-house scrutiny of Adams' findings. Second, he arranged a meeting with Sherman Kent, James Graham (the CIA Office of National Estimates officer in charge of the Vietnam Estimate), and a Pentagon representative and asked them to work out an agreement on the figures. It was too important a matter to be footnoted; it was central to the war on the ground, and its domestic political dangers were well appreciated. In addition, the CIA under Raborn and then Helms, faced with White House pressure, was concerned not to rock the boat on the war more than it had to. For Helms this meant that if agency analysts concluded that the enemy in Vietnam was stronger than had originally been estimated and that therefore winning the war would be more difficult, he wanted their findings copperbottomed to withstand the bureaucratic, bloody fight that would inevitably ensue. To put it mildly, President Johnson would not like what he heard.

The third thing Helms did was to send George Carver, Sam Adams, and William Hyland (a senior analyst) to Saigon in September to see what MACV's sources were and to try to reach an agreement on the figures. A consensus number was demanded by the White House so that debate and plans would have a common basis, and it was Helms's job to obtain agreement on one from the military. "It's a political war," Desmond FitzGerald, deputy director for plans from 1965 until his sudden death in 1967, once remarked to Robert McNamara, and he was right.[58] Completely aware of these tensions, Helms delayed the Estimate, waiting for his people to report back to him.

---

*Interview, Sam Adams, November 20, 1983. Within the Johnson administration there was more concern about the cost of the war than there was about American public opinion. Opinion polls up to the 1973 withdrawal of American forces demonstrated a majority in favor of winning the war and getting out only if the war could not be won. The decline in popular support for the war and in Johnson's own popularity as President was not in itself crucial to the U.S. war effort. (See Stanley Karnow, *Vietnam: A History* [New York: The Viking Press, 1983], pp. 545–546.)

For three days in Saigon, from September 10 to 13, Carver, Adams, and Hyland argued with the MACV analysts about the enemy order of battle. Finally Carver came to an agreement—the "Saigon agreement"—which MACV, the Pentagon, and the CIA accepted. They would all agree on a common figure for the enemy regular and Vietcong self-defense units and would leave the other order-of-battle forces in separate categories with "no aggregates"—that is, they would not be added to the official order-of-battle figures. The previous Vietcong self-defense unit figure was reduced by taking militiamen out of it, leaving in only the guerrilla-strength estimate. It was a compromise in the interests of agreeing on an Estimate and not rocking the boat. A range of 299,000–334,000 enemy combatants was privately accepted. Everyone was free to differ over the forces in the separate categories, but the effective enemy strength would not exceed 334,000.

At the end of the Saigon meeting on September 13 Carver cabled to Helms that he had made a major concession in not quantifying the irregular forces, because this had been MACV's major sticking point. "MACV juggling the figures," Carver went on, "all point to the inescapable conclusion that General Westmoreland, with Komer's encouragement, has given instructions tantamount to direct orders that the VC strength will not exceed 300,000 ceiling. A rationale seems to be that any higher figure would not be sufficiently optimistic and would generate an unacceptable level of criticism from the press."[59] Seventeen years later in a lawsuit over a CBS documentary, *Vietnam: The Uncounted Enemy,* Carver modified his "inescapable conclusion," explaining: "I had had two extremely frustrating days, very difficult discussions where I felt the people with whom I was talking, discussing, were being singularly unreasonable since they were not doing things my way. I was tired, I was irritated, and I lapsed into slightly purple prose trying to convey a mood and impression, having no thought that I would be discussing this in detail seventeen years later in a lawsuit."[60]

Two months after the Saigon agreement MACV rearranged numbers within the 334,000 ceiling figure, reclassifying particular groupings in the process. Up until then MACV was claiming that the enemy was 285,000 strong. On November 22, 1967, Westmoreland gave a press conference to announce that "the enemy has declined from 285,000 down to 248,000." What was not mentioned was that during the rearrangement and reclassification of the enemy that had taken place over the previous two months, the whole basis of calculation had changed and two whole categories contained in previous order-of-battle figures, and amounting (as Colonel Gains Hawkins and Sam Adams both agreed) to between 250,000 and 350,000, were no longer being counted: they were in the separate categories of the Saigon agreement. For the 1967 Estimate, however, the 299,000–334,000 range was used. "Sam," Sherman Kent said to Adams after the Board of National Estimates had agreed to the new ceiling, "have we gone beyond the bounds of reasonable dishonesty?"[61] On

November 13 Helms signed the Estimate. The overall enemy-strength figure it gave was 500,000 to 600,000 (the combination of the effective enemy-strength ceiling of the Saigon agreement and separate categories), but it conceded to the Pentagon that the effective fighting force MACV faced was fewer than 334,000.*

The internal examination of Sam Adams' findings ordered by Helms was inconclusive. It was not easy to count the enemy strength in Vietnam, since so much of it, by Adams' own analysis, consisted of undeclared soldiers, village cadres, informants. The Vietcong did not come through turnstiles, so estimates of their strength were based on intercepted radio traffic, captured documents, prisoner interrogations, and body counts. The senior agency analysts who studied Adams' work quickly concluded that the evidence was a set of assumptions and extrapolations, which meant that any skilled analyst could arrive at a number that might be completely different from that of someone else working with the same material.

What the analysts also concluded, however, was that Adams' work was very valuable in one respect: he had come up with about as authoritative an estimate as was possible of the militia, irregular, part-time enemy strength, and this estimate was double the number estimated by MACV. Since the Vietnam War was a guerrilla war, the investigators agreed with Adams on this point: his analysis was both sustainable and important within the limits set by the assumptions and extrapolations involved. The single biggest weakness in Adams' work, they considered, was that he had studied one Vietnamese province, Bin Dinh, in detail, and extrapolated his findings and applied them to the whole country. And although Bin Dinh was the largest and most populous province in South Vietnam, containing one million of the country's total population of

*Central Intelligence Agency, "Capabilities of the Vietnamese Communists for Fighting in South Vietnam," Special National Intelligence Estimate, 14.3.67, November 13, 1967. The Estimate began with an introductory note saying that "in many instances our numerical estimates of Communist forces, other than for the Regular units, were too low. Our information has improved substantially in the past year or two, but the unconventional nature of the war poses difficult intelligence problems, the more so in a social environment where basic data is incomplete and often untrustworthy." This was an indication that the methodology involved in estimating the enemy strength did not claim to be foolproof:

> For the purposes of this estimate, we consider the following elements of the Communist organization in South Vietnam: the Regular forces (NVA and VC Main and Local forces), the administrative service units which support them, the VC guerrilla forces, the political cadres, the self-defense forces, the secret self-defense forces, and the "Assault Youth." The contribution of these diverse elements to the Communist effort in South Vietnam differs widely in value....
>
> We believe that, with the exception of the Regular forces, we have previously underestimated the strength of these elements. The figures carried in this estimate for these elements reflect new information and analysis rather than an increase in actual Communist strength. Furthermore, our information on the strength and organization of the different elements varies widely. For the Regular forces it is good; for other components it is much less reliable, less current, and less detailed.

sixteen million, it was not safe to say that what applied to it applied nation-wide. Adams was alive to this point but felt that his evidence on Bin Dinh was exceedingly important and that there was circumstantial evidence indicating that the methodology he had employed was applicable to other provinces; therefore he pressed ahead with it. At the same time he began working through the other provinces, and by the time of the Tet offensive in January 1968 he had readings on three-quarters of them, all of which sustained his original estimate.

Before this, however, further evidence supporting Adams' numbers came in the form of more captured documents in May 1967. One document, a Vietcong accounting document, indicated that there had been about 170,000 irregulars in South Vietnam in early 1966 and that while Bin Dinh Province was a special case because the ratio of guerrilla units to militia there was untypical, nevertheless this did not substantially alter Adams' numbers. It did alter the categories within which the numbers fell, which meant that his origi-

---

This was a cautious tribute to Sam Adams' work. Regular forces were

about 118,000 troops who are generally well-armed. . . . We estimate that there are now at least 35,000–40,000 administrative service personnel in South Vietnam who are performing essential administrative support functions. In addition, almost anyone under VC control can be and is impressed into service to perform specific administrative or support tasks as local conditions require. . . .

Information from captured documents leads us to believe that we have previously underestimated the guerrilla strength. Certain Communist documents, which date from early 1966, assert that there were then about 170,000–180,000 guerrillas. This figure was almost certainly exaggerated [and] we estimate that the current strength of the guerrilla force is 70,-000–90,000. . . .

The political apparatus . . . : Its numbers are large—with a hard core estimated at about 75,000–85,000. . . .

Our current evidence does not enable us to estimate the present size of [the] self-defense, secret self-defense, the "Assault Youth," or other similar VC organizations with any measure of confidence. Some documents suggest that in early 1966 the aggregate size of the self-defense force was on the order of 150,000. This force and the other groups, however, have unquestionably suffered substantial attrition since that time. . . .

Though in aggregate numbers these groups are still large and constitute a part of the overall Communist effort, they are not included in the offensive military forces. Hence they are not included in the military order of battle total. . . .

The VC/NVA Military Force (Main and Local forces, administrative service elements and guerrillas) can be meaningfully presented in numerical totals and, as indicated above, we estimate that this Military Force is now at least 223,000–248,000. It must be recognized, however, that this Military Force constitutes but one component of the total Communist organization. Any comprehensive judgment of Communist capabilities in South Vietnam must embrace the effectiveness of all the elements which comprise that organization, the total size of which is of course considerably greater than the figure given for the Military Force.

Adams was dissatisfied with the Estimate. Just over a year later he declared, "The portion in NIE 14.3.67 having to do with southern manpower represents one of the low points in US intelligence history." (Samuel Adams, "Intelligence Failures in Vietnam: Suggestions for Reform," memorandum, January 24, 1969)

nal estimate carried more self-defense militia and fewer guerrillas than was probably the case. With this in mind, the internal examiners decided that while Adams was probably more accurate than MACV in his findings and that there might well be 600,000 Vietcong of one sort or another, it was not possible to be certain about the categories. R. Jack Smith put it in simple terms:

> The result was that when you added Sam's number you got almost double the number of opposing forces. Suppose we had roughly $10 in money and of that $5 was in pennies, you'd have 500 units in pennies and the rest in dollar bills—505 units. If you suddenly discovered you'd miscounted the pennies and there were actually 1000 pennies, you would then still have $10, but you wouldn't have the same quality. They're not the same quality of forces—pennies versus dollars. You're not talking about conventional forces that can strike the U.S. army: you're talking about people who can do dreadful things with sabotage and sniper fire. Not quite the same, nonetheless.[62]

When it came to the Estimate on Vietnam, SNIE 14.3.67, therefore, the Saigon agreement was deemed by the agency to be a proper compromise. Said Smith:

> We never left agreement with the military on conventional forces or regular units of the Vietcong to any major degree. In Saigon, Carver came up with what in retrospect was a very intelligent proposal. Taking the cases where there was no major disagreement, they used numbers; where there was some disagreement they used ranges—"between 3000 and 5000"—and where they had real disagreement they used words, describing the forces involved in phrases. This was the compromise they finally reached. The next paragraph said that the total number of forces facing the U.S. and the South Vietnamese was "in the order of half a million people"—again in words. The numbers Sam Adams was pushing for were there, but they're not stipulated precisely. It was a compromise demanded by people who had the right to demand it, and even then we did not back away from our position in terms of numbers but instead expressed it in terms others could agree with.[63]

Jack Smith's point was the important one about the figures. The Estimate did not shy away from presenting difficult, unpopular information, and it made clear that whatever public pronouncements on enemy strength were, the probability was that there were at least as many Vietcong and North Vietnamese forces in South Vietnam as there were American. What was more, the Estimate demonstrated (and so did the MACV figures) that the enemy possessed considerable fighting strength—up to 600,000 in all the various categories.

In contrast, observers estimated American forces in a very different way: "Approximately 70 percent of the men in Vietnam cannot be considered combat soldiers except by the loosest of definitions," said one foreign expert. In addition, only about 14 percent of American soldiers were actually involved in combat. In mid-1966 this meant that only about 30,000–35,000 American, Korean, and Australian soldiers were available for operations away from base.[64] The CIA-MACV consensus figure of Vietcong fighting strength was used to satisfy the public need to quantify the enemy. It also had a bureaucratic value; it reduced the dangers of double counting and talking at cross purposes. It gave all those involved in estimating the enemy a common basis, and if there was disagreement among them, another figure could be worked out, bearing in mind that the separate enemy categories gave everyone room to maneuver and to come up with widely different overall estimates.

The CIA's estimate of up to 600,000 enemy was confirmed as essentially accurate by the launching of Giap's Tet offensive of January–March 1968. MACV and the South Vietnamese army found themselves up against enemy forces, both regular and irregular, in much greater strength and with much better organization than they had publicly conceded. At Khe Sanh alone—the isolated American stronghold besieged by Vietcong and North Vietnamese army units—over 10,000 enemy were killed. Many more were killed around Saigon.

On November 24, 1967, Joe Hovey, a CIA analyst stationed in Saigon, concluded from captured documents, communications intercepts, and photographic intelligence that an enormous flood of infantry was coming down the Ho Chi Minh Trail. He wrote an extremely detailed memorandum predicting what turned out to be the Tet offensive. His warning was not heeded for two reasons. First, everyone realized than an offensive was coming, but no one knew precisely when it would take place: Hovey's warning was one of several, each giving different dates for the offensive. Second, everyone was concentrating on the numbers debate and its resolution in the interests of bureaucratic peace and politics. Edward Behr, a *Newsweek* journalist, spoke to Robert Komer six weeks before Tet. "Ed," Komer said, "our information is that they can't put more than a company-sized unit into the field anywhere in South Vietnam."[65] As a result, Tet came as a surprise. It was another example of the CIA providing accurate intelligence that was not properly read or was not heeded.*

After the Tet offensive started, it was immediately clear that the numbers game was on again, and Helms accepted the inevitable fight. On February 11, 1968, George Carver called up Sam Adams, who was on the point of resigning in fury and frustration. Adams was convinced that if his numbers had been accepted by MACV and pressed even more by the agency, Tet would not have

---

* Behr recounts a story told, apparently, by Ellsworth Bunker, who was the U.S. ambassador in Saigon in January 1968. The surprise of Tet was experienced by Bunker personally. "The first thing I knew about Tet," he said, "was when a fucking great big black MP sergeant burst into my bedroom in the middle of the night and said, 'Mr. Ambassador, we're going to get you the fuck out of here,' and hustled me away to safety in my pajamas in an armoured car" (Edward Behr, *"Anyone Here Been Raped & Speaks English?"* [London: Fontana, 1981], p. 268). Bunker was a mandarin of the old school, and such language was unusual for him.

come as a surprise and the military defeat of Giap's forces would have been more severe. "Sam," said Carver, "maybe you better send a cable to Saigon saying that we're going to reopen the numbers dispute." President Thieu of Vietnam helped force the issue when he made a speech declaring unambiguously that the Vietcong were much more numerous than had been admitted.[66] Although reopening the numbers dispute caused a major row, the agency had little choice. Adams had obviously been more accurate than MACV. Hovey had accurately predicted that Tet would be the occasion of the expected Vietcong-North Vietnamese attack. The enemy strength demonstrated during the Tet offensive, the shock Americans felt with the surprise of the attack, and the sight of an enemy swarming all over the American Embassy in Saigon—and, for that matter, all over Vietnam—forced a public reckoning.*

One of the principal reasons CIA analysts attempted to provide accurate enemy counts, in spite of pressures to conform, was the awareness that if they compromised the news would soon be all over town and their reputations for integrity would be ruined. They especially wanted to maintain their image within academia, where they might one day seek future jobs. For this reason, and because the public demanded to know the bitter truth, it was important that the numbers dispute be settled convincingly. It was also suddenly easier than before to be frank about the numbers because Tet had demonstrated that President Johnson's drive to resolve the war in 1967 had failed. Understanding that Johnson had probably lost the presidency with the failure, the agency now had an opportunity to call all the shots as accurately as possible in the hope of a new beginning. Helms was prepared to have the CIA lead the way.

"What happened during the Vietnam war," said R. Jack Smith, "was that some of the issues were so divisive that it was almost senseless to try for an Estimate. There were not many Estimates about the Vietnam war for that reason. Instead, CIA took over the load and did unilateral analysis. I came more and more to believe that the country would be better served if we did a great deal more of that and a great deal less of trying to get everybody together."[67] By unilaterally establishing crucial facts in an important argument about the war,

---

* U.S. television coverage of the Tet offensive did convince Johnson and many Americans that the war could not be won, and at this point, despite majority public opinion which remained in favor of the war, Johnson determined that withdrawal was America's only option. In fact, Vietcong commanders considered Tet to be a catastrophic defeat for them. Regular North Vietnamese troops had to be thrown into the fight much earlier than intended in order to relieve the Vietcong, most of whose elite troops were decimated during the offensive. Tran Van Tra, a senior Vietcong general, in 1982 admitted, "During Tet of 1968, we did not correctly evaluate the specific balance of forces between ourselves and the enemy, did not fully realize that the enemy still had considerable capabilities and that our capabilities were limited. . . . We suffered large losses of matériel and manpower, especially cadres at various echelons, which clearly weakened us. . . . We were not only unable to retain the gains we had made but had to overcome a myriad of difficulties in 1969 and 1970 so that the revolution could stand firm in the storm" (quoted in Karnow, *Vietnam: A History*, p. 544). Vietcong General Tran Do conceded, "As for making an impact in the United States, it had not been our intention—but it turned out to be a fortunate result" (quoted ibid., p. 545).

the CIA could become what Donovan had hoped for but which no director had achieved: truly preeminent within the intelligence community.

When Adams was told by Carver that the agency was going to reopen the numbers dispute, he was joyful. "I went 'whoo-ee!' and dashed downstairs and wrote a cable to Saigon. And then all hell broke loose."[68] The dispute was going to the top. On February 4, 1968, six days after the Tet offensive had been launched, Robert McNamara called in George Carver. McNamara had been going over the reports from Vietnam about enemy activity and had noticed that about half the identified units were not listed in the consensus order of battle. Thus at least one man at the top was prepared for the dispute, but he was about to retire. At the end of February, with MACV pressing for an additional 206,000 troops, President Johnson asked Clark Clifford, his new secretary for defense in succession to McNamara, who had returned to private life, to call together a special study group to consider the request. On February 28 Helms met the group and over the next three days supplied them with a series of agency studies, the conclusion of which was "our best estimate is that . . . the overall situation ten months hence will be no better than a standoff."[69] Clark Clifford and his study group came to the same conclusion, and he reported to the President on March 4 that further escalation would not make any difference; more troops would not make winning the war more likely, and MACV's request should be turned down.

This was the moment when Johnson accepted the proposition that the war could not be won, and over the next three weeks he wrestled with the question of what to do. He was not angry that the CIA's pessimistic analysis was now widely accepted or that Helms had convinced Clifford and his study group that a standoff in the war was the best hope. Rather, he saw that the votes were going against him, and as a practical politician he needed either a standoff policy or a policy of withdrawal from the war. At the end of March he asked his Senior Informal Advisory Group, known as "The Wise Men," what to do. They had already decided: although they had until now favored the war, they now considered that the United States should disengage and withdraw. They too had been influenced by CIA briefings stating that the pacification program under Robert Komer and MACV was not working.* R. Jack Smith said about this episode:

> Never before had a civilian intelligence organization challenged an army in the field about its order of battle. There is one principle which military men hold dearest to their hearts, and it is the security-of-forces principle. Any time you presume to tell them their forces are or are not in danger to the extent they say they are, they get outraged. Their job is to keep their forces secure.

---

* Thomas Powers, *The Man Who Kept the Secrets, Richard Helms and the CIA* (New York: Knopf, 1979), p. 193. This group was fluid, but had a core membership of Dean Acheson, George Ball, General Omar Bradley, McGeorge Bundy, Arthur Dean, Douglas Dillon, Henry Cabot Lodge, Robert Murphy, General Matthew Ridgway, and Cyrus Vance.

But here were a bunch of civilians telling not only the Pentagon but also the forces in the field that the number they were facing was higher. That created a very difficult position: it was their war. They were the ones getting killed. There was a lot of emotion involved in that.[70]

Logic rather than emotion colored the Wise Men's conclusions. On March 25 they called in Philip Habib, who was covering Vietnam at the State Department, Major General William E. DePuy of the Joint Chiefs of Staff, and George Carver from the CIA to present their respective views. Habib spoke about the diplomatic, logistic, and political problems that would result from a withdrawal or the collapse of the South Vietnamese government, focusing on the likelihood of floods of refugees. George Carver spoke for about seventy-five minutes. "You can't tell the people in Keokuk, Iowa, you want to get the hell out and tell the North Vietnamese you're going to stick it out for two decades and make them believe you,"[71] he said. The pacification program started by de Silva and taken over by Komer and MACV in the Civilian Operations Revolutionary Development Staff organization in Saigon was, Carver declared, a shambles.* The war was definitely being lost. On top of this, Carver presented Adams' analysis of the enemy order of battle. The enemy should be estimated at up to 600,000 strong, said Carver. Bombing, desertions, body counts, and the failure of the Tet offensive notwithstanding, the enemy was still powerful. The Pentagon's and MACV's classification had been shot to hell. Factors other than military concerns had distorted factual reporting.

General DePuy presented the Pentagon's assessment: "Gentlemen, I would like to give you the MACV assessment. There were 230,000 enemy in the order of battle. We have killed approximately 80,000 of them. We're not doing badly. There's been a bit of a shock with Tet but we're doing okay."

Then Arthur Goldberg, one of the Wise Men, who had been in World War II and knew about military support requirements from his days in the Labor Division of the OSS, questioned DePuy. "Wait a minute. Would you hold the phone here a second, General. Would you please go over the first part of that again?"

---

*For a year the monthly report on the progress of pacification efforts in each of South Vietnam's forty-four provinces had been routinely written up in the "Monthly Pacification Report" and circulated within the administration. In February 1968 William Colby, who was about to leave Washington for reassignment to CORDS to run the Phoenix program, studied the latest report and immediately pressed a panic button. The report said that in forty provinces pacification efforts had failed. Colby had the two or three hundred copies of the report withdrawn and destroyed, keeping only six under tight security.

Richard Helms asked the Board of National Estimates in mid-March for a Special National Intelligence Estimate on the pacification program. It was produced in time for Carver's briefing and concluded that pacification was not working; the program had failed. This was of major importance, because in the wake of the failure of the Rolling Thunder bombing to weaken Hanoi's resolve or Vietcong activity, the common wisdom in Washington by 1968 was that the CIA had been correct: the war would be won or lost in the South by the South Vietnamese. Now the CIA was saying the war was being lost by the South Vietnamese.

"Yes, sir," said DePuy.

"You said there were 230,000 in the order of battle, is that right?"

"Yes, sir, that's right," said DePuy.

"And you said we've killed about 80,000. Is that right?"

"Yes, we killed about 80,000. Yes, sir, that is correct."

"General," Goldberg then asked, "I realize the Vietcong have a different method of accounting than we do vis-à-vis the wounded, but how many seriously wounded would you say there were for every one killed? You've been in combat, General, haven't you?"

"Yes, sir."

"Well, what's the ratio of seriously wounded to killed?"

"About ten to one, sir."

"Wait a minute now, General," said Goldberg. "You say there's 80,000 killed, is that right?"

"Yes, sir, that's right."

"That's a big figure. Let's assume that the enemy are not as solicitous of their wounded as we are, and put their slightly wounded back into combat, can we consider three to one as a conservative figure for those rendered ineffective by wounds? Is that all right, General?"

"Yes, sir, that's all right."

"Okay. I'm not much of a mathematician, but by my count if you have 240,000 seriously wounded plus 80,000 killed, for a total of 320,000 out of an order of battle of 230,000, General, who the hell are we fighting out there?"*

While DePuy stood there, the two senior generals among the Wise Men,

---

*Interview, Sam Adams, November 20, 1983, and Herbert Y. Schlandler, *The Making of a President: Lyndon Johnson and Vietnam* (Princeton, NJ: Princeton University Press, 1977), pp. 259–261: The meeting took place over dinner at the State Department. Dean Acheson, George Ball, General Omar Bradley, McGeorge Bundy, Arthur Dean, Douglas Dillon, Abe Fortas, Arthur Goldberg, Henry Cabot Lodge, John J. McCloy, Robert Murphy, General Matthew Ridgway, General Maxwell Taylor, and Cyrus Vance were the Wise Men. They met with Dean Rusk, Clark Clifford, Averell Harriman, Walt Rostow, Richard Helms, General Earle Wheeler, Paul Nitze, William Bundy, and Nicholas Katzenbach. Over dinner the Wise Men questioned the government officials about the war. The government officials left after dinner, and the Wise Men were briefed on conditions after Tet (corruption, refugee problems), on the military situation, and on the CIA's estimate of conditions in the war zone. When Arthur Goldberg was interviewed by Schandler he recalled that he felt the briefings were designed to show that Tet had been a great victory, which he did not accept as the case.

SNIE 14.3.67 gave a much lower ratio of killed to wounded than DePuy and Goldberg:

Total Communist losses have been rising sharply over the past 2 years. On the basis of the latest data, we estimate that total losses for 1967 will amount to about 170,000—an increase of about two-thirds compared with 1966. The bulk of these losses are killed-in-action as reported from body count. Our estimate of permanent losses from wounds is based on evidence indicating that for every 100 killed there would probably be 150 wounded, and that, of these, at least 35 die or are permanently disabled.

General Maxwell D. Taylor, *Swords and Plowshares* (New York: W. W. Norton, 1972), p. 390, records in contrast to Goldberg that in his opinion the briefings were temperate and thoughtful presentations.

General Matthew Ridgway and General Omar Bradley, started laughing. Soon the whole table was laughing, and the meeting broke up. On the following day, March 26, the Wise Men formally recommended to President Johnson that MACV should not be given more troops and that the United States should get out of Vietnam. Johnson, not surprisingly, wanted to hear for himself what the Wise Men had heard that had brought about their change of mind. What had the CIA told them? On March 28 Richard Helms, George Carver, and General DePuy were summoned to the White House to repeat their briefings to the President, Vice-President Hubert Humphrey, General Creighton Abrams (about to succeed General Westmoreland in Vietnam), and General Earle G. Wheeler, chairman of the Joint Chiefs of Staff.

Carver followed DePuy, and throughout his talk Johnson fidgeted, interrupted him, made telephone calls, and asked several times, "Are you finished?" "Are you finished yet?" Helms smiled quietly, amused by Johnson's restless irritation. When Carver was finished, Johnson quickly left the room, immediately coming back in to shake Carver's hand, and then left again, saying nothing at all.[72] Three days later Johnson announced on television that he would not seek the presidency again but would devote the remainder of his term to finding a way to end the war.

A number of factors contributed to Johnson's decision, including the unpopularity of the war and the realization that America could not win it. The frustration of the U.S. effort—the occupation of the U.S. Embassy, the fall of Hue—was brought into every American home on the television nightly news.* It was clear to Johnson that if a real military victory—Tet—was nevertheless seen by Americans as a defeat, he would have no military "success" to look forward to that could swing the tide of popular opinion and that he would lose the election in November 1968.

This marked Johnson's personal political defeat as well as the major turning point in the war. Behind it lay the CIA's consistency of analysis and Richard Helms's political ability to stay on the inside, to be a regular at the Tuesday lunches, and to keep Johnson's confidence despite being a no-sayer. It was a moment when, although late in the day, the CIA's message was finally heeded. "The Tet offensive represented a victory over the guerrillas," reflected one senior agency officer, "but as a result the North Vietnamese upped the ante and faced us with having to put more chips in the pot by entering the war directly themselves. The Chinese had done the same thing in Korea. At no point was the extent of the communists' blind resolution to do their thing realized. At no point was there any evidence that they were pragmatic people. They were

---

*Walter Cronkite of CBS News, the most respected television newsman in the United States, made a telling newscast on February 27, 1967, following a visit to Saigon. He rejected official forecasts of victory and stated that it seemed "more certain than ever that the bloody experience of Vietnam is to end in a stalemate." The newscast shocked and depressed Johnson (Karnow, *Vietnam: A History,* pp. 547-548).

going to do it to the point of suicide."[73] Nearly four years earlier John McCone had warned the President that in the North Vietnamese and the Vietcong the United States faced a fanatical, irresponsible foe "in a military effort that we cannot win."[74]

The CIA's record of advice on Vietnam was now vindicated. This generated a renewed bitterness toward the agency on the part of the military. Military leaders believed the CIA had such a vested interest in its view that the war was not winnable that it suppressed or took insufficient account of other evidence. The agency's willingness to go along with MACV's order-of-battle estimates in 1967 modified this view. There was, however, definite opposition to the war within the CIA, not on grounds of principle but for pragmatic reasons. In the agency's view the war in Vietnam was not winnable and therefore should not be fought. Fighting it would not only produce other serious domestic and foreign problems but would also drain valuable resources that could be put to better use elsewhere. Moreover, the agency questioned the domino theory: there might be other, natural stops—Thailand, for instance—which would resist communist incursions without hundreds of thousands of American troops being involved. CIA analysts pointed out that there were a host of national antagonisms within Indochina which would also counteract the expansion of Chinese and Vietnamese communism throughout the whole subcontinent.* They had also reached the conclusion that there was no monolithic world communist movement, controlled from Moscow, dominating China.[75]

To the CIA the U.S. position as the world's greatest power meant that its power should be committed only when it was clear that by doing so American objectives would be met. Domestic and international political considerations should never be more important, once American power was committed, than

---

*The domino argument went thus: if Vietnam fell to the communists, the other countries of Indochina, Thailand, and the Malay peninsula would fall next, followed by Indonesia. Behind the theory lay the assumption of monolithic communism, which is now seen to have been wrong. The Sino-Soviet split meant that Russia and China were at odds in Indochina (reflected in Soviet support for Vietnam against Chinese interests) and that Vietnam was not a stalking horse for China, as was demonstrated by the 1979 war between Vietnam and China following Vietnam's invasion of Cambodia.

American intervention in the 1960s acted to strengthen the resolve of anticommunists in the region and took communist pressure off Thailand, Malaysia, Singapore, Indonesia, and the Philippines. In 1965 a communist coup in Indonesia collapsed, with an estimated three hundred thousand communists being massacred in the following months without China (the coup's backers) being able to do anything about it. In addition, the prosperity of the noncommunist countries during the 1960s and 1970s increased domestic resistance to communism. In the 1980s the comparison between capitalist and communist Indochina put the noncommunist countries ahead on every social and economic count. The per capita income of Indonesia, the poorest noncommunist country, at $440 (1983) compared with $189 (1985) in Vietnam, the richest communist country. Former Defense Secretary James Schlesinger, however, still sounded a warning note: "For the theory to be valid, the dominoes don't have to fall in a compressed period of time. If I were the Thais, I wouldn't be all that comfortable" (Newsweek, "The Legacy of Vietnam," April 15, 1985, p. 26D).

the objectives that had called forth that commitment. If only a handful of professional troops could hold (i.e., prevent the loss of) Vietnam for decades, but
it was politically unacceptable to do so, then the troops should not be sent.
Similarly, if a politically unpopular effort involving more than five hundred
thousand troops could not be won, the troops should be withdrawn before unrest and political dissent erupted at home. By committing the United States
militarily and then not being able to achieve a complete military victory over a
five-year period—longer than the United States had ever fought before—the
governing elite was condemning itself to an extremely severe public backlash.
To its credit, the CIA had seen this prospect more clearly than most.

The role of the CIA had also generated a bitterness in Sam Adams for different reasons. He had never been a centrally important figure in the high-level
enemy-strength debates, although his work was basically important. He was a
middle-level analyst and as such protected from the pressures that Richard
Helms and his close colleagues faced. But within the agency Adams' frustration spilled over. He had become, as Lawrence Houston described him, somewhat "fanatique" about the order-of-battle debate.[76] And while it turned out
that he was more right in his estimates than MACV, his methodology—extra-
polating from one province to others and making intelligent guesses—was not
certain. "He went off at half-cock," said George Carver.[77] He jeopardized the
tightrope walk the agency was conducting with the Johnson administration to
persuade the President that the war was not winnable in conventional terms.

Adams felt that if only the policy makers would listen to him, the war
might be won.* He considered that while the agency had finally mustered its
courage and backed his order-of-battle figures, Richard Helms had put politics
ahead of integrity and had not pressed his arguments hard enough or in time.
In Adams' view, if Helms had acted sooner, the Tet offensive would not have
taken America by surprise or cost thousands of American lives. He had no tolerance for the arguments that it was better to have some influence than none at
all and that if Helms had pressed Adams' case during 1967, it was likely that,
out of annoyance, Johnson would have cut Helms out just as he had McCone.
Adams believed that thousands of Americans had died because of Helms's failure to force the truth about the enemy strength on the policy makers. His conviction was so strong that on April 1, 1968, he told the CIA inspector general

*Interview, Sam Adams, November 20, 1983. Interestingly, postwar opinion polls show that
Americans blame politicians and political restraints for preventing U.S. victory in Vietnam. A
Veterans' Administration survey in 1980 showed that 82 percent of veterans who had been involved in heavy combat in Vietnam believed the war was lost because they were not "allowed" to
win, and 66 percent said that they would be willing to fight again. General William C. Westmoreland in his memoirs blamed political restraints for failure in Vietnam. In his view, Johnson
intensified the war too slowly and then did not pursue it energetically enough. He blamed Johnson for not being honest with the American public and for bowing to the pressure of public opinion (although, in fact, majority opinion throughout supported fighting the war if it could be won).
He also blamed television and newspaper reports for distorting the war and muddying the issues
(General William C. Westmoreland, *A Soldier Reports* [New York: Dell, 1980], pp. 538–562).

that he would file a formal complaint against Helms in an attempt to get him dismissed.

Adams delivered his evidence at the end of May and requested the inspector general to investigate his charges.[78] Helms willingly agreed (his agreement was not necessary since the inspector general is empowered to make his own investigations) and was very relaxed about the whole affair. The inquiry was completed on August 1, 1968, three months before the presidential election. Since his own conduct was the subject of the investigation, Helms appointed a three-man review board to hear the case, including Lawrence Houston, CIA general counsel; John A. Bross, assistant to the DCI; and the deputy director, Admiral Rufus Taylor, as chairman. The board conducted more of an informal, in-house affair than a formal inquiry, and it considered not only Adams' evidence but also his conduct: there was considerable pressure in some quarters to have Adams fired instead.

The board decided that while Adams was probably more accurate in the order-of-battle debate than anyone else, he had not produced absolutely certain evidence. It also decided that Adams had followed correct procedure, carefully checking on every step he took and obtaining permission for his actions. He had, they considered, been given a fair opportunity to present his case, and they recommended that he be given one more opportunity to do so to General Maxwell Taylor, then chairman of the President's Foreign Intelligence Advisory Board. Adams' case and the inspector general's report were sent to the White House in September. Nothing further was heard of his charges or attempt to have Helms fired, and Adams resigned from the CIA.[79]

One senior CIA officer said:

> When you've got poor evidence, it's very hard to stand up and shout, "I'm going to insist on this number here!" None of us was persuaded of that number to the extent Sam Adams was. It was a very tricky kind of methodology that he used. Our retrospective analysis of the Tet offensive showed that they did not have many more people than we had thought. The Tet offensive was a terrible disaster for their forces. It created great havoc. They tried to get everything accomplished in one great blow, and they didn't carry it off. We were able to get a good idea of the units involved: they surfaced. In terms of effectiveness—those who made a contribution to the offensive—the number was somewhere between the CIA and the military position. That's not a point I would want to rest an awful lot on, but it certainly does not prove that we had grossly underestimated their strength. And in this particular case— counting tactical units in a hot war with the military involved—it was not strategic intelligence as we were schooled to think of it.
>
> I don't think the writ of the director of the CIA runs that far. I don't think he ever possessed any rights in that matter really. What was needed was a workable number, and we were simply the resource used by the President and McNamara to find common ground among military people in the field and analysts in Washington. It was certainly not a clear-cut case of abandoning a position. Helms, as far as he knew, had not given up anything. He sim-

ply took the compromise wording, as had every DCI when it was impossible to arrive at a fair statement of exactly what the capabilities were of a given weapon.[80]

DISSENT WITHIN

Vietnam and the question of whether or not the CIA had compromised its analysis to an undue extent were not the only issues facing the President and the agency. As the war in Vietnam became more unpopular, opinions about it within the CIA began to vary widely. John Huizenga recalled:

In the early 1960s, before we had a heavy involvement in Vietnam, there were more people who would have said that by a minimal effort we could have contained the situation. But the number of people who continued to believe that dwindled very rapidly once we had our own heavy involvement. Some were true believers, some were not. There was a breaking up of the consensus. People who followed the subject had their beliefs about it matured by events. In the Office of National Estimates in the late 1960s and early 1970s, the people who actually worked the subject were themselves as passionate in their minds and in their instincts about it as the people demonstrating in the streets. I made speeches to them, saying let's not be intemperate about this matter. They thought it was a loser. But you can't do a professional job on a subject if you're going to be passionate about it.[81]

Out of this passion and out of the widespread sense that the CIA's shadowy hand was involved in unsavory activities (rumors of agency involvement in the assassination of President Kennedy and of the agency's invisible—but all-powerful—hand in government led to public paranoia about the CIA as the "invisible government" of the United States)* came a closer scrutiny of CIA activities in the press and there emerged a number of whistle-blowers from the agency itself.

A series of articles in *Ramparts* early in 1967 revealed the CIA's support of and connection with the National Student Association. These exposés were followed by articles in *The New York Times* and elsewhere revealing CIA connections with corporations, trusts, individuals, research centers, and universities. Perhaps most damaging, however, was the revelation that came from

---

*Sustaining this impression later on was some of the work the CIA undertook at Johnson's direction. In particular, the 1967 study entitled "International Connections of US Peace Groups" involved the agency in domestic surveillance and connections with American citizens, the FBI, and police forces in the United States. In the mid-1970s, when details of this work came out in the investigations of the agency following Watergate, it seemed to many as if the agency had spearheaded an "invisible government" as well as a secret police force in America. The study, presented to President Johnson on November 15, 1967, found that there was no foreign funding of U.S. peace groups and that the anti-Vietnam War movement was a genuine American protest movement (Central Intelligence Agency, "International Connections of US Peace Groups," November 15, 1967).

Philip Agee, who resigned from the agency in 1969 for "personal reasons," having served as a DDP officer in Latin America. With the help of the Cuban government Agee wrote an account of the CIA entitled *Inside the Company: CIA Diary*, which was published in 1974. The book named several hundred CIA officers and informants and identified cover organizations and relationships with governments and companies. Agee said in his book:

> At last I am finding the proper course. Behind these decisions have been the continuation of the Vietnam war and the Vietnamization programme. Now more than ever exposure of CIA methods could help American people understand how we got into Vietnam and how our other Vietnams are germinating wherever the CIA is at work. . . .
>
> I have also decided to seek ways of getting useful information on the CIA to revolutionary organizations that could use it to defend themselves better. . . .
>
> Increasingly, as the oppressed in capitalist society comprehend the myth of liberal reform, their ruling minorities have no choice but to increase repression in order to avert socialist revolution. Eliminate CIA stations, US military missions, AID Public Safety missions and the "free" trade-union programmes and those minorities would disappear, faster perhaps, than they themselves would imagine.[82]

Names of agents were also revealed in *CounterSpy*, an anti-CIA newsletter published by radical American journalists. The name and home address of Richard Welch, who in 1975 was chief of station in Athens, where he was serving under State Department cover as a first secretary of the embassy, were published in the English-language *Athens News* on November 25. On December 23, 1975, Welch was shot dead on his own doorstep. In the edition of *CounterSpy* that identified Welch, Agee wrote: "The most effective and important systematic efforts to combat the CIA that can be taken right now are, I think, the identification, exposure, and neutralization of its people working abroad. . . . Having this information, the peoples victimized by the CIA and the economic exploitation that CIA enforces can bring pressure on their so-often compromised governments to expel the CIA people. And, in the absence of such expulsion, which will not be uncommon, the people themselves will have to decide what they must do to rid themselves of CIA."[83] Not surprisingly, most people in the CIA connected Agee directly with Welch's murder (a point Agee vehemently contests) and came to regard him as possibly a penetration agent, someone who worked for the interests of the Soviets after he resigned and who might have been working for the Soviets before that point as well.* In January 1981 the United States Supreme Court ruled that Agee no longer had the right to hold a U.S. passport.

---

*In the review of Agee's book in *CIA, Studies in Intelligence*, n.d., an "Editor's Note" prefaced the review: "The following is primarily a review of the book, and does not purport to exam-

PRUDENT PROFESSIONALS

Although the Vietnam War consumed a great deal of agency energy during this period, the rest of the world was no less a problem, with the result that considerable demands were placed on the agency's operations and analytical activities, which continued unabated. A notable success was scored by the agency analysts in the June 1967 Arab-Israeli war. During May, as tensions in the Middle East were obviously advancing toward outright conflict—the Egyptian and Syrian armed forces had been mobilized; Nasser was making increasingly bellicose anti-Israel speeches; Soviet aid to Egypt and Syria had been stepped up—Arthur Goldberg pressed Johnson to give more support and military supplies to Israel. Goldberg claimed that CIA estimates of Israeli strength were overly optimistic. In Goldberg's view, the United States should put aside its evenhanded treatment of the Arabs and Israelis in favor of support for Israel, which was facing well-armed and far more numerous enemies on three of her four borders. (Jordan had joined with Egypt and Syria in the anti-Israel Arab alliance.)

Johnson asked the CIA to report on Goldberg's warning and produce a study of Israeli military strength. Within twenty-four hours of this request, a Special National Intelligence Estimate (SNIE) was produced by Sherman Kent's Board of National Estimates and presented to the President by Richard

---

ine the possibility or extent of Soviet involvement in Agee's actions, from the start or at an early stage." The review itself starts: "Phillip Agee's 600-page story of his career and views as a junior and middle-level case officer in Quito, Montevideo, and Mexico City will anger all those who have worked for the Central Intelligence Agency because he is its first real defector in the classic sense of the word." Later the review states: "The book will affect the CIA as a severe body blow does any living organism: some parts obviously will be affected more than others, but the health of the whole is bound to suffer. A considerable number of CIA personnel must be diverted from their normal duties to undertake the meticulous and time-consuming task of repairing the damage done to its Latin American program, and to see what can be done to help those injured by the author's revelations."

"Agee wrote that most 'special assistants' to ambassadors were really CIA chiefs of station," recalled the widow of the CIA chief of station in Brazil at the time *Inside the Company* was published. "After the CIA's Dick Welch was assassinated in Greece, a worldwide shuffling of titles took places. We were in Brazil, where Joe was chief of station. His name was dropped to sixteenth place on the embassy's diplomatic list, the better to bury his importance" (Bina Kiyonaga, "Remembrances of a CIA Wife," *The Washingtonian*, March 1985, p. 207).

Agee said about the Dick Welch charges that they were an example of CIA disinformation. Several years earlier the house in which Welch lived was well known as the home of the CIA chief of station in Greece. Agee said that Welch was warned about this by the agency, but "he replied that he preferred living there." *CounterSpy*, in a press release published on December 28, 1975, declared that since Welch was well known as a CIA man (he was identified as such as early as 1967 in an East German publication, *Who's Who in the CIA*), "if anyone is to blame for Mr. Welch's death, it is the CIA that sent him to Greece. . . . When the *Athens News* publicly identified him, there was no excuse for the CIA to keep him there" (Philip Agee and Louis Wolf, *Dirty Work—The CIA in Western Europe* [Secaucus, NJ: Lyle Stuart, 1978], pp. 79–80, 92).

Helms on the evening of May 26. Hours before, the Israelis sent an estimate of their own strength to the CIA, confirming Goldberg's warnings and indicating that Israel would be defeated by the Arabs if American assistance were not immediately forthcoming. Taking all this into account, the CIA analysts nevertheless declared in the SNIE that Israel would win a war within two weeks without any American aid. Richard Helms defended the Estimate's categoric prediction of Israeli victory despite the Arabs' numerical superiority. It was a brave stand, demonstrating that once Helms was convinced of a case and satisfied by the evidence, he would act with integrity despite the risks.* In this particular case Helms was taking on the strong and influential pro-Israeli lobby and recommending in effect a course of action that, if wrong, could have disastrous consequences not only for Israel but also for the President, the agency, and himself.

The temptation for Helms to hedge his bet must have been enormous, but he resisted. The President listened and decided not to step up aid to Israel. Within weeks the June war was over, Israel was victorious, the CIA was vindicated, and the President was relieved and impressed. With justifiable pride Helms looked back on this episode:

> The estimating process did much better on what became known as the June war of 1967, but there the analysts had military statistics and known weapons systems to deal with. As war clouds gathered in the Middle East during May, the Israeli government finally sent an estimate to Washington designed to demonstrate that Israel might well be defeated by the Arabs without U.S. assistance. Within five or six hours of receiving this estimate, the Agency produced a written estimate of its own contending that Israel could defeat within two weeks any combination of Arab armies which could be thrown against it no matter who began the hostilities. When Dean Rusk read this commentary, he asked me if I agreed with it. I replied that I did. Then with a wry grin he commented, "Well, in the words of Fiorello La Guardia, if this is a mistake, it's a beaut!" Later at the request of President Johnson the estimate was reworked or, to use his words, "scrubbed down." The new version had the Israelis winning in one week. In fact, they took six days.[84]

The strategic and tactical questions the agency addressed in the 1960s had changed subtly from the 1950s, as had America's outlook on the world and its role in it. The Vietnam War, the Cuban missile crisis, and the Bay of Pigs all contributed to this change in perceptions. So had the survival of the agency under several different presidents as it found a place in U.S. foreign-policy making with a tactical, practical approach to the great questions of the day, no-

---

*The agency had been asked a specific set of questions and had come up with specific answers. This was not a continuing matter—Arab-Israeli wars did not happen every year—and so was different from questions about the Vietnam War, where things were changing all the time and a long view as well as a political awareness were essential to the agency if it wanted to have some influence.

tably relations with the Soviet Union and the collapse of the old empires. The brilliant intellectuals of genuinely wide-ranging philosophic mind involved in U.S. foreign policy since 1947 had concentrated on reformulating American interests in ways that had incidentally secured a place for the CIA. George Kennan's Moscow telegram, his "Mr. X" article, his talk to American ambassadors in Rio de Janeiro clarified the view that American interests did not exist simply in emergencies but were there all the time. It was a reassessment recognizing that after World War II, emergency had become permanent.

What resulted was a juggling of intense idealism with intense national interest, with the CIA moving in to identify, maintain, and protect the expanding national interest across a host of issues. This was one of the great motivating forces in the agency as it wrestled with other agencies and itself over Vietnam. It saw earlier than most that conflict as a safety valve for permanent emergency was a mistake. In a world of neither war nor peace, America should not seek war, although it would have to be prepared for war in order to protect the peace. This awareness became more widespread in the 1960s, generating an intense atmosphere that mobilized people emotionally and intellectually; a pride in clear-mindedness, seeing that things might not be black and white but also gray; and an acceptance of impersonal, ruthless management methods as a substitute for conflict.

The agency was very often the touchstone for this approach, since the State Department could not act in a ruthless manner on the big questions of the day (official ruthlessness at the international level might produce conflict), and the Defense Department had not thought things through intellectually, as President Kennedy rightly complained. The Defense Department thought that if there were a nuclear war, massive attack and retaliation would take place, both sides would be hurt, but ultimately the United States would win. The sense of there being other choices, of political movement being possible, of a world behind the world of appearances, was the agency's territory, and in this it meshed with the world of the 1960s.

Despite the Bay of Pigs, the CIA entered the 1960s as closet heroes, emerging as public heroes in the missile crisis only to become public villains as a result of Vietnam. When William Colby returned to Washington after overseeing Phoenix in Vietnam, he was met by posters and handbills saying, "Colby—Wanted for Murder." Philip Agee was not the only person who considered the CIA a hidden monster that must be stopped.

The agency was sustained through all these episodes and changes of public mood because it was never what it was accused of being—heroic or villainous; and it was never invisible.* It was at all times a body made up of the

---

*In 1951, for example, the CIA gave $300,000 to finance the Massachusetts Institute of Technology's Center for International Studies. CIA funding for the Center continued into 1966, ending with the start of public revelations about its secret funding activities (although its support for the Center was never secret). "The number of my friends around here who have swallowed

President's men. The agency was aggrieved over its association with two public disasters—the Bay of Pigs and the shooting down of the U-2 over Russia. It felt—with justification—that the public's impression of its functions was based solely on these incidents and that there was no understanding of agency achievements. The feeling was especially strong over the U-2 flights. The gaining of intelligence information from the flights was among the agency's greatest achievements, but the public knew only about the plane that was shot down. The Bay of Pigs and the forced departure of Allen Dulles also labeled the agency a failure, although many in the agency knew that Dulles' firing was a cover for a failure of nerve in the Oval Office.

Despite these setbacks, the agency remained a collection of elite professionals with a remarkable track record, with a pool of experts to work for it and the ability to attract a new generation of talented people who were committed to preserving America's position in the world. The wartime enthusiasm had died away, and people of talent could make fortunes in the professions and on Madison Avenue and Wall Street, but still the agency attracted a remarkably high caliber of persons. Many were drawn by what the agency did for America and by its position as a presidential arm. They were interested in the organization of complex information into comprehensible statements for senior policy makers; the ability to mount operations and analytical studies quickly, and the rapid response to presidential wishes. Professionals who turned to the agency might surrender the opportunity to become really rich, but they gained instead the experience of exercising power and powerful influence.

The founding generation of the agency, the generation that had grown up during the Depression, was a little startled to find that a lot of able people were willing to make genuine financial sacrifices for their country and still saw the CIA as a place to work to improve the world. These people found their wealth in the performance of the agency and in the secrets they held: they knew things about countries and individuals that no one else knew; they were on the inside of power in America. This special position gave people who worked for the CIA a distinctive aura, which was perceived both inside and outside the agency. It also kept morale high despite public disasters. Peer de Silva reflected later:

> Throughout my many years abroad I was invariably known as a CIA official and I was intrigued by the remarkable way the CIA was regarded by foreigners. Whether in Europe or in Asia, the local chieftains in government, the military establishments, the trade-union hierarchy, and the so-called intellectuals, in dealing with me, clearly felt they were in touch with the really

---

this 'invisible government' line is disturbing," said Max Millikan, the Center's director. "They think there is an entirely separate foreign policy being concocted by people in dark corners. When they say that this kind of work is immoral, what they're saying is that it's immoral to have anything to do with telling the President what the world's really like" (*Time*, February 24, 1967, p. 16).

direct and significant route to the American decision makers in Washington. . . . The CIA connection was looked upon as a less formal, more confidential, and more rapid means of dealing with the U.S. government. This fact was recognized, perhaps ruefully, by every ambassador with whom I ever served.[85]

The "prudent professional" image of the CIA also plugged into the sense of the 1960s. President Kennedy's concern with the management of industrial society as a problem of administration was something the agency had been aware of since the mid-1950s. Born in the cold war as an elite service, it was a vital arm for those who were piecing the world back together again after the chaos of World War II. The agency prided itself on its professionalism and on being a complete service in itself. Its responsiveness to the vast range of possibilities in the post–World War II period made it attractive to those who wanted to create a better world. It sustained this image by having a definite world view of its own, a view that helped the agency clarify issues, avoid conflict and commitment, and be in accord with the Wilsonian vision of the second-generation New Dealers who created the CIA. Liberal democracy was seen as a desirable but difficult management problem and American power and ingenuity as forces to be harnessed to remake the world in a liberal democratic mold.

All institutions tend to cement the attitudes that color their birth, and the CIA was no exception. At the agency's heart were the attitudes of the generation that had fought World War II and had then come to power in the 1960s. The agency's cool professionalism was demonstrated to this generation in two forms. First, it was good at managing. The U-2 had been a triumph of management in comparison to air force management procedures. Its Estimates managed information effectively. Its operations, though by no means all successful, usually worked. Second, its people were the right people, connected in all sorts of ways to money and influence. There was always someone in the agency who knew the right person to call to get a decision changed or made, a favor granted, an argument advanced or set aside. What was more, its people were usually correct in their assessments. The Arab-Israeli Six-Day War was a startling confirmation of how accurate the agency could be in a difficult and emotive situation.

There were mistakes too, of course, but none that really damaged the U.S. (the Bay of Pigs had hurt the agency rather than the United States), and on the two great issues of the 1960s—the continuing estimate of Soviet capabilities and intentions and the Vietnam War—the agency was considered by Kennedy and ultimately by Johnson to be more accurate and consistent than anyone else. Although it might not have helped the agency at the time to point out to President Kennedy that there was no missile gap, since he had just won the election with a statement that there was a gap, the accuracy of the analysis ultimately proved the agency's worth, and it was not surprising that the President turned to the CIA for information and help.

Richard Helms was the epitome of the agency professional: "The word 'professional' is invariably used by CIA men to assess Richard Helms," wrote Stewart Alsop in 1968. " 'Dick's a *real* old pro,' they say. 'He really knows where the bodies are buried.' Helms is certainly prudent as well as professional. 'There will be no Bay of Pigs under Dick Helms,' a colleague said shortly after Helms had taken over from Bissell as DDP, 'but there'll be no U-2 either.' "[86] According to Alsop, by 1968—the CIA's twenty-first birthday—Helms and his "Prudent Professionals" had completely replaced such men as Richard Bissell, Frank Wisner, and Ray Cline. These "Bold Easterners" from the best private schools and colleges had had their day. "All in all," Alsop concluded, "a sensible assessment of the CIA would give the Agency a kind of solid B-minus rating. The CIA is not really a very dramatic organization. It is not a 'secret government' or a '*Stadt in Stadt.*' Neither is it a brilliant nest of daring spies, in the James Bond manner. It is a prudently professional bureaucracy, run by prudent professionals."[87] In 1968 this was high praise.

—14—

On the Edge
1968–1972

The growing public awareness of the agency brought about by the disclosures of its activities during the later 1960s reopened the question of congressional control. This was first proposed in 1955 when Senator Mike Mansfield tried to push through the Senate a bill that would have given Congress oversight of the CIA. Although Mansfield's bill gained the support of twenty-six senators, it was defeated decisively on the Senate floor after Allen Dulles convinced the ranking senators of the security dangers involved in formal oversight. Committee staffers might leak intelligence data, he said; foreign security services would object to sharing information. Allen Dulles always argued that the manner in which Congress organized its oversight arrangements was entirely its affair. Equally, he saw his job as protecting the security of intelligence methods and operations. The senior members of both houses of Congress who determined the oversight arrangements were very conscious of the need to maintain security. Accordingly, they used their influence to keep oversight at an essentially informal level.

A compromise followed whereby CIA subcommittees were created in the Armed Services and Appropriations committees in the Senate and in the Armed Services Committee in the House. In 1961, after the Bay of Pigs, Senator Eugene McCarthy tried to convince the Senate of the need for a formal oversight committee, but again the proposal was defeated. In the mid-1960s, as the Vietnam War intensified and as nuclear proliferation, advances in space technology, and increased international tension pulled congressional attention away from domestic issues, Richard Helms responded by increasing the number of CIA briefings to committees. In 1967 a total of seventeen congressional committees received detailed briefings about the agency's plans and activities. These briefings remained within the informal structure of reporting operated by the senior senators and representatives since the inception of the agency. By the mid-1970s the director or deputy director was averaging thirty to thirty-five committee appearances annually.

Most of these presentations were made before intelligence subcommittees of the House and Senate. However, to an increasing degree, the director was also invited to give world-roundup intelligence briefings to the full Armed Services Committee and Defense subcommittees of each House. The director also made several appearances before other committees, such as Foreign Relations in the Senate, Foreign Affairs in the House, and the Joint Committee on Atomic Energy. The agency was also often asked for more specialized briefings—for example, on Soviet weapons development for Senator Muskie's subcommittee on arms control. In addition to committee briefings, individual congressmen would ask for briefings on intelligence and related subjects. In 1973 there were 175 such requests.[1]

In 1966 Senator McCarthy again tried and failed to have a formal Senate oversight committee. The personal relations established with ranking committee members in both the Senate and the House by John McCone and Richard Helms (Raborn was liked but was soon perceived to be professionally inadequate) had a lot to do with the continuation of the informal information-sharing procedures and the avoidance of formal scrutiny.[2] Despite this, the sands were shifting. Senator Richard Russell, an important Senate power, was one of the key people involved with the CIA on Capitol Hill. From the 1950s until his death in 1971 Russell was a friend of the agency and defined his role in the Senate as protector of the security and position of the CIA, in relation to Congress and other government agencies as well.

When in 1963 President Johnson ordered the CIA to release to the press data recently gathered by Ray Cline's Office of Research and Reports showing that the Soviet Union's economic growth had come almost to a halt, Senator Russell, unaware of the President's order, let John McCone know that he disapproved. Russell made sure McCone understood that if this sort of thing continued he would withdraw his support of the CIA in the Senate. The press conference—which was the first the agency ever held—went poorly because of press suspicion of CIA motives. *The New York Times* headlined a front-page story to the effect that the agency was conducting psychological warfare against the Soviet Union by releasing dubious statistics about the Soviet economy. Although other evidence confirming the CIA's findings emerged in the following weeks, the CIA was never given credit by the press. This experience and Russell's objection meant that the agency did not give another press conference for ten years.[3]

Senator Henry Jackson of Washington State was another Senate power involved with the agency. Like Russell, Jackson was a Democrat and a strong supporter of President Johnson and the Vietnam War. He was a member of important Senate committees and was one of those trusted by the CIA. Although the agency objected in practice to oversight, it did not object in principle. Indeed, it was always anxious to find senators and congressmen who, like Jackson, could be trusted to keep sensitive information to themselves and not use it for immediate political advantage.* These relationships had very practical advantages for the agency, particularly when it came to appropriations and budget scrutiny. For example, whenever an important appropriations vote came up, Jackson would call an executive session of the Armed Services Committee and reveal apparently up-to-the-minute secret information supporting the request for funds.[4]

As a result, the agency had a far easier ride in Congress at the nuts-and-bolts level and had much greater financial flexibility than other agencies and the armed services. While Curtis Le May had to account for every dollar he spent on the Strategic Air Command and the B-52, the CIA did not have to account in the same detail for the money it spent on the U-2, the satellites, the SR-71, or the covert operations it conducted during the 1960s. Richard Helms was the last director of Central Intelligence to enjoy this freedom, and to keep it he had to work harder at cultivating Congress than any of his immediate predecessors. He also had to work hard to deal with congressional committees that considered the agency's internal matters to be of direct concern to them. Helms's chief antagonist was Senator William Fulbright, who chaired the Senate Foreign Relations Committee. Among the things Fulbright demanded to know were the embassy slots abroad occupied by agency officers and agency involvement with multinational corporations in Latin America.[5]

One of the unspoken elements in the good relations between the agency and Congress was the awareness that members of the CIA were the President's men. The ease with which the agency passed congressional inquiry reflected the perception of its closeness to each particular President and the popularity

---

*Where operational details were involved, especially those relating to sensitive sources and methods, the agency followed the guidelines laid down by the chairmen of the oversight subcommittees. Generally no exceptions were made to the strict rule against passing operational information without the approval of the chairmen. Where disputes occurred, compromise was preferable to confrontation. One analogy cited by Jack Maury was that if a senator expressed concern over the agency's activities in a foreign capital, the chairman of one of the oversight committees might take him directly to one side and explain the facts, or he might arrange for the senator to be briefed privately by the agency. Although there were cases where this confidence was breached, such infringements were more often inadvertent than deliberate. Maury thought it was a worthwhile price to pay and recalled what Senator Russell once said to an agency official: "There isn't a single member of this Senate that's so lowly that he can't make life unbearable for you fellows if he decides he wants to do it" (Jack Maury, "CIA and the Congress," *Congressional Record*, Vol. 130, No. 117, September 18, 1984).

of that President. In 1966, when Senator McCarthy proposed formal oversight for the second time, Johnson was still reasonably popular in Congress and in the country, but the agency under Raborn was perceived as having lost ground with him. This also happened with Dulles and Kennedy when McCarthy tried to push through his first oversight proposal in 1961. When in 1968 it became clear to Helms that Johnson would not win the presidency again, he asked John A. Bross to survey intelligence users, the people who read the CIA's Estimates, to gauge the performance of the agency. In Helms's view it would be useful to know the opinions of these people, because they would inevitably influence the next President. It was a measure of how dependent the agency was on informed opinion and on the climate of opinion in the White House and the government.

Bross found that White House people and Robert McNamara appreciated and supported the agency's work. Senior officials wanted completely objective Estimates and expected to receive them from the agency. They were not, Bross found, particularly interested in coordinated views.[6] There was another side to the question of outside opinion about the agency as well. Unlike John McCone and Allen Dulles, Helms was not a rich man, and he lacked an outside financial base. This made Helms dependent on his job in a way that neither McCone nor Dulles was, and even if this did not influence his decisions in tricky situations, it was bound to be something others wondered about. So gauging outside opinion about the agency's performance must also have helped Helms gauge opinion about himself as he addressed the prospect of the next President, whose right it would be to appoint a new DCI.

THE GENTLEMAN FROM CALIFORNIA

On November 11, 1968, just after winning the presidential election, Richard Nixon visited President Johnson in the White House. Nixon was briefed by senior government officials, including Richard Helms, about the state of the country, Vietnam, and the world. A couple of days later Nixon invited Helms to the President-elect's headquarters at the Hotel Pierre in New York. Helms was Johnson's appointee but he had proved himself an effective administrator and an effective director on the Hill. Moreover, he had a reputation in Washington for not trying to make policy but to serve it. In part this was a consequence of the tightrope that he walked over Vietnam with Johnson. Now his balancing skills began to pay off, because while Helms was not a Nixon man, he was perceived as being competent and professional. Again, unlike Allen Dulles and John McCone, he had no personal political base and so was no threat to Nixon. Allen Dulles had fought to put the agency in a nonpolitical position, and the agency as a whole regarded this as extremely important: it would give the CIA an autonomous position in the Washington infrastructure and a leg up in the bureaucratic hierarchy.

When Helms and Nixon met at the Hotel Pierre, this was on both men's minds. Nixon told Helms that both Helms and J. Edgar Hoover would remain during his administration. More than a month went by, and then on December 18, 1968, Nixon publicly announced his decision. "I think he regarded me as one of those Georgetown types," said Helms. "I have never lived in George-town and I didn't associate with Georgetown, but I was sort of one of that type, I suppose. One has to make a distinction between not liking a type of person and yet getting along with that individual even though you don't like his type."[7] It was not just a matter of being a Georgetown type, however, that was important; it was that Nixon was both angry and suspicious about the agency and was probably glad to have someone there who was clearly depen-dent on his favor.

Nixon's suspicions came from his deep-seated social sensitivities. A Georgetown type would be fashionable and well connected. He would have at-tended the right schools and colleges and would be at ease socially. In addition, he would be a Washington insider, familiar with the lobby systems and the key bureaucrats in the different agencies. A Georgetown type was the sort of person popularly imagined to have surrounded Jack Kennedy; he was a courtier of Camelot, a successor of the "Oh So Social" set of the OSS. Nixon was well connected entirely through his own efforts, and he had none of the other quali-ties. "I won the 1968 election as a Washington insider," said Nixon, "but with an outsider's prejudices. The behind-the-scenes power structure in Washington is often called the 'iron triangle': a three-sided set of relationships composed of congressional lobbyists, congressional committee and subcommittee members and their staffs, and the bureaucrats in the various federal departments and agencies. These people tend to work with each other year after year regardless of changes in administrations; they form personal professional associations and generally act in concert."

He urged his cabinet members not to recruit their staffs solely from east-ern schools and companies but to look to the South, the West, and the Mid-west. "We can't depend on people who believe in another philosophy of government to give us their undivided loyalty or their best work," he told them. "For some reason this is something that the supposedly idealistic Demo-crats have always been better at recognizing than the supposedly hard-nosed Republicans. If we don't get rid of those people, they will either sabotage us from within, or they'll just sit back on their well-paid asses and wait for the next election to bring back their old bosses." The new President di-rected that holdover bureaucrats should be replaced as quickly as possible with people who believed in the new administration.[8] Richard Helms was very lucky to have avoided this purge, but the pressure was on him to be a loyal member of the new team. Once, in 1970, when Helms had been instructed by Nixon to do something about Allende in Chile, David Atlee Phillips, who was involved in the agency's plans, turned to a colleague and said, "I don't understand. Why should we be doing this, especially when we believe it won't work?"

"Understand?" said his colleague. "Some time ago I returned with Dick Helms from a meeting downtown. On the way back the car was tied up in traffic for almost half an hour, and Helms and I talked about the assignment he had just been given. I ended by saying to Helms, 'I don't understand.' Well, you know what Helms said? He looked at me and said, 'Abe, there's something I've had to learn to understand. I've had to learn to understand Presidents.' "[9]

In complete contrast to Johnson, Nixon did not enjoy talking to other people. He liked to think, to work, to write, to read. He was uneasy with strangers and stiff on social occasions, finding it particularly difficult to make small talk. When it came to work and to administration, rather than deal directly with the heads of agencies and departments himself, he preferred to go through his close and trusted aides John Ehrlichman, H. R. "Bob" Haldeman, and, later, Alexander Haig. He also depended a great deal on Henry Kissinger, who first served as his national security adviser and then as his secretary of state as well. Helms found himself talking nearly every day to Kissinger or Haig (who was originally Kissinger's deputy), informing them of developments and decisions that needed to be made, and they would say to him, "We need that for the President."[10] Nixon protected himself and bought more time for work by using his assistants and advisers to deal with the outside world, including cabinet members and organizations.

In contrast, Johnson bought time by carving two working days out of each twenty-four hours. He would get up early in the morning and work through until after lunch. Then he would have a nap—he had started this habit well before he became President, after he had had a heart attack and was ordered by doctors to rest. At about 4 P.M. he would get up, take a shower, change his clothes, and start a second day, working through until about midnight. Helms recalled:

> Nixon liked to read his intelligence. So did Johnson. Johnson also liked to hear it once in a while. Nixon would pay more attention and listen longer than Johnson would. These were all things you had to learn if you were going to get along with them. Also, different directors have different views of their job. McCone used to have his "two hats" theory, one hat as an intelligence adviser, another as a policy adviser. I didn't believe in that. I believed I was an intelligence adviser. I did that with both Johnson and Nixon. Nixon was very conscious of this. He had the feeling when he came into office that the agency had had too much of a say in policy in earlier years.[11]

"What the hell do those clowns do out there in Langley?"[12] Nixon would ask when something happened that the CIA had not predicted. He also had a personal anger about the CIA from his days as Eisenhower's Vice-President and from his own presidential campaign in 1960, when the agency briefed both him and Jack Kennedy on what would later become the Bay of Pigs operation and on the missile gap with the Soviet Union. The missile gap had figured prominently in Kennedy's campaign, and Nixon felt that the agency had failed to convince Kennedy that the gap was a myth. Had they really shown Jack Kennedy all their evidence? Or had they soft-pedaled, happy not to convince him, effectively encouraging him to make political mileage at Nixon's expense? "In the 1960s and early 1970s," wrote Nixon, carefully avoiding direct reference to Kennedy's campaign,

> for eleven years in a row, the Central Intelligence Agency underestimated the number of missiles the Russians would deploy; at the same time the CIA also underestimated the totality of the Soviet strategic program effort and its ambitious goals. . . . Throughout the critical period of the mid-1960s, when McNamara decided to curtail unilaterally U.S. nuclear programs and the Russians moved massively to catch up, and in the early 1970s, when the first concrete steps toward arms control were taken, American Presidents were being supplied by the CIA with figures on Russian military spending that were only half what the agency later decided spending had been.[13]

SHIFTING GROUND

The analytical side of the house was not Richard Helms' familiar territory. He had come from the DDP, the operations and espionage side, and his expertise lay in running agents, guiding and controlling covert actions and espionage activities. On becoming director he concentrated on learning the methods of the analysts until he was completely comfortable with the Estimates. When in 1965 Lyndon Johnson decided to send the marines into the Dominican Republic following a rebellion there against a military-backed junta (Johnson feared that the rebellion might produce another communist satellite in America's backyard), the CIA was not involved at all. The CIA chief of station designate in Santo Domingo was taken completely by surprise.[14] Two developments followed from this experience: first, the CIA established a permanent operations center in Langley manned twenty-four hours a day—called the "War Room" (not to be confused with the "War Room" set up by Kennedy in the White House)—to report on, and if necessary deal with, crises as they happened around the world. Second, it brought the realization that the days of massive covert operations, such as the Bay of Pigs, that were too big to hide were over.

Between 1947 and 1965 there was an assumption in governing circles that no matter what happened anywhere in the world, the CIA would be ready and able to deal with it at a moment's notice. The CIA's history was dotted with brilliant, rapid operations that contained or forestalled problems and changed events. The Italian elections; the overthrow of Mussadegh in Iran; the seduction of the oil sheiks of the Middle East; the overthrow of Arbenz in Guatemala; the support for the noncommunist left in Europe, and the Berlin Tunnel all showed the CIA's capability under pressure. After 1965, when the shock of the Cuban missile crisis had shown that brilliant opportunist action (in this case on the part of the Russians) could easily lead to war, the CIA came to see its role in more long-range terms. It would no longer simply respond to events but rather seek to control and ordain them, and it would do everything it could to avoid direct confrontation. No matter what was happening on the edge or in secret, there must never be war.

At the same time the opportunities that had determined the agency's early nature diminished. The world was settling down. The old empires were relics of the past. The ex-colonies—now independent countries in their own right—were beginning to organize for themselves. The Third World, once thought to be the ground for competition between Kennedy and Khrushchev, was considered—with some exceptions—not worth fighting over. The emergence of China was believed to be far more important and interesting. The agency's role in the Bay of Pigs and the Cuban missile crisis gave it a much higher profile (published U-2 photographs of Soviet emplacements in Cuba impressed the world), with the result that it could no longer easily slide in and out of an operation with nobody noticing.

Johnson recognized this when he sent the marines into the Dominican Republic; it was so obvious that America was involved that there was no point in trying to pretend that it was not by using the CIA. Moreover, the agency's involvement in Vietnam was no secret to any journalist covering the war. The low-profile, efficient operation that characterized Kermit Roosevelt's effort in Iran was no longer possible by the mid-1960s. Vietnam was already demonstrating that a Third World conflict was no longer just a set of dirty tricks carried out by a handful of people away from the spotlight but was more likely to be a full-scale slugging match in the bright light of publicity.

Until the mid-1960s the agency had an extraordinary run of luck. A perfectly presentable shah ruled in Iran. (Although he had an unsavory secret police, he possessed a healthy anticommunism and a wish to modernize his country in all respects.) Castillo Armas, who replaced Jacobo Arbenz in Guatemala, had courage and dash and, despite the considerable inequities of his government, was no out-and-out dictator. In Italy the government changed every six months, but nonetheless it was a democratic country and none of the governments was communist. The strikes that plagued France and Germany were crippling, but at least none of the labor unions were Communist party pawns. Even in its failures the agency had a chilling effect. Although Sukarno had not been overthrown in Indonesia, he had been frightened, and he behaved with greater circumspection toward the Soviet Union in the 1960s than had seemed likely in the late 1950s.

After the Bay of Pigs, however, the ordinary run of bad luck began to catch up with the CIA. For an outfit that is expected to succeed every time it performs a major operation, it did not take many failures or setbacks to diminish its reputation. Thus the CIA itself was happy to cut down on covert action. Also contributing to the shift in emphasis from operations was the decay of the consensus on America's world role brought about by Vietnam and the reassessment of cold-war assumptions forced on the public by the missile crisis. While the liberals, the agency's natural constituency as it battled against imperialism and totalitarianism, were prepared to accept an intensive cold war under John Kennedy because he involved them in its management, they were not prepared to take part in a scaled-down cold war under Lyndon Johnson.

Kennedy excited liberals with his idealism and his appeal for new frontiers everywhere. Kennedy was bold and challenging. Johnson was not. Johnson preferred to limit things, and he had no grand theory. He saw himself as continuing the basic foreign policy of his three predecessors, which he interpreted as simply keeping communists out of places they were not already in. His actions in Vietnam and the Dominican Republic were as blunt as his policies. He had no concept of how to use such a finely strung instrument as the CIA in such matters and treated the agency as yet another support unit for the big battalions.

These changes in assumptions and in world politics contributed to the changes in the nature of the CIA. It was in the ordinary cycle of things no longer an emergency institution. Also, as Truman used to say, "If you keep on playing block, sometime you'll get beaten," and in the mid-1960s the agency had been playing block for nearly twenty years. Then it found itself confronting a public that no longer shared the attitudes of 1947, that no longer saw Russia as a relentlessly expanding power and communism as totally evil. People were more sophisticated, more aware of the complexities in the world, more reflective about the use of power and worried that in the nuclear age confrontation might lead to annihilation. They wanted cold negotiators, not cold warriors. They were not interested in an agency that defined itself in terms of dazzling services crucial to a suddenly changed world. Rather, they preferred a prudent, professional agency that was well aware it was operating in a dangerous world. They also preferred to focus on domestic policies, an emphasis they shared with Lyndon Johnson, who constantly bemoaned the demands of Vietnam.

The false optimism surrounding involvement in Vietnam, and the bitter, painful truth on nightly television of America's failure to win, brought a new mistrust of government. As one CIA analyst put it, people felt they had been lied to:

> "The enemy is running out of men" is what everyone was saying in the latter part of 1967 and into 1968. There was a chorus of officials telling the American people that we were winning the war and that the enemy was running out of men. Then, whammo! The Tet offensive hits and the sons-of-bitches are coming out of the woodwork everywhere. The American people were not thinking "We're winning" or "The enemy is running out of men." They were thinking "Jesus Christ! They're into the embassy compound! They're into every goddamned city in Vietnam! They've taken Hue!" And what the American people concluded was that they were being lied to, that the American government was not telling them the truth. Nobody trusted anything the administration said.[15]

Bound firmly in the public's mind to the growing public disclosures of its secret activities, the CIA was a casualty of this mistrust, with few choices open to it. The agency pulled in its horns and sought a reputation for competence and professionalism in bureaucratic terms. Richard Helms was a man who had risen through the ranks of the agency because of his competence and professionalism. He understood the changes that were taking place in the public mood and the changes each President wanted. He knew that President Johnson was determined to learn from Kennedy's Bay of Pigs fiasco and that as a result the CIA's days of exploits and covert operations were over. The agency's security in the bureaucracy lay in its analytical activities, and from the mid-1960s, putting aside special Directorate of Plans activities in Vietnam, the proportion of the CIA budget allotted to the four or five thousand analytical staff steadily increased. Helms' comfort with this changed environment was fortunate, for both Nixon and Henry Kissinger had an avid interest in written intelligence.

A REAL MISSILE GAP

The annual Estimate of the capabilities and intentions of the Soviet Union was the agency's big set piece each year. After the Cuban missile crisis the Soviet Union began a massive program to equal and if possible surpass the United States in the whole range of weapons and armed forces. They began building up their arsenal of nuclear missiles and conventional weapons, and ships, airplanes, and submarines. They also sought superiority in their manned space program. Khrushchev and his successors were determined never again to be in a position in which on military calculations alone they could be outfaced by America. When Willard Mathias, an analyst with the Board of National Estimates, wrote a paper summarizing the comparative strengths of Russia and the United States in the wake of the missile crisis, he forecast that in all probability there would be a major increase in the Soviet arms program.

In 1962 Colonel Oleg Penkovsky reported to his British contact that "Khrushchev boasts that we are ready, we have everything. This is just so much idle talk. He himself probably does not see the whole picture. As far as launching a planned missile attack to destroy definite targets is concerned, we are not yet capable of doing it. We simply do not have any missiles that are accurate enough.... Many of our big missiles are still on the drawing-boards, in the prototype stage, or are still undergoing tests. There are altogether not more than a few dozen of these, instead of the 'shower' of missiles Khrushchev has been threatening the West."[16] This confirmed U-2 and satellite reconnaissance photographs, which showed that while the Russians were building and testing an assortment of missiles, they were beset by teething problems and were far from accurate. After Cuba, Khrushchev claimed that the Soviet Union had between 80 and 120 Intercontinental Ballistic Missiles (ICBMs). The 1962 CIA Estimate put the number at 75. The following year, 93 Soviet ICBMs were counted. These, however, were the SS-6 variety, which was plagued by problems of inaccuracy and unreliability. In addition, preparing them for firing took a great deal of time. Another ICBM, the SS-7, was first deployed in 1962. However, it did not replace the SS-6 and was itself vulnerable to the U.S. Minuteman missile.

Altogether, the evidence amassed by the analysts indicated that, despite its efforts, the USSR was far behind the United States qualitatively and quantitatively. By 1967, Estimates put Soviet strength at between 423 and 484 Soviet ICBMs and 21 Submarine-Launched Ballistic Missiles (SLBMs). The actual numbers were 570 ICBMs and 27 SLBMs, discovered soon afterward from satellite and other technical intelligence. Based on previous Estimates of Soviet strength, Robert McNamara, who had argued for an acceptance of rough parity in nuclear missiles in the interests of deterrence and the mutual-assured-destruction theory, held back some U.S. weapons systems. He now acknowledged, however, that the Soviet rate of construction had been faster than anticipated. At the same time he stressed that by their very nature Estimates were uncertain and required revision as additional information became available. Ironically, a missile gap developed under the Democrats, who had falsely accused Eisenhower of presiding over one.

Between 1967 and 1969, the analysts developed a new theory of Soviet intentions. They expected that the Soviets would construct enough missiles to give them parity with the United States. At most, they believed, the Russians would build a few more missiles than were necessary in order to claim superiority for prestige purposes, but then they would be satisfied. This judgment, while entirely rational, also proved to be wrong. The Soviets had put so much into their missile program that the institutional momentum had broken through the dam of restraint. A halt to the buildup was called only after Nixon and Kissinger successfully negotiated the first Strategic Arms Limitation Treaty—SALT I—in 1972. After 1967 the CIA Estimate of Soviet strength was revised upward until by 1971 actual Soviet missile strength compared to what was being estimated in Washington.*

Dealing with McNamara's acknowledgment of inaccurate Estimates and Nixon's anger about the inaccuracy was one of Richard Helms's main jobs throughout his tenure as director. Melvin Laird, Nixon's secretary of defense, publicly attacked the accuracy of the Estimates on Soviet forces in 1970. "The situation caused by the continuing rapid expansion of Soviet offensive forces is a matter of serious concern," he said to Congress. "For some time, the Soviet forces which became operational in a given year have often exceeded the previous intelligence projections for that year."[17] It was the mark of a bitter battle between the agency and the Department of Defense over estimated Soviet military capabilities.

THE MIRV DEBATE

In 1962 John McCone decided to set up a separate directorate to deal with scientific and technical intelligence matters—the Directorate of Science and Technology (referred to as "DDS&T" after the title of its head, the Deputy Director of Science and Technology). He was convinced by Bissell's U-2 and Cosmos programs that technical collection of intelligence was one of the most important aspects of the CIA's development. He offered the job of run-

*The actual numbers of Soviet missiles compared to American missiles and to the CIA Estimates were as follows:

Year	Actual numbers		CIA Projections of Soviet strength for:				
	United States	Soviet Union	1967	1968	1969	1970	1971
			ICBMs				
1966	904	292	420–426	514–582	505–695	509–792	499–844
1967	1054	570	423–484	670–764	805–1010	775–1027	805–1079
1968	1054	858	536–566	848–924	946–1038	949–1154	939–1190
1969	1054	1028	570	858	1038–1112	1158–1207	1181–1270
1970	1054	1299	570	858	1028	1262–1312	1360–1439
			SLBMs				
1966	590	27	24–30	24–42	24–78	24–114	30–138
1967	628	27	21	29	37–53	61–85	85–117
1968	656	43	24–27	43–46	75–94	123–158	187–238
1969	656	120	27	43	94–110	158–238	222–366
1970	656	232	27	43	110–126	184–248	296–376

SOURCES: John Prados, *The Soviet Estimate: U.S. Intelligence Analysis and the Soviet Military Threat* (New York: Dial Press, 1982), pp. 183–199; Lawrence Freedman, *U.S. Intelligence and the Soviet Strategic Threat* (London: Macmillan, 1978), pp. 107–108. By 1972, while U.S. ICBMs remained at 1054 and SLBMs at 656, Soviet ICBMs numbered 1527 and SLBMs 440.

ning the new directorate first to Bissell, who declined and left the agency, and then to Dr. Herbert Scoville. Scoville soon left after some internal disagreements about organizational arrangements, and Albert ("Bud") Wheelon was appointed to head the directorate.

Wheelon was a masterly bureaucratic infighter who had joined the Office of Scientific Intelligence in the late 1950s from the technical research firm Thompson-Ramo-Wooldridge. He quickly gave coherence to DDS&T, pulling it together from the Development Projects Division in the Directorate of Plans (this was Bissell's "baby," and Bissell's departure certainly made the reorganization a lot easier), the Office of Scientific Intelligence—which came into the new directorate from the Directorate of Intelligence—and the Office of Electronic Intelligence from the DDP.

Ray Cline was furious with the shift of the Office of Scientific Intelligence, especially since he was consistently outmaneuvered by Wheelon in this bureaucratic empire building. "Ray had an uncontrollable ability to make enemies," remembered one colleague. "He and Bud Wheelon were at daggers drawn. When you take on Bud Wheelon, you're taking on a bureaucratic master, and Bud Wheelon ripped Ray to shreds."[18] When Ray Cline left the agency in 1966 he was succeeded as deputy director for intelligence by R. Jack Smith, who managed to get along with Wheelon. In 1963 Wheelon moved into the missile debate by creating the Foreign Military Space Analysis Center within DDS&T. As a matter of policy, he involved his directorate with outside research centers on a large scale, giving it quite a different feel from that of the directorates of Intelligence and Plans, which remained relatively closed worlds.[19]

In 1967 R. Jack Smith began drawing together offices in the agency involved in space analysis to create the Office of Strategic Research, which monitored and reported on Soviet military activity in space. Together with Wheelon's DDS&T, this office renewed the struggle for influence with the military, who were always reluctant to share their secrets with civilians. In one way, Raborn did his successor as director a great service by resolving the feud between the DDS&T and the air force over control of reconnaissance. But he also compromised his successor by not being an effective chief intelligence officer, tending personally to side with the military in debates on the Estimates. In addition, the recognition that the CIA Estimates on Soviet missile capabilities had underestimated the threat in the mid-1960s played into the hands of the military. In retrospect, despite the military's tendency to overestimate threats, they were perceived as being more accurate than the CIA on the issue of Soviet missile strength in the 1960s. As a result, Melvin Laird was able to disregard CIA Estimates and rely instead on his own Defense Intelligence Agency analysis.

This new struggle first came to a head in 1969 over the issue of the Soviet SS-9 ICBM, given the NATO code name Scarp. The military and the CIA differed over the question of whether the SS-9 had a Multiple Independently Targeted Reentry Vehicle (MIRV) capability. The first suspicions that such a new-generation ICBM was being developed appeared in 1964 through satellite reconnaissance, telemetry (the radio transmission and recording of devices within missile systems) eavesdropping from stations in Iran, Turkey, and Pakistan and from ships at sea, and in Soviet writing in scientific and technical journals.* A year later more was known. It had a loaded weight (with fuel and warhead[s]) of about fifteen thousand pounds.

Armaments experts in the United States did not understand why the Soviets were building such a large missile. In the past, ICBMs such as the U.S. Titan and Jupiter missiles had been large because fuel and engine systems were less advanced. But in 1964 the Soviets had progressed to the point where their missiles no longer needed to be large to have the desired intercontinental capability. There were two possible reasons for the size: the Soviets might want to deliver a massive nuclear warhead with enormous destructive power in order to compensate for inaccuracy. Or they might intend the SS-9 for MIRVing.

In the mid-sixties MIRVing was clearly the next step in the arms technology race. In 1964 the *Polaris* A-3 SLBM became the first missile with more than one independently targeted warhead (it had three). This was only a half step forward, however, because the three warheads combined carried less throw-weight—effective destructive capacity—than the original single warhead on the *Polaris* and were able to do significantly less damage to their three targets. The first successful MIRVs were developed for the U.S. Minuteman III missile in 1968. Therefore, many Washington analysts believed, the SS-9 could well be intended for a MIRV system. This view was embraced by the Pentagon, which pressed not only for a larger American MIRV program but also for improved antimissile defenses.

Clearly MIRVing was still in its infancy, and there was a large question as to whether the Soviets had the skills and the technology to complete a MIRV system paralleling the American one. In 1967 the issue was confused further when the Soviets tested and began deploying two hundred single-warhead SS-9s, almost certainly targeted at U.S. Minuteman sites, two to each site for reliability. At the same time the CIA reported that the Soviets were also developing a fractional orbital bombardment system with the SS-9. In this system the warhead would be launched at its target from an orbiting missile rather than from a missile having a conventional ballistic trajectory. The fact that MIRV-

---

* Telemetry was one of the major operating skills of the DDS&T, providing the CIA's listening stations with very accurate information about the operating characteristics not only of Soviet missiles but of a wide range of Soviet military systems. It could accurately indicate the reliability of a missile, its in-flight attitude, the amount of fuel it consumed, and its trajectory and accuracy. Wheelon gave his old firm, Thompson-Ramo-Wooldridge Corporation, so much consultancy and contracting work in telemetry intelligence that the company formed a telemetry analysis group to work with the air force and CIA.

MIRVing a missile in effect made it into several missiles. Each "reentry vehicle" could be programmed to strike a separate target. The result of MIRVing the U.S. ICBM force increased the number of reentry vehicles from 1054 ICBMs and 656 SLBMs to a total of 7274 warheads.

ing was not involved in these cases raised doubts about whether the SS-9 had this capability.

At this point the CIA thought that it did. In 1967 the Soviets published a book in which two of their military analysts considered targeting strategies for multiple-warhead systems. Also in 1967, the Pentagon publicly acknowledged the U.S. MIRV program and decided to deploy the Sentinel antiballistic missile defense system, which was capable of countering MIRV missiles. All this suggested that whether or not the Soviets had originally planned to MIRV the SS-9, they would now almost certainly do their best to develop a MIRV system with the SS-9 or another missile. A National Intelligence Estimate late in the year thought that the Soviets were already developing MIRV capability for their larger missiles and would probably have an operational system in place between 1971 and 1975.

Robert McNamara concluded, however, that there was still no evidence that the SS-9 was being MIRVed. He was being cautious, unwilling to spend vast amounts of money on top of the costs of the Vietnam War. He also wanted to avoid any action that could start a major arms race, negating his efforts to reach a reassuring deterrence with the Soviet Union based on approximate parity of nuclear strength. Checking the facts, however, was always Richard Helms's priority, and during the first 181 days of 1968, U.S. reconnaissance satellites were over the Soviet Union's missile-testing sites for 117 days. It was not until August 1968—220 days into the year—that the CIA obtained sufficient evidence to decide whether it or McNamara had been correct about the SS-9.

Satellite reconnaissance and telemetry intelligence showed that the Soviets were developing a MIRV program, that they had not yet achieved MIRV capability, that they were testing a multiple-warhead system that did not have independently targetable warheads (and so was not yet a MIRV system), and that their system was for the SS-9. So McNamara had been right after all: the SS-9 was not in fact being MIRVed. In a more important way, however, the CIA was correct: the SS-9 was not being MIRVed, not because the Soviets had decided against MIRVing it but because they could not MIRV it; they did not have the technology to do so. Otherwise, it was now clear, the SS-9 would have been MIRVed, and the Soviets were hard at work to develop their own MIRV capability.

Clark Clifford, McNamara's successor as secretary of defense, adhered to McNamara's judgment on the SS-9, and the CIA now agreed. On October 2, 1968, a CIA National Intelligence Estimate, NIE 11.8.68, concluded without any dissent that the SS-9 was not MIRVed. It also noted that there was progress in Soviet development programs. Intelligence indicated that the SS-9 might have a crude system by which its separate warheads, while not being independently targetable, would encompass a larger target area giving them the potential to damage or destroy different Minuteman sites in the United States. Richard Nixon, Melvin Laird, the air force, and the Defense Intelligence

Agency went against the McNamara reasoning and decided that the SS-9 was effectively MIRVed after all (to use their language, the SS-9 was "functionally equivalent to a MIRVed missile") and that the Sentinel defense system should be redirected from the defense of American cities to the defense of Minuteman sites. In their view the Soviets might be able to inflict a damaging first-strike attack on United States missile sites unless American defenses were speedily geared to meet this threat.

The stakes concerned in the SS-9 debate were now extremely high. The issues involved spending huge amounts of money to meet this possible Soviet threat and crucially important decisions about the nuclear defense of the United States and America's own next step in offensive nuclear capability. In addition, President Nixon and the CIA were rapidly becoming aware that in 1969 there *was* a dawning missile gap—and this time it was real. It soon became clear that the agency was in a weak political position if it continued to argue that the SS-9 was not MIRVed. Against this position was the weight of powerful administration opinion and the opinion of an increasingly nervous American public deeply suspicious of Soviet intentions. The pressure on the agency to hedge its conclusions and revert to its pre-August 1968 position must have been enormous. At this moment Congress was also debating whether or not to ratify the Nuclear Non-Proliferation Treaty.

The Pentagon, the CIA, and the new administration all had to argue their cases, present their projections, state their judgments and outline their proposals. "The spring of 1969," one student of American analysis of Soviet military strength has stated, "should be seen as a major postwar watershed of nuclear strategic doctrine."[20] The CIA, however, stuck to its position and continued to maintain that the SS-9, while being a threat, was not a threat of the same order as a MIRV system. A wide divergence was developing on a matter of fact just as it did in the Vietcong order-of-battle dispute. Henry Kissinger decided that his National Security Council staff should examine the evidence and the arguments in an effort to secure a consensus position that brought together CIA and Pentagon views. When the October 1968 National Intelligence Estimate was reexamined by Kissinger's staff and CIA analysts were questioned, the analysts reacted in the same way the military had reacted to CIA analysis in Vietnam—as if their professional integrity had been questioned and as if close questioning by nonexperts was improper.[21]

While this examination was under way, pressure on the CIA to agree that the SS-9 was effectively MIRVed increased still more. In April President Nixon publicly declared that the Estimates on the SS-9's capability had been wrong. In March and again in April, Melvin Laird declassified and released detailed intelligence findings on the SS-9 which alarmed Congress and supported his argument for more sophisticated antiballistic missile systems. "From the point of view of the CIA," recalled John Huizenga, then deputy director of the Office of National Estimates, "the game was being played because the Soviet MIRV was necessary as a threat to justify the Safeguard

[ABM] system. There's no doubt that the White House was determined that there should be an intelligence finding that the Soviets were engaged in MIRV testing."[22] All through this period the Senate Armed Services Committee and the Foreign Relations Committee were conducting hearings on the nature of the Soviet nuclear threat and the measures, including various antiballistic missile systems, being formulated to meet it. On May 17, 1969, Richard Helms confirmed to the Senate that serious disagreements existed within the intelligence community on the SS-9's capabilities.

Despite these pressures, the CIA analysts were satisfied that the SS-9 was not MIRVed, that its multiple warheads were not very accurate and depended entirely upon their explosive power (rather than targeting accuracy) for their effect, and that the Soviets were far behind the United States in deploying an accurate MIRVed strike force. In effect, the CIA was saying that the request for increased defense spending and the worries that caused it were premature. This development swept aside Kissinger's examination, placing the SS-9 debate firmly in the political arena.

No longer at issue was the technical question of the SS-9 and MIRVing. The "functionally equivalent" argument had turned into an argument about whether the Soviets were proceeding toward an effective first-strike capability. By opting for the view that the SS-9 had MIRV equivalency, the administration and the Pentagon were saying that the Soviets were moving in this direction and that therefore new weapons systems had to be rapidly developed and deployed. The CIA believed that the Soviets were a long way from having a MIRV capability and that therefore a Soviet first-strike capability should not be feared. In its view there was no need for panic defense measures. Jack Smith and Bud Wheelon prepared a paper on this question for the National Security Council in June 1969, updating the October 1968 Estimate but not altering the conclusions. The Soviets, they said, were not seeking and did not have a first-strike capability.

At the National Security Council meeting that discussed the CIA judgment, Henry Kissinger asked Helms to go over the analysis again. It was not in anyone's interest that a public fight should break out between the agency and the administration. Helms went back and decided on a new Estimate, which would go through all the arguments and evidence again and be fully coordinated with the other interested parties. Abbott Smith, chairman of the Board of National Estimates in 1968, was in charge. Two weeks later, on June 23, before the board had time fully to reexamine the question, the differences between the CIA and the administration spilled out in front of the Senate Foreign Relations Committee when both Laird and Helms were questioned together. The judgment as to whether or not the Soviets were developing or planning a first-strike capability was the focus of committee attention.

"What do you mean when you use that term 'first strike capability'?" Senator Albert Gore asked Melvin Laird.

"I mean . . . that I want to be in a position where we can take a first blow and still retaliate," replied the secretary of defense, "and I want the potential enemy to know that we can do that."

"Yes, but what is a first-strike capability?" pressed Gore.

"A first-strike capability is a blow delivered against the United States—"

"That makes it impossible to retaliate," interrupted Senator Fulbright, pinpointing the question. In banging the drum about the SS-9's capabilities and the prospect of a successful Soviet first strike, the administration had given everyone the impression that a first strike would be final, and this was why Congress had to approve the increased Defense estimates. Now Laird was telling the senators that this was not quite the case: America could sustain a Soviet first strike and then retaliate.

"Oh no, not that it makes it impossible to retaliate," continued Laird, and he reached for the deterrence argument to justify his position, "but which makes it impossible to retaliate beyond any question of doubt."[23] Laird was now saying that even though there was doubt about Soviet capabilities, America should react as if the Soviets had a first-strike capability whether they actually did or not, simply because the risk of not doing so was too dangerous. This position was a major modification of Laird's previous statements, and it left him open to the question of why America should spend billions of dollars on antiballistic and other defensive systems to protect itself against a threat that might not actually exist. The ball was firmly back in the CIA's court; was the agency's judgment correct? Richard Helms gave the committee members the CIA's evidence and analysis and convinced them that the SS-9's capabilities and Soviet intentions were by no means as clear-cut as the secretary of defense maintained.

"What Laird was trying to do," observed R. Jack Smith, "was upset our judgment, which was a guiding one, that the Soviets were not proceeding to a first-strike capability. We had said this repeatedly. It had become the standard statement about the SS-9. Laird had a tremendously exaggerated idea of the capability of the weapon, and he was dead wrong. The Pentagon was dead wrong too—they were trying to promote the antiballistic missile system at the time. In June 1969 Laird and the White House indicated that they were not happy with our judgment, but Helms consulted his people and he stuck with it."[24]

The position of Jack Smith, Bud Wheelon, and Richard Helms on this issue was sustained by Abbott Smith and the Board of National Estimates in the new Estimate, which came up for discussion at the United States Intelligence Board in August. What was more, most of the other agencies involved now agreed with the CIA's conclusions in this new report, which were unequivocal:

We believe that the Soviets recognize the enormous difficulties of any attempt to achieve strategic superiority of such order as to significantly alter the strategic balance. Consequently, we consider it highly unlikely that they will attempt within the period of this estimate to achieve a first strike capability, i.e., a capability to launch a surprise attack against the U.S. with assurance that the USSR would not itself receive damage it would regard as unacceptable. For one thing, the Soviets would almost certainly conclude that the cost of such an undertaking along with all their other military commitments would be prohibitive. More important, they almost certainly would consider it impossible to develop and deploy the combination of offensive and defensive forces necessary to counter successfully the various elements of U.S. strategic attack forces. Finally, even if such a project were economically and technically feasible the Soviets would almost certainly calculate that the U.S. would detect and match or overmatch their efforts.[25]

Once again, this was in direct conflict with the view of Laird and the administration, and its bluntness caused problems. "I think the people who wrote the Estimate were perhaps at fault for stating things so starkly and letting it get to such a naked head-on clash," said R. Jack Smith. "The point could have been made without making it a black-or-white issue."[26] Laird reacted by telling Helms that the Estimate intruded into the policy area and that it subverted administration policy. He wanted the concluding paragraph out. "On this issue of the first-strike capability," recalled Helms, "one of the things that occurred in connection with that was a battle royal over whether it was the agency's job to decide definitely whether the Soviet Union had a first-strike capability or did not have a first-strike capability. And this thing seemed so contentious that it seemed impossible to resolve."[27]

This conflict was certainly a far cry from running agents and double agents; finding and making secure safe houses; and organizing efficient and dependable communications with agents and sizing up their products, which were the skills Helms knew best. He acceded to Laird's pressure and dropped the conclusion. Thomas L. Hughes, outgoing head of the Bureau of Intelligence and Research at the State Department, thought this was wrong. In his view the conclusion was the best judgment not only of the CIA but also of the intelligence community as a whole and, despite the political pressures, should not be dropped. Hughes exercised his right to insist on a dissent and put the paragraph back in as a footnote.

Abbott Smith was stunned by Helms's decision, seeing it not only as a cave-in on a matter of high principle—the integrity of the CIA's analytical work and of the Board of National Estimates—but also as a public slap in the face from his director, a vote of no confidence in his work. "I probably should have resigned," said Abbott Smith about the incident. "It was such a shock. Things were never the same." But he did not complain at the time, taking what he felt to be a seriously damaging interference quietly. "Abbott was a New Englander, very reticent, very stoical," said R. Jack Smith. "I think the conversation he had with Helms was like ships passing in the night. I don't think Helms saw the problem in the terms that Abbott did, and I don't think Abbott saw it in the terms that Helms did. Helms had no awareness that the chairman of the Board of National Estimates was so upset."[28]

The consensus among agency analysts was that Dick Helms had not covered himself with glory this time. The Estimate was the director's Estimate; his signature went at the bottom; he presented it to the President. He should have been satisfied that his Estimate was accurate, particularly since in this case he had checked it all so carefully, aware that his agency's judgment was at odds with the administration's wishes. Now Helms had backtracked and modified his Estimate, not because he was satisfied that its factual analysis was wrong, but because of political pressure. Nevertheless there was also sympathy for his position. Jack Smith pointed out some things in defense of Helms:

> History is replete with instances where intelligence people have come to conclusions as best they possibly could, and policy people have ignored them. Winston Churchill's record is full of instances where he ignored what intelligence people thought. It's a policy person's right to do so. Laird had every right to do so. The Estimate was a judgment—it turned out to be entirely right—but still a judgment. The factors and information leading to it, which had been included in the earlier Estimate, were compressed or removed in this one, leaving the judgment all by itself. Helms in the circumstances dropped it; it may be that he thought it didn't sustain itself or that it wasn't necessary for the purpose of that particular Estimate. Laird was wrong, but all the same I think we should have found a way to express the judgment in some way.[29]

"I would say that by and large the impact of the paper was pretty much the same," said John Huizenga, who had been involved in writing the Estimate. "The negotiation and coordination of Estimates is very much a battle over words. The SS-9 was about MIRV really, and despite some intervention by Laird and Kissinger, the paper was not really altered."[30] Helms himself probably saw the episode as having more to do with getting on with the new administration than with challenging the integrity of the agency's analysis. When the director of Central Intelligence "clashes with the secretary of defense, he isn't a big enough fellow on the block," explained Helms to the Senate Intelligence Committee in 1978.[31]

The actual Soviet MIRV program became clearer by 1972, and its progress vindicated the position the CIA had taken. The SS-9 missile was never MIRVed. The first Soviet MIRV system was tested in August 1973 with the successor to the SS-9, the SS-18. The SS-9's accuracy was never improved, so the fear that its three warheads were "functionally equivalent" to a MIRV system receded. When the Soviets actually deployed their MIRV system in December 1974 it was not even with the SS-18 missile but with the SS-19, a much smaller missile of a new generation with only one-third of the throw-weight of the SS-18 and having no developmental connection with the SS-9. In retrospect, the best guess about the SS-9 was that the Soviets saw it as their most suitable missile for MIRVing because of its large throw-weight and then found that they were unable to develop MIRV capability for it. "On balance the CIA performed admirably," said John Prados. "Its early predictions were accurate, the agency showed a healthy suspicion that the Soviets were considering multiple-warhead development in 1967–1968, and also a healthy skepticism in 1969 and after on the Russian MIRV 'functional equivalent' argument. . . . It is striking that, nevertheless, the initial judgment foresaw a Soviet MIRV in the 1970–1975 period—exactly on the mark."[32]

As usual, being correct offered no guarantee of being heeded or of maintaining a position with the White House and the bureaucracy. Despite admitting in 1972 that the Soviets were behind in the MIRV race and that they had not yet flight-tested a MIRV system, Laird refused to use the CIA to any great extent in preparing his plans, preferring instead the intelligence and analysis of the Defense Intelligence Agency. President Nixon and Henry Kissinger did not like the independent stand the CIA had taken, and Helms found himself at the White House much less often than during the Johnson days. "We'd just come from a marvelous period," recalled one deputy director of intelligence:

> We'd had Robert McNamara and LBJ, both of whom understood and had confidence in what we were trying to do and were very receptive. We had tremendous access to both of them. It was a very heady period—the most satisfactory period I can remember. Then along came Nixon, Kissinger, and Laird. And it was just as though the shades in the White House were pulled down all of a sudden. They came in with the assumption that everybody outside the White House was partisan to one degree or another, on one side or another, and was trying to grab a slice of the White House power. They were antagonistic right from the outset. If the CIA has any work to do at all, it is work on behalf of the President. The President is the man the agency serves. If the President feels that we are just another of the contenders out there with policy axes to grind, then it is hard for the agency to do its work. We suddenly had to work in this chill compared to what we had had before.[33]

FALLING OUT

Nixon and Kissinger, just like Kennedy, wanted to control foreign policy—and all those involved in foreign-policy information—from the White House. They wanted intelligence presented in their terms—not as a set of prejudices—in order to serve the immediate needs of their policies. They were much less interested in having their opinions confirmed than in having their view of things presented to others. They wanted to manage intelligence in the way that all administrations want to manage the news—that was what the battle over the SS-9 was in part about. Nixon was obsessed with setting up his own establishment in Washington. "I've got Chuck Colson's law firm announcement in the mail," one Nixon White House staffer remarked in 1973. "Nixon is determined to have his own Clark Clifford."[34]

The Washington "fat cats" who sat on "their well paid asses" were associated in Nixon's mind with the State Department as well as with the CIA, and he never really expected them to become part of "his" establishment. As a result, the agency was not involved in the full policy picture; it was simply left out. With Nixon in the White House, the agency had no real chance to be in the center of the action; someone in the White House—usually Henry Kissinger—would be there calling the shots instead. Nixon, Kissinger recalled, "felt it imperative to exclude the CIA from the formulation of policy; it was staffed by Ivy League liberals who behind the facade of analytical objectivity were usually pushing their own preferences. They had always opposed him politically."[35]

Very early in the Nixon administration it became clear that the President wanted Henry Kissinger to run intelligence for him and that the National Security Council staff in the White House, under Kissinger, would control the intelligence community. This was the beginning of a shift of power away from the CIA to a new center: the growing National Security Council staff. It was both a personal shift of power by the President in his own interests and an institutional shift as well. From this point on, under successive presidents, the agency began to lose influence to the NSC staff under the President's special assistant for national security affairs, who in turn has paralleled and at times challenged the director of Central Intelligence as the President's chief intelligence officer.

The technique Kissinger employed was never to say directly what he or the President wanted but instead to ask for analysis generally, taking out of it what was of particular interest to him. He did make particular requests from time to time, but these were the exceptions rather than the rule. "Send me what you've got, and I'll know what I like when I get it," was the Kissinger line. This was matched by procedural and administrative changes that enhanced the position of the White House—and Kissinger—in intelligence matters. In December 1968, before Nixon's inauguration, Kissinger informed Helms that things would be different in the new administration. In the past the director of Central Intelligence was expected to open National Security Council meetings with a briefing on the subject being considered and then to attend the rest of the meeting to answer questions or deal with points as they came up. In the future, Kissinger said, Helms would leave after his briefing. This was a serious challenge to the position of the DCI and the CIA in the Washington bureaucracy. The National Security Council was the foremost policy body in intelligence matters, and the CIA received its approvals and directives through it. The NSC was also the body that discussed intelligence and foreign policy. For the DCI not to be present would limit his knowledge of the policy picture and possibly result in less effective CIA activities.

Helms took the Kissinger proposal up with Melvin Laird, secretary of defense designate, who agreed that the CIA should not be excluded from the NSC in this way. All this took place before the SS-9 battle, and Laird no doubt considered that it would be useful to have Helms indebted to him, so he took the matter up with Kissinger. If Helms was excluded, the President would be vulnerable to criticism from a statutory point of view and from the point of view that he was making strategic decisions without the advice of his chief of intelligence. Helms stayed at the NSC meetings.[36]

During National Security Council meetings Helms had to deal with a host of put-downs from Nixon himself. "Nixon considered the CIA a refuge of Ivy League intellectuals opposed to him," Kissinger wrote in his memoirs, "and he felt ill at ease with Helms personally, since he suspected that Helms was well-liked by the liberal Georgetown set to which Nixon ascribed many of his difficulties."[37] Backed by the President, Kissinger insisted on being given the raw material of intelligence analysis—the cables, agents' reports, the communications intercepts, the photographs, and the technical intelligence. With his NSC staff, he made his own interpretation of this material, separate from the one he received from the CIA. Nixon, who prided himself on his grasp of foreign policy and knowledge of other countries, always read the detailed briefing books that circulated before NSC meetings. As a result, at meetings Helms faced a President and a national security adviser who were well informed about the CIA's sources and analysis.

Helms was often interrupted on points of information. Less than a month after Nixon's inauguration the NSC discussed the war between Nigeria and its secessionist Biafra province. Helms opened with his briefing, listing the countries that had recognized Biafra, and then, as one man present recalled,

> Nixon stopped him and said, "Look, Dick, you've left out a couple of countries—Zambia and the Ivory Coast." Helms sort of stopped a moment and looked slightly shaken. Helms then said something else, about tribal rivalries within Nigeria being part of the origin of the civil war and a complicating factor in the politics of the war, and Nixon stopped him and said, "Yes. And this is a problem which really goes back in the history of that country. The British colonial policy favored the Moslem Hausas in the north and that aggravated the tensions and there's cultural as well as economic and political factors here. It's a very, very tragic problem." I was sitting there in utter amazement: "My God, this man has actually read his briefing papers—and he's not only read it but he's understood it." . . . I had become accustomed in the Johnson Administration to a sort of scatter-shot approach. Whatever you sent up you never assumed that Johnson necessarily assimilated it.[38]

The note of condescension in the voice, the patronizing attitude of Nixon toward his director of Central Intelligence, was lost on no one present.[39]

Just in case the agency as a whole missed the point, John Ehrlichman, on Nixon's orders, started to badger Helms for reports on the Bay of Pigs and Diem's death, which could be used to embarrass the agency through press leaks and in bureaucratic battles. (This was not exactly the way the President was expected to treat his men.) After a long battle Helms personally presented some files to Nixon in 1971. "There is only one President at a time," said Helms to Nixon, "and I only work for you."[40] On another occasion Helms was asked by Nixon to break the CIA charter and organize domestic surveillance of Nixon's brother, Donald, but he managed to avoid it.[41]

There were other criticisms of Helms and the agency. Nixon did not want DCI briefings at National Security Council meetings to spend so much time on such matters as the population of a country or its area and geography. Helms tended to provide this sort of information as a matter of course, much to Nixon's obvious impatience. Nixon wanted to know what was going on in Moscow and Peking and in Sino-Soviet relations, and he wanted to know the sources of CIA judgments. Kissinger, as well as Nixon, requested detailed written intelligence. "He told us precisely the form he wanted it in," said Jack Smith. "Very Germanic and extravagantly articulated."[42]

Out of this came two factors that limited the CIA's ability to perform for the President. First, as a result of the more detailed written briefings, the President and Kissinger knew a tremendous amount about each subject themselves, frequently demonstrating this knowledge while arguing with the CIA about its judgments. This kept the agency on the defensive and helped center intelligence debates in the White House rather than in the bureaucracy. Second, with the White House curtains drawn to exclude outsiders from the intimate policy making of the administration, the CIA, along with other agencies and departments, very often did not know what policy was being followed. While Nixon was involved in his "madman theory," the CIA, the Joint Chiefs, and the State Department simply did not know what the President wanted or planned and consequently found themselves in disfavor.

The madman theory came out of Nixon's determination to end the war in Vietnam on favorable terms. Accordingly he wanted to convince the North Vietnamese, the Soviets, and the Chinese that he was capable of anything so that they would believe his threats. "I call it the madman theory," he told Bob Haldeman. "I want the North Vietnamese to believe I've reached the point where I might do *anything* to stop the war. We'll just slip the word to them that, 'for God's sake, you know Nixon is obsessed about Communists. We can't restrain him when he's angry—and he has his hand on the nuclear button'—and Ho Chi Minh himself will be in Paris in two days begging for peace."[43]

While Nixon, Haldeman and Kissinger understood this theory, they were too cautious to tell anyone else about it. (If word got out, it would not work.) So when on April 14, 1969, a North Korean air-force jet shot down a USAF EC-121 electronic spy plane without any provocation (apart from its spying) over international waters, killing all thirty-one men aboard, Nixon and Kissinger argued for ruthless retaliation. Helms, Laird, William P. Rogers, and the Joint Chiefs argued for a moderate, measured nonmilitary response. They knew from communications intercepts that the North Koreans had not shot down the plane as a deliberate act of provocation; it had been a command-and-control error. The combined weight of these senior officials against military retaliation first caused a delay in determining what the U.S. response to the incident should be and then made it very difficult for Nixon to implement his madman theory, which depended upon immediacy for its success. The delay meant that whatever he decided to do would be seen as deliberate and considered, not mad. Moderate response was the only choice, but Nixon was furious that his hands had been tied, and he spoke about getting rid of Laird and Rogers at the earliest opportunity. For their part, Helms, Laird, Rogers, and the Joint Chiefs never understood what they had done wrong; they had offered their best advice from the facts available and exerted their influence accordingly.

No military action was taken against North Korea. Instead a second secret bombing of Vietcong refuges in Cambodia was authorized (the first secret bombing raid had occurred a month earlier, in March). "If we strike back, even though it's risky," Kissinger said in support of Nixon's wish for a tough response, "they will say, 'This guy is becoming irrational—we'd better settle with him.' But if we back down, they'll say, 'This guy is the same as his predecessor, and if we wait he'll come to the same end.' " "I remained troubled by the response we had made," said Nixon, "or, as I saw it, that we had failed to make. I told Kissinger, 'They got away with it this time, but they'll never get away with it again.' "[44] Behind the hyperbole was a serious point: apart from Henry Kissinger, the President's senior officials and the heads of the great agencies and departments of government did not know that the President felt this way or that calculated irrationality was now part of American policy.

Policy issues in intelligence and foreign affairs always held more interest for Nixon than operations, and he emphasized three in particular: ending the war in Vietnam, the nature and consequences of the Sino-Soviet rift, and the prospects of an arms-limitation treaty with the Soviet Union. Ending the Vietnam War did not involve the CIA beyond its finding that the war was unwinnable on terms that lay within the bounds of practical politics. There was nothing the agency could do that was not already being done by the State Department, the Pentagon, or MACV. Moreover, because the issue held such political importance, Nixon naturally wanted to keep it in his own hands—in the White House. The CIA was much more involved in the Sino-Soviet rift and arms-limitation issues.

CHINA

Both the Soviet Union and Red China had supported North Korea during the Korean War, presenting the West with evidence of a communist monolith stretching from the middle of Germany to the Pacific, from the North Pole's

ice cap to the steaming jungles of Indochina. The Soviet Union had supplied
North Korea with weapons and raw materials; the Chinese had supplied them
with men, tens of thousands of whom had been killed in the war, including one
of Mao Tse-tung's own sons. Behind this apparent Sino-Soviet bloc, however,
lay deep-rooted differences, suspicions, and competition. In fact, Chinese and
Soviet support for North Korea represented an incipient rivalry between the
two communist giants: neither was prepared to let the other dominate North
Korea or be seen as North Korea's sole sponsor. In 1955 Ray Cline, then in
the Office of Current Intelligence (OCI) as chief of the Sino-Soviet area analytical staff, changed the basis of OCI's analysis of the communist states. Said
Cline:

> I took most pleasure in my new job because of having persuaded OCI to look
> at the whole world of Communist states from a single analytical viewpoint,
> that of my Sino-Soviet staff, so that we could detect similarities, and more sig-
> nificantly, differences among the various dictatorships that confronted us. . . .
> The free world–Communist world conflict—perceived to be the key strategic
> issue confronting the United States—demanded, in my view, the application
> of rigorous common standards of political and economic analysis to all parts
> of this vast totalitarian empire, which I was certain could not be the monolith
> of which it was then fashionable to speak.[45]

Within a year Cline's staff were cautiously suggesting a Sino-Soviet split
based on analysis of their different reactions to the riots in Poland and the
Hungarian revolt. According to Cline, "This staff compiled the data that permitted the CIA to lead the way—against furious opposition elsewhere—in
charting the strategic conflict between Soviet and Chinese styles of dictatorship and doctrine that was basic to the definitive split in 1960."[46] In essence,
the split came about because the Soviet Union demanded to be the leader of
world communism, while China refused to suppress its own interests in favor
of Russian ones in the name of unity. The USSR had become the voice of "developed" world communism, while China was the leader of Third World communism. China's was a peasant communism that forced itself on the cities.
Russia's was a city communism that had spread outward with a simulacrum of
a Marxist working class. When China wanted more help in developing its nuclear capabilities, the Russians delayed at first and then, in 1960, abruptly
withdrew their technicians from China; Russia did not want China to be a nuclear power. China had claims to vast areas of the eastern USSR, which the
Soviets refused to discuss despite their protestations that they were comrades
unwedded to national boundaries.

There was also ideological rivalry between Chinese and Russian versions
of communism, with each claiming orthodoxy. While the Chinese wanted to
spread communism throughout the world, by 1960 the Soviets were more concerned with keeping the communist states they already had. (Of course the
Russians were also quite willing to seize opportunities for expansion, as they

had done in Cuba.) History governed the split as well: for centuries the Chinese and the Russians had despised each other. Richard Nixon recalled:

> The Soviet leaders constantly denigrated the Chinese. Russian leaders as far back as Khrushchev privately warned their American counterparts against the Chinese disregard for human life—which, given the Soviet record, invites its own wry commentary. Brezhnev repeatedly warned me against the Chinese threat, and described the Chinese leaders as brutal and barbaric in their treatment of their own people; he urged that "we Europeans" should unite, to contain the potential great threat from China. The Chinese, for their part, make clear in their private conversations that they consider the Russians crude, ruthless barbarians.[47]

Starting in the 1950s, the CIA accurately monitored the Sino-Soviet conflict. As the rift became more apparent during the 1960s, the agency's record on the Sino-Soviet relationship strengthened its position in foreign-policy debates in Washington, particularly since during the fifteen years after McCarthy's attacks on it the State Department had made only the most circumspect analyses of China. The agency, however, was not involved in Nixon's successful effort to reach a diplomatic accommodation with China; Nixon kept this close to himself and conducted directly with the Chinese leadership in secret through Henry Kissinger. It did mean, however, that even with Nixon's suspicions of the agency and his determination to keep everything secret, he maintained a grudging respect for the ability of the analysts.*

DÉTENTE DREAMING

The desire for arms limitation provided the agency with another opportunity to prove its worth to Nixon. There were several reasons why Nixon was anxious to secure a limitation agreement with the Soviet Union. The arms race was expensive and by 1969, after eight years in Vietnam (from 1965 very intensively), the American economy was feeling the strain of paying for a major military effort out of peacetime fiscal measures. Moreover, as the war became more and more unpopular, politically it was not possible to reduce domestic welfare spending or increase taxes to pay for it. The result was growing inflation. Also involved was the awareness that an arms-limitation agreement would help demonstrate to the American public and to the world that despite Vietnam, Nixon had peaceful interests. He wanted to be a great peacemaker, and

---

*In mid-1969 Helms presented evidence to Nixon that the Soviet Union was planning both a preemptive military strike into China and a nuclear attack on China's nuclear installations. In November the agency presented an Estimate on the Sino-Soviet split which Nixon and Kissinger said they found impressive. Kissinger used CIA communications facilities to maintain the secrecy of the negotiations with Peking (Henry Kissinger, *White House Years* [Boston: Little, Brown, 1979], pp. 738, 757).

to this end he tried to gear domestic policies to give him elbowroom in foreign policy. It would help defuse antiwar feeling as well. Finally, an agreement would at least quantify the differences between American and Soviet capabilities, and it might help maintain some sort of parity of forces. The difficult question was how to monitor any agreement. The Russians had always refused to allow on-site inspections, probably because they feared that such examinations might reveal more about Soviet strengths and weaknesses than American. Satellite reconnaissance and electronic surveillance were the principal methods of monitoring an agreement, but were they good enough? Could the defense of the United States depend on the accuracy of technical intelligence devices, which, in the final analysis, were nothing more than extremely sophisticated gadgets? These were questions the CIA addressed with the utmost seriousness.

The first suggestion that America and Russia might reach an arms-limitation agreement was made by the United States in 1967. It came out of the desire of the Kennedy and Johnson administrations to control the use and the proliferation of nuclear weapons by concentrating them in the hands of the United States and the Soviet Union while simultaneously agreeing to bilateral limits. It was both an idealistic idea and a selfish one; its achievement would reduce the danger that a third country might start a nuclear war and would also mean that America and Russia would be the only two superpowers. If another country entered the list of nuclear powers, Russia and America, acting in concert, would always be able to limit the interloper's nuclear capability through their far superior force. Superpower cooperation in this respect would also emasculate the small nuclear powers like France and Britain. The multilateral Nuclear Non-Proliferation Treaty of 1968 was the culmination of one aspect of this desire. A strategic arms-limitation agreement with the Soviet Union was more difficult, presenting a challenge that Nixon accepted when he continued, as he put it, "the SALT negotiations initiated by the Johnson administration—in part because we hoped to reach long-term equitable limitation agreements that would provide greater strategic stability with fewer arms. Congress and the country were clearly not receptive to costly new strategic force programs, as demonstrated by the fact that the Senate approved the Safeguard ABM system by a margin of only one vote, and it took the heaviest pressure we could muster to manage even that."[48]

Part of the pressure depended on the CIA's ability to verify an agreement. Nixon was determined to believe that the agreement was verifiable. The CIA remained skeptical. Here the disagreement over the SS-9's capabilities and the Soviet MIRV program cast a long shadow and was at the core of Nixon's antagonism toward the CIA. If there was disagreement about the SS-9, how could the United States be certain that it could verify exactly what the Russians were and were not doing across the whole range of nuclear weapons? The agency found itself in a classic dilemma: on the one hand the White House wanted the CIA to support its views of the Soviet nuclear threat and denigrated its analysis when they refused to do so; and on the other hand the White

House wanted the CIA to deploy exactly the same skills required in the SS-9 investigation to convince Congress and the country that a strategic arms-limitation treaty with the USSR could be verified. The agency was confident throughout this conflict: it was certain that technical intelligence methods could verify a treaty. Kissinger, seeking to undermine the agency, spread the story that the CIA was taking this view because if it had to verify a treaty its power and influence would grow. The Joint Chiefs, for other reasons, were equally suspicious, and when on June 25, 1969, Helms presented to the National Security Council the CIA's judgment that all the elements being considered by the administration for inclusion in a treaty could be verified, his position was attacked by General Earle Wheeler.

The division of opinion over verification was used by Nixon and Kissinger to obtain still more personal control of policy. On July 21 Kissinger created a new group, the National Security Council Verification Panel, which he chaired. Although the job of the panel was to assess the CIA's claim that SALT could be verified, it rapidly became the group that dealt with all SALT matters, by-passing the National Security Council. Ultimately both the panel and the NSC (and the official negotiators) were ignored by Nixon and Kissinger, who conducted personal diplomacy and negotiations directly with the Soviet Ambassador in Washington, Anatoly Dobrynin.*

The secrecy with which Nixon and Kissinger surrounded their policy objectives and their efforts to achieve them isolated the White House from the bureaucracy and made every major department and agency in Washington resort to intrigue to discover what was really going on. Nixon wanted this isolation because it acted to center power in his hands; Kissinger, naturally a gregarious soul, went along with it because it also enhanced his position and because he realized that his tenure depended entirely on keeping Nixon happy. In one instance, Admiral Thomas H. Moorer, chairman of the Joint Chiefs of Staff, turned to Charles E. Radford, a navy yeoman, working in the Joint Chiefs' liaison office in the White House, for copies of Kissinger's cables and other secret documents. A naval officer monitored telephone calls between Nixon and Kissinger and Haig and reported on the conversations to the chairman. From these, as one of the Joint Chiefs recalled, "It was clear that Haig was running to Nixon and shooting down Kissinger. Kissinger was running to Nixon and shooting down Haig. Nixon from time to time would cut Kissinger off totally and not see him, whereupon Kissinger would become totally paranoid. It all made it totally impossible to carry out structured policies."[49]

As the secret backchannel negotiations proceeded between Kissinger and

*Seymour M. Hersh, *The Price of Power: Kissinger in the Nixon White House* (New York: Summit Books, 1983), pp. 157–158, 340–344. When in 1971 it looked as if an agreement were going to be reached in the formal SALT negotiations, Nixon and Kissinger were seriously alarmed that this would circumvent their secret "backchannel" negotiations. As a result Dobrynin was summoned to the White House and told to stop the official Soviet negotiators from making serious proposals.

Dobrynin, it became clear in 1971 that the Soviets were also anxious to reach an arms-limitation agreement. The expense of the arms race was proportionately far greater for the Soviets, and they needed resources to prop up their dismal agricultural performance. Accordingly, the question of being able to verify an agreement—rather than being able to reach an agreement—became the central issue. Because of the differences of opinion about America's ability to verify that the Russians were sticking to an agreement, Nixon and Kissinger decided that they would confine verification to quantitative matters—numbers of missiles and so on—rather than to qualitative ones—missile accuracy, MIRV development. The advantage of this plan was that all parties agreed that quantitative verification was possible. The disadvantage was that although the United States was well ahead qualitatively (American technology was far superior to Soviet technology at the time), the Russians could catch up and still remain within the terms of the agreement.

After the arms-limitation treaty, SALT I, was signed on May 26, 1972, one of the main problems the Nixon administration faced was to disguise the fact that the agreement did not prevent the Soviets from continuing to develop qualitatively. Having reaped tremendous political reward from achieving a breakthrough in arms limitation, the administration found it politically difficult to admit that SALT I was not really that big an advance. As a result, a feeling rapidly developed that the Soviets had hoodwinked the United States and that Nixon and Kissinger were trying to cover up a mistake. The secrecy of the Nixon White House intensified this feeling. The CIA, along with the other intelligence agencies, was caught up in a debate shot through with deceit and suspicion.

On July 1, 1972, the Defense Intelligence Agency, the National Security Agency, the heads of the service intelligence departments, and the Central Intelligence Agency formed a Steering Group on Monitoring Strategic Arms Limitations, under the chairmanship of the DCI, Richard Helms. The purpose of the group was to coordinate American verification of Soviet compliance with SALT I, and it found itself the focus of attention. Negotiations for a second limitation agreement, SALT II, had begun immediately after SALT I was signed, so the Steering Group's reports assumed an even greater importance. If the Soviets were adhering to the terms of SALT I, then the prospects of SALT II were good and President Nixon, facing reelection in November, would look good too. The problem was that because verification was limited to quantitative matters, the Soviets could stay within the agreement while at the same time developing, testing, and deploying new weapons systems. This, of course, would leave the President with a major political headache.

There was little doubt that the reports of the Steering Group would be political dynamite, since they would inevitably confirm continuing Soviet weapons development and not the strict limitation Americans thought SALT I had established. Eleven weeks after the formation of the Steering Group,

Henry Kissinger directed Helms to send the group's reports to only the National Security Council; the council would decide what information to release and whether the Soviets were adhering to SALT I or not. In addition, SALT intelligence was put on "hold"—meaning that it was not only highly classified but also not distributed. The White House was going to use the backchannel to warn the Soviets about any violations of SALT I that were spotted but was not going to tell anyone else about them.* In 1975 the House Select Committee on Intelligence, chaired by Congressman Otis Pike, questioned William Hyland, a senior CIA analyst and subsequently Kissinger's deputy on the NSC staff, about this procedure. The committee asked Hyland, if the Russians were told of violations, whom are we keeping them a secret from? "We are keeping a hold item secret from people who might read the Central Intelligence Bulletin that is disseminated in several hundred copies," explained Hyland.[50] The CIA was in the middle of a political thicket.

The backchannel and hold procedures worked well in the short term, enabling Nixon to capitalize on SALT I and his visit to China in February 1972 and present a set of glowing foreign-policy successes to the electorate in November. But all the secrecy ultimately caught up with Nixon and Kissinger and the bureaucrats they controlled. After Nixon's landslide victory for his second term as President, the contradictions between public statements and secret realities began to emerge, especially as more and more information about the Watergate break-in became known during 1973. Entwined in this web of secrecy and deceit were the CIA, the FBI, the White House, and the President.

---

*To an important degree the Soviets had an advantage over Nixon. He had made a deal with them—SALT I—and his political fortune would be affected by public perceptions of Soviet adherence to the terms of the deal. If the Soviets were seen not to be sticking to SALT I, then Nixon (and Kissinger) would be shown up as gullible. So the subtext of SALT I was that the Soviets should be able to grow in strength without being accused of breaking the agreement. Pressing ahead with the opening to China was the Nixon/Kissinger reply. It infuriated the Soviets and gave Nixon something to bargain about with them over SALT I.

—15—

The President's Men?
1970–1972

For Richard Nixon, as for Jack Kennedy, the presidency was an opportunity to do everything he wanted. Kennedy wanted to know about people and to dominate domestic policies and agencies in ways that would secure his political influence after he left the presidency. He wanted his family to have an impressive presidential legacy that would amount to nothing less than an inside track on power in America. Nixon wanted something similar (he did not have his own family in mind but, instead, his close supporters) in the area of foreign policy, and he also wanted to make money and achieve personal power and position. His interest was not in establishing the power of domestic bureaucracies but rather in centering influence, which would endure after he left office, in great Republican law firms.

Nixon's expectation was that he would leave office rich and healthy in 1977 at the age of sixty-four, having presided over America's bicentennial celebrations and withdrawal from Vietnam. He clearly expected that by the time he left office he would set the stage for the continuing influence of his brand of Republicanism. He was willing to act like a street fighter as he used the tremendous powers and patronage of the presidency to put his people in place and to put other people out of business. Just like Kennedy, he was a keen reader of J. Edgar Hoover's salacious FBI reports and was not above letting titbits out around town. To him power was akin to war: it could be effective only if it was used energetically and ruthlessly.

On September 15, 1972, the day that a grand jury indicted the seven men accused of illegally entering the Democratic National Committee's offices in the Watergate building in Washington, Nixon's reaction was to express his concept of power to John Dean, counsel to the President. "This is a war," he said. "We take a few shots and it will all be over. We will give them a few shots and it will be over. . . . They are asking for it and they are going to get it. We have not used the power in this first four years as you know. We have never used it. We have not used the Bureau and we have not used the Justice Department but things are going to change now. And they are either going to do it right or go."[1] Nixon's reaction to the news of the Watergate break-in was extreme. Indeed, the question has to be asked whether any other President would have responded in the same way. How many other men who have occupied the office of the presidency would have been so exercised—or for that matter involved—at such a basic level? And, more important, how many would have used presidential power with such energy to cover it up?

Nixon's willingness to exercise power so ruthlessly and to hide behind a wall of secrecy came at a pivotal moment in the history of the CIA. At the time Nixon moved into the White House in 1969 the agency prided itself on being calm and unenthusiastic. It also prided itself on its special bureaucratic position and on the enormous congressional appropriations it received. (Although CIA budgets are secret, its estimated budget at the time was about $800 million within the overall defense budget.) The agency wanted to do its business in a quiet way, attracting no attention to what it did or the amounts of money it spent. Vietnam War protests proved to agency officials that people were now more squeamish than they had been in times past. As a result, they feared a tremendous public backlash if news of their worldwide activities leaked out. Nixon's request for agency files on the Bay of Pigs and Diem's assassination was designed to let CIA people know that he would use their fears against them if they did not get in line behind his leadership and give him their full support. As professionals, agency people also realized that the world was a complicated place within which even America had to tread carefully as Americans no longer trusted the political leadership that was to do the treading.

Distrust of government and politicians was one of the great changes in attitudes of the 1960s, and agency people were among the first to spot it. By 1969 the CIA's conception of itself had also changed. It was no longer a brilliant wartime improvising agency but a medium-sized bureaucracy doing long-term work for America. Top agency officials had made the break with the OSS. The CIA had ceased to be an elite, dashing, distinguished agency, conceived and dedicated to emergency operations. The Bay of Pigs and the long-term satellite and electronic intelligence programs helped make this break. So did the long slog of the Vietnam War. But more important was the awareness that the emergency of the early cold war was here to stay. The job was to contain the emergency, make it normal, and prevent emergency from blossoming into war.

The ambition of the agency was to gauge a more complicated world accurately rather than to soften up the border countries of eastern Europe, making them receptive to U.S. advances in another war. Under Raborn and then Helms the agency was quietly withdrawing from the subversion emphasis of the 1940s and 1950s. It was seeking instead a larger part in foreign-policy formation as it tried to become more gray, less palpable, and more prudent, while still overseeing operations. It was a bureaucracy maturing, no longer taking pride in meeting the pace set by its political masters, preferring instead to set its own pace. At this point in its development the agency was engaged in defining and conquering its bureaucratic territory in Washington in competition with the State Department, the Pentagon, the armed forces, and the other intelligence agencies.

"If there was a real fault in the organization," said Lawrence Houston, looking back at the CIA's first twenty-five years, "I would say it was the too great willingness to say, 'Yes, we can do it' instead of pointing out dangers."[2] By the late 1960s the agency was defining its targets with much greater care and was much less concerned with redefining issues with each new administration and each new emergency. In many ways the U-2 had presaged this change. It was a development involving a long-term assessment of the Soviet Union and the commitment of resources to a set of very specific, nonemergency questions. The purpose of the U-2 was to answer questions about Soviet strategic plans, not whether Soviet armies were about to invade western Europe. Its flights were across the heartland of the Soviet Union, not along the border with the West.

In the late 1940s the CIA had used whatever planes were available for reconnaissance; with the U-2 it had created its own and, with it and the subsequent satellite programs, was beginning to seek its own niche in the world. It no longer wanted simply to fit into the particular cracks that opened up. The people rising in the agency were ever less the kind of people who could go anywhere and do anything. In the twenty years before he became director, Richard Helms spent very few days outside the United States, despite the fact that he was in the operations side of the agency. The vitality with which Kennedy had entered the war in Vietnam was gone by 1967. No longer was there glamour in injecting America into things: Vietnam had made that all go sour. The United States was still the world's major power, but the mystique of its power had gone.

Under Truman the CIA had been a useful adjunct of foreign policy which, nevertheless, held little fascination for the President. In contrast, Eisenhower had a field commander's respect for intelligence: nothing was more important than knowing the enemy's capabilities and intentions. As a result he established the CIA and the National Security Council at the core of his policy making. The CIA's role changed dramatically between 1961 and 1974. Two out of the three presidents who served during this period were fascinated by secrets and secrecy. The agency found itself entwined with the machinations and fantasies of presidents, no longer being treated with respect and admiration as a fine instrument of presidential power but as hit men and spies and wiretappers and blue-movie makers and gumshoes. Its intellectual brilliance was only occasionally recognized by Kennedy (notably during the Cuban missile crisis) and was consistently ignored by Nixon. As Ray Cline observed:

> A Vietnam-obsessed President Johnson and a secretive President Nixon never gave Dick Helms much of a chance to be the kind of DCI that Dulles was for Eisenhower and McCone was for Kennedy. They both viewed Helms and the CIA primarily as an instrument for the execution of White House wishes by secret methods. They neither seemed to understand nor to care about the carefully structured functions of central intelligence as a whole, and increasingly under Nixon and his principal assistant, Dr. Kissinger, disregarded analytical intelligence except for what was convenient for use by Kissinger's own small personal staff in support of Nixon-Kissinger policies. Incoming intelligence was closely monitored and its distribution controlled by Kissinger's staff to keep it from embarrassing the White House, and the national estimates function fell into comparative disrepute and neglect. I doubt that any could have done better than Helms in these circumstances. One thing is clear, however; the CIA was deteriorating in its influence and its capability to influence policymaking by objective analysis.[3]

"When intelligence producers have a general feeling that they are working in a hostile climate," said John Huizenga, the last director of the Office of National Estimates, "what really happens is not so much that they tailor the product to please, although that's not been unknown, but more likely, they avoid the treatment of difficult issues."[4]

There was also a wish to avoid difficult operations. In 1970, when it looked as if the Marxist Salvador Allende would win the Chilean presidential election, Nixon ordered the CIA to intervene, in a covert action, in an attempt to prevent Allende from winning. Ten years earlier the agency would have risen to the challenge with enthusiasm. Now it responded with long faces and a calculation of the risk. "One in 10 chance, perhaps, but save Chile!" read Helms's note of his meeting with Nixon on September 15 when he was given his orders. "Worth spending. Not concerned risks involved. No involvement of embassy, $10,000,000 available, more if necessary. Full-time job—best men we have. Game plan. Make the economy scream. 48 hours for plan of action." Henry Heckscher, the CIA station chief in Santiago, had to be ordered to cease cabling his doubts to Washington about the agency's ability to stop Allende. He was finally ordered by the DDP, Thomas Karamessines, to return to headquarters, where he was dressed down for not understanding that this was something the CIA *had* to do even though it did not want to. When Heckscher returned to Santiago he told his staff that they had no choice. "Nobody," said Karamessines, "was going to go into the Oval Office, bang his fist on the table, and say we *won't* do it."[5]

CHILE

Nixon's concept of "saving" Chile was more complicated than Kennedy's concept of "saving" Cuba. Nixon did not order the CIA to kill anybody. It had a successful history of political manipulation in Chile, and he wanted it repeated. President Kennedy had launched a massive secret program to make Chile the showcase of democracy and capitalism in Latin America, a counterpart to the model of Castro's Cuba. In 1962 and 1964, when Allende had previously sought election, the CIA had spent a total of $4 million supporting the opposing Christian Democrats.[6] Funds were given directly to the Christian Democrats, and propaganda campaigns—using leaflets, newspaper stories, posters—were financed depicting Allende and his Socialist Workers party as antidemocratic and suggesting that an Allende victory would result in a terror-filled police state. Although the 1962 election saw a Christian Democrat victory, there was a strong Allende vote. The 1964 election was much more successful from the American point of view. The Christian Democrat, Eduardo Frei, won handsomely, due in large measure, it was thought, to CIA backing; it was estimated that the CIA paid half the total costs of his campaign.[7]

In Washington, Frei's success was seen as putting Chile firmly on the road toward becoming a successful democracy. The CIA was felt to have done an effective job. Chile, it was considered, was safe with Frei and no longer needed the same close attention it had received in the past. For the next six years, Frei instituted a series of land reforms and wealth-redistribution measures, along with reforms in education and the social services. He enjoyed the strong support of Edward M. Korry, the U.S. ambassador to Chile from October 1967 to October 1971.

As the 1970 election approached, however, Allende was back again, gaining support for his argument that Frei's measures were halfhearted and that an Allende government would legislate a fairer society quickly. Since December 1969 the White House had again considered plans to stop Allende, and in March 1970 the 40 Committee had approved the first anti-Allende propaganda campaign. In June 1970, as indications grew stronger that Allende's challenge might succeed, the 40 Committee began to consider what the CIA should do in addition to its low-key support for the Christian Democrats.

The 40 Committee was the successor to Kennedy's Special Group. It was renamed the 303 Committee in 1965 under Johnson and became the 40 Committee in February 1970. As the interdepartmental committee established by the National Security Council to review CIA covert operations, it consisted in 1970 of the mandatory members—a senior State Department official (the undersecretary of state for political affairs), a senior Defense Department official (the deputy secretary for defense), the chairman of the Joint Chiefs of Staff, and a White House representative of the National Security Council itself—as well as the attorney general, John Mitchell. "I don't see why we need to stand by and watch a country go Communist due to the irresponsibility of its own people," said Henry Kissinger, the NSC representative to the committee, on June 27 as the decision was made once more to increase the American effort to influence the Chilean elections.[8] The CIA was authorized to conduct a poll of the Chilean electorate before the election took place on September 4. Based on these polling results, the agency predicted that Jorge Alessandri, the right-wing candidate, would beat Allende, with the Christian Democrats in third place. However, despite another propaganda campaign against Allende, on September 4 he, and not Alessandri, gained the largest vote. As the last ballots were counted, alarm bells were ringing in Washington.

Separately from the CIA's efforts to prevent Allende from winning, several large American companies with substantial investments in Chile had financed Alessandri and the Christian Democrats, fearful of Allende's promises to nationalize industry. The International Telephone and Telegraph Corporation (ITT) and Anaconda Copper were the two leading companies involved. In May 1970 John McCone, now a member of the board of ITT, approached Richard Helms privately and proposed a joint CIA-ITT effort to prevent an Allende victory. The chairman of the board of Anaconda had already offered the State Department $500,000 in corporate funds (several companies contributed) to be used against Allende. ITT offered the CIA $1 million. All along, the CIA had been doubtful of its ability to influence the 1970 elections to any great extent; a 1968 National Intelligence Estimate on Latin America concluded that forces for social reform in the Latin countries were too strong to be manipulated from outside.[9] As a result, Helms decided that it was better for ITT to spend its own money directly, and he simply provided the corporations with the names of useful contacts.

There was a feeling of desperation in corporate boardrooms and within some military circles in Chile at the prospect of Allende becoming president. These fears were expressed to Henry Kissinger, John Mitchell, and Richard Helms, who in turn passed them on to President Nixon. What Nixon learned convinced him to order the CIA to attempt to secure Allende's defeat in the confirmation election for president to be held in the Chilean Congress on October 24 and to start planning to "make the economy scream" in the event of Allende's continuing success. Helms followed orders and put some of his best men on the job. David Atlee Phillips was appointed head of a new Chilean Task Force and was given the mission of preventing Allende from assuming the presidency of Chile.

"I couldn't believe it," said Phillips. "Why me?" he asked.

"We're supposed to put the very best people we have on it," explained Jim Flannery, the deputy head of the Western Hemisphere Division in the DDP.

"And we don't involve the embassy? Does that mean that Ambassador Korry and Harry Shlaudeman [the deputy chief of mission at the Santiago Embassy] in Chile won't be told?" Phillips inquired.

"Yup, and Secretary of State Rogers won't be told either. That's what the man wants. Korry and Rogers will participate in diplomatic and economic efforts, which we are going to call Track I, but CIA is to try Track II, a second way, all by itself." Nixon's secrecy was at work again. The CIA's involvement in Track I would be known, but Track II was to be super secret. Phillips was told that the 40 Committee had approved Track I but that the committee did not know about Track II and the order to thwart Allende's inauguration by whatever means possible.

"There is only one way," said Phillips. "A military coup."

"Yup," said his chief. "It'll probably come down to that in the end."

"And the odds against that working are very long indeed," replied Phillips. The commander of the Chilean armed forces, General René Schneider, was known to be a strong democrat and opposed to any unconstitutional action to prevent Allende's election. "What do you think?" Phillips asked.

"I agree. Problem is, Helms has his marching orders."[10]

Track II was conducted in the greatest secrecy, even within the CIA. In order to disguise the fact from even senior agency officers that after ten years the agency was involved in a major covert action again, Phillips was given an unprepossessing office in an old mail room. His problem, and the problem of Track II, was not simply the agency's own skepticism and dislike of the operation but also the subversion of a democratically elected leader. "Salvador Allende had been the world's first avowed Marxist freely elected to the highest office in his country," said Phillips. "Should the CIA, even responding to a President's ukase, encourage a military coup in one of the few countries in Latin America with a solid, functioning democratic tradition?"[11] Phillips also worried that the CIA had no one to work with in Chile who might be a realistic alternative to Allende. This was demonstrated on October 24 when, despite the expenditure of $250,000 as part of Track I by the CIA to prevent Allende's confirmation as president, the Chilean Congress elected him to the post. The effort of Track II to secure a military coup was equally ill-fated, involving the CIA once again indirectly in an assassination.

The lines between Track I and Track II were often blurred. Both envisaged the possibility of a military coup; Ambassador Korry, who did not learn of Track II until five years later, made it clear to President Frei and senior Chilean military commanders that if Allende became president, American military aid to Chile would stop and that "not a nut or bolt will be allowed to reach Chile under Allende."[12] The real difference was that Track II was an attempt to organize a military coup without anyone but the plotters knowing. Here again, however, the CIA found that hardly anybody was willing to plot a coup. Thomas Karamessines, who had overall charge of Track II in the agency, told

President Nixon that "the Chilean military seemed to be disorganized and un-willing to do anything. And without their wanting to do something, there did not seem to be much hope."[13] The best the CIA could do in October 1970 was to develop a three-point plan to "collect intelligence on coup-minded officers," recognizing that both Schneider and President Frei were constitutionalists who were unwilling to take illegal action to prevent Allende's inauguration; to "cre-ate a coup climate by propaganda, disinformation, and terrorist activities in-tended to provoke the left to give a pretext for a coup"; and to "inform those coup-minded officers that the U.S. Government would give them full support in a coup short of direct U.S. military intervention."[14]

The U.S. military attaché in Santiago, Colonel Paul Wimert, who had excellent personal contacts within the Chilean military, was enlisted to help carry out this three-point program. The Defense Intelligence Agency was also enlisted to provide the names of key Chileans who would be helpful in orga-nizing a coup.[15] The names these sources came up with included Robert Viaux, a retired Chilean army general who had led a minor insurrection osten-sibly over military pay in 1969, and General Camilo Valenzuela, the com-mander of the Santiago garrison. Everyone agreed, however, that the highest levels of the Chilean armed forces would not support a coup and that General Schneider's resistance to unconstitutional action carried great weight within the military as a whole. Viaux, upon whom the CIA decided "to continue to focus our attention" because he "appears to be the only military leader willing to block Allende," was simultaneously described by Henry Heckscher as "a General without an army."[16]

The limited support for Viaux within the Chilean military drew attention back to Schneider. His resistance to coup plans was noted as making it "more important than ever to remove him."[17] At all times, however, Helms made it plain that assassination was not an option. "When I became Director," said Helms, "I had already made up my mind that we weren't going to have any of that business when I was Director, and I had made that clear to my fellows."[18] On October 13, mindful of this ban, Heckscher cabled Langley that "Viaux intends to kidnap Generals Schneider and Prats [Schneider's deputy] within the next 48 hours in order to precipitate a coup."[19] On October 15 Thomas Karamessines met Henry Kissinger and Alexander Haig at the White House to reach a decision on how far to go with Viaux:

> It was decided by those present that the Agency must get a message to Viaux warning him against any precipitate action [the memorandum of the meeting recorded]. In essence the message should state: "We have reviewed your plans and based on your information and ours, we come to the conclusion that your plans for a coup at this time cannot succeed. Failing, they may re-duce your capabilities in the future. Preserve your assets. We will stay in touch. The time will come when you with all your other friends can do some-thing. You will continue to have our support."

The meeting concluded, according to the CIA record, "on Dr. Kissinger's note that the agency should continue keeping the pressure on every Allende weak spot in sight—now, after the 24th of October [the date the Chilean Congress would elect the president], after November 5 [the day the new president would be inaugurated], and into the future until such time as new marching orders are given. Mr. Karamessines stated that the Agency would comply."[20]

In Chile, General Viaux had already decided to go it alone, and while postponing his planned kidnap of Schneider, told the CIA that it would now take place on October 22 as "the first link in chain of events to come."[21] On the evening of October 17 Colonel Wimert met a Chilean army officer and a navy officer and passed back to the CIA their request for eight to ten tear gas grenades, three .45-caliber submachine guns and five hundred rounds of ammunition for self-protection. It was suspected that these might be used to kidnap Schneider, but since the officers concerned were not part of Viaux's group this was not certain. On October 19 the weapons were sent to Chile in a diplomatic bag and handed over to these officers in the early hours of October 22.* Meanwhile General Valenzuela informed the CIA that, together with some senior officers, he was prepared to mount a coup, also beginning with the kidnapping of Schneider. Although Viaux and Valenzuela knew about each other's plans, they were not willing to combine efforts. Each, apparently, was ambitious to head a military junta.

Valenzuela attempted to kidnap Schneider on October 19 but failed because Schneider drove to a dinner in a private car rather than in his official one, and his police guard was alert. At this point, apparently, the CIA tried to discourage the plotters and then broke off contact. Viaux nevertheless went ahead with his attempt on October 22 as planned. Shortly after 8 o'clock in the morning Schneider was stopped in his car on his way to work and mortally wounded when he drew his handgun in self-defense. Subsequently Viaux was arrested and tried by a Chilean military court which found that handguns had been used by the kidnappers, although one unloaded submachine gun was also found at the scene. The court sentenced General Viaux to twenty years in prison and a five-year exile for his involvement in Schneider's death and imposed a three-year exile on General Valenzuela for plotting a coup.[22]

The CIA was satisfied that its guns had not been used, even though it was never very clear whether some of the same officers had been involved in both the Valenzuela and Viaux kidnap plans. Hearing the news of Schneider's death, Phillips had

immediately assumed that CIA was involved somehow with the assassination, because the Santiago station had passed three machine guns the night

---

*What was the CIA expecting them to do with the weapons? Small weapons in a diplomatic bag were for a "small" crime—a murder, most probably. A revolution would not be staged with small weapons. Gas grenades and submachine guns were not weapons of self-protection either.

before to a cabal of military officers who considered Schneider the principal stumbling block to their plans to block Allende's confirmation. Later reports indicated, however, that Schneider had been killed by men carrying hand guns; it had been their intention to kidnap him, but he died in the firefight which ensued when he drew his own gun to defend himself. The Schneider assailants were later convicted of the crime. They had been contacted previously by CIA agents—then discouraged by CIA and contact severed. Thank God, I said to myself, for at least that small favor.[23]

In the judgment of the Chile Task Force, Schneider's fatal wounding (he died on October 25) had changed things, making the possibilities of a coup brighter if only the military would stage one. The problem was, as Henry Heckscher had foretold on October 9, that Schneider's death would "rally the army firmly behind the flag of constitutionalism." On October 23 Richard Helms reviewed Track II and decided "that a maximum effort has been achieved, and that now only the Chileans themselves can manage a successful coup. The Chileans have been guided to a point where a military solution is at least open to them."[24]

There were no further coup attempts. Already, a week or so earlier, the CIA had informed the President that all had been done that could be done, and, as Nixon recalled, "I instructed the CIA to abandon the operation."[25] Which operation had been abandoned was not clear, however. The CIA understood that only Track I had been abandoned and that Track II should continue until they were given new marching orders, as Thomas Karamessines understood Kissinger had said to him on October 15. Later Kissinger and Haig both testified that something quite different had occurred on October 15: that Kissinger had told Karamessines that Track II was "being turned off by the White House, after which Track II was dead as far as my office was concerned, and we never received another report on the subject. In my mind Track II was finished on October 15th." Alexander Haig concurred about the meeting. "I left with the distinct impression that . . . they were to cease and desist."[26]

In any event, Track II went on trying to secure the overthrow of Allende's government. Perhaps the confusion about whether only Track I or Track II as well had been turned off was the result of Kissinger and Haig being out of favor with Nixon at the time and thus being kept out of the secret. Or perhaps the entwined nature of Track I and Track II meant that Nixon, Kissinger, and Haig were all under the impression that they were one and the same by mid-October or that by then Track II had subsumed Track I. It was the same sort of thing the agency had faced under Eisenhower and Kennedy: plausible deniability was assumed to be in the President's mind, and the agency acted accordingly until given explicit new marching orders. As far as Thomas Karamessines was concerned, Track II continued, becoming a long-term effort to change the government in Chile. He testified to the Church Committee in 1975:

I am sure that the seeds that were laid in that effort in 1970 had their impact in 1973 [when Allende was killed or committed suicide in a successful military coup]. I do not have any question about that in my mind. . . . As far as I was concerned, Track II was really never ended. What we were told to do in effect was, well, Allende is now President. So Track II, which sought to prevent him from becoming President, was technically out, it was done. But what we were told to do was to continue our efforts. Stay alert, and do what we could to contribute to the eventual achievement of the objectives and purposes of Track II. That being the case, I don't think it is proper to say that Track II was ended.[27]

"Everybody's very down on Helms for failing to take drastic action to stop Allende," John McCone told John Bross in December 1970, and the word was around town that Helms had slipped and that Nixon and Kissinger blamed the CIA for bungling the attempt to stop Allende.[28] Helms and the agency rode the storm. "We're there as the whipping boy," said one CIA man involved with Track II. "Kissinger and Nixon left us holding the bag, but that's what we're in business for. And if you don't like it, don't join up."[29]

Meanwhile the planning of Allende's downfall revived. A National Security Council Decision Memorandum, "Policy Toward Chile," was issued on November 9 authorizing economic sanctions against Chile, much like the ones Ambassador Korry had warned his Chilean contacts about earlier, and in the weeks that followed, the CIA was instructed to disrupt secretly the Chilean economy. Between Allende's inauguration as president in November 1970 and his death in September 1973, the CIA officially reported spending $8 million on anti-Allende plotting. Track II, paralleling this new subversion effort, focused on stimulating "the military coup groups into a strong unified move against the government" and gathering intelligence on Allende's plans in the event of a military uprising.[30]

When a successful coup by Chilean army officers took place in September 1973 the CIA, through undercover agents and with the help of the Australian Secret Intelligence Service, knew in detail about the plot and had a direct hand in encouraging the plotters. Neither the agency nor its agents were actually involved in the coup or in Allende's death. Inevitably, however, as paranoia—much of it justified, as it turned out—and suspicion raged about the activities of the Nixon administration, the CIA, because of the continuation of Track II, was perceived by the public as having helped to overthrow democracy in Chile in favor of a brutally repressive military dictatorship.

WATERGATE

In the middle of the CIA's anti-Allende operation Nixon's own efforts to be reelected President of the United States boomeranged with Watergate and with his overconfidence after winning his second term in November 1972 with the biggest majority of states and electoral college votes since Franklin Roosevelt's victory in 1936. Evidence slowly accumulated after the June 17, 1972, break-in of the Democratic National Committee headquarters in the Watergate building that White House staffers and then Nixon himself might be involved in covering up both their connections with the intruders and their knowledge of the break-in. Nixon, concerned about the impact of the break-in on the election, tried to use the CIA to stop the Department of Justice investigation on the grounds of national security. It was this early attempt to deflect the investigation that ultimately cost Nixon the presidency, forcing him to resign two years later. Less than two weeks after the break-in John Dean, Nixon's general counsel, told General Vernon Walters, the new deputy director of Central Intelligence, that he was worried that the intruders—most of whom had worked for the CIA in one way or another in the past—might start talking, to the disadvantage of the CIA and the White House.

"My wife picked up the paper after the break-in and it listed the names of the people who broke in," said Lawrence Merthan, married to an ex-CIA employee, "and she said, 'If Jim McCord is involved in this, he got orders from the President of the United States. I know Jim McCord so well—he's the most decent, compassionate man I've ever known. He would never break the law. If they broke in and did this, they were ordered by the President of the United States to do it, otherwise Jim McCord wouldn't do it.' That was my wife after reading the news item on day one."[31] James McCord had been a senior officer in the CIA's Office of Security. He had retired from the agency in 1970 and early in 1972 had offered his services to the Committee to Re-elect the President.

Another of those implicated in the Watergate break-in, E. Howard Hunt, had also retired from the CIA in 1970. Hunt had been a DDP operator, acting at one point under the name "Eduardo" as the CIA's contact with exiled Cubans in Miami during the Bay of Pigs operation. In 1971 he began to work for the Nixon White House and was one of those who started Nixon's "plumbers" unit, which conducted secret (and illegal) break-ins and political espionage operations. Watergate was one such break-in, and Hunt had recruited McCord for the job. Four Cuban-Americans, all recruited by Hunt through his contacts with the Cuban exile community in Miami, were arrested with McCord. One, Eugenio R. Martinez, was on the CIA payroll at the time, being paid a hundred dollars a month for information about the Miami Cuban community. (By June 20 Martinez had been dropped from the agency's books.)

In the secret and suspicious atmosphere of Nixon's Washington, such connections were enough to convince even Washington insiders that the CIA was behind the break-in—that the agency had given itself fully to Nixon's machinations. This was compounded by what James McCord—throughout loyal to his old employer, the CIA—termed "pressure on the defendants to blame the Watergate operation on CIA and other matters." The pressure, said McCord, was coming from the White House, and he "sought to head it off by sending a letter to [John J.] Caulfield," a former colleague in the White House who had offered McCord the prospect of a presidential pardon if he took the blame for Watergate. McCord considered that this would simply be a step toward blaming the CIA, rather than himself, and in any case he no longer trusted Nixon or his emissaries. He wanted to stress that he would not let the CIA take the blame. The letter, sent in December 1972, was recalled from memory by McCord on May 22, 1973, during the Senate Watergate hearings: "If Helms goes and the Watergate operation is laid at CIA's feet, where it does not belong, every tree in the forest will fall. It will be a scorched desert. The whole matter is at the precipice right now. Pass the message that if they want it to blow, they are on exactly the right course."[32] As it turned out, a lot of people were on the right course, and although the CIA was not involved in the Watergate break-in, a great deal of information came out about it and "other matters," some of which had nothing to do with Watergate, some of which was associated with Watergate, and all of which would lead to a massive public Senate investigation of the agency.*

Within twenty hours of the Watergate break-in Howard Osborn, head of the CIA's Office of Security, telephoned Richard Helms at home to tell him that a former employee, McCord, and four other men had been arrested at

*There had been a constant rumor of much greater CIA involvement in Watergate, with the implication that the agency's most senior officers arranged the whole affair, including the discovery of the intruders, in a successful effort to discredit and topple Nixon. Such speculation is too farfetched, taking no account of the obvious: that the agency itself could be severely damaged simply by the slight connection it had had in the past with most of the intruders. Jim McCord was alive to this point; thus his anonymous attempts to protect the agency. Had McCord been a CIA agent all along—as has been suggested—then he was not a successful one, and his attempts to protect the agency merely drew attention to his connection with it.

Jim Hougan in *Secret Agenda: Watergate, Deep Throat and the CIA* (New York: Random House, 1984) advances a thesis that high-level Washington blackmail was involved, including a CIA call-girl ring that gave the agency the "goods" on a number of congressmen and officials. The break-in, Hougan suggests, may have been to retrieve files in the office of Larry O'Brien (the head of the Democratic National Committee) compromising Nixon people. Hougan indicates that Jim McCord may have actively sought to ensure that the break-in was discovered so that the information in O'Brien's files would not reach the White House but would remain the exclusive property of the CIA.

All this seems farfetched. Surely Nixon or John Dean or Bob Haldeman or John Ehrlichman (Nixon's top advisers) would have used such an allegation in their own defense? Ehrlichman wrote a novel, *The Company* (New York: Simon & Schuster, 1976), in which he suggested that the DCI had monitored the illegal activities of the "plumbers" and had used the evidence to blackmail the President, forcing him to protect the CIA's most sensitive secrets. This is a thesis that makes Helms—the DCI during Watergate—visibly angry. He was never in the business of blackmailing his President. Ehrlichman did not make any such suggestion in his own defense. And what sort of information about Washington people could possibly be so important or sensitive? Washington is a small town where sooner or later everybody knows who is doing what and seeing whom. See J. Anthony Lukas, "A New Explanation of Watergate," a review of *Secret Agenda*, in *The New York Times Book Review*, November 11, 1984, pp. 7–9.

2:30 A.M. planting wiretaps in the offices of the Democratic National Committee. Another ex-agency man, E. Howard Hunt, continued Osborn, was also implicated. The call did not mean that the agency had kept a close eye on McCord and Hunt after they had left it; it was standard procedure for Helms to be informed whenever someone connected with the CIA ran afoul of the law.[33]

Helms, whose antennae were as good as anyone else's in Washington, took immediate action to check that the agency was not involved and to ensure that it would not be. At his 9 o'clock meeting on Monday, June 19 (he followed the practice established by John McCone of having a meeting every morning with his deputy directors to review events and stay in touch), Helms had the break-in and the agency's connections with McCord and Hunt at the top of the agenda. "Hell, Osborn tells me that Hunt was involved," he said. "How can that be? I haven't seen Hunt's name in the papers."[34] It was not in the papers yet, but it was in the notebooks of two of the arrested intruders, and Osborn's police contacts had come through with the news. Hunt's connection was particularly worrying because the CIA had helped him with equipment and disguises while he was working for Nixon. Some of the trees in the CIA's forest were already feeling the breeze.

A year earlier John Ehrlichman, Nixon's assistant for domestic affairs, had called the then deputy director of Central Intelligence, General Robert B. Cushman, Jr. "I received a call on the 7th of July, 1971, from Mr. Ehrlichman," recalled Cushman, "who said that Howard Hunt had been hired as a consultant to the White House on security matters, that he would be coming to see me, and could I lend him a hand." Two weeks later Hunt came to Cushman's office at the CIA's headquarters in Langley and asked the agency to give him an office and a monitored telephone system and answering service in New York. Cushman felt Hunt's request was improper—it might involve agency people in domestic surveillance, an area specifically outside the agency's statutory guidelines—and it was turned down. Subsequent requests by Hunt for camera and recording equipment, disguises (which were probably used in Hunt's September 1971 burglary of Dr. Lewis Fielding's office in Los Angeles where Daniel Ellsberg, who had leaked *The Pentagon Papers* to the press, was receiving psychiatric care), and a CIA psychiatric profile of Ellsberg—the first the agency ever did on a U.S. citizen—were met.*

The Watergate Hearings: Break-in and Cover-up (New York: Bantam/A New York Times book, 1973), pp. 608–611, and Thomas Powers, *The Man Who Kept the Secrets: Richard Helms and the CIA* (New York: Knopf, 1979), p. 253. The first request met by the CIA was made on July 22, 1971, for a wig, a speech-altering device, and some false identification papers. These were approved by Richard Helms personally. Then came the profile of Ellsberg; two were completed because the first was too vague. A CIA polygraph expert was lent to Hunt to help question a State Department official suspected of leaking information about the SALT negotiations. Hunt asked for his old secretary at the CIA to come and work for him (she was with the CIA station in Paris at the time), but Helms refused the request. In August, Hunt was given a tape recorder, false

It was all part of the agency's attempt to hammer out a working relationship with the Nixon White House. At the end of August 1971, because Hunt's requests caused a growing number of agency people to express surprise and concern (Thomas Karamessines even took Hunt to lunch in an attempt to find out why he wanted all the material and information he was being given; for "political work," Hunt cryptically responded), Helms put a stop to further CIA help for Hunt. All of this must have stared Helms and the CIA's deputy directors in the face that Monday morning as they considered the implications of McCord's arrest and the link with Hunt. William Colby, back from Vietnam and now the number-three man in the agency as executive director-comptroller, was put in charge of dealing with Watergate and protecting the agency. Concerning the CIA's fears that Monday, he recalled:

> There was a real danger that the flame of suspicion about the agency would ignite into blazing headlines, making it seem that Watergate and all that rubric would come to stand for was at bottom yet another dastardly CIA operation. To prevent that from happening, Helms spelled out a fundamental strategy with which all his associates, myself included, agreed. To protect itself from even the appearance of involvement in Watergate, the agency was to distance itself from the event to every extent possible. "Stay cool, volunteer nothing, because it will only be used to involve us. Just stay away from the whole damn thing." That was the gist of Helms' advice.[35]

Staying away from Watergate was not something Nixon wanted the CIA to do. On June 23, a week after the break-in, Nixon decided to use the CIA to cover up White House connections with the intruders. Two days earlier Helms had denied any CIA connection with the break-in to the new FBI director-designate, L. Patrick Gray III, but Gray nevertheless wondered to John Dean if there was, in fact, CIA complicity, and Nixon played on this doubt. Richard Helms and General Walters were summoned to the White House at the Presi-

---

credit cards, a false driving license, false business cards, a spy camera, more disguise materials, and a telephone number for a false business that the CIA would cover, confirming its legitimacy to any inquirers. This seems to have been the sum total of CIA help to Hunt.

In March 1972, using a CIA-supplied disguise, Hunt visited an ITT lobbyist, Dita Beard, in a hospital in Denver where she was recovering from a heart ailment. A memorandum Beard had apparently written in June 1971 had been made public. It stated that ITT's support for the Republican Convention at San Diego "had gone a long way" to facilitate negotiations with the government over ITT's plans to merge with the Hartford Insurance Group. In July 1971 an antitrust suit against ITT was settled out of court, generating suspicions that the Republicans had made a deal with ITT on the merger in exchange for ITT's defraying the cost of their convention. The memorandum seemed to confirm this suspicion and also indicated that Nixon and the attorney general, John Mitchell, knew about the deal. This was clearly very embarrassing to Nixon, facing reelection, and to the Justice Department for dropping a case under political pressure. After meeting Hunt, however, Beard announced that the memorandum was "a forgery, a fraud and a hoax," and she stuck to this statement. So did ITT, and nothing was ever proved to the contrary.

dent's direct instruction and were met by John Ehrlichman and H. R. Haldeman, Nixon's chief of staff.

The White House plan, which had been discussed in detail with the President before the CIA men arrived, was to get Walters "to call Pat Gray and tell
him to 'stay the hell out of this . . . business here. We don't want you to go any
further on it.' The FBI and the CIA had a longstanding agreement not to interfere in each other's secret operations," Nixon later elaborated. "Haldeman
said this call would not be unusual. He said that Pat Gray wanted to limit the
investigation but simply didn't have a basis on which to do so; this would give
him his basis. Haldeman said that this would work well because the FBI agents
on the case had already come to the conclusion that the CIA was involved in
some way." Nixon's own contribution was to observe:

> We had protected CIA Director Richard Helms from a lot of things.
> Helms had rarely approached me personally for any kind of assistance or in-
> tervention, but I remembered the visible concern on his face less than a year
> earlier over the possible publication of a book by two disaffected CIA agents.
> Helms had asked if I would back up legal action by the CIA, despite the fact
> that there would be cries of "suppression." I had told him that I would.
>
> I mentioned Hunt; he had been involved in a lot of earlier CIA opera-
> tions, including the Bay of Pigs. I postulated an approach by which we would
> say to Helms and Walters, "You open that scab and there's a hell of a lot of
> things." I told Haldeman to say that we felt it would be very detrimental to
> have the investigation go any further, alluding to the Cubans, to Hunt, and
> to "a lot of hanky-panky that we have nothing to do with ourselves."
>
> . . . I thought back again to the time I had instructed Ehrlichman to ask
> for the CIA's files on the Bay of Pigs, and the Diem assassination. I remem-
> bered how [Helms] had been unwilling to give them up. Even after I had per-
> sonally requested that he do so, the Bay of Pigs report he turned over to us
> was not complete. I saw that Howard Hunt would give us a chance to turn
> Helms' extreme sensitivity about the Bay of Pigs to good advantage.*

---

*Richard Nixon, *RN: The Memoirs of Richard Nixon* (New York: Grosset & Dunlap,
1978), pp. 640–641. By June 20 Nixon had already started to think of a CIA connection. The
"Cuban angle" was a link that might work, he said to Haldeman, and "Tell Ehrlichman this
whole group of Cubans is tied to the Bay of Pigs." On June 23 he told Haldeman:

> Well, we protected Helms from one hell of a lot of things. . . . When you get these people
> in, say, "Look, the problem is that this will open the whole, the whole Bay of Pigs thing, and
> the President just feels that"—ah, without going into details . . . don't lie to them to the
> extent to say there is no involvement, but just say this is a comedy of errors, bizarre, without
> getting into it—"the President believes that this is going to open the whole Bay of Pigs thing
> up again. And . . . they should call the FBI in and say that we wish for the country, don't go
> any further into this case. Period!" (quoted in Leon Jaworski, *The Right and the Power*
> [New York: Pocket Books, 1977], pp. 256–257).

Later, about half an hour before Helms and Walters arrived for the meeting, Nixon added to
Haldeman, "Tell them that if it gets out . . . it's going to make the CIA look bad, it's going to

Helms and Walters lunched together before the meeting—Colby was not invited—and concluded that it was bound to be about Watergate. Walters, only six weeks into the job of DDCI, and specifically required by Ehrlichman to be at the meeting, was something of an unknown quantity to Helms. No doubt he wondered if Walters, a Nixon appointee, would go along with a White House effort to involve the CIA. He must also have been reminded of his own relationship with the Johnson White House when he had been Raborn's DDCI.

The meeting took the course Nixon had outlined. Haldeman did most of the talking. Was there a CIA connection with the Watergate break-in? Helms said there was not. FBI investigations in Mexico, Haldeman next suggested, were throwing up connections with the Bay of Pigs. Helms said he did not know what Haldeman was talking about and that "I had no interest in the Bay of Pigs that many years later, that everything in connection with that had been dealt with and liquidated as far as I was aware and I did not care what they ran into in connection with that." Despite this, according to Helms, Haldeman went on, the President wanted General Walters to call Patrick Gray and tell him "these investigations of the FBI might run into CIA operations in Mexico and that it was desirable that this not happen and that the investigation, therefore, should be either tapered off or reduced or something."

The message was stark: Nixon wanted the CIA to contain the Watergate break-in so that nobody else would be charged by the FBI and so that even those charged might be able to plead "national security," with CIA backing in their defense. It was also clear that if Helms and Walters did not go along, they would doubtless be fired at some point. Helms, not surprisingly, paused. "At this point," he later testified, "the references to Mexico were quite unclear to me. I had to recognize that if the White House, the President, Mr. Haldeman, somebody in high authority, had information about something in Mexico which I did not have information about, which is quite possible—the White House constantly has information which others do not have—that it would be a prudent thing for me to find out if there was any possibility that some CIA operation was being—was going to be affected and, therefore, I wanted the necessary time to do this."

The meeting ended with the understanding that Walters would talk to Gray. On their way back to their cars as they were leaving the White House,

<hr />

make Hunt look bad, and it's likely to blow the whole Bay of Pigs, which we think would be very unfortunate for the CIA" (quoted in ibid., p. 257).

The book by "two disaffected CIA agents" Nixon had in mind was *The CIA and the Cult of Intelligence*, by Victor Marchetti and John D. Marks, which was eventually published in 1974 after a long legal wrangle with the agency and after the CIA had secured the right to make cuts in the book in the interests of national security. Marks was never in the CIA but had worked as staff assistant to the intelligence director at the State Department. Thomas Powers, in *The Man Who Kept the Secrets*, p. 370, states that Helms was aware of only one "favor" from the President: offering him the use of Camp David one weekend, an offer Helms did not take up.

Helms told Walters that he should confine himself to reminding Gray, who might not be familiar with things (Gray had been nominated on May 3, 1972, the day after J. Edgar Hoover's death), that the CIA and the FBI had an understanding that if they ran into each other's agents they would immediately notify each other.* Helms was buying time to find out if there was some connection after all with the Watergate intruders and a CIA operation in Mexico or with the Bay of Pigs and to decide whether or not to go along with the President's expressed wish that he head off the FBI investigation.

Walters saw Gray and told him that "while investigation of this matter in Mexico had not yet touched agency projects, continuation of it there might expose some assets. I reminded him of the agreement between the two agencies as Helms had suggested." After that Walters reported his conversation with Gray to Helms and checked whether there were, in fact, any CIA assets in Mexico that might be jeopardized; there were not.[36] Meanwhile, acting on Walters' statement, Gray (who seemed to have a good understanding of where the Watergate investigation might really lead and seemed sympathetic to the White House's predicament) told his agents not to question two men who had written checks on a Mexican bank that were used to pay the intruders.† On Monday, June 26, Walters was called by John Dean to the White House for another meeting about Watergate. The deputy director was now considered to be Nixon's man in the agency, the one who was going to pull the President's chestnuts out of the fire. But Walters disappointed Dean, and in three meetings that week he told Dean that the CIA had no connection with Watergate, and that there was no CIA operation in Mexico that might be compromised by the FBI investigation. "Fire everyone connected with this," he advised.

"No one is going to be fired," Dean replied in a low voice.

"Then, Mr. Dean, what is now a small conventional painful explosion will become a multi-megaton hydrogen bomb and those who are not now touched by the matter certainly will be," said Walters, meaning the President.

There had been an almost pleading look in Dean's eyes during these meetings, Walters remembered. "What shall we do? What shall we do?" Dean had whispered.[37]

---

* See *The Watergate Hearings*, pp. 603–604, for Helms quotes above. See also Powers, *The Man Who Kept the Secrets*, pp. 261–262; and Haldeman, *The Ends of Power* (London: Star, 1978), pp. 53–62: according to Haldeman, after he suggested that the FBI's Watergate investigation might go back to the Bay of Pigs, the atmosphere changed and Helms became compliant: "The two CIA officials expressed no concern that Walters go to see Gray. . . . I went back to see the President and told him his strategy had worked. I had told Helms that the Watergate investigation 'tracks back to the Bay of Pigs.' So at that point . . . he said, 'We'll be very happy to be helpful.' "

† Gray was clearly acting as a result of being called by the White House and told, "Stay the hell out of this business here." See Jaworski, *The Right and the Power*, pp. 253–254. See also Powers, *The Man Who Kept the Secrets*, p. 262.

After each meeting Walters reported in full to Helms. Both men knew that Watergate could become an enormous scandal, and every conversation, every letter, memorandum, telephone call had to be not only carefully considered but tightly coordinated. "Play it tough," Nixon had instructed Haldeman on June 23 before the meeting with Helms and Walters. "That's the way they play it and that's the way we are going to play it."[38] Playing it tough with Helms and Walters did not work for very long. On June 28 Helms decided that "we still adhere to the request that [the FBI] confine themselves to the personalities already arrested or directly under suspicion and that they desist from expanding this investigation into other areas which may well, eventually, run afoul of our operations."* This was the last time Helms went along with the White House plan, although already he had built in safeguards; it was quite reasonable for the agency to ask the FBI to concentrate on the break-in and not to use past CIA connections of the intruders to investigate past or present CIA operations. On the same day Helms went off for a prearranged three-week tour of Australia and New Zealand, leaving Walters in charge.

At the FBI, Patrick Gray had become nervous about his position in the developing cover-up, and he asked Walters to put in writing what he had said on June 23. Gray wanted the record to show that the CIA had formally asked the FBI to restrict the Watergate investigation in the interests of national security. Walters, however, as he had already demonstrated to John Dean, was not prepared to cooperate any longer. He accepted that he, and not William Colby (who only days before had been appointed by Helms as the agency's point player on Watergate), had become the CIA's principal actor in the drama as far as the White House was concerned, and he now worked for the best interests of the agency. He expressed his decision to Dean, telling him: "I was sure there was no agency involvement in this matter, that any attempt to involve it would be a grave disservice to the President, to the Congress and to the nation. The value of the CIA to the nation arose from the fact that it was a non-partisan organization. It did not support either of the parties. It served the United States government regardless of the personal opinions of those who served

---

* Haldeman, *The Ends of Power*, pp. 58–59. Haldeman was convinced that the CIA had prior knowledge of the Watergate break-in from their agent, Martinez, who "almost certainly was reporting to his CIA case officer about the proposed break-in," and that the Mexican connection was not the fabrication by Nixon's men that Helms later told the Watergate prosecutor it was:

> If the Mexican Bank connection was actually a CIA operation all along, unknown to Nixon; and Nixon was destroyed for asking the FBI to stop investigating the bank because it might uncover a CIA operation . . . the multiple levels of deception by the CIA are astounding. At that time I knew nothing of this serpentine intrigue. What I did know was that the CIA was an agency hostile to Nixon, who returned the hostility with fervor.

It all seems a bit too complicated to be tenable. Too many people, including the FBI investigators, would have realized it if the Mexican Bank was a CIA front, and constitutionally Helms and Walters would have been forced to tell the President, even if they did not like him. Thomas Powers, in *The Man Who Kept the Secrets*, p. 263, suggests that Helms wanted to stick to the concession they had made on June 23.

there. If it were to become involved in any partisan political activity, it would lose all value to the President and the nation."[39]

This rather self-serving statement overlooks the fact that Helms's orders to General Walters were unambiguous in their insistence that the agency would put up no money as bail for the Watergate intruders or be involved with their trial in any way. Helms warned Walters repeatedly that he should not compromise and that under no circumstances should he consider making himself personally a sacrificial lamb for the administration. Any action of this kind would hurt the agency grievously, no matter what Walters' motives might be.[40]

On July 6, Walters visited Gray at his office in the Justice Department. He informed him that "I could not tell him to cease further investigations in Mexico on the ground that this would compromise the security interests of the United States or the CIA. Even less could I write him a letter to that effect."[41] Walters "had regained his capacity for indignation," as the Watergate special prosecutor, Leon Jaworski, put it.[42] He had also firmly detached the CIA from the White House cover-up. Ten months later Walters was given the Distinguished Intelligence Medal, the agency's highest honor for "non-valor activity." He was told by James Schlesinger, who succeeded Helms as director, that "a single misstep by me could have destroyed the agency and I did not make it. . . . The citation recognized that I had resisted great pressures on me and by so doing had avoided even more serious consequences for the agency."*

For several weeks in July, Walters remained in touch with Gray about the investigation. Gray had come to the same conclusion as Walters—that the President should dismiss everyone connected with Watergate—but was still willing to do his best to protect the President and his immediate staff from involvement. Ultimately this was Gray's undoing, and he resigned in April 1973 as acting director of the FBI after it emerged that he had burned some of Howard Hunt's files containing cables forged by Hunt implicating President Kennedy and the CIA in Diem's assassination.†

By August 1972, however, James McCord, awaiting trial for his part in the break-in, reported to an old friend, Paul Gaynor, in the Office of Security, that pressures were being put on the defendants to claim they had been on a

---

* Vernon A. Walters, *Silent Missions* (New York: Doubleday, 1978), p. 610. One of the pressures had been for the CIA to come up with money to pay off the Watergate intruders, who were indicating that they would take complete responsibility for the break-in if they were paid handsomely to do so. This seems to have been Howard Hunt's line in particular. Walters told Dean that any such expenditures from secret funds would have to be reported to the congressional oversight committees, and this greatly lessened Dean's enthusiasm for pressing the matter further.

† There is no evidence that Hunt actually saw the Bay of Pigs and Diem files that Helms gave Nixon in October 1971, but he had suggested to Haldeman that those particular files be obtained by the White House. The implication is that they did provide him with the information he needed to make convincing forgeries. The forgeries were to be used if Teddy Kennedy had been the Democratic candidate against Nixon in 1972. Hunt, unlike McCord, was not "a loyal CIA alumnus" (Colby's phrase).

CIA operation. Some photocopies of pictures Howard Hunt had taken with his agency-supplied camera while planning the Fielding break-in were also in the agency's possession. (Hunt had asked the CIA to develop the photographs for him.) William Colby instructed the Office of Security to make a detailed investigation of what the photographs might signify; he was worried that they might tie the agency into Watergate or some other potential scandal. His caution paid off. In December, Howard Osborn was able to identify the photographs as those of a particular building in Los Angeles, the offices of two well-established psychiatrists, one of whom was Dr. Fielding.[43] This meant nothing to Colby or anyone else in the CIA at the time—Hunt's burglary of Fielding's office was not yet known—and after a week or so of rumination, Colby sent the photographs to the FBI. This caused another alarm in the White House, and on February 9, 1973, John Dean suggested to the CIA that it have the FBI return to the agency photographs and all CIA memos about Watergate. Walters and Colby both recommended against doing so. "The only result," said Walters, "would be to leave an arrow in the Department of Justice files pointing directly at the CIA,"[44] and so on behalf of the agency, Walters said no to Dean again.

McCord's anonymous letters persisted throughout the period and were considered by Helms and the CIA's general counsel, Lawrence Houston. What should be done with them? Should the CIA report McCord's allegations to the FBI or stay away and let McCord do it himself if he chose to? Houston and Helms decided that they should stick to the policy of volunteering nothing, only responding in precise terms to specific requests.[45] Looking back at this period a few years later, Colby said:

> The strategy was to ensure that CIA avoid getting involved in Watergate or any other improper activity, but to do this without taking a hostile position toward the White House. . . . But this cautious, "distancing" strategy proved to be a double-edged sword, cutting the Agency in two ways. On the one hand, the CIA was perceived as withholding evidence as long as it possibly could. . . . On the other hand, each disclosure wrung or leaked from the reluctant agency during this period caused a greater sensation than it would have done if the information had been volunteered.[46]

Nevertheless, as even severe agency critics admitted, CIA officials were the only people in town who, when asked, said "No" to the Nixon White House. Watergate sundered traditional perceptions of government and resulted in Nixon's disgrace and resignation from the presidency in 1974.

CONSEQUENCES

Watergate and the congressional investigations that followed were symptoms of a number of trends converging in a narrow period of time. The reaction to Watergate was symptomatic of the distrust of government regenerated by Vietnam. It forced Americans to consider the purity of their political idealism in the light of what everyone knew—but few admitted—were the political realities of Washington and the world. During Watergate, for example, it emerged that Franklin Roosevelt had started the bugging of conversations in the Oval Office and that Jack Kennedy had installed the basic secret recording system that Nixon had used and that provided the evidence that finally brought him down.* Generations of White House security people knew about these secret buggings and so did five Presidents, but it was not until Watergate that the American public was told.

The transcripts of Nixon's Watergate conversations, with all the "expletive deleted" brackets in them, were probably more shocking to most Americans than the actual content of the conversations. But many presidents had used expletives frequently in their private conversations. George Ball, for example, recounted that "Not only was Lyndon Johnson's language colorful, it was scatological—a habit he shared with John F. Kennedy. . . . The only problem was that the secretaries who took down my conversations were gently brought up. Thus, conversations with either Presidents Kennedy or Johnson tended to be spotted with asterisks. Fortunately, the girls were not only well-bred, they were also precise; because they included the exact number of asterisks, translation required little imagination."[47] Still, the awareness that presidents could and did use bad language helped confirm another trend: the suspicion that came with the Vietnam War that presidents were not omniscient and omnicompetent after all and should be challenged.

Arthur M. Schlesinger, Jr., who, under Kennedy, was one of the principal hierophants in the cult of the presidency, described the office of the President as having progressed toward "imperial" status. He said that, with Watergate, "Nixon's Presidency was not an aberration but a culmination. It carried to reckless extremes a compulsion toward presidential power" arising out of the decay of traditional institutions and America grappling with its place in the world. "Watergate," said Schlesinger, "was potentially the best thing to have happened to the presidency in a long time." The three elements in the checks and balances of the Constitution had become distorted, with congressional power being overshadowed by an increase in the power of the executive branch

---

* The most damaging conversation that was released was held between Nixon and Haldeman on the morning of June 23 as they discussed what should be said to Helms and Walters later in the day. It came to be called the "smoking gun" conversation because it directly implicated the President in the cover-up attempt only days after the break-in. It also fueled popular suspicions, which still linger, that if Nixon and Haldeman at that stage thought of the CIA, and thought that the CIA had secrets it would be desperate to hide, then perhaps the CIA really was involved in Watergate somehow, and perhaps it still has some secrets that it has managed to hide. However, neither Nixon nor Hunt nor anyone else in the White House knew about the assassination plans of 1960–63 (Eisenhower, it seems, had kept his involvement from his Vice-President) or about Lyman Kirkpatrick's Bay of Pigs report. They simply assumed that the CIA had something to hide—and would have on file embarrassing information that could be used to twist its arm to do things for them.

over several decades. Watergate put the executive on the defensive, giving Congress a chance to reassert itself. "Corruption appears to visit the White House in fifty year cycles," Schlesinger warned wryly. "Around the year 2023 the American people would be well advised to go on the alert and start nailing down everything in sight."[48]

In the early 1970s people were also reacting to the attitudes of the 1940s and 1950s, which required that they accept authority unchallenged. They were no longer prepared to do this, and the growing prosperity of the 1960s gave many the ability to say "no." Unlike their parents, who were forced to take whatever jobs they could find in the 1930s and 1940s, young people of the 1960s were freed from the same restraints and could protest violently against a war they did not want to fight. Dreams seemed possible, and prosperity buttressed the widespread assumption of personal freedom. Americans did not like the idea of a secret authority, engaged in secret activities carried out by a secret "police," which would circumscribe their birthright and constitutionally guaranteed freedom. As more and more was learned about intelligence, people found themselves liking it less.

It was not by any means just the CIA they scorned. J. Edgar Hoover's FBI was also under intense pressure as information emerged about its activities. Members of the civil rights movement had come up against Hoover's hostility and dirty tricks throughout the 1950s and 1960s. Liberals in the Kennedy administration had been horrified by his right-wing views. While investigating the murder of President Kennedy, the Warren Commission showed the American public that Hoover had an edge on smut. Hoover frightened a great many people who never abused the limits of the law. Legendary in Washington, for example, were the dirt-filled files he collected on anyone engaged in activities of which he did not approve. After his death on May 2, 1972, the nature of his abuse came out—his taping of Martin Luther King's extramarital sexual activities, his pornographic campaigns to ruin the reputations of left-wing activists.

The CIA was tarred with the brush of suspicion too. It was not that the agency had not made a blue movie in its time or had not distributed compromising photographs; it was that Hoover's activities made that sort of thing seem the routine of American intelligence rather than the exception. Novels, magazine articles, and films emerged in abundance in the early 1970s, focusing on the abuses of American intelligence. These in turn reawakened concern about the Warren Commission report, leading to a spate of books and films, some closely argued, suggesting CIA involvement in Kennedy's death.* Other books revealed inside information on agency operations, including its covert ac-

---

* The suggested connections center on the agency's contracts with Cubans and the Mafia in the effort during the early 1960s to have Fidel Castro killed; the contacts Lee Harvey Oswald (who shot Kennedy) and Jack Ruby (who shot Oswald) had with some of the same people; and on the contacts Oswald had with the KGB and the CIA's knowledge of them.

tivities. William Colby summarized what all of this meant to the CIA: "In a time of growing distrust of government, [the CIA] found itself regarded as an exemplar of the repugnant clandestine methods and secret manipulations that were seen as characteristic of the Johnson and Nixon administrations."[49] Clearly, the view of the CIA as a group of "honorable men" expressed earlier by Richard Helms would no longer stand.[50] After the early 1970s the nation was prepared to take precious little on faith about anything.

CHAOS UNCOVERED

As the assessment of what was known of the Nixon White House and the scandal of Watergate generated increasing fear and suspicion in Congress and the bureaucracy (a White House staffed by ruthless young men in the service of a President without honor), and as it became clear that Watergate was but a symptom of corruption that existed at all levels of government, more and more began to emerge about the activities of the CIA. The Vietnam War brought the first real press interest in the agency's secret activities, but it was in the 1970s that most of the secret stories were told.

In July 1971 William Colby gave testimony to a congressional committee on the Phoenix program, revealing the number of people killed by Phoenix teams, and found it followed up by articles stating that the CIA was the only U.S. agency authorized to assassinate people. Despite the fact that Phoenix was not a CIA operation, Americans were already prepared to believe that the agency's secrecy hid assassinations. When Colby became DCI in 1973 and decided formally to investigate the allegation within the agency he realized he "was onto a volatile subject, with a number of ambiguities, and I found that no one would discuss it with me in any detail."[51] No doubt he felt he was preempting an outside investigation; after nearly twenty years in the CIA he was no boy scout. He must have known in general terms about what he was now investigating officially. Only the details would have been new to him.

Colby's investigation brought other agency activities into question. The CIA had been instructed to conduct surveillance on the newspaper columnist Jack Anderson, who had published stories obviously based on classified material. Nixon and Kissinger were furious about the leaks (the stories dealt with foreign-policy issues) and used the gray area in the CIA charter to make the agency cooperate in the surveillance operation. This gray area gives the director responsibility for "protecting intelligence sources and methods from unauthorized disclosure." About fifty people were involved in the surveillance. "Let's face it then," said Colby to Howard Osborn. "There's not one chance in a million that this is going to stay a secret. Sooner or later, this is going to make the headlines."[52] And it did—in 1975. Colby also found a similar operation, code-named Chaos (technically, MHChaos), in full swing and causing concern to many CIA people who knew about it.

The operation had started in 1967 in James Angleton's Counterintelligence Staff in response to a directive from President Johnson that the CIA determine whether the anti–Vietnam War movement enjoyed any foreign financing or manipulation. From the beginning, Chaos was clearly on the fringe of the gray area in the CIA charter. The operation was mounted jointly with the FBI, which acted to give it legitimacy, but as it progressed, it involved the compilation by the agency of thousands of files on individual Americans who lived and worked in the United States, not out of it. Although Chaos showed that there was no foreign financing or manipulation of the antiwar movement, Johnson refused to accept this, and the operation continued into the Nixon presidency. By 1971 CIA agents were operating inside America, infiltrating protest groups to provide authentic cover stories they could use while traveling abroad and joining foreign antiwar groups.[53]

All these activities had the potential for embarrassing the agency, just as publicity over the CIA connection with the National Student Association had done four years earlier. In 1972 Helms instructed that Chaos be turned from an investigation of the antiwar movement into an investigation of international terrorism—an area that was well within the agency's legal operating guidelines. Nevertheless by the time the details of Chaos were made public by Congress in 1975, rumors of it—often distorted—had circulated widely, and the facts seemed to confirm suspicions that the CIA and the FBI had been laws unto themselves, spying on Americans as much as on Russians or anyone else. The country's sense of violation from within was made more powerful by the fact that despite the 1972 official change in the purposes of Chaos, an associated operation, Project Resistance, conducted by the Office of Security, had continued surveillance of American domestic dissent until it was terminated in June 1973.[54]

Colby was not the only person in the agency who was worried by these various activities. Many of the younger officers who knew about Chaos, for example, repeatedly expressed concern that the CIA was acting outside its charter and that American domestic dissent was not the CIA's province. In the autumn of 1972 William Broe, the CIA inspector general, reported on these internal worries:

> Even though there is a general belief that CIA involvement is directed primarily at foreign manipulation and subversive exploitation of U.S. citizens, we also encountered general concern over what appeared to constitute a monitoring of the political views and activities of Americans not known to be or suspected of being involved in espionage. Occasionally, stations were asked to report on the whereabouts and activities of prominent persons . . . whose

comings and goings were not only in the public domain but for whom allegations of subversion seemed sufficiently nebulous to raise renewed doubts as to the nature and legitimacy of the MHCHAOS program.[55]

People within the CIA were no different in their personal attitudes from people outside. Protests against the Vietnam War echoed inside the agency, forcing Abbott Smith and then John Huizenga, consecutive heads of the Office of National Estimates, to lecture their analysts on the need for impartiality and close reasoning. Passion that might cloud judgment would not be tolerated no matter what the analysts felt about the war; it was not their job to proclaim these feelings. They had to respond professionally at all times.

Nevertheless, internal dissent with government policies continued within the agency and simmered on throughout the Nixon years. This fact became abundantly clear to the Nixon administration as the agency distanced itself from Watergate. It was not that the CIA was politically opposed to Nixon or to any particular administration; it did not see itself as a political operator linked to a particular party. It served the President, not the politician, and sought constantly to establish a tradition that the CIA was apart from domestic politics. To cement this in the bureaucratic structure, neither Dulles, McCone, nor Helms offered his resignation as each new President entered the White House. Vernon Walters once estimated that there were "probably more Democrats there than Republicans" in 1972 but that "it would be absolutely impossible to use the agency for partisan political purposes without it flying apart at the seams."[56]

There was a feeling, however, that Nixon, at least, wanted to use the agency for partisan political purposes and that Chaos was an example of the agency prostituting itself to this end. Out of this came a frustration, because the position of the agency in law and in the Washington scheme of things made it very difficult to refuse a presidential directive, even when the DCI thought it might be illegal. Although Helms wondered about the agency's role in Chaos, he found that it was probably within the CIA charter. The Rockefeller Commission and the Church Committee agreed. In 1975 both bodies investigated Chaos and decided that it was within the CIA's operational mission but recommended that in the future presidents refrain from directing the CIA to perform what were essentially internal security tasks.*

---

* In January 1962 the CIA general counsel, Lawrence Houston, made a report to the new DCI, John McCone, entitled "Legal Basis for Cold-War Activities." It was prompted by Senator Eugene McCarthy's questions about congressional oversight of the CIA and "the juridical or constitutional right of CIA to carry out covert activities directed towards the imposition of a particular line of political thought on a foreign country." Houston stated:

The President, with his responsibility for the conduct of foreign relations, as Commander in Chief of the Armed Forces, and with the powers inherent in the Presidency, has authority to take such executive actions as he deems appropriate to protect the national interest which are not barred by the Constitution or other valid law of the land. . . . It would appear, there-

"The jurisdiction is divided at the water's edge," said Helms, discussing the CIA/FBI roles. "When you are dealing with something that has both foreign and domestic aspects to it, I don't recall anybody having come down, I mean any President come down hard and say, all of this is for the FBI and all of this is for the agency. I mean the line has to be wavy. There is no other way to do it that I know of. It is like cutting a man down the middle."[57]

WHISTLE-BLOWERS

Helms's practical if somewhat theological dilemma (like that of the man who is asked how many angels can dance on the head of a pin; there is no question about the pin or the ability of angels to dance on it, just how many) was not appreciated by some of his colleagues or by many outsiders. "The fact of the matter," said Colby, looking back at this period, "was that the crisis of confidence in government over Vietnam, which was sweeping the nation at large, was beginning to infect the faith of the intelligence community in itself. Just how serious the infection was soon became clear when a publisher passed along a copy of the outline of a book on the CIA being circulated by Victor Marchetti, a former CIA employee."[58]

Marchetti, "disenchanted and disagreeing with many of the agency's policies and practices, and, for that matter, with those of the intelligence community and the U.S. government," as he explained, had resigned from the CIA in 1969 after fourteen years of service.[59] He had joined the agency straight out of Pennsylvania State College, becoming first an analyst specializing in Soviet military affairs (he dealt with Soviet military aid to the Third World, Soviet preparations to place nuclear missiles in Cuba, and Soviet antiballistic missile

---

fore, that cold-war activities not involving an act of war and not within such legal limitations would be within the executive prerogative. (Lawrence R. Houston, General Counsel, Memorandum for the Director of Central Intelligence, January 15, 1962, OCC 62–0083)

This view of the legal basis for CIA activities was sustained by the Church Committee and the Rockefeller Commission. Each made the point that if Congress wanted to change the situation, it was up to Congress to do so. On Chaos, the Rockefeller Commission concluded:

Some domestic activities of Operation CHAOS unlawfully exceeded the CIA's statutory authority, even though the declared mission of gathering intelligence abroad as to foreign influence on domestic dissident activities was proper. Most significantly, the Operation became a repository for large quantities of information on the domestic activities of American citizens. This information was derived principally from FBI reports or from overt sources and not from clandestine collection by the CIA, and much of it was not directly related to the question of the existence of foreign connections. It was probably necessary for the CIA to accumulate an information base on domestic dissident activities in order to assess fairly whether the activities had foreign connections. . . . But the accumulation of domestic data in the Operation exceeded what was reasonably required to make such an assessment and was thus improper (*Report to the President by the Commission on CIA activities within the United States* [Washington, DC: U.S. Government Printing Office, 1975], pp. 24–25).

programs) and then, from 1966 until shortly before his resignation, a staff officer in the Office of the Director of Central Intelligence. As an insider Marchetti knew some of the agency's top secrets. Unlike previous writers on the CIA—notably the journalists David Wise and Thomas B. Ross, whose book *The Invisible Government** had been the first to give accurate details of some CIA operations, and the more academic Alfred W. McCoy's *The Politics of Heroin in Southeast Asia,*† which linked the CIA with the heroin trade—Marchetti was a whistle-blower.[60]

Marchetti was telling everything he knew and, in collaboration with John D. Marks, an ex-State Department Intelligence and Research Bureau officer who resigned in 1970, disillusioned with American policy in Southeast Asia and in protest against the April 1970 invasion of Cambodia, he put his knowledge to use in surmising a lot more. The CIA general counsel, Lawrence Houston, and his deputy, John Warner, pointed out that Marchetti had signed the standard contract when he joined the CIA in 1955, stipulating that he would not reveal anything he learned in his job, and that therefore the book was in breach of contract. They did not argue that Marchetti could not publish his book, only that he could not use the classified information he had gained while in the CIA's employ.

When Houston and Warner suggested that the agency take Marchetti and his publishers to court, Richard Helms agreed. He went to see Nixon to secure support for this step (presidential support would be crucial when the court case became public) and to press the need for vigorous and serious Justice Department action. Nixon backed Helms, and for two years the agency pursued Marchetti in the courts, and won.‡ The two authors (Marks, never an agency employee, was not prosecuted) were required to drop 168 passages from their book *The CIA and the Cult of Intelligence* when it was finally published in 1974. (Blank spaces indicated the excised passages in the published work.) The first excision on the grounds of endangering national security was made on the eleventh page of the manuscript. It was Henry Kissinger's statement at the 40 Committee meeting of June 27, 1970, on Chile—"I don't see why we need to stand by and watch a country go Communist due to the irresponsibility of its own people"—and it was followed by other excisions ranging from a whole paragraph to one word. What remained, however, still gave readers a good idea of the workings of the CIA and the extent of its operations.

Over the next six years many of the passages originally excised were allowed back into print as the information became public through congressional hearings and investigations and as the Freedom of Information Act, passed in 1967, was amended in 1974 to give individuals greater access to government

---

* New York: Random House, 1964.

† New York: Harper Torchbooks, 1972.

‡ The constitutional issue involved was enormous: the restraint of publication and therefore of an individual's freedom. The courts had established a right of prepublication suppression.

records, books, and articles. By 1983, 65 of the passages had been printed in whole or in part, leaving 574 lines (approximately 6000 words) still deleted. In retrospect, these subsequent revelations did not in any way diminish the sensitivity of the book to the CIA at the time. "There were breaches of security in the book which would have turned your hair gray," said one CIA officer on the case. "The naming of principal agents in six or seven cases, for example; the naming of one head of government who helped us; the relationships with another government. The least that would have happened apart from blowing agents and getting some of them killed, was certainly our ouster from a number of countries. Possibly the overturning of a couple of governments. It was dynamite."[61] A year later another ex-insider, Phillip Agee, published his exposé of the CIA, *Inside the Company: CIA Diary*,* in England. Although he avoided the problems Marchetti had experienced, the publication of his book ultimately resulted in his self-exile from America.

Marchetti and Agee were both affected by the mood of dissent that characterized the moment. Agee's sympathy with Marxist ideals was successfully exploited by Cuban agents, who persuaded him to name everyone he knew in the CIA and associated with the CIA. Marchetti was disillusioned and disaffected. He was an idealist plagued with doubts about Vietnam, which in turn made him doubt the agency and the government he worked for. Money, no doubt, also played a part. Books "exposing" the CIA, revealing political plots and covert actions—the news behind the news, America's secret policies—sold well. Neither author, however, knew the deepest secrets—the assassination plots; these were to come out only in congressional testimony some years later.

LOSING GROUND

Matching the domestic unease affecting the agency in the early 1970s was its growing exclusion from the mainstream of foreign policy. This situation also affected the State Department; both organizations found themselves squeezed out of foreign policy by the White House, and Nixon's and Kissinger's substitution of the National Security Council Staff for them. Ray Cline, who left the CIA in 1969 to become director of the State Department's Intelligence and Research Bureau (John D. Marks had worked there as an assistant to Cline), resigned from his job in 1973 in dismay at the concentration of power in the White House. "The White House almost totally disregarded the State Department in the Nixon era," said Cline, "subordinating it to carrying out White House directives and keeping crucial policy information out of State hands, just as crucial intelligence was often suppressed to insure that only Nixon and Kissinger had the full body of information on which to make broad

---

* Harmondsworth, England: Penguin, 1975.

judgments. The whole interagency bureaucracy was emasculated to provide a monopoly of power for the White House."[62]

The same thing happened to the CIA. "At one point," said Cline about the Chilean Track II, "the President and Dr. Kissinger even took matters out of the hands of the 40 Committee of the NSC and directed the CIA, much against its officers' judgment, to try to stage a military coup. . . . The White House was using the CIA for what it conceived the CIA to be good for: fighting covert military campaigns in Southeast Asia and large-scale intervention in political elections in Chile and Italy."[63] This concentration of power in the White House at the expense of the agency was backed up by various administrative measures.

Nixon and Kissinger had given a clear indication of how they planned to control policy before Nixon's inauguration. Helms had managed to forestall the first attempt to sidestep him through the intervention of Melvin Laird, but the determination to run American foreign policy straight from the Oval Office was still part of Nixon's plans. In December 1970 Dr. James Schlesinger, assistant director of the Bureau of the Budget, was directed by Nixon to review the agencies and the organization of American intelligence. Three months later Schlesinger reported back with a paper, "A Review of the Intelligence Community," in which he criticized the Estimates as tending to the anodyne in their attempt to reach a consensus and argued that the role of the director of Central Intelligence as head of the intelligence community was a fiction. Intelligence, the report stated, cost a great deal more than was realized by Congress, but the big expense—technical intelligence collection—was worthwhile and produced far better information than old-fashioned political intelligence.

Richard Helms brought John A. Bross, who had recently retired from the agency, back to advise him on his response. Bross found that there was no practical suggestion for action in the report that had not already been thoroughly considered and implemented years before. The office of National Intelligence Programs Evaluation, set up by John McCone in 1963 to review organizational and program efficiency, had succeeded by 1970 in giving visibility to the component parts of the murky jungle of intelligence-community budgets. Helms had overseen the development of the United States Intelligence Board committee structure and CIA procedures for rationalizing resource allocations within the intelligence community. The National Intelligence Resources Board, which reviewed all community programs and generally was effective in focusing and controlling community budgets, had been established by Helms and was responsible directly to the director of Central Intelligence. It was a multifaceted coordinating system that enabled differences to be resolved without constantly risking loss of face within the bureaucracy.

Casper Weinberger, then Schlesinger's boss as director of the Bureau of the Budget, had written to Helms not long before Schlesinger's report was commissioned by Nixon to compliment him on the way he conducted the intelligence community. The effect of the Schlesinger report was to destroy the inconspicuous but effective way in which the intelligence community was managed under Helms. Helms had gained a large degree of practical superiority through his organization of the intelligence community committee and liaison structure. Schlesinger's report cast this achievement into high relief, encouraging bureaucratic challenges to the status quo.*

On November 5, 1971, a presidential directive was issued implementing Schlesinger's principal recommendations. In particular, a National Intelligence Committee was established, under the chairmanship of Henry Kissinger, as a subcommittee of the National Security Council, to coordinate and review the activities of the intelligence community. It removed the coordinating structure from the personal entourage of the director of Central Intelligence and created, as a more or less separate edifice, a coordinating staff largely composed of military officers of increasingly clanking seniority. The director retained responsibility for reviewing only the overall intelligence budget.[64] The effect of this, when coupled with the Verification Panel created in 1969 to monitor SALT, was to make Henry Kissinger the President's chief intelligence officer, and it shouldered aside the National Security Council and the DCI, and the DCI's role as head of the intelligence community.

Helms set up an Intelligence Resources Advisory Committee with the other intelligence agencies to fulfill his responsibilities under the new directive. It was just a new committee, and Helms did not try to press himself on the other agencies as a financial controller. Nixon did not try to give the DCI's new role meaning either, and submitted no legislative proposals to give the arrangement strength, leaving Helms to arbitrate on financial matters without any statutory back-up. In January 1972 Helms established an Intelligence Community Staff in the CIA as a replacement for the National Intelligence Programs Evaluation Staff created by John McCone in 1963. Both staffs had the purpose of advising the DCI in his role as head of the intelligence community, and both failed for the same reasons. The other agencies constantly resisted outside direction; there were no regular procedures for coordination among the agencies (they all preferred to leave that to the National Security Council or *ad hoc* arrangements); the staffs were composed entirely of CIA personnel rather than community-wide representatives, thus limiting access to other agencies; and the job was full-time. If the DCI was to coordinate the intelligence community, he would not be able to run the CIA as well.[65]

Every DCI, whatever thoughts he might have about coordination when he started, soon came to the conclusion that it was better to run the agency with its tangible power than to attempt to run the confederacy of the intelligence community, each component of which had powerful friends and inter-

---

* The DCI's supremacy in the intelligence field had always been a fiction. Individual DCIs, notably Bedell Smith and, to a significant extent, Richard Helms had managed to establish a degree of supremacy.

ests in the bureaucracy and in every administration which might combine to place any aspiring coordinator on the fringes of power. Helms was no different, and he did not attempt to do more than use the Intelligence Community Staff to collect the various budgets and views of the other agencies and present them to the President. It would have required a revolution in the bureaucracy for the agencies to agree to one overall budget and gear themselves to its requirements; it is in the nature of organizations to define budgets in terms of institutional needs and perceptions, not in terms of principles or to achieve coordination with others.

The effect of these changes was to cement the big change in the agency's role as perceived from the White House since the mid-1960s. The standard set-piece Estimates continued. The quality of the analysts continued to impress. But the agency's role was no longer to innovate or pronounce upon the great foreign-policy issues of the day; it was to support and to serve the military in Vietnam and to take specific actions within the big picture of foreign policy without ever quite knowing the frame within which the big picture was set. Nixon had made up his mind to achieve détente with the Soviet Union, which meant making compromises and angering allies, and he did not want anybody to see the big picture until he was ready.

Typical of the subjects the analysts were asked to address during Nixon's presidency were "The Soviet Defense Council and Military Policy Making" (April 1972) and "The Soviet Decision Making Process for the Selection of Weapons Systems" (June 1973).[66] The focus was on particulars, on quantifiable elements, and not on the big questions Nixon and Kissinger were considering in private. They did not ask the agency to estimate the effect on Sino-Soviet or Soviet-American relations of the opening to China: this was kept entirely within the Oval Office. Nor did they ask the agency to consider the implications of SALT I before they agreed on it with the Soviets.

Nixon hated the sort of argument the CIA gave him over the SS-9, although at the time no one in the agency realized this. He had not told them that a tailored Estimate was an element in his strategy to bring the Russians to the negotiating table and ultimately to frighten people sufficiently about the prospects of a Soviet nuclear strike to enhance the magnitude of his achievement for peace and give the impression that he had secured major concessions from the Russians after twenty years of cold war. Following that, the agency was asked to examine smaller questions by Kissinger, who became the agency's White House controller and only avenue to the President.

CAMBODIA AND LAOS

Apart from his opening to China and SALT, Nixon's major effort was to secure peace (or at least honorable U.S. withdrawal) in Vietnam. In early 1970, having decided that in order to reach a negotiated settlement in Vietnam he had to demonstrate his willingness to fight the war ferociously despite large-scale domestic dissent, Nixon sent troops into Cambodia to destroy Vietcong centers there. As Nixon was making this decision, Paul Walsh, an analyst in the Office of Current Intelligence, used communications and photographic intelligence to estimate that between December 1966 and January 1970 about 6000 tons of supplies for the Vietcong had come through the Cambodian port of Sihanoukville. MACV disagreed, estimating that closer to 18,000 tons had come through. Another battle broke out about numbers, with the President inclining toward the MACV view because it suited his plans better and because he suspected that the CIA had a built-in bias against the war that colored its judgments against any proposal to widen it or increase the U.S. effort.

In March the agency came up with evidence that four Vietcong/North Vietnamese divisions were in Cambodia, where there was an extensive network of supply depots, hospitals, and camps for them. On April 13 the Board of National Estimates completed its first draft of an Estimate, "Stock-taking in Indochina: Longer Term Prospects," which considered the benefits of invading Cambodia to attack the communist forces there. An invasion would do damage, the Estimate said, but would be unlikely to disrupt the Vietcong or North Vietnamese permanently. Eight days later Nixon and Kissinger told Richard Helms that they were planning to invade Cambodia but that he must tell no one, including his own people. On April 29 Helms returned the draft Estimate to Abbott Smith. "Let's take a look at this on June 1st," he said, "and see if we would keep it or make certain revisions."* The following day Nixon announced that U.S. troops were invading Cambodia to clean out communist sanctuaries.

The invasion drove American antiwar protesters to fury. Nearly five hundred college campuses went on strike. The National Guard was called in to control students at Kent State in Ohio and Jackson State in Mississippi and some protesters were shot dead. Thousands demonstrated in Washington, and troops took up positions around and inside the White House. Public opinion was evenly divided about the invasion, but less than half of those polled thought the invasion would work, instinctively reaching the same conclusion as the CIA, something Nixon did not thank either the agency or the American

---

* William Shawcross, *Sideshow: Kissinger, Nixon and the Destruction of Cambodia* (London: Fontana Paperbacks, 1980), pp. 137–138, 414. The draft Estimate was suppressed (Powers, *The Man Who Kept the Secrets*, pp. 216–218). Helms backed Walsh in the argument, although as it progressed it became apparent that he might be wrong. A spy, recruited in Hong Kong and working in Sihanoukville, sent detailed reports about the quantities of supplies actually being unloaded from ships. MACV captured an unopened crate of Chinese AK-47 machine guns in the Mekong Delta early in 1970, and the serial numbers showed they had been recently manufactured. How did they get there? asked MACV and supplied the answer: through Sihanoukville. With the bombing of the Ho Chi Minh Trail there was no way the AK-47s could have reached the Mekong Delta within the time periods involved except by ship through Sihanoukville and Cambodia. Paul Walsh argued that the guns could have come down another particular track, but MACV pointed out that this track was not suitable for trucks and was overgrown—how could a two-hundred-pound case have been carried down it in the time available?

people for. His anger with the CIA increased when the invasion did not work but captured a lot of supplies, revealing that the 6000-ton estimate had been far out of line, just as Nixon suspected and MACV claimed. The tonnage was more like 23,000, and the President demanded to know why the CIA had been so wrong. Helms appointed a committee to investigate the misjudgment. Paul Walsh and R. Jack Smith, the deputy director for intelligence, attended a President's Foreign Intelligence Advisory Board meeting to explain. In their view, the difference could have been the cargo of just one freighter that had slipped through their net. It was, nevertheless, a fourfold error of magnitude.[67]

A year later Nixon planned another invasion, this time of Laos, and the CIA again blotted its book with him. The analysts judged that the North Vietnamese in Laos were too weak to put up more than sporadic resistance, encouraging not only the invasion plan in Nixon's mind but also the application of the "Nixon Doctrine"—called "Vietnamization" in Vietnam—which involved giving others arms and material with which to fight, rather than having American troops do the fighting themselves. It was containment "on the cheap," because the other countries doing the fighting would buy their supplies from America.* It also provided Nixon with a rationale for pulling out of Vietnam.

In February 1971 Operation Lam Song 719 commenced as the South Vietnamese army invaded Laos with only backup support from MACV. It was a disaster. The North Vietnamese presence in Laos was strong, not weak, and television showed U.S. helicopters shot down and under attack as the South Vietnamese fled in disorder. Nixon then ordered a massive series of bombing attacks, and within four months Laos became the most heavily bombed country in history. In 1972 the agency reported a build-up of North Vietnamese forces on the border with South Vietnam but did not predict the offensive that was launched on March 30. (The analysts assumed that intensive bombing had dispersed forces and that after Tet the North Vietnamese would not seek a conventional confrontation.) Nixon was angry with the CIA again.

All these instances of presidential disfavor arose out of limited matters, almost battlefield intelligence—an area of responsibility the CIA never sought for itself or wanted; the agency recognized the legitimate and preeminent interest of the service intelligence departments and local military commanders in such matters. The agency tried hard to stay up front as a major player in Southeast Asia, arguing that it should "run" Cambodia, just as it had "run" Laos, by having a few hand-picked operatives in key places and by advising the government on counterinsurgency programs. "Arm the population," William Colby had advised in Cambodia in 1970. "Like an oil spot gradually spreading out. Don't worry about killing the enemy. Get your own people involved. Build a political base in communities anxious to defend themselves."[68] But this argument was not accepted. Nixon wanted to get out of Indochina, not

* From about $2 billion of U.S. arms sales in the mid-1960s, sales reached $10 billion in 1974. (In 1972–73 Iran alone bought $2.5 billion worth of U.S. arms and equipment.)

stay there, and chose the conventional military approach instead, restricting the CIA to reporting and analysis.*

In March 1970, General Lon Nol, the Cambodian prime minister, seized power, overthrowing the government of Prince Norodom Sihanouk. The agency tried hard to work with Lon Nol and make his government effective— all to no avail. Several intelligence operations were run by the agency in Cambodia, coordinated by the Saigon station Cambodian Reports Division, and the CIA knew about the coup plot. Frank Snepp, an analyst at the station, later wrote about his experience there.[69] He recalled that in 1970 the CIA believed that if Lon Nol came to power "he would welcome the United States with open arms and we would accomplish everything."[70] The problem with Sihanouk, it was felt in Saigon, was that his determination to keep Cambodia out of the Vietnam War gave too much succor to the communists, to the detriment of the U.S. effort.

There is nothing but circumstantial evidence to suggest that the CIA was behind Lon Nol's coup. The same sort of evidence exists to suggest that the CIA might have tried to help Sihanouk instead. When Lon Nol's coup took place, Elliot Richardson, undersecretary of state until June 1970, told congressmen privately that "it was only Sihanouk's overthrow" that had allowed the April invasion of Cambodia even to be "considered."[71] The CIA was given no credit by the Nixon administration for this change of circumstances and no doubt deserved none. After the coup the CIA station chief in Phnom Penh was among the first to predict the consequences accurately. Lon Nol was a "fantasist," unwilling to deal with reality; his pro-American coup had resulted in an increase in communist guerrilla activity in Cambodia; his tolerance of corruption and inefficient administration rapidly brought the Cambodian economy to the point of collapse.

"There are several reasons for pessimism about the situation in Cambodia," the station chief cabled to Langley five months after the coup. He listed Lon Nol's personal failings, the lack of enthusiasm for the government, and the multitude of economic and political problems the government seemed incapable of grasping, let alone solving.[72] A special National Intelligence Estimate was prepared by Abbott Smith and his Office of National Estimates after the April 30 invasion, arguing that it had actually worsened the situation, jeopardizing the future of Cambodia. Again, none of this was music to the President's ears, and by the time of his reelection for a second term in 1972, Nixon had decided that there were going to be changes at Langley.

---

* Laos was no advertisement for the CIA to run anything. By 1970 large parts of Laos were controlled by the communist Pathet Lao and the North Vietnamese. The agency had been slipping throughout the 1960s in its operational objectives in Southeast Asia. Monitoring whole societies was one kind of operation; covertly running even portions of whole societies was another matter and was not really practicable. Just as the Bay of Pigs should have been a U.S. Marines operation, running Laos and Cambodia required major and long-term military, economic, and political involvement beyond the resources of any agency. It would have meant America becoming, in effect, an old-fashioned colonial power.

—16—

Power Plays
1972–1975

"I had not been given any warning that I was scheduled to leave," said Richard Helms after Nixon had called him up to Camp David on November 20, 1972, and fired him. "I don't have any doubts that Nixon all along in the back of his mind had a time for how long I was going to be there. After all, I was not his personal friend or choice or political favor or anything like that, so I always thought he would change me at some point. I just didn't realize it was going to be at that point." Helms had gone up to see the President at the retreat expecting to discuss the CIA's budget and was surprised to find that he was discussing his job instead. "At the time of the election," Vernon Walters said, "I had suggested to Helms that I submit my resignation. . . . Helms replied that he did not want me to do this. He felt that such resignations should be submitted only for normal political posts. He did not wish the CIA to be in this category. He did not intend to submit his own resignation and he did not wish me to submit mine. I deferred to his wishes."[1]

"There had been a sort of tradition," said Helms, "that the FBI and the CIA were the two things that should not be political in government, and the way you told the public you did not intend to be political about internal security or about intelligence was by not rushing in and appointing your own guys." When the blow came, it was not just his own career that Helms considered, it was the implications for the agency, his agency, with the coils of Watergate thrashing around it. "Upon his return [from Camp David]," observed Walters, "it was quite clear to me that he would be leaving. He did not tell me this, but I could see it from his face."[2] "Dick Helms paid the price for that 'No' [to the White House over Watergate]," said William Colby with hindsight. "What happened at Camp David had nothing to do with the budget. It had to do with Helms' careful distancing of the agency from Watergate, his refusal to allow it to be used in the cover-up. And for that Nixon fired him as DCI, sent him packing to Iran as ambassador and named James Schlesinger as the agency's new chief."[3]

Helms' action was preserving the agency as a *bureaucracy*, not as a powerful instrument of presidential policy. Helms was probably correct in his "No" if he calculated that Watergate was going to break and that a "Yes" from him would make no difference. It was apparent within days of the break-in that Nixon was arrogant in his belief he could cover it up, and that his close aides had lost their nerve. The obvious step for the White House to have taken was to say, "Yes, these are our people, and they have overstepped the mark. We shall prosecute them." But any institution that wants power has to be prepared to do grubby things (just like J. Edgar Hoover's FBI), and so Helms' "No" firmly removed the agency from power under Nixon.

In a wider sense, Nixon saw Helms as a bureaucrat who was forever building. Nixon wanted action *now*. For him, intelligence was not a question of perpetuity, but of immediate activity. There was a lot of the 1950s cold warrior in Nixon. For him, the struggle for the world was as intense as ever. What had changed, in Nixon's view, was Soviet power and America's ability to respond quickly, to seize opportunities. The CIA, he felt, was too complacent, too content with containment, and not sufficiently alive to the world still being in the melting-pot. He sensed that for the agency, secret work and secret objectives had become predictable, with the good guys and the bad guys already labelled in the world that was still, in fact, in flux. He saw the agency as being no longer prepared to take risks, preferring to be prudently professional.

Schlesinger wasted no time in establishing himself. His appointment was announced within days of Helms' firing. He moved into the director's office in Langley on February 2, 1973, after being sworn in. Helms knew that the ordeal of Watergate was going to writhe on, and he was anxious that his successor continue to keep the agency out of it. In his farewell speech delivered in the main entrance hall at Langley he stressed that the CIA honestly had had nothing to do with Watergate. His people believed him and were themselves anxious about their agency's future. As an old colleague put it:

> Dick Helms was a fellow who by and large gave the people who worked with him his confidence, and if they did a piece of business he was expected to approve, such as a National Estimate, his instinct was to trust them and not try to do it himself or to insert his own preferences in judgments. That was his style. The question he would tend to ask himself on an issue was "Is there something about this that is going to make it difficult for me? Is this going to trigger political reactions that are going to be unpleasant?" That was something he always had to think about, because after the Nixon administration

began he was always in a somewhat tenuous position. I think he tried very hard to be honest in the system. He tried to be honest with his own people. He was a career bureaucrat. When he was fired, I don't think Nixon had been happy with him for a long time.[4]

Throughout his years as director of the CIA Helms depended on efficient staff work. He delegated authority and expected the hierarchy of command and responsibility within the organization to function properly. He managed the agency well. He had the respect of his staff, the admiration of other bureaucrats, but the affection only of his family and personal friends.

David Atlee Phillips polled retired colleagues in the mid-1970s on how they rated five directors of the CIA, starting with Allen Dulles. The first question in the survey was: "If I were to be shipwrecked on a desert island, a pleasant one with abundant food, good climate, a supply of scotch and every hope a ship would pass by, I would choose to be with . . . " Allen Dulles was the first choice of three-quarters of those polled. Dulles was a great storyteller, his best yarn being the one of opportunity lost when he skipped the chance of talking with Lenin. Other CIA people remarked that Dulles was a comfortable, old-shoe type. Several noted that he was somewhat more inclined to be a supervisor than a doer: "What a schemer! He would devise a plan to get us off, but arrange it so I would have to implement the plan." Another said, "Dulles would be selecting all the places *I* should be digging for clams to keep us both alive."

The second question was: "If I were to be shipwrecked on a terrible desert island, with little food and no amenities, with scant hope for survival and I wanted to escape badly, I would choose to be with . . . " Helms came out on top of the poll this time. "Helms would also be selecting places to dig for clams," continued the mollusk fancier, "but I would have a better chance of persuading him he darn well better dig with me. . . . " A few noted that Helms would be aloof and keep his distance. One said, "I credit myself with enough skepticism to not let him get off the island alone." The eleven who worked most closely with the ex-directors voted this way for the pleasant island: six wanted to share it with Dulles, four with Helms, one with McCone. For the terrible desert island, the eleven votes were split: four for McCone, four for Helms, three for Colby.[5]

THE POLITICAL DIRECTOR

James Schlesinger was not included in this poll, and although he was director for only five months (February–June, 1973), he was probably the most unpopular DCI the agency had experienced in its first twenty-five years. He was a politicized intellectual who was available for any job. He was the agency's first "comer"—young (forty-eight years old in 1973) and going places. For him the agency was just another job, another stepping-stone. William Colby, whose admiration for Schlesinger was unusual, said of him:

> James Schlesinger came on strong. On the direct orders of President Nixon, he had conducted a comprehensive review not only of the agency but of the entire intelligence community. So he was no neophyte when he was sworn in as CIA chief in February 1973. Indeed, quite to the contrary; he knew a great deal about it. More to the point, he had developed some strong ideas about what was *wrong* with it and some positive ideas as to how to go about righting those wrongs. So he arrived at Langley running, his shirt tails flying, determined, with that bulldog, abrasive temperament of his, to implement those ideas and set off a wave of change both in the practice of intelligence generally and in the organization and operation of the CIA specifically.[6]

In practice this had three effects. First, Schlesinger was fully aware of Nixon's dislike of the agency (which did not recognize that the CIA of the 1970s was different from the CIA Nixon had known in the 1950s) and knew that part of his job—politically, the most important part—was to bring the agency onto Nixon's team. He was the agency's first *political* director, and he welcomed it. "The deterioration in the climate of civility within the government from the late 1960s onward is a phenomenon in itself," reflected John Huizenga from his vantage point as head of the Office of National Estimates. "It happened to all sorts of agencies that had been expected to do objective, professional jobs. Everything became highly politicized. It was a question of 'If you're not with us, you're against us.' There was a fellow who came out to the agency with James Schlesinger, and he said to me: 'The trouble with you fellows is that you're not on the team.' "[7]

It was understood that Schlesinger was Nixon's revenge. Nixon considered that the agency had to be changed from being an established bureaucracy and brought back as a presidential instrument. He did not feel that it should possess the same separate standing as the State and Defense departments. His perspective was a historical one: he saw the agency as a secret presidential arm, just as it had been when he had first encountered it in 1953 as Eisenhower's Vice-President. Until he felt he had succeeded in changing CIA views, he would let the CIA know it had lost its "protector" and was no longer secure.

Second, Schlesinger's arrival signaled Nixon's determination that *his* DCI should become the real head of the intelligence community and not just the titular head. Nixon did not intend Schlesinger to be a long-term head of the agency and was therefore prepared to allow him great power. As someone who depended on political patrons, Schlesinger understood that his political clout as an outsider in Washington derived from two sources: his relationship with the White House and the size of the budgets under his control. Eighty percent of the money spent on American intelligence was under the control of the Department of Defense, giving every secretary of defense real power in Congress and the administration.

One of the criticisms leveled at Helms from outside the agency during and after his tenure as DCI was that although he sought security through professional integrity, personally and institutionally he did not have the financial resources needed to be properly independent. Helms, it was felt, had not been above massaging an Estimate in the face of political pressure because he was anxious to cling to office, and a DCI—as Helms himself declared—never had the institutional resources for the same "fix" in the Congress as the secretary of defense. Also without personal wealth, Schlesinger, unlike Helms, saw political arrangements as his means of advancement and was happy to massage as his patrons wished. He did not see any particular office as offering him security, and he did not seek to be independent. He knew how important large budgets and demonstrable influence were for political survival. He convinced Nixon of his loyalty and ability and was rewarded with power. Nixon not only appointed him as DCI but also made him chairman of the Intelligence Resources Advisory Committee, with authority over the National Security Agency and the Defense Intelligence Agency. He was in a position to be the most powerful DCI ever, as long as he followed his patron's wishes.

Finally, the change in direction also brought about a housecleaning of the agency. About 7 percent of the CIA's total staff were either fired or forced to resign or retire early. The largest proportion of these came from the clandestine side of the house. (Schlesinger changed the name from Directorate of Plans to Directorate of Operations, recognizing the real nature of the activities and demonstrating his "new realism.")[8] About fifteen hundred people were involved (with about a thousand coming from operations), and while the process was painful, most agreed it was long overdue. There was more concern about Schlesinger's reason for making the cuts than for the cuts themselves. It was not that he thought the CIA had become too bureaucratized or set in its ways (he probably did think this), nor did he want to encourage those who remained to stay on their toes. Rather, he was convinced that the future, first perceived by Bissell nearly twenty years earlier, had now arrived.

Schlesinger believed that the day of the clandestine operator was passing. He was determined to place technical collection, in the form of spies in the skies and in the airways, computers, and telemetry in the forefront of agency activities. The days when the agency's greatest ambition was to find more Popovs and Penkovskys were past. Even Penkovsky had been most useful in enabling photographic interpreters to analyze more quickly and accurately information already obtained from U-2 and satellite reconnaissance. Biased by his background in clandestine operations, Richard Helms had refused to acknowledge the change that had taken place in intelligence, and while he gave more prominence to analysis while he was director, he kept on the old operators. Schlesinger was having none of this. Although he too saw the importance of first-rate analysis, he was determined to tie it directly to technical intelligence.* He was also determined to pare down the agency's operational capability to the bare bones. He was saying something Nixon longed to hear: that all those Europeanized Americans in the CIA were out of date and had not kept up with material developments. From now on, he said, the CIA was going to be a twenty-year career, behind a desk.

Schlesinger did not care that he was unpopular in the agency. He had a job to do—he intended to shake up Langley—and a mission: he wanted a better agency, more in tune with the realities of Washington, on the team. Schlesinger's goals were a stark and brutal statement of the changes that had taken place in the CIA and in America. The agency was no longer an elite service serving the elite. It was an institution with its own ways and its own imperatives, still dominated by the attitudes of its founding fathers. As dissent grew over America's involvement in Vietnam, employees at all levels in the agency had to justify themselves to their wives and husbands, their families and friends.

Often they were asked questions they could not answer. How could the agency do all those things in Vietnam? How can you work for a secret agency serving a corrupt government? Is it true that the agency tried to thwart democracy in Chile? Is it true that you heartlessly calculated the effect of bombing strikes in Vietnam? In one way or another their answers were always the same: *Don't you understand? We're fighting the cold war.* The trouble was that Americans no longer understood or wanted to understand. They wanted to believe in a different world, in which moral distinctions were not that great and in which the moral prerogative of government had disappeared. If the cold war meant wars like the one in Vietnam, they did not like it. Realizing this, Nixon launched his drive for détente. And in an age of détente, cold warriors could be embarrassing.

Schlesinger brought more than a feel for intelligence to his new position. He had come to Nixon's attention in the first place because of his managerial expertise, gained in the Rand Corporation and applied effectively in government since 1967. While at the Bureau of the Budget he had earned a reputa-

---

* The focusing on technical collection suited Nixon's desire to keep policy to himself. It also suited many in the CIA and elsewhere because the pressure on them to make judgments could be deflected by collecting vast quantities of intelligence information, which not only would tend to make clear judgments difficult to arrive at but also would impress intelligence consumers by its sheer volume. A case in point was the OPEC oil embargo of 1973. Arab experts in 1972 had warned of the likelihood of the boycott and had pointed out that the economic power of the oil-exporting countries had implications for U.S. national security. The oil crisis hit America and the West early in 1973, and the fact that the CIA's analysts had not predicted the embargo gave Schlesinger a rod to beat the agency with, although he did not accept the real lesson: that he should strengthen the analytical side rather than concentrate on technical collection.

A year after the oil embargo, India exploded its first nuclear device, catching the U.S. intelligence community unaware: no one had thought India was so advanced in its nuclear program. It raised the whole question of high-technology exports which was to become a major national security question by the end of the decade.

tion as a "budget cutter" and a "bureaucracy tamer," reducing the Defense Department's running costs by $6 billion. In 1971 Nixon appointed him chairman of the Atomic Energy Commission, which he completely reorganized. At the commission he also revealed an impressive political determination to incorporate environmental considerations to a greater extent than his predecessors in nuclear power planning while simultaneously pressing ahead with the construction of nuclear power plants (much to the concern of environmentalists and many in Congress).

Schlesinger applied the same determination to the reorganization of the CIA, not always to the best effect. The CIA's "Contact Division"—the overt intelligence-collection operation responsible for debriefing Americans who had useful information gained abroad—lost its separate status within the agency and became part of the clandestine side under the Directorate of Operations. The board and the Office of National Estimates were reviewed with the intention of abolishing them (a move effected later under William Colby) and in the meantime lost their right to choose what to analyze; Schlesinger instructed that the main purpose of the analysts was to write papers to order for the National Security Council staff. This move was designed to force the analysts onto the White House team. It meant that Estimates could be more easily controlled by Henry Kissinger and the President. Altogether, these changes hit the agency like a whirlwind, marking the start of an uneasy decade in Langley. There was no respite when the White House announced on May 11, 1973, that Schlesinger was to be the next secretary of defense and that William Colby would be the next DCI.

Schlesinger's departure from the agency after seventeen weeks was prompted by Nixon's growing entanglement in Watergate. It was part of a reconstruction designed to win more support for the administration in Congress. In effect, Colby's appointment and the restrictions on his authority (Colby's authority never came close to the authority exercised by Schlesinger) were Nixon's way of saying, as a sop to his critics, that he did not intend the CIA to be political after all. Colby was expected to be a competent, professional DCI, and the agency was expected to continue its reputation for nay-saying in the administration. Ironically, these were now seen by Nixon as being positive advantages: if Nixon promoted professionals and encouraged nay-sayers, how could the White House be as paranoid and secretive as everybody was saying? As it turned out, Nixon gained little mileage from these changes, for as more and more was learned about White House activities, more and more suspicion was directed at the CIA as a presidential arm as well.

Richard Nixon's fundamental problem was that he was a cat that walked by himself, and this frightened everybody. He had primitive appetites—thus his ruthless domination of the CIA through Schlesinger. But while being manipulative, he was not very original. Faced with Watergate, he strove to be ordinary in an effort to reduce antagonism toward himself. This meant foregoing the ability to appoint "his" people. Just before announcing Colby as DCI, he had fired Haldeman, Ehrlichman, the attorney general, Richard Kleindienst, and withdrawn L. Patrick Gray's nomination to head the FBI. For Nixon, appointing Colby was much safer than appointing another outsider. If Nixon had been the head of a Washington bureaucracy instead of being a politician, he would have given J. Edgar Hoover a run for his money, and this was what people recognized in him.

Nixon was different from his immediate predecessors: he was not part of the governing consensus. He rejected the language of Wilsonian ideals in favor of pragmatic dealing of an Old World type—his "madman theory" of diplomacy was an extreme statement of this. He did have a streak of idealism (Wilson was one of Nixon's heroes), and the ideal of peace was close to him. He was also a president who exercised to the full the prerogatives of his office, thrilled with power, determined to mold a Nixonian elite and thrust aside the old Wilsonian, East Coast, Ivy League, liberal Establishment—all the elements the CIA had in abundance. He knew that the agency would never really be "his," and he treated it accordingly. Nixon was an adventurer, and was seen as such in the agency. An enshrined wisdom is that you can get anything you want in Washington as long as you don't mind who gets the credit: Nixon wanted the credit. His noncollegiality alienated insiders. He wanted a freer but lesser America. The "Nixon Doctrine" was his expression of this, implicitly taking the view that America had been carrying Europe and Japan long enough. Nixon wanted to break free.

For the CIA, this involved a new set of priorities and a massive change in objectives. Nixon wanted the agency to take a more hostile view of the world in general—just like his own "plumbers." It would have to serve a foreign policy that was fast, aggressive, and unfriendly, as exemplified by Nixon's overnight severing of the dollar from the gold standard and simultaneous temporary surcharge on imports which he announced on a Sunday—August 15, 1971— when everyone was away for the weekend. These actions had really shocked Japan and alarmed Europe. As far as Nixon was concerned, there was no need for the CIA to protect the United States from surprises when the United States was surprising everyone else. Nixon wanted offensive policies, not defensive ones. He was a radical who wanted to sit in the eye of the storm.

The CIA had found itself in the position of any bureaucracy faced by a radical leader: it burrowed into the mechanics of its work, surrendering the substance of policy formation until Nixon went away. The willingness of the agency to accept an emphasis on technical collection as opposed to analysis was a symptom of this awareness.

SKELETONS

Apart from the "insider" challenge by Nixon to its position, the agency simultaneously faced a challenge from the American people. On January 7,

1973, *The New York Times* carried a profile of Cord Meyer—"One Man's Long Journey: From a One World Crusade to the Department of Dirty Tricks"—that was a token of a major shift in attitude toward the agency. Americans had changed from thinking that the world would corrupt America to thinking that America would corrupt the world. On February 6 a blaze of publicity surrounded the revelation that the CIA had trained police from twelve domestic agencies. Critics perceived this as a breach of the CIA's charter and demanded a congressional investigation.[9] Articles flourished about the Marchetti case, arguing that prior restraint of publication set a dangerous precedent for civil liberties. On March 21 Schlesinger's staff cuts were announced, making it seem as if something very wrong had been going on in the CIA, spurring further suspicions and investigations.

On January 18 the trial of Daniel Ellsberg for leaking *The Pentagon Papers* began. Sam Adams, testifying on Ellsberg's behalf, asserted on April 8 that MACV had falsified its reporting of Vietcong strength in late 1967. Comparisons were drawn with the CIA estimates of enemy strength prior to the April 1970 invasion of Cambodia, it being stated that there had been a massive underestimate. On April 10 the CIA announced that it was discontinuing its training programs for domestic police forces except in certain special cases, implying an acceptance of the charge that it had overstepped its statutory limits. On April 19 a book by David Wise, *The Politics of Lying,** revealed that between 1958 and 1961 the CIA had trained Tibetan guerrillas at a base near Leadville, Colorado. Again the implication was that the agency was in breach of its charter and that it was engaged in a vast number of dirty tricks, some of which might even jeopardize the developing rapprochement with China. On April 27 Judge Matthew Byrne, Jr., presiding over the Ellsberg case, revealed that two of those convicted for the Watergate break-in (Howard Hunt and an ex-FBI man, G. Gordon Liddy) had also burgled the office of Ellsberg's former psychiatrist, Dr. Lewis J. Fielding, in September 1971. On May 11 Judge Byrne declared a mistrial and dismissed all the charges against Ellsberg.†

William Colby, on a trip to Bangkok, read the news of the Fielding break-in in the newspapers, which also carried the story of the CIA's profile of Ellsberg:

> This was a shocker and I couldn't understand how I had never heard of it before, when I was supposed to have been in charge of assembling all the CIA material relevant to Watergate. But more disturbingly, I wondered how the news had hit Schlesinger; for I had assured him that I had told him the full

* New York: Random House, 1973.

† The Fielding break-in was the major element in Byrne's decision. He discovered that John Ehrlichman had ordered the break-in and that the FBI had tapped telephone conversations between Ellsberg and Morton Halperin, who had headed the *Pentagon Papers* study while at the NSC. When Byrne ordered that the transcripts of these conversations be turned over to his court, he was told that they had been lost. He was furious. When he announced his mistrial decision he also revealed that in the middle of the trial Ehrlichman had offered him the post of director of the FBI. He accused the government of "gross misconduct" disgracing the system of justice.

story of CIA's relationship to Watergate on virtually the first day he had arrived at Langley. . . .

Schlesinger said he assumed that the news was as much of a surprise to me as it was to him. But then he went on to say that he would tear the place apart and "fire everyone if necessary," but we had to find out whether there were any other questionable or illegal activities hidden in the secret recesses of the clandestine past that we didn't know about and that might explode at any time under our feet.[10]

On May 9, two days before it was announced he would be leaving the agency, Schlesinger issued a directive, which he drew up with Colby, ordering "all the senior operating officials of this agency to report to me immediately on any activities now going on, or that have gone on in the past, which might be construed to be outside the legislative charter of this agency. . . . I invite all ex-employees to do the same."[11] It was the start of what was to be called in the press "The Family Jewels" and within the agency "The Skeletons."

It fell to Colby to assemble "The Skeletons," and it was a task he pursued with diligence. Like many other CIA people, he had been affected by the mood of dissent and the questioning spirit of the times. There was a degree of moral fatigue involved as well. When there had been a ten-year horizon on the "world crisis" in the late 1940s, it had been acceptable to support every anti-Soviet venture and watch while brave men and women lost their lives. But after twenty-five years this was far more difficult. The "world crisis" was still there. Russia and America had broken a lot of crockery but had not changed the world. Colby's effort—the American effort—had been like nectar in a sieve. Colby had given his best in Vietnam, and Vietnam had been lost. He had believed in a sunshine world of American victory and a dark night of American defeat. He had discovered it was neither: just a twilight of combat. The remarkable element was that this discovery had not disrupted the integrity of his character. He was a Roman Catholic, and after his eldest daughter's death in April 1973 from a combination of epilepsy and anorexia nervosa, he seemed to change, becoming more religious and more reflective.

He had been a dedicated cold warrior, in many respects a model clandestine-services officer. He had been a brave and resourceful OSS officer, parachuting twice into Nazi-occupied France and Norway. He joined the CIA in 1950 in Frank Wisner's Office of Policy Coordination, and apart from his temporary reassignment to the Phoenix program, he had been on the clandestine side of the house ever since. But the Colby who had run Phoenix was not the Colby who became director of Central Intelligence in 1973. In Vietnam his reputation had been as a tough man, a hardball player, dedicated to his job and with little imagination.

Edward Behr, a senior *Newsweek* correspondent in 1970, had gone on a trip with Colby while he was in Vietnam. They flew to Quang Ngai, to the south of Da Nang, an area effectively controlled by the Vietcong, spending some days with the province chief. As Behr remembered it:

There were only a few days to go until Christmas, and our schedule included endless church services and hymn singing. The GIs attached to the province chief's HQ were also, by some strange coincidence, Baptist Fundamentalists, and the result was that we seemed to be in the midst of a singularly well-armed, militant, and uniformed missionary outpost. One evening, Colby and I had hymnbooks pressed into our hands and prepared ourselves for yet another interminable service. Inevitably, one of the hymns was all about "Peace on earth" and "goodwill towards men." Our singing was entirely covered by the regular sound of artillery shells being fired off into the surrounding jungles only yards away from the school building the service was being held in. "Don't you think," I hissed to Colby over my hymnbook, "that there's something particularly grotesque about all this?"

He looked at me with astonishment. "No, I don't," he said. "What's wrong with it?"[12]

"Colby was one of the old school," said a colleague who worked with him in the agency in the 1960s, "but a different kind of old school. He was Catholic. His father was in the military. He wasn't 'family.' He was also a lot meaner and nastier, and a lot dirtier. A prick. Colby changed quite a bit. The Colby today is a different Colby. The Colby I knew in the agency was a real sonofabitch. Very intense. Very hardworking."[13] Victor Marchetti remembered that it was Colby who had gone after him over his book. "Colby really went wild. He wanted to put me in jail."[14]

When his appointment as DCI was announced the press focused on this Bill Colby, the man behind Phoenix. In a profile of Colby in *The New York Times* on July 1, 1973, David Wise singled out this part of his career, presenting Phoenix as a program of systematic murder and torture devised by Colby, emphasizing the figures he himself had provided in congressional testimony of the number killed under the program. Not one of Colby's friends, said Wise, could imagine him torturing people with his own hands—he had a "boy scout" image—but as a true believer in America's policy in Vietnam, Colby condoned whatever it took to win the war. With profiles like this appearing in different newspapers throughout the country, Colby soon found himself in a protracted series of Senate hearings on his appointment.

The Senate Armed Services Committee (responsible for confirming the appointments of directors of Central Intelligence) also in July investigated assertions that Colby, who had been station chief in Saigon from 1959 until 1962, had slanted intelligence data to show that the Diem family was successfully grappling with the Vietcong and winning broad support. On July 20, newspapers carried reports that the committee was going to reopen its hearings on Colby's appointment, as a result, in part, of representations by Senator Edward Kennedy that Colby's work in Vietnam had involved unacceptable activities. Colby was able to refute the specific allegations made against him and the Phoenix program to the committee's satisfaction, and on August 2 his appointment was approved. In the period between Schlesinger's departure in

June and Colby's swearing-in on September 4, 1973, Vernon Walters was acting DCI. He agreed with Colby and Schlesinger that Colby should inform the chairmen of the congressional committees to which the agency reported about "The Skeletons." The idea was to prevent Colby's confirmation hearings from going off into an anti-CIA extravaganza by telling all in private and giving assurances that full compliance with the CIA charter would be observed in the future.

The list of "Skeletons" drawn up by the agency covered 693 closely typewritten pages and contained everything that could be construed as CIA "dirty tricks." The list opened with a summary of CIA contacts with Egil Krogh, John Ehrlichman's assistant at the White House and head of the White House Special Investigation Unit, the "plumbers." Krogh also oversaw antidrug-traffic operations for the White House as secretary of the Cabinet Committee for International Narcotics Control. In all these capacities Krogh had dealings with the CIA. None was illegal, but all could be embarrassing in the anti-Nixon atmosphere of Washington in 1973. CIA employees working elsewhere in government agencies and departments were listed. Although CIA people being employed elsewhere in the government was also legal, publicity about it was potentially embarrassing because of the suggestion that the agency was spying on the White House and on the Washington bureaucracy.

"Contacts with Watergate figures" was another item in the list, as was "Activities directed against U.S. citizens," with the Chaos operation outlined. Project Mockingbird was revealed: "During the period from March 12, 1963, to June 15, 1963, the Office of Security installed telephone taps on two prominent Washington-based newsmen who were suspected of disclosing classified information obtained from a variety of governmental and congressional sources." Nixon was by no means the only President who had used the CIA to spy on newsmen and to track down leaks. Project Mudhen—the surveillance of columnist Jack Anderson in 1971 and 1972—was listed. So were Projects Butane, Celotex I, and Celotex II, which involved the surveillance of other newsmen. Project SRPointer was sketched out:

> Since 1953, the Office of Security has operated a mail intercept program of incoming and outgoing Russian mail and, at various times, other selective mail at Kennedy airport in New York City. This operation included not only the photographing of envelopes but also surreptitious opening and photographing of selected items of mail. The bulk of the take involved matters of internal security interest which was disseminated to the Federal Bureau of Investigation. This program is now in a dormant state pending a decision as to whether the operation will be continued or abolished.

Project Redface I, the "surreptitious entry of an office" in Washington in July 1970, was on the list. So too was information about the agency's penetration of the Bureau of Narcotics and Dangerous Drugs (with the agreement of the director of the bureau) "to monitor any illegal activities of other BNDD employees." Project Merrimac, which ran from February 1967 until November 1971, was detailed. It had "the purpose of covertly monitoring dissident groups in the Washington area considered to be potential threats to agency personnel and installations. In addition, during this period, the Office of Security field offices were tasked with collecting available intelligence on dissident groups." The details of various domestic police support programs were also given. "Polygraphing of employees of other government agencies," and "Influencing human behavior" were other headings. The assassination plots against Lumumba, Castro, and Trujillo were included.[15]

Emerging along with "The Skeletons" list was the other Bill Colby—a man with a driving determination to cleanse the agency and make it acceptable once more. His confirmation hearings were

> a pretty rough experience. All throughout Washington, mainly on the hoardings around the new subway construction sites, anonymous posters appeared, showing an unflattering photograph of myself superimposed on the Ace of Spades and accusing me of assassinating 20,000 people in Vietnam.... At the same time, my telephone at home—which I insisted remain listed—frequently rang with abusive or obscene callers.... I took only one step with regard to the phone calls. It was against one that persisted after most of the others had stopped, the phone ringing at various odd hours but no one speaking when we answered it.... I noted the times of the calls [and told] the phone company and soon learned the name under which the calling phone was registered. Again I told the security officers to do nothing; I did not wish to add another CIA surveillance to the jewels. But the next time the phone rang, I picked up the receiver and, as soon as I realized that it was our silent harasser, I said, "Mr. John Doe," using his name. He gasped and hung up, and never called again, probably terrified at what retribution CIA might be about to inflict on him.[16]

While all this was happening Colby's colleagues noticed a change in him and put it down to his daughter's death and the harassment he faced over Phoenix. In retrospect they felt that he had "got religion," that he was a "soldier priest," and that in his own way he was trying to do the best for the agency, convinced that if he made a clean breast of the CIA's secrets, they could be put in the past and a cleaner future would thus be guaranteed. He may have sensed that he had people under him desperate to "confess" and that by taking on the responsibility himself, he would be taking a lot of weight off them and the agency. He can be seen as making a planned evacuation from an exposed position. Implicit in his decisions was a recognition that the agency's secrets were going to come out anyway. So he contrived to involve America's political leadership in the embarrassment of discovery as the best hope for the survival of the agency. He was not prepared to allow the agency to appear to have been a rogue elephant at any time: if things had been done that now would be condemned, he would demonstrate that the agency had acted under orders. Colby never lost his nerve over the next three years as his plan unfolded, nor did he go to the "confessional," which would have meant an acceptance by him that the agency was to blame.

Bitter debate surrounded Colby's decision to go public over "The Skeletons," especially when his revelations at various congressional hearings reflected adversely on Richard Helms, who had been deputy to the director for plans, director for plans, deputy director and then director when most of "The Skeletons" were buried. "Helms never forgave Colby for the disclosures," said one retired clandestine-service chief. "Helms could never have done what Colby did. There are two camps among CIA people: pro-Colby and anti-Helms and vice versa, and they'll never really come together."[17] "We all find what Colby did incomprehensible," said one of Helms's supporters, refusing to concede the skill with which Colby compromised the attacks on the agency, and he continued:

> I just have a feeling about Bill Colby that he is quite lacking in the qualities that enable most of us to be introspective about our behavior. As far as I can judge his mind, I have a feeling it's a pretty blunt mind that has certain fixed points in it. I have this feeling that he has the ability to reduce quite complicated questions to points that just won't do with the real world. One of his friends and admirers said to me, "The thing you have to understand about Bill Colby is that he's intransigent." Everybody I've ever talked to who worked with Bill said that they would go in and talk to him, and he would smile and listen to them, and nine times out of ten they would come out persuaded that he would think about it, but he never swerved. He had a total incapacity to compromise. That's the judgment I've come to.[18]

"I think the most important issue is the one Bill walks up to and doesn't really deal with," said R. Jack Smith:

> How does a secret espionage agency operate in what is an open society? I think Americans in our era have gone childish about the question of an open society. The values they have are those of a kindergarten—"I'll be fair to you; you be fair to me." It's banal. The ethics of personal relationships do not apply to international affairs. And I don't think Bill recognizes that if you follow his argument to its conclusion, you cannot have an intelligence service. You've got to allow room for it somehow, as the British have done for centuries as "the business of the Crown." The Crown has its rights, and people in Britain know that it needs to do certain things in certain ways, and they do not question it. You've got to have some sort of sanctuary in a society's set of values in which secret things take place. America has never grown up in its thinking about it.[19]

William Colby, naturally, felt differently. The investigations and suspicions brought to a head by Watergate revealed the paradoxes of the CIA's operations which, according to Colby, at times

> ran straight into the Constitution. In a typically American way, this was resolved messily and in public. Until this happened it was never clear what was legal and what was illegal. I didn't rush to volunteer anything. It had to be dragged out of me. But it did have to be dragged out of me: there was no other choice. I was teased one time about going to confession. But no; I came to a very deliberate decision. We were under attack. I had to be responsive to the committees on the larger question in order to protect the real secrets. The real secrets are the sources, the people. The fact that we were involved in some adventure in Chile—you wish it did not have to come out, but if it does, the damage isn't that great. I took the position very strongly that we should protect the secrets, the people and some of the technology, and that we should try not to stonewall on anything else. That's the argument, and it's a good argument.[20]

It was an argument that colored Colby's whole period as director. Helms had kept things secret, pursuing a policy of volunteering nothing and answering questions with precision, avoiding elaboration. Under his directorship the CIA's "Skeletons" had stayed in their closets. Everyone knew while Helms was DCI that there were some things he would not talk about, some things that he would talk about if pressed but better not to, and some things it was fine for the public to know. He had operated within the understandings of the 1950s and 1960s with Congress and had held the line even when those understandings began to slip.

Schlesinger and Colby did not have the same experience, the same fund of trust on the Hill, and they did not believe that the agency could keep its secrets and stay in business in the atmosphere of Watergate. The days of the powerful chairmen of Senate and House committees were over—Senator Richard Russell, who died in January 1971, had been the last real power broker on the Hill. Moreover, Watergate coincided with a large influx of new senators and representatives, many of whom had no patience with the established committee system. These young Turks rose up against committee chairmen, demanding to know what was going on, anxious to make their own names quickly. "We had absolute security in Congress in the old days," said one senior CIA officer who had testified on the Hill frequently over the years. "We could tell them anything, and nothing leaked. There was a system, and it operated with absolute candor. Not a thing was held back on a question—how much money we spent—nothing was held back. Then the discipline went. We never had the power to tell Congress whom we were going to talk to—they told us. And after men like Russell had gone, with Watergate a lot of glory boys saw us as their publicity."[21]

Starting with "The Skeletons," the people in the agency looked on as their new director revealed one by one the agency's secrets, some of which only a handful of people had previously known. Schlesinger's cuts could be understood in terms of Nixon's revenge on the agency for the Watergate "no." But Colby's revelations were an enigma. After all, CIA people reasoned, *he is one of us!* A few people were deeply suspicious of what Colby was doing. He did not clear his first revelations with the White House before he made them, no doubt believing (probably correctly) that Nixon would prefer not to be involved as the noose of Watergate tightened around his neck.* Colby's loyalty was also in question. Some officers on the Counterintelligence Staff, convinced that the CIA had been penetrated by the Russians, wondered if Colby might not be their man.

The Counterintelligence Staff had another reason for not liking their new DCI: as part of the Schlesinger cuts and reorganization, Colby as executive director-comptroller and DDO had urged the firing of James Angleton, the longtime head of Counterintelligence, and a number of other senior members of the staff. He had also recommended a general housecleaning. As far as Colby could see, Angleton and his people had tied up resources, seriously mistreated one defector, and were no longer doing their job effectively.[22]

> To my surprise [said Colby], there was one senior officer who escaped the purge, and that was Jim Angleton. I make no secret of the fact that I recommended to Schlesinger that Angleton ought to be moved, reiterating my long-held feeling that his supersecretive style of operation had, at least in recent years, become incompatible with the one I believed essential. But Schlesinger wasn't sure. He was clearly fascinated by Angleton's undoubted brilliance and couldn't help wondering if there just might be something to his complicated theories that deserved further exploration. It may also have been that Angleton's unbending Cold War view towards the Soviets appealed to Schlesinger's own fierce anti-Communism. So he refused to let me move him.[23]

When Schlesinger went, however, this restraint no longer applied.

The mail-opening operation was the first issue leading to a confrontation between Colby and Angleton. The CIA Office of Security actually conducted the openings; the Counterintelligence Staff processed the information and acted as the liaison with the FBI. At various points since the operation had started in 1953, postmasters general were informed of its existence and their permission was obtained. "The Skeletons" list brought the operation to the

---

* Colby, by masterminding the publicity, preempted the involvement of anyone else in the bureaucracy. He was playing a very heavy card, trumping the White House by bringing the American people into the secret world. As a result, there were so many people investigating and reporting that no one could blow the referee's whistle. And Colby got what he wanted: no President could put the CIA in a bottle and throw it away.

attention of Schlesinger and Colby. So did the chief postal inspector, an ex-CIA man who knew about the operation and in his new job felt he could not let it continue without specific approval from the White House—something that Nixon was not likely to agree to as he battled for his own survival. Colby was particularly bothered by the operation: "First was the fact that opening first-class mail was a direct violation of a criminal statute. I looked it up in the law library to make sure. And secondly, I could get nothing beyond vague generalities from the Counterintelligence Staff when I asked what the operation had actually accomplished of any value over the years."[24] So Colby recommended termination of this operation. Angleton countered with a strong appeal for its continuation, citing more evidence of its value to Schlesinger than he had given to Colby, and urged that President Nixon's personal approval be obtained. Face was saved all round when Schlesinger decided to "suspend" the operation, neither ending it nor keeping it going.

As director, Colby did not take immediate action against Angleton, feeling that the Directorate of Operations (within which Counterintelligence nominally existed; it was more like a self-contained fiefdom) had suffered enough turbulence with Schlesinger's cuts and the removal from Counterintelligence of FBI liaison and responsibility for keeping tabs on international terrorism. Angleton remained with a smaller staff to work on counterintelligence operations. "I spent several long sessions doing my best to follow his tortuous theories about the long arm of a powerful and wily KGB at work, over decades, placing its agents in the heart of allied and neutral nations and sending its false defectors to influence and undermine American policy," recalled Colby. "I confess that I couldn't absorb it, possibly because I did not have the requisite grasp of this labyrinthine subject, possibly because Angleton's explanations were impossible to follow, or possibly because the evidence just didn't add up to his conclusions."[25]

By 1973 Angleton had been in counterintelligence for nearly thirty years and had concluded that the CIA, and through the CIA American policy, in certain respects, had been influenced and misdirected by the KGB. His principal source for this was the December 1961 defector from the KGB, Anatoly Golytsin, who backed up assertions of KGB disinformation plots with information on Soviet spy networks and methodology. His principal example was the other subsequent defector from the KGB in February 1964, Yuri Nosenko, who had volunteered the statement that the KGB had nothing to do with Lee Harvey Oswald's assassination of President Kennedy.

Counterintelligence had become consumed with the implications of the Nosenko case (which was handled by the Soviet Russia Division). Was Nosenko telling the truth or was he—as Golytsin suggested—a disinformation agent whose denial of KGB involvement in Kennedy's death meant that the KGB had almost certainly been involved? The complex of arguments, facts, judgments, and personalities concerned in this question and others like it were at the nub of Colby's complaint about Angleton and his staff.* What was more, Angleton's pursuit of the ever elusive truth in the case involved nearly every single "Skeleton": he was a one-man minefield as far as Colby was concerned. "I feared that Angleton's professional integrity and personal intensity might have led him to take dire measures,"[26] said Colby disturbingly and obscurely in explaining afterward why he delayed forcing Angleton out.

Angleton was a legend in his own lifetime within the CIA. He was reputed to be omniscient, with eyes and ears all over the world, let alone Washington. He was known to have excellent contacts with the intelligence services of Italy and Israel. He seriously shook the agency's China analysts in the early 1960s by forcefully representing that the Sino-Soviet split was a sham, an example of communist duplicity, designed to ensnare the West into thinking that there was more likelihood of conflict between the two communist giants than there was of communist world domination. It was a smokescreen, he was convinced, to distract the West from guarding against the real intentions of the communist powers.† The complexities and levels of deceit involved in the Nosenko case intrigued him enormously, and from them he concluded that the CIA faced a very sophisticated KGB plot to discredit defectors and the agency itself.

For ten years, starting in 1964, Angleton devoted a substantial part of the resources of the Counterintelligence Staff to investigating the charges and counter-charges surrounding Nosenko, suspecting that the CIA harbored a Soviet double agent. In the eyes of many—including William Colby—Angleton's suspicions caused enormous damage within the CIA and to relationships between the CIA and foreign intelligence agencies:

> What really turned me off [said Colby] was the discovery that counterintelligence theories were actually hurting good clandestine operational officers. One had come under suspicion through a gross leap in logic. A defector had remarked that the Soviets were in contact with a CIA officer in a particular city. By a process of elimination, suspicion had settled on this one. But absolutely no other evidence was ever found to support it, even after careful check. Nonetheless, the officer was sent off to a distant and dead-end post for a number of years as a result.[27]

* In due course, paranoia will overwhelm every counterintelligence officer, and this fact is taken advantage of in every conflict with them. All forms of reality begin to blur in such conditions.

† This was the view of Golytsin (referred to as "Mr. X" by the House Select Committee on Assassinations) which he had pressed upon Angleton: "One of his contentions was that the schism between the Soviet Union and China, Communist China, was simply a KGB disinformation ruse, designed to confuse the West," Peter Bagley testified. "He offered this theory quite seriously, and in some limited quarters within the agency, it came to be taken seriously" (House Select Committee on Assassinations, *Investigation of the Assassination of President John F. Kennedy*, Vol. II [March, 1979], p. 495). While public perceptions at the time shared Golytsin's and Angleton's suspicions about Sino-Soviet relations, analysts in the CIA had for years known that a serious and real rift between the two countries was growing.

On another occasion Angleton informed the head of French intelligence that David Murphy, the CIA's station chief in Paris, was a Soviet agent. The French checked with Colby. "After I had recovered from the shock and looked into the case, I discovered that similarly vague coincidences had once been used to bring him under suspicion. But the matter had been exhaustively investigated several years before, and the officer, a brilliant and effective one at that, was given a totally clean bill of health. But our counterintelligence had never accepted the conclusion."[28] The basis of Angleton's charges in each case had come from Golytsin.

BACK THROUGH THE LOOKING GLASS

Anatoly Golytsin had defected to the CIA in December 1961 from Finland, where he had been working as a KGB major in the First Chief Directorate (responsible for foreign operations), concentrating on NATO targets. He had been planning to defect for some time and had collected all the information he could on Soviet operations and agents in the West. This was to be his "treasure" for a new life once he had defected. His knowledge was vast, and he provided leads to over one hundred Russian spies and sources within the NATO alliance, as well as information about the KGB and its personnel. "The amount of information we got from Golytsin in the first forty-eight hours of his interrogation established in most people's minds that he was for real," a CIA officer who interrogated him said. "We knew quite a bit about the Soviet Embassy in Helsinki, and we were able to check his information against what we already knew."[29]

Golytsin used his extensive knowledge to back up an ever-increasing range of allegations about Soviet disinformation and scheming against the West, finding a ready acceptance of his theories at senior levels in the Counterintelligence Staff. James Angleton was particularly supportive of Golytsin's arguments and predictions about KGB intentions. One of the first predictions Golytsin made was that the KGB would spare no effort to discredit him. Within a few months three Soviet disinformation agents defected to other countries and then made contact with the CIA and the FBI ("Fedora"— J. Edgar Hoover's informant who had confirmed some of Nosenko's story— turned out to be one of them). Nosenko was suspected of being another—Golytsin was convinced of it—trying to mislead investigations started as a result of Golytsin's information. It was taken as convincing evidence that Golytsin's claims were genuine, and it gained the defector access to the top levels of the agency before he was fully debriefed.

Controversy began, as a result, within the CIA over the handling of Golytsin. Some questioned whether he was an *agent provocateur* himself, since he accused nearly every other defector of being one, and whether his information about Soviet intentions was accurate. One CIA officer who dealt with him presented his view of Golytsin and his dealings with the CIA:

> Golytsin is a very suspicious, very withdrawn, very difficult man. He saw his information as his only real capital in the West. Among defectors there are often two kinds of attitudes. One is that the West is a great opportunity, and they think they have this one chunk of gold, and every time they tell something they are cutting another piece off from it, and they feel when they finish they'll be thrown away. Golytsin from the beginning was bargaining about information. Part of his idea was that he should be made head of a NATO security service, a kind of Western Cheka, with a free hand. He was bitterly disappointed when this didn't happen.
>
> He had a lot of problems in getting along with people, and he was not handled very well. He was not confronted with the voice of authority. He was confronted with an awful lot of people in high positions, and none of them ever sat him down and said, "Tolya, this is the way it is. You do it our way or you're out as far as we're concerned." Somebody should have said that. Among other things, it is very characteristic if you've been brought up in Soviet officialdom always to seek the authoritative superior. A good bureaucrat anywhere, but particularly in that kind of system, will keep pushing until he finds the resistance of true authority.
>
> But that is not how Golytsin was handled. Instead he was introduced to one more level of authority, and it was hoped he would be overawed by position, but that was not what he was looking for. He was looking for someone who would tell him how to behave, essentially, and what his situation was and what he could expect. The trouble was he got out of the control of people who knew how to handle Russians and got higher and higher. In consequence, he got into the position of bargaining about information. Some of his initial information was very good, but after a while he came to realize he didn't necessarily have to tell the truth in order to get attention. His later information, from the fall of 1962, lacked an element of veracity. It was about that time that Angleton took over, apologized to him for the behavior of people who had tried to get him to straighten up a little bit, and Golytsin at that point realized he had a nice situation he could control, and he's traveled with it ever since.
>
> Being a colleague is very difficult for anyone trained in Soviet officialdom to understand. A successful worker in that system has to understand that it is very much a question of being servile and being dominant. Cooperation is not part of it. So if you find yourself a situation where you can dominate a boss, that's almost the ideal position, and that was the position Golytsin was in from that time on.[30]

At the heart of Golytsin's claims was the warning that the KGB had a massive, highly organized, coordinated, and sophisticated plan, backed up by enormous resources and highly placed agents inside Western governments and intelligence agencies, to mislead the West. Golytsin had enough information about Soviet agents to lend weight to his warnings. He provided leads to three

Soviet agents in England which resulted in their arrests and warned about a "Ring of Five" highly placed Soviet agents in Britain. Philby, Burgess, and Maclean had been three, but there were two more, said Golytsin, starting a twenty-year hunt for a Soviet spy in British intelligence.

In 1964 Anthony Blunt confessed to a British MI-5 interrogator that he had been a Russian spy and had tipped off Burgess and Maclean that they were under suspicion, prompting their flight to Moscow. Blunt had been tracked down not through information supplied by Golytsin but through the evidence of an American communist sympathizer Blunt had tried to recruit for the Soviets at Cambridge University in the 1930s, Michael Whitney Straight. Straight was undergoing security clearance by the FBI for the post of chairman of the Advisory Council on the Arts, offered to him by President Kennedy in 1963, and had thought it best to detail his communist past at Cambridge, implicating Blunt. This left Golytsin's fifth man, and suspicion eventually fell on Sir Roger Hollis, director general of MI-5 from 1956 to his retirement in 1965. No proof was ever found that Hollis had been a Soviet agent, and he was cleared on two separate occasions, first by an internal inquiry and then posthumously by his successor as director general and the prime minister in 1981.* But the search created turmoil in the British security services, and many of those affected believed that Golytsin could not have done more harm if he had been a Soviet agent.

Golytsin's information and James Angleton's belief in it also led to a similar experience in France. Golytsin revealed that there was a network, called Sapphire, of Soviet spies in the French government, including one on the staff

---

* The argument that Hollis was a Soviet agent stems from a mass of circumstantial evidence. In July 1984 Peter Wright, a former MI-5 officer who chaired the "Fluency" committee—a joint MI-5/MI-6 committee investigating KGB penetration of MI-5—stated that "intelligencewise it was 99 percent certain that [Sir Roger] was a spy" (*The Times* [London], July 16, 1984). Golytsin revealed that the KGB did have an agent in British intelligence up to the early 1960s and that as a KGB officer he had seen the contents of a document written by Wright in the possession of the British department of the KGB in Moscow.

This disclosure came at a time when British suspicions that there was a Soviet agent in their midst had been rearoused, said Wright, "because all the operations against the Russians, whether they were double agent or technical operations, failed fairly soon after they were started." Shortly before Hollis retired in 1965 he spoke to Wright. "Why do you think I am a spy?" he asked. "I pointed out that he was by far the best suspect," said Wright. "His reply to that was: 'Peter, you have got the manacles on me. . . . I can only tell you that I am not a spy' " (*The Times* [London], July 17, 1984).

Philby's defection to Moscow in 1963 prompted an internal MI-5 inquiry that pointed to Hollis' deputy, Graham Mitchell, as a Soviet agent. A subsequent MI-5 review pointed to Hollis as a spy. In 1974 the former cabinet secretary Lord Trend concluded that Hollis had not been a Soviet agent. Chapman Pincher, *Too Secret Too Long* (New York: St. Martin's Press, 1984), argues that Hollis was a Soviet agent from the 1930s until his death, but much of Pincher's case is tendentious. The suspicion that there may have been a high-level Soviet agent in British intelligence into the 1960s does not mean that it had to be Hollis. Maurice Oldfield, director general of MI-6 during 1973–78, thought that Guy Liddell, at one time Hollis' deputy, was more likely than Hollis to have been a Soviet agent (Richard Deacon, *"C"—A Biography of Sir Maurice Oldfield* [London: Macdonald, 1985], p. 86). The highest level Soviet defectors to the West all have denied that Hollis was a Soviet agent.

of the French cabinet. President Kennedy wrote a personal letter to President de Gaulle, warning him of the spy, thus starting another inconclusive hunt.* At the same time, however, Golytsin gave precise information: he exposed a senior French official at NATO as a Russian spy.

An earlier defector, Michael Goleniewski, corroborated much of Golytsin's initial information, lending further weight to Angleton's decision to act on virtually everything Golytsin said.† The trouble was that while some of Golytsin's information was accurate, some was not, and a good part of it fell into that murky category of information that could not be conclusively proved either way. It was a safe enough bet that the Soviets had a spy ring in France; ten years earlier Bedell Smith and Allen Dulles had decided that they could not trust the French with top-secret information because of this suspected penetration. It was also a safe enough bet that there was a "fifth" man in Britain, that German intelligence was penetrated, and so on. In all cases, some of the allegations were true and spies were caught as a result. It was just that the spies that were caught were almost secondary to the effort involved, which was directed at great plots and spy rings that were never proved.

The problem with Golytsin's information was that its benefits were matched by gnawing suspicions and disruptions within Western intelligence services. "It would be inaccurate to say that counter-Soviet operations ground to a halt," said one of those involved in tracking down Golytsin's leads, "but doing things like telling the French that Dave Murphy is a Soviet agent don't contribute to organizational smoothness. The Counterintelligence Staff was deeply divided with suspicion, but the fact is that at the same time there was a great deal going on that had nothing to do with that or with the debate over Nosenko."[31]

A great deal of the suspicion within the agency was generated by Golyt-

---

* Jacques Foccart, on de Gaulle's personal staff and an adviser to the president on intelligence matters, was accused of being the "French Philby" as a result. He sued a newspaper that published the accusation and was awarded damages.

† Goleniewski was a Polish intelligence officer who had been recruited by the KGB to report to them on the activities of his service. In 1960 he defected to the CIA in West Berlin, giving the names of several hundred Polish and Russian agents in the West. He revealed that Gordon Lonsdale, apparently a Canadian businessman living in London, was actually a Russian with false identity running a spy ring in England. This led to Lonsdale's arrest and eventual imprisonment (he was exchanged in 1964 for Greville Wynne, the English businessman and MI-6 agent who had acted as Penkovsky's contact) along with the capture and imprisonment of his ring, which included Peter and Helen Kroger, who turned out to be Morris and Lona Cohen of New York City. The Krogers/Cohens had been on the FBI wanted list since 1951 as suspected accomplices of the Rosenbergs.

Goleniewski provided the information that led to the arrest and conviction in 1961 of George Blake, a senior MI-6 officer serving in Berlin, for spying for the Soviets. Goleniewski also pointed to Heinz Felfe in West German intelligence as a spy; he was, and in tracking him down, another Russian spy, Hans Clemens, also in the Bundesnachrichtendienst (Federal Intelligence Service), was discovered. With many of Golytsin's leads meshing with Goleniewski's, and in the atmosphere of suspicion generated by the revelation of so many successful Soviet agents working in Western intelligence services, it was not surprising that Golytsin's information and allegations made the impression they did.

sin's statement that the KGB had a source they code-named "Sasha" who had penetrated the CIA's German operations and that there was a high-level Soviet agent in Langley. The pursuit of these agents—none was ever found—gradually made the Counterintelligence Staff paranoid about their own agency colleagues. It also caused Angleton to become increasingly reluctant to discuss his work with anyone but the director of Central Intelligence, and then only in terms of the strictest secrecy. In itself this was perfectly understandable and proper, given the sensitivity of counterintelligence operations. It was also proper to wonder why the agency had never found a Soviet agent in its midst although every other Western intelligence service had been penetrated, and Angleton diligently pursued this line of thought.

But by the time William Colby became DCI, the careers of too many people had been hurt and, in Colby's view at least, Angleton's suspicions had become too extreme. Despite the fact that Michael Goleniewski's information meshed with Golytsin's, and despite the fact that Goleniewski had revealed high-level Soviet agents in British and German intelligence (George Blake and Heinz Felfe respectively) and had given a crucial lead to an American, Sergeant Robert Lee Johnson, who while serving in Paris at NATO's Armed Forces Courier Station had supplied the Russians with priceless NATO strategy documents, Angleton came to believe that Goleniewski was a Soviet disinformation agent. There was evidence to support this hypothesis. Before he defected, Goleniewski had sent information to the CIA by letter. "The key to the Goleniewski case," a member of the Counterintelligence Staff said, "is that the Soviets became aware that somebody was writing these letters. There was a feedback in Goleniewski's later letters of things he'd learned from the Soviets. . . . The Soviets began inserting corrections into his previous information."[32]

An investigation determined that Goleniewski had probably been used by the KGB without his knowledge but that most of his information was genuine. One of Angleton's critics saw it this way:

> It seems to me that the Angleton et al. argument is one that people who do not know anything about the significance of strategic and military intelligence can come to because of their own narrow focus on counterintelligence. The Sergeant Johnson case caused an enormous redoing at the cost of hundreds of millions of dollars of the SIOP [Single Integrated Operating Plan], our major strategic plan, when it was realized that very likely it had been exposed to the Soviets. To have pretended our ignorance of the fact that we knew they had the plan, as Angleton argued because he wanted to mislead the Soviets as to our knowledge, would have meant having to keep the plan, because changing it would be obvious to the Soviets, and this would have been intensely valuable to the Soviet High Command. This, apparently, cut no ice at all with Angleton. He said that the Soviets were prepared to have Johnson revealed because he had been reassigned back from Paris to Washington and was no longer in a key position and they already had the docu-

ments, so what did they care? But what that argument omits is the enduring significance of having all of the basic planning documents for targeting which, presumably, Johnson delivered.[33]

With Nosenko's arrival in 1964, Golytsin's suspicions were fueled again, and through him, Angleton's. "Golytsin came to have a hypnotic effect over Jim and two or three other people," said a colleague. "Once in this position, having created the division in the staff and having fed Angleton's chronic suspicions, part of proving his case right was to show up disinformation agents and find the penetration of the agency."[34] Over the next few years, at least three CIA officers found their careers blighted as a result of suspicion falling on them from Golytsin's accusations. At one stage the search for "Sasha" affected an unfortunate officer whose name was Sasha until the point was made that the KGB was very unlikely to give an agent his real name as a code name. Then Golytsin remembered that "Sasha's" real name began with a K, and for several months officers unlucky enough to have names starting with K and who had served in Germany found themselves under embarrassing scrutiny. One officer resigned in frustration. Another was fired because he could not prove his innocence. Richard Helms, then DDP, took the view, quite correctly, that the agency could not afford to keep on someone who *might* be a Soviet agent. Although this was hard on the man concerned, it was, nevertheless, prudent.

COLBY DECIDES

None of this, however, was conducive to good morale or harmonious working relationships. "I doubt if the agency was ever penetrated at a significant level," said Donald Jameson, a longtime Soviet Russia Division officer, and went on to explain:

The basic reason that I don't think it was, because logically it should have been, is the polygraph. I respect it. I acquired that respect because I did a lot of interrogation, and I've seen what the machine can do. It provides a very substantial barrier. There are one or two funny cases that went awry in that period, and one explanation is that someone on the inside tipped off the opposition. But there are other explanations too—penetration at a low level; insecurity of the operation. I don't know of any serious evidence against a CIA officer that has ever come out of any of the defectors or anyone else. It does not mean that there has not been a penetration, just that I don't think there has been and that none has been found.*

* Interview, Donald Jameson, November 16, 1984. Others did not agree that the polygraph was a substantial barrier. Richard Helms, in discussing the Nosenko case, said:

We discovered that there were some Eastern Europeans who could defeat the polygraph at any time. Americans are not very good at it, because we are raised to tell the truth and when

In 1967 the Counterintelligence Staff conducted a survey of the number of defectors who actually confessed to being disinformation agents as opposed to those who were simply suspected of being ones since the start of the agency's defector-handling system in 1951. Between 1951 and 1967 there were fewer than thirty confessed disinformation agents. A subsequent survey some years later showed that only one defector confessed to being a disinformation agent in the period from January 1968 to January 1973. This coincided with a change in the handling procedures: instead of being brought straight to Washington, defectors were first interrogated and given a polygraph test locally. If they did not pass they were put in a refugee camp and kept away from the agency and the mainstream of American intelligence, while a decision was made on whether or not to return them. If not, they would be allowed to resettle in the West, but with no agency help.

The KGB's obvious interest in sending witting or unwitting disinformation agents to the United States naturally lent weight to suspicions of every defector. But when it came to Nosenko and the way he was handled, there was a general sense that Angleton had overreached. As one man involved with the Nosenko and Golytsin cases, said:

> I do not believe that in November/December 1963 an agent being briefed in Moscow to go as a phony to the United States would have been told anything at all about Oswald in the Soviet Union, because they would have to assume that their agent would be doubled and that whatever they told him would be explained by him as part of his briefing. So whatever they said, particularly from their own point of view, about such things would be subject to the interpretation that somehow the KGB was behind the assassination of President Kennedy, which is something I was convinced they would be at great pains to avoid. If Nosenko had come out and said, "Yes, I was briefed that we had nothing to do with it," then, aha! Or suppose, "I was briefed that we

---

we lie it is easy to tell we are lying. But we find a lot of Europeans and Asiatics can handle that polygraph without a blip, and you know they are lying and you have the evidence that they are lying. . . .

There is an occasional individual who lives in that part of the world who has spent his life lying about one thing or another and therefore becomes so good at it that he can pass the polygraph test. But this would be one individual in maybe 1 million or a 100,000, something of that kind. I imagine Americans, if they set their minds to it, could do it as well. I meant no offense to Eastern Europeans as a category or any individual Eastern European. (*Investigation of the Assassination of President John F. Kennedy*, Vol. IV, pp. 98–99, 118

Helms had come to realize that cultural differences really were differences, and that people from different cultures could fool machines. The question of moral fatigue after decades of constant conflict and unchanged "world crisis" is again raised. Despite massive effort, Helms was admitting that American culture had not been able to dominate other cultures, and was itself vulnerable to penetration by other cultures. Interestingly, the first long-term penetration of the CIA was by an analyst, Larry Wu-Tai Chin, arrested in November 1985 for spying for China since the early 1950s.

did." There is nothing you can say about it if you assume your agent will confess.[35]

After nearly ten years of internal wrangling over the conundrums of counterintelligence and disinformation theories, Colby simply decided to cut through it all and have the Counterintelligence Staff concentrate on their main task of penetrating rival and enemy intelligence organizations.

Angleton had many supporters within the agency as well. Richard Helms was one because he appreciated Angleton's skill and intellectual agility, although he never accepted Angleton's theory that there was a Soviet agent in the CIA. Said Helms in 1983:

> I don't think the core of the agency was ever penetrated, at least while I was there. Nobody has ever demonstrated that it has been. There may have been somebody on the fringes or there might have been some contact agent doing translations downtown, but nothing in the core. As director I was aware every day when I went to work that somebody might come up on the elevator and say, "My God! We've found that so-and-so is a penetration agent right in the heart of the agency!" That is a director's nightmare. Other things may be unpleasant, but that's his nightmare because that's what he's meant to be able to prevent.[36]

Angleton was the director's preventer, and many recognized that he had to pay a penalty for the position: his suspicions would always be matched by the suspicions of others about him, and since his job was about suspicion, it was inevitable that some suspicions would be wrong and hurtful. He represented a lesser disease inoculating against a greater one, but a disease despite that. There was also an inevitable tension between those who were doing the recruiting for the agency and those, like Angleton, who were attempting to see to it that those recruited were not penetration agents.

Angleton's role was akin to that of the Grand Inquisitor: if he were not there, the defense would run away with the case. If counterintelligence was not sustained, the enthusiasm of the recruiters would inevitably lead to the recruitment of some dubious people and the greater chance of the agency's being penetrated. Many people felt that there had to be somebody like Angleton in the agency—someone who distrusted everything and virtually everyone and was willing to tread on anyone in his way in his search for penetration agents—even if at times the effect was overdone.

Colby, however, felt that Angleton had taken his efforts to an extreme and that it was time for him to go. Describing how he finally asked Angleton to leave, Colby said:

> Angleton had one major responsibility other than counterintelligence—Israel—which he had traditionally handled in the same totally compartmented fashion as counterintelligence. . . . I called Angleton into my office to talk the

matter out with him, saying that I had come to the conclusion that a change was necessary in both jobs, the Israeli liaison and counterintelligence, but that I wanted to retain his talents for the agency, and especially his experience. I offered him the prospect of a separate status, where he could summarize for us the many ideas he had and conclusions he had reached about counterintelligence, and where he would be consulted on, but no longer be in charge of, our Israeli liaison.*

While Angleton went off to think about the offer a storm broke around Colby's, Angleton's, and the agency's heads.

THE CLOSET OPENS

On December 18, 1974, the day after his conversation with Angleton, Colby received a telephone call from Seymour Hersh, a leading investigative reporter on *The New York Times* who in 1970 had won a Pulitzer Prize, a Polk Award, and the Worth Bingham Prize for uncovering and reporting the My Lai massacre.† He had, he said to Colby, "a story bigger than My Lai" about illegal CIA domestic activities. Some of "The Skeletons" were now coming out, and it was Colby's situation to be the director of Central Intelligence during the time the agency's innermost secrets were revealed in public. Hersh said he had details of Operation Chaos' surveillance of American antiwar groups— the wiretaps, mail openings, and so on—and his view was that it had all been in breach of the CIA charter.

On December 20 Colby met Hersh in his office and attempted to clarify the story. He said that it was right and proper for the CIA to investigate the antiwar movement to see if a foreign power were involved. When this investigation revealed that there was no foreign involvement, the operation ended. The mail interception and wiretaps were another matter, Colby explained, and were not connected to the antiwar movement; they were part of the CIA's proper effort to protect intelligence sources and techniques against leaks. Then Colby went on to admit that "on some few occasions in its twenty-eight-year history [the CIA] had used such surveillance techniques in the United States and in so doing had overstepped the boundaries of its charter. But the impor-

---

* William Colby and Peter Forbath, *Honorable Men: My Life in the CIA* (New York: Simon & Schuster, 1978), pp. 365, 387. Angleton was right to act in this way. Israel was a naturally compromised country because of its connections with the Soviet bloc through mass Jewish immigration from Eastern Europe and the Soviet Union. Several high-level Israeli officials over the years had been revealed as Soviet spies. There were sound historical reasons for compartmentalizing Israeli-CIA relations.

† The My Lai massacre took place in Vietnam on March 16, 1968, and was first reported (by Hersh) on November 16, 1969. American infantrymen under the command of Lieutenant William L. Calley, Jr., killed at least 450 unarmed South Vietnamese civilians—men, women, and children. On November 24, 1969, Calley was court-martialed and in March 1971 convicted of the premeditated murder of 22 Vietnamese civilians.

tant point, I emphasized, was that the agency had conducted its own review of such activities in 1973 and had issued a series of clear directives making plain that the agency henceforth must and would stay within the law."[37]

He had confirmed the essence of Hersh's story, agreeing that the agency had broken the law—something that none of his predecessors had ever conceded and something that no court of law or Congress had ever held. In so doing he effectively admitted that his predecessors, particularly Richard Helms, during whose directorship the antiwar surveillance was conducted, had exceeded their powers and acted illegally. He sat as judge, jury, and court, giving Hersh authoritative support for a headline-grabbing story. Immediately after his conversation with Hersh, Colby called Angleton (who had been responsible for the "illegal" surveillance) and told him that he had to go, that Colby's decision was firm, and that the news of Angleton's mail openings was about to break in the press.

Angleton and his senior assistants resigned, in their view having been "purged" and convinced that Colby had leaked the evidence of the mail openings to Hersh in order to get rid of them.* Some harbored even darker thoughts: that the high-level Soviet penetration of the agency suggested by Golytsin ten years earlier had finally succeeded in ousting the trackers.[38] On Sunday, December 22, 1974, Hersh's story was front-page news in *The New York Times*: "Huge CIA Operation Reported in U.S. Against Anti-War Forces, Other Dissidents in Nixon Years," was the banner headline. "The Central Intelligence Agency," the article began, "directly violating its charter, conducted a massive illegal domestic intelligence operation during the Nixon Administration against the anti-war movement and other dissident groups in the United States, according to well-placed Government sources."

This was the start of the public scrutiny of the history of the CIA, giving onlookers the extraordinary spectacle of a secret service having its secrets re-

---

* "Colby had opposed the role of the Counterintelligence Staff for some years," said Edward Jay Epstein in his book *Legend* (New York: Ballantine Books, 1981):

His dispute with Angleton had come into the open when Colby headed the CIA mission to Vietnam in the late 1960s and decided to terminate all counterintelligence activities in that country. This meant, in effect, that the CIA could not question or evaluate the sources of information in Vietnam. By routinely questioning the validity of information supplied to the CIA by double agents and continually suspecting that the data might be disinformation, Angleton had tended to inhibit the collection of information from the Soviet Union and Eastern Europe. It made the CIA's task of measuring the intentions of the Soviet Union that much more difficult.

After Hersh left his office, Colby called in Angleton and his chief assistants. . . . He asked for Angleton's resignation and made it clear to the assistants that they would not be promoted within the CIA. All accommodated him by resigning. . . . Among those "purged," as Angleton put it, were the authors of the counterintelligence reviews and evaluations of the Nosenko case (Ibid., pp. 268–277).

Colby had not, in fact, opposed the role of the counterintelligence staff: he had opposed its scope. His criticism was CI's lack of specificity. He wanted CI to pinpoint problems, not simply to be suspicious of everyone and everything.

vealed by the nation on whose behalf it operated. The withdrawal of Johnson from politics in 1968 and the fall of Nixon in 1974 had encouraged people generally to withdraw support for everything that had been part of the status quo in the late 1960s and early 1970s. The fact that the agency had not been operating "against" the antiwar movement, but had given the movement a clean bill of health and had acted entirely professionally in its investigation, was ignored. Colby had warned Nixon's successor, Gerald Ford, that a difficult story was about to break after he had spoken to Hersh, and "when the story came out, I got on the phone to the President and said: 'Nothing like that happens now. Whatever happened in the past, it's not going on now.' And then I said, 'I'll give you a report in a day or two.' "[39]

The result was the "Vail Report" on the CIA's domestic activities, which Colby produced from his earlier "Skeletons" survey in an unclassified form so that it could be released by the White House to the press. "My thought was that the easiest way to cut this off was to release the true story. Other people prevailed in a decision not to release anything on the grounds that it would just get out of hand. Then the House Armed Services Committee and the Senate Appropriations Committee held a joint hearing in closed session, and I presented essentially the same report to them. They said they didn't see anything classified in it, and I was forced to say there wasn't, so they said they'd release it."* There was no prior consultation with the White House this time: it was the start of the Congress asserting that its rights to control and review the CIA were equal to those of the President. Colby stuck to his decision that the only way to save the agency, as the storm of Watergate churned overhead, was to reveal many of its secrets, making it clear that they related to days past and would not be repeated.

This attitude placed Colby squarely in the middle of controversy. President Ford certainly did not want responsibility for broadcasting America's secrets publicly or for accusing, by implication, his predecessors of dirty tricks and illegal actions. Colleagues in the CIA, past and present, were naturally alarmed at the prospect of their secrets being revealed, particularly when their director was saying that some of their past activities had moved beyond the boundary of law. Many feared that they just might end up convicted of crimes they never realized they were committing. For Congress the prospect that the CIA's secrets would be revealed meant that it would have to address its respon-

---

* Interview, William Colby, July 25, 1983. Vail, Colorado, was where President Ford was spending Christmas. Colby had taken the report and "The Skeletons" to Henry Kissinger, who had been a loud critic of Colby's "reveal all" approach. "When he came to the part about the assassinations he slowed down," Colby recalled. "Well, Bill," said Kissinger, "when Hersh's story first came out I thought you should have flatly denied it as totally wrong, but now I see why you couldn't" (Colby, *Honorable Men*, pp. 394–395).

By his candor, Colby had made the question of revelation a matter of U.S. government policy, and had entwined the whole government with responsibility. The U.S. government would now have to look hard at how it had done business for decades.

sibility for the laws under which the CIA operated; it would have to reconsider the system of reporting that had operated with the CIA since 1947; it would have to take a clear position with regard to the CIA in relation to the executive branch (this was possibly a constitutional issue); and it would have to do something—exactly what was not clear—about the CIA. It was a mess for everyone.

The matter was complicated further by the view taken by Larry Silberman, the acting attorney general: "What else have you boys got tucked away up your sleeves?" he asked Colby after the Hersh story broke. "What's this one all about, Bill?" Colby told him what he had told the President and also about the existence of "The Skeletons" list. "That's very interesting. Tell me, did you turn that list over to the Justice Department?"

"No."

"You know what that amounts to? You're a lawyer, Bill. You have had in your possession evidence of illegal actions. As a public servant, you're obliged to turn such evidence over to the proper authorities, in this case the Department of Justice. In withholding that evidence for a year and a half, Bill, you may have committed a crime yourself."

"The thought that the Jewels should have been reported to Justice never crossed my mind," said Colby, shocked by Silberman's statement. "I reported the list to the chairmen of our appropriate congressional committees and issued the directives that corrected the situation. I thought that was sufficient."

"Well, maybe. But in any case you better let me have that list and I'll see what we should do about it." After the Hersh article, the matter was actually out of Colby's hands: Silberman had taken it into the remit of the Justice Department.

Within the agency a different view was put to Colby. One retired officer asked him rather pointedly if he was going to try to save the agency. "Yes," said Colby, "but I won't lie and I won't do anything illegal."

"Does that mean I would?" said his questioner sharply.

"No, I don't mean that, but I want my limits to be clear."

"What am I going to tell my children?" said CIA people as the revelations of questionable activities began to mushroom in Congress and the press. Colby called a meeting of the agency's officers in the main auditorium at Langley five days after Christmas to try to reassure them that he was trying to protect the agency. He briefed them on "The Skeletons," the exaggerations of the Hersh article, and the 1973 directives ending dubious operations. The agency would survive, he argued, if it could get the true story across. He believed that "no fair jury would convict CIA officers for these long-past activities, which had been undertaken in totally different circumstances and atmospheres than today's." "How a nation that has assigned them difficult and dangerous work in the past could be discussing prosecuting them for doing it today" was a question asked in fury by many there that day.[40]

One senior Directorate of Operations officer went to see Colby privately in his office. "You just don't go down to Congress and tell them all," he said. "If you do it to one committee, you're going to have to do it to another. Just turn up your coat collar and don't say anything. Live it through. Don't make apologies." Colby refused to accept this view: he had determined his course of action. He was going to "kick out the Eastern Establishment" (of which he, as a graduate of Princeton and Columbia, was part), which he identified with the Directorate of Operations. "I want an American service," he declared. "I am going to make the Clandestine Service part of the CIA, and the CIA part of the intelligence community." The officer, who strongly disagreed, argued that by doing this Colby would destroy the covert operations section which had to remain small, flexible, and elite, separate from the rest of the agency, if it was to function as a human intelligence espionage service. Colby dismissed this argument, and the officer resigned from the agency soon afterwards.[41]

Colby had taken a moralist position, in tune with the intense moralism of the times. He was genuinely affected by the attitude that the agency had apparently become dangerously self-directed and not oriented toward the country's wishes and needs. He was probably tired of the deceptions, and doubted whether human intelligence and covert operations had been worthwhile. His course was a reductionist one, making both the DDO and the CIA less than what they had been. He realized that the nation did have an opinion, and was intent on making himself (and the agency) an American-of-the-moment, willingly surrendering a longer view of American intelligence in the process. An "American" agency would be one that felt good and had no real secrets, rather than an agency that had unpleasant secrets and sometimes dirty hands. Colby, in a completely different way from Helms, was saving the bulk—the bureaucracy—of the CIA, not its purpose or spirit.

The Hersh article was a turning point for the CIA—and for the American public.

> Overnight CIA became a sinister shadow organization in the minds of the American people [said David Atlee Phillips reflectively]. Visions of a CIA payroll swollen with zealous and ubiquitous cloak-and-dagger villains impervious to good judgment and outside control arose throughout the country. CIA was seen as what the detractors had been so long claiming: unprincipled spooks threatening American society. That was not the CIA I knew, but I realized that any image less sinister would never really be believed by Americans still stunned by Watergate. . . . The Hersh story, I found on returning to Langley after the Christmas holidays, had produced massive cracks in what had been up to that time a fairly monolithic intelligence establishment.[42]

One of the biggest cracks was the difference in attitude of Colby when compared to that of his predecessors. He had, as he saw it in the interests of the agency, become a boy scout determined to do good regardless of cost, convinced that his decision was the only one that would secure salvation. In contrast, Richard Helms, seeing the dangers of investigation looming in 1972 as Watergate stirred, had ordered that all the original records of the MKUltra programs be destroyed. His approach had been to limit and to contain, using closed hearings and executive sessions in Congress to detail to the appropriate committees and chairmen the activities that might be considered dubious. The understandings had operated for him, and he was never under the same pressure as director that Colby was to be, but the difference was clear. Helms would never have agreed that the CIA had ever operated illegally. Helms would never have compiled a "Skeletons" list that might get out. It was to be both men's fate that they would from now on be compared to each other as competitors for the real heart of the agency, as its best defender.

Was Colby right? Was it his job to try to save the agency? If the agency was the President's men, wasn't it up to the President to save them? And if the President made no move to do so, wasn't it the CIA's duty to accept the consequences silently as one of those things that the President wanted but could not say he wanted? As a presidential appointee, shouldn't Colby have checked with the President to make sure that it was all right to reveal "The Skeletons"? Shouldn't he have checked with his own general counsel before admitting that the agency had acted illegally? In addressing this point, Colby said:

> I think that in our society, not just in our government, if you take a number of people and put them in a career position, they'll fight to maintain it. They'll differ as to how to maintain it, but they'll fight to maintain it. Everybody will fight to maintain the integrity of the career they've adopted, and in that sense if the President wanted to get rid of it, yes, he could do it. Truman got rid of OSS with the stroke of a pen. I think the people in the White House for a long time were delighted that I was doing it and keeping it out of the White House. I certainly didn't get any criticism from them along that line. What I got was some criticism that I was being too generous with some of the information. I had a sense that they wished it wouldn't happen—I wished it wouldn't happen myself—but if it happened, I was the head of the organization and took the rap for it.[43]

The imperatives of the organization had taken over. The integrity of careers, the nature of the institution of the CIA were now at the forefront, rather than the job it was meant to do. The whole concept of covert action in peacetime enshrined in the agency was new to the United States. It was going to have growing pains no matter what happened, and some of the pains would be severe. With Watergate the CIA placed itself within American society as just another government agency, staffed by people with a healthy sense of their career interests, involved in foreign affairs, no longer with its most acute growing pains. Symptomatic of this was the fact that William Colby saw the President alone only three times in the two years and five months he was director; the CIA by 1973 was no longer close to the President or the President's principal men. It had matured into a forthright service, forthrightly keeping an eye on America's opponents, operating fairly quietly abroad. If it were to become involved in another Bay of Pigs or Iranian operation, everyone would know, and everyone would judge.

The agency's operations in El Salvador, Nicaragua, and Honduras in the 1980s are known in some detail. If Congress does not like them, Congress can stop them, unless the President is prepared to use discretionary funds. If Congress wants to know anything about the operations, Congress is told in full. If the President wants the agency to do something that Congress does not like, the agency can do it, but ultimately Congress has to agree or else the activity stops. All this came out of the Watergate atmosphere and the publicity about the CIA's first twenty-eight years. If America was to have a shadowy monster, Americans would accept it as long as they knew it was *their* monster, not just the President's, and as long as they knew its basic shape.

GUARDIANS OF THE TEXT?

Despite the fact that the role of the agency had changed from being "can do" and generalist at the President's instruction to being "can't do unless it's clearly legal" and "as long as Congress knows," the analytical side of the house maintained its position within the bureaucracy and with the presidency. Its technical-collection expertise commanded attention and now rapidly became the agency's other principal element (rather than covert actions and clandestine functions) as people found comfort in the quantifiable and the agency's ability to detect patterns. They no longer wanted to face the moral questions and problems of judgment inherent in clandestine activity.

Colby oversaw the reorganization of the Office and the Board of National Estimates first planned by Schlesinger. The membership of the board (composed of academics and experts) had dropped to six by June 1973, when Colby took over as director. The reduction (from an average of twelve members) came about because of retirements that occurred at the same time. In this respect the board mirrored a more widespread change in the agency which was not directly related to Schlesinger's firings. Matching the changes in the agency that flowed from intense congressional interest, was the natural change that came from personnel turnover. The founding generation was rapidly retiring. The Schlesinger cuts had compounded the sense of moral fatigue following nearly three decades of strenuous operation which had not produced a manifestly better world. In the space of three years, as a result, there was a higher rate of retirement than usual as many officers, disenchanted with government policy and the diminution of the agency in the bureaucratic framework, chose to leave despite the fact that they had not reached retirement age.

Colby wisely tried to take advantage of the resulting personnel changes to draw new people into the middle levels of the agency. He also had specific ideas about the analytical work of the agency, and he wanted to make it more immediate, faster, and less academically conscious. "I had sensed an ivory-tower mentality in the Board," Colby elaborated. "Its composition had tended to shift to a high proportion of senior analysts who had spent most of their careers at Langley and who had developed a 'mind-set' about a number of the issues. . . . I was convinced that change was needed if their inclination toward fixed positions was not to lead to trouble." As for the Office of National Estimates, "I was troubled over how badly the machinery was organized to serve me. If I wanted to know what was happening in China, for example, I would have to assemble individual experts in China's politics, its economics, its military, its personalities, as well as the clandestine operators who would tell me things they would tell no one else. Or I could commission a study that would, after weeks of debate, deliver a broad set of generalizations that might be accurate but would be neither timely nor sharp."[44]

He decided to replace the board with experts on the major issues of concern, expanding upon what Richard Helms had done with his special assistant for Vietnamese affairs and Schlesinger had copied with the appointment of a second special assistant for Mideast affairs. A trouble spot or troublesome issue would have one national intelligence officer (NIO) familiar with all aspects of the problem. John Huizenga resisted Colby's proposals to the utmost, resigning from the agency rather than accept them, on the grounds that the independence of the Estimates would be compromised because individual experts would find it far more difficult to stand up to White House pressures. "You can't take the position that it's never good to reorganize," said Huizenga. "I don't have an opinion if the things McCone did were useful or damaging. But by the time you get to Colby's period, reorganization for reorganization's sake became the thing, and by and large it was destructive." As far as he was concerned, there had been enough reorganization under Schlesinger, and by further interfering with people's accustomed ways of doing things and of relating to each other, serious disorientation would result. "It's a human structure. People are accustomed to certain relationships. If you start mucking around with them, people get uncomfortable and worried, and it affects their capability."[45] (See Appendix VI.)

As usual, however, once a bureaucratic reorganization is implemented, it develops its own momentum and gathers its supporters. The system of national intelligence officers was far more personalized than the old system, and the Estimates experienced some changes as a result. Whereas the Office of National Estimates had regarded itself as the custodian of the text, the guardians of the independence of the Estimates, Colby insisted that this was his responsibility as director. The Estimates were *his* Estimates. In the old system the principle of footnoting allowed dissent to be expressed on important matters and was part of an overall effort to achieve consensus within the intelligence community. There was no room for petty disagreements over words or formulations.

The text of an Estimate was scrubbed down by the analysts and the board, trimmed of qualification whenever possible. Estimates under the national intelligence officer system were not subjected to the same testing process and tended to reflect the qualities of the NIO concerned. Dissent was now incorporated in the text rather than footnoted.

To many this was another indication of the decline in the status of the agency. When it had been responsible for divining and expressing the intelligence community's consensus on a subject, the onus was on those who footnoted their disagreements to make their case. In the new system those disagreements were seen as being given equal weight with the agency's view, making the CIA judgment simply one of the several judgments competing for favor with the President. On the other hand, each NIO had a strong interest in maintaining his reputation personally and in writing clear and effective Estimates. The officers were not plagued with the job of having to write Estimates by committee and could—as Colby had wanted—react more quickly to events.

The United States Intelligence Board remained as a scrutinizing committee, which now no longer competed with the board for the role of "Wise Man." In 1977 there was a partial return to the old system in one respect: the national intelligence officers were grouped to form a National Intelligence Council and were separated from the Directorate of Intelligence in the same way the old Board of National Estimates had been. But the idea of single specialists with an overview of their subject area, protected from a mushrooming of committees, survived.

The new arrangements reflected a shift in the demands of the intelligence consumer. In the early days, considered, wide-ranging assessments were digested by presidential advisers. During the 1960s the previous hunger for scarce information, which had characterized the early intelligence consumers, was replaced by a lesser fear of the other side and a tendency for decision makers to fly to places to see for themselves. This reduced the significance of the Estimates. The NIO structure represented a diminished faith in analytic intelligence and was an institutional change reflecting a serious failure in political intelligence on the Middle East.

BLOOD AND OIL

Early in 1973, as Schlesinger's cuts took place and Colby's plans took shape, the agency was hit by another important intelligence failure, which for a time weakened its best asset, the respect for its analysis. The subject was the likelihood of war starting in the Middle East again. In 1967 the Israelis had launched their preemptive strike against Egypt and had gone on to win the Six-Day War, occupying the Sinai to the banks of the Suez Canal and taking the West Bank of the Sea of Galilee and the Arab section of Jerusalem from Jordan. One of the results of the war was a heightening of tensions in Soviet and American interest in the Middle East. It was obvious from the moment of cease-fire that the Israeli occupation of parts of Egypt and Jordan could not last without either further conflict or a negotiated settlement. In preparation for these alternatives the Soviet Union stepped up its aid to Egypt and Syria, while the United States increased its aid to Israel.

The year before, one of Richard Helms's first jobs for President Johnson had been to provide a statement of "how we have helped Israel." In a succinct report the CIA stated that "U.S. aid through F[inancial] Y[ear] 66 will total $1.1 billion," with "around $40 million for this year's slice of the tank and plane sales—the highest yearly total since FY 58," and "on the diplomatic front, the preservation of Israel is one of our three top objectives in the Middle East." Aid to Jordan, considered a moderate buffer on Israel's longest border and in Israel's interest, amounted to $520 million in 1965, including the payments by the agency to King Hussein of Jordan, started fifteen years earlier.[46]

When the Six-Day War came in 1967, Helms was confident that Israel would win. Moreover, the war was seen by Walt Rostow and President Johnson's foreign-policy advisers as presenting an opportunity to reach a definitive settlement in the Middle East. On June 6, 1967, the day after the Israeli pre-emptive strikes, Rostow wrote to the President, "If the Israelis go fast enough, and the Soviets get worried enough, a simple ceasefire might be the best answer. This would mean that we could use the *de facto* situation on the ground to try to negotiate not a return to armistice lines but a definitive peace in the Middle East."[47] It was, thought Rostow, a perfect time for American diplomatic initiatives to encourage the Arabs and the Israelis to settle their differences themselves by negotiation. Within two days of the war's starting, Israel had already gained enough ground and weakened the Egyptians sufficiently for the Arabs to feel that they might have something to gain, after all, from talking to the Israelis across the conference table.

The consensus in Washington was that a stronger Israel would hasten a peaceful Middle East settlement. This consensus soon changed, however, and American support for Israel, almost regardless of its effect in the Middle East, became the policy. Domestic American political considerations and an emotional sympathy for the small state of Israel, with the harrowing history of its people, surrounded by aggressive and populous neighbors, played a greater part in determining America's approach. After the Six-Day War, U.S. military and economic aid to Israel soared, with over 99 percent of the more than $17 billion in military aid in the period 1946–83 being provided after 1965.* One of

---

* The CIA has been reported as helping to develop Israel's nuclear-weapons program, and the cooperation between the Israeli intelligence services, particularly Mossad (the Israeli equivalent of the CIA), and the U.S. intelligence community became very close (Stephen Green, *Taking Sides: America's Secret Relations with a Militant Israel* [New York: Morrow, 1984], pp. 250–253). This seems unlikely. The CIA has no known nuclear-weapon manufacturing expertise of its own, and it is improbable that the United States would risk being associated with an Israeli program. Israel has the scientific and engineering talent required: the Technion is one of the world's leading technological institutes.

the things that annoyed President Nixon about the agency was its close connections with foreign intelligence services, notably the British, German, and Israeli services, which, he felt, the CIA relied on to an excessive extent. This was all in the background in 1973 as war clouds loomed once more in the Middle East.

President Anwar Sadat of Egypt, who succeeded President Nasser after his death in 1970 (it was rumored that Nasser had been poisoned), immediately attempted to reach a negotiated settlement with Israel, insisting that a necessary precondition was the withdrawal of Israeli forces to the pre–Six-Day War frontier. This was something the Israeli government would not accept. Withdrawal in part was possible (and eventually achieved in 1979), but Israel would not accept the return of Jerusalem or the West Bank previously held by Jordan. Faced with this impasse, Sadat decided that war was his only hope of regaining the Sinai and achieving a breakthrough toward a settlement with Israel. He made no secret of his intentions, but few believed him. The comparative strength of Israel after five years of massively increased American aid, and the prevalent view that what the Israelis had done in the Six-Day War they could always do again, meant that analysts in all the intelligence agencies in Washington, and not just in the CIA, tended to downplay Sadat's threats of confrontation.

The CIA was the first to suggest in a National Intelligence Estimate on the Middle East on April 20, 1973, that Sadat might have begun to take his own talk seriously but that there was no evidence of specific military operation plans for a specific time. It concluded that Sadat would continue to try for a political and diplomatic solution with Israel, but if that did not work he would probably go to war.[48] On May 5 James Schlesinger sent Henry Kissinger (soon to be secretary of state as well as national security adviser) a report that Sadat had ordered the preparation of military plans for crossing the Suez Canal and attacking the Israeli army in the Sinai. He added that the CIA did not believe that the plan described matched up with Sadat's objectives: the plan was for psychological rather than practical purposes. "Overall the CIA did not believe that an outbreak of hostilities was likely before the next UN debate (scheduled for mid-summer). Similarly, an interagency report of mid-May noted that even if the UN debate passed without useful results, 'this does not mean that hostilities will then become inevitable or even probable,' " Kissinger recalled.

Ten days later Schlesinger said that Egypt's military capabilities were limited to "a sneak air attack on Israel," which would be a move "extremely ill-advised," and that if the Egyptian army did cross the canal, it would not be able to hold "even a small amount of territory . . . for as much as one week." These later conclusions were an example of bad analysis: that the Egyptians, because they were outclassed technically, would not attack because they would be beaten. Sadat was pursuing *political* objectives, and the political incentives for him to attack were great: it would accelerate a solution. After April, the CIA had not analyzed the politico-military combination well. Only Ray Cline,

as head of the State Department's Bureau of Intelligence and Research, disagreed with the CIA's later assessment, reasoning that Sadat must be strongly
tempted to resort to arms if diplomacy proved fruitless, concluding that the
"resumption of hostilities by autumn will become a better than even bet."[49]

By September 1973, however, even the Bureau of Intelligence and Research agreed with all the other intelligence agencies that the political climate
in the Arab states was not conducive to a major war. Everyone assumed that
the Arabs were not ready to make war and thought that they would be defeated
even more seriously than in 1967 if they did go to war. Retrospective analysis
of this intelligence breakdown conducted by the CIA determined that the
whole system had failed. The National Security Agency had intercepted thousands of Arab communications indicating war and detailing plans, but because
of the sheer volume of these messages, many key intercepts were never analyzed. In addition, some of the more sensitive of the NSA's intercepts (revealing cryptographic success or unexpected monitoring ability) were held back
from analysts for security purposes. The secret methods of Henry Kissinger and
President Nixon prevented analysts from having access to their conversations
with heads of state and high-level diplomatic connections. A CIA source, who
accurately reported Egyptian preparations for war, was disbelieved.

The Israelis themselves thought war was unlikely, and when, on October
6, Egypt and Syria launched the Yom Kippur War, the Israeli armed forces
were caught entirely by surprise. It was seen by Nixon as being another example of the CIA getting things wrong because they depended too much on a foreign intelligence service and not on their own sources and assessments. Private
Soviet warnings that war was likely were also set aside. The rumor that went
round Washington, reaching the ears of the Israeli military attaché, General
Mordechai Gur, was that Ray Cline's bureau had alone warned that Sadat was
preparing an attack, that the CIA had concluded the same thing, but that
Schlesinger had watered down the Estimate at an earlier stage during his period as director, because it would have forced Nixon to take a more interventionist role in the Middle East. The U.S. domestic situation was important:
Nixon did not feel he had the political capital to take an initiative in the Middle East. The war was a relief for him. But until Sadat attacked, by staying with
the common wisdom—shared by the Israelis—that he was trying for a diplomatic solution, the U.S. policy of trying to encourage both sides to come to
terms was maintained.[50] It was a perfectly reasonable position to take, except
that if this actually were the case, it meant suppressing information and not
presenting the agency's full judgment. "My own view of intelligence is that the
problem is not one of quality, but of the inability of the system to digest it,"
said Lawrence Eagleburger, at the time on Henry Kissinger's staff. "The intelligence had clearly demonstrated that Sadat was going to begin the '73 war,
but the fact of the matter was that this did not penetrate the system. Interestingly enough, Henry reading some fairly raw intelligence came to the conclu-

sion that Sadat was going to start a war before the intelligence community itself did, but too late all the same."[51]

The year 1973 was one of turmoil for the CIA at almost every level. President Nixon was increasingly involved in trying to fend off Watergate. Congress had its antennae up, clearly sniffing intolerable conspiracy and deceit in the White House and becoming aware of dubious activities elsewhere, notably in the CIA. Within the agency the year saw the departure of Richard Helms, the arrival and departure of James Schlesinger, and the appointment of William Colby. It saw the voluntary and involuntary retirement of over two thousand officers coinciding with a generation change in the middle and senior levels of the agency. It saw a whole series of administrative changes, from the whittling down of the clandestine side to the complete reorganization of the analytical side. It had a director—Colby—convinced that the very survival of the agency was in jeopardy—an attitude that shocked nearly everyone's confidence. In the world at large, events in the Middle East and in Chile, where Allende had finally been overthrown and killed in a military coup, embroiled the CIA in further domestic investigation and suspicion. The agency failed to foresee the OPEC oil embargo. It was concentrating on detail, on specifics, having hunkered down under Nixon away from the big picture. The world was changing faster than the CIA. At home, critics would not have been snapping at its heels if they felt the agency was doing essential work. Additionally, the agency was seen as being involved with unsavory types: in 1953 the CIA had restored the shah of Iran to power; in 1973 the shah was Mr. OPEC, leading an oil embargo which affected every American. People remembered that he was the CIA's friend with a CIA man—Richard Helms—as ambassador to him. Altogether, 1973 was not a good year for the agency. Accurately, Ray Cline characterized it as the "Time of Troubles,"[52] and by 1975 the analytical "failure" involved was a major element in the public and congressional challenge to the agency.

—17—

Survival
1974–1976

"To this day," said General Vernon Walters, "I believe Mr. Nixon harbors the idea that someone in the CIA tried to do him in, or acted in some way against him." If the President felt this, especially a President with a reputation for acting against people himself, it was not surprising that many others harbored dark thoughts about the agency as well.* Walters went on to say that he was absolutely certain that Nixon was wrong in his belief. The problem that faced the agency, however, was no longer what Nixon thought—he had done his worst, many considered, in wreaking his revenge with Schlesinger—but what Congress and the average American thought. "Americans have always had an ambivalent attitude toward intelligence," Walters reflected. "When they feel threatened they want a lot of it, and when they don't, they tend to regard the whole thing as somewhat immoral."[1]

On August 9, 1974, Gerald Ford replaced Richard Nixon as President. Congressional pressure, backed up by overwhelming public support, had forced Nixon's resignation because of his involvement in the cover-up of

---

* Nixon no doubt thought this because, far more than the State Department, the CIA was the custodian of the post–World War II settlement which Nixon saw as unsettled. He saw the contest with the Soviet Union as no longer a matter of containment, but as a chessboard of movement. Nixon, the disrupter of the postwar settlement, was resisted by the CIA, its keeper. Agency people reciprocated Nixon's view of them: they were angry and contemptuous of him. They considered theirs to be the most rational and coherent approach to the Soviet Union and China: to counter and to contain every move within the borders agreed in 1945, but not to launch attacks or seek to change the borders with guerrilla action. The agency in the 1950s, when Nixon was Vice President, was closer to Nixon's view, but in the intervening eight years before Nixon became President the agency had changed while Nixon had not.

White House connections with the Watergate intruders. Ford had himself succeeded Nixon's Vice-President, Spiro Agnew, who resigned on October 10, 1973, after he was implicated in income-tax evasion and payoffs from construction companies while governor of Maryland. Nixon had chosen Ford, the House minority leader, to follow Agnew, because he "was the first choice among members of Congress, and they were the ones who would have to approve the man I nominated."[2] Nixon had not wanted another problem with Congress, increasingly united across the parties, against him.

Ford was very much closer in all sorts of ways to the "average" American than Nixon or Agnew, and he shared the American public's ambivalence toward intelligence. As one of the twelve congressmen in the 1950s and 1960s involved in the informal oversight of the CIA, he had been diligent in ensuring that the understandings between Congress and the agency worked well. He strongly supported the principle of congressional oversight but in practice was happy for the agency to tell him what it thought he should know. It was not until January 3, 1975, for example, that Ford as President learned of all "The Skeletons," including the assassination plots of the early 1960s, when he had been a congressional overseer.[3] Ford was one of those who had been happy to operate within the pre-Watergate system that was built on the understanding that the agency would not embarrass the President or other elected representatives with unpleasant knowledge—the old idea of "plausible deniability." The system had a great deal to recommend it, not the least of which was its encapsulation of the ambivalence toward intelligence. But after Watergate, and with Ford as President, all this changed.

Ford himself was the first to institute a detailed investigation of the agency. "The Skeletons," or Family Jewels, list, which William Colby had given to Henry Kissinger and sent to the President over Christmas 1974, was finally addressed by Ford at a special meeting:

> On January 3, I met with Colby in the Oval Office and learned—for the first time—about what agency executives referred to as the "family jewels." These were highly classified documents that provided details about unsavory and illegal CIA practices. In the 1950s and 1960s, the CIA had plotted to assassinate foreign leaders, including Fidel Castro. Although none of these assassinations had been carried out, the fact that government officials had even considered them was distressing. In the aftermath of Watergate, it was important that we be totally aboveboard about these past abuses and avoid giving any substance to charges that we were engaging in a "cover-up."[4]

For Ford, it was politically too risky to be anything but aboveboard and so he sought to distance the presidency from everything. He fired James Schlesinger, now secretary of defense, a man who had obviously been a ruthless Nixon servant, as an indication that the Ford presidency would be more accommodating.

For Colby this meeting was vitally important because it would dictate his future actions as well as the future of the agency. Over Christmas he had felt left out of affairs. Press reports had been full of speculation about the "CIA crisis" and the President's deliberations while at Vail. Said Colby, looking back at these tense days:

> I was not included. I felt myself increasingly out in left field while the infield was making decisions well out of my hearing. I concluded that the White House planned to "distance" itself from the CIA and its troubles (as the CIA had distanced itself from the White House during Watergate), that it was going to draw the wagons around—and leave me isolated and exposed on the outside. I felt very lonely, but I saw a certain logic in the Ford administration's determination not to take on almost thirty years of CIA's sins.[5]

The feeling was justified. It was another mark of the agency's changed place. It was no longer close to the President, no longer so responsive to presidential wishes that the wishes did not have to be clearly expressed. Rather, the agency was a bureaucracy out of favor and in the one place it should not be: the political limelight. It was being confirmed as just another Washington bureaucracy with turf to defend and aging perspectives, no longer formidable or the main channel for the President's will. In September 1973, the popular perception was that the agency had toppled Allende; in November 1973 that it had failed to predict OPEC and the oil embargo. It was seen as faded, dilapidated, and an embarrassment from the past. Americans did not want its "successes" (Allende) or its "failures" (OPEC). From this point on, the CIA was on the defensive.

Richard Helms's "no" had had a resounding echo.

It was probably a correct "no," encapsulating a judgment that far from protecting the agency, a presidency under attack might pull the CIA down: the "Imperial Presidency" of four decades was over. The chances that the true story of Watergate would emerge were always high. Any attempt by the CIA to intervene would simply have been another cover-up, with another set of problems. But Helms's "no" had also been a declaration of independence from the President. It had been a statement that the agency had its own idea of what it should and should not do, that it was responsible for itself first and the President second. It was a serious act of self-preservation, recognizing that Nixon's request had sought overtly to politicize the agency. Enlightened self-interest dictated the "no." Helms established the agency as having a greater duty than to passing presidents: its prime duty was to maintain the national security, he was saying, and the agency itself would decide best how to discharge this duty.

Ford's response—he had little choice, for the train of events had already been set in motion by Nixon—was to be aboveboard with the agency, whose role was below board, leaving Colby and his colleagues to fend for themselves without any favors from him. Ford conceded:

I realized that unnecessary disclosures could cripple the agency's effectiveness, lower its morale and make foreign governments extremely wary about sharing vital information with us. Such unnecessary disclosures would almost certainly result if I let Congress dominate the investigation. I decided to take the initiative. On January 4, I announced that I was establishing a blue-ribbon Commission on CIA Activities within the United States to look into the allegations, determine the extent to which the agency had exceeded its authority and make recommendations to prevent such abuses in the future. "It is essential," I declared, "that we meet our security requirements and at the same time avoid impairing our democratic institutions and fundamental freedoms. Intelligence activities must be conducted consistently with both objectives."[6]

There was no mention, no hint in this statement that the activities of the agency were conducted on the President's authority; it was as if Ford wanted the country to think that the agency was somehow independent, acting on its own. And again, without any proper hearing or legal opinion, he too was clearly implying that some of these activities were illegal. From the moment he became President, Ford was running for election, and everything was calculated to give him his best chance. He was also attempting to defend the presidency—this was why he pardoned Nixon. He did not want deep investigation of the executive branch. His dealings with Colby and the CIA were shaped by political considerations. Above all, Ford was running "against" Washington. The CIA had been brought into being in an age of hero leaders when presidents were clothed with public veneration. After Nixon the presidency no longer possessed this aura. Ford sought to remake the presidency by turning it into another people's tribune against Washington, against the government. The CIA under Ford was distanced from the presidency and presented as epitomizing the dark side of government. Ford's approach, coupled with Colby's response, conceded that the agency was another expendable bureaucracy.

Nelson Rockefeller, Ford's Vice-President, was appointed to head the blue-ribbon commission investigating the CIA. On January 21 the Senate voted to create a Select Committee to Study Governmental Operations with Respect to Intelligence Activities. A month later the House of Representatives established by resolution a Select Committee on Intelligence.* For the next two years revelations about the CIA spilled out, notably to the Senate com-

---

* The House Select Committee was first chaired by Representative Lucien Nedzi (D-Michigan), who was also chairman of the House Armed Services Intelligence Subcommittee. Since the subcommittee had for years been responsible for monitoring the CIA, and, in the opinion of many of Nedzi's colleagues in 1974, had not done a very good job of it, his chairmanship of the Select Committee was controversial. When *The New York Times* on June 5, 1975, published details of "The Skeletons/Family Jewels" and revealed that Colby had briefed Nedzi about them in 1973, Nedzi resigned as chairman. The full House refused to accept his resignation, and Nedzi refused to act as chairman. On July 17 the House abolished the Select Committee and voted for a new one with Representative Otis Pike (D-New York) as chairman.

mittee chaired by Frank Church. The first to report was the Rockefeller Commission on June 6, 1975, and it concentrated on the charge Seymour Hersh had leveled in his December 22, 1974, article: that the CIA had conducted illegal activities within the United States, violating the rights of private citizens.

At the same time, as it stated in the preface to its report, the commission was well aware that "many persons have voiced alarm that public controversy and exposure would seriously impair the CIA's ability to function—which in turn could seriously undermine the national security."* The commission, therefore, in accordance with President Ford's wishes, took it upon itself to conduct its investigation in private. It also reported back directly to the President. "I was convinced that the blue-ribbon commission would not be the end of the matter," said Colby, "and that the President's carefully circumscribed investigation of CIA's domestic affairs would not stop Congress from conducting its own probe."[7] He saw the commission as an ambivalent effort by Ford to meet public demands for an investigation of the agency while protecting as many embarrassing secrets as it could. The assassination plots, for example, were not likely to surface in a commission report on the agency's domestic activities. However Ford might have felt about the agency in his congressional days, from the perspective of a presidency severely damaged by his predecessor he recognized that public exposure of the plots would reflect badly on the presidency and would not simply hurt the agency.

Colby, on the other hand, had reached the conclusion that he stood alone and that, although the thought was unspoken, the agency was expected to fight for itself. He saw this fight as one of survival and determined that the only way to survive was to come clean about all past deeds. This was Colby controlling publicity by being the source of information. He was trying to become a star rather than let the stars of the White House or of the Congress obscure the CIA's value and merit. It was for what Colby considered the good of the agency that he made his revelations to the commission. It was obvious to Washington insiders that the commission was a news management effort, and in a daring coup Colby effectively took it over. He considered that the agency would be destroyed by prolonged involuntary exposure and that immediate voluntary exposure might save it. He made his revelations in a way that made it

---

* *Report to the President by the Commission on CIA Activities Within the United States* (Washington DC: U.S. Government Printing Office, June 6, 1975). The members of the commission were Nelson Rockefeller, chairman; John T. Connor, chairman of the board and chief executive of Allied Chemical Corporation, former secretary of commerce under President Johnson; C. Douglas Dillon, a managing director of Dillon, Read & Company, Inc., an investment banking firm, former secretary of the treasury under Presidents Kennedy and Johnson and former ambassador to France and undersecretary of state under President Eisenhower; Erwin N. Griswold, former solicitor general under Presidents Johnson and Nixon, and former dean of the Harvard Law School; Lane Kirkland, secretary-treasurer of the AFL-CIO; Lyman L. Lemnitzer, former chairman of the Joint Chiefs of Staff; Ronald Reagan, former governor of California and former president of the Screen Actors Guild; and Edgar F. Shannon, Jr., Commonwealth Professor of English and former president of the University of Virginia.

quite clear that the whole executive apparatus of the United States was compromised and that the agency had acted under orders. He was outdoing the White House:

> I discovered that I was being somewhat too open and candid for some people's tastes. After my second or third appearance, the Commission's Chairman, Vice President Rockefeller, drew me aside into his office at the Executive Office Building and said in his most charming manner, "Bill, do you really have to present all this material to us? We realize that there are secrets that you fellows need to keep and so nobody here is going to take it amiss if you feel that there are some questions you can't answer quite as fully as you seem to feel you have to." I got the message quite unmistakably, and I didn't like it. The Vice President of the United States was letting me know that he didn't approve of my approach to the CIA's troubles, that he would much prefer me to take the traditional stance of fending off investigation by drawing the cloak of secrecy around the agency in the name of national security. So I mumbled something appropriate and went on to give the Commission what it needed to get a fair picture of CIA's history.[8]

Colby played brilliantly to the public mood. He went over the heads of the President and Congress and appealed to the majority in the country, presenting himself as a representative American (which he was not) making the same journey as the majority had made. The majority had favored the agency and the Vietnam War; now the majority doubted both. Colby quantified the doubt about the agency, making it specific by detailing plots and admitting that it had made mistakes. But now, he was saying, the agency is different because it is wiser. This was how the majority of Americans also felt about themselves. And it was therefore hard to strike Colby for being "open" and American.

Ten years earlier Allen Dulles or John McCone or William Raborn would not have mumbled something appropriate and gone on to do what they thought should be done. They would have spoken up sharply with a "Yes, sir!" and done what the White House wanted. They would have been President's men. And if they felt they could not do something the President wanted, they would have behaved in the way Rockefeller wanted, in the way Richard Helms would have behaved—volunteering nothing, responding in precise terms to specific questions.*

As a result of Colby's forcing the commission to hear what he wanted it to hear, he effectively determined the nature of the commission's report. The

---

* Richard Helms provided an example of this in the way he dealt with the Warren Commission in 1964. He was asked in testimony before the House Select Committee on Assassinations, "As a general rule, did you wait to receive an inquiry from the Commission prior to passing information on to the Warren Commission?" "Yes, I believe so," Helms replied (House Select Committee on Assassinations, *Investigation on the Assassination of President John F. Kennedy,* [1979] Vol. IV, p. 12).

commission could not pretend it had not heard what the director of Central Intelligence was telling it about CIA misdeeds, and it could not ignore Colby's argument that "the previously unacknowledged contradiction between the old tradition of intelligence and the Constitution" needed to be resolved even if it meant the reduction of the President's power and greater congressional power.[9] It might have struck the President and the Vice-President as odd that a presidential nominee—Colby—responsible for an agency related directly to presidential authority should be telling them and the country what to do in a way that forced their hands. "Colby drove the White House, and in particular three rather senior people, namely Ford, Rockefeller, and Kissinger, straight up the wall," said one CIA man watching Colby from the sidelines.[10]

"Allegations that the CIA had been involved in plans to assassinate certain leaders of foreign countries came to the Commission's attention shortly after its inquiry was under way," was how the commission's report put it. "Although it was unclear whether or not those allegations fell within the scope of the Commission's authority, the Commission directed that an inquiry be undertaken. The President concurred in this approach." They had no choice, but there was still a last-ditch attempt to prevent the allegations from being publicly confirmed. "The Commission's staff began the required inquiry," the report explained, "but time did not permit a full investigation before this report was due. The President therefore requested that the materials in the possession of the Commission which bear on these allegations be turned over to him. This has been done."[11]

It was in part a cover-up, and in part a desperate effort to keep America from being embarrassed in the court of world opinion. The Vietnam-inspired isolationist revival would feed off the revelations to an even greater extent. Once Colby had told the commission of the assassination plots, it was inevitable that the information would become public. Apart from anything else, at least fifty people with no allegiance to the CIA now knew about them. Ford's effort was to have the plots investigated privately again, hoping that something of the old understandings in Congress would still work in exchange for an undertaking to publicize the corrective and preventative measures that would result.*

The findings of the Rockefeller Commission were in many ways the last gasp of the old understandings. The report gave emphasis to the dangers the United States faced from an estimated 500,000 or more communist-bloc intel-

---

* In a sense, Colby was doing the obvious. There had been a steady increase in the discretion of the executive in international affairs as reaction time had narrowed and as the world became more complicated. Colby was striking back at the endeavor to particularize intelligence as an illegitimate activity. He proposed to show its importance in foreign policy and its connection with government *at all levels.* The country was becoming "antigovernment," and preparing for ritual washing. Colby accurately sensed this and strove to ensure that the agency was not seen as a piece of ritual defilement to be cast aside. By doing this, Colby produced a new awareness: if the CIA was a rogue elephant, it had a rogue mahout—the President for the time being.

ligence officers, nearly 2000 communist-bloc diplomats in the United States, and the technical intelligence of the Soviet Union and its allies. "We believe that these countries can monitor and record thousands of private telephone conversations. . . . This raises the real specter that selected American users of telephones are potentially subject to blackmail that can seriously affect their actions, or even lead in some cases to recruitment as espionage agents." * With this combination of the threat without and the threat within, the report fundamentally exonerated the agency:

> A detailed analysis of the facts has convinced the Commission that the great majority of the CIA's domestic activities comply with its statutory authority. Nevertheless, over the 28 years of its history, the CIA has engaged in some activities that should be criticized and not permitted to happen again—both in light of the limits imposed on the agency by law and as a matter of public policy. Some of these activities were initiated or ordered by Presidents, either directly or indirectly. Some of them fall within the doubtful area between responsibilities delegated to the CIA by Congress and the National Security Council on the one hand and activities specifically prohibited to the agency on the other. Some of them were plainly unlawful and constituted improper invasions upon the rights of Americans. The agency's own recent actions, undertaken for the most part in 1973 and 1974, have gone far to terminate the activities upon which this investigation has focused.[12]

The plainly unlawful and improper activities, in the commission's view, were: the mail openings; some of the domestic activities of Operation Chaos—specifically "the use of agents of the Operation on three occasions to gather information within the United States on strictly domestic matters. . . . In addition the intelligence dissemination and those portions of a major study prepared by the agency which dealt with purely domestic matters"; the investigation of newsmen "simply because they have published leaked classified information"; some domestic electronic eavesdropping; the involuntary solitary confinement of a defector; providing equipment and disguises to Howard Hunt and the making of psychological profiles of Daniel Ellsberg; the administering of drugs to unsuspecting persons; the involvement with the Bureau of Narcotics and Dangerous Drugs; payment of stationery and other costs for replies to people who wrote to the President after the invasion of Cambodia.[13]

Various recommendations were made in each case, usually involving some statutory amendment to the 1947 act or a clarification in the directives from the National Security Council. The commission also investigated claims

---

* There was a paradox in this: as the importance of the CIA diminished, Soviet intelligence was gaining and growing. This really worried Rockefeller, and this section of the commission's report was a cry from his heart. At the same time, it was not the job of the CIA to monitor the scale of Soviet intelligence in the United States: it was the job of the FBI. What to do in the intelligence war was seen as separate from what to do about the CIA.

that the CIA had some involvement with President Kennedy's assassination and concluded that "there is no credible evidence of CIA involvement." Not surprisingly, William Colby was pleased with the report, since it was a confirmation of what he had said to the President after the Hersh article in December 1974: that no activities of the sort Hersh had described were going on under Colby.

THE CLAWS OF CONGRESS

The Senate and House investigations of the agency were another matter altogether. In the Senate, Frank Church made no bones about his personal ambition to run as the Democratic presidential candidate in 1976 or 1980, and he saw the congressional investigation as a major plank in his campaign, taking advantage of the reaction against secrecy and duplicity in the wake of Watergate. In the House, the chairman of the Select Committee, liberal Democrat Otis Pike, also saw the CIA investigation as a possible step up the political ladder. Both select committees demanded to know everything about the CIA. They were not restricted to the agency's dubious domestic activities, and after the Rockefeller Commission report was published, they both raced for the evidence of assassination plots, which President Ford had retained. The extent of CIA archives (as of October 31, 1980, amounting to at least 470 million pages of documents)[14] meant that the investigations had to be judgmental. The resulting reports were strictly impressionistic in their portraits of the agency: they focused on the drama, not the nature or the purpose of the CIA. As Colby later wrote:

> The lesson was clear. The old power structure of the Congress could no longer control their junior colleagues and hold off their curiosity about the secret world of intelligence. In this new era, CIA was going to have to fend for itself without that long-time special Congressional protection. Indeed, as it became ever more obvious that the nation's attention and the media's limelight were now to be focused mercilessly on the agency, a number of other Congressional committees discovered that they too had some jurisdiction in the intelligence area and moved quickly to get their share of the headlines. CIA's former Congressional protectors helplessly asked me to go ahead and testify before those committees and not claim any exclusive responsibility to the old watchdogs. In this fashion I ended up adding such audiences as the House Post Office Committee to the groups I had to tell about CIA's past activities and the fact that they would not be repeated. . . .
>
> But I must say that, unlike many in the White House and, for that matter, within the intelligence community, I believed that the Congress was within its constitutional rights to undertake a long-overdue and thoroughgoing review of the agency and the intelligence community. I did not share the

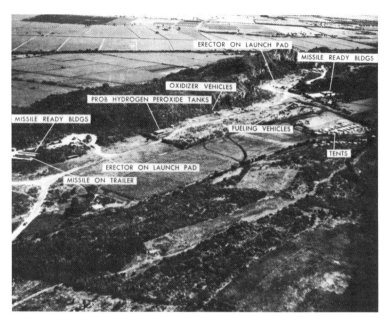

ERECTOR ON LAUNCH PAD

MISSILE READY BLDGS

OXIDIZER VEHICLES

PROB HYDROGEN PEROXIDE TANKS

MISSILE READY BLDGS

FUELING VEHICLES

TENTS

ERECTOR ON LAUNCH PAD

MISSILE ON TRAILER

The Missiles of October: The photographic evidence provided by U-2 and low-level reconnaissance flights confirmed the Soviet missile build-up in Cuba in October 1962, leading to the thirteen days of the Cuban missile crisis. This photograph of a Soviet-Cuban medium-range missile base only days away from being operational was released by the Pentagon on October 24, 1962, two days after President Kennedy publicly announced the facts of the Soviet build-up. *(Wide World Photos)*

$53 million: At 6.06 p.m. on Sunday, December 23, 1962, twenty months after the Bay of Pigs, these first invasion prisoners returned to America, arriving at Homestead Air Force Base, Florida. Their freedom had been negotiated by Robert Kennedy, who had secured the $53 million of food and drugs demanded by Castro for their release. The following Saturday, President Kennedy accepted the invasion force's flag and promised the survivors in front of forty thousand people in the Orange Bowl stadium: "I can assure you that this flag will be returned to this Brigade in a free Havana." *(Wide World Photos)*

Fidel Castro was the target of more Kennedy-CIA assassination plots than any other person. One involved chemicals to make his beard fall out. Here Castro is at the battlefront during the Bay of Pigs invasion. *(Wide World Photos)*

Richard M. Bissell, Jr.: Intelligence as a science was his brilliant concept. The man behind the U-2, the first satellites and the SR-71, Bissell here receives the National Security Medal from President John F. Kennedy in April 1962. *(Wide World Photos)*

Above: Richard Helms (center), having just been sworn in as director of Central Intelligence, chats with former director Allen Dulles (left) and Admiral William Raborn (right), the outgoing DCI, on June 30, 1966. *(Wide World Photos)*

Below right: James Schlesinger, director of Central Intelligence, February 2 to July 2, 1973. *(Wide World Photos)*

Below left: William Colby, director of Central Intelligence, September 4, 1973 to January 30, 1976, photographed near Hué in Vietnam on January 31, 1969, while on leave from the CIA as director of Civilian Operations Revolutionary Development Staff, Saigon, where he was one of the oversees of Operation Phoenix. He is examining the shotgun of a member of the Vietnamese self-defense forces. *(Wide World Photos)*

Zbigniew Brzezinski (left), President Carter's national security adviser, and Stansfield Turner, Carter's director of Central Intelligence, photographed together at the White House in an attempt to play down rumors of conflict between them. The rumors were true. *(Wide World Photos)*

Company headquarters: Avant garde in the 1950s when it was designed but dated today, the headquarters building of the CIA (called "The Company" by insiders) in Langley, Virginia, was never satisfactory. Under William Casey a $46 million extension was approved. In front of the building by the awning stands a statue of Nathan Hale, executed as a spy by the British during the War for Independence, whose last words were: "I only regret that I have but one life to lose for my country." This was a garbled quote from Joseph Addison's play *Cato:* "What pity is it that we can die but once to serve our country!"

William Casey, Reagan's director of Central Intelligence, arriving at a Senate Armed Services Committee hearing in February 1982. *(Wide World Photos)*

The technological shield: Electronic intelligence systems, ranging from spy and communications satellites to ground-based radar and telemetry stations, have become America's primary defense, reducing the need for spies and agents but enhancing the importance of technical and political analysis. The tracking and data relay satellite system represented here was made possible by the space shuttle and is used both for commercial and defense purposes. It provides advanced tracking and telemetry services for a number of users. Behind the deployment of this system lay a fierce bureaucratic battle in the 1970s when the decision in favor of real-time, nonphoto system development was made. The Air Force wanted high-resolution photographic satellite systems which would assist identification of weapons systems and order of battle. William Colby and the National Security Agency favored telemetry collection. Jimmy Carter and Stansfield Turner resolved the issue and chose the telemetry system, finally deployed in the mid-1980s. *(UPI/Bettmann)*

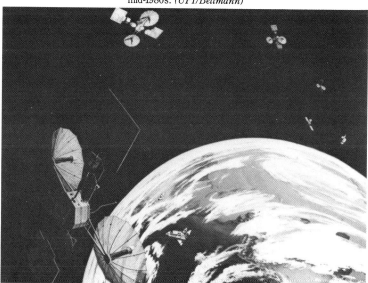

The Contras: An officer in the Sandinista army holds a copy of the CIA-edited "Psychological Operations in Guerrilla Warfare" on how to "neutralize" Sandinista leaders. The Sandinistas captured this copy of the manual from a Contra named "Lester." The manual was evidence of the CIA's involvement in covert warfare in Nicaragua. *(UPI/Bettmann)*

Reagan and Casey: The Presidential connection, all-important to the DCI and the CIA. *(Wide World Photos)*

view that intelligence was solely a function of the Executive Branch and must be protected from Congressional prying. Quite the contrary.[15]

Colby knew he was paying a high price for having a "legitimate" agency, supervised and controlled to the same degree as any other Washington bureaucracy. Nor was he behaving like a man who expected to be DCI very long: there was a kamikaze quality to his effort. He knew he was expendable, and never deluded himself with hopes of keeping his job. President Ford did not like this turn of events, nor did he agree with Colby that Congress should have a greater say in intelligence matters. He *knew* Congress, he *knew* what would happen: leaks, leaks, and more leaks. "Back in the 1950s and early 1960s," he fumed, "when I was on the House Appropriations Committee, no more than ten or twelve members of Congress were fully and regularly informed about the budget and the activities of the CIA. For eight years prior to January 1965, I was one of this group. . . . We met with the CIA director and his top staff people on a regular basis. No staff members ever joined us and there were no leaks. . . . By 1975, however, that number had swollen to between fifty and seventy-five. Inevitably, there were leaks."[16] Ford also knew that Congress, eyeing the CIA as wheat for its publicity mill, could do real damage to the United States abroad and to the security interests of the nation. It could also circumscribe some of the powers exercised by presidents since Franklin Roosevelt; and now that Ford was President, he had a healthy interest in the powers of the presidency.

Ford's fears were confirmed. The Rockefeller Commission, despite its careful language, was the first officially to acknowledge the assassination plots.*

---

* Earlier, massive publicity had accompanied Colby's testimony to the intelligence subcommittees of the Senate Armed Services and Appropriations committees meeting in joint session on January 15, 1975. That is when he gave them his Vail Report—the watered-down version of "The Skeletons"—and was forced to admit that there was nothing classified in it and that it could be released to the press.

I was, of course, privately delighted. Ever since I had prepared the Vail report I had been hoping to get it out—believing it to be the most effective way to counter the misconceptions fostered by Hersh's article. But on my way down from the Hill that afternoon, I realized that I had not told the White House what was coming in the press next day, so I stopped there to give Brent Scowcroft [deputy assistant to the President for national security affairs] a copy of the statement the Committee had released; the substance was well known to them, but the fact of its public release was a new bombshell (William Colby and Peter Forbath, *Honorable Men: My Life in the CIA* [New York: Simon & Schuster, 1978], p. 402).

The difference between the Vail Report and the information indicated in the Rockefeller Commission report was the assassination plots. Together, these releases encouraged a sense that only the tip of an iceberg was being revealed and that there was much more to come. It is also interesting to note that Colby had not thought to clear his actions with the White House beforehand and was dealing with Scowcroft rather than with Kissinger. (Scowcroft succeeded Kissinger as assistant to the President for national security affairs in November 1975.) This was yet another indication of the agency's fall from grace at the White House.

The first public rumors that the CIA had been involved in assassination plots surfaced on February 28, when Daniel Schorr broadcast on CBS that President Ford had reportedly expressed

On June 5, just before its publication, the commission's report leaked. *The New York Times* ran a story about the assassination plots and the fact that Colby had revealed them over a year earlier to the chairmen of the congressional committees responsible for overseeing the agency. From then on there was no stopping the wide-ranging investigation of the agency planned by Senator Church and Representative Pike. On June 10 President Ford stated at a press conference: "I will make available to the Senate and House Select Committees these [Rockefeller Commission] materials, together with other related materials in the executive branch. . . . So there's not going to be any possibility of any cover-up because we're giving them the material that the Rockefeller Commission developed in their hearings, plus any other material that is available in the executive branch."[17]

In the post-Watergate atmosphere of a Congress with its blood up, having successfully flexed its muscles and brought down a President, and with a revived intensity about morality in government, the President had no choice but to be totally aboveboard with anything that was even speculated about in public. Many Americans as well as many foreigners considered the United States in general to be intemperate and a failure after Vietnam and in the wake of Watergate. The months in which the revelations tumbled out saw the fall of Saigon, marking the end of a decade of massive American effort, resources, and over fifty thousand American war deaths, all of which was seen to have achieved nothing.

Americans did not like failure and were not used to it. To a whole generation foreign policy meant Vietnam—not NATO or the Marshall Plan or Third World aid. The CIA was to this generation a shorthand symbol for a view of the world in perpetual conflict with the United States, and they did not see why this should be so. They did not accept a role for America as watchman on the walls of freedom. They were isolationist in reaction to failure and had anger and dislike for the rest of the world. Ford was determined not to be associated with failure. Colby shared this determination and forced the President down his path. He was not prepared to risk the consequences of stonewalling, and as the source of most of the information about past misdeeds, he was giving the President no choice but to tell all.

Colby was successfully calling the shots in his effort to save the CIA from disbandment or emasculation by Congress. When the Senate Select Committee was established, Colby telephoned Frank Church "and offered him and his staff my full cooperation, saying that I was fully available for discussions on how we could go about assisting in the comprehensive investigation he had in

concern that if the investigations of the CIA went too far, they would reveal assassination plots. Ford had said this at an off-the-record lunch for the publisher and senior editors of *The New York Times* in late January, and inevitably the news spread. Schorr had asked Colby about the rumor on February 27 and had received the reply that there had been no such plots for assassinations "in this country."

mind while at the same time protecting the necessary secrets of intelligence work."[18]

Otis Pike's committee did not fare as well, in part because it operated in a politically partisan manner and was perceived as having made its mind up to secure the dismantling of the agency before it heard the evidence. President Ford paid particular attention to the demands for documents and information made by Pike, bringing in the attorney general on several occasions to advise if the demands should be met. When the attorney general said no, Ford withheld the requested information. The House Select Committee finally imploded with internal rivalries, its unfinished report being leaked to the press in January and February 1976.

This caused a bureaucratic furor, with President Ford, Secretary of State Henry Kissinger and William Colby all stressing to Pike and the House leadership that the leaks and the uncensored nature of the information were damaging national security. The House responded to these representations and on January 29 voted to suppress publication of the Pike Committee's report until it had been cleared by the White House for security purposes. The murder in Athens of the CIA station chief, Richard Welch, on December 23, 1975, widely ascribed to his public identification by anti-CIA activists, was an important element in the changing attitude of Congress toward the nation's secrets and without doubt had influenced the House. So had the surprise of the 1973 oil embargo following the creation of the Organization of Petroleum Exporting Countries. The fascination with intelligence was beginning to wear off. Both the public and Congress were beginning to accept the fact that America had to have secrets and that to be a secret, something had to be kept secret.

On February 17, 1976, President Ford addressed this point head on. "It is essential that the irresponsible and dangerous exposure of our nation's intelligence secrets be stopped," he said at a press conference. "Openness is a hallmark of our democratic society but the American people have never believed that it was necessary to reveal secret war plans of the Department of Defense, and I do not think they wish to have true intelligence secrets revealed either."[19] The revelation of the assassination plots, however, changed the mood. Secrets were accepted as a necessity in the terms that Ford described, but planning to kill people in peacetime was not considered necessary, and many Americans found it shocking.

There was another level of thought involved as well: if we seek to defeat our enemies on their terms, we shall become like our enemies, and they shall have won. So it was very important for Americans not to become what they beheld but to be American and either withdraw into the United States or publicize what had been done and so seek a democratic sanction for maintaining America's worldwide engagement.

Within a year of its establishment the Church Committee published its definitive report, *Alleged Assassination Plots Against Foreign Leaders,* the first subject addressed by Church and his colleagues. It confirmed that the CIA had tried to secure the assassination of Patrice Lumumba and of Fidel Castro and other members of the Cuban leadership but had not planned the deaths of General René Schneider in Chile, Ngo Dinh Diem and his brother Ngo Dinh Nhu in Vietnam, or President Rafael Trujillo of the Dominican Republic. The committee could not satisfactorily establish whether the plots were authorized by American presidents or other senior governmental officials above the CIA but found that administration officials had clearly not ruled out assassination as an acceptable course of action. The CIA had not tried to assassinate foreign leaders on its own initiative. The most that could be said against the agency and its senior officers was that they had misunderstood presidential instructions, but in all cases there was good ground for their misunderstanding—just not quite good enough to blame the President concerned.

Interestingly, the committee itself did not rule out assassination as unacceptable in certain cases, echoing in its findings the practical considerations it had heard in the testimony of CIA people. In his preface to the report Frank Church said:

> It is sometimes asked whether assassination should be ruled out absolutely, such as in a time of truly grave national emergency. Adolf Hitler is often cited as an example. Of course, the cases which the committee investigated were not of that character at all. Tragically, they related to Latin leaders and black leaders of little countries that could not possibly have constituted a threat to the security of the United States.
>
> The only time when Fidel Castro permitted his island to become a base for Russian missiles, the only time during which it might have been said that he had become a threat to the security of the American people, was the one time when all assassination activity, plans, and plots against his life were stood down.
>
> So we are not talking about Adolf Hitler or anything of that character, nor are we condemning actions taken in a grave national emergency when the life of the republic is endangered.[20]

When three directors of Central Intelligence—John McCone, Richard Helms, and William Colby—were questioned by the committee about the assassination plots, they expressed two different views. McCone and Colby declared that assassination was wrong: "With respect to assassination, my position is clear" declared Colby. "I just think it is wrong. And I have said so and made it very clear to my subordinates." McCone said much the same: "I didn't think it was proper from the standpoint of the US Government and the Central Intelligence Agency." Neither man considered the Hitler example or admitted the question of the lesser of two evils. War, somebody might have pointed out (and did not), is wrong too. Were Colby and McCone saying that because something was wrong or not proper, it should never be done? Were they pacifists? These questions were not put to them—the crusading spirit of the inquirers prevented sophisticated points from being made. Richard Helms's reply was more complicated. It wasn't that assassinations were wrong—they were—but that they didn't work at a practical level. Helms told the committee:

> As a result of my experiences through the years, when I became Director I had made up my mind that this option . . . of killing foreign leaders, was something that I did not want to happen on my watch. My reasons for this were these:
>
> There are not only moral reasons but there are also some other rather practical reasons.
>
> It is almost impossible in a democracy to keep anything like that secret. . . . Somebody would go to his Congressman, his Senator, he might go to a newspaperman, whatever the case may be, but it is just not a practical alternative, it seems to me, in our society.
>
> There is another consideration . . . if you are going to try by this kind of means to remove a foreign leader, then who is going to take his place running that country, and are you essentially better off as a matter of practice when it is over than you were before? And I can give you I think a very solid example of this which happened in Vietnam when President Diem was eliminated from the scene. We then had a revolving door of prime ministers after that for quite some period of time, during which the Vietnamese Government at a time in its history when it should have been strong was nothing but a caretaker government. . . . In other words, that whole exercise turned out to the disadvantage of the United States. . . .
>
> There is no sense in my sitting here with all the experience I have had and not sharing with the Committee my feelings this day. It isn't because I have lost my cool, or because I have lost my guts, it simply is because I don't think it is a viable option in the United States of America these days.[21]

The assassination report of the Church Committee was its key publication. There were others on mail opening, on the performance of the intelligence agencies generally and over the assassination of President Kennedy, and on intelligence activities and the rights of Americans. All essentially agreed with the earlier findings of the Rockefeller Commission. The Church Committee also published two surveys of the history of American intelligence development, one concentrating on the CIA, drawn from the agency's own official history. Nearly every single secret—apart from the identification of sources and methods and current operations—of the CIA was revealed. William Colby, in welcoming this extensive investigation, had realized what it would mean: a change in the relationship between Congress and the agency on the one hand, and Congress and the President on the other. He was turning his face to the rising sun: he saw that power was moving from the President to Congress. He had therefore prepared for this change diligently, reaching back to his experiences as a lawyer:

> Drawing on my legal experience at Donovan and Leisure many years before, I explained to my CIA associates that the investigation we now faced was like a major antitrust action. In those cases, an enormous number of documents are demanded by the prosecution, meticulously examined and then three or four specific papers are extracted to prove the case. The only real defense in such actions, I pointed out, was not to fight over the investigators' right to obtain the documents, as the courts would almost invariably rule against you, but to come forward with the documents selected by the investigators and explain that they had another significance than guilt. Since this strategy often required the revelation of even more material then the investigators sought, it was greeted with very little enthusiasm within both the administration and the intelligence community. . . .
>
> As in the White House, many long-time professionals in the Agency were anything but happy with my approach. Raised in the old tradition, some argued that intelligence was inherently a Presidential function and that the Congress should be kept out of it. Others warned that the Congress could not be trusted with intelligence secrets, that release to it was the equivalent to release to the world at large. And still others, while eschewing such extreme stances, asserted that each item that the investigators requested should be fought over tenaciously and turned over only when there was no alternative. . . . I remain satisfied that [mine] was the correct approach, pragmatically and constitutionally, and eventually resulted in the Church Committee coming to fair conclusions about American intelligence.[22]

What actually happened was slightly different. Colby had taken a lawyer's approach to a case and had therefore not argued on general grounds but on specific charges, marshaling evidence to refute false charges and put others into context. It was a quantitative rather than a qualitative approach, depending, as he himself pointed out, on the volume of documentation. Rather than theorize about the place of intelligence in American society and the Constitution, he was content to reveal its place and its method of operating, leaving others to make overall judgments. This was terribly important, because it enabled the investigations to hold the CIA to its image of itself: a finely tuned agency operating under presidential direction in foreign affairs. There might be aberrations from time to time, lapses into domestic activities, which were not proper, some illegalities, but nothing serious. Particular clandestine operations and failures of intelligence analysis could be picked out and examined.

No real operational changes were effected by the revelations. Secrets tend to be valuable as secrets for only a narrow stretch of time. Nearly all the secrets revealed were "dead." The exercise was a file clearing, an emptying of the lumber room. This was matched by the attitude of the American public: it never tried to make its opinion of the CIA felt. There was no surge of telegrams to congressmen or the White House about the agency. There was neither a concentrated nor a generalized set of representations to Congress by the public. It was all a very in-house debate. The big questions were never really addressed. Should the United States have a secret, centralized, unfragmented intelligence service? When should the United States break international law and the laws of other countries? (Everyone knew that America would break international law on occasion; everyone else does.) Should there be an area, within a democracy, of absolute secrecy where only experts and a few public representatives were in the know?

Because these questions were not tackled, a new understanding mushroomed in the mid-1970s as the investigations wore on: there was a secret place as long as it was not examined too closely. It existed by implication rather than by outright statement. Specifics could be spotlighted, but people were not willing to expand upon those specifics to the general picture. This was Frank Church's and William Colby's most important contribution to American intelligence. It had found a new place, between the President and Congress and definitely for foreign consumption.

An important set of American questions was involved. The European countries have secret services that are expected to be in the murder/kidnapping business—that is why they are secret services. It went against the national genius of the United States, however, to have anything that was secret and concealed for all but short periods of time, so the problem when it came to American secrets has always been the choice between hypocrisy and dishonesty. The CIA is an extremely obvious organization that cannot speak about the obvious things it does.

Addressing this problem was an important shift in the attitudes of the mid-1970s. If the Church Committee had been confronted by a CIA that said, "Yes, we do engage in assassinating people down dark alleys and in keeping people in 'safe' houses in 'spartan' conditions if they do not tell us what we want to know—what do you think presidents have been authorizing for decades?" Frank Church would have been faced with the problem of saying, "Well, it has been all right for decades, but it isn't all right now." Instead, all Church had to do was hold the agency to its myth: everything was in the past; we do not need more stringent controls to ensure that those operating in the name of the American people act as anything but Americans or only in ways that Americans act. The trick was that Americans act like everybody else, and implicitly, therefore, the CIA could too. Church gave its actions democratic sanction.*

---

* The Pike Committee also exonerated the CIA from the charge of operating on its own authority as a band of mutinous mercenaries:

The origin of many covert action projects is murky at best.

The CIA, as the prospective implementation arm, is often directed to produce proposals for covert action and is, therefore, incorrectly seen as a plan's original proponent. It is

LAST SECRETS

Despite the fears of Gerald Ford, Henry Kissinger, Colby, and most of the officers of the agency, the CIA's intelligence activities did not come to a halt with the investigations. Morale suffered, and agency analysts were soon known around town to be reluctant to commit themselves to controversial positions for fear of publicity and possible investigation. David Atlee Phillips, chief of Latin American and Caribbean operations, took early retirement from the agency in May 1975 to create, with ex-colleagues, the Association of Former Intelligence Officers, to speak up for the CIA record, in effect as an outside pressure group, and to educate the American public about the need for and nature of intelligence. "There was some discussion about whether, instead, it might not be better for me to remain in CIA. I said that I had already made the decision. 'In that case,' Colby said, 'I wish you well.' I had the feeling the soldier-priest was not completely unhappy."[23]

Colby was not. He was glad to have support for the agency outside and another voice defending it as he grappled with one of the most active periods in the agency's analytical and operational history as well as the constant round of appearances before various congressional committees. The year 1975 saw the fall of South Vietnam to the Vietcong and North Vietnamese (April 30); the fall of Cambodia to the Khmer Rouge (April 17); the *Mayaguez* crisis (May 12–15), in which President Ford ordered the marine rescue of thirty-nine sailors from the SS *Mayaguez*, which had been hijacked by Cambodian patrol boats;* the launching of a major covert-action program in Angola (July); the secret supply of arms to Kurdish rebels in Iraq (May); another debate about SALT verification; the Turkish withdrawal of intelligence cooperation and bases in retaliation for Congress's refusal to lift an arms embargo on Turkey following its occupation a year earlier of northern Cyprus (July); and the revelation in the press in February of what was described within the agency as the "last secret," the *Glomar Explorer* operation to salvage a sunken Soviet nuclear-weapon submarine (1969–75).

---

clear that on several occasions involving highly sensitive projects, CIA was summarily ordered by the President or his National Security adviser to carry out a covert action program. It is further clear that CIA has been ordered to engage in covert action over the Agency's strong prior objections.

All evidence in hand suggests that the CIA, far from being out of control, has been utterly responsive to the instructions of the President and the Assistant to the President for National Security Affairs. It must be remembered, however, that the CIA Director determines which CIA-initiated covert action projects are sufficiently "politically sensitive" to require Presidential attention. (*CIA: The Pike Report* [Nottingham, England: Spokesman Books, 1977], p. 189).

---

* Before the marines landed in Cambodia, the Khmer Rouge had released the sailors. However, if the operation had not been launched, given what we now know about the Khmer Rouge regime, it is likely that the sailors would have been kept and tortured to death.

Project Jennifer was the code name given to the *Glomar Explorer* operation. It was reminiscent of the U-2 program; the agency once again found itself in business at the most advanced levels of technology and engineering. Unlike the U-2, however, the Jennifer Project was something the CIA undertook without objections from the military service concerned once it was in operation, in this case the navy. The navy had suggested the operation in the first place and had brought it to the 40 Committee. On the face of it, the whole idea of retrieving a Soviet submarine that had sunk at over 16,000 feet in the mid-Pacific in March 1968 was a navy operation. But the sophisticated electronic tracking of Soviet submarines, by satellite and by a network of underwater monitoring devices, involved not only the navy but also the National Security Agency and the CIA, giving the intelligence agencies an interest in the project. The need for secrecy pushed the project toward the CIA. In 1969, when Richard Helms was told that the plan to raise the Russian submarine was being seriously investigated by his people, he was very surprised. "You must be crazy!" he said, instinctively certain that the project was too complicated to be feasible.[24]

But as the evidence accumulated that the project might work, Helms became interested, and the Directorate of Science and Technology settled down to make plans. It came up with a proposal that the Hughes Tool Company, in association with another Hughes company, the Summa Corporation, should be commissioned to design a recovery ship that could be operated as part of the well-established Glomar Marine Corporation's fleet. Howard Hughes took a personal interest in the commission. His companies had been used in the past by the agency for contract work, and he must have recognized not only the potential commercial importance of the proposed ship but also the gratitude that would come from the White House and elsewhere following a successful effort. By mid-1970 the Summa Corporation and Glomar Marine had submitted their proposals, with total expenditures of about $30 million for the construction and fitting of a ship and a separate submersible. The *Glomar Explorer* was to be a 36,000-ton, self-stabilizing, deep-sea drilling ship which would also be a mother ship for a deep-sea exploration vehicle called *Hughes Mining Barge I* (HMB I).

The plans were accepted, and by the spring of 1974 the *Glomar Explorer* was ready for the attempt to lift the Soviet Golf II class submarine, with its missiles, code books and operational systems, from the seabed 750 miles west of Hawaii. The ship's components had been constructed in separate dockyards and its real purpose kept secret. Completed, its final cost was $70 million. It was regarded in the press and by most of those involved in its construction as another of Howard Hughes's eccentricities, in the tradition of his flying boat, the world's largest, built during World War II and flown only once. Glomar Marine and the Summa Corporation publicized the *Glomar Explorer* as a deep-sea mining/drilling/exploration ship intended to search the Pacific Ocean bed for minerals, oil, and precious metals.

After its successful sea trials, in the summer of 1974 it sailed on its first voyage, ostensibly on a commercial mining mission. Just off the coast of the California island of Santa Catalina, the HMB was taken aboard through the open-and-close hull of the ship. From there the *Glomar Explorer* sailed to the area where the Russian submarine had sunk six years earlier and quickly went to work. The HMB went down and soon found the submarine, its television cameras showing the operators in the surface ship that the submarine was intact. Despite the explosion that had caused the submarine to sink (probably a hydrogen gas leak that had been ignited by heat from the engine exhaust system) and the pressure under which it had lain—over 7000 lbs per square inch at 16,000 feet—it had not broken up into separate pieces.

The HMB, with its mechanical hand of six claw grips, fastened to the submarine. The initial connection was too far forward, and in adjusting the grip, two of the claws were bent. The lifting operation was started, and all went well until about 5000 feet from the surface, when the submarine broke in half, leaving only the front section in the claw grips. With this section the *Glomar Explorer* returned to California, and valuable information was obtained about Soviet nuclear submarine technology. Two nuclear torpedoes were recovered as well. The bodies of six Russians were in the hull, one of them being the submarine's nuclear-weapons officer. He had kept a detailed journal of his training and assignments, and this was salvaged too. It gave analysts a wealth of knowledge about Soviet naval nuclear-systems operation and procedures.

The following year—the year in which the true story of the *Glomar Explorer* and its mission broke in the press—plans were made for the ship to return to the site and recover the rear section of the submarine. Before a second trip could take place, however, the first press story leaked in the *Los Angeles Times* on February 7, 1975. William Colby threw himself into the effort of trying to convince newspaper owners and journalists not to publish the story in the interests of the operation. Their information, it seemed, had come from the Los Angeles Police Department, some of whose officers had been briefed about Project Jennifer following a burglary of Summa Corporation's Los Angeles headquarters in which documents about the operation had been stolen.

When the *Los Angeles Times* published the story on page one, Colby immediately telephoned the editor and managed to convince him to move the story in later editions of the paper back to page eighteen and to order his reporters not to do any follow-up pieces. *The New York Times* also had the story planned for February 8, but after a call from Colby it was moved to page thirty in the first edition and dropped entirely from later editions. Press cooperation did not last, however, and on March 18 Jack Anderson reported the story of the *Glomar Explorer* on national television.

This was the end of the intelligence use of the *Glomar Explorer*, but by then it had been very successful. Its retrieval operation had failed to secure the Russian codes and nuclear missiles and the steering and transmission devices in the aft section of the sunken submarine but had retrieved a wealth of other information.* The bodies recovered were buried with full military respect according to the rites of the Soviet navy. "A close CIA source," wrote an investigator of the project, "when questioned about why such a service had been held, reported there had been a lot of discussion on the matter, and the decision had been reached based on a concern for negative public opinion if the operation was ever blown and the recovery became public knowledge. No one wished to be thought of as callous, and the interment ceremony was designed to show proper respect for the fallen men."[25] The idea of secret activities by a secret agency remaining secret in all areas was over for the CIA in 1975; it had to conduct itself with an eye to publicity, no longer able to depend on the security of all its operations.

There was something else as well. Publicity in the United States has always been associated with power. Powerful people are held publicly accountable for the exercise of power by newspapers and congressional committees, in contrast to the European ethos of power as secret. Newspapers and parliaments in Europe that try to investigate powerful people rarely find them forthcoming unless they are forced to be. In America powerful people tend to welcome publicity because it is accepted as enhancing their power and respect within the community at large. In 1945 Donovan had reached for publicity as his best chance of securing the peacetime continuation of the OSS. In 1975 the attractions of publicity for one of the CIA's highly successful operations in the midst of hostile investigations into the agency's past were not denied. The television film of the recovery operation was kept, and the burial of the Russian seamen was filmed. William Colby personally telephoned all the journalists who had knowledge of the story just before Jack Anderson broke it, to tell them they could go ahead and publish because Anderson was going to reveal all anyway. Everyone knew that Project Jennifer was a CIA operation and a successful one. It was a great technological achievement. It was Yankee know-how at its best. The ideas that the agency was corrupt and sinister could not be applied to this story. It was an extremely popular success. The "no comment" from the agency and the White House that followed fooled no one.†

---

* When Colby's autobiography, *Honorable Men: My Life in the CIA*, was in typescript stage it reached a French publisher before it had been screened by the CIA. As a result, certain passages that were deleted on national security grounds in the book as published in the United States appeared in the French version. They revealed that the *Glomar Explorer* had failed to retrieve nuclear missiles, steering and transmission devices, and codes (William Colby, *30 Ans de CIA*, trans. Jean-Pierre Carasso [Paris: Presses de la Renaissance, 1978], pp. 331–335).

† Colby, *Honorable Men*, pp. 416–418. Colby denies that he welcomed publicity for the operation or that the retrieval was completely successful:

There were those who were convinced that the *Glomar* project was completely successful and that then, in order to keep this a secret, I deliberately went around to all those newsmen to plant on them a false story that it wasn't, fully aware that if I told enough people the story was bound to leak eventually. And there are others who are sure that I put the story out solely for public-relations reasons. According to this view, I reckoned that it would do the agency's image a world of good at a time when the headlines were scourging it for assassina-

VIETNAM AFTERSHOCK

Just as the dust was settling over the *Glomar Explorer* publicity, the fall of South Vietnam took over the front pages. Nixon and Kissinger in their secret Paris peace negotiations with the North Vietnamese, concluded in January 1973, had secured an agreement enabling the withdrawal of U.S. troops from Vietnam to take place without the immediate fall of the South Vietnamese regime. This was matched by a massive increase in American military and economic aid (totaling $3.2 billion in fiscal year 1973–74) to South Vietnam in accordance with the principles of the Nixon doctrine of selling friendly governments weapons and training to defend themselves rather than America providing them itself. For the first year and a half after the Paris agreement this approach worked. Despite a major increase in the number of North Vietnamese troops in the South, there were no major changes in territory during 1973 and most of 1974.

Then, late in 1974, Congress, in line with popular disenchantment with the continuing involvement with South Vietnam, voted to reduce U.S. aid by half. It was the signal that prompted the collapse of the South, which was no longer even confident of continuing U.S. financial support. Nixon and Kissinger had secured the acceptance of the Paris agreement by President Thieu of South Vietnam by secretly promising him full support if the North Vietnamese launched another offensive. The value of this promise was steadily eroded, however, by the progressive steps taken in Congress to restrict presidential power to undertake another war without its formal approval; the War Powers Act, passed in November 1973, legislated this principle. When Nixon argued that Congress was effectively supporting his actions in the various military and bombing campaigns of 1972 that helped to secure the Paris agreement from the North Vietnamese, because the military appropriations for South Vietnam were passed by Congress, the legislators reacted by reducing those appropriations. By April 1975 it was clear to everyone that the South Vietnamese government was in its last days. On April 28 President Ford ordered the evacuation of all Americans remaining in the country, and on the following two days 1373 Americans and 5595 Vietnamese (a small proportion of those who wanted to escape) were taken by U.S. Navy helicopters to American ships off the coast. On April 30 South Vietnam surrendered to the "Provisional Revolutionary Government of South Vietnam," the Vietcong.

---

tion attempts and illegal domestic activities to get the press to report on a project of such daring and brilliance as the *Glomar* certainly was. I must say, that this is all nonsense. The *Glomar* project stopped because it was exposed [ibid., p. 418].

The total cost of the operation was in the region of $300 million, according to President Ford (Ford, *A Time to Heal*, p. 132).

The last American ambassador to the South, Graham Martin, resisted suggestions during 1974 that Americans and their Vietnamese coworkers should be evacuated on the ground that this would prompt a panic. The CIA's analysts estimated after the Paris agreement that the North Vietnamese would probably make a push to take over the country in 1976 unless an opportunity to do so opened earlier, and Martin used this judgment to back his point. It was a controversial decision, fiercely debated in Washington as well as in Saigon. William Colby pressed for as many of his men and CIA informants as possible to be removed from Saigon during 1974 and early 1975, pointing out the dangers that would face them if they fell into Vietcong or North Vietnamese hands and arguing that the collapse of South Vietnam was inevitable.

Colby's case was accepted by Henry Kissinger, who, however, also argued that the man on the spot—Ambassador Martin—had to be free to make the decision on evacuation. Kissinger therefore backed Martin while simultaneously pressing him on the question. The consequence was a last-minute rush as Martin accepted the inevitable: approximately 120,000 South Vietnamese got out during April 1975. In retrospect, William Colby regarded this as a tribute to Kissinger's approach, because, he considered, fewer would have escaped in the panic that would have followed any earlier attempt at evacuation.[26]

Frank Snepp, a CIA analyst who served two tours in Saigon (the first from 1969 to 1971, the second from 1972 until 1975), violently disagreed and ultimately broke with the CIA in his determination to publicize what he regarded as a series of terrible decisions about evacuation. He believed that an earlier, orderly evacuation would have saved the lives of tens of thousands more Vietnamese coworkers and would also have maintained CIA security, which, he believed, was seriously compromised by the capture of Vietnamese informants and CIA documents following the April collapse. Snepp wrote later:

Only about 537 of the Station's 1,900 "indigenous employees" were finally evacuated, together with 2,000 others—including family members—who had enjoyed privileged contacts with the agency over the years. . . .

Large categories of Vietnamese who faced untold danger from the Communists or whose capture could prejudice American intelligence interests were left behind. Among them: the 400 members of the Special Police Branch, whose training the CIA had financed and supervised; 400 working echelon members of the Central Intelligence Organization, also our protégés; a large staff of clerks and computer operators which the Station had set up to keep book on PRG personalities; the young Vietnamese who served as our clandestine radio operators at the Embassy; the staff which maintained our special radio links with Vietnamese police headquarters; the hundred or more Vietnamese, including maids, waitresses and agents, who had collected at the Duc Hotel on the final day; several agents from Bien Hoa; the 70 translators whom [a colleague] had tried to rescue; literally hundreds of high-level defectors who had worked closely with the Station over the years to pinpoint and hunt down their former Communist comrades; and countless counter-terrorist agents—perhaps numbering as high as 30,000—specially trained to operate the Phoenix Program.

Then too, to compound our errors and their costs, we committed that unpardonable mistake of failing to ensure the destruction of the personnel files and intelligence dossiers we had helped the government assemble.[27]

According to Snepp, a serving CIA officer was left behind, captured, and inter-rogated by the new government. So was an ex-CIA officer, Tucker Gougel-mann, a giant of a man who had lost a foot some years earlier in a mine explosion in Vietnam but who had returned to Saigon to try to rescue Viet-namese friends. He was interrogated not only by the North Vietnamese but also by the KGB, and he died in captivity a year later. It was, altogether, a har-rowing story.

Without doubt, many people who had helped the CIA in Vietnam were left behind, and intelligence documents in the hands of the South Vietnamese authorities which compromised some CIA informants were captured by the new regime. On the other hand, thousands of Vietnamese who had helped the U.S. effort were rescued (an estimated 250,000 in all; about 130,000 managed to leave the South before the April 1975 rush), and the argument that panic might have set in earlier if a full evacuation had been put into operation was no doubt true.

As in all such cases, what happened was the result of decisions made on the spot, and the postmortems are always judgments and debates. As Saigon fell, however, it seemed symbolic of a humbling of America, of a loss of self-confidence at the time when the CIA, the agency presented as being there to protect America from surprises, was in the dock undergoing public scrutiny. Joseph Burkholder Smith, a CIA officer who became disillusioned with the agency at this stage, ascribed his new attitude to American involvement in Vietnam. "Without apology," he wrote, "I believed in the American Cen-tury. . . . It began in April 1950 when Harry S Truman signed NSC 68 and the Clandestine Services became a vital part of the resources that document called for to help America protect the Free World. It ended in April 1975, when we withdrew our support and the weak, corrupt and ineffective client state we had propped up in Saigon since 1954 collapsed almost before we could get out of town."[28]

The attitude of such people as Smith in the mid-1970s reflected a popular view of them and other whistle-blowers as representative casualties of the intol-erable and growing demands of power. A simple and paradoxically more "in-nocent" earlier republic of self-governing citizens was counterposed to a vision of an "invisible" government of cool experts, who were not so much wicked as remote and hard, seeing individual people as commodities to be bartered and manipulated. No serious examination of the American past was likely to justify so vulgar a distinction, but this did not prevent its being made. For many

Americans their country had been humbled and debased by its global involvements. There was a feeling that the CIA somehow bore a responsibility for this humbling, with a set of contradictory accusations being made: that the agency was simply inefficient; that if the agency had spent as much time tracking America's real enemies as it did tracking domestic dissent, there might have been a different end to the war; that the CIA had not made any difference in Vietnam, so why should it be kept?

When governments are defeated or are thwarted in major policy objectives, there is a natural quest to place blame. Presidents perceived to have failed or to have been inadequate are rarely elected for second terms. Generals who lose major battles are usually replaced. In 1975, in the wake of Saigon's fall, many people inside the agency agreed with William Colby that the CIA was fighting for its survival against the additional threat of being saddled in the public mind with the failure in Vietnam.

No one blamed the military for the Vietnam failure in the same way. There was no suggestion, for example, that West Point or the army should be abolished. The CIA was suspect because, unlike the military, whose actions had been clear and clearly understood, the CIA's actions were largely unknown and unclear. It was shadowy, an easy scapegoat. Its sophistication had not "won" the war or secured an honorable withdrawal. It had powerful bureaucratic enemies who were happy to expose it to public scrutiny. And it had powerful ideological enemies in government and elsewhere who, like Jimmy Carter, did not like shadows or dirty work, and did not know its role in convincing President Johnson to reassess America's involvement in Vietnam, tending instead to blame the agency for weakening his resolve at a crucial moment. Many saw the agency as an engine of misplaced efficiency: good at dealing with the wrong people—the shah in Iran, President Somoza in Nicaragua—and bad at dealing with American interests.

IRAQ AND ANGOLA

In the middle of the attack on the agency an Iraq covert-action operation was under way at the direction of the White House and the National Security Council. CIA help for rebel Kurd tribesmen in Iraq dated from 1972, when the shah of Iran secured President Nixon's agreement to joint U.S.–Iranian support for the Kurds in their struggle to secure independence. Iran had a long-standing dispute with Iraq over the border between them and saw the Kurds as a useful ally, keeping Iraq occupied. The support (in the form of weapons, food, and medical supplies) was channeled to the Kurds through Iran. In March 1975 the shah decided to withdraw his support (and effectively U.S. aid as well) from the rebels because the Kurds were losing their fight with the Iraqi army and he thought it wiser to settle his differences with Iraq. Colby had the unenviable task of explaining the sudden change in Iranian policy to a surprised President and State Department, who expected that the CIA (and Richard Helms, ambassador in Tehran) would have given earlier warning.

At about the same time the CIA was involved in another operation, in Angola, which was also under the direction of the White House and the National Security Council. Late in 1974, after Portugal announced that it would grant independence to its colony of Angola but before independence occurred, intelligence reports and satellite surveillance revealed that the Soviet Union was secretly arming the Popular Movement for the Liberation of Angola (MPLA). CIA analysts concluded that the purpose of this move was to give the MPLA the capability of annihilating its rival nationalist groupings, the National Front for the Liberation of Angola (FNLA) and the National Union for the Independence of Angola (UNITA). Both the State Department and the CIA took very seriously the prospect of Soviet domination of Angola. Angola had considerable wealth in the form of raw materials, oil refineries, and distribution systems (roads, railways, ports) connected to the Congo, Zambia, and Rhodesia. The country was also strategically placed in southern Africa, bordering on Namibia, where South Africa's control was increasingly being challenged by nationalist guerrillas. Under Portuguese rule, Angola was seen as a bastion of stability in the area, providing a base from which to counter—if necessary—Soviet influence.

By September 1975 the 40 Committee had approved $24.7 million for a CIA covert operation to support the FNLA and UNITA against the Soviet-backed MPLA in the civil war between the groups following Portugal's agreement to Angola's independence. The CIA stations in Pretoria (South Africa), Luanda (Angola), Lusaka (Zambia) and Kinshasa (formerly Congo-Leopoldville) were strengthened, and by 1976 eighty-three CIA officers were in the Angolan Task Force in the field, attached to these different stations.[29] Close cooperation was effected with the South African security services—South Africa had a direct interest because of Namibia—and with the Chinese, who joined in supporting UNITA and the FNLA to counter the Soviets, with whom they were competing for influence in Africa.

After the Portuguese left Angola in November 1975 the civil war intensified. At first the FNLA and UNITA forces dominated, then the MPLA, and then back again, at which point the Soviets, correctly reading opinion in the U.S. Congress and the effect of the legislation circumscribing presidential powers, organized the dispatch of twelve to fifteen thousand Cuban soldiers with tanks and aircraft to support the MPLA. The Russians calculated, accurately, that Congress would not support any greater American involvement. With the backing of the President, Colby formally requested the congressional appropriations committees for an increase in funding for the Angolan operation and maintained his frequent background briefings to congressmen on the operation. The fears of another Vietnam, only months after the fall of Saigon, dominated the thoughts of Congress, however, and Colby was rebuffed and the operation leaked to the press.

> The operation [Colby recalled] exploded into the public print a few months after the fall of Vietnam and in the middle of the Congressional investigations and hearings on CIA—and was sensationalized to suggest that a new terrible Vietnam-like American involvement, not mere assistance to black nationalists who wanted to fight for their own version of liberation, was being cooked up in far-off Africa. The Congress turned down our requests for more aid, and in a short time the MPLA's victory over its opponents was plain.[30]

While Colby was arguing for more funds for Angola from Congress he was also in the middle of the most sensational revelations about CIA activities over the years. He was filmed before the Church Committee with an electric pistol capable of firing dissolving poison pellets. He was giving evidence to the committee about part of the MKUltra program involving the secret filming of unwitting Americans to test the effects of drugs given them by prostitutes hired by the agency. He admitted that the agency had held stocks of deadly shellfish toxin after President Nixon had ordered them destroyed. Everyone in the agency felt very isolated, very much on his own. John Stockwell, chief of the Angola Task Force, described feelings within the CIA:

> We inside the agency reacted to these disclosures differently. The hard core was untroubled by their substance: "Are you kidding?" they would say. "Maybe we could straighten things out if the director had the balls to let us do more of that. . . . After all, the other side . . . " Others felt betrayed, by the CIA directors who had led the CIA into such activities, and by the changing rules which in one decade had us superpatriots and in another suggested we were enemies of the people. But, as the CIA's public image slipped, even the hardest cases felt insecure. If we were still the good guys, the elite of the American foreign service, we ourselves seemed to be the only ones who appreciated the fact. We drew closer into our little world, working with agency people, playing tennis with agency people, socializing with agency people. It was not a happy time to conduct a clandestine war.[31]

The sense of isolation and insecurity permeated every echelon of the agency. James Potts, the Africa Division chief, who briefed Colby for his meetings with Congress, the 40 Committee, and the National Security Council when the Angolan operation was discussed, found himself clinging to a smile. "One day Kissinger smiled at Colby, Colby returned to tell Potts about it, and Potts repeated it to us in his staff meeting, then instructed me to tell the task force," remembered Stockwell. "He also told his secretary to spread it around. It was, Potts felt sure, a favorable judgment of our early efforts that Kissinger had smiled at Colby during a National Security Council meeting. Everyone agreed."[32]

IN THE DOCK

Whether or not Kissinger's smile was important, the Senate and the House of Representatives were not smiling. And as President Ford, Henry Kissinger, and the CIA discovered over Angola, Congress' smile was important. Apart from the almost daily press headlines from the Church and Pike committees, there was also new legislation. The Hughes-Ryan Amendment to the 1961 Foreign Assistance Act required the director of Central Intelligence to brief no fewer than eight separate congressional committees in advance on any CIA action apart from intelligence collection. The effect of this, as seen over Angola, was that everything was leaked to the press, either through the members of the committees or through the committee staffs. "It was," said Senator Barry Goldwater ten years later, "a period of time when anyone working for the CIA had good reason to feel angry at the activities of the Congress towards the intelligence family."[33]

The Hughes-Ryan Amendment to the 1961 Foreign Assistance Act had been passed in 1974 following revelations in *The New York Times* that the agency had tried to prevent Salvador Allende's election in Chile during the six weeks between his winning a plurality of the popular vote and his election to the office of president by the Chilean Congress in 1970. The amendment meant that the CIA could not engage in covert operations without informing the various appropriate committees, with the inevitable press leaks following, and that it could not respond or act quickly with covert operations. It also meant that for the first time Congress had given legislative recognition to the CIA's covert-action function. The most serious problems in the relationship between the agency and Congress generally arose out of covert political and paramilitary actions, Laos being the prime example.*

There was a widely held feeling, shared not only by members of the Foreign Relations and Foreign Affairs committees but also by the intelligence subcommittees, that such operations should not properly be the responsibility of a covert-intelligence organization at all. Congressional sensitivity was particularly acute about efforts to influence foreign elections and about meddling with the media. "It's hard to generalize about the basis for this persistent con-

---

* In the opinion of Jack Maury, most of the congressional huffing and puffing was for public consumption only. "Some of these same members privately congratulated the agency for having done such an effective job in helping the Meo tribes to tie down such a large number of Communist troops on a budget that, in terms of the costs of the overall U.S. involvement in southeast Asia, was infinitesimal" (John Maury, "CIA and the Congress," *The Congressional Record*, Vol. 130, No. 117, September 18, 1984).

gressional sensitivity," wrote Jack Maury. "Perhaps it springs in part from a gut feeling that any attempt to influence the course of events abroad should be under close and continuing congressional scrutiny, and that the President and his immediate staff should not have at their disposal politically potent instruments which they can use without congressional knowledge and approval, and the misuse of which might produce serious consequences or embarrass the national image."[34]

Secret operations were not prohibited; Congress simply wanted to know about them. This was almost a contradiction in terms: if Congress knew about operations, they were very unlikely to stay secret. Congress was, in fact, taking up a spurious position. In part this was in reaction to the Nixon-Kissinger technique of "backchanneling," and not informing the officials and negotiators about the details of policy in their own highly secret negotiations over Vietnam, SALT, and China. It was also, paradoxically, a reaction against the idea of secrecy and of a secret agency outside of congressional oversight—something that Congress had been anxious to create during the previous twenty-seven years but now decided should be brought under far stricter control.*

On February 7, 1973, Helms had publicly testified during the hearings for his nomination as ambassador to Iran and on March 6, 1973, in executive session before the Senate Foreign Relations Subcommittee on Multinational Corporations that the CIA had not tried to overthrow the Chilean government (true; Track II was against Allende and not the government as such), and had not given money to candidates opposing Allende (true; money had been given to parties and organizations, not to individual candidates), and had not cooperated with ITT in either venture (again technically true; the effort had been to prevent Allende's being elected president). However, the news of Track II— which leaked as a result of Colby's informing members of the subcommittee on Inter-American Affairs of the House Foreign Affairs Committee—resulted in Helms' facing misdemeanor charges. On the day Jimmy Carter was elected President, President Ford announced that Richard Helms would resign as ambassador on January 1, 1977. In Washington, the Justice Department had decided to prosecute Helms for lying in his testimony.[35] The understandings that had operated in 1973 were now regarded as inadequate and, as such, unofficial. The only secrets that could be official were now not secrets at all but in effect public property as a result of the inevitable leaks.

Helms had done his best to keep the secrets, to protect the agency and its people from the real dangers of publicity. Dick Welch had been murdered because of publicity; John Rosselli and Sam Giancana were both murdered in

---

* It was senators and representatives themselves who voted against the various proposals to strengthen congressional oversight of the CIA. As CIA officers repeatedly point out, they spoke to the senators and representatives (the chairmen of the key committees, in effect) to whom they were told to speak by Congress itself. When Colby was required by the Hughes-Ryan Amendment to brief eight committees, he did; he had no right to refuse.

1975, almost certainly because other Mafia people were worried about what they might say to congressional committees, which had called for their testimony in the assassination-plot hearings. Publicity could do more than damage and embarrass, it could kill; and Helms was very aware of this. Now the public mood rejected the idea that the American government should have secrets that it kept back from the public's representatives, and Helms became a fall guy. He was seen as having collaborated with Nixon, as having covered up a dirty Nixon operation in Chile. The mood was for retribution. Giving evidence to the Senate Foreign Relations Committee in January 1975 about Track II, Helms said:

> I realize, sir, that my answer was narrow, but I would like to say something here. I didn't come to the Multinational Committee hearing to mislead you, but I have had as Director . . . a lot of problems, and one of the principal problems was who in the Congress [I] was really to divulge all of the details of covert operations to, and I must say this has given me a great deal of difficulty over the years. . . . If I was less than forthcoming it wasn't because I was being bloody-minded, it was simply because I was trying to stay within what I thought were the congressional guidelines.[36]

On October 31, 1977, Helms appeared in court, having made a deal with the Justice Department that he would plead *nolo contendere* to two misdemeanor charges arising from his testimony to the Senate Foreign Relations Committee in February and the Subcommittee on Multinational Corporations in March 1973. (The Latin phrase translated, "I do not wish to argue [or contend]," means in terms of law that a defendant in a criminal case does not admit guilt but is subject to conviction without impairing his right to deny the charges against him in a subsequent or parallel case.)* The Justice Department explained to the court that it had agreed to the deal in order not to have a contested case that would be bound to reveal and jeopardize national secrets during trial.

---

* In a congressional hearing in 1978 Helms was questioned about this charge by Representative Harold S. Sawyer:

"Well, you did, in fact, plead guilty to having withheld information from the Senate committee, didn't you?"

"No, sir, I did not, " Helms replied.

"I thought you had."

"I did not. I pleaded *nolo contendere.*"

"So that you just don't contest it, then, which is the legal equivalent of a plea of guilty, is that correct; except that it can't be used as an admission against you in a civil case; right?"

"I am not a lawyer, Mr. Sawyer."

"But I am sure you were advised by a lawyer before you entered a *nolo contendere;* were you not?"

"I was advised by lawyers."

(*Investigation of the Assassination of President John F. Kennedy,* Vol. IV, p. 245.)

In 1973, Spiro Agnew had pleaded *nolo contendere* in the corruption scandal that brought him down. The implications of the plea were well known.

Richard Helms had been worried that his pension might be affected by the plea but had been reassured on this point by the Justice Department. In court he explained his reason for making the deal. "I found myself in a position of conflict. I had sworn my oath to protect certain secrets. I didn't want to lie. I didn't want to mislead the Senate. I was simply trying to find my way through a very difficult situation in which I found myself."[37]

Helms had found himself in humiliating circumstances. His question about his pension testified to this. It was also a significant political event, showing that the agency by the late 1960s was led by people who were anxious about job security. Allen Dulles had always had Sullivan and Cromwell to return to. John McCone had great personal wealth and the Joshua Hendy Corporation to return to. William Raborn had a full admiral's pension and a lucrative consultancy with Aerojet General Corporation to return to. Helms had only the secret world, and he was out of it now.

The Rockefeller Commission had sensed this change in the agency's leadership from people who had other sources of income to CIA professionals who had only what the agency gave them. It had recommended that "Persons appointed to the position of Director of Central Intelligence should be individuals of stature, independence, and integrity. In making this appointment, consideration should have been given to individuals from outside the career service of the CIA, although promotion from within should not be barred. Experience in intelligence service is not necessarily a prerequisite for the position; management and administrative skills are at least as important as the technical expertise which can always be found in an able deputy."[38] By having directors with outside sources of income, the commission thought, there would be less danger that the independence and objectivity of the agency would be compromised. "The best assurance against misuse of the agency," the commission declared, "lies in the appointment to that position of persons with the judgment, courage, and independence to resist improper pressure and importuning, whether from the White House, within the agency or elsewhere."[39]

There was, however, a malassumption behind this recommendation. Wealth and outside sources of income are no guarantees of moral strength. Helms had as much moral strength as any of his predecessors, and his "no" over Watergate had been uttered in the face of enormous political and personal pressure. Colby, the only other CIA careerist to become director, had also demonstrated moral strength and independence in the way he dealt with the investigations of the agency. What the commission did not fully realize, and what Helms's question about his pension revealed, was that the CIA as an agency designed for improvisation was manned by people who were no longer able to improvise in their private lives.

In all senses, the agency was shown to be a mature bureaucracy. It was manned by a cadre of people who were just as much outside the mainstream of life as are any group of government officials. The people who had started the agency and who had been political operatives during World War II, who were well placed and well connected, had gone. There was no new agency cadre that had similar experience. "Do we establish a trust fund of $10 million for every director and thus ensure his judgment, courage, and independence?" was the revealing question the Rockefeller Commisssion effectively asked. The answer was not what the commission recommended. It was what Helms's anxiety had revealed: if anything, the CIA had triumphed too well—its professionalism was an isolating factor. The prospect of life after the institution was worrying to men and women whose only experience was secret government service. As professionals they could be depended upon to provide their best judgments. As Americans, they knew that other Americans had still not come to terms with secrecy in government.

Four days after the court appearance Judge Parker of the Federal District Court sentenced Helms to a two-thousand-dollar fine—the maximum—and a two-year suspended jail term. In sentencing Helms, Parker said:

> You considered yourself bound to protect the agency whose affairs you had administered and dishonor your solemn oath to tell the truth. If public officials embark deliberately on a course to disobey and ignore the laws of our land because of some misguided and ill-conceived notion and belief that there are earlier commitments and considerations which they must observe, the future of our country is in jeopardy.
>
> There are those employed in the intelligence security community of this country . . . who feel that they have a license to operate freely outside the dictates of the law and otherwise to orchestrate as they see fit. Public officials at every level, whatever their position, like any other person, must respect and honor the Constitution and the laws of the United States.

Leaving the court, Helms drove to the Kenwood Country Club in Bethesda, Maryland, where four hundred retired CIA officers gave him a standing ovation and within minutes collected cash and checks to the amount of the fine.[40]

For years real bitterness and anger soured relations between Helms and Colby as a result of the case. They represented two opposing views of the place and function of intelligence in the United States. Helms was of an older, traditional school, founded by Donovan during World War II, which recognized the need for America to have effective intelligence and secrecy and sought a place for it under the mantle of the President as commander in chief. When appointed director in 1966 Helms had commented: "I think there's a tradition that the CIA is a silent service, and it's a good one. I think the silence ought to begin with me."[41]

William Colby had served in the same school but accepted the fact that the nature of American democracy demanded that secrecy be agreed to democratically, with the consequence that people and secrets might be hurt in the inevitable public debate until the place and nature of secrecy was determined publicly. The European concepts of gentlemen whose understandings and personal loyalties could supersede public duties had no place in America. In February 1976 the Lockheed Aircraft Corporation was caught in exactly the same way when it was forced by law to admit to the Senate Subcommittee on Multinational Corporations that it had paid over $22 million in bribes to foreign leaders to secure contracts. To be European gentlemen, several Lockheed executives would have had to face the prospect of jail if they had not betrayed the confidences of these relationships. It wasn't that Helms was a gentleman in a European sense, it was that conflicts in United States laws precluded the effective operation of understandings and personal considerations of loyalty.

William Colby had a greater sense of being an American gentleman: his instinct was to reach for the law and be guided by the letter of the law when in crisis, rather than to reach for friends and private arrangements. It was the contrast between the journalist, Helms, with a concept of "off-the-record" and "deep background briefing," and the lawyer, Colby, who knew that ultimately everything was on the record under law. For Colby the effect of the Track II revelations on Helms was personally painful. As he wrote later:

> Here I was in the middle of another conflict between the past and the future. Helms as a totally loyal servant of his President and his intelligence profession had manfully tried to keep the secret he had been directed to keep. But that middle-grade CIA officer [who in 1973 had brought to Colby's attention the possibility of Helms being guilty of perjury because of his Chile testimony] had equally properly reacted to my very specific instructions that he should present to me anything about whose propriety he had the slightest doubt. If I accepted the one, I repudiated the past; if I accepted the other, I compromised the future.

After consulting Lawrence Silberman, the acting attorney general, Colby determined to repudiate the past:

> I did what I had to do. Times had truly changed since 1954 [when an agreement had been struck that the CIA, because of the secrecy of its operations, could decide on its own whether or not to report possible criminal charges to the Justice Department]. . . .
> Besides, I was convinced that no fair jury in the land would conclude that Helms had committed perjury, and that therefore he would not be indicted for it. And the subsequent long silence from the Justice Department [Colby had sent them the Track II file in December 1974; they decided to prosecute Helms in January 1977], despite occasional press rumblings, seemed to confirm my original assessment. Indeed, the final outcome, with Helms avoiding a show trial by not contesting a lesser misdemeanor that he had not "fully, completely and accurately" testified to Congress, specifically eliminated the perjury charge. One can only wonder how often that "fully, completely and accurately" standard is breached in Washington, and consequently whether the Justice Department's using it against Helms reflected

more of a political than a legal attack on his directorship of CIA. But some would say, therefore, that I should never have presented the matter to Silberman, since that started the process, and I accept blame for that as the cost of my belief that intelligence must operate according to new rules.[42]

The new rules were more than the Hughes-Ryan Amendment. In June 1976 Congress approved the Tunney-Clark Amendment to the Arms Export Control Act specifically forbidding covert action in Angola. Both these amendments, combined with the establishment of a Senate Intelligence Oversight Committee in 1976 and a similar House committee the following year, meant that for the CIA, part of whose function was covert actions, it was as if they were in the position of the medical staff in a hospital waking up one morning to find their board of governors consisted of Christian Scientists and herbalists. It was a hopeless situation, driving the agency more and more into analytical work. "Few major covert action programs were proposed for a number of years for many reasons," observed Ray Cline, "one of which was the absurd requirement by Congress that members of eight separate committees be briefed on any CIA action."[43]

Gerald Ford, reviewing the actions of Congress in the mid-1970s, explained:

> When I served in the House the system we had for monitoring the CIA worked well. Under that arrangement, eight Representatives and six Senators were designated as overseers. We met with the CIA director and his top staff people on a regular basis. No staff members ever joined us and there were no leaks. It was in one of those sessions, for example, that I was informed about our plans to build the U-2 and I was kept abreast of every development from the inception of the program. Only a handful of people knew about the planned overflights of the USSR and we kept the secret to ourselves. That couldn't happen today.
>
> The reason is the Hughes-Ryan amendment of 1974. Congress decided that the "appropriate committees" that had to be informed of CIA activities totalled eight with a combined membership of 163 Senators and Representatives. That's not including the dozens of top staff members who would be privy to reports. Anytime you tell some 200 people in Washington, D.C., the details of a "secret" operation, the odds are overwhelming that they'll be in the media soon. Rather than risk exposure and embarrassment, the intelligence agency will simply decide not to undertake the operation it planned. That's what happened to the CIA.[44]

ESTIMATING PROBLEMS

Focusing on its analytical work, the agency did not escape attacks on its Estimates. The Pike Committee singled out several of what it termed "intelligence failures" on the analytical side: a failure to forecast the Tet offensive, which it most unfairly blamed on the CIA; failure to detect the Warsaw Pact's arrangements for the invasion of Czechoslovakia in 1968; failure to predict the 1973 Mideast War; failure to predict accurately the nature of the 1974 Portuguese revolution; failure to monitor effectively India's progress toward its successful testing in 1974 of a nuclear device; and the failure, also in 1974, to forecast the coup in Cyprus and the following Turkish invasion of the island.[45] At the same time, another conflict over SALT involving the agency's judgment of Soviet capabilities mushroomed again.

The problem over SALT in 1975 was similar to the problem that had faced the agency six years earlier when the accuracy of its analysis was seen as jeopardizing the Nixon administration's effort to achieve an arms-limitation agreement with the Soviets. This time the subject was monitoring Soviet adherence to SALT. It was of great political significance because President Ford hoped to agree to a second arms-limitation agreement—SALT II—in time to improve his chances of gaining the Republican party's nomination for the 1976 presidential election. SALT I was made possible because Richard Helms had assured Congress that the United States could monitor Soviet compliance and because the CIA had been able to supply Nixon, Kissinger, and the SALT negotiators with accurate information about Soviet intentions and weapons capabilities. CIA figures had been used as the basis of SALT I negotiations.

Throughout 1975, however, there were mounting charges in Congress and in newspapers that the Soviets were violating SALT I, with the implication that the CIA and the rest of the intelligence community was not, in fact, able to monitor the Soviets effectively. If the Soviets were violating SALT I, questioned critics, then why didn't the CIA say so? The reason for the CIA's silence on the question of violations was not that it did not know about them (it did, and reported them in detail to Henry Kissinger and to a closed session of the Senate Armed Services subcommittee hearings on Soviet compliance with SALT) but that it was governed by domestic politics. The "hold" procedure that was used to disguise the limited nature of SALT I when it was oversold to the American public before the 1972 presidential election was still being followed in 1975, with the result that CIA reports of violations were not circulated.

This contributed to a very messy set of arrangements about intelligence reporting and an atmosphere laden with suspicion, which was damaging to the CIA on one hand and to Henry Kissinger on the other. Since Soviet weapons development had not been prohibited by SALT I—although most Americans thought that it had—Kissinger and Nixon and then Kissinger and Ford tried to avoid the problems that might arise from public discovery that SALT I was not an agreement that prevented the Soviets from gaining a weapons advantage over the United States and was simply an agreement to limit specified weapons.* The "hold" procedure and a vigorous attempt to secure a second, more comprehensive SALT agreement were the results. As the attempt dragged on, however, charges of a "cover-up" were made against the administration along-side allegations that the Soviets were violating SALT I and deliberately deceiving the United States.

By 1976 this was an election issue with Ronald Reagan, the leading Republican challenger to Ford for the party's presidential nomination, making the removal of Kissinger and the review of the policy of détente main planks in his campaign. Jimmy Carter also made use of these themes in his campaign. Included in his argument were charges that the Russians were cheating; that Henry Kissinger had made a hatful of bad deals; that the CIA was good only for spying illegally on Americans and couldn't tell what the Soviets were really up to. The intelligence community as a whole was trapped in the debate because of its central role in monitoring and reporting Soviet adherence (or the lack of it) to SALT I.

The difficulty for the intelligence community was that its reports, enshrined in the CIA's National Intelligence Estimates, were perceived by policy makers as dangerous because of their accuracy. It was the same old problem: being right wasn't good enough—being on the inside was far more important. In the middle of all the fury surrounding the CIA, Colby sensed that this time the agency had to get the presentation of its analysis, and not simply the analysis itself, right. Both he and the CIA were in a political maelstrom, and Colby reacted by trying to simplify every problem and deal with things as they came up. Unlike Dulles or McCone or Helms, who had all had the luxury of being able to develop strategies to enhance the agency's influence and power, Colby had time only for crude tactics.

Dulles had been able to establish the CIA firmly as a principal player in foreign policy. McCone had placed the agency solidly in the world of technical intelligence. Helms had made the agency a powerful bureaucratic player. Each had been able to act because of the agency's friends in the White House and the Congress. But once the agency lost its most important friend, the President, during Nixon's term of office, it found its other friends melting away like ice in a furnace. Its natural allies, the liberals, regarded it with fear and disappointment. The credit the agency might have had with them for its stand on the Vietnam War was lost by the agency's simultaneous effort to stay inside the reservation and dampen its criticisms of policy.

The revelations of the Rockefeller, Church, and Pike investigations drove the agency into psychological isolation: CIA people played tennis with each other because no one else wanted to play with them. The enemies the agency

---

* America wanted to "go home," to isolate itself again, and so it was politically very difficult for Ford or Nixon to declare that the Soviets had obtained more from SALT I than the United States had. To admit this would have involved a call for reinvigorated engagement, fueling isolationist instincts at home.

had made along the way—the congressmen like Senator Eugene McCarthy who felt left out; the State Department, which did not like competition on its turf; the armed services, which, particularly over Vietnam, resented civilians with access to military information who argued with them over strategy and tactics as well as their appropriations—all saw the White House's cutting off and the public onslaught on the agency as their opportunity to settle scores and gain advantages. Colby had to face it all. He was the most beleaguered director of Central Intelligence ever.

The bureaucratic and political enemies of the agency centered their attempts to reduce the CIA's power and influence on the Estimates. The breach in the CIA's analytical wall came as a result of an error on the calculation of Soviet military expenditure. The effort to quantify everything, including the proportion of gross national product the Soviet Union devoted to defense, originated during Robert McNamara's period as secretary of defense. The amount of money the Soviets spent on their weapons and armed forces was interesting and useful for overall economic analysis of the Soviet economy, but it was not as important as information about the actual strength and effectiveness of the Soviet military. Ten percent of the USSR's GNP was substantially less than 10 percent of the USA's, and the differences of efficiency in the use of resources and of weapons would also have to be calculated. Cost, in other words, did not equate with strength.

Nevertheless, once the effort started to quantify everything, from the labor cost of a Soviet worker to the comparative unit cost of a tank, it did not stop. The difficulties of accurately quantifying elements in the economic arena, however, gave the agency an Achilles' heel. Within the CIA in the mid-1960s there had been a debate about whether or not the effort should be made, with some members of the Board of National Estimates questioning the real use of the exercise, arguing that what mattered was accuracy about numbers and capabilities of soldiers and weapons. The Office of Research and Reports within the DDI had been working since the mid-1950s on methods of calculating the cost of the Soviet defense effort. This, coupled with the demand from McNamara for quantifiable data and the new importance of economic reporting, brought about by the emergence of Third World countries and demands for specific information about their economies, carried the day.

Entering the field of economic forecasting and military spending represented a bureaucratic success for the agency, although the focus on foreign economies was another reminder that the power of the United States was diminishing: America had to take serious account of more and more countries. In March 1965 John McCone worked out an agreement with the secretary of state, Dean Rusk, giving the Office of Research and Reports the right to be the primary source of economic analysis on noncommunist countries. It was an area that the State Department was weak in, and McCone had seen and taken the opportunity to extend the agency's area of influence. In a similar vein, as a result of the Cuban missile crisis in October 1962, McCone (who had played a central role throughout the crisis) successfully argued that the agency needed access to U.S. strategic plans in order to provide full intelligence support to the President.

After the crisis the agency, with McNamara's support, continued to receive regular reports on U.S. strategic planning, bolstering its claims to provide strategic research in all areas. Early in 1965 this was recognized by the Department of Defense in an agreement negotiated by McCone which established the CIA's primary responsibility for research into the cost of foreign military and space programs. This agreement resolved the residual military opposition to the CIA's having access to U.S. military capabilities and opened the way for the agency to try to meet McNamara's constant requests for comparative assessments of Soviet and American military capabilities. Part of the resistance to this development by Sherman Kent and other members of the Board of National Estimates was that they feared that by incorporating assessments of U.S. forces in the National Intelligence Estimates they would be drawn into conflicts about U.S. military programs. They also questioned whether a proper basis for cost comparisons could be established.[46] They understood that a major problem in Soviet estimates was gauging the *quality* of Soviet units, weapons systems, soldiers, labor, and so on.

A straightforward ruble-dollar conversion was inadequate; no one believed that the announced figures of Soviet military spending were accurate or that the Soviet definition of their defense spending was comparable to U.S. categories. In the SALT negotiations, Soviet military negotiators were always anxious that their civilian colleagues should not hear American statements and assessments of Soviet military capabilities; they showed more concern for their own domestic political considerations than for the accuracy of U.S. intelligence. So it was fair to assume that their published figures were inaccurate. There was also a problem in setting a true value in dollar terms on the ruble. The Soviet economy is closed, trading with the outside world in goods and services or in gold rather than in cash transactions, and it was therefore very difficult to gauge the value of the ruble in relation to its comparative purchasing power. It was more effective to examine the whole Soviet budget as published and redefine its categories to see how much was being spent on defense as defined in the U.S. budget, thus providing an overall percentage of GNP in ruble terms. Another method was to examine the figures and categories of Soviet industrial output and estimate through a comparison with the U.S. output how much was military.

A combination of these two approaches was chosen by the Office of Research and Reports (renamed the Office of Economic Research in 1967 when it focused on international economic analysis). A "building-block" method was developed in which actual output was costed in U.S. terms. If the Russians produced a hundred new tanks, for example, they were counted at what it would cost the U.S. to produce a hundred comparable tanks. Then this U.S. cost would be projected in rubles to assess the impact on the entire Soviet economy. Done over the whole range of Soviet military ouput (which was constantly monitored by satellite surveillance) in the context of the Soviet economy as a whole, this provided what was thought to be a reasonably accurate assessment of Soviet-American comparative defense spending. There was a central vulnerability in the method, however, which was seized on by the Defense Intelligence Agency: an American tank was not comparable to a Russian tank. American weapons were much more sophisticated.* Even in terms of the overall economies of both countries, the costs of different weapons systems were not comparable. The economies were not comparable.

Major General Daniel Graham, who became director of the Defense Intelligence Agency (DIA) in 1974, came to the post after a stint on the order-of-battle estimates in Vietnam and having served as Colby's deputy for the national intelligence community (rather than the CIA). He was an energetic enthusiast. He stood out in the intelligence community because he did not project prudence. He was a man who believed every moment was a battle for the world. By 1974, Graham was the senior zealous anticommunist in intelligence, and he had a highly political view of the struggle with the Soviets. He knew the CIA and its methods well and in his new job used this knowledge in an effort to strengthen the DIA. One of the first things he did was to challenge the CIA's "building block" method of comparing American-Soviet military expenditures. Since 1970 DIA analysts had used a different method for costing the Soviet defense effort and had come up with consistently higher figures than the CIA. It seemed—and was presented by the agency as such—that this was the old battle between the military and the civilian analysts, in which the military were really eyeing their appropriations rather than realistically estimating the Soviet threat. Graham, however, had identified the vulnerability of the "building block" method and was satisfied that the DIA analysts were more accurate than the CIA.

Edward Proctor, who joined the CIA as a young economist with a Ph.D. from Harvard in the early 1950s and who was heavily involved in developing the "building block" method, had been appointed deputy director for intelligence by Richard Helms in 1971. He too began to sense that the "building block" approach might not be as accurate as had been thought in 1972 when it was obvious that Soviet military production was much larger than the CIA's estimate of the proportion of GNP it was taking up. This was supported by

* Does an American tank which, if it works as planned, is the best in the world, but which because of its complexity may break down often, compare to a Russian tank of primitive construction but which, if it is not destroyed, may still be operating on the second day of battle? Does a Soviet soldier who fights on despite being wounded and who will wait silently for days until rescued, compare to an American soldier who will fight bravely, but whose morale will crack if a wounded colleague is not rescued right away? Qualitative as well as quantitative judgments were involved all the time.

evidence from defectors who had worked in Soviet economic planning and by a copy of the Soviet Politburo's Statistical Handbook obtained by the CIA which gave the "real" figures of Soviet military spending. By mid-1975 everyone realized that the CIA's January 1975 estimate—that Soviet spending was only 20 percent more than American spending—was a substantial underestimate.[47]

With this internal doubt and external attack on the "building block" method, Colby had to make an assessment. He appointed a joint CIA-DIA study group, giving for the first time a non-CIA team of analysts equal weight with the agency's own. It was a major bureaucratic victory for the DIA, cemented when the CIA analysts accepted that their estimates of Soviet spending had been about half of what the Soviets had actually spent. In February 1976 the agency's estimate was revised upward: the Soviet Union was spending much more than the United States on defense, Proctor now said, and 10 to 15 percent of Soviet GNP was consumed by military spending as opposed to the 6 to 8 percent previously thought. The Russians, in other words, were more militarist than the CIA had reported, and the cries of alarm from the U.S. military and the concern about SALT I and Soviet violations suddenly seemed far more serious. To many the CIA's performance in this most important area of American concern was dangerously disappointing. Once again Colby had behaved correctly and the agency had been hurt.

A TEAM/B TEAM

The upshot of the CIA's admission of error was a further dilution of its monopoly of National Intelligence Estimates. With Colby's dissolution of the Board of National Estimates in October 1973, all the final assessors of CIA Estimates were outside the agency. National Intelligence officers submitted their draft Estimates to the United States Intelligence Board (consisting of the heads of the intelligence community), where they were vulnerable to bureaucratic alliances against the agency. The President's Foreign Intelligence Advisory Board (PFIAB), the civilian overseers of the intelligence community for the President, independently reviewed Estimates and made recommendations about intelligence activities and organization. Ever since its creation by Eisenhower, the PFIAB had pressed for more power for itself in controlling U.S. intelligence; this remained a constant drive despite the fact of changing membership with each new administration.

Again competing interests and the CIA's vulnerability resulted in a reduction of the CIA's autonomy. In August 1975 the chairman of the PFIAB, George W. Anderson, Jr., wrote to President Ford suggesting that there should be "competitive analysis" of the CIA's Estimate of Soviet intentions and capabilities. Such an analysis would, of course, develop a competitor of equal significance to the CIA's Soviet experts and would place the PFIAB in a position of judgment over the director of Central Intelligence, whose role that had so far been. One Estimate would be the director's Estimate; another of equal weight would be someone else's. The bureaucratic consequences of scrapping the effort to achieve consensus in National Estimates was catching up with Colby. He saw the dangers to the agency and to the position of the director of Central Intelligence in Anderson's proposal and tried to stave it off. He assured President Ford that the forthcoming National Intelligence Estimate would meet the criticisms being made about costing Soviet military expenditure and that he himself was taking a personal interest in the Estimate.

Ford acceded to Colby's representations, but the following year, after the 1975 Estimate had been published, Anderson renewed his pressure for a retrospective analysis. He was not satisfied that the CIA, which had seriously underestimated the economics of the Soviet defense effort for a decade, should be the prime national estimator on the Soviet Union. It was an argument that made sense in the light of experience, and Ford agreed. The CIA was now just one of several competing agencies, and the director of Central Intelligence was no longer the President's chief intelligence officer in practice. Donovan's argument for central, coordinated intelligence was being swept away.

Two teams were formed by the National Security Council: the "A Team," of CIA analysts under Howard Stoertz, the agency's national intelligence officer for the Soviet Union, who when Ford made his decision in favor of retrospective analysis was already preparing the 1976 Estimate, and the "B Team," consisting of a number of specialized study groups of outside experts and a senior review group responsible for an overall assessment. The B Team was headed by Professor Richard E. Pipes, professor of Russian history at Harvard, and was weighted toward critics of the CIA's "building block" method and of the SALT process.* Not surprisingly, the B Team in its report at the end of 1976 concluded that CIA Estimates had underestimated Soviet strength and that, in consequence, the United States had not prepared sufficiently to meet the possible Soviet threat.

The Soviet Union, the B Team held, was intent on a first-strike, war-winning capability against the United States, and was pursuing a policy geared to achieving global domination through economic leverage (control of world shipping; control of gold prices; control through development and distribution of Third World resources) backed by military might. The A Team, while

* Other members of the senior B Team group were General Daniel Graham; General John Vogt, former USAF Chief of Staff; William R. Van Cleave, a SALT negotiator; Colonel Thomas Wolfe, a Rand Corporation analyst and former air attaché in Moscow during the mid-1950s; General Jasper A. Welch, Jr., head of USAF systems analysis; Paul Wolfowitz from the Arms Control and Disarmament Agency; Seymour Weiss from the State Department; and Paul Nitze, one of the Washington insiders, having served as McNamara's deputy at the Defense Department and having chaired or been on several commissions of inquiry into intelligence and foreign-policy matters.

amending the estimate of Soviet defense spending, maintained the CIA's established view that the Soviets were less efficient but were all the time improving their weapons systems. The essential difference between the two teams related to Soviet intentions, with the B Team taking a very pessimistic view and the A Team remaining in the tradition of containment attitudes.

Both teams presented their reports to the PFIAB and argued their respective cases, and, according to the B Team, their arguments had a direct effect on the 1976 CIA Soviet Estimate. "We just licked them on a great number of points," said one B Team member. "Sometimes we left them speechless," said another. "We had men of great prestige, some of them with memories going back twenty-five years or more, and they made devasting critiques of agency estimates." The 1976 Estimate (which was not actually addressed by the B Team) was sent back to the CIA three times for redrafting, and was not approved until January 1977.[48]

COLBY'S BOAT

As the A Team/B Team competition started, William Colby was fired as director of Central Intelligence by President Ford. Protesting that he liked and respected Colby very much and that he supported him fully in his policy of full disclosure of CIA secrets to Congress, Ford explained that "this did not alter my conviction that the agency needed a change at the top. Colby had completed his exhaustive Capitol Hill testimony about past CIA activities. Drawing essentially on the excellent recommendations of the Rockefeller Commission, we had proceeded with plans to reorganize and reform the agency. If that reorganization was to have the substance as well as the image of a significant change, we had to appoint a new man to preside over it."[49]

Most observers thought that Colby's directorship had represented both the substance and the image of a significant change, witnessing a secret agency itself revealing its secrets—a sign that the CIA was becoming a technical institution, removed from covert action. Colby had driven the Rockefeller Commission to its conclusions and recommendations. It was far more likely, despite his claims to the contrary, that President Ford had had enough. He had a limited time in which to create an image for himself and his administration that would enable him to overcome his association with Nixon and his pardoning of Nixon for any crimes he may have committed in office. The pardon had struck millions of voters as smacking of a behind-the-scenes deal, and although it was not, Ford lost considerable credibility and support. The continuing revelations of CIA activities kept the shadow of the Nixon administration across the Ford White House. A new man at the CIA could only help to create a better atmosphere as Ford entered 1976, the presidential election year.

"I had a great respect for President Ford," said Colby, "and he fired me.

He had to indicate politically that he was taking control. He chose a very good man, George Bush, his man, and he put him in to take control and show that the misery was all over."[50] Colby was told the news by the President in person in the Oval Office, and he had known it was coming:

> To a large degree, the circus that the Church committee and the media made out of the poisons and dart gun was the last straw for the White House. From the outset I had been, of course, aware that many in the administration did not approve of my cooperative approach to the investigations, and I had felt myself increasingly isolated from the White House "team" as the year progressed. I had been blamed for not categorically denying Hersh's story at the very beginning; I had been criticized for turning material on Helms over to the Department of Justice; I had been chided for being too forthcoming to the Rockefeller Commisssion; I had been scolded for stonewalling at every Congressional hearing. But the impact of the toxin spectacular, and especially the fact that I had delivered the dart gun when Congress demanded it, blew the roof off.[51]

At 8 o'clock on Sunday morning, November 2, 1975, Colby was told he was going. It was the start of Ford's "Halloween Massacre," when he shuffled his administration, chiefly to cover the fact that Nelson Rockefeller was not going to run as his vice-presidential candidate in 1976. Ford had decided to drop Rockefeller because he was unpopular with the Republican right wing, and if Ford wanted the party's nomination himself he had to make concessions to the right. He wanted his men in place as he prepared for the election, and his men were those who would best help him win it. Henry Kissinger was removed from his post as national security adviser and replaced by his deputy, Brent Scowcroft.

Kissinger remained secretary of state; politically, Ford had no alternative but to ride out the opposition to Kissinger and take the equal benefits accruing from having so brilliant a person in his cabinet. He had kept Kissinger in his posts after becoming President, and to lose him now would be seen as a complete turnaround by Ford on foreign policy. Dropping him as national security adviser was enough to indicate that Kissinger was not supremely powerful and that Ford had a mind of his own. James Schlesinger, with whom neither Kissinger nor Ford got on, was fired as secretary of defense and replaced by Donald Rumsfeld, Ford's principal assistant. Some other changes were made as well, but for the CIA the appointment of George Bush as Colby's successor was the most important.

Everyone recognized that Colby's departure was meant to mark an end to revelations and investigations of the CIA. They were damaging to America's image abroad and politically embarrassing at home. This was tacitly accepted in Congress, where several senators and representatives had been hurt when the investigations turned up their relations with the agency in the days of the old understandings. Representative Lucien Nedzi, for example, had lost the chairmanship of the House Committee on Intelligence early in 1975 when it became known that he had been informed of covert actions by the CIA in the past. Throwing stones in glass houses is always likely to break some glass, and the congressional investigations were matched by journalistic revelations of the private lives of congressmen, often with scandalous results.

Altogether, there was a sense of enough being enough, and during 1976 the investigations of the CIA were ended and new revelations of CIA activity dwindled away. People wanted to forget the past, to draw a veil over it and certainly over those associated with revealing the murkier secrets. "It looks like Dick Helms outlasted both of us," said James Schlesinger to William Colby as they dined together on the evening of the "Halloween Massacre."[52] It was an innocent portent of the future. Ford, seen as a Washington insider, narrowly beat Ronald Reagan for the Republican nomination, but then narrowly lost the election to an outsider, Jimmy Carter. The revelations, not the actions revealed, became what people wanted to forget. There had been a blooding of America in Vietnam and with Watergate, and Americans in the main seemed to have decided, reluctantly, that although America's place was in the world— not aside from it—the world was a tough and dangerous and dirty place. It needed a capability that could play the world's games and win for America. Eight years later, in another presidential election year, President Reagan would gain popular support for a public statement that there had been a "near destruction" of U.S. intelligence capability before he came to office in 1981 as a result of the investigations and revelations.[53] The wheel had come full circle, and the ethos of Dick Helms had indeed outlasted the two diners.

The twelve most senior ex-CIA officers polled by David Atlee Phillips on which director they would like to share a pleasant island with voted six for Allen Dulles; four for Richard Helms; one for John McCone, and none for William Raborn or William Colby. Phillips kept his own vote back. When it came to sharing the terrible desert island, however, it was a different story:

> Dulles did not receive a vote. Nor did Raborn. The eleven votes were split: four for McCone, four for Helms, three for Colby. I could have broken the deadlock by voting for either McCone or Helms. But I thought about Chesterton and his island. What if a volume of How to Build a Boat for One Passenger should float ashore on my desert island? With that in mind, my vote did not break the deadlock, but created a three-way tie. I selected Colby. He would get us both off that island. Certainly he would never entertain the notion of building a boat for one or, if he did reach that point, he would later stand in the surf and wave good–bye—a faint smile on his thin lips after pushing me out to sea.[54]

—18—

Secrecy in the Republic 1976–1980

"No employee of the United States Government shall engage in, or conspire to engage in, political assassination," declared President Ford on February 18, 1976, in Executive Order 11905. It was the first time a President had declared such a policy, and it was to be repeated by his successors. In itself the declaration represented no change from the position under any previous President. It was a political statement, made for political purposes: the President was publicly responding to Colby's revelations and the recommendations of the Rockefeller Commission. It reflected an entirely American approach to relations with the world in its guiding assumption that Americans have the right to know what their government does and that there always comes a time when government activity is made public. The executive order also reorganized the structure of foreign-affairs coordination procedures, reducing the role of the director of Central Intelligence. Covert operations were removed from the DCI's direct responsibility and placed with an Operations Advisory Group, which also replaced the 40 Committee.*

Intelligence coordination was made the province of a three-man Commit-

---

* The OAG consisted of the secretaries of state and defense, the chairman of the Joint Chiefs of Staff, the DCI, and the President's national security adviser. The attorney general and the director of the Office of Management and Budget attended the group's meetings as observers. Although a group of this nature could not be expected to run covert operations—it had no effective staff—its existence meant that the DCI would have to consult far more widely *before* any operation was started. The Intelligence Oversight Board maintained responsibility for looking into matters of illegality and impropriety. Jimmy Carter followed Ford's prohibition of assassination with Executive Order 12036 on January 24, 1978, and Ronald Reagan continued the prohibition with Executive Order 12333 on December 4, 1982.

tee on Foreign Intelligence chaired by the DCI and reporting to the National Security Council. The committee would "control budget preparation and re-source allocation for the National Foreign Intelligence Program"—previously a function of the DCI but now to be shared by him with a deputy assistant to the President for national security affairs and a deputy secretary of defense for intelligence (a new post created for this purpose). A new director, George Bush, appointed four weeks earlier, was to oversee this change and to run the CIA during the election year.

Bush's appointment and the earlier removal of Henry Kissinger from his post as national security adviser marked an important bureaucratic move on the part of Ford. He was opening up his own foreign-policy channels, which did not include the CIA. He looked instead to the National Security Council staff, an extremely bright group of people whose work would no longer be hampered by Kissinger interposing himself between them and the President. (Kissinger's successor, Brent Scowcroft, was very much a general in the service of his commander in chief.) Bush's job was to hold the fort and smother prob-lems, not to unleash the controversial agency and court additional trouble. He was able to impart tone to the agency and the administration. He was a social cut above the ambitious bureaucrats who had characterized Nixon's presi-dency. "A quasi-aristocrat on the one hand and a self-made Texas businessman on the other," was how one senior agency official described him.[1] Self-conscious rectitude was to be Bush's hallmark.*

Ford was also taking account of a sea change in Congress and in its rela-tionship with the presidency. Arthur M. Schlesinger, Jr.'s "imperial presi-dency" was a buoy marking a wreck. The urge to see a diminution of government now affected Congress. With Vietnam came a demystification of

---

* Bush's success in this respect is demonstrated by the paucity of information about his year as DCI. There were neither major intelligence successes and failures nor colorful tales to be told about him. He concentrated on improving morale and was good at it, thus making agency people happy and keeping both himself and the agency out of the news. When Stansfield Turner came in as Bush's successor, he found no major scandals bubbling beneath him. Bush's principal legacy was an agreement with the British under which the U.S. intelligence community would provide them with important elements of satellite surveillance not only of the Soviet Union but of other parts of the world. Turner considered the intelligence to be too secret and vulnerable to leaks to be shared with anyone, so he balked at implementing the deal. Finally, after the British prime minister, James Callaghan, had personally intervened about the matter on two occasions with Carter, Turner was compelled to implement the agreement.

Cord Meyer fingered Bush's hallmark as director. "He was initially viewed with suspicion as an ambitious politician who might try to use the agency for partisan purposes. However, he quickly proved by his performance that he was prepared to put politics aside and devote all his considerable ability and enthusiasm to restoring the morale of an institution that had been bat-tered enough by successive investigations. Instead of reaching outside for defeated Republican candidates to fill key jobs, he chose from within the organization among men who had demon-strated their competence through long careers in intelligence work. He leaned over backward to protect the objectivity and independence of the agency's estimates and to avoid slanting the re-sults to fit some preconceived notion of what the President wanted to hear" (Cord Meyer, *Facing Reality: From World Federalism to the CIA* [New York: Harper & Row, 1980], pp. 225–226).

public authority, and with Watergate came a multiplication and intensification of the change in public attitudes toward politics and politicians. The 1974 midterm elections witnessed a Democratic surge of new, young senators and representatives. Impatient with the traditions of congressional seniority, they blamed the old guard, both Democrats and Republicans, at least in part, for the apparent collapse of political standards.

Carl Albert, the Speaker of the House, was a reformed alcoholic; his predecessor, John McCormack, was fading intellectually during the last five years of his speakership, and McCormack's principal assistant had been jailed for taking bribes; Representative Wilbur Mills, who for a generation was the most respected master of the governmental process, was found drunk with a stripper, Fanne Fox, "The Argentinian Firecracker," in Washington's Tidal Basin. Mills, who was serving as chairman of the powerful Ways and Means Committee at the time, was also suspected of financial irregularities. Representative Wayne Hays was deposed by the 1974 intake of new members of Congress as chairman of the House Committee because of his vindictive ways and mean-mindedness: he had, for example, secured the removal of seats for elevator operators in the Capitol building on the grounds that they should not be able to sit while others stood. While the old boys had gone ahead by going along, the new boys said no. They supported Senator Frank Church in his drive to open the CIA to congressional scrutiny. Congress was demanding the right to enter even those areas traditionally left to the President;* there were no sacred cows. An operation such as the one in Iran in 1953 was no longer possible, because Congress would demand to know every phase of the plan as it unfolded.

Underpinning this new congressional attitude was the awareness that the great offense in a democracy is to act without debate. If the people feel that the pros and cons of a policy have been aired, they will make allowances. But they will react in anger if they learn that immense sums of money have been spent and action taken without prior debate. Suspecting that this was the case with the CIA, Congress acted. No longer limited by the same sense of emergency that held them back in 1947, congressional leaders demanded public—not private—rationalizations for CIA actions. The justification of the moment was no longer a sufficient explanation for the public. This was one of the appeals of Jimmy Carter as he waged his successful 1976 presidential campaign.

The new mood in Congress also had a direct bearing on the CIA, now seen as the embodiment of secrecy in the democracy. There was a congressional—and public—sense that secrecy was the mask for disgrace. Many Americans, both in Congress and outside, feared that the CIA was training

---

* When Ford announced George Bush's appointment as DCI, the congressional leadership insisted that he give them a commitment that Bush would not be his vice-presidential running mate or else they would block his confirmation as director. This was the first time that such a demand had been made, and although Ford and Bush objected to the requirement, they accepted (Gerald Ford, *A Time to Heal* [New York: Berkley Books, 1980], p. 326).

mavericks who, when they left the agency, would be able to use their knowledge and skills for nefarious purposes. This was a real and founded fear. Howard Hunt was an example. So was Edwin P. Wilson, a former CIA contract agent and arms dealer, eventually convicted and sentenced to a fifty-two-year prison term for conspiring to trade in arms with Libya and for conspiring to murder two U.S. prosecutors and six other people. The Wilson case resulted in several dismissals and resignations from the agency. Wilson himself was described by a senior retired agency officer who had known him for years as "our bad one."[2] Such people gave weight to the popular revulsion from the Kennedy glorification of secrecy to the discovery by Rockefeller, Church, and Pike of how dirty, grubby, and unsuccessful so much of the secret world was.

In the wake of this change in attitudes, the agency faced a reinforced American reluctance to grant unquestioned power to anyone except in extreme emergency. Even in the height of the cold war in the years after the CIA was formed, Congress placed firm restrictions on the agency's domestic operation. Now, during an era of reduced tensions, its hitherto unquestioned power to operate abroad was being questioned. Congress felt it had been patronized by the agency for a generation. There was a subtext to the interrogation: Congress was determined to assert its authority in relation to the executive branch in general. The CIA, as an arm of the executive, was a natural target.

Many congressmen also sensed that they would have to pay for the CIA's secrecy in one way or another at some time in the future. The implication of running a secret organization was clear: future commitments were being made that would embroil the United States in unexpected and unwanted quagmires. Congress wanted a precise accounting of where U.S. national interests lay. Until this was provided, it (and to a much lesser extent the average American—a point misjudged by most politicians) was unwilling to allow the CIA to stand behind a cloak of secrecy that would block congressional inquiries. Ford's effective promotion of the National Security Council as the main presidential secret arm and his isolation of the CIA were hard-nosed decisions, given this congressional mood.*

Ford was essentially an orderly man, so in his fight for political survival he reached for bureaucratic and institutional protection. He was a man who lived in and by the organization—in his case the Republican party and those middle-class values of competitive success and elementary principle which it embodies. He was the child of a broken home, the first President not to bear his real father's name (King). His career was always better than average: university football star; Yale Law School (he graduated in the top third of his class); Navy PT instructor. He was a model young congressman for the postwar Republican

---

* Members of the NSC staff are regarded as part of the White House Staff and are not questioned formally by Congress unless the President agrees. So Ford's promotion of the NSC— a process started under Nixon and Kissinger—had the advantage of protecting presidential secrets.

party with a safe district, an affable manner, and few ideas of his own. He moved steadily up the House party system. He was partisan enough to encourage others and unmemorable enough to have no major enemies. When Nixon started looking for a replacement for Agnew, he wanted to appoint his fellow adventurer, John Connally. Warned by congressional Republicans that this was not possible, he chose someone acceptable to the nation: Gerald Ford. Eight months after being appointed Vice-President, Ford was President of the United States. He knew he would not hold authority through political or intellectual flair, so he chose to hold it by developing the quality of being a representative man. Just as a new Pope has to be different from his predecessor, Ford had to be as visibly simple as Nixon had been visibly complex.

In this effort Colby outflanked him by complicating affairs with the release of The Skeletons. But Ford had the prime presidential attribute of being cold when it counted: the pardon of Nixon; the *Mayaguez* response; the dismissal of Betty Ford's social secretary six hours after her husband committed suicide were all part of a piece. He had to convince the public to trust him for what he was, not for what he was going to do. No one thought Ford really had his own foreign policy: cool heads recognized how much of it was Nixon's—a hand reaching from the grave for the levers of power—and Ford saw how dangerous to him this perception was. Kissinger was the symbol of Nixon's hand. No one believed Ford would not be taken prisoner by those subtle fellows out at Langley: Colby cornered him in public. By releasing The Skeletons, Colby was emphasizing that Ford could not get away from long-term nastiness that easily. It was a slap in the face for reform generally. To go after the CIA, Colby was demonstrating, Ford would have to go after the reputations of predecessors in the White House, in Congress, in the agency, and in the government generally. Colby was rubbing Ford's nose in the fall of man. So the very least Ford could do was break the DCI who was setting the pace and reduce Kissinger in rank: this was a strong element in the Halloween Massacre. He had to show he was boss, and he did so by forbidding, by firing, and by reorganizing. He was an uncreative man prepared to be constructive.

The dismissal of Colby, the appointment of Bush, and Executive Order 11905 were all part of Ford's efforts to distance the presidency from the CIA (and from as much else as possible) for political purposes. He knew he had to be a reform President if he was to have any chance of winning in 1976. He was not going to defend an agency that had lost its public standing. George Bush understood this and also understood that his real job was to ensure that the CIA gave Ford no more surprises. Most important, however, Bush believed that there was a need for the CIA, and he wanted to rebuild and strengthen the agency.[3] Of course, such an aim was part of the "no surprises" mission. To fire people, as Schlesinger had done, or to reveal CIA deeds, as Colby had done, would have been to continue the surprises—but to Bush this aim was still a serious desire. On an entirely different level, Bush, who had just reached military age at the time of Pearl Harbor, felt keenly that America—and not just Ford—needed protection from surprises and that the CIA's job was to provide it.

Bush was a man more capable than he looked. From a wealthy Republican Connecticut family—his father, Prescott Bush, had been a U.S. senator—Bush had proven himself as a navy pilot during the war and then, after graduating from Yale with a degree in economics in 1948, as a successful entrepreneur in the oil-equipment business in Texas. As DCI he had a fundamental loyalty to the agency and its people even though he was an outsider. He was a man with a strong sense of obligation downward. Under him the people of the CIA soon realized that they were not going to be served up piecemeal. He probably did more for agency morale and standing in Congress than any DCI since Allen Dulles. Unlike Colby, who was loyal to the ideal of the CIA rather than to the people, Bush was committed to both. He was a genuine conservative in his politics and his approach, conveying no touch of originality, and was not a man to take initiatives. People knew exactly where they stood with him. He was a classic custodian, and it was this quality that Ford had recognized in appointing him. For Bush being DCI was "the best job in Washington."[4] "He was pretty popular with the pros in the CIA," a senior analyst later observed. "He worked hard in the job and learned a great deal about how intelligence is collected and analyzed. He was a good listener. He seemed to be an intelligent person. I guess they contrasted him with the people who came before and after him whom they disliked rather strongly. Neither James Schlesinger nor Stan Turner was very popular with the pros because both of them set out with antagonism to the CIA. Bush didn't."[5]

Less than ten months after Bush's appointment Jimmy Carter defeated President Ford in the 1976 presidential election. Carter's winning platform centered on the condemnation of what he termed three national disgraces—"Watergate, Vietnam, and the CIA."[6] Carter's victory spelled the end of Bush's tenure as DCI; the new President had a vested interest in demonstrating that more changes were needed at Langley and that there were still secrets that ought to be revealed; Bush stood for secrecy. Carter had run against the CIA and Washington; he was an outsider, suspicious of Washington sophistication, and so he stood fast against the corrupting compromises that informed people have to make. Bush was an insider.

Carter was a man of images rather than of structured intellect. He consciously modeled himself on his image of Jack Kennedy, carefully shaping his hair in Kennedy's style and his manner on Kennedy's public persona—although the real Kennedy was unknown and alien to him. Carter thought all involvement could be minimized and was essentially concerned with the posture rather than the process of America's dealings with other countries. He did not understand the need for secret intelligence—a failing that contributed to the Iranian crisis at the end of his administration. He was a profoundly ignorant (though by no means unintelligent) American, especially in the areas of economics, international affairs, and history,* who assumed that the economic and moral strength of the United States meant that it did not have to behave like other countries or protect itself in hidden ways. He saw no real use for the CIA. He had a view of intelligence as order of battle—about detail. He saw issues in narrow categories, and his mind was inhospitable to events that did not fit into these categories. As an ex-naval officer, he translated the distancing function of the navy—the perception that U.S. warships could keep enemies far away from continental America—to this isolationist attitude.

By the end of his administration four years later Carter had begun to change his views as grim experience bore down on him and religious zealots in Iran came, in effect, to imprison him in the Oval Office at the same time that they held the U.S. diplomats hostage in Tehran. The alteration in perceptions that flowed from this event was to sweep Carter aside and put Ronald Reagan in the White House: the bunker that Carter had sought to hide away in was neither deep enough nor well protected enough to serve its purpose.

Despite Carter's views, George Bush wanted to stay on as director of Central Intelligence for some months so that the principle that the office should be above elective politics might be maintained, thus helping to remove the CIA from the political arena, but Carter had no interest in protecting the agency. For the first time there was to be a change of DCI simply because of a change in administration.† Congress, it turned out, had more of an interest in defending the agency. Senators and representatives on both sides of the aisle had a better understanding of the value and purpose of the CIA than Carter, and were prepared to be far more "hands on" in intelligence matters than he was. They had been especially impressed by the quality of CIA officials, and by George Bush in particular, during their investigations of the agency. Carter seemed unaware that the investigations had exonerated the CIA from most of the accusations against it, and in the process had made the agency far more responsive to Congress. Having established its right to know any secret, Congress had also recognized its responsibility to establish what should remain secret.

---

* In 1979 Carter admitted to reading more history since entering the White House than in all the rest of his life before (interview by Don Oberdorfer, *The Washington Post*, February 18, 1979). Carter had risen in a world in which he was the most intelligent person. As President he discovered that there were many people more intelligent than he was, and this made him insecure about his own abilities and vacillating in policy. Stansfield Turner found Carter to have an enormous capacity for information. "Carter was one for absorbing facts and data. My fear was every time I briefed him that I was engraving something on his mind. He would play it back to me four or five weeks later. He'd say, 'Wait a minute, that statistic doesn't match with the one you gave me four weeks ago.' It was terrifying!" (interview, Stansfield Turner, July 29, 1983).

† After the 1952 election, Eisenhower announced that he would appoint Allen Dulles as DCI. Richard Helms was fired by Nixon after the 1972 election. Bush was not the first DCI to change with a President or after an election, but he was the first to be changed for the sake of change. Bush first tried hard to convince Carter to keep him on as DCI for six months to ease the transition, promising to renounce his own political ambitions for that period in exchange.

Ever since the late 1940s Congress had never been against the principle of engagement in the cold war, even though it was critical at times of the management of government and the implementation of policy. It had looked suspiciously at Vietnam after 1967, but it had no love for pacifism. It had prevented engagement in Angola but more as a signal to the White House that its power was real and that congressional participation in important decisions was necessary. When Carter's choice for Bush's successor, Theodore Sorensen—who had been a Kennedy aide—was found to have been a conscientious objector to military service and to have taken classified documents with him when he left the government in 1964, the Senate hearings on his nomination promised to become so hostile that Sorensen withdrew.

Carter's next choice for DCI was Admiral Stansfield Turner, a man comfortable with machines, statistics, and technical concerns, but without a reflective sense. He was coldly affable, disguising his own uncertainties and lack of interest in people: very much the opposite of George Bush. Turner—like Carter—possessed the naval officer's view of the world in which systems and facilities are most important. More than this, he wanted to create an agency as close as possible to a functioning machine, with each part replaceable. The problem was that he never had a clear vision of the agency's purpose. There was no unifying hypothesis about Turner's view of the world. He just wanted the agency to collect information. As a result, he was content to be Carter's man, every bit as much a "political" director as James Schlesinger had been. A member of Carter's inner advisory team said:

> Carter had this disaster with Sorensen, and he thought he had better get a military man for the job and hit the pacifism in the neck. The person he turned to was Bernie Rogers who had been the commander at Fort McPherson in Atlanta. Bernie had just been made army chief of staff and wanted to stay in the job, but he said he had a friend who had been a Rhodes Scholar at Oxford with him in 1947, Stan Turner. Stan was not going to make it to the top of the navy—he had a lot of enemies. But he had a background suitable for the CIA job. And Carter remembered him too: he'd been in Carter's class at Annapolis. He'd been the big man on campus—in the brigade of midshipmen, on the football team, that sort of thing—and he'd won a Rhodes Scholarship which Carter had tried for and hadn't got. So Carter remembered him favorably and he called him back from Naples where he was the NATO South commander and offered him the job.[7]

"One of my first and most urgent concerns was to put the CIA's much criticized past behind us," Turner said, neatly ignoring the work Colby, Church, Ford, and Bush had successfully completed in this regard but following Carter's wish to vindicate his election campaign.[8]

Turner was an outsider in political Washington who was determined to become an insider and who thought that managerial professionalism would provide him with the key. "I came to Washington in 1954 as a lieutenant in the navy. I was a liaison officer between the navy and the State Department. It was addictive. There was nothing I wanted more than to be in Washington from then on. I almost quit the navy at that point I loved it so much. I wanted to stay in this milieu. I didn't want to go back to sea and all that—fortunately for me I did. 'Potomac fever' they call it. Intangible, but it's very real. Twenty years later when I came back and into the CIA, I found Bush was tops for CIA people. They loved him. He was just the kind of director they want. He did exactly what they wanted him to do. They run the agency. That's what I came up against. But I can't run something without being in charge. The place was a shambles in administration and needed somebody to take charge of it, and they didn't want that."[9] "One of Turner's problems was that he was a military man and didn't like anybody looking over his shoulder," one White House intelligence adviser recalled. "He'd get a little edgy at times and you'd have to say to him, 'Look, Stan, I don't want to have to go back to the President on this.' I often said to him, 'Stan, you've never run an operation. I have. And let me tell you, when somebody gives orders that don't make any sense you have to do what's best for the operation.' It's important to have people who know about the business."[10]

Five months after being sworn in as DCI, Turner—who made it his business to let the agency know it was a "disgrace"—found some residual evidence about CIA–owned houses in San Francisco and New York where some drug testing had been carried out in the 1950s. He immediately reported it to the newly formed Senate Committee on Intelligence, and, predictably, publicity ensued. A year later, when called before the House committee investigating the assassination of President Kennedy, Turner excoriated his own agency for its treatment of Nosenko and its handling of the case.* More publicity resulted. "There was a feeling on Capitol Hill that the CIA answered questions satisfactorily," Turner recalled of his confirmation hearings, "but only if Congress knew what questions to ask. I believed that I could assure them on that one, and did."[11]

Within the CIA, Turner was soon to become the most disliked and distrusted director. To a man, every CIA officer who dealt with him felt that he made up his mind without considering what they had to say or what the con-

---

* Turner genuinely believed that there was no way of establishing facts in the Nosenko case, so that the agency simply had to make a decision one way or the other and follow it through. He was not interested in psychological assessment or Chinese boxes. He wanted to keep the CIA out of anything it could not control (thus his lack of interest in human intelligence).

Robert ("Rusty") Williams, a civilian with whom Turner had worked on analyses of naval problems and whom he had brought into the CIA as a special assistant, investigated the Nosenko case for Turner. Williams also investigated the Directorate of Operations and reported after six months that the directorate engaged in no improper practices and that its decision-making procedures were sound (Stansfield Turner, *Secrecy and Democracy—The CIA in Transition* [Boston: Houghton Mifflin, 1985], p. 197).

sequences might be for them or for the agency. He accepted the resignation of Hank Knoche, his able and respected professional deputy, four months after becoming DCI. He brought in several naval staff officers who protected him from direct dealings with CIA staffers. "Employees said he thought the CIA was like a battleship, with replaceable crew members on call when needed," reported Ray Cline, who, like many ex-CIA people, now looked on with worry and concern. "He seemed genuinely fearful of being outwitted by the old CIA hands," Cline observed.[12] He concentrated on technical intelligence and attempts to run the intelligence community, ruthlessly disbanding what remained of the clandestine service: 820 positions were abolished, including those of approximately 200 experienced covert operation staffers and more than 600 backup officers and staff in covert action and espionage.[13] "Turner had to cut back. He had to carry out a reduction of forces in the CIA," observed Thomas Farmer, who was on the Intelligence Oversight Board created by Ford to examine cases of illegality and impropriety in the intelligence community as a whole. "The agency had expanded tremendously during the Vietnam War, as had the military, and the military had cut back and the CIA had not. Several study groups had recommended cutting back. Turner decided to look at it in navy terms, and there was a great overhang of older men which was making it difficult to promote the forty-year-olds, so he concentrated the firing on this over-fifty group. I'm not sure it was the right thing to do, but the rationale was not bad in the sense of long-term promotion possibilities. Turner's trouble came from the fact that these were the guys with influence and contacts in town, and because he did it all in a rather impersonal way."[14]

Turner earned his dislike also because he was threatening: he was the most informed DCI ever on technical matters. He had in effect an ideology of intelligence in which he saw technology as the wave of the future, but to the agency his ideology seemed like the flag of the Department of Defense. It meant that under him the professional technical experts would gain ascendancy over the "daring," more colorful operators. The mystique of CIA people like the ones who killed a thirty-foot-long Bolivian snake in the early 1960s was of men and women who went to specific places for specific purposes, made personal friendships through which in large part they operated, and had a "feel" for their jobs. This Turner did not want.

Was I relying on the technical too much? That the DDO's nose was out of joint because I didn't pay as much attention to them as they would like—as Helms and Colby paid—is true. But one of the things that threw these people into such a tizzy is that technical intelligence has become so much more important. It's taking a lot of money, and the decisions that you make today on technical systems may take years to come to fruition. I thought those were pretty momentous decisions because once you get a family started you're stuck with them. And so you sweated those. You were called up to Congress because it was billions of dollars. Whereas here's the DDO running along with much less money and not as great a need for future planning and so on. So, yes, you gave a lot more attention to the technical.

Another factor is that in crisis management you turn to the technical systems because it's almost pure happenstance when you can turn to the human systems in a crisis. You can't turn the DDO on and off. You cannot suddenly say, "I want information about the financial tradings in gold being conducted by the Soviets on the German exchanges." If you haven't thought ahead to get a man inside the German gold ministry, you're out of luck for this week at least. You can now make a start and try and get a man inside for next week. But you can turn the National Security Agency loose right away and say to them, "Somebody communicates out of the gold ministry and I want you to get on that." That's why you turn to the technical people first in a crisis. But you also always ask the human, "Do you happen to have a fellow in the gold ministry?" And the answer is generally no. Understandably.

The human people have not understood the revolution in intelligence collection brought on by the technical systems. It means they have got to change. You can't have this enormous flow of data coming into the system without it changing the way you go about all your intelligence. One, you never send a spy when you can get the information you want by technical means. Two, you now focus the human collector on the missing pieces: there's always going to be an element that isn't obtainable by the technical systems. But that means that you recruit differently and that you target differently, and they're not willing to do that. They don't understand that the role of human intelligence has got to be different in an environment where you've got huge quantities of data available from the technical systems.

I once played quarterback on a football team, but I can't pass a football. Today there isn't such a thing as a quarterback who can't pass. Why? Football has evolved. It's a different game today. And it's the same thing here: spying has evolved. It doesn't mean that the kind of quarterback that I was is less important—they call him a blocking back today. They change the name, but somebody has to do the job. But there is another guy who has come along and is the real quarterback today who does a job that wasn't done very much in my time because football has changed. It's too bad, but they're going to drive themselves out of business if they're not careful.[15]

Turner wanted an agency suited to any job, in tune with the nature of the modern world where the United States could not rely on handcrafted intelligence. Part of his formative knowledge was the Cuban missile crisis when a technical collection system, the U-2, rather than agent reports, had provided the conclusive evidence that the Soviets intended siting missiles in Cuba. So Turner was, in effect, telling an agency shaped by the cultural and political apprehensions of the 1940s and 1950s that technology would be the focus of the last twenty-five years of the twentieth century. Like Richard Bissell, Turner saw that complex societies are incredibly leaky, so why go to the trouble and danger of trying to secure agents in place when those societies are literally broadcasting detailed information about themselves which gadgets can collect? As an admiral, if Turner had ever had to fight a Soviet fleet, he would not have relied upon being able to place agents on the Soviet flagship! He would have looked to weapons systems and technical devices. The whole history of the United States in large part is the substitution of technology for human effort and intellect, and Turner was saying that this should extend to intelligence. "I'm a naval officer, and when you tell a fellow to take his ship off and do something, you don't tell him how to put the rudder over because he's the expert on his ship and with his rudder. My feeling with the DDO was to tell them I wanted to know when they were planning to take a risk above a certain threshold. And when they did, I'd ask what was the percentage risk of them or their agent getting caught. I wouldn't then say, 'Use a different technique.' I didn't know techniques. I don't know how you put rudders over for spies. But I would say I was willing or unwilling to take the risk."[16] He was bringing to intelligence a military view of not chalking up any black marks. He was cautious about taking risks; he would take them, but only after nailing down everything he could.* He saw technical intelligence as how to stay alive and win in both combat and career terms. It was also a very American point of view.

One of the immediate effects within the CIA of Turner's becoming DCI was a renewed emphasis on the polygraph, that symbol of human distrust.† "I eventually urged regular polygraphing," he said. "I took it myself. I didn't have

---

* "You suggest I was cautious about taking risks in the clandestine collection process. In four years there was only one risk the espionage branch asked me to take that I did not approve—sometimes we debated and refined the operation—but the spooks got all the support they asked for. The problem was they didn't have enough risky proposals" (letter, Stansfield Turner to author, December 11, 1985). This was an acknowledgment of the agency's preference for prudence and coolness, and a mark of the organization as a bureaucracy. The contrast with the CIA of the 1950s could not be greater.

† "I came in very skeptical of the polygraph. In fact I had several studies done in my first few months before I decided not to cancel all polygraphing" (letter, Stansfield Turner to author, December 11, 1985).

> The most important specific tool of counterintelligence is the polygraph. . . . Civil libertarians loathe the polygraph because of the potential for injustice. . . . I believe that potential definitely exists. . . . I view the polygraph only as a supplementary counterintelligence device when used on our own personnel.
> There are two situations in which such use is called for: the screening of new applicants for employment (the CIA and the National Security Agency both use this) and the periodic, unscheduled retesting of employees. What I found extremely helpful was the confessions that were elicited during retesting. . . .
> Largely because of the confessions and the inhibiting effect, I felt the polygraph had its usefulness, and I attempted to extend its use to civilian contractors and to certain other government personnel. . . .
> [T]he CIA uses the polygraph on foreign agents whenever feasible. In such cases it is an even more useful tool. . . . Perhaps the best evidence that the polygraph does help separate true agents from false is that we know the KGB has made determined efforts to develop techniques for "beating the machine." Although there is a risk that some professionals will fool the polygraph, there is the greater one that our intelligence agencies will rely on it too heavily (Turner, Secrecy and Democracy, pp. 69–70).

to, but I felt, being a military man, that you don't ask the troops to do what you won't do yourself."[17] "When they polygraph you, they ask, 'Are you a homosexual and have you ever taken drugs?' " recalled an ex-agency analyst who had been through the test under Turner:

> They ask, "Are you under the control of a foreign intelligence organization and have you ever been?" They tell you beforehand what the questions are as part of the technique. The whole procedure of the polygraph is very intrusive into your constitutional rights. In fact, you sign away your constitutional liberties when you join the agency and allow that kind of access into you. But in another sense you are becoming part of a very sensitive and special government organ, and I don't begrudge them the necessity for that kind of technique.
>
> I think that polygraphing is a tool. It's not the ultimate tool—it's one of many. It's hard to lie to it. I've never lied to it. I've never tried. You have to train to overcome it. It just shows physical reactions. The time of the test depends on your reactions to the questions, and they'll refine the questions and ask you new questions. You never know if you've passed or failed. Even when you're hired, your initial entry polygraph may have been an ambiguous test. You passed it in a sense because you were hired, but five or ten years later you may find that your career pattern was guided by that test.[18]

Another ex-CIA man who left during Turner's time as DCI said:

> Admiral Turner thought it was magic. It is very powerful, but it's not magic. In oriental culture, deception and lying are part of their social and cultural heritage, which they aren't for us. So that's a problem for a start. But there's another problem too. Theoretically, the information stays private. Your security file in the agency, which contains the results of your polygraphs, is separate from your personnel file. You're never given access to your own security file. You can see parts of your personnel file. Your line superiors are not supposed to see your security file either. Only at the very top, the theory goes, can the two files be brought together. So there is reasonable protection of your privacy. But I have found in my own case that this did not happen, the theory was not applied, and some polygraph information from me was leaked. It appeared in *The New York Times*, and I'm still as angry as a lion at the agency about that.[19]

Resentment about Turner's emphasis on polygraphing surfaced elsewhere for another reason: the whole experience was humiliating and encouraged a sense of vulnerability in those being tested. "Theoretically, you have to go through it once every five years," said one CIA man, "and whenever one returns from a foreign posting. It's called 'fluttering.' Turner claims he was polygraphed, but if he was, it was not in the same way as the rest of us. The fact of polygraphing itself is not something that anyone would like particularly." [20] Turner never seemed to understand that the human emotions which technology and gadgets could generate need, at times, to be taken very seriously for the overall health of the organization involved.

Coming into the job doubting the value of human intelligence efforts, Turner was not convinced otherwise by anything the agency did, and this was the weakness of his assumptions. Wearing blinders, he failed to ask—and answer—the key questions of what U.S. intelligence preparation should be in a world returning to disorder. The issue was not whether technical intelligence was preferable to human intelligence. What was required was a reappraisal of a changing, unsettled world, and this Turner completely failed to perceive.

Turner's appraisal was consistent with the widespread loss of confidence after Vietnam, reflected in a general distrust of traditional methods. By the mid-1970s America's "magic" had clearly disappeared. With U.S. power apparently diminished, technical intelligence represented minimum risk, and technology operating with a minimum of human interference was less risky still. It was impossible to achieve subversion with a satellite, for example. When politicians are scared, they look for certainty. This need for certainty was fed by the dual blows of Watergate and Vietnam; public confidence in politics and politicians had reached an all-time low. It was now clear that America's political leadership had been indecisive, unable to react expediently to Watergate or to resolve the commitment to South Vietnam. Two Presidents had walked into the morass of the Vietnam War, where the South Vietnamese themselves increasingly had little will to win, while at home America was undergoing a great cultural upheaval involving blacks, women, youth, and sexuality. World economics increased the uncertainty. The United States had been forced by the OPEC oil embargo to recognize its dependence on raw-material imports and its connections with the rest of the world, which now meant that other countries had hooks in America. "Interdependence" and "linkage" were the new watchwords of foreign policy.

A new agenda was presenting itself, encouraging America to withdraw from personalized engagement behind a wall of systems, machines, and technology that could provide the certainty the politicians wanted. It was led by the dramatic coming of age of the computer in the early 1970s and the subsequent push to computerize. (Although computers had been around for many years, suddenly they were accessible to individuals because of the development of the microchip.) With computers came a new world of technology. An item on the agenda was the need to come to terms with the economic power of the Arab world and Japan. The United States, which had effortlessly been the world's first power in 1945, now had to gauge the cost of leadership. Americans also had to gauge how to handle the pervasive loss of faith in government, reflected in the sense that whenever America sought to improve or to help, it actually caused further damage. Altogether, this new agenda signified a more disordered, uncontrollable world of greater complexity than ever before. Impersonalized technology was of enormous attraction in these circumstances as Americans defensively reacted to this "new" world.

Neo-isolationism was a further element in their reaction. George McGovern's great cry at the 1972 Democratic Convention had been "Come home, America." He represented the deeply ingrained American instinct to pull back.* His defeat by Nixon in the presidential election masked the strength of this instinct. Carter's lack of knowledge of the world outside America was isolationism in another form. His emphasis on human rights in international dealings came from an assumption that America was more moral, more pure than the rest of the world—that America was separate from other countries and should remain so. Commenting on this, a member of Carter's intelligence Oversight Committee said:

> We were not in the business of saying that the overthrow of country X was a good idea or a bad idea. Basically, our effort was to estimate the risks involved and the political issues involved and see if there were clear violations of the law and give our view whether we thought something was ethical or not. It was very clear that we had no authority to terminate anything, but we did give our judgment if things were questionable in terms of ethical or legal concerns. That's what Carter said he wanted. There were a few that were clearly illegal. Most were gray areas. Carter was essentially a very ethical man. He was interested in that aspect of things. He would often say, "This is pretty dirty stuff. Do we really want to do this?" His feeling was "We're not the Russians." That was very definite.[21]

Behind the glittering shield of Carter's public expression of his principles, and behind the emphasis on technology, America was quietly withdrawing from involvements.

LOSING FAITH?

This new direction and these new concerns transformed intelligence priorities and encouraged the steady shift to technical collection. Intelligence concerns were also transformed by an unrecognized increase in the scope of conflict with the Soviets. In 1947 the conflict involved a battle for people's minds in the relatively narrow geographical areas of Europe, Turkey, and China. Thirty years later the intellectual battle was still under way, but now the entire continent of Africa, the Caribbean basin, the Middle East, and the Far East were also involved. There were additional concerns as well centering on the control of high technology exports, illegal drugs, and terrorism. Conflicts of any kind were more complex than they had ever been. Traditional problems had also become more sophisticated: what had happened in Cuba in

---

* McGovern, however, also represented a missionary impulse to settle a problem—or at least to declare it settled—and then go home. He had won the Distinguished Flying Cross as a bomber pilot in World War II and thus had a healthy sense of the costs of involvement. But he was not a knee-jerk isolationist.

1959–1960 was repeated in slow motion in Nicaragua in the late 1970s; the ability of the Soviets to gain allies was a new phenomenon compared to the early years of the cold war.

The inevitable result of the withdrawal behind a human-rights-directed foreign policy and the termination of covert-action capability was a quiet American disengagement that produced some noisy American "failures." These failures were blamed on the CIA because of two earlier experiences of effective interventionism in Iran and Guatemala. There was a dilapidation of world order, much as Nixon had perceived. The fear that nuclear weapons would one day be used added to general world demoralization and the reassertion of disorder. The United States had lost a sense of purpose in international affairs after the failure of the massive economic, military, and idealistic effort in Vietnam. Moreover, the CIA did not have the authority of recent stunning successes. Nor did it embody a view of the world that could rally governing opinion.

The changes in analytical arrangements within the agency instituted by James Schlesinger and followed through by William Colby also meant that, under Turner, people and systems were still settling down. "The CIA had gone so far along the road of leaning backwards and not getting involved in policy that the analysis was often irrelevant," said Turner. "They were doing analysis on one thing while the policy makers wanted to know about something else. I used to have trouble with that. I would say I needed some analysis by tomorrow afternoon and they would say, 'But we'll have some new information next week. Can't it wait?' And I would then have to say, 'I don't care. The President has to make a decision the day after tomorrow. I don't care what you're going to have next week. After the train has left the station is no time to give the conductor your itinerary!' "[22]

One senior analyst who came into the agency under Turner remembered the strong emotions still running in the wake of the Schlesinger/Colby changes:

> The National Intelligence Estimates were meant to be the cream of the intelligence community's product. They were worked over by interagency groups. They had contributions from all the agencies in the intelligence community, and of course they were the great product of the old Board of National Estimates which had a reputation going back to Bill Langer and Sherman Kent. But it had been scheduled for abolition by Jim Schlesinger in a very ruthless and arbitrary way, everybody thought. He made a crack, I'm told, which is not apocryphal: "That's a gentleman's club, and I don't think intelligence is any place for gentlemen." And he swept it away. But an awful lot of people in the CIA thought that it had become a little ossified in its procedures, a little bit mechanical, a little too detached from the collection of intelligence and a little too detached from the concerns of policy makers. Nonetheless, it had a lot of merit to it.[23]

Turner commented:

> I don't know much about why the Board of National Estimates and that system was disestablished, but what I heard when I came in was that it had become encrusted and was a parking place for people. The replacement national intelligence officer system was all right but was inadequate in some respects. It wasn't large enough to do anything of its own, and I don't think you can hold your head up in an analytic community when you're only an administrator, when you're only telling other people what to analyze. Yes, you're smart, and you can talk and argue with them, but you don't get your hands dirty doing the work yourself. And sometimes you do not know enough to be able to pinpoint the areas of sensitivity in a subject for an Estimate.[24]

Turner's observation was another indicator that the agency had become just another intelligence contributor. It was no longer *the* intelligence agency, and the DCI's coordinating role was clearly being successfully challenged. Turner had some success as overseer of the intelligence community budget, but even there he could be—and was—overruled by cabinet members who had the President's ear: "Particularly when Carter gave me the authority to make out the budgets, I didn't have to take votes, I decided. On the first budget I had to get everyone to agree. By the second one, the rules had been changed by Carter. Sometimes the Secretary of Defense got the President to overrule me on budget decisions, but otherwise I was in charge."[25]

The agency had lost the quality of being special, and the views that Jimmy Carter and Stansfield Turner associated with it were the opposite of what they thought they wanted. "I was deeply troubled by the lies our people had been told," explained Carter, "our exclusion from the shaping of American political and military policy in Vietnam, Cambodia, Chile, and other countries; and other embarrassing activities of our government, such as the CIA's role in plotting murder and other crimes. . . . I was familiar with the widely accepted arguments that we had to choose between idealism and realism, or between morality and the exertion of power; but I rejected those claims. To me, the demonstration of American idealism was a practical and realistic approach to foreign affairs, and moral principles were the best foundation for the exertion of American power and influence."[26] "There is one overall test of the ethics of human intelligence activities," declared Stansfield Turner. "That is whether those approving them feel they could defend their decisions before the public if the actions became public. . . . American intelligence, operating in the past in confidence that it would not be held accountable, committed errors that both disgraced our nation and, in the longer run, imperiled our very intelligence capabilities."[27]

Both men placed idealism before U.S. needs and interests, and they refused to accept the possibility that America itself needed anything but technical secrets. In addition, most of the secrets that America needed about others were, after all, best obtained by technical means.* The problem was that they took no precautions to avoid human surprises. When the Soviet Union invaded Afghanistan in December 1979, Carter was horrified to discover that Brezhnev, who had assured him for months that he did not intend to invade, had "lied" to him.† With a President who was so limited, the CIA had little chance of being properly used or appreciated.

In addition to the dislike and distrust of the agency in the White House and in its own director's office, the CIA under Turner no longer had quiet authority with the press or with Congress. Its impressive founding generation had gone. Bureaucratically the agency was no longer preeminent in the intelligence community either at home or abroad. Horrified by the publication of CIA secrets, foreign-intelligence agencies downgraded their assessment of what the agency could do. Colby's effort to make it an "American" service, with "affirmative action" requirements and an assumption that everything it did would soon become public, may have saved the agency as a bureaucracy, but it also sacrificed it as a unique intelligence organization.

When Turner reduced the DDO by 820 positions in two years—losing

---

* An example of this was given by Arkady Shevchenko, the most senior Soviet diplomat to defect to the United States, working with the CIA and the FBI while he was under secretary general of the United Nations in New York. His spying lasted several years before he publicly defected in April 1978, and it had been to interpret information rather than to obtain it: "What kind of information should I bring?" Shevchenko asked his CIA contact, Bert Johnson. "Johnson said I would be the best judge of what was important and of how much time to give to any subject, but that it would help to have a basic pattern. He suggested I start with the most recent cables received in the Mission, the date, the time they were sent, the text as fully as I could get it." This clearly indicated that Shevchenko's information was of use for cryptographic purposes. Shevchenko continued:

> I was startled. What did he mean, the full text of cables? . . . To copy a code cable inside the Soviet Mission would invite almost certain detection. . . .
> He quickly responded that they did not expect full copies, just whatever I could remember of the important messages. . . .
> "The big developments will stick out a mile," Johnson said, "you'll spot them right away." What might be of more interest to Washington might be difficult for me to identify at first. Something that seemed completely routine to me because it was so familiar might be absolutely novel to them. I should try to read as if I were seeing the information for the first time. I must try to think of its value to outsiders, what it might reveal to someone without my background and experience.
> Johnson particularly wanted me to be on the lookout for nuance, new shades of meaning signalling a change in policy or indicating debates on certain issues (Arkady M. Shevchenko, *Breaking with Moscow* [New York, Knopf, 1985], pp. 27–28).

Inferentially Johnson was saying that the United States already had access to the texts of documents and cables but needed interpretation—that spies were no longer needed as collectors.
According to some critics, Shevchenko's book contains inventions to boost its sales. In particular, his accounts of his work for the CIA are singled out in this respect.
† Jimmy Carter, *Keeping Faith: Memoirs of a President* (London: Collins, 1982), pp. 471–474. Carter saw the invasion as a brutal act, not as a threat to the Indian Ocean area or as a Soviet move toward a warm-water port. He possessed the naval officer's view of the Soviets as a continental power and did not consider that they might be positioning themselves to be a global power. He recognized that the invasion was a sign that world order was collapsing, but for him the prospect of having to deal with a liar state was almost intolerable. He depended upon empiric discipline.

many experienced operators in the clandestine service—he eliminated the agency's special-project capability, forcing it to compete with specialized agencies in the burgeoning field of technical intelligence collection and analysis.*
The director of Central Intelligence was now only nominally the President's chief intelligence officer: the real power was in the hands of the national security adviser, who received the full support of the National Security Council staff and who to an increasing degree both collated and synthesized the intelligence received from the various agencies—the role once performed by the DCI—and was protected from formal congressional probing and oversight by being within the executive branch. Although still very powerful, the DCI in contrast was relegated to the position of harmonizer of the conflicting bureaucratic interests within the intelligence community. Congress, in the wake of the Church and Pike committees, began to enter the day-to-day world of intelligence activities and policy by establishing controls and oversight committees and expressing a (usually) negative interest.

Implicit in what Carter and Turner were doing to the agency were certain important questions: Since there are secrets, how should they be handled? Was there a secret world? Or was there simply a set of secret topics? Should there be an elite group empowered to do what ordinary citizens and policemen cannot do in a democracy? During peacetime should people be asked to make sacrifices without knowing the details of conflict? The American Revolution itself had been about these very questions. For a democracy to function there has to be some degree of public approval. But most ordinary citizens never ask for more than a general understanding of how democracy protects itself. They do not want to know the gory details of battle nor to have a specific understanding of how an antipersonnel mine tears a person apart. People also accept the need for secrecy for negotiating purposes. No country can deal with others on matters of national security without withholding vital information that, if known, could threaten its very existence.

Nations essentially behave in the same way as homeowners who keep the secrets of their burglar alarm systems from strangers. Understanding the need for self-protection, a practical public does in fact endorse the existence of spe-

---

* Turner's reorganization also signified that a covert-action arm was necessary only if the United States was prepared for a prolonged presence anywhere. The effective closedown of the clandestine service was another indication of U.S. withdrawal. The whole history of America in the world is one of intervention followed by departure, and Turner was ensuring that the CIA mirrored this.

The principal competing agencies with the CIA were the National Security Agency, the chief cryptographic institution; the National Reconnaissance Office, run by the CIA and the air force, responsible for most space intelligence collection systems; the various military intelligence offices and agencies; and elements of the Department of Energy intelligence office, the intelligence arm of the FBI, the Treasury intelligence office, and the Bureau of Intelligence and Research at the State Department. All these agencies are technically coordinated by the DCI, but in practice they are autonomous in significant ways. It would, for example, be very difficult if not impossible for the DCI to interfere with an FBI investigation, even if he cited "national security" as his reason.

cial groups with special powers in the form of elite democratic bodies—elite military units, for example. In effect, they give certain information the status of democratically sanctioned secrets. People may not like secrets in a democracy, but they want an economy of confidence as well: they do not want to agonize with the elected government over what to do all the time. Carter and Turner understood that some secrets could indeed be democratically sanctioned,* but they confused a temporary degree of shock in the mid-1970s with a settled popular determination not to have secrecy. They never connected the fact that the investigations of the agency had been closed-door affairs, with the public's accepting the secrecy. Complicating this approach was the American preoccupation with *winning,* which often conflicted with American idealism. Carter's lack of popularity among the people and in Congress grew out of his use of idealism as an excuse for not winning.

The Carter/Turner approach raised questions about the ethics of CIA tactics. What about bribing fifty people instead of risking one life? Is bribery more ethical? "It is impossible to set absolute standards of ethics," Turner maintained as he argued for a political approach in which everything that might be done in secret had to be unembarrassing. "Overseers should be so convinced of the importance of the actions that they would accept any criticism that might develop if the covert actions did become public, and could construct a convincing defense of their decisions."[28] To Turner, therefore, bribery was more responsible than risking a life and was certainly preferable despite its costs.

Decimating the clandestine service was also a statement that covert action was not wanted under any circumstances. It was a gesture of no-confidence in the CIA's capacity for skilled manipulation. If covert action was ever needed again, then America should respond as best it could through military intervention, not secret CIA activity. America should never assume the necessity for covert action by being prepared for it. "The stipulation by Congress in the 1974 Hughes-Ryan amendment that covert actions must be '. . . important to the national security,' " said Turner, "was put into the law so that we should not bypass the normal processes of government for less than important benefit."[29] Undefined in this statement is exactly what the "normal processes of government" are. Do they include, for example, the need for the average congressman to know exactly how every dollar in the CIA's budget is being spent? As Turner recalled:

> I once testified before one of the [congressional] committees on the CIA's budget, knowing that one of the figures in the budget had been intentionally

* They had outstripped Congress in their wish to illuminate the secret world. On July 21, 1980, for example, declaring that "There are secrets the U.S. Congress needs to know," the House Foreign Affairs Committee voted 14 to 10 to allow a President to ignore rules on notifying Congress in advance about any covert operation. This happened not because Carter or Turner had pressed for leeway but because more and more congressmen were concerned by Carter's ineffectiveness and his emasculation of the CIA. It was a formal democratic sanction of secrecy.

falsified. The amount of money was not for one project, which was described; it was for two projects, one not described. But I could not knowingly present something to the Congress that was deceitful, so in a secret session I told the committee about the second, hidden project. I said, however, that I could not discuss it; that the project was one of which they would be very proud; that it did not involve any degrading activities or very much money; that if one hint of its existence got out, the United States would lose a very valuable source of information; and that fewer people in the CIA knew about this program than those sitting in the committee room at that time.[30]

Neither Turner nor Carter seemed to understand how illogical or unrealistic his position was. Although congressmen did know how much money they were voting for intelligence, they knew only the broad terms of intelligence operations; they left the details to the CIA. Clearly it was impossible for the system to function in any other way. A democracy would collapse under the weight of full disclosure; decision making would be paralyzed. Inevitably, trust in a democracy must mean—as Richard Helms suggested a decade earlier—trusting its servants to have secrets.

Carter and Turner claimed the contrary: that in a democracy people want to know everything and can be told everything as it happens. What Americans really felt was resolved in the 1980 presidential election. Ronald Reagan's victory was an overwhelming mandate to make America forceful again, not to be a patsy, and not to emote about toughness. Reviving the mystique of the CIA was in the forefront of Reagan's campaign. The relationships between the CIA and Congress and between the President and Congress were also fundamentally resolved in 1980. Having accepted the need for secrecy, Americans recognized that Congress was not secure. To tell Congress—as Carter and Turner had urged—was to tell the nation, and to tell the nation was to tell the world. Even Turner, after two years as DCI, in practice had come to endorse the older system of informing and gaining approval from trusted (and powerful) congressional leaders, instead of seeking wider congressional (and public) approval. "Some fine lines had to be drawn, and tolerance, understanding, and trust were needed on both sides," he observed in retrospect. "Finding the right balance between secrecy and disclosure will always be part of the DCI's task."[31]

The wish of Congress to protect secrets—one of the hallmarks of the relationship from the 1940s to the early 1970s—also reasserted itself, as Turner discovered:

The residual feeling on the Hill that the Church and Pike Committees had done harm to our capabilities made the new committees [on intelligence: the Senate Committee established in mid-1976 and the House Committee a year later] eager to establish a constructive relationship with the Intelligence Community. To achieve that, Majority Leader Robert C. Byrd and Minority Leader Howard H. Baker in the Senate, and Speaker Thomas P. (Tip) O'Neill, Majority Leader James C. Wright, and Minority Leader Robert H.

Michel in the House took special care in appointing the first chairmen of the committees. Senator Daniel K. Inouye, on the Senate side, had the liberal credentials necessary to assure critics that the committee would be inquiring and investigative. His war record, patriotism, and proven support for national security reassured others that the committee would be constructive. Speaker O'Neill's strong endorsement of the House committee was reflected in the appointment as chairman of his close friend and companion in the House, Edward P. Boland of Massachusetts, who was seen as an impeccably fair man. The same kind of care went into selecting the members. . . .

On one occasion I went to Chairman Inouye privately to tell him we were going to do something very risky: if it failed there would be adverse publicity and I didn't want him taken by surprise, but if it succeeded we would need more money to follow up with the next step. I pointed out that this case was unusual in that the life of one of our CIA case officers would be at stake. I could not look that officer in the eye and tell him I was going to inform two entire committees and their staffs about what he was going to do. I was, in effect, asking Dan Inouye to take it on his shoulders for his entire committee. He agreed to do that as long as we also informed the ranking minority member of the committee, Barry Goldwater.[32]

The lessons of experience, however, were something Turner's idealism could not accept. He maintained his insistence that telling Congress did not mean telling the nation, although, in fact, by telling Inouye and Goldwater he had simply told two senators and passed the buck.*

IRAN

Events in Iran exploded the Carter/Turner approach to intelligence (and to foreign affairs). The religious fundamentalist revolution that overthrew the shah in 1979 succeeded in part because Carter demonstrated that he had no wish to support the shah—there would be no Kermit Roosevelts sent to bolster his regime—and in part because the shah's attempt to propel Iran into modern times generated widespread domestic resentment and fear. Most Iranians found modernization upsetting to old religious ties. The seventy thousand or so young Iranians educated abroad returned home with liberal, anti-shah ideas.

---

* Left unanswered by Congress or any DCI were certain fundamental questions: How long are matters to be kept secret? Are secrets tactical? Or are they strategic—to be buried for a lifetime or longer? What level of secrecy is involved? How long could the United States keep its involvement in anything secret? Were those CIA people and politicians who were privy to the secrets fit to be trusted? Was secrecy a tool of incompetence rather than of national security? From whom were secrets to be kept—did not the Russians actually know what the secrets were?

The appointment of Senator Inouye as chairman of the intelligence committee was a signal of self-criticism by the Senate for Church's exposing investigation. Inouye had demonstrated his toughness during the Watergate hearings and would be prepared to take responsibility for secrets. It was a sign that Congress wanted to come to terms with the CIA and with secrecy.

Instead of supporting and being prepared to implement the shah's modernization plans, they formed another nucleus of dissent.

Both the CIA and the State Department were slow to gauge the extent
and force of opposition to the shah. At the shah's demand, there was virtually
no contact between the CIA and opposition groups in Iran. Neither Turner,
the CIA analysts, nor the State Department noticed any gathering storm in the
country.* Five years later a presidential intelligence adviser reflected:

> I think the problem in Tehran was that we had long ago decided to rely on
> the shah. We didn't have a CIA station there that tried to do anything do-
> mestically. Our understanding was that the deal with the shah was, "You rely
> on me for what goes on here, and I'll let you have all the telemetry and mon-
> itoring equipment up north that you want." Most people decided that was
> not a bad deal—it was more important to monitor Soviet missiles and so
> forth than to have agents keeping tabs on the political situation inside Iran.
> We thought we could rely on the diplomats for that. This is part of the prob-
> lem with American intelligence—it isn't just a reflection of Stan Turner's ap-
> proach. It is very cost-efficient and short-term. We're bound to have a
> problem in every country sometime, and what we have to do is simply stash
> away people for the day that things may go wrong. I remember the day that
> the Tehran thing started and Brzezinski [Carter's national security adviser]
> saying, "We've now got to go in there and do something," and we said,
> "With what?" You don't mount an intelligence operation overnight. That
> goes way, way back. We have never taken long views. It's very expensive to
> have people in countries which are in pretty good shape because we think one
> day they may go sour and we had better be ready to do something. I wouldn't
> be that hard on Turner.†

* No one who dealt with pre-Khomeini Iran came out well. Nixon had been buffaloed by the
shah—supposedly America's great friend in the Middle East—with OPEC. The British and
French intelligence and diplomatic services did not have any greater sense of the impending collapse of the shah than the CIA or the State Department. The Peacock Throne impressed everyone with its wealth and glamour.
  The shah's resistance to CIA activity in Iran, it should be noted, did not stop it from happening. No restrictions were placed on CIA operations in the country by Jimmy Carter or Stansfield Turner. Still, a 1978 National Intelligence Estimate on Iran held that the shah would stay in
power for another ten years and would be prepared to use whatever force was necessary to do so.
  † Interview, November 17, 1983. The British played an instrumental part in the intelligence
side of the crisis. "The British are very clever. There's no doubt about it. They have one very good
thing: people all around the world who are very smart. They may not have many sources, but they
do good reports from unclassified material. They're street smart. People like Sir Anthony Parsons.
He was giving us first-rate reports from Iran in the middle of the crisis when we had nobody reporting from there. He was the primary source of intelligence from there for a while. When we
had to abort the rescue mission we were trying to assess how good we were at piecing together
fragments of information we were getting on Iran and how good British intelligence was in its
current intelligence analysis" (interview, Stansfield Turner, July 29, 1983). "There was a certain
amount of rivalry with British intelligence when I was there," recalled one of Carter's intelligence
advisers. "I must say that I was impressed by the British on the whole. They were very seat-of-
the-pants. They had very good people but very few resources. Amateur hour. There was a good
deal of rivalry but pretty good cooperation as well. My guess is that the British were beginning to

By late 1978 it was obvious that the shah was facing a genuine revolution that had caught both him and the Carter administration by surprise. It was a colossal intelligence failure all round, and it was compounded by shilly-shallying and lack of resolve in the White House.

There was a seesawing relationship between Carter and his two principal foreign-affairs specialists, Cyrus Vance, the secretary of state, and Zbigniew Brzezinski. Vance took a "soft" line in foreign affairs, placing great faith in the value of negotiation and diplomacy and refusing to see any crisis necessarily as a challenge. Brzezinski was the opposite, seeing the Soviets as presenting a constant challenge in a bipolar world and any crisis not dealt with firmly as a potential flash point for still greater trouble. Carter veered from one view to the other, favoring Vance or Brzezinski accordingly but never finally deciding between the two approaches. When each man sent him diametrically opposed drafts for a speech on Soviet foreign policy, he resolved the difference by incorporating both into his speech.[33]

This situation made life difficult for Turner, who was originally seen by Carter as one of his team of core advisers. "In my first substantive meeting with the President—it was over lunch—it was my intention to ask him for twenty minutes a week on his schedule for a briefing session with me, and I came out of the meeting with his having taken the initiative before I could ask him, telling me that I was to have three one-half-hour meetings a week with him. This stayed the case in the first year, then we scaled it back to two, and in the election campaign it was once every other week."[34] But while Turner set the agenda for these meetings with the President, other advisers—especially Brzezinski, whom Turner regarded as a bureaucratic adversary competing with him for the President's ear—were also present. "Brzezinski was almost always there at the President's invitation, and Mondale was always invited. Mondale came when he could, but as Vice-President he traveled a great deal and so he wasn't there all that much. There were occasions when I asked for a one-on-one with the President when I wanted to say something I didn't want Brzezinski to be in on. There was never any problem about that. The President made it clear it was my prerogative any time I wanted, and Brzezinski and Mondale both understood that."[35]

When Iran came to the boil, Carter could not decide whether to give the shah America's support because he would probably win, as Brzezinski urged, or to deal with the army or revolutionary leaders as men justified by the shah's oppression. (SAVAK, the shah's secret police, which had close ties with the CIA, relied on torture and had had about fifty thousand Iranians imprisoned for opposition to the shah.)[36] Gary Sick, the specialist on Iran of the National Security Council staff, briefed Brzezinski that "the most fundamental problem at

---

feel a bit hard done by being displaced by the big boys. Very understandable: all that money and all those people. Their operations were like putting smelling powders in people's pants!" (interview, November 17, 1983). In Iran as the crisis mounted, Parsons was invited by the shah to attend virtually every meeting he had with the American ambassador, William H. Sullivan.

the moment is the astonishing lack of hard information we are getting about developments in Iran. . . . This has been an intelligence disaster of the first order. Our information has been extremely meager, our resources were not positioned to report accurately on the activities of the opposition forces [or] on external penetration."[37]

The consequences of terminating the clandestine services and taking too much on trust from the shah's government were coming home to roost, encouraged by a nervous White House willing to leak everything that indicated weakness elsewhere in the government. On November 11 Carter sent a handwritten note to Vance, Brzezinski, and Turner: "To Cy, Zbig, Stan: I am not satisfied with the quality of our political intelligence. Assess our assets and as soon as possible give me a report concerning our abilities in the most important areas of the world. Make a joint recommendation on what we should do to improve your ability to give me political information and advice. J.C."[38] The consequence of depending on machines and therefore not hearing the tone of voice and the nuances of information was at last slowly being recognized by Carter.

Turner still did not see all this. "I suspected that Zbig Brzezinski was behind [this note]," he wrote later. "My suspicions were strengthened a few days later, when, despite the precautions taken to deliver the note privately, a story about it appeared in three newspapers simultaneously. I knew I had been set up as the scapegoat. When the shah did fall two months later, the easy explanation was that it was an 'intelligence failure.' "[39] Brzezinski had, in fact, urged Carter to write the note in the first place,[40] but not in an attempt to make Turner or the CIA a scapegoat: he wanted to make the President understand the consequences of his indecisiveness and of his isolationist instincts. By making Carter call for *political* information, Brzezinski was taking an important step toward forcing a recognition that the United States was dependent on other countries (in this situation the United States was dependent not only on Iranian oil but also on the location in Iran of important electronic, telemetry, and communications intelligence-monitoring stations) and toward the understanding that what went on in other countries was important for the United States to know. He was trying to emphasize the fragility of arrangements and the danger of disorder that made it foolhardy for the United States to try to bury its head in the sand.

Three months later, on February 20, 1979, the Ayatollah Ruhollah Khomeini, who had been in exile in Paris for many years before returning to Iran on February 1, led the overthrow of the shah and the establishment of an anti-American, anticommunist Islamic revolutionary state. Just over eight months later, on November 4, 1979, after the shah—now in exile—had been permitted to enter the United States for cancer treatment, Khomeini militants occupied the U.S. Embassy in Tehran, holding hostage 69 diplomats, marines, and staff. Although Khomeini released 16 women and blacks, the remaining 53 remained hostage for 444 days. Their release came on the day of Ronald

Reagan's inauguration, a gesture asserting Iran's defiance of the United States.

Six months after the hostages were seized (along with some secret CIA documents revealing that three of the hostages were CIA men)* Carter authorized a secret military raid to release them. Not surprisingly, the agency was not expected to conduct the rescue mission. To have had the capability would have meant a transformation of the CIA; it had never had—not even in the days of OPC—an elite special-forces arm. It was now full of analysts, administrators, and technical intelligence collectors. Its involvement in the rescue mission was minimal: a retired CIA operative was called back to go into Iran (the agency had no operatives or agents in place in the country), and "when the U.S. Navy provided the helicopters for the Iranian hostage mission," Turner related, "they did not have a suitable overland navigation system for the helicopters. The CIA's paramilitary branch did, and installed them in the Navy aircraft, thus making the mission feasible."† The paramilitary branch of the agency was

---

* Documents so far published by the Iranians include material on the connection between Israeli intelligence and SAVAK; reports to the embassy from Iranians seeking to act as intermediaries between the shah and Khomeini, and later between Khomeini and the first post-shah government; cables about the political situation in Iran to the State Department in Washington; and "Cover Considerations" for (CIA) operatives along with examples of forged passport stamps. Thomas Ahern, the station chief, organized the successful destruction of most CIA papers when the militants invaded the embassy, but most of the papers in the defense attaché's office were captured. They apparently included (they have not been published by the Iranians) virtually all the defense attaché's intelligence reports during 1978 and 1979; a list of the true identities of all Defense Intelligence Agency sources and agents in Iran; records of Operation Gray Pan, a joint CIA-DIA plan to steal a Soviet antiaircraft gun sold to the Iranian army in 1978; the October–November 1979 intelligence reports on Soviet naval movements by the U.S. Pacific and European commands; and a list of DIA top priority intelligence targets worldwide. Some of the material Ahern shredded was reported to have been pieced together again (*Newsweek,* December 28, 1981, pp. 33–34).

† Stansfield Turner, *Secrecy and Democracy,* pp. 176–177. See also Col. Charlie A. Beckwith and Donald Knox, *Delta Force: The U.S. Counter-Terrorist Unit and the Iranian Hostage Rescue Mission* (London: Arms and Armour Press, 1984), pp. 199–200, 221:

> Without "stay-behind assets," intelligence agents, information gathering was slow and tedious. That's where America was in November 1979—without anyone in Tehran working for it. The Central Intelligence Agency was working to locate someone in the area, but that process would take some time. Hell, it takes five to seven years just to train and emplace an agent. He or she has to be spotted, recruited, trained, assessed, and introduced into a country. Then he or she can become productive only after they've lived their cover for a reasonable period of time.
>
> The Carter administration had made a serious mistake. When retired [sic] Admiral Stansfield Turner went into the CIA, a lot of the old whores—guys with lots of street sense and experience—left the Agency. They had been replaced with younger, less experienced people or, worse, not replaced at all. Why this happened I don't know. But I do know that in Iran on 12 November 1979 there were no American agents on the ground. Nothing could be verified. At the end of December . . . the CIA managed to introduce an agent into the Iranian capital. Given the code name Bob, he was brought out of retirement for this mission.

In all probability the Iran network of agents had been in disrepair for some time, otherwise more than Bob would have been called in.

full of useful equipment for rescuing hostages but had no people it could train for the task. The mission was properly one for military special forces.

All the weaknesses of technical intelligence were demonstrated in the April 1980 rescue mission. The strengths of technology—quantifiable information, "safe" collection, immediacy—were not appropriate to the mission. Nevertheless, having decided to make the rescue attempt, Carter had no alternative but to rely on technology. In practice, he looked to technology to provide him with the impossible—perfection. No room was allowed for error or for loss. The rescue plan and its implementation involved a pathological unwillingness to accept losses. It was a classic instance of a politician's handling of a problem, without imagination; underlying it was the determining view that there could be no embarrassment by waste: every helicopter, every radio, every member of the rescue team was to do a vital job. Carter did not realize that by insisting on accuracy he was increasing risk. If one element failed, the whole mission would be jeopardized—which is exactly what happened. Two helicopters crashed into a transport plane, killing eight soldiers, and the mission was aborted. The failed rescue attempt reflected an overreliance on technology that assumed certainty, a mirror image of what had already happened to the CIA.

Turner remembered the effect of the Iranian crisis on Carter's last year as President:

> We were totally consumed by Iran. If the politicians don't understand the mechanism they're operating, they are either going to ask it for things it can't produce or for things it can't produce well. It may try to produce them, and it won't do a good job, and they won't know. Carter had an understanding of technology and of what it could do. In my briefing sessions with him, I took him capacitors and resistors and stuff. I tried to inform him about how intelligence operates with details of intelligence collection techniques, to give him a feel for how much he could rely on it and what he could call on us for. If he hadn't had some understanding when we were sitting there at night and there were fires burning on the deserts of Iran with airplanes crashed, it might have been another real problem. The questions were, "How soon are the Russians going to know about this? How soon are the Iranians going to know?" And somebody comes running in with an intercept of an Iranian communication, he had to have something to judge the value of that intercept and what it meant.[41]

In the middle of the technical nightmare of the failed rescue mission, the human element gave rise to additional tensions and problems. Cyrus Vance had opposed the rescue mission from the start, arguing for purely diplomatic moves instead to bring pressure on the Iranian government to secure the release of the embassy personnel. When he found that the decision had been taken to go ahead with the rescue mission, and that it had been taken while he was away for a weekend break, he penned his resignation letter. He was prepared to stay on as secretary of state until the Iranian crisis was over, but then he was determined to go. He was not prepared either to be excluded from foreign policy decisions or for his advice to be set aside in what seemed to him such a scheming way. So he kept on repeating his advice throughout the crisis, and this caused Turner some anxious moments. "I was sitting there saying to the President that I did not want him to go public on the failure until I could notify my people and get them out. But Vance was saying, 'We can't let the Iranians find out about this through their normal channels. We've got to tell the world about it ourselves because they'll think it's an invasion if they uncover it themselves. And we don't want the Russians to misinterpret it.' And I'm saying, 'But I've got people!' "[42] "I admired the way Turner fought for his agents," Brzezinski wrote later, "and we agreed to delay the public announcement."[43]

In most situations technology avoids the need to depend on people and to cope with their surprises.* It is a minimalist option; it helps America remain informed about the rest of the world without having to place its agents and soldiers where personal and national risk is great. It also allows both the agency and the United States to keep their hands clean, even in potentially compromising situations. Through electronic eavesdropping, for example, the CIA knew which girl President Tubman of Liberia was sleeping with on any particular night.[44] Technical intelligence is predictable. Arguing against reliance on human intelligence, Stansfield Turner stated:

> Technical systems cost infinitely more money than human ones, [but] once the Congress appropriates the money for something like a new satellite, the commitment is set; you cannot modify a satellite once it is launched, and it may be up there for years. . . . The DCI is called on almost daily to make decisions concerning technical collection, because it has become such an integral part of crisis management. . . .
> Uncovering intentions is the strong point of human espionage, but it is an exaggeration to say that only espionage can do that. Reading another country's messages through intercepts or listening to its leaders talk to each other through a concealed microphone can reveal intentions, often with greater accuracy than an agent's reporting.[45]

Although all this is true, it somehow misses the mark of what the United States actually needed in Iran. Technical intelligence could not foresee the revolution or the hostage seizure, nor could it organize and plan the rescue mission with-

---

* Distrust is a disease of all technique. In 1914, for example, the German general staff successfully argued that mobilization (which led to war) had to be geared to the railway timetables; the discipline had run away with objectives it was meant to serve. It is not the technical means that should be criticized but the nature of its use, consumption, and support, which often gives the means an ascendancy over its nominal masters.

out the help of a retired CIA agent. Alone it was inadequate. To be effective, human intelligence was needed as well.*

The debate about technical versus human intelligence and the decision to concentrate on technical intelligence masked a greater change in American foreign policy and America's view of itself and the world. By 1977—the thirtieth anniversary of the CIA and the sixtieth anniversary of the Russian revolution—both the United States and the CIA had lost their mystique. The assumption born of a proper sense of urgency—and opportunity—in 1947 that a few people could combine and act for America and let events justify them was over. The diffusion of power and authority meant an increasing involvement in CIA activities by those outside the agency; the increase in congressional attention, the assertion of congressional authority, and the mushrooming of congressional staffs emphasized this change.†

Public scrutiny also intensified. Foreign affairs played a large part in almost every presidential election since World War II, signifying widespread interest in America's world role. In the wake of Watergate the country wanted a greater check on the formless scope of executive-branch power (this was an element in increased congressional supervision). The perception that the bureaucracy was pursuing a policy of its own—that it was transacting business with world powers while the American people stood powerless on the sidelines—motivated Americans to reduce the size and scope of government as well as America's involvement with the rest of the world. It also spurred many Americans to take a greater interest in governmental affairs. These moves were not resisted by the technical elites, who by this time had lost confidence in their ability to control intelligence. Preferring impersonal systems that concentrated on technical collection rather than analysis, they were always ready and willing to let others (and machines) make policy.‡

---

* The failure was a general one in Iran. There was no evidence, even in the high days of human intelligence, of an agent infrastructure there, an indigenous network capable of smuggling the hostages out. Intelligence networks are specialized, and the more generalized they are, the more easily they are wrapped up. There was no way that anyone could have planned for (as opposed to foreseen) the hostage situation. The failure was the lack of any agents in Iran, not the lack of an agent infrastructure. The substantial failure was in Washington: it did not require intelligence to know that Iran was in ferment and that the embassy staff should be moved out. Everyone in Iran knew that the embassy had coordinated the overthrow of Mussadegh—losers have long memories—but the U.S. did not recognize the connection.

† As of October 1, 1985, 3.8 million Americans had secret military or intelligence clearance; 115,000 had sensitive departmental clearances, and 700,000 were cleared for top-secret. One hundred million secret documents were on file, and 16 million secret documents were being created annually. There were 14,000 defense contractors cleared for specific secrets (General Richard G. Stilwell, USA [Ret.], chairman, Department of Defense security review committee, speaking at the eleventh annual convention of the Association of Former Intelligence Officers, Rockville, Maryland, October 5, 1985).

‡ Under Turner, for example, the number of National Intelligence Estimates fell to about twelve a year. Subsequently, under Casey, they increased to about sixty a year.

—19—

In Search of Magic
1980-1987

Carter's defeat by Ronald Reagan in 1980 held the promise of a new dawn for the CIA. There was hope that Reagan would understand the need for a secret instrument in foreign policy. What few realized at the time was that this did not necessarily mean that the CIA would be the secret instrument Reagan might choose.

The Iranian crisis had marked the sands running out not only for Jimmy Carter, but also for the CIA. People saw that by a combination of bad luck, bad judgment, emotional exhaustion, a refusal to think clearly, and an assumption that the United States could muddle through, the President and those who served him had achieved an effect comparable to that of Suez for the British in 1956. But whereas the British elites in 1956 had concluded that the will at the center had gone and that therefore foreign policy should be aimed at withdrawing to a smaller perimeter, the American elites remained hopeful and saw the crisis simply as events going wrong. They understood that unlike Britain twenty-four years earlier, America was not seriously weak or weakened. The United States may have lost confidence and felt helpless in the face of their diplomats' being held prisoner in Iran by captors who were supported by chanting, fanatical mobs, but this was a tactical matter and could be blamed on specific administrative and intelligence failures and on particular people, starting with Jimmy Carter. However unfair the apportioning of blame might be, the fact was that it could be apportioned and it provided a reasonable rationale for the temporary frustration of the crisis. If people were not content to accept this explanation, then they could reflect that America had undergone in the 1960s and 1970s a social revolution which had been paralleled by the collapse of the economic expectations of the early 1960s, and that it was therefore somehow inevitable that there should be a loss of confidence, a steady falling away of the popular acceptance of the government's ability to manage domestic and foreign affairs successfully.

The facts supported this two-tier analysis. The 1970s were a decade which saw little increase in the personal incomes of Americans. In the 1960s the U.S. economy had grown by about 50 percent; in the 1970s it grew by about 30 percent, but this growth had been diluted by the entry of the postwar "bulge" generation and a larger number of women and blacks into the job market. Americans were far more uncertain of themselves and their values: More people were divorcing than ever before. There were more people addicted to drugs than ever before. America's international standing was seen as diminished after Vietnam. There was an acute sense as the decade came to an end that the world was hostile and was closing in on America. OPEC and the first oil crisis of 1973 had crystallized much of America's self-doubt. The fall of Saigon eighteen months later confirmed the Vietnam War as a national humiliation. Carter's Panama Canal treaty (ratified in 1978 and effective from October 1, 1979) was regarded by many Americans as another national humiliation. It was "our" canal and no "banana republic" should control it. Reflecting this sense, the Senate passed the treaty by only one vote. Then there was the second oil shock of 1978–1979, with further price increases and limitations of supply, and the continuing spectacle of national leaders whom America had thought of as friends and allies (and had in some cases—for instance the shah—helped to power and helped to keep in power) enjoying tweaking the eagle's beak. On top of all this, the 1970s had witnessed the emergence of Japan as a major economic competitor to America, possessed of at least as much dynamism and flexibility as the United States.

Just as Jimmy Carter had capitalized on popular perceptions in 1976, so in 1980 Ronald Reagan capitalized on the change in awareness. He appealed to a revived, angry, and anxious national pride, and the acceptance that there was no return to isolation because the rest of the world, as the oil crises and foreign economic competition had shown, would not leave the United States alone. Like Jimmy Carter and Gerald Ford, Reagan also ran on an anti-Washington platform, benefiting enormously from being able to portray Carter as synonymous with governmental failure. Behind this, however, Reagan felt strongly that nobody had warned of these changes and the effect they would have on America, and his finger pointed at the CIA. On November 4, 1979, when the embassy and the diplomats were seized in Tehran, it was an event to which every American could relate. It was highly illegal, highly dramatic, and riddled with the sense that high incompetence was involved. Suddenly, everybody wondered why the embassy had not been evacuated or only skeletally staffed months earlier: the shah had fled in January, and in retrospect the seizure seemed inevitable. The failure to destroy sensitive embassy documents in time compounded this sense of incompetence. When three days after the failure of the rescue mission the secretary of state resigned without giving the public any clear reason, it seemed as if there was a general failure of nerve in the Establishment. Canada, the poor American relation, managed to smuggle some U.S. diplomats out of Iran while America itself could only look on.

And where was the CIA? It had not warned of OPEC in 1973. It had not foretold the effects on the American economy of the rise of Japan. It had not predicted the shah's fall. There is no evidence that it had recommended reducing the Tehran embassy staff before the diplomats were seized. On this last point alone, if the agency had made such a recommendation, it would have been the hero of the time. Instead, the CIA was seen in governing circles as having been saved by William Colby's preemption of the morality of secrecy, only to be reduced in effectiveness in consequence. In 1980, millions of Americans would have welcomed Khomeini's assassination.

Reagan probably thought this. He also probably saw the agency as having grown long in the tooth, satisfied with the triumph of the prudent professional, no longer exciting or innovative or flexible and not wanting to be—as an organization glad of the star quality of its founding generation, but anxious not to have that quality in it anymore.

One of the elements that most worried Reagan staffers as they prepared for government after Reagan's victory was the quiet way in which the agency had bowed down to Stansfield Turner's policies. Out of concern that Carter's policies (or rather lack of them) were seriously weakening United States security, the Committee on the Present Danger, formed by Paul Nitze and members of Team B—the group that had reviewed CIA analysis of Soviet strategic forces in 1976—and the Madison Group, another similarly concerned organization, provided Reagan with his campaign panels on military and foreign policy.* Both groups voiced deep worry that the CIA had not only been reduced to operational ineffectiveness but had also become too partisan under Turner in its analytical support for the view that the Soviets were prepared to deal honestly.

The experience of SALT I, and Carter's abortive attempts to work out SALT II in the face of mounting evidence of Soviet aggression in Afghanistan and massive defense expenditures, had eroded public support for détente.† CIA efforts to maintain a moderate view of the Soviets and not to be rushed into accepting "worse case" scenarios was out of tune with the incoming ad-

---

* The Madison Group, made up of young political Washington insiders, was named after its meeting place in the Madison Hotel.

† Some leading members of the Committee on the Present Danger supported détente but felt that SALT II was going too far.

ministration. So Reagan set out with two objectives for the agency as he entered the White House in January 1981: to restore its morale and operational ability and to make it more activist and enthusiastic. In effect, his goal was an ideological housecleaning.

THE TRANSITION TEAM REPORT

The Reagan transition team for the CIA (the change of administration was marked by hand-over teams, consisting of new administration advisers consulting with the outgoing leadership and senior staffers in all government agencies and departments) was considered to be an especially important one. The CIA was the focus of a great deal of worry and concern. The resulting pressure on the team was matched by tensions within it. Shortly after being appointed, the team head, Lawrence Silberman, who had dealt with Colby in 1974 when he was acting attorney general, and now a Reagan supporter, learned that Stansfield Turner had managed to see Reagan without his being present. When this was followed by an accident at home that resulted in a broken foot for Silberman, he resigned. His place was taken by Bill Middendorf, more of a hard-liner than Silberman and a Reagan loyalist. Middendorf, however, had another job, which took more of his time and attention—arranging the inaugural balls for Reagan. Accordingly, he delegated most of his responsibility to retired Lieutenant General Edward Rowny, viewed by Reaganites as a sensible, no-nonsense soldier who concentrated on administrative tasks. (Rowny had resigned from the army in protest at the SALT II negotiations.)

The other members of the team included Ed Hennelly, a friend of William Casey's (Reagan's DCI designate) from Mobil Oil; three ex-CIA officers—John A. Bross, Walter Pforzheimer, and George Carver; and "three hooligans from the Hill," as one team member described them—Angelo Codevilla, Mark Schneider, and Kenneth deGraffenreid, all from the staff of the Senate Committee on Intelligence and all enthusiastic supporters of the views of the Madison Group and the Committee on the Present Danger.[1] At the end of November 1980 Roy Godson, a student of intelligence from the National Strategy Information Center in Washington, was also brought in. Others were brought in on a part-time basis to complete the team.

With Middendorf's strong support, Angelo Codevilla led the ideological assault. His proposals, according to one colleague, amounted to "firing every officer above GS-14."[2] William Casey—in an unusual position, since within days of the election it was known in top Republican circles that he would be Reagan's director of Central Intelligence (normally, there would be a jockeying for position, and the decision would not be made public for several weeks)— sat in on some of the team's deliberations before it was officially announced that he would be the next DCI. The proceedings were acrimonious, with

Rowny and the ex-CIA men arguing against any wholesale housecleaning, which rapidly focused on the DDI's Soviet Russia Division.* Codevilla led an effort to break up the CIA and create three new organizations in its place: a new counterintelligence agency composed of CIA and FBI staffs in this field; an analytical agency made up of people from the Estimates side of the agency; and an operations agency to perform the functions of the old CIA clandestine service. Donovan's original concept of centralized intelligence was being challenged yet again.

Behind these dramatic proposals were the findings of the Senate Intelligence Committee over the previous four years and the anxiety among Reagan supporters about U.S. national security. The transition team's working papers and final report summarized this concern over the agency's current plight. The findings and recommendations contained in the final report were so sensitive that the CIA sent its only copy to the White House for safekeeping, preferring to cut itself off from such a politically worrisome document.

"The fundamental problem confronting American security is the current dangerous condition of the Central Intelligence Agency and of national intelligence collection generally," the November 1980 outline transition-team report declared in an opening statement. "The failure of American intelligence collection has been at the heart of faulty defense planning and a vacillating and misdirected foreign policy."[3] The decades-old rivalry between the CIA and the State Department and the Nixon/Kissinger détente policy were singled out as prime causes of this disarray: "The unhealthy symbiosis between the Central Intelligence Agency and the Department of State is the chief underlying cause of the eroded security position of the United States. . . . Decisive action at the CIA is the keystone in achieving a reversal of the unwise policies of the past decade." This assertion was not really tenable, however. Vacillating

---

* Many of the people who worked in the Soviet Russia Division could not speak Russian, and it was generally felt that the quality of its analysis was not very good. Carter's note "To Cy, Zbig, Stan" in November 1978 was an important indicator of this. Stansfield Turner, looking back on the division's opposition to his publication of unclassified information, said:

> Like the espionage people, the analysts were trying to avoid criticism. They were, though, subjected to more of that when we published a second study on energy, in the summer of 1977. This one concluded that oil production in the Soviet Union would start declining in the early 1980s. The outside experts who differed were eventually proved right. . . . Our report was wrong not because of faulty work, but because the Soviets changed their tactics after the report came out. They found ways to postpone the decline (Stansfield Turner, *Secrecy and Democracy—The CIA in Transition* [Boston: Houghton Mifflin, 1985], pp. 119–120).

The analysts should have considered the possibility of Soviet policy changing in the way he later described. The change in Soviet "tactics" was always a likely response to the problem: any politician facing a major deficit will seek ways of postponing and softening the reckoning.

After such discussion between the CIA and the new administration, the 250-strong Directorate of Intelligence division charged with Soviet analysis was moved from the Langley headquarters to a satellite office in nearby Vienna, Virginia, and some of its officers were reassigned. This had far more to do with internal debates, however, than with anything the transition team recommended.

and unwise foreign policies were the result of bad political leadership, not bad intelligence. The CIA has never been better than the nation's political leaders. As U.S. foreign-policy formation became more complex, placing increasing demands on U.S. presidents, the clarity and certainty of command dissolved, affecting the CIA as much as any other agency of government. If there was, in fact, any identity with the State Department, this was the extent of it.

Some team members felt strongly that "the self-described professionals at CIA" were more concerned about their job security than national security and more interested in preserving the agency as a bureaucracy than in developing effective intelligence and policy coordination. In the view of these team members, the agency had been effectively politicized during the 1970s and was no longer capable of unbiased reporting: "The next Director of the Central Intelligence Agency . . . will be told repeatedly by virtually everyone in policy positions at the Agency that the CIA is a highly professional, non-political agency that produces 'objective' intelligence. Those assertions are arrant nonsense. . . . In part out of a mutual drive for individual and corporate self-preservation, the CIA has become an elitist organization which engenders incredible loyalty among its staff and retired personnel. . . . An immediate effort will be made by top CIA personnel to capture and co-opt the next Director."

As a result of this perception, which, in fact, was a statement of the ordinary condition of institutional history to be expected in any bureaucracy, some members of the team recommended that a host of agency officials be fired and that some specific replacements be made. Stansfield Turner, a "lame duck" DCI who "actually believes that he has done a good job as Director and genuinely thinks that there is some prospect that he will be retained," had no chance of survival. In addition, nearly every top agency staff officer was recommended for dismissal as "Carter Administration protégés who advanced in grade and position during the past four years because of their willingness to support leftist-oriented perceptions and programs." There was an almost McCarthyesque tone in some cases: "The present Legislative Counsel of the CIA, Fred Hitz, was a member of [Presidential chief of staff] Hamilton Jordan's White House working group for selling SALT II. Hitz is closely identified with the Carter Administration and is known to have stated within the last week, 'It is vital that conservatives not be permitted access to the CIA.' Hitz should be removed effective January 21, 1981." Proposed replacements for Hitz and other top staff members included William Schneider (who was on the staff of Representative Jack Kemp); Roy Godson; Kenneth deGraffenreid; Sven Kraemer, a Republican Policy Committee staff member; Amron Katz, from the Rand Corporation; Norman Friedman, from the Hudson Institute, and several other "conservatives" from outside the agency.*

---

* These people were proposed in an early team paper before the team's membership was completed. The full team determined that personnel changes were not a transition team job and belonged to the new DCI. William Schneider was later in charge of the CIA's budget in the

The transition team also recommended reversing Carter's abolition of the President's Foreign Intelligence Advisory Board. Carter had taken this action because of the board's record of support for covert actions and the clandestine service and because he was anxious to establish direct lines of authority over the CIA and the intelligence community as a whole. He did not consider that he needed more advice than he was getting through the National Security Council, its staff, and the heads of the intelligence agencies. Moreover, he knew the board would almost certainly disagree with his views. "The President's Foreign Intelligence Advisory Board should be reestablished and its watchdog function should be strengthened," the transition team held. "The board should be given a quality control mission over the product of the agency and should be permitted wide-ranging authority to review the intelligence product of the last four years to identify erroneous information and to locate the individuals chiefly responsible for those areas."

The concern over CIA analysis and the Estimates had been building up for several years. Stansfield Turner was partially responsible for bringing the problem to a head by his practice of writing some Estimates himself. Although he had every right to do so—the Estimates were still under the purview of the DCI—his actions generated deep resentment within the agency's analytical staff as well as occasional leaks. One analyst, David Sullivan, was fired by Turner for giving a copy of a highly classified report to Admiral Elmo Zumwalt, who was no longer in government. Turner had disagreed with Sullivan's conclusions and insisted that the report be amended accordingly.[4] But, more significant, there was a widespread feeling that the CIA's analysis had been seriously wrong in several key instances and that reform was necessary. Once he was out of the agency, Sullivan played an important part in lending weight to criticism of the CIA and Carter's foreign and defense policies.

Air force General George Keegan also played a major part in securing a public reassessment of the CIA's analytical performance. After his time in Vietnam, Keegan had risen to become assistant chief of staff for air force intelligence. His advancement was somewhat unexpected because he was an intellectual officer, interested in ideas and their practical application and an articulate and aggressive debater. He was regarded by many as a self-promoter and self-publicist. He was controversial. By 1977 he had over thirty years' experience of military intelligence.

Keegan was convinced that détente was a mistake, that SALT I and the attempt to reach SALT II were serious miscalculations, and that the Soviet Union was manipulating public opinion the world over as it quietly secured increasing military strength. He became convinced that the Soviet Union had

---

Office of Management and Budget. Throughout the Reagan administration Kenneth deGraffenreid was the National Security Council's liaison with the working level of the CIA. Sven Kraemer was also a National Security Council staffer under Reagan.

overtaken the United States in military power and that in the drive for détente, the intelligence community, led by the CIA, had refused to acknowledge the military imbalance. He advanced a simple argument: the United States must enjoy, for its own national security, superiority in every military area over the Soviet Union. The Soviet Union was intent on world domination, and the Soviet military buildup was evidence of their determination to secure this objective regardless of what they said or what agreements they signed. The United States was burying its head in the sand if it believed and acted otherwise.

In 1975 the CIA had attempted to reach a community-wide consensus on Soviet objectives in response to pressure from Keegan within the intelligence community and the Ford administration. The report, "Understanding Soviet Strategic Policy," was written by a national intelligence officer, Fritz Ermath, who could obtain no consensus. There were three broad views of Soviet policy within the intelligence community, Ermath said. There was the Keegan view; the CIA view that the Soviets were not aiming for world domination but were engaged in a standoff battle with America, constantly seeking to maintain and improve their existing interests; and a State Department view that the Soviets were interested in military parity with—not superiority over—the United States and would be opportunistic expansionists. In other words, Ermath was saying, the United States did not know what the Soviets really wanted or intended. His report was seen as a major admission of analytical weakness and overall doctrinal confusion.*

The Team A/Team B controversy over Soviet policy objectives proceeding in 1975–1976 also fueled the sense that the CIA's analysis needed an overhaul in the direction Keegan was urging. The revision in 1976 by the CIA of their Estimates on Soviet military spending after General Daniel Graham's Defense Intelligence Agency analysis of the question was an additional element in the growing criticism of the agency within governing circles. In 1977 Keegan resigned, retiring from the air force, following a run-in with Carter's secretary of defense, Harold Brown, about the nature and size of the Soviet threat. Keegan then went public in a series of articles and lectures, setting into motion the public apprehension of Soviet intentions and capabilities that Ronald Reagan exploited so successfully in 1980.

---

* An insight into the problem of gauging Soviet intentions can be gained by comparing it with the analysis of the United States that the American Indians could have debated in the nineteenth century. The Indians could have realized what we realize today: One group of Americans wanted to annihilate the Indians; a second group was happy to live and let live; a third group were opportunists, expanding at the expense of the Indians whenever the chance arose. Now, turning this awareness back on the Soviet Union's intentions toward the United States, we can see that Ermath's description of the different American arguments was probably an accurate mirror image of the arguments and tensions on the subject within the Soviet Union's leadership. Since the United States had no way of knowing for certain which argument was receiving favor in the Soviet Union, it had to be prepared for all possible eventualities. The only way to do this was through a detailed world analysis. But, Ermath was indicating, the CIA was not providing this analysis.

The transition team debated what was, in effect, Keegan's—and to an important though less well-known extent, David Sullivan's—agenda. Reagan's people were looking for failures, because, along with most Americans, they assumed that America caused everything in the world and that when something was wrong, America had failed in some respect. Twelve "intelligence failures" were discussed, including "the general and continuing failure to predict the actual size and scope of the Soviet military effort and military sector of the Russian GNP"; "the consistent gross misstatement of Soviet global objectives"; "Iran"; "the wholesale failure to understand and predict the nature of so-called wars of national liberation in Africa and Central and South America"; and "the consistent miscalculation regarding the effect of and general apology for massive technology transfer from the West to the East."*

* The other "intelligence failures" listed in the November 1980 report were:

a. Abject failure to predict the massive Soviet buildup of ICBMs and SLBMs;
b. The wholesale failure to understand the characteristics of Soviet missiles under development prior to SALT I;
c. The failure to predict (coupled with, in fact, predictions to the contrary) the major improvements in accuracy of Soviet ICBMs in the late 1970s;
d. The general failure to explain the characteristics of Soviet conventional weapon systems and vessels—for example, the Soviet T-64 and T-72 tanks and the new Russian guided missile cruisers;
e. The apparent internal failure of counterintelligence generally;
f. The wholesale failure to understand or attempt to counteract Soviet disinformation and propaganda;
g. The failure to detect the Soviet brigade in Cuba.

Designating the last item a "failure" was, in fact, nonsense. In 1979 Senator Richard Stone, casting around for an election issue (he faced a difficult election campaign in Florida the following year), declared that there was a Soviet brigade in Cuba and that steps must be taken to make the Soviets remove it. Although this position was popular with the right and with the substantial Cuban exile community in Florida, Stone was not reelected. However, there was no Soviet brigade in Cuba—air force intelligence had suggested that there was on the basis of the layout of Soviet camps—and the CIA, correctly, argued the point. There were Soviet troops in Cuba—there had been since 1961—but not a combat brigade. There was a subsidiary debate about the purpose of the Soviet troops, some arguing that they were there to defend secret Soviet nuclear installations, others that they were there for training purposes. The consensus was that they were there for training and to replace Cuban troops based in southern Africa.

The "internal failure of counterintelligence" could not be blamed solely on the CIA, and objectively there was a question of whether it was a failure at all, since a great many Soviet spies were being uncovered. Between 1965 and 1975 seven Americans were arrested for spying; in contrast, forty-three Americans were arrested on espionage charges during the decade that followed.

The allegation that the CIA had failed in a propaganda battle was also misplaced. The agency is a silent service, and propaganda is not its job. This was more of a State Department and United States Information Agency failure.

Behind all these allegations was the sense that the CIA's tendency toward moderation was being overtaken by events, in particular the decision of the Soviets after the Cuban missile crisis to increase their military strength enormously.

One of William Casey's first Estimates was on "Soviet Acquisition of Western Technology," responding to the need to monitor technology transfer. The Estimate was completed in August 1981, and according to the deputy director of Central Intelligence, Admiral Bobby Ray Inman, "the results were startling to those of us inside the intelligence community." The Soviet

The mood of Reagan's followers brooked no excuses for what were, in many cases, reasonable disagreements and matters of opinion. Their assumption was that the Soviet Union had a plan (as opposed to a settled desire) for global domination and that international anarchy was part of this plan rather than a historic feature of world relations. They represented an American insistence on thinking in terms of "friends" and "enemies" rather than in terms of conflicting interests. (This friend/enemy framework was at the heart of the real shock that occurred when the shah, a "friend," led the 1973 OPEC raid on the U.S. economy and on U.S. wealth.) The collapse of the shah and the hostage seizure in Iran in 1979, on the other hand, had certainly been an intelligence failure, and the CIA had been slow to pinpoint the dangers of technology transfer.

The argument over Soviet objectives was reasonable, however, and the CIA's long history of moderation on the subject had been vindicated many times during the 1950s and 1960s. The building of the Berlin wall was symbolic of the standoff approach of the Soviets in Europe, just as the CIA had argued. The invasion of Afghanistan was an example of possible Soviet opportunism or of world-domination objectives, just as Keegan or the State Department argued. There can never be absolute certainty in estimates or judgments, just best guesses. But there was no room for such considerations in the wake of Reagan's election. "These failures are of such enormity," declared the Reaganite team members, "that they cannot help but suggest to any objective observer that the agency itself is compromised to an unprecedented extent and that its paralysis is attributable to causes more sinister than incompetence."

Focusing on the analysis, some team members were determined to review the whole intelligence-collection effort. The "sinister" way in which the CIA's analysis was "compromised" was thought to be the result of an ossified bureaucracy ("The National Intelligence Estimate process is itself a bureaucratic game," said the report) and inadequate espionage: "Only in one area can the CIA offer a rational excuse for its inaccuracies and faulty predictions. Collection systems generally, both human and technical, have been grossly underfunded during the Carter years. . . . The failure of a single launch in the early to mid-1980s could negate all of our capability for a particular type of collector for a protracted period of time. A failure of the space shuttle could be disastrous for the entire technical intelligence collection effort."

The blame was placed squarely on Carter for a barely adequate American intelligence-collection capability (a point generally agreed on by the members of the team). As a result of his decision to terminate various collection projects

Union and its allies, the Estimate said, had and were obtaining large quantities of up-to-the-minute American military and computer technology by both legal and subversive means (Permanent Subcommittee on Investigations, Senate Committee on Governmental Affairs, *Transfer of United States High Technology to the Soviet Union and Soviet Bloc Nations* [Washington, DC: U.S. Government Printing Office, 1982]).

(primarily because of their cost but also as a unilateral gesture to the Soviets in an attempt to secure comparable moves by them in the SALT II process), "high-quality technical intelligence with maximum measurement capability is no longer available on a regular basis. Moreover, the new follow-on medium-to-high-resolution [satellite photoreconnaissance] system is planned for only one per year ... but for full coverage, three launches per year are necessary and, at a minimum, there should be two."*

In area-search satellite photoreconnaissance—wide coverage rather than high-resolution technology—"the United States is in a position now to launch only one per year through 1984. As a result, in any given year during that period, there will be a five- or six-month gap in which the United States has no significant area search resources. Moreover, the decision to fly the [successor] system in its high-resolution mode has reduced the potential of that system for area search."† High-altitude telemetry system satellites were considered by the team to be planned at only one-third of actual requirements. "Moreover," the report continued, "any problem in the space shuttle could prevent the launch of the improved system on schedule, and since there is no backup whatsoever, the United States could be completely blinded with no overhead photo-reconnaissance capability at all in the mid-1980s. ... As presently planned, all satellites in the new system must work or the United States will be blind." The only way to "catch up for losses," concluded the report, would be an annual increase of $1.5 billion in the intelligence-collection program through 1985.[5]

Out of this dire reading of the situation came recommendations for improvement under Reagan. "A long-endurance (up to two days), high-altitude reconnaissance aircraft" should be developed. There should be a review of "the feasibility of a follow-up SR-71 type aircraft, perhaps developed to fly in the hypersonic (Mach-5 or above) range as an atmospheric skimmer. This system

* The principal satellite reconnaissance systems through to the mid-1980s were the Keyhole systems: the KH-9 ("Big Bird") operated by the air force, and the KH-11 operated by the CIA. Satellites in both systems were maneuverable. The KH-11 was first introduced in December 1976 and represented a major technological advance. It was able to transmit images electronically in real time, thus providing accurate minute-by-minute information. It had an average twenty-five months of life and possessed both television cameras giving very high resolution and electronic sensors capable of picking up terrestrial communications. According to one report, it was a KH-11 satellite that revealed Soviet construction of a new super submarine and a new mini-aircraft carrier in 1984.

The KH-9 system provided pinpoint resolution through a camera with an eight-foot focal length. Film from the KH-9 satellites was sent back to earth in capsules recovered either in air by planes or from the sea by frogmen. For details of these and other systems see *Aviation Week and Space Technology*, September 29, 1980; James Canan, *War in Space* (New York: Harper & Row, 1982), pp. 85–106; Curtis Peebles, *Battle for Space* (Poole, Eng.: Blandford Press, 1983), pp. 23–26; and Jeffrey T. Richelson, *The U.S. Intelligence Community* (Cambridge, MA: Ballinger, 1985), pp. 112–115.

† The successor system is DRM-4, operational in 1986. In many ways it is an improved KH-11 system, providing the same real time information as the old system with the same pinpoint resolution capability of the KH-9 system. The transition-team report suggested that by going for super resolution, the less detailed but very wide area "footprint" of the KH-11 system would be lost (Richelson, *The U.S. Intelligence Community*, p. 115).

should also be examined for its potential use against ballistic missiles."* "Remotely piloted vehicles (RPVs) possibly using stealth technology [the technique by which an airplane's identification by radar is prevented] should be reviewed for possible tactical intelligence collecting value and for strategic intelligence collection." Ground telemetry and monitoring stations should be increased, and "a plan for establishing telemetry collection stations in Pakistan" should be prepared:

> In that connection, the team should examine present agreements with the People's Republic of China to determine if better operational results could be obtained through Pakistan at less risk and at lower cost in terms of technology transfer and other forms of payment. In general, the number of ground collection stations should be roughly doubled to compensate for a reduction by one-half during the Carter years. An additional COBRA JUDY collection ship should be constructed at a cost of about $70 million. As matters now stand, the Soviet Union can be expected to wait until the one vessel on station moves out of the area and then launch a test missile. COBRA DANE in Alaska should also be upgraded and adequately funded.†

The team's summary of the state of American technical intelligence collection was succinct: "Technical collection for the United States reached its peak in 1965. Since then the quality of technical intelligence has declined steadily. That fact is a result of general underfunding of necessary systems, outright collection-system compromises by Soviet agents within the CIA (for ex-

---

* Clarence Robinson, former military editor of *Aviation Week and Space Technology*, has said about this follow-on system:

> We have a requirement in order to be able rapidly to perform a mission in space in low earth orbit for the military. We can do that for a number of reasons. One is to use it as some sort of space fighter. You could arm it with a kinetic-energy kill missile system. You could use it to service a spacecraft in orbit. In the case of high-energy lasers that might be space based, that plane could be used to haul tanks of chemical propellants up to refurbish those lasers once they'd engaged targets and expended their chemical propellants (interview, *Spaceflight*, TV documentary, by Blaine Bagget, c/o Producer Services Group, Brookline, MA, 1985).

† Cobra Dane and Cobra Judy are phased-array electronic radar stations (that is, they electronically scan the full field of view rather than only part of the field at any one time). Cobra Dane is situated on Shemya Island in the Aleutians; Cobra Judy is a ship based at Pearl Harbor. Their purpose is to track Soviet missile tests and satellites and to obtain telemetric information on Soviet weapon systems. Cobra Judy can also monitor the near-earth trajectories of Soviet reentry vehicles.

The intelligence relationship with China is an example of the sort of secret deal that worries many Americans because of the potential encumbrance on future action and policies. It is an example of the hidden links and interdependencies of the modern world. Along with the equally secret (but much older) intelligence relationship with Pakistan, it is also an example of the derivative quality of the agency, functioning as a consequence of diplomacy conducted by the State Department. The relationship dates from 1979 and consists of an information exchange between the U.S. and China. Additionally, the Chinese agreed to the construction by the CIA Directorate of Science and Technology of two signals intelligence stations, one at Qitai and the other at Korla in western China near the border with the Soviet Union, which were then manned by the Chinese. CIA arrangements for arming Afghan guerrillas were also in part conducted through China.

ample, Kampiles and Boyce), Carter administration leaks in its efforts to sell SALT II as verifiable, and probable general penetration of the CIA and high-level intelligence posts throughout the government." This was a most serious allegation.

Over the years there had been successful Soviet penetrations of American intelligence agencies but none of the CIA (or at least, none that were detected) until the mid-1970s. David H. Barnett, a career CIA officer, resigned from the agency in 1970 after twelve years of service. In 1976, by his own admission, he began spying for the Soviets. Not only did he pass on to them his knowledge of the agency and various operations but he also agreed to become an active Soviet agent. His target was the Senate Intelligence Committee; his Soviet controllers wanted him to gain a position on the staff of the committee. His motive appeared to be money. He was arrested in 1980, tried and convicted for espionage, and sentenced to ten years in prison.

In January 1977 Christopher Boyce, a young college dropout working as a clerk with TRW Corporation in California, was arrested along with a friend, Andrew Lee, for passing secret satellite information to the Soviets. TRW Corporation was doing contract work for the CIA on the Pyramider satellite system, and Boyce passed to the Soviet Embassy in Mexico City operating manuals detailing the system's construction and operation. Again, Boyce's motive appeared to be money for drugs, though a wish for excitement was also discernible. The damage he did was enormous, as Leslie C. Dirks, chief of the CIA's technical branch, testified at his trial. Dirks explained:

> Project Pyramider is a system to provide a means for communicating with CIA agents, foreign agents, emplaced sensors, and provide backup communications for overseas facilities. The key distinction is covert communications as opposed to standard, routine satellite communications. It also has to do with communications with what we call emplaced sensors—these are pieces of equipment left behind in various parts of the world which collect data remotely and later relay that data back to stations that we man. One example would be a seismic sensor. There are seismic sensors all over the world for the purpose of detecting earthquakes and also for the purpose of detecting underground nuclear explosions.[6]

Boyce and Lee were convicted of espionage. Boyce received a sentence of forty years and Lee of life. Their spying (and the general funding restrictions on intelligence under Carter) led to the cancellation of the Pyramider system.

William Kampiles joined the CIA in March 1977. He apparently had a James Bond image of the agency and was disappointed to find that his work was unexciting. He tried to transfer to the clandestine service just as Turner was cutting it back, but his requests were rejected. He resigned from the agency after only eight months, taking with him a copy of the manual for the KH-11 photoreconnaissance satellite system, which he sold to the Soviets for three thousand dollars. He was arrested and, like Boyce, sentenced to forty years in jail.

These cases, like the Walker family navy spy ring exposed in May 1985, exemplified a resurfacing of isolationism. Behind the activities of these American spies was the assumption that the United States was separate, removed, unendangered, that the Soviet Union, distant from American shores, posed no real threat. Underlying this misconception was the fact that none of the spies had ever been to Russia, and consequently none had firsthand experience of the Soviet system that was reaping the benefits from their espionage activities. The common denominator, besides money, in each of these cases was the sense that technical intelligence was unreal and incomprehensible, that it was nothing more than a game played by a huge complex of institutions in which the revelation of technical secrets mattered little if at all, and that if big corporations could apparently break the law and get away with it, why shouldn't an individual make some money by ripping off a corporation or the government too?

In every instance spying for the Soviets (as far as the CIA and the courts could determine) had commenced after service in the agency; there still was no evidence that the agency itself harbored a Soviet spy. Now, in November 1980, the earlier certainty that the CIA and "high-level intelligence posts" had not been penetrated by the Soviets no longer prevailed.* Whether true or not, the significance of the accusation was that it could be made. It was final and conclusive testimony that the agency had become ordinary in every sense. The whole tenor of the transition team's papers and reports demonstrated this. The CIA was a bureaucracy; it was at the level of other intelligence bureaucracies in government; its staff were as interested in their careers and job security as anybody else in government service; it was no longer flexible or risk-taking.

The need for an improved and expanded counterintelligence effort was stressed in the transition report (although Codevilla's separate counterintelligence agency idea was rejected). Trained people rather than money was the real deficiency. Overall, the team was saying that something had gone wrong with the agency, that it had the wrong people and the wrong methods, that it had a historical commitment to containment and an understated view of the world, that it was inward-looking and lacked internal debate, that Richard Bis-

---

* In 1984 Karl Koecher, a naturalized American who did contract translation work for the CIA between 1973 and 1977, was arrested for spying for his native Czechoslovakia during the time he worked for the agency. In June 1985 a CIA clerk who was still working in the agency was arrested for spying for Ghana. In October 1985 a former CIA officer, Edward L. Howard, was reported to have sold information to the KGB after he left the agency in 1983 when he failed a polygraph test for drug-taking and petty theft."I put the fact that so far we haven't had a Soviet penetration of the agency proper down to the polygraph," said William Casey. "Nobody says it's perfect, but it's a damn good safeguard to have" (interview, October 8, 1985). In November 1985 a retired analyst named Larry Wu-tai Chin was arrested for spying for China while working for the CIA.

sell's brilliance was still being used nineteen years later to support its reputation in technical intelligence collection, that it lacked resources but was itself partly responsible for this, that it had failed to stay abreast of intelligence developments by ignoring the human factor to such a great extent, and that its pervasive lack of urgency had resulted in a major failure to recognize Soviet advances.

The strong Reagan supporters added to this assessment the accusation that the CIA had assimilated a liberal perspective on the world and that its bureaucratic impulse to find favor with presidents and Congress had made it passive to ignorant political pressure. In turn, they sensed, the agency no longer wanted to be in the business of monitoring the Soviets, preferring to monitor its own systems and assessments instead, and thus was no longer able to live with the real tensions of the present time. Secrecy, this view held, was being used as a crutch to protect the agency and its staff from criticism and overhaul and was maintained for U.S. national security in only a secondary way.

The transition team's final report, submitted to William Casey on December 22, 1980, was a contentious document. Not only did it comprehensively condemn the agency's performance during the Carter-Turner years, it also questioned the future of the agency. Angelo Codevilla's view that the CIA should be broken apart was supported by some very serious and pointed arguments: the agency's analysis had been found wanting; the agency's counterintelligence branch—along with the clandestine service—had been reduced to such an extent that it was no longer able to deny the charge of probable Soviet penetration of the CIA; the agency's movement away from covert action meant that it could be only a passive observer of events with a minimal ability to influence or change events as they unfolded elsewhere in the world. Based on these three points, Codevilla's arguments had merit, but they ran against the underlying trend toward American disengagement from world affairs and the institutionalized logic that stressed technical over human intelligence methods.

There were also practical problems in Codevilla's approach, including where to put the agency's component parts. With their authority over intelligence collection stripped away, and with their participation blunted, the analytical operations would soon be far less effective. The operational and research and development components, each with an extremely specialized nature, had no natural home elsewhere. Who would defend their budgets, represent them at congressional hearings, ensure their access to the highest levels of decision and policy making in the executive branch, or police their requirements? The agency's reconnaissance program, for example, would certainly vanish into the caverns of the Pentagon within minutes. The espionage and counterintelligence functions would quickly follow as soon as their new chief started looking for room space, facilities, budgetary support, and so on. Before long most intelligence information would emanate unchallenged from the Defense Department. A separate counterintelligence agency would not necessarily improve American counterintelligence and would have to struggle with the National Security Agency, the FBI, the counterintelligence and investigative agencies of the Department of Defense, to say nothing of the other new operations agency that Codevilla had also proposed. It was, in the opinion of other team members, a recipe for disaster. George Carver led the argument against Codevilla, but before there was any resolution, William Casey terminated the transition team.

Casey's move was not unexpected for several reasons. In the first place, he was personally convinced of the value of centralized intelligence. In 1975 he had been a member of the Murphy Commission on "The Organization of the Government for the Conduct of Foreign Policy," which had, among other things, looked at the organization of the CIA and the intelligence community. Thus he was familiar with the arguments for and against centralization and had already resolved them once in favor of centralization. He believed that American national security would be weakened by fragmenting the CIA. Second, he did not want to be director of an agency that had no bureaucratic clout. His interests lay in expanding the agency's powers in certain ways, not in reducing them. Despite this, Casey did not aggressively go after his objective. His old-fashioned, nontechnical orientation made him comfortable with what he had. He was suspicious of the difficulties and complexities that a bigger technical agency would give him and the fact that he would be obviously out of place and time in such an agency. Had Casey been a different kind of person, significant expansion would have been quite likely; in 1981–82 he probably had the bureaucratic clout with the President to convince him that expansion was essential to meet the country's intelligence needs. Reagan's respect for Casey was such that one of his first acts as President was to give Casey cabinet rank, a position no other DCI had held.

The third reason for Casey's decision to terminate the team was based on the emphasis placed by Reagan's election campaign on the importance of the national security organizations, so it would not have been politic to start the administration by breaking up the leading security agency. Fourth, the transition team had been far more radical and detailed in its investigation and recommendations than expected, making its report a political hot potato. If the report's analysis was accepted, then Reagan and Casey would have had to politicize the agency in a more obvious way than had ever been done before, which would almost certainly expose the new administration to charges of being an "American Gestapo" and to unnecessary difficulties with Congress. These considerations, rather than the thought, harbored darkly by agency opponents, that Casey had been reached by senior agency professionals, carried the day.

RONALD REAGAN AND WILLIAM CASEY

Within the transition team's deliberations, however, was the germ of a "new" CIA. Until Reagan's election the CIA's strength—and identity—lay in its voice of expert moderation, which usually favored caution in the face of complexity. Now this was to become its weakness as everyone became lukewarm and moderation became reflexive rather than imaginative.

In 1947 the CIA had been different. Emergency gave it credentials. It contained a large group of people who possessed rare expertise for their unusual mission. Their talent and accomplishments made the agency the single most important intelligence body in the country. Thirty years later, when the direct threat to the United States was much greater, the agency was no longer viewed as a line of defense. At best it was simply an observer, and at worst it was a possible source of embarrassment. Its special people had gone, and emergency was now commonplace. It had distanced itself from its beginnings by urging caution and seeking to become a bureaucracy comparable to other great Washington agencies. Its own move to technical intelligence cemented this transformation: the core of secrecy was now in the cryptographic and communications intelligence agencies and the National Security Council staff.[7]

The CIA had become one of several competing institutions and was outclassed in the most important areas: communications and signals intelligence gathering. In the 1970s the United States had begun to return to its instinctive role as an "offshore" power, and thus intelligence had a special emphasis placed upon its preventative function—to forewarn and to enable resources to be effectively deployed and used. By accommodating itself to this change (and, in effect, by foretelling it in the 1960s), the CIA accurately reflected America's diminished role and was itself reduced in turn.

This lessening of America was Reagan's complaint, and the CIA seemed, therefore, to be in an obvious position to benefit from his election because of its early history of enthusiasm. The change that had taken place in the agency and in the American role was much more than surface deep. Once in the White House, Reagan, who had clearly suspected that this was the case (thus his appointment as DCI of the dynamic, risk-taking, and successful William Casey), had his suspicion confirmed. But what Reagan had not considered was the objective of rekindled enthusiasm. A go-getting DCI was to find that there was not much to go and get any more. Reagan's campaign pressure to make America strong and proud again in government became a policy of massive defense spending and operational restraint. The advice of caution, of moderation, was taken by Reagan, but no one was thanked for uttering it.

Like FDR, to whom he has been compared, Reagan possessed enormous courage. It was an unmistakable mark, even though it might have been the valor of ignorance. He demonstrated this courage to the world in March 1981 when he was shot by John Hinckley as the television cameras looked on. He was also a man of coolness. In October 1983 when 241 U.S. Marines were killed by a massive terrorist bomb in Beirut, he acted with calm deliberation. His decision to go into Lebanon was a measured statement of strategic intentions; his decision to withdraw after the marine deaths demonstrated steadiness and judgment under pressure. During the invasion of Grenada in 1983 he stayed with his decisions because he saw that he would win. In 1976 when he decided to run against President Ford for the Republican nomination, he had demonstrated a willingness to endure great unpopularity within his own party (the Republican left and center were furious with him, and all Republicans realized that his decision meant the Democrats would probably win) and a willingness to take risks. He knew that if Ford won, he would have little chance of ever being President himself, and he acted so that he might win in 1980.

Reagan was a very tough political animal, untroubled by doubt. He had an astounding ability to charm, to be liked, and to accumulate goodwill. He was an eternal optimist, and this made people feel he was on their side. There was a deceptive modesty to him: he claimed no special truth and played off the mistakes and miscalculations of others. Right or wrong, he was a simplifier. He might change his mind, but his second or third thought about a subject was unlikely to be more complex or better than his first. He held the opinions of a common man with the powers of an uncommon one. He was originally a liberal Democrat but left the party in the early 1950s as he discovered in himself a distaste for leftist temperament.

Ronald Reagan was an extremely good-natured man but not a generous one. Like Roosevelt, the President who had dominated Reagan's formative political years, he held the view that America had the right to preeminence in the world. Reagan considered that this right had been squandered. It was his deep conviction, formed by the experience of the early cold war, that the United States had had its hopes destroyed after the moment of victory. For the CIA, Reagan's presidency meant much less emphasis on secrecy—Reagan was a very public man—and on analysis. He knew what he thought, and analytical complexity did not engage him.

Once Reagan stepped into the presidency and realized that the appearance and the real nature of America's role diverged, he made few changes in the CIA's role. Those he did make were surface changes involving atmosphere and morale.* Reagan was good at creating moods and, as it turned out, at se-

---

* One of Reagan's early acts as President in 1981 was to issue Executive Order 12333, under which the CIA is permitted to operate domestically for the first time in order to collect "significant" foreign intelligence within the United States as long as the effort does not involve spying on the domestic operations of U.S. citizens and corporations. The order also empowered the CIA to conduct "special activities" within the U.S.A. as long as they were approved by the President and did not involve efforts to influence U.S. political processes, U.S. media, or U.S. public opinion. The order was not matched by any CIA staff buildup or by the creation of new CIA director-

curing legislation but not at fine-tuning the great institutions of government. He was not interested in mastering the details of the federal machinery. He sounded more belligerent and activist than he in fact was. Little action was taken, for example, on the recommendations of the minority of the transition team, and instead William Casey was allowed to run the agency in his own way. Since Casey was very much like Reagan, this in turn meant that the agency's professionals were able to organize themselves and set their own bureaucratic priorities while fulfilling the new administration's expectation of them to act as a stalking horse for the intelligence community and to administer the "public" secrets, in particular the overt-covert wars that became a Reagan hallmark.

William Casey played a major role—perhaps, as campaign manager, the most important role—in Reagan's election campaign. When he became DCI on January 28, 1981, he was the oldest man (sixty-seven) ever to be appointed to the post. He was tough, practical, effective, and a smart Republican New York lawyer. He was also a very Irish American and a devout (though flexible) Roman Catholic. He was unhaunted by ideals. He was highly intelligent. He had served in London in the OSS during the war, managing espionage penetrations of Germany. He had strong nerves, which he demonstrated during the confirmation hearings for his appointment as DCI. As the public watched, he refused to be stampeded into hasty action when the propriety of his continuing to control his own investments while being privy to national secrets was questioned.

Casey was not an elevated man, as this behavior showed. Nor was he dishonest—just insensitive. His stand had not been motivated by any consideration of financial profit but was a pure gesture of defiance. He had complied with the disclosure laws, and he felt he was a political target, so he decided to thumb his nose at his opponents. A Senate intelligence committee staffer said:

> I think what you have here is a personality issue rather than a philosophical one. Casey is not comfortable with Congress. He doesn't like Congress personally. He doesn't like us and what we have to do. He has an instinctive reaction that we are politicians and he and his guys are experts. So it's often better to have his deputy, John McMahon, up on a sensitive issue rather than to get off the track with Bill Casey and argue peripherals. That's why we often deal with John McMahon, because it's a better way to accomplish things. When we ask Bill Casey up, he comes. He does not make a good witness. He tends to read his statements, which are usually very long. It works out to mutual benefit.[8]

---

ates, however, and it should be seen as largely having to do with CIA morale boosting through the easing of legal obstacles to the pursuit of operational objectives, demonstrating that Reagan trusted the agency and did not consider it likely to be a rogue elephant under him. The order was also a direct response to the recommendations for an expanded counterintelligence effort made by the transition team.

"Secrecy is a problem for democracy," Casey observed. "We sustain a lot of damage. But what is one to do? Resist it? Where we really have a problem is with the congressional staffs, not subject to the security standards we require, seeking sensitive information."[9]

In an administration of successful men of narrow opinions Casey was particularly narrow, possessing a notably conventional (though very acute) understanding of politics, business, and people. His guidelines were not to return to the CIA of 1961 but to create a "can do" agency for a President of energetic opinions but also of simple and conventional mind. He was to provide a bureaucracy for the President. He inherited a bureaucratic agency and did not seek to change it, despite public and political claims to the contrary. Casey did not have his own agenda. He was simply interested in making the CIA work well; and the problem, as he saw it, was the agency's competence.

Casey was also an ex-spook who was going no further. His understanding of intelligence was fundamentally forty years old. He did not feel that everything was possible. He had wanted to be appointed secretary of state or of defense but had been outclassed by Alexander Haig and Casper Weinberger. Reagan made him DCI and a cabinet member because his campaign work deserved recognition, because Casey's political views largely coincided with Reagan's own, and because Reagan needed to make a number of appointments to console old-line Republicans worried by some of the younger members of the team. Casey was not appointed to make the CIA new but to energize it, although to what purpose was never made clear. In turn, Casey played it day-to-day, with no big objectives, just a sense of exploitation. But having forsworn publicity (he said he wanted "a no-profile agency"[10] and, as his own life showed, had found that publicity could be damaging),* he was not able to back up secrecy with secret successes.

---

* It emerged in June 1981 that during the 1980 election campaign, the Reagan team had been leaked briefing papers prepared for Jimmy Carter for the television debate between the two candidates. Casey maintained that he had no knowledge of such a leak (*The New York Times,* July 6, 1981). The fuss about the incident—referred to as the "Debategate" affair in the press— coincided with another fuss about Casey's appointment of a New England Reagan campaign manager, Max Hugel, to the post of deputy director for operations at the CIA. Hugel was first appointed deputy director for administration at the agency by Casey, but was then moved over. Without any intelligence experience, Hugel was a most unpopular choice among DDO officers and the CIA's old guard. Following a press campaign that alleged improper stock-trading practices on his part, Hugel resigned. Hard on the heels of these incidents came the Senate Intelligence Committee investigation of Casey's fitness to serve as DCI. In December it reported that he was, but he continued to make people uneasy. One senior ex-CIA officer and former OSS colleague of Casey's was reported as saying, "We pay lip service to the idea of support, for the sake of the agency. In fact, Casey is regarded as a bad choice" (quoted in Brian Freemantle, *CIA: The 'Honourable' Company* [London: Michael Joseph/Rainbird, 1983], p. 75).

Admiral Bobby Ray Inman, Casey's first deputy director of Central Intelligence, was an early casualty. He came straight from being director of the NSA with a reputation for being good with Congress and a superior administrator. He was given his fourth star by Reagan—the first intelligence officer to become a full admiral. He devoted himself to securing larger budgets for the CIA and the intelligence community, and insiders regard the sizable increases in intelligence ap-

CONGRESSIONAL RELATIONS

In the behind-the-scenes world of power relationships within the intelligence community, those between Congress, the National Security Council, and the CIA stand out as most important—Congress because it makes and oversees the law and determines financial appropriations; the National Security Council because it is the group in which the President determines national security policy and objectives; and the CIA because of its wide range of functions with the director of Central Intelligence as its head.

The technical role of the NSC is often misunderstood. It is not another intelligence agency. Its staff is small (about 250 in 1985) and advisory, not operational. It does not spend large amounts of money. Most importantly, it is under the umbrella of the executive branch and is chartered to provide the President with advice on the analysis and the intelligence developed elsewhere (most often by the CIA). Its power lies in its relationship with the President, conducted on a day-to-day basis by the national security adviser, whom the staff of the NSC effectively serve. This gives the adviser and the staff a vitally powerful position in any administration. Zbigniew Brzezinski gave quiet emphasis to this fact on the front and back endpapers of his book *Power and Principle*,* where he reproduced Carter's schedule for his first and last days as President. On both days, Carter's first appointment was with Brzezinski.

Since its creation, the CIA has provided a power base for the director of Central Intelligence as head of the agency, sustaining him in the separate effort over the years of exercising more and more coordinating authority over the intelligence community. By making Casey a cabinet member, Reagan added to the authority of the DCI and the position of the CIA among the competing bureaucracies. Bernard McMahon, who had been a naval assistant to Stansfield Turner for some time, including the latter's period as DCI, before becoming staff director of the Senate Select Committee on Intelligence, pointed out:

> Casey is a cabinet member as director of Central Intelligence, not as director of the Central Intelligence Agency. It's a very important distinction. Being a

---

propriations as his—rather than Casey's—success. Inman had benefited from changes in congressional attitudes when in the last year of Carter's administration and later, Congress often pushed for more funds for intelligence. In the middle of Casey's 1981 difficulties with the press and Congress, several senators made it clear to Reagan that they would prefer to see Inman as DCI. The White House was loyal to Casey, however, and put it about that Inman would never be made DCI: if Casey were not ratified, it was indicated, then Lt. Gen. Daniel Graham, the leading advocate of the "High Frontier" and the Strategic Defense Initiative, would be nominated instead. Inman, who had a career of public service, decided that he might as well retire to the private sector and earn some money if he had no hope of advancement. He left the CIA on June 10, 1982, and was succeeded as DDCI by a career CIA officer, John McMahon, who had been DDO under Turner.

  * *Power and Principle: Memoirs of the National Security Adviser 1977–1981* (New York: Farrar, Straus & Giroux, 1983).

cabinet member has advantages. His view as an intelligence officer is provided at the highest levels at which decisions are made, whereas previously this would have been done by the national security adviser. It also fundamentally changes the relationship Casey has with people like the secretary of defense. Before, the secretary was a cabinet member and the DCI wasn't. The DCI was running a service organization, and to have a service guy equal to the customers is not how these things are supposed to work. If your laundryman has an equal voice with you, and you don't like the way your laundry is being done, and it's your opinion against his, you'll continue to get it the way *he* thinks it ought to be done.[11]

As the principal intelligence agency, the CIA itself has a large budget (about $1 billion annually). The DCI, in his coordinating role, sustained under Reagan by being a cabinet member, has a much larger financial reach over the budgetary plans and disbursements of the whole intelligence community.* In the past, unless the President consistently and clearly backed the DCI in this respect, he would be outvoted and outmaneuvered by secretaries of large spending departments (most often the secretary of defense) using their congressional pull to secure the appropriations they wanted. In the cabinet, Casey could argue the case as an equal and would be present with a vote whenever intelligence budget decisions were being reviewed by Reagan.

Unlike the NSC and its staff, both the DCI and the CIA have to report to Congress and have to secure financial appropriations from both the Senate and the House. With the exception of decisions on covert action, Congress is not privy to the internal decision-making process of the National Security Council. The protection of executive privilege extends to the NSC. Bill Casey, on behalf of the President, notified both the Senate and House intelligence committees within forty-eight hours of the President signing a "Finding" approving covert action. This was a self-imposed time limit. Both committees also required that they be notified of any intelligence failure. These stipulations came from the Hughes-Ryan amendment of 1974, which legislated that Congress be informed "in a timely manner" of any new covert action and that the President had to

---

* The columnists Jack Anderson and Dale Van Atta have reported that the CIA's annual budget is "close to $1 billion"; the National Security Agency's budget is "about $10 billion a year"; the National Reconnaissance Office "spends at least $2 billion and possibly as much as $4 billion a year on spy satellites." The Defense Intelligence Agency and the intelligence arms of the four military services, and the State, Defense, and Treasury departments come to "at least $2 billion" a year. The total intelligence community budget was therefore about $15–17 billion a year. The Information Security Oversight Office, they went on to report, listed 881,943 "original classification decisions" by all government agencies as to whether a document should be confidential, secret, or top-secret; 17,789 were classified top-secret. "Even making the unlikely assumption that all 881,943 decisions involved foreign secrets, it would factor out at $20,409.48 per secret, according to our calculator. But if we rate intelligence-gathering agencies only by the hottest stuff they get—the top secrets—the cost works out to a little more than $1 million each" (*The Washington Post*, October 14, 1985). What Anderson and Van Atta failed to say was that a document can vary from one page to thousands.

"find" that the action was "important to the national security of the United States." Thus, in addition to its crucial appropriation power, Congress also had an operational role (discharged through the two intelligence committees) in the execution of intelligence activities. "We do play a very active role," said Bernie McMahon, "and we feel it is our responsibility to go out and actively seek information about what is going on and not just wait to be told."[12] If a Finding is very sensitive, the President can decide that instead of the full intelligence committees of the Senate and the House being informed, only the respective chairmen and vice-chairmen and the majority and minority leaders of both the Senate and the House need be told. "The Hughes-Ryan amendment requires that the oversight committees be briefed on Findings," Casey pointed out. "I have a responsibility for protecting sources and methods in law. The President has rights as commander-in-chief. When Jimmy Carter decided on the Iranian rescue mission, he told nobody. He acted under his authority as commander-in-chief."[13]

This combination of roles and requirements produced, under Reagan, new channels for secret activities centered on the National Security Council staff. The CIA in the wake of the investigations and legislation of the 1970s was too exposed to congressional—and therefore public—scrutiny for Reagan to be able to use it as his secret arm.

OPERATIONS AGAIN

Afghanistan and Central America were the sites of the new administration's first confrontation with the nature of the CIA and what America's world role should be. Nicaragua and El Salvador provided two case studies of how Reagan would act when faced with traditional problems, and Afghanistan of how he would respond to Soviet expansionism as well as to the new perceptions of America's apparently reduced world role. In Nicaragua, after twenty years of resistance to the greed and corruption of Anastasio Somoza, revolutionary Sandinista forces were clearly overthrowing his regime in 1979. Carter, declaring that democracy and freedom did not need dictators to defend it, refused to intervene on Somoza's behalf.* Then, just before Somoza was over-

---

* The Sandinistas were named after Augusto Sandino, a legendary peasant guerrilla who had fought U.S. Marines in Nicaragua between 1927 and 1933. Somoza personally owned approximately one-quarter of Nicaragua, and the terror tactics of his National Guard, combined with his family's greed, eventually alienated most sections of Nicaraguan society.

Nicaragua had provided the jumping-off point for the CIA's Guatemalan and Bay of Pigs operations. Anastasio Somoza was a graduate of West Point—he had been sent there by Roosevelt as a favor to his father. This was the degree of interlock between the Somoza regime and the United States from which Carter wanted to break away.

thrown, Carter reversed himself and sought unsuccessfully to mobilize the Organization of American States to help sustain the regime.* With Somoza's departure, Carter next attempted to win over the Sandinistas with $75 million in aid. Within the Sandinista movement the Marxist element that favored close ties with Cuba secured dominance and began to reject American overtures.

The United States had supported the Somoza regime with aid and diplomatic backing for over forty years, and that regime had become brutal in its suppression of opposition. Cuba had helped the Sandinistas in the last months of their struggle, and now thousands of Cuban military advisers, health experts, teachers, technicians and political advisers began flooding into the country, soon followed by Soviet economic and military aid. A new Cuba had appeared within the historic American "reservation" of Central America. When Nicaraguan soldiers began to advise revolutionaries in El Salvador, and the Sandinista government began sending these revolutionaries supplies, the break with the United States was confirmed.

El Salvador in 1980 existed under one of the most brutal and repressive military governments in the history of Central America. When that year four American Roman Catholic missionary women were murdered by El Salvadoran soldiers and the government took no action to find the murderers, Carter cut off American aid.† But when revolutionaries followed this with a major offensive in January 1981, Carter reversed himself again and began to supply the military government with aid once more. In both cases Carter had finally opted for aid packages rather than direct intervention. He never contemplated any attempt to launch a military or guerrilla invasion of Nicaragua or the involvement of anyone but a handful of advisers in El Salvador. At the same time he tried to maintain pressure for democratic procedures to operate in both countries.

---

* The OAS might well have backed Carter if he had sought a new non-Somoza, non-Sandinista regime. But Carter had veered from one unpopular extreme to another.

† Stansfield Turner had accurately predicted that El Salvador was likely to boil over. "In 1978 I briefed the President on El Salvador in one of my regular meetings with him. I told him that although it was a small country and of no particular immediate significance, it had problems. It had overpopulation. It had a terrible social structure. It had a terrible economic plight for most of the population. It was controlled by four hundred people. And it was going to blow up some day. We were worried then about Nicaragua, but we could see that El Salvador was coming down the pike too" (interview, Stansfield Turner, July 29, 1983).

The murder of the nuns had a major effect on the attitude of House Speaker Tip O'Neill. The incident colored his total view of policy in Central America, and he was a strong influence behind the Boland amendment, passed on December 21, 1982, forbidding the CIA or the Department of Defense to fund military equipment, military training or advice, or other support for military activities aimed at overthrowing the Sandinista government. In turn, this amendment added push to the transfer of power and influence in intelligence to the National Security Council, which could advise on the use of executive funds without congressional interference.

In Afghanistan, neither aid packages nor appeals for democracy were applicable. After the Soviet invasion of the country on December 27, 1979, a Vietnam situation soon faced the Red Army as thousands of Moslem nationalist guerrillas emerged. But was the invasion the first move in a more ambitious Soviet plan? The U.S. Embassy in Tehran had been seized seven weeks earlier. It looked as if Iran might disintegrate and the Soviet Union might achieve control, fulfilling Russia's historic ambition of a warm-water port. Carter's reaction was to embark on a policy of rebuilding American defenses and adopting a more confrontational approach to the Soviet Union.

From the summer of 1979 the outside world was hammering at Carter with repeated blows—Nicaragua, El Salvador, Iran, a second oil crisis as a result of the fall of the shah, Afghanistan—forcing him to respond traditionally at last. Apart from withdrawing from SALT II, he ordered registration for the draft (which he had abolished in 1978) to recommence, put an embargo on the export of U.S. wheat to the Soviet Union, promised to increase defense spending by 5 percent annually in real terms, approved more secret CIA operations than Reagan later did, and forbade American athletes to attend the 1980 Olympic Games in Moscow. He left the pot simmering when Reagan took office in 1981.

Rather than revive the clandestine service and ask the CIA to mount a "secret" invasion of Nicaragua (which, after the December 1982 Boland amendment, was prohibited by Congress), and rather than ask the U.S. military to enter El Salvador in support of the military government there, Reagan chose the far more cautious approach of supporting indigenous resistance to the Sandinistas (through Argentina in an entrepreneurial move of international right-wing alliance, which was broken by U.S. support for Britain in the 1982 Falklands War) and the revolutionaries in El Salvador. While publicly maintaining (and providing photographic and other intelligence evidence from Nicaragua supporting his view) that the burgeoning conflict with the Sandinistas and El Salvadoran rebels was part of the East-West battle for the world and that the Soviet Union was actually behind both groups, Reagan refused to provide any direct military or large CIA involvement. Undoubtedly he was taking into account the mood in Congress, which probably would have made any medium- or long-term intervention impossible. (Congress was determined that there should be no more Vietnams.) But he did secure from Congress substantial aid packages, including CIA advisers and bases in Honduras and Costa Rica for the anti-Sandinista "Contra" guerrillas. Many people within the agency felt he was putting the CIA at risk by reasserting covert action so strongly, but Casey, completely behind the President, argued that the CIA was strong enough to survive criticism and that it was the agency's job to take the risk. Reagan also secured a relatively fair democratic election in El Salvador in 1982 which saw the success of the center and right-wing opponents of the Marxist guerrillas.[14]

Reagan, accepting the demand for less secrecy made by Congress in the 1970s and accepting the widespread reluctance of Americans to risk another Vietnam, like Carter opted for aid packages. In many ways he was following a version of the "Nixon Doctrine." Under Reagan, anticommunists would be supported, but few if any Americans would ever be directly engaged. "There are fewer than thirty covert-action specialists in the agency today," said one congressional staffer close to the CIA in June 1985, "and they would have trouble in doing anything in even a banana republic that had more than two hundred gendarmes."[15] That was six months into Reagan's second term. "In Central America," said Lawrence Eagleburger, Reagan's undersecretary of state for political affairs until 1984, "the CIA is far less a military manager than the newspapers say, and certainly is not in the same class as the Bay of Pigs."[16]

Despite the public performance, Reagan did not emphasize the need for a covert-action agency because, unlike every President since Truman, he was not embarrassed to be seen waging unofficial wars. This was where the relationships between the CIA, the NSC, and Congress came into play. What Nicaragua and El Salvador showed Reagan was how he could use the CIA and, specifically, how it provided him with more flexibility than he would otherwise have had. It had this simple utility value: for two decades linked to no triumph that might justify it in the public mind, it was always expendable. This tethered-goat quality of the "new" CIA revealed a certain callousness and lack of proprietorial affection on the part of the administration.

The CIA's vulnerability to public scrutiny compounded this, and two developments followed. The first was operations by proxy where the agency worked with guerrillas or the forces of other countries to secure mutually desired objectives. (Thus aid and training were provided to the Contras through the Argentinian defense forces in exchange for other forms of aid from the U.S. to Argentina.) This arrangement neatly avoided detailed congressional scrutiny and public explanations, and also effectively hid the cost in various aid budgets for Argentina.

Reagan's approach to the guerrilla war in Afghanistan was an example of the second development: Congress's operational interest. Afghanistan became the site of the largest covert operation mounted by the CIA since Vietnam. The difference between CIA operations in Vietnam and Afghanistan was that very few CIA people were involved in Afghanistan as Reagan pursued his policy of distanced support. He was prepared to spend money and send weapons, not U.S. fighting forces or CIA operatives. What was particularly interesting about Afghanistan, however, was that Congress rather than the President was in the driver's seat, nearly tripling Reagan's original request for funding Afghan rebels. About $250 million a year was voted by Congress—more than 80 percent of the CIA's annual covert-operation expenditure. Congress, not the President, was in the vanguard when it came to action against the Soviets, and it did more than simply press for a defense buildup and utter warnings about Russia's "evil empire." *

For the CIA the Afghan operation provided another much-needed and much-welcome boost to morale. It was the first time the agency had everything served up to it on a platter. The Soviet Union was seen the world over as a wanton aggressor. The guerrillas led a very brave people capable of enduring immense suffering. Afghanistan adjoined Pakistan, a strong military dictatorship friendly to the United States, and anti-Soviet China, and both facilitated the passage of supplies. If the Soviet invasion had occurred thirty years earlier, it would have been the most incredible opportunity for the CIA. ("Be careful of what you want in your youth," wrote Goethe, "because you will achieve it in your old age.")

There was one very important difference, however, in operations under Reagan. Following through the one-among-equals philosophy of decision making in the administration, the agency most interested in or affected by a covert operation chaired the operational oversight group. "There is always a member of the State Department or the Defense Department involved whenever a covert operation is agreed," said Bernie McMahon. "This is new. We never used to have that. Now the State Department has to say what the policy objective is, and the CIA is responsible for the mechanics of the operation."[17] In Nicaragua, for example, the agency became in effect an executive arm for a decision taken by the National Security Council and overseen by the State Department.

Only one serious question was raised about the Afghan operation and that involved the morality of covert activity: while virtually every American decried the Soviet invasion, few thought the Afghans would win. There was, therefore, a moral conundrum about encouraging the Afghan guerrillas to fight at great cost to themselves and the Afghan people. The operation might be technically satisfying to the CIA as it effectively used its resources, and it might be of political advantage to America, but it might also wind up costing the lives of thousands. The Soviet Union found itself in a situation reminiscent of Vietnam, facing the courage and determination of the Afghan guerrillas; but even so, the CIA did not come away with clean hands. Rather, it was seen as an agency of blood as it helped fuel a hopeless struggle.† The fact was, however, that the

---

* "It was a windfall to [the administration]," said one congressional official. "They'd faced so much opposition to covert action in Central America and here comes the Congress helping and throwing money at them, putting money their way and they decided to say, 'Who are we to say no?' " (*The Washington Post,* January 13, 1985). Aid to the rebels through the CIA was about $30 million in 1983.

It no doubt suited Reagan that the executive branch was being driven by the legislative branch in intelligence matters and covert operations, a relationship that made Congress complicitous. Equally, it made it impossible to say that Reagan had established any leadership in intelligence.

† "The question was, do we give [the insurgents] weapons to kill themselves, because that is what we would be doing," said a senior Carter official. "There is no way they could beat the Soviets. The question here was whether it was morally acceptable that, in order to keep the Soviets

agency was simply carrying out the wishes of the American people as expressed by Congress and the President. After thirty-five exhausting years the CIA, like America, had accepted that problems might change but would never go away. It also knew that as choices became more complicated, ambiguous, and depressing with knowledge and experience, its founding objectives and ideals had become more remote.

CHANGING ANALYSIS

Throughout the changes and the batterings of the 1970s, everybody had recognized the importance of the CIA's analytical work. Turner had overseen some administrative refinements to the national intelligence officer system, reorganizing the officers as a National Intelligence Council and retitling the Directorate for Intelligence the National Foreign Assessment Center. It was headed by Robert Bowie, who had service in several government posts (including heading the Policy Planning Staff in the State Department under John Foster Dulles) and had a distinguished academic career as director of the Center for International Affairs at Harvard. Bowie was very much somebody lending tone and seriousness to the estimating process under Turner; he was also an adept administrator. A distinguished senior colleague remembered:

> Early on in Bob's tenure of the job, he became distressed with both the quality of the National Estimates and with the extent to which they were used. They used some periodic informal surveys of readers to discover if these

---

off balance, which was the reason for the operation, it was permissible to use other lives for our geopolitical interests." "I don't know anyone who believes we will overthrow the Soviet-supported regime in Afghanistan," said Senator Malcolm Wallop (R-Wyoming) in January 1985, "so what does anyone define as success? You have got to have in mind what you want to do, and we don't in this case." "This whole thing is conceived as a supply operation, not a war operation," a well-informed official was reported as explaining. Another official went further: "Our policy is to get the Soviets out basically . . . [we] have tied up about 1 percent of their Army . . . and the cost to the Soviets is about $4 billion a year [and the] total cost since 1979 is about $16 billion." "One of the important things is restraint," yet another official said, "and that includes restraint on our part . . . and restraint by the Soviet Union. You've got to consider what they haven't done to Pakistan and others. . . . Afghanistan is on their border, and you have to believe the Soviets could, if they chose, march in with sufficient troops to do the job." "That's ludicrous," said a congressional official. "This represents the kind of self-delusion according to which the Soviets and we have an unspoken gentleman's agreement to never go for the jugular. Since the Soviets have disproven this constantly, this view can only be held through a heroic effort at self-deception" (all quoted in *The Washington Post*, January 13, 1985).

The CIA's institutional memory included others who had been friends only to be abandoned. Carter and Reagan probably did not know all about the Albanians, Ukrainians, Estonians, Latvians, Lithuanians, Poles, Czechs, Hungarians, Germans, Laotians, Kurds, and Vietnamese who had been supported and then forgotten. With Afghanistan, the agency went to its task with a cold knowledge of the consequences for the guerrillas.

things were just being dropped into the wastepaper baskets or if they were being used and paid attention to. He found that the wastepaper basket was the most common destination. So he decided that in order to improve their quality and their usefulness he would institute a senior review panel. Senior, not only on the theory that years bring wisdom, which obviously can be argued, but also on the theory that senior people—people in their sixties— would not be regarded as rivals by the NIOs. They would be friendly, constructive critics who had also had some policy experience and who would therefore help the analysts present their conclusions in ways that would be most useful to policy makers. And because of their experience they would be able to identify the gaps in subjects that policy makers needed to have answered in order to have sensible policy making.[18]

"The senior review panel," said Bowie, "was basically designed to improve the quality of the analysis. One problem it addressed was the lack of a critical review of past Estimates. It was to test retrospectively the Estimates' conclusions in the light of events and experience. In addition, there was no systematic way of reviewing the terms of reference of Estimates to see if they were focusing on the relevant issues. The panel also looked at the drafts of Estimates to see what they thought of their adequacy. It was a critique group to advise me personally."[19]

With the senior review panel, Bowie created a system that withstood the change of administration and the test of time. In many ways, the four-man panel performed a function similar to that of the old Board of National Estimates in its heyday, although it lacked the institutional authority of the Board.* Bruce Clarke, Bowie's successor, and Bob Gates, Clarke's successor (under Casey, the National Foreign Assessment Center again became the Directorate for Intelligence), both maintained the panel and its original members—Klaus Knorr, a political economist and professor at Princeton; Bill Leonhart, a retired senior State Department officer and ex-ambassador to Tanzania and Yugoslavia who had served on the Policy Planning Staff under Bowie; Herb Rothenberg, an applied scientist with fifteen years of CIA work behind him and before that a sonar specialist with General Electric; and General Bruce Palmer, a broad-minded, intellectual West Pointer who had been army vice-chief of staff before joining the panel. Knorr retired in 1980 and was replaced by Lincoln Gordon, who had been a professor at Harvard, president of Johns Hopkins, ambassador (Brazil) and State Department officer; like Knorr, he was a political economist. "I have a working definition of the

---

* "The old Board of National Estimates had to approve the text before any National Intelligence Estimate was 'published' (i.e., circulated for internal governmental use). The Senior Review Panel had (and has) no such authority. It reviews drafts and makes comments and suggestions. The NIO in charge can disregard them, although he knows that a copy has gone to the DCI. The authority rests with the NIO and ultimately with the Director, not the Panel" (letter, Lincoln Gordon to author, November 22, 1985).

term 'political economist,' " Gordon jokingly observed, "because it doesn't mean today what it meant once. At first it meant an economist or an applied economist. Today my operational definition is that it is somebody who can pretend to be an economist among political scientists, and pretend to be a political scientist among economists, and get away with it in both places!"[20] Rothenberg retired in 1985 and was not immediately replaced.

As Bowie had intended, the panel tried to make the Estimates more pertinent and effective by a combination of reviewing drafts and retrospective analysis. But the inertia of the system, despite the changes, limited their effectiveness. "Getting through to policy makers is just potluck," a CIA analyst reflected wryly. "The big frustration is the difficulty of publishing, in fact. There are so many layers of review that it stifles publication of intelligence, not only because of the time and effort, but because review stifles creativity. Somebody changes 'happy' to 'glad' and somebody else changes 'glad' back to 'happy' and so on, and it goes up through the layers. So the smart analyst learns how to play off the review process to get his original creation through as much as possible. It's completely bureaucratic."[21] "The climate in the agency is liberal/academic," said a former analyst. "Very few people on the analytical side had military experience. They had very little foreign experience. They didn't understand Washington politics, and therefore they didn't understand international politics. We were babes in the wood out there. Ivory-towered. In some ways it is good to be away from the politics of Washington, but in another way it made everyone naïve. We were so far removed from the realities of the world that we looked through rosy glasses. Our analytical record, I am afraid, speaks for itself on this. All too often we underestimated Soviet capabilities and intentions, right across the board."[22]

The intelligence performance on the question of the Soviet Union's oil production was an early Casey review conducted by the panel. That this subject should be chosen for a detailed study was symbolic of the growing concern in Carter's last year that the agency was failing to predict developments which might affect America economically. Another early retrospective study under Casey was on the agency's performance with regard to the Soviet Alfa submarine.* Again, the choice of subject spoke volumes about the Reagan administration's interests and concerns: Reagan and Casey wanted specifics. They

---

* In 1978 satellite intelligence provided evidence that the Soviets were well on the way to launching their Alfa submarine. Hearsay evidence from emigrés and satellite photographs showing a shiny metal made some analysts think that the submarine might have a titanium hull. This conclusion was discounted on two grounds, the first being that American technology had not yet succeeded in perfecting the welding techniques required for titanium hull construction, and that therefore the Soviets could not be using titanium because their technology, it was assumed, was behind America's. The second reason for discounting the titanium hull was that a combination of camouflage and cloud cover over the shipyard at Leningrad where the submarine was under construction prevented extended satellite surveillance. Only when the submarine was launched and undergoing sea trials near the north pole was its titanium hull confirmed. Charting the analysis that had resulted in this surprise was the task of the panel.

wanted to simplify. Thus they were anxious to concentrate on the "evil empire" of the Soviets in a traditional way when it came to intelligence, uninterested in the complexities of sophisticated propaganda or long-term analysis. A review of agency analysis of Soviet oil production would inform a judgment about Soviet economic prospects which could be used to score political points. A review of the agency's work on the Alfa submarine would help the administration's efforts to persuade Congress to fund its defense plans.

The National Intelligence Council—the NIOs collectively—reported to the DDI separately from the panel and acted to coordinate the work and the responsibilities of the NIOs. Casey sought to improve the whole estimating process in part by re-creating the Directorate for Intelligence and in part by reorganizing the analytical side of the house on a geographical basis with each area covering the whole gamut of studies. Thus area divisions and country desks were blended with the subject responsibilities of the NIOs, whereas previously there had been considerable overlaps. So, under Casey, the Office of Strategic Research (the office responsible for Soviet studies) was abolished. Instead the NIO responsible for the Soviet Union theoretically coordinated the work previously conducted by the office as well as the work on the USSR going on elsewhere in the agency and the intelligence community (see Appendix VII). In addition, Casey added to the number of NIOs (to a total of about fifteen) in order to cover new subjects, particularly drugs and international terrorism, and in order to have some NIOs "at large" as a kind of flexible reserve to cover emergencies and new subjects on an *ad hoc* basis. "The NIOs perform a staff function," said Casey. "The NIO for Soviet strategic forces chairs the group of people who do the Estimates on strategic forces. I review it and make whatever changes I think are needed. I've sought to create a more cooperative feeling. If someone has significant and substantiated views on a subject, I'll try to see that the Estimate will reflect them. That's what policy makers need. The policy maker is developing policy for the future, and he's got to be able to review the alternatives. It's no use having something where the real differences do not emerge."[23]

The NIOs' staff function reflected a wider emphasis on coordination within the intelligence community as a whole under Reagan (see Appendix VIII). A Senate intelligence committee staffer observed:

This particular President is a strong believer in equal representation in the forums in which major governmental decisions are made. The various agencies that might be affected by a decision are all involved as equals in making it. This committee approach is different from that of previous administrations, in which the National Security Council acted as a broker amongst the various baronies. In this administration, the NSC is more of a coordinator and it speaks as one of several voices. It is more a staff to prepare the President or McFarlane [Robert McFarlane, National Security adviser during Reagan's second term until December 1985] for meetings than people who knock heads together to get a common determination. The President lays out his policy on an individual basis, and each person interprets it his way. That's the reason why we have differences between the Secretary of State and the Secretary of Defense. But these differences, this give-and-take quality, is a specific design feature of Reagan's governmental organization. It isn't that everybody is out of control fighting with each other: it's how he does it. One of the disadvantages is that it makes it hard to get agreement on implementing a common policy. But the other side of that coin, from Reagan's point of view, is that for every glitch there are all the other cases where he's got all the views represented to their fullest and not filtered, and out of that has come the right decision. Reagan likes to deal with the principals in cabinet. This is the ultimate cabinet administration, in fact.[24]

Within the intelligence community, Casey and his NIOs worked on an intelligence issue in a similar fashion, through a series of meetings organized according to subject. The first was an interagency working group (called "IGs") which met at whatever agency had the predominant interest in a subject (see Appendix IX). A former member of the DCI's staff described the procedure:

They all used to meet at the NSC, but now, if it's Central America, say, they'll meet over at the State Department. The meeting will consist of the assistant secretary for Latin American affairs, a representative from the Joint Chiefs of Staff, somebody from the National Security Council staff, somebody from the CIA, and maybe somebody from Commerce. If it's on strategic arms—SDI—it'll be at the Defense Department. Those are the IGs. They try to distill issues and bring up subjects for the next highest level, the Senior Agency Group, where those involved each have a member: these are the deputy secretaries. Then, finally, it goes to a National Security Planning Group, and those are the President's. Usually the President is ready at that point to sit in on that meeting and make his decision. At each step of the way there's an intelligence person from the CIA, and at the top it's either Casey or his deputy, to weigh in as a provider of unvarnished truth.[25]

Despite fears that Casey would politicize the Estimates, and despite some early reports that he had said that he wanted to bring the Estimates into line with administration policies, the general conclusion among analysts was that he had not done so. "The Estimates are my Estimates," said Casey. "I'm a little bit looser about that when it comes to putting in other views. But they're my Estimates. I'm responsible for drawing the conclusions and presenting them. But I feel I have a concomitant obligation to the user to see that any well-substantiated alternative view is also laid on the table. So we have a lot of facets in the Estimates now. When we do an Estimate we bring it to the Intelligence Board and put it on the table and give everybody a chance to express any differences they may have and encourage them to reflect that difference when it seems significant, to give an alternative view, and that ends up in the Estimate."[26]

An ex-director of the Defense Intelligence Agency confirmed:

> Casey has really lowered the boom on arrogant treatment of other points of view. DIA people now feel that if they've got a point, Casey will take it. It's very encouraging. The power of the draft out there is enormous, and they've got really clever people, wordsmiths, able to write an Estimate so that you really don't have a place to hang a dissent. No matter how objective someone tries to be doing an analysis, if someone else comes along and challenges it and the person who has done the work thinks he's done pretty well and doesn't want to change it and he has the power of the draft, he can say "Go fly a kite" to the challenger. And sometimes he shouldn't. Since Casey has taken over there has been a transition to a more give-and-take attitude. There will always be a bureaucratic urge in the CIA, however, to be less alarming than the Pentagon. That will always be there.[27]

Casey himself voiced a similar thought. "The most frequent criticism is that our interpretations and assessments have shown a tendency to be overly optimistic, to place a benign interpretation on information which could be interpreted as indicating danger. It's our obligation to present conclusions which emphasize hard reality undistorted by preconceptions or by wishful thinking. . . . I found in SALT I, for example, that some of the judgments were soft. They leaned toward a kind of benign interpretation rather than a harder interpretation of assessing or viewing a situation as being more dangerous."[28]

Without politicizing the Estimates, Casey cleverly meshed the agency's analytical work with administration policies through his choice of subject. Drugs and international terrorism were two such examples: both had been proclaimed as targets by Reagan, so instead of pulling together the agency's work on the subjects in a regular way, Casey created NIOs for each, in one fell swoop putting an additional fifteen percent of the agency's analytical effort into them.* He was ruthlessly fashionable in choosing subjects, ensuring that each one was a Reagan preoccupation (this is not to say that each one was not important—it was just that each one loomed large in the President's mind), so that both he and the agency would stay in tune with the administration.

Casey's achievement in this respect was an important one. The DCI's degree of closeness to the Oval Office—and Casey was always close—had a marked effect on the morale of the agency and its (and the DCI's) position in the bureaucracy. But the closeness had a long-term detrimental consequence.

---

* There are NIOs for the geographic areas of the Middle East, Latin America, Africa, Western Europe, East Asia, and the Soviet Union. Then there are NIOs for subjects: strategic forces (by tradition a civilian), general purpose forces (i.e. non-nuclear—by tradition a military officer detailed from Defense), nuclear proliferation, high technology, drugs, terrorism, and international economic problems. There are also assistant NIOs.

Casey himself was not comfortable with the intricacies of technical intelligence collection systems and was content to administer what Turner had organized and planned. The 1985 space shuttle launches on intelligence missions had been planned as early as 1978 by Turner. Under Casey, no great technical intelligence rearrangements or breakthroughs were made. This personal blinker was compounded by the nature of the Reagan administration's preoccupations, essentially a single preoccupation in every major subject. In technology, it was the Strategic Defense Initiative or "Star Wars," involving one of the largest combinations of financial and intellectual resources in the history of mankind. And the CIA was out of SDI with a director who was not even fighting to be in on it.

COVERING THE WATERFRONT

One particular quality which everybody admired about Casey was his energy. One retired senior agency officer said in 1985:

> I must say that although I dislike some of his policies I admire his energy. He's seventy-two now and he shows no sign of slowing down whatever. But even with a man as energetic as that—I think he's even more energetic than Stan Turner was, and Turner is much younger—he has the problem of becoming emotionally involved with operations and not seeing the analytical side of it clearly. How could Casey today look objectively at the Nicaraguan situation? It's just humanly impossible. If the CIA had been in charge of the whole Vietnam War, they would have suffered from the same syndrome that the military did. That's one of Casey's big problems. But his capacity for work is enormous—the amount of stuff he reads, the way he works himself on trips—and he shows no sign of stopping.[29]

An extension of this energy was the way he encouraged the DDI to try to cover everything that might conceivably have a bearing on national security and the future development of the United States.

Bob Gates, who under Turner had been the NIO for the Soviet Union, became DDI in January 1982. "Bob Gates has all of Casey's energy plus a little bit more," said a colleague. "He is, of course, very much younger—in his early forties. He is exceptionally young for that job."[30] Gates threw himself into the job of extending the range of analysis undertaken by the agency, defining ten major areas of investigation and concern in the development of the estimating process in the future. The trends that would dominate intelligence to the year 2000, said Gates in October 1985, were going to be a mixture of new, specific problems, and a greater complexity of existing ones. He saw them all and defined them all in the terms of a bureaucrat seeking to identify with the other important government bureaucracies. His imagination was reserved for methodology, not objectives or opportunities.

The first trend Gates saw was "the coming revolution in the way intelligence is communicated to policy makers." The electronic dissemination of finished intelligence from the analysts to the policy makers was already being planned. There would be computer terminals on the desks of key people, which, it was thought, "would speed current intelligence to real time should a policy maker want it," and which might have a talkback capacity that would improve the relationship between policy makers and analysts. Such a system would have security advantages, it was argued, because there would be much less paper and access to the information could be by handprint or other means specific to the individual. The terminals would be designed so that they could not be connected to other terminals or to printers.[31] The weakness of this scenario was that it is not just how fast information reaches a policy maker that matters, but how it may be buried by what else is on his or her desk. The telephone already provides the same basic access as a terminal, but it is not often used by policy makers contacting analysts, which suggests that the terminal-on-the-desk future would simply be more clutter. For it to be otherwise, intelligence recipients would have to be taught how to see information through intelligence eyes—much as Stansfield Turner attempted with Jimmy Carter.* The education of the consumer is as important as the information received. Even the argument of security improvement was suspect: people will always doublecheck by looking over each other's shoulders and by speaking to each other. Information is separate from the way it is recorded.

The second trend foreseen was that "the data we need will be more difficult to obtain." Soviet camouflage and disguise techniques were already reducing the effectiveness of telemetry in monitoring missile tests, quite apart from the traditional Soviet refusal to divulge information about their weapons systems development even when it came to arms reduction and limitation talks. Compounding this, information that was once available about the Soviet economy was no longer published and was increasingly restricted within the Soviet governing elite. Further afield, other countries were increasingly picking up American intelligence techniques and improving their own methods of camouflage and deception.[32]

The increasing difficulties of intelligence collection, however, also contained important benefits. It was not a one-way street. For example, by denying

---

* Speaking in general terms, Stansfield Turner observed:

Each President has to work out his own system. He's got to learn about intelligence. He has to have tutorials. He can read a book, he can get briefing papers, he can listen to people. But he has to understand that satellites stay over Moscow only for three minutes a day, and that every other day there are clouds, and that therefore he should not call up the DCI and say, "Get me a picture of the Olympics in Moscow today. I want it by three o'clock!" The probability of doing this is only about 25 percent. The chances of getting it by three o'clock are directly related to the satellite schedule—it may pass over Moscow at ten o'clock, and you can't change that. The President has got to understand these things. Each President has to have some technique for absorbing enough mechanical intelligence to know how to manage it (interview, Stansfield Turner, July 29, 1983).

economic information that until recently was published, the Soviets were preventing levels of their own government from having it, thus increasing both the
chances of mismanagement and fueling an increase in espionage as Russians,
in effect, had to spy on themselves to discover facts about their own economy.
And with more people trying to obtain information, it would be easier for the
United States to "lose" its informers in the general activity. Any society pays a
heavy price for the degree of secrecy sought by the Soviet Union, because it is,
in fact, seeking to keep information from itself.

The third future trend identified by Gates was that "recruitment would
become more difficult." The number of people of the right standard to be CIA
officers, and who could pass the polygraph, was declining. The overall pool of
talent for intelligence work was diminishing, and the effort to recruit people
was enormous. Additionally, government service was becoming less attractive,
although once people joined the agency they tended to stay. Among professionals, there was a less than 4 percent attrition rate, better than anywhere else
in the government or in industry.[33] The principal reason for polygraph failure
was drugs, a strictly cultural problem which was likely to be accommodated in
some way eventually.* All societies learn how to adapt to themselves: in the
1920s the consumption of alcohol would have been a disqualification, but
American law changed. A question behind the low attrition rate was, "Do you
want twenty-year people in the CIA?" The length of tenure was a clear statement of the agency as an established bureaucracy rather than the fast-moving
and flexible creation of 1947. And the pride in the low attrition rate was a demonstration of contentment with this position.

Fourth, there was already "a revolution in relations with Congress,"
which would continue. Beginning in the mid-1970s, the flow of finished intelligence to Congress had come to mean that Congress had as much intelligence
as the executive branch. Building on this, observed Gates, the huge number of
staff on Capitol Hill had enabled Congress to ask tougher and better-informed
questions of often hard-pressed officials. In turn, he suggested, this had resulted

---

* In the early 1950s, China started to cultivate its traditional drug production with a view to
affecting American troops in Japan and Korea. In 1960, Castro apparently signed a secret agreement with the Soviet Union to help distribute Soviet-produced drugs in America in cooperation
with elements of Czechoslovak intelligence. In 1962, the intelligence forces of the member countries of the Warsaw Pact joined this effort. In 1965, Chou En-lai was reported to have told Nasser
that China was manufacturing heroin to spread addiction among U.S. servicemen in Vietnam
and through them back to young people in the United States. In 1975, Warsaw Pact efforts to
distribute drugs in the United States and Western Europe were stepped up, with Cuba acting as
the coordinator for America. It was an estimated $200-billion-a-year operation (interview, Octo-
ber 12, 1985).
Thus, in an important sense, the Soviet Union and China as drug suppliers were effectively
damaging the CIA by affecting potential agency recruits. "Drugs are the secret weapon of the
KGB," observed one analyst. "In the last two years they've targeted Ireland to get at the British
forces there. We could cut the legs from under it by doing two things: address the alienation in
our society in the first place, and secondly, legalize drugs. But instead we treat drugs with a Jerry
Falwell approach. There is no rhyme or reason based on fact about it" (interview, October 14,
1985).

in Congress playing a larger and more effective role in foreign policy.[34] While this was certainly true, the important point was ignored: Congress has never *initiated* foreign policy. The result of what Gates described was simply more *business* of foreign policy. Further, the developing relationship with Congress was seen as a demonstration that Congress was a partner to the agency. In the 1970s the agency had lost its special place as the President's secret arm; in the 1980s it was seeking a special place with Congress. What, it might be wondered, would have been said if Gates had observed that, despite the flow of intelligence, Congress was not effective in policy-making terms?

The fifth trend was "the use by the executive branch of intelligence for public education." It had begun under Carter and Turner with the release in 1977 of the agency's detailed analysis of the performance and prospects of the Soviet economy,* and had subsequently expanded to include up-to-the-minute analysis which required special declassification. In the summer of 1985, for example, the agency's "key judgments" (the summary conclusions of an Estimate) on Soviet strategic forces had been published in a sanitized form at the insistence of the Executive branch.† It was part of the Reagan administration's effort to win support for its defense policies in the press and in Congress.[35]

This public education aspect held serious implications not only for the CIA but for the intelligence effort of the United States. Public education used to be done through background briefings to journalists and congressmen, but the suspicions surrounding the intelligence community as a whole during the 1970s forced more openness, and the publication of sensitive reports was a consequence. This development gave analysts, collectors, and secret informants a headache. Still more, it betokened the isolationism which underpinned both Carter and Reagan, since it was saying that America was strong enough (or unconcerned enough) to reveal its secret intelligence assessments and withstand any consequent damage delivered to its collection and analytical abilities (for example, by disinformation ploys) by the Soviet Union. Finally, the use of sensitive information for public education in this way was political, and the more involved politically intelligence becomes, the more vulnerable it is to the small change of politics where superior information can put someone on the "inside" and where leaks are commonplace. "That's always been a fear," Bernard McMahon agreed. "The design of the oversight committee, the composition of the staff, the nonpartisan nature of the effort, are all geared to

---

* This was *Soviet Economic Problems and Prospects* (Washington, DC: CIA, 1977). It was followed by supplementary reports on *Prospects for Soviet Oil Production* (Washington, DC: CIA, 1977) and *USSR: Some Implications of Demographic Trends for Economic Policies* (Washington, DC: CIA, 1977).

† *Soviet Strategic Force Developments*, testimony before a joint session of the subcommittee on strategic and theater nuclear forces of the Senate Armed Services Committee and the defense subcommittee of the Senate Committee on Intelligence, by Robert M. Gates, Chairman, National Intelligence Council, and Deputy Director for Intelligence, Central Intelligence Agency, and Lawrence K. Gershwin, National Intelligence Officer for Strategic Programs, National Intelligence Council, June 26, 1985.

reduce temptation. But it is a natural tendency because there is a sense in the executive branch that the secrets belong to them and not to Congress because intelligence belongs to the executive branch. Then there is the insider's fear that the outsider is going to use that information against him—a political means to a political advantage. What people talk about less is the power of the executive branch to declassify information. Take the publication of the report on *Soviet Strategic Defense Programs:* is that a glossy leak on legitimate declassified data? A skeptic could say that it is sophisticated leaking for political purposes because the President is down to the wire on SDI. The committee takes an interest in this process, because Congress has paid for the systems that collected the information and it does not like to see leaks done for partisan political purposes when the appropriation of funds was nonpartisan and for the good not of any particular administration but for the country as a whole."[36]

"The *Strategic Defense Programs* release was an almost word-for-word replication of the National Intelligence Estimate," said a senior CIA official. "A lot of it was declassified just for the purpose of putting out that document. Somebody made the decision for political purposes. It was released by the White House. They had obviously decided that now was the time to inform the American people that the Soviets were doing SDI too, even though Gorbachev denies it."[37] "We have had little choice about the intelligence we provide to Congress," said Gates. "*So far* it has provided us with no serious problems. *So far.*"[38] "I would contrast what Bob Gates and Bill Casey want to do with what Colby and Turner tried to do," said a congressional intelligence staffer. "Colby and Turner wanted to declassify stuff just for university, academic use—basic encyclopedic knowledge—not so much to educate the public in the political sense about the Soviet threat, but just to have CIA as a massive storehouse and disseminator of encyclopedic information, noncontroversial for the most part. What Bob and Bill want to do is make intelligence public and use it as part of the political process."[39]

"The increasing use of intelligence by the policy community to show the rectitude or the efficacy of our foreign policy to our allies" was the sixth trend Gates identified. Dissemination of U.S. intelligence had also expanded beyond the United States' traditional allies.[40] This development was a secondary event in the much bigger show of changing world opinion. The receptivity of allies—and others—to U.S. intelligence marked a shift in attitudes toward both the United States and the Soviet Union by those allies. Policy makers are power seekers, and they will always use intelligence for what they want and need, so this use was to be expected. An institutional worry would always be that agency intelligence distributed in this way would inevitably be double-checked wherever possible by the recipients, with possible beneficial or detrimental results for the CIA depending on whether the double-checking was done with a cooperative interest or not.

The seventh prospect already discernible was "the dramatic increase in the diversity of subjects the community is required to address," said Gates.

The main subjects used to be the Soviet Union, China, and Southeast Asia. While the Soviet Union and China were still major subjects, they had been joined by a range that included foreign technology developments; genetic engineering; trends in food, population, and resources worldwide; religion; human rights; arms control; drugs; terrorism; and high-technology transfers.[41]

This was a key observation by Gates. The list of subjects alone showed that the agency was thinking of itself not so much as a partner in policy, but as a manager and a servant of policy. This had always been its formal position, but its founding fathers had in fact established an agency role in the policy-making area. Now, with the overwhelming balance of CIA interest and attention reserved for its analytical and collection work, its intelligence effort was following the general direction of the social sciences. The agency was becoming an instrument for applied social science, ever less operational and ever more seeking to fill in the blank spaces in forecasting. The range of subjects showed an agency terrified of missing anything. It was another bureaucracy saying it covered the waterfront, the reverse of its starting attitude of being the worthy challenger to the State Department or the Department of Defense, of being the agency that identified a few essential themes and mastered them. Now it was, in effect, a secret extension of the Library of Congress.

"That's very true," said Bernard McMahon:

> When you ask the agency what they're doing and why they're doing it, there are two responses. The first is that more intelligence is better than less, and who can argue with that? The second is that they never know what questions they'll be asked, and they feel they have to be ready. So there's a limitless approach on their part. The National Intelligence Requirements document has nine thousand listings. You can find a home for anything there. That's why we say to them that they need a strategy. Apart from the fact that without a strategy there's no way to tell where the money is going, if all they do is provide a library of material that nobody draws much out of, the CIA, the intelligence community as a whole, will be a machine driven to its own perfection. Some requirements they are the best people to determine because they know what they need for their data base. And somebody has to perform a role as Cassandra. But they should identify these requirements, and then we will be able to see if all the intelligence goes into a library or goes into the product.[42]

"No, I do not feel that the agency has become a secret annex of the Library of Congress," William Casey declared:

> We have the kind of data that does not get into a library. The big surprise for me coming back into intelligence was the breadth and the depth of the analytical work. Donovan did start that element with a formidable bunch of people, and they did range beyond the military, but they weren't into things like drugs or terrorism or international trade competition or oil flows or currency movements like we are today. In the OSS days, all you had to do was figure out where a German division was. It was far more tactical than strate-

gic, which is the change today. We make a great effort to make every product practical. But the important thing is that the analysis and assessing have been done. The fact that it's been done. The fact that it's there. The fact that somebody did it. That's what is important.[43]

"An increasing growth in the diversity of the users of intelligence" was the eighth trend identified by Gates. Use in the early days was concentrated in the White House, the State Department, and the Department of Defense. Now, in addition to these, principal users included the Treasury and the Departments of Commerce and Energy.[44] Again, the agency saw this as a welcome challenge, defining its nature in the process. It was welding itself to the bureaucracy, just as with Congress, seeking allies and support. For all the talk about the speed with which intelligence should reach the policy makers' desks, the agency was no longer being defined by its ability to respond, but by its ability to meet its quota of information and to drown questions with an enormous volume of intelligence rather than with farsighted and accurate political analysis. Secret intelligence is rarely general in its application. In 1973, for example, it was obvious that the Egyptians were considering attacking the Israelis across the Suez Canal in the Sinai. But the enormous defensive sandbanks the Israelis had built on the east bank of the canal were regarded by analysts in Washington (and by the Israelis) as major impediments to a successful Egyptian attack. So, like the French in 1940, who thought that their Maginot line would prevent a successful German attack, the Israelis placed undue confidence in their sandbanks. Secretly, the Egyptians bought fire hoses, nozzles, and compressors. They had worked out that they could blast through the sandbanks with water from the canal. This knowledge, coupled with the purchase of the necessary equipment, was the secret. For the CIA to extend its effort to cover such specialized intelligence analysis as would have been involved in estimating Egyptian intentions and capabilities in 1973 (and it had failed to do this then, much to Nixon's fury), so that it was providing specialized and useful information combined with accurate forecasting on a wide range of subjects such as Egyptian fire-hose purchasing as well as international currency markets, trade, and energy to the respective government departments, would involve a gargantuan effort very unlikely to be speedy. Ultimately, accurate forecasting depends far more on the caliber of the forecaster than on the quantity of information.

Gates' ninth trend was that "intelligence is becoming steadily more central to the foreign policy process of the government." In certain areas, policy itself depends on intelligence. In technology transfer, drugs, terrorism, there would, he suggested, be no effective policy without intelligence. In some other areas, notably arms control, policy had become more dependent on intelligence.[45] In effect, this was another way of saying that police work had become more international. Technology transfer could be seen as involving a superior form of patent law; drugs, a superior form of prohibition and traditional police/customs work; terrorism, a superior deterrent and police work for kidnapping and murder. In these areas, a superior FBI might be better suited to informing policy than the CIA. Indeed, in many of the subject areas along the waterfront being covered under Casey, other government agencies might be more appropriate and expert in the work required.

The last trend that Gates saw expanding in the future lay in the fact that "intelligence is the only arm of government looking to the future." As the world became more complex and as policy makers needed more data, the intelligence community was the only government sector looking two, five, ten or more years ahead. This threw up the perennial working challenge of "having to go to a policy maker whose hands are full and convince him to do something which will benefit the future—a successor's successor's successor—at a time when the cost of doing it is still low, but when there is no immediate benefit."[46] It was a problem of democracy's short horizons and brief attention spans which all of Bob Gates' predecessors had faced and all of his successors would face.

Lt. General Lincoln D. Faurer, who retired as director of the National Security Agency in 1985, made a further point about future planning:

> People like to think that we are in competition with the Japanese. We are, in fact, in competition with ourselves to provide systems that suit our needs in a controlled manner for specific purposes. Our technological ingenuity creates a threat to us by encouraging the pursuit of new, more, and costly systems all the time. We can always find ways of making things better, but we should not continue to pursue perfection. We must be more disciplined in deciding what to pursue and sticking to it. We need to go back to basics in identifying requirements. As a nation, we have always failed to be modest and austere in identifying our requirements. And as resources become more scarce, as money becomes tighter, a reduction in our requirements will enable us to release money for the task.[47]

Faurer was voicing a major truth (although, of course, the United States was also in competition with Japan). All nations face the danger of strangling themselves by self-competition and becoming uncompetitive with the outside world, as happened to Britain. At the same time, self-competition is vital to a vibrant political and market economy, as it generates efficiency and focuses effort on important problems. In Aesopian language, Link Faurer was identifying the fact that in intelligence there are few operations anymore where two or three elite people can be effective. The United States was engaged in an intelligence siege, not a battle, with the other countries of the world, a siege in which what was involved was massive and would date very quickly.

INTERNATIONAL TERRORISM

The growth of international terrorism exemplified the disordered world of the 1980s. The nihilistic quality of terrorism worried everybody interested in the orderly arrangement of international relations and domestic tranquility. It particularly worried the United States because it paved a destructive path *into* America and because American terrorists might be encouraged by outsiders.

There are three forms of terrorism, all of which zero in on the United States as the leading capitalist country and the big boy on the block. Indigenous terrorists—the Irish Republican Army, the Red Brigades in Italy, the Baader-Meinhof group in Germany—all claim political programs and objectives and exist in communities that nourish them. Terrorists driven by deranged thinking rather than ideology usually lack this community support and are often nipped in the bud before they do extensive harm. The Move group in Philadelphia, who in May 1985 barricaded themselves in a house and fired at police and firemen, ultimately causing millions of dollars of damage and their own deaths by fire, might well have turned to terrorism had their movement lasted. Such terrorist states as Qaddafi's Libya also pose a considerable threat. These states are characterized by secret and armed forces that operate in terrorist fashion abroad.

As a dynamic and heterogeneous society, the United States has large numbers of "marginal" people.* The American middle class has far more alienated members than any other such class anywhere else in the world. There is also a slice of every ethnic group in the United States, providing a two-way street with every country in the world. During World War II and the early cold war these connections were used effectively by America. By the 1980s, however, such connections seemed of more use to other countries, with their own agents within their American ethnic communities and with pressure groups operating in their interests. In addition, America's fascination with the outlaw created a distinct ambivalence about terrorism in many Americans. All these factors combined meant that the problem of international terrorism in the mid-1980s attracted attention not only because of what terrorists might do (one day a terrorist group will have a nuclear device) but also because of what it signified for and about America.

Early on, the CIA was involved in gauging the nature of international terrorism and its threats to America. Accordingly, one of William Casey's early Estimate requests was on terrorism. He had been attracted to the question by *The Terror Network: The Secret War of International Terrorism*, a book by the journalist Claire Sterling.† Sterling claimed that the growth of international terrorism was controlled by the Soviet Union. Her book was also, apparently, read in galley-proof by the incoming secretary of state, Alexander Haig, who incorporated some of her arguments in one of his first speeches, in which he referred to international terrorism as the "new enemy" facing the

---

* If the United States can produce nearly one thousand people who go off to another continent, murder a visiting congressman, and commit mass suicide, as James Jones and his followers did in Guyana in 1979, then there is a proper worry about the extent of aberrant behavior in America.

† London: Weidenfeld & Nicolson, 1981.

United States. The overall impression Haig gave was that this phenomenon "was a sort of Wurlitzer being played by the people in the basement of the Kremlin," as a CIA analyst put it.[48] The head of the Bureau of Intelligence and Research at the State Department, Ron Spiers, went to see Haig in the wake of this speech and, courageously for a professional foreign service officer with a new and fiery secretary of state, told him that he had overstated the case. There was some evidence, Spiers said, that the Soviets had discouraged certain forms of international terrorism—particularly some of the Palestinian groups—and they had often declared both in public and in private that they were opposed to it. As a result, Haig went to Casey with a request that the CIA produce a National Intelligence Estimate on the subject.

The CIA analyst who drafted the Estimate came to no clear conclusion on whether or not the Soviet Union was the terrorist manager, and he defined terrorism narrowly as acts of violence committed by people who liked violence for its own sake. It was a difficult definition because it explained terrorism not only by terroristic acts, but also by the intentions and motivations of the perpetrators. "That was a very difficult thing to work with because who knows what the motivations of those involved really are?" a member of the senior review panel observed. "Most of them will say that they have a cause, if you get a chance to ask them, and that would have excluded them from the definition. It was so narrowly drawn that it was pretty easy to find that the Soviet Union didn't have much to do with them—they obviously had little interest in groups that were just violence-prone."[49] The Defense Intelligence Agency also took exception to this definition and went to the opposite extreme, seeking to define terrorism as including practically any kind of violence or use of force by anybody for any purpose other than declared war. It was a definition, the CIA pointed out, that would have included George Washington, Robert E. Lee, and Simón Bolívar.[50]

Casey then turned to Ambassador Lincoln Gordon to produce a decisive Estimate.* Gordon decided to work from what the man in the street thought terrorism was—acts such as kidnapping, assassination, blowing up airplanes, hijacking, tossing bombs into marketplaces and movie theaters—and that whatever the motivations of the perpetrators, analysis should proceed from such acts. Gordon's Estimate concluded that while some particular terrorist groups did have connections with Moscow, and that while the USSR along with East Germany and Bulgaria supported various terror training camps, international terrorism was not controlled by the Soviets, and indeed the relations with Moscow of many terrorist organizations were ambiguous.†

---

* Lincoln Gordon was a man of impalpable influence. He was very lucid and to the point, possessing a broad perspective and great competence. By going to him Casey was trying to obtain bipartisan support for the resulting report (Gordon had been favored by Democratic administrations) and a certain *gravitas* for his DCI-ship. Gordon was no crank, and he had no ax to grind.

† Interview, June 16, 1985. Four years after Gordon's findings, something had changed. On October 14, 1985, William Casey made a speech in which he declared that the Soviet Union and its allies allowed terrorist groups to maintain offices in Eastern Europe and granted free passage to

For the CIA, dealing with terrorism had the attraction of a problem that was hypothetically solvable. Good detective work and psychological assessments—two of the principal requirements for success—could be conducted. The agency's range of technical intelligence capabilities could also be effectively deployed against terrorist groups. Human intelligence would be of value once more since well-placed agents and counterintelligence work were central to monitoring and staying abreast of terrorist contacts and activities. Additionally, dealing with terrorism put the agency back in the center of governing concerns. America was undergoing a period of intense frustration and needed "successes" such as the October 1983 Grenada invasion (which, significantly, had no direct CIA involvement and was coordinated by Robert McFarlane, the national security adviser, and the National Security Council staff). Counterterror action also offered the CIA popular support, with the prospect of regaining lost ground with the American public. But despite these attractions, looking to the CIA as the counterterror agency was a classic misuse of an intelligence capability, and Reagan's willingness to use it for this purpose worried many CIA people.

Counterterror was a police or special military function that an intelligence agency could usefully and effectively support but that it could not engage in

operatives traveling to commit terrorist acts. He said that the USSR itself trained about six hundred people in terror and paramilitary methods. "A Soviet connection may seem very shadowy to some, but it seems very close to me," he said. "Where are these training facilities located? They are heavily concentrated in the Soviet Union itself, in Bulgaria, Czechoslovakia, and East Germany, in South Yemen, Cuba, and increasingly Nicaragua, and in the radical entente countries of Syria, Libya, and Iran." He went on to outline the CIA's counterterror effort of increased intelligence collection and foreign cooperation, strengthening legal measures to deal with terrorism and isolating "terrorist states and gangs that sponsor terrorism." Since January 1, 1985, U.S. intelligence combined with effective police work had successfully thwarted about eighty terrorist incidents around the world, he said (*The Washington Times*, October 15, 1985).

Casey's personal interest in the Estimates had other repercussions. In 1984 the National Intelligence Officer for Latin America, John Horton, resigned from the agency in protest over what he considered to be Casey's political interference with an Estimate on Mexico. Horton explained:

> I resigned because of the pressure put on me by the Director of Central Intelligence to come up with a National Intelligence Estimate on Mexico that would satisfy him. This is not the first time that pressure has been put on intelligence officers to come up with what their superiors consider to be the right answers. A previous director not long ago remarked that he was considered a "traitor" because the Estimates on Southeast Asia that were being written under his direction were not pleasing to the policy makers at the time—the Estimates didn't say that our policy in Vietnam was working. In my own case, it was not that the policy makers were putting pressure on the director, but rather that the pressure on me and others working on the Mexico Estimate came from the director himself" (*The Washington Post*, January 2, 1985).

Horton was expressing a real concern about the general diminution of the Estimates. Sherman Kent used to insist that the Estimates had to be drafted by the agency: that way, he argued, they would be controlled by the agency. During the 1970s, Kent's system collapsed, with the agency becoming in effect a member of an Estimates committee arrangement whereby the military supplied the portions on military matters, the State Department on foreign policy, and so on. It meant less bureaucratic infighting and clearer Estimates with fewer footnotes (Casey's willingness to accommodate different views in the text facilitated this too), but less intellectual coherence and more compromises.

itself without completely changing character. With Congress' firm grip on the CIA, it was no longer in a position to move silently and secretly against terrorists (or anyone else). The parasitic relationship between terrorists and their host state(s) meant that more than an intelligence agency was required to deal with them: the mobilization of all America's diplomatic police and intelligence capabilities was required, including close cooperation with the police and intelligence agencies of other countries—and not necessarily only those of friendly countries. Terrorists represented the personalization of politics and international affairs and were symptomatic of growing international disorder. They were far more than simply an intelligence problem: to crack down on the Lebanese terrorists who hijacked a TWA airliner in July 1985, for example, at the very least would have required extensive U.S. naval and air actions and would have involved the deaths of many men, women, and children who were uninvolved. It would all have happened in the full view of television cameras.

Intelligence is about discovering hidden facts, about analyzing information, and about acting in secret. To be effective an intelligence agency has to be able to conduct its important work in secret. To deal with terrorists is ultimately a very public affair, from the shoot-out on an airport tarmac to convincing a whole people or society not to give terrorists shelter. Domestic public opinion also has to be strong in its support of counterterror activities since they can often invite great unpopularity (as the Israelis have found when they attack Palestinian camps hosting terrorist groups). An intelligence agency such as the CIA can pinpoint terrorists and predict their next moves, but it cannot do much more; recognizing this, William Casey said in a speech in October 1985 that effective action to prevent terrorist incidents does depend on a *combination* of intelligence and police work.[51]

When in May 1985 *The Washington Post* ran a story (categorically denied by Casey, the CIA, and the White House) that the agency had trained and directed terroristic Lebanese security forces that were combating anti-American terrorist groups in the Middle East (including those held responsible for the bombing of the U.S. Embassy in Beirut in October 1983), there was no public outcry, nor was there substantial congressional protest. The democratic sanction for covert activities that had emerged in the 1970s was being reaffirmed.[52] The effectiveness of those activities was not of public concern. The agency and the things it does had been accepted. It was another Washington bureaucracy, and taxpayers knew about it.

DOUBLE TROUBLE AGAIN

It was not just the U.S. taxpayers who were made aware of the CIA in the summer of 1985 by the spate of defections, arrests, and a redefection within the world of the intelligence agencies themselves. The Walker family spy ring uncovered early in the year had traded in U.S. Navy secrets, not the secrets of the CIA or of the KGB. But starting in June 1985, a series of interconnected discoveries, reminiscent of the "wilderness of mirrors" that James Angleton had surveyed in the 1960s, promoted the secret world to headline status once more.

The first of these discoveries began in 1979 when Norwegian counterintelligence began to suspect that Arne Treholt, the son of a socialist ex-cabinet minister and himself a rising star in the Norwegian Labor Party, was working as an agent for the KGB. Over the next five years, suspicion of Treholt hardened to certainty, and in 1984 he was arrested at Oslo airport on his way to Vienna for a meeting with his Soviet case officer. In his briefcase were sixty-six secret documents which he intended to hand over. A year later, in June 1985, he was convicted and sentenced to twenty years in prison for spying for the Soviet Union. A crucial witness at his trial was a KGB officer who was a Western double agent.

In Moscow, the discovery of Treholt aroused concern that he might have been betrayed to the West by just such a double agent. This was a routine thought: every intelligence organization considers the possibility that when one of its agents is "blown," it is because there is an agent of a foreign intelligence organization in its midst. And as a matter of routine, every KGB officer who had knowledge of Treholt was investigated.

Oleg Gordievsky, who in 1984 had been appointed acting KGB resident in London—the senior Soviet intelligence post in any country—was one suspect. He had been in the KGB for over twenty years, starting in the early 1960s when he worked with East Germans being trained to assume false identities in the West. In 1972 he was posted to Copenhagen as a diplomat. It was the same time that Treholt was being recruited, although it was unlikely that Gordievsky would have known this then. Paradoxically, Gordievsky was recruited as an agent by Danish intelligence at the same time. He was a very religious man, and had become entirely disaffected from the Soviet regime by the conflict between its public pronouncements on détente and what he knew to be its real policies from his position in the KGB. From Denmark he was posted back to Moscow, where he rose further in the KGB, all the while acting as an agent for the British, to whom he had been passed by the Danes (they did not consider that they had the skills or the resources to run Gordievsky as a double agent). In 1982 he was assigned to the Soviet Embassy in London, and two years later filled the top KGB post there. As acting resident, he would have full information on all Soviet agents in the British Isles, on all those whom the Soviets hoped to recruit as agents and informers, on all KGB officers in the embassy and elsewhere in the country, and on the policy objectives and decisions of the Politburo. In addition, he would have detailed working knowledge of KGB efforts in western Europe and North America, and of "Moscow Center," the KGB headquarters. He was, in short, one of the most valuable and important spies the West had ever had.

In the summer of 1985, Gordievsky had returned on his annual leave to

Moscow with his wife, and there apparently had alerted the British that he had to flee immediately—probably because of growing KGB suspicion that he was a double agent. In June 1985, it was reported, he left the Soviet Union in a "black" operation (the clandestine exfiltration of a person from a country) mounted by MI-6. Close on his heels in July came another senior KGB defector, Colonel Vitali Yurchenko, at first described as the "number five man in the KGB," and subsequently as a much lower-level official. For a time it seemed as if Yurchenko was an even better catch than Gordievsky. He told the CIA about the KGB's method of tracking foreign diplomats and visitors in Moscow by dusting their cars, rooms, and doorhandles with radioactive powder. He also identified an ex-CIA officer, Edward L. Howard, as someone who had sold information to the KGB after he left the agency and as the person who had identified an important CIA source in Russia, A. G. Tolkachev, an aviation electronics expert who had worked on Soviet aircraft development, electronic countermeasures, and radar and "stealth" (i.e., radar-avoiding) technologies.[53]

After three months of debriefing in a CIA house in Virginia, Yurchenko caused a sensation by redefecting to the Soviet Union. He had become increasingly unhappy as a defector, it was reported, because his girlfriend, the wife of a Soviet diplomat in Canada, refused to join him. The first months of any defector's new life are fraught with psychological difficulties, and Yurchenko, it seemed, suffered more than most from homesickness and the dawning realization of the enormity of his defection. On the evening of Friday, November 1, 1985, out at dinner with his CIA handlers at the Au Pied du Cochon restaurant on Washington, DC's Wisconsin Avenue in the old Georgetown section of the city, Yurchenko turned to one of the CIA men and asked, "What would you do if I got up and walked out? Would you shoot me?"

"No," the CIA man said, "we don't treat defectors that way."

"I'll be back in fifteen or twenty minutes," said Yurchenko. "If I'm not, don't blame yourself."[54] He left the restaurant and went to the Soviet diplomatic compound not far away.

Of course, although that particular CIA man might not be culpable, the CIA was to be blamed for this redefection. Yurchenko had obviously been mishandled. His psychology had not been properly assessed, at the very least. Three days later at the Soviet Embassy in Washington he gave a televised press conference, claiming that he had been kidnapped in Rome, where he was organizing security for a forthcoming Russian cultural visit, drugged, flown to the United States, and for three months kept in a drugged state and questioned by the CIA.* It was a propaganda coup for the Soviets on the eve of the Reagan-

---

* Yurchenko's drug claims resonated on two points. First, they acted as propaganda to counter to a small extent the documented Soviet misuse of drugs to control political prisoners and dissidents. Second, in 1985 more details of CIA drug experiments in the 1950s were emerging in the press, so Yurchenko's claims were less likely to be dismissed automatically.

Gorbachev summit, making the CIA look incompetent (although, in fact, Yurchenko had voluntarily provided the agency with information). "After he'd been here for a few months," commented William Colby from the sidelines, "they'd begin to try to get him used to living in America. You take him out to movies. You take him out to dinner . . . And then he got up and walked away, which was a little disappointing. But remember, his walking away was exactly what he had every right to do."[55] "We did our best," said President Reagan about the affair. "I think it's awfully easy for any American to be perplexed by anyone that could live in the United States and would prefer to live in Russia."[56] "The Spy Who Went Back to the Cold" and "Soviet Spy's Double Cross Shakes West" was how the world press front-page headlines read.[57]

The headlines disguised a far more serious matter. In the years following the Nosenko case, the CIA's counterintelligence arm was generally agreed to have declined significantly in effectiveness. Some argued that James Angleton's pursuit of every rumor and his conviction that the agency harbored a high-level Soviet mole had done the damage. Others considered that Angleton's dismissal marked the moment of decline. Reagan's CIA transition team had singled out counterintelligence as requiring particular attention. Now, with the headlines about Yurchenko, attention within the intelligence community focused on counterintelligence, which had very publicly just "lost" a defector.

William Casey was very much on the firing line with the Yurchenko affair. His own interests and aptitudes were geared to human rather than technical intelligence. He had taken a personal interest in the case and had gone so far as to have Yurchenko to lunch in his office and to assure various congressional committees that the Russian was a valuable defector. He might have been, but events prevented the assertion's being proved. Deeper than the embarrassment of the case (added to by the FBI's failure to arrest Howard who, reportedly, had managed to reach the Soviet Union before they knew he had gone) lay the whole debate about human and technical intelligence. Casey, by promoting human intelligence in contrast to Stansfield Turner's promotion of technical intelligence, was seen as paying the price of human vulnerability with Yurchenko's redefection. Was Yurchenko a clever Soviet plant, some wondered, to embarrass the CIA?[58] And if so, had not the agency taken the bait too quickly and too well? A *Washington Post* editorial on November 6, 1985, summed up this view. "From the first exultant leaks to the press about the catch of a blue-chip defector, to the glee freely expressed in the resultant sure discomfort of the KGB, the CIA and those influenced by its briefings in Congress and elsewhere have acted in a strangely incautious and amateurish way. . . . Somehow, a ranking Soviet officer still in the stage of debriefing was watched so laxly that he could make his way to a Soviet haven in Washington. . . . [Americans] need to know how the CIA let itself be made a fool of in so incredible a fashion and how responsibility for it is to be assumed—and by whom."*

The problem about counterintelligence was that America had never had any strong sense of the need for it. The gung-ho mentality of the Reagan administration as a whole tended to ignore counterintelligence. America has never recognized the extent to which it is vulnerable to its own specific weakness: people who are not crazed ideologues but who, like the Walker family, want to buy a second home or car. Indeed, the members of the Walker family might well have voted for Reagan in 1984 because they wanted a bigger slice of the good life. The frustration about human intelligence and counterintelligence stems in part from the fact that it is much easier for the Soviets to "buy" Americans than vice versa. And even if the United States markedly improved its human effort, it would have to be prepared for far more incidents. There might be more embarrassing revelations of Americans spying for the Soviet Union. There might be more cases like that of Tolkachev—American agents caught by the Russians. There would always be the likelihood, because of societal differences, of more American than Russian agents and informants being discovered. By the same token, infiltration of the Soviet Union would be far more difficult. Technical intelligence would always be more reliable, and it would always have the advantage of offering politicians precise control. The spy headlines of 1985 were, in the longer term, powerful allies of the technocrats.

THE MISSING PATH

Technocracy and bureaucratic expertise were the rocks upon which the Reagan administration built. It coasted on the restraint of professionals, and it willed a simple world. The shift to quantitative from qualitative analysis on the

---

* The Washington Post was in a 1960s liberal tradition when it came to intelligence (and political) issues. In the intelligence war, once the headlines were set aside, the West was winning hands down, as Casey was quick to point out:

> I happen to think that in the intelligence arena we are probably ahead. We had to develop technical capabilities in order to penetrate their closed society. I don't think they have been notably successful in their operations in this country. They have had successes, but most of these were with people who volunteered to work for them. They were individuals at low levels within Government organizations who, after they left, for money or revenge reasons, gave information to the Soviets. We don't think we have moles within our own system. Over the past three years, the Soviets have lost 200 of their intelligence officers, arrested or expelled from 20 to 25 countries. A number of their most senior people gave up and turned against them. What rating do you give that combination of factors? I wouldn't mark it very high [Time, October 28, 1985].

"Two hundred of their officers exposed is an intelligence disaster of major proportions," said a retired CIA station chief. "It means they can never operate in the West again: their photographs and other details will be on file. All their experience and training has become a waste— they might be able to operate in Third World countries, but that's it. It will take years for the Soviets to replace them" (interview, October 16, 1985).

part of the CIA mirrored the administration's whole atmosphere and indicated its weakness: as everything rapidly became more complex, the President and his advisers acted as if the opposite were the case. Quality was the keynote of the agency's early years. Detail and volume were not so important. Was Arbenz a communist? Well, he's close enough. Was Castro a communist? He might as well be. Questions and answers in those days were more general, but as the world position of the United States deteriorated to approximate that of the Soviet Union, the mobilizing magic of American power faded and so did America's uniqueness. In 1947 if the Soviet Union had put a brigade into Cuba and refused to withdraw it, America would have taken military action. In 1977 this was no longer possible. So the agency had to address the more focused questions of equality, just as the United States as a whole did, and consequently it ran the inevitably greater risk of more serious consequences if it got details wrong. This need for focus was largely ignored by the Reagan team.

Instead, what Reagan sought was an administration of tone. His themes were resistance to enemies, support of allies, trade, relief for natural disasters, and resistance to terrorism and subversion. They were all relatively "easy" issues: very few people are for terrorism or subversion, or against support for allies, disaster relief, or trade. Also, the issues did not involve success or failure, just simple and cost-effective action. Even wars were thought of as simple problems requiring that some action be taken in a given amount of time. The Contra war with Nicaragua, the Afghan guerrilla war, were simple ways of exacting a price from opponents. For relatively small expenditures, Reagan was able to force large expenditures of money and resources on the part of the Soviet Union and its allies when they did something America did not like.

Reagan had no bundle of doctrines when he came into the White House in 1981. Doctrine was for the people who wrote transition reports and had no clout upstairs. Reagan had a 1930s model of optimism for domestic issues, and an early cold-war model for foreign affairs. He was an armed isolationist. His vision was of an ideal America whose strength lay in being apart from the rest of the world. He liked to explain himself anecdotally, and one of his favorite anecdotes was about a German-American immigrant he met who had left Berlin during the period of the Weimar Republic in the 1920s. "Why did you leave Germany under Weimar?" asked Reagan. "I would have expected you to leave under Hitler, but Weimar was a democracy." "Well," said the immigrant, "when I arrived in New York, I was met by a relation, and he said to me, 'Here you are on the east coast of America, and there are three thousand miles to the west, and you can live anywhere you want to.' In Berlin, I had to get police permission to move from one street to another."[59] Reagan's America was a country of midwestern virtues, where good guys wore white hats and bad guys wore black hats, and where a muscular Christianity ordained the day. His intelligence doctrine was that communism was responsible for all the troubles in the world. This was false: some troubles are caused by Bolshevik intrigue, but many are not. The KGB will always try to manipulate discontent to Soviet advantage, but this is separate from the cause of the discontent. It was false, for example, to see the anger of Palestinians as communist-inspired or to think that because Qaddafi and Khomeini were anti-American that they must therefore be communists too.

At the same time, Reagan recognized that a greater degree of conflict was to be expected in the 1980s; thus he was preoccupied with subversion and countersubversion. The guerrillas in Afghanistan would probably have been supported in some way by any American government, but the Contras? Jimmy Carter, had he won a second term, might very well have preferred a deal with the Sandinistas. Having talked loud and clear about the "evil empire" of the USSR, Reagan in practice showed that he had a moralist reflex rather than a moral vision and that his reflex was to contain, not to undertake thoughtful engagement. He took pride in accurately insulting the Soviets (William Casey did too), but to what purpose? Attitudes alone do relatively little to alter what happens. It was an administration that had not mastered command and control, that was more interested in visible responses than in intimate, commanding responses. Thus when Palestinian terrorists hijacked the Italian cruise ship *Achille Lauro* and murdered a Jewish American passenger in October 1985, Reagan chose to capture the terrorists very publicly at the expense of U.S. relations with Egypt and Italy, causing the fall of the Italian government and seriously undermining the popularity of President Mubarak of Egypt's regime. In April 1986 Reagan ordered an air raid on targets in Libya as retaliation against Qaddafi's support for and involvement with terrorist groups. The raid was carried out against the wishes of Egypt and U.S. allies in Europe (with the exception of the United Kingdom—some of the planes used were based in England) who feared that it would only generate sympathy for Qaddafi in the Arab world and that it might trigger greater terrorist activity in response. Vengeance was Reagan's, but the long-term interests of the United States may not have been best served. It was the mark of a fundamentally isolationist sensibility similar to Jimmy Carter's, and of an administration relating to a public not concerned with detail.

Significantly, both operations were managed by National Security Council staff under the direction of Lieutenant Colonel Oliver North, USMC, an assistant to the national security adviser. From the White House, North played a vital operational role in supplying the Contras; mining Nicaraguan harbors in early 1984; combatting death squads in El Salvador; preparing plans for the release by force of the Trans World Airlines passengers and crew taken hostage by Arab terrorists in Beirut in the summer of 1985; and the Libyan bombing in the spring of 1986. The CIA might be taking the heat for covert operations, but the NSC apparatus—originally set up and widely assumed merely to be a staff function completely removed from direct involvement in operations—was providing the Reagan administration with the means to act secretly without congressional scrutiny. Congressmen were suspicious, but like most people they assumed that the CIA was the only agency that conducted secret operations, although this had not been true for years. This gave the NSC staff additional cover behind the CIA, which acted as a magnet for attention. A marked decline in the real status and authority of the CIA, as opposed to public and congressional perceptions about it since the 1960s, was demonstrated by this shift in operational management.

Reagan was less obviously in the tradition of Carter in being suspicious of the agency. Carter's interest was that the CIA should be highly moral and give him no shocks, and he sent Stansfield Turner into the agency to control it. Casey, Reagan's man, was also sent in to control the agency but with an entirely different interest: Reagan was not too worried about shocks. He wanted Casey to make the CIA more enthusiastic and less bureaucratic; his suspicion was that the agency was bureaucratic and unenthusiastic about anything except itself. Distrust by the national leadership of the agency for whatever reason was a mark of the 1970s and 1980s.

The CIA did little to help itself. Because of the problems of qualitative analysis, it was seen by successive administrations as having "failed" on the "big" questions—OPEC, the rise of the Arab world, Japan's economic advance—and in turn this meant that its value as a forecaster was lessened considerably. The quality of its political analysis (which technology could not do) had not withstood the test of time. On quantitative questions the agency remained authoritative; on qualitative ones it no longer figured. Another major mark of change in the CIA's position compared to its early period was that it was no longer close to the presidency or central to anyone. When Nixon and the CIA had quarreled, people wondered if the agency was stalking Nixon. Had it masterminded the Watergate episode? Had it been "Deep Throat"? If the CIA fell out with Reagan, people would say, "Poor CIA." It was a very significant change. There had been an institutional displacement between Nixon and Reagan: secrecy in qualitative terms had moved toward the National Security Council, and the nature of what was secret had altered, leaving the CIA behind. Monitoring whole societies and having an enormous quantity of information remained CIA territories, but the key element of analysis had moved in practical terms to the NSC staff. The technical intelligence agencies, notably the National Security Agency and the National Reconnaissance Office, along with that part of the CIA involved in technical intelligence collection, was where secrets were, locked up in spools and disks, away from people and paper. The terms on which the Contra war was conducted and discussed showed that deniability, considered so important in the 1950s and 1960s, was no longer a factor. This was another major change in the political and institutional culture of the agency. Sources and methods, and dealings with other intelligence services (although both the National Security Council staff and the National Security Agency were in the driving seat on such relationships), were the areas of secrecy left to the CIA.*

* "They Didn't Laugh When I Invited CBS to Film the CIA" was the headline of a profile of Herbert E. Hetu, head of the CIA's public affairs office from 1977 to 1981 (*The Washington*

Casey—like any of his predecessors—could have made a difference. The question he in particular faced when he came in as DCI in 1981 was one of emphasis, energy, and regeneration in intelligence priorities and interpretations: had the CIA become, in effect, a sleepwalker? In answering this question he could have brought in new people, not people of the center or left or right, but people to crack routine. That was the way to shake up the bureaucracy. He could have improved technical intelligence even more by reaching into his own experience for creative financing, or by going after Nobel laureates to contribute directly to the agency's effort rather than indirectly through consulting and advisory arrangements. But instead of going after the very best, he was content to go after the very good. He could have sought to command the relationship with Congress by pressing for a secret committee of named senators and representatives only, with no staff, but he preferred to pretend that Congress did not deserve his attention. He could have taken a view about the structure of the intelligence community as a whole, from how much duplication there should be between the various agencies of military intelligence to the question of whether the DCI should also be head of the CIA, but he did not. He was happy to inherit the DCI's established role and to enjoy what was clearly a personal status symbol of cabinet membership. He could have sought a clear decision on whether the CIA should be the specialist agency it was conceived to be or the generalist agency it had become in the 1980s. Instead he tried to ride both horses, achieving distinction on neither. He could have determined what was needed that the agency alone could do. Was guerrilla activity a proper CIA function? Were covert operations generally something it should do, rather than, say, military special forces? Where should intelligence techni-

---

Post, July 15, 1984). A headline like this—let alone the office—would have been inconceivable even ten years earlier. It was a mark of the dilapidation of the agency. Now it was valued as much for publicity for political purposes as it was for analytical skill. Justifying the job, Hetu said, "I don't think any agency, department or instrument of government can succeed without the public knowing what they're doing and giving their support. . . . [Even] the NSA. But the things they do are so technical that it's pretty hard to even talk about what they do. Everything they do is classified, I'm sure. . . . We never said 'No Comment.' I thought it was important, even if we couldn't comment, to tell the reporter why" (ibid.).

This development was by no means popular with old agency hands, especially in the DDO. "I remember early in the first year," said Hetu:

I went to a meeting of all the DDO office chiefs. . . . The DDOs. The operations directorate. The clandestine part of the house. The *spies*. I went to a meeting with all the senior office chiefs in this dark conference room and showed a slide show that I had put together for all the educational classes they had at CIA. It was fairly simplistic. I was trying to show them what I was showing the other people. After I turned on the lights I started to answer questions to explain what I had in mind. I never have met such hostility in my life. It wasn't me, it was apparently what I was doing. . . . I went out visibly shaken and I was shaken for several days. Their rationale was that agents and potential agents might either leave the service of the CIA or would never join us because of what I was doing. That they'd be afraid that if the CIA was mad enough to have somebody dealing with the press that someday I would blow their cover [ibid.].

Under Casey, the briefings and the press contacts continued with an average of 385 telephone calls a week from the news media (*The Washington Post*, April 29, 1983).

cal development and research be conducted? Should it be contracted out? Should it be done in-house by each agency? Should there be one agency responsible? But none of these questions was asked.*

Despite William Casey's professed interest in human intelligence, and despite the fact that he undoubtedly engineered an improvement in the morale of the agency, technical intelligence was at the core of the U.S. intelligence effort. And Casey's interests and achievements were, essentially, outside the mainstream. This was not to say that Stan Turner had been "right" after all and that Bill Casey was "wrong." It was simply that technical intelligence involved far more money (and therefore had more supporters), was far more reliable, was far less risky, and was far more easily controlled than spies and covert operators. Technology operating technically (for example, satellites operated by computers from the moment of their launch to the end of their use) was even more certain, and this was the strength of its attraction. The Reagan administration's concentration on the Strategic Defense Initiative was a massive indicator of this appeal. Reagan's was another technological administration when it came down to it, and the CIA—because of its fundamental human intelligence history—paid the price.

MAGIC?

Congressional oversight and concern about secrecy exacted another price from the agency and the Reagan administration. The isolationist desire for distance from the rest of the world that technological systems represented was mirrored by the Ninety-ninth Congress' frequent assumption that the United

* The simmering concern with Casey in Congress surfaced in November 1985 in the wake of the Yurchenko affair. Senator David F. Durenberger (R-Minn.), chairman of the Senate Select Committee on Intelligence, on November 13 was reported as saying that the CIA under Casey lacked "a sense of direction" and an adequate knowledge of long-range trends in the Soviet Union. The CIA's failure to maintain a high quality of political analysis was again being attacked. Inferentially, Casey's commitment to human intelligence was being condemned as well. Contrasting with what Bob Gates maintained, Durenberger said that the intelligence process prevented CIA analysts from looking "five years down the road" or analyzing effectively such problems as Shiite fundamentalism or the political deterioration in the Philippines. He also said that he would consider a "recommendation" restricting the DCI to intelligence work with no policy role.

The following day Casey replied, reaching for the archetypal bureaucratic response of accusing Durenberger of undermining CIA morale. "What are they to think," he said, "when the chairman of the Senate Select Committee offhandedly, publicly and inaccurately disparages [CIA officers'] work?" He accused the committee of "repeated compromise of sensitive intelligence sources and methods" and declared that Durenberger's criticisms were "tragically wrong. . . . The intelligence community has produced an enormous number of long-range studies over the last six years or more where we have been far out in front." Then Casey went on, "Public discussion of sensitive information and views revealed in a closed session of an oversight committee is always damaging and inadvisable. As we have discussed many times, if the oversight process is to work at all, it cannot do so on the front pages of American newspapers. The cost in compromise of sources, damaged morale and the effect on our overall capabilities is simply too high" (*The Washington Post*, November 15, 1985).

States did not need secrets and that CIA—or any other U.S operatives—should not be covertly engaged abroad. This assumption was given additional weight by the administration's lack of command and control.

Depending on the professionalism and restraint of bureaucrats was one thing, controlling the bureaucracies to blend easily with the administration's policies was another. And since it was an administration of atmosphere rather than of substantive policies, it was rare for a coherent set of objectives around which the bureaucracies could gather to emerge in any area. One of the principal results of this was the way in which senior administration figures were constantly to be found contradicting each other in public and in secret congressional hearings. Another was the way in which Congress set negative parameters for foreign policy in certain areas, such as its refusal to support the Contras in Nicaragua, or with South Africa where it also set the pace of foreign policy by acting against the regime of State President Pieter Willem Botha as an extension, in effect, of U.S. equal rights domestic policy.

In November 1986 the weaknesses of the administration tumbled out. There was a set of extraordinary revelations about arms deals with Iran, money for the Contras, hostage releases, cooperation with Israel, and CIA and National Security Council staff roles that threw into high relief the nature of the administration, some of its most secret activities, its relationship with Congress, and the real situation of the CIA. Lack of coordination was publicly demonstrated. The administration had been able to get away with so much for six years that when an upset came along it was not prepared for it. In particular, a foursquare administration that projected a tough image and had proclaimed war on terrorism was found to have been dealing with terrorists. It was a self-inflicted wound that did real damage to U.S. foreign policy.

What came to be called "Irangate" or "Iranscam" developed from an attempt to achieve something: exactly what was never worked out. When Iranians opened a channel to the administration by suggesting an arms-sales-for-hostages deal, the Reagan team could not resist going in. Various justifications were later given, the hope of securing hostage releases being the most consistent. It was true that it was not in Western interests to see Iran enter the Soviet orbit since it was a major oil supplier to the West and the only country between Soviet troops and the Indian Ocean, but this in no way justified the arms-sales-in-exchange-for-hostages deals. Nor did the Iranian political situation. While Khomeini was in charge, Iran would follow an independent line against both the United States and the Soviet Union. Less certain was what Khomeini's successors might do. The ayatollah, in his mid-eighties and unwell, was considered unlikely to live very much longer. His country was fighting a seemingly endless, vicious, and costly war with neighboring Iraq. His successors might well be tempted to turn to the Soviets for military and economic help, particularly because Iran's failure to secure victory under Khomeini would raise the question of the effectiveness of the noncommunist Muslim state he sought to establish. There was a real concern in Washington that post-Khomeini Iran might go communist, possibly permanently denying Iranian oil to the West. This would also provide Russia with its centuries-old ambition of having a warm-water port. But arms sales and hostage deals in no way advanced U.S. interests and were far more likely to set them back by alienating American, Iraqi, and antiterrorist opinion worldwide.

It was the desire for stunning successes on the part of the administration that sparked a decision by President Reagan in July 1985 to see whether it might be possible to sell U.S. arms to Iran as a swap for U.S. hostages held by pro-Iranian militant Muslim groups in Lebanon. This idea came from Manucher Ghorbanifar, an ex-senior officer in the shah's secret police, SAVAK, living as an arms dealer in the south of France. Despite his association with the shah and the hated SAVAK, Ghorbanifar had links to the Khomeini regime and felt he could act as a middleman. In November 1984 he floated the swap proposal to an ex-CIA officer, Theodore Shackley. This happened in West Germany where both men had business interests. Shackley passed the message back to Washington where it was considered by NSC staffers and the CIA. Ghorbanifar was understood to speak with the support of the Khomeini regime in this matter. He was also known to have close ties with Israel. And central to his proposal was that all U.S. hostages held in Lebanon would be released in exchange for two arms shipments.[60] Paralleling Ghorbanifar's move, Israeli officials were involved in discussions along similar lines with Robert C. McFarlane. Six months later, reportedly, the agency suggested that selling arms to Iran might improve relations immediately, and could seed important future friendships with Iranians.

The secretary of defense, Caspar Weinberger, who was one of those involved at this stage, dismissed the whole idea with the words "This is absurd."[61] Ever since the embassy hostage affair of 1979–81, the United States had placed an embargo on arms sales to Iran and had sought to prevent other countries from selling arms to the Khomeini regime too. Additionally, Reagan had stated publicly that the United States would not deal with terrorists over hostages. To swap arms sales for hostages, therefore, would not only be hypocritical, but would also nullify the arms embargo.

The proposal nevertheless had attractions for Robert McFarlane and for Reagan. They saw it as offering hope both for the release of hostages in Lebanon and for better relations with Iran. They also tended to dismiss Weinberger's view as being a departmental one, and to see him as having been captured by the bureaucracy. The Department of Defense was getting all the money it wanted and was meeting its objectives under Reagan, so it naturally saw the initiative as "absurd" because it was satisfied. Weinberger did not recognize that in terms of foreign policy, as opposed to military policy, the administration faced frustration. He did not want bother, and he could see the risks.

Frustration was the keynote to the affair. Reagan came into office in 1981 thinking, like most new Presidents, that things were going to be easier than they seemed. It was a common form of wishful thinking at the highest political level. It was the combination of the intoxication of victory and Reagan being a simple man. In particular, he thought that the Soviets only had to be confronted for them to withdraw. That was accurate as far as it went. The Soviets, when confronted by equal or stronger powers, have always pulled in their horns. When facing weaker powers they have always sought to advance. One of Reagan's successes was the marked drop in aggressive Soviet behavior during his presidency: at the 1986 Reykjavik summit, the Soviet leader, Mikhail Gorbachev, for the first time seriously addressed the prospect of substantial reductions in nuclear weapons; in the months after the summit, Gorbachev announced his intention to scale down Soviet involvement in Afghanistan and he also instituted a policy of less domestic secrecy, culminating with the December 1986 release of the Nobel prizewinner Andrei Sakharov and his wife, Yelena Bonner, from internal exile.

But there was another side to confrontation. The Soviets have always been good at spinning things out, at organizing opinion, at dropping delay fuses. By the summer of 1985, with the exceptions of Grenada and the capture of some of the *Achille Lauro* hijackers, Reagan had achieved no victory either.

A great feeling of frustration was the consequence. Reagan sensed that he had reversed nothing and that his successes were like fingers in a leaking dike, preventing some leaks while all the time the pressure was building up. As he looked forward to the remaining years of his last administration, he wanted victories. The factor of time, however, was now working against him. The Sandinista regime in Nicaragua was settling in, happy to be the center point of a Soviet plan for securing communism in Central America. It was a triumph of Soviet diplomacy: the Sandinistas considered it to be their plan, forgetting that it was bankrolled by the Soviets before 1979. Mexico was obviously going to become a future social and economic catastrophe. Spanish-American immigration could easily become a massive political lever in the hands of America's opponents. The 1986 Simpson-Mazzoli Immigration Control Act enabled millions of illegal immigrants to become legal, signaling that if the United States could not control its own borders it was unlikely to control its own destiny. Reagan had cut taxes, but an incredible budget deficit had built up. There had been a domestic economic revival, but it was overshadowed by a historic trade deficit. Postponement and loss of control underlay his administration.

So, as his last term started, Reagan was looking for opportunities for victory, and the Iran arms-sales-swap proposal opened up a remarkable congruence of limited objectives that, taken together, offered him several chances: securing the release of hostages and developing a pro-American faction in Iran. Later, support for the Contras was added.

Because of high-level dislike of the swap proposal within the administration, McFarlane kept it within the NSC staff. His assistant, Oliver North, was put in charge of developments. Already the CIA was being cut out, in keeping with the shift of power and of some covert operations to the NSC staff. As

William Casey was to testify later, the agency was never told the full story and did not know many of the details. "I don't know everything that occurred on the Iranian side among and between the people who were working with the Iranians," he said later. "I don't know everything the NSC did. The NSC was operating this thing; we were in a support mode."[62] Secrecy within the administration was already working against coordination and control among the various agencies that might be expected to be involved—notably the CIA, the State Department, and the Department of Defense—if a swap deal was pursued and reached with Iran.

Events now began to move quickly. On July 3, 1985, the director general of the Israeli Foreign Ministry, David Kimche, met McFarlane. The two men had previously discussed the idea of a joint U.S.–Israel effort to improve relations with Iran, and at the meeting, arms sales were discussed as a way of achieving this objective. Separately, Kimche had been in touch with arms dealers, including Ghorbanifar, and the Saudi financier, Adnan Khashoggi. From such contacts, Kimche said, the Israeli government believed that it might be possible for the United States, by agreeing to arms sales, to befriend people in Iran who would eventually win the power struggle that had started for the succession to Khomeini.

McFarlane discussed the Israeli view with the secretary of state, George Shultz, with Caspar Weinberger, and with William Casey, and then relayed the proposal to the President, who was in Bethesda Naval Hospital where he had had a colon operation. Reagan saw the danger that an arms-sale-for-hostages deal, if it became public, would make U.S. policies in relation to Iran and hostages look hypocritical, but he considered that the chance of building bridges to "moderates" in Iran who might be Khomeini's successors and who might stop Iranian support for terrorist groups was worth taking. George Shultz had warned that Israel's objectives in the Gulf war were different from those of the United States, and that the deals could hurt U.S. relations with the Arab world, but his view was set aside.[63] McFarlane called Kimche in Israel and said that the United States was interested in exploring possibilities. The project was with the NSC staff and Israel: discussing it with the three cabinet members (who were also members of the National Security Council) was quite separate from involving their respective departments and the CIA.

Not analyzed was the nature of the Iranians involved. They were called "moderates" but no one established what that meant. Lenin did not become a moderate when he asked the West for economic help. Stalin did not become a moderate when he was an ally in World War II. All, in fact, the Iranians were doing was demonstrating their practicality. They needed arms. They had no shortage of money. They had hostages in Lebanon. They correctly calculated that they could pressure the United States into selling them arms. They saw only an arms-sales-for-hostages deal. And Khomeini was almost certainly behind the proposal from the start.[64]

On August 2, Kimche flew to Washington for another meeting with

McFarlane. He said that his contacts in Iran were not sure that they could secure the release of U.S. hostages in Lebanon, but that they needed an arms sale for their own credibility at home. Israel, said Kimche, was willing to ship arms to Iran if the United States would undertake to replace them. This meant that America would have no direct contact with the Iranians and thus its public statements would not be compromised; Israel, not the United States, would be selling the arms. No U.S. arms embargo would be broken, no hostages would be seen to have been ransomed. Four or five days later, McFarlane presented the Israeli proposal to Reagan, Shultz, Weinberger, John McMahon, the deputy director of Central Intelligence, and Donald Regan, the President's White House chief of staff.

Shultz and Weinberger were strongly opposed to the deal. The outcome of the Persian Gulf war, in this context, could be affected with Iraq being pushed further into the Soviet camp and the USSR being, in effect, encouraged to counteract U.S. attempts to build up influence in Iran. How, they asked, could anybody be sure of the good faith of the Iranians? What would happen if the deal was made public? Might not the Iranians take the arms and then publicize U.S. involvement to score propaganda points? After all, Iran constantly referred to the United States as "The Great Satan" and had never lost an opportunity to embarrass the United States. Or why should it be assumed that Iran was able to keep secrets? Shultz was particularly concerned not to supply arms, even indirectly, to a country that was supporting terrorism. Nevertheless, the group decided that the United States would resupply Israel with any arms it sold to Iran. McFarlane communicated this decision to Kimche. It was noteworthy that Israel, a country with a remarkable sense of self-preservation, thought it had all but full clearance to pursue the proposed deal at this stage. McFarlane later said that he stressed that the U.S. was not looking for a hostage swap, but only for influence in Iran. Oliver North was to be the U.S. liaison man.

Adnan Khashoggi, Manucher Ghorbanifar, and some Israeli arms dealers now went into action. The Israelis and Ghorbanifar negotiated the sale of Israeli arms to the Iranians. Khashoggi organized a consortium including some Canadian businessmen to guarantee the deal—indemnify the United States if Iran defaulted; indemnify Iran if the arms were not as specified—in exchange for a share of the profit. His political function, and that of the arms dealers, was to act as a cutout so that none of the governments had to deal directly with one another. It seemed, later, that the Iranians trusted him more than the U.S. government. His involvement was also to guarantee no political or technical double crosses: there would be no photographs and his business reputation depended upon square dealing.

In August and September two planeloads of arms arrived in Tehran from Israel. On September 14 a U.S. hostage in Lebanon, the Reverend Benjamin Weir, was released. In November a third arms shipment was arranged, this time with more direct U.S. involvement organized by North. He secured CIA planes from Casey, telling him that they were needed for secret shipments of oil-drilling equipment to Iran. In fact they flew arms from Israel to Iran. The use of CIA planes confirmed to the Israelis that the deals had White House approval. Casey, who did not check North's story, was thereby showing willingness in a general sense, and was accepting a displacement of the CIA by the White House. The center of the presidency's most exciting operations was now firmly in the NSC staff and far away from Langley. In the perpetual battle for presidential favor and confidence, the agency was losing. The President's chief intelligence officer, William Casey, and the Central Intelligence Agency were no longer chief or central.

After this third shipment, McFarlane considered the time had come to contact the Iranians directly. He understood that all the hostages would be released in exchange for the first arms sales, and was increasingly worried when this did not happen. Dealing directly would help prevent misunderstanding. Additionally, he himself had decided to leave government, and before he went he wanted to wrap up the operation either by ending it or by the United States taking it over completely. His resignation as national security adviser was announced on December 4. On December 6, at a National Security Council meeting, Reagan decided that the operation should end: efforts should be made to build upon the Iranian contacts, but there should be no more arms sales. McFarlane, now in his last three weeks in office, and Oliver North were sent to London to meet David Kimche to tell him the decision. In London, Kimche brought them to meet Ghorbanifar, who, they found, was obsessed with arms deals and was, McFarlane considered, a man without integrity.*

Returning to Washington, McFarlane reported back to the NSC. George Shultz, traveling in Europe, was contacted. He urged that the United States "not have anything more to do with this."[65] The council agreed. McFarlane left the White House believing that the arms deals were over.

They were not. Opinion was divided within the council, the NSC staff, and the CIA, which, following the December 6 council meeting, now officially knew about the Israeli arms-sales-for-hostages deal. The new national security adviser, Vice Admiral John M. Poindexter, who had been McFarlane's deputy, ensured that the debate that took place about continuation was based on the assumption that he and North would be in control. Poindexter was a more impressive man than he projected. He was one of only two men in the history of the service academies to be head of his class and commandant of cadets (Douglas MacArthur had achieved the same distinction at West Point). He was the only U.S. fleet commander to hold a doctorate in nuclear science. He was a more remarkable man, stronger of purpose, more disciplined, harder, more of a leader, than his appearance suggested. By appointing him, Reagan

---

* At about this time the Israeli arms dealers dropped out, apparently on orders from their government. One, Yaacov Nimrodi, an ex-Israeli intelligence officer, claimed to have arranged one of the arms deals for $5 million of which he kept $1 million as commission (*The Economist*, December 20, 1986).

was appealing to the powerful can-do qualities that Poindexter possessed. Poindexter would follow through for "the boss."

On January 2, 1986, Amiram Nir, an Israeli counterterrorism expert and aide to the Israeli prime minister, met Poindexter and North in Washington. The Israeli government, said Nir, was satisfied that all remaining U.S. hostages in Lebanon would be released if the United States agreed to sell Iran 4000 TOW antitank missiles. The hostages would be released after 1000 missiles were shipped to Tehran. Despite the fact that the hostages had not been released after the Israeli arms shipments, the Israeli government urged that this new deal be accepted by the United States. On January 7, 1986, another council meeting found opinion more favorably disposed to continuing the arms sales. Poindexter, in a memorandum, set out the Israeli proposal:

> The Israeli plan [for arms sales to Iran] is premised on the assumption that moderate elements in Iran can come to power if these factions demonstrate their credibility in defending Iran against Iraq and in deterring Soviet intervention . . . If all the hostages are not released after the first shipment of 1,000 weapons, further transfers would cease.[66]

Along with North, he also pushed the argument that the remaining hostages might be murdered unless arms sales continued. The U.S. government should be prepared, they were saying, to cave in to blackmail and appease a terror regime. Along with everybody else involved in the White House, they were blinded by their dreams of achieving a notable success—the hostages released, the Contras victorious, a new friendship with Iran—and did not see the mess they were actually getting into. Once they discovered that they could make deals, they just started making them, losing sight of the wider issues.

Shultz, still opposed, did not pay much attention at this point, believing that no new decision was being made. "I rack my brains about that, kick myself here and there," he told the House Foreign Affairs Committee eleven months later after the deals had become public. "I'm probably more critical of myself than you are."[67] A secretary of state can expect to be informed, so Shultz blaming himself for not being so was odd. It suggested that he later thought he might have been told and that he should have pressed for clarification. His statement was another sign of incoherence at the highest levels of the administration. About ten days later Reagan changed his mind and signed a finding, at Casey's urging, that authorized the CIA to support a NSC staff operation headed by Poindexter and North to continue arms sales to Iran. The finding declared that the United States would "act to facilitate efforts by third parties and third countries to establish contact with moderate elements within and outside the Government of Iran by providing these elements with arms, equipment and related material, in order to enhance the credibility of these elements in order to achieve a more pro–U.S. government."[68]

Casey had pressed for a finding in November 1985 that would retrospectively authorize any "prior actions taken by government officials" in the affair.

He was anxious that the use of CIA planes in November might have been illegal.[69] The January finding was not retrospective, but it was the result of Casey attempting to get on the record any angle he knew about in a legally satisfactory way, and it was a mark that he was concerned to play things by the book. It strongly suggested that he suspected that more was involved than he had been officially told.

Throughout, Reagan was personally concerned to secure the release of hostages, and this remained his strong motivation. William Buckley, the CIA station chief in Beirut, had been taken hostage there in March 1984, and both Reagan and Casey, for emotional reasons, were anxious to see him released (for security purposes, it must have been assumed that he had been broken after being taken hostage). However, in October 1985, a month after Benjamin Weir's release, Islamic Jihad, the pro-Iranian Lebanese terrorist faction, announced that Buckley had been killed. Photographs and other information indicated that Buckley had been tortured before his death. Such a fate was a real prospect for the other hostages and was a strong reason for continuing the effort to secure their release. The President determined that Weinberger and Shultz, the two leading opponents of the scheme, should not be informed and he also ordered Casey not to tell Congress about the operation.

Feeling that he could not confide in his own senior cabinet members, and running the operation out of the White House, Reagan was demonstrating a fundamental inability to orchestrate his own administration. He was implying that the bureaucracy had captured Shultz and Weinberger and that they were speaking for their departments. In Weinberger's case, arms were being obtained from the secretary of defense who was then being misled as to their intended destination. More than this, the NSC staff was now keeping secrets from the NSC. The council, which had started as the coordinator of the highest level of government in national security matters, was being hijacked by the presidency. This represented a steady contraction of the presidency: It felt it had to stay within the White House to achieve its objectives and that it could not bend the bureaucracies or its own senior officials to its will. Deceit had become an operational system.* It must be said, however, that congressional interest in intelligence matters and covert operations, and restrictions on them, made it very difficult legally and politically for the presidency to rely on people outside the White House.†

---

* It was not surprising that when the affair became public both Casey and Shultz showed that they were uncertain about the facts. Apart from any determination there might have been not to know, subordinates had been systematically encouraged to deceive their superiors.

† Laws broadly fall into two categories. Those on national policy, like the Boland amendment barring aid to the Contras, are often imprecise (e.g., the amendment never specified what constitutes aid) and carry no specific penalties if broken. Laws dealing with procedure, in contrast, are usually precise and carry penalties. Congressional restrictions on intelligence and covert operations are in the national policy category and are full of loopholes. The President can, for example, waive certain restrictions on arms sales to states that support terrorism. He can also waive the requirement on the DCI to inform Congress of covert operations.

In late January, Amiram Nir again met North in Washington. Arms, North explained, would be flown from the United States via Israel to Iran. The Iranians would pay considerably more than their book value into a Swiss bank account set up by the CIA. Adnan Khashoggi would act as middleman and collect the money from Iran. Part of the profits would be used to buy arms for the Contras. According to the December 1986 Senate Intelligence Committee investigation into the affair, the idea of helping the Contras in this way came from the Israelis—an allegation the Israeli government denied.[70] Nir told the Iranians the arrangements and gave them the Swiss account number.

In February the Department of Defense sold TOW missiles to the CIA at North's behest. The Pentagon had said it would have to notify Congress if arms were sent to Israel, so North went to Casey. Casey agreed that the CIA would buy arms from the Pentagon. North undertook to ensure the agency was repaid. This transaction helped obscure the destination of the weapons, and kept the Department of Defense (and Congress) officially ignorant of the whole operation, although it was a flimsy cutout since not many people were using TOW missiles in 1986 and the Pentagon knew them all. More people than William Casey were happy to record their ignorance (although Casey privately knew much more than he ever admitted). Eventually, the CIA was repaid from the arms sales the book value of the arms it bought from the Pentagon, leaving its accounts complete. The missiles were flown in CIA planes to Israel and then to Iran. The Iranians paid Khashoggi $10 million for this shipment of which he kept about $6.25 million, depositing about $3.75 million—the approximate book value of the missiles—in the Swiss account. Part of the profit, North arranged, was used to buy arms for the Contras.

Following the enactment of the Boland amendment by Congress, private funding became the Contras' principal source for arms and the CIA was effectively prevented from continuing its support of the Contras. In July 1985, Congress had agreed to $27 million in nonmilitary and humanitarian aid to the Contras, but refused repeated presidential requests to vote money to support the Contras' military effort. In order to maintain this effort, therefore, North and other administration officials encouraged groups like the Council for National Policy and the National Endowment for the Preservation of Liberty in fund-raising efforts for the Contras. North was much in demand as a speaker at pro-Contra meetings. "Ollie let you know what is really going on in Central America," said Bradley Keena, political director of the Leadership Foundation. "Nobody really knew like Ollie knew."[71]

The profits from the arms sales retained by North were channeled through a shadowy, private network to purchase arms for the Contras.[72] USAF Major General Richard Secord, an ex-deputy assistant secretary of defense, who retired from the air force and government in 1983 to become president of Stanford Technology Trading Group International based in Vienna, Virginia, was called in by Poindexter and North to help get military supplies to the Contras with the profits. Together with his partner, Albert Hakim, an Iranian-born arms dealer, Secord arranged with a Geneva firm that shared an address there with a Stanford subsidiary in Switzerland, Compagnie de Services Fiduciaires, for it to take the profits and buy arms for the Contras.[73] It was another cutout device distancing the U.S. government from direct funding and avoiding the congressional ban.

In May, two more arms shipments, using CIA planes, were sent to Israel and from there to Iran. At the end of May, Poindexter asked McFarlane to fly secretly to Iran: he was completely disillusioned and wanted to resolve the release of all U.S. hostages in Lebanon or else end the shipments. McFarlane was given a background briefing by the CIA on the Iranian political scene and the personalities he would meet. On May 28 he left for Tehran together with North, an NSC staff expert on the Middle East, Howard Teicher, and George Cave, a retired CIA veteran who had served as deputy station chief in Tehran during the shah's regime, and had been a member of Kermit Roosevelt's team that had engineered the overthrow of Mussadegh in 1953. Cave had been acting as a consultant on Iran for North. McFarlane carried a cake in the shape of a key to his contacts in Iran.

It was an extraordinary risk to put such senior U.S. officials in Tehran: they could easily have been kept hostage and then what would Reagan have done? It was a mark of the amateur, naive quality of the whole operation.

The group spent three days in Tehran and met several leading figures in the Iranian government and parliament, but no hostage release deal was achieved. The Iranians made further demands, including the release of all political prisoners in Israel. On their return to Washington, McFarlane reported back to the National Security Council. On the flight back from Tehran, North had told him that profits from the arms sales were going to help the Contras, but McFarlane's pessimistic account to the NSC of his mission to Iran, it seemed to him, convinced the council to end contacts with the Iranians. George Shultz later said that at about this time both Poindexter and Casey told him that the effort had been "stood down."[74]

All that had been ended, however, was that obviously deluded part of the operation to build up U.S. influence with some Iranians by selling arms to them so that they could demonstrate to other factions in Iran their ability to deliver military supplies, despite the U.S. embargo, vital to Iran's war effort against Iraq.* The determination was being met in full to keep the whole operation secret and away from all but the handful of people in the White House who knew all the details. Again, the DCI and the CIA were being kept out, despite the fact that CIA resources—planes and secret communication networks—were being used. Casey doubtless suspected that a top secret operation

---

* For the United States to be involved with either Iran or Iraq was to invite the long-term hostility of the other, and to encourage the Arab world as whole to see the U.S. as cynical: helping one group of Muslims to kill another, and working in concert with Israel, seen in the Arab world generally as the enemy. The thinking through of the affair was nonexistent. It was an operation determined by a craving for action, for success: a dream for magic.

was being run by Poindexter and North—after all, the use of CIA planes and the use of a CIA proprietary account in Switzerland must have alerted him—but he was content to ask no questions: the operation was being conducted out of the White House, and that was good enough for him. "I think we knew in a general way that money was being raised and probably [we] could have put a report together on it if we wanted to, but we didn't," he declared later. "We were not running the operation. We were supporting that. That was done by a few fellows in the NSC. It was their operation; they were in charge of the operation."[75]

Casey was revealing his general assessment of the agency's place in the Washington scheme of things. He was saying, in effect, that the real action was in the White House and that the CIA was so far out of it that ignorance of the operation would not result in the agency inadvertently stumbling across it and compromising it, or being compromised by it. He was saying that the CIA was just another bureaucracy.

The release of hostages and funding for the Contras by now had become the operational objectives. The Iranian contacts had not secured the expected hostage releases. At no stage were the contacts objectively assessed. The excitement of dealing, of breaking into the wilderness of relations with Iran, had become as thrilling a prospect to the White House as the opening to China had been for Nixon. But the Iranians throughout operated through the most junior people they could. When McFarlane and his team flew to Tehran, they were kept waiting on arrival and were met not by any official, but by Manucher Ghorbanifar. The Iranians jacked up the price of hostages at every step. Yet, while McFarlane and Poindexter had become increasingly disenchanted with the whole deal, it went on.

Further arms sales were halted. The Iranians responded by withholding payment for the last delivery, leaving Adnan Khashoggi and his consortium in debt: having underwritten the deal, they now owed the U.S. government the book value of the arms involved. The standoff lasted until July 26 when another hostage in Lebanon, the Reverend Lawrence Jenco, was released. The Iranians gave Khashoggi part of what they owed, and he contacted North to arrange two more arms deliveries in exchange for more hostage releases. After the deliveries were made, however, again no hostages were released. North threatened that there would be no more sales unless the Iranians came through with releases. It was standoff once more: the Iranians withheld payment for the deliveries, three more Americans were taken hostage in Beirut in September, and once more Khashoggi, and his consortium, were in debt.

Fearing for his investment, one of Khashoggi's Canadian partners and an ex-legal client of Casey's, Roy Furmark, met the DCI in his office on the third floor of the Executive Office Building beside the White House on October 7 and told him that he suspected a Contra connection; that Casey should check the Swiss bank account of Lake Resources, a CIA proprietary into which arms-sales money had been paid, and that he and his partners were considering legal action against the U.S. government in order to recover their money. The inference was that the capital and profit that should have been returned to the Khashoggi consortium was being sidetracked to the Contras. It was also that Khashoggi and his partners thought the CIA knew much more than Casey admitted, and that the Contra connection was outside their particular deal. "He said he knew nothing about the arms deal with Iran," Furmark recalled. "He asked me whether I knew Poindexter, and I said no. He then picked up the phone and tried to reach Poindexter, but couldn't."[76] This, Casey insisted, was the first time he was made aware of the financial ramifications of the arms sales and of the Contra funding. He reported the conversation to Poindexter the next day and advised him to get a lawyer:

> I told Poindexter I had learned that people had put money up to finance this, and they were not getting paid and were very upset about that and were trying to figure out how to get their money back . . . He said he was surprised. He was concerned about it. I advised him that I thought he ought to get prepared to pull the whole story together and make a public statement of some kind. He said he didn't want to do that until—because it was an ongoing operation. They were hoping to get some hostages out.[77]

Casey also telephoned North and asked if any CIA people had been involved in the Contra funding. North assured him that no CIA people had been involved.

It was interesting that Casey assumed that no one in the CIA could tell him if CIA people were involved. By speaking to North instead, he was showing that he did not believe that the agency had pride and autonomy. He recognized that Reagan's people might have instructed people in the CIA to keep Casey in the dark, and that Reagan himself was not going to interfere; otherwise, he would have spoken to the President directly and complained about what was going on. By not doing this, Casey was acknowledging the diminished real position of the agency and of the DCI.

The operation was now obviously unraveling. In a last attempt to resolve matters, North arranged a final arms shipment on October 26. A week later on November 2 a third hostage, David Jacobsen, was released. By this point there had been seven arms shipments from Israel and the United States for three hostages. Jacobsen's release had taken three shipments. The deals had simply demonstrated a pathetic dependence on a White House will for a better result when all that was actually happening was that Iran was securing more and more arms supplies for each hostage release. If this was the action of a tough administration, what, it might be wondered, were appeasers like? Then, on November 4, a Beirut magazine, *Al Shiraa*, broke the story of McFarlane's visit to Tehran. The magazine had been told by the Iranians. Publicity would provide a propaganda victory against Reagan. The likelihood of this happening had always been high; it was part of the risk inherent in dealing secretly with Iran. Within two weeks, newspaper headlines all over the world carried details. The

Iranian Speaker of Parliament, Hashemi Rafsanjani, one of the people McFarlane met in Tehran, confirmed McFarlane's visit and that he had come with a planeload of spare parts for Hawk antiaircraft-missile batteries. On November 19, President Reagan in a national telecast confirmed the bare bones of the story and expressed the hope that while there would be no more arms sales to Iran as a country that supported terrorism, that the contacts made with Iranian "moderates" would not be destroyed by publicity and would be developed further. On November 25, the attorney general, Edwin Meese, called in by Reagan to investigate the legalities of the operation, disclosed the Contra connection. Only Oliver North knew about the entire operation, Meese held.* The President had not known. Poindexter resigned as national security adviser and North was fired from the NSC staff. Frank Carlucci, who had served as deputy secretary of defense in 1981–82 after leaving the CIA, succeeded Poindexter. He promised to return operations to the CIA, and restrict the NSC staff to their coordinating and clearinghouse role.

Carlucci was a man on good terms with both Republicans and Democrats. He represented the accommodating bureaucracy with no strong opinion on any subject. He was a senior expediter, removed from identification with any particular policy. He was a "sound" man, proud of being cool, professional, and unexciting. He was known for his friendships with people rather than his alliances with people. His appointment represented a defeat for the ideologues in the administration and a statement that Reagan had lost confidence in activism. For Reagan, appointing Carlucci was an acknowledgment that disillusion would now underpin the desire to postpone problems in his last years in the White House.

Americans were distressed by the story. Many thought that Reagan was lying about it, and his popularity dropped. The great tone setter had failed. Frank Mankiewicz, who had been Robert Kennedy's press secretary, summed up early feelings when he said, "I think people are horrified by the idea that Reagan had been helping the Ayatollah. About three months into the Presidency, Clark Clifford said about Reagan: 'He's an amiable dunce.' We've been able to live with that, but now the situation has taken a turn that's very bad for Ronald Reagan. People are feeling, 'If he *hasn't* been out of touch, then he's a liar.' In either case it's a no-win situation."[78] "Ronald Reagan . . . gave us an image of someone who was comfortable with himself, and 49 out of 50 states voted for his doctrine," said Mark Shields, a *Washington Post* commentator. "Now, since he's made anti-terrorism a hallmark of his Presidency, and we see who was responsible for blowing up the Marine barracks in Lebanon, and then find that Reagan's selling arms to the Ayatollah—I think that leads to a terrible feeling of let-down."[79]

---

* In view of the large amounts of money that Ghorbanifar and Khashoggi stood to receive from the deals, it was probable that they knew about the entire operation too; Roy Furmark, at one remove, seemed to know more than the director of Central Intelligence.

Questions were immediately raised about the money trail in the affair. How much money was involved? Who had it? How had it been spent? Khashoggi and Ghorbanifar said in an ABC News interview that Iran was supposed to pay between $30 million and $35 million for the arms it had received, that they and the other investors had raised $12.2 million to pay the CIA for the arms, and that the Iranians had paid $10 million less than agreed, leaving them and the other investors short.[80] The amount of money involved in the deals was enormous. Iran was reported to have paid about $42 million for the Israeli arms shipments and about $20 million for the direct U.S. shipments. At one stage Khashoggi and his partners made a $3 million agreed profit for depositing $15 million for thirty days in the Lake Resources account. Even more was involved in associated financial deals by which the Saudi royal family and the Sultan of Brunei acted as cutouts in Contra funding. In January 1987 the Senate Intelligence Committee could not discover what had happened to as much as $24 million involved in the various deals.[81]

Conflicting statements were frequent. At first they were thought to be contradictions, but then it became clear that they were a mark of the administration's incoherence. Each person knew a different, partial story. In his November 19 telecast, Reagan had referred to only one planeload of arms, a "really minuscule" quantity. Then it emerged that there had been four arms shipments direct from the United States, and three shipments from Israel. Robert McFarlane said that the President had approved the Israeli shipments. Presidential spokesmen said that Reagan did not learn about the Israeli shipments until after they had taken place. Later Reagan said he might have been told about them when he was recuperating from his colon operation, but that he could not remember. Edwin Meese announced that "representatives of Israel" deposited profits from the sales in Swiss accounts for the Contras. Israeli spokesmen denied this and claimed that payments were made into Swiss accounts directly by the Iranians at U.S. instruction. Reagan said that the United States was not involved. The ambassador to Lebanon, John Kelly, revealed that in August 1986 he had seen Robert McFarlane for a private briefing before taking up his post. McFarlane had told him that the United States was selling arms to Iran, mainly to obtain the release of hostages, and that although Shultz was opposed, the President had authorized the deals. In October, using CIA communications channels, Poindexter had instructed Kelly to cooperate with North and Secord who were coming to Beirut with an arms shipment (the last one) tied into the release of David Jacobsen. Kelly did not inform the secretary of state about any of this because, he said, he assumed from what Poindexter said that Shultz knew and because his instructions were straightforward. Shultz was furious when he only learned about Kelly's involvement two months later, after the affair had broken. "I am, to put it mildly, shocked to learn this after the event from an ambassador," Shultz declared.[82] But since ambassadors are appointed by and are responsible to the President, Shultz's anger was tempered. He understood that Kelly's tale was just another example of the administration's lack of coordination and coherence, and of the amateur nature of the affair, rather than a mark of lack of confidence in him. John Poindexter and Oliver North, called to give evidence about the operation to the Senate Intelligence Committee, unprecedentedly for serving U.S. officers, took the Fifth Amendment.

Great suspicion surrounded Bill Casey and the CIA. The two were by no means identical. There was the suspicion that Casey knew or had worked out what was going on, and that the agency did not know. There was the opposite suspicion that the agency knew or had worked it out, and that Casey did not know, as his call to North after speaking to Furmark indicated. The vulgar suspicion that Casey and the CIA both knew and were working together was the most dated. The same fragmentation that had overtaken the executive branch as a whole (as demonstrated by the cutting-out of Shultz and Weinberger) had overtaken the agency and the DCI: that call to North showed that the DCI could not trust the CIA and vice versa. The unarticulated general theme was that in the Reagan administration everything was done through personal contacts and not through institutional channels. Still, some congressmen were convinced that the operation was a CIA one and the agency and Bill Casey had broken the law. They did not believe that the CIA was not in the driving seat, and they ridiculed Casey's claim that

> The CIA role was to provide support to an activity under the direction of the NSC. All the activities were entirely properly conducted and fully authorized. We received $12 million to pay for the Defense Department weapons shipped to Iran. It has been meticulously accounted for. We facilitated the movement of these weapons in three separate flights, and none of the $12 million reaching us has been diverted for any other purposes.[83]

After Casey testified to the House Foreign Affairs Committee on December 11, 1986, the committee chairman, Dante Fascell (D-Florida), described his evidence as "incredible."[84] Representative Samuel Gejdenson (D-Connecticut) said, "If Casey really knows as little as he tried to portray, he ought to be fired for incompetence. And if he knew more, he ought to be fired because the President instructed his people to be forthcoming."[85] Gejdenson's implication was that Casey should have spied on the presidency. The irony was that people were still trying to blame the CIA for a monopoly position it had lost more than a decade previously. Jokes in Washington, more accurately, reflected the NSC staff and White House in the affair:

> Q.: What's the difference between a children's home and the National Security Council?
> A.: A children's home has adult supervision.
> Q.: How many White House aides does it take to turn on the lights?
> A.: None. They like to keep Reagan in the dark.

Days later Casey collapsed at his desk in Langley, was rushed to Georgetown University Hospital, and had an emergency operation for the removal of a cancerous tumor in the brain.

To some people, the affair seemed like another Watergate. "This is the most fun we've had since Watergate," Ben Bradlee, *The Washington Post's* editor (and editor at the time of Watergate) was quoted as saying.[86] But Watergate had been about cover-ups, and Reagan moved quickly to ensure that the attorney general, Congress, and the independent counsel, Lawrence E. Walsh, appointed to investigate the affair, should have full access to all the documents and people available (Oliver North, it was reported, had shredded documents in his office just before leaving the White House). For the first time, a White House chief of staff testified to Congress under oath. The Vice-President, George Bush, publicly called upon Poindexter and North to tell Congress all they knew and not to take the Fifth Amendment. Few people imputed moral nastiness to Reagan, but many wondered if he was in control. The question that lingered was, had he talked tough but in fact taken the line of least resistance all the way through?

The real significance of the affair went much deeper. The Gulf war between two countries antipathetic to the United States presented only dangers and difficulties. Its continuation was not in long-term Western interests, but there was also no prospect of an early peace. Electronic and satellite intelligence (later claimed to have been doctored) was given to both Iran and Iraq. By playing both sides, the United States was making its diplomats and ordinary Americans vulnerable to reprisals. The U.S. government was saying to both sides: "Go ahead, kill each other. We'll help you." And each side would resent being treated so cynically. The best hope for a resolution to the war that did not favor the Soviet Union and did not see a communist Iran or Iraq, the Natinal Security Council seemed to be implying, was to keep it going until domestic changes in either Iran or Iraq made a settlement in Western interests possible. But this was entirely inaccurate. Israeli, not American, interests were better served by the continuation of the Gulf war—Iran and Iraq were both violently anti-Israel.* American interests were in fact done great harm by the war and by U.S. involvement. Anti-Americanism was built up in the Muslim world. Relations with Arab countries were set back. Egypt declared that a promise not to repeat arms sales to Iran was not enough to restore U.S. credibility among Arabs.[87] European allies were disconcerted. Giovanni Spadolini, Italy's foreign minister, hoped that despite "the great confusion demonstrated by White House aides, who thought they could fight extremism by fortifying the Iranians," joint European-American efforts to combat terrorism would not be damaged.†

---

* A cynic might also point out that the greater the chances of communism increasing in the Middle East, the more valuable Israel becomes to the United States. And if both Iran and Iraq bleed themselves dry in a war, the principal winner is Israel.

† *International Herald Tribune*, January 12, 1987. Spadolini resigned as minister of defense

A more immediate factor was the role of Israel which had acted as a middleman throughout.

The security of Israel depends almost completely on U.S. support, so in the Israeli involvement in the affair a large element of realpolitik was evident. For the United States and the Reagan administration in particular, the Israelis were the only people to have emerged with real toughness, a worldwide range, a democratic sensibility, and an ability to keep things secret. Working with Israel was a way of circumventing congressional restrictions.

Israel's demonstrated close relationship with America reflected an acute awareness that the United States could easily go into a deep isolation. The Israelis' willingness to work for U.S. objectives was a hardheaded and successful attempt to weave themselves into the fabric of U.S. policy-making so as to reduce the risk of ever being discarded. They were able to offer a high-level, voluntary set of services to the presidency. They acted as potentiators of skill and quality. "The reason the NSC was put in charge of [the operation]," said Casey, "is that it started between the NSC adviser and the adviser to the Israeli Prime Minister."[88] In contrast, the Contras suffered the experience of dependence without connection.

The White House's embrace of Israel demonstrated marked self-awareness on the part of the U.S. national leadership and the intelligence leadership in particular. They were admitting that the United States had not produced an effective, truly covert service, and the political cadre to go with it.

For the presidency, the affair was very serious. Reagan's Nicaragua policy was never thought through. The Contras were given a certain support—never sufficient to give them a real chance—and the President was never able to convince Congress to back the Contras to victory. As the congressional hearings following the arms sales / Contra funding revelations demonstrated, the Contras became a Trojan horse for Congress into the workings of the executive branch. One apparent consequence of the affair was the general feeling that the arms sales cheapened and humiliated the United States, and that the United States had also been taken for a ride. "It became an arms-for-hostages deal, and that was wrong," commented Richard Nixon.[89] Additionally, because of congressional restrictions, the presidency found itself in a situation where it was impossible for it to do much about the Sandinistas. Congress had prevented the United States from having a secret and coherent and effective policy in Central America. The presidency, in consequence, was like Gulliver tied down by the Lilliputians. To try to break away was natural.

The power of the executive branch is like a great water pressure. If it cannot fountain in Washington, it will travel great distances underground to break out far away. As it does so, it leaves the great Washington bureaucracies dry,

---

after the *Achille Lauro* affair in protest at the Italian government's decision to release the terrorist leader, Abul Abbas. He had agreed with Reagan that Abbas' release was an attempt by Italy to appease terrorists. His resignation caused the fall of Bettino Craxi's government. Craxi subsequently formed a new government with Spadolini as foreign minister.

reducing each in scale and status. The CIA and William Casey were notable victims in this respect with Iranscam. Wrangling at senior levels is the frequent symptom, and leaks are commonplace. But as the second generation of Americans called to administer a world role for their country found that the world order was synonymous with the will and dispositions of the United States, the Iranscam affair highlighted the need to resolve the place of secrecy in the democracy. Having to spend time and effort keeping things secret from its own people, whether justified or not, was publicly shown to be counterproductive and to reduce the chances of policies being pursued capably. The bureaucratic displacement and decline of the CIA since the late 1960s was symptomatic of the failure to address this need.

THE INVISIBLE DIRECTORS

On January 29, 1987, William Casey resigned as DCI. Robert Gates, who had succeeded John McMahon as DDCI in April 1986, and had been acting-director since Casey's collapse in mid-December, was nominated to succeed him. Gates had been promoted by Casey and he came from the analytical side of the house. His nomination represented general recognition of the agency as a source of information rather than as an action-oriented institution. It also represented an overall withdrawal of the agency from Casey's early determination to have a revivified CIA in the mold of its founding generation (or at least what Casey and Reagan believed that mold to have been).

Apart from being backed by Casey, Gates owed his nomination to his distance from Iranscam and his virtual invisibility to opinion formers and politicians. (He was the administration's third choice for the post.) His intellectual ability was acknowledged, but there went with it a reputation for abrasive arrogance. His range was strikingly narrow: he had never run agents, had never been in the field, and was considered "academic." At 43 he was the kind of bright young officer who advances in an army that has long been at peace. In the midst of Iranscam, Reagan reached for uncontroversial people. Iranscam was the product of amateurs and idealogues. Bob Gates, like Frank Carlucci, who came in in January as Vice Admiral John M. Poindexter's replacement as national security adviser, was cautious, professional, institutional and safe.

Unfortunately for Gates, he was not safe enough. Iranscam had been a bipartisan insult to Congress. It occurred when Republicans controlled the Senate, but Reagan had not sought to confide even an outline of his purposes to senior Republican senators. Gates himself was worried on this score, and approached his nomination hearing in the Senate with trepidation. His fears were confirmed when despite his assurances and undertakings, senators of both parties made clear their reluctance to confirm him as DCI. Theirs was an impersonal rejection aimed at the White House. They were signaling that in the wake of Iranscam, Congress intended to be far more active in clipping Presidential wings; also, that the security and the future of the CIA now lay in its relationship with Congress rather than in its connections with the Presidency. On Monday, March 2, Gates withdrew his nomination.

Days before, the Tower Commission, appointed by the President to look at the working of the National Security Council and its staff after Poindexter's resignation, reported back. It found that Iranscam had been an arms-sales-for-hostages deal, and that despite Reagan's protestations, there had been enormous incompetence and incoherence at the top of the Reagan administration, but that the President himself had been unaware of many of the details of the Iranscam deals. Donald Regan, the President's long-time chief of staff, charged with responsibility for the management of the presidency and White House staff, resigned. The Tower Commission's report had directly challenged his competence and that of the President. Reagan appointed former Senator Howard Baker as his new chief of staff.

Baker was a vital addition to the President's team. He was respected in Congress and in the Republican Party, and in accepting the post he surrendered his own declared ambition to be the Republican presidential candidate in 1988. His principal task in the remaining twenty-two months of the Reagan administration was to demonstrate that the President was, in fact, a competent administrator and strategist. Together with Frank Carlucci, he moved swiftly to find a new DCI candidate. Two days after Bob Gates withdrew his nomination, the President nominated William Webster, the director of the FBI, to serve as director of Central Intelligence.

Webster's nomination was a dramatic one. Congress found it difficult to quarrel with Webster's nomination because to do so would have been to question his conduct of the FBI. Over the years, Webster had won substantial respect in Congress. His was a totally domestic appointment (prior to the FBI post he had been a judge), and it signified that the White House understood that the CIA had to be kept "safe" in domestic terms. There were to be no more exciting excursions or thumbing-of-the-nose at Congress. The imputation was that after Iranscam, someone of known integrity had to be appointed to succeed William Casey. Webster was "Mr. Domestic" and "Mr. Safe." During his FBI days he had been associated with no surprises and nothing sensational. He had been an "invisible" director of the bureau, priding himself on effective administration. He was an ally of the office of the presidency while, in complete contrast to Casey, not close to the President himself. His appointment acknowledged that the agency was, at last, an independent, established bureaucracy no longer looking to the presidency for its main support.

Nor did anyone, least of all agency professionals, think of the agency as a lion pacing its cage under Webster. As Bob Gates had implied some years earlier, it was more like an annex of the Library of Congress. The excitement, the headlines, the attention of the myth-makers, now focused on individual figures in the White House and the bureaucracy. The wheel had come full circle, and so far from being the secret police that Truman and many thoughtful people had feared only half a lifetime earlier, the CIA was now almost universally taken for granted as a moderate and constitutional arm of the American state.

Epilogue

The KGB embraces every area of intelligence: subversion, lying, corruption, killing, spying, analysis. It is the classic espionage service of a great continental power to whom neighbors are enemies, and of an ideological power to whom disagreement is infidelity. The United States, in contrast, is the classic "off-shore" power that has been able to intimidate its neighbors. It has been able to live in an Edenic state of foreign policy, and this is reflected by the CIA's emphasis on technical intelligence collection, which serves to distance America from other countries. When a satellite over 100 miles in space can pick out in minute detail a new Soviet submarine being constructed in the top-secret Leningrad naval yards, there is little need for American agents or spy ships to be involved. Technology, in this respect, is a means of economizing manpower and substituting devices for danger. It also provides a "feel good" quality to intelligence: CIA people do not have to replicate every KGB activity when they have gadgets to do many intelligence jobs. And as Americans, they have never wanted to.

The old empires accumulated intelligence over centuries. The United States had to force-grow intelligence in a few years after 1941. It had to depend upon its cultural genius—organizational and technological—and its tradition of capital intensity: American intelligence has always been characterized by huge expenditures of money and a dependence on quantity rather than quality. If Britain had to create an intelligence capability from scratch, it would devote a proportion of its elite to the task. The French would seek to produce a new cadre of intellectuals to provide a philosophy of intelligence to counteract other philosophies of intelligence. But with the CIA, the United States achieved an American service that assumed a community with the countries it was dealing with and combined toughness and goodwill. The guiding perception was that the United States did not enter other countries as a ruler. Bobby Kennedy entitled one of his books *Just Friends and Brave Enemies*,* summarizing in five words America's wish for the world. American intelligence has always been designed to find things out, not to rule secretly. Only in times of

---

* New York: Harper & Row, 1962.

intense emergency has the CIA been seriously engaged in more than information collection: otherwise, the U.S. always gravitates back to wanting intelligence agencies to gather intelligence and no more.

Behind this American wish lies a powerful American instinct to be isolated from the rest of the world. Preventing surprises has been perhaps the single most important task of the CIA. The shock of Pearl Harbor lay not simply in the immorality of the attack, but in the discovery that the outside world could shatter American complacency, could determine and force American response. At the agency's start, therefore, it was not surprising that to an important degree no questions were asked in Congress about what it was doing. Then, in the years that followed, it was understood that the CIA was the cold-war arm of the United States and was involved in unsavory activities that Americans wanted for America as long as they did not know the details. But once the agency had been going for decades, once intelligence had become a business, attitudes about it inevitably altered. As problems remained unresolved over long periods, the CIA (along with the rest of government) was blamed. It was seen as causing surprises, as being an avenue for the outside world to enter the United States rather than a barrier to prevent entry. This opened windows for the enemies it had created: junior congressmen who had been kept out by the understandings; young media people simultaneously envious and contemptuous of their elders who were "on the team"; elements in the military and competing Washington bureaucracies jealous of the influence and power and budgets of the CIA. The move to technical intelligence was also a way of shielding the agency from such critics by depersonalizing it.

The change in attitudes toward the CIA matched the change in America's position in the world since 1945. Victory in World War II was seen by the United States not in a tactical but in a strategic sense. The world's militarist tyrannies had been broken. China had been "saved." Russia had destroyed its invaders. The oppressed civilized peoples of Europe had been liberated. There was no popular fear of another great despotism being formed. Then, within a year, as America prepared to return to normality, there were two enormous shocks. First, there was a colossal disillusion with Russia. It was seen as standing unmasked and terrible, marching with Mao Tse-tung, pushing Chiang Kai-shek into the sea, terrorizing the brave peoples of Eastern Europe into submission, creating a new and tyrannical empire almost overnight. Second, the technological revolution speeded up by the war meant that pre-1941 normality was no longer possible. The invention of the missile, the intercontinental bomber, the atom bomb, made this the case.

After 1946 there were more shocks. The illusory security of sole possession of the atom bomb soon broke down. The costs of reconstruction in the rubble and ashes of Europe demonstrated that Britain and France were through as great powers. All the major props of the prewar world order began to fall away. There was the discovery that any American technological triumph might pass into other hands that could improve on it. As the years passed swiftly, Japan's economic power, guided and sustained by the United States, demonstrated this finding. Japanese technology by the 1980s had come to beat American ingenuity with ominous regularity. Finally, there was the hard and cold truth, manifest after Vietnam, that America no longer enjoyed the dominating world power it had had in 1945.

Out of these changes came a great anger. America had to face the fact that, instead of a mountain climbed, victory in 1945 was just a number of ledges scaled, and that there were ledges and precipices ahead as far as the eye could see. But in the white heat of this anger, the American governing elite held to their liberalism and created, in the CIA, an extraordinary weapon—both shield and sword—for the inevitable U.S. engagement with the Soviet Union and the rest of the world. They behaved with great restraint and caution. To the present the CIA is an echo of its founders. Its job is not to find enemies, but to define them. Its theme is the substitution of intelligence for force.

Understanding the background atmosphere at the CIA's creation is vital. The perceptions of the later 1940s have been maintained by the agency, despite political and cultural changes, and despite directors of Central Intelligence who have been as varied as the Washington political scene. The CIA has never been the creature of one man. From the very start it was the superior agency of the U.S. government, intimately connected to the national security and foreign policy establishments of America. William Colby demonstrated the strength of these connections when he successfully fought the White House and the Congress to convince Americans of the nature of and the need for the agency.

By the 1980s, the CIA as the child of one disillusion found itself in the process of dealing with another. While it always argued that time was on the side of democracy and that the effort of each day should go into buying time and being tactical, weak political analysis in the 1970s worried both its political masters and Americans generally. The nature of the individual who was DCI became far more important than before because the agency's institutional view was undermined. People were no longer sure that time was on the side of democracy. From James Schlesinger on, the DCI was more and more instrumental in defining the CIA and making it effective. In the early days, DCIs were important because of the CIA. During the 1970s, the CIA became important because of the DCI. William Casey epitomized the change. He was much more than just a director, he was an ambassador for the agency (thirty years earlier the agency did not need one), and he personally gave the CIA access to the president. In short, he was the most important thing about the agency.

The evolving nature of the CIA reveals evolving U.S. attitudes toward the world. That the world could be saved by a combination of American wealth and good impulses was the characteristic sense at the agency's start. Then there was a long period of way-seeking and attention to detail as America fueled and managed the world recovery. As the dreams of idealism faded, and as wealth and goodwill were seen as insufficient without a matching willingness to engage physically and for the long term, there was a search for a new institution in the 1970s which culminated in the technical option. By 1985 the CIA appeared, to a new generation without the experience of post-1945 recovery, as not having enabled the United States to keep up; America had "lost" to Japan and was losing to the USSR. For every American who felt that America was better, prouder, and stronger, there was an American who felt threatened and frightened by external forces.

As an institution of the golden age of U.S. foreign policy, the CIA suffered from the relative decline of America since 1945. Then America had enormous effects and was very flexible. In the 1980s, America's secondary enemy in World War II—Japan—was seen as making a new world. In 1945, a handful of agents in a place could make a permanent difference. In the 1980s, as Nicaragua, Afghanistan, Namibia, Angola, El Salvador all showed, they could not. They could keep the pot boiling but could not serve the meal. A clandestine, skill-intensive organization like the CIA was bound to suffer from these changes and from the short attention span of elective politics. In 1947 the CIA had the magic of U.S. victory, of youth, of social cachet, of technical supremacy over foreign rivals. In the 1980s none of these qualities applied. The CIA, like the United States, was just the biggest competitor in a much more complicated world.

The agency was founded in the full confidence of a democracy undertaking the burden of what John F. Kennedy called "a hard and bitter peace." No one really contemplated how long, how hard, and how bitter that peace would be. The CIA remained and all else changed, except perhaps the Soviet Union. Great institutions prove themselves great by not yielding to every zephyr of opinion in the societies that have established them. But if they set themselves apart, locking themselves into unchanging goals and attitudes, they are in danger of being smothered, like a knight in his armor, unhorsed and forgotten on the battlefield. The struggle that America engaged in with Russia in full consciousness and determination in the 1940s continues still, but the determination, the conscious effort, are ever increasingly the properties of one side only. The CIA has shifted from being a welcome response to bad news to being an unwelcome reminder of bad news. In its beginning the agency was seen as doing hard things for hard reasons. Thirty years later it was seen as a contaminating agency. In the 1980s the nation does not want to be rid of it but is not proud of it.

The CIA has become a bureaucracy of repetitive deeds. It is no longer seen as saving the world; nor is it now seen as corrupting the world. It is seen as a reminder of how old and corrupt and incorrigible the rest of the world is, and Americans in general have accepted it in these terms. Containment in the

1940s and 1950s had seemed a policy of courage, maturity, and moderation. But the long view required for containment brought the agency into disfavor. When presidents wanted action, the CIA cried "Danger!" When the electorate wanted the reassurance of tangible success in world affairs, the agency asked, "To what purpose?" When latent cold warriors warned about Soviet expansionism and military strength, the agency—from its experience—said, "Are you sure the Soviets are about to expand and attack? Are you sure that they are as strong as you say?" By the mid-1980s its restraint was unfashionable.

The foundation of the agency in 1947 was an emblematic part of the extraordinary few years in which America built a new world. The agency was one of the guarantors of this achievement. But as the fires burned down, as the confidence of America waned with Vietnam, and as America was no longer so welcome abroad, the energy and freshness of the early years—when great power was married to generosity, moderation, and apparently limitless resourcefulness—began to diminish. The mission became a task, although the necessity that brought that mission into being remained as great. Today, after forty years of unparalleled achievement, America feels somehow less than she was among the nations that owe so much to her forbearance and goodwill.

The story of the CIA is the story of an American secret, great but simple, public very soon. In a true democracy, people, in order to exercise their rights of choice, demand to know—at least in outline—what choices there are. What was secret was usually grim, sometimes terrible, sometimes repugnant. But in its moments of achievement as well as condemnation, the agency was a reminder that it was a faithful instrument of the most decent and perhaps the simplest of the great powers, and certainly the one that even in its darkest passages practiced most consistently the virtue of hope.

Appendices

Appendix I: Heads of CIA Directorates, 1947–1987

Deputy Director for Intelligence
National Foreign Assessment Center
Deputy Director for Intelligence

	Year Appointed
Loftus Becker	1952
Robert Amory	1953
Ray Cline	1962
R. Jack Smith	1966
Edward Proctor	1971
Sayre Stevens	1976
Robert Bowie	1977
Bruce Clarke	1979
Robert Gates	1982

Deputy Director for Research
Deputy Director for Science & Technology

Herbert Scoville	1962
Albert Wheelon	1963
Carl Duckett	1967
Leslie Dirks	1976
Evans Hineman	1982

Deputy Director for Administration
Deputy Director for Support
Deputy Director for Management & Services
Deputy Director for Administration

Murray McConnel	1950
Walter Wolf	1951
Lawrence White	1953
Robert Bannerman	1965
John Coffey	1971
Harold Brownman	1973
John Blake	1974
Donald Wortman	1979
Max Hugel	1981
Harry Fitzwater	1981

Deputy Director for Plans
Deputy Director for Operations

Allen Dulles	1950
Frank Wisner	1951
Richard Bissell	1958
Richard Helms	1962
Desmond FitzGerald	1965
Thomas Karamessines	1967
William Colby	1973
William Nelson	1973
William Wells	1976
John McMahon	1977
Max Hugel	1981
John Stein	1981
Clare George	1984

Appendix II: Coordinator of Information, 1941

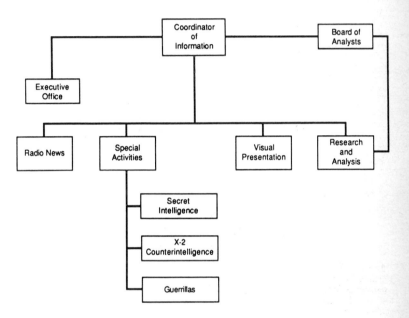

Appendix III: Office of Strategic Services, 1945

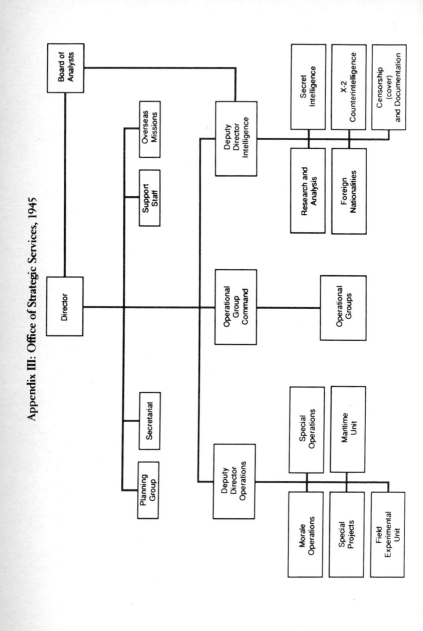

Appendix IV: CIA Organization, 1950

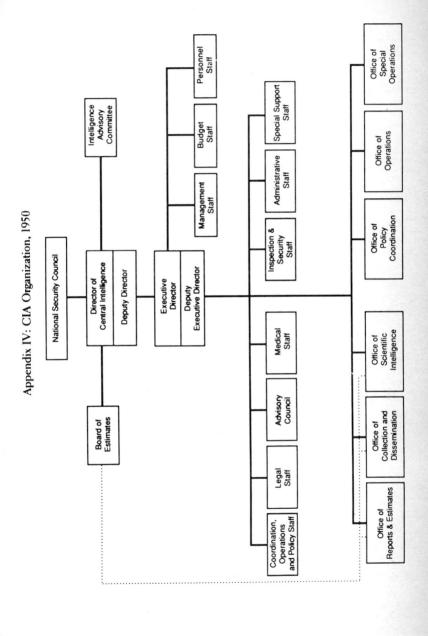

Appendix V: CIA Organization, 1964

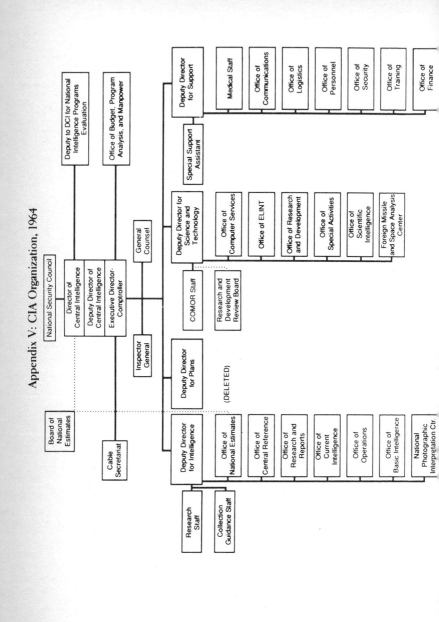

Appendix VI: CIA Organization, 1975

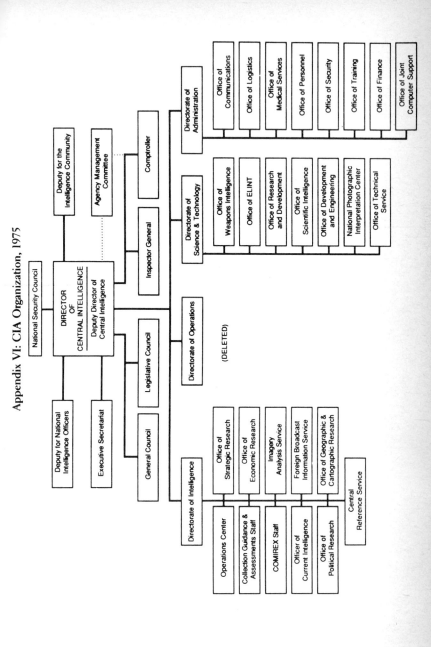

Appendix VII: CIA Organization, 1985

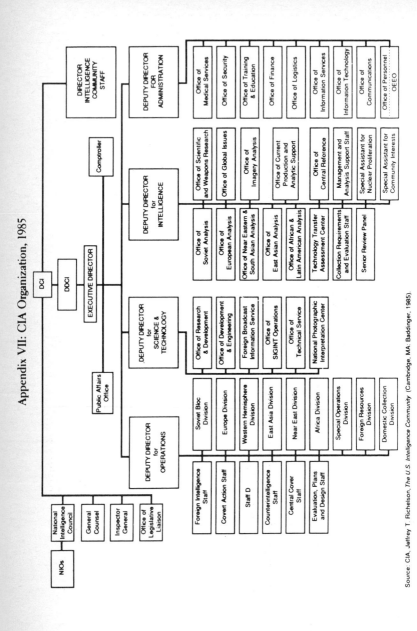

Source: CIA. Jeffrey T. Richelson. *The U.S. Intelligence Community* (Cambridge. MA. Baddinger. 1985).

Appendix VIII: The Intelligence Community

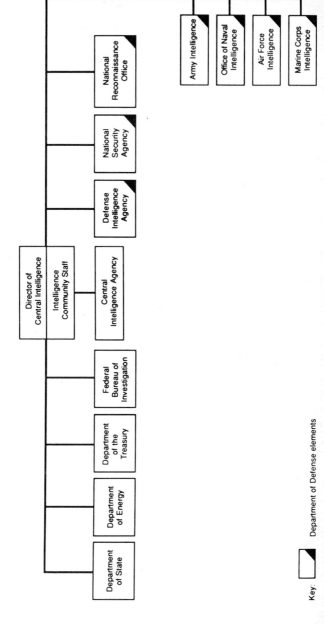

Key: ◣ Department of Defense elements

The Director of Central Intelligence (DCI)—the DCI is the primary adviser to the President and the National Security Council on national intelligence matters. He is the head of the Central Intelligence Agency and of such other staff elements as are required for the discharge of his Intelligence Community responsibilities.

An Executive Order gives the DCI authority to develop the consolidated National Foreign Intelligence Program budget and to direct the analytic and collection tasking of all Intelligence Community elements.

In addition to staff elements of the Office of the DCI, the Intelligence Community consists of the Central Intelligence Agency; the National Security Agency; the Defense Intelligence Agency; the offices within the Department of Defense responsible for collection of specialized national foreign intelligence through reconnaissance programs; the Bureau of Intelligence and Research of the Department of State; and the intelligence elements of the military services, the Federal Bureau of Investigation, and the Departments of Treasury and Energy.

The DCI also serves as chairman of the NSC's Senior Interagency Group when it meets to consider intelligence matters. This committee establishes requirements and priorities, relates these priorities to resources, and reviews the intelligence product for quality and responsiveness.

Intelligence Community Staff—provides primary staff support to the Director of Central Intelligence in his role as senior intelligence officer responsible for a coordinated intelligence effort. The staff carefully coordinates the collection activities of all agencies and departmental elements to minimize duplication and to ensure coverage of major targets and to assure that emphasis is placed on topics of priority interest. It also monitors the dissemination of collected intelligence and consumer satisfaction. The staff provides advice on all matters pertaining to the National Foreign Intelligence Program budget prior to its presentation to Congress. It develops the actual presentation for Congress and monitors the implementation of the budget process.

Central Intelligence Agency (CIA)—has primary responsibility for the clandestine collection of foreign intelligence, for conducting counterintelligence abroad, and for the research and development of technical collection systems. CIA exploits new technology for this purpose. Further, it is responsible for the production of political, military, economic, biographic, sociological, and scientific and technical intelligence to meet the needs of national policymakers. CIA also supports the Director of Central Intelligence in his role as coordinator of the Intelligence Community.

Department of Defense (DOD) Defense Intelligence Agency—satisfies the foreign intelligence and counterintelligence requirements of the Secretary of Defense, the Joint Chiefs of Staff, the Unified and Specified Commands, Defense Department components, and other authorized agencies and provides the military intelligence contribution to national intelligence. It is also responsible for coordinating the intelligence activities of the military services and managing the Defense Attache System, which assigns military attaches to U.S. embassies around the world.

National Security Agency—is responsible for the centralized coordination, direction, and performance of highly specialized technical operations in support of U.S. Government activities to protect U.S. communications and produce foreign intelligence information.

Army Intelligence—provides specialized intelligence support to the Army worldwide and to DOD. Responsibilities include: the collection, production, and dissemination of military and military-related foreign intelligence, including information on indications and warning, capabilities, plans, and weapon systems and equipment; the conduct of counterintelligence activities and the production and dissemination of counterintelligence studies and reports; and the development, procurement and management of tactical intelligence systems and equipment.

Naval Intelligence—works to fulfill the intelligence, counterintelligence, investigative and security requirements and responsibilities of the Department of the Navy. It also provides highly specialized collection and analysis related to the Naval environment.

Air Force Intelligence—conducts and manages collection, processing and analysis, and dissemination activities to meet worldwide Air Force and national intelligence needs. Among the Services, the Air Force has the largest intelligence program, and its Foreign Technology Division is a leading national source of analysis of foreign aircraft and missiles.

National Reconnaissance Office—is run jointly by the CIA and the Air Force. It manages satellite reconnaissance programs for the whole intelligence community. It is responsible for the operation, control, scheduling and assignment of reconnaissance systems, and is supervised by the National Reconnaissance Executive Committee chaired by the Director of Central Intelligence.

Marine Corps Intelligence—focuses on providing responsive intelligence support to Marine Corps tactical commanders, primarily in the amphibious warfare mission area, but also across the full spectrum of Marine Corps worldwide contingency missions. Marine Corps intelligence coordinates closely with and receives extensive support from other Service, theater, and national agencies but, particularly, Naval Intelligence elements, both at the Fleet and National levels.

Department of State—the Department of State's Bureau of Intelligence and Research produces political and some economic intelligence to meet the State Department's needs. It also coordinates State's relations with other foreign intelligence operations, disseminates reports received from U.S. diplomatic and consular posts abroad, and participates in the preparation of National Intelligence Estimates.

Department of Energy (DOE)—openly collects political, economic and technical information concerning foreign energy matters. While DOE does produce and disseminate some foreign intelligence and provides technical and analytical research capabilities to other intelligence operations, it remains primarily a consumer of intelligence.

Department of Treasury—openly collects foreign financial and monetary information and assists the Department of State in collecting economic data. It provides analysis to support the Secretary of the Treasury in carrying out his responsibilities for U.S. economic policy and assists in the production of national intelligence for the President and other senior U.S. officials.

Federal Bureau of Investigation (FBI)—has primary responsibility for counterintelligence *within* the United States. This includes the detection, penetration, prevention and neutralization, by lawful means, of espionage, sabotage and other clandestine intelligence activities directed against the U.S. by hostile foreign intelligence services. FBI works closely with the Central Intelligence Agency, which has primary responsibility for counterintelligence *outside* the United States.

Source: CIA; Jeffrey T. Richelson, *The U.S. Intelligence Community* (Cambridge, MA: Ballinger, 1985).

Appendix IX: The President's Intelligence Organization

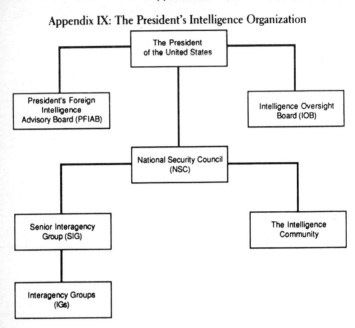

A Presidential Executive Order assigns to the Director of Central Intelligence the responsibility to act as the primary adviser to the President and the National Security Council on national foreign intelligence. To discharge this and other assigned duties, the Director is the appointed—with the advice and consent of the Senate—head of both the Central Intelligence Agency and the Intelligence Community. These relationships and the mechanisms established to sustain them are as follows:

President's Foreign Intelligence Advisory Board (PFIAB)—The PFIAB is maintained within the Executive Office of the President. Its several members serve at the pleasure of the President and are appointed from among trustworthy and distinguished citizens outside Government who are qualified on the basis of achievement, experience, and independence. They serve without compensation. The Board continually reviews the performance of all Government agencies engaged in the collection, evaluation, or production of intelligence or in the execution of intelligence policy. It also assesses the adequacy of management, personnel, and organization in intelligence agencies; and advises the President concerning the objectives, conduct, and coordination of the activities of these agencies. The PFIAB is specifically charged to make appropriate recommendations for actions to improve and enhance the performance of the intelligence efforts of the United States; this advice may be passed directly to the Director of Central Intelligence, the Central Intelligence Agency, or other agencies engaged in intelligence activities.

Intelligence Oversight Board (IOB)—The President's Intelligence Oversight Board functions within the White House. The IOB consists of three members from outside the Government who are appointed by the President. One of these, who serves as chairman, is also a member of the President's Foreign Intelligence Advisory Board. The IOB is responsible for discovering and reporting to the President any intelligence activities that raise questions of propriety or legality in terms of the Constitution, the laws of the U.S., or Presidential Executive Order. The Board is also charged with reviewing the internal guidelines and direction of the Intelligence Community. The IOB is a permanent, non-partisan body.

National Security Council (NSC)—The NSC was established by the National Security Act of 1947 to advise the President with respect to the integration of domestic, foreign, and military policies relating to the national security. The NSC is the highest Executive Branch entity providing review of, guidance for, and direction to the conduct of all national foreign intelligence and counterintelligence activities. The statutory members of the NSC are the President, Vice President, the Secretary of State, and the Secretary of Defense. The Director of Central Intelligence and the Chairman of the Joint Chiefs of Staff participate as advisers. The same 1947 Act also established the CIA as an independent agency subordinate to the NSC.

Senior Interagency Group (SIG)—This committee of the NSC is composed variously of the Director of Central Intelligence, the Assistant to the President for National Security Affairs, the Deputy Secretary of State, the Deputy Secretary of Defense, the Chairman of the Joint Chiefs of Staff, the Deputy Attorney General, the Director of the Federal Bureau of Investigation, and the Director of the National Security Agency. The SIG chairman varies according to the meeting agenda, e.g., the Director of Central Intelligence is chairman when the body addresses intelligence matters. The SIG (Intelligence) is charged to advise and assist the NSC in discharging its authority and responsibility for intelligence policy and intelligence matters. It ensures that important intelligence policy issues requiring interagency attention receive full, prompt, and systematic coordination. It also monitors the execution of previously approved policies and decisions.

Interagency Groups (IGs)—To assist the SIG (Intelligence), Interagency Groups have been established to consider individual policy issues. Each IG consists of representatives of the SIG members and, upon invitation of the IG chairman, others with specific responsibilities for matters being considered. A representative of the Director of Central Intelligence chairs meetings dealing with national foreign intelligence. A representative of the Federal Bureau of Investigation chairs meetings dealing with counterintelligence, except for international terrorism, which is divided between a State Department representative for terrorism abroad and an Attorney General representative for terrorism in the U.S. An indeterminate number of IGs may be designated by the SIG to address such policy issues. The IGs, in turn, may establish working groups as needed to provide support to the approved mechanisms of the NSC for such matters.

The Intelligence Community—The concept of an Intelligence Community is unique in the Government in that it is composed for the most part of elements which have their primary institutional homes in various departments and agencies of the Executive Branch. Many of these elements differ from each other in significant ways. Together they conduct the variety of activities that add up to the entire U.S. national foreign intelligence effort. What binds these diverse components is their common goal: to provide national leaders with the most reliable and accurate intelligence to serve as a sound basis for making timely, informed decisions.

It is the job of the Director of Central Intelligence to make certain that this goal is constantly and successfully pursued. Members of the Intelligence Community advise the Director of Central Intelligence through their representation on a number of specialized committees that deal with intelligence matters of common concern. Chief among these is the National Foreign Intelligence Board, which the Director chairs and which is composed of the heads of Community components and, as observers, heads of the military intelligence services.

Source: CIA.

Appendix X: Directors of Central Intelligence
SIDNEY WILLIAM SOUERS DCI-1
Rear Admiral, U.S. Naval Reserve

Tenure As DCI	23 January 1946–10 June 1946
Birth	30 March 1892, Dayton, Ohio
Education	Attended Purdue University; Miami University (Ohio), B.A., 1914
Appointment	Appointed by President Harry S Truman and sworn in on 23 January 1946*
Relieved	Resigned, effective 10 June 1946
Deputy Director	Kingman Douglass (Acting)
Earlier Career	Private business
	Commissioned Lieutenant Commander in the U.S. Naval Reserve, 1929
	Volunteered for active duty, July 1940
	Promoted to Rear Admiral and made Deputy Chief of Naval Intelligence, 1945
Later Career	Executive Secretary of the National Security Council, 26 September 1947–15 January 1950
	Returned to private business
	Died 14 January 1973

* Before the National Security Act of 26 July 1947, the Director of Central Intelligence served by executive authority as a member of the National Intelligence Authority and head of the Central Intelligence Group.

HOYT SANFORD VANDENBERG DCI-2
Lieutenant General, U.S. Army (Army Air Forces)

Tenure as DCI	10 June 1946–1 May 1947
Birth	24 January 1899, Milwaukee, Wisconsin
Education	Graduated U.S. Military Academy, 1923; Army War College, 1936
Appointment	Appointed by President Harry S Truman, 7 June 1946; sworn in 10 June 1946*
Relieved	Reassigned as Deputy Commander, U.S. Army Air Forces, 1 May 1947
Deputy Director	Kingman Douglass (Acting) until 11 July 1946; Brigadier General Edwin Kennedy Wright, U.S. Army, from 20 January 1947 for remainder of tenure
Earlier Career	Commanded 9th Air Force in Europe during Word War II
	Assistant Chief of Staff, G-2, War Department General Staff, January–June 1946
Later Career	Appointed Vice Chief of Staff of U.S. Air Force with rank of General, U.S. Air Force, effective 1 October 1947
	Chief of Staff, U.S. Air Force, 1948–1953
	Retired from Air Force and Joint Chiefs of Staff, 30 June 1953
	Died 2 April 1954

* See footnote above.

ROSCOE HENRY HILLENKOETTER DCI-3
Rear Admiral, U.S. Navy

Tenure as DCI	1 May 1947–7 October 1950
Birth	8 May 1897, St. Louis, Missouri
Education	Graduated U.S. Naval Academy, 1919 (Class of 1920)

Appointment	Appointed by President Harry S Truman, 30 April 1947; sworn in 1 May 1947

Appointed by President Harry S Truman, 30 April 1947; sworn in 1 May 1947
Recess appointment under new law,* 29 August 1947; sworn in 26 September 1947
Reappointed under new law by President Harry S Truman, 24 November 1947 and confirmed by U.S. Senate, 8 December 1947

Relieved Returned to Navy sea command, 7 October 1950
Deputy Director Brigadier General Edwin Kennedy Wright until 9 March 1949†
Earlier Career Several tours as Assistant Naval Attaché or Naval Attaché, France, 1933–1935, 1938–1940, 1940–1941 (Vichy), and 1946–1947
Officer in Charge of Intelligence, on the staff of Commander in Chief, Pacific Ocean Area (Admiral Chester W. Nimitz), September 1942–March 1943
Promoted to Rear Admiral, 29 November 1946
Later Career Commander, Navy Task Force in the Korean War, November 1950–September 1951
Promoted to Vice Admiral, 9 April 1956
Inspector General of the Navy, 1 August 1956
Retired from Navy, 1 May 1957
Private business
Died 18 June 1982

* The Central Intelligence Agency was established by the National Security Act of July 1947, effective 18 September 1947. It replaced the Central Intelligence Group (CIG).
† There was no Deputy Director from 10 March 1949 to 7 October 1950.

WALTER BEDELL SMITH DCI-4
General, U.S. Army

Tenure as DCI 7 October 1950–9 February 1953
Birth 5 October 1895, Indianapolis, Indiana
Education Attended Butler University briefly
Appointment Appointed by President Harry S Truman, 21 August 1950
Confirmed by U.S. Senate, 28 August 1950
Sworn in, 7 October 1950
Promoted to General, U.S. Army, effective 1 August 1951
Relieved Resigned to become Under Secretary of State, 9 February 1953
Deputy Director William H. Jackson, October 1950–August 1951; Allen W. Dulles for remainder of tenure
Earlier Career During World War II served as Chief of Staff of the Allied Forces in North Africa and the Mediterranean, and then as Chief of Staff to General Eisenhower, Supreme Headquarters, Allied Expeditionary Forces
Promoted to Lieutenant General, 13 January 1944
U.S. Ambassador to the Soviet Union, 1946–1949
Commanding General of the First Army, 1949–1950
Later Career Retired from Army, 9 February 1953
Private business
Died 9 August 1961

ALLEN WELSH DULLES DCI-5

Tenure as DCI 26 February 1953–29 November 1961
Birth 7 April 1893, Watertown, New York
Education Princeton University, B.A., 1914, M.A., 1916; George Washington University, LL.B., 1926

Appointment	Appointed by President Dwight D. Eisenhower, 10 February 1953 (served as Acting Director pending confirmation)
	Confirmed by U.S. Senate, 23 February 1953
	Sworn in, 26 February 1953
	Requested by President-elect John F. Kennedy to continue as Director of Central Intelligence, 10 November 1960
Relieved	Retired, 29 November 1961
Deputy Director	General Charles Pearre Cabell, U.S. Air Force
Earlier Career	U.S. Diplomatic Service, Department of State, 1916–1926
	Practiced law in New York, 1926–1942 and 1946–1950
	Head of Office of Strategic Services office in Berne, Switzerland, 1942–1945
	Previous service in CIA as Deputy Director for Plans, December 1950–August 1951, and Deputy Director of Central Intelligence, 23 August 1951–26 February 1953
Later Career	Retired to private life and writing
	Served on President's Commission on the Assassination of President Kennedy, 1963–1964
	Died 28 January 1969

JOHN ALEX McCONE DCI-6

Tenure as DCI	29 November 1961–28 April 1965
Birth	4 January 1902, San Francisco, California
Education	Attended University of California
Appointment	Appointed by President John F. Kennedy, 27 September 1961
	Sworn in as recess appointee, 29 November 1961
	Confirmed by U.S. Senate, 31 January 1962
Relieved	Resigned, effective 28 April 1965
Deputy Director	Lieutenant General Marshall A. Carter, U.S. Army
Earlier Career	Private business
	Member of President's Air Policy Commission, 1947–1948
	Deputy to the Secretary of Defense, March–November 1948
	Under Secretary of the Air Force, 1950–1951
	Chairman, Atomic Energy Commission, 1958–1960
Later Career	Private business
	Counselor to the President's Commission on Strategic Forces, 1983

WILLIAM FRANCIS RABORN, Jr. DCI-7
Vice Admiral, U.S. Navy (Retired)

Tenure as DCI	28 April 1965–30 June 1966
Birth	8 June 1905, Decatur, Texas
Education	Graduated U.S. Naval Academy, 1928; Naval War College, 1952
Appointment	Appointed by President Lyndon B. Johnson, 11 April 1965
	Confirmed by U.S. Senate, 22 April 1965
	Sworn in, 28 April 1965
Relieved	Resigned, 30 June 1966
Deputy Director	Richard M. Helms
Earlier Career	Director, Special Projects Office, U.S. Navy (developed Polaris missile for Fleet Ballistic Missile System) 1955–1962
	Deputy Chief of Naval Operations (Development), 1962–1963
	Retired from Navy, 1 September 1963
	Private industry, 1963–1965
Later Career	Private business

RICHARD McGARRAH HELMS   DCI-8

Tenure as DCI	30 June 1966–2 February 1973
Birth	30 March 1913, St. Davids, Pennsylvania
Education	Williams College, B.A., 1935
Appointment	Appointed by President Lyndon B. Johnson, 18 June 1966
	Confirmed by U.S. Senate, 28 June 1966
	Sworn in, 30 June 1966
Relieved	Retired, 2 Februry 1973
Deputy Director	Vice Admiral Rufus L. Taylor, U.S. Navy, 13 October 1966–31 January 1969; Lieutenant General Robert E. Cushman, Jr., U.S. Marine Corps, 7 May 1969–31 December 1971; Lieutenant General Vernon A. Walters, U.S. Army, 2 May 1972 for remainder of tenure
Earlier Career	Journalist
	Commissioned into U.S. Naval Reserve, 1942
	Served with Office of Strategic Services and its successors, 1943–1946
	Career in CIA
	Deputy Director for Plans, 1962–1965
	Deputy Director of Central Intelligence, 28 April 1965–30 June 1966
Later Career	Ambassador to Iran, March 1973–January 1977
	Private consultant since 1977
	Member of President's Commission on Strategic Forces, 1983

JAMES RODNEY SCHLESINGER   DCI-9

Tenure as DCI	2 February 1973–2 July 1973
Birth	15 February 1929, New York, New York
Education	Harvard University, A.B., 1950, A.M., 1952 and Ph.D., 1956
Appointment	Appointed by President Richard M. Nixon, 21 December 1972
	Confirmed by U.S. Senate, 23 January 1973
	Sworn in, 2 February 1973
Relieved	Resigned, effective 2 July 1973, to become Secretary of Defense
Deputy Director	Lieutenant General Vernon A. Walters, U.S. Army*
Earlier Career	Assistant and Associate Professor of Economics, University of Virginia, 1955–1963
	Rand Corporation, Senior Staff Member, 1963–1967; Director of Strategic Studies, 1967–1969
	Assistant Director and Acting Deputy Director, Bureau of the Budget, 1969–1970
	Assistant Director, Office of Management and Budget, 1970–1971
	Chairman, Atomic Energy Commission, 1971–1973
Later Career	Secretary of Defense, 1973–1975
	Secretary of Energy, 1977–1979
	Private consultant since 1979
	Counselor to the President's Commission on Strategic Forces, 1983

---

* General Walters served as Acting Director from the departure of Schlesinger, 2 July 1973, until the swearing in of William E. Colby on 4 September 1973.

WILLIAM EGAN COLBY   DCI-10

Tenure as DCI	4 September 1973–30 January 1976
Birth	4 January 1920, St. Paul, Minnesota
Education	Princeton University, B.A., 1940; Columbia University, LL.B., 1947
Appointment	Appointed by President Richard M. Nixon, 10 May 1973
	Confirmed by U.S. Senate, 1 August 1973
	Sworn in, 4 September 1973
Relieved	Retired, 30 January 1976
Deputy Director	Lieutenant General Vernon A. Walters, U.S. Army
Earlier Career	Commissioned into U.S. Army, August 1941
	Served with Office of Strategic Services, 1943–1945
	Attorney in private practice, New York, 1947–1949; with National Labor Relations Board, Washington, D.C., 1949–1950
	Career in CIA
	Chief, Far East Division, 1962–1967
	On leave from CIA, assigned to Agency for International Development as Director of Civil Operations and Rural Development Support, Saigon (with rank of Ambassador), 1968–1971
	Executive Director–Comptroller, 1972–1973
	Deputy Director for Operations, 1973
Later Career	Private law practice

GEORGE HERBERT WALKER BUSH   DCI-11

Tenure as DCI	30 January 1976–20 January 1977
Birth	12 June 1924, Milton, Massachusetts
Education	Yale University, B.A., 1948
Appointment	Appointed by President Gerald R. Ford, 3 November 1975
	Confirmed by U.S. Senate, 27 January 1976
	Sworn in, 30 January 1976
Relieved	Resigned, 20 January 1977*
Deputy Director	Lieutenant General Vernon A. Walters, U.S. Army, until 2 July 1976; E. Henry Knoche for remainder of tenure
Earlier Career	Served in World War II as naval aviator in the Pacific
	Private business
	Member of Congress, 7th District, Texas, 1966–1970
	Ambassador to the United Nations, 1971–1972
	Chairman, Republican National Committee, 1973–1974
	Chief, U.S. Liaison Office, People's Republic of China, 1974–1975
Later Career	Private business and politics
	Sworn in as Vice President of the United States, 20 January 1981

* E. Henry Knoche, Deputy Director of Central Intelligence, served as Acting Director until 9 March 1977, when Admiral Stansfield Turner became Director.

STANSFIELD TURNER   DCI-12
Admiral, U.S. Navy (Retired)

Tenure as DCI	9 March 1977–20 January 1981
Birth	1 December 1923, Highland Park, Illinois
Education	Attended Amherst College, 1941–1943; graduated U.S. Naval Academy, 1946 (Class of 1947); Rhodes Scholar, Oxford University, B.A., 1950, M.A., 1954
Appointment	Appointed by President Jimmy Carter, 8 February 1977
	Confirmed by U.S. Senate, 24 February 1977

	Sworn in, 9 March 1977
	Retired from active duty in U.S. Navy, 31, December 1978
Relieved	Resigned, 20 January 1981
Deputy Director	E. Henry Knoche, until 1 August 1977; Frank C. Carlucci for remainder of tenure
Earlier Career	Director, Systems Analysis Division, Office of the Chief of Naval Operations, 1971–1972
	Promoted to Vice Admiral, 1972
	President, U.S. Naval War College, 1972–1974
	Commander, U.S. Second Fleet, 1974–1975
	Promoted to Admiral, 1975
	Commander-in-Chief, Allied Forces, Southern Europe (NATO), 1975–1977
Later Career	Private consulting and writing

WILLIAM JOSEPH CASEY   DCI-13

Tenure as DCI	28 January 1981–29 January 1987
Birth	13 March 1913, New York, New York
Education	Fordham University, B.S., 1934; St. John's University, LL.B., 1937
Appointment	Appointed by President Ronald Reagan, 13 January 1981
	Confirmed by U.S. Senate, 27 January 1981
	Sworn in, 28 January 1981
Deputy Director	Admiral Bobby Ray Inman, U.S. Navy, 12 February 1981–10 June 1982, John N. McMahon 10 June 1982–18 April 1986, Robert M. Gates, 18 April 1986–
Earlier Career	Lawyer and businessman
	Commissioned into U.S. Naval Reserve, 1943
	Wartime service with Office of Strategic Services, becoming Chief of the Special Intelligence Branch in European Theater of Operations, 1944
	Associate General Counsel at the European Headquarters of the Marshall Plan, 1948
	Chairman of the Securities and Exchange Commission, 1971–1973
	Under Secretary of State for Economic Affairs, 1973–1974
	President and Chairman of the Export-Import Bank of the United States, 1974–1976
	Member, President's Foreign Intelligence Advisory Board, 1976–1977
	Campaign Manager for Ronald Reagan, 1980
Later Career	Private law practice.

WILLIAM HEDGECOCK WEBSTER   DCI-14

Birth	6 March 1924, St. Louis, Missouri
Education	Amherst College, 1947; Washington University Law School, 1949
Appointment	Appointed by President Ronald Reagan, 3 March 1987
Deputy Director	Robert M. Gates
Earlier Career	Private attorney, 1949–1959
	Federal attorney, Eastern District of Missouri, 1959–1961
	Private attorney, 1961–1970
	District court judge, Eastern District of Missouri, 1970–1973
	Judge, U.S. Court of Appeals, 1973–1978
	Director, Federal Bureau of Investigation, 1978–1987

DEPUTY DIRECTORS OF CENTRAL INTELLIGENCE

KINGMAN DOUGLASS   DDCI-1

Tenure as DDCI	2 March 1946–11 July 1946*
Birth	16 April 1896, Oak Park, Illinois
Education	Yale University, B.A., 1918
Appointment	Appointed Assistant Director and Acting Deputy Director by Director of Central Intelligence, Admiral Sidney W. Souers, 2 March 1946
Relieved	Transferred to Office of Special Operations, 11 July 1946
	Resigned from Central Intelligence Group, September 1946
Earlier Career	Investment banking
	Military service in World War II: Senior U.S. Army Air Force intelligence liaison officer in the British Air Ministry; Allied Intelligence Group in Pacific Theater
Later Career	Returned to CIA as Assistant Director, Current Intelligence, 4 January 1951–11 July 1952
	Private business
	Died 8 October 1971

* There was no Deputy Director from 11 July 1946 to 20 January 1947.

EDWIN KENNEDY WRIGHT   DDCI-2
Brigadier General, U.S. Army

Tenure as DDCI	20 January 1947–9 March 1949*
Birth	28 December 1898, Portland, Oregon
Education	Attended Oregon State College
Appointment	Appointed by Director of Central Intelligence, General Hoyt S. Vandenberg, effective 20 January 1947
	Promoted to Brigadier General, U.S. Army, 3 February 1947
Relieved	Returned to Army, 9 March 1949
Earlier Career	Served with General Bradley's 12th Army Group during World War II
	Executive Director of the Intelligence Division, War Department General Staff, February–June 1946
	Executive to the Director of Central Intelligence (Central Intelligence Group), 26 June 1946–20 January 1947
Later Career	Assigned to the Far East Command, U.S. Army, 1949–1952
	Promoted to Major General, U.S. Army, 8 March 1952
	Commander, Military District of Washington, 1952–1954
	Retired from Army, 30 September 1955

* From 10 March 1949 to 7 October 1950, there was no Deputy Director. Second in the Agency's command line was the Executive: Captain Walter C. Ford, U.S. Navy, to 1 June 1949; Captain Clarence L. Winecoff, U.S. Navy, to 7 June 1950; and Lyle T. Shannon (Acting) to 7 October 1950.

WILLIAM HARDING JACKSON   DDCI-3

Tenure as DDCI	7 October 1950–3 August 1951
Birth	25 March 1901, Nashville, Tennessee
Education	Princeton University, B.A., 1924; Harvard University, LL.B., 1928
Appointment	Appointment announced by Director of Central Intelligence, General Walter Bedell Smith, 18 August 1950
	Sworn in, 7 October 1950
Relieved	Resigned, 3 August 1951

Earlier Career	Lawyer
	Served with the U.S. Army, 1942–1945
	Served on intelligence (G-2) staff of General Omar Bradley, 1944
Later Career	Law and private business
	Part-time Special Assistant and Senior Consultant to the Director of Central Intelligence, 23 August 1951–18 February 1956
	Special Assistant to President Eisenhower with various assignments in national security field, 1956–1957
	Died 28 September 1971

ALLEN WELSH DULLES*   DDCI-4

Tenure as DDCI	23 August 1951–26 February 1953
Appointment	Appointed by Director of Central Intelligence, General Walter Bedell Smith, effective 23 August 1951
	Elevated to Director of Central Intelligence, 26 February 1953

* For further information, see entry under DCI-5.

CHARLES PEARRE CABELL   DDCI-5
General, U.S. Air Force

Tenure as DDCI	23 April 1953–31 January 1962
Birth	11 October 1903, Dallas, Texas
Education	Graduated U.S. Military Academy, 1925
Appointment	Appointment announced 24 January 1953 by President Dwight D. Eisenhower
	Nominated under new law by President Eisenhower, 10 April 1953*
	Confirmed by U.S. Senate, 20 April 1953
	Sworn in, 23 April 1953
	Promoted to General, U.S. Air Force, 11 July 1958
Relieved	Resigned as Deputy Director and retired from Air Force, effective 31 January 1962
Earlier Career	Director of Intelligence for U.S. Air Force, 1948–1951
	Director, Joint Staff, Joint Chiefs of Staff, 1951–1953
	Appointed Special Consultant to CIA, 1 February 1952
Later Career	Private consultant
	Died 25 May 1971

* On 4 April 1953 Congress amended the National Security Act of 1947 to establish the position of Deputy Director of Central Intelligence to "act for, and exercise the powers of, the Director during his absence or disability." This amendment also prohibited both Director and Deputy Director positions from being occupied simultaneously by commissioned officers of the armed services, whether in active or retired status. The Deputy Director would henceforth be appointed by the President and confirmed by the U.S. Senate.

MARSHALL SYLVESTER CARTER   DDCI-6
Lieutenant General, U.S. Army

Tenure as DDCI	3 April 1962–28 April 1965
Birth	16 September 1901, Fort Monroe, Virginia
Education	Graduated U.S. Military Academy, 1931; Massachusetts Institute of Technology, M.S., 1936; National War College, 1950

Appointment	Appointed by President John F. Kennedy, 9 March 1962
	Confirmed by U.S. Senate, 2 April 1962
	Sworn in, 3 April 1962
Relieved	Resigned to become Director, National Security Agency, 28 April 1965
Earlier Career	Chief of Staff, North American Air Defense Command, 1957–1959
	Chief of Staff, U.S. 8th Army, Korea, 1959–1960
	Commanding General, Army Air Defense Center, 1961–1962
Later Career	Director, National Security Agency, 1965–1969
	Resigned as Director, National Security Agency, and retired from Army, 28 March 1969

RICHARD McGARRAH HELMS*   DDCI-7

Tenure as DDCI	28 April 1965–30 June 1966
Appointment	Appointed by President Lyndon B. Johnson, 11 April 1965
	Confirmed by U.S. Senate, 22 April 1965
	Sworn in, 28 April 1965
	Elevated to Director of Central Intelligence, 30 June 1966

* For further information, see DCI-8 entry.

RUFUS LACKLAND TAYLOR   DDCI-8
Vice Admiral, U.S. Navy

Tenure as DDCI	13 October 1966–1 February 1969
Birth	6 January 1910, St. Louis, Missouri
Education	Graduated U.S. Naval Academy, 1933
Appointment	Appointed by President Lyndon B. Johnson, 20 September 1966
	Confirmed by U.S. Senate, 7 October 1966
	Sworn in, 13 October 1966
Relieved	Resigned as Deputy Director and retired from Navy, 1 February 1969
Earlier Career	Director of Naval Intelligence, 1963–1966
	Promoted to Vice Admiral and made Deputy Director, Defense Intelligence Agency, June 1966
Later Career	Retired to private life
	Died 14 September 1978

ROBERT EVERTON CUSHMAN, Jr.   DDCI-9
Lieutenant General, U.S. Marine Corps

Tenure as DDCI	7 May 1969–31 December 1971
Birth	24 December 1914, St. Paul, Minnesota
Education	Graduated U.S. Naval Academy, 1935
Appointment	Appointed by President Richard M. Nixon, 6 March 1969
	Confirmed by U.S. Senate, 22 April 1969
	Sworn in, 7 May 1969
Relieved	Resigned to become Commandant of the Marine Corps, 31 December 1971
Earlier Career	Assistant for National Security Affairs to Vice President Richard M. Nixon, 1957–1961
	Commanding General, 3rd Marine Division on Okinawa, 1961–1962
	Assistant Chief of Staff (G-2 and G-3), U.S. Marine Corps, 1962–1964
	Commanding General, Marine Corps Base and 4th Marine Division,

Camp Pendleton, California, 1964–1967
Promoted to Lieutenant General, June 1967
Commander, III Marine Amphibious Force, Vietnam, 1967–1969
Later Career   Commandant of the Marine Corps, 1 January 1972 until retirement, 30 June 1975

VERNON ANTHONY WALTERS   DDCI-10
Lieutenant General, U.S. Army

Tenure as DDCI	2 May 1972–2 July 1976
Birth	3 January 1917, New York, New York
Education	Attended Stonyhurst College, England
Appointment	Appointed by President Richard M. Nixon, 2 March 1972
	Confirmed by U.S. Senate, 10 April 1972
	Sworn in, 2 May 1972
Relieved	Resigned as Deputy Director, effective 2 July 1976, and retired from Army, 31 July 1976
Earlier Career	Member, NATO Standing Group, Washington, 1955–1960 (with additional duties as Staff Assistant to President Eisenhower and Interpreter to the President, Vice President and high officials of the Department of State and the Department of Defense)
	Army Attaché, Italy, 1960–1962; Brazil, 1962–1967; and Defense Attaché, France, 1967–1972
	Promoted to Lieutenant General, March 1972
Later Career	Private consultant
	Appointed Ambassador-at-Large by President Ronald Reagan, June 1981

ENNO HENRY KNOCHE*   DDCI-11

Tenure as DDCI	7 July 1976–1 August 1977
Birth	14 January 1925, Charleston, West Virginia
Education	Graduated Washington and Jefferson College, 1946
Appointment	Appointed by President Gerald R. Ford, 22 April 1976
	Confirmed by U.S. Senate, 30 June 1976
	Sworn in, 7 July 1976
Relieved	Resigned, 1 August 1977†
Earlier Career	Served as naval officer in World War II and Korean War
	Career in CIA
	Director, Foreign Broadcast Information Service, 1972
	Director, Office of Strategic Research, 1973
	Assistant Deputy to the Director for the Intelligence Community, 1975
Later Career	Private business

* Usually styled E. Henry Knoche.
† John F. Blake served as Acting Deputy Director of Central Intelligence, 1 August 1977–10 February 1978.

FRANK CHARLES CARLUCCI   DDCI-12

Tenure as DDCI	10 February 1978–20 January 1981
Birth	18 October 1930, Scranton, Pennsylvania
Education	Princeton University, B.A., 1952; graduate study, Harvard University, 1956

Appointment	Appointed by President Jimmy Carter, 22 December 1977
	Confirmed by U.S. Senate, 9 February 1978
	Sworn in, 10 February 1978
Relieved	Resigned to become Deputy Secretary of Defense, 20 January 1981
Earlier Career	Foreign Service Officer, 1956–1971
	Director, Office of Economic Opportunity, January–September 1971
	Associate and Deputy Director of the Office of Management and Budget, 1971–1972
	Under Secretary of Health, Education and Welfare, 1972–1974
	Ambassador to Portugal, 1974–1977
Later Career	Deputy Secretary of Defense, 1981–1982
	Private business
	Assistant to the President for National Security, 1986–

BOBBY RAY INMAN DDCI-13
Admiral, U.S. Navy

Tenure as DDCI	12 February 1981–10 June 1982
Birth	4 April 1931, Rhonesboro, Texas
Education	University of Texas, B.A., 1950; National War College, 1972
Appointment	Appointed by President Ronald Reagan, 1 February 1981
	Confirmed by U.S. Senate, 5 February 1981
	Sworn in, 12 February 1981
Relieved	Resigned as Deputy Director, 10 June 1982, and retired from Navy, 1 July 1982
Earlier Career	Director of Naval Intelligence, 1974–1976
	Promoted to Vice Admiral, 1976
	Vice Director, Defense Intelligence Agency, 1976–1977
	Director, National Security Agency, 1977–1981
	Promoted to Admiral, 1981
Later Career	Private business

JOHN NORMAN McMAHON DDCI-14

Tenure as DDCI	10 June 1982–18 April 1986
Birth	3 July 1929, East Norfolk, Connecticut
Education	Holy Cross College, B.A., 1951
Appointment	Appointed by President Ronald Reagan, 26 April 1982
	Confirmed by U.S. Senate, 9 June 1982
	Sworn in, 10 June 1982
Earlier Career	Career in CIA
	Associate Deputy Director of Central Intelligence for the Intelligence Community, 1976–1977
	Acting Deputy to the Director of Central Intelligence for the Intelligence Community, 1977–1978
	Deputy Director for Operations, 1978–1981
	Deputy Director for National Foreign Assessment, 1981–1982
	Executive Director of the Central Intelligence Agency, 4 January–10 June 1982
Later Career	Private Business

ROBERT MICHAEL GATES   DDCI-15

Tenure as DDCI	Since 18 April 1986
Birth	25 September 1943, Wichita, Kansas
Education	College of William and Mary, B.A., 1965; Indiana University, M.A., 1966; Georgetown University, Ph.D., 1974
Appointment	Appointed by President Ronald Reagan, 4 March 1986
	Confirmed by U.S. Senate, 18 April 1986
	Sworn in, 18 April 1986
Earlier Career	Joined CIA in 1966
	Current intelligence analyst
	Staff of the special assistant to the DCI for Strategic Arms Limitation
	Assistant National Intelligence Officer for Strategic Programs
	National Security Council Staff, 1974–1979
	Administrative positions in CIA
	National Intelligence Officer for the Soviet Union, 1981–1982
	Deputy Director for Intelligence, 1982–1986
	Chairman, National Intelligence Council, 1983–1986
	Acting Director of Central Intelligence, 15 December 1986–March 1987

Source Notes

Introduction

1. David Atlee Phillips, *The Night Watch: 25 Years of Peculiar Service* (New York: Atheneum, 1977), pp. 190–191, and telephone interview with Phillips, May 20, 1985.
2. Phillips, *The Night Watch*, pp. 189–190, 202, 239–240.
3. Thomas Powers, *The Man Who Kept the Secrets: Richard Helms and the CIA* (New York: Knopf, 1979), p. 337.
4. Interview, July 12, 1983.
5. Interview, November 16, 1984.
6. Phillips, *The Night Watch*, p. 123. James Schlesinger, DCI for some months in 1973, is also credited with coining the term "Knights Templar" as a derogatory phrase to characterize the operational staff. By the time he left the agency, however, he came to have a higher regard for them than for the analysts.
7. Richard Helms, affidavit, *General William C. Westmoreland v. CBS, Inc., et al.*, United States District Court, Southern District of New York, November 23, 1983.
8. Interview, Major General George Keegan, July 16, 1984.
9. Interview, John Waller, November 18, 1983.
10. Winston Spencer Churchill, *The Second World War: The Grand Alliance* (Boston: Houghton Mifflin, 1950), Vol. III, p. 606.
11. Jack Valenti, *A Very Human President* (New York: W. W. Norton, 1975) pp. 317–319, quoted in Larry Berman, *Planning a Tragedy: The Americanization of the War in Vietnam* (New York: W. W. Norton, 1982), p. 111. The example of Munich was even more important during the Kennedy administration, being invoked frequently during the Cuban missile crisis.

1. Cruel Necessity: 1939–1941

1. Interview, James R. Murphy, July 12, 1983.
2. Thomas F. Troy, *Donovan and the CIA* (Frederick, MD: University Publications of America, 1981), p. 29. Troy has given a definitive account of Donovan's career and the birth and development of American intelligence in the 1930s and 1940s. The published book consists of all but about six still secret pages of his history of U.S. intelligence in the decade before World War II and up to 1947. Troy was on the agency's training staff and wrote the history after years of exhaustive research. It is a treasure trove of documents, recollections, and detail.
3. F. H. Hinsley, E. E. Thomas, C. F. G. Ransom, and R. C. Knight, *British Intelligence in the Second World War* (London: Her Majesty's Stationery Office, 1979), Vol. I, pp. 311–312.
4. H. Montgomery Hyde, *The Quiet Canadian: The Secret Service Story of Sir William Stephenson* (London: Hamish Hamilton, 1962), p. 24. Stephenson was instructed in particular "to establish relations on the highest possible level between the British SIS

organization and the U.S. Federal Bureau of Investigation." (Hyde's book was published in America as *Room 3603: The Story of the British Intelligence Center in New York During World War II* [New York: Farrar, Straus & Giroux, 1962].)

5. William Stevenson, *A Man Called Intrepid* (London: Sphere, 1977), p. 121. This book is generally unreliable but does have material from Sir William Stephenson himself, such as the text of the cable he sent to London with this phrase in it.

6. See Hyde, *The Quiet Canadian*, pp. 38–39, for Lothian's remark; see also Anthony Cave Brown, *Wild Bill Donovan: The Last Hero* (New York: Times Books, 1982), pp. 151–152. It is clear that the British realized that Donovan's trip was important, and since he was personally pro-British and anti-Nazi, his report to Roosevelt was likely to be favorable to the British war interest. Accordingly, they opened their doors to him, giving him better access than Ambassador Kennedy ever had and strengthening the credibility of his report in advance.

7. See Brown, *The Last Hero*, p. 151, for a discussion of Donovan's legal device; see Troy, *Donovan and the CIA*, p. 34, for Lothian's hint.

8. Stevenson, *A Man Called Intrepid*, p. 185, makes this assertion.

9. Ibid.

10. See Hyde, *The Quiet Canadian*, pp. 34–41, for a description of the working relationship between Donovan and Stephenson.

11. Brown, *The Last Hero*, p. 152. See Hyde, *The Quiet Canadian*, p. 43, and Troy, *Donovan and the CIA*, p. 36, for an account of the background of Donovan's second trip.

12. Quoted in Troy, *Donovan and the CIA*, p. 40.

13. Brown, *The Last Hero*, p. 161.

14. For a detailed discussion of the power and influence of communists in America during the 1940s, see Harvey Klehr, *The Heyday of American Communism: The Depression Decade* (New York: Basic Books, 1984).

15. Hyde, *The Quiet Canadian*, p. 152.

16. Ibid.

17. Ibid., p. 153. For particulars of the advice Donovan received in this period, see Ray S. Cline, *The CIA Under Reagan, Bush and Casey* (Washington DC: Acropolis Books, 1981), pp. 32–33. Brown, *The Last Hero*, p. 161, and Troy, *Donovan and the CIA*, pp. 419–421, detail the reports Donovan submitted to the President. The British director of Naval Intelligence, Rear Admiral Godfrey, and his aide Commander Ian Fleming—later to be world-famous as the creator of James Bond—traveled specially to Washington in May 1941 to urge the U.S. government to coordinate U.S. intelligence. Godfrey later recalled that "he and Fleming overrated at the time their part in briefing and boosting Big Bill, while underrating the skilful preparatory work done by Little Bill Stephenson" (Troy, *Donovan and the CIA*, p. 59). In his second report to the President, Donovan continued to stress that "the proposed centralized unit will neither displace nor encroach upon the FBI, the Army and Navy Intelligence, or any other department of the Government" (ibid., p. 56).

18. Quoted in William Manchester, *The Glory and the Dream: A Narrative History of America, 1932–1972* (New York: Bantam Books, 1974), p. 191. A Princeton University study subsequently identified the "war scare in Europe," Depression insecurity, and intellectual and emotional immaturity as some of the principal causes of the panic the broadcast generated.

19. Interview, James R. Murphy, July 12, 1983.

20. Interview, Herschel Williams, July 8, 1984. Williams lived at 1 Beekman Place, the apartment building in which Donovan lived. Donovan asked him to run the COI office in Switzerland (the post Allen Dulles later took in OSS), and when Williams refused—because he wanted a regular army post—Donovan offered him the job as head of operations in Morocco.

21. Interview, James R. Murphy, July 12, 1983.

22. David K. E. Bruce, "The National Intelligence Authority," *Virginia Quarterly Review* (July 1946). The COI office in London was set up as a result of a request from President Roosevelt to Winston Churchill on October 24, 1941. A ten-man COI mission

arrived soon after. By 1944 this office, by then OSS, had increased to 2100 people and was the largest overseas mission.

23. Bruce, "The National Intelligence Authority."

24. U.S. War Department, Strategic Services Unit, *War Report of the OSS* (New York: Walker & Co., 1976), exhibit W-18, Brigadier General Donovan to Major General W. B. Smith, September 17, 1943 (hereafter referred to as *War Report of the OSS*).

25. Bruce, "The National Intelligence Authority."

26. Lieutenant General Hoyt S. Vandenberg, director of Central Intelligence. Statement before the Armed Services Committee of the United States Senate on "The National Security Act of 1947," April 27, 1947.

27. Bruce, "The National Intelligence Authority." Later on, when he was in retirement, Donovan made a study of the history of American intelligence. He planned to write a book on George Washington as the country's first spy master, showing that espionage was not un-American (and, no doubt, that if action had been taken earlier along the lines he had proposed, Pearl Harbor might not have happened).

2. In the Service of a Republic: 1942–1945

1. Thomas Braden, "The Birth of the CIA," *American Heritage* (February 1977).

2. Bradley F. Smith, *The Shadow Warriors* (New York: Basic Books, 1983), pp. 100–103. The President was sent the idea about bats by a Mr. Adams of Irwin, Pennsylvania. On February 9, 1942, Roosevelt sent Donovan Adams' memorandum with a covering note saying, "This man is *not* a nut." Despite his refusal to see the pretender Otto von Habsburg, as late as 1944 Roosevelt seriously considered the restoration of the Habsburgs to the Austrian throne. "While considering these frequently bizarre post-Pearl Harbor schemes of Donovan," says Bradley Smith, "it is germane to remember that in such a game there is a catcher as well as a pitcher. Franklin Roosevelt thrived on genteel intrigue . . . In such an environment, it was easy for Roosevelt to give free rein to his imagination and that of William Donovan."

3. Thomas F. Troy, *Donovan and the CIA* (Frederick, MD: University Publications of America, 1981), p. 131.

4. Quoted in Smith, *The Shadow Warriors*, p. 102. Roosevelt was talking to Adolf Berle.

5. Quoted in Troy, *Donovan and the CIA*, p. 109.

6. Ibid.

7. *War Report of the OSS*, memorandum from Donovan to Roosevelt, March 30, 1942. Donovan was excited by the prospect of being in the army again. In February he had sent Roosevelt "an appeal from a soldier to his Commander-in-Chief" that he "be permitted to serve . . . in any combat capacity."

8. Beatrice Bishop Berle and Travis Beal Jacobs, eds., *Navigating the Rapids 1918–1971: From the Papers of Adolf A. Berle* (New York: Harcourt, 1973), pp. 396–397.

9. Ibid., p. 404.

10. Quoted in Troy, *Donovan and the CIA*, p. 153.

11. JCS 155/11/D, directive: "Functions of the Office of Strategic Services," October 27, 1943. See also JCS 155/4/D, directive: "Functions of the Office of Strategic Services," December 23, 1942, and JCS 155/7/D, directive: "Functions of the Office of Strategic Services," April 4, 1943. All are reproduced in Troy, *Donovan and the CIA*, pp. 36–42, 431–434.

12. Richard Harris Smith, *OSS: The Secret History of America's First Central Intelligence Agency* (Berkeley, CA: University of California Press, 1972), pp. 227–228.

13. Ibid., pp. 6–7. See also Charles Thayer, *Hands Across the Caviar* (New York: Lippincott, 1953), p. 119.

14. Interview, Peter Karlow, April 3, 1984. See also Robert Hayden Alcorn, *No Banners, No Bards* (New York: David McKay, 1965), p. 182.

15. Quoted in Robert Hayden Alcorn, *No Bugles for Spies: Tales of the OSS* (New York: David McKay, 1963), p. 134.

16. Quoted in Smith, *OSS*, p. 11.
17. Ibid., p. 17.
18. Ralph de Toledano, *Lament for a Generation* (New York: Farrar, Straus & Giroux, 1960), pp. 78–79.
19. Quoted in Smith, *OSS*, p. 18.
20. Richard Helms, "Remarks at Donovan Award Dinner," May 24, 1983. This was about as close as Richard Helms himself ever came to physical danger.
21. Interview, James R. Murphy, July 12, 1983.
22. Interview, Lawrence Houston, July 8, 1983.
23. This and the previous quote are from an interview with James R. Murphy, July 12, 1983. Despite Ultra, the great intelligence failure of the war was not alerting Eisenhower to the German plan to attack in the Ardennes in 1944. Neither the British nor the American intelligence services managed to analyze accurately the information they had and so to predict the attack. For the OSS, Donovan's emphasis on operations had not paid off.
24. Helms, "Remarks at Donovan Award Dinner," May 24, 1983.
25. Ibid.
26. Anthony Cave Brown, *Wild Bill Donovan: The Last Hero* (New York: Times Books, 1982), pp. 428–431.
27. Brown, *The Last Hero*, p. 681. The OSS was Nazi-proof but not communist-proof. There is some question whether the Bishop traffic was compromised by a leak to the Russians from within OSS. As to the information in the Bishop traffic, it should have surprised no one that the Russians intended to swallow up Rumania. Rumania had fought with the Germans against Russia until 1944. King Michael was not being democratic or liberal when he changed sides; he was trying to join the winning side.
28. Thomas Powers, *New York Review of Books*, May 12, 1983.
29. David Wise and Thomas B. Ross, *The Espionage Establishment* (New York: Random House, 1967), p. 14.
30. Brown, *The Last Hero*, p. 275.
31. Ibid., pp. 271–273.
32. Kim Philby, *My Silent War* (London: Macgibbon & Kee, 1968), pp. 61–62. Philby's book is a masterpiece of deception, having been written with close attention to fact in order to give credibility to damaging interpretation. Thus he indicates that Dansey rejected the Kolbe/Dulles material because Dansey was jealous of Dulles for having scored an intelligence coup that SIS had failed to respond to. Philby suggests that Dansey and Dulles did not like each other—which, according to other accounts, was not the case—and in general attempts to plant suspicions about Anglo-American relations and to sow discord between the intelligence services of both countries.
33. Anthony Cave Brown, *Bodyguard of Lies* (New York: Bantam Books, 1976), pp. 312–313. The Russians had their own German underground, the Rote Kapelle, and were anxious to put rivals out of business. Philby (*My Silent War*, p. 62) claims to have been the person who demonstrated that the Kolbe/Dulles material was genuine by checking it against Ultra information. This may be true; a check of the material was done in this way—although it is not certain that Philby did it. For more background, see Anthony Read and David Fisher, *Colonel Z: The Secret Life of a Master of Spies* (London: Hodder & Stoughton, 1984), pp. 319–321.
34. Brown, *The Last Hero*, p. 280.
35. Quoted ibid., p. 283. The OSS analyst was Ferdinand Lammot Belin.
36. Ibid., p. 285.
37. Interview, Gerhard Van Arkel, November 11, 1983.
38. Ibid.
39. Ibid. Molden was in Hungary in 1956 at the time of the Russian invasion. He was a newspaper publisher and then a publisher of books in Vienna.
40. Quoted in Leonard Mosley, *Dulles: A Biography of Eleanor, Allen and John Foster Dulles and Their Family Network* (New York: Dial Press/James Wade, 1978), p. 138.
41. Interview, Gerhard Van Arkel, November 11, 1983.

42. Quoted in Mosley, *Dulles*, p. 175.
43. Wilhelm Hoegner, *Der Schwierige Aussenseiter* (Munich: Isar Verlag, 1959), pp. 172–173, quoted in translation in Smith, *OSS*, p. 221.
44. Troy, *Donovan and the CIA*, p. vi. Roosevelt, it seems, was not enamored of a peacetime intelligence organization comparable to the OSS, and in any case he felt he could deal with Stalin and achieve a postwar settlement amicably.
45. *Washington Times-Herald, New York Daily News, Chicago Tribune,* February 9, 1945. Donovan immediately wrote to Roosevelt refuting the charges, stating that personnel would be trained analysts and removed from the policing realm. His refutation was published in *The New York Times*, February 13, 1945. See Troy, *Donovan and the CIA*, p. 255.
46. Interview, Gerhard Van Arkel, November 11, 1983. By 1945 there should have been enough information to tell if the massive deployment of resources required to build the Redoubt was taking place. Falling for the story was naïve.
47. Allen W. Dulles, *The Secret Surrender* (New York: Harper & Row, 1966), pp. 77, 87.
48. Quoted in Mosley, *Dulles*, p. 178.
49. Quoted in Brown, *The Last Hero*, p. 732.
50. Quoted in Dulles, *The Secret Surrender*, p. 162.
51. Ibid., p. 165.
52. Ibid., pp. 167–217.
53. Quoted in Troy, *Donovan and the CIA*, pp. 280–281.
54. JCS 155/11/D, directive: "Functions of the Office of Strategic Services," October 27, 1943, reproduced in Troy, *Donovan and the CIA*, pp. 439–442.
55. Corey Ford, *Donovan of OSS* (Boston: Little, Brown, 1970), pp. 202–203.
56. FNB Papers, memorandum by Donovan, April 24, 1942. The FNB was created under the auspices of the COI and continued under the OSS.
57. FNB Papers, N. 147, September 1, 1943.
58. Ford, *Donovan of OSS, pp.* 148–152. Interview, Peter Karlow, July 28, 1983. U.S. locomotive manufacturers who had sold locomotives overseas had plans and precise information about the railway systems for which the locomotives were designed. Locomotives had to be built for the system they were to serve, so manufacturers had to know the gauge of the track, the minimum and maximum gradients, the size of the tunnels and their length, the distance between fueling and watering points, the signaling system, the maximum weight the rail could take, the number of cars the locomotive would be expected to pull, and so on.
59. Ray S. Cline, *Secrets, Spies and Scholars: Blueprint of the Essential CIA* (Washington, DC: Acropolis Books, 1976), p. 76.
60. *The New York Times*, April 26, 1966.
61. *The New York Times*, June 2, 1963, interview with Jack Raymond.
62. Between 1941 and 1943 Casablanca was one of the busiest airports in the world. It was not idly chosen as the setting for the film of its name. It was a leading jumping-off point to the Americas from Europe.
63. Brown, *The Last Hero*, p. 310. Donovan instructed Doering to establish the FBQ Corporation in New York to buy two commercial radio listening posts and to operate as a cryptanalytical department for COI without publicly disclosing the fact.
64. Interview, James R. Murphy, July 12, 1983.
65. Ford, *Donovan of OSS*, p. 127.
66. Richard Helms, "Remarks at Donovan Award Dinner," May 24, 1983.
67. Interview, Lawrence Houston, December 2, 1983. On August 29, 1944, an OSS team led by Frank Wisner arrived in Bucharest to organize the repatriation of 1350 allied airmen who had been prisoners in Rumania. In Bucharest Wisner carried out a top secret OSS mission, codenamed Bughouse, to collect as much information as possible about German and Rumanian anti-Soviet intelligence efforts. Out of Bughouse came the Bishop traffic. It was the first American operation with the Soviets as the intelligence target.
68. David Kahn, *Hitler's Spies* (London: Arrow Books, 1980), pp. 418–422.

69. Quoted in Mosley, *Dulles*, p. 232.
70. Quoted ibid., p. 234.

3. *Fear and Emergency: 1945–1947*

1. George Kennan, interviewed in *Children of Violence*, TV documentary (1984), a Bill Jersey and Jim Belson Production for the Corporation of Public Broadcasting, 4560 Horton Street, Suite 420, Emerville, CA 94608.
2. Joseph Alsop, *FDR: A Centenary Remembrance* (New York: Pocket Books, 1982), p. 151. The Ukraine famine occurred in the early 1930s and was accurately reported by another Moscow correspondent, William Stoneman, of the *Chicago Daily News*. After his report was published, the Soviet authorities arranged for Duranty to go on a guided tour of the Ukraine, and "he sent back word that there were no real signs of horrors."
3. Thomas F. Troy, *Donovan and the CIA* (Frederick, MD: University Publications of America, 1981), pp. 219–221. There was an ideological view inherent in Smith's question: the war would soon be over and the concerns of peace and domestic politics would soon be paramount. Smith was an ardent New Dealer, and his instinct, therefore, was for a return to the isolationist America of the New Deal.
4. *The New York Times*, September 5, 1945.
5. For the background to this struggle, as well as the texts of documents, see Troy, *Donovan and the CIA*, pp. 226–227. Otto C. Doering, Jr., was the senior OSS officer who advised Donovan to refute Carter's allegation in regard to the British. He had joined Donovan's law firm in 1929 and later served as general counsel, executive officer, and assistant director of OSS. Along with Colonel G. Edward Buxton, Doering was one of Donovan's principal assistants.
6. Bradley F. Smith, *The Shadow Warriors* (New York: Basic Books, 1983), pp. 403–404.
7. Thomas Braden, "The Birth of the CIA," *American Heritage* (February 1977).
8. Troy, *Donovan and the CIA*, p. 280.
9. Donovan said that he wanted to wait until the "entire case" against OSS was made "before we take any obvious countermeasures" (Troy, *Donovan and the CIA*, p. 281).
10. Troy, *Donovan and the CIA*, pp. 287–290. Arthur Krock argued along the same lines in an article in *The New York Times* on August 19, 1945. He pointed out that since America was now taking its place as a leader in world finance, world diplomacy, and world peace, an active intelligence service looking to the outside was crucial to avoid prewar mistakes.
11. Interview, Tom Braden, November 14, 1983.
12. Interview, James R. Murphy, July 12, 1983.
13. Interview, Lawrence Houston, July 8, 1983.
14. Smith, *The Shadow Warriors*, p. 408, and Troy, *Donovan and the CIA*, p. 303. Anthony Cave Brown, *Wild Bill Donovan: The Last Hero* (New York: Times Books, 1982), pp. 786–787, gives a figure of "about 16,000 men and women" as the OSS's strength in September 1945. Accurate figures are hard to establish because there were so many transfers between the regular services and the OSS. In 1946, SSU was budgeted on the basis of 2500 staff.
15. Smith, *The Shadow Warriors*, p. 409.
16. Troy, *Donovan and the CIA*, pp. 464–465.
17. Braden, "The Birth of the CIA."
18. He was also Admiral William Leahy's nominee. See Harry S Truman, *Memoirs: Years of Trial and Hope* (New York: Doubleday, 1956), p. 57.
19. For Donovan's comments on Truman's directive, see *The New York Times*, January 23, 1946.
20. This was a point picked out by *The New York Times*, January 23, 1946, in its treatment of the directive and Donovan's views.
21. The Eberstadt Committee's chapter on intelligence was apparently written by the then Captain Sidney W. Souers, Office of Naval Intelligence planning chief. Eberstadt singled out the importance of coordinated "joint intelligence" among the various departments. For the details, see Troy, *Donovan and the CIA*, pp. 315–316.

22. Quoted ibid., p. 318.
23. Interview, Lawrence Houston, July 8, 1983. At his retirement from the CIA in 1974 Houston in his farewell speech said: "I don't know how many of you remember the work of the Lovett Committee in December of '45, which, after bitter debate for weeks, got acceptance of the concept of a central intelligence entity as an independent function. There was still a long way to go. But again I wonder how many people now working for the Agency remember the first Director of Central Intelligence, Rear Admiral Sidney W. Souers, who drafted the directive of January 22, 1946, that set up the Central Intelligence Group. CIG was technically illegal. You cannot have an operating agency going on for more than a year without a statutory basis" (quoted in Central Intelligence Agency, "Lawrence Houston," *Studies in Intelligence*, 1974).
24. Troy, *Donovan and the CIA*, p. 369.
25. Quoted in Charles W. Kegley, Jr., and Eugene R. Wittkopf, *American Foreign Policy—Pattern and Process* (New York: St. Martin's Press, 1979), p. 41.
26. Truman, *Memoirs: Years of Trial and Hope*, p. 2.
27. Vandenberg was the most eminent Republican convert from isolationism.
28. See pp. 144–49. Stories of Soviet spy rings operating in the United States turned out to be true. Unknown to the American public, military and FBI code-breakers had discovered that the Soviet Embassy in Washington was coordinating spying in America.
29. *Christian Science Monitor*, April 14, 1947.
30. See, for example, Trohan's article in the *Chicago Tribune*, June 15, 1947, with the headline "CIG Secretly Creates U.S. 'Gestapo' of 1500 Agents."
31. See pp. 133–38 for a discussion of the merging of the Office of Policy Coordination into the CIA. The Office in effect became the agency's covert operation arm, being integrated with the agency's own smaller Office of Special Operations. See also Harry Rositzke, review of Chapman Pincher, *Too Secret Too Long* (New York: St. Martin's Press, 1984), in *The New York Times Book Review*, February 17, 1985, where he says that the covert operation function did not really come aboard the CIA until 1952 when the OPC and the OSO merged. The covert operation function came aboard the agency in 1950 when Bedell Smith took control of OPC, two years before the OPC-OSO merger.
32. *The New York Times*, July 27, 1947. Also interview, Lawrence Houston, July 8, 1983.

4. Dawn Like Thunder: 1947–1948

1. *The New York Times*, July 20, 1948.
2. Ibid., July 22, 1948.
3. Ibid., April 16, 1948.
4. Ibid., July 22, 1948.
5. Quoted in Leonard Mosley, *Dulles: A Biography of Eleanor, Allen, and John Foster Dulles and Their Family Network* (New York: Dial Press/James Wade, 1978), p. 112.
6. *The New York Times*, July 23, 1948.
7. Interview, Lawrence Houston, July 8, 1983.
8. The Office of Special Operations was the renamed Strategic Services Unit that Vandenberg had brought into the Central Intelligence Group from the War Department in August 1946. See Thomas Powers, *The Man Who Kept the Secrets: Richard Helms and the CIA* (New York: Knopf, 1979), p. 29, and *Final Report of the Select Committee to Study Governmental Operations with Respect to Intelligence Activities*, United States Senate (Washington, DC: U.S. Government Printing Office, 1976), 94th Congress, 2d Session, Book IV, "History of the Central Intelligence Agency," by Anne Karalekas, p. 14. The Church Committee is hereafter referred to as *Final Report*.
9. "Memorandum Respecting Section 202 (Central Intelligence Agency) of the Bill to Provide for a National Defense Establishment," submitted by Allen W. Dulles, April 25, 1947, in U.S. Congress, Senate Committee on Armed Services, *National Defense Establishment (Unification of the Armed Services)*, Hearings on S. 758 (Washington DC: U.S. Government Printing Office, 1947), 80th Congress, 1st Session, p. 526.
10. Ray S. Cline, *Secrets, Spies and Scholars: Blueprint of the Essential CIA* (Washington, DC: Acropolis Books, 1976), p. 120.

11. Interview, November 21, 1984.
12. Arnold A. Rogow, *James Forrestal: A Study of Personality, Politics and Policy* (New York: Macmillan, 1963), pp. 155–156. On August 19, 1944, for example, Forrestal met de Gaulle in Algiers and told him that there were widespread fears in America that a Russian menace would be substituted for a German one after Hitler was defeated.
13. *The Washington Post*, May 27, 1982. Church had served in military intelligence in China during World War II and had there witnessed a country in the process of being grabbed. In the Senate, Church was one of the leading opponents of gun-control legislation; his perspective was one of tough individualism and tough cold war.
14. See, for example, Joseph Alsop, *FDR: A Centenary Remembrance* (New York: Pocket Books, 1982), pp. 115–117, for a discussion of the relationship between Roosevelt, public opinion, the press, and government policy in 1940.
15. Interview, November 18, 1984.
16. William Manchester, *The Glory and the Dream: A Narrative History of America, 1932–1972* (New York: Bantam Books, 1974), pp. 433–434. Manchester credits this as the moment when "the flag of world leadership began to pass from the dying British Empire to the United States." This is debatable. Ever since the 1880s the United States had had the world's most powerful economy. In 1919 the role of world leadership had, in effect, been offered to America, which had declined to accept. Within two years of Pearl Harbor it was obvious to everyone that U.S. economic and military strength were winning the war. More realistically, the flag of world leadership had passed to the United States after World War I but was not unfurled until after 1945.
17. Dean Acheson, *Present at the Creation* (New York: W. W. Norton, 1969), p. 219. For an insight into Acheson's instrumental role in U.S. foreign policy under Truman, see pp. 217–219.
18. Michael Charlton, *The Price of Victory* (London: British Broadcasting Corporation, 1983), p. 15. This is a fairly sweeping statement by Jebb. Roosevelt was more of a hegemonist than a world divider. He did not want a power comparable to the United States. He wanted to see an end to the old empires. He felt if he and Uncle Joe could get together, they could settle the running of the world rather than its division.
19. Speech to U.S.–Soviet Friendship Rally, Madison Square Garden, New York, September 12, 1946 (reported in *The New York Times*, September 13, 1946).
20. Quoted in Daniel Yergin, *Shattered Peace* (London: André Deutsch, 1978), pp. 253–254, as diary entry on September 19, 1946. Truman dismissed Wallace the following day.
21. Ibid., p. 254.
22. *USSR: Policy and Information Statement* (Washington, DC: Department of State, May 15, 1946).
23. Quoted in John L. Gaddis, *The United States and the Origins of the Cold War* (New York: Columbia University Press, 1972), p. 299.
24. Quoted ibid., p. 300.
25. Quoted ibid., p. 300.
26. Quoted ibid., p. 300.
27. Quoted in James F. Byrnes, *All in One Lifetime* (New York: Harper & Bros., 1958), pp. 401–402. For Truman's overall position see Harry S Truman, *Memoirs: Years of Trial and Hope 1946–1952* (New York: Doubleday, 1956), pp. 93–109. Between 1942 and 1945 the Soviet Union received Lend-Lease aid worth $10.982 billion from the United States.
    Truman was already rewriting history. The British/Soviet presence in Iran dated from the war and had occurred in order to ensure that Iran did not side with the Axis powers.
28. Walter Bedell Smith, *My Three Years in Moscow* (Philadelphia: J. B. Lippincott, 1950), p. 53.
29. *Foreign Relations of the United States: The Conference of Berlin (The Potsdam Conference)* (Washington, DC: Department of State, 1960), Vol. 1, p. 9. See also Winston S. Churchill, *Triumph and Tragedy* (Boston: Houghton Mifflin, 1953), pp. 489–490. Churchill was speaking for himself and Britain; the United States did have some idea of

what was going on behind the iron curtain because of its Jewish/Russian/Ukrainian / Latvian / Estonian / Lithuanian / Polish / Czech / German / Hungarian / Rumanian/Bulgarian/Yugoslav/Bylorussian ethnic community connections.

30. Interview, Lawrence Houston, July 8, 1983.
31. Harry S Truman, *Memoirs: Year of Decisions* (New York: Doubleday, 1955), p. 421.
32. *The New York Times*, February 17, 1946.
33. "For eighteen long months I had done little else but pluck people's sleeves, trying to make them understand the nature of the phenomenon with which we in the Moscow embassy were daily confronted and which our government and people had to learn to understand if they were to have any chance of coping successfully with the problems of the postwar world" (George F. Kennan, *Memoirs 1925–50* [New York: Pantheon Books, 1967], p. 293).
34. Ibid., p. 550. Excerpts from the telegram are given ibid., pp. 547–559.
35. Ibid., p. 554.
36. Ibid., p. 557.
37. Ibid., pp. 294–295.
38. *The New York Times*, March 6, 1946. The speech implied that there must not be full-scale war and so there must be containment organizations.
39. *Time*, March 18, 1946.
40. Gaddis, *The United States and the Origins of the Cold War*, p. 315.
41. Dewey W. Grantham, *The United States Since 1945* (New York: McGraw-Hill, 1975), p. 20. For Truman's own explanation, see his *Memoirs: Years of Trial and Hope 1946–1952*, pp. 105–110:

> Never before in history has one nation faced so vast an undertaking as that confronting the United States of repairing and salvaging the victors as well as the vanquished. The complete surrender of the Axis powers did not bring any relaxation or rest for our people. They had to face and were ready to make whatever new sacrifices were necessary to insure the peace. This was the most destructive of all wars. There were no battle fronts, and civilian populations were, unhappily, military targets as much as were the armed forces, because they were part of the industrial and economic centers involved in a total war. . . .
>
> Nations, if not continents, had to be raised from the wreckage. Unless the economic life of these nations could be restored, peace in the world could not be reestablished.
>
> In the first two years following V-J Day the United States provided more than *fifteen billion dollars* in loans and grants for the relief of victims of war. We did everything humanly possible to prevent starvation, disease, and suffering. We provided substantial aid to help restore transportation and communications, and we helped rebuild wrecked economic systems in one major country after another.
>
> For the first time in the history of the world a victor was willing to restore the vanquished as well as to help its allies. This was the attitude of the United States. But one of our allies took the conqueror's approach to victory.

U.S. deaths in World War II were about 300,000; Soviet war deaths were on the order of 20–25 million. The Soviet view should not have been unexpected. Truman was expressing a lack of imagination that was later to have expensive consequences in the unimaginative, brutal pursuit of the cold war: the assassination plots; the support of ex-Nazis; some of the covert operations. For a severe critique of the U.S. Army's willingness to do deals with ex-Nazis after 1945, see John Loftus, *The Belarus Secret*, Nathan Miller, ed. (New York: Knopf, 1982). Loftus blames the State Department, arguing that from 1948 the Office of Policy Coordination (see pp. 166–69) under Frank Wisner actively tried to recreate Nazi networks in eastern Europe.

42. Rogow, *James Forrestal*, pp. 4–6, 17.
43. See Kennan, *Memoirs, 1925–50*, pp. 325–342, for the background and thinking that went into the recommendations of the Policy Planning Staff.
44. Quoted in Thomas Powers, *The Man Who Kept the Secrets: Richard Helms and the CIA* (New York: Knopf, 1979) p. 31.

45. Interview, July 8, 1983. Relations between OPC/CIA and the FBI formed a further subplot. On September 22, 1948, Frank Wisner and J. Edgar Hoover reached an agreement that has remained effective:

> It is understood that in the discharge of the duties and obligations laid upon the Office of Policy Coordination by the National Security Council, it is necessary for this Office to have dealings with individuals and groups of foreign nationalities within and without the United States and to sponsor the movement from time to time of such individuals and representatives of such groups between the United States and foreign countries. The Office of Policy Coordination recognizes the primary responsibility of the FBI in the field of United States domestic security, and the FBI acknowledges that it is essential for the Office of Policy Coordination to have direct dealings with the individuals and groups aforementioned. (Frank G. Wisner, Memorandum for the Record, "Cooperation and Liaison Between Federal Bureau of Investigation and Office of Policy Coordination, CIA," draft)

Behind this lay OSS practice of interviewing refugees and Americans with experience abroad. This was translated into the CIA's Contact Division, which operates openly within the United States, dealing with anybody who volunteers information that may be of intelligence use.

46. Quoted in Mosley, *Dulles*, p. 243.
47. Interview, July 8, 1983.
48. *Final Report*, IV, pp. 6–9.
49. E. H. Cookridge, *George Blake: Double Agent* (New York: Ballantine Books, 1982), pp. 60–62.
50. Ibid., pp. 61–63.
51. Ibid., pp. 63–64.
52. Sanche de Gramont, *The Secret World* (New York: Putnam's, 1962), p. 454.
53. For the story of the Ukrainian resistance and various other covert operations that took place at the time, see Harry Rositzke, *The CIA's Secret Operations* (New York: Reader's Digest Press, 1977). For Wisner's and the U.S. Army's use of ex-Nazis, see Loftus, *The Belarus Secret.*
54. By 1948 the Gehlen organization had taken shape under U.S. Army auspices, and when West Germany was established as independent in 1949, Gehlen was appointed head of the Federal Intelligence Service, a position he held until his retirement in 1968. His agent close to Ulbricht was Hermann Kastner, who became a member of the East German cabinet. Another agent, Walter Gramsch, was in the East German intelligence service.

When the CIA became responsible for liaison with the Gehlen organization, a CIA officer in Austria, Henry Pleasants, who was later to become station chief in Switzerland, was sent to Frankfurt to deal with Gehlen. He established an office within the Gehlen organization's headquarters at Pullach, outside Munich, under James H. Critchfield, who was transferred to the CIA from the army and went on to become a senior CIA operative. Urged by Pleasants and Critchfield, Gehlen expanded his organization's activities from concentrating on order-of-battle intelligence to espionage (Gehlen had a few contacts from the war period in the Eastern bloc, which he activated), research, and analysis.

Gehlen's work always depended far more on signals intelligence and radio monitoring than on reports by agents in the field. The U.S. Army and, initially, the CIA, hoped for more from Gehlen than he was equipped to provide. He was also bedeviled by the same sort of bureaucratic in-fighting that plagued the OSS. Not to be outdone by the CIA, Britain's foreign espionage organization, MI-6, backed Gehlen's principal rival for the laurels of German intelligence, Otto John, head of the Bundesamt für Verfassungsschutz (BfV), the West German counterintelligence and security service. (The Federal Republic of Germany did not come into being until May 23, 1949; until then the Western Allies were legally responsible as occupying powers in the West; the Russians in the East.)

Otto John, who had been active in the bomb plot against Hitler in July 1944, defected (or so it was believed) to the East in 1954. MI-6 and the CIA were appalled. The evidence suggested that John defected not for ideological reasons but because he was losing the bureaucratic battle for dominance to the CIA's Gehlen. He broadcast for the East Germans and then came back to the West claiming that he had been kidnapped. He was charged with treason and found guilty by a federal court. He was released from jail in 1958. Subsequently the CIA considered that there were adequate grounds for accepting the view that John had been kidnapped and had not been a Soviet or East German agent. For the British view of the affair, see *The Observer*, January 6, 1985. One of Gehlen's agents, Horst Eitner, was hired by MI-6 to obtain information about the Gehlen organization and its contacts in the East. Eitner worked with George Blake, and in 1961 both were exposed as Soviet agents.

55. See David C. Martin, *Wilderness of Mirrors* (New York: Ballantine Books, 1980), pp. 74–77, for the details of Silver.
56. Quoted ibid., p. 75.
57. Ibid., p. 75.

5. Double Trouble: 1945–1951

1. Harry S Truman, *Memoirs: Years of Trial and Hope* (New York: Doubleday, 1956), p. 306.
2. Central Intelligence Agency, "Estimate of the Effects of the Soviet Possession of the Atomic Bomb upon the Security of the United States and upon the Probabilities of Direct Soviet Military Action," ORE 91-49, April 6, 1950. The title of the Estimate indicates the sense of tension and emergency at the time—everything was seen in terms of Soviet aggression and possible war. The work on the Estimate began in October 1949 and was submitted for coordination with the other agencies in February 1950. The foreword to the Estimate stated:

   It was apparent that no early agreement could be reached. In view of the time already elapsed and the broader significance of many of the issues that emerged during the study, CIA considered that it was more important to publish this paper at this time than to attempt the time-consuming, if not impossible, task of obtaining agreement. It considered, furthermore, that it would be more useful to publish a straightforward point of view, accompanied by contrary opinions, than to present a watered-down version.

   This was a clear statement of CIA confidence. Inherent in the CIA's conclusions in the paper was an explanation of why the agency was expected to monitor whole societies and engage at all levels of activity: it had to counter Soviet subversion, which was considered to be the first step in the Soviet takeover of the world in ways that involved neither war nor peace.
3. Quoted in Daniel Yergin, *Shattered Peace: The Origins of the Cold War and the National Security State* (London: André Deutsch, 1978), p. 154.
4. Quoted in David C. Martin, *Wilderness of Mirrors* (New York: Ballantine Books, 1980), p. 10. The journalist Isaac Don Levine related this story to Chambers.
5. Allen Weinstein, *Perjury—The Hiss-Chambers Case* (New York: Knopf, 1978), p. 356.
6. Martin, *Wilderness of Mirrors*, p. 41.
7. Quoted in ibid., p. 150.
8. For a detailed treatment of the Rosenberg case, see Ronald Radosh and Joyce Milton, *The Rosenberg File—A Search for the Truth* (London: Weidenfeld & Nicolson, 1983).
9. Quoted in Martin, *Wilderness of Mirrors*, p. 11.
10. Nigel West, *MI5: British Security Service Operations, 1909–1945* (London: Triad/Granada, 1983), pp. 88–90.
11. Krivitsky's death was officially given as suicide and referred to as such by Kim Philby in

My Silent War (London: Grove Press, 1968), p. 78. See also Weinstein, *Perjury*, p. 331, and West, *MI5*, p. 88.

12. Interview, James Angleton, January 13, 1983. See also Bruce Page, David Leitch, and Phillip Knightley, *Philby: The Spy Who Betrayed a Generation* (London: Sphere, 1969), p. 210.
13. Quoted in Martin, *Wilderness of Mirrors*, p. 47.
14. Quoted ibid.
15. Michael Burke, *Outrageous Good Fortune* (New York: Little, Brown, 1984), p. 145.
16. Philby, *My Silent War*, p. 126.
17. Ibid., p. 114.
18. Ibid., p. 128.
19. The "third party rule" has so far precluded any public statement of the facts of the Philby case. This rule is that no intelligence service will discuss an allied service's affairs with a third party. In documents released under Freedom of Information legislation, the unreleased portions frequently refer to the involvements of other intelligence services, especially the British service. For a fascinating discussion of the layers of deceit in the Philby case, see Page, Leitch, and Knightley, *Philby: The Spy Who Betrayed a Generation*. For an authoritative discussion of the relationships between Philby, Burgess, and Maclean and their importance, see Robert Cecil, "The Cambridge Comintern," in Christopher Andrew and David Dilks, eds., *The Missing Dimension: Governments and Intelligence Communities in the Twentieth Century* (London: Macmillan, 1984), pp. 169–198. For some informed speculation about Philby and his relationship with British intelligence, see Harold Evans, *Good Times, Bad Times* (London: Coronet, 1983), pp. 72–85: "A message from Beirut said that in his final years there [Philby had become a journalist for the London *Observer*, 1956–63] he loved displaying a large photograph of the double-humped Mount Ararat on the Turkish-Soviet border. Its uniqueness lay in the fact that it could have been taken only from the Soviet side. The conclusion we drew was that SIS had allowed him to be a double agent in Turkey." Harold Evans was editor of *The Sunday Times* and oversaw the Page, Leitch, and Knightley investigation.
20. Martin, *Wilderness of Mirrors*, p. 51.
21. Kim Philby, *My Silent War*, pp. 130–131.
22. Page, Leitch, and Knightley, *Philby: The Spy Who Betrayed a Generation*, p. 266.
23. Philby, *My Silent War*, p. 131. Page, Leitch, and Knightley, *Philby: The Spy Who Betrayed a Generation*, p. 271.
24. Martin, *Wilderness of Mirrors*, p. 56.
25. Page, Leitch, and Knightley, *Philby: The Spy Who Betrayed a Generation*, p. 271.
26. *U.S. News and World Report*, September 30, 1955.
27. Roy Medvedev, "Requiem for a Traitor," *The Washington Post*, June 19, 1983.
28. Truman, *Memoirs: Years of Trial and Hope*, p. 362.
29. Andrew and Dilks, eds., *The Missing Dimension*, pp. 191–192. For an interesting insight into the attitude of the Truman administration toward Attlee and Britain at this time, see Dean Acheson, *Present at the Creation* (New York: W. W. Norton, 1969) pp. 480–485. Attlee was "suave . . . he soon led the President well onto the flypaper." Britain, Acheson felt, was cleverly seeking American economic and military support for British interests and was using the crisis in Korea as a bargaining counter for British political support in the United Nations. Attlee wanted joint Anglo-American control of atomic weapons, but despite the fact that Truman at one point essentially agreed to this, the American team contrived to get out of making such a commitment. For Truman's view, see Truman, *Memoirs: Years of Trial and Hope*, pp. 396–413.
30. Evans, *Good Times, Bad Times*, p. 76. See also Page, Leitch, and Knightley, *Philby: The Spy Who Betrayed a Generation*, pp. 211–216. The first seaborne infiltration into Albania was in October 1949. The first American airborne drop was in November 1950. One of the serious errors made over Philby by OPC and the CIA was that even after he was suspected, and after he left SIS, the Albanian operation continued, because its American planners could not accept that Philby had compromised it fully. The Brit-

ish, convinced that Philby had betrayed the operation, pulled out of it in 1951. Of course, by then Philby was no longer informed about operational details, but by revealing the plans at an early stage, he had made Albanian counterespionage work almost routine.

31. Page, Leitch, and Knightley, *Philby: The Spy Who Betrayed a Generation*, pp. 217–221. For a detailed account of the Albanian operation, see Nicholas Bethell, *The Great Betrayal: The Untold Story of Kim Philby's Biggest Coup* (London: Hodder & Stoughton, 1984), p. 199, where Bethell concludes:

> Philby was in the author's view one of the main causes of the disaster. He betrayed the plan for nearly two years. He alerted the Soviet Union about the first seaborne landings in October 1949. He gave them details too about the cross-frontier infiltrations of mid-1950 and the first American parachute drop in November 1950. These first operations did not succeed, but they were not disastrous. They would have been more successful if Philby had not betrayed them and perhaps provided a basis for real success. As it was, he gave the communists a crucial advantage.

For the Ukrainian operation, see Harry Rositzke, *The CIA's Secret Operations* (New York: Reader's Digest Press, 1977), pp. 167–169. Rositzke explains American involvement with the Albanian exiles very much in the same terms as Dean Acheson had argued to the congressional leaders in 1947: "By 1949 Albania had become an attractive target for the military planners in Washington. The rebels in Greece were on their last legs, Tito had isolated himself from Moscow, and the Russians were working hard to stabilize the shaky Hoxha regime in Tirana. The tide in the Balkans appeared to be running against Moscow. Albania looked soft, and a breakthrough there might unsettle the other satellites" (p. 172).

32. Rositzke, *The CIA's Secret Operations*, p. 173. He was talking about Europe rather than Latin America, where covert operations soon demonstrated their validity.

33. Burke, *Outrageous Good Fortune*, pp. 152–153. Ken Downs was a professional colleague.

6. Among the Ruins: 1947–1951

1. Interview, Richard M. Bissell, Jr., July 18, 1983.
2. Cord Meyer, *Facing Reality* (New York: Harper & Row, 1983), p. 37.
3. Ibid., pp. 51–55. At the time there were strong reports that the Trotskyites helped swing the balance against the communists, suggesting that it was not a simple victory of democrats over communists.
4. Ibid., p. 55.
5. See Harvey Klehr, *The Heyday of American Communism: The Depression Decade* (New York: Basic Books, 1984), p. 261: "For two short years, from 1936 to 1938, the Party enjoyed a status it had never before attained in any American state. The People's Front in Minnesota did not achieve as large a mass base as in Washington, nor did as many Communists, concealed or open, rise to positions of political influence. Yet, in no other state in the Union did the Communists have so intimate a relationship with the executive branch and the political party that controlled it." During the 1930s an estimated 250,000 Americans joined the Communist party—many of them for less than a year (ibid., p. 413).

As for the OSS, see Bradley F. Smith, *The Shadow Warriors* (New York: Basic Books, 1983), pp. 330–331:

> Conservative and cautious United States ambassadors such as Carlton Hayes in Spain and Lincoln MacVeagh in Greece thought during the war and immediately after that that O.S.S. was "slanted toward the left" and was indulgent of communism. Both Winston Churchill and Chiang Kai-shek believed that some O.S.S. activities in their countries aided Communists. During the great postwar Red Scare, rightists contended that since O.S.S. included veterans of the Spanish Civil War Abraham

Lincoln Brigade in its ranks, and employed prominent Marxists, including Herbert Marcuse, Noel Field, Maurice Halperin, and Paul Sweezy, Moscow at all times must have been calling the tune.

OSS counterespionage identified one OSS man as a Soviet agent during the war.

For a political angle on the struggle with communists in the labor unions, see Carl Solberg, *Hubert Humphrey—A Biography* (New York: W. W. Norton, 1984), pp. 111–123, 156–159:

> In Minnesota, though he never said so, Humphrey had been a Popular Front man. He had worked quite comfortably with the Communists and their sympathizers to unify the Left in the 1944 Democratic-Farmer-Labor party merger. . . .
> Neither Humphrey nor his other friends were prepared for what happened next. As the party's most prominent officeholder, Humphrey was expected to deliver the keynote address. But when he arrived he was jeered at and spat upon. His wife was refused admission until Humphrey got his police driver to escort her in. His supporters had to muscle their way in. As Humphrey rose to speak, there were cries of "fascist" and "warmonger." A beefy sergeant at arms shouted at him, "Sit down, you son of a bitch, or I'll knock you down." He was not allowed to finish his speech.
> It was an outright coup. The totally organized left wing took command of the DFL convention, its rules, its procedures. They passed resolutions excoriating Winston Churchill for his "iron curtain" speech, Truman for "betrayal" of Roosevelt's war aims and peace plans. They put through their platform, their party nominees, the election slate. (Ibid., pp. 112–113)

6. Quoted in Daniel Yergin, *Shattered Peace: The Origins of the Cold War and the National Security State* (London: André Deutsch, 1978), pp. 401–402. The directive was drafted by an NSC working party of State and Defense department officers during February and March 1949. The perspective and the language of the directive owed a great deal to George Kennan's 1946 telegram and James Forrestal's awareness of the Soviet Union. The guiding force behind the directive in 1949 was Dean Acheson, who succeeded George Marshall as secretary of state in January 1949. Acheson and Secretary of Defense Louis A. Johnson disliked each other intensely. Until Johnson resigned in 1950 this had the effect of making the Defense Department oppose the State Department, and vice versa, almost as a matter of principle. When NSC-68 came to be debated within the administration, Johnson and the Defense Department strenuously opposed it, despite the fact that it argued for an increase in defense spending from $15 billion a year to $35–$50 billion a year.

7. Central Intelligence Agency, "The DCI Historical Series: Organizational History of the Central Intelligence Agency, 1950–53" (May 1957), Chapter 11, pp. 30–36.

8. Interview, Lawrence Houston, July 8, 1983.

9. Ibid.

10. Vannevar Bush's memoirs, *Pieces of the Action* (New York: Morrow, 1970), bring out the close connection between government, industry, and the great centers of learning and engineering that developed in the United States during World War II and became cemented afterward. Interestingly, Bush makes no mention of his involvement with intelligence work.

11. Interview, Lawrence Houston, November 9, 1983. The DCI, of course, has never had the power to hire and fire people throughout the intelligence community, and so his power was never that great. It was far more dependent upon personal relationships. A strong DCI such as Bedell Smith had his way as DCI because he was Bedell Smith, not because he was DCI.

12. Ray S. Cline, *The CIA Under Reagan, Bush and Casey* (Washington, DC: Acropolis Books, 1981), p. 132.

13. Office of Reports and Estimates Evaluation, August 8, 1947.

14. Memorandum for the President, July 6, 1948. The memorandum concluded: "The above report was delivered to the Joint Congressional Atomic Energy Committee of which Senator Hickenlooper is the Chairman and in addition has also been dissemin-

ated to the Armed Services and the Department of State. This report, although prepared by the Central Intelligence Agency, was examined and concurred in by the intelligence agencies of the State, Army, Navy and Air Force Departments as well as by the Atomic Energy Commission." See Chapter 5 for the part played by Soviet espionage in the more rapid development of the Soviet atom bomb than was expected.

15. John Prados, *The Soviet Estimate: U.S. Intelligence Analysis and Russian Military Strength* (New York: Dial Press, 1982), p. 19.
16. Central Intelligence Group, "Soviet Bomber Production," ORE 3/1, October 3, 1946; see also Leslie C. Stevens, *Russian Assignment* (Boston: Little, Brown, 1953), p. 141, and Asher Lee, *The Soviet Air Forces* (New York: Harper & Row, 1956), p. 87.
17. Central Intelligence Agency, "Soviet Capabilities and Probable Courses of Action Through 1960," NIE 11-3-55, May 17, 1955.
18. Ibid. See also Central Intelligence Agency, "Main Trends in Soviet Capabilities and Policies, 1957–1962," NIE 11-4-57, November 12, 1957.
19. Central Intelligence Agency, "Policy Governing Concurrences in National Intelligence Reports and Estimates," DCID 3/2, September 13, 1948.
20. National Security Council, "The Central Intelligence Agency and National Organization for Intelligence" (Dulles/Jackson/Corea report), January 1, 1949.
21. Walter Millis, ed., *The Forrestal Diaries* (New York: Viking, 1951), p. 387. Clay was writing to James Forrestal, the secretary of defense.
22. Yergin, *Shattered Peace*, p. 353.
23. *Congressional Report*, March 17, 1948.
24. Prados, *The Soviet Estimate*, p. 11.
25. See p. 172–73.
26. Central Intelligence Agency, "Norway," September 1, 1947, pp. 5–6.
27. Central Intelligence Agency Office of Reports and Estimates, "The Current Situation in Italy," ORE 47, October 10, 1947, pp. 3–4.
28. This and the material on the following pages is from Central Intelligence Agency, "Review of the World Situation as It Relates to the Security of the United States," CIA 3, December 17, 1947.
29. See pp. 143–44 for CIA awareness in this respect. George Kennan in his *Memoirs, 1950–1963* (New York: Pantheon Books, 1977), recalled the expectation of the war in the late 1940s:

> In 1948, I had had the impression that American opinion, official and otherwise, recovering from the pro-Soviet euphoria of the period around the end of World War II, had been restored to a relatively even keel. True: it was hard to get the Pentagon to desist from seeing in Stalin another Hitler and fighting the last war all over again in its plans for the next one. True: we still had a vigorous right-wing faction which called for war with Russia—usually over China. But by and large, the moderate Marshall Plan approach—an approach aimed at *creating* strength in the West rather than *destroying* strength in Russia—seemed to have prevailed; and I, like those others who went by the name "Russian experts," felt that our view of the Russian problem—a view that accepted Russian-Communist attitudes and policies as a danger at the political level, but did not see either a likelihood or a necessity of war and did not regard the military plane as the one on which our response ought to be concentrated—seemed to have found general acceptance.
>
> Two years later, all this was rapidly changing. . . .
>
> The German–Nazi syndrome still dominated people's minds. The attack in Korea, even though Soviet troops were not involved, was viewed as another "Austria"—as the first move in a supposed "grand design" of world conquest. And by virtue of this misimpression on our part, more, actually, than by the North Korean attack itself, the peace of the world now seemed to me to be in real, and needless, danger.
>
> This was not because I supposed that the Soviet leaders wanted such a war or would intentionally provoke it. It was because I thought we ourselves might inadvertently convince them that it could not be avoided. I could not forget that even prior

to the Korean War our military—and to some extent our political—planners had adopted for military planning purposes, against my anguished objections, the year 1952 as the probable "peak" of danger which our preparations should be designed to meet. They did not themselves intend to start a war at that time, but they assumed there would be real danger of the Russians doing so as soon as their current program of military preparations was completed—and for this, 1952, apparently, seemed to them the most likely date [ibid., pp. 90–92].

30. Central Intelligence Agency, "Review of the World Situation as It Relates to the Security of the United States," CIA 4–48, April 8, 1948.
31. Central Intelligence Agency, "Possible Program of Future Soviet Moves in Germany," ORE 29–48, April 28, 1948.
32. Ibid.
33. Central Intelligence Agency, "The Strategic Value to the USSR of the Conquest of Western Europe and the Near East (to Cairo) Prior to 1950," ORE 58–48, July 30, 1948. The conclusions were presented on July 15 and, together with detailed reports forming an appendix, published on July 30.
34. Rear Admiral R. H. Hillenkoetter to Sidney W. Souers, executive secretary, NSC, April 20, 1949.
35. Office of Scientific Intelligence, Central Intelligence Agency, Nuclear Energy Branch, "Status of the USSR Atomic Energy Project," OSI/SR–10/49, July 1, 1949.
36. Central Intelligence Agency, "The Emergency Capabilities of the German Railway Systems," ORE 14–49, August 2, 1949.
37. Central Intelligence Agency, "The Tudeh Party: Vehicle of Communism in Iran," ORE 29–49, July 18, 1949.
38. Central Intelligence Agency, "China," SR–8, May 1948. It should be said that it was questionable whether Soviet sympathies did lie with the Chinese in this way, but this kind of analytic question was not really addressed in the atmosphere of the period.
39. Central Intelligence Agency, "Survival Potential of Residual Non-Communist Regimes in China," ORE 76–49, October 19, 1949:

    It is concluded, therefore, that even with extensive US support (short of major armed intervention involving the use of US combat forces), none of the non-Communist regimes in China can survive beyond 1950 except on Communist sufferance. Taiwan is the only non-Communist area of China where limited US military action in support of other measures might be effective in preventing Communist control. At the same time, such US action with respect to Taiwan could serve other important US security interests.

40. Central Intelligence Agency, "The Possibility of Britain's Abandonment of Overseas Military Commitments," ORE 93–49, December 23, 1949.
41. Cline, *The CIA*, p. 129.
42. Rear Admiral R. H. Hillenkoetter, memorandum on Korean situation, June 29, 1950.
43. Rear Admiral R. H. Hillenkoetter, memorandum on Korean situation, July 2, 1950.
44. Rear Admiral R. H. Hillenkoetter, memorandum on Korean situation, July 3, 1950.
45. Interview, William Bundy, July 21, 1983.
46. *The New York Times*, July 22, 1948.
47. Rear Admiral R. H. Hillenkoetter, memorandum, August 3, 1950. The material on the following pages is from this memorandum.

7. *Terra Nostra: 1950–1953*

1. Ray S. Cline, *The CIA Under Reagan, Bush and Casey* (Washington, DC: Acropolis Books, 1981), pp. 130–131.
2. Interview, July 18, 1983.
3. Interview, Lyman B. Kirkpatrick, Jr., July 19, 1983.
4. Interview, William Bundy, July 21, 1983.
5. Central Intelligence Agency, "The DCI Historical Series: Organizational History of

the Central Intelligence Agency, 1950–53," chapter 2, p. 1. These remarks were made by Truman to Smith, probably in December 1952 or early January 1953, at the end of Truman's presidency. They were quoted by Smith in his farewell letter to all CIA personnel on February 9, 1953.

6. Interview, William Bundy, July 21, 1983. So successful was the Smith–Langer partnership in establishing effective Estimates and procedures that Langer was able to leave after a year and return to Harvard. He was succeeded by his deputy, Sherman Kent.

7. *The New York Times*, March 8, 1949.

8. Interview, Lyman B. Kirkpatrick, Jr., July 19, 1983.

9. Central Intelligence Agency Act, 1949, Section 8 (a), (b).

10. Interview, Tom Braden, in Granada Television program, *World in Action: The Rise and Fall of the CIA* (Manchester, Eng., June 1975), Part I.

11. Lawrence R. Houston to the director of Central Intelligence, memorandum, May 25, 1949, p. 2.

12. *Final Report*, I, p. 493.

13. William L. Langer, *In and Out of the Ivory Tower* (New York: W. W. Norton, 1977), p. 220.

14. *Final Report*, I, p. 257.

15. Cline, *The CIA*, p. 141: "Some of these employees got involved in real cloak-and-dagger work [but] . . . not 5 percent of the CIA's employees ever had any significant contact with this world of spy fiction, and most of the agency employees had absolutely no first-hand knowledge of any activity more hazardous than driving to work each morning."

16. William E. Colby and Peter Forbath, *Honorable Men: My Life in the CIA* (New York: Simon & Schuster, 1978), pp. 86–87.

17. Quoted in *Time*, August 3, 1953.

18. Cline, *The CIA*, p. 134.

19. Interview, Lawrence Houston, July 8, 1983.

20. Interview, Richard M. Bissell, Jr., July 18, 1983.

21. William R. Corson, *The Armies of Ignorance: The Rise of the American Intelligence Empire* (New York: Dial Press, 1977), p. 311.

22. Ibid., p. 310; see also *Final Report*, IV, pp. 6–9.

23. Interview, Richard Helms, July 26, 1983. There was lingering rivalry between individuals formerly with the two offices, and the primary task of the DDP was to consolidate the two personnel groups into a common, disciplined service. With some exceptions, Wisner had achieved this by 1954. The major internal bureaucratic battle then shifted to the jockeying for superiority between the staffs and the seven area divisions within the DDP. The battle was "won" by the divisions, with one or two exceptions. They gained control of operational activity and personnel assignments in their respective geographic areas, with the staffs relegated to essentially advisory positions.

24. Interview, Lyman B. Kirkpatrick, Jr., July 19, 1983.

25. Cline, *The CIA*, p. 153: "As a result of the burgeoning political effort in Europe and the skyrocketing paramilitary programs in Asia, CIA's covert action arm grew by leaps and bounds. . . . The sums of money grew even larger as costs mounted and they accounted for the largest part of the CIA's budget down until the 1970s, which saw the divestiture of the big radio projects and the collapse of the last big paramilitary efforts in Laos."

26. NSC 68 pulled together elements of NSC 4 and NSC 4A and a later directive, NSC 10/2, which superseded NSC 4A on June 18, 1948, in the midst of the war scare of that year. NSC 10/2 was the charter of OPC, adding to NSC 4A's psychological-warfare approvals with authority for political and economic warfare and for direct action in the national security interests of the United States. It was the umbrella under which sabotage, guerrilla activity, and support for foreign political parties and front organizations took place. NSC 68 consolidated them all.

27. For an indication of these concerns, see a CIA internal memorandum on the MKUltra program in the Joint Hearing before the Select Committee on Intelligence and the

Subcommittee on Health and Scientific Research of the Committee on Human Resources, United States Senate, 95th Congress, First Session, *Project MKUltra: The CIA's Program of Research in Behavioral Modification* (Washington, DC: U.S. Government Printing Office), August 3, 1977, pp. 123–125.

The program was to discover "substances which will promote illogical thinking and impulsiveness to the point where the recipient would be discredited in public"; "substances which increase the efficiency of mentation and perception"; "materials which will prevent or counteract the intoxicating effect of alcohol"; "materials which will promote the intoxicating effect of alcohol"; "materials which will produce the signs and symptoms of recognized diseases in a reversible way"; "materials which will render the induction of hypnosis easier"; "substances which will enhance the ability of individuals to withstand privation, torture and coercion"; "materials and physical methods which will produce amnesia for events preceding and during their use"; "physical methods of producing shock and confusion over extended periods of time and capable of surreptitious use"; "substances which produce physical disablement"; "substances which will produce 'pure' euphoria with no subsequent let-down"; "substances which alter personality structure in such a way that the tendency of the recipient to become dependent upon another person is enhanced"; "a material which will cause mental confusion of such a type that the individual under its influence will find it difficult to maintain a fabrication under questioning"; "substances which will lower the ambition and general working efficiency of men"; "substances which promote weakness or distortion of the eyesight or hearing faculties"; "a knockout pill"; "a material which can be surreptitiously administered [in food and drink and cigarettes] which in very small amounts will make it impossible for a man to perform any physical activity whatever."

28. Central Intelligence Agency, memorandum, "An Analysis of Confessions in Russian Trials," 1950.
29. Report of the Inspector General, Department of the Army, "Use of Volunteers in Chemical Agent Research," 1975.
30. John Marks, *The Search for the "Manchurian Candidate": The Story of the CIA's Secret Efforts to Control Human Behavior* (London: Allen Lane, 1979), pp. 6–7.
31. Central Intelligence Agency internal memorandum, n.d., A/B, 2, 10/48.
32. Interview, Tom Braden, November 14, 1983.
33. Central Intelligence Agency internal memorandum, n.d., A/B, 2, 10/48.
34. See pp. 210–16 for details of some Artichoke experiments.
35. Central Intelligence Agency, memorandum for director of Central Intelligence, "Sensitive Research Programs," June 1964.
36. Robert Harris and Jeremy Paxman, *A Higher Form of Killing: The Secret Story of Gas and Germ Warfare* (London: Triad/Granada, 1982), p. 206.
37. George F. Kennan, *Memoirs, 1950–1963* (New York: Pantheon Books, 1977), pp. 158–159. The chief of the Medical Staff in CIA wrote a memorandum on January 25, 1952, setting out the rationale of the behavior-control programs:

> There is ample evidence in the reports of innumerable interrogations that the Communists were utilizing drugs, physical duress, electric shock, and possibly hypnosis against their enemies. With such evidence it is difficult not to keep from being rabid about our apparent laxity. We are forced by this mounting evidence to assume a more aggressive role in the development of these techniques, but must be cautious to maintain strict inviolable control because of the havoc that could be wrought by such techniques in unscrupulous hands. (Joint Hearing, *Project MKUltra*, p. 73)

A year later, in a memorandum to Allen Dulles, "Memorandum from ADDP Helms to DCI Dulles, March 4, 1953, Richard Helms described the purpose of the various programs as

> research to develop a capability in the covert use of biological and chemical materials. This area involves the production of various physiological conditions which could support present or future clandestine operations. Aside from the offensive potential, the development of a comprehensive capability in this field of covert chemi-

cal and biological warfare gives us a thorough knowledge of the enemy's theoretical potential, thus enabling us to defend ourselves against a foe who might not be as restrained in the use of these techniques as we are. (Joint Hearing, *Project MKUltra*, p. 70)

38. Kennan, *Memoirs, 1950–1963*, p. 162. Kennan himself levelheadedly ascribed his loss of temper to the strain of life in Moscow.
39. J. S. Earman, inspector general, CIA, to director of Central Intelligence, memorandum, "Report of Inspection of MKUltra," July 26, 1963; see also Lyman B. Kirkpatrick, inspector general, CIA, to director of Central Intelligence, memorandum, "The Suicide of Frank Olson," December 18, 1953.
40. Richard Helms, deputy director for plans, CIA, to director of Central Intelligence, memorandum, "Sensitive Research Programs (MKUltra)," June 1964.
41. Joint Hearing, *Project MKUltra*, p. 67. Chatter was terminated shortly after the end of the Korean War in 1953.
42. Joint Hearing, *Project MKUltra*, pp. 68–69. The specific purposes of the MKNaomi program included "to stockpile severely incapacitating and lethal materials for the specific use of TSD [Technical Services Division]," clearly indicating that assassination was contemplated. The program was terminated in 1970:

> On November 25, 1969, President Nixon renounced the use of any form of biological weapons that kill or incapacitate and ordered the disposal of existing stocks of bacteriological weapons. On February 14, 1970, the President clarified the extent of his earlier order and indicated that toxins—chemicals that are not living organisms but are produced by living organisms—were considered biological weapons subject to his previous directive and were to be destroyed. Although instructed to relinquish control of material held for the CIA [by the Army Chemical Corps Special Operations Division at Fort Detrick], a CIA scientist acquired approximately 11 grams of shellfish toxin from SOD personnel at Fort Detrick which were stored in a little-used CIA laboratory where it went undetected for five years. (Joint Hearings, *Project MKUltra*, pp. 68–69)

> In 1975, when the then director of Central Intelligence, William Colby, discovered that this toxin had been kept, he was furious and ordered it destroyed immediately. However, this did not happen because several scientific research organizations requested the toxin for research purposes. The scientist concerned had kept it largely because the toxin had been enormously expensive to produce.

43. Joint Hearing, *Project MKUltra*, p. 71. According to the CIA, MKDelta and the MKUltra programs were all terminated in "the late 1960s."
44. "Prepared Statement of Admiral Stansfield Turner, Director of Central Intelligence," to the Joint Hearing, *Project MKUltra*, pp. 4–8. Turner in his statement specifically referred to "antipersonnel harassment and assassination delivery systems including aerosol generators and other spray devices." See also Church Committee, *Final Report*, I, pp. 201–209, 385–422.
45. Central Intelligence Agency, "Memorandum for the Record," Project MKUltra, Subproject No. 142, May 22, 1962. Again, assassination was obviously contemplated.
46. Central Intelligence Agency, "Memorandum for the Record," Project MKUltra, Subproject No. 94, October 18, 1960.
47. Ibid. The total cost of the program in fiscal year 1961 was estimated to be $40,858; the next year the program was estimated at $57,431.82 (Central Intelligence Agency, "Memorandum for the Record," Project MKUltra, Subproject No. 94, November 22, 1961).
48. Central Intelligence Agency, " 'Guided Animal' Studies," memorandum for the deputy director (Plans), April 21, 1961.
49. Interview, Victor Marchetti, November 22, 1983.
50. J. S. Earman, inspector general, CIA, to director of Central Intelligence, memorandum, "Report of Inspection of MKUltra," July 26, 1963.
51. Ibid.
52. Lyman Kirkpatrick, inspector general, CIA, to director of Central Intelligence, memo-

randum, "The Suicide of Frank Olson," December 18, 1953. The chief of the Technical Services Staff was Willis Gibbons; the deputy chief was James Drum. Marks, *The Search for the "Manchurian Candidate,"* pp. 82–86, details the initial attempt at a cover-up by Robert Lashbrook, Olson's CIA companion; Gottlieb's deputy in the Chemical Division of TSS; Dr. Harold Abramson, the New York psychiatrist Olson was taken to see, and Lieutenant Colonel Vincent Ruwet, Olson's boss at Fort Detrick. However, the point needs to be made that within the agency Kirkpatrick, Houston, and Dulles were not party to this and actively sought to discover the truth about what had happened. This was kept to "eyes only" and "one copy only" reports within the agency.

53. Lawrence R. Houston, general counsel, CIA, to inspector general, memorandum, "Frank R. Olson," January 4, 1954.
54. Marks, *The Search for the "Manchurian Candidate,"* p. 82.
55. Church Committee, *Alleged Assassination Plots Involving Foreign Leaders* (New York: W. W. Norton, 1974), pp. 20–21.
56. Ibid., pp. 79–83.
57. Ibid., p. 181.
58. Interview, Richard M. Bissell, Jr., July 18, 1983.
59. Central Intelligence Agency, memorandum, "Artichoke," special comments, November 26, 1951, A/B, 4, 3/20.
60. Ibid.
61. Central Intelligence Agency, security officer, CIA to assistant director, SI, Memorandum Bluebird, April 6, 1951. This refers to all six tests mentioned on pp. 213–14.
62. Central Intelligence Agency, memorandum, October 21, 1951.
63. *The New York Times*, May 4, 1951; May 5, 1951.
64. *Time*, December 11, 1950.
65. *Final Report*, I, p. 141.
66. David Wise and Thomas B. Ross, *The Invisible Government* (New York: Random House, 1964), pp. 109–110.
67. *The New York Times*, April 14, 1966; April 27, 1966; May 14, 1967. See also Victor Marchetti and John D. Marks, *The CIA and the Cult of Intelligence* (New York: Knopf, 1974), p. 153. The center received $300,000 in 1950.
68. William Colby, statement before the Senate Armed Services Committee, January 16, 1975.
69. Interview, Tom Braden, November 14, 1983; see also *The New York Times*, May 8, 1967.
70. William Colby, statement before the House Foreign Affairs Committee, *The Washington Post*, October 21, 1973. See also *The New York Times*, August 2, 1974: George Papadopoulos, the Greek army colonel who led the military coup in Greece in 1967, had received a CIA subsidy since 1952. Marchetti and Marks, *The CIA*, p. 40, show that similar support was given in Germany.
71. *Ramparts* (March 1967).
72. *The New York Times*, March 14, 1967. Marchetti and Marks, *The CIA*, pp. 152–156.
73. See Marchetti and Marks, *The CIA*, pp. 105, 128; Wise and Ross, *The Invisible Government*, pp. 106–107; David Wise, "Colby of CIA—CIA of Colby," *The New York Times Magazine*, July 1, 1973, p. 9.
74. Marchetti and Marks, *The CIA*, pp. 25–26; 105.
75. *Final Report*, I, p. 146.
76. Interview, Victor Marchetti, November 22, 1983.
77. *Final Report*, I, p. 146.
78. Cline, *The CIA*, pp. 133–134.
79. Corson, *The Armies of Ignorance*, p. 320. The overall staffing of CIA increased from about 5000 in 1950 to about 15,000 in 1955.
80. *Final Report*, I, p. 22.
81. David Atlee Phillips, *The Night Watch: 25 Years of Peculiar Service* (New York: Atheneum, 1977), pp. 59–60.
82. John M. Maury, "CIA and the Congress," *Congressional Record*, Vol. 130, No. 117,

September 18, 1984. Charles ("Chip") E. Bohlen was a career diplomat. He succeeded George Kennan as ambassador to the USSR in 1953. He served as ambassador to France, 1962–68, and retired in 1969 as deputy undersecretary of state for political affairs.

83. David Halberstam, *The Best and the Brightest* (Greenwich, CT: Fawcett Crest, 1972), p. 497.

84. Cline, *The CIA*, p. 237. Cline was station chief in Taiwan from 1958 to 1962, during which time he was in command of CIA activities and operations on the island. Fitz-Gerald would have consulted Cline as a matter of courtesy on a host of matters, but as a division head he also possessed a large degree of autonomy. In a conflict between a station chief and a division head, the division head usually won.

85. Colby, *Honorable Men*, p. 104.

86. Joseph B. Smith, *Portrait of a Cold Warrior* (New York: Ballantine Books, 1976), p. 95.

87. Ibid.

88. L. Fletcher Prouty, *The Secret Team—The CIA and Its Allies in Control of the United States and the World* (New Jersey: Prentice-Hall, 1973), p. 34.

89. *The New York Times*, September 17, 1953; see also Smith, *Portrait of a Cold Warrior*, pp. 97–103. Magsaysay was elected president of the Philippines with 1,688,172 votes to the 708,398 of his opponent, Elpidio Quirino.

90. Harry Rositzke, *The CIA's Secret Operations* (New York: Reader's Digest Press, 1977), p. 170.

91. Interview, David Atlee Phillips, July 6, 1983.

8. The Wounded Peace: 1953–1956

1. Interview, McGeorge Bundy, July 21, 1983.

2. Quoted in Richard Deacon, *"C"—A Biography of Sir Maurice Oldfield* (London: Macdonald, 1985), p. 90.

3. Richard Nixon, *RN—The Memoirs of Richard Nixon* (New York: Grosset & Dunlap, 1978), pp. 135–136.

4. Quoted in Walter LaFeber, *Inevitable Revolutions—The United States in Central America* (New York: W. W. Norton, 1983), p. 88.

5. Quoted ibid., p. 51.

6. Quoted ibid., pp. 51–52.

7. National Security Council, *A Report to the President by the National Security Council on US Objectives with Respect to Greece and Turkey to Counter Soviet Threats to US Security*, NSC 42/1, March 22, 1949.

8. Quoted in Walter LaFeber, *America, Russia and the Cold War*, 4th ed. (New York: John Wiley & Sons, 1980), p. 30.

9. Quoted ibid., p. 32.

10. Leonard Mosley, *Dulles: A Biography of Eleanor, Allen and John Foster Dulles and Their Family Network* (New York: Dial Press/James Wade, 1978), pp. 32–35. Robert M. Lansing was State Department counsel in 1914. He was more of an Anglophile than the rest of his family and conspired with British intelligence agents to thwart American neutrality during World War I. He became secretary of state after the sinking of the *Lusitania*. He also took elocution lessons to perfect a British accent.

11. Quoted in LaFeber, *America, Russia and the Cold War*, p. 149: from the Dulles Oral History Project, Princeton, interview with George Humphrey and Herbert Hoover, Jr.

12. Dwight D. Eisenhower, *The White House Years: Mandate for Change, 1953–56* (New York: Doubleday, 1963), pp. 148–149. Eisenhower credits American intelligence for the information presented to him through the National Security Council by the director of Central Intelligence as the coordinator of intelligence material.

13. U.S. Senate, *Nomination of John Foster Dulles*, 1953, pp. 10–11.

14. Richard Rovere, *Senator Joe McCarthy* (London: Methuen, 1959), p. 42.

15. *The New York Times*, September 30, 1952.

16. Lyman B. Kirkpatrick, Jr., *The Real CIA* (New York: Macmillan, 1968), p. 138.

17. Letter, Robert Amory, Jr., to author, February 22, 1985.
18. Interviews, William Bundy, July 21, 1983; Robert Amory, November 9, 1983; Walter Pforzheimer, April 2, 1984. Letters, Robert Amory to author, February 22, 1985; William Bundy to author, March 6, 1985.

   The initial press reaction to Dulles' stand was unfavorable, taking the view that he had capitulated and that the CIA was going the way of all the other agencies attacked by McCarthy. This was because Dulles had agreed that Bundy would be reinvestigated and subjected to a new loyalty and security hearing. As the days went by and it was seen that Bundy, back from "leave," was still working at his desk, the agency was able to point out that his reinvestigation was not a very serious concession, and comment swung around to the view that the agency had managed to stand firm on not letting its people be interrogated by McCarthy.
19. Nixon, *RN*, pp. 139–140. "But what about his contribution to Hiss?" McCarthy asked. "Joe," said Nixon, "you have to understand how those people up in Cambridge think." Bundy graduated from Harvard Law School, and Hiss was one of its most famous graduates. I think he probably just got on the bandwagon without giving any thought to where the bandwagon was heading" (ibid., p. 140).
20. *Time*, July 27, 1953. Cohn later asked Bedell Smith to try and arrange an army commission for David Schine, another McCarthy henchman, with the possibility of a transfer for Schine to the CIA. Cohn changed his mind when Bedell Smith offered to speak to Allen Dulles. "The CIA," Cohn was reported as saying, "was too juicy a subject for future investigation and it would not be right to ask them to get Mr. Schine commissioned and then investigate the organization later" (*The New York Times*, June 3, 1954).
21. Interview, William Bundy, July 21, 1983.
22. Ibid.
23. Ibid.
24. Ibid.
25. Cord Meyer, *Facing Reality* (New York: Harper & Row, 1980), p. 65. Dulles' reputation for loyalty to his subordinates was well established. Gerhard Van Arkel recalled his time with Dulles in Switzerland during World War II: "I was very fond of him. I had great admiration for him—I think mostly because he never gave me an order, never told me what to do. But if I ran into a problem and needed help, he was always ready to give it. All I had to do was go in to him and explain what the trouble was, and he'd usually work it out. If not, he'd certainly do his level best to work it out" (interview, November 11, 1983).
26. Meyer, *Facing Reality*, p. 80. However, his brush with McCarthyism proved a traumatic incident in Meyer's life. After he was cleared, "friends say that he was irremediably scarred by the experience . . . he seems to have decided that never again would he leave room for the slightest doubt about the totality of his commitment to the hardest of hard anticommunist lines" (Godfrey Hodgson, "Cord Meyer: Superspook," in Philip Agee and Louis Wolf, *Dirty Work: The CIA in Western Europe* [Secaucus, NJ: Lyle Stuart, 1978], pp. 63–64).
27. Interview, Tom Braden, November 14, 1983. Large amounts of money were passed to Lovestone and Brown by the CIA. The counterintelligence arm under James Angleton did its best to monitor the expenditure of these funds, opening mail between Lovestone and Brown in the process. There was always a fuss about this funding, because at times enormous amounts were involved and there was no way to be sure that all of it would go where it was intended. This issue surfaced after the *Ramparts* articles in 1967 (see p. 251). The CIA–labor connection was discussed at length in *The New York Times*, February 21–28, 1967.
28. *The Washington Post*, December 30, 1965. Lovestone had been an ambitious communist and was closely associated with the Third International (the Comintern) established by Lenin and Trotsky in 1919 to work for communist revolutions. (It was disbanded in 1943 by Stalin as a gesture to his new allies.) He was being groomed to become a major American voice in world communism.

29. See Thomas Powers, *The Man Who Kept the Secrets: Richard Helms and the CIA* (New York: Knopf, 1979), p. 59, for a discussion of this point. He quotes Charles McCarry, an early CIA officer who subsequently became a speech writer for Eisenhower and then a thriller writer, as saying there were two things he had never met in the CIA: an assassin or a Republican.
30. Thomas W. Braden, "I'm Glad the CIA Is 'Immoral,' " *Saturday Evening Post*, May 20, 1967.
31. Meyer, *Facing Reality*, p. 99.
32. This and the previous extract ibid., p. 101.
33. *The New York Times*, February 14, 1967.
34. Meyer, *Facing Reality*, p. 103.
35. Ibid., pp. 88–94, 103–105. This is a point stressed by Meyer. The other view is that the CIA's funding and support were corrupt and corruptive, and not until 1967 did someone of sufficient moral strength come forward and make the story public.
36. See especially *The New York Times*, February 14–28, 1967.
37. *The New York Times*, February 15, 1967.
38. *The New York Times*, February 20, 1967. Makinen was sentenced to eight years in prison on espionage charges by a court in Kiev.
39. *The New York Times*, February 21, 1967. William Hobby, president of the Hobby Foundation, said of the news of his foundation's involvement with the CIA: "We are glad to have been of service to the Federal Government. We would help again any time they ask us."
40. *The New York Times*, February 21, 1967. Spokesmen for the World University Service and the Institute for Public Administration, both identified as receiving CIA funding through various channels, declared that they never knowingly accepted CIA funds and had no reason to disbelieve that their funding was coming from private sources.
41. *The New York Times*, February 22, 1967. The institute had schools in Costa Rica and the Dominican Republic.
42. *The New York Times*, February 21, 1967.
43. *Final Report*, I, p. 169.
44. William V. Kennedy, David Barker, Richard S. Friedman, and David Miller, *The Intelligence War* (London: Salamander, 1983), pp. 24, 46. The authors quote secret CIA analyses, stolen from the American Embassy in Tehran in 1982, concerning Israeli attempts to penetrate the U.S. diplomatic corps and U.S. intelligence. "The extensive formal and informal intelligence-sharing arrangements are not seen as any reason by the Israelis to spare the United States from the sometimes brutal Israeli intelligence-gathering and counter-intelligence methods" (p. 46).
45. Interview, Ray Cline, July 25, 1983.
46. Ray S. Cline, *The CIA Under Reagan, Bush and Casey* (Washington, DC: Acropolis Books, 1981), p. 147.
47. *Final Report*, I, p. 166.
48. William Hood, *Mole—The True Story of the First Russian Intelligence Officer Recruited by the CIA* (New York: W. W. Norton, 1982), p. 26.
49. Allen Dulles, *The Craft of Intelligence* (Westport, CT: Greenwood Press, 1977), pp. 134–135.
50. Hood, *Mole*, p. 13.
51. Ibid., pp. 108, 111.
52. Interview, Peter Karlow, July 28, 1983.
53. Lord Moran, *Winston Churchill: The Struggle for Survival, 1940–1965* (London: Sphere, 1968), pp. 377, 380.
54. *The New York Times*, May 12, 1953. "The Prime Minister was trying to bring the United States into an East-West detente while, at the same time, cutting back his ties with Americans as he dealt with the whirling problems of nationalism in the newly emerging nations," commented the paper in its editorial. See also Walter LaFeber, *America, Russia and the Cold War*, pp. 150–154 for a discussion of the Anglo/American/Russian triangle in 1953.

55. *The New York Times,* May 15, 1953.
56. Dulles Papers, Princeton University: conference dossiers, "Conclusions on Trip," May 9–May 29, 1953, quoted in LaFeber, *America, Russia and the Cold War,* p. 157.
57. Dean Acheson, *Present at the Creation* (New York: W. W. Norton, 1969), p. 506.
58. Kermit Roosevelt, *Countercoup: The Struggle for the Control of Iran* (New York: McGraw-Hill, 1981), p. 3. Roosevelt was an intelligence man's dream: charming, resourceful, understated, possessing great energy and a phenomenal range of contacts without making a cult of either.
59. This and the previous extract from Roosevelt, *Countercoup,* p. 18.
60. Steven Schlesinger and Stephen Kinzer, *Bitter Fruit: The Untold Story of the American Coup in Guatemala* (New York: Doubleday, 1982), pp. 110, 112. The authors argue that Arbenz's government was not so much left-wing as reformist and that in toppling it the CIA were in effect pawns of the United Fruit Company rather than defenders of democratic liberalism against communist threats.
61. David Atlee Phillips, *The Night Watch: 25 Years of Peculiar Service* (New York: Atheneum, 1977), pp. 49–51. "Brad" is the pseudonym Phillips uses for Colonel Albert Haney. "Hector" is his pseudonym for Rip Robertson, a CIA paramilitary trainer who worked with Haney in Korea and acted as his aide during Operation Success.
62. *Final Report,* IV, p. 45.

9. Cry Havoc: 1956

1. Thomas W. Braden, "I'm Glad the CIA Is 'Immoral,'" *Saturday Evening Post,* May 20, 1967; see also *The New York Times,* May 7 and 8, 1967.
2. William Colby, Senate Armed Services Committee statement, January 16, 1975.
3. Central Intelligence Agency, Memorandum for the Record, "DCI's Meeting Concerning HTLingual," May 19, 1971. U.S. Senate, *Intelligence Activities,* Senate Resolution 21, *Hearings Before the Select Committee to Study Governmental Operations with Respect to Intelligence Activities,* Vol. 4, *Mail Opening,* October 21, 22, and 24, 1975. The HTLingual project developed from an earlier operation, SGPointer, begun in 1952 by the CIA's Office of Security. This project involved collecting the names of senders and receivers of mail to and from the Soviet Union. In 1955 the project was transferred to the Counterintelligence Staff and expanded under the name HTLingual.
4. Interview, Tom Braden, in Granada Television program, *World in Action: The Rise and Fall of the CIA* (Manchester, Eng., June 1975), Part I.
5. *Final Report,* IV, pp. 45–46.
6. Richard Helms, "Remarks at Donovan Award Dinner," May 24, 1983.
7. Minutes of meeting, January 12, 1953, quoted in Walter LaFeber, *Inevitable Revolutions—The United States in Central America* (New York: W. W. Norton, 1983), p. 111.
8. U.S. Congress, Senate Committee on Foreign Relations, *Nomination of John Foster Dulles,* 1953.
9. Quoted in LaFeber, *Inevitable Revolutions,* p. 107, "2nd Regional Conference of U.S. Chiefs of Mission, Rio . . . 1950," Inter-American Economic Affairs Committee, 1945–50. George F. Kennan, *Memoirs 1950–1963* (New York: Pantheon Books, 1977), pp. 65–70, refers to this meeting but does not give any details, concentrating instead on his trip to Mexico City on his way to Rio.
10. See A. L. Langguth, *Hidden Terrors: The Truth About U.S. Police Operations in Latin America* (New York: Pantheon, 1978).
11. David Wise and Thomas B. Ross, *The Invisible Government* (New York: Vintage, 1974), pp. 119–120. David Atlee Phillips, *The Night Watch: 25 Years of Peculiar Service* (New York: Atheneum, 1977), pp. 62–63. Figueres and Phillips became friendly in 1955, and Phillips spent three days with the Costa Rican president as a guest. Both Figueres' first wife and his second wife, Karen, were American, and Figueres himself had been at MIT. Phillips, who had played an important part in toppling Arbenz in Guatemala, was not involved in trying to topple Figueres and gives no impression that there was any need to in 1955.

12. Quoted from "Conference with Doolittle," October 19, 1954, Eisenhower Library, Ann Whitman Administration Series Papers, in Stephen E. Ambrose, *Eisenhower the President* (New York: Simon & Schuster, 1984), pp. 226–227.
13. *Final Report*, IV, p. 50.
14. Wise and Ross, *The Invisible Government*, p. 264. See pp. 283–84 for the role of the Hoover Commission in this step.
15. *Final Report*, IV, pp. 62–63.
16. Cord Meyer, *Facing Reality* (New York: Harper & Row, 1980), pp. 364–366; see also Wise and Ross, *The Invisible Government*, pp. 187–188. The PBCFIA resigned on President Kennedy's inauguration, since its members saw themselves as being personal appointees of the President. (All had been nominated by Allen Dulles, but technically they held political, not administrative, positions.)
17. *Final Report*, IV, p. 52.
18. Interview, Senator J. William Fulbright, July 7, 1983.
19. Interview, Lawrence Houston, July 8, 1983.
20. Quoted in *Final Report*, IV, pp. 53–54. The *History* states that Senators Russell, Bridges, and Byrd "essentially . . . held full responsibility for Senate oversight of the CIA."
21. Robert Amory, Jr., "Hungary '56—A Subjective/Objective Account," delivered before the Literary Society of Washington, DC, March 15, 1975.
22. Ray S. Cline, *The CIA Under Reagan, Bush and Casey* (Washington, DC: Acropolis Books, 1981), p. 186.
23. *The New York Times*, November 30, 1976.
24. Cline, *The CIA*, p. 187.
25. CIA, CS Historical Paper, Clandestine Services History, "The Berlin Tunnel Operation," August 25, 1967.
26. Interview, Peter Montagnon, January 10, 1985.
27. David C. Martin, *Wilderness of Mirrors* (New York: Ballantine Books, 1980), p. 78, quoting from a CIA document. Martin, pp. 74–92, provides a detailed account of the whole operation.
28. CIA, "The Berlin Tunnel Operation."
29. Martin, *Wilderness of Mirrors*, p. 83.
30. CIA, "The Berlin Tunnel Operation."
31. Cline, *The CIA*, p. 185.
32. CIA, "The Berlin Tunnel Operation."
33. Martin, *Wilderness of Mirrors*, p. 87.
34. CIA, "The Berlin Tunnel Operation," paraphrasing a memorandum prepared on August 15, 1956, which examined in detail all evidence available as of that date on the reasons for the discovery.
35. *The New York Times*, May 12, 1953.
36. John Foster Dulles stated this at his opening address to the NATO Foreign Ministers' meeting in Paris on December 15, 1955.
37. Kermit Roosevelt quoted in Leonard Mosley, *Dulles: A Biography of Eleanor, Allen and John Foster Dulles and Their Family Network* (New York: Dial Press, 1978), p. 349.
38. Ibid., p. 349.
39. Miles Copeland, *The Real Spy World* (London: Sphere, 1978) p. 62.
40. U.S. Senate, Committee on Foreign Relations, February 24, 1956.
41. Robert H. Ferrell, ed. *The Eisenhower Diaries* (New York: W. W. Norton, 1981), p. 333.
42. Mosley, *Dulles*, pp. 350–351.
43. Amory, "Hungary '56."
44. Ibid.
45. Meyer, *Facing Reality*, p. 119.
46. Amory, "Hungary '56."
47. Ibid.
48. Ibid.

49. Mosley, *Dulles*, p. 420.
50. Meyer, *Facing Reality*, p. 118.
51. Ibid., p. 119.
52. Ibid., pp. 126–130.

10. *Planes, Plans, Plots: 1955–1961*

1. Interview, Richard M. Bissell, Jr., July 18, 1983.
2. This was the reason that Eisenhower insisted on exercising closer personal control of U-2 operations. "Well, boys," he said when he approved the project, "I believe the country needs this information and I'm going to approve it. But I'll tell you one thing. Someday one of these machines is going to get caught and we're going to have a storm" (quoted in John Prados, *The Soviet Estimate: U.S. Intelligence Analysis and Russian Military Strength* [New York: Dial Press, 1982], p. 31).
3. John Kenneth Galbraith, *A Life in Our Times—Memoirs* (London: André Deutsch, 1981), p. 396.
4. Central Intelligence Agency, NIE 11-7-60.
5. Robert Keith Gray, *Eighteen Acres Under Glass* (New York: Doubleday, 1962), p. 25.
6. Interview, Richard M. Bissell, Jr., July 18, 1983.
7. Ibid.
8. Leonard Mosley, *Dulles: A Biography of Eleanor, Allen and John Foster Dulles and Their Family Network* (New York: Dial Press/James Wade, 1978), p. 367, and interview, Richard M. Bissell, Jr., July 18, 1983: "The old J-57 used to flame-out. We had a flame-out once or twice a week. I was prepared to lose a whole lot of sleep if we had that power plant flying over hostile territory."
9. The J-57 engine developed 11,200-lb. thrust; the J-75 had 17,000-lb. thrust. By 1959, J-75 engines had been installed in most U-2s.
10. The first deployment was to Lakenheath, England, in April 1956, shortly redeployed to Wiesbaden, then Giebelstadt, West Germany, by June 1956. A second detachment was based in Incirlik Air Force Base at Adana, Turkey, from June 1956.
11. Interview, Richard M. Bissell, Jr., July 18, 1983. Eisenhower was always worried that a U-2 would be shot down over Russia sooner or later, thus increasing American-Soviet tension or else ruining an attempt to reach agreement over nuclear weapons, which was something Eisenhower was particularly anxious to secure. His hopes were pinned to satellite surveillance, still in the future but in 1955 clearly not far distant. He wanted U-2 flights kept to a minimum, "pending the availability of this new equipment," as he put it. The flights were very useful both in terms of information valuable for strategic planning and in terms of bargaining with the Russians, who of course knew that they were taking place. This was the reason, at the 1955 Geneva Summit, that Eisenhower presented a mutual overhead reconnaissance proposal to the Russians (in the process effectively alerting them to the existence of an American overflight capability).

   If the Russians had accepted, mutual confidence would have been built up and there would have been an end to the American politics of "bomber gaps" and "missile gaps." When they rejected the proposal, Eisenhower knew that the overflights could take place anyhow, because the Russians did not have the antiaircraft technology necessary to shoot them down, and he hoped that by the time the Russians did have the technology, satellites would be doing the job instead. For the background, see Stephen E. Ambrose, *Eisenhower the President* (New York: Simon & Schuster, 1984), pp. 513–515, and Prados, *The Soviet Estimate*, pp. 32–35.
12. The first U-2s, fitted with the J-57 engine, had a maximum speed of 494 mph and a ceiling of 70,000 feet. The second series of U-2s, the U-2B, fitted with J-75 engines, had a maximum speed of 528 mph and a ceiling of 85,000 feet. Gary Powers flew a U-2B.
13. Interview, Richard M. Bissell, Jr., July 18, 1983. Robert F. Kennedy, *Thirteen Days* (New York: Signet, 1969), p. 68, describes the volume of U-2 photographs during the Cuban missile crisis as being "more than twenty-five miles long." Much more was obtained by flights over the USSR.

14. Interview, Lawrence Houston, July 8, 1983.
15. Interview, Richard M. Bissell, Jr., July 18, 1983. On April 11, 1959, Eisenhower approved some U-2 flights. The following day he changed his mind and called in Richard Bissell and the secretary of defense, Neil McElroy, to explain himself. "We cannot in the present circumstances," he said, "afford the revulsion of world opinion against the United States that might occur—the U.S. being the only nation that would conduct this activity." Bissell clearly took the point. See Ambrose, *Eisenhower the President*, p. 515.
16. Interview, Richard M. Bissell, Jr., July 18, 1983.
17. Ibid. See also Mosley, *Dulles*, pp. 369–370.
18. Interview, Richard M. Bissell, Jr., July 18, 1983.
19. Ibid.
20. Nikita Khrushchev, *Khrushchev Remembers*, ed. Strobe Talbott (New York: Bantam Books, 1971), pp. 212–213.
21. Francis Gary Powers with Curt Gentry, *Operation Overflight: The U-2 Spy Pilot Tells His Story for the First Time* (New York: Holt, Rinehart & Winston, 1970), p. 82.
22. For details of his experience see Powers with Gentry, *Operation Overflight*; see also Edward Jay Epstein, *Legend* (New York: Ballantine Books, 1979), pp. 116–120.
23. *Final Report*, IV, p. 59.
24. The requirement for the SR-71 was as successor to the U-2. Once Powers was shot down, altitude was no longer sufficient protection, so speed had to be added. The plane was fitted with two Pratt & Whitney J-58 continuous-bleed afterburning turbojets, each developing a 32,500-lb. thrust. Its top speed was about 2200 mph and range about 3000 miles. The first flight of the plane took place on April 26, 1962. It was the most advanced plane at the time. Titanium and its alloys were used in the construction of the airframe, creating unprecedented engineering problems, since this metal had never before been used in this way. The SR-71 could also be used as a bomber.
25. In his diary on February 29, 1956, Eisenhower noted that the American missile program was stressing accuracy, not distance. "If we stopped guiding and other things," he said, "we could get all sorts of distances that would scare them to death." Eisenhower saw no sense in what would later become the Kennedy administration's policy of "mutual assured destruction," which placed no emphasis on accuracy, and he considered that the Russians would see no sense in it as well. So throughout the 1950s' "missile gap" argument Eisenhower's expressed view was that accuracy rather than quantity was the vital factor.

    "Now, I just want to ask you one thing," he said to reporters at a 1956 press conference, "and if there is anyone here that has got the answer to this one, you will relieve me mightily by communicating it to me here or in private: Can you picture a war that would be waged with atomic missiles . . . ?" Missiles were inaccurate (then); there would have to be vast numbers of them to be effective, each with a heavy payload; there would be indiscriminate destruction, not "war" in any recognizable sense, "because war is a contest, and you finally get to the point with missiles where you are talking about race suicide, and nothing else." "After a certain point," he said on another occasion, "there is no use in having more, no matter what the quantity. If we have all we need to create the devastation we know we can create, what the hell is the use of more?" (quoted in Ambrose, *Eisenhower the President*, pp. 313–314).
26. Quoted ibid., p. 314.
27. Central Intelligence Agency, "Main Trends in Soviet Capabilities and Policies, 1957–1962," NIE 11-4-57, November 12, 1957. See also Prados, *The Soviet Estimate*, p. 114.
28. Prados, *The Soviet Estimate*, pp. 85–96, 113. The 1960 Estimate, NIE 11-4-60, included the air force estimate that there would be about 700 Soviet intercontinental ballistic missiles by 1963, giving 200–700 as the range of deployment.
29. Prados, *The Soviet Estimate*, p. 106.
30. Interview, Richard M. Bissell, Jr., July 18, 1983. The first Corona launches took place at Vandenberg Air Force Base. On January 21, 1959, a procedural error in the count-

down forced a postponement of the first launch. A similar error postponed the second on February 25.

31. Quoted in Mosley, *Dulles*, p. 432.
32. George B. Kistiakowsky, *A Scientist at the White House: The Private Diary of President Eisenhower's Special Assistant for Science and Technology* (Cambridge, MA: Harvard University Press, 1976), p. 45. It seems that Samos was not as successful as Kistiakowsky was led to believe and that its photographs were of poor quality. See Lawrence Freedman, *U.S. Intelligence and the Soviet Strategic Threat* (London: Macmillan, 1977), p. 72. One report, however, maintains that Samos provided excellent intelligence in 1961, leading to a reduction in the estimate of Soviet ICBM strength from 120 to 60 (Philip Klass, *Secret Sentries in Space* [New York: Random House, 1971], pp. 104–106).
33. Quoted in Mosley, *Dulles*, pp. 432–433.
34. Richard Helms, "Remarks at Donovan Award Dinner," May 24, 1983.
35. Ray S. Cline, *The CIA Under Reagan, Bush and Casey* (Washington, DC: Acropolis Books, 1981), pp. 181–182.
36. *Final Report*, IV, pp. 59–60. See also Cline, *The CIA*, pp. 178–180, and Thomas Powers, *The Man Who Kept the Secrets: Richard Helms and the CIA* (New York: Knopf, 1979), p. 97.
37. Cline, *The CIA*, p. 180.
38. Interview, Richard M. Bissell, Jr., July 18, 1983.
39. Interview, Richard Helms, July 26, 1983.
40. Cline, *The CIA*, pp. 183–184.
41. Interview, Richard M. Bissell, Jr., July 18, 1983.
42. Powers, *The Man Who Kept the Secrets*, pp. 98–100. This is a very good account of the relationship between Helms and Bissell, clearly based on extensive interviews with both men and others.
43. William V. Kennedy, David Baker, Richard S. Friedman, and David Miller, *The Intelligence War* (London: Salamander, 1983), pp. 20–22; see also Powers, *The Man Who Kept the Secrets*, pp. 100–103.
44. Bill Jersey and Jim Belson, *Children of Violence*, television documentary (1984), production for Corporation for Public Broadcasting (4560 Horton Street, Suite 420, Emeryville, CA 94608).
45. *The New York Times*, April 14 and 15, 1966. See also Victor Marchetti and John D. Marks, *The CIA and the Cult of Intelligence* (New York: Knopf, 1974), p. 197.
46. Joseph B. Smith, *Portrait of a Cold Warrior* (New York: Ballantine Books, 1981), pp. 216–230. Victor Marchetti and John D. Marks, *The CIA and the Cult of Intelligence* (New York: Knopf, 1974), p. 254, date the start of the operation to early 1958.
47. Smith, *Portrait of a Cold Warrior*, pp. 230–231.
48. Ibid., p. 232. Robert Maheu, an ex-FBI officer, was responsible for making the film. Maheu later became Howard Hughes's chief assistant.
49. Ibid., p. 272.
50. Ibid., p. 240.
51. Marchetti and Marks, *The CIA and the Cult of Intelligence*, pp. 26, 101, 122.
52. Ibid., p. 102.
53. Ibid., p. 103.
54. Cline, *The CIA*, p. 211, and interview, Richard M. Bissell, Jr., July 18, 1983: " 'Executive Action'—I think that came from someplace else. It may have been European, possibly even British MI-6 terminology."
55. Church Committee, *Alleged Assassination Plots Involving Foreign Leaders* (New York: W. W. Norton, 1976), p. 256. This was the published interim report of the Select Committee of the United States Senate to study governmental operations with respect to intelligence activities—the Church Committee. See also *Final Report*, IV, pp. 121–142. There is an unconfirmed story that Gamal Nasser was also the target of a CIA assassination attempt in 1957. It is said that the CIA was acting at the request of the British prime minister, Sir Anthony Eden, smarting after the Suez debacle, and with

the consent of President Eisenhower. A CIA agent in Egypt, Miles Copeland, apparently was given cigarettes injected with botulism poison for Nasser to smoke. These cigarettes, Copeland said, were furnished by Dr. Sidney Gottlieb, head of the Technical Services Division. Copeland did not go through with the attempt (Miles Copeland, *The Game of Nations* [New York: Simon & Schuster, 1969], p. 202). Apart from Copeland's account, there is only hearsay evidence about any attempt on Nasser's life by the CIA. While the Church Committee did look into allegations of CIA attempts on Nasser's life, it could not establish satisfactorily if any attempt or attempts had in fact been planned or made, and it did not list Nasser as ever having been an assassination target.

The Church Committee investigated allegations that the agency had tried to assassinate Chou En-lai (termed in the committee's report, "an East Asian leader") in 1955. An Air India plane on which Chou was scheduled to fly to Bandung, Indonesia, for the Afro-Asian Conference in April that year, blew up in flight. Chou had changed his plans at the last minute and was not on board. A detonating mechanism was found in the wreckage. On November 21, 1967, an alleged American defector, John Discoe Smith, claimed in the Moscow *Literaturnaya Gazeta* that he had delivered a CIA bomb to a Chinese Nationalist in Hong Kong for the purpose of killing Chou in the plane. Some CIA officers in the Far East had recommended Chou's assassination to headquarters, but it had been firmly rejected by Allen Dulles. "A reply cable was received immediately from CIA headquarters disapproving the recommendation to assassinate the East Asian leader . . . [T]he cable 'strongly censured' the station and indicated 'in the strongest possible language this Agency has never and never will engage in any such activities.' The cable added: 'Immediately proceed to burn all copies of any documents relating to this request.' . . . [A] senior representative from CIA headquarters arrived shortly at the station to reprimand the officers involved in the incident" (*Final Report*, IV, p. 133). See also W. R. Corson, *The Armies of Ignorance* (New York: The Dial Press/James Wade, 1977), pp. 365–366, and Arthur M. Schlesinger, Jr., *Robert Kennedy and His Times* (London: Futura, 1979), p. 517.

56. *Alleged Assassination Plots*, p. 256.
57. Interview, William Colby, July 25, 1983.
58. Powers, *The Man Who Kept the Secrets*, pp. 335–336.
59. *Alleged Assassination Plots*, p. 93.
60. Ibid., p. 93.
61. Cline, *The CIA*, p. 209.
62. *Alleged Assassination Plots*, p. 263.
63. John A. Bross, review of Powers, *The Man Who Kept the Secrets*, in Central Intelligence Agency, *Studies in Intelligence*, 1980.
64. Interview, Richard M. Bissell, Jr., July 18, 1983.
65. Cline, *The CIA*, p. 211; see also *Alleged Assassination Plots*, pp. 93, 181–187, 274.
66. *Alleged Assassination Plots*, p. 263.
67. Ibid., p. 60: Special Group minutes, August 25, 1960.
68. Ibid., p. 62: National Security Council minutes, September 21, 1960.
69. Richard D. Mahoney, *JFK: Ordeal in Africa* (New York: Oxford University Press, 1983), p. 37.
70. *Alleged Assassination Plots*, p. 56. The NSC staff member who recalled this was Robert H. Johnson, in testimony to the Church Committee fifteen years later.
71. Ibid., pp. 15–16. This ties in with Robert Johnson's memory—"high quarters" clearly means the President—and sustains the point that Allen Dulles, Richard Bissell, and all those involved understood that they were acting at the direction of the President.
72. Quoted in Ambrose, *Eisenhower the President*, p. 226, "Conference with Knowland," November 23, 1954.
73. See *Alleged Assassination Plots*, pp. 11–12, for a discussion of the concept of plausible denial. The point made is that this concept is generally recognized and accepted in Washington and is not something invented by the CIA.
74. Interview, Richard M. Bissell, Jr., July 18, 1983.

75. *Alleged Assassination Plots*, p. 22. In the report Gottlieb is referred to by a cover name, "Scheider."
76. Ibid., p. 38. In the report O'Donnell is referred to by a cover name, "Mulroney."
77. *Alleged Assassination Plots*, p. 39.
78. Ibid., pp. 39–40.
79. Powers, *The Man Who Kept the Secrets*, p. 108.
80. Mahoney, *JFK: Ordeal in Africa*, pp. 69–70. On October 7 the Leopoldville CIA station cabled headquarters that Gottlieb had "left certain items of continuing usefulness" and that they would "continue try implement op" (*Alleged Assassination Plots*, p. 29). On October 15 headquarters cabled Leopoldville: "Possibility use commando type group for abduction [Lumumba], either via assault on house up cliff from river. . . . Request your views" (ibid., p. 32). Leopoldville replied on October 17: "Not been able to penetrate entourage. . . . Recommended HQS pouch soonest high powered foreign make rifle with telescopic scope and silencer. Hunting good here when lights right. However as hunting rifles now forbidden, would keep rifle in office pending opening of hunting season" (ibid., p. 32). On January 13, 1961, worried that Lumumba might escape from Mobutu, Leopoldville cabled headquarters: "The combination of [Lumumba's] powers as demagogue, his able use of goon squads and propaganda and spirit of defeat within [government] coalition which would increase rapidly under such conditions would almost certainly insure [Lumumba] victory in Parliament. . . . Refusal to take drastic steps at this time will lead to defeat of [United States] policy in Congo" (ibid., p. 49). On January 19, after Lumumba's murder, the CIA base chief in Elisabethville cabled headquarters: "Thanks for Patrice. If we had known he was coming, we would have baked a snake" (ibid., p. 51). The will to see Lumumba dead was certainly there.
81. *Alleged Assassination Plots*, p. 92. On December 11, 1959, Colonel J. C. King wrote a memorandum to Allen Dulles using these statements. Dulles approved the memorandum.
82. Ibid., p. 92. Again the point being made by Bissell was that a plan was one thing, its implementation another. On January 13, 1960, for example, Dulles was recorded at a Special Group meeting as insisting that "a quick elimination of Castro" was not contemplated by the CIA, "but rather actions designed to enable responsible opposition leaders to get a foothold" (p. 93).
83. This and the following quotes are from interviews, McGeorge Bundy, July 21, 1983; Richard Helms, July 26, 1983. Letters, McGeorge Bundy to author, February 26, 1985; Richard Helms to author, February 27, 1985.
84. Interview, R. Jack Smith, July 15, 1983.
85. *Final Report*, IV, p. 62.

11. On the Beach: 1961

1. Church Committee, *Alleged Assassination Plots Involving Foreign Leaders* (New York: W. W. Norton, 1974), p. 138.
2. Ibid., p. 139. Kennedy said this to Richard Goodwin, special assistant to the President, who was present at both of Szulc's conversations with the Kennedy brothers. Goodwin recalled the President's words corroborating Szulc.
3. Ibid., p. 317.
4. Ibid., p. 316.
5. William Manchester, *One Brief Shining Moment* (London: Michael Joseph, 1983), pp. 39–43. None of the Kennedy sons wanted to be like their father; it was left to the brother-in-law Sargent Shriver to manage the family fortune. Businessmen were "beneath" them. They were determined to show they were not just rich—or thin-blooded. All of this was wrapped up in the language of public purpose. Father was content; he wanted his sons to be better than he was.
6. Ibid., pp. 119–120.
7. Ibid., p. 120.

8. Harris Wofford, *Of Kennedys & Kings: Making Sense of the Sixties* (New York: Farrar, Straus & Giroux, 1980), p. 358.

9. Stewart Alsop, *The Center: People and Power in Political Washington* (New York: Harper & Row, 1968), p. 213.

10. Interview, R. Jack Smith, July 23, 1983. We now know that the Soviets train their interceptor pilots to ram enemy aircraft if necessary; the cool professionalism of CIA analysis was always vulnerable to the cult of coolness. The bomber, not the aircrew, was the object of sacrifice; the aircrew could always parachute.

11. New York *Herald Tribune*, August 1, 1958.

12. John Prados, *The Soviet Estimate: U.S. Intelligence Analysis and Russian Military Strength* (New York: Dial Press, 1982), pp. 75–95.

13. George B. Kistiakowsky, *A Scientist at the White House: The Private Diary of President Eisenhower's Special Assistant for Science and Technology* (Cambridge, MA: Harvard University Press, 1976), p. 219.

14. Richard M. Nixon, *Six Crises* (New York: Doubleday, 1962), p. 351.

15. Joseph Burkholder Smith, *Portrait of a Cold Warrior* (New York: Ballantine Books, 1981) pp. 316–317.

16. Arthur M. Schlesinger, Jr., *A Thousand Days: John F. Kennedy in the White House* (Boston: Houghton Mifflin, 1965), pp. 208–210.

17. *Alleged Assassination Plots*, pp. 93–96.

18. Ibid., pp. 74–77.

19. Judith Campbell Exner, *My Story* (New York: Grove Press, 1977), pp. 102–103.

20. Memorandum, Director of Security, CIA, "Robert Maheu," April 10, 1963. The CIA requested the Justice Department not to prosecute Maheu. Prosecution "undoubtedly would lead to exposures of most sensitive information relating to the abortive Cuban invasion in April 1961 and would result in most damaging embarrassment to the United States Government."

21. *Alleged Assassination Plots*, p. 78.

22. Ibid., p. 79.

23. Ibid., pp. 181–187.

24. Interview, Richard M. Bissell, Jr., July 18, 1983.

25. Ibid.

26. Ibid.

27. Robert H. Ferrell, ed., *The Eisenhower Diaries* (New York: W. W. Norton, 1981), pp. 379–380.

28. Quoted in Lucien S. Vandenbroucke, "The 'Confessions' of Allen Dulles: New Evidence on the Bay of Pigs," *Diplomatic History* (Fall 1984), Vol. 8, No. 4, p. 367.

29. Thomas Powers, *The Man Who Kept the Secrets: Richard Helms and the CIA* (New York: Knopf, 1979), pp. 106–111, 330.

30. Interview, Peter Karlow, July 28, 1983. Interview, November 18, 1984.

31. Ernst Halperin, *National Liberation Movements in Latin America*, Center for International Studies, MIT (June 1969), p. 51.

32. Interview, Richard Helms, July 26, 1983.

33. Schlesinger, *A Thousand Days*, pp. 593–594. Powers, *The Man Who Kept the Secrets*, p. 133. Later it was alleged that had the spadework on the proposed Cuban operation been done in the more structured bureaucratic channels of the Eisenhower administration, the results might have been different, and that, in particular, the abolition of the OCB was a major contributory factor in the Bay of Pigs fiasco. But even if the OCB had been retained, it would not necessarily have continued to work effectively, because there would have been an almost total change in its composition as Kennedy made his appointments.

34. David Atlee Phillips, *The Night Watch: 25 Years of Peculiar Service* (New York: Atheneum, 1977), pp. 101–102. "Colonel Alcott" is Phillips' pseudonym for Hawkins.

35. Powers, *The Man Who Kept the Secrets*, p. 331. Admiral Arleigh Burke, navy Chief of Staff, took precautionary steps on his own initiative, placing two marine battalions on a

navy task force off Cuba, ready to invade if the President were to order it, or to relieve "La Brigada" if necessary.

36. Schlesinger, *A Thousand Days*, p. 177.
37. Interview, July 6, 1983.
38. David Halberstam, *The Best and the Brightest*, (Greenwich, CT: Fawcett Crest, 1972), p. 87.
39. Schlesinger, *A Thousand Days*, p. 262. Eighteen months later, during the Cuban crisis, Kennedy emphasized this point. When someone suggested that each of his advisers write down his recommendation, Kennedy said "he did not want people, if things went wrong, claiming that their plans would have worked" (ibid., p. 691).
40. Phillips, *The Night Watch*, pp. 102–109, and Schlesinger, *A Thousand Days*, pp. 591–597. Peter Wyden, *Bay of Pigs* (London: Jonathan Cape, 1979), pp. 93–288, gives a comprehensive account of the operation from all sides.
41. Interview, David Atlee Phillips, July 6, 1983.
42. Interview, Richard Helms, July 26, 1983.
43. Interview, Richard M. Bissell, Jr., July 18, 1983.
44. Quoted in Vandenbroucke, "The 'Confessions' of Allen Dulles," p. 368; see also Richard M. Bissell, Jr., "Response to Lucien S. Vandenbroucke," *Diplomatic History* (Fall 1984), Vol. 8, No. 4, pp. 377–378.
45. Phillips, *The Night Watch*, p. 110.
46. Ibid., p. 109.
47. Wyden, *Bay of Pigs*, p. 240.
48. Quoted in Vandenbroucke, "The 'Confessions' of Allen Dulles," p. 368.
49. See Bissell, "Response to Lucien S. Vandenbroucke," p. 378.
50. Interview, Richard M. Bissell, Jr., July 18, 1983.
51. Schlesinger, *A Thousand Days*, p. 692.
52. Interview, Richard M. Bissell, Jr., July 18, 1983.
53. Bissell, "Response to Lucien S. Vandenbroucke," p. 377.
54. Wyden, *Bay of Pigs*, p. 160.
55. Bissell, "Response to Lucien S. Vandenbroucke," p. 380.
56. Phillips, *The Night Watch*, p. 109.
57. Interview, Richard M. Bissell, Jr., July 18, 1983. See also Wyden, *Bay of Pigs*, p. 322, and Powers, *The Man Who Kept the Secrets*, pp. 115, 117–118, 331. Some versions of the story have Kennedy saying this to Dulles, not to Bissell. Bissell remembers the President saying it to him. It could be that Kennedy made the same remark to both men.
58. Quoted in Manchester, *One Brief Shining Moment*, p. 137.
59. Quoted in Schlesinger, *A Thousand Days*, p. 250.
60. Quoted in Arthur M. Schlesinger, Jr., *Robert Kennedy and His Times* (London: Futura, 1979), p. 493.
61. Ibid. National Security Council Action Memoranda 55 and 57 transferred some paramilitary operations to the Defense Department and restricted the DDP.

CIA's budget now exceeded State's by more than 50 percent (even if it was less than half that of the intelligence operations of the Defense Department). Its staff had doubled in a decade. In some areas CIA had outstripped the State Department in the quality of its personnel, partly because it paid higher salaries and partly because Allen Dulles' defiance of McCarthy enabled it to attract and hold abler men. It had almost as many people under official cover overseas as State; in a number of embassies CIA officers outnumbered those from State in the political sections. Often the CIA station chief had been in the country longer than the ambassador, and had more money at his disposal and exerted more influence. CIA had its own political desks and military staffs; it had in effect its own foreign service, its own air force, even, on occasion, its own combat forces. . . .

The Bay of Pigs stimulated a wide variety of proposals for the reorganization of CIA. The State Department, for example, could not wait to separate CIA's overt from its clandestine functions and even change the agency's name. . . . The Agency itself suffered from doubt and gloom after Cuba, and it was feared that drastic measures would cause total demoralization. Instead, Kennedy moved quietly to cut down the CIA budget in 1962 and again in 1963, aiming at a 20 percent reduction by 1966. At the same time, anticipating the resignation of Allen Dulles, he began looking for a new director (Schlesinger, *A Thousand Days*, pp. 381– 382).

The CIA budget—always secret—in 1967 was about $700 million (Victor Marchetti and John D. Marks, *The CIA and the Cult of Intelligence* [New York: Laurel, 1980], p. 297). Schlesinger's allegation that there were "almost as many people under official cover overseas as State" is contested by CIA insiders (Samuel Halpern, letter to author, August 11, 1986).

62. Phillips, *The Night Watch*, p. 112.
63. Quoted in Schlesinger, *Robert Kennedy and His Times*, p. 493.
64. Ibid., p. 493. Something may have been lost in this story. Lovett was one of the most experienced power brokers in the United States, famous for his coolness and patience. If, after eight years on the Board of Consultants, his allegation of amateurism was accurate, something very serious was wrong. It would have called for a major overhaul of the agency. Three years earlier, with the success of the U-2 and Guatemala, could this have been said?
65. Ibid., pp. 493–494. The significance of this episode is that it shows that the Kennedys wanted to be their own spy masters. Dulles went in part because of this; McCone was chosen in part because he was not interested in spying or operations, which now came under Bobby's control.
66. Wyden, *The Bay of Pigs*, pp. 317–322.
67. Quoted in David C. Martin, *Wilderness of Mirrors* (New York: Ballantine Books, 1980), p. 119.
68. Ibid., p. 120.
69. Powers, *The Man Who Kept the Secrets*, pp. 116, 332. This was a guess: two years before, the army had been fighting Castro, and Latin American armies have never been renowned for loyalty. Castro's popularity was more important.
70. Lyman B. Kirkpatrick, Jr., "Paramilitary Case Study—The Bay of Pigs," *Naval War College Review* (November-December 1972). See also Wyden, *The Bay of Pigs*, pp. 322–324, for a discussion of Kirkpatrick's article and view that incompetence marked the whole operation.
71. Quoted in Martin, *Wilderness of Mirrors*, p. 120.
72. Quoted in Halberstam, *The Best and the Brightest*, p. 85.
73. Quoted in ibid., p. 91. See also Schlesinger, *A Thousand Days*, pp. 296–298.
74. Wyden, *The Bay of Pigs*, p. 318.
75. Quoted in Halberstam, *The Best and the Brightest*, p. 84. Carl Kaysen was a disarmament expert from Harvard then working on the National Security Council Staff as McGeorge Bundy's deputy.

12. *Touch Football: 1961–1965*

1. Church Committee, *Alleged Assassination Plots Involving Foreign Leaders* (New York: W. W. Norton, 1974), p. 182.
2. Ibid., p. 330. There is conflicting testimony as to whether or not Bissell had already informed Robert Kennedy of the CIA-Mafia link. Hoover clearly thought he had. What is definite is that with this memorandum, Hoover ensured that Kennedy knew, and that this would be on the record. The Justice Department decided not to prosecute Maheu for the bugging.
3. Ibid., p. 333.
4. Ibid., p. 333.
5. Ibid., p. 334.
6. Ibid., p. 334.
7. Ibid., p. 334.
8. Ibid., p. 336.

9. Harris Wofford, *Of Kennedys & Kings: Making Sense of the Sixties* (New York: Farrar, Straus & Giroux, 1980), p. 386.
10. This story is told in Thomas Powers, *The Man Who Kept the Secrets: Richard Helms and the CIA* (New York, Knopf, 1979), pp. 139–140.
11. Ibid., pp. 137–141. Powers gives a detailed account of the way Robert Kennedy operated and the pressure he put on Harvey and Helms.
12. *Alleged Assassination Plots*, p. 105.
13. Ibid., p. 104.
14. See pp. 415–16.
15. Powers, *The Man Who Kept the Secrets*, pp. 141–142.
16. *Alleged Assassination Plots*, pp. 59, 89. See also George Crile, "The Riddle of AM/LASH," *The Washington Post*, May 2, 1976, and Powers, *The Man Who Kept the Secrets*, pp. 148–152, 343. AM/LASH was Cubela's CIA cryptonym. Edward Jay Epstein, *Legend* (New York: Ballantine Books, 1979), pp. 232–234, 241–243, 255, links President Kennedy directly with Cubela's plans to assassinate Castro:

> Desmond FitzGerald decided to meet with Cubela himself, as a "personal representative" of Kennedy's. The risk of possibly compromising the President was apparently outweighed in his opinion by the gains in advancing the coup d'état. . . . About two weeks later [about November 12, 1963] FitzGerald managed a further "signal" for Cubela and his followers in Cuba. He wrote a section of the speech President Kennedy was to deliver in Miami on November 18. It described the Castro government as a "small band of conspirators" that, "once removed," would ensure United States assistance to the Cuban nation. (Ibid., p. 241)

17. Quoted in Arthur M. Schlesinger, Jr., *Robert Kennedy and His Times* (London: Futura, 1979), p. 665. Bobby was commenting on allegations being made in 1967 by the New Orleans district attorney, Jim Garrison, that the CIA was behind his brother's death. He seems to have thought Garrison was a sensationalist, and he did not believe Garrison's charges. He also seems to have thought that the Warren Commission had conducted an inadequate investigation but that nevertheless its conclusions were probably correct and that there had been no conspiracy behind his brother's death (ibid.).
    The thought that there might have been a conspiracy also crossed the mind of Richard Helms. When news came of the assassination, Helms was lunching with McCone. "Suddenly Mr. McCone's aide came through the door and said that the president had been shot. And I realized very quickly that my responsibility was to get the lines out as rapidly as possible to see if there was anything going on anyplace else in the world. Could this be part of a conspiracy? . . . It became manifest within 24 or 48 hours that this was not the case" (*Newsweek*, November 28, 1983).
18. Wofford, *Of Kennedys & Kings*, p. 411.
19. Quoted in Schlesinger, *Robert Kennedy and His Times*, p. 700. Johnson's thought that Kennedy's death was "divine retribution" was expressed to Pierre Salinger. Johnson must have known that Salinger would tell Bobby, which is precisely what happened.
20. Leo Janos, "The Last Days of the President," *Atlantic Monthly* (July 1973).
21. Quoted in Schlesinger, *Robert Kennedy and His Times*, p. 701.
22. Quoted ibid., pp. 599–600. Castro went on to say, "I'll tell you one thing: at least Kennedy was an enemy to whom we had become accustomed. This is a serious matter, an extremely serious matter." In 1978 Castro told members of the House Select Committee on Assassinations that killing Kennedy would have been "tremendous insanity . . . the most perfect pretext for the United States to invade our country which is what I have tried to prevent for all these years" (ibid.).
    In 1967 Marvin Watson of Johnson's White House staff told an FBI agent that Johnson "was now convinced there was a plot in connection with the assassination. Watson stated the President felt that CIA had something to do with this plot" (ibid., p. 665). In 1967 Johnson asked the CIA to prepare an exhaustive report on its assassination efforts, perhaps in an attempt to discover for himself if there was any truth in allegations of possible CIA involvement in Kennedy's death. In 1975 the Rockefeller

Commission asked the agency for a report "regarding allegations of Castro Cuban involvement in the John F. Kennedy assassination." In all cases no evidence was found of CIA involvement.

23. Richard Nixon, *Leaders* (New York: Warner Books, 1982), p. 179.
24. Nikita Khrushchev, *Khrushchev Remembers*, ed. Strobe Talbott (New York: Bantam Books, 1971), pp. 544–546. These memoirs are generally considered to be authentic although published after KGB censorship.
25. Central Intelligence Agency, "The Military Buildup in Cuba," SNIE 85-3-62.
26. Ibid.
27. David Halberstam, *The Best and the Brightest* (Greenwich, CT: Fawcett Crest, 1972), pp. 96–97.
28. *New York Review of Books*, April 14, 1966, p. 12.
29. Ray S. Cline, *The CIA Under Reagan, Bush and Casey* (Washington, DC: Acropolis Books, 1981), pp. 219, 220.
30. Interview, R. Jack Smith, July 23, 1983.
31. Central Intelligence Agency, "Soviet Reactions to Certain US Courses of Action on Cuba," SNIE 11-18-62, October 19, 1962.
32. Central Intelligence Agency, "Major Consequences of Certain US Courses of Action on Cuba," SNIE 11-19-62, October 20, 1962.
33. Arthur M. Schlesinger, Jr., *A Thousand Days* (Boston: Houghton Mifflin, 1965), p. 688. The knowledge that the United States' nuclear weapons far exceeded the strength of those of the Soviet Union must have been a constant (although unspoken) deterrent to Khrushchev throughout and must have been a source of reassurance to Kennedy and his advisers.
34. Robert F. Kennedy, *Thirteen Days: A Memoir of the Cuban Missile Crisis* (New York: Signet, 1969), p. 31.
35. Schlesinger, *Robert Kennedy and His Times*, pp. 546–551. See also George W. Ball, *The Past Has Another Pattern* (New York: W. W. Norton, 1982), pp. 290–310, and Cline, *The CIA*, pp. 220–222. The Excom group consisted of Secretary of State Dean Rusk, Secretary of Defense Robert McNamara, Secretary of the Treasury Douglas Dillon, Special Assistant to the President McGeorge Bundy, Presidential Counsel Theodore Sorensen, Undersecretary of State George Ball, Deputy Undersecretary of State U. Alexis Johnson, Maxwell Taylor, Assistant Secretary of State for Latin American Affairs Edward Martin, Ambassador Llewellyn Thompson, Deputy Secretary of Defense Roswell Gilpatric, Assistant Secretary of Defense Paul Nitze, Director of Central Intelligence John McCone. Vice-President Lyndon Johnson, Ambassador Adlai Stevenson, Special Assistant to the President Kenneth O'Donnell, and Deputy Director of the United States Information Agency Donald Wilson attended intermittently. Dean Rusk, who as secretary of state might have assumed the position of chairman of the group, did not, and—along with Lyndon Johnson—had other duties that kept him from attending all the meetings.
36. Cline, *The CIA*, p. 222. The CIA's photographic analysis was especially impressive to the President and Excom. The Office of Current Intelligence had developed "crateology," an extremely specialized form of photo-interpretation involving the study of Soviet methods of crating weapons for shipment. From a photograph of a crate they could tell what weapon it was probably carrying. They produced the first hard intelligence that the Russians were shipping missiles to Cuba from analysis of crates photographed on the decks of Russian cargo ships. Cline asked Bundy and Kennedy to evaluate the October 14 U-2 photographs and their analysis, "and they each said it fully justified all that the CIA had cost the country in all its preceding years" (ibid., p. 221).
37. Ibid., p. 221.
38. In the summer of 1962 the agency had rejected the likelihood of the Russians' installing medium- and intermediate-range missiles in Cuba. In the CIA view, the Russians would not want to upset the balance of power with the United States so directly, since American nuclear and conventional forces were superior (Schlesinger, *A Thousand Days*, p. 682). Kennedy shared this view. The day before the missiles were discovered

McGeorge Bundy said on national television that there was "no present evidence" and in his judgment "no present likelihood" of a "major offensive capability in Cuba" (quoted in Schlesinger, *Robert Kennedy and His Times*, p. 552).

39. Kennedy, *Thirteen Days*, p. 62; see also Schlesinger, *Robert Kennedy and His Times*, pp. 537–554.

40. Interview, R. Jack Smith, July 23, 1983. The British, French, and German governments had all been informed before Kennedy formally told his cabinet about the crisis on October 22. Also on October 22 the Excom group was formally constituted under National Security Council Action Memorandum 196. Until then it had all been informal, "touch football."

41. Ball, *The Past Has Another Pattern*, p. 291.

42. Greville Wynne, *The Man from Odessa* (London: Robert Hale, 1981), p. 201.

43. Ibid., pp. 202–204.

44. Ibid., pp. 202–203.

45. Ibid., p. 206.

46. For an interesting discussion of Penkovsky and the doubts about him, see Richard Deacon, *"C"—A Biography of Sir Maurice Oldfield* (London: Macdonald, 1985) pp. 130–138. Penkovsky also revealed two Soviet agents in MI-5, Britain's counterespionage service; the identities of several KGB agents working under Soviet diplomatic cover; the deployment patterns of Soviet missile sites; over 5000 photographs of documents; information about Soviet military personnel; economic intelligence; and scientific and technical intelligence on Soviet weapons systems. He was, according to Oldfield, "The answer to a prayer. What he provided seemed like a miracle, too. That is why for so long he was mistrusted on both sides of the Atlantic. It seemed incredible that he could take such risks—not merely photographing top secret documents, but actually giving us the original documents in some instances" (ibid., p. 131).

47. House Select Committee on Assassinations, *Investigation of the Assassination of President John F. Kennedy*, Vol. II (1979), pp. 444–445.

48. Ibid., Vols II, IV, and XII. See also Edward Jay Epstein, *Legend: The Secret World of Lee Harvey Oswald* (New York: Ballantine Books, 1979), and David C. Martin, *Wilderness of Mirrors* (New York: Ballantine Books, 1981). Epstein's book is seen as Angleton's version of the Nosenko case; Martin's book is regarded as the other view.

49. *Final Report*, IV, pp. 67–68, 70–72.

50. Victor Marchetti and John D. Marks, *The CIA and the Cult of Intelligence* (New York: Laurel, 1983), pp. 234–236.

51. *Final Report*, IV, p. 73. In a sense, however, this specification was a major setback for the agency. It was no longer a very special agency within the presidency but a cabinet-level bureaucracy. Kennedy's letter was in effect a demotion.

52. Interview, McGeorge Bundy, July 21, 1983.

53. Cline, *The CIA*, p. 217.

54. Ibid., pp. 217–218.

55. Ibid., pp. 216–217.

56. Martin, *Wilderness of Mirrors*, p. 119.

57. Richard Helms, "Remarks at Donovan Award Dinner," May 24, 1983.

58. Ibid.

59. Interview, R. Jack Smith, July 15, 1983.

60. Stephen E. Ambrose and Richard H. Immerman, *Ike's Spies* (New York: Doubleday, 1981), pp. 256–257, and Andrew Tully, *The CIA—The Inside Story* (New York: Morrow, 1962), p. 110; also interview, Lawrence Houston, July 16, 1984.

61. Peer de Silva, *Sub Rosa—The CIA and the Uses of Intelligence* (New York: Times Books, 1978), pp. 209–210, 230.

62. *The New York Times*, July 5, 1971, "The Pentagon Papers."

63. Cline, *The CIA*, pp. 222–223.

64. Ambrose and Immerman, *Ike's Spies*, pp. 252–256.

65. David Wise and Thomas B. Ross, *The Invisible Government* (New York: Vintage Books, 1974), p. 236.

66. Cline, *The CIA*, pp. 225–226.
67. Interview, April 2, 1984.
68. Interview, July 15, 1983. Raborn's swearing-in ceremony was attended by leading members of the CIA Establishment. For some unknown reason the White House press release included all their names and identified many of them for the first time, including, besides Dulles and McCone, Helms, Cline, Kirkpatrick, R. Jack Smith, Desmond Fitz-Gerald, Albert Wheelon, Sherman Kent, John A. Bross, Lawrence Houston, Walter Elder, Cord Meyer, William Colby, J. C. King, and Bronson Tweedy (David Wise and Thomas B. Ross, *The Espionage Establishment* [New York: Random House, 1967], p. 137).
69. Interview, April 2, 1984.
70. *Final Report*, IV, p. 66.
71. *Final Report*, IV, p. 68.

13. Agency Agonistes: 1965–1968

1. Quoted in David Wise and Thomas B. Ross, *The Espionage Establishment* (New York: Random House, 1967), p. 138.
2. Quoted, ibid., p. 139.
3. Interview, Lawrence Houston, November 7, 1984. Wisner was head of OPC at the time.
4. The OSS had urged support for Ho and Vietnamese communism, but OSS links with Ho were broken off after 1945 and its advice set aside. See William Colby and Peter Forbath, *Honorable Men: My Life in the CIA* (New York: Simon & Schuster, 1972), p. 52, and Archimedes L. A. Patti, *Why Vietnam? Prelude to America's Albatross* (Berkeley, CA: University of California, 1980).
5. Quoted in Sherman Adams, *First-Hand Report* (New York: Harper & Bros., 1961), p. 124.
6. "Communist Capabilities and Intentions with Respect to the Offshore Islands and Taiwan Through 1955, and Communist and Non-Communist Reactions with Respect to the Defense of Taiwan," National Intelligence Estimate, NIE 100.4.55, March 16, 1955, discussed various courses of action, giving an insight into the sense of emergency governing this cold-war period. It was colored by an assumption of a monolithic, Soviet-controlled communist bloc. It also revealed the extent of dissensions within the intelligence community about the precise courses of action to take, as the footnotes demonstrated. "The Chinese Communist regime appears firmly committed to the seizure ('liberation' as they call it) of the offshore islands and Taiwan. . . . We believe that the Chinese Communists with the forces now in place or readily available in the east China area have the capability to seize the Quemoy and Matsu groups assuming that these islands were defended by the Nationalists alone and the Chinese Communists were willing to risk heavy casualties."

   The first dissension came over the next paragraph:

   > The Chinese Communists will probably undertake air, naval, and artillery attacks against the Quemoy and Matsu groups and will probably attempt to seize lightly defended island outposts within these groups. They will seek to erode Nationalist ability and determination to hold these islands, and, more importantly, to probe US intentions. If the Chinese Communists should become convinced that the US was determined to prevent the seizure and retention of these islands, taking whatever military action was necessary, including, if required, all-out attacks on any part of China, they would probably be deterred from attempting an outright seizure during 1955. However, they would make every effort to render the Chinese Nationalist position on the offshore islands untenable by bombardment, interdiction of supplies, and subversion.

   The Assistant Chief of Staff of the army's G-2 insisted on a footnote to this paragraph. In the army's view, it underestimated "the willingness of the Chinese Communists, supported by the USSR, to assume the risks of war to attain their objectives." The army argued that "even though the Chinese Communists were convinced that the US is determined to prevent the seizure of these offshore islands, it is believed they will attempt to seize them, although not necessarily during 1955."

Two dissensions were registered over another paragraph:

> If the US used nuclear weapons against Communist China, the predominant world reaction would be one of shock. These reactions would be particularly adverse if these weapons were used to defend the offshore islands or destroy military concentrations prior to an all-out Communist Chinese attempt to take the offshore islands. However, certain Asian and European allies might condone the US use of nuclear weapons to stop the actual invasion of Taiwan.

The first dissension was registered by the deputy director for intelligence of the Joint Staff, who "believes that this sentence should read: 'Certain Asian and European allies would probably condone US use of nuclear weapons, particularly if used tactically, as firm evidence of US determination to put a halt to further Communist expansion wherever occurring.'" The second dissension came from the Assistant Chief of Staff, G-2, who "believes that this sentence should read as follows: 'However, certain Asian and European allies might condone the tactical use of nuclear weapons by the US provided that they were convinced such weapons were necessary to stop an actual invasion to Taiwan and that the US was exercising the utmost restraint and attempting to spare civilians.'"

7. Diem received about 89 percent of the total vote, which amounted to an estimated 93 percent of the eligible voters. The election, held on April 9, 1961, was the subject of a CIA Office of Current Intelligence memorandum on November 14, 1961: "An assessment by the American Embassy in Saigon in May concluded that the election was conducted 'with a reasonable degree of honesty' and almost certainly represented the will of the majority of the people. . . . British Intelligence officials in London, noting the large voter turnout and high percentage of votes for Diem, have concluded that the President secured a clear mandate apparently without resorting to any blatant manipulation or corruption."

8. *The New York Times*, October 27, 1961.

9. Quoted in Arthur M. Schlesinger, Jr., *Robert Kennedy And His Times* (London: Futura, 1979), p. 762.

10. Quoted in Stephen E. Ambrose and Richard H. Immerman, *Ike's Spies* (New York: Doubleday, 1981), pp. 257–258.

11. "Communist Reactions to Certain US Courses of Action with Respect to Indochina," Special National Intelligence Estimate, SNIE 10.4.54, June 15, 1954. See also Ambrose and Immerman, *Ike's Spies*, pp. 257–258.

12. Ambrose and Immerman, *Ike's Spies*, pp. 259–261, and David Wise and Thomas B. Ross, *The Invisible Government* (New York: Vintage, 1974), p. 158. Later, when Diem and his brother, Nhu, cracked down on opposition, Lansdale warned that this would result in increasing instability within South Vietnam. Lansdale gradually lost influence with Diem, however, as the U.S. government continued its support for Diem's regime despite the crackdown.

13. Ambrose and Immerman, *Ike's Spies*, pp. 261–262.

14. George Ball, *The Past Has Another Pattern* (New York: W. W. Norton, 1982), p. 370.

15. Church Committee, *Alleged Assassination Plots Involving Foreign Leaders* (New York: W. W. Norton, 1974), pp. 218–219. The cable read:

> We must at the same time also tell key military leaders that US would find it impossible to continue support GVN [Government of South Vietnam] militarily and economically unless above steps are taken immediately which we recognize requires removal of Nhus from the scene. We wish give Diem reasonable opportunity to remove Nhus but if he remains obdurate, then we are prepared to accept the obvious implication that we can no longer support Diem. You may also tell appropriate military commanders we will give them direct support in any interim period of break-

down central government mechanism.... Concurrently with above, Ambassador and country teams should urgently examine all possible alternative leadership and make detailed plans as to how we might bring about Diem's replacement if this should become necessary.

The Pentagon Papers (New York: *New York Times*/Bantam, 1971), pp. 158–233, disclosed that President Kennedy knew and approved of plans for the overthrow of Diem.
16. Quoted in *Alleged Assassination Plots*, p. 217.
17. Ibid., pp. 217–223.
18. Interview, Richard Helms, July 26, 1983.
19. *Alleged Assassination Plots*, p. 223.
20. William Colby, *Honorable Men*, p. 229.
21. Interview, November 20, 1983.
22. Interview, Barton Osborne, in Granada Television program, *World In Action: The Rise and Fall of the CIA* (Manchester, Eng., June 1975), Part III. Osborne later worked for the CIA.
23. Interview, Sam Adams, November 20, 1983.
24. Thomas Powers, *The Man Who Kept the Secrets: Richard Helms and the CIA* (New York: Knopf, 1979), pp. 181–183, 287.
25. Quoted in Victor Marchetti and John D. Marks, *The CIA and the Cult of Intelligence* (New York: Knopf, 1974), p. 245.
26. William Colby, *Honorable Men*, pp. 270–271.
27. Ibid., pp. 270–272.
28. Interview, Major General George Keegan, July 16, 1984.
29. *Final Report*, IV, p. 75.
30. Ibid., pp. 74–76.
31. Interview, Major General George Keegan, July 16, 1984.
32. Ibid. In June 1967 the CIA drafted a Special National Intelligence Estimate, "Capabilities of the Vietnamese Communists Fighting in South Vietnam." The draft stated that bombing had "caused extensive destruction and damage of trucks" and had "restricted cargo movements largely to hours of darkness to minimize losses to air attacks." Despite this, however, the draft argued that North Vietnam had mobilized an enormous repair and construction force that effectively counteracted the destruction caused by U.S. bombing: "In terms of logistical supply capabilities, the net effect of these countermeasures is that North Vietnam is actually in a better position than before the bombing because of the forced draft effort to expand the road system and alternative routes." This conclusion was removed from the final version of the SNIE presented in November 1967. It was an example of an Estimate being "massaged" so as not to alienate its readers.

Similar softening of conclusions occurred elsewhere in the Estimate. In the July draft, for example, it held: "The overall system of supplies delivered into Laos from North Vietnam and Cambodia during the current dry season exceed the total volume estimated to have been delivered last year.... We cannot estimate the actual amount forwarded to South Vietnam, but as far as capabilities are concerned, for the first time a motorable road has been extended directly into South Vietnam." In the final version this passage read: "The capacity of the entire system for delivery of supplies to South Vietnam through Laos continues to be limited by the capabilities of the routes in Laos rather than by those in North Vietnam." The ineffectiveness of the bombing was still being maintained, but less forcefully. No doubt Keegan's intelligence had made a difference to CIA assessment between June and November 1967, but also the need to assert only what was definite is apparent: any conclusion that was not sustained by a wide range of evidence might be successfully attacked by the military, and respect for the agency's analysis in the White House would be undermined.

The Estimate in its final version concluded forcefully: "The Communists have apparently succeeded in creating a strong base for moving supplies at a high level despite air interdiction. The adequacy of the system of course depends on actual requirements for supplies for forces in South Vietnam. But on the basis of raw capabilities, it does not seem likely that the logistical system will pose any significant limitations on the Communist ability to sustain the present war effort."

33. Peer de Silva, *Sub Rosa—The CIA and the Uses of Intelligence* (New York: Times Books, 1978), p. 238.
34. Ibid., p. 239.
35. Ibid., p. 261.
36. Ibid., p. 264.
37. Interview, R. Jack Smith, July 15, 1983.
38. Interview, John A. Bross, July 14, 1983. Joe Kiyonaga was the CIA chief of station in El Salvador for four years from 1966. In 1969 he learned before the ambassador did that El Salvador planned a war with neighboring Honduras. His widow described what happened next:

> Joe told the American ambassador, who was incredulous because he said he had information from the government contradicting that. Joe cabled the agency with the news. The CIA notified the State Department, which queried the ambassador. One of the most delicate tasks a CIA chief of station must perform is to avoid undercutting the ambassador—he must always keep the ambassador apprised of critical happenings. . . . The ambassador was not to forget that loss of face. His next post was Guatemala, which was also supposed to be Joe's next assignment. Joe told me the ambassador nixed that. (Bina Kiyonaga with Rudy Maxa, "Remembrances of a CIA Wife," *The Washingtonian* [March 1985], p. 207)

In November 1960, following long-running friction in the field between the CIA and the State Department, Eisenhower issued an executive order assigning ambassadors "affirmative responsibility" for the activities of other government agencies in foreign countries, "to the extent permitted by law and in accordance with instructions as the President may from time to time promulgate" (quoted in Wise and Ross, *The Invisible Government*, p. 268).

39. John Richardson's recall a month before the coup aroused the suspicion that the CIA had been following its own policy in Saigon in defiance of Washington. Richardson had been close to Diem and Nhu—Lodge considered too close. On October 17 Nhu (who had good contacts with the North Vietnamese and the Vietcong and was suspected by the CIA and the State Department of being a communist agent) claimed that the CIA was conspiring with Buddhists to overthrow the Diem government (Wise and Ross, *The Invisible Government*, p. 163).

40. De Silva, *Sub Rosa*, pp. 210–212.
41. Interview, April 2, 1984.
42. Interview, Richard Helms, July 26, 1983.
43. When his nomination was being approved by the Senate Armed Services Committee, Helms made it clear that the CIA did not try to make foreign policy. The agency never acted without the appropriate official approval, he declared, and he offered to provide any information the committee might request within the limits imposed on his authority by the President and the demands of national security (*The New York Times*, June 24, 1966).
44. Ball, *The Past Has Another Pattern*, pp. 319–321.
45. Interview, Richard Helms, July 26, 1983.
46. Arthur M. Schlesinger, Jr., *A Thousand Days: John F. Kennedy in the White House* (Boston: Houghton Mifflin, 1965), p. 559.
47. Interview, Richard Helms, July 26, 1983. See also Ball, *The Past Has Another Pattern*, p. 321. When Helms became DCI, he took a particular interest in relations with the press. He had worked for United Press before World War II and would say that he understood journalists and their problems. Marvin Kalb of CBS News thought that Helms "had the capacity for astonishing candor but told you no more than he wanted to give you. He had this way of talking, of suggesting things with his eyes; yet he usually didn't tell you anything" (Marchetti and Marks, *The CIA and the Cult of Intelligence*, p. 310).

48. Interview, Ray Cline, July 25, 1983.
49. John McCone to the secretary of state, secretary of defense, special assistant to the President for national security affairs, and Ambassador Maxwell Taylor, memorandum, April 2, 1965, quoted in Larry Berman, *Planning a Tragedy: The Americanization of the War in Vietnam* (New York: W. W. Norton, 1982), pp. 58–59, from National Security File, National Security Council History, "Deployment of Major U.S. Forces to Vietnam, July, 1965."
50. The differences in the order-of-battle estimates in Vietnam and the differences over the effect of the bombing were so great that McNamara asked the President if he could request Helms to set up a special group in the CIA to estimate these questions. The Defense Intelligence Agency, McNamara felt, was reflecting an unconscious bias in being optimistic (telephone interview, Robert McNamara, July 11, 1983).
51. Interview, R. Jack Smith, November 16, 1983.
52. *The Pentagon Papers*, p. 128.
53. Powers, *The Man Who Kept the Secrets*, p. 174.
54. Quoted ibid., p. 177.
55. Interview, John Huizenga, July 25, 1983.
56. Interview, Sam Adams, November 20, 1982. Samuel Adams to chief, Indochina Division, memorandum, "The Strength of Viet Cong 'Main Force Support Personnel,' " December 2, 1966: "The evidence in captured documents and POW reports is beginning to indicate that the so-called 'Main Force Support Personnel' listed in MACV's OB on the Viet Cong are carried at a strength far below their actual numbers. These personnel are separate from the category of VC irregulars, also believed to be listed well below actual strength by MACV." Adams went on to give examples of enormous disparities and suggested that "The probable total strength of Main Force Support Personnel could be as high as 100,000, if Assault Youths are included." This was more than double MACV's estimate of just one category in the order of battle (OB).
57. Powers, *The Man Who Kept the Secrets*, pp. 187–188, and interview, Sam Adams, November 20, 1983.
58. Interview, July 7, 1983.
59. George Carver to Richard Helms, director of Central Intelligence, September 13, 1967. Carver used the cryptonym "Funaro" and Helms the cryptonym "Knight." These were their agency code names. See also *The Washington Post*, November 10, 1984.
60. Quoted in *The Washington Post*, November 10, 1984. The lawsuit was *General William C. Westmoreland* v. *CBS, Inc., et al.*, United States District Court, Southern District of New York, 1984.
61. Quoted in Powers, *The Man Who Kept the Secrets*, p. 188.
62. Interview, R. Jack Smith, July 23, 1983.
63. Interview, R. Jack Smith, July 23, 1983. SNIE 14.3.67 nowhere mentions an overall enemy strength "in the order of half a million people."
64. John Keegan and Richard Holmes with John Gau, *Soldiers* (London: Hamish Hamilton, 1985), p. 239.
65. Edward Behr, *"Anyone Here Been Raped & Speaks English?"* (London: New English Library, 1982), p. 248.
66. Interview, Sam Adams, November 20, 1983.
67. Interview, R. Jack Smith, November 16, 1983.
68. Interview, Sam Adams, November 20, 1983.
69. Powers, *The Man Who Kept the Secrets*, p. 352.
70. Interview, R. Jack Smith, July 23, 1983.
71. Powers, *The Man Who Kept the Secrets*, p. 192.
72. Ibid., pp. 192–193.
73. Interview, John Waller, November 18, 1983.
74. John McCone, memorandum, April 2, 1965, quoted in Larry Berman, *Planning a Tragedy*, pp. 58–59.
75. By the early 1960s the China experts in the agency had concluded that there were, in fact, serious divisions of purpose and opinion between China and the Soviet Union and

that these differences could be exploited by the United States. Ray Cline, head of the Office of Current Intelligence Sino-Soviet analytical staff from 1955 to 1957, early on suspected that China was not part of a Russian empire:

> During my tenure in OCI, I designated a few analysts with detailed familiarity with Soviet political leaders, doctrines, and daily policy pronouncements to work alongside others who were equally knowledgeable about Mao's China. With a few East European and other Asian Communist specialists, they began an intensive search into the Sino-Soviet relationship that has not ended to this day. I insisted that they write nothing for current publication but instead devote themselves to becoming the greatest experts in the world concerning Communist states' behavior patterns.
> This special research staff, elevated to high bureaucratic levels and expanded in size later on, was beginning cautiously to suggest the Sino-Soviet split as early as 1956, when the different Moscow and Peking reactions to disorders in Poland and Hungary were noted. This staff compiled the data that enabled the CIA to lead the way—against furious opposition elsewhere—in charting the strategic conflict between Soviet and Chinese styles of dictatorship and doctrine that was basic to the definitive split in 1960 (Ray S. Cline, *The CIA Under Reagan, Bush and Casey* [Washington, DC: Acropolis Books, 1981], p. 173).

Part of the furious opposition to this conclusion came from James Angleton, convinced that the Sino-Soviet "split" was simply a clever ruse to tempt the United States into commitments and aid to China, which would then be used to weaken and exploit the United States. Angleton's conviction on this point delayed acceptance of the findings of Cline's staff and those of the OCI Sino-Soviet staff within the CIA as well as outside. The normally level-headed British Intelligence officer Maurice Oldfield, for example, for several years in the early 1960s refused to accept the reality of the Sino-Soviet split because of Angleton's suspicions (Nigel Clive, reviewing Richard Deacon, *"C"—A Biography of Sir Maurice Oldfield* [London: Macdonald, 1985], in *The Times Literary Supplement*, April 5, 1985, p. 374).

76. Lawrence Houston, Affidavit, *General William W. Westmoreland v. CBS, Inc., et al.* (1984), United States District Court, Southern District of New York, December 22, 1983. "He was a man obsessed with a cause who believed that he was right and that no one could honestly disagree with him. He seemed to be unable to compromise or to acknowledge that people could honestly differ with him" (ibid.).

77. Quoted in *The Washington Post*, November 9, 1984.

78. On April 2, 1968, Adams wrote a Memorandum for the Record, "History of Strength Estimates of the Communist 'Administrative Services,'" in which he detailed the progress of the numbers debate, culminating with:

> The MACV OB holding for Administrative Services dropped from 37,650 on January 31, 1968 to 33,725 as of February 29, 1968. The decline was apparently justified by an estimate of losses suffered during the Tet offensive. An internal CIA memorandum produced on March 30, 1968 estimated there were 75–100,000 Administrative Service troops in South Vietnam prior to the Tet offensive. This estimate did not include sappers, engineers, intel-recon, or special action personnel (which the CIA carries in the Main and Local Forces), or Assault Youths.

> On May 2, 1968, Adams produced another Memorandum for the Record, "The Case for Higher Guerrilla Strengths Based on Shortcomings in the MACV RITZ Reporting System, August and September 1967," in which he summarized: "On the basis of the omissions [of categories by MACV in compiling their order of battle], it is probable that the overall study, which estimated that there were 65,200 guerrillas in South Vietnam in mid-1967, was short by at least 24,300, and probably many more."

> On January 24, 1969, Adams submitted a forty-six-page indictment of CIA and MACV analysis of enemy order-of-battle figures to his superiors. It was entitled "Intelligence Failures in Vietnam: Suggestions for Reform" and summed up his feelings and arguments. Accepting MACV's rationale that its prime concern was the enemy Main

and Local Forces, Adams argued that the other categories had been underestimated both in numbers and as effective fighting forces. "The Viet Cong Security Service," he stated, "poses the central threat to the CIA, just as the Viet Cong Army is MACV's principal adversary." He recommended that "the Executive Branch of the Government appoint a Board of Inquiry to investigate thoroughly the conduct of the U.S. intelligence community in Vietnam and elsewhere."

79. Interviews, Lawrence Houston, November 9, 1982, and Sam Adams, November 20, 1983. See also Powers, *The Man Who Kept the Secrets*, pp. 193–195.
80. Interview, R. Jack Smith, July 23, 1983.
81. Interview, John Huizenga, July 25, 1983.
82. Philip Agee, *Inside the Company: CIA Diary* (Harmondsworth, Eng.: Penguin, 1975), pp. 563–567.
83. Quoted in David Atlee Phillips, *The Night Watch: 25 Years of Peculiar Service* (New York: Atheneum, 1977), pp. 287–288.
84. Helms, "Remarks at Donovan Award Dinner," May 24, 1983.
85. De Silva, *Sub Rosa*, p. 232.
86. Stewart Alsop, *The Center: People and Power in Political Washington* (New York: Harper & Row, 1968), p. 234.
87. Ibid., p. 251.

14. On the Edge: 1968–1972

1. John M. Maury, "CIA and the Congress," *Congressional Record*, Vol. 130, No. 117, September 18, 1984. The briefings were certainly needed, especially on more technical subjects. Maury recalled:

> I have seen my colleagues wince when asked questions about how many missiles an hour can be launched from an SS-9 silo, or whether our estimate of the number of Soviet Y-Class submarines is based on anything more than a wild guess. One distinguished member apparently has never been quite clear on the difference between Libya, Lebanon, and Liberia, and when answering his questions on what's going on in these countries, a witness can only guess as to which of them he has in mind.

Nor was technical or geographical ignorance the only problem:

> The older members also occasionally suffer from a decreasing attention span, and particularly in afternoon sessions are prone to intermittent dozing. Also, failing faculties sometimes take their toll. I recall one elderly chairman [who] when shown a chart of various categories of covert action, reacted sharply and demanded to know "What the hell are you doing in covert parliamentary operations?" When it was explained that the box on the chart he was pointing to was "paramilitary operations" he was much reassured, remarking, "The more of these the better—just don't go fooling around with parliamentary stuff—you don't know enough about it."

2. *Final Report*, IV, pp. 51–55, 72.
3. See Ray S. Cline, *The CIA Under Reagan, Bush and Casey* (Washington, DC: Acropolis Books, 1981), pp. 228–229; Thomas Powers, *The Man Who Kept the Secrets: Richard Helms and the CIA* (New York: Knopf, 1979), pp. 276–277; *The New York Times*, January 10–16, 1964.
4. Interview, Senator J. William Fulbright, July 7, 1983.
5. John M. Maury, "CIA and the Congress." It is probably no coincidence that Maury specifically names Senator Fulbright with regard to another possible conflict: "Senator Fulbright may want to know whether the Agency has contact with Soviet émigré groups to an extent that might jeopardize détente."
6. Interview, John A. Bross, July 14, 1983.
7. Interview, Richard Helms, July 26, 1983.
8. Richard Nixon, *RN: The Memoirs of Richard Nixon* (New York: Grosset & Dunlap, 1978), pp. 351–352.

9. David Atlee Phillips, *The Night Watch: 25 Years of Peculiar Service* (New York: Atheneum, 1977), pp. 222–223.
10. Interview, Richard Helms, July 26, 1983.
11. Ibid.
12. Nixon, *RN*, p. 447. In this case Nixon was complaining that Lon Nol's coup in 1970 against Prince Sihanouk in Cambodia came as a complete surprise to the CIA.
13. Richard Nixon, *The Real War* (London: Sidgwick & Jackson, 1981), pp. 283–284.
14. Phillips, *The Night Watch*, p. 144.
15. Interview, November 20, 1983.
16. Oleg Penkovsky, *The Penkovsky Papers* (London: Collins, 1965), p. 241. This book, while collated and edited by British and American intelligence officers, does consist of Penkovsky's own statements and views delivered during his debriefings.
17. Quoted in John Prados, *The Soviet Estimate: U.S. Intelligence Analysis and the Soviet Military Threat* (New York: Dial Press, 1982), p. 193.
18. Interview, April 2, 1984. Cline also was at loggerheads with Sherman Kent, who had worked with him from OSS days. Kent managed to break away from the DDI and, with McCone's approval, secured separate status for his Board of National Estimates.
19. *Final Report*, IV, pp. 77–79. "CIA advocacy of its own scientific collection techniques became mixed up with its objective analysis of all scientific and technical developments," Cline maintained. "Without deprecating the excellent work of this Directorate, I have always felt it violated a cardinal rule of sound intelligence organization in allowing the same unit to conduct intelligence operations and then evaluate the results" (Cline, *The CIA*, p. 224).
20. Prados, *The Soviet Estimate*, p. 209.
21. Ibid., p. 211.
22. Quoted in Seymour M. Hersh, *The Price of Power: Kissinger in the Nixon White House* (New York: Summit Books, 1983), p. 159.
23. Quoted in Prados, *The Soviet Estimate*, pp. 214–215, and U.S. Senate Foreign Relations Committee, "Hearing: Intelligence and the ABM," 1969, pp. 53–54.
24. Interview, R. Jack Smith, July 15, 1983.
25. Quoted in *Final Report*, I, p. 78.
26. Interview, R. Jack Smith, July 15, 1983.
27. Quoted in *Final Report*, I, p. 79.
28. Interview, R. Jack Smith, July 15, 1983.
29. Ibid.
30. Interview, John Huizenga, July 25, 1983.
31. United States Senate Intelligence Committee, "Hearings: National Intelligence Reorganization and Reform Act of 1978," p. 21.
32. Prados, *The Soviet Estimate*, p. 223.
33. Interview, R. Jack Smith, July 15, 1983. "While [this] may be true as far as Nixon, et al., relations with DDI was concerned, it was *not* true for relations with DDP which was involved in numerous activities in various areas around the world at the direction of Nixon, et al." (Samuel Halpern, letter to author, August 11, 1986).
34. Interview, November 21, 1984. Charles ("Chuck") Colson liked to describe himself as a "flag-waving, kick-em-in-the-nuts, antipress, antiliberal Nixon fanatic," and once said to some astonished journalists, "I would walk over my grandmother if necessary" to ensure Nixon's reelection in 1972. He was a special assistant to the President in 1970–72 and masterminded the "plumbers" unit as well as drawing up the "enemies list" of people perceived as antipathetic to Nixon. He was an out-and-out Nixon loyalist.
35. Henry Kissinger, *White House Years* (Boston: Little, Brown, 1979), p. 11. In this passage Kissinger seems to be saying that Nixon felt the agency had worked against him rather than simply "voted" against him. He also seems to be saying that Nixon felt that the preferences of agency people were for accommodation rather than confrontation with the Soviet Union. This is interesting if it is based on Kissinger's considered opinion of Nixon's views, telling us a great deal about Nixon and his perspectives.

The agency was not to the left of Nixon and Kissinger, although it may have been composed of people who, in the main, were. The difference between the agency and

Nixon/Kissinger was that while Nixon insisted on arguing that the Soviets would maintain their agreements honestly, the agency embodied a tradition of distrust, doubting Nixon's wisdom in pressing agreements which, if observed by the U.S. but not by the Soviets, would weaken the U.S. SALT I gave an example of this divergence, with the agency being subsequently vindicated as it emerged that the Soviets had not adhered to the precise terms of the agreement. Nixon's signing of the treaty banning chemical weapons was another example: as we know now, despite the treaty the Soviets have used chemical weapons against guerrillas in Afghanistan.

The Nixon/Kissinger line has always been that they were conservatives in a liberal town, with the CIA being a typical liberal institution. In fact, Nixon and Kissinger were more like adventurers, pragmatic in the extreme, in a hurry to be great. The CIA battened down its hatches, waiting for the Nixon/Kissinger storm to blow over.

36. Powers, *The Man Who Kept the Secrets*, p. 202. Kissinger's proposal was the brain-child of Morton Halperin, one of his young assistants, who would soon join the National Security Council staff. Similar proposals were made to other heads of agencies, all designed to concentrate power and authority in the White House.
37. Kissinger, *White House Years*, p. 169.
38. Hersh, *The Price of Power: Kissinger in the Nixon White House*, p. 105. The witness was Roger Morris, who had handled Africa on the NSC staff under Walt Rostow.
39. Powers, *The Man Who Kept the Secrets*, pp. 202–203.
40. Ibid., p. 255.
41. H. R. Haldeman, *The Ends of Power* (London: Star Books, 1978), pp. 59–61.
42. Interview, R. Jack Smith, July 15, 1983. The big change came with the annual Soviet Estimate, which was converted from a single volume of perhaps 100 pages to three or four volumes, with copious appendices and containing a great deal of raw material. This, of course, also helped make other users less willing to read the Estimate, thus concentrating more power in Nixon's and Kissinger's hands.
43. Haldeman, *The Ends of Power*, p. 109.
44. Nixon, *RN*, pp. 384, 385.
45. Cline, *The CIA*, pp. 172–173.
46. Ibid., p. 173.
47. Nixon, *The Real War*, p. 147.
48. Ibid., pp. 181–182.
49. Interview, Admiral Elmo Zumwalt, July 27, 1983.
50. *CIA: The Pike Report* (Nottingham, England: Spokesman Books, 1977), p. 68.

15. The President's Men? 1970–1972

1. *The White House Transcripts* (New York: Bantam/A *New York Times* book, 1974), p. 63. J. Edgar Hoover had died on May 2, 1972, and Nixon's appointee as director of the FBI, L. Patrick Gray, was obscure. He was an ex-navy captain practicing law in New London, Connecticut. The presumption was that Gray was Nixon's man and that Nixon was now able to use "the power" of the FBI.
2. Interview, Lawrence Houston, July 16, 1984.
3. Ray S. Cline, *The CIA under Reagan, Bush and Casey* (Washington, DC: Acropolis Books, 1981), p. 240. More happened to the agency than a change of presidency and a change of director. Dulles was not the same kind of DCI for Eisenhower that McCone was for Kennedy. Dulles was fleshing out an institution; McCone was managing one.
4. Quoted in Seymour M. Hersh, *The Price of Power: Kissinger in the Nixon White House* (New York: Summit Books, 1983), p. 159.
5. Thomas Powers, *The Man Who Kept the Secrets: Richard Helms and the CIA* (New York: Knopf, 1979), p. 235, and David Atlee Phillips, *The Night Watch: 25 Years of Peculiar Service* (New York: Atheneum, 1977), p. 221.
6. Richard Nixon, *RN: The Memoirs of Richard Nixon* (New York: Grosset & Dunlap, 1978), p. 489.
7. Powers, *The Man Who Kept the Secrets*, p. 223. Victor Marchetti and John D. Marks in *The CIA and the Cult of Intelligence* (New York: Laurel, 1980), p. 14, quote

Laurence Stern in *The Washington Post* to the effect that total U.S. funding of anti-Allende groupings was $20 million in 1964. CIA support for the Christian Democrats had been alleged in 1968. These allegations were seen as a communist move to play on general nationalist fears of American intervention, with the object of uniting the Chilean left. *The New York Times*, November 19, 1968, headlined one story "Chile's Reds Open Drive Against the U.S."

8. Quoted in Marchetti and Marks, *The CIA and the Cult of Intelligence*, p. 12. See also Powers, *The Man Who Kept the Secrets*, pp. 227–228. The 40 Committee also approved a $500,000 contingency fund to bribe members of the Chilean Congress (the Chilean president was actually elected by the Congress) in the event Allende won at the polls.
9. Marchetti and Marks, *The CIA and the Cult of Intelligence*, p. 14.
10. Phillips, *The Night Watch*, pp. 220–221.
11. Ibid., p. 222. Church Committee, *Alleged Assassination Plots Involving Foreign Leaders* (New York: W. W. Norton, 1976), pp. 223, 235.
12. *Alleged Assassination Plots*, p. 231.
13. Ibid., p. 233.
14. Ibid., p. 234.
15. Ibid., pp. 235–238.
16. Ibid., p. 241.
17. Ibid.
18. Ibid., p. 228.
19. Ibid., p. 242.
20. Ibid. Neither Truman nor Eisenhower would have expected to be told that the agency would comply with their wishes. It was an indication of how far the CIA was now distanced from the presidency and of its sense of being a separate institution.
21. Ibid., p. 243.
22. Ibid., p. 245.
23. Phillips, *The Night Watch*, p. 223.
24. *Alleged Assassination Plots*, p. 246.
25. Nixon, *RN*, p. 490.
26. *Alleged Assassination Plots*, p. 247.
27. Ibid., p. 254. Tom Karamessines retired from the agency in February 1973 and so did not have firsthand knowledge of the period between his retirement and the coup in September.
28. Quoted in Powers, *The Man Who Kept the Secrets*, p. 238.
29. Quoted in Hersh, *The Price of Power*, pp. 287–288.
30. Ibid., p. 295. In 1971 CIA expenditures for subversive activities in Chile totaled more than $3.5 million and in 1972, $2.5 million.
31. Interview, Lawrence Merthan, November 21, 1983.
32. *The Watergate Hearings: Break-in and Cover-up* (New York: Bantam/A *New York Times* book, 1973), p. 167. McCord's letters were anonymous, and their origin was not immediately apparent to those who received them.
33. Powers, *The Man Who Kept the Secrets*, p. 250.
34. Ibid.
35. William Colby and Peter Forbath, *Honorable Men: My Life in the CIA* (New York, Simon & Schuster, 1978), p. 323.
36. Vernon A. Walters, *Silent Missions* (New York: Doubleday, 1978), pp. 589–590.
37. Ibid., pp. 590–594.
38. Quoted in Leon Jaworski, *The Right and the Power* (New York: Pocket Books, 1977), p. 256.
39. Walters, *Silent Missions*, p. 591.
40. Letter, John A. Bross to author, October 5, 1984.
41. Walters, *Silent Missions*, p. 599.
42. Jaworski, *The Right and the Power*, p. 258.
43. Colby, *Honorable Men*, pp. 326–327.

44. Walters, *Silent Missions*, p. 604.
45. Colby, *Honorable Men*, p. 327.
46. Ibid., pp. 327–328.
47. George Ball, *The Past Has Another Pattern: Memoirs* (New York: W. W. Norton, 1982), p. 320.
48. Arthur M. Schlesinger, Jr., *The Imperial Presidency* (New York: Popular Library, 1974), pp. 395–396.
49. Colby, *Honorable Men*, p. 309.
50. Ibid., p. 310. People did not question the honor of CIA men. But honorable men had bombed Dresden and Hiroshima, so why should they not be doing comparable things in secret in the CIA? The question was not whether they were honorable men; it was about what honorable men are capable of doing.

   The phrase "honorable men" has Shakespearean resonance; it occurs in Mark Antony's speech after the murder of Caesar by Brutus and his supporters. "So are they all, all honourable men," cried Mark Antony dissolving the murderers' pretensions.
51. Ibid., p. 312.
52. Ibid., p. 313.
53. The "Restless Youth" study of domestic student dissent was part of the Chaos operation. An internal memorandum to the DCI gave details:

   In the late spring of 1968, Walt Rostow, then Special Assistant to the President for National Security Affairs, tasked the DCI with undertaking a survey of worldwide student dissidence. Confronted by tumult at campuses like Columbia and mindful of the violence accompanying student outbursts at Berlin's Free University and elsewhere, Rostow sought to learn whether youthful dissidence was interconnected: spawned by the same causes; financed and hence manipulated by forces or influence hostile to the interests of the U.S. and its allies; or likely to come under inimical sway to the detriment of U.S. interests. (Memorandum for Director of Central Intelligence via Deputy Director for Intelligence, from Richard Lehman, Director of Current Intelligence, "Activity Related to Domestic Events," May 7, 1973)

   Chaos, another CIA internal memorandum records, started in October 1967 when "President Johnson expressed interest" in "foreign connections of U.S. organizations and activists involved in the anti-war movement. The main purpose of these reports, prepared at the request of the White House, was to determine whether any links existed between international Communist elements of foreign governments and the American peace movement" (ibid.).
54. Colby, *Honorable Men*, pp. 310–317, and *Final Report*, III, pp. 681–732. Chaos was formally terminated in March 1974.
55. *Final Report*, III, pp. 705–706.
56. Walters, *Silent Missions*, p. 592.
57. *Final Report*, III, p. 710.
58. Colby, *Honorable Men*, p. 317.
59. Marchetti and Marks, *The CIA and the Cult of Intelligence*, pp. xx–xxiv. Marchetti's disaffection was also prompted by his strong sense of being kept outside the CIA's inner circle because he was not eastern Establishment.
60. The CIA considered buying the first printing of the Wise/Ross book. Cord Meyer visited Random House and was told that the agency was welcome to purchase as many printings as it liked but more copies would always be printed for public sale. See *The New York Times*, "CIA Shaper of Public Opinion," December 25, 26, 27, 1977. David Wise in his review of *The Agency* (*Washington Monthly*, August 1986) says that Cord Meyer did not visit Random House and that *The New York Times* was in error.
61. Interview, April 2, 1984.
62. Cline, *The CIA*, p. 242.
63. Ibid., p. 250. Despite Henry Heckscher's opposition, the agency top brass had pursued Track I and Track II diligently. Cline is implying that the administration was acting

against agency advice, but the evidence actually indicates that the agency, while alarmed, kept its doubts to itself.

64. *Final Report*, IV, p. 84, and Powers, *The Man Who Kept the Secrets*, pp. 207–208.
65. *Final Report*, IV, pp. 76, 84.
66. Jeffrey T. Richelson, *The U.S. Intelligence Community* (Cambridge, MA: Ballinger, 1985), p. 247.
67. Powers, *The Man Who Kept the Secrets*, p. 219.
68. Quoted in William Shawcross, *Sideshow: Kissinger, Nixon and the Destruction of Cambodia* (London: Fontana Paperbacks, 1980), p. 182.
69. Frank Snepp, *Decent Interval* (New York: Random House, 1977).
70. Ibid., p. 115.
71. Quoted in Shawcross, *Sideshow*, pp. 112–127.
72. Ibid., pp. 182–183.

16. Power Plays: 1972–1975

1. Interview, Richard Helms, July 26, 1983, and Vernon Walters, *Silent Missions* (New York: Doubleday, 1978), p. 604.
2. Interview, Richard Helms, July 26, 1983, and Walters, *Silent Missions*, p. 604.
   The difference between the CIA and the FBI is and was enormous. The FBI was in the hands of one man—J. Edgar Hoover—for forty-eight years. It was independent fundamentally because Hoover had seen to it that both he and the bureau were of service to successive presidents. Hoover was a rancid man, and it quickly became difficult to get rid of him. Directorships of Central Intelligence, on the other hand, changed repeatedly. Events shaped the course of the CIA; Hoover shaped the course of the FBI.
3. William Colby and Peter Forbath, *Honorable Men: My Life in the CIA* (New York: Simon & Schuster, 1978), p. 328.
4. Interview, November 9, 1983.
5. David Atlee Phillips, *The Night Watch: 25 Years of Peculiar Service* (New York: Atheneum, 1977), pp. 279–280. The five directors in the poll were Allen Dulles, John McCone, William F. Raborn, Richard Helms, and William Colby. No one voted for Raborn.
6. Colby, *Honorable Men*, p. 329.
7. Interview, John Huizenga, July 25, 1983.
8. *Final Report*, IV, p. 85: Colby, *Honorable Men*, p. 333; Ray S. Cline, *The CIA under Reagan, Bush and Casey* (Washington, DC: Acropolis Books, 1981), p. 243; and Phillips, *The Night Watch*, pp. 233–234.
9. *The New York Times*, February 6, 1973. The CIA had trained some city and county police forces in the handling of explosives, detection, wiretaps, and the organization of intelligence information—all of it, in fact, perfectly legal. Training people in America was quite different from operating in America. But behind this was the awareness that the CIA was alert to the prospect of terrorism in the U.S.A. Part of the outcry following the revelation of its police-training activities was because the CIA was bringing bad news and was not popular for it. In the ancient world, messengers with bad news were often executed: in the modern world, the impulse has remained although the action has been denied.
10. Colby, *Honorable Men*, pp. 337–338.
11. Quoted in ibid., p. 338.
12. Edward Behr, *"Anyone Here Been Raped & Speaks English?"* (London: New English Library, 1982), pp. 288–289.
13. Interview, November 22, 1983.
14. Interview, Victor Marchetti, November 22, 1983.
15. CIA internal memorandum, William V. Broe, Inspector General, to Mr. Colby, "Potential Flap Activities," May 21, 1973. This was the official title of the list.
16. Colby, *Honorable Men*, pp. 346–347.
17. Interview, July 6, 1983.

18. Interview, July 15, 1983.
19. Interview, R. Jack Smith, July 23, 1983.
20. Interview, WIlliam Colby, July 25, 1983.
21. Interview, July 23, 1983.
22. See pp. 402–9.
23. Colby, *Honorable Men*, p. 334.
24. Ibid.
25. Ibid., p. 364.
26. Ibid., p. 365.
27. Ibid.
28. Ibid., pp. 365–366.
29. Quoted in David C. Martin, *Wilderness of Mirrors* (New York: Ballantine Books, 1981), p. 109.
30. Interview, November 18, 1983.
31. Interview, November 16, 1983. See also Edward Jay Epstein, *Legend: The Secret World of Lee Harvey Oswald* (New York: Ballantine Books, 1979), pp. 267, 367.
32. Quoted in Martin, *Wilderness of Mirrors*, p. 106.
33. Interview, November 14, 1983.
34. Interview, November 7, 1983.
35. Interview, November 14, 1983.
36. Interview, Richard Helms, July 26, 1983.
37. Colby, *Honorable Men*, pp. 390–391.
38. Epstein, *Legend*, pp. 266–267, 367.
39. Interview, William Colby, July 25, 1983.
40. Colby, *Honorable Men*, pp. 395–397.
41. Interview, Carleton Swift, May 9, 1985.
42. Phillips, *The Night Watch*, pp. 262–264. It should be stressed that Colby sacrificed past events. No current operation was in "The Skeletons" list. Colby made a cold assessment of the balance of forces and acted accordingly.
43. Interview, William Colby, July 25, 1983.
44. Colby, *Honorable Men*, pp. 351–352.
45. Interview, John Huizenga, July 25, 1983.
46. CIA memorandum, "How We Have Helped Israel," May 19, 1966.
47. Stephen Green, *Taking Sides, America's Secret Relations with a Militant Israel* (New York: William Morrow, 1984), p. 203.
48. Henry Kissinger, *Years of Upheaval* (London: Weidenfeld & Nicolson, 1982), pp. 225–226, and interview, R. Jack Smith, November 23, 1983.
49. Kissinger, *Years of Upheaval*, pp. 461–462, and *CIA: The Pike Report* (Nottingham, England: Spokesman Books, 1977), pp. 141–148.
50. Interview, Mordechai Gur, August 17, 1983.
51. Interview, Lawrence Eagleburger, July 12, 1983.
52. Cline, *The CIA*, p. 247.

17. Survival: 1974–1976

1. Vernon Walters, *Silent Missions* (New York: Doubleday, 1978), pp. 609, 611.
2. Richard Nixon, *RN: The Memoirs of Richard Nixon* (New York: Grosset & Dunlap, 1978), p. 925.
3. Gerald Ford, *A Time to Heal* (New York: Berkley Books, 1980), pp. xxii–xxiv, 223. William Colby and Peter Forbath, *Honorable Men: My Life in the CIA* (New York: Simon & Schuster, 1978), pp. 394–398, say that Colby informed Kissinger of the details of "The Skeletons" list and that Kissinger went to Vail and briefed the President. In his memoirs Ford maintains that he did not know about the details—especially the assassination plans—until January 3, 1975, about ten days after Colby spoke to Kissinger. Kissinger's memoirs do not mention the incident; they end with the resignation of Nixon.

4. Ford, *A Time to Heal*, pp. 223–224.
5. Colby, *Honorable Men*, p. 398.
6. Ford, *A Time to Heal*, p. 224.
7. Colby, *Honorable Men*, p. 399.
8. Ibid., p. 400.
9. Ibid., pp. 453–454.
10. Interview, April 2, 1984.
11. *Report to the President by the Commission on CIA Activities Within the United States* (Washington, DC: U.S. Government Printing Office, June 6, 1975), p. xi.
12. Ibid., pp. 8–9.
13. Ibid., pp. 9–42.
14. Central Intelligence Agency, "Freedom of Information Act: Administrative Problems Experienced by the Central Intelligence Agency," 2, 1981.
15. Colby, *Honorable Men*, pp. 403–404.
16. Ford, *A Time to Heal*, pp. xxv, 258.
17. *The New York Times*, June 11, 1975.
18. Colby, *Honorable Men*, p. 404.
19. *The New York Times*, February 18, 1976.
20. Church Committee, *Alleged Assassination Plots Involving Foreign Leaders* (New York: W. W. Norton, 1976), p. xix.
21. Ibid., pp. 281–282.
22. Colby, *Honorable Men*, pp. 406–407.
23. David Atlee Phillips, *The Night Watch: 25 Years of Peculiar Service* (New York: Atheneum, 1977), p. 271.
24. Quoted in Clyde W. Burleson, *The Jennifer Project* (London: Sphere Books, 1979), p. 47.
25. Ibid., p. 125. The Soviet Golf II class submarine carried a crew of 12 officers and 74 seamen. Reports of the number of bodies retrieved vary from 6 to 70, but between 50 and 60 is most generally accepted. The bodies were unrecognizable from decomposition and misshaping from sea pressure over six years.
26. Colby, *Honorable Men*, p. 419.
27. Frank Snepp, *Decent Interval* (Harmondsworth, Eng.: Penguin, 1980), pp. 472–473.
28. Joseph Burkholder Smith, *Portrait of a Cold Warrior* (New York: Ballantine Books, 1981), p. 427.
29. John Stockwell, *In Search of Enemies* (New York: W. W. Norton, 1978), p. 162. The title of this book encapsulates a whole body of criticism of the agency. Was the CIA really in search of enemies? Or was it more true of the KGB? After 1941 America never needed to search out enemies; it had plenty.
30. Colby, *Honorable Men*, p. 423. UNITA has continued. The MPLA did not secure victory, it just became the official government.
31. Stockwell, *In Search of Enemies*, p. 173.
32. Ibid., p. 162.
33. *The Congressional Record*, Vol. 130, No. 117, September 18, 1984.
34. Stockwell, *In Search of Enemies*, p. 162. Also John Maury, "CIA and the Congress," *The Congressional Record*, Vol. 130, No. 117, September 18, 1984.
35. Interview, Lawrence Houston, November 7, 1984. Helms had agreed with Church that the questions he would be asked by the Senate Foreign Relations Committee's Subcommittee on Multinational Corporations would be limited, with restricted parameters. Church's staff opposed this arrangement, but Church himself saw it through. During the actual hearing, however, Symington, innocent of the arrangement, asked other questions. Church tried to keep the proceedings limited all the same. Helms answered Symington within his understanding of the arrangement. In the parking lot, after the hearing, Houston said to Helms that he thought Helms might have a problem and that "You should not be so didactic in your answers."
36. Quoted in Thomas Powers, *The Man Who Kept the Secrets: Richard Helms and the CIA* (New York: Knopf, 1979), p. 239.

37. Quoted in ibid., p. 304.
38. *Report to the President*, p. 17.
39. Ibid.
40. Powers, *The Man Who Kept the Secrets*, pp. 301–305.
41. Quoted in *Newsweek*, June 27, 1966.
42. Colby, *Honorable Men*, pp. 383–387. If everyone agreed that Helms had probably not committed perjury, everyone was playing safe at his expense. The general counsel of the CIA, John Warner, whom Colby asked for guidance, had said that Helms was not guilty of perjury, and Colby could have rested on that: no case, no charge.
43. Ray S. Cline, *The CIA Under Reagan, Bush and Casey* (Washington, DC: Acropolis Books, 1981), p. 293.
44. Ford, *A Time to Heal*, p. xxv. "Ford's memory is faulty in that the chiefs of the committee staffs usually sat in on the meetings referred to" (Samuel Halpern, letter to author, August 11, 1986).
45. *CIA: The Pike Report* (Nottingham, Eng.: Spokesman Books, 1977), pp. 130–167.
46. *Final Report*, IV, pp. 79–82.
47. John Prados, *The Soviet Estimate: U.S. Intelligence Analysis and Russian Military Strength* (New York: Dial Press, 1982), p. 247.
48. Ibid., p. 252. A congressional investigation of the different perspectives of the Soviet threat concluded that the 1976 National Intelligence Estimate had not been dramatically changed by the B Team's arguments.
49. Ford, *A Time to Heal*, p. 315.
50. Interview, William Colby, July 25, 1983.
51. Colby, *Honorable Men*, pp. 443–444.
52. Quoted in ibid., p. 445.
53. *The Times* (London), September 24, 1984.
54. Phillips, *The Night Watch*, p. 280.

18. Secrecy in the Republic: 1976–1980

1. Interview, October 4, 1985.
2. Interview, October 12, 1985.
3. Gerald Ford, *A Time to Heal* (New York: Berkley Books, 1980), p. 326.
4. Quoted in Stansfield Turner, *Secrecy and Democracy—The CIA in Transition* (Boston: Houghton Mifflin, 1985), p. 24.
5. Interview, October 4, 1985.
6. Ray S. Cline, *The CIA Under Reagan, Bush and Casey* (Washington, DC: Acropolis Books, 1981), p. 268. See also Jimmy Carter, *Keeping Faith: Memoirs of a President* (London: Collins, 1982), p. 143.
7. Interview, November 17, 1983.
8. Turner, *Secrecy and Democracy*, p. 39.
9. Interview, Stansfield Turner, July 29, 1983.
10. Interview, November 17, 1983.
11. Turner, *Secrecy and Democracy*, pp. 27–28.
12. Cline, *The CIA*, p. 270. Turner's fear of being outwitted was linked to his awareness that human intelligence activity was outside his control and experience.
13. Cline, *The CIA*, p. 270. See also Turner, *Secrecy and Democracy*, pp. 196–202:

   I remembered Jim Schlesinger's telling me that the Agency was still overstaffed. That was surprising, since Schlesinger had slashed the Agency by more than 630 people during his five-month tenure. I had been impressed by the emphasis he had used when mentioning the problem to me.
   It was at this point that I learned about a study the espionage branch itself had done on its personnel situation in mid–1976, while George Bush was DCI. It called for a reduction in the size of the branch by 1350 positions over a five-year period. No action had been taken. Bush had not rejected it, but neither had he faced up to it. . . .
   I finally turned to James Taylor, the comptroller. Taylor had come to the CIA

with Schlesinger and was enough of an outsider to look at the subject objectively. He cautioned me not to go ahead with the entire cut of 1350, but proposed instead that I reduce staff positions by only 820. He pointed out that in the time it would take to effect that reduction, we could determine whether we wanted to go further. I decided to do as he recommended but to accomplish the reduction over two years instead of the five suggested in the original plan. I didn't want the organization beset for five years with uncertainty about who might have to leave. I also wanted to restore incentive to those bright, impressive younger people who now had too many supervisors. The future of the CIA depended on them.

Accomplishing the reduction in two years rather than the five made one big difference. The reduction was to be 820 *positions* (not people), most of which would be vacated as people left through normal retirement, resignation, or death. The estimate was that 820 posts would be vacated by this kind of attrition if we took five years to accomplish the reduction. But there would not be enough attrition in merely two years to eliminate 820 positions, so we would have to push some people into early retirement or out of a job. The press has repeatedly reported that anywhere from 820 to 2000 *people* were summarily fired as a result of the decision. The actual number of people fired was 17. An additional 147 were forced to retire early (and most were actually better off financially for doing so, owing to anomalies in the government's retirement system). The remaining positions were vacated by normal attrition or by the transfer of people to other branches in the Agency. In short, the espionage branch's authorized number of people shrank by 820: all of the reduction except the 147 forced into early retirement and the 17 dismissed was effected by attrition.

The point is that Turner chose to act on an internal report—he did not have to—and that his action signified a major policy decision away from human intelligence capability and covert action, effectively removing the agency from covert operations.

14. Interview, Thomas C. Farmer, November 18, 1983.
15. Interview, Stansfield Turner, July 29, 1983.
16. Ibid.
17. Ibid.
18. Interview, October 14, 1985.
19. Interview, David S. Sullivan, October 14, 1985.
20. Interview, October 13, 1985.
21. Interview, November 17, 1983.
22. Interview, Stansfield Turner, July 29, 1983.
23. Interview, October 9, 1985. The abolition of the Board of National Estimates was planned under Schlesinger but carried out by Colby. Schlesinger's crack about "gentlemen" was directed at the DDP/DDO, not the Board. The interviewee probably confused the remark because toward the end of his period as DCI, Schlesinger seemed to have changed his mind and developed a partiality for the operational people, reserving his derogatory remarks for the analysts.
24. Interview, Stansfield Turner, July 29, 1983.
25. Ibid.
26. Carter, *Keeping Faith*, p. 143.
27. Stansfield Turner, "Secrecy and Democracy," *Newsweek*, May 20, 1985.
28. Ibid.
29. Ibid.
30. Turner, *Secrecy and Democracy*, pp. 147–48.
31. Ibid., p. 148.
32. Ibid., pp. 146–147.
33. James Fallows, "Zbig Without Cy," *New Republic*, May 10, 1980.
34. Interview, Stansfield Turner, July 29, 1983.
35. Ibid.
36. Zbigniew Brzezinski, *Power and Principle: Memoirs of the National Security Adviser 1977–1981* (New York: Farrar, Straus & Giroux, 1983), pp. 355, 388–393.

37. Gary Sick, *All Fall Down: America's Tragic Encounter with Iran* (New York: Random House, 1985), p. 90.
38. Quoted in Turner, *Secrecy and Democracy*, p. 113.
39. Ibid., p. 114. The failure, which Turner did not comprehend, was not simply one of analysis or reporting. Rather, it was one of isolationism. Neither the White House, the State Department, nor the CIA understood what was happening in Iran. Turner rejected the allegation that the CIA had a responsibility for this failure by arguing that, "In the case of Iran's Islamic revolution, for instance, there was relatively little secret information that was pertinent. There was no master revolutionary plan that spies could steal, no single revolutionary headquarters in which to place an agent" (ibid., p. 117). If information was so open it was all the more serious that the CIA had not analyzed it correctly.
40. Brzezinski, *Power and Principle*, p. 367.
41. Interview, Stansfield Turner, July 29, 1983.
42. Ibid.
43. Brzezinski, *Power and Principle*, p. 499.
44. Interview, May 9, 1985. The knowledge that Tubman's amorous activities were being electronically monitored by the CIA soon spread through Washington; it was the sort of information about which people could not resist gossiping.
45. Turner, *Secrecy and Democracy*, pp. 206–207.

19. In Search of Magic: 1980–1987

1. Interview, June 17, 1985.
2. Interview, June 14, 1985.
3. Unless otherwise specified, this and the quotations following to the end of the section are from the November 1980 "Top Secret" transition-team outline report. The team's final report was delivered on December 22, 1980, with three specialized reports at weekly intervals preceding this—December 1, 15, and 18. The outline report was an early document, and not a full report agreed to by the transition team.
4. Stansfield Turner, *Secrecy and Democracy—The CIA in Transition* (Boston: Houghton Mifflin, 1985), pp. 122–123. Zumwalt, who agreed with Sullivan's findings, told Sullivan to give the report to Richard Perle on Senator Henry Jackson's staff. Sullivan did so. Then Turner said that Sullivan, in a random polygraph test, admitted he had leaked the report, which led to his dismissal.
5. See p. 677, for estimated CIA budget under Reagan.
6. Quoted in Turner, *Secrecy and Democracy*, p. 64.
7. The transition team report stated: "COMINT in general is too sensitive for discussion in this memorandum." This was where the "magic" was.
   Ambassador Charles W. Yost, a career Foreign Service officer who retired in 1971, has argued that the growth in the power and influence of the National Security Council occurred throughout the 1960s and demonstrated presidential distrust of the State Department (Charles W. Yost, *The Conduct and Misconduct of Foreign Affairs* [New York: Random House, 1973]).
8. Interview, October 11, 1985.
9. Interview, William Casey, October 8, 1985.
10. Quoted in *The Washington Post*, April 29, 1983.
11. Interview, Bernard McMahon, October 10, 1985.
12. Interview, Bernard McMahon, October 11, 1985.
13. Interview, William Casey, October 8, 1985.
14. Raymond Bonner, *Weakness and Deceit: U.S. Policy and El Salvador* (London: Hamish Hamilton, 1985), pp. 290–319, gives a critical account of the conduct of the election. The centrist Christian Democrats received 35 percent of the votes—the largest single share—and the ultraconservative Nationalist Republican Alliance (ARENA)

received 26 percent. The official military party, the National Coalition party (PCN), came third with 17 percent (p. 306).

15. Interview, June 18, 1985.
16. Interview, Lawrence Eagleburger, July 12, 1983.
17. Interview, Bernard McMahon, October 11, 1985. "Bernie McMahon is in error or simply does not know the history of covert operations. Except for the extremely few and rare covert operations ordered by the President not to be divulged to State or Defense (e.g., Track II in Chile), covert operations from their beginning in the late 1940s *always* had State or Defense input. When McMahon says 'we never used to have that' he may be referring to his time as an assistant to Admiral Turner in CIA under Carter. But State's involvement is *not* new before that" (Samuel Halpern, letter to author, August 11, 1986).
18. Interview, October 4, 1985.
19. Telephone interview, Robert Bowie, October 8, 1985.
20. Interview, Lincoln Gordon, October 4, 1985.
21. Interview, October 14, 1985.
22. Interview, October 14, 1985.
23. Interview, William Casey, October 8, 1985.
24. Interview, October 10, 1985.
25. Interview, October 11, 1985.
26. Interview, William Casey, October 8, 1985.
27. Interview, October 8, 1985.
28. Quoted in David S. Sullivan, *The Bitter Fruit of SALT: A Record of Soviet Duplicity* (Houston, Texas: Texas Policy Institute, 1982), p. 76. Casey was talking about his time in the 1970s as a member of the General Advisory Committee on Arms Control, during the SALT I negotiations; he considered some of the *intelligence* judgments soft (letter, William Casey to author, December 18, 1985).
29. Interview, October 16, 1985.
30. Interview, October 4, 1985.
31. Robert M. Gates, "The Future of the Intelligence Community," Association of Former Intelligence Officers, Eleventh Annual Convention, October 5, 1985.
32. Ibid.
33. Ibid.
34. Ibid.
35. Ibid.
36. Interview, Bernard McMahon, October 11, 1985.
37. Interview, October 5, 1985.
38. Robert M. Gates, "The Future of the Intelligence Community."
39. Interview, October 14, 1985.
40. Robert M. Gates, "The Future of the Intelligence Community."
41. Ibid.
42. Interview, Bernard McMahon, October 11, 1985.
43. Interview, William Casey, October 8, 1985.
44. Robert M. Gates, "The Future of the Intelligence Community."
45. Ibid.
46. Ibid.
47. Lt. Gen. Lincoln D. Faurer, "The Future of the Intelligence Community," Association of Former Intelligence Officers, Eleventh Annual Convention, October 5, 1985.
48. Interview, October 4, 1985.
49. Interview, October 3, 1985.
50. Interview, October 4, 1985.
51. *The Washington Times*, October 15, 1985.
52. *The Washington Post*, May 12, 14, 1985. Both the CIA and the State Department denied the alleged involvement. On May 13 the CIA issued a statement saying that it had "never conducted any training of Lebanese security forces related to the events described and had no foreknowledge of the Lebanese counterterrorist action mentioned."

Representative Don Edwards (D-California) commented: "The use of proxies to avoid executive order prohibitions against assassinations is fraught with problems. . . . Such groups are inherently uncontrollable. With a license to kill from the United States government, they serve only to escalate the problems of international terrorism and further tarnish our reputation abroad." The CIA stated that it "scrupulously observes the requirements to keep all the congressional oversight committees appropriately informed" (ibid., May 14, 1985).

53. *The Washington Post*, October 18, 1985.
54. *The Observer*, November 10, 1985.
55. Interview, William Colby, BBC TV, *Panorama: The Year of the Spy*, November 11, 1985.
56. Quoted in *Daily Telegraph*, November 7, 1985.
57. *Daily Mail*, November 5, 1985; *Daily Express*, November 5, 1985.
58. *Daily Mail*, November 7, 1985. "This might have been a deliberate ploy," Reagan said, linking the affair to two other incidents—a Russian soldier who defected to the U.S. Embassy in Afghanistan and then decided to redefect, and a Russian seaman who twice jumped ship on the Mississippi River before deciding to return to Russia. "I have to say that in the coming together of the three incidents you can't rule out that this might have been a deliberate ploy. You just have to accept that we did our best in giving the three men a chance to stay" (ibid.).

   Oleg Bitov, foreign culture editor of the Soviet *Literary Gazette*, defected to Britain from the Venice Film Festival in September 1983. A year later he went back to Russia claiming that he had been kidnapped by British intelligence agents and forced to write articles for the *Sunday Telegraph* newspaper. He was back at work on the *Literary Gazette* in November 1984, and there is a lingering suspicion that he was a "plant" to secure redefection publicity.

59. Interview, November 18, 1985.
60. *The Washington Post*, January 11, 1987.
61. Quoted in *Time*, December 22, 1986.
62. Interview, *Time*, December 22, 1986.
63. *The Washington Post*, January 11, 1987
64. *The New York Times*, January 8, 1987. In a front-page headlined article, "Iran Seen Easing Hostility to U.S. in Shift of Policy on Superpowers," Elaine Sciolino noted how the Ayatollah Khomeini had acted to quell criticism of the Iranians who had dealt with the United States, and went on to quote experts on Iran to the effect that "Hojatolislam Rafsanjani, who has emerged as the regime's foreign policy spokesman since the arms deal revelations, could not enunciate policy regarding the United States and the Soviet Union without at least the tacit approval of Ayatollah Khomeini." Gary Sick, the NSC staff expert on Iran during the embassy hostage crisis, was quoted as saying "Their silencing of those who criticized the American arms deals is an on-going strategy, not a passing fancy."
65. Quoted in *Time*, December 22, 1986.
66. Quoted in *The Times* (London), January 12, 1987.
67. Ibid.
68. Quoted in *Newsweek*, December 22, 1986.
69. *The Washington Times*, January 9, 1987, and *The Washington Post*, January 8, 1986. In calling for a retrospective finding, Casey was following some very odd legal advice from the CIA general counsel, Stanley Sporkin, that since the President has constitutional powers to grant pardons he could therefore declare an action legal after the fact. It was not clear if Sporkin had statutes or executive orders in mind. If he was referring to orders, then he was probably correct. But if he was saying that the retrospective presidential power applied to statutes, as it seemed from what Sporkin said to the Senate Intelligence Committee and the press after the affair broke, then he was wrong. Casey, as a lawyer, must have known this. It was another indication of his determination to know as little as possible and to cloak with whatever legality he could that which he did know about. For his part, Sporkin testified that he "was given fragmentary information

at the time which led me to the conclusion that we needed a presidential finding to authorize the agency's activity, and ratify all action that had been carried out."

Good lawyers tend to keep their statements as focused as they can. The reaching for Sporkin's thesis by Casey suggests that he knew the White House was trying to start up its own operations, working outside the bureaucracies, and that he was quietly helping this development along.

70. *The Washington Post*, January 11, 1987.
71. Quoted in *Time*, December 29, 1986.
72. In December 1986, the Senate Intelligence Committee investigating the affair found evidence that arms deals involving Ghorbanifar in 1983 may have been the genesis of Iranscam, and may have provided North with the private network he used. Obsolete and surplus U.S. armaments were sold in 1983 to shell companies, refurbished in Israel, and then sold on to Iran despite the U.S. embargo. Reportedly, hundreds of millions of dollars were paid by Iran for such weapons (*The New York Times*, January 11, 1987).

In September 1985, Robert McFarlane asked Charles Allen, the national intelligence officer on counterterrorism, to monitor, using National Security Agency facilities, the financial transactions being conducted by Ghorbanifar. He also asked the CIA for a briefing on the Iranian (*The Washington Post*, January 11, 1987). This indicates a belated suspicion on McFarlane's part that he had stumbled into an existing web of deals, involving those with whom he was dealing, and that they might have seen him coming. The NSA was reported to have amassed a substantial documentation of Ghorbanifar's deals that demonstrated that millions of dollars were slipping through cracks all over the place (ibid). Allen became increasingly concerned about such evidence and on October 1, 1986, brought his worries to the attention of Bob Gates who, about ten days later, ordered a CIA inquiry into what was going on. Allen had not been told about the arms-sales-for-hostages operation, or the arms supplies to the Contras, and thus did not know (although by October he clearly suspected) that a possibly illegal set of deals was involved. Gates had not been told either.
73. Before Secord retired, he was involved in an inquiry into possible conflict-of-interest deals and was cleared.

Two U.S Army colonels, William Mott and Ralph Broman, serving as attachés at the U.S. Embassies in London and Paris respectively, were questioned in 1983 about possible conflict-of-interest and illegal arms deals with Iran involving a vast array of weapons ranging from tanks and fighter jets to submarines and missiles (*The New York Times*, January 11, 1987).
74. Quoted in *Time*, December 22, 1986.
75. Interview, *Time*, December 22, 1986.
76. Quoted in *Time*, December 22, 1986.
77. Interview, *Time*, December 22, 1986.
78. Quoted in *Los Angeles Times*, January 4, 1987.
79. Quoted in ibid.
80. *Newsweek*, December 22, 1986.
81. *The Washington Post*, January 11, 1987.
82. *The New York Times*, December 14, 1986.
83. Interview, *Time*, December 22, 1986.
84. Quoted in *The Washington Post*, December 12, 1986.
85. Quoted in *Time*, December 22, 1986.
86. Quoted in *Time*, December 29, 1986.
87. *The Times* (London), January 12, 1987.
88. Interview, *Time*, December 22, 1986. But how things start do not dictate how they finish. There was no reason not to hand over the operation to the CIA unless the agency was not trusted or trusted only minimally by those involved.
89. Quoted in *Time*, December 22, 1986.

Select Bibliography

Abernathy, M. Glenn, Dilys M. Hill, and Phil Williams, eds. *The Carter Years: The President and Policy Making*. London: Frances Pinter, 1984.

Acheson, Dean. *Present at the Creation*. New York: W. W. Norton, 1969.

Adams, Sherman. *Firsthand Report*. New York: Harper & Brothers, 1961.

Agee, Philip. *Inside the Company: CIA Diary*. Harmondsworth, Eng.: Penguin Books, 1975.

———— and Louis Wolf, eds. *Dirty Work: The CIA in Western Europe*. Secaucus, NJ: Lyle Stuart, 1978.

Alsop, Joseph. *FDR—A Centenary Remembrance*. New York: Washington Square Press, 1982.

Alsop, Stewart. *The Center: People and Power in Political Washington*. New York: Harper & Row, 1968.

———— and Thomas Braden. *Sub Rosa: The OSS and American Espionage*. New York: Harvest Books, 1964.

Ambrose, Stephen E. *Eisenhower the President*. New York: Simon & Schuster, 1984.

————. *Ike's Spies: Eisenhower and the Espionage Establishment*. New York: Doubleday, 1981.

————. *Rise to Globalism: American Foreign Policy Since 1938*. 3d rev. ed. Harmondsworth, Eng.: Penguin Books, 1983.

Anderson, Jack, with James Boyd. *Confessions of a Muckraker: The Inside Story of Life in Washington During the Truman, Eisenhower, Kennedy and Johnson Years*. New York: Ballantine Books, 1980.

Andrews, Christopher, and David Dilks, eds. *The Missing Dimension: Governments and Intelligence Communities in the Twentieth Century*. London: Macmillan, 1984.

Anson, Robert Sam. *Exile: The Unquiet Oblivion of Richard M. Nixon*. New York: Simon & Schuster, 1984.

Ashman, Charles. *The CIA-Mafia Link*. New York: Manor Books, 1975.

Bailey, Thomas A. *The Pugnacious Presidents: White House Warriors on Parade*. New York: The Free Press, 1980.

Ball, George W. *The Past Has Another Pattern: Memoirs*. New York: W. W. Norton, 1982.

Bamford, James. *The Puzzle Palace: A Report on America's Most Secret Agency*. Boston: Houghton Mifflin, 1982.

Baral, Jaya Krishna. *The Pentagon and the Making of US Foreign Policy: A Case Study of Vietnam, 1960–1968*. New Delhi: Radiant Publishers, 1978.

Barnaby, Frank, ed. *Future War: Armed Conflict in the Next Decade*. London: Michael Joseph, 1984.

Barnet, Richard J. *The Alliance—America, Europe, Japan: Makers of the Postwar World*. New York: Simon & Schuster, 1984.

Barron, John. *KGB: The Secret Work of Soviet Secret Agents*. London: Corgi Books, 1975.

————. *KGB Today: The Hidden Hand*. New York: Reader's Digest Press, 1983.

Bartlett, C. J. *The Rise and Fall of the Pax Americana: United States Foreign Policy in the Twentieth Century.* London: Paul Elek, 1974.

Beckwith, Col. Charlie A., and Donald Knox. *Delta Force: The U.S. Counter-Terrorist Unit and the Iranian Hostage Rescue Mission.* London: Arms and Armour Press, 1984.

Beevor, J. G. *SOE: Recollections and Reflections 1940–1945.* London: The Bodley Head, 1981.

Behr, Edward. *"Anyone Here Been Raped & Speaks English?"* London: New English Library, 1982.

Berle, Adolf A., Jr. *The 20th Century Capitalist Revolution.* New York: Harcourt Brace & World, 1954.

Berle, Beatrice Bishop, and Travis Beal Jacobs, eds. *Navigating the Rapids 1918–1971: From the Papers of Adolf A. Berle.* New York: Harcourt, 1973.

Berman, Larry. *Planning a Tragedy: The Americanization of the War in Vietnam.* New York: W. W. Norton, 1982.

Bernikow, Louise. *Abel.* New York: Ballantine Books, 1980.

Bernstein, Carl, and Bob Woodward. *All the President's Men.* New York: Simon & Schuster, 1974.

Between the Wars. An Alan Landsburg TV Production with commentaries by Eric Sevareid. New York: Berkley Books, 1978.

Bittman, Ladislaw. *The Deception Game.* New York: Ballantine Books, 1981.

Blakey, G. Robert, and Richard W. Billings. *The Plot to Kill the President.* New York: Times Books, 1981.

Blaufarb, Douglas S. *The Counterinsurgency Era: US Doctrine and Performance, 1950 to the Present.* New York: The Free Press, 1977.

Bloch, Jonathan, and Patrick Fitzgerald. *British Intelligence and Covert Action: Africa, Middle East and Europe Since 1945.* Ireland/London: Brandon/Junction Books, 1983.

Blumenthal, Sid, and Harvey Yazijian, eds. *Government by Gunplay: Assassination Conspiracy Theories from Dallas to Today.* New York: Signet, 1976.

Bohlen, Charles E. *Witness to History.* New York: W. W. Norton, 1973.

Bonner, Raymond. *Weakness and Deceit: U.S. Policy and El Salvador.* London: Hamish Hamilton, 1985.

Bowart, Walter. *Operation Mind Control.* London: Fontana/Collins, 1978.

Bown, Colin, and Peter J. Mooney. *Cold War to Detente 1945–80.* 2d ed. London: Heinemann Educational, 1981.

Boyle, Andrew. *The Climate of Treason: Five Who Spied for Russia.* London: Hutchinson, 1979.

Bradley, Omar N., and Clay Blair. *A General's Life: An Autobiography.* London: Sidgwick & Jackson, 1983.

Brandt, Willy. *People and Politics: The Years 1960–1975.* Trans. J. Maxwell Brownjohn. London: Collins, 1978.

Brogan, Patrick, and Albert Zarca. *Deadly Business.* London: Michael Joseph, 1983.

Brook-Shepherd, Gordon. *The Storm Petrels: The Flight of the First Soviet Defectors.* New York: Ballantine Books, 1982.

Brown, Seyom. *The Faces of Power: Constancy and Change in United States Foreign Policy from Truman to Reagan.* New York: Columbia University Press, 1983.

Brzezinski, Zbigniew. *Power and Principle: Memoirs of the National Security Adviser 1977–1981.* New York: Farrar, Straus & Giroux, 1983.

Buranelli, Vincent and Nan. *Spy/Counterspy: An Encyclopedia of Espionage.* New York: McGraw-Hill, 1982.

Burke, Michael. *Outrageous Good Fortune.* Boston: Little, Brown, 1984.

Burleson, Clyde W. *The Jennifer Project.* London: Sphere Books, 1979.

Byrnes, James F. *All in One Lifetime.* New York: Harper & Brothers, 1958.

Caldwell, Dan, ed. *Henry Kissinger: His Personality and Policies.* Durham, NC: Duke Press Policy Studies, 1983.

Campbell, Christy. *Weapons of War.* New York: Peter Bedrick, 1983.

Canan, James. *War in Space*. New York: Harper & Row, 1982.

Caputo, Philip. *A Rumor of War*. London: Macmillan, 1977.

Carter, Jimmy. *Keeping Faith: Memoirs of a President*. London: Collins, 1982.

Cave Brown, Anthony. *Bodyguard of Lies*. New York: Bantam Books, 1976.

———. *The Last Hero: Wild Bill Donovan*. New York: Times Books, 1982.

Center for National Security Studies. *The Consequences of "Pre-Publication Review": A Case Study of CIA Censorship of the CIA and the Cult of Intelligence*. CNSS Report No. 109 (September 1983).

Charlton, Michael. *The Price of Victory*. London: BBC Publications, 1983.

——— and Anthony Moncrieff. *Many Reasons Why: The American Involvement in Vietnam*. New York: Hill & Wang, 1978.

Chester, Lewis, Cal McCrystal, Stephen Aris, and William Shawcross. *Watergate: The Full Inside Story*. London: André Deutsch, 1973.

Churchill, Allen. *The Roosevelts*. London: Frederick Muller, 1966.

Churchill, Winston Spencer. *The Second World War*, Vols. 1–6. Boston: Houghton Mifflin, 1948–53.

CIA: The Pike Report. Nottingham, Eng.: Spokesman Books, 1977.

The CIA's Nicaragua Manual: Psychological Operations in Guerrilla Warfare. New York: Vintage Books, 1985.

Cline, Ray S. *The CIA Under Reagan, Bush and Casey*. Washington, DC: Acropolis Books, 1981.

———. *Secrets, Spies and Scholars: Blueprint of the Essential CIA*. Washington, DC: Acropolis Books, 1976.

——— and Yonah Alexander. *Terrorism: The Soviet Connection*. New York: Crane Russak, 1984.

Colby, William. *30 Ans de CIA*. Trans. Jean-Pierre Carasso. Paris: Presses de la Renaissance, n.p., 1978.

——— and Peter Forbath. *Honorable Men: My Life in the CIA*. New York: Simon & Schuster, 1978.

Collier, Peter, and David Horowitz. *The Kennedys: An American Drama*. New York: Summit Books, 1984.

Colson, Charles W. *Born Again*. London: Hodder & Stoughton, 1977.

Commager, Henry Steele, ed. *Documents of American History*. 7th ed. New York: Appleton-Century-Crofts, 1963.

Constantinides, George C. *Intelligence and Espionage: An Analytical Bibliography*. Boulder, CO: Westview Press, 1983.

Cook, Blanche Wiesen. *The Declassified Eisenhower: A Divided Legacy*. New York: Doubleday, 1981.

Cooke, Alistair. *Talk About America 1951–1968*. Harmondsworth, Eng.: Penguin Books, 1981.

Cookridge, E. H. *George Blake: Double Agent*. New York: Ballantine Books, 1982.

Copeland, Miles. *The Game of Nations*. New York: Simon & Schuster, 1969.

———. *The Real Spy World*. London: Sphere Books, 1978.

Corson, William R. *The Armies of Ignorance: The Rise of the American Intelligence Empire*. New York: Dial Press/James Wade, 1977.

——— and Robert T. Crowley. *The New KGB*. New York: Morrow, 1985.

Dallin, Alexander. *Black Box: KAL 007 and the Superpowers*. Berkeley, CA: University of California Press, 1985.

Davis, John H. *The Kennedys: Dynasty and Disaster 1848–1983*. New York: McGraw-Hill, 1984.

Deacon, Richard. *"C"—A Biography of Sir Maurice Oldfield*. London: Macdonald, 1985.

———. *A History of British Secret Service*. London: Granada, 1980.

Dean, John W., III. *Blind Ambition: The White House Years*. New York: Simon & Schuster, 1976.

Deconde, Alexander. *A History of American Foreign Policy*. 3rd ed. Vol. 2: *Global Power (1900 to the Present)*. New York: Scribner's, 1978.

de Gramont, Sanche. *The Secret World*. New York: Putnam's, 1962.

Deriabin, Peter, and Frank Gibney. *The Secret World*. New York: Ballantine Books, 1982.

De Silva, Peer. *Sub Rosa: The CIA and the Uses of Intelligence*. New York: Times Books, 1978.

de Toledano, Ralph. *Lament for a Generation*. New York: Farrar, Straus & Giroux, 1960.

Detzer, David. *The Brink: Cuban Missile Crisis, 1962*. London: J. M. Dent, 1980.

Dinges, John, and Saul Landau. *Assassination on Embassy Row*. New York: McGraw-Hill, 1980.

Divine, Robert A. *Eisenhower and the Cold War*. New York: Oxford University Press, 1981.

Dobson, Christopher, and Ronald Payne. *The Dictionary of Espionage*. London: Harrap, 1984.

Domhoff, G. William. *The Higher Circles: The Governing Class in America*. New York: Vintage Books, 1971.

Donner, Frank J. *The Age of Surveillance: The Aims and Methods of America's Political Intelligence System*. New York: Vintage Books, 1981.

Dorschner, John, and Roberto Fabricio. *The Winds of December: The Cuban Revolution 1958*. London: Macmillan, 1980.

Drew, Elizabeth. *Portrait of an Election: The 1980 Presidential Campaign*. London: Routledge & Kegan Paul, 1981.

———. *Washington Journal: The Events of 1973–74*. New York: Random House, 1975.

Dulles, Allen. *The Craft of Intelligence*. Westport, CT: Greenwood Press, 1977.

———, ed. *Great True Spy Stories*. New York: Ballantine Books, 1982.

———. *The Secret Surrender*. New York: Harper & Row, 1966.

Dulles, Eleanor Lansing. *Chances of a Lifetime: A Memoir*. Englewood Cliffs, NJ: Prentice-Hall, 1980.

Ehrlichman, John. *Witness to Power: The Nixon Years*. New York: Simon & Schuster, 1982.

Eisenberg, Dennis, Uri Dan, and Eli Landau. *Meyer Lansky: Mogul of the Mob*. London: Corgi Books, 1980.

———. *The Mossad: Israel's Secret Intelligence Service Inside Stories*. New York: Signet, 1979.

Eisenhower, Dwight D. *The White House Years: Mandate for Change 1953–1956*. New York: Doubleday, 1963.

Epstein, Edward Jay. *Legend: The Secret World of Lee Harvey Oswald*. New York: Ballantine Books, 1979.

Etzold, Thomas H. *The Conduct of American Foreign Relations: The Other Side of Diplomacy*. New York: New Viewpoints, 1977.

Evans, Harold. *Good Times, Bad Times*. London: Coronet Books, 1983.

Eveland, Wilbur Crane. *Ropes of Sand: America's Failure in the Middle East*. New York: W. W. Norton, 1980.

Ewald, William Bragg, Jr. *Eisenhower the President: Crucial Days, 1951–1960*. Englewood Cliffs, NJ: Prentice-Hall, 1981.

Exner, Judith. *My Story: As Told to Ovid Demaris*. New York: Grove Press, 1977.

Fairbank, John King. *The United States and China*. 3d ed. Cambridge, MA: Harvard University Press, 1971.

Famous Soviet Spies: The Kremlin's Secret Weapon. Washington, DC: US News and World Report, 1973.

Farago, Ladislas. *Burn After Reading*. New York: Macfadden, 1963.

Ferrell, Robert H., ed. *The Eisenhower Diaries*. New York: W. W. Norton, 1981.

Fitzgerald, C. P. *A Concise History of East Asia*. Harmondsworth, Eng.: Penguin Books, 1974.

Ford, Corey. *Donovan of OSS*. Boston: Little, Brown, 1970.

Ford, Gerald R. *A Time to Heal*. New York: Berkley Books, 1980.

Forrestal, James. *The Forrestal Diaries*, ed. Walter Millis. New York: Viking, 1951.

Frazier, Howard, ed. *Uncloaking the CIA*. New York: The Free Press, 1978.

Freed, Donald, with Fred Simon Landis. *Death in Washington: The Murder of Orlando Letelier*. Westport, CT: Lawrence Hill, 1980.

The Freedom Fighter's Manual. New York: Grove Press, 1985.

Freedman, Lawrence. *US Intelligence and the Soviet Strategic Threat.* London: Macmillan, 1977.

Freemantle, Brian. *CIA.* London: Michael Joseph/Rainbird, 1983.

———. *KGB.* London: Michael Joseph/Rainbird, 1982.

Gaddis, John Lewis. *The United States and the Origins of the Cold War, 1941–1947.* New York: Columbia University Press, 1972.

Galbraith, John Kenneth. *The Age of Uncertainty.* London: Book Club Associates, 1977.

———. *A Life in Our Times: Memoirs.* London: André Deutsch, 1981.

Ganster, Jacques S. *The Defense Industry.* Cambridge, MA: MIT Press, 1982.

Gehlen, Reinhard. *The Service: The Memoirs of General Reinhard Gehlen.* New York: Popular Library, 1972.

Geraghty, Tony. *Who Dares Wins: The Story of the Special Air Service 1950–1980.* London: Arms & Armour Press, 1980.

Godson, Roy, ed. *Intelligence Requirements for the 1980s.* 5 vols. Washington, DC: National Strategy Information Center, 1979–84.

Gordon, Kermit. *Agenda for the Nation.* Washington, DC: Brookings Institution, 1968.

Goulden, Joseph C. *Korea: The Untold Story of the War.* New York: McGraw-Hill, 1983.

Grantham, Dewey W. *The United States Since 1945: The Ordeal of Power.* New York: McGraw-Hill, 1976.

Gray, Robert Keith. *Eighteen Acres Under Glass.* New York: Doubleday, 1962.

Green, Stephen. *Taking Sides: America's Secret Relations with a Militant Israel.* New York: Morrow, 1984.

Gulley, Bill, with Mary Ellen Reese. *Breaking Cover.* New York: Warner Books, 1981.

Haig, Alexander M., Jr. *Caveat: Realism, Reagan, and Foreign Policy.* London: Weidenfeld & Nicolson, 1984.

Halberstam, David. *The Best and the Brightest.* Greenwich, CT: Fawcett Crest, 1972.

———. *The Powers That Be.* New York: Knopf, 1979.

Haldeman, H. R. *The Ends of Power.* London: Star, 1978.

Halperin, Morton H., Jerry J. Berman, Robert L. Borosage, and Christine M. Marwick. *The Lawless State: The Crimes of the U.S. Intelligence Agencies.* Harmondsworth, Eng.: Penguin Books, 1976.

Harriman, W. Averell, and Elie Abel. *Special Envoy to Churchill and Stalin 1941–1946.* London: Hutchinson, 1976.

Harris, Robert, and Jeremy Paxman. *A Higher Form of Killing.* London: Triad/Granada, 1983.

Haswell, Jock. *Spies and Spymasters: A Concise History of Intelligence.* London: Thames & Hudson, 1977.

Henze, Paul B. *The Plot to Kill the Pope.* London: Croom Helm, 1984.

Herring, George C. *America's Longest War: The United States and Vietnam, 1950–1975.* New York: John Wiley, 1979.

Hersh, Seymour M. *The Price of Power: Kissinger in the Nixon White House.* New York: Summit Books, 1983.

Higgins, George V. *The Friends of Richard Nixon.* New York: Ballantine Books, 1976.

Hilsman, Roger. *Strategic Intelligence and National Decisions.* Glencoe, IL: The Free Press, 1956.

Hinckle, Warren, and William W. Turner. *The Fish Is Red: The Story of the Secret War Against Castro.* New York: Harper & Row, 1981.

Hinsley, F. H., E. E. Thomas, C. F. G. Ransom, and R. C. Knight. *British Intelligence in the Second World War: Its Influence on Strategy and Operations.* 3 vols. London: Her Majesty's Stationery Office, 1979, 1981, 1984.

Hodges, Andrew. *Alan Turing: The Enigma.* New York: Simon & Schuster, 1983.

Hohne, Heinz, and Hermann Zolling. *The General Was a Spy.* New York: Coward, McCann & Geoghegan, 1977.

Holmes, W. J. *Double-Edged Secrets: U.S. Naval Intelligence Operations in the Pacific During World War II.* Annapolis, MD: Naval Institute Press, 1979.

Hood, William. *Mole.* New York: W. W. Norton, 1982.

Hougan, Jim. *Secret Agenda: Watergate, Deep Throat and the CIA.* New York: Random House, 1984.

———. *Spooks: The Private Use of Secret Agents.* London: W. H. Allen, 1979.

Howarth, Patrick. *Undercover: The Men and Women of the Special Operations Executive.* London: Routledge & Kegan Paul, 1980.

Howe, Ellic. *The Black Game: British Subversive Operations Against the Germans During the Second World War.* London: Michael Joseph, 1982.

Howe, Russell Warren, and Sarah Hays Trott. *The Power Peddlers: How Lobbyists Mold America's Foreign Policy.* New York: Doubleday, 1977.

Hurt, Henry. *Shadrin: The Spy Who Never Came Back.* New York: Reader's Digest Press, 1981.

Hyde, H. Montgomery. *The Atom Bomb Spies.* New York: Atheneum, 1960.

———. *Room 3603: The Story of the British Intelligence Center in New York During World War II.* New York: Ballantine Books, 1962. (Originally published as *The Quiet Canadian: The Secret Service Story of Sir William Stephenson.* London: Hamish Hamilton, 1962.)

Isaacs, Arnold R. *Without Honor: Defeat in Vietnam and Cambodia.* Baltimore: Johns Hopkins University Press, 1983.

Jeffreys-Jones, Rhodri. *American Espionage: From Secret Service to CIA.* New York: The Free Press, 1977.

Johnson, Paul. *A History of the World from 1917 to the 1980s.* London: Weidenfeld & Nicolson, 1984.

Jones, R. V. *Most Secret War.* London: Coronet Books, 1979.

Jordan, Amos A., and William J. Taylor, Jr. *American National Security: Policy and Process.* Baltimore: Johns Hopkins University Press, 1981.

Jordan, Hamilton. *Crises: The Last Year of the Carter Presidency.* New York: Berkley Books, 1983.

Kahn, David. *The Codebreakers.* London: Sphere Books, 1973.

———. *Hitler's Spies.* London: Arrow Books, 1980.

Kalb, Madeline G. *The Congo Cables.* New York: Macmillan, 1982.

Kaplan, Fred. *The Wizards of Armageddon.* New York: Simon & Schuster, 1983.

Karnow, Stanley. *Vietnam: A History.* New York: Viking Press, 1983.

Kegley, Charles W., Jr., and Eugene R. Wittkopf. *American Foreign Policy: Pattern and Process.* New York: St. Martin's Press, 1979.

Kennan, George F. *Memoirs* Vol. 1. 1925–1950; Vol. 2. 1950–1963. New York: Pantheon, 1967 and 1972.

———. *Russia and the West Under Lenin and Stalin.* New York: Mentor Books, 1960.

Kennedy, John F. *Profiles in Courage.* Memorial ed. New York: Harper & Row, 1964.

Kennedy, Robert F. *To Seek a Newer World.* London: Michael Joseph, 1968.

———. *Thirteen Days: A Memoir of the Cuban Missile Crisis.* New York: Signet, 1969.

Kennedy, William V., et al. *The Intelligence War: Penetrating the Secret World of Today's Advanced Technology Conflict.* London: Salamander Books, 1983.

Kerr, Walter. *The Secret of Stalingrad.* New York: Doubleday, 1978.

Khrushchev Remembers. With an introduction, commentary, and notes by Edward Crankshaw. Trans. and ed. Strobe Talbott. New York: Bantam Books, 1971.

Kirkpatrick, Lyman. *The Real CIA.* New York: Macmillan, 1968.

Kissinger, Henry. *For the Record: Selected Statements 1977–1980.* London: Weidenfeld & Nicolson/Michael Joseph, 1981.

———. *The White House Years.* Boston: Little, Brown, 1979.

———. *Years of Upheaval.* London: Weidenfeld & Nicolson/Michael Joseph, 1982.

Kistiakowsky, George B. *A Scientist in the White House.* Cambridge, MA: Harvard University Press, 1976.

Klare, Michael T., and Cynthia Arnson. *Supplying Repression: U.S. Support for Authoritarian Regimes Abroad.* Washington, DC: Institute for Policy Studies, 1981.

Klass, Philip. *Secret Sentries in Space.* New York: Random House, 1971.

Klehr, Harvey. *The Heyday of American Communism: The Depression Decade.* New York: Basic Books, 1984.

Kowet, Don. *A Matter of Honor.* New York: Macmillan, 1984.

Kumar, Satish. *CIA and the Third World: A Study in Cryptodiplomacy.* London: Zed Press, 1981.

LaFeber, Walter. *America, Russia, and the Cold War 1945–1984.* 5th ed. New York: Knopf, 1985.

―――. *Inevitable Revolutions: The United States in Central America.* New York: W. W. Norton, 1983.

Langer, William. *In and Out of the Ivory Tower.* New York: Random House, 1977.

Langguth, A. L. *Hidden Terrors: The Truth About U.S. Police Operations in Latin America.* New York: Pantheon, 1978.

Leary, William M. *Perilous Missions: Civil Air Transport and CIA Covert Operations in Asia.* University, AL: University of Alabama Press, 1984.

Ledeen, Michael, and William Lewis. *Debacle: The American Failure in Iran.* New York: Vintage Books, 1982.

Lee, Asher. *The Soviet Air Forces.* New York: Harper & Row, 1956.

Lefever, Ernest W., and Roy Godson. *The CIA and the American Ethic: An Unfinished Debate.* Washington, DC: Ethics and Policy Center, Georgetown University, 1979.

Lernoux, Penny. *In Banks We Trust.* New York: Anchor Press/Doubleday, 1984.

Lewin, Ronald. *The American Magic: Codes, Ciphers and the Defeat of Japan.* Harmondsworth, Eng.: Penguin Books, 1983.

―――. *Ultra Goes to War.* New York: McGraw-Hill, 1978.

Liddy, G. Gordon. *Will: Autobiography.* London: Sphere Books, 1981.

Lindsey, Robert. *The Falcon and the Snowman: A True Story of Friendship and Espionage.* New York: Simon & Schuster, 1979.

Lodge, Henry Cabot. *As It Was: An Inside View of Politics and Power in the '50s and '60s.* New York: W. W. Norton, 1976.

Loftus, John. *The Belarus Secret,* ed. Nathan Miller. New York: Knopf, 1982.

Lorain, Pierre. *Clandestine Operations: The Arms and Techniques of the Resistance, 1941–1944.* New York: Macmillan, 1983.

McCormick, Donald. *Who's Who in Spy Fiction.* London: Sphere Books, 1979.

McCoy, Alfred W. *The Politics of Heroin in Southeast Asia.* New York: Harper Torchbooks, 1972.

MacEoin, Gary. *Chile: The Struggle for Dignity.* London: Coventure, 1975.

McGehee, Ralph W. *Deadly Deceits: My 25 Years in the CIA.* New York: Sheridan Square Publications, 1983.

McGhee, George. *Envoy to the Middle World: Adventures in Diplomacy.* New York: Harper & Row, 1983.

Maclear, Michael. *The Ten Thousand Day War: Vietnam 1945–1975.* New York: St. Martin's Press, 1981.

Mahoney, Richard D. *JFK: Ordeal in Africa.* New York: Oxford University Press, 1983.

Manchester, William. *The Glory and the Dream: A Narrative History of America 1932–1972.* New York: Bantam Books, 1975.

―――. *One Brief Shining Moment: Remembering Kennedy.* London: Michael Joseph, 1983.

Marchetti, Victor, and John D. Marks. *The CIA and the Cult of Intelligence.* New York: Laurel, 1980.

Marks, John. *The Search for the "Manchurian Candidate": The CIA and Mind Control.* London: Allen Lane, 1979.

Martin, David C. *Wilderness of Mirrors.* New York: Ballantine Books, 1981.

Maury, John. "CIA and the Congress," *The Congressional Record,* Vol. 130, no. 112, September 18, 1984.

Mayer, Martin. *The Bankers.* New York: Ballantine Books, 1974.

―――. *The Diplomats.* New York: Doubleday, 1983.

Medved, Michael. *The Shadow Presidents: The Secret History of the Chief Executives and Their Top Aides.* New York: Times Books, 1979.

Mee, Charles L., Jr. *The Marshall Plan: The Launching of the Pax Americana.* New York: Simon & Schuster, 1984.

Meyer, Cord. *Facing Reality: From World Federalism to the CIA.* New York: Harper & Row, 1980.

Moran, Lord. *Winston Churchill: The Struggle for Survival.* London: Sphere Books, 1968.

Morgan, Richard E. *Domestic Intelligence: Monitoring Dissent in America.* Austin, TX: University of Texas Press, 1980.

Morgan, William J. *The OSS and I.* New York: W. W. Norton, 1957.

Morris, Richard B., ed. *Encyclopedia of American History.* 6th ed. New York: Harper & Row, 1982.

Morris, Roger. *Uncertain Greatness: Henry Kissinger and American Foreign Policy.* London: Quartet Books, 1977.

Moses, Hans. *The Clandestine Service of the Central Intelligence Agency.* Mclean, VA: Association of Former Intelligence Officers, 1983.

Mosley, Leonard. *Dulles: A Biography of Eleanor, Allen and John Foster Dulles and Their Family Network.* New York: Dial Press/James Wade, 1978.

Moynihan, Daniel Patrick. *Loyalties.* New York: Harcourt Brace Jovanovich, 1984.

Mr. X, with Bruce E. Henderson and C. C. Cyr. *Double Eagle: The Autobiography of a Polish Spy Who Defected to the West.* New York: Ballantine Books, 1983.

Myagkov, Aleksei. *Inside the KGB.* New York: Ballantine Books, 1981.

Neff, Donald. *Warriors at Suez: Eisenhower Takes America into the Middle East.* New York: Linden Press, 1981.

Nixon, Richard. *Leaders.* New York: Warner Books, 1982.

———. *No More Vietnams.* New York: Arbor House, 1985.

———. *Real Peace.* London: Sidgwick & Jackson, 1984.

———. *The Real War.* London: Sidgwick & Jackson, 1980.

———. *RN: The Memoirs of Richard Nixon.* New York: Grosset & Dunlap, 1978.

Nye, R. B., and J. E. Morpurgo. *A History of the United States.* Vol. 2. *The Growth of the United States.* Harmondsworth, Eng.: Penguin Books, 1965.

The Official Warren Commission Report on the Assassination of President John F. Kennedy. With an analysis and commentary by Louis Nizer and a historical afterword by Bruce Catton. New York: Doubleday, 1964.

Opotowsky, Stan. *The Kennedy Government.* New York: Popular Library, 1974.

OSS Assessment Staff. *Assessment of Men: Selection of Personnel for the Office of Strategic Services.* New York: Rinehart, 1948.

Paddock, Alfred H., Jr. *US Army Special Warfare: Its Origins—Psychological and Unconventional Warfare, 1941–1952.* Washington, DC: National Defense University Press, 1982.

Page, Bruce, David Leitch, and Phillip Knightley. *Philby: The Spy Who Betrayed a Generation.* London: Sphere Books, 1977.

Page, Joseph A. *Peron: A Biography.* New York: Random House, 1983.

Palmer, Jr., Gen. Bruce. *The 25-Year War: America's Military Role in Vietnam.* New York: Touchstone, 1985.

Parmet, Herbert S. *JFK: The Presidency of John F. Kennedy.* Harmondsworth, Eng.: Penguin Books, 1984.

Patti, Archimedes L. A. *Why Vietnam? Prelude to America's Albatross.* Berkeley, CA: University of California Press, 1980.

Peebles, Curtis. *Battle for Space.* Poole, Dorset, Eng.: Blandford Press, 1983.

Penkovsky, Oleg. *The Penkovsky Papers.* London: Collins, 1965.

Perrault, Gilles. *The Red Orchestra.* New York: Pocket Books, 1970.

Persico, Joseph E. *Piercing the Reich: The Penetration of Nazi Germany by OSS Agents During World War II.* London: Michael Joseph, 1979.

Persky, Stan. *America, The Last Domino: U.S. Foreign Policy in Central America Under Reagan.* Vancouver, Canada: New Star Books, 1984.

Pforzheimer, Walter. *Bibliography of Intelligence Literature.* 8th ed. Washington, DC: Defense Intelligence College, 1985.

Philby, Kim. *My Silent War.* London: MacGibbon & Kee, 1968.

Phillips, David Atlee. *The Night Watch: 25 Years of Peculiar Service.* New York: Atheneum, 1977.

Pincher, Chapman. *Inside Story: A Documentary of the Pursuit of Power.* London: Sidgwick & Jackson, 1979.
———. *Their Trade Is Treachery.* London: Sidgwick & Jackson, 1981.
———. *Too Secret Too Long.* New York: St. Martin's Press, 1984.
Plate, Thomas, and Andrea Darvi. *Secret Police: The Inside Story of a Network of Terror.* New York: Doubleday, 1981.
Poelchau, Warner, ed. *White Paper Whitewash: Interviews with Philip Agee on the CIA and El Salvador.* New York: Deep Cover Books, 1981.
Powell, Jody. *The Other Side of the Story.* New York: Morrow, 1984.
Powers, Francis Gary, with Curt Gentry. *Operation Overflight.* New York: Holt, Rinehart & Winston, 1970.
Powers, Thomas. *The Man Who Kept the Secrets: Richard Helms and the CIA.* New York: Knopf, 1979.
Prados, John. *The Soviet Estimate: US Intelligence Analysis and Russian Military Strength.* New York: Dial Press, 1982.
Prange, Gordon W. *At Dawn We Slept: The Untold Story of Pearl Harbor.* Harmondsworth, Eng.: Penguin Books, 1982.
Pringle, Peter, and William Arkin. *SIOP: The Secret US Plan for Nuclear War.* New York: W. W. Norton, 1983.
Prouty, L. Fletcher. *The Secret Team: The CIA and Its Allies in Control of the United States and the World.* Englewood Cliffs, NJ: Prentice-Hall, 1973.
Radosh, Ronald, and Joyce Milton. *The Rosenberg File: A Search for the Truth.* London: Weidenfeld & Nicolson, 1983.
Ray, Ellen, William Schaap, Karl Van Meter, and Louis Wolf, eds. *Dirty Work 2: The CIA in Africa.* Secaucus, NJ: Lyle Stuart, 1979.
Read, Anthony, and David Fisher. *Colonel Z: The Secret Life of a Master of Spies.* London: Hodder & Stoughton, 1984.
———. *Operation Lucy: Most Secret Spy Ring of the Second World War.* London: Sphere Books, 1982.
Richelson, Jeffrey T. *The U.S. Intelligence Community.* Cambridge, MA: Ballinger, 1985.
Ritchie, David. *Spacewar.* New York: Plume, 1983.
Robbins, Christopher. *The Invisible Air Force: The Story of the CIA's Secret Airlines.* London: Macmillan, 1979.
Rohmer, Richard. *Massacre 007: The Story of the Korean Air Lines Flight 007.* London: Coronet Books, 1984.
Rogow, Arnold A. *James Forrestal: A Study of Personality, Politics and Policy.* New York: Macmillan, 1963.
Roosevelt, Kermit. *Countercoup: The Struggle for the Control of Iran.* New York: McGraw-Hill, 1981.
Rositzke, Harry. *The CIA's Secret Operations.* New York: Reader's Digest Press, 1977.
———. *The KGB: The Eyes of Russia.* New York: Doubleday, 1981.
Rostow, W. W. *The Diffusion of Power, 1957–1972.* New York: Macmillan, 1972.
Rovere, Richard H. *Senator Joe McCarthy.* London: Methuen, 1960.
Sakharov, Vladimir, with Umberto Tosi. *High Treason.* New York: Ballantine Books, 1981.
Salisbury, Harrison E., ed. *Vietnam Reconsidered: Lessons from a War.* New York: Harper & Row, 1984.
Sampson, Anthony. *The Sovereign State: The Secret History of ITT.* London: Coronet Books, 1974.
Schell, Jonathan. *The Time of Illusion.* New York: Vintage Books, 1976.
Schlesinger, Arthur M., Jr. *The Imperial Presidency.* New York: Popular Library, 1974.
———. *Robert Kennedy and His Times.* London: Futura Publications, 1979.
———. *A Thousand Days: John F. Kennedy in the White House.* Boston: Houghton Mifflin, 1965.
Schlesinger, Stephen, and Stephen Kinzer. *Bitter Fruit: The Untold Story of the American Coup in Guatemala.* New York: Doubleday, 1982.
Schoenebaum, Eleanora W., ed. *Profiles of an Era: The Nixon/Ford Years.* New York: Harcourt Brace Jovanovich, 1979.

Scott, Peter Dale, Paul L. Hock, and Russell Stetler, eds. *The Assassinations: Dallas and Beyond—A Guide to Cover-ups and Investigations.* Harmondsworth, Eng.: Penguin Books, 1978.

Seagrave, Sterling. *Yellow Rain: A Journey Through the Terror of Chemical Warfare.* London: Abacus, 1981.

Sergeyev, F. *Chile: CIA Big Business.* Trans. Lev Bobrov. Moscow: Progress Publishers, 1981.

Seth, Ronald. *The Executioners: The Story of Smersh.* New York: Tempo Books, 1970.

Shawcross, William. *Sideshow: Kissinger, Nixon and the Destruction of Cambodia.* London: Fontana Paperbacks, 1980.

Shevchenko, Arkady N. *Breaking with Moscow.* New York: Knopf, 1985.

Shirer, William L. *Berlin Diary: The Journal of a Foreign Correspondent 1934–1941.* New York: Popular Library, 1961.

————. *20th Century Journey: A Memoir of a Life and the Times.* Vol. 2. *The Nightmare Years 1930–1940.* Boston: Little, Brown, 1984.

Sick, Gary. *All Fall Down: America's Tragic Encounter with Iran.* New York: Random House, 1985.

Sirica, John J. *To Set the Record Straight: The Break-in, the Tapes, the Conspirators, the Pardon.* New York: W. W. Norton, 1979.

Smith, Bradley F. *The Shadow Warriors: OSS and the Origins of the CIA.* New York: Basic Books, 1983.

Smith, Hedrick. *The Russians.* London: Sphere Books, 1976.

Smith, Joseph Burkholder. *Portrait of a Cold Warrior.* New York: Ballantine Books, 1976.

Smith, Richard Harris. *OSS: The Secret History of America's First Central Intelligence Agency.* Berkeley, CA: University of California Press, 1972.

Snepp, Frank. *Decent Interval: The American Debacle in Vietnam and the Fall of Saigon.* Harmondsworth, Eng.: Penguin Books, 1980.

Sobel, Robert. *ITT: The Management of Opportunity.* London: Sidgwick & Jackson, 1982.

Solovyov, Vladimir, and Elena Klepikova. *Yuri Andropov: A Secret Passage into the Kremlin.* Trans. Guy Daniels. London: Robert Hale, 1983.

Steel, Ronald, *Pax Americana.* New York: Viking Press, 1967.

Steele, Jonathan. *Soviet Power.* New York: Simon & Schuster, 1983.

Sterling, Claire. *The Terror Network: The Secret War of International Terrorism.* London: Weidenfeld & Nicolson, 1981.

Steven, Stewart. *The Spymasters of Israel.* London: Hodder & Stoughton, 1981.

Stevens, Leslie C. *Russian Assignment.* Boston: Little, Brown, 1953.

Stockholm International Peace Research Institute. *The Arms Trade and the Third World.* Harmondsworth, Eng.: Penguin Books, 1975.

Stockwell, John. *In Search of Enemies: A CIA Story.* New York: W. W. Norton, 1978.

Sullivan, David S. *The Bitter Fruit of SALT: A Record of Soviet Duplicity.* Houston, TX: Texas Policy Institute, 1983.

Summers, Anthony. *Conspiracy.* London: Fontana Paperbacks, 1980.

Suvorov, Viktor. *Soviet Military Intelligence.* London: Hamish Hamilton, 1984.

Talbott, Strobe. *Endgame: The Inside Story of Salt II.* New York: Harper Colophon Books, 1980.

Taub, William L. *Forces of Power.* New York: Grosset & Dunlap, 1979.

Taubman, William. *Stalin's American Policy: From Entente to Detente to Cold War.* New York: W. W. Norton, 1982.

Thomas, Gordon, and Max Morgan-Witts. *Ruin from the Air: The Atomic Mission to Hiroshima.* London: Sphere Books, 1978.

Tobias, Sheila, Peter Goudinoff, and Stefan and Shelah Leader. *What Kinds of Guns Are They Buying for Your Butter: A Beginner's Guide to Defense, Weaponry and Military Spending.* New York: Morrow, 1982.

Toland, John. *Infamy: Pearl Harbor and Its Aftermath.* London: Methuen, 1982.

Tompkins, Peter. *The Murder of Admiral Darlan.* London: Weidenfeld & Nicolson, 1965.

Troy, Thomas F. *Donovan and the CIA: A History of the Establishment of the Central Intelligence Agency.* Frederick, MD: University Publications of America, 1981.

Truman, Harry S *Memoirs.* Vol. 1. *Year of Decisions;* Vol. 2. *Years of Trial and Hope.* New York: Doubleday, 1955–56.

Tsipis, Kosta. *Arsenal: Understanding Weapons in the Nuclear Age.* New York: Simon & Schuster, 1983.

Tully, Andrew. *CIA: The Inside Story.* New York: Morrow, 1961.

———. *The Super Spies: More Secret, More Powerful than the CIA.* New York: Morrow, 1969.

Turner, Stansfield. *Secrecy and Democracy—The CIA in Transition.* Boston: Houghton Mifflin, 1985.

Tusa, Ann and John. *The Nuremberg Trial.* London: Macmillan, 1983.

U.S. Commission on CIA Activities Within the United States. *Report to the President.* Washington, DC: U.S. Government Printing Office, June 1975.

U.S. Commission on the Organization of the Government for the Conduct of Foreign Policy. *Report.* Washington, DC: U.S. Government Printing Office, June 1975.

U.S. Congress. Church Committee. *Alleged Assassination Plots Involving Foreign Leaders. Interim Report of the Select Committee to Study Governmental Operations with Respect to Intelligence Activities.* New York: W. W. Norton, 1976.

House Permanent Select Committee on Intelligence. *Compilation of Intelligence Laws and Related Laws and Executive Orders of Interest to the National Intelligence Community.* Washington, DC: U.S. Government Printing Office, April 1983.

House Permanent Select Committee on Intelligence. *Hearings* and *Reports.* Washington, DC: U.S. Government Printing Office, October 1978.

House Select Committee on Assassinations. *Investigation of the Assassination of President John F. Kennedy, Hearings,* Vols. II, IV, XII. Washington, DC: U.S. Government Printing Office, 1979.

House Select Committee on Intelligence. *Recommendations of the Final Report of the House Select Committee on Intelligence.* Washington, DC: U.S. Government Printing Office, 1976.

House Select Committee on Intelligence. *Hearings:* (1) *U.S. Intelligence Agencies and Activities—Costs and Fiscal Procedures;* (2) *U.S. Intelligence Agencies and Activities—The Performance of the Intelligence Community;* (3) *U.S. Intelligence Agencies and Activities—Domestic Intelligence Programs;* (4) *U.S. Intelligence Agencies and Activities—Committee Proceedings;* (5) *U.S. Intelligence Agencies and Activities—Risk and Control of Foreign Intelligence;* (6) *U.S. Intelligence Agencies and Activities—Committee Proceedings II.* Washington, DC: U.S. Government Printing Office, 1976.

Joint Economic Committee. *Soviet Economy in the 1980's: Problems and Prospects,* Parts 1 and 2. Washington, DC: U.S. Government Printing Office, December 31, 1982.

Joint Economic Committee. *Studies: USSR—Measures of Economic Growth and Development, 1950–80.* Washington, DC: U.S. Government Printing Office, December 8, 1982.

Joint Hearings Before the Select Committee on Intelligence and the Subcommittee on Health and Scientific Research of the Committee on Human Resources: Project MKULTRA, the CIA's Program of Research in Behavioral Modification. Washington, DC: U.S. Government Printing Office, 1977.

Senate Permanent Subcommittee on Investigations of the Committee on Governmental Affairs. *Transfer of United States High Technology to the Soviet Union and Soviet Bloc Nations.* Washington, DC: U.S. Government Printing Office, November 15, 1982.

Senate Select Committee on Intelligence. *Hearings* and *Reports.* Washington, DC: U.S. Government Printing Office, May 1977–.

Senate Select Committee to Study Government Operations with Respect to Intelligence Activities. *Final Report:* (1) *Foreign and Military Intelligence;* (2) *Intelligence Activities and the Rights of Americans;* (3) *Supplementary Detailed Staff Reports on Intelligence and the Rights of Americans;* (4) *Supplementary Detailed Staff Reports on*

Intelligence and Military Intelligence; (5) *The Investigation of the Assassination of President John F. Kennedy—Performance of the Intelligence Agencies;* (6) *Supplementary Reports on Intelligence Activities.* Washington, DC: U.S. Government Printing Office, 1975–1976.

Senate Select Committee to Study Governmental Operations with Respect to Intelligence Activities. *Hearings:* (1) *Unauthorized Storage of Toxic Agents;* (2) *Huston Plan;* (3) *Internal Revenue Service;* (4) *Mail Opening;* (5) *The National Security Agency and Fourth Amendment Rights;* (6) *Federal Bureau of Investigation;* (7) *Covert Action.* Washington, DC: U.S. Government Printing Office, 1975–1976.

Senate Select Committee to Study Governmental Operations with Respect to Intelligence Activities. *Staff Report: Covert Action in Chile, 1963–1973.* Washington, DC: U.S. Government Printing Office, 1975.

Studies Prepared for the Use of the Joint Economic Committee: USSR—Measures of Economic Growth and Development, 1950–80. Washington, DC: U.S. Government Printing Office, 1982.

U.S. Department of Defense. *The "Magic" Background of Pearl Harbor,* Vols. I–V. Washington, DC: U.S. Government Printing Office, 1979.

U.S. War Department, Strategic Services Unit. *War Report of the OSS,* Vols. I and II. New York: Walker, 1976.

Valenti, Jack. *A Very Human President.* New York: W. W. Norton, 1975.

Van Der Rhoer, Edward. *The Shadow Network.* New York: Scribner's, 1983.

Verrier, Anthony. *Through the Looking Glass: British Foreign Policy in an Age of Illusions.* New York: W. W. Norton, 1983.

Volkman, Ernest. *Warriors of the Night: Spies, Soldiers and American Intelligence.* New York: William Morrow, 1985.

Walters, Vernon A. *Silent Missions.* New York: Doubleday, 1978.

The Watergate Hearings: Break-in and Cover-up. Proceedings of the Senate Select Committee on Presidential Campaign Activities as Edited by the Staff of The New York Times. New York: Bantam Books, 1973.

Weinstein, Allen. *Perjury: The Hiss-Chambers Case.* New York: Knopf, 1978.

West, Nigel. *A Matter of Trust: MI5 1945–72.* London: Weidenfeld & Nicolson, 1982.

———. *MI5: British Security Service Operations 1909–1945.* London: Triad/Granada, 1983.

———. *MI6: British Secret Intelligence Service Operations 1909–1945.* London: Weidenfeld & Nicolson, 1983.

Westmoreland, Gen. William C. *A Soldier Reports.* New York: Dell, 1980.

The White House Transcripts. Submission of Recorded Presidential Conversations to the Committee on the Judiciary of the House of Representatives by President Richard Nixon. Staff of *The New York Times.* New York: Bantam Books, 1974.

White, Richard Alan. *The Morass: United States Intervention in Central America.* New York: Harper & Row, 1984.

White, Theodore H. *Breach of Faith: The Fall of Richard Nixon.* New York: Dell, 1978.

Whiting, Charles. *Gehlen: Germany's Master Spy.* New York: Ballantine Books, 1972.

Wills, Garry. *The Kennedy Imprisonment.* Boston: Little, Brown, 1982.

Winterbotham, F. W. *The Ultra Secret.* New York: Dell, 1975.

Wise, David. *The American Police State: The Government Against the People.* New York: Random House, 1976.

———. *The Politics of Lying.* New York: Random House, 1973.

——— and Thomas B. Ross. *The Espionage Establishment.* New York: Random House, 1967.

——— and Thomas B. Ross. *The Invisible Government.* New York: Vintage Books, 1974.

Wofford, Harris. *Of Kennedys & Kings: Making Sense of the Sixties.* New York: Farrar, Straus & Giroux, 1980.

Woodward, Bob, and Carl Bernstein. *The Final Days.* London: Secker & Warburg, 1976.

Wyden, Peter. *Bay of Pigs: The Untold Story.* London: Jonathan Cape, 1979.

Yakovlev, Nikolai. *CIA Target—The USSR.* Moscow: Progress Publishers, 1982.

Yardley, Herbert O. *The American Black Chamber*. New York: Ballantine Books, 1981.

Yergin, Daniel. *Shattered Peace: The Origins of the Cold War and the National Security State*. London: André Deutsch, 1978.

Yost, Charles W. *The Conduct and Misconduct of Foreign Affairs*. New York: Random House, 1973.

Index

Index

CHRISTOPHER ANDREW

SECRET SERVICE

The Making of the British Intelligence Community

'Scholarly, balanced and highly entertaining'
Hugh Trevor-Roper

'The first serious and reliable history of Britain's Intelligence Service, most carefully researched and also very funny indeed. Dr Andrew succeeds admirably in demythologizing the history of Intelligence. Splendid and astonishingly good value'
Keith Jeffrey in History Today

'Dr Andrew's determined research and admirable prose, besides giving working historians much that is new, provide the amateur *aficionado* of history with an irresistible brew: a record of exciting successes laced with ludicrous ineptitude . . . As well timed as it is well executed'
Peter Calvocoressi in the Sunday Times

'A history of the Secret Service as exciting as any spy novel, and which also makes the most powerful case I have seen for greater public accountability'
David Cannadine in the New York Review of Books

'Excellently informed, well researched, compulsive reading . . . A fascinating story of triumph and failure'
D. Cameron Watt in the Daily Telegraph

'A great deal of military and diplomatic history will have to be rewritten in the light of some of these revelations . . . remarkable'
Robert Blake in The Illustrated London News

NIGEL HAMILTON

MONTY:
The Field-Marshal 1944–1976

The award-winning biography of the victor of the Battle of Alamein, of D-Day and of Normandy

'. . . well balanced, well planned and well written, put together on a basis of enormous research meticulously and critically conducted . . . gives a fresh account of one of the outstanding, most significant and most complicated men of our time'

Sir John Hackett

'As a memorial to the Field-Marshal, a comprehensive and minutely detailed record, Nigel Hamilton's biography can never be surpassed – magisterial in its shape and scope, brilliantly woven, and a joy to read'

Richard Hough in the Sunday Times

'There can never be a definitive life of anyone, but these three volumes come as near to that achievement as possible. It is safe to say that they are most unlikely to be superseded in the foreseeable future . . . An indispensable work of reference . . . Nelson was a great man and so was Monty. He deserves a great biography and he has got it'

Lord Blake in the Financial Times

MONTY: THE FIELD-MARSHAL 1944–1976 is the third of three volumes, all published in Sceptre.

A. ALVAREZ

OFFSHORE

Since 1969, when oil was first struck in the North Sea, Britain has become one of the world's major oil producers. We now take for granted the science fiction high technology which allows men to work in some of the most brutal conditions on earth, but how the treasure is extracted from far beneath the sea bed remains a mystery. Al Alvarez travelled offshore and talked to divers, helicopter pilots, oil engineers, crane drivers and roustabouts, geologists, administrators and businessmen. His evocative account of life on the stormy 61st parallel paints a unique picture of a brave new world and the men who work there.

'Exciting as well as informative'
The Observer

'Alvarez' sturdy enthusiasm is to be prized'
The Sunday Times

'OFFSHORE reads spot on as a true chronicle of one of the monumental endeavours of our times'
Melvyn Bragg in Punch

'Alvarez captures the sensations and rhythms of North Sea life . . . his strength is that he can build up a rapport with men such as these, penetrate the laid-back image and catch the emotions behind the mask'
The Scotsman

BERNARD LEVIN

HANNIBAL'S FOOTSTEPS

In the winter of 218 BC, Hannibal marched to war across the Alps with 60,000 infantry, 9,000 cavalry and 37 elephants. His journey 'captured the imagination of the world'.

2,000 years later, Bernard Levin retraces his hero's steps. With great reluctance he abandoned the idea of taking elephants. The story of his travels is a marvellous blend of history, travel, anecdote and personal philosophy.

'The benign, inquiring spirit of ENTHUSIASMS is still present in HANNIBAL'S FOOTSTEPS, still enjoying and seeking something "beyond the next mountain"'
Bel Mooney in the Listener

'Who could be a more amusing or provocative cicerone on a journey from the Rhône across the Alps towards Turin, following Hannibal's legendary elephantine dash of 218 BC into Italy?'
Peter Jones in The Times

'He had a ball, and so will the reader'
Daily Express

Current and forthcoming titles from Sceptre

CHRISTOPHER ANDREW

SECRET SERVICE

NIGEL HAMILTON

MONTY: VOLUME 1 THE MAKING OF A GENERAL 1887–1942

MONTY: VOLUME 2 MASTER OF THE BATTLEFIELD 1942–1944

MONTY: VOLUME 3 THE FIELD-MARSHAL 1944–1976

A. ALVAREZ

OFFSHORE

BERNARD LEVIN

HANNIBAL'S FOOTSTEPS

BOOKS OF DISTINCTION